MONTAIGNE

MONTAIGNE

A Life

PHILIPPE DESAN

Translated by Steven Rendall and Lisa Neal

Avec le soutien du
CNL
Centre national du livre

PRINCETON UNIVERSITY PRESS

Princeton & Oxford

First published in French under the title *Montaigne: Une biographie politique* by Philippe Desan. © Odile Jacob, 2014

Copyright © 2017 by Princeton University Press

Requests for permission to reproduce material from this work should be sent to Permissions, Princeton University Press

Published by Princeton University Press, 41 William Street, Princeton, New Jersey 08540

In the United Kingdom: Princeton University Press, 6 Oxford Street, Woodstock, Oxfordshire OX20 1TR

press.princeton.edu

Cover art: Portrait of Montaigne, c. 1590, School of Fontainebleau, anonymous. Private collection. Oil on copper plate. 8.8 cm. diam.

First paperback edition 2018
Paper ISBN: 9780691183008

The Library of Congress has cataloged the cloth edition as follows:

Names: Desan, Philippe, author. | Rendall, Steven, translator. | Neal, Lisa (Lisa Dow), translator.

Title: Montaigne : a life / Philippe Desan ; translated by Steven Rendall and Lisa Neal.

Other titles: Montaigne: Une biographie politique. English

Description: Princeton : Princeton University Press, [2017] | Includes bibliographical references and index.

Identifiers: LCCN 2016012378 | ISBN 9780691167879 (hardback : acid-free paper)

Subjects: LCSH: Montaigne, Michel de, 1533-1592. | Montaigne, Michel de, 1533-1592—Political and social views. | Authors, French—16th century—Biography. | BISAC: BIOGRAPHY & AUTOBIOGRAPHY / Political. | BIOGRAPHY & AUTOBIOGRAPHY / Literary. | PHILOSOPHY / Political. | LITERARY CRITICISM / Renaissance. | LITERARY CRITICISM / European / French.

Classification: LCC PQ1643 .D39513 2017 | DDC 844/.3 [B] —dc23
LC record available at https://lccn.loc.gov/2016012378British Library Cataloging-in-Publication Data is available

This book has been composed in Garamond Premier Pro and Stancia

Printed on acid- free paper. ∞

Printed in the United States of America

CONTENTS

PART TWO — PRACTICES

PART THREE—POST MORTEM

ACKNOWLEDGMENTS

Some books take a long time to write. That is the case for this biography of Montaigne, which draws on many investigations I have published in various books and journals over more than twenty-five years. But a book is also a conversation with specialists. There is no lack of specialists on Montaigne, and unfortunately I cannot mention them all here. However, I want to thank those who have allowed me to present the various stages of my research at colloquia and in lectures and seminars in France and abroad, and also those who have offered valuable suggestions and criticisms, notably Katherine Almquist[†], Jean-Robert Armogathe, Celso Martins Azar Filho, Anna Bettoni, Telma Birchal, Claude Blum, Concetta Cavallini, Anne-Marie Cocula, Denis Crouzet, Jean-Charles Darmon, Emiliano Ferrari, Véronique Ferrer, Philip Ford[†], Thierry Gontier, Rosanna Gorris, Olivier Guerrier, Dorothea Heitsch, George Hoffmann, Neil Kenny, Ullrich Langer, Chiara Lastraioli, Alain Legros, Frank Lestringant, Juan Lluís Llinàs Begon, Peter Mack, Hassan Melehy, Jan Miernowski, John O'Brien, Gianni Paganini, Nicola Panichi, Loris Petris, Michel Simonin[†], Paul J. Smith, José Alexandrino de Souza Filho, Richard Strier, and especially Jean Balsamo, a learned expert on Montaigne and a long-standing friend, whose enlightened advice enabled me, from the beginning of this project, to avoid many a slipup. In addition, I thank my editors at Princeton University Press, Ben Tate, Sara Lerner, and Dawn Hall, for their attentive readings of the manuscript and their judicious editorial suggestions. The English translation of this book by Steven Rendall and Lisa Neal surpasses my best expectations and in many ways renders the reading more fluid. Thanks to their careful reading and editing, many blunders and ambiguous passages present in the French edition have been corrected. Any remaining errors are, of course, entirely my own. I am grateful for the University of Chicago's Humanities Visiting Committee, which subsidized in part the translation of this book. I am also indebted to my students (graduate and undergraduate) who, over the last three decades, have participated in my seminars on Montaigne at the University of Chicago. They often served as a testing ground for new approaches and interpretations, and I have greatly benefited from their comments and reactions.

Finally, there are the faithful friends: François, Giovanni, Nicole, Pierre, Francine, and Pessel. Their generosity and goodwill have eased the completion of this work. Not to forget Eriko, who continues to put up with my deficient sociability and who has long since accepted Montaigne as a member of the family. I dedicate this book to her.

FIGURE 1. Antoine-Jean Gros, *Charles Quint venant visiter l'église de Saint-Denis, où il est reçu par François Ier, accompagné de ses fils et des premiers de sa cour, 1812.* Photo © RMN-Grand Palais (musée du Louvre) / Michel Urtado.

PROLOGUE

Who wouldn't have liked to see Montaigne with Francis I and Charles V? This meeting, which never took place, was nonetheless made possible in 1812 thanks to Baron Antoine-Jean Gros (1771–1835), a painter of historical and military subjects and of religious compositions. His painting, *Charles Quint venant visiter l'église de Saint-Denis, où il est reçu par François Ier, accompagné de ses fils et des premiers de sa cour* (figure 1),[i] depicts Montaigne as a child.[1] It is the painter himself who identifies Montaigne and gives a list of the men and women represented in the framework of his composition.[2] The young Michel stands alongside the platform, on the right. The magnificence of the event seems hardly to impress him; he is concentrating his gaze on a detail we cannot see. The scene is supposed to date from January 1540, so that the Montaigne in the picture would be seven years old.

In the nineteenth century, Montaigne specialists argued about his exact place in this picture, as if Gros might have been mistaken about the identity of his figures. Dr. Payen, an eminent and erudite "Montaignologist" of his time, preferred to identify Montaigne not with the young man near the platform, but with a gentleman standing just behind the monarchs. Payen ignored the painter's designation of the figure and unhesitatingly replaced Henri d'Albret with the author of the *Essais*. The argument he gave to justify this iconological correction has to do with figure's physiognomy and a few details of the clothing. We note that the necklace on the gentleman's dove-gray vest vaguely resembles the chain and medal of the Order of Saint Michael conferred on Montaigne in 1571, more than thirty years later. Other Montaigne specialists also disagreed with the painter's idea of respecting the dates and representing Montaigne as a child. All this seems to ignore the fact that the figure supposedly representing Montaigne is as tall as Charles V and looks like he is closer to twenty than seven. They preferred to see Montaigne standing, behind the sovereigns, himself a noble and an important political actor. Disregarding chronology, they opted for a Montaigne who was *already* in full possession of his abilities as a negotiator; in that way they wanted to indicate that the essayist would no doubt

---

[i] Commissioned in 1811 for the new sacristy at Saint Denis, and transferred to the Royal Museum in 1820, this painting inspired several artists and was the subject of several engravings during the Romantic period, notably by Sisco (1812), Forster (1826), and Réveil (1827). Let us also mention Norblin de la Gourdaine's version (1837), another copy of Gros's painting by Dehay, and a Gobelins tapestry that represents the same scene. The young Montaigne appears in all these representations.

have been one of the kingpins at a meeting between Charles V and Francis I, had he been lucky enough to have been born twenty years earlier. Never mind the dates, here we are in the order of the possible; it was better to broaden the picture's temporal framework a little in order to insert Montaigne into it as a wise philosopher and accomplished author.

1812 is not an insignificant date so far as judgments regarding Montaigne are concerned; in that year he received his literary canonization. The First Empire consecrated the author of the *Essais*, whom the French Academy had designated for the *concours des éloges* in 1810. The genre of "eulogies" contributed to the rediscovery of many authors who had been forgotten in the course of the eighteenth century. Thirty-seven candidates entered this prize competition. Ten of the eulogies were published in 1812, and most of them served as introductions to one of the many editions of the *Essais* printed in the first half of the nineteenth century. In most of the eulogies of Montaigne, as in Antoine-Jean Gros's painting, no distinction was made between the author and the politician. It was taken for granted that a great writer would participate in the public life of his time and, even at a young age, in historically memorable events.

As a precursor of French Romantic painting, Gros brought the young Montaigne into the history of France by placing him amid the sovereigns of the Renaissance. Exhibited at the Salons of 1812 and 1814—climactic years for Napoleon I and the Empire—this canvas was favorably received by the critics. The painter considered it "his crowning achievement." All the historical actors of the period between 1530 and 1550 are represented in it, along with great literary men and artists of the time. Influential women, even if their names are less well known today, also occupy prominent places in the composition. Despite a few approximations, Gros does not take liberties with chronology; there is no real anachronism that would spoil the verisimilitude of the scene. The artist also respected, on the whole, the biography of the figures represented, with one notable exception: that of Montaigne.

Traveling through the Low Countries to put down the revolt of the people of Ghent, Charles V was invited by Francis I to cross France. He made his entrance into Paris on January 19, 1540, and asked permission to pay his respects to the tombs of the sovereigns buried in the church of Saint-Denis. The scene chosen to represent this event emphasizes the reconciliation of these powerful monarchs known for their long-standing rivalry, and their shared choice of Catholicism in the age of the "new religion." The comparison with Napoleon I at the apex of the Empire and just before the Russian campaign is not innocent. In a moment of respite, the two sovereigns stand side by side. Charles V appears as the master of Europe. The emperor of Germany and king of Spain, he dominates his neighbors and has extended his reign as far as the Low Countries. Francis I is accompanied by his sons, Crown Prince Henry, the future king, who is painted in profile and occupies the left side of the picture, and Charles II of Orléans, who is not yet eighteen years old and stands behind his father. Dressed in black, Charles V expresses the mastery and self-assurance of a soldier, he is sizing up his host. The king of France establishes himself in another register, more tranquil and reposed. In accord with his image as the father of the rebirth of the arts and letters, he is surrounded by architects, painters, poets, and men of letters, who constitute a necessary counterpoint to the great military leaders.

Reconciled for the moment, the two sovereigns are moving toward a stairway that leads to the tombs of the kings of France. A chaplain holding two torches waits for them under an arch, ready to guide them into the church's crypt. With his left hand, Francis I is directing Charles V's attention to the tomb of Louis XII, which only the young Montaigne seems to be looking at. Facing the sovereigns and accompanied by two priests, the Cardinal of Bourbon, abbot of Saint-Denis, wears the miter and carries the crosier. On the steps of the stairway, Constable Montmorency holds his sword raised, with Henri d'Albret, son of Catherine de Foix and Jean III d'Albret, king of Navarre, on his right, and the duke of Guise on his left, next to the pillar. Antoine de Bourbon, a prince of the blood who favored the introduction of Calvinism into France while remaining faithful to the Catholic religion and to his king, stands on the same step. In 1562, he was to be fatally wounded during the siege of Rouen, at which Montaigne might have been present. The father of Henry IV, Antoine de Bourbon, here supplies the historical continuity between the last Valois and Henry of Navarre, the first French sovereign from the Bourbon branch of the royal family. Montaigne was later to serve as a political intermediary between Henry III and Henry of Navarre, who had not yet been born at the time of the imagined meeting of Francis I and Charles V.

Behind these princes of the blood, we can recognize the legate, with his long, flourishing beard, as well as Cardinal Du Bellay and the Cardinal of Lorraine, with their red cardinals' hats. And, behind these representatives of the clergy, we can see the Marquis of Astorga, a Spanish grandee, dressed in black like his king. Swiss guards with pikes and halberds stand in the background. The whole political history of the years between 1530 and 1550, along with an anticipation of the civil wars waged in the time of Montaigne, is suggested by the Empire-period painter.

The balcony located above the platform is occupied by Catherine de Medici, on the left. We know her political influence and the role she was soon to play as Henry II's wife, and then as the mother of the kings of France, Francis II, Charles IX, and Henry III, of Elisabeth of France, and of Margaret of Valois, also called "Queen Margot." In perfect symmetry with Montaigne, on the opposite side of the picture, Catherine casts a benevolent but perhaps already calculating look on the unprecedented scene taking place before her eyes. She was the person who held the keys to the new alliances and religious conflicts that divided the kingdom. Montaigne intermittently associated with her right up to her death in 1589. Alongside the future queen, on the same level, we see Louise de Clermont-Tonnerre, Duchess of Uzès; Catherine's lady-in-waiting; Charlotte Le Sueuer d'Esquetot, Countess of Brissac and wife of Charles I of Cossé, who was raised to the dignity of Marshal of France in 1550; Diane de Poitiers; and "la Belle Ferronière," Francis I's mistress. Behind these influential women, Jacques Amyot, the translator of Plutarch, seems to be conversing with the Duchess of Uzès and Jean Goujon, the sculptor of the bas-reliefs at the château of Écouen. The latter dominates the others by his height. Men of letters, artists, and ladies-in-waiting share this historical moment so that it might be perpetuated on monuments, books, and salons.

The second balcony, to the right of the platform, shows Claudine de Rieux, known as Madame d'Angelot, the wife of François de Coligny, one of the Protestant leaders at the beginning of the Wars of Religion; Anne de Polignac, Countess de la Rochefoucauld; and Marie-Marguerite de Lorraine-Guise, called Mlle d'Elbeuf, who was to become queen and regent of Scotland. In this moment of apparent peace, Protestants and Catholics are still side by side, caring little about the religious inferno that was about to divide them and tear the kingdom apart.

Finally, to complete this impressive list of queens and princesses, and perhaps to bring the scene up to date, Gros added the portrait of his wife to the left of Montaigne, as if it were she who had rediscovered the author of the *Essais* at the beginning of the nineteenth century and made him join the canon of French letters. In the second row, le Primatice, a painter in the service of Francis I and one of the masters of the first School of Fontainebleau, cranes his neck to see around the pillar that is preventing him from viewing the scene. To his left, Pierre Lescot, the architect of the Louvre, is trying to look over women to see the sovereigns. Jean Bullant, the architect of the château of Écouen, also leans forward to gain a better view. Above Montaigne, Clément Marot and François Rabelais are whispering to each other. We can imagine what they are saying. . . . In the third row, an unidentified figure dominates the scene. Still very young, he may be the painter himself. He has succeeded in getting around the pillar and is leaning dangerously over le Primatice. Like a dwarf on the shoulders of a giant—Gros on the shoulders of le Primatice?—the painter remains outside the scene. Moreover, it is hard to understand how he can stand so high above the other spectators. He is the only one who has a bird's-eye view. Both a witness and a reporter, the painter looks out from his own canvas.

The scene Gros chose to depict is unstable and temporary. Reality and illusion merge. The people depicted are soon going to separate and will be rediscovered in other situations. Some will go back to Spain, others to Italy or Scotland. Most will be involved in wars. The moment of peace and hope Gros suggests was to vanish in Montaigne's time. For this is a *foreshadowing* canvas: the only thing that counts is what is going to happen after the meeting of Francis I and Charles V. The painting is to be read from left to right, from Catherine de Medici to Montaigne. To Catherine's political hyperrealism we should perhaps oppose a more idealist vision of politics. The scene reflects an assemblage that is too historical, and only Montaigne-as-a-child could give it a naiver dimension to reestablish a semblance of balance between the forces that were soon to oppose one another. The future author of the *Essais* offers an innocent but optimistic vision of politics, in harmony with Napoleon I's indefectible confidence during the First Empire. The child is not yet capable of understanding the intrigues that were to come and that constitute the real stakes involved in this picture, far beyond the formal setting. He is the only guarantor of a candid vision of the situation. At least, that is the image of Montaigne that the early nineteenth century liked to project.

As if marked by this imaginary scene of his youth, Montaigne held several public offices. He was a member of the parlement of Bordeaux,[ii] mayor of the same city, and served as a negotiator for Henry III, Catherine de Medici, and Henry of Navarre. In turn, he frequented the Court and proposed a different approach to politics after Machiavelli. As an author, he developed the project of describing himself and leading his life differently from his contemporaries, advocating transparency rather than dissimulation. To the end of his life, he insisted that "pure naturalness and truth, in whatever age, still find their time and their place."[3] This optimistic approach to the events of his time allowed him to serve his king for a time and to develop his own political ambitions, basing himself on his moral integrity. However, like many others, he ended up having doubts about this "childish view" of politics and finally lost his illusions regarding the kinds of action allowed by official functions. Having experienced that, he became a full-fledged author. Gros's painting symbolizes the political man's hope at the same time that it announces his failure.

Montaigne belonged to history even though he had not yet joined the literary canon suggested by the "good" Marot and the "simple and pleasing" Rabelais. All the figures in Gros's painting were chosen with care, in order to maintain a balance between arms and letters, those two complementary elements of the history of the Renaissance. But in the end, one has to be realistic—and Montaigne was, in his own way. His encounter with the political and artistic elite suggests a historical project rather than an objective description, and he

---

[ii] Under the Old Régime, the "parlements" were provincial appellate courts, not legislative bodies. Laws and edicts issued by the crown were not official in a jurisdiction until they had been registered by the respective parlements. [Trans.]

was barely able to slip into this idealized construction. Gros's representation of him as a child ultimately corresponds to his quite minor place in the history of the events of the sixteenth century. This foreshadowing of Montaigne among the great names of the Renaissance may be more accurate than we imagine, and on this point our history painter had only to stretch historical fact a little. His view of the reign of Francis I is valid in a way for the whole century. It is also a resolutely political conception of the Renaissance dominated by the last Valois and the Habsburgs. Just one thing is absent from this canvas: the Wars of Religion. But we nonetheless find here the duke of Guise, a Catholic extremist, and Admiral Coligny's sister-in-law, Madame d'Andelot. The Protestant evangelism of Clément Marot and François Rabelais is suggested by their whispering together. In this sumptuous scene in which a temporary peace prevails, we can already find all the reasons for which the tempest of the Wars of Religion broke out twenty years later, in Montaigne's time.

Montaigne's biography has always been flexible enough to allow men of letters and historians to adapt history a little and insert the author of the *Essais* into almost all the significant events of his time. However, Montaigne's place in history—as in Gros's painting—remains problematic. Rather than a self-portrait in a romantic context and framework, we propose here a different picture of Montaigne in order to evaluate his various careers as a member of parlement, mayor, and negotiator, as the translator of Raymond Sebond, the editor of La Boétie's works, and finally as a full-fledged author—in short, a portrait of Montaigne in politics.

INTRODUCTION

Over the centuries, Montaigne's *Essais* have gradually lost their historical character. It could certainly be said that this is the fate of great texts that enter the cultural patrimony of modern societies. Universality demands the erasure of temporality, and in the case of Montaigne we have to recognize that the author saw to it that all that remained was the famous literary portrait of himself (*peinture du moi*), the model and "pattern" (*patron*) of "the human condition."[i] Lord Michel de Montaigne, knight of the Order of Saint Michael, gentleman of the chamber of the kings of France and Navarre, mayor and governor of Bordeaux—titles and offices duly mentioned on the title pages of the first editions of the *Essais* in 1580 and 1582—has slowly given way to the generic Montaigne—without a first name or a social status—to which we are now accustomed: a Montaigne dissociated from history.

Philosophers and specialists in literary studies emphasize this universal, atemporal Montaigne, but too often they ignore the royal servant and public official, just as they underestimate the role played in his conduct by professional choices and career strategies. But for all that let us not condemn the critics. Montaigne himself demands that a distinction be drawn between the private and the public: "The mayor and Montaigne have always been two, with a very clear separation."[1] This famous declaration has caused much ink to flow and has often been taken at face value. When he wrote, the author of the *Essais* is supposed to have laid aside the mayor's finery and at the same time the social dimension that made him a political actor in his time. However, a long study of the *Essais*, illuminated by the historical context, teaches us that we must not always take Montaigne at his word. As he himself recognizes, the perception and interpretation of events and human actions is often adapted to the circumstance and to subjective considerations that emanate from the moment at which they are experienced or reported. That is why one's "history needs to be adapted to the moment."[2] Writing often reflects an adjustment that has to do with the social practices of a period, and the artificial separation of the private from the public sometimes results in a failure to take them into account.

Setting out to write a biography of Montaigne requires us to look into the historicity of the *Essais*, that is, into their situation in the political and social

---

[i] This expression is not a hapax legomenon, as has been claimed, because it appears six times in the *Essais*, including three times in the 1580 edition.

practices of the late French Renaissance. Must we disregard history in the name of an atemporal objectivization of the man and his work in order to facilitate the constitution of a philosophical object? Or are we, on the contrary, obliged to restitute the political dimension of a text that, while claiming that it does not take up the problems of its time, can nonetheless not escape them? In short, is it possible to provide a political reading of the *Essais* while at the same time preserving the philosophical and literary dimension of this text that is foundational for modernity? Here I have not focused on Montaigne's genius or wisdom, because it would be very difficult to situate in his period concepts that were popularized and propagated only in the nineteenth and twentieth centuries. Instead, I have concentrated solely on Montaigne's career as an author in relation to his ambitions and political activity.

Without denying the aesthetic and stylistic value of the *Essais*, I will approach Montaigne's work on the basis of the functions it might have had at various points in the author's life. Written over a period of twenty years, the *Essais* were published four times during Montaigne's lifetime, in different cities and in different formats. Each edition differs from the preceding one not only in its content and form but also in the publishing and political project that accompanies it. Rather than an evolution of Montaigne's thought, we note, on the contrary, successive transformations of a text that refer to conceptions, distinct and sometimes contradictory, of political commitment and public service. To understand these mutations of the text in the course of the various editions, we must therefore approach it—without neglecting the other works—on the basis of a sociopolitical analysis that will allow us to grasp these separate objects in their specific historical contexts and to discern their respective functions over time.

Did Montaigne create a book so unique and imbued with such a marked idiosyncrasy that it eludes sociological analysis? No, because the *Essais* also bear witness to a period. Can this book be situated within a social group or order that influenced its literary and philosophical production? Does it bear the trace of its author's social origins, his upbringing, and his career expectations? I think it does. Such a proposition will appear dangerous to literary scholars, because it tends to chip away at the pedestal on which Montaigne has stood since the early nineteenth century. My goal is not to praise his judgment or to make him an author in quest of freedom, but rather to evaluate the way in which the writing and publication of the *Essais* were the result of more worldly concerns and intentions. It is possible to become a great writer while at the same time pursuing more frivolous and material ends, because literature inevitably passes through the social and the political.

Questions of Method and the Politics of a Book

The literary and philosophical constitution of the *Essais* was influenced by Montaigne's need to realize his political ambitions and aspirations. We have to demystify the conventional image of the essayist isolated in his tower, far from the agitations of his time, playing with his cat and inquiring into the human condition. Even when he retired from society, the author of the *Essais* aspired to rejoin it and resume his political service. Every retirement implies the taking of a position and a reaction with regard to a particular conjunctural situation in which the individual concludes that he no longer has a place. This conclusion is political in nature. Writing is conceived in its social context, which necessarily includes the people with whom the writer spends time and who directly or indirectly influence his projects for publication as a translator, editor, and author. From his relatives and friends to the king, by way of his colleagues in the parlement, neighboring lords, humanists in Bordeaux, Protestant and Catholic military leaders, members of the Bordeaux *jurade*,[ii] and the highest officials of the kingdom—all these influenced, at one time or another, the conception and composition of the *Essais*. In its literary expression, Montaigne's self exists only in relation to others, that is, in a system of interactions that are certainly singular, but multiple, and of which the *Essais* provides the right measure.

Montaigne's philosophical thought—which, moreover, he refuses to define as such—is part of what he calls a "comedy," more a social than a human comedy, because its rules are temporal. Montaigne cites Petronius: "The whole world plays a part."[3] All occupations are merely "farcical," and each person has to play his role. Life itself is a comedy in four acts, or in four seasons, as Montaigne reminds us: "And at worst, the distribution and variety of all the acts of my comedy runs its course in a year. If you have taken note of the revolution of my four seasons, they embrace the infancy, the youth, the manhood, and the old age of the world. It knows no other trick than to begin again. It will always be just this."[4] Human actions are repeated over time and are thus foreseeable. Politics is transformed into a social science insofar as it takes an interest in the recurrence of behaviors in time and tries to define rules in the service of the prospect of gaining or maintaining power. That is the whole project of Machiavelli, a counselor and historian in the service of the prince. Montaigne distantly echoes the discourse of the time and takes cognizance of the multiple roles that everyone has to play in life.

The world is the theater of our actions, and Montaigne—who we know was interested in theater while he was studying at the College of Guyenne—was on

---

[ii] The name given to Bordeaux's municipal council under the Old Régime. [Trans.]

several occasions in the forefront of the political arena, acting before a local, regional, and then national audience.[5] Like many of his contemporaries, he also knew how to playact, even if he repeatedly warns the reader against masks and appearances. Public responsibilities require one to play a role.[6] These stagings are the matter of the *Essais*, even if Montaigne later chose to accord them less value, or even to forego any reference to them. From 1560 to 1592, during the Wars of Religion, Montaigne tried out several roles—offices that he called "borrowed" or "temporary" when he passed on to other projects, other responsibilities, other stages. But we have the feeling that when Montaigne occupied a public office, he believed in it fully, at least at first. It was only later on, with the appropriate distance, that he analyzed the success or failure of his tryouts. These political experiences provided him with an opportunity to define more clearly the moral boundaries of public service: "I am called to a more worthy role; so if anyone wanted to employ me to lie, to betray, and to perjure myself for some notable service, even to if not to assassinate or poison, I would say: If I have robbed or stolen from any man, send me rather to the galleys."[7] The "more worthy role" Montaigne mentions is the product of a later assessment made possible only in light of the experiments he carried out in various public offices.

It seems illusive to approach the *Essais* as if it were a fixed philosophical or literary object, without taking into account the historical context of its writing over two decades. What interests us here is the production of the *Essais* and other works by Montaigne in their immediate relationship to the market, considering them as objects conceived in a network of exchange and consumption. The works Montaigne translated, edited, and wrote corresponded to particular expectations at the time, but they were also perceived as "novelties" that allow their author to distinguish himself from others and to innovate with respect to codified social practices. These objects had multiple functions and were all, in their own way, part of essentially political strategies. The publication of the *Essais* in 1580 represents a literary event, to be sure, but it must also be approached as a *social fact*, that is, a way or mode of being and appearing.

The various works Montaigne published will be analyzed here as "social objects" that sometimes go beyond individual intentions and have to do with collective behaviors. Montaigne's particular choices regarding publication have to be understood in the framework of the political conditions and practices of his time. Similarly, the personal opinions expressed in a book—even one with the innovative title of *Essais*—participate in the dialogue of a period, with the beliefs, tendencies, and inclinations peculiar to a group, order, or social class. The conditions and modalities of these collective habits are transmitted and perpetuated by ideologies. At the end of the nineteenth century, in a passage that foreshadows Pierre Bourdieu's analyses, the sociologist Émile Durkheim wrote: "Collective custom does not exist only in a state of immanence in the successive actions which it determines, but, by a privilege without example in the biological kingdom, expresses itself once and for all in a formula repeated by word of mouth, transmitted by education and even enshrined in the written word."[8] We will examine Montaigne's works in the context of the social and cultural practices of the late Renaissance, all of which are connected with social orders—clerics, nobles, magistrates, bourgeois—but are also illumined by corporatist and clientelist behaviors, notably in parlementary, diplomatic, and administrative milieus (the *jurade* of the city of Bordeaux for example), not to mention the middle-level nobility of Guyenne.

The private is transformed into objective reality for others. In fact, the dichotomy that seems to exist between the private and the public disappears as soon as one considers that every social fact is also the realization in time of apparent "individual facts." Studying Montaigne and his thought consists in looking *around* the author to understand the milieu from which he came, his family's social itinerary, the upbringing he received, and the ideological and political convictions of the circle of friends and nobles that facilitated his entry into the Cour des Aides[iii] in Périgueux and then the parlement of Bordeaux, and that placed him at the head of that city and propelled him to the royal Court. His first writings (the translation of Raymond Sebond in 1569, the edition of La Boétie's works in 1571, and the publication of the first edition of the *Essais* in 1580) served as springboards for gaining access to careers as a member of the parlement and as an ambassador or diplomat. Each publication allowed him to develop a conversation with a restricted group and to assert that he was a member of it. As Durkheim notes, the individual always acts as part of a group, because every personal act is situated in "collective *modes of being*."[9] Similarly, Montaigne and the *Essais* have modes of being. These represent various roles for different audiences; they are based on shared ideologies. The flagrant contradictions in the *Essais* acquire meaning if they are seen in light of the preceding careers or professional choices. In Montaigne's case, these modes of being are fundamentally political, because they seek to shape and control the social image fashioned by the individual in a precise conjunctural framework. Therefore I will emphasize the political dimension of what has been called the "self-fashioning" (another mode of being) of late Renaissance authors.[10] The representation of the political can sometimes resemble a poetics, that is, it can facilitate the adaptation of the episodes of a life to the topoi prescribed by current literary genres.[11]

If the seventeenth century can be defined as a stage in the process of civilization marked by the appearance of a Court society, the sixteenth century was

---

[iii] The *Cours des Aides* were appellate courts dealing primarily with fiscal and financial matters. [Trans.]

similarly characterized by the emergence of another kind of Court society—that of the parlement. It was the transfer of the culture of the magistrates of the late Renaissance to the milieu of the middle-level nobility—by means of complex but clearly defined strategies of passage—that forced the high nobility of the sword to turn in on itself and concentrate its distinctive behaviors in a single place (the Louvre or Versailles), which Louis XIV later transformed into a unique space of sociability. The decline of the low and middle nobility throughout the sixteenth century and the regrouping of the values of the nobility in a system of even more regulated etiquette made it possible for a time to produce the illusion of a sociability that led to the civilizing process Norbert Elias analyzed.[12] However, the sociogenesis of modern sociability obliges us to consider the parlements of the sixteenth century as essential spaces in the period's social and political relationships, because simply by circumventing the strict rules of membership in the Old Régime's three orders, they helped redefine the very idea of nobility and changed forever the social relationships that emerged from the Middle Ages.

In a system of mutual dependency with regard to the nobility and in accord with the codes and behaviors specific to members of the parlements, the culture of the magistrates gave rise to new strategies of social ascent. Montaigne's case in particular allows us to study the passage from one court society to the other. In fact, his first career as a member of a parlement, with its rules of etiquette and its logic of prestige inherited from its corporatist organization, soon gave way to a system of values expressing a nobility that revealed itself more in its way of life than in the signs usually displayed by that order. The *Essais* have a sociological interest insofar as they bear the mark of this shift from one culture to the other and allow us to retrace, by studying their publication history, the steps that eased the transition from a parlementary court society to a Court society proper.

Without being aware that his acts were part of a *habitus* (to borrow Bourdieu's term), which does not mean that he could not have identified with a group or clientele, or even opted for alliances that were temporary and sometimes unnatural, Montaigne nonetheless expresses himself in the name of a constituted entity, and thus it is possible to approach his particular acts from a sociological point of view. Beneath the veneer of institutions and sometimes in contradiction with the orders, groups, or clienteles to which they belong, individuals also have personal aspirations that must not be underestimated.[13] Montaigne learned to adapt to the worlds he joined, and he knew how to incorporate himself into networks, but he did hesitate to assert his independence with regard to his models when his models no longer corresponded to his expectations. We might say that Montaigne spent a large part of his life distinguishing himself from groups he had nonetheless avidly sought to join, or from individuals with whom he had at first felt a certain intellectual or political affinity. He became expert at justifying his choices, his errors, and himself in general.[iv]

In the case of Montaigne, no philosophical reflection extracted from the *Essais* can be dissociated from a relationship to the collectivity; Montaigne's way of life and his way of thinking express and also determine a collective life and thought. For this reason, it seems to me difficult to dissociate literature, philosophy, and politics. Traditional history has often highlighted a few "exceptional" thinkers who, thanks to their writings, are supposed to have made possible the emergence of capitalism and modern science (Luther, Calvin, Copernicus, Galileo), as if the two automatically went together in a broader conception of modernity. According to this approach, a teleological or theological discourse characteristic of the Renaissance gave rise to new economic and scientific behaviors. Simple *qualitative* changes in the spiritual domain are even supposed to have made it possible to redefine and reorient society's economic and political organization. This form of psychological determinism, which gives priority to the individual as the motive force in history seems inadequately founded when past centuries are being studied. Rejecting this idealist view of history, I have not made Montaigne a genius or a sage. On the contrary, he was a man like others, with dreams and desires that were to be expected in his period.

The typical career course of other individuals belonging to the same collective way of life helps us imagine Montaigne's aspirations. His discourse, which at first seems unusual, follows socially coded guidelines and forms that are observable in the "social facts" (and not only in the historical events) of his time. Montaigne's particular type of consciousness—his way of life and his point of view—produces common practices. So Montaigne's sense is also common sense. Our approach here understands the discourse and actions of a single agent as revelatory of the expression of a group. For example, we will have to ask whether the private character of Montaigne's opinions was shared by other members of the group to which he belonged. It is in that perspective that we will interpret his adhesion to (and then rejection of) the magistrates' ideology (Montaigne's

---

[iv] The works of Luc Boltanksi and Laurent Thevenot (*De la justification: Les économies de la grandeur*. Paris: Gallimard, 1991) have made it possible to foreground this construction on two levels—collective will and particular interest—which leads to a "common superior principle" in which individuals constantly adapt to the new situations they encounter in different worlds and thus arrive at a compromise that satisfies them. The justification for this compromise inevitably leads to a relativization of the common good because of the individual's questioning and detachment vis-à-vis the norms and values of the common good. Montaigne constantly practiced this mode of social interaction, which allowed him to free himself from the authorities and dogmas that limited his possibilities of societal and political action.

first career was as a member of the Bordeaux parlement), his activity as mayor in the service of the Bordeaux nobility, and finally the aristocratic aspirations made visible through the noble values he declares in his writings.

These social and political groups—in the regional milieu of Guyenne and the city of Bordeaux in the late sixteenth century—express ideologies that are sometimes contradictory but are nonetheless connected when they are analyzed in relation to the production of the *Essais*. Montaigne's thought is obviously paradoxical if it is reduced to a text presented in a homogeneous way, in a single edition, but the divergences among the three "strata" of the *Essais* (1580, 1588, 1595) are no longer abnormal or paradoxical if they are considered in the unstable, changing historical and political climate of the Wars of Religion. Thus in my analysis I will seek to take into account the temporality of writing and publishing the *Essais*. Many of the peremptory and often discordant statements acquire a very different meaning when they are seen in their immediate social and political context. It does not suffice to study Montaigne's political thinking in his writings—that has been done many times;[14] instead, we need to see how this thinking is articulated with social and professional practices related to particular periods in Montaigne's life. In this sense, Montaigne's political thought often responds to punctual situations. That is why I have given priority to the study of the relations between immediate history and the publication of the different editions of the *Essais*. Sociological and historical approaches help us understand the rather complex publication history of the *Essais*, particularly in their relation to the works of Raymond Sebond and Estienne de La Boétie. Montaigne's publications are closely linked with his professional ambitions and his political career. I will argue that Montaigne actually tried his hand at politics by developing his activities as translator, editor, and author.

The various printings of Montaigne's books exist as objects independent of one another: first his translation of Raymond Sebond's *Theologia naturalis* (1569 and 1581); then his editing of La Boétie's works (1571)—including the *Discourse on Voluntary Servitude*, which Montaigne initially intended to publish, and the *Memorandum* on the edict of January 1562, which he preferred not to discuss; the journal of his journey through Germany, Switzerland, and Italy (written in 1580 and 1581); the editions of the *Essais* published in 1580, 1582, and 1588; and finally the manuscript additions in the Bordeaux Copy,[v] which

---

[v] What is now commonly called the *Exemplaire de Bordeaux* (Bordeaux Copy) is a printed copy of the last edition of the *Essais* published during Montaigne's lifetime, brought out by Abel L'Angelier in 1588. This copy is annotated in the author's hand and includes numerous additions, suppressions, corrections, typographical modifications, substitutions of words, changes in punctuation and spelling, and stylistic variations. But it is above all the textual developments, which Montaigne calls the last *allongeail* ("extension," "prolongation"), written between autumn 1588 and September 13, 1592 (the date

extend from 1588 to 1592. All these texts respond to specific publishing strategies and were influenced by political considerations. The Sebond and La Boétie
"affairs" showed Montaigne how necessary it was to clear away potential dangers in matters of publication politics. How could he say things without giving
the impression that he was committing himself too much to one side or the
other? The very form of the essay might be a response to this great question of
political engagement that marks the end of the French Renaissance. In this
sense, Montaigne is indeed a *politique*—in the sixteenth-century meaning of
the term, but also in its modern sense—in the successive politics of publishing
he adopted. His writing never claims to be definitive; it remains tentative while
waiting to be confirmed or disconfirmed by the events of his time.

A reading of the *Essais* in light of their author's successive political engage-
ments does not put in question the originality of the work. Montaigne often
distances himself from the political practices of his time, but the reactions and
judgments expressed in the *Essais* sometimes led him to develop an idealist view
of politics. All the same, the quest for universals does not dispense one from
assuming political responsibilities, and Montaigne recognizes that political responsibilities cannot be avoided by those who occupy administrative or military
offices. Morality results from an ongoing construction and cannot be fixed. The
temporality of public life was a reality that Montaigne never ignored.

Before working out the theory of politics, Montaigne passed through the
practice of politics. The goal of this study is to relate the two inseparable aspects
of his life: literature and political action. Private life and public life cannot be
detached from each other in a permanent way. If the *Essais* are now an essentially philosophical or literary object, we still have to understand the relationship that this allegedly private object entertained, through its successive editions, with events or political positions taken by its author and other political
actors of his time. When Montaigne takes an interest in ancient philosophers,
he considers first of all their lives, drawing no dividing line between the private
and the public. Plutarch's *Parallel Lives*, in Jacques Amyot's French translation,
remained his favorite book, and he tells us why: "those who write biographies,
since they spend more time on plans than on events, more on what comes from
within than on what happens without, are most suited to me."[15] This movement
that begins "from the inside" and rejoins the social and political world is the
object of the present biography of Montaigne.

Montaigne specialists long refused to take an interest in the author's life. It
was Dr. Payen, an avid collector of everything that had to do with Montaigne,
who best formulated this position when he asserted, in the middle of the nine-

---

of his death), that make the Bordeaux Copy a unique object whose peculiarity is to be
both a manuscript and a printed text.

teenth century, that "Montaigne's biography does not have to be written in order to know his character, his genius, the influence he received from his time and the influence he exercised. . . . Montaigne's life is all in the *Essais*."[16] There we find an interpretive credo that long remained dominant in Montaigne studies: it is pointless to look outside the *Essais*, because the book itself constitutes the author's biography. The *Essais* have even been approached as a full-fledged autobiography.[17] Couldn't the man's character, his passions, convictions, and frustrations, all be found in it? This biographical reading of the *Essais* was long based on the sincerity and honesty Montaigne claimed. His life, reconstructed on the basis of information gleaned from the *Essais*, made it possible to discern a unity of the man on the basis of a *uniform text*. Everything tended toward a single project, that of the fully realized man. The "last Montaigne" was already present in the "first Montaigne," in accord with a logic of the evolution of the text that is founded on a synthetic, unifying model. The two great specialists on Montaigne in the twentieth century, Pierre Villey[18] and Hugo Friedrich,[19] remained the prisoners of this illusion of a "finished" text and of the "consubstantiality" of the man and his work, basing their interpretations on ideas present *in* the *Essais* and discerning in them successive stages that led ineluctably to a kind of successful realization of a life, generally called "wisdom" (*sagesse*). Confronting a "finished" text—namely, the posthumous edition of the *Essais*—critics still tend to approach Montaigne through an evolutionary schema: Stoic, Epicurean, Skeptic, and finally sage—the order of this progression varying depending on the period.

Would Montaigne's name be known to history without the publication of his *Essais*? The answer is no. We are accustomed to seeing in him the creator of a new genre, the essay, rather than as a political man. Most of what we know about Montaigne is extracted from his *Essais*, because the documents that present him as a political actor are relatively rare. For that reason, it is difficult to speak of Montaigne's life without drawing on his writings. Most of Montaigne's biographers have succumbed to this easy solution and have borrowed heavily from the *Essais* in attempting to reconstruct his career as a public man. A large majority of these studies are content to adduce—often at second hand—a few public "moments" in Montaigne's life, such as the time he spent as mayor of Bordeaux, his conversations with Henry III and Henry of Navarre, his imprisonment, and such. But the goal is always a better understanding of the text of the *Essais*—which, we have to recognize, offer a view of the Wars of Religion and of many of the major events of his time attenuated by forgetfulness or by omission.

The argument advanced to make Montaigne an important political actor is the following: Montaigne (the sixteenth-century author), being Montaigne (the author incorporated into our modern literary canon), must necessarily have known the great men of his time and was undoubtedly admired by his contemporaries. How could it be otherwise? Who wouldn't want Montaigne to be at the royal Court, conversing with De Thou, Duplessis-Mornay, and Pasquier, or in regular correspondence with princes and military leaders? A few of these meetings and conversations actually took place, but they were almost always conjunctural and relatively exceptional. That does not mean, however, that Montaigne did not try to make his way into the closed milieus that were the Bordeaux parlement or the royal Court. Montaigne's personal ambition has not been granted the place it deserves. He has often been compared with other great writers and poets of the sixteenth century by attributing an exuberant sociability to him. This may be a retrospective illusion, for what critic would not have liked to meet the author of the *Essais* to speak with him about his book? At the opposite extreme from this approach we find the proponents of a Montaigne retired to his tower and silent about the political and religious tribulations during the Wars of Religion.

Today, the technique that consists in browsing through Montaigne's writings in order to extract the important moments of a life is still the point of departure for most biographies of him. Since the nineteenth century, biographers of Montaigne have emphasized the private character of the man, and they have invariably seen his work against the same background. His service as a member of the Bordeaux parlement, mayor, and negotiator are not forgotten, but they hardly influence the construction of the author's literary persona. Public life and private life usually remain separate. However, we must mention a few exceptions to this rule, notably the biographies by Alphonse Grün,[20] Bayle Saint John,[21] Théophile Malvezin,[22] and Donald Frame,[23] which accord politics an important place and try to free themselves from an essentially literary perspective on Montaigne's life.[24]

Nonetheless, the great majority of biographies of Montaigne use history as a background, a decorative mural that serves to bring out the author's singularity. The important stages in Montaigne's life, corresponding to historical events, strengthen a reading that is primarily literary or philosophical, in which the different "Montaignes"—those of childhood, youth, maturity, and wisdom—fit nicely into one another. The goal is to demonstrate the coherence and unity of the text by playing down the role of political and religious turmoil, which are supposed to have left the essayist indifferent. The events or experiences of a life, insofar as they correspond to stages, have meaning only in the apotheosis of a last Montaigne: wise, moderate, and tolerant. Thus the first Montaigne merely offers us a preparatory reading of the last Montaigne, the only one truly worthy of study because he is the objectified sum of the preceding Montaignes. This cumulative reading of Montaigne and his writings expresses the main difficulty the modern reader confronts, a difficulty accentuated by editorial choices that often amalgamate the various printings of the *Essais*, of which the posthumous edition of 1595 is supposed to be the logical outcome. I shall propose, on the contrary, that readings of the editions of the *Essais* that are distinct and separate in time are better to gauge the multiple printings from 1572 to 1592.

The way in which Montaigne approaches politics has little to do with what the *Essais* have become for us in the twenty-first century. When he translated Raymond Sebond, edited Estienne de La Boétie, or composed his *Essais*, Montaigne was far from imagining a renown that was ultimately rather slow in coming and was essentially posthumous. For him, writing and publishing led to an immediate *benefit* that we can try to quantify. This gain is economic for the printer and symbolic for the author. Getting published corresponds to expectations, because we always write for someone else. The various editions of the *Essais* emanate from strategies elaborated on the basis of logics that differ in time; they take into consideration the ideology of the period; for example, what is "outside the book" (the *hors-livre*), the social function it occupies both for the author and for the reader. For instance, we have to ask what the author's expectations were. Publication strategies are typically constructed on an anticipation of the impact the book will have on the readers targeted and the possible "returns" on this investment. For that reason, an analysis of Montaigne's readership is indispensable for interpreting the books he translated, edited, or wrote. Similarly, the reception of a cultural object implies positioning its author in a social, political, or professional network and requires that others be able to identify this object. The categories and genres current in the Renaissance certainly influenced the subjective choices Montaigne made. It would be paradoxical to offer a biography of Montaigne solely in the light of what the author was willing to tell us about his public life, because this political experience necessarily transforms the idea that the individual can have of his private life. His particular remarks are inevitably part of a period's discourse on the same subject.

This biography of Montaigne closely connects him with the political activity of the groups, orders, or social classes with which he was associated at various times in his life. Whether it was the milieu of the parlement, the Bordeaux bourgeoisie, the middle-level nobility of Guyenne, or the royal Courts in Paris and Nérac, Montaigne understood his publication enterprises in relation to objective expectations on the part of the groups to which he was attached at certain points in his life. Always aware of his reader, Montaigne used him/her as a means of achieving goals that were initially political before they became literary. However, we must not overestimate Montaigne's importance on the historical level. He was a member of the minor nobility, and his "château" was far from being among the most sumptuous of his region. In Montaigne's time, "nobility" was a diluted term. It was also a status—or rather a way of life—that Montaigne was later to claim. Until 1580, when he was approaching fifty, he had achieved nothing noteworthy on either the public or private level. The testimonies of his contemporaries and the memoirs written at the time accord the author of the *Essais* only a small place. No one presents him as a major political actor of the end of the sixteenth century. We find references to Montaigne in the archives, but they are not as important as biographers have claimed. Montaigne played a political role between 1580 and 1588, but that was the case for many other minor lords in Guyenne. His name was hardly on everyone's lips, and we have to keep his political influence in proportion. Thus it is important to avoid the anachronisms resulting from an a posteriori evaluation of Montaigne's place in the history of philosophy and literature.

Some critics have tried to restore a historical dimension to Montaigne, but the studies that have taken this path have been interested only secondarily in publication history, and thus ignore the particular functions of each publication, not only of the *Essais* but also of other texts with which Montaigne is associated. Moreover, biographers who make Montaigne a moralist often adopt an idealistic bias. According to that way of reading, Montaigne always offers a truer and more accurate view of his period. Holed up in his observation tower, he is supposed to have attained an objectivity never equaled by his contemporaries. In my view, this is an error in judgment and method, because the position that claims that the *Essais* express moral truths inevitably leads to an essentialization of Montaigne's thought. On the basis of a "wisdom" present in the *Essais*, there is then a risk of transforming Montaigne's declarations and judgments into maturely considered axioms. That is the whole danger of formulas, aphorisms, and maxims. Hence we will seek to qualify personal judgments by always integrating them into social and cultural practices. Moreover, this approach is in accord with what Montaigne recommends when he says he prefers to project the image of a man devoted to "the moderate measure."[25] We will see that he anticipates and pursues his ambitions, maneuvering and intriguing in the same way as those in his cohort. Our procedure will therefore seek to contextualize Montaigne's remarks as much as possible and to situate them in the practices of orders, groups, networks, and clienteles.

Is the notion of the self useful for understanding a work in its social and historical context? To the specialist in literature, the answer seems obvious. Yes, clearly, the expression of the self intrigues and fascinates us. As if this concept allowed us to capture the essence of an author and transform it into a model. But in my view this quest for Montaigne's self is both deceptive and doomed to fail, because it confines the author *to his book*, while at the same time making it seem that his experience of people and the world exist only in his difference from others. What do we find, in the end? A genius who admits of no generalization and is distinguished by his exception. It is tempting to classify in this category authors like Shakespeare, Cervantes, Descartes, and others of the same caliber who form the literary and philosophical canons. Montaigne, on the contrary, interests us by his predictable side when he acts in a codified system of social and professional possibilities, when he acts and thinks like others. Distinguishing oneself from colleagues and companions is not always in good taste, and one has to assert in a timely way one's membership in the group or the order that has allowed one to occupy a place in a social and political network, or to attain a position or an office. If Montaigne often differentiates himself from his neighbors and fellow citizens when he presents himself in the *Essais*, he also shared their ideas when he confronted in his turn the same practical problems. Like many of his contemporaries, he knew how to take advantage of his political options, adapted to the current situation, and took responsibility for his allegiance to the powerful.

There are two ways of proceeding in order to connect the events in a life with a literary or philosophical object. The first is accepting a form of psychological determinism, a variant of the "the man and his works" syndrome. This approach had its adepts in the early twentieth century, and whole series of books were even created on this model, which interprets a text on the basis of a reconstructed psychology (what was then called "the writer's character"), or even in certain cases on the basis of a psychoanalysis. According to this interpretive schema, the text is explained by the writer's strength of character, his personality, emotions, and feelings. The second approach brings biographical elements to bear on the understanding of the text: this is by far the most widespread method today. The goal is to elaborate a relatively vast tableau that makes it possible to place a work in its historical and political context. The author thus becomes the interpreter of a weltanschauung. His particular experiences can be understood only in the framework of an epistemology. Liberated from the problems of psychologism, this second way of seeing things falls, however, into another trap, that of reflection. In fact, according to this type of analysis, the literary work is part of the ideological superstructure, which is itself the result of the mode of production and the society's economic infrastructure. This positivist reductionism generally makes the author and the artist simply agents caught in the implacable mechanism of the abstract functioning of power, classes, and the state. The captive of an ideology of which he is not conscious, the author is supposed to merely reproduce a discourse or ideas that are in the air at the time. The biography of an author is assumed to be representative of a group, or even of a social class, which is the only thing worth studying.[26]

A happy medium between these two approaches is obviously desirable. That is what both Durkheim and Bourdieu sought to produce in their own ways. How can a place be restored to the individual and to the expression of his subjectivity without losing sight of his membership in the social, political, and ideological structures that shape him? This "middle road" seems particularly pertinent for the study of Montaigne. The two methods described above are a problem that concerns the author of the *Essais*. Tracing the contours of Montaigne's character does not allow us to understand a book written over almost a quarter of a century. Montaigne's celebrated "self" cannot be seen as a fixed object—whence the impossibility of speaking of a character or personality of Montaigne. Movement—that is, the successive transformations of a multifaceted text and its author—has to be taken into consideration.[27] However, the notion of movement can lead to a new critical difficulty, because we have to reject the idea of a dialectic of Montaigne's thought based on a quantity of experiences that, when added to one another, would objectively define a future behavior. Montaigne sweeps that methodological premise away with a single sentence: "Myself now and myself a while ago are indeed two; but when better, I simply cannot say."[28] No wisdom accumulated through experience, no self that establishes itself. Whence the necessity of approaching the composition of the *Essais* via a biographical approach that is limited in time and based on a schema that gives priority to the *moyenne durée*.[vi] The problem raised here is that of the limits of the biographical approach that tends to accumulate the important events in a life on the basis of a simple chronology, adding up the experiences and connecting them to one another in an implacable logic that leads to a form of good sense and intellectual maturity. When studying Montaigne, it is impossible to talk about an *accumulated value* of the past. His various experiences do not form a kind of multilayered pastry, because they belong to different worlds. The parlement, the Court, the embassy to Rome, and the mayor's office in Bordeaux do not necessarily fit into a unique and rectilinear itinerary. Montaigne played several different roles, and his publications correspond to differing life scenarios that often contradict one another.

A biography of Montaigne must therefore be anchored in the political practices of the time. Without denying their philosophical and literary contribution, I have chosen to give a predominant place to Montaigne's political experiences *outside* the *Essais*. In fact, retrospective readings that seek to discover in the *Essais* the traces of a public life are too often impressionistic. As Pierre Bourdieu wrote, "nothing is more misleading than the illusion created by hindsight in which all the traces of a life, such as the works of an artist or the events at a biography, appear as the realization of an essence that seems to pre-exist them."[29] This remark applies to the reception of Montaigne and to his biography. Such a retrospective reading can only bring out the formative moments—which are usually the only ones known—of a life that invariably tends toward the realiza-

---

[vi] "Middle length of time," as opposed to *longue durée* and *courte durée* ("long-term" and "short term"). *Longue durée* and *courte durée* are widely used in French historiography. [Trans.]

tion of a project conceived at the outset. Here I refer, of course, to Montaigne's political ideas, but especially to his career objectives *in politics*, to his ambitions, which were not always realized. In this way we reject any cumulative reading of the *Essais* and give, for example, an important place to the short chapters in the first two books of the *Essais*, which allowed Montaigne to make his entrance on the political stage.

In a book that constantly claims to be consubstantial with a body of flesh and blood, it is hard to distinguish between the public man and the private man—which sometimes fuse, no matter what Montaigne says.[30] Toward the end of his life, the author of the *Essais* tried to impose on his reader a sharp separation between introspection, on the one hand, and on the other, conjunctural remarks connected with political events that he underwent without approving of them. To be critical, one has to have an opportunity to express oneself. This remark applies to past centuries as well as to our own period. Keeping silent is not always a sign of impotence or acquiescence; sometimes it is also a strategic decision, and thus fundamentally a political act. Montaigne's failure to mention certain things has been seen as proof of his detachment with regard to society. Despite a few studies that have proposed a systematic reframing of the *Essais* in their political and social context, Montaigne's silence concerning the events of his time still impresses the contemporary reader, who sees in this silence a proof of wisdom. Some have even gone so far as to read between the lines of the *Essais* in order to show that Montaigne could not have expressed himself overtly regarding the bloody and calamitous events that punctuated the civil wars in France. This is to ignore the fact that pamphlets, diatribes, factums, and other forms of politically engaged literature proliferated in the sixteenth century. Others have argued that Montaigne must have necessarily expressed his views in anonymous publications, as if he had no other choice. This is far from reality. Like many authors of the late Renaissance, Montaigne spoke up when he felt like it and did not mince his words. If he sometimes chose to keep silent, it was not out of fear of censorship or possible repression, it was a political choice, that is, a choice made on the basis of precise interests that had to do primarily with career strategies.

Montaigne thought that the political events of his day would not stand the test of time. Let us quote, for example, his curious analysis of the Wars of Religion in France: "It will be a lot if a hundred years from now people remember in a general way that in our time there were civil wars in France."[31] This way of distancing himself from religious and political upheavals must, however, be interpreted with caution, because Montaigne then had political pretensions that he abandoned only after 1588. His château was located at the heart of a zone of civil conflict, and his desire to forget the Wars of Religion may also testify to a will to write a history as seen by a man who was enduring events while deploring his failure to participate in them to a greater degree. It is this kind of *political questions* that are asked here. Without totally abstracting from the literary work, I focus on Montaigne's engagement and his political accommodations, a series of careers that he envisaged at the international and national levels, but which were essentially local—or rather, regional. There were eight civil wars in France during Montaigne's lifetime, the first seven of which—from 1562 to 1580—preceded the first publication of the *Essais*. We can imagine how much these wars might have weighed on the conception, composition, and publication of the book that made Montaigne famous. His public and political careers were also marked by thirty years of religious conflict. Episodes of increasingly violent confrontations, moments of relative civil peace and stubborn negotiations, and lapses back into even more bloody incidents form the background of his activity as a man of letters.

Like many of his contemporaries who came from the same milieu, Montaigne could dream of rising to the most elevated offices of the state, perhaps even becoming a royal steward or ambassador. He obtained only municipal responsibilities, except when he served briefly as an intermediary between Henry III and the king of Navarre. His political itinerary underwent several ups and downs caused by reversals of situations that were impossible to foresee. Confronted by the events that marked his period, Montaigne was a prudent, level-headed, wait-and-see kind of man who emphasized these character traits as advantages in politics. Immoderate and extreme engagement was not in Montaigne's nature. Throughout his life he maintained an indefectible loyalty to the established authority, whatever it was. He was born a Catholic and remained one, refusing to confuse religion and politics—a very paradoxical approach at this period. In a region where religious and ideological conversions were frequent, not so much for reasons of personal belief but rather out of political opportunism or economic interest, Montaigne was a man of convictions. On the basis of his own experiences, he finally fell back on a conception of politics that ran counter to the practices current in his period. His failures in politics nonetheless allowed him to find the right tone for a new literary and philosophical genre that he built on the ruins of his career in public service. He made several attempts at politics before his book transformed him into a literary monument.

In the end, Montaigne's *Essais* constitute an attempt to reappropriate politics in the wake of the Saint Bartholomew's Day massacre. This attempt was not unique; it was situated in a more general intellectual enterprise in which we could classify Jean Bodin's *Six Livres de la République* (1576) and François de la Noue's *Discours politiques et militaires* (1587). Following some of his contemporaries, Montaigne refused to fall into the excessive reaction of the supporters of Innocent Gentillet's *Discours . . . contre Nicolas Machiavel* (1576) and proposed in his own way an innovative configuration of politics in which actors could serve the king and their country with full transparency. For Montaigne, there were too many words, too many speeches, too many books. In these Wars of Religion, politics had to take the high ground and do what it could to slow a course of events marked by constant acceleration. The *Essais*—in their different editions published during Montaigne's lifetime—represent political moments dissociated from one another, but they also reminded their author of the misfortunes of his public life. One can often learn from mistakes, and Montaigne's book never claims to be a dogmatic political treatise at a time when what had to be done was to reinvent a dynamic conception of government and of power in general. Negotiation was necessary, even if it was often doomed to fail. That mattered little; what counted was to preserve, at any price, the civility necessary to maintain society. In their own way, the *Essais* helped decenter political discourse in order to give it a new aim that was more private and less dependent on the effects of belonging to a group, a clan, or a faith. That is certainly why Montaigne belonged to no alliance, no league, no brigade.

As conversations seeking to expose humans' political dimension, the *Essais* also explore the possibility of an ethics reconciling private morality in its universal dimension (both ancient and Christian) with a practice of government founded on compromise and jurisprudence. Montaigne does not like the model of political affiliation proposed by Machiavelli in chapter XVIII of *The Prince*; he prefers transparency and candor. Pretense is sometimes necessary, but it must not be taken for a philosophy. Ideally, Montaigne's political project corresponds to his literary project and can be summed up in this confession: "Had I been placed among those nations which are said to live still in the sweet freedom of nature's first laws, I assure you I should very gladly have portrayed myself here entire and wholly naked."[32] The pluperfect subjunctive Montaigne uses here and sometimes elsewhere expresses a perplexity, if not an impossibility. We can doubt this claim and turn against Montaigne the same reproach he makes, not without irony, against the Indians of the New World: "All this is not too bad—but what's the use? [He] doesn't wear breeches."[33] This passage contradicts the principle enounced in the preface "To the Reader" and demonstrates the contradiction inherent to Montaigne's task as a writer. At the Court as in Rome, it would have been impossible to show himself "naked"—a fact that Montaigne, as a political man from Aquitaine, knew very well. Aware of this fracture between an ideal but impossible world and an all-too-pragmatic world in which intrigues and barbarity reigned, Montaigne always remained on the side of political realism, but a realism tempered by a constant critique of its excesses.

All political people know the euphoria of victory and the loneliness of defeat and disgrace. As did Henri de Mesmes who, after having served the king as a *podestà* in Siena and refused an ambassadorship in Rome, returned to France after the defeat at Saint-Quentin in order to "enjoy a repose that he placed above all the goods conferred by fortune."[vii] His disillusionment with politics "led him to abandon the court and live henceforth in retirement."[34] Here we have the feeling that we are reading Montaigne. Political life consists of withdrawals and returns. Princes pass, and their counselors and servants have to find new positions or adapt to the new requirements of the established power. In politics, one spends a large part of one's time awaiting favors and benefits that do not always come. Under the Old Régime, there was not enough room for all the ambitious people at the Court, and only a few favorites succeeded in gaining access to the restricted circle of the princes. The others were forced to wait for better days. The change in France's rulership following the death of Henry II was hardly propitious for Henri de Mesmes, who was also a brilliant jurist and a skilled diplomat. His career testifies to a series of ups and downs that were inevitable in the religious and political turbulence of his time.

With each new king, each new chancellor, positions were redistributed. In Montaigne's case—at a lesser level of service to the state—we find a similarly functioning of political life. Henri de Mesmes evaluated his own situation at the time of the death of Henry II: "I was disposed, after his death, to travel less and court less, and I thought that it would be better for me to stick to my books and my office."[35] A wise decision on the part of this contemporary of Montaigne. The author of the *Essais* pondered this question in turn after the assassination of Henry III. An exit from political life can represent a new departure. Can one merge Henri de Mesmes the member of the Council of State and servant of the king with Henri de Mesmes the author of memoirs? What are the points of intersection between these two careers that were, nonetheless, conceived as linear and distinct in time? I have asked the same questions about Montaigne, councillor in the parlement, mayor of Bordeaux, and essayist.

[vii] *Biens de fortune.* According to Brunetto Latini (thirteenth century), there are three of these: wealth, power, and glory ("richece, signourie, et gloire"). [Trans.]

PART ONE

Ambitions

CHAPTER I

The Eyquems' Social Ascension

"And if I were to live a long time, I do not doubt that I would forget my own name."[1] Montaigne's name constitutes the author's memory and incarnates the history of a family and its social ascension, but we still need to know what name Montaigne is talking about. Is it Michel Eyquem, his patronymic, or Michel de Montaigne, the name of his estate and his seigneury? The answer to this question differs over time, and the passage from Eyquem to Montaigne is a textbook case for the study of the social history of the class of wealthy merchants and bourgeois who became gentlemen at the end of the fifteenth and throughout the sixteenth centuries. The author of the *Essais* was the first member of his family to give up the name of his ancestors and retain only the name of his seigneury. In fact, the biography of "Michel, seigneur Montaigne" begins long before his birth. To understand his familial milieu, we have to study the social ascension of the house of Montaigne that started in the middle of the fourteenth century. The economic transformations of the fifteenth and sixteenth centuries favored the emergence and domination of well-off merchant families who had settled in the great European cities.

Political power slowly but surely shifted toward centers of exchange and commerce, particularly cities built on navigable waterways or at the mouths of rivers. Bordeaux was ideally situated to become a hub serving most European ports. Its access to the ocean gave a major advantage to those whose main activity consisted in warehousing merchandise and sending it on by sea to new markets. In the fifteenth century, during the decline of the English presence in the region, Bordeaux was a land of opportunity, and a significant number of merchants emigrated there from other parts of France and also from Spain and Portugal. For example, an edict of 1464 authorized emigrants to settle in Bordeaux in houses they found empty and to obtain letters of naturalization. Very early on, the wheels of commerce and the administrative control of the city were concentrated in the hands of a few families that had been able to benefit from the commercial development of Guyenne after the departure of the English.

In the fourteenth century, the name Eyquem was quite common in the Bordeaux region. It was spelled "Ayquem" and "Aiquem" as well as "Eyquem" and is found in several localities, including Mérignac, Taillan, Pessac, Camblanes, Blanquefort, and Langon. The Eyquems of Blanquefort—from whom the Montaignes descended—settled in Bordeaux in the early fourteenth century and joined the *jurade*[i] as early as 1358, a sign that they had already achieved a significant economic success. Wealthy Bordeaux families formed a bourgeoisie that was little inclined to discuss its origins. Focused on the future, they practiced endogamy to increase their status in the city and to favor their access to municipal political power. Their goal was to advance their social position by means of marriages with other great bourgeois families. In the city, a political void allowed these families to take control of the administration in order to manage the regulation of their economic and commercial activities. By the middle of the fifteenth century, English power had grown considerably weaker in Guyenne, and in 1453 the battle of Castillon put an end to three centuries of English domination in Aquitaine. A parlement[ii] was established in 1462, and the city's privileges were approved and confirmed by Charles VIII in 1483. The king was generous toward the bourgeois of Bordeaux, declaring them free and exempt from having to pay subsidies and land taxes or make compulsory loans. Troops could not be billeted in the city without the consent of the mayor and the magistrates, and the city's guard as well as its police were entrusted to the citizens. However, after the English left, Guyenne's share of the land tax to be collected in Aquitaine was doubled. In this context of European expansion and political reforms, the city of Bordeaux underwent an unprecedented economic growth at the end of the fifteenth and the beginning of the sixteenth centuries.

Under Francis I the *Anciennes Coutumes de Guyenne* ("ancient customary laws of Guyenne") were reformed to take into account the local bourgeoisie's demands. The three estates of the sénéchaussée of Guyenne assembled in February 1520 to modify the old *Coutumier*. Several articles were suppressed or changed and new ones were added. The work lasted five months and the reformed *Coutumier* went into effect toward the end of 1527. Its territory was extended to include the former sénéchaussée of Bordeaux. The new customary law of Guyenne, which heavily favored the bourgeoisie, consisted of 117 articles written in a rather disorderly fashion and without much equity. Questions of inheritance and testamentary succession strongly recentered customary law around the transmission of property, and the goal of the great majority of the

---

[i] Roughly, the city council; its members were called "jurats." [Trans.]

[ii] Under the Old Régime in France, the *parlements* were provincial appellate courts (not legislative assemblies). They heard cases of all kinds, especially relating to taxation, and the Crown's laws and edicts were not official in their respective jurisdictions until the parlements had granted their assent by publishing them. [Trans.]

articles was to provide better protection for private property and to favor bour-geois property owners over the feudal territorial rights of noble landlords.[iii] The first article sets the tone of this rewriting of customary law. It stipulates that every son of a merchant family engaged in commerce or other business (bank-ing, brokerage, purchasing) "can make commitments without his father's con-sent, in matters concerning merchandise or business."[2] For example, children had the right to do business under their own names without depending on the authority of their fathers. In the same spirit of liberalizing mercantile law, Ar-ticle V reorganized the law governing the legacy of goods to descendants by specifying that lineal transmission henceforth always had priority over feudal law. Inheritances, successions, transmissions, and donations of buildings, as well as the regulation of rents and mortgages, were subjected to new interpreta-tions favorable to the rising bourgeoisie and represented more than sixty articles in the *Coutumes générales de la ville de Bordeaux et de la sénéchaussée de Guy-enne* between 1520 and 1527. The revision of customary law at the beginning of the sixteenth century was the end result of a long process of political redistribu-tion in Bordeaux and in Guyenne.

The Eyquems were among the small number of families that very soon came to hold the reins of the city's administration. Montaigne's ancestors made a for-tune selling woad[iv] and smoked herring. The Eyquems followed the social trajec-tory typical of wealthy merchant families and used their economic success to gain access to political power. No matter what Montaigne says about it, his fam-ily's past in Guyenne is not of noble origin, but is instead associated with com-merce and merchandise, which may explain why the historical periods men-tioned in the *Essais* are mainly Antiquity and the immediate present. The last hundred years are not referred to anywhere in the text, because for obvious rea-sons Montaigne is not interested in retracing the history of his family. There are only vague remarks about his grandparents and great-grandparents, on both the paternal and maternal sides. Of course, Montaigne talks about his father and brothers, but he remains almost completely silent about his earlier ancestors. We are told only that he was born of "a race famous for integrity,"[3] and that his nobility goes back "more than a hundred years before me."[4] The limit of one hundred years is not chosen by accident. In the sixteenth century, the rules gov-erning membership in the nobility varied depending on the region.[5] In his

---

[iii] The oldest text of this *Coutume* was printed in Bordeaux in 1528 by Jean Guyart. The *Coutume* was reprinted by Simon Millanges in 1611 and 1617, and again by Jacques Mongiron Millanges in 1661 and 1666. A new, more rigorous and systematic edition was published in the eighteenth century by Alexis and Delphin de Lamothe, *Coutumes du ressort du Parlement de Guyenne; avec un commentaire pour l'intelligence du texte, et les arrest rendus en interprétation*. Bordeaux: Chez les Frères Labottiere, 1769.

[iv] A blue dyestuff and/or the plant from which it is made. [Trans.]

Traité des nobles et des vertus dont ils sont formés, François de L'Alouëte proposes that nobles be forced to produce "once in their lives a description and genealogy of the race from which they come and descend from father and from mother to the fourth degree, and beyond as far as they can go and extend themselves,"[6] and to deposit these descriptions in the hands of the bailiffs or seneschals so that they could be consulted in case of need. In Aquitaine, custom required a person to have "lived nobly" for one hundred years on his land before he could claim to be noble "by prescription."[v] Usually leaving aside this quantitative conception of nobility, Montaigne prefers a qualitative definition, reminding his reader repeatedly that he behaves as a lord and lives nobly on his lands.

Belonging to the nobility of the sword,[vi] the only noble race,[7] also meant performing military service. Montaigne wholeheartedly adhered to what was called the "soldierly" spirit of the nobility,[8] even if he did not wear the sword into combat as his father had done. This correspondence between the social order and the main activity of the members of the nobility is often foregrounded in the *Essais*. In contrast, the world of commerce and merchandise remains a taboo subject. For Montaigne, money distorts human relations, corrupts traditional values, and injures the spirit of the nobility. He prefers battlefields to markets. It suffices to see the way in which he talks about the Indians of the New World and projects onto them his idea of nobility to see that he fully adheres to the military and chivalric principles that defined the noble ideal. Marked by this idealization of military values and their transformation into virtues, Montaigne reminds us that his father participated in the military campaigns in Italy during Francis I's conquest and then loss of Milan. He describes himself as a soldier even though he took part in no battles and witnessed only one military siege—perhaps two—as an observer and not as a knight in the service of the king. If Montaigne is proud to be a Gascon, that is partly because of the military reputation the young men of his region enjoyed at the time. He repeatedly emphasizes this origin that made him an excellent horseman and indirectly authorized him to assert his membership in the French nobility. In his *Essais* Montaigne always distinguishes himself from the mercantile class (*mercadence*) and the world of the bourgeoisie.

---

[v] A legal term referring to the right to something on the ground of long-established use. [Trans.]

[vi] The term *noblesse d'épée* was rarely used to qualify nobility and became widespread only in the seventeenth century, almost always in opposition to the *noblesse de robe*. Here this expression will nonetheless be used as a social category valid in the time of Montaigne, because it illustrates quite well the structural difference that opposes the "nobles de race," that is, those who carried a sword, from the "nobles de service," who wore a long robe and were associated with a parlement or occupied an administrative office they had received or purchased.

A Family Matter

Montaigne's great-grandfather, Ramon Eyquem, was born in 1402; Ramon's father was Martin (?) Eyquem and his mother was Jeanne de Gaujac, the daughter
of a family that exported wine, salted fish, and woad in Bordeaux. Ramon took
over the business of his uncle Guillart Eyquem, and around 1440 he married
Isabeau de Ferraignes, the sister of Henri de Ferraignes, one of the first members of the Bordeaux parlement. The latter was connected, by his first marriage,
to the noble Madeleine de La Mothe, the daughter of Jean de La Mothe, lord of
Cambes, and by his second marriage, to the noble Jehanne du Puy, the daughter
of Hélie du Puy, lord of La Jarthe. The marriage linking the Eyquems to the
Ferraigneses marks the starting point of an alliance that was profitable for the
Eyquems both financially and as a way of cultivating useful relationships.
Thanks to her brother, Isabeau also offered her husband an opportunity to gain
access to new power groups. From the middle of the fifteenth century on, the
bourgeois family of the Eyquems signed its notarized documents with the title
"honorable man Ramon Ayquem, merchant in the parish of Saint-Michel and
bourgeois of Bordeaux." He was among the city's influential merchants and
joined the *jurade* in 1472.

Ramon Eyquem's everyday life was completely focused on pecuniary matters. Like many bourgeois who had grown rich, he invested his profits in real
estate. In a logic of accumulating lands and houses, he reasoned and acted as a
merchant would and was not yet cut out to be a noble. He left this concern
about nobility to his children; his role was limited to preparing the terrain for
the generations to come. Everything he did had as its aim to make his family's
name known and respected. Ramon was a prosperous merchant, and he rapidly
made himself known as an "entrepreneur" in all sorts of commercial projects.
He established his home on the Rue de la Rousselle in Bordeaux and began by
exporting mainly salted fish, but he soon diversified his activities and began
selling wine and woad, depending on the market opportunities. Like other big
merchants of the time—the Carles, the Le Ferrons, the Pontacs, and the
Makanams—Ramon Eyquem took an active part in the city's political life,
which greatly helped him in his personal affairs. At the end of the fifteenth
century, the wine trade had supplanted that in woad and had become the main
source of income for the bourgeois of Bordeaux and the region.[9]

In 1477, one year before his death, Ramon Eyquem bought the noble houses
of Montaigne and Belbeys, in the barony of Montravel, along with their lands,
vineyards, woods, and mills, from Guillaume Duboys, for 900 Bordeaux
francs.[10] This transaction made it possible to move from "Eyquem" to "Montaigne." The estate of Montaigne is located on a hill between the Dordogne
River and a stream called the Lidoire, and is now situated within the depart-

ments of Gironde and Dordogne, about forty-five kilometers due east of Bordeaux. The buildings and lands of Montaigne and Belbeys had first been sold to Thomas Pons, Lord of Clermont, for 300 gold royals and an annual income of thirty *livres tournois*. But Pons was unable to raise the sum asked and Guillaume Duboys had the sale canceled on October 10, 1477. The same day, he sold his lands to Ramon Eyquem and promised to transmit to him the list of the *esporles*[vii] for the past six years. The payment of this fee was required when there was a change of owner. The amount of the *esporle* was generally modest, but this tax had an important symbolic function because it made it possible to anticipate the prescription of the landed seigneury and to assert the new lord's right over the property in the event of a challenge. On November 30, 1477, Ramon Eyquem took possession of his land and the noble house of Montaigne, 103 years before the first publication of the *Essais*. In accord with the custom associated with the transmission of property, Ramon had traveled to his lands in the company of the former owner, who entered his former home in Ramon's company and then left alone, witnessed by all the neighbors who had gathered there for the occasion. Ramon spoke a few words before a notary and then sat down to table, which allowed him to be officially recognized as the new master of the estate.[11]

Around 1450, two children had been born to Ramon and Isabeau Eyquem: Grimon, Montaigne's grandfather, and Pey (Pierre), their second son. In documents notarized in the 1470s, Grimon and Pey are described as "honorable men . . . merchants of the parish of Saint-Michel." Ramon also had two daughters, Pérégrina and Audeta. In a process of marriage and mixture between the rising bourgeoisie and a nobility in decline, Ramon married his daughters to Jean de Lansac and Bernard de Verteuilh, respectively; Lansac and Verteuilh were the heirs of noble families that had found it necessary, for financial reasons, to connect themselves with families from the bourgeoisie. In 1473, while he was getting ready to go on a pilgrimage to Saint James of Compostela, Ramon wrote a testament in which he left his wife a large number of buildings and lands, provided monetary dowries for his two daughters, and designated his two sons, Grimon and Pey, as universal heirs.[viii] He died in June 1478, less than a year after acquiring the seigneury of Montaigne. In 1488, after the death of his brother, who had no children, Grimon remained alone to turn the Eyquems' affairs to good account. Thanks to his acute business sense, especially in exports, his fortune grew considerably. He specialized in the trade in wine and salted fish with England and Spain, which led Scaliger to say, not without irony,

[vii] A payment due by a vassal to his lord in order to obtain his approbation before a sale.

[viii] In sixteenth-century France, a "universal heir" was not (as is today the case) the sole heir, but rather the "principal heir." [Trans.]

that Montaigne's father was a fishmonger. A document from 1477 presents Grimon as a ship owner who is chartering a caravel, the *Nicholas de Saint-Paul*, to transport fifty casks of wine to the port of La Crotoy in Picardy.[12] His commercial profits allowed him to increase his real estate holdings and to buy more and more forests, houses, and lands around his noble house of Montaigne.[13]

Like his father, Grimon became a Bordeaux notable: elected to the *jurade* in 1485, at the age of thirty-five, he continued in that office for eighteen years before becoming provost of Bordeaux in 1503. Around 1490, he married Jeanne Dufour, the daughter of a merchant and *jurat*[ix] of the city. They had three daughters and five sons, including Pierre, Montaigne's father, who was born on September 20, 1495. In 1485, Grimon Eyquem was still signing official documents as an "honorable man," "merchant and bourgeois," or "bourgeois of Bordeaux." Ramon had enabled his family to acquire a noble land, but Grimon made the Eyquems' fortune and consolidated their patrimony in real estate. However, for professional reasons he continued to reside in the ancestral house on the Rue de la Rousselle, where the Bordeaux bourgeoisie had settled.[14] The Eyquems had owned this house since the middle of the fifteenth century. It remained their main domicile, and even Montaigne lived there for at least three years, after his marriage to Françoise de La Chassaigne in September 1565, and until the death of his father in 1568, before he returned to live in the château of Montaigne, whose owner he had become as his father's universal heir. The "château" in question was a middle-sized building that did not yet have its towers or surrounding walls. There were far more imposing châteaus in the region than the one Ramon Eyquem had bought.

During the last years of the fifteenth century, Grimon Eyquem was split between two ways of life: that of a commoner residing in Bordeaux and that of a new noble who seldom visited his lands, but who had already begun to let time do the work of attaching the new name (Montaigne) to his family. The best way of being considered noble, without belonging to the nobility of the sword, was to "live nobly" on one's lands in order to be recognized one day as a noble by prescription. Grimon could not claim to be "noble" without ceasing his mercantile activities, a step he hesitated to take. To do that he had to break all ties with a commoner's life and spend more time on his estate in order to establish his reputation as a noble. That is what he finally did in 1508, when he handed his business over to one of his employees, Peyrot de Brusselay, and left the world of commerce and merchandise. He had not been able to decide to take this step earlier because he feared that he might lose his noble house and the title associated with it. As a result of an administrative and judicial suit, the sale of the noble house of Montaigne was contested for thirty years by the Duboys heirs.

[ix] A sworn municipal magistrate. [Trans.]

The transaction between the descendants of the former owner of the estate of Montaigne and Ramon Eyquem was ratified only in 1509, after Grimon paid 120 *livres* to seal the sale contract of 1477 with children of Belbeys.[15]

This belated agreement between the Duboyses and Grimon Eyquem played a decisive role in the Montaignes' acquisition of nobility. The notarized documents bear the mark of Grimon's evolution and testify to his social ambitions at the beginning of the sixteenth century. In fact, when he was on the point of giving up the commoner's life, Grimon no longer hesitated to strike out the word "honorable," replacing it with that of "noble," as is shown by a document dated April 17, 1509.[16] Before a notary, Grimon had the descendants of the former owner promise to "hand over and deliver the papers and information" about the two houses of Montaigne and Belbeys. He had to have proofs attesting to his recent social status. At this point Grimon began to present himself as the "noble man[x] Grimon Ayquem, squire, lord of the noble houses of Montaigne and Belbeys." He lived on the income from his investments after he had consolidated the revenues from his domains, which came to 300 Bordeaux francs a year. The Eyquems had risen from the rank of well-off bourgeois to that of "country gentlemen" living on their assets. The cession of the noble house of Montaigne was legally settled, but the nobility of the family was not yet established. At that time, the title of "noble man . . . lord of . . ." referred to a series of different social realities: members of the nobility of the sword who had acquired their status on the battlefield over several centuries; country noblemen from prosperous peasant families; wealthy merchants who had bought their lands (and even the corresponding coats of arms)—that was the case for the Eyquems; the minor nobility ruined by wars and the movement of populations toward the cities; and councillors, lawyers, and magistrates who, thanks to the acquisition of their offices and their membership in the parlement, had been ennobled and sought in their turn to purchase noble lands where they could settle their families.[17]

In 1517, Grimon was actively trying to make his recent nobility recognized. In this effort to gain public recognition of his new status, he obtained a mandate from the parish priest of Blanquefort, Jean de Vivant, an honorary protonotary apostolic. In a document dating from the same year, Grimon signed himself "noble man lord of Montaigne and Mathacolom." He died in early 1519, leaving to his four sons the task of following the long road to nobility by prescription. His eldest son, Pierre, had three brothers: Thomas, who was a lawyer before becoming canon of the church of Saint-André in Bordeaux and parish

---

[x] Not to be confused with "nobleman"; *noble homme* designated a broader social category. For details, see below. [Trans.]

priest of Montaigne; Pierre Eyquem, lord of Gaujac, who, after having also had a go at being a lawyer, finally opted for the clergy and became canon of Saint-André upon the death of his brother Thomas; and Raymond, lord of Bussaguet, who had a long career as a councillor in the parlement of Guyenne. In conformity with the rules of succession in force at that time, the noble house of Montaigne went to Pierre, the eldest of the four brothers. The house on the Rue de Rousselle was divided up, but Pierre retained the largest share. Grimon had wished to give his eldest son the means of casting off the title of "bourgeois" in order to climb a further rung up the social hierarchy. Full of these aristocratic ambitions—revived by old age and the fear of dying while still labeled a merchant—he had decided to break with his business activities and make his eldest son a military man. Pierre would be a noble and a soldier; there was no better way of accelerating the family's ennoblement. Spending time on a battlefield was an expedient way of proving the nobility of an individual who had up to that point had only the title of a "gentleman on parchment," as the poet Tabourot des Accords put it in his *Bigarrures*. The sole nobility recognized was the nobility of the sword, which was won on the battlefield.

Grimon Eyquem began the transition from "Eyquem" to "Montaigne," but ridding himself of the status of bourgeois was not easy; it was probably for that reason that he took advantage of his meetings with the notary to sign his name as "Lord of Montaigne" every time he bought a new property, trying to erase the appellation "bourgeois" that appears in all his commercial transactions. Grimon was far from being a lord, but he continued the slow process begun by his father. He played by the rules so well that toward the end of his life he moved unhindered from "honorable man" to "noble man"—a few notarial documents even describe him as "squire" (*écuyer*), not without exaggeration. Slowly but surely, people forgot his mercantile origins. The various titles given Grimon allow us to understand better the slow development toward nobility and the transition, so delicate and important, from the title of "honorable man" to that of "noble man" in the sixteenth century. There is a subtle distinction between these two attributes. The "noble man" is still a bourgeois who lives on his investment income after having retired from commerce; he belongs to a class in transition that no longer wants to be bourgeois, but is not yet entirely noble. The noble man comes from an urban elite and aspires to political office, seeing in the parlement and in municipal responsibilities a means of social ascent. In Bordeaux, for example, "noble men" had a good chance of ending up on the *jurade*, an administrative entity that ran the city. Even though it did not yet have either a name or political representation at the regional level, this new class constituted a genuine gentry.[18] At the beginning of the sixteenth century, the Eyquems were steadfast members of the Bordeaux gentry. Their real estate holdings had greatly increased, and they were about to leave the status of commoners.

Pierre Eyquem played a crucial role in the Eyquems' slow but certain social transformation into Montaignes. We do not know exactly where he was educated. Montaigne tells us that his father had only a mediocre knowledge of letters and was "a man of very clear judgment for one who was aided only by experience and nature."[19] He is proud that his father embraced the military profession, the sole occupation worthy of the nobility. After his years at school, Pierre Eyquem was initially employed as a page in the noble house of Jean de Durfort, viscount of Duras,[20] before leaving for Italy, where he served in a company of archers that accepted only gentlemen. For ten years, he pursued the military profession, most of the time outside Guyenne and abroad. Montaigne writes that his father had "taken a very long part in the Italian wars."[21] He tells us how his father left a diary in which he noted in great detail all the military campaigns in which he had participated. Pierre Eyquem fought in Francis I's armies and returned to live in the château of Montaigne only in 1528, almost ten years after his father's death. He retained the military spirit all his life and was able to convey his sense of chivalric virtues and his taste for the art of war to his son Michel. But he was the only true soldier in the family.

By 1558 Pierre Eyquem could no longer meet his military obligations as a lord, as he acknowledged in a statement made before the assembly of the barons and vassals of the sénéchaussée of Périgord. He sought to transmit his passion for arms to his youngest son, Pierre Eyquem, lord of La Brousse, who was serving as a man-at-arms in the company of Burie, governor of Guyenne. In 1561, he ordered military equipment for his son from an armorer in Bordeaux, including a plastron, a saddle, and a head protector for a horse, "the front capable of resisting an arquebuse."[22] After many years spent fighting, the elder Pierre Eyquem could claim the title of "noble Pierre Eyquem, lord of Montaigne, squire" without anyone daring to doubt the well-foundedness of his titles, even if on his return from Italy he resided most of the time in the family's old house on the Rue de la Rousselle in Bordeaux. In a patrimonial document from 1531, he declared that he lived in Bordeaux. He did the same in 1543, when he bought another house on the Rue Gensan.[23] Moreover, he chose, perhaps in accord with a family tradition, to follow the path laid out by his father and grandfather by getting involved in the city's affairs, but without departing from his status as a noble, since at this time it was preferable, though not yet obligatory, to elect a mayor who came from the nobility. Despite their aristocratic pretensions, the Eyquems never separated themselves from the Bordeaux political milieu and continued to take an active part in the administration of the city. Their political engagement was constant from one generation to the next.

"Nobilibus parentibus"

On January 15, 1529, Pierre Eyquem married Antoinette de Louppes (Lopez)—
born in 1514—the daughter of Pierre de Louppes (Pedro Lopez) of Toulouse
and the niece, or perhaps the god-daughter, of Antoine de Louppes de Villeneuve (Villanueva), a Spanish merchant who had gotten rich by trading in
woad. The Louppes family may have descended from Jewish converts to Christianity, so-called Marranos or new Christians who had settled in London, Antwerp, Toulouse, and Bordeaux. In 1527 an arbitrage between Antoine de
Louppes and Martin de Castille mentions a delivery of 764 sacks of woad to the
port of Antwerp, ordered by "Pierre Loppes" merchant, residing in Antwerp.[24]
A little later on, we find Pierre de Louppes in Toulouse, where he joined the
capitoulat[xi] in 1542. In Bordeaux, Jean de Villeneuve, the son of Antoine de
Louppes, was ennobled when he gained a seat on the Great Council in 1553. The
Louppeses specialized in trading in woad, chiefly among the cities of London,
Antwerp, Bilbao, Bordeaux, and Toulouse.

The marriage of Pierre Eyquem and Antoinette de Louppes has caused
much ink to flow, and we have to linger on it for a moment. Antoine de Louppes belonged to the Bordeaux bourgeoisie and signed notarized documents
with the name "Anthoine de Louppes de Villeneufve." After marrying his
daughters to notables in the city, Antoine de Louppes saw in Pierre Eyquem, a
young gentleman who had recently won glory by his military exploits, a fine
husband for the daughter of his brother Pedro, who also traded in woad in
Toulouse. The Louppeses belonged to the class of nouveaux riches who did not
shrink from making use of any means of giving their children access to nobility. They generally chose the fastest way of achieving that end, namely, marriage with families that had recently been ennobled or were about to be ennobled. Thus in 1525 Étienne Eymar, the king's advocate in the sénéchaussée of
Guyenne, married Béatrix, the daughter of Antoine de Louppes, who was
Pierre de Louppes's brother. Eymar's new father-in-law used his influence to
secure Eymar a position in the sénéchaussée. Antoine de Louppes saw placing
his daughter in a good family as an investment, especially since his new son-in-
law was a lawyer who might someday become a parlement member (*parlementaire*). Étienne Eymar did join the parlement eight years later, in 1533. In accord
with the same logic, the Louppeses married another daughter to another future *parlementaire*, Pierre Ferrand.[25] The noble land of Montaigne promised
Antoinette an attractive future.

The bourgeois origins of Montaigne's mother—who became noble through

---

[xi] The municipal council in Toulouse. [Trans.]

her marriage, but whose ancestors were not at all noble—seemed a little too close and thus problematic for the author of the *Essais*, who is constantly preoccupied with asserting his own nobility. The mercantile branch on his mother's side, which was still very present in the collective memory, might explain Montaigne's famous failure to mention his mother. The evidence he adduces to show that his mother came from a noble family is far from corresponding to reality. Thus the well-known entry in his almanac (*livre de raison, Ephemeris historica*) in which he declares that he was born of noble parents (*nobilibus parentibus*) has never been taken seriously by scholars. It has even been suggested that Montaigne's silence regarding his mother probably indicates that his father's marriage was considered "unfortunate." Let us be clear: "unfortunate" socially, not religiously. This hypothesis gains even more validity if we take into account Montaigne's constant concern to emphasize his noble origins. Antoinette's dowry nonetheless allowed Pierre Eyquem to escape worries about money, to spend major sums on his lands, and to undertake the renovation of his noble house, which at the beginning of the sixteenth century hardly resembled a château. However, his marriage in no way helped to confirm or accelerate his accession to "noble" status. It might even have been counterproductive insofar as the Louppeses had not yet left the world of commerce.

Although it is possible, Antoinette de Louppes's Jewish origin has never been demonstrated with certainty and does not allow us to conflate Montaigne's familial origins with his cultural and religious identity.[26] In fact, the Louppes family's establishment in Toulouse goes back to a time long before the expulsion of the Jews from Spain in 1492 or from Portugal in 1496. The fact that they settled in southern France is explained by the economically viable trade in woad in that region. All through the fifteenth century, fiscal opportunism led many Spaniards to settle in Toulouse. Nonetheless, Montaigne's ancestry on his mother's side remains an interesting problem in the *Essais*, but although we do not have the slightest documentary certitude—except by textual cross-checking—the remarkable absence of references to his mother can be plausibly explained by his desire to avoid mentioning her ancestry. Although time had made it possible to erase Montaigne's bourgeois ancestry on his father's side, this was not the case for his mother's side. Dowries are soon forgotten, but social origin leaves a more persistent mark on people's minds.

In his marriage contract with Antoinette de Louppes, Pierre Eyquem signed his name as "noble Pierre Eyquem de Montaigne, bourgeois of Bordeaux." In 1530, at the age of thirty-five, he was named first *jurat* and provost of Bordeaux; once again, after paying homage to the archbishop of Bordeaux during a ceremony that provided him with an opportunity to take his oath publicly, to promise to lease his lands instead of working them himself, and to list within a period of forty days all the fiefs, *cens*,[xii] and revenues that he possessed, he presented himself as "noble Pierre Eyquem," "lord of the noble house of Montaigne." Bernard de Villiers, lord of Canican and governor of Armaignac; Jean de Martin, lord of La Roque; Bertrand de Mendosse, lord of Montlaur; Bernard de Saint-Genez; and Johan de Peutotz, lord of Cugnac, were the noble witnesses to this ceremony. They made it possible, in accord with the custom, to confirm Pierre Eyquem's nobility by their simple presence at his side.[27] This symbolic homage was supposed to leave a memorable mark on the inhabitants of the region who might then report the event. Pierre Eyquem considered himself to be a member of the minor nobility, and his neighbors confirmed his title. The eldest of his children was to inherit the family patrimony; to that end Pierre wrote a testament that stipulated the terms of his legacy.[28]

Shortly after their marriage, Pierre and Antoinette set up housekeeping in the château of Montaigne and begin to "live nobly." Following an already well-established family tradition, Pierre did not abandon his municipal responsibilities and divided his time between Bordeaux and his estate of Montaigne. The official change in his residence, which was more symbolic than real, marked an important step toward the final ennoblement of the Eyquems.[29] Pierre behaved as a lord, and noble life was all the more agreeable to him because he could boast of having fought in Italy at the side of the king. He drew attention to his military service and "dragged his sword" (*traînait l'épée*), as people said at that time. He liked to receive on his estate local scholars or strangers who were passing through. In April or May 1542, Pierre Bunel, a scholar from Toulouse who wrote esteemed Latin letters, spent some time at the château of Montaigne. When he left, he gave his host a copy of Raymond Sebond's *Theologia naturalis*, a gift that shaped the intellectual evolution of the young Michel de Montaigne, who was not yet ten years old. A few years later Pierre asked his son to translate this Latin work into French, as a simple schoolboy's exercise. Fifteen years later, still inclined to receive erudite humanists who were stopping in Bordeaux or in Guyenne, Pierre Eyquem played host to John Rutherford, a classmate of Montaigne's at the College of Guyenne, who took advantage of his stay at the château to write the opening epistle for his *Commentarium de arte disserendi libri quatuor* (published in Paris in 1557), a treatise in which he proved to be a bitter enemy of the Ramists.[xiii] Rutherford even supervised the studies of Michel's young brother, Thomas.[30] Pierre Eyquem's benevolent hospitality toward men of letters also allowed him to draw attention to his noble way of life and to

---

[xii] The *cens* was a fee payable to a landlord. [Trans.]

[xiii] Adherents to theories of rhetoric, logic, and pedagogy based on the work of Petrus Ramus, a Huguenot convert who was murdered in 1572 during the Saint Bartholomew's Day massacre. [Trans.]

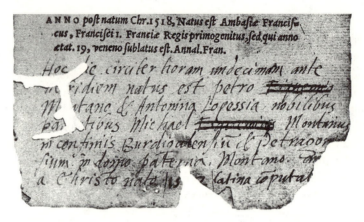

FIGURE 2. Michel Beuther, *Ephemeris historica*, Paris, 1551, p. 61, February 28. Image courtesy of Bibliothèque municipale de Bordeaux.

imbue his sons with the doctrines of the glorious humanism of the first half of the sixteenth century.

Pierre and Antoinette's first surviving child, Michel Eyquem de Montaigne, was born in the noble house of Montaigne on February 28, 1533, between 11:00 a.m. and noon.[xiv] In his almanac (*Ephemeris historica*), Montaigne notes that his father and mother were noble by birth: "natus est Petro ~~Eiquemio~~ Montano & Antonina Lopessia nobilibus parentibus, Michael ~~Eiquemius~~ Montanus"[31] (figure 2). Montaigne later modified this first inscription in his hand—probably after 1570, because in the early 1560s he was still using his Latinized name— doing away with "Eyquem" by twice striking out the patronymic. In another entry in his almanac, Montaigne's father's name is again struck out, leaving only the name of the noble land: "in 1495 Pierre ~~Eyquem~~ de Montaigne my father was born at Montaigne"[32] (figure 3).

A few days after his birth, Michel was held at the baptismal font by four persons "of the most abject fortune," in accord with an aristocratic practice that consisted in having a child baptized by beggars or impoverished people. The child was immediately taken to a wet nurse in a hamlet near the château where he was brought up to "the humblest and commonest way of life."[33] In his *Essais*, Montaigne mentions this nurse whose milk, "moderately healthy and temperate,"[34] is supposed to have given him a "heavy, lazy, and do-nothing nature"[35] and a "soft" (*molle*) disposition. Montaigne even goes so far as to insinuate that a person's character is not hereditary but is transmitted by his nurse.[36] The following year, 1534, Antoinette de Montaigne gave birth to her second son,

[xiv] Before Michel, Antoinette de Louppes had given birth to two children who died in infancy.

16

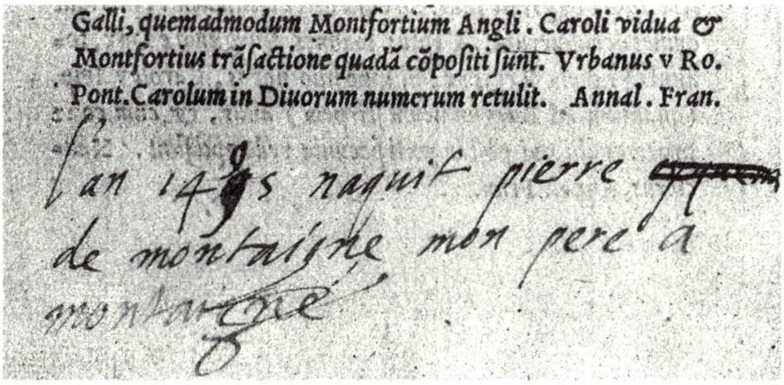
Galli, quemadmodum Montfortium Angli. Caroli vidua & Montfortius trāſactione quadā cōpoſiti ſunt. Vrbanus v Ro. Pont. Carolum in Diuorum numerum retulit. Annal. Fran.

l'an 1495 naquit pierre de montaigne mon pere a montaigne

FIGURE 3. Michel Beuther, *Ephemeris historica*, Paris, 1551, p. 284, September 29. Image courtesy of Bibliothèque municipale de Bordeaux.

Thomas (1534–1602), who became the lord of Arsac after marrying his second wife, Jacquette d'Arsac, Estienne de La Boétie's stepdaughter. Thomas joined the Protestant cause, thereby incurring his elder brother's disapproval. Montaigne's second brother, Pierre (1535–1595), was born the next year. Montaigne's father had ensured the transmission of the name of the seigneury of Montaigne by producing three sons in less than three years. In 1536 his first daughter, Jeanne (1536–1597) was born; she married Richard de Lestonnac in 1555. After having opted for Protestantism as well, Jeanne gave birth to a daughter, Jeanne (1556–1640), a devout Catholic who founded the Convent of Notre-Dame in Bordeaux.[xv]

Six years later, Pierre and Antoinette had another child, Arnaud (1541–1569), who died shortly after his father of an apoplexy resulting from being struck in the head by a court-tennis ball. He had inherited 1,700 *livres* and property on Macau, an island in the estuary of the Gironde. Montaigne pays homage to his late brother in the 1580 edition of his *Essais*. A second sister, Léonor, was born eleven years later, in 1552. She married Thibaud de Camain, lord of Tour-Carnet and a councillor at the parlement of Bordeaux. Like her brother Thomas, she also converted to Protestantism. In 1555, Montaigne had a third sister, Marie, who married Bertrand de Cazalis, lord of Frayche, in 1579, shortly before her sudden death in 1580.

Although he made a point of "living nobly," Pierre Eyquem did not cut himself off from the urban world, because Bordeaux remained the center of power. Remaining on his lands would have been tantamount to political and social suicide for him and his family. Therefore, he went regularly to Bordeaux, where he had become the owner of several houses. Like his father, he rapidly acquired an important position in the municipal government and became Bordeaux's deputy mayor in 1536. He was also reelected to the *jurade*. Pierre Eyquem had

[xv] Jeanne was beatified in 1900 by Pope Leo XIII and canonized in 1949 by Pius XII.

established himself as an administrator of the city, but the time was not propitious, because it was still too close to the salt-tax revolt of 1548, which had cost Bordeaux dearly. After this revolt, the city was summarily deprived of its privileges and severely sanctioned by Henry II. To make amends and to speed the reestablishment of the city's privileges, Pierre Eyquem traveled to Paris with "twenty casks of wine to make gifts to lords favorable to the city of Bordeaux." His devotion to the city's service got him elected mayor of Bordeaux in 1554. This office marked the culmination of a local political career begun three generations earlier. Pierre took advantage of his success in public life to transform his noble house of Montaigne into a genuine château. On December 8, 1554, he obtained from the archbishop of Bordeaux, François de Mauny, the authorization to fortify it.[37] In 1555, he had towers and a surrounding wall constructed, thus giving his home a more imposing appearance. The religious disturbances that had begun to rage in Guyenne made such fortifications indispensable. The lands and buildings his grandfather and father had bought now formed a fairly respectable seigneury, without being among the most opulent of the region. Five years later, Pierre and Antoinette had their last child, Bertrand (1560–1627), lord of Mattecoulon, Montaigne's fourth brother, twenty-seven years younger than he. Although he was a fervent Catholic and devoted to the Virgin Mary, Bertrand became, like his brother Michel, a gentleman of Henry of Navarre's chamber in 1584. He accompanied Montaigne to Italy and remained in Rome to take fencing lessons there.

At the time, Bordeaux was a city in transition. The authority of the jurats and the mayor had been seriously reduced after the revolt of 1548, and in the early 1550s the provost appointed by the king had more actual power than the mayor. On May 25, 1556, while Pierre was mayor, letters from Henry II and a decision by the parlement of Bordeaux defined the respective rights and powers of the provost, the mayor, and the jurats. Following a difference of opinion regarding jurisdictional questions, a suit concerning the supervision of the city's political police was filed by the mayor and the jurats against the provost of the city, Pierre d'Estignoulx. The king demanded that the parlement issue a ruling reasserting the provost's authority. On this occasion he reminded the parlement that in conformity with the decrees of August 1550, the representative of the political authority was the lieutenant general, Thomas de Ram. Forced to recognize that this representative of royal authority in the sénéchaussée of Guyenne had the right to intervene in matters of political justice, the parlement nonetheless decided that the provost of the city could take no part in them. This represented a small victory for Pierre Eyquem and the jurats, even if they did not yet recover the authority they had exercised earlier. It was in this climate of the slow reestablishment of municipal powers that Pierre performed his functions as mayor.

During his term as mayor of Bordeaux, Pierre Eyquem lent a sympathetic ear to the grievances the city's rich merchants expressed. He quickly understood that only the bourgeois could ensure the economic security necessary for the everyday management of the city. The price of wine was a central preoccupation, because a decline in prices had set in after the revolt of 1548 and lasted until the end of the 1560s. A petition filed by the jurats and the mayor of Bordeaux, dated June 11, 1568, reminded the king that "the country of the Bordelais is more sterile and infertile than any other in your kingdom."[38] Charles IX had been able to observe this firsthand during his journey through the region in 1565. According to the jurats, it was impossible to "sow and grow grains or fruits other than grapevines." The producers and merchants of wines from the Bordeaux region deplored the increase in expenses connected with the production and transportation of wine, and in particular the increase in the cost of a day's work by a "laboring man." They drew the sovereign's attention to the fact that despite the rise in prices for other products, the price of wine had not risen for almost ten years. They also complained about the fees for transportation and storage, which they considered excessive. In addition, there were the increasing taxes for the maintenance and wages of the military forces. To compensate the wine merchants' losses, the jurats asked to be exempted from the tax of five *sols* per hogshead of wine stored inside the city walls. To make up for this deficit, they proposed to pay the king a fixed sum of 10,000 *livres tournois* instead of the 33,234 owed to the Crown, referring to various misfortunes and calamities, past and present. There followed a disguised form of blackmail that reminded the sovereign of Bordeaux's strategic position as the capital of Guyenne and a "frontier and maritime" city that had to be kept loyal at any cost "in order to avoid the surprises that might occur [as a result of] the pernicious conspiracies that everyone has seen being covertly formed in the sermons of those belonging to the so-called reformed religion."[39] The jurats promised the king that they would see to it that "the so-called reformed religion"—as the Catholics called it—did not establish itself in their region, in exchange for which they expected a decrease in taxes on the storage and sale of wine. The political and religious argument did not remain a dead letter.

As an elected municipal official, Montaigne's father was at the center of the negotiations with the king seeking to reestablish the city's privileges, which left him little time to visit his lands or to display before his neighbors his status as a noble lord. The author of the *Essais* preferred to keep silent about his father's and his grandfather's various municipal responsibilities, emphasizing instead the noble land of Montaigne and considering his château his ancestors' sole place of residence. Although Bordeaux remained the political and economic center of the region, he chose to depict himself on his estate. Speaking of his ancestors' château, he presents it as "my birthplace and that of most of my ancestors; they set on it their affection and their name."[40] After 1588 Montaigne added: "and of my father," but changed his mind and ended up striking out this manuscript notation on the Bordeaux Copy. It was now his château, and after all, his father was, like Ramon and Grimon, relegated to the status of ancestor. However, few of these ancestors had lived at Montaigne, and the author of the *Essais* is obviously inclined to transform this brief history of the lords of Montaigne into an immemorial reality. Montaigne was only the second member of his family to have been born at Montaigne. To compensate for his family's recent accession to nobility, he describes selected moments when his ancestral nobility is revealed in all its dignity and even creates memorable events that show off his noble way of life.

Establishing his nobility required him to present documents relating to his house and to leave records that could be used by future generations. On the matter of these records, we know that Pierre Eyquem had the habit of keeping a diary (*papier journal*) in which he was accustomed, according to Montaigne, to "insert in it all occurrences of any note, and the memorabilia of his family history day by day."[41] At one point in his life, Montaigne had the same habit, and we now have the first page of an old manuscript on which we read: "1568. Memoir of the affairs of the late Messire Michel de Montaigne, after the death of Monsieur his father."[42] This "diary" still existed at the end of the seventeenth century, because an inventory drawn up by a notary named Claveau on October 21, 1697, mentions a "Livre d'heures" written by Montaigne. Unfortunately, the rest of this precious document later disappeared. The use of a diary was never a practice diligently pursued by Montaigne, who nonetheless regards it as "an ancient custom, which I think it would be good to revive, each man in each man's home. And I think I am a fool to have neglected it."[43] We know that Montaigne accorded great importance to everything that had to do with his name, his titles, his lands, and his "family history" in general, without for all that deigning to elaborate on that history in his *Essais*.

Living Nobly

In his *Discours de la noblesse, et des justes moyens d'y parvenir*, which dates from 1584, Loys Ernaud describes the grave malady then afflicting the French nobility. He notes with annoyance that it is very hard to distinguish noble lords because "one does not know by what marks a Gentleman can be recognized: this title being today so vague in France."[44] From a strictly legal point of view, in the Renaissance there were only two social categories: the nobles and the commoners. The jurist Jehan Bacquet explains, in his *Quatriesme traicté . . . des droicts du Domaine de la Couronne de France*, published in 1582, that "under these kinds are included all the inhabitants of the kingdom."[45] In reality, things were more complex, and a large number of "gentlemen" took advantage of the ambiguity that prevailed at the end of the sixteenth century regarding the definition of nobility.[46] Wealthy merchants achieved noble status more and more frequently by buying noble lands and houses, which were sold to them by minor lords or impoverished barons in need of money. All they had to do was pay the franc-fief [xvi] fee.[47] Then these "nobles on paper" sought to be exempted from paying this fee and thus gain equal footing with nobles from ancient families. This practice rapidly became general, and the mercantile bourgeoisie knew how to exploit a legal possibility that opened the door to nobility for them. Some foreign bourgeois even occasionally succeeded in having themselves naturalized by the king in order to no longer be subject to the *droit d'aubaine*,[xvii] but to do so they had to obtain letters of ennoblement. This required them to follow a rather tricky but effective procedure that allowed them to procure legal documentation that was then religiously transmitted from one generation to the next.

Montaigne's grandfather had demanded such written records of his new nobility from the former owner of the noble house he had acquired. But these letters had to be verified, and everything depended on contacts made with the royal chancellery. The second and better means of being ennobled was based on the condition, dignity, and service of the person in question. The Eyquem family chose to take this route to ennoblement through performing official functions. In France, several conditions and responsibilities then guaranteed the ennoblement of persons who fulfilled responsibilities for the king. This was the case for the Chancellor of France, the Keeper of the Seals, the members of the king's Privy Council, and the members of the Council of State, that is, the members of the high nobility of the parlements. Similarly, the presidents, councillors, attorneys, and state prosecutors of the Paris parlement were considered noble and thus exempt from the franc-fief fee. The provincial parlements soon followed this practice, basing themselves on the principle that they too belonged, in a statutory fashion, to the Paris parlement, on which they depended. On this principle, all councillors, no matter in what city they performed their duties, were themselves attached to the Paris parlement and thus should enjoy the same prerogatives.

The Paris parlement served as a model for the kingdom's other parlements. Bacquet notes that the prerogatives of the various provincial parlements were comparable to those of the capital's: "The same can be said of the other Courts of Parlement in the Kingdom of France."[48] This possibility of ennoblement via

---

[xvi] A franc-fief was a fief owned by a commoner, with the concession and permission of the king, contrary to the usual rule that reserved fiefs for nobles. [Trans.]

[xvii] A right that allowed a lord to appropriate the property of a foreigner if the foreigner died on the territory the lord ruled. [Trans.]

parlementary office also applied to the councillors of the Cours des Aides and of any court sovereign in its jurisdiction. The reasoning went like this: since the members of parlement dispense royal justice, they must themselves belong to the nobility. There can be only one justice, that of the sovereign, and it can be dispensed only by nobles. The nobility of the "long robe" was transmitted to descendants, like the nobility of sword.[49] Both were hereditary. The children of the councillors of the courts of parlement could "enjoy all the rights, authorities, privileges, freedoms, and immunities that nobles of the sword enjoy."[50] François de L'Alouëte testifies to this with regard to royal officers: "Such is the force of the nobility's privilege and right that the king grants those who hold these positions, responsibilities, and offices. And the merit of their service is so prized and esteemed that if their children want to follow the vocation of nobility, they will be immediately received into the rank of nobles, even if they hold it [only in] the first degree, and from then on all those who descend from them will be nobles."[51] However, no one was deceived, and tensions rapidly appeared between the nobility of sword and the nobility that had emerged from the law courts. The courts of parlement could not be confused with the true court, that of the king. Those who had succeeded in retiring to their lands after occupying offices in parlements preferred to forget their pasts as magistrates.

Probably for the same reasons, Montaigne does not dwell on his family's lineage, and he also prefers to emphasize his noble way of life. He does not expand on the origin of his nobility, and he was not the only one who found for himself ancestors of elevated extraction. Unable to trace their families back more than a hundred years to find ancestors of lofty extraction, most of these new nobles preferred to stress their way of living in retirement on their lands, free from any visible commercial activity. In this way, "living nobly" is a leitmotiv and a genuine social aspiration in the *Essais*. Family history is usually not mentioned, to the advantage of the present and everyday preoccupations. According to this credo, the merchant class that sought to join the nobility preferred to ignore its history the better to glorify itself by emphasizing its present service. This ideological choice led to a preference for writing about everyday life, a new category of modernity into which the form of the essay inserts itself. Montaigne quickly learned to use his book as a proof of nobility and to make it an object of memory. It could be argued that the *Essais* are substituted for a lacking documentation and constitute the proof par excellence through which the author establishes his own nobility.

In the sixteenth century, the surest way for a wealthy merchant to achieve nobility was to purchase a public office and join a provincial parlement. A royal councillor at the court of a parlement automatically became noble, and so did his children. The rising bourgeoisie, including that in Bordeaux, made extensive use of this way of moving from one order to the other. One then had to "live nobly" for two or three generations before this nobility was no longer subject to challenge. A decree issued by the Paris parlement in 1573 confirmed this condition. In his "Seventh Plea," titled "That to justify nobility of blood, it has to be shown that the father and grandfather lived nobly,"[52] Cardin Le Bret asks whether the children of councillors enjoy the same privileges as their parents. Are they, for example, exempt from the land tax? Taking as his model the Romans, who ennobled ministers and magistrates, Le Bret indicates that "the appellants must set forth their genealogy and demonstrate it" before the court in order to benefit from the same rights as their parents.[53] A decree of 1593 endorsed this system of verbal verification, which appealed solely to the collective memory. Families in possession of an office in the magistracy were exempted from the requirement of a hundred years (of living nobly) or three quarterings (of noble blood); the possession of an office, including that of councillor in the parlement, over three generations could usually be substituted for any other proof of nobility.[54]

In a chapter on the law of ennoblement taken from the *Trois premiers traictez ... des droits du domaine et de la couronne de France*, published in 1580, Jehan Bacquet explains that there are five ways of proving nobility: by "common reputation," that is, by proving that one's parents were themselves "considered" noble by their neighbors; by "noble and decent conversation," the best proof of which consisted in demonstrating that one's ancestors were accustomed to wearing noble clothes or devices; by showing that one of one's ancestors had borne arms and served in the military profession; by demonstrating that one of one's parents had previously owned a château or a "terre forte"; and finally, by attesting that members of one's family had ancient coats of arms painted in "lofty places" such as churches and burial sites. Bacquet explains that when combined, the first two of these means make it possible to demonstrate an individual's nobility, while the other three do not suffice by themselves to establish nobility irrefutably. In any case, one had to present documents or rely on witnesses whose role Bacquet seeks to explain: "To prove that a man is noble, it suffices that the witnesses state that they knew his grandfather and father, saw them living nobly, following the profession of arms, going off to war, ... consorting with Gentlemen, wearing Gentlemen's clothes, their wives wearing the garments of ladies, and performing other noble acts, without being subject to the land tax, as nobles, and that they have been considered, esteemed, and reputed to be noble by all the inhabitants of the area."[55] Thus a bourgeois could not claim to be transformed into a gentleman from one day to the next. Purchasing land and obtaining the title that was attached to it did not suffice to be ennobled. To enjoy the privilege we have just enumerated, the "new noble" had to live nobly for an indeterminate and variable period. This temporal tribute was the only way of being recognized as noble. The procedure consisted in patiently displaying one's way of life before the largest possible number of people. In order to do that, one had to organize and participate in events whose function was to exhibit the noble life of these lords-on-paper.

"Living nobly" became a necessity for every gentleman who wanted to be recognized as such and thus confirm his status. Although this expression generally had a legal value in the sixteenth century, it was not based on any specific criterion and remained rather vague on the legal level.[56] For example, "living nobly" was not self-evident and had meaning only in the eyes of others, mainly one's neighbors. Once his rank was established, the new noble had to give up all commercial activity. Those who did not risked losing their status. In reality, however, this seldom happened during the second half of the sixteenth century, and a large number of new nobles continued to pursue hidden commercial activities through intermediaries.

Officially, a gentleman had to live solely on the income from his assets, espouse a military career, or belong to the nobility of the robe[xviii] through his office. Commercial activity and nobility did not go together, which implied a radical modification of the former bourgeois's way of life. Being noble designated a mode of life extending over a limited time, because genealogical research to prove nobility seldom went back more than three generations. At the end of the sixteenth century, being noble implied being perceived as such by the community and by the collective memory. Every lord worthy of the name had to live in a way that respected noble values. Nobility could be summed up as a question of reputation, which was established by multiplying "representations of nobility" that could mark the minds of the nearby peasants and neighbors. Public opinion and appearance were determining factors in claiming a nobility that was still poorly established. Consequently, many of these bourgeois gentlemen had become experts at communication and applied literally one of Machiavelli's political principles: only appearances matter. Human memory has an unfortunate tendency to register only what is displayed in an ostentatious way. Therefore, what was important was to be "notoriously noble," to use Bacquet's expression. Montaigne invariably sought to demonstrate his notorious nobility. The necklace of the Order of Saint Michael was for him a godsend because it was a constant reminder of his status as a gentleman, and he followed rigorously all the rules set forth in the order's statutes.

Without always being able to present letters of nobility, it was nonetheless possible to prove that nobility went back several generations. But abuses were frequent, and the courts sometimes intervened to decide cases involving the

---

[xviii] Under the Old Régime, the *noblesse de robe* consisted of aristocrats whose rank was based on holding judicial or administrative posts. They were commonly called (usually pejoratively) *robins*. In this translation, *robin* will be used in this sense. [Trans.]

false attribution of nobility. Thus a judgment handed down on July 30, 1575, against the lord of La Motte de Mar-Fontaine stipulates that "nobility must be proven back to the great-grandfather, having lived nobly, otherwise one is not acceptable without letters of ennoblement, even if one is considered noble from father to son." Another decree, dated August 8, 1582, prohibits "anyone to call himself noble if he is proven to be a commoner, on pain of corporal punishment."[57] However, these cases were relatively rare, and few of the new nobles were ever bothered. Montaigne had no difficulty defending himself against his detractors who accused him, when he was reelected mayor of Bordeaux in 1583, of having usurped his title of nobility. Accusations of this kind were difficult to prove, and nobles on parchment had ample means of defending themselves when a suit was brought against them.

The shortest path to the recognition of nobility was, as we have said, to show that one's ancestors had lived nobly on their lands. For example, membership in this rank could be demonstrated by gathering all the local inhabitants at a parish high mass in order to attest publicly to one's good faith. The approval of one's neighbors served as a legal proof. But the converse could also occur, and sometimes made it possible to unmask a false noble. For example, a community meeting at which Pierre Doignet was denounced before the parishioners of his quarter in Paris on March 10, 1581, made it possible to begin a procedure of liquidating his right of franc-fief. Generally speaking, if it was established that a man's father and grandfather had lived nobly on their lands, then his title of nobility was verified and his status as a gentleman was confirmed. On this point Montaigne felt invulnerable, and he was. His strategy consisted in combining the three means that highlighted his nobility: first, by acquiring an office as councillor at the parlement of Bordeaux, he was assimilated to the nobility of the robe; then he created a reputation and a "common renown" on his lands; and finally he successfully proved his father's military service in Francis I's royal army. Montaigne had little to worry about. Descended from a "noble lineage," "living nobly," and a member of parlement since the end of the 1550s, he had all the assets mentioned and commented upon by the jurists of his time. After 1575—that is, after having obtained his title of knight of the Order of Saint Michael and after his appointment as a Gentleman of the Chambers of the Kings of France and Navarre—he really no longer needed to pursue the parlementary path to claim to be noble. The triple strategy of the 1560s was no longer necessary, and he preferred to count on his family's true nobility of blood.

Most of the time, bourgeois who had conformed to a certain mode of noble life over several generations became noble by prescription. They had succeeded in making productive use of the lands and seigneuries purchased from the bankrupt minor nobility and felt themselves to be legitimate members of the aristocracy. They had also been able to infiltrate the administrations of cities and still participated indirectly in the economic activity of their region. The process of ennoblement begun by the Eyquem family toward the end of the fifteenth century began to bear fruit, and Montaigne was the first to enjoy it fully. Others quite frequently followed his family's course of action. Ennoblement by prescription was not rare in the Renaissance, even though we have very few texts relating to this means of entering the nobility. As one scholar has put it, "prescription consists above all of silence. It is based on oblivion or on a complicity of interests."[58] We can easily see why this increasingly widespread practice was not based on any legal text, because it was in everyone's interest to leave no written trace of this form of ennoblement. The vaguer the term "prescription" was, the more it could be exploited. In practice, the "oblivion" covered a period of three generations or, in certain parts of France—including Guyenne—a period of about a hundred years. The noble whose status was recognized after the third generation or one hundred years then had a right to the title "noble."

In the *Essais*, Montaigne points to his nobility by referring to his own title's right of prescription: "All her [Fortune's] gifts that my house enjoys were there more than a hundred years before me."[59] With this apparently trivial remark, Montaigne intends to distinguish himself from those who have not followed this sacred rule: he does not want to be confused with the nouveaux riches who ignored temporal prescription and tried to cut corners. By informing the reader that his lands and his seigneury date back more than three generations, he reminds him that he has the right to consider himself a true gentleman. Let us note that in Brittany, for example, the period of a century was often mentioned as a proof of nobility.[60] In any case, the gentleman by prescription seeks to show that a necessary and "legal" period of time separates him from commoner status and from the mercantile world to which his ancestors formerly belonged.

Marriage also allowed new nobles to consolidate economic alliances and to carry members of other merchant families along in the wake of their recognized nobility. For the minor, newly established nobility, marriage was above all an economic and social matter that favored both the increase of its patrimony and the transmission of its name. L'Alouëte observes that most of the new nobles obtained their titles "by marriage through the alliances and conjunctions of the Nobles with the aforementioned commoners, through inheritances, divisions, gifts from the King or the Princes, or other similar means."[61] He recommends prohibiting marriages between commoners and nobles in order to preserve "the Condition of the nobility." In the Renaissance, marriage was a matter of social or economic advancement and not a matter of the heart.[62] As Montaigne writes, "Let us choose the most necessary and useful action of human society; that will be marriage."[63] When in 1565 he wed Françoise de La Chassaigne, the daughter of Joseph de La Chassaigne, *soudan*[xix] of Pressac, and Marguerite Douhet, the granddaughter of the late vice president of the parlement, Geoffroy de La Chassaigne, lord of Pressac, he made a good marriage on the social level, at least in the context of his first career in the parlement of Bordeaux. This was not, moreover, the first alliance between the Eyquems and the La Chassaignes, who had long shared political ambitions and pretensions to nobility.

Twenty years earlier, taking advantage of the king's expansion of the number of members of parlement, Montaigne's uncle, Raymond Eyquem, lord of Bussaguet, had entered the parlement of Bordeaux as a councillor. In 1546, he married Adrienne de La Chassaigne, the daughter of Geoffroy de La Chassaigne, who was also a councillor at the parlement.[xx] They had four children: Geoffroy, Jeanine, Jeanne (married to the lord of La Taulade), and Robert, the lord of the noble house of La Salle de Brielhan and of the parish of Blanquefort. The family of the La Chassaignes of Guyenne was a branch of the La Chassaignes that had long been established in Berry.[xxi] Settled in Poitou and Périgord since the beginning of the sixteenth century, this family rapidly made a place for itself in the political and judicial administration of these regions. We find the name La Chassaigne in Guyenne for the first time in 1512.[64] The family established itself permanently in Bordeaux by holding the office of general prosecutor of the parlement. The La Chassaignes very quickly contracted powerful alliances and made the acquisition of several titled lands, including the *soldanerie*[xxii] of Pressac attached to their house of Ségur. The registry of nobles for Gascony and Guyenne indicates that, in the sixteenth century, there were only two *soudans* in Guyenne: that of Pressac and that of La Trau. The *soldanerie* of Pressac was inscribed on the rolls of the nobility of Basadois in 1557. Harassed during the salt-tax revolt of 1548, Geoffroy de La Chassaigne lost the exercise of his office of president but nonetheless retained a significant political influence.

Geoffroy's son, Joseph de La Chassaigne, also served as a councillor at the parlement of Bordeaux from 1543 to 1569 before becoming vice president of this law court in 1569. He had inherited by testament the land and seigneury of

[xix] In the municipal law of Bordeaux, the title of *soudan* indicated a rank equivalent to that of count, viscount, or baron.

[xx] From his first marriage to Catherine de Lescours, Geoffroy de La Chassaigne had had five children: Joseph, Nicolas, Guillaume, Lucrèce, and Adrienne. Catherine died in 1556, and shortly afterward Raymond Eyquem married the rich Renée de Belleville, viscountess (*vigière*) of Cosnac, in Saintonge. Raymond Eyquem died in 1563, the same year as Estienne de la Boétie. He had named his two brothers, Pierre Eyquem, lord of Montaigne, and the other Pierre Eyquem, lord of Gaujac, as the executors of his will. Estienne de la Boétie, Michel de Montaigne, and Jehan de Saint-Maure had served as witnesses.

[xxi] A historical province in central France; its capital was Bourges. [Trans.]

[xxii] An estate associated with a *soudan* (see note above). [Trans.]

Pressac. From his marriage with Marguerite Douhet he had five children: Geof-froy II, who became squire and *soudan* lord of Pressac, gentleman of the king's chamber; François; Nicolas; Jeanne; and Françoise, who inherited 7,000 *livres tournois* from her father and was to be Montaigne's future wife. The enviable political trajectory of Joseph de La Chassaigne, lord of Pressac, did not go un-noticed in Bordeaux, and his daughter, Françoise, was a fine match for someone who sought a parlementary career in Bordeaux. The La Chassaignes were not nobles by blood, but in the early 1560s the Eyquem family had not yet reached the hundred years necessary for nobility by prescription. An alliance with the La Chassaignes offered other, more immediate advantages, and might permit Michel de Montaigne to join a well-established parlementary clientele that was sufficiently powerful in Bordeaux to allow him to envisage a promising career in the parlement.

From the La Chassaignes' point of view, the Montaignes were an equally ideal alliance, because the two families were pursuing similar strategies, as members of the parlement, as administrators of the city, and as potential new nobles. For Michel de Montaigne, a marriage with a La Chassaigne—after that made by his uncle—had the advantage of increasing the social and political vis-ibility of the name Eyquem in Bordeaux, thanks to the La Chassaignes' rich connections and political influence. This marriage also allowed him a chance to ensure that he had children and could hand down a name. On this point, Mon-taigne was less fortunate, because his wife never gave him a male child; we can imagine the frustration of the man who was the first "noble by prescription" in his family, but was incapable of transmitting the new name of Montaigne to his descendants. Françoise de La Chassaigne gave birth to six children, all girls, of whom only one survived, Léonor. The nobility of the Eyquems thus began and ended with Michel.

"We Latinized Ourselves"

Pierre Eyquem wanted to give his son the best of educations, in accord with the pedagogical precepts of the humanism of the time of King Francis I. From birth, Montaigne was instructed and brought up as the heir of a noble family. It was he who would ensure in a definitive way the conversion of the Eyquems into Montaignes. It was necessary to lavish on him an upbringing worthy of his fu-ture responsibilities. After having been put out to a wet nurse, he was brought back to the château, where in early 1535 his father decided to make Latin his son's native tongue, a practice Erasmus had recommended in his *De pueris* (1529). Thus in his early childhood Montaigne was instructed in Latin. His fa-ther forced even the château's servants to speak to him only in Latin: "it was an inviolable rule that neither my father himself, nor my mother, nor any valet or housemaid, should speak anything in my presence but such Latin words as each had learned in order to jabber with me."[65] Montaigne relates that his parents learned enough Latin to be able to communicate with him. As he notes, not without exaggeration and irony: "Altogether, we Latinized ourselves so much that it overflowed all the way to our villages on every side, where there still remain several Latin names for artisans and tools that have taken root by usage."[66]

The young Montaigne was entrusted to a tutor whom his father "had sent for expressly, and who was very highly paid," "a German, who has since died a famous doctor in France," but who did not know a word of French.[67] Two "less learned" assistants helped the tutor perform his pedagogical task; everyone, including Montaigne's mother and the servants, avoided speaking French or Gascon in Michel's presence. In his *Essais*, Montaigne asserts that French was a foreign language for him. However, we can presume that in his contacts with servants and the peasants who worked the seigneurial land, he was exposed to numerous Gasconisms that later studded his writings. Montaigne's education had begun in the château with his tutors, according to the principles of the noble tradition. Influenced by humanist education as it is described, for example, in Gargantua's famous letter to his son in Rabelais's *Pantagruel*, Pierre Eyquem wanted to send Michel to the best school to learn the humanistic disciplines. In the region, only one institution then offered an education that combined both the gentleness "without rigor or constraint" of the Erasmian system and the methodicalness of a Scholastic education. In 1539, at the age of six, Montaigne entered the College of Guyenne as a boarder, joining immediately the third grade (or maybe even fourth grade)[xxiii] class, because he already had sufficient knowledge of Latin.

Established in February 1533, the College of Guyenne had been founded specifically to meet the demands of the well-off bourgeois of the region who wanted to give their children a humanistic education as early as the age of six or seven.[68] Under the presidency of the deputy mayor Pierre Dagès, the Bordeaux jurats had met as a committee in February 1533 to discuss the creation of a college in their city. Shortly afterward, they recommended to the parlement the foundation of a college in Bordeaux. Jean de Tartas, the principal of the College of Lisieux, had proposed a model that was not likely to displease the wealthy merchant families or the members of the parlement.[xxiv] The instruction in Latin and

---

[xxiii] In the French system, which began with tenth grade, these are *huitième* or *septième* respectively.

[xxiv] Twenty years later, on March 10, 1555, the principal of the College of Guyenne came to present the *Statuta gimnasii aquitaniae* before the parlement to have them approved. The ties between the college and the parlement had grown permanently stronger.

humanist training proposed by the committee was supposed in particular to prepare students for the examinations required to join the magistracy.[69] A solid education at the college could also allow the students to go to a university as prestigious as the one in Toulouse. The record of the foundation of the College of Guyenne thus proposes to "found and endow a College, similar in form and manner to the Colleges of the city of Paris, in order that the children of the said city and other neighboring cities and places, and all countries, might be able to study and benefit at lower cost and expense."[70] The college opened on May 15, 1533, the year of Michel de Montaigne's birth. The program proposed by Jean de Tartas was so successful that the college had to enlarge its premises and recruit more teachers.

However, less than a year after he had created the College of Guyenne, Jean de Tartas was dismissed and replaced by André de Gouvéa, who had been the principal of the College of Sainte-Barbe in Paris since 1530.[71] Although he retained Tartas's main ideas regarding the educational *cursus*, Gouvéa wanted to improve the quality of the teaching. He personally brought to Bordeaux Guillaume Guerente, Nicolas de Grouchy, Gentian Hervet, Élie Vinet, Marc-Antoine Muret, and George Buchanan, with whom Montaigne studied. Gouvéa and his teaching staff arrived in Bordeaux on July 12, 1539, the same year that the young Montaigne began his studies there. Called in by Gouvéa, Vinet was among the most famous members of the college's faculty. A passionate scholar of antiquities, he even became one of the first archaeologists of Bordeaux. George Buchanan also began teaching at the college in 1539 as professor of rhetoric; he too had taught in the past (1528–29) at the College of Sainte-Barbe in Paris. Nicknamed the "prince of poets," Buchanan was one of the most remarkable figures at this institution and soon acquired a reputation as a free thinker. It was probably he who introduced the young Michel to poetry, and Montaigne declared his admiration for "that great Scottish poet."[72] A nonnegligible part of the curriculum consisted of an introduction to the Greek and Latin poets, and also to poets who wrote in neo-Latin and French. Several teachers openly sympathized with the ideas of the Reformation, and Buchanan belonged to a new intellectual movement that was one of the most critical of the dogmas of the Catholic Church.[73] Other teachers embraced the ideas of the Reformation more covertly. This was the case for André Zébédée, Nicolas de Grouchy, Claude Budin, and Mathurin Cordier. Montaigne was exposed to these ideas at a very young age, but always within a strictly Catholic framework punctuated by the sacraments of the Roman church. The college remained Catholic.

Montaigne began his studies at the College of Guyenne in 1539. He was destined one day to succeed his father as lord of Montaigne, and Pierre Eyquem spared no expense to procure the best education possible for his descendants.

Subsidized in part by the city, which put municipal premises at its disposal, the College of Guyenne still had to find the money necessary to defray its operating costs. Each boarding student had to pay the teacher and the director of the room where he was lodged the sum of four *écus* (twelve *livres*) per trimester for his bed, linens, heat, candles, and the recital of his readings. The annual salary of the regents varied between thirty and sixty *livres* a year for the most popular teachers, such as Nicolle and Zébédée. However, an exception was made for master Guillem, who was by far the best-paid professor, since he received ninety-two *livres* per annum. Discipline was an integral part of the education given the children, and on this point Gouvéa had set up a less punitive system that was essentially based on the model of the College of Sainte-Barbe. The principal had the authority to punish and discipline the children "in the Paris manner," that is, "decently and humanely." In 1533, the college had eighteen rooms with fifteen regents and three public readers. The number rapidly rose to twenty-one regents. In addition to the boarders there were the day pupils, who were called "*martinets*." The teachers did not give lectures, but rather "readings," and were for that reason hired as public readers in accord with the practices current in Paris and with the model of the royal readers.

In the *Essais*, Montaigne speaks on several occasions about his stay at the college, which he judges "the best in France," and in particular about André de Gouvéa, whom he also considers "incomparably the greatest principal of France."[74] He nonetheless admits that he completed his studies at the age of thirteen without having really acquired any practical knowledge. His knowledge of Latin before entering the college had allowed him to skip two grades—perhaps three—and to finish his studies of grammar in seven or eight years rather than ten. On the whole, Montaigne's assessment of his time at the College of Guyenne is rather negative; he declares that he derived from it "[not] any benefit that I can place in evidence now."[75] If the educational program left something to be desired, Montaigne judged more positively the college's readers and the teaching staff. Among the teachers, he especially liked Turnebus, who had, however, left Bordeaux in 1547 after accepting the chair of Greek at the College Royal in Paris. At the end of the year 1549, a plague epidemic forced Jean Gelida—the college's administrator after Gouvéa left for Portugal—to send his pupils away from the college and dismiss his teachers. Gelida wrote to La Taste, his contact in the capital, to ask him to recruit a new grammar teacher. He explained that Horstanus, Montaigne's tutor, did not want to continue to teach his class, being too frightened by "the calamity of the times."[76] In the end, Horstanus agreed to remain in Gelida's service for another year. He may have been Montaigne's tutor but, contrary to what has been suggested, certainly not when he was a little child. Having arrived in Bordeaux after Montaigne's entrance into the College of Guyenne, Horstanus was not the German tutor

Montaigne talks about, telling us that he became a famous doctor in France. On the other hand, it has been shown that Horstanus was indeed the house tutor of Montaigne's brothers Thomas and Pierre, and perhaps Michel's as well, but only toward the end of his studies at the College of Guyenne. Another letter from Gelida dated October 1 encourages Horstanus to come back to the college "with his Montaignes."[77]

We know little about Montaigne's early childhood, and any attempt to describe his youth can be no more than speculation. But we know in detail the curriculum of the College of Guyenne at that time, and we can reconstruct quite precisely the pupils' school day for each grade. In his *Schola Aquitanica* (1583), Élie Vinet sketches a rather complete picture of the instruction Montaigne might have received. These formative years had a major influence on the conception and development of the *Essais*. It is therefore useful to examine briefly the educational program that Montaigne experienced in Bordeaux from 1539 to 1547.

Instruction at the College of Guyenne was divided into ten grades. Between 1534 and 1583, the number of years of teaching varied between nine and twelve. The school day began at 8:00 a.m., with lessons from 8:00 to 10:00 a.m., from noon to 1:00 p.m., and from 3:00 to 5:00 p.m. on days when school was in session. All the morning and afternoon lessons were followed by half an hour of "disputations," or debates, which at the time were considered the means of instruction most effective for training young minds, and which over the years occupied a growing part in the program of studies. Saturday was a school day like the others, but classes were given only in the morning and from noon to 1:00 p.m. The fourth and fifth grades were generally divided into "advanced" and "less advanced" sections, fifth grade receiving the most advanced students.

The children began their studies in "tenth grade" (*Decimus ordo*), at the age of six. The beginners' class was called that of the *alphabétaires*, because in it they learned essentially the twenty-three letters of the sixteenth-century alphabet. It was by far the largest class, and pupils frequently had to repeat it. Élie Vinet tells us that parents sent their children to the college to learn Latin letters, "because the principal object of this school was the knowledge of the Latin language."[78] The college's goal was not to provide practical training but rather to teach its pupils humanist principles and prepare them for debating in the Latin language. Those who envisaged an administrative or judicial career considered the program Gouvéa offered to be the best possible training for their children, because they were destined, when the time came, to take over the responsibilities and offices that their parents had acquired. Two school booklets were used to teach pupils the rudiments of spelling. The *cursus* for this first year concentrated on learning the alphabet on the basis of the paternoster and the seven penitential psalms.

The classroom had ten benches arranged in rows, and the most gifted pupils sat in the first row. At noon and 3:00 p.m., the same subjects were recited in the same order. Each lesson lasted one hour. As soon as they knew the alphabet, the children learned to copy the letters in a notebook. To do that they had to buy a writing case. Toward the end of the first year they were given a few examples of Latin declensions and conjugations; that was the subject of the second manual, *Livret des Enfants*. Although classes were taught chiefly in Latin, the young pupils were allowed to speak French during their first year at the college. Those in the advanced classes had to express themselves in Latin to the children in the first two classes, and then translate into French what had not been understood.

Second grade students were introduced to an entirely new space, with the intention of socializing them. Instruction took place in a large hall, the *aula*. Second-year pupils were thus called *aulani*. They occupied only part of this vast hall that was also called the *theater*, because it was supposed to resemble an ancient theater. Built of wood, this hall made it possible to gather the pupils together in an enclosed space. It had eleven tiers of seats and enabled pupils to become familiar with various forms of representation and staging, both theatrical and social. The declared goal of this grade was to learn to read and write "well and rapidly in Latin and in French." The pupils were also introduced to the first *Elements* of grammar using a Latin edition accompanied by a French translation. They learned to recite longer and longer speeches by Latin authors.

In third grade, pupils studied Cicero's letters, a few scenes from Terence's comedies, and Mathurin Cordier's *Colloquies* on the Holy Scriptures. These three works were divided into lessons to be learned by heart. The children had to buy all the books used in the courses as well as a blank notebook. They began to learn the conjugation of Latin verbs in the present indicative, the imperfect, and so on for all the moods and tenses. At the end of the year, the teacher introduced the pupils to figures of speech on the basis of a few Latin examples. After six months, if the teacher noticed some students who were more advanced than the others, he notified the principal of the college, who, after checking, might send them directly into fourth grade. Montaigne's good knowledge of Latin must have gotten him exempted from third grade. In his *Essais* he congratulates himself on having completed his grammar classes at the age of thirteen (in fact, probably fourteen).

The pupils in fourth grade spent most of the year studying Cicero's *Letters to His Friends* (*Epistulae ad Familiares*). They were asked to explicate selected passages. They were also taught the basics of commentary and copied out passages of the Latin author in their notebooks, leaving a space of at least half an inch between the lines where their grammatical explication could be written in French. The teacher then explained the different parts of speech. This exercise took place in the morning. The students read their explications out loud in class, before their schoolmates. They were also trained in translation (chiefly from French into Latin). At noon, they learned the gender of nouns according to Despautère,[xxv] two or three points in his grammar book being explained each day.

The purpose of fifth grade was to consolidate the knowledge gained in fourth grade, and the most gifted pupils, including Montaigne, might be permitted to pass directly to sixth grade. The college's regulations stipulated that "each one, depending on his progress, will move up or fall back, or remain in the same grade, pursuant to our order, in accord with the result of the examination that we have given him."[79] Cicero continued to be the main object of study. The texts chosen for the morning were memorized during the day and recited in the afternoon or the next morning, if the teacher's text explication had taken place the preceding day. The pupils continued to work on genders, declensions, the perfect tense, and Latin syntax in their copies of Despautère. The *cursus* was the same in sixth grade: Cicero in the morning, Despautère at noon, and a comedy by Terence at 3:00 p.m. At the end of the year, the pupils studied selected texts by Ovid.

In seventh grade, the pupils began their day with Cicero's *Letters to His Friends* or his *Letters to Atticus*. Despautère's genders, declensions, and various other matters were quickly reviewed. The teachers introduced one of Cicero's simpler speeches and a few summaries of rhetoric. At noon, the pupils were introduced for the first time to the art of versification and tried their hands at composing verses. At 3:00 p.m., they read a comedy by Terence and then moved on to Ovid's *Tristia*. The Latin compositions became more numerous and longer. Eighth grade resembled seventh but accorded a greater place to rhetoric.[80] The pupils also read Ovid's *Metamorphoses* and recited by heart whole pages of Cicero and Ovid. The teachers then favored poetry for compositions. In ninth grade, the teacher explicated in the morning a speech by Cicero and the parts of rhetoric. In the afternoon, he made the pupils familiar with ancient history, and at 3:00 p.m. he asked them to read Virgil, a few passages from the *Metamorphoses*, or extracts from Lucian's *Pharsalia*. At 5:00 p.m., the tutor handed out the subject for a text in verse that had to be submitted before the end of the day. During this year the pupils were introduced to declamation, in private and in public.

This education, which was very structured and representative of humanist values, led to the final year of grammar classes. In this class, almost the only

---

[xxv] Born around 1460 or 1480, Jean Despautère was a Flemish grammarian who wrote in Latin and had published *Commentarii grammatici* in 1537. This book served as the basis for teaching Latin in the colleges of Montaigne's time and continued to be used until the eighteenth century.

subject was rhetoric and Latin grammar, based on texts by Suetonius. In the morning, the pupils studied the rules of the oratorical art according to Cicero and Quintilian. Starting at 9:00 a.m., they analyzed a speech by Cicero to check whether they had learned the rules they had studied earlier; they also put them into practice by trying their hands at public speaking, which allowed the best minds to display their skills at eloquence. We know that these oratorical competitions were not Montaigne's strong point. At noon, they were read ancient history according to Livy, Justin, Seneca, and Pomponius Mela. At 3:00 p.m., the tutor gave them a lesson in poetics on the basis of texts by Virgil, Lucian, Juvenal, Horace, Ovid, and Persius, "but in the places where they respect morals."[81] At 5:00 p.m., the pupils received a passage in verse that they had to translate before the evening was over.

Public exercises were given priority, especially on Saturday morning, when the pupils in tenth grade had to address an audience composed of pupils in the lower classes. The celebration of Ludovicales—August 25—marked the end of the school year. This day, Saint Louis's feast day, was an opportunity to show the progress made during the year. The Ludovicales allowed the best pupils to display their brilliance. Speeches in verse and prose were hung on the walls, and a theatrical representation completed this festive day. Prizes were awarded and the pupils were granted a vacation until October 1 for the grape harvest. During the Ludovicales of 1547, Montaigne played one of the main roles in a tragedy by Marc-Antoine Muret, *Julius Caesar*,[82] during Antoine Gouvéa's brief term as principal. Gouvéa's brother, André, had left in March 1547 to found a college in Coimbra at the behest of the king of Portugal, John III, taking with him almost all his teaching staff, including Buchanan, Grouchy, and Guerente. The College of Guyenne's apogee coincided with the end of Montaigne's studies in the grammar classes, probably in 1547.

Montaigne claims that around 1544–46 he was the pupil of Nicolas de Grouchy, Guillaume Guerente, and George Buchanan, who had left the college in 1543,[83] and also of Jean Binet.[84] Although he had a low opinion of the instruction he received, he held his teachers at the College of Guyenne in high esteem. He mentions in particular: "Nicholas Grouchy, who wrote *De Comitiis Romanorum*, Guillaume Guerente, who wrote a commentary on Aristotle, George Buchanan, that great Scottish poet, my private tutors, have often told me that in my childhood I had that language so ready and handy that they were afraid to accost me. Buchanan, whom I afterward saw in the suite of the late Marshal de Brissac, told me that he was writing on the education of children and that he was taking my education as a model."[85] Muret is not on this list in 1580; only in the 1588 edition of his *Essais* did Montaigne add his name, explaining in the Bordeaux Copy that "France and Italy recognize him as the best orator of his time."[86] Montaigne was proud to have listened to the readings of these famous tutors and places himself on an equal footing with them when he boasts of having been as fine a Latinist as they were.

After ten years of grammar classes—probably eight for Montaigne—the pupils followed an intermediate *cursus* for two years: they entered the Faculty of Arts run by the College of Guyenne, a sort of preparatory program preceding the university. The students no longer belonged to a class, and instead of being under the authority of a teacher, they received instruction by the most famous teachers at the College of Guyenne, one after the other. The two teachers of philosophy dealt with the students leaving tenth grade. The first-year students were called "dialecticians" or "logicians," while second-year students were called "physicians." This distinction was based on the progression in the philosophy program. The courses generally began with Porphyry's *Isagoge* and Aristotle's *Categories, Prior* and *Posterior Analytics, Topics, Physics,* and *On the Heavens.* Only Aristotle's treatises, Porphyry's *Isagoge*, and Nicolas de Grouchy's *Préceptes de la Dialectique* were explicated. Starting on October 1, the students attended public lessons, as at the College Royal founded by Francis I. They acquired basic knowledge of Greek. The professor explained the Greek grammar book by Théodore de Gaza (*Introductivae grammatices libri quatuor*) or that of another author of his choice. Demosthenes and Homer were read in Greek. Montaigne never excelled in Greek, even though he had an adequate competence in writing it. Although he had complete mastery of the Latin language, his acquaintance with Greek remained rather rudimentary, and he went so far as to admit that he had "practically no knowledge at all"[87] of it. However, we have to qualify that claim. In fact, despite his linguistic shortcomings in that language, Montaigne's library contained a respectable number of books in Greek.[xxvi] Dionysius of Halicarnassus, Diogenus Laërtius, Cassius Dio, Eusebius, and Strabo were among his readings in Greek. [88]

Montaigne completed his grammar classes in August 1547. In October he began his first year as a "dialectician." In 1548, the year of the salt-tax revolt in Bordeaux and the terrible repression that followed it, he probably studied philosophy under Mathieu Béroalde the Elder, who was Vatable's nephew and a famous Aristotelian. In addition, he attended the classes given by Marc-Antoine Muret and by Jean Gelida, a Spaniard from Valencia who had become the principal of the college after Gouvéa's departure. Gelida also came—like Gouvéa and Buchanan—from the prestigious College of Sainte-Barbe in Paris. We know almost nothing about the end of Montaigne's studies, except that in January 1549 he bought a Latin edition of Virgil published in Venice, on which he wrote down his age. The same year, he also purchased, for 19 sols, a Caesar in the edi-

---

xxvi Of the hundred books that have been found up to this point with Montaigne's signature (ex libris), sixteen are entirely or partially in Greek.

tion by Vascosan and Roigny. Montaigne seems to have spent time reading Latin authors, perhaps at the château in the company of his brothers Thomas, Pierre, and Arnaud, who were fifteen, fourteen, and eight years old, respectively.

In 1583, forty-four years after the beginning of his studies at the College of Guyenne and while he was mayor of Bordeaux, Montaigne saw to it that the College of Guyenne's *cursus* proposed by his former professor, Élie Vinet, was adopted by the municipality. For the occasion, the mayor had brought together in the city's common building the jurats—Geoffroy d'Alesme, Jean Gallopin, Pierre Régnier, Jean de Lapeyre, and Jean Claveau—as well as the prosecutor-syndic, Gabriel de Lurbe, and the secretary of the city, Richard Pichon. In accord with the custom, the prosecutor-syndic presented the cycle of instruction recommended by Vinet. The members of the council, supported by Montaigne, adopted the proposed program unanimously and decided to publish it "as soon as possible, in order that the rule observed up to the present day in their College of Bordeaux might be well known and never easily altered."[89] In fact, as the city officials emphasized, the College of Guyenne's program of teaching had hardly changed over half a century. The main role of this institution was to receive and train the Bordeaux elite that had been sending its children there for half a century to establish their social status and thus show that Bordeaux could compete with the best colleges in Paris. In 1583, the accent was put more than ever on a general education in Latin that could lead to a career in the magistracy, the track preferred by the class—the *robins*—ennobled by their parlementary responsibilities. However, in 1583 humanism was in decline and its pillars—notably Aristotle and Cicero—had lost some of their splendor.

The Balance Sheet of a Humanist Education

Montaigne does not say a word about his university studies, and perhaps for good reason. Although he gives the names of his professors at the College of Guyenne, he mentions only Turnebus and Sylvius among those with whom he studied in Paris. Specialists have always wondered if he did his university studies in Paris or in Toulouse; there is little evidence either way. Both these cities had many famous professors, but there was no law *cursus* in Paris, except for public lectures and readings by famous jurists who were at the parlement of Paris or were passing through the capital. However, these lectures and readings were always given in the faculty of theology. So if Montaigne studied law—and that remains to be proven—it was probably in Toulouse, where there was a rich, long tradition of instruction in the subject. A large number of the members of the Bordeaux parlement had been trained in Toulouse. For example, Montaigne's uncle had studied in that city, and his mother still had family there.

Even if he intended to study in Toulouse and had been able to begin his study of law there, Montaigne seems not to have completed it. Moreover, the entrance examination at the Cour des Aides in Périgueux did not require any diploma, only a good knowledge of Latin and of ancient authors. On that point, Montaigne's education at the College of Guyenne was amply sufficient. Montaigne's silence in the *Essais* regarding his training in law, or the lack of it, can be explained in two ways: first, because he rejected a tradition of the *robins*, which he preferred not to mention after 1570, since he had abandoned that profession; or second, because he did not finish his studies and became a councillor without having a diploma in law. Thus he would logically have preferred not to comment on this period in his life.

In 1546, after finishing his studies at the College of Guyenne, Montaigne registered for the course for *artiens* (the first two years of study preparatory to entering the university) that was offered in the quarters of the College of Guyenne. Whereas his brothers were still boarders at the college, the young Michel could stay at the château. He had completed his course of studies in two years, that is, during the summer of 1548, four days before the feast of Ludovicales. Revolt was brewing in Bordeaux. Francis I had increased the salt tax to 24 *livres* per hogshead in 1542, and then two years later raised it again to 48 *livres*. Tristan de Moneins, a Basque gentleman, governor of Navarrenx and sénéschal of Béarn, had been called to Bordeaux as lieutenant general to make sure that the fiscal measures decreed by the king were carried out.

Taking advantage of the revolt against the salt tax, rebels had slipped into the city, and Moneins tried to meet with them. The insurgents assassinated him. Other royal officers were hunted down, and the building where they had taken refuge was set afire. Moneins's body suffered the insults of the people, who, in mockery, filled it with salt. Bordeaux had risen in revolt, and the bourgeoisie was considered responsible for this, because it had taken part in the rebellion and had not taken action to free Moneins, even though it controlled the city's police. Looting ensued, and the city was taken over by a raging mob.

Royal repression was not slow in coming, and the Constable of France, Montmorency, was ordered to punish the city and those responsible for the riots. He had part of the city walls demolished in order to enter the city. The bourgeois had to lay down their arms, and an inquiry into the murder of Moneins was begun. Montmorency had also forbidden the parlement to meet, and its president, La Chassaigne, was arraigned before the parlement of Toulouse to answer to the accusation of high treason. Pierre Eyquem certainly preferred that Michel take refuge in the security of the family château, far from Bordeaux and the political tumult. The College of Guyenne was indirectly affected by the revolt, and most of the pupils were sent home. It is possible that this revolt of October 1548 upset the young Montaigne's plans, and that he decided, perhaps at his father's behest, to occupy himself with the education of his brothers immediately after completing his *artiens* courses in late summer 1548.

The people of Bordeaux were judged guilty of the crime of lèse-majesté, the city's privileges were canceled, and the right to elect jurats and to assemble was suspended. The parlement could no longer exercise any jurisdiction and its future was uncertain. On October 26, 1548, in reprisal for the revolt of the people of Bordeaux, royal commissioners passed judgment on the "Commune of Guyenne in Bordeaux" and deprived the city of its "privileges, city hall, jurats, and council, common purses, seal, bells, justice and jurisdiction, artillery, and arms."[90] The judgment against the city mentioned "rebellions, disobediences, crimes of lèse-majesté, seditions, popular uprisings at the sound of the warning bell, murders, and homicides."[91] The letters and charters of privilege were even burned, and the city hall was razed and replaced by a chapel. The punishment the king ordered was disproportionate with regard to the events, and more than five hundred people were condemned to death and executed. The people of Bordeaux had to make amends, and history (that of the first historians of the city) tells us that the jurats were forced to exhume Moneins's body with their own hands in order to give him a burial more worthy of a representative of the king.[92] Henry II did not pardon the assassination of the lieutenant general of Guyenne, and the Bordeaux oligarchy that had held the reins of the city and the parlement since the departure of the English paid a high price for having rebelled against its sovereign. The extreme violence of Montmorency's repression marked people's minds, and the Bordeaux political class withdrew wherever it could in order let time repair its image. It was a bad time to begin studying law, and Montaigne certainly felt the repercussions of this political crisis.

We know next to nothing about Montaigne's life between 1548 and 1556, a period that has been called "Montaigne's lost years."[93] We know that he read the ancients and that he probably did not travel between 1548 and 1550. Similarly, his interest in medicine is undeniable, and he seems to have been sufficiently familiar with anatomy and physiology to allow us to say with certainty that he had probably read and studied several treatises on these subjects. In addition, the *Essais* contain many references to physicians of his time, notably Jean Fernel, Pierre Pichot, and Jacques Dubois, known as Sylvius.

Given the absence of documents regarding his university career, we can only suppose that he followed a track similar to that of other men of his time, origin, and rank. We would like, for example, to find evidence that Montaigne studied in Toulouse, whose university then enjoyed a great reputation. The most elevated servants of the state had studied at the prestigious Faculty of Law in that city. Henri de Mesmes, Paul de Foix, and Guy du Faur de Pibrac all studied there. Montaigne probably spent some time there as well, and he seems to have known the city fairly well. Later, in 1560, he attended in Toulouse the famous appeal proceedings in the case of the imposter Martin Guerre. He mentions this trial in the chapter "Of cripples" (III: 1). The case had had a great impact on the kingdom. While he was already a councillor at the parlement of Bordeaux, this famous case of the usurpation of identity that ended with the condemnation of the imposter, Arnaud du Tilh, symbolized a "textbook case" sufficiently interesting to cause Montaigne to make the trip to Toulouse. However, his presence in Toulouse in 1560 in no way proves that he sojourned there in the early 1550s. Moreover, in a rather strange way, Montaigne begins his account of the appeal proceedings with the expression "In my youth,[xxvii] I read about the trial of a strange case . . ." whereas he was already twenty-seven years old at the time.[94] As we see, the dates of his passage through or stay in Toulouse remain rather vague.

On the other hand, it has been established that Montaigne attended some kind of public course in Paris, where he is supposed to have stayed several times in the early 1550s. His uncle, Raymond Eyquem de Bussaguet, might have taken Montaigne with him when he went to the capital in the spring of 1551, where he remained for forty days as a representative of the parlement of Bordeaux. At that time, the parlement was trying to regain from the king the trust it had lost in 1548, and members of the Bordeaux parlement were often sent to deliver messages of submission and goodwill to the king. Montaigne bought a copy of Michel Beuther's *Ephemeris historica* there in 1551, proving his presence in the capital; the book had just been published by Michel Fezandat and Robert Granion ("In Taberna Gryphyiana").[xxviii] Montaigne used it as a record book and noted in it all kinds of family episodes: births, marriages, the deaths of children, relatives, and friends, and memorable events that affected him directly.

Five of the entries in his *Ephemeris* are written in Latin, the language that Montaigne preferred to use at that time. They were certainly all written between 1551 and 1555. Montaigne wrote down in this almanac—retroactively—

[xxvii] *"dans mon enfance."* Montaigne's text suggests that he read about this trial while still a child.

[xxviii] Michel Beuther was born in Carlstadt and died in Strasbourg in 1587. A German philosopher, man of letters, and theologian, he studied under Luther and Melanchthon. Later he taught history in Strasbourg. The work he published in 1551 in Paris is in reality a perpetual calendar, a kind of almanac or *ephemeris*, 432 pages in length. The historical memento of this work occupies page 1 to 382, that is, one page per day with a title page for each month and a few blank pages. The top of each page includes chronological indications, the month of the year and date, with their correspondences for the Latin (in calends, nones, and ides), Greek, and Hebrew calendars. This *ephemeris* could be used for any year. On most of the pages there is also a list of the most remarkable events that occurred on that day of the year, whether they are past facts, contemporary events, or even biblical episodes. Some pages have only a few lines, while others have summaries that fill almost three-quarters of the space.

the important events in the history of his family, and also the recent deaths of princes and great intellectual figures of the time. He registered, notably, the deaths of François Vatable (March 16, 1547) and Jacques Toussaint (March 31, 1547) as well as the death of Margaret of Angoulême, queen of Navarre (December 21, 1549). At the same time, Montaigne also attended the lectures on Galenic medicine given by Jacques Dubois, a reader at the College Royal of Paris between 1550 and 1555.

It was perhaps at this same time that he translated Sebond's *Theologia naturalis* for his father, since he had no other full-time activity and seems not to have pursued with assiduity any university *cursus*. From 1548 to 1556, we imagine that he divided his time between Paris and his father's château. He probably sojourned in Paris several times between 1551 and 1556. Buchanan's poem dedicated "To Michael, Thomas, and Pierre Eyquem de Montaigne, from Bordeaux" in memory of his pleasant stay at the château de Montaigne in the company of Michel and his two brothers was perhaps composed in Paris on the occasion of an encounter with Montaigne during which they recalled the years they had spent together at the College of Guyenne and at the château de Montaigne. Buchanan had returned to France in 1552 after an unhappy period in Portugal, where he had narrowly escaped prosecution by the Inquisition. He remained at the College of Boncourt until 1554 and could have met Montaigne in the capital and written his poem on this occasion. It is also possible that, back in Bordeaux, the Scottish humanist visited the three young Montaignes on their estate between 1554 and 1556.[95]

Montaigne at this time may have frequented the salon of Jean Morel and Lancelot de Carle, a relative of Estienne de La Boétie. This salon was also attended by Aymar de Rançonnet, Élie André, Paul de Foix, Guy du Faur de Pibrac, Arnaud du Ferrier, and Guillaume de Lur Longa, a group of Gascon intellectuals who had immigrated to Paris.[96] Lur Longa had recently taken up residence in the capital after accepting a post of councillor-clerk, ceding his place in the parlement of Bordeaux to Estienne de La Boétie, who, to celebrate Lur Longa's departure for Paris, dedicated to him a "declamation," soon to be known under the title of *Discourse on Voluntary Servitude*. The nomination of Lur Longa as well as the composition of La Boétie's *Discourse* have been studied in the context of the battle over of the edict of the Semester (April 28, 1554). Henri de Mesmes, who had recently been named *maître des requêtes*; Guillaume de Lur Longa, who had just joined the parlement of Paris; and Estienne de La Boétie, who was entering the parlement of Bordeaux, were each in their own way the object of political and professional pressure to commit themselves to the king's party, which was trying to regain control over councillors who were demanding more and more independence from royal authority.[97] We know that Lur Longa was a personal friend of Montaigne's uncles.

Pierre Eyquem was already foreseeing a parlementary career for his son. Knowing that Michel was very strong in Latin, and to keep him from losing his competence in this subject, he asked him, probably around this time, to translate into French the *Theologia naturalis* of the Catalan theologian Raymond Sebond. This book had been given to him ten years earlier, in 1542, by Pierre Bunel, a scholar from Toulouse whom he had put up at his château. A translation of this kind would be well regarded by Montaigne's examiners, when the time came, if he entered the magistracy. This translation exercise, considered as a good apprenticeship for the profession of councillor, was above all a "study assignment" imposed by a father concerned about his son's future.

What remained to Montaigne from his humanistic education? More than a simple veneer, contrary to what some have said. His education at the College of Guyenne and the courses he attended in Paris as a "free auditor" allowed him to gain confidence in his own judgment and to be less dependent on the authority of the ancients. Montaigne was to continue to cite Greek and Latin authors throughout his life, but only as decorations to frame and illustrate his own reflections. He moved from the gloss to the quotation with a disconcerting ease. His way of reasoning became mainly comparative and critical. The "debates" from his time at the college turned out to be not very effective in a political world in transition where it was less and less advisable to lay one's cards on the table and keep one's word. Montaigne preferred to develop a model of knowledge founded on experience rather than on authority. But with time he realized that even the best arguments rarely make it possible to change people's minds.

Montaigne began his studies at the College of Guyenne not long after Petrus Ramus (Pierre de la Ramée) launched the anti-Aristotelian movement in France. To gauge the import of Ramus's criticism, let us recall what he said at the Sorbonne in 1536: *"Quaecumque ab Aristotele dicta essent, commentitia esse"* ("everything Aristotle said is mere falsity"). In his turn, Montaigne judged the father of Western philosophy with skepticism. Although always invoked when philosophical questions were involved, Aristotle was no longer regarded as an infallible authority. His method was questioned and it was rapidly perceived that numerous premises of the *corpus aristotelicum* no longer corresponded to the lived experience of people at the end of the Renaissance. However, despite these critical examinations of the very foundations of the knowledge drawn from the ancients, the Aristotelian order still survived. Montaigne's education is located precisely at the crucial intersection between the challenge to the Aristotelian system of knowledge and the introduction of new methods of investigation based on dialectics, on the one hand,[98] and on the constant negotiation of the idea of truth, and especially the idea of jurisprudence, on the other. It is in this sense that Montaigne declares that when he was young he never gnawed his nails "over the study of Plato or[xxix] Aristotle."[99]

Montaigne remained outside philosophical quarrels, taking an interest in more concrete questions such as the art of governing. The situation in Bordeaux, where his father participated in the everyday management of the city, probably allowed him to form a more realistic and more practical idea of the influence of politics on human relations. During the Renaissance, Aristotle's texts had been disseminated by Scholastic authors, thanks to compilations augmented by commentaries. In the *Essais*, these "savants" of the Middle Ages repeatedly provoke Montaigne's irony: "Anyone who does not know Aristotle, according to them, by the same token does not know himself."[100] He also mocks those who run everything through the *étamine* (a cloth used as a sieve or filter) of Aristotle. Montaigne compares Aristotelian philosophy to a mercantile operation, desacralizing it and making it seem banal; he takes philosophical argumentation as "a coin which human stupidity readily accepts as payment,"[101] adding after 1588 that "the learned employ, like conjurors, [this coin] in order not to reveal the vanity of their art." This anti-intellectual view, often present in the *Essais*, is perhaps the sign of a truncated or unfinished education.

Montaigne systematically criticizes the Aristotelianism he encountered in his schooling, but remains deeply influenced by Aristotelian morality, for lack of a better one. His rejection of philosophy nonetheless reveals a profound respect for studies that he had not been able to complete. This kind of autodidactic work remains frustrating when one secretly continues to harbor ambitions to succeed. Aristotle and most of the other philosophers are always present, even if they are roundly criticized in the *Essais*. When one sets out to struggle against the abuse of the ancients' authority, there is no more perfect example than Aristotle: "The god of scholastic knowledge is Aristotle; it is a religious matter to discuss any of his ordinances, as with those of Lycurgus at Sparta. His doctrine serves us as magisterial law, when it is peradventure as false as another."[102] The definition Montaigne gives of Aristotelianism as a "Pyrrhonism in an affirmative form"[103] produces an oxymoron that reflects rather well his view of the Greek philosopher after his years of study at the College of Guyenne and in Paris. From his education and his apprenticeship in logic and the human sciences, he retained the memory of a "clatter of so many philosophical brains."[104]

The humanistic education Montaigne received at the College of Guyenne and in Paris was out of sync with the scientific and ethical transformations of his time. Montaigne was exposed to all sorts of questionings that undoubtedly

---

[xxix] The words "Plato or" were deleted on the Bordeaux Copy, and thus do not appear in Frame's translation. [Trans.]

favored his skepticism and relativism. What is lacking in the thinkers of this period—and what distinguishes them, for example, from the authors of the eighteenth century—is a powerful awareness of the relativity of all knowledge. The humanist movement merely strengthened the fixity of Western knowledge by advocating a moral and political universalism. After successfully combining Aristotelianism with religious dogma, the sixteenth-century intellectual began in turn to produce facile glosses on the ancients. On this point, the College of Guyenne's *cursus* is revealing. It sometimes departed from Aristotelian doctrines but hardly dared to distance itself completely from the *corpus aristotelicum*. The questioning of the purpose of all knowledge inevitably involved the destruction of the two great specters of the Renaissance: Aristotle and the dogma of the Catholic Church. All truth, whether ecclesiastical or secular, was inevitably inspired by these two dogmas, which limited any criticism and any judgment.

The works of Nicholas of Cusa, Copernicus, Thomas Digges, and Giordano Bruno contributed to the collapse of Aristotelian ideas, advanced the heliocentric conception of the cosmos, favored the idea of an open-ended world, and eventuated in the acceptance of a universe in permanent movement. These successive stages led to what has been so judiciously called the "dissolution of the cosmos."[105] When Montaigne was writing his first essays, this dissolution was not yet complete, but the process was advancing and our essayist easily discerned the first cracks in the Aristotelian edifice. That is probably why Montaigne declares science to be unstable, "useless," "sterile or thorny," and sees in it only "dreams and fanatical follies," "fantasies," "twaddle and lies," preferring for his part a form of empirical and even experimental knowledge.

The ideas set forth by Copernicus in his *De revolutionibus orbium caelestium* (1543) slowly spread, but as early as 1560 the notion of a heliocentric cosmos was already sufficiently well known to allow Montaigne (who had no scientific pretensions and shared the views most common in his time) to make reference to it in his *Essais*. Imagine Ptolemy and Aristotle, who had been pillars of Western civilization for more than fifteen centuries, suddenly being shaken; it was the whole humanistic edifice that was about to topple. Montaigne was a witness to his time: "Ptolemy, who was a great man, had established the limits of our world; all the ancient philosophers thought they had its measure."[106] Everything collapsed in a moment. So who should be believed? What can we know? These two questions constantly recur in the *Essais*. Montaigne's scientific relativism is almost always situated in an opposition between bookish knowledge and the concrete experiences it pleases him to adduce. His education had given him only an indirect knowledge of human beings and the world; the *Essais* ended up concentrating on their author's own experience.

In the 1550s, Copernicus's ideas also raised other problems of a religious nature. How could man and God be situated in an infinite universe? If man was no longer the center of the universe, what became of the divine relation between the microcosm and the macrocosm? If the Earth was a planet just like the other planets, it was no longer a privileged place. Were these other planets inhabited? If they were, were their inhabitants also children of Adam and Eve? How could they have inherited original sin? If the universe was infinite, where would the throne of God be located? These were all awkward questions for the ecclesiastical authorities, who took no official position until 1616, when Copernicus's theory was deemed dangerous and harmful to the faith, and Galileo was condemned by the Inquisition for promoting it, and then again in 1633, when it was finally forbidden to teach or believe that the sun was the center of the universe and that the Earth was a planet. Although during the twelfth and thirteenth centuries it had been possible to integrate Aristotle and Ptolemy into Catholic dogma, by the end of the sixteenth century the questions Copernicus and his followers raised had become unacceptable to the Church and met with even more violent opposition among Protestants.

After challenging Aristotle's physics, metaphysics, and ethics, the Renaissance found itself facing a void. The Aristotelian idea of the "natural place" in a finite universe, where everything had its place and where there was a place for everything, was now obsolete. Ernst Cassirer observes that after Copernicus "there is no absolute 'above' or 'below,' and, therefore, there can no longer be just one direction of influence. The idea of the world organism is here expanded in such a way that every element in the world may with equal right be considered the central point of the universe."[107] Things wander about in an infinite cosmos, everything is in motion, and man himself is astonished by his ontological nakedness. Everything has to be done over. Montaigne is once again a witness to this time and offers a pessimistic assessment of the state of scientific knowledge: "there is no existence that is constant, either of our being or of that of objects. And we, and our judgment, and all mortal things go on flowing and rolling unceasingly. Thus nothing certain can be established about one thing by another, both the judging and the judged being in continual change and motion."[108]

The man of the late Renaissance was credulous; the world was suddenly falling away under his feet, and he was ready to believe all sorts of things. People marveled at the discovery of the New World, and fabulous stories were told about the human beings and animals living on those lands. Montaigne shared this interest in the marvelous. To use Alexandre Koyré's expression, the man of the Renaissance was the prisoner of a "magic ontology";[109] he got lost on countless paths that led nowhere. This apparent disorder nonetheless allowed a multitude of ideas to arise and develop on the basis of a critique of the ancients. This skeptical questioning constituted the ground on which it became possible to construct the science and philosophy of the seventeenth century. It is in the middle of this transition between two conceptions of the world that Montaigne and his *Essais* are situated. His education served to open his eyes, so to speak. The *Essais* became a disillusioned testimony to a period that was tired of being Latin and ancient. People doubted because they could no longer do otherwise, and relativism was not yet a philosophy but simply a necessity.

Montaigne nonetheless refused to adhere to Copernicus's ideas and those of his disciples. After all, "who knows whether a third opinion, a thousand years from now, will not overthrow the preceding two?"[110] Science did not really interest him, because he considered it "in motion" and, especially, he never had the means to reconstruct a fallen order. This position has rightly been called "ignorance."[111] In fact, Montaigne declares that "there is nothing I treat specifically except nothing, and no knowledge except that of the lack of knowledge [*inscience*]."[112] Montaigne's *inscience* may have its origin in his conception of chance and fortuity. Moreover, what point is there in taking an interest in science, since any explanation will always be only provisional? Edifices, which fall victim to the erosion of time, end up disappearing sooner or later, as do political systems.

From the years he spent at the College of Guyenne, Montaigne derived a single precept that soon established itself as a method: "What matters is not merely that we see the thing, but how we see it."[113] The instruction in politics he received from his father during the salt-tax revolt made him understand that society can pass from stability into chaos at any moment. No system can last very long without undergoing profound upheavals that are intrinsic to it. The Wars of Religion are probably the best example of this. From that moment on, any perception of human beings and the world could only be relative. History, science, and truth acquired a previously unknown malleability. Reason manifested itself only as a flexible and distortable artifice: "I always call reason that semblance of intellect that each man fabricates in himself. That reason, of which, by its condition, there can be a hundred contradictory ones about one and the same subject, is an instrument of lead and of wax, stretchable, pliable, and adaptable to all biases and all measures."[114]

Why is Montaigne so little inclined to talk about the years following his study at the College of Guyenne? Probably for the same reason that he does not talk about his experience at the Cour des Aides in Périgueux or at the parlement of Bordeaux. The *Essais* is a book written by a noble, and Montaigne preferred to keep silent about his first career as a member of parlement and the education that led to that profession. Montaigne's memories of his years as a student were bitter and even negative. We know the recommendation he gave Diane de Foix regarding the choice of a tutor capable of instructing her child: "I would also urge that care be taken to choose a guide with a well-made rather than a well-filled head."[115] However, he was able to benefit from his studies; this humanist education, challenged by his own experiences and observations, led to the feeling that knowledge was unstable and relative and to a salutary doubt. Much later, in 1588, he admits that at first he regarded education as a means of showing off before later returning to a more playful conception of knowledge and teaching. But he adds that he never saw his studies as a way to succeed and earn a living: "In my youth I studied for ostentation; later, for recreation, never for gain."[116] It remains to be seen what use he made of his education during his initial career in the parlement. One thing is certain: despite what he says, this education made it easier for him to obtain an office. The Eyquems' social ascent led Montaigne to hope he had a bright future in the parlement.

CHAPTER 2

A First Career as a Magistrate (1556–1570)

In 1556, when Montaigne was about to join the parlement of Bordeaux, that prestigious institution still remained an exclusive domain. The Palais de l'Ombrière, where it was located, was a site of power, the highest judicial authority in Guyenne. The Bordeaux parlement, the fourth oldest in France, was a kind of supreme court that considered only cases on appeal and was the final authority. The parlements' jurisdiction had been limited by the introduction of the présidial courts created by Henri II in 1552 in order to reinforce his judicial power and replenish the royal coffers with the sale of new offices, but in practice these civil and criminal tribunals, which were intermediary between the parlements and the sénéchaussée, increased the prestige of the parlements and the magistrates, because with the creation of a supplementary level within the structure of the judiciary, the members of the parlements considered their position still more elevated and their authority greater. In Montaigne's time, most of the councillors "inherited" their offices from generation to generation and came principally from the wealthiest families of Bordeaux and Guyenne. The members of the parlement constituted a veritable patriarchy and dispensed justice without being answerable to any superior authority. Until 1550, all Bordeaux's magistrates were appointed directly by the parlement, in accord with its recognized competence in jurisdictional matters. The majority of the offices were filled by members of merchant families who saw in the parlement a means of social ascent. The judicial system was slowly transformed into a plutocracy and had reached a level of hereditary monopoly such that the local elites engaged in ruthless battles to keep control of judicial positions within their families and defend themselves against other families that were also trying to make their way into the parlementary milieu in order to show their local or regional success. We need only consider one incident to see how political consanguinity prevailed in Bordeaux in Montaigne's time. This affair reveals the tensions and internal battles that divided these parlementary lineages as they defended their social and political prerogatives.

In late 1559, the jurats of the city of Bordeaux presented a request to the parlement with the goal of challenging no less than fifty-one of its members who had more or less direct family connections with one another and shared narrow economic interests with the defendant in a trial, Came de Sagle, a bargeman who had illegally brought wine inside the city walls.[1] These challenges were actually equivalent to refusals to recognize the authority of a member of the parlement on the grounds that he was suspected of partiality; the best way of contesting the integrity of a judge was to invoke parental ties with one of the parties involved in a trial. The documents collected for the hearing claim that it was a matter of ensuring that the statutes and privileges of the city of Bordeaux were respected; in reality, it was chiefly a question of protecting the economic advantages of the bourgeoisie of Bordeaux. Numerous attorneys and councillors of the parlement were directly involved in defending the interests of the winemakers of Haut Pays, thus opposing the commercial protectionism of the city's bourgeois. In Bordeaux and the surrounding region, the wine trade was the main source of revenue, and the stakes involved would be considerable if the monopoly on wine and the regulations concerning its storage within the city's walls were to be put in question. The trial of this bargeman from Toulouse could have acquired a significant economic importance, because the judgment on the appeal would have created a precedent and made laws regarding the right to bring wine from the Haut Pays into Bordeaux. This case, which was otherwise ordinary enough for the tribunal, reveals the political and economic interests not only of the members of the jurade but also of those who had to judge this case on appeal, that is, of the members of the Bordeaux parlement who were Montaigne's contemporaries.

The mayor at the time, Pierre Geneste, who was also a crier at the chancellery, joined the complaint alongside the jurats in this case. Because of its composition—two bourgeois, two nobles, two *robins*[i]—the jurade often endorsed the positions defended by the representatives of the bourgeoisie, since the decisions made by nobles of the robe who were members of the jurade were frequently in line with the views of the bourgeois. Coming from the same great families, they generally shared a common ideology, but they sometimes clashed because of specific interests, notably regarding the sale, transportation, and storage of wine. The jurats mainly defended the city's interests, and the members of the parlement—including a large number of them who had commercial interests in the region, and not solely in Bordeaux—sometimes opposed the economic protectionism advocated by the city's bourgeois. We do not know exactly the origin of the conflict (in the first trial), but it seems to have divided the jurade and the parlement in this case. A class analysis or a simple opposition between the two orders does not suffice to understand the stakes involved in this litigation. In

---

[i] I remind the reader that this term, which will be frequently used, refers to a member of the nobility of the robe. [Trans.]

any event, a majority of the jurats turned against their mayor, whom they accused of being in cahoots with the parlement and of not doing enough to defend the city's interests. The petition presented by the jurats denounced a flagrant conflict of interest and held "as suspect" most of the presidents and councillors of the parlement, who were accused of protecting their own economic interests in a trial that could have had repercussions on the circulation and sale of wine in the region, thus putting in question the privileges of the bourgeois of Bordeaux regarding the production and sale of wine. A list was drawn up with the names of the members of the parlement to be challenged and the reason for which their competence was contested in this trial.

A rapid examination of this list shows the family interdependence of the members of the parlement and their common interests. The parlement was composed of presidents, advocates, judges, and reporters who belonged to families that had been intermarrying for several generations. The members of the Bordeaux parlement constituted an *extended family* in the literal sense of the term. However, these professional and family alliances did not do away with career conflicts, which became even more visible when the disputes concerned the economic basis of these families. Over the long term, the personal confrontations were, of course, attenuated by class interests common to the generations, but in practice personal dissensions sometimes led to very violent conflicts. In the Old Régime, the members of the parlement were more than a milieu; they were already more like a constituted body whose steps toward social recognition were not solely symbolic but also revealed a stubborn struggle for control of the local political organization.

In Bordeaux, the career of a member of the parlement inevitably passed through the bottleneck of promotions to the Great Chamber and to the two investigative chambers. It was in connection with these professional promotions that the bitterness and hatred became most visible. Too many applicants were seeking the same rare promotions and, in the confusion of family ties, many members of parlement found it difficult to accept seeing a cousin in the fourth degree promoted ahead of them. Each member kept his own secret account of the alliances that guaranteed him a promotion, but he was also wary of other parlementary phratries that nourished similar ambitions. Although the bourgeoisie did not have direct access to political power, the *robins* took control of the judicial apparatus and used their influence on the municipal administration to increase the power they had succeeded in gaining. The collusion between these two groups was common currency. Thanks to their status, the councillors belonged to the "nobility of service" and often sold their competence to those of the merchant class eager to take advantage of their judicial expertise. Their alliance was natural, because they had common economic interests. This social interdependence produced resentment on the personal level and often led to accusations that took the form of challenges during deliberations in the parlement.

In the petition presented during the case of the Toulouse bargeman who had had the bad idea of unloading his wine on the banks of the Garonne, the collusion of interests reached its apex because the president, Christophe de Roffignac, is described as the close friend of the general prosecutor, Bernard de Brachs, who represented the mayor in this trial. The mayor's affairs, we are told in the decree issued by the parlement following this petition, are considered as "his own," thus revealing a complicity between the parlement and the jurade. The prosecutor was a cousin of the mayor "in the fourth degree." The second president of the parlement, Pierre de Carle, was married to the sister of another councillor, Arnoul Le Ferron, a descendant of a rich family of merchants[2] who had married one of the daughters of the advocate Bertrand Duplessis, the son of one of Pierre Geneste's nieces.

The numerous challenges invoked in this trial, almost all of them based on family ties among members of the parlement, are dizzying. We cannot enumerate all of them here without confusing the reader. It will suffice to note that archival documents implicate an impressive number of members of the parlement. It is easy to get lost in these complex parlementary lineages, but the councillors of the period knew the history of these families inside out and did not hesitate to resort to challenges at every moment. These endogamous practices were frequent in Bordeaux during the first half of the sixteenth century. The conflict of interest in the procedure targeting Came de Sagle referred chiefly to the financial profits connected with the transportation and sale of wine. Many members of the parlement had every interest in seeing to it that the wine produced on their property could enter Bordeaux without too much difficulty, and that was what the city's bourgeois wanted to prohibit. Despite the great number of challenges, the trial of the Toulouse bargeman was not an exception; on the contrary, it reveals a well-worn practice and a habitual way of proceeding at the parlement of Bordeaux in Montaigne's time.

Montaigne's family was also involved in this affair. The petition of recusal actually names Montaigne's uncle, Raymond Eyquem de Bussaguet, whose first wife, Adrienne, was the daughter of the president, Geoffroy de La Chassaigne. The judicial procedure notes in particular that Raymond Eyquem was a first cousin "in the fourth degree" of Le Ferron. The La Chassaignes tried to play their cards well on this occasion. They were one of the three great parlementary families in Bordeaux, and they had deliberately infiltrated the various chambers of justice, constantly intervening in the administrative machinery of the city and the parlement. In December 1560, the president, Christophe de Roffignac, warned his colleagues by declaring before the parlement that "the alliances of the aforementioned president Lachassaigne [*sic*] in the court were great."[3]

Montaigne himself had also joined this little world of presidents, council-lors, and advocates bound together by family ties; within only three genera-tions, they had transformed themselves into a veritable parlementary nobility. The Eyquems had no lack of relatives in the parlement. It suffices to recall that Richard de Lestonnac was Montaigne's brother-in-law, Antoine de Belcier, his first cousin, Joseph de La Chassaigne, his father-in-law, Raymond Eyquem de Bussaguet his uncle, Étienne Eymar a distant cousin, and Jean du Faure de La Roderie a relative by marriage with one of Montaigne's cousins. All these rela-tives of Montaigne were among the people most influential at the parlement of Bordeaux in the early 1560s. In November 1561, before the whole court, Mon-taigne recognized that several members of his family were members of the par-lement, as were still others "he did not know about."[4] Thus the Eyquems were connected with the Valiers, the Maisonneuves, the Carles, the Baussays, and the Le Ferrons; the La Chassaignes were connected with the Beaulnes and the Pon-tacs. Examples of these family and professional ties were certainly numerous throughout the kingdom, but they were particularly frequent in Bordeaux.[5] The privileged relationships that united the Eyquem and Le Ferron families are re-vealing on this point.

The Le Ferrons' social trajectory is almost identical with that of the Ey-quems. A merchant, then treasurer of the city in 1486 and jurat in 1490, Jehan Le Ferron married his two daughters to councillors at the parlement.[6] One of his sons, Arnoul, was appointed lay councillor in 1535 when his father resigned. The same social and professional course was followed by the councillors Étienne Eymar and Pierre Ferrand, who became brothers-in-law after marrying, respec-tively, Béatrix and Catherine de Louppes, who were relatives of Montaigne's mother. Antoine de Louppes, the father of Béatrix and Catherine, was the uncle of Antoinette, the wife of Pierre Eyquem, Montaigne's father.[7] To complicate the situation still further, one of the cousins of their two wives was herself the sister-in-law of Raymond Eyquem. The Eyquems had been able to exploit these matrimonial connections in order to break into the closed circle of the members of the parlement.

But the story of our Toulouse bargeman does not end there. The quarrel over the transportation and storage of wine in Bordeaux caused the deliberations in the parlement to develop into a veritable fistfight worthy of a schoolyard, in which the names of Montaigne and La Boétie were soon involved in the numer-ous altercations and the insults exchanged on both sides. Several jurats de-nounced Antoine de Belcier, the judge of the royal provostship and a councillor at the parlement, and also the nephew of Raymond Eyquem as well as Le Fer-ron's cousin in the fourth degree. The sister of Raymond and Pierre Eyquem, Blanquine, had married Martial de Belcier, an advocate at the parlement and the son of the president, François de Belcier. Richard de Lestonnac, an advocate at the court who had married Raymond Eyquem's niece, was also attacked. Jehan de Ciret, Joseph de Valier, and Denis de Baulon, all advocates, were the target of a demand for recusal on the same grounds as Estienne de La Boétie, who, because of his marriage to the sister of the president, de Carle, and his family tie "in the fourth degree" with the Belcier, did not seem likely to deliberate impartially regarding the case. Jean de Calvimont, an advocate at that time, was himself one of Belcier's cousins. It was also mentioned that La Boétie had an uncle, Léonard Amelin, who was also an advocate at the parlement and was implicated even more directly in this case because of his commercial ties with several Bordeaux bourgeois. All these members of the parlement were accused of conniving with Joseph Eymar, who was the nephew of a secretary to the king, Bertrand de Villeneuve. Three generations of intermarriages had created a veritable caste that placed the city and parlement in the hands of a few families. The blood relationships between judicial officials were so prevalent that it was common to begin the parlement's sessions with a series of challenges that had become a ritual.

The family relationships binding together the councillors, presidents, advocates, and royal secretaries were so complex that it proved impossible to take an objective position concerning the infraction committed by the Toulouse bargeman. In fact, it was soon forgotten and gave way to a squabble between clans determined to see their interests prevail. Although the list of challenges was still long, we will not mention all the sons-in-law, cousins, uncles, stepbrothers from the same mother, and children from various marriages. In 1560, the parlement had become a "matter of families" with its immemorial quarrels and economic conflicts that flared up anew in each generation. This little world closed in on itself could favor an entrance into the magistracy through the support of relatives who were themselves members of the parlement, but this system of political nepotism also showed its limits because of the competition between the families to keep the upper hand. Montaigne also suffered from these internal quarrels among the great parlementary families. In the case of the transporter of wine from Toulouse, we see that a large proportion of the members of the Bordeaux parlement used their offices to deflect the prohibition on importing wine to the city and took advantage of their positions as magistrates to make a decision in their own favor, which was denounced by the French chancellor, Michel de L'Hospital, as will be seen later. Moreover, this tradition that made it possible to gain economic advantages from public offices was not limited to the parlement. We will see how during his two terms as mayor of Bordeaux, Montaigne used his political power to make his private affairs prosper and to "illegally" store wine from his lands within the city walls.

A few members of the parlement had every interest in having the monopoly on wines and the prohibition on storing casks from other regions lifted. The

Pontacs were several times involved in suits against the jurats "because of the honors and preeminences of their estates," which they exploited in the form of special privileges. The Bordeaux bourgeois distrusted the parlement's officers, who used their power to get around the regulations on bringing merchandise inside the city walls, and in general they thought they were superior to the jurats on the pretext that they represented the king's justice. For example, the advocate Antoine Gaultier owned vineyards at La Réole where he "received large quantities of wine" and repeatedly ignored municipal ordinances concerning its transportation and storage. Agreements between the bourgeois and *robins* were rather common, and bribes generally ended up in the pockets of members of the parlement. Thus Louis de Pontac, a relative by marriage of the Lestonnacs, bourgeois of Bordeaux, often defended the economic interests of merchants in exchange for generous payments. The Pontacs were descended from a wealthy family of businessmen and had retained precious contacts in the mercantile world. Arnaud de Pontac, a bourgeois and merchant in Bordeaux who owned a vineyard in Haut-Brion, had been ennobled at the very beginning of the sixteenth century and had received patent letters of nobility in 1514 as a reward for services rendered.[8] He was mayor of Bordeaux in 1505 and was generally recognized for having developed and transformed the wine trade there, allowing numerous businessmen to get rich and the city to prosper.[9] On the strength of his success, in 1523 Jehan de Pontac had bought an office as clerk of the parlement, and Louis de Pontac entered the parlement in his turn in 1543.[10] The first wife of the clerk Jacques de Pontac, Louis's brother, was an Eyquem niece. Raymond de Pontac, Jehan's son, also became a councillor at the parlement in 1567 and a president in 1570; a brilliant career thanks to an excellent marriage with Ysabeau de La Chassaigne, who had been widowed.[ii] We see that the same family names constantly recur all through the sixteenth century. The quarrels between jurats and magistrates were frequent, and "retributive" suits often opposed municipal elected officials and the families of members of the parlement who came from Guyenne.

On the fringes of the Toulouse bargeman's case, other attorneys were accused of being too close to the merchant Jean Rignac—Came de Sagle's agent in Bordeaux—who was in conflict with the jurats "because of certain legal proceedings," and was accused of having violated the city's statutes and ordinances. The advocate Pierre du Duc—who became a councillor shortly afterward and worked with Montaigne—was also denounced by the bourgeois members of the jurade because he owned "large properties" in Mas d'Agenois and other places in the Haut Pays. Half the parlement was involved in one way or another in this

---

[ii] In the culmination of a rapid social ascent, in 1632 Arnaud de Pontac married Henriette-Gabrielle-Louise de Thou, the daughter of Jacques-Auguste de Thou.

simple case of commercial transgression. In the end, more than half the names listed on this document were recused for the trial, including Raymond Eyquem. The other half of those whose names appeared on the list were absolved, and the court even judged certain accusations to be frivolous. After deliberation, the decree promulgated allowed most of the members of the parlement to intervene in the trial, speaking and "opining" as they wished. This was notably the case for La Boétie, La Chassaigne, and Alesme. In the end, it was a tempest in a teapot. However, more important than the judgment on the appeal was the quarrel itself, which is significant here because it sketches a not very advantageous portrait of the parlementary milieu in the time of Montaigne. The parlement and the jurade were at daggers drawn, and justice too often gave way to considerations of a commercial and mercantile order.

Nonetheless, we have to distinguish between nepotism and conflicts of interest. Relations between rival families were far from harmonious, and members of the parlement found it very difficult to weigh the merits of the relative claims of family ties and punctual political alliances that could bring them the most immediate benefits. Private interests were not always in accord with a family tradition that went back several generations. The sale of public offices encouraged a form of political nepotism, but conflicts of interest soon led to denunciations and exposed members of the parlement to increased supervision on the part of royal authority. By the early 1560s demands for recusals had become systematic in Bordeaux, and every time family ties—direct or indirect—were invoked to prove that the judicial system was corrupt and in the pay of whoever paid most. The case of the bargeman from Toulouse shows that the relations among the great bourgeois families were so closely intertwined that it had become relatively easy to point out a connection in the third or fourth degree. Members of the parlementary "extended family" that had appropriated judicial offices in Bordeaux spent a large part of their time denouncing one another. The Eyquem family had made a major contribution to this *consanguine judicial system*, thanks to its patrimonial marriages with the Lestonnacs and the La Chassaignes. But what had initially benefited these families soon turned against those who had joined the parlement more recently. Montaigne was later to pay the price for this familial proximity that made more difficult the prospects of having a prestigious career and rapid professional advancement within this institution.

Parlementary Habitus

The sale of judicial offices, which had been legal since 1524, had allowed the king to reduce a budget deficit that was increasing from year to year, and to replenish his treasury. But this rushing into the trade in offices was rather ill received by the sitting magistrates. During the second half of the sixteenth century, criticisms of the cost of judicial proceedings and the corruption connected with these offices became more and more numerous.[11] Jean Savaron fulminated against the outrageous multiplication of offices in the late sixteenth century and objected to the proliferation of honors. He complained about "subjects burdened by a countless number of officials who live at their expense and make them incapable of paying your [the king's] taxes and contributions."[12] Savaron's argument expresses well the liberal ideology defended by the great merchant families; the bourgeois burdened by the costs incurred during the trial would find it easier to pay their direct taxes if they were not spending such large sums on defending themselves in the various courts of justice created by the king. People were already complaining about excessive regulations and legal proceedings. Judicial offices increased in number at an enormous pace and everyone was encouraged to take his neighbor to court, no matter how trivial the complaint. The judicial machine had to have something to do.

All through the sixteenth century, there was a slow but effective patrimonialization of judicial offices, which were transformed into businesses that could be handed down from one generation to the next, because dispensing justice brought in income. Let us cite a few figures for Bordeaux. In 1515, the parlement of Bordeaux had only twenty-five members. In 1533, it had five presidents and thirty-one councillors. This figure was practically doubled in less than a decade, because the number of members of parlement increased to seven presidents and fifty-five councillors in 1543, then leveled off at between sixty-two and sixty-six councillors from 1543 to 1585. A second Chambre des Enquêtes (Chamber of Investigations) was created in 1543 in order to cope with this rapid increase in the number of judicial officials—an increase that directly benefited the Eyquem family and Montaigne. Members of the parlement were exempt from the requirement to perform military service for their lords, and were also exempt from certain taxes. Their power continued to be primarily economic, and it has been estimated that by the end of the sixteenth century more than half the city's wealth was in the hands of the members of the parlement of Bordeaux.[13] The parlement had such authority that the king himself said that "if he wasn't king, he would want to be a councillor at the parlement of Bordeaux."[14] In addition to this economic power there was also the prestige associated with the status of a member of the parlement.

The sale of offices had been officially condemned under Charles IX, at the meeting of the Estates General held at Blois in 1560. Another condemnation was decreed in 1576 under Henry III. However, nothing had really changed, because, as we have said, these offices represented a considerable source of revenue for a crown whose coffers were emptying faster than they were filling up. At the beginning of the 1560s there was, as Savaron put it, "an enormous number of officials so great that it is almost easier to encounter an official than to find a man who does not hold an office."[15] Despite Savaron's exaggeration, it nonetheless remains that by their very numbers the nobility of the robe constituted a new political force that ended up weakening royal authority. Of course, officially justice was not for sale, and the historian Natalie Zemon Davis reminds us that under the Old Régime obtaining an office was not seen as a sale, and that the payment was made in the form of a friendly loan to the king.[16] The purchase of an office was not in itself sufficient to enter the parlement; the aspirant also had to be sponsored and examined by the professional group that he wanted to join. But no one was deceived by this ethical posture. It was purely conventional and the "loan" was, of course, never repaid by the king. Public offices were an effective means of cutting oneself off from mercantile practices and taking a first step toward the nobility of the robe, which, although it was decried by the nobility of the sword, nonetheless had a genuine political power at the regional level. The transmission of offices to their descendants allowed *robins* to keep symbolic and financial capital within their own family.[17]

The sociologist Pierre Bourdieu analyzed the way the conditioning to which particular groups are exposed gives rise to transmissible *habitus*. The parlementary *habitus* allowed the individual to perceive career possibilities structured in time. The councillor internalized a system organized from within and agreed to respect judicial practices founded on a strong hierarchical organization of offices. In Montaigne's time, the parlementary *habitus* was characterized by career expectations that governed and determined individual behaviors: it favored a hierarchical progression that took place within clearly defined structures, but in which each individual could also express his difference with regard to his colleagues through strategies of advancement that were more rapid but also more dangerous because they risked producing conflictual relationships with his peers. The example of the bargeman from Toulouse is a symptom of these structural tensions that characterized the parlementary *habitus*. According to Bourdieu, the expectations of a particular agent are defined "by the relationship between, on the one hand, his *habitus* with its temporal structures and dispositions towards the future, constituted in the course of a particular relationship to a particular universe of possibilities, and on the other hand a certain state of the chances objectively offered to him by the social world."[18] It is a question of accepting the rules governing the parlement's functioning while at the same time trying to transgress them in order to benefit from the system more than others do. This *habitus* can be discerned in the social behavior of a single individual whose professional course serves as a model and a reference point for a larger group, but it also denotes deviations with respect to the norms of behavior possible within a career. In Montaigne's case, the parlementary *habitus* authorizes us to imagine a typical behavior where archival documents are often lacking.

The social ascent of the De Thou family offers a good example of the parlementary *habitus* and remains a model of the kind. Jacques-Auguste de Thou's career sheds light on this ideal career path of a *robin* whose individual strategy nonetheless corresponded to a typical behavior. In the Renaissance, the magistracy led to social recognition.[19] Although Jacques-Auguste distinguished himself from other members of the parlement and succeeded in establishing himself by showing more elevated aspirations to claim to be assimilated to families of the nobility of the sword and of the "high robe" (*haute robe*),[20] he nevertheless had to go through these stages without overturning the rules that structured the framework of promotions within an established hierarchy, and thus without arousing the resentment of other members of the parlement. Whatever the level one occupied in an administrative organization, one still had to show consideration for one's peers until one had risen to a more elevated status. This typical and successful path—successful since De Thou finally attained the "high robe," that is, the highest summit of the state—is worth recalling because it incarnates the ideal career to which every member of the parlement in the second half of the sixteenth century aspired.

In 1562, Christophe de Thou, Jacques-Auguste's father, held the office of first president of the parlement of Paris and placed his children in key positions at the upper levels of the state administration.[21] Christophe de Thou's career served as a model for other presidents of the regional parlements. His daughters played roles as important as those of their brothers in this rapid ascent of a merchant family. In 1566 Jacques-Auguste's sister Anne married Philippe Hurault, the lord of Cheverny and Chancellor of France; two years afterward his other sister, Catherine, married the first president, Achille de Harlay; in 1568 one of his brothers, Jean, became "Master of Requests" (*maître des requêtes*)[iii]; another brother, Christophe, held the post of "Master in the Courts of Finances" (*maître des comptes*) and then that of "Grand Master of Waters and Forests" (*grand maître des Eaux et Forêts*). Jacques-Auguste's career represents far more than an individual success, because the terrain had been largely prepared for him by the family trajectory characteristic of wealthy merchant families that had recently been ennobled thanks to their membership in the parlement: a fortune accumulated in the world of commerce (fabrics), the offices of advocate, *président à mortier*,[iv] councillor in the parlement, *maître des requêtes, grand maître des Eaux*

[iii] A "Master of Requests," is a counsel of the Council of State (*Conseil d'État*), a high-level judicial officer of administrative law in France. [Trans.]

[iv] A title used for presidents of the Great Chamber to mark their preeminence with regard to the presidents of the other chambers—"mortier" being the name of the velvet cap they wore.

et Forêts, and finally state councillor. Jacques-Auguste de Thou had passed through all these stages before becoming a great servant of the king and the state. His family symbolizes the success of a strategy whose goal was to insinuate itself into the administrative machinery of the parlement and then of the "high robe," in order to cross social barriers and move from one order to the next.

During the second half of the sixteenth century, the office of *maître des requêtes* enabled a person to gain access to the antechamber of power. For a member of a parlement, it was a necessary stage on the way to the Council of State. The *maîtres des requêtes* were responsible for receiving petitions presented to the king, but La Roche Flavin considers them to be "the Chancellor's assessors and advisers,"[22] that is, men close to the source of power. In 1558 there were twenty-six of them,[23] but this number grew steadily throughout the 1560s and exceeded one hundred by 1575. This office was an obligatory transition to approaching the royal Court and gaining access to more important royal offices. That was the chief objective of members of parlements who had to make themselves noticed in the halls of justice while at the same time doing their best to keep on the good side of their colleagues who were playing the same game and nourished the same hopes. Despite the multiplication of *maîtres des requêtes*, these positions were still expensive in Montaigne's time. In the past, seven councillors at the parlement of Bordeaux had succeeded in rising in the hierarchy and joining the parlement of Paris. That was the case for Christophe de Roffignac, who left the parlement of Bordeaux and was received as a councillor-clerk in the parlement of Paris in February 1544.[24] The same year, he became *président des requêtes* of the same court. In 1555, he returned to Bordeaux as president of the parlement. Other people joined the Great Council, a judicial formation whose purpose was to relieve the Council of the King of judicial petitions:[25] Annet de Plas in 1527, Jehan Bagis in 1536, Geoffroy Couillaud in 1538, and Ogier Hunault de Lanta in 1542 followed this path.[26] These members of the Bordeaux parlement who had been called to the Great Council served as models for young councillors eager to have a brilliant career.

It was not easy to approach the court. But it was there that the most important posts were handed out. Organizing and joining networks was indispensable for penetrating powerful circles. On this strategy for approaching the court, we have the testimony of Philippe Hurault, count of Cheverny.

In 1586, when he began writing his *Mémoires*, Cheverny retraced a career that sheds light on the way in which one gained access to the Court. Born in 1528 to a "good, noble, and ancient family" of Brittany, Cheverny was intended to become a churchman. Confronted by the difficulty of obtaining a benefice that would lead to a comfortable life, he undertook studies in Poitiers and Padua. Through his mother, he entered the service of his cousin, the archbishop of Tours, who accompanied Henry II when he went off to Germany to battle the emperor's armies. But his protector, the archbishop, suddenly died and Cheverny found himself without employment. He briefly sums up the rest of his fortune: "Being at that time twenty-four years old, I resolved to acquire an ability to get along by myself and a certain experience in the parlement of Paris, where I recognized that great people had made themselves. By good fortune, this intention happened to coincide with a decision made by my lord Michel de L'Hospital, later Chancellor of France, who wanted to resign from his position as Councillor of the Church at the said parlement, in order to take the position of chancellor to Madame Margaret of France, the sister of King Henry II . . . so that by his resignation I was given the aforesaid position of councillor to the aforementioned parlement by King Henry."[27] These events occurred in 1553, at almost the same time that Montaigne joined the Cour des Aides in Périgueux, under rather similar circumstances. It was essential to remain vigilant and constantly on the watch for opportunities that might present themselves.

These discretionary appointments were relatively frequent. Cheverny was named to the parlement on March 9, 1553. He held this office for nine years, content to have joined the parlement without even having studied law, "which is very unusual," according to him. Montaigne benefited from a similar conjunction of circumstances favorable to his entrance into the magistracy. A loyal servant of the state, Cheverny received advancement in his career, soon rising to the Great Chamber thanks to friends with influence at Court. In 1562, being "suitable and courageous [enough] to do more," he got himself named, "through the counsel and help of [his] friends, *maître des requêtes ordinaire de l'Hôtel du roi*. He was then thirty-three years old. Thereupon he undertook to present himself at the Court, where he was "lucky enough" to win the affection of the Cardinal of Lorraine, who was "then greatly favored and employed." On the strength of this support, Cheverny approached Catherine de Medici, who had "all the power in that state."[28] Employed by the queen mother to make the people of Paris obey and see to it that the royal edicts were respected, Cheverny was soon sent to the Dauphiné, to Provence, and to Languedoc in order to bring the regional parlements into line. Following these commissions, he returned to the Court in Poitiers to accompany the king on his tour of France. When this great journey was over, there were two diplomatic missions, one to England, the other to Venice, that he "considered accepting."[29] But the queen mother had other plans for him, and Cheverny was made the duke of Orléans's chancellor, a promotion. What we must remember about this illustrious itinerary are the stages that follow one another almost logically: the establishment of a clientele-like dependency within a powerful network, the initial career as a councillor, the approach to the royal Court, the assignment to a diplomatic mission, and finally the appointment as state secretary or *maître des requêtes*. Cheverny symbolizes the royal way of the parlementary *habitus* during the second half of the sixteenth century.

Promotion thanks to local support, the broadening of one's political and clientele network, marriage with the daughter of a first president, missions at the court as a representative of the parlement: these are all ways of seeking an advancement of one's career and hoping later to leave the regional political space and obtain an office in the capital, closer to the king's first circle. It was in this same way—but with less luster—that the Eyquems established themselves at the Bordeaux parlement. A series of strategic marriages allowed them to multiply parlementary alliances while at the same time strengthening aristocratic behaviors that could make people forget their social origins. The attitude and aristocratic pretensions of the nobility of the robe were still more marked within the regional parlements. They operated on two levels simultaneously: country gentlemen on their lands and magistrates used to legal wrangling in the city. On this point, Montaigne waited patiently for the prescription that could make him a noble of the sword after a hundred years, as was required by the customary law of Guyenne. However, this desire for nobility did not grip him until after his father's death, when he received the noble land of Montaigne as his heritage. Before 1568, he was fully invested in a career in the parlement, and was not yet preoccupied with living nobly. He envisaged his future as being in the magistracy, if possible in the Great Chamber, and—why not?—as a *maître des requêtes* or a councillor on the Great Council in Paris. Although he still had to wait twenty years to claim that he could declare himself noble by prescription and definitely abandon the patronymic of Eyquem, his entry into parlement accelerated the process of social ascent by way of the stage of the *purgatory of the nobility*, which his membership in the world of the long robe authorized him to do.

Unlike the bailiffs, royal advocates, présidial councillors, tax collectors, clerks, lieutenant generals, and provosts, who—if they were not already nobles of the sword or ennobled by the kings thanks to letters of nobility—were taxed like other commoners, the members of parlements were considered to be nobles by the simple fact that they represented the king and dispensed justice in his name. However, they were not exempt from paying a franc-fief fee. In his *Quatriesme traicté des droicts des domaines de la couronne de France* (1582), Jehan Bacquet remarks that the rich and opulent merchants "sought by every possible means at their disposition to exempt themselves from paying the Francs-Fiefs fee."[30] They were concerned not so much to avoid the tax as they were to distinguish themselves symbolically; being exempted from the franc-fief fee was one of the best proofs of membership in the nobility. The magistracy also escaped the land tax and the *aides*. At that time, the franc-fief was a fee for the use of royal property and not a tax on land ownership. There were two ways of getting

oneself ennobled: by patent letters of ennoblement obtained from the king or
by holding a public office legitimately granted that guaranteed ennoblement
"by estates, dignities, and offices."[31] As we have seen, royal offices and other
functions at the summit of the hierarchy of public offices were the only ones
exempt from the franc-fief fee. Those who held them were considered full-
fledged nobles. Consequently, the magistracy represented an expedient for acceding to nobility, even if true nobility—that of the blood or of the sword—was
by far preferable to it.

The officials at the second rank had a more ambiguous form of nobility. Thus
the presidents of the parlements, councillors, advocates, and the king's general
prosecutors at the parlement of Paris were exempted from the franc-fief fee, because they were also considered as "descended from a noble race,"[32] but only on
condition of retaining their office. They could, for example, transmit the title of
"noble" to their descendants so long as they held an office. In the 1560s, when
his family had not yet been living "nobly" on its lands for a hundred years, Montaigne became noble by entering the Bordeaux parlement. That city had history
on its side. The parlements had a rank and a reputation that were linked to the
date of their creation. After Paris and Toulouse, the parlements of Bordeaux
and Grenoble competed for third place as to their antiquity. During the Wars
of Religion, the Bordeaux parlement acquired considerable political importance
because its jurisdiction included the Bordeaux area, Gascony, Guyenne, Agenais, Périgord, Limousin, Landes, Bazadais, and Saintonge; Saintonge was to
become crucial for the king during the armed conflicts with the Huguenots.

There was an esprit de corps and an equality on the administrative level that
did not legally permit the establishment of a hierarchy among the parlements.
That was, at least, the position defended by the regional councillors, who rejected any supervision by their Parisian counterparts, even though it had been
confirmed during official ceremonies. The members of the parlement of Paris
were certain of their superiority over the other parlements, and on this subject
Bacquet notes that "the other Courts of Parlement are not equal in authority
and dignity to the Court of the Parlement of Paris, which is the true seat and *lit
de justice*[v] of our Kings, and the only Court of the Peers of France."[33]

The members of the regional parlements constantly reaffirmed their nobility
in the name of a centralized conception of royal justice. However, in practice
everyone was fully aware that they constituted a third *ban*, or a third nobility,
but time was on their side. Those who had been *anoblis* (ennobled) by their offices were less respected than the nobility of the sword, but they knew how to

---

[v] Under the Old Régime, the *lit de justice* (lit., "bed of justice") was a special session
of the parlement presided over by the king in person, at which royal edicts were registered. [Trans.]

62

maintain the ambiguity and were especially more active when it was a question of having their nobility of the robe recognized.[34] Since they were responsible for verifying letters of nobility, the parlements pointed out, for example, that it "would not be decent that such letters be verified by non-nobles."[35] The king needed them too much to register his edicts and exercise his power; he did not want to alienate them. It was in this power relationship based on a mutual exchange of services and prerogatives that the *robins* who exercised their offices in the regional parlements were able to get themselves exempted in turn from the franc-fief fee, and were thus legally able to display their nobility. Montaigne's professional advance in his initial career as a *robin* was governed by this logic, even though the *Essais* remain silent regarding this nobility deriving from his office as a parlementary councillor. But it is true that Montaigne had several strings to his bow. The *habitus* of the members of the parlement prevented him from asserting his difference, which will ultimately become his literary enterprise.

A veritable parlementary aristocracy was set up during the second half of the sixteenth century.[36] Starting around the middle of the century, the Bordeaux parlement included an increasing number of members who came from rich mercantile families that had been "ennobled" by their offices only one or two generations earlier. In 1550 the parlement was still controlled by the old nobility of the sword. Out of forty-one members, thirty-five were nobles by blood and only six came from the mercantile milieu.[37] However, during the period between 1550 and 1570 this proportion was reversed in favor of the merchant families, who appropriated (purchased) almost all the offices newly created by the king. The bourgeois who joined the parlement decked themselves out with titles such as *messire*, *écuyer* (squire), *chevalier*, *noble homme*, and *noble*. They were authorized to use these titles, or at least the presidents of the courts were, during the first stage. On this subject, La Roche Flavin writes that at the end of the sixteenth century "the title of chevalier belonged to all the Officers constituted in eminent dignity, such as the Officers of the Crown, the heads of the offices of the King's Household, the Councillors of the Council of State, the heads and presidents of the sovereign Courts, the Governors and lieutenants of the King in the Provinces."[38] Despite these restrictions, it was not rare for members of the parlements, whatever their function, to take the title of "*chevalier*" or "*chevalier de loix*" ("knight," "knight of the laws"). In *Le Miroir politique* (1555), Guillaume de La Perrière lists "six kinds of people," nobles and priests, but also "Magistrates, bourgeois, artisans, and laborers." Although these last four categories were officially grouped together in the Third Estate when the Estates General was held, we see that the magistrates provided by far the largest number of representatives and were organized as a veritable corps. In less than two generations, they succeeded in forming a powerful political force. For example, whereas in 1576 the nobility of the robe provided 35 percent of the representatives of the Third Estate during the assemblies of the Estates General, this figure increased to 44 percent in 1588 and to 47 percent in 1593.[39] The title of *"chevalier de loix"* was considered insufficient to account for their status, and a growing number of judicial officials even went so far as to call themselves *"seigneurs"* or *"sieurs"* ("lords"), using their recently acquired lands to mark their social distinction. The members of the parlements were slowly but surely making their way into the order of the nobility.

The Bordeaux parlement had a few cases of rapid advancement, but careers were frequently blocked by members who were concerned to maintain a balance between the great families of the nobility of the robe. When these families succeeded too quickly, this sometimes worked against them. The internal competition was often brutal in this autarkic system that was marked by a nepotism based on complex political expectations. A councillor who had strong supporters could hope to enter the Great Chamber or even be received as a fourth president after only about ten years of service, but to do that he had to submit to a corrupt system, and above all accept the rules of a very structured clientelism. Without drawing attention to themselves, most councillors patiently waited in the background a good part of their lives before joining the Great Chamber.

That was the case for Jean de Calvimont, lord of Cros, who waited for twenty-one years before becoming a second president. The role of the presidents was to call the chambers into session and to pronounce the edicts during audiences. Historically, the edicts deliberated upon and written in the Chambre des Enquêtes were read out in the Great Chamber, but the considerable number of matters to be dealt with led to the Chambres des Enquêtes being given the right to make decisions directly regarding the cases they had examined. Thus, de facto, the councillors played the role of full-fledged judges. They could also receive commissions to represent the judiciary when the parlement was making the circuit of the various cities in the jurisdiction of the parlement of Bordeaux. Unpredictable combinations of circumstances might sometimes cause a councillor's ambitions to vacillate. Nothing was guaranteed in advance, and chance played a non-negligible role in advancements and promotions. The surest way to succeed was to join a faction and to wait one's turn. It was not in Montaigne's character to remain in the background of a constituted group or to let himself be forgotten for too long. To wait for a departure, a resignation, or a withdrawal was to put oneself at the mercy of imponderables. On the whole, the system did little to compensate the value of individuals and generally gave priority to political alignment and membership in a clientele.

Such a system of family interdependencies and hierarchical submission increased the possibility of challenges on the grounds of conflicts of interest, and blocked the advancement of careers. Most of the time, the reasons given when such challenges were made were judged to be without foundation by a majority of the members of the parlement, who had hardly any interest in denouncing a system to which they belonged. Political power infringed on economic power, and the conflicts were almost always settled through a compromise that was supposed to avoid bad publicity that might harm the whole parlementary caste that was confident in its political power. The three orders of the medieval imagination—the priest, the lord, and the peasant[40]—were gradually replaced by the merchant, the magistrate, and the royal secretary.[41] In Montaigne's time, the center of power had shifted toward the state secretariats and the regional parlements. The vast majority of the masters of the administration belonged to families that had succeeded in buying official responsibilities. Thanks to an education received in the best colleges of France, this political caste had succeeded in taking control of the regional parlements. Hence the number of officials, which had risen to about 4,000 under Francis I, reached 25,000 under Henry IV.[42] The state thus endowed itself with a bureaucracy that it was far from dominating.

The kingdom's large cities were now in the hands of a few families that, thanks to marriages with the local nobility, were able to strengthen their hold on the parlements and their administrative control of the cities. The magistracy facilitated rapid participation in local political decisions (the only ones that really counted for the urban bourgeoisie) and created, at the beginning of the seventeenth century, a genuine opposition between the nobility of the sword and the nobility of the long robe.[43] If the former scorned the *robins*, it still had to cope with them. The situation in Bordeaux was characteristic of these circumstantial ententes that transcended ideologies. Composed of six members—two jurats belonging to the nobility, usually including the mayor, two bourgeois, and two *robins*—the jurade had weakened the nobility's power. This kind of equilibrium greatly favored the *robins*, who were not only better educated but also served as intermediaries (and thus frequently played the role of decision makers) between the bourgeoisie and the nobility of the sword. Naturally, this new class of former merchants—who had become nobles by being included in the parlement—tried to make its origins forgotten in order to accede to true nobility.[44] The compartmentalization in force during the Middle Ages, which structured society by dividing it into three orders, was suddenly put in question, and the *robins* were the first to benefit from this social mobility.

Another way of distinguishing oneself from other members of parlement consisted in presenting oneself as a man of letters. A small group of councillors—of whom the best example is La Boétie—managed to enjoy a reputation as learned scholars. More detached from contemporary events, they found in Antiquity models and recipes applicable to the problems of their time. By remaining above the fray, Montaigne also sought to make a reputation for himself as a learned and humanistic member of parlement. The publication of his translation of Raymond Sebond's *Theologia naturalis* in 1569 was part of this strategy, because the publication of works on law, translations, or compendia on customs corresponded to the parlementary *habitus*. The *Coutumes generalles de la ville de Bourdeaulx sénéchausée de Guyenne et pays Bourdeloys*, published in 1528 by Jean Guyart, the University of Bordeaux's printer, were part of this publishing work that could single out a councillor destined to have a brilliant career. The president Nicolas Bohier, Geoffroy de La Chassaigne, and the advocate general Thomas de Cousinier had all helped draw up this inventory of the customs of Guyenne, which allowed them to acquire a certain prestige among their colleagues. We could also count among this research on local antiquities La Boétie's book (now lost) on the *Description du Médoc*, or Gabriel de Lurbe's *Chronique bordeloise* (Bordeaux: S. Millanges, 1594) and *De viris illustribus Aquitaniæ* (Bordeaux: S. Millanges, 1591).

By showing their erudition and knowledge, especially when they were written in Latin, these collections of antiquities increased the esteem their authors enjoyed. In 1559, Jehan d'Alesme had a text by the president Bohier—accompanied by a biography—printed by Gabiano in Lyon. The *Decisiones aureae in Burdigalensi senatu discussae ac promulgatae . . . cum Boerii vita, authore Jo. Alesmio* made a major contribution to the reputation of the father of Léonard d'Alesme, a colleague of Montaigne's in the first Chambre des Enquêtes. Jehan d'Alesme had limited himself to editing Bohier's collection of jurisprudence, but that had sufficed to distinguish him from his colleagues. In turn, his son, Léonard d'Alesme, published two works: *Leonardi Alesmii tractatus in materiam substitionum eiusdem regulae in eaudem materiam* (Poitiers: Marnef, 1540), and *Leonardi Alesmii juniris, Lemovicensis, in Sancto Leonardo Nobiliaco nati, jureconsulti prudentissimi Lucubrationes videlicet ennaratiorum in titul. De Triente . . .* (Toulouse: J. Colomies, 1552). Thanks to these publications, within the parlement, the Alesmes won a reputation as intellectuals.

Historical works were also a good way to acquire respectability as an author or editor. This was the choice made by Arnoul Le Ferron, who continued Paul Émile's *Histoire de France* from 1488 to 1547 under the title *De rebus gestis Gallorum libri IX: ad historiam Pauli Aemylii additi, perducta historia usque ad tempora Henrici II. Francorum regis* (Paris: Vascosan, 1550). This work, which recounted the history of the period from the reign of Charles VIII to that of Henry II, allowed Le Ferron to pass for a man of letters. He also wrote a commentary (*Consuetudinum Burdigalensium commentarii*, Lyon: Gryphe, 1538) on the customs of Bordeaux; translated a few short works by Plutarch (*Plutarchi Chaeronei Pro nobilitate libri fragmentum*, Lyon: Gryphe, 1566); and even published, in 1557, a work titled *De inscriptiones particulae hujus Ei pro foribus Delphici templi*.[45] These translations were particularly prized in a time when humanistic values continued to be appreciated. Christophe de Roffignac distinguished himself by publishing *Commentarii omnium a creato orbe historiarum* (Paris: Jean Bienné, 1571), which earned him great respect among his peers.[46]

In Bordeaux, many other magistrates cultivated belles lettres and aspired to become authors, notably the presidents François de Belcier, Jehan d'Ybarolla, and Sauvat de Pomiés. Similarly, a number of councillors devoted themselves to Latin poetry: Briand de Valée; Jean and Geoffroy de La Chassaigne; Pierre Bouchier; Jehan de Ciret; Guillaume de Lur Longa; Geoffroy de Malvyn, the author of a Latin poem titled *Gallia gemens*; the advocates Jean de Lauvergnac and Estienne de Maisonneuve, the author of the *Premier Livre de la plaisante et delectable histoire de Gerileon d'Angleterre* (Paris: Jean Borel, 1572); Pierre de Métivier; the first advocate-general, Jean de Lahet; and of course Estienne de La Boétie. All these men were proud of their erudition and dreamed of getting their work published.[47] The notable rulings written by the councillors of the parlement were also part of this literary tradition, which took an interest in the most remarkable judgments and reproduced them in narrative form.[48] The goal was to impress other members of the parlement and to distinguish oneself from colleagues who had not published anything.

Montaigne, who was certainly influenced by this tradition of erudite publications within a regional parlement, took from a chest in the château, where it had lain for almost fifteen years, his translation of Raymond Sebond, and had it printed in Paris in 1569. The French translation of a large volume written in Latin by a theologian was no small achievement and suggested a significant scholarly effort. Besides, the Wars of Religion required both a new approach and a reformulation of theological questions, and Montaigne was able to demonstrate that he not only had an excellent knowledge of Latin but was also not afraid to get involved in the debates of his time. But he too was mainly interested in acquiring the label of a scholar. His translation of Raymond Sebond's *Theologia naturalis, sive liber creaturarum* fit perfectly into the practice of belles lettres in the milieu of the Bordeaux parlement, and he expected to benefit from this youthful exercise that might have a major impact on·his career there.

From the Cour des Aides in Périgueux to the Parlement in Bordeaux

In 1553 Henry II decided to create a Cour des Aides in Guyenne. Several cities saw this step as a political opportunity that could increase their prestige and fame. The citizens of Périgueux sent a request to the king asking that he establish this new court in their city, but the members of the Bordeaux parlement were displeased by this competition and registered a protest with the king.

Henry II had already created a *présidial*[vi] in Périgueux in 1552,[49] and the Bordeaux parlement, still weakened by the erosion of its authority after the salt-tax revolt of 1548, rightly feared seeing its jurisdiction reduced once again. Its members explained that the court in Périgueux would soon cast umbrage not only on the Parisian magistrates who formerly dealt with these cases, but also on themselves insofar as they would thereby lose an opportunity to enlarge their jurisdiction.[50] These arguments defending the maintenance of spheres of influence had little weight compared to financial considerations, the only ones that mattered to the king: creating a new Cour des Aides was an excellent way to fill the Crown's coffers by selling new offices to the highest bidders.

The function of the Cour des Aides was to judge both civil and criminal cases involving the collection of taxes such as the *aides*, the *taille*, the *octrois*, and the *Gabelle*.[vii] They were also used to restore a modicum of order in regions where revolts against taxation were frequent. The king expected to gain several advantages from this administrative creation: he hoped to obtain new funds by the sale of offices and also to strengthen the collection of taxes in Guyenne. The Bordeaux parlement wanted its competence, both judiciary and fiscal, to be recognized. Thus the Cour des Aides in Périgueux was positioned as a rival of Bordeaux. It was also perceived as a danger to the Cours des Aides in Paris and Montpellier, which were deprived of part of their revenues and which sent strong protests to the king. At first, the complaints filed by the members of the Paris and Bordeaux parlements bore fruit, since an edict issued in May 1554 canceled that of March 1553 concerning the creation of the Cour des Aides in Périgueux. The citizens of Périgueux immediately protested in their turn, sending a delegation composed of Fronton de Béraud, advocate general at the parlement of Bordeaux, and Antoine de Poynet, lieutenant general at the seat in Bergerac. These magistrates sought the offices of first and second president in the Cour des Aides and enjoyed great political influence in Périgord. Their argument emphasized the central location of Périgueux for the generalities[viii] of Guyenne, Auvergne, and Poitou.

The Paris parlement had succeeded in getting the edict creating the Cour des Aides in Périgueux revoked, and its members agreed to come to Guyenne to hear cases so that the defendants would not have to travel to the capital. However, the king did not find this solution convincing; in July 1554 he changed his mind again and confirmed the creation of a Cour des Aides in Périgueux. On

---

[vi] The *présidial* courts' functions differed from those of the sénéchaussée; they were intended to relieve the parlements of less important cases.

[vii] The *aides* were indirect taxes on property, crops, etc.; the *taille* was a direct tax on land; the *octrois* were indirect taxes on the importation of merchandise; and the *Gabelle* was an indirect tax on salt. [Trans.]

[viii] Under the Old Régime, the *généralités* were administrative districts. [Trans.]

December 16, 1554, Pierre de Carle, president at the parlement of Bordeaux and royal commissioner, established a Cour des Aides in Périgueux at the city's expense. The city paid 50,000 *écus* (150,000 *livres*) to the king and promised to sell the new offices to the highest bidders, in order to replenish their coffers. This advantageous solution for the crown was decisive, and in August 1554 another edict had confirmed the first edict issued in March 1553.

This court allowed the king to get around direct taxation, which was very unpopular. The sale of offices also made it easier to bring new subsidies into the royal treasury. In the context of the revolt of 1548, this court offered the additional advantage of judging authoritatively and definitively all civil and criminal cases concerning taxation. In fact, this institution was not really necessary, since for trials concerning taxes, the people of Guyenne fell within the purview of the Cours des Aides in Paris or Montpellier. The Bordeaux parlement wanted to obtain this jurisdiction in fiscal matters, but since the revolt of 1548 its members no longer enjoyed the good grace of the king, who preferred to kill two birds with one stone: raising funds by selling offices, and also sidelining the members of the Bordeaux parlement, who were too interested in defending their privileges in matters of judicial purview.

The early 1550s were also the time when the privileges lost during the revolt in Bordeaux in 1548 were regained. The king had officially restored Bordeaux's statutes in 1550, but the city's administration was still far from having the political and juridical authority it had previously enjoyed. The jurats and the mayor engaged in a veritable lobbying operation and went regularly to Paris to remind the king of their allegiance. Montaigne might have had an opportunity to see Henry II at the Court during one of his father's official visits to the capital in 1555.

Montaigne's father, Pierre Eyquem, had been mayor of Bordeaux since August 1, 1553. His brother, Raymond Eyquem, had been a councillor at the Bordeaux parlement since 1535. He had bought his office for 6,000 *livres*, paid with "a hundred gold écus and 45 sous."[51] Pierre Eyquem immediately thought of his son when the offices in Périgueux were put up for sale. Périgueux had the advantage of being far enough way from Bordeaux for little arrangements among notables to go more or less unnoticed. Not being able to acquire an office for himself—because of his lack of legal education and his insufficient knowledge of Latin—in order to transmit it directly to his son, to buy this office Pierre Eyquem decided to go through his younger brother, the lord of Gaujac, whose first name was also Pierre.[ix] Montaigne's uncle had studied at the university in Toulouse. With a diploma in law, he held a position as advocate in the parlement.

[ix] Bearing the same first name, this younger brother of Pierre Eyquem has often been confused with Montaigne's father.

He agreed to play the role of intermediary and keep the office for his nephew. Montaigne had just turned twenty and was pursuing vague studies in Paris, but he had never completed his *cursus* in law. His father saw in the creation of a Cour des Aides in Périgueux a way for Michel to join, without too much difficulty, the judicial profession, even if by the back door and in a court that was highly contested both in Bordeaux and Paris. The new offices nonetheless represented an opportunity for a father who was concerned about his son's future.

The offices in Périgueux were quickly sold and the tribunal promptly set up. An extract from the mayor's office in Périgueux lists the statutes of this tribunal and names its officers. Montaigne's uncle figures among the new councillors and is presented as "the aforesaid Eyquem, lord of the house of Montaigne in Périgord."[52] As planned, Béraud and Poynet were appointed first and second presidents, and the positions of councillor were filled by Bertrand de Makanam, Pierre de Montaigne, Bertrand Lambert, Jean de Saint-Angel, Estienne d'Aringiès, François Fayard, Jacques Brusac, and Jean Barbarin. The family origins of these officials were extremely varied. Descendants of merchant families, some of these officers of the court—Bouchier and Guérin, for example—had openly declared their support for the Reformation. Pierre de Saint-Angel was named advocate general, Léon de Merle royal prosecutor, François Vigouroux clerk, Pauly Chaumette paymaster, Poncet de Champagne collector of fines, and François Saunier and Claude Brosson bailiffs.[53] Shortly afterward, three new councillors, Jean du Faure, François de Merle, and Pierre Blanchier, were added to this first list.

The court officially went into session on December 16, 1554, under the aegis of Pierre de Carle, president of the parlement of Bordeaux. Eighteen months later, in 1556, Pierre Eyquem resigned his office as councillor general at the Cour des Aides in Périgueux, ceding it to his nephew, Michel de Montaigne. The office Montaigne obtained had been handed down to him by his uncle through one of those family arrangements that the bourgeois and the *robins* knew how to make. We do not know the financial details of this transaction between Pierre Eyquem and his brother, but we can imagine that the initial sum had been advanced by Montaigne's father and that the lord of Gaujac had served only as a mediator in this affair. It had been necessary to get around the rule regarding the age of the officials, since Montaigne was still too young in 1556. Officially, one had to be at least twenty-five years old to hold an office in the parlement, but dispensations were common. Letters of dispensation were accorded with greater or lesser indulgence depending on the political connections enjoyed by the person concerned. This was the case for Estienne de La Boétie, who became a councillor at the Bordeaux parlement at the age of twenty-three,[54] and for Arnoul Le Ferron, who was named a lay councillor at twenty when his father resigned, and was received less than a year later. This practice had illustrious precedents. Let us mention only Henri de Mesmes, who became a councillor at the Cour des Aides in Paris at the age of twenty, "because I was so young that I would not have been admitted elsewhere."[55] Such a dispensation was more easily granted when an office was ceded to a family member.

Contrary to the custom—at least in the Bordeaux parlement—Montaigne seems not to have been examined. There is no record in Périgueux regarding this matter, and the procedure required for applicants for an office of councillor was probably not followed at the time when the court was being hastily created. Practices varied considerably from one court to another. We also know that under certain conditions, councillors could be received without examination on the strength of a simple testimony attesting to their studies and debates in law in Toulouse or Paris. For example, Joseph de La Chassaigne had benefited from a dispensation after having shown that he had studied law and attended the lectures of the best jurists of his time. These under-the-table arrangements made it possible to get around the examination that had, nonetheless, been made obligatory since 1500. Those who applied for offices were questioned on texts that were relatively easy, but almost always in Latin.[56] Even if the candidates failed, they were put to the test for a year, like Jean Mérignac, who failed in 1554 but was admitted the following year. It had been decided that he would be admitted only after he had studied "theory and practice for the space of a year, and that year over, he shall present himself before the aforementioned court to be examined again."[57] On May 17, 1554, La Boétie had no difficulty passing this test and was judged "suitable and satisfactory."[58]

Montaigne's father's influence may have allowed him to escape this test. In any case, his knowledge of Latin and ancient authors would have sufficed to apply for an office as a judicial official. It is probable that his translation of Raymond Sebond from Latin into French dates from the year 1554, at a crucial point in his career as a magistrate. Pierre Eyquem might have asked Michel to undertake this exercise the better to prepare himself in the event that he had to be examined. Similarly, Montaigne's uncle might have arranged for the young man to do an internship with his lawyer, Fronton de Béraud, to prepare him for the post that he was soon to cede to him. This on-the-job training with an advocate general at the parlement is supposed to have lasted two years, from 1554 to 1556. As mayor of Bordeaux, Pierre Eyquem had enough connections in Périgueux to facilitate the transmission of the office from his brother to his son. Besides, Montaigne was far from being the only one to benefit from this kind of special privilege. Henri de Mesmes also joined the Great Council through "the diligence, mediation, and means" of his father-in-law, Oudart Hennequin, a councillor and *maître des comptes*. Henri de Mesmes was admitted to the parlement of Paris in 1533, without being examined. These examples tell us much about political influences and the traffic in offices at this time.

In 1557, the Bordeaux parlement's delegates tried to argue that they should examine the councillors coming from Périgueux, but the king made it clear that he was opposed to these councillors "being examined on their admission to the court, not that he intends and wishes that those who will later come to be granted such positions be examined as they are in Paris."[59] The argument rested on the fact that they had already been admitted as "members of the Cour des Aides and judged with full authority," and could not be examined again when they arrived in Bordeaux. Montaigne began his career as a magistrate at the Cour des Aides in Périgueux in 1556, without holding a degree in law and probably without having been examined, any more than he was in Bordeaux. But this Cour des Aides existed for only a short time, because a new royal edict of May 1557 eliminated it and transferred its officials to the parlement of Bordeaux. Naturally, the councillors of the Bordeaux parlement opposed this fusion, because the increase in the number of officials in Bordeaux significantly reduced their salaries and *épices*.[x] It has to be understood that a significant portion of their compensation came from the presents they received for each decision they made, in addition to their annual salaries as officers of the court. These presents represented payment for the councillor's individual work; they were received not by those who judged during the sessions of the council in the parlement, but solely by the reporters for the work they had done during the classification, analysis, and rendering of an opinion regarding the documents in a file. Thus councillors who did not report cases did not share in the *épices*.

Unhappy about seeing their ranks increased, the sitting councillors drew up protests that were delivered to the king by the president Christophe de Roffignac and the councillor François de La Guyonnie.[60] At the last minute, the third president, Pierre de Carle, was subrogated for Roffignac. Ultimately, the officers of the Cour des Aides were all assigned to the Chambre des Requêtes. This transfer was an extraordinary stroke of luck for Montaigne, who retained throughout his life a fascination with these manifestations of chance that smiled on him more than once in his various careers.[61] However, moving to Bordeaux was not without difficulty for him. His uncle, Raymond Eyquem, already held an office as councillor in the second Chambre des Enquêtes, and the appointment of members of parlement who had family ties in the first, second, or third degree with other members was theoretically prohibited, but once again dispensations were frequently granted. Antoine Gaultier benefited from such a dispensation in 1543 when he married a niece of the first president, Antoine de Belcier, who was also a relative of the second president, Jean de Calvimont. Finally, we may mention the case of Joseph de La Chassaigne, who also received a dispensation from this rule, even though his father was a president.[62]

---

[x] Presents made directly to judges by the parties to a suit. [Trans.]

Nothing was impossible, but the Eyquem-Montaigne family was exposed to the jealousy and criticism of other great Bordeaux families.

When Montaigne joined the Chambre des Requêtes of the Bordeaux parlement in 1557, the endogenous system of family interdependencies raised problems of promotion. There were many candidates for a few positions. Thus, as we have seen, as soon as the Cour des Aides in Périgueux was eliminated, the members of the Bordeaux parlement strongly opposed the king's decision to increase the number of councillors in their parlement. Montaigne was part of the group of new arrivals who found themselves marginalized when they arrived in Bordeaux. The Chambre des Requêtes occupied the lowest position in the jurisdiction of the parlements, and its members were not considered full-fledged members of parlement, even though La Roche Flavin—himself a first president of the Chambre des Requêtes of the Toulouse parlement—recalled that the presidents and councillors of the Chambre des Requêtes enjoyed the same "rank, right to sit, right to speak, and deliberative opinion" as the other members of parlement during assemblies of the court, "without anyone contradicting or challenging" them.[63] However, in reality, and especially in Bordeaux, the councillors of the Chambre des Requêtes were far from being considered the equals of their colleagues in the two Chambres des Enquêtes.

Since the 1540s, the number of councillors in the Bordeaux parlement had steadily increased. Four new offices had been created in 1536, fifteen in March 1542, and five more lay offices five months later. Two offices of second president for the two Chambres des Enquêtes were also created in the early 1540s. Of course, such an increase in the number of offices displeased those who already had a magistrate's office and thus saw their *épices* reduced. The presidents in the Chambres des Enquêtes received both their salaries as councillors and their remunerations for serving as presidents. The short existence of the Cour des Aides in Périgueux is explained above all by the rather tarnished prestige of the members of the Bordeaux parlement after the salt-tax revolt of 1548. The members of the Bordeaux parlement did not like having their judicial power infringed upon, but they were still under the surveillance of a king who distrusted them and was little inclined to listen to them when they loudly and forcefully proclaimed their judicial independence.

The thirteen councillors who came from Périgueux, including Montaigne, were very badly received on their arrival in Bordeaux. Antoine de Poynet, the second president of the Cour des Aides and of the Chambre des Requêtes in Bordeaux, was admitted only as a simple councillor when these other bodies were dissolved. The councillors of the Cour des Aides were sworn in before the parlement of Bordeaux only as members of the Chambre des Requêtes, and not as full-fledged members of the parlement. They were authorized to make final judgments only in cases concerning *aides* and *tailles*; in other kinds of cases they could make judgments only in the first instance. The first president of the Cour des Aides became the fifth *président à mortier*, and the thirteen councillors were divided among diverse chambers. They sat, "for cases involving *aides* and what is related to them, as the Cour des Aides of Bordeaux; with regard to the purview of the Requêtes, as the Chamber dealing with petitions at the Court in Bordeaux." For example, Montaigne joined the first Chambre des Enquêtes only in 1562, after suffering many unpleasant ups and downs.[64] The parlement's *Registres secrets* make it possible to follow the councillors' service. Thus Montaigne appears on the list of councillors in the first Chambre des Enquêtes only in November 1561. It has to be emphasized that the judiciary's prestige was established mainly on the basis of its ability to judge cases on appeal, which Montaigne did not do when he was beginning his career in the parlement of Bordeaux.

On October 23, 1557, the assembled chambers were still deliberating on the incorporation of councillors from the Cour des Aides of Périgueux into the Bordeaux parlement's Chambre des Requêtes. They found it "strange that the said generals want to negotiate and traffic and consult one another in the court, which has been given sovereign authority only to decide matters concerning the King's subjects and to advise only the King."[65] It was only four years later, after the edict of August 1561, that the Chambre des Requêtes was dissolved in Bordeaux and its officers finally incorporated into the parlement's two Chambres des Enquêtes. By a royal edict, Charles IX had abruptly done away with the Cour des Aides as well as the Chambre des Requêtes in Bordeaux.[xi] These constant reforms of the judicial map of the kingdom rather irritated the caste of the *robins*, who considered themselves to have been mistreated by the royal power. The integration of the councillors of the Chambre des Aides and the Chambre des Requêtes into the two Chambres des Enquêtes disturbed the functioning of these two chambers enough to produce an uprising on the part of the members of the parlement who sat in them.[66] Further protests were sent to Charles IX to denounce once again the increase in the number of councillors.

Ostracized by their colleagues, the councillors from Périgueux also complained to the king. An order issued by the parlement and dated November 14, 1561, echoed their discontent. Various considerations concerning the interest of the general legal service, as well as that of the defendant, had led to the suppression of the Chambre des Requêtes. In actuality, after the protest made by the

---

[xi] The Bordeaux parlement was to be forced to accept the creation of a Chambre des Requêtes in 1580, after several fruitless attempts made by the royal authority. The *lettres de jussion* (letters addressed by the king to the courts, enjoining them to register an ordinance or edict) and their registration by the court were approved on April 14, 1581, when the king was regaining control over the Bordeaux parlement, and before Montaigne took office as mayor of Bordeaux.

already established members of parlement, it was only two years later, after the edict issued in a *lit de justice* on September 20, 1563, and the registration of that edict on November 13 of the same year, that Montaigne was finally able to consider himself a full-fledged councillor. It was only after La Boétie's death that Montaigne *officially* became a councillor in one of the two Chambres des Enquêtes, without for all that being considered by his peers to be a member of the parlement. He had begun to serve in the first Chambre des Enquêtes in 1562, alongside La Boétie, but until 1563 his role was very limited. His arrival in the parlement of Bordeaux was far from being unanimously welcomed, and throughout his life Montaigne retained a certain resentment against the judicial system and the *robins*. This less than cordial reception on the part of his colleagues was connected with the fact that the integration of the Cour des Aides into the parlement had greatly reduced the already sitting councillors' revenues. Montaigne was, for example, authorized to report investigations only starting in 1562, or five years after his arrival in the parlement of Bordeaux.

The councillors of the Chambre des Requêtes and the Chambre des Aides had to join the ordinary chambers of the parlement. Thus it was not until 1562 that Montaigne officially moved into a Chambre des Enquêtes. The chambers were constituted in mid-November of each year, when decisions on promotion to the Great Chamber were also decided upon. This career advancement was decided solely on the basis of seniority. The Great Chamber included four presidents and nineteen councillors, whereas the "Tournelle"[xii] had two presidents and twelve councillors. Created in 1519, the Tournelle judged crimes that required a punishment inflicted on the condemned's body. Its members were recruited alternately from the other chambers, and access to this chamber was in no way a promotion. Montaigne seems not to have served in it during his years in the parlement, but the archival records are incomplete.[xiii] On the other hand, his uncle, Raymond Eyquem, frequently served as its president when he was detached from the Great Chamber. In Montaigne's time, the first Chambre des Enquêtes had two presidents and seventeen councillors, while the second chamber had two presidents and thirteen councillors. A member of the parlement traditionally began his career as a councillor in one of the Chambres des Enquêtes. It was then possible to be detached to serve on the Tournelle before finally ending up in the Great Chamber, but only by rank of seniority.

[xii] The Tournelle only handled criminal cases. Contrary to the Chambres des Enquêtes, the Tournelle had no permanent councillors. Its members were taken from the two Chambres des Enquêtes by rotation. In Bordeaux they were appointed for a year.

[xiii] The *Registres secrets* are missing between August 30, 1566, and November 13, 1569. Thus we do not know the formation of the chambers for the years 1567 and 1568. Some scholars believe Montaigne might have served in the Tournelle Chamber on a few occasions during these years.

The councillors in the Chambres des Enquêtes were promoted on the basis of their seniority and in order to replace councillors in the Great Chamber who had departed (these were quite rare) or died. The presidents of the Chambres des Enquêtes and of the Tournelle were themselves chosen among the councillors of the Great Chamber. Parlementary protocol was governed by well-established hierarchy, and access to the Great Chamber amounted to a symbolic recognition of a councillor's status. In the parlement of Bordeaux, the Great Chamber incarnated the site of power par excellence and a necessary springboard if one hoped to be called to Paris. It was the only place where pleas and defenses were presented orally when the case was heard on appeal. Every case that was the object of procedure that contradicted it and required a preparatory procedure and an oral debate was within its purview. It was the Great Chamber that heard the pleas of the king's advocates and agents. Once the oral debate was over, the court could choose to judge the case on that basis and before the whole chamber, or it could ask, in more complicated cases, for additional evidence *en faits contraires* (of contrary facts), which would be the point of departure for the work of investigation done in the Chambres des Enquêtes.[67] The case file was transmitted to one of the two Chambres des Enquêtes only once the hearing had been completed in the Great Chamber. The defense lawyers and public advocates spoke only in the Great Chamber. The Chambres des Enquêtes judged cases that were appealed to the parlement after they had been transmitted by the Great Chamber, which had ordered that the investigation be "received to be seen and judged." Each case transmitted to the Chambre des Enquêtes included an *intendit* (the complaint and the conclusions of each of the parties) and *articles* (facts that the parties were adducing in the procedure). In addition to these items there were also the depositions of the witnesses, which were recorded in a transcript. Once the evidence had been assembled and the investigation completed, the inquest was closed and the files put in a sealed bag in the presence of the plaintiff and the defendant. Once he was in the parlement, the appellant (the person contesting a jurisdictional decision) tried to show that he had been incorrectly judged in the first trial. At this point the work of the reporter of the Chambre des Enquêtes began. This role fell to a councillor named by the president of one of the two Chambres des Enquêtes who assigned a reporter or *relator* for each investigation; the other councillors of the chamber judged the case but did not intervene in the study of the evidence.

What do we know about Montaigne's work in the Bordeaux parlement? Not much, in the end,[68] but it is nonetheless possible to imagine his work on the basis of the Bordeaux parlement's judicial practice while he was a member of it. The different transcriptions of the *Registres secrets* of the parlement for this period give us a fairly good idea of the everyday work of the various chambers.

Every civil procedure presented before the parlement was introduced by a *demandeur* or an *appellant*, that is, a plaintiff, by means of a petition (*requête*) presented to a competent judge. Roland Mousnier sums up a civil procedure this way: "The defendant offered his defense orally, denying the facts alleged by the plaintiff, and contested the legal point. The judges heard the pleas and if they thought they knew enough, they could give their decision before the court."[69] The councillor's work was therefore preparatory to the hearing before the Great Chamber. It consisted principally of drawing up written reports after having studied the testimony of the witnesses and the pleas of the parties. If the case was sufficiently clear, a judgment could be handed down immediately by the Great Chamber; if not, the judges limited themselves to "receiving for judgment" and transmitted the file to one of the Chambres des Enquêtes. Investigations were ordered to prepare "extracts" and sometimes to ask for additional evidence to be added to the file. The depositions were recorded by the reporter, who was then responsible for presenting them in a session with his fellow councillors. Montaigne became a reporter for the first time in 1562. His work consisted in sifting through the evidence in the file, organizing it, and producing a synthesis of it.[xiv]

After receiving a bag containing an investigation or case file, the reporter took it home to study it. The study of the evidence bags was carried out in the councillor's home and not in the Palais de l'Ombrière.[xv] The reporter numbered each item in the bag and wrote in the margins of the articles as well as on the records of the witnesses' depositions. This writing in the margins of the articles makes us think, of course, of the way Montaigne later wrote his *Essais*, a kind of brief commentary on a text (book) from which he extracted the essential point. The reporter's task consisted in "extracting" from the case file whatever seemed to him pertinent on the sides of both the accusation and the defense. This work of reduction (to extracts) required a synthetic mind. The reporter had to judge what was essential in a file and to that end made two kinds of extracts, first in the margins of the documents that he had before him, and then in a separate document, a kind of recapitulation of the articles contained in the evidence bag. He evaluated the probative potential of the arguments presented or of a testimony by writing *op[time]*, *be[ne]* or *par[rum]* (*parvum* ?) in the margins of the documents. These reading notes were intended to refresh his memory when he later had to come back to the whole of the file. These temporary, provisional

---

[xiv] André Tournon's work (*Montaigne: La glose et l'essai*. Lyon: Presses Universitaires de Lyon, 1983) has shown how Montaigne's activity in the first Chambre des Enquêtes as an investigator and reporter influenced the form of the essay, notably in the practice of paradox and contradiction, forms of exposition widely used in the *Essais*.

[xv] The former residence of the Dukes of Aquitaine, this palace had served since 1462 as the seat of the parlement of Bordeaux (or Guyenne). [Trans.]

judgments naturally remind us of a practice of writing connected with the form of the essay as it was soon to be conceived by Montaigne.

Once the appeal had been "seen and examined" by the reporter, it could finally be judged by the Chambre des Enquêtes during a plenary session. The extracts were verified and the report cited the parties' facts as well as the testimonies, indicating what he regarded as the convincing proofs. The reporter's work was not limited to analyzing the written evidence because he also had to offer a judgment. After having completed his extracts, he was called upon to express an opinion, because his role as a *relator* speaking before the Chambre des Enquêtes was to "opine" (*opiner*). When he was before the assembled chamber, he was playing the role of a *partiteur*, that is, he expressed a clear position that served as a prejudgment. This kind of temporary judgment presented by the reporter, who thus became the defender of his opinion, might become the object of a contrary opinion expressed by a councillor-judge belonging to the same chamber, who served as a *contretenant*, *contrepartiteur*, or *compartiteur*. The president went around the room and listened to the opinions of the other councillors. After deliberating, the *partiteur* and the *compartiteur* were supposed to agree on the ruling to be written. Several treatises from the time offer precise and detailed opinions regarding the reporter's work, the way and the style in which he was supposed to produce extracts and make attentive comparisons.[70] After hearing the opinions and after deliberating, the president of the Chambre des Enquêtes asked for a vote with a "plurality of voices" (that is, with a majority of at least two votes).[71] The reporter then wrote the sentence, subject to the other judges' approval. The judgment (*judicium*) was rendered and signed by the councillors present. After being deposited at the registry office, the ruling (*arrêt*) was finally pronounced by the Great Chamber. However, in Montaigne's time, faced with a new increase in the number of appeals, it seems that certain rulings were tendered directly by the Chambres des Enquêtes.

In 1562–63 Montaigne was finally able to judge a case on appeal in one of the two Chambres des Enquêtes, even if he had been sitting in the first Chambre des Enquêtes since 1561. Despite the difficulties he had in making himself accepted by other members of the parlement, his family ties had allowed him to weave a network of allies, and he was in a far better position than most of his colleagues from the Cour des Aides in Périgueux who had no political support in Bordeaux.[72] Shortly before he was incorporated into a Chambre des Enquêtes, the councillors in Bordeaux raised the thorny question of precedence during assemblies. The court's protocol reflected its members' prestige and symbolic power. Regarding the question of precedence between the collectors of the *aides* and the members of the Bordeaux parlement, the councillor Sarran de Lalanne presented a petition asking that the councillors coming from the Cour des Aides not be accorded precedence over him during sessions of the parlement.[73] Montaigne was assigned to reply to Lalanne on behalf of his colleagues from Périgueux. The young councillor reminded his audience that the councillors from the *aides* had been received in parlement in an equal way and on the same basis as all other councillors, and that there was no statutory precedence for officials holding the same title. He argued that the councillors of the Cour des Aides that had been dissolved had all been received by the Cour des Requêtes after being "examined" by the same Lalanne and that they should therefore not be considered second-rate members of the parlement.

However, Lalanne prevailed and the parlement decided that during official ceremonies he would have precedence over the presidents and councillors from the former Chambre des Requêtes in Périgueux. In a supremely painful affront, the court went even further, specifying that the order relating to this right of precedence could be inscribed in the secret registers "without making any mention of it by the publication of this incorporation."[74] The hierarchical distinction among the members of the parlement was not accorded even an official debate, it was part of an arbitrary but no less real tradition. Montaigne and his colleagues from the Cour des Aides were doomed to remain on the lowest rung of the ladder with respect to protocol. This episode illustrates the difficulties Montaigne encountered between 1557 and 1563. He had entered the parlement of Bordeaux in a roundabout way, and for several years he was considered a foreigner—despite his family's political power—by members of parlement insisting on their privileges and disinclined to share them. Financial reasons were also invoked, and the court was "reminded that, given the large number of councillors who were now in the Chambre des Enquêtes, little profit was to be made there."[75] Montaigne had attained his objective, inclusion in the parlement thanks to the recognition of his competencies by his peers, but this simple confirmation of his membership in the judicial world was not enough to achieve his social entry into this closed milieu. Frictions were constant, and the new arrivals (who had already been there six years!) from Périgueux were treated like dogs in a game of skittles. They were made to understand that career promotions were not going to come any time soon and that access to the Great Chamber was out of the question.

The little affronts and quarrels over precedence were almost daily occurrences during Montaigne's first six years at the parlement of Bordeaux. Its members considered themselves injured by the sudden increase in the number of colleagues in direct competition with them for promotions. They also feared a decrease in their wages and *épices* because they had to share the reports on the rulings with the newcomers. To show their discontent, they forbade the magistrates of the *aides* to have ushers precede them when they passed through the halls of the palace. A profound contempt reigned toward the former councillors of the Chambre des Requêtes, who were stigmatized in most of the provincial parlements. Roland Mousnier notes that "the councillors of the Chambres des Requêtes were hardly part of the parlement";[76] that was certainly the case in Bordeaux. The hierarchy among the chambers was strongly marked and created a strictly established order within the parlement.

The failure of the Cours des Aides and the Cours des Requêtes in Bordeaux represented a personal defeat for the king, who had not succeeded in imposing his own officials, and who constantly collided with the power of a close-knit class of *robins* determined to defend its system of access to the traffic in offices and promotions within the parlement. The members of the parlement, especially in Bordeaux, were about to set up a veritable counterpower and lost no opportunity to ignore or get around the rulings handed down from Paris. Everything became a pretext for distancing oneself from royal decisions and for reasserting one's own independence. The members of parlement insisted on their autonomy and did not accept being told what they should or should not approve. Royal edicts were no longer systematically registered in the Bordeaux parlement, and the king had constantly to call its members to order. Montaigne made his debut in the parlement of Bordeaux in this context of almost permanent confrontation with royal power. He nonetheless found a few supporters in the parlement, notably among his numerous relatives, but he very often had to recuse himself in cases in which his uncle, Raymond Eyquem de Bussaguet, a first cousin of his mother, Jean de Villeneuve, or the son of another cousin, Richard de Lestonnac, the husband of Montaigne's sister Jeanne, were involved.

The councillors who had entered the parlement of Bordeaux retained their salaries from the Cour des Aides. As a councillor, Montaigne received around 500 *livres* a year at that time, compared to 1,300 *livres* for the first president, 1,000 *livres* for the second president, and 600 *livres* for the advocates and the general prosecutor.[77] The councillors' meager salaries were compensated by the *épices* received directly by the magistrates from the defendants or the plaintiffs. In the *Treze livres des parlmens de France*, La Roche Flavin remarks that "although probity and learning are the qualities most required of a Magistrate, nonetheless it is very good and appropriate that he have decent means."[78] Thus people often turned a blind eye to the corruption that had been institutionalized to compensate for the low salaries. An edict of December 2, 1545, condemned the excesses committed in the Palais de l'Ombrière by the pages and valets of members of the parlement of Bordeaux who extorted bribes from the parties to a suit. This edict forbade them to "beat or strike anyone, or to extort money, whether for wine or other things; or to play cards or dice on the premises of the aforesaid palace" on pain of being whipped and compelled to pay heavy fines.[79] The Palais de l'Ombrière was so dilapidated in 1545 that 2,000 *livres tournois* were allocated to refurbish the criminal law chamber of the Tournelle as well as the second Chambre des Enquêtes.[80] It was only after 1586 that a Mercurial[xvi] forbade councillors, prosecutors, and advocates to receive *épices* directly from the parties to a suit. Starting from that date, only the clerks of the registry serving the chambers were authorized to receive *épices*. The office of councillor represented more a symbolic distinction than a genuine source of revenue.

A receipt dated August 27, 1567, and signed by Montaigne, gives us some precious information regarding his emoluments as a councillor:

> Sr Michel Eyquem de Montaigne Councillor of the King in his court of the Parlement of Bord[eaux] and previously in the court of the tax collectors acknowledges having received in cash from M[r] Nicolas Lebeauclerc, and in payment of the wages and fees of the officers of the law 93 *livres ducats* and 15 *sols tournois* for my wages because of my office during one quarter (beginning the first day of January and ending on 15 March and the following and ten past). This sum was counted out and paid to me and I have acquitted and release M. Lebeauclerc receiver-general of it and certify by the present, signed by my hand, in Bordeaux 27 August one thousand five hundred sixty-seven. Michel de Montaigne.[xvii]

Officers of the king exercised their offices by "quarters," that is, they were paid every trimester, often with considerable delay. This sum (93 *livres*) must be multiplied by four because it corresponds to quarterly payments, or about 375 *livres* a year. Montaigne received a little less than 400 *livres* in 1567, that is, a sum inferior to what he had received at the Cour des Aides in Périgueux ten years before.

Other benefits were added to this salary, notably exemption from direct taxes and the *épices*, that is, the costs of dispensing justice that were evaluated by the president of the parlement for each chamber and paid directly by the parties to the magistrates who served as reporters. It is hard to determine the exact amount of the *épices* paid for each case presented on appeal in one of the Chambres des Enquêtes. Everything depended on the number of written reports made by each councillor. These represented a considerable labor of writing and presentation, and some councillors were not eager to volunteer for it. As we shall see, starting in 1563 Montaigne did not balk at this task. Serving as a re-

---

[xvi] A speech, usually made by the first president of the parlement, against abuses and disorders in the judicial system.

[xvii] This receipt was part of the marquis of Aigle's original collection; it takes the form of an oblong, quarto piece of vellum whose right edge has been eaten away, causing the loss of the ends of the lines in the text. This document is currently in a private collection.

porter was a way of making oneself better known and gaining the respect of other members of the parlement. On average, and taking into account the fact that Montaigne wrote more reports than his colleagues did, we can estimate that he received supplementary payments amounting to 300 *livres* a year.

What corresponded to this remuneration? A few figures will allow us better to evaluate this salary. For example, Montaigne's marriage to Françoise de La Chassaigne in 1565 had brought him a dowry of 7,000 *livres tournois*, or the equivalent of about ten years of salary at the parlement. In comparison, before 1550 the mayor of Bordeaux received annual emoluments in the amount of 1,383 *livres* and 15 *sols* (from 1550 his only payment was two ceremonial robes in the colors of the city). In 1584, while Montaigne was mayor of Bordeaux, the city gave him 200 *livres* to buy his mayor's robes and 900 *livres* for the robes of the six jurats. For their part, the city's jurats were paid 1,000 *livres* a year, but this sum was supposed only to compensate them for lost income. Thus a jurat was paid twice as much as a councillor in the parlement.[81] During his lifetime, Montaigne had been able to make his land productive and had amassed a considerable fortune. Let us give a last example. In 1570, Montaigne sold his office as a councillor to Florimond de Raemond for 6,000 *livres*, or the equivalent of about ten to twelve years of salary. In comparison, Élie Vinet earned 1,200 *livres tournois* as the head of the College of Guyenne, but teachers' salaries were generally augmented by fees paid by their boarding students. Montaigne's salary at the Bordeaux parlement was far from high in 1567, even taking into account the supplementary income from the *épices*.[82] He obviously did not become a magistrate in order to get rich; the prestige of the office and the status of nobility it provided far surpassed financial considerations.

Toward the middle of the 1560s, Montaigne seems to have finally accepted the rules of the parlementary milieu: he yielded to protocol and accepted the constraints associated with his profession. Starting in 1565, the *Registres secrets* of the parlement offer a portrait of him as a councillor relatively well integrated into the parlement. He then enjoyed the respect of his peers and was sufficiently familiar with the machinery of this very complex institution to be able to draw a few advantages from it. Like many of his colleagues, he was preoccupied with his career and thus his promotion to the Great Chamber. Having the necessary seniority, he could even foresee becoming president of one of the chambers, indeed, making himself known at the royal Court and perhaps being called to Paris. He frequently volunteered when there was an opportunity to go there in a delegation or to represent the parlement. In fact, he liked any mission that kept him away from the Palais de l'Ombrière.

In 1560, in Toulouse, Montaigne witnessed the judgment on appeal of the famous trial of Martin Guerre. This case of usurping identity had, as we have already said, been widely discussed and fascinated the jurists of the time. Jean de Coras and Guillaume Le Sueur wrote detailed accounts of the trial,[83] and Montaigne offers the following commentary on this case that left most jurists perplexed:

> In my youth, I read about the trial of a strange case, which Coras, a councillor of Toulouse, had printed, about two men who impersonated one another. I remember (and I remember nothing else) that he seemed to me, in describing the imposture of the man he judged guilty, to make it so marvelous and so far surpassing our knowledge and his own, who was the judge, that I found much rashness in the sentence that had condemned the man to be hanged. Let us accept some form of sentence which says, "The court understands nothing of the matter," more freely and ingenuously than did the Areopagites, who, finding themselves hard pressed by a case that they could not unravel, ordered the parties to come back in a hundred years.[84]

This distant memory of a memorable ruling—Montaigne claims that he was a youth, whereas he was already a councillor at the parlement of Bordeaux—allows the councillor to reflect on the difficulty the judicial system has in producing decisions that are both incontestable and just. Departing from a universal conception of Roman law, he resolutely places himself alongside Jean de Coras, who never lost sight of the fact that justice was best served by jurisprudence, and that his goal was to maintain the public welfare and civil peace. Keenly interested in humanism, Coras was able to influence Montaigne, who also boasted that he knew and read the classical authors.[85] Although Montaigne had not yet succeeded in gaining a seat as a councillor in the first Chambre des Enquêtes, this trip to Toulouse to attend the trial of the false Martin Guerre shows that he learned about things by observing the most famous councillors, and that despite the difficulties he had in making a place for himself, and while he was patiently waiting until he, too, could render judgments, Montaigne still had a high opinion of the magistrate's profession. In spite of his initial enthusiasm, and after almost ten years of reports and deliberations in the first Chambre des Enquêtes, no "memorable" case led him to recount his notable experiences as a member of the parlement.

In the 1560s, the marriage of Michel de Montaigne and Françoise de La Chassaigne consolidated his already considerable influence in the parlement. However, despite his family connections, Montaigne still had more than a little difficulty in becoming integrated into this closed milieu. The fact that he had entered it through the back door did not help him make his way in this profession. Logically, the union of two families that were among the most powerful in Bordeaux should have facilitated the broadening of his sphere of influence, since marriage is, as Montaigne puts it, "a bargain . . . ordinarily made for other ends"[86] than love, such as "procreation, alliances, wealth." Despite this calculation that gives priority to social alliances and relegates feelings of love to the second rank, Montaigne did not truly benefit from his marriage, because his career as a member of parlement did not succeed in really taking off until after 1565.

The years between 1560 and 1569 are important, because they mark a turning point in Montaigne's professional ambitions; he focused his efforts entirely on his work in the first Chambre des Enquêtes. He accumulated judicial documentation to complete his knowledge of the law. A recently discovered manuscript, bearing his handwritten ex libris, shows that he took notes in a course, *De principiis iuris*, given by François Bauduin in Paris in 1561.[87] This manuscript was not inherited from La Boétie, who had bequeathed his books (and manuscripts) on law to his uncle. Montaigne made a serious effort to immerse himself in the parlementary milieu and quietly waited for his promotion to seniority. He was careful not to take sides and to avoid attracting attention to himself; his name does not often appear in the conflicts that continued to divide his colleagues. Montaigne had almost ten years of experience behind him—if we count the time he spent at the Cour des Aides in Périgueux—and he had learned to avoid confrontations. In fact, his name appears relatively infrequently in the *Registres secrets* of the parlement, and his participation in its debates relating to questions of procedure or protocol is practically nonexistent.

Michel de Montaigne, Royal Councillor

When he arrived at the parlement of Bordeaux, Montaigne benefited from the experience of his uncle, Raymond Eyquem de Bussaguet, who gave him access to various power groups in Bordeaux. We also know that he accompanied this uncle to Paris in the hope of meeting high-ranking individuals at the Court and making himself noticed. Thus in 1559, on the occasion of the preparations for the royal marriages,[xviii] Montaigne may have had an opportunity to make one of his first stays at the court as a councillor.[88] He noted Henry II's inability to name the gentlemen of Gascony without making mistakes: "I have observed that King Henry II could never call by his right name a gentleman from this part of Gascony."[89] On July 31, 1559, after Henry II's death, the parlement of Bordeaux assured Francis II of its loyalty and announced the dispatch of a del-

---

[xviii] In accord with the Treaty of Cateau-Cambrésis, which was signed by Henry II and Philip II of Spain on April 3, 1559, the duke of Savoy married Margaret of France, Henry's sister, and Philip married Elisabeth, Henry's daughter. [Trans.]

egation composed of the president, Christophe de Roffignac; the president of a Chambre des Enquêtes, Guy de Brassac; the general prosecutor Antoine Lescure; and the councillor Raymond Eyquem de Montaigne.[90] Michel was bored in the Chambre des Requêtes and probably benefited from an exceptional leave to accompany his uncle on this official journey. In early September, the presidents of the Chambres des Enquêtes tried to fill out their chambers, which had been short of councillors since Jean de Mabrun and Mathieu de Masparaulte had declared that they were ill and "the said Eyquem is not present in the city, given that he is absent for the service of the King and on leave from the court."[91] Despite his absence, the court ruled that Montaigne would be among those who would serve during the examination of a case, "provided that he begins during the week's [sick] leave that Auzaneau has taken." Shortly afterward, we find Montaigne in Bar-le-Duc, with Francis II,[92] even though it is impossible to determine exactly what role he was playing "in the service of the King."

Back in Bordeaux, Montaigne resumed his work at the Chambre des Requêtes, serving as an intermediary between the advocates and the prosecutors who filled the halls of the parlement. His role was to see to it that the legal actions expressed in the form of petitions were executed. The councillors of the Chambres des Enquêtes sometimes declared that they were sick; they were then excused and were not expected to attend deliberations. The practice was to replace them with councillors requisitioned from the Chambres des Requêtes. That is how Montaigne began to sit in the Chambres des Enquêtes, starting toward the end of 1561. In late November of that same year, a report was presented to the parlement denouncing the attack on the convent of Marmandes by Protestants assembled in a force of 5,000 to 6,000 men. The parlement deliberated an appropriate response after the destruction of sacred images in the church of Saint-André in Bordeaux. To that end they recommended, after deliberation,

> that the King be informed of the breaking of the images and of the warning of the said Vidal and that of the said Desportes, his companion, and of the warning that he has received regarding La Reolle and in the same way the said lord of Burie, to whom it will be written [to tell] him to come as soon as possible, and the president Messire Christophe de Roffignac has been assigned to draw up the said missives. [It is] ordered that the court shall assemble at one in the afternoon to read and consent, and those who fail to be there will be deprived of their wages for a month. The aforesaid missives will be sent by way of Maître[xix] Michel Eyquem de

---

[xix] Randle Cotgrave's *Dictionarie of the French and English Tongues* (1611) says, "*So were the* Conseillers du Parlement *called in old time.*" [Trans.]

Montaigne, royal councillor at the court, who is going to the court for other business.[93]

After Emery de Gasc's report, the president, de Roffignac, wrote a letter in which he asked the lieutenant general in Guyenne, Charles de Coucy, lord of Burie, to return to Bordeaux immediately. Montaigne was assigned to transmit the parlement's official correspondence to the queen, the chancellor, the king of Navarre, and to Burie, who was at the Court at that time. This role as messenger and emissary certainly suited him better than the subtleties of protocol that the members of the Chambre des Requêtes and the parlement wrangled over.

Starting in 1561, Montaigne had regular access to the royal Court, even if it was only as a messenger and subordinate of the Bordeaux parlement. Carrying letters to the queen of Navarre was not displeasing to him:

> Thus in the said assembly the letters from the king of Navarre and from the said lord of Burie were read and agreed to, and when they had been deliberated upon it was ruled that they would be written, as the aforesaid president de Roffignac had formulated them and as for those of the Queen and Monsieur the Chancellor the clerk was ordered to draw them up and send them the same day because the aforesaid Montaigne wanted to leave that night as he said in accord with the letters of the king and the Queen of Navarre.[94]

Montaigne seems to have found an activity that he was excited about and that gave him considerable influence in the parlement, far greater in any case than the influence offered him by his position in a discredited Chambre des Requêtes. Urged to leave at nightfall and to carry out the missions entrusted to him, he transformed his repeated journeys to the Court into a "political experience" that later served his ambitions. His encounters at the Court allowed him to discover a different world. As a simple member of a parlement, he did not have access, of course, to the inner circle of the courtiers, but he quickly became familiar with the functioning and decorum of the king's entourage. Fifteen years later, he returned to the same Court (with a different monarch) as a *gentilhomme ordinaire de la chambre du roi*.

In the southwest it was still thought that the Protestants could be quickly eradicated. In Bordeaux, assurances of allegiance to the Catholic faith multiplied, and the parlement clearly sided with the Roman Apostolic Church. The city's jurats reiterated their loyalty to the king of France and to the "old religion." It was in this context that Montaigne conducted the investigations for his first trials as a member of the parlement's first Chambre des Enquêtes, of which he had just become a member at last.[95] He appears to have been rather selective in choosing those with whom he associated, and he was rapidly identified as an inflexible Catholic. The king thought he had acted with enough firmness in Guyenne, but his authority was soon to be contested. Monluc was sent to the region to reestablish order. In this climate of hatred and suspicion justice had to be dispensed by a parlement that was itself divided. In reality, the councillors of the Bordeaux parlement acted out of political and religious conviction and were no longer much concerned with respecting or applying the laws.

Conflicts between merchants and litigations over inheritances constituted the majority of the cases appealed. There was also a considerable number of judgments concerning the rights of succession or unpaid rents. Most of the time, the appeals resulted from new evidence introduced by the defendant in the initial trial. The court assigned councillors to conduct the investigations and write up reports after examining the files; other councillors—usually members of the same chamber as the reporter—were responsible for presiding over the trial and delivering the ruling. If a question regarding the customary regional practices was raised during a trial, the court sent one of its members to look into the usage in the place concerned. The Chambres des Enquêtes had the authority to make decisions concerning all the clauses that had led to an appeal.

Montaigne began to prove himself in the parlement in 1562, under the presidency of Léonard d'Alesme, who had been the first president of the first Chambre des Enquêtes since 1556. At that time, he was particularly close to Jean Rignac, a councillor since 1554, and François Fayard, one of his former colleagues at the Cour des Aides in Périgueux. Montaigne began to work actively for the first Chambre des Enquêtes in 1562, even though some members of the parlement continued to consider him as a councillor in the Chambre des Requêtes. Starting in the summer of 1562, he was finally able to boast that he had joined the court of justice, and he signed his first rulings at the end of that year, along with Bertrand de Makanam, Pierre de Saint-Angel, Antoine Beringuier, and Henri de La Taste. He sometimes worked, but rarely, for the second president of his chamber, François de La Guyonnie. On the documents, he was now presented as "Maître Michel de Montaigne, royal councillor in the aforesaid court." We almost always find him associated with Alesme, who took him under his wing and taught him the trade.[xx]

Montaigne voted in more than three hundred rulings distributed in the following manner: five rulings between December 12 and the end of December 1562; sixty-three rulings in 1563; seventy-five in 1564 (up to August 19); eighty-

---

[xx] The parlement's rulings based on Montaigne's reports were transmitted to me by Katherine Almquist in 2007. Almquist died suddenly in 2012, and these rulings and the book she was writing on Montaigne's years at the Bordeaux parlement have not been published.

eight in 1565 (up to September 7; then he was at the court, and on December 27, at the château of Hauterive in the Agenais, as a witness to the marriage of Jean Belot's niece);[96] eighty-seven for the year 1566 (but only starting on March 23; he was absent from August 24 to December 4); sixty-seven in 1567 (starting in mid-July). These figures show an altogether respectable activity for a councillor in the parlement. The years between 1563 and 1567 provide an image of a Montaigne who was fully engaged in the everyday work of the parlement. He rather willingly agreed to conduct investigations outside Bordeaux. Thus at the end of February 1562, the parlement sent him on a mission to the présidial of Périgueux. A good horseman and younger than most of his colleagues, he repeatedly served as a courier, and, in the parlement's *Registres secrets*, it is not rare to find him "going to the Court for other business."

Between January 1563 and December 1567, Montaigne served as a reporter for thirty-seven rulings, far more than any of his colleagues.[xxi] We see that Montaigne was very active and always ready to serve as a reporter, almost exclusively under the presidency of Léonard d'Alesme. The other four councillors who had been transferred from the Cour des Aides in Périgueux—Makanam, Fayard, Merle, and Brusac—tried to earn respect as he did and made numerous reports, but they never achieved the level of Montaigne.

Between May 1560 and May 1562, La Boétie served as reporter in twenty-two rulings, several of which also bore Montaigne's name.[97] He was without any doubt the rising star of the first Chambre des Enquêtes, and would probably have been able to join the Great Chamber in 1565 had he not died before he could do it. Montaigne had grown close to him in the spring of 1562, while they were both serving in the first Chambre des Enquêtes. The councillor from the Sarlat area, who was only two years older than Montaigne, was already one of the most experienced members of the parlement and was able to serve as Montaigne's mentor. On April 6, 1562, a ruling of the parlement of Bordeaux on Montaigne's report also bears the name of Estienne de La Boétie as councillor;[98] it was the first time they had worked together on a case. In this judgment on appeal, the ruling reversed the ruling of the présidial court of Périgueux and, amending its judgment, found the other party guilty. On March 15 of the following year, we find Montaigne and La Boétie dealing with a similar case brought by Catherine d'Abadie, the plaintiff appealing before the seneschal

---

[xxi] This figure should be compared with those of his colleagues in the parlement: Joseph d'Alis (thirty-six rulings under his authority), Bertrand de Makanam (thirty-three), Joseph Eymar, Jean Rignac, Bertrand Duplessis (twenty-seven), Léon de Merle, François Fayard (sixteen), Jean de Massey, Jean du Duc (fifteen), Mathurin Gilibert (nine), Bertrand Arnoul (seven), Henri de La Taste, Antoine Beringuier, Hugues Casaulx (six), Estienne de La Boétie (five, but he died in 1563). Several other councillors reported fewer than four rulings (Jacques Brusac—formerly in Périgueux—Berthon, Le Comte, et al.).

d'Albret a decision made in favor of the defendants, Marie Ducom and her husband, Simon d'Abadie. Once again, Montaigne signs the ruling as the reporter and the name of La Boétie appears on the same ruling as councillor.[99]

In 1563 Montaigne established himself as a reporter, an important responsibility that was entrusted to him by the president of his chamber, Léonard d'Alesme, with whom the name "Montaigne" was henceforth almost always associated, especially in the thirty-six appeals that have now been counted between December 17, 1562, and August 8, 1567. Alesme and Montaigne sometimes summoned the parties to explain themselves in person, as in the case of the ruling issued on June 6, 1563: Jeannette, Léonard, and Jean du Boiret, the heirs of a man named Meynard, were sued by a woman who claimed that she had been deprived of her share of the goods sold by the heirs. She had to prove her lineage and show that her husband had earlier filed a suit against Meynard to recover his property. After proceeding to judgment, Montaigne and Alesme summoned the parties to appear before the court after the feast of Saint Martin to demonstrate the truth of the facts "before a commissioner." The investigations conducted by Montaigne and his colleagues in the first chamber were very respectful of the judgments made earlier by the judges of the présidial courts, and the rulings in Montaigne's report generally confirm that there was "no relevant new evidence, and that it was correctly judged by the aforementioned présidials and wrongly appealed by the aforementioned appellants."[100]

A ruling issued on December 12, 1563, refers to a statement reported by "Maître Michel Eyquem de Montaigne, Commissioner" dated August 11 and notes that "Montaigne's report was heard in this [court]." Montaigne was a reporter of statements that were recorded "in front of" him. He was a reporter at the court on April 21 and May 10 and 16, 1564, regarding an appeal of a judgment before the seneschal of Périgueux. Alesme and Montaigne once again confirmed the earlier judgment. On several occasions, Alesme and Montaigne reduced the fines, but confirmed the initial judgment; in another case, they verified a signature and ratified the présidial court's decision. Very rarely, they decided to institute a new trial—for example, in the dispute between Buyrault and Pierre Lhommeau, two bourgeois merchants in Bordeaux. In a judgment handed down on April 29, 1564 (the ruling is dated March 2, 1565), we learn that the two parties had appealed an initial court decision. After hearing new witnesses, the judgment was reversed and Montaigne and Alesme decided on a new trial. But this was a rather unusual case. The two merchants were asked to present themselves before the reporter (Montaigne) within two weeks so that they could explain contradictions noted in their initial statements.

A ruling dated August 23, 1566, reports how Jehan Boudin, the son of the late Guilhaume Boudin, who had been a prosecutor at the présidial court in Périgueux, appeared before "Maistre Michel de Montaigne royal councillor in the aforesaid Court." It was a question of real estate that had been seized by the defendant in payment for a debt owed by his mother, and that he refused to give back even though he had received the payment of the principal and interest. The defendant claimed that he had obtained royal letters annulling the sale of the goods at auction. The court ignored these letters, refused to hear the appeal, and assented to the request in documents that seemed more like an arbitration. The court forbade the defendant to resell the property to the plaintiff, who was for his part ordered to pay within one month both the capital and the court costs, and if he did not the plaintiff could receive the sum deposited in the defendant's hands, plus interest, starting from the date it was deposited. This rather technical case certainly required a good knowledge of property law. The rulings Montaigne signed show that from 1564 to 1568 he was fully involved in his profession as a magistrate and dispensed justice with increased experience in this kind of litigations. Many rulings bearing his name attest to his maturity as a judge.[101]

Technical work as a councillor and reporter was sometimes influenced by religious considerations, and councillors had a hard time keeping their distance from the political negotiations going on in the Palais de l'Ombrière. In 1561 an association was formed to combat heresy, anticipating the leagues of 1576 and 1585. A few members of the parlement had taken this political opportunity to set out on a veritable witch-hunt. The only policy supported by the Catholic extremists consisted in ruthlessly repressing the Protestants. The assassination of François de Guise in early 1563 strengthened the cohort of intransigent Catholics in the parlement of Bordeaux. At the beginning of the 1560s, that is, before the first War of Religion broke out, Montaigne and La Boétie had taken the side of religious intransigence, even though they had never recommended prosecuting the members of the parlement who sympathized with the Protestants. The situation in Bordeaux had been tense since the edict of June 1560 according Protestants the freedom to worship in the city's suburbs, and many cases on appeal before the parlement were tinged with religious considerations.

Catholics saw in the parlement and its first president, Benoît Lagebaston, a perfect target for putting an end to dangerous compromises and thus opposing the edicts of tolerance by legal means. On July 25, 1562, the parlement applied a law dating from 1543 that required all its members to belong to the Catholic faith. On November 12, 1563, the lieutenant general of Guyenne, François de Peyrusse d'Escars, created a scandal by bursting into the hearing hall with his armed men. A defender of civil liberties and the autonomy of the parlement, Lagebaston ordered them to leave immediately. Threats were exchanged. D'Escars was already considered a *ligueur*,[xxii] while Lagebaston had a reputation

---

[xxii] Members of the leagues (*ligues*) formed to defend the Catholic faith were called *ligueurs*. [Trans.]

for sympathizing with the Reformation. This confrontation also revealed the opposition between the parlement and the city's military power, represented by the lieutenant general. Lagebaston came to the aid of several councillors who had been accused by the king's lieutenant general, but he recused others, including Montaigne, who was very offended by this sidelining and abruptly left the court in a cold fury, challenging in his turn "the whole Court." He was called back by the president, who demanded that he explain his violation of parlementary decorum and asked him to say precisely what he intended by this general challenge.

Montaigne thought better of it:

> When it came Michel de Montaigne's turn to speak, he expressed himself with all the vivacity of his character, and said that there was no reason they [the lieutenant general and his armed men] should leave, and that the first president had no right to propose to recuse anyone as a remonstrance or otherwise, when he himself had been recused; then he left, saying that he named the whole Court. He was recalled. The Court ordered him to say what he meant by these words, whereupon the aforementioned Eyquem said that he had no bias with regard to the present case, nor any hostility to the first president, since they were friends and the first president had been the friend of all those of the house of the aforesaid Eyquem; but in view of the bad beginning that justice had made, that *jagabecta erat alea* [*sic*] [probably *alea jacta est*], and that the accusations were accepted against the rules of the Court, to recuse other judges who were no more interested than he was; he had said that if that was allowed, he could also recuse the whole Court, but did not mean thereby to name any individual, and renounced what he had said only insofar as he had named the whole Court.[102]

This account shows us an angry Montaigne who didn't like having his feet trod upon, even by his superiors in the parlement.

We can understand his irritated reaction, even if he rapidly backpedaled. He was used to these frequent recusals, which often prevented him from participating in the parlement's debates. His parental ties with other members of parlement did not allow him to express his opinions without being systematically sidelined. He emerged from this incident looking somewhat foolish, but once is not always, and it had nonetheless given him an opportunity to express publicly his feelings about the way the parlement operated. Lagebaston had accused him of partiality, but this kind of recusal was common, and Montaigne should have considered this procedure as normal. This much-talked-about incident was undoubtedly the straw that broke the camel's back, whereas for more than five years he had kept out of the internal controversies in the Palais de l'Ombrière. It was three months after La Boétie's death and Montaigne had few supporters in the Great Chamber. He seems to have sided with the *ligueur* d'Escars, without, however, being considered an extremist. He had also succeeded in displaying the difference between him and his colleagues in the parlement, whom he considered too inclined to protest against a royal authority that in his opinion should not be disavowed publicly. He was not convinced of the parlement's independence with regard to a representative of the king, in this case the lieutenant general of the province. Throughout his life he maintained this respectful attitude toward the king's representatives.

Montaigne was a loyalist from the outset, and on this point he never budged. His views on the religious question were on the whole quite similar to the positions defended by the members of the Catholic high nobility in the early 1560s. He recommended firmness in dealing with the Protestants and was annoyed by the growing power in the Bordeaux parlement of a group of their hidden partisans whose most active members were the councillors Jean Guilloche, Pierre Sevin, François Bouchier, Bertrand de Makanam, Arnaud Guérin, Bertrand Arnoul, and Jean Dupont, all of whom sympathized with the reformed religion. Montaigne remained a friend of Lagebaston—he supported him later on—but he could not accept the interference of religion in judicial matters. He considered himself, perhaps wrongly, above all suspicion and could hardly imagine that one might doubt his integrity. Against his will, this incident exposed his political affinities to public scrutiny, and it attracted the approval of Catholics who were much more committed than he was, notably Antoine de Prévost de Sansac, the archbishop of Bordeaux; Christophe de Foix-Candale, bishop of Aire; his brother Frédéric de Foix-Candale;[xxiii] and Montaigne's all-powerful neighbor, Germain-Gaston de Foix, Marquis of Trans, who recognized in this young member of the parlement a potential ally who could serve the Catholic cause. These *ligueur* leaders were sworn enemies of Lagebaston, and the notorious altercation between Montaigne and the president of the parlement might have made them think that the hot-headed councillor was openly on their side.

This political quarrel sheds light on the way in which Montaigne was viewed politically within a parlement that was increasingly divided between, on the one hand, a first president rather inclined to make concessions to the Protestants and, on the other hand, the royalist Catholic party committed to a policy of repression.

[xxiii] The Foix-Candale family had long been part of the political power in Bordeaux. Henri de Foix-Candale even served briefly as mayor and governor of Bordeaux in 1571. He died in February 1572 during the siege of Sommières.

One month later, d'Escars once again opposed the president of the parlement by pointing out that even Henry of Navarre had once asked that Lagebaston be dismissed because of his excessive tolerance. Lagebaston replied violently, denouncing a conspiracy between d'Escars and certain members of parlement who supported him and who "often went to drink and eat with the lord d'Escars, which made them contemptible to the point that the lord d'Escars sent for them at all hours, and used them in whatever affairs he pleased."[103] He was asked the names of those whom he accused of serving d'Escars's interests. He named the presidents Roffignac and La Chassaigne, the archbishop of Bordeaux, Prévost de Sansac, as well as the councillors Fauguerolles, Malvyn, Gaultier, Belot, La Guyonnie, Eymar, Le Comte, and Montaigne; in short, all those who had a reputation of being resolute and inveterate Catholics.

It was Montaigne who spoke up to defend himself against the president's accusations. In a way rather unusual for him, he thus appeared as a leader. Without any possible ambiguity for the other members of the parlement, in the early 1560s he gave the impression of being politically aligned with the Catholic extremists. The excuses he gave reveal a genuine fracture between the camps in the parlement that were divided on denominational questions. At that time Montaigne and his friends were in the minority: in the early 1560s people who sided with the ideas of the Reformation had begun to infiltrate the parlement and represented a force that was still silent.

Montaigne counted Lagebaston among his friends, but the majority of the members of the parlement who were present recalled that on that day Montaigne had declared himself the spokesman of the Catholics who were seen as close to d'Escars. The ties that he maintained with the magistrates Lagebaston mentioned also indicate the denunciation of a familial network. Eymar was Béatrix de Louppes's husband, and Raymond Eyquem was the husband of one of the La Chassaigne daughters, not to mention Montaigne himself, who also married a La Chassaigne two years later.

At a time when ties of proximity were just as important as family ties, and in a region divided by religion, Montaigne had every interest in maintaining good neighborly relations with the powerful Catholic lords who controlled the lands surrounding his own, and the Marquis of Trans, who was soon to serve as his political godfather. For this reason, he could hardly oppose d'Escars, which seems to have been a genuine political choice on his part. Whether he wished it or not, for most of his colleagues Montaigne belonged to a political clan whose pro-*Ligue* ideology was clear. Moreover, he never repudiated his political affinities in the 1560s, even though he preferred not to mention them in his *Essais*.

A letter dated December 1567 reveals Montaigne's Catholic zeal. This letter, addressed to his friend Jean Belot, a councillor at the parlement since 1557, was to be read at the court, before the assembled chambers. When the second civil war had just broken out, and while Montaigne was on the way to his château, he had noticed suspicious troop movements in the area near Castillon. He wanted to inform the parlement of this as soon as possible, and from his château he wrote a detailed report of the situation that warned the Bordeaux authorities:

> Five or six days ago, a group of people on horseback, as many as twenty five sent by the Duke of Orléans's party... in such a way that groups are being formed to rise up and take arms, on the pretext of going to find M. the Prince of Navarre, who they say is descending toward Montauban.... Those responsible for guarding the neighboring cities would be well-advised to keep an eye on their gates, without getting excited or frightened.[104]

Montaigne was good at spotting the Protestants who were hanging around his lands. Later on, when he was mayor of Bordeaux, he made similar reports to Marshal Matignon to warn him of troop movements in the region. Acting as an informer for the established power, Montaigne had chosen his camp, and his involvement on the terrain did not change over twenty years. His practice of politics in its most everyday form must not be confused with the ideas of tolerance frequently expressed in his writings.[105] Theory and practice do not always coincide, and Montaigne's actions often contradict his declarations regarding liberty and toleration in the *Essais*. Administering a city, a region, or a country is rarely compatible with the high idea one may personally have concerning power and politics.

Montaigne's marriage to Françoise de La Chassaigne on September 22, 1565, strengthened his support in the parlement and helped him expand his sphere of influence. This marriage was arranged by the parents of the young couple. Françoise was the daughter of the councillor Joseph de La Chassaigne and the granddaughter of the president Geoffroy de La Chassaigne. The marriage brought Montaigne a dowry of 7,000 *livres* payable in two installments:[106] 4,000 *livres* plus interest were to be paid at the end of six months, and the rest four years after the first installment, in addition to interest at the rate of 7.5 percent per annum, payable each trimester.[107] In the marriage contract, Montaigne associated his wife with one-third of the property acquired during their marriage, up to 7,000 *livres*. From his father he received one-fourth of the revenues from the land of Montaigne stretching from Castillon in the Bordeaux region to the stream of Lestros in the jurisdiction of Montravel, with the exception of the château and a few other buildings on the estate retained by Pierre Eyquem. In actuality, the La Chassaigne family never paid Montaigne the 7,000 *livres*, and in 1588 he was still demanding that his brother-in-law, the lord of Pressac, pay the balance of this sum.[108] Montaigne's marriage brought him next to nothing financially.

However, on the political and social level Montaigne could hope to gain from his marriage. In 1565 his marriage confirmed his commitment to the side of the La Chassaignes, who were declared enemies of the Reformation, members of the Catholic group in the parlement, and very influential in Bordeaux. The two families were already linked by the marriage of Adrienne de La Chassaigne with Raymond Eyquem, Montaigne's uncle, who had died in 1563, a few weeks before La Boétie. The three years following his marriage gave Michel an opportunity to devote himself fully to his career as a councillor. At that time, he resided chiefly in Bordeaux. After a rather lackluster debut in the parlement and the sudden death of La Boétie, who might have been able to help him find his true place among his colleagues in the first Chambre des Enquêtes and get promoted, Montaigne's marriage to a La Chassaigne offered him a promising outlook for his career in the parlement. However, contrary to all expectations, his promotion within the parlement was not accelerated by this marriage. On the contrary. This disappointment might well explain Montaigne's silence about his wife in the *Essais*. Moreover, the La Chassaignes were still close to the world of the merchant class, and after 1570 Montaigne did all he could to avoid references to his past as a member of parlement and to the social origins of his wife's family.

One of the most important moments in this period came just before his marriage to Françoise de La Chassaigne. A few weeks earlier, Montaigne had gone to Saintonge on a mission for the parlement. This journey to another province undoubtedly fed his future ambitions. From mid-May to mid-July 1565, in accordance with a decision made by the king and along with eight other councillors from the Bordeaux parlement, he was attached to a special chamber in Saintonge presided over by Henri de Mesmes, who had been sent there from Paris.[109] Montaigne was given the same treatment as Henri de Mesmes, and probably ate his meals with the already famous jurist who had refused an ambassadorship at the age of twenty-four. The two men were almost the same age (Mesmes was born in 1531). Working together for two months, the two magistrates had plenty of time to get to know each other. We shall see that a few years later Montaigne recalled his meeting with the lord of Roissy and Malassise, the great servant of the state. The parlement's registers mention that Montaigne made another stay at the royal Court in November 1565.

The death of Pierre Eyquem on June 18, 1568, at the age of seventy-three, marked a decisive turning point in his son's career in the parlement of Bordeaux. Montaigne chose this symbolic date to dedicate to his father his translation of Raymond Sebond's book. Pierre Eyquem's estate was probated in accord with the rules of inheritance in force at that time. Pierre Eyquem's five sons and three daughters shared various lands and goods, but the eldest child, Michel, received the seigneurie of Montaigne as the universal heir. Thomas inherited the noble house of Beauregard in exchange for the sum of 2,600 *livres tournois* paid to Michel by testamentary disposition. In accord with another testamentary clause, Michel ceded to his other brother, Pierre, the fief of La Brousse. Arnaud, Montaigne's youngest brother, obtained all the goods and possessions on the island of Macau in the estuary of the Gironde as well as the sum of 1,750 *livres*.[110] As for Jeanne, she had already received a dowry. The three other children were still minors at the time of their father's death.

After the notary, Guillaume de Lanyn, had confirmed the authenticity of the will for the parties, and before the judge attested that the document had been properly collated and was in conformity with the original,

> the noble Micheau de Montaigne, holding his cap in his hand and with his head uncovered, addresses his mother; he declares at length the very humble obedience he intends to render her, promising to cherish her all his life; he gives her, for the sums that he is supposed to pay her, the properties and incomes he has in Mattecoulon to use as much as she likes, and he enumerates his other various gifts. Finally, turning to his brothers Thomas, Pierre, and Arnaud, he expresses to them the fraternity and affection he intends to have for them, offering them all the favors, aid, and help in his power.[111]

The father's wish to see his son have a prestigious career as a magistrate was having a hard time being fulfilled. The facts had to be faced: although he had shown his aptitude for the quibbles involved in the administration of justice, Montaigne was not ready to add political considerations to them. The recent political events in the parlement could also have frightened him, probably making him feel that he was embarking upon a policy of repression without limits. The Bordeaux parlement was engaged in a hunt for Protestants of which Montaigne, despite his strong Catholic convictions, did not necessarily approve. He had never adhered to the politics of terror, being well aware that concern for his own security made a certain form of moderation indispensable.

In what can be called a total war against the partisans of the new religion, a ruling issued by the parlement of Bordeaux on April 6, 1569, condemned 579 Protestants to death.[112] Artisans, workers, soldiers, monks, nobles, judges, even women, inhabitants of the regions of Bordeaux, the Landes, Saintonge, the Agenais, the Angoumois, and Périgord were judged *in absentia*. Montaigne was present during the court's deliberations. Aghast at a parlement gone mad, he silently rejected these condemnations. The judgments issued give many details regarding the application of the punishments, which varied depending on the order and rank of the accused. Nobles were to be dragged on a hurdle, and their coats of arms attached to the tail of a horse before being broken and burned. In front of the Palais de l'Ombrière, a large number of people were sentenced to have their heads cut off and placed on the point of a lance at the gates of the city.[113]

On January 17, 1570, seventy-five Protestants were sentenced to death in almost identical terms, and another 563 on March 6 of the same year. Their bodies were quartered and hung from the forks of the gallows. Their goods and possessions were confiscated by further rulings of the parlement.[114] These excesses of zeal on the part of the parlement created a genuine terror among judicial officials, who feared their colleagues would denounce them as Protestant sympathizers. Montaigne remained impassive and participated in these decisions, but he did so grudgingly and without any political conviction. His name is not found on these rulings, whereas those of his colleagues and friends Malvyn, Mabrun, Eymar, and Pontac are, along with those of many others. The followers of the Reformed religion had to flee, and others were forced to resign their offices. Although he was recognized as a loyal and devoted servant of the king, the president Lagebaston's exercise of his functions in the parlement was suspended from June 18, 1570, to November 12, 1571. Ten councillors suspected of having gone over to the Protestant cause were excluded from the chambers in which they sat. Among these councillors was Bertrand de Makanam, with whom Montaigne had long worked at the Cour des Aides in Périgueux and then in the first Chambre des Enquêtes of the parlement.[xxiv] The councillor Joseph de Valier, also suspended as a Huguenot, was executed in effigy, as a rebel, on January 8, 1569, before being reinstated on September 9, 1570. The same was true for the councillors Jehan de Ciret, Arnaud Guérin, Jean Berthon, Pierre Sevin, Jean Guilloche, Jean Dupont, and Raymond Bouchier, all of whom were accused of heresy or "false religion."[115] The tempest was at its height around the middle of 1570, and it was better to keep away from the parlement. This was precisely the moment when Montaigne decided to retire.

In the course of 1570, the parlement gained ascendancy over the jurats and the mayor. It meddled increasingly in the affairs of the city on the pretext that a large number of the bourgeois were Huguenots. The king had to intervene on several occasions to regain control of his parlement. As a result of the jurats' repeated complaints, he ended up forbidding the parlement to interfere in the administration of the city's public moneys.[116] At this point, Montaigne became

---

[xxiv] Makanam was suspended on January 11, 1569, and reinstated in office on September 9, 1570.

a father: on June 28, 1570, two years after his father's death, his first daughter, Thoinette, was born; she died two months later.[xxv] The following year, Léonor, his second daughter, was held at the baptismal font by her uncle, the lord of Gaujac, and by his sister, whose name was also Léonor. There had been too many deaths over these last two years. Montaigne had lost a father and a daughter, and he had also abandoned any hope of a successful career, which had been compromised by the religious fever that had seized the Palais de l'Ombrière.

His numerous trips back and forth between Bordeaux and his château made him realize how vulnerable he was when he was crossing the region on horseback. A long-standing neighbor could suddenly be transformed into an enemy, and the public positions taken by Montaigne, who bore the label of a Catholic member of the parlement, exposed him to reprisals on the part of the Huguenots who had constituted themselves as a military force and were roaming the roads of Guyenne. In the parlement, more and more countermeasures against the Protestants were being taken toward the end of 1569. On December 3, the court learned that four of its members had been arrested and taken to Blaye, where they were held prisoner under the guard of Bérard Ségur de Pardaillan. They were the president La Chassaigne, at that time president of the Tournelle, the councillors Gabriel Gentil and Antoine de Poynet, as well as François de la Roche, the king's advocate-general. Montaigne was a notorious ally of these judicial officials seen as die-hard Catholics. Determined to avenge its officers, the parlement approved a series of reprisals that took the form of arbitrary arrests. It was in the midst of this frenetic escalation of violence that Montaigne is supposed to have begun to ask himself questions about his position as a member of parlement. The general political situation at the beginning of the second War of Religion, the bellicose climate in the parlement, and the vulgar and execrable quarrels among the different parlementary factions led Montaigne to think that he would find it increasingly difficult to accept partisan and irrational decisions.

Confronted by a judicial system in the pay of particular interests and locked up by a few individuals whose decisions and judgments were strictly political, Montaigne ended up forming a poor opinion of the justice system in general. In the *Essais*, he openly criticizes the parlement's Byzantine ways: "We give legal

---

[xxv] *Éphéméride*: "[June 28] 1570, a daughter was born to Françoise de la Chassaigne and me, whom my mother and President La Chassaigne, my wife's father, named Thoinette. This is the first child from my marriage. And [she] died two months later," p. 85. Pregnant again after the death of her first daughter, Françoise gave birth to Léonor on September 9, 1571: "[September 9] 1571, at two o'clock in the afternoon, Françoise de La Chassaigne, my wife, gave birth at Montaigne to my daughter Léonor, the second child from our marriage, whom Pierre Eyquem de Montaigne, lord of Gaujac, my uncle, and Léonor, my sister, baptized," p. 85.

authority to numberless doctors, numberless decisions, and as many interpretations. Do we therefore find any end to the need of interpreting? Do we see any
progress and advance toward tranquility? Do we need fewer lawyers and judges
than when this mass of law was still in its infancy?"[117] The kingdom's judicial
apparatus had been rapidly transformed into an uncontrollable machine. This
judgment of Montaigne's dates from 1588, when his political enemies were precisely his former colleagues in the parlement. Montaigne knew what he was
talking about, because he later found the same cleavages at the mayor's office in
Bordeaux. The parlementary milieu had allowed him to assess at their true value
the excesses of procedural disputes that often focused on a mere detail and lost
sight of the essential point. In the *Essais*, he refers on several occasions to the
"chicanery of the palace of justice,"[118] as if this mode of discourse were peculiar
to members of the parlement. As he remarks, it is always possible to quibble over
the interpretation of events, because "the diversity of human events offers us
infinite examples in all sorts of forms."[119] The Palais taught him at least one
thing: "Our truth of nowadays is not what is, but what others can be convinced
of."[120] Most of our convictions are merely quibbles and often result from an ideology that precedes us.

The frequent oppositions between "justice," "our justice," and "their justice"
in the *Essais* led Montaigne to define a middle path that makes it possible to
better "regulate justice" between the reason of the cases and the reason of judicial forms. For Montaigne, justice is a *happy medium*. Thus in the *Essais* there is
an essential distinction between justice "in itself" (*en soy*), an ideal conception
of universal justice, and justice "for oneself" (*pour soy*), the temporal application
of the idea of justice, which is realizable only through the deployment of a political and police apparatus that is controlled by the executive branch of the
government. The idea of a justice "in itself" is supposed to be an atemporal universal, whereas the everyday practice of justice can only be national and temporal. On several occasions Montaigne distinguishes these two levels of justice
(universal and public) and never confuses them in his writings. Jean Bodin, in
his *Six Livres de la République* (1576), and then in his *Tableau du droit universel*
(1580), theorized this essential difference between two levels of justice. However, what is new in Montaigne is the awareness that our actions can be judged
only in relation to public justice. After 1588, he applied this principle to kings:
"And those who out of respect for some private obligation unjustly espouse the
memory of a blameworthy prince, do private justice at the expense of public
justice. Livy says truly that the language of men brought up under royalty is always full of foolish ostentation and vain testimonies, each man indiscriminately
raising his king to the highest level of worth and sovereign greatness."[121] Public
justice is all "show" and serves to reinforce the morality promulgated and reproduced by the established power. Wouldn't it be better, for instance, to rapidly

carry out an execution after a man has been found guilty of a crime, even if the true culprit later confesses and thus exonerates the man condemned? That was what the case of Martin Guerre made it possible to verify. The question is whether the particular errors made by public justice weaken the very idea of universal justice:

> There is nothing subject to more continual agitation than the laws. Since I was born I have seen those of our neighbors the English change three or four times; not only in political matters, in which people want to dispense with constancy, but in the most important subject that can be, to wit, religion. At which I am shamed and vexed, the more so because that is a nation with which the people of my region formerly had such intimate acquaintance that there still remain in my house some traces of our old cousinship.[122]

We have to note that laws generally remain flexible. Justice and injustice are really two sides of the same coin, and are liable to be reversed at any time, and still more easily during religious conflicts: war has the unfortunate power to reverse moral values within a single society. As Montaigne writes: "here at home I have seen things which were capital offenses among us become legitimate; and we who consider other things legitimate are liable, according to the uncertainty of the fortunes of war, to be one day guilty of human and divine high treason, when our justice falls into the mercy of injustice, and, after a few years of captivity, assumes a contrary character."[123]

In 1569, Montaigne no longer had the necessary will power to commit himself or to rally behind the extremist phalanxes that were fighting each other mercilessly in the name of a truer religion. His accession to the upper levels of the nobility of the robe was largely compromised in a provincial parlement that was increasingly alienated from the capital. We shall see that interpersonal conflicts may also have influenced his decision and hastened his renunciation of a profession that had, after all, been imposed on him by his father. Now that his father was dead, Montaigne no longer felt the need to pursue a career full of traps that he could scarcely control. In fourteen years he had not even succeeded in climbing the first step in the parlementary hierarchy by joining the Great Chamber. Access to the upper levels of the nobility of the robe seemed to him so distant that a position as state councillor or *maître des requêtes*, the first step toward an aristocracy of the robe, had become inconceivable in the political and religious context of the parlement of Bordeaux.[124] His membership in the minor nobility of the robe could go on for a long time still without anything portending an opening in the bedlam that the Palais de l'Ombrière had become.

In 1559, Montaigne's parlementary career had begun with a series of recusals that had laid bare the blood ties that bound the councillors and the presidents of the two Chambres des Enquêtes, the Great Chamber, and the Tournelle. Ten years later, on November 14 and 15, 1569, our councillor had had enough; he had endured all the pettiness of a parlement characterized by countless quarrels. The prestige of the members of the parlement was particularly great at the time, but Montaigne was aware that he was not sufficiently erudite to become an eminent jurist of his time. He was doomed to listening to plaintiffs and defendants, to writing reports and judging cases of a disconcerting banality. The everyday work of the judicial system was far from corresponding to his idea of the jurist's profession. His meager skills as an orator might have been another reason to leave a profession that was all eloquence and representation. Moreover, access to the Great Chamber depended on co-optation. Montaigne would have had to cultivate a constant proximity to his peers in order to hope for promotion, and he had ended up getting weary of these restrictive steps. After the death of his father, he had seigneurial responsibilities on his lands and spent less time in the Palais de l'Ombrière. His repeated sojourns on his estate cut him off from the parlementary milieu and finally made him an officer too isolated to climb the steps of his profession. It was time for him to change careers.

The Religious Question

From the beginning of the Wars of Religion on, Montaigne's parlementary experience was intrinsically linked with the religious question. The 1560s witnessed a series of attempts to make peace that failed one after the other. The unexpected death of Henry II in July 1559 had allowed Catherine de Medici to accede to power as Queen Mother. The Treaty of Cateau-Cambrésis, signed in April of the same year, legitimated the Guises' counterpower, but it also gave the Protestants time to make the Lorraine family its designated enemy. The marriage of the French crown prince, Francis II, to Mary Stuart (née Marie de Guise) on April 24, 1558, gave the house of Lorraine a supreme European stature and allowed it to impose itself on the European political chessboard. Catherine managed the country from one crisis to the next during the short reign of her son Francis II. Charles IX mounted the throne in 1560 at the age of ten. His mother had become regent and was served by Michel de L'Hospital, the Chancellor of France, for almost ten years. The Estates General held in Orléans led to a reorganization of the election and appointment of members of the clergy. But this was an empty gesture that in no way quieted the Protestants' increasingly pressing criticisms. Article 1 of the *Ordonnance sur les plaintes, doléances et re-*

montrances des députés des Trois États ("Order on the complaints, grievances, and remonstrances of the deputies of the Three Estates") stipulated the order of ecclesiastical nominations as well as the presence of the nobility and of twelve bourgeois notables elected in archepiscopal or episcopal city halls. One year later, in September 1561, a new religious conference was held with a view to keeping peace in the kingdom.

Catherine de Medici assembled forty-six Catholic prelates, twelve Protestant ministers, and about forty theologians to enter into dialogue and try to bring them closer together. The goal of the Colloquy at Poissy was above all to satisfy the Protestants and Catholics.[125] Michel de L'Hospital, trying to guide the debate toward political questions, emphasized the right and the duty of the monarch to provide for the needs of the Church. But the discussions quickly got lost in controversial points of theology. Théodore de Bèze imposed a rigid theological framework on the colloquy and spoke at length about the doctrine of the Reformation. The Cardinal of Lorraine focused the debate on the nature of the Eucharist. Everyone seemed to ignore the political foundations of the religious controversy, and after almost three weeks, the conference ended in failure. Spain kept an eye on the situation, ready to intervene at the Guises' request, whereas for their part the Huguenots had begun to look for allies in Germany.

From these deliberations emerged the edict of January 1562 that forced the Protestants to return to Catholics the churches they had seized, to cease overturning statues and destroying images of saints, and to stop disturbing the public peace. Anyone contravening these orders would be punished by death. Freedom of religion was accorded to the Protestants, but the debate immediately got off track by taking up the freedom of worship and Protestants' right to build churches and gather inside the cities.[126] The Protestants were no longer authorized to assemble within cities, and preaching was allowed only outside the walls. They were also forbidden to choose new magistrates, to raise troops, or to form leagues. In Guyenne, disturbances had flared up again. In July 1562, the Catholic party commanded by Blaise de Monluc defeated Protestant troops at Targon.

The eight Wars of Religion that were fought between 1563 and 1594 are always discernible in the background of the *Essais*.[127] Some chapters are even directly inspired (at least in their titles) by events or denominational problems related to these wars: "We should meddle soberly with judging divine ordinances" (I: 32), "Of the battle of Dreux" (I: 45), "Of freedom of conscience" (II: 19), and "Of prayers" (I: 56). Others take up moral questions in relation to the religious disturbances: "Parley time is dangerous" (I: 6), "Of a lack in our administrations" (I: 35), "Of the inequality that is between us" (I: 42), "Of evil means employed to a good end" (II: 23). The twenty years during which Montaigne wrote his *Essais* were deeply marked by these wars that succeeded one another and resembled one another, and whose chronology punctuates the book. Montaigne refers to "our first troubles," then to "our third troubles or the second ones." Finally, he speaks of the eighth war—fought at the time of the Catholic League—which serves as the backdrop to the third book of the *Essais* and finds a particularly virulent description in "Of physiognomy," (III: 12) a chapter in which Montaigne gives vent to his revulsion and his shame: "Monstrous wars," he exclaims with despair. Ruin, rage, venom, popular ills, words are not strong enough to describe the events that touch him most closely.

Montaigne has the feeling of belonging to a time that has reached an unprecedented degree of barbarity; his very existence might be completely overturned at any moment. "In this confusion that we have been in for thirty years every Frenchman, whether as an individual or as a member of the community, sees himself at every moment on the verge of the total overthrow of his fortune."[128] By the geographical situation of his home, he resided at the center of the storm and saw himself as "situated at the very hub of all the turmoil of the civil wars of France."[129]

These wars were constantly on Montaigne's mind, and we can observe an evolution in the way he talks about them or remains silent about them in the *Essais*. In fact, he takes three different stances with regard to them: up to the battles of Jarnac (March 1569) and Moncontour (October 1569), Montaigne takes an interest in the war and openly opposes the "new religion." At that point he is still a member of the parlement and feels close to Catholic positions, without for all that being an extremist. After 1572—in the wake of the Saint Bartholomew's Day massacre—when he considers himself a member of the middle-level nobility of Guyenne, he prefers to keep silent about the religious conflict, even though it still forms the backdrop for his reflections. Thus in the first edition of the *Essais*, published in 1580, Montaigne resorts seventeen times to the expression "civil wars," twenty-three times in the 1588 edition, and twenty-five times in the posthumous edition of 1595. After 1585, when his participation in the political life of his time seemed compromised, he sought to be more critical toward the Wars of Religion. His tone is still vehement, but he makes use of allusion and takes care not to blame either side.[130] This evolution in his thinking concerning the civil wars in France expressed his growing desire to distance himself from the atrocity surrounding him and to create a personal comfort zone for himself. For him, the horror and violence of the Wars of Religion had become an almost inevitable malady with which he had learned to live.[131] The armed conflicts produced a "horrible corruption of morals,"[132] a medical metaphor that makes war seem almost natural.

The civil wars mocked the notion of honor because no pact was respected. Words were depreciated to the advantage of a mercantile pragmatism that Montaigne considers contemptible. The periods of negotiation were often taken as an opportunity for belligerent stratagems: "there is no time ... when a leader must be more on the watch than that of parleys and peace treaties."[133] Montaigne devotes a whole chapter to the problem of dangerous negotiations (*parlemens*) and recognizes the importance of compromises. The Wars of Religion also disturbed the proper functioning of everyday life in particular villages, and even in particular families. Nothing—neither language nor bearing—distinguished those who were prepared to kill to defend their opinions and their religious beliefs. Montaigne tells a story that reveals his helplessness and the distrust that he has to show to stay alive. He reports the apprehensiveness that gripped him during a trip on horseback with his brother, the lord of La Brousse, when they met a gentleman who was "of the opposing party" but who spoke French and was dressed in the same way. Montaigne hesitated to flee, not knowing whether this horseman, who had no apparent distinguishing mark and had been "brought up in the same laws and customs and the same atmosphere,"[134] was going to attack them. One had to be wary all the time and always remain on one's guard. Even at home, one could hardly feel safe. After 1585, Montaigne considers religious conflicts worse than other wars: "Civil wars are worse in this respect than other wars, that they make us all sentinels in our own houses."[135] He felt like a prisoner on his own estate.

Confronted by the religious troubles and social disorders, Montaigne recommended the security of present institutions and thus implicitly the status quo. His famous conservatism is a logical reaction to the excesses that marked his time.[136] Maintaining the religion is the only remaining solution when faced by the Protestants' ardor:

> The soundest side is undoubtedly that which maintains both the old religion and the old government of the country. However, among the good men who follow that side (for I speak not of those who use it as a pretext either to wreak their private vengeances, or to supply their avarice, or to pursue the favor of princes; but of those who follow it out of true zeal toward their religion and a holy concern for maintaining the peace and the status of their fatherland).[137]

Religious zeal drives the majority of the Protestants beyond the bounds of reason and makes them accept "unjust, violent, and even reckless courses."[138]

However, Montaigne is aware of the political and religious relationships that helped make his region a Protestant area. Bordeaux remained profoundly Catholic, at least in its institutions and administration, but when one was riding on horseback through Périgord and Guyenne, it was possible to form a more sophisticated opinion of the power relationships operating in this religious conflict. For example, Montaigne accuses in a scarcely veiled manner the Roman church of intellectual sectarianism and of having done great harm to letters, and thus to humanism, by putting books considered pagan on the *Index*. We shall see that he himself had to submit to a moderate form of censorship during his visit to Rome. Nonetheless, he tried to situate religion in a history that went back several centuries, which led him to defend even acts that might at first seem reprehensible. He relativized the "novelties" of his time by situating them in the broader context of the history of civilizations. Antiquity gave him an opportunity to emphasize and comment on several historical examples that led him to conclude that in matters of religion it is never possible to "give free rein" without at the same time promoting division. This criticism was also addressed to his own time.

In 1561, there were about two thousand Protestant churches in France. This figure continued to increase until the end of the 1570s. The Amboise conspiracy (March 1560) was the spark that set the kingdom on fire. Several of Montaigne's neighbors converted to the Reformed religion and armed themselves to join the Huguenot forces—the majority of them certainly more out of opportunism than religious conviction. Others took the law into their own hands and organized themselves into militias. Near Bordeaux, Bertrand d'Aix, lord of Meymy and La Feuillade, had assembled a group of harquebusiers to resist the royal troops. The lords of La Feuillade and Meymy were the first to introduce Protestantism in Périgueux. Two canons associated with this family who had embraced Calvinism had succeeded in convincing Bertrand d'Aix, their elder brother, to join them. On August 18, 1560, the parlement of Bordeaux had complained to the king about the wrongs being committed by the lord of Meymy, who was hindering the proper functioning of the judicial system. Another of Montaigne's neighbors, François de Gontaut-Biron, lord of Salignac, had also joined the Protestants, along with his brothers, Armand and Antoine. Other nobles rallied to the Protestant banner and conspired against the Guises.[139] The king of Navarre threatened to leave Paris if the princes of the house of Lorraine were not sent away from the Court. The response was not slow in coming. On April 7, 1561, the three most powerful men in the kingdom, the constable Anne de Montmorency, the marshal Jacques de Saint-André, and the duke of Guise, joined together to form a triumvirate and defend the Catholic faith. They opposed the Queen Mother's policy of religious harmony. Confident of their military forces, they pursued the Protestants who did not follow the letter of the January edict.

The judicial zeal of the triumvirs led to one of the most infamous blood baths of the Wars of Religion. The massacre of Vassy (March 1, 1562) had repercussions throughout the kingdom and served as a detonator for a generalized armed conflict that was now inevitable. Occurring six weeks after the signature of the edict of January 1562, this massacre marked the beginning of an escalation of violence. The Protestants took the cities of Rouen, Dieppe, Cherbourg, Bayeux, Le Mans, and Le Havre. The largest cities in Normandy were henceforth in the hands of the Huguenots, and the military situation was hardly propitious for the proper functioning of a parlement that was supposed to render in all serenity an independent justice. Montaigne kept his distance from the events that punctuated the first three civil wars, which were waged during his parlementary career, though he never concealed his conviction that the Catholic religion had to be maintained. He did not mention the Vassy massacre. When he had not yet begun writing his *Essais*, religious questions were already at the heart of parlementary debates. The implication of the duke of Guise and his men in this affair made commentary on it rather delicate, and Montaigne preferred to retain an ambivalent attitude toward the Guises, as we shall see in his commentary on the Battle of Dreux. Vassy and Saint Bartholomew's Day were not the kind of events that he liked to report, contrary to more traditional sieges and confrontations that raised strategic and technical questions regarding the art of war. Encirclements, blockades, frontal assaults, and pitched battles corresponded better to his conception of armed conflict, whereas skirmishes, assassinations, massacres, and other brief and underhanded acts revolted him. The Guises also occupy an important place in the history of the civil wars, and Montaigne preferred to keep his distance from a family of military leaders who, although Catholics, never ceased to destabilize royal power.

Vassy can serve as a model of the violence that confined Montaigne to the role of a witness, what he expressed using the formula "j'ay veu de mon temps . . ." (in my time I have seen . . ."). Montaigne uses this formula forty times in his *Essais*. Most of the time, he creates a distance from the events of his time, presenting himself as a simple passive observer. Occasionally, as in the case of Vassy, he prefers to remain silent. The massacre was, however, widely commented upon[140] and was the object of several iconographic representations, including Tortorel's famous engraving (figure 4).[141] On his way to Paris, François de Guise had stopped in Vassy, in Champagne. He learned of an assembly of Protestants who had gathered for a religious service inside the city's walls, which constituted a violation of the edict of January that authorized Protestants to gather only outside cities. He sent emissaries to verify the information and was badly received by the Huguenots assembled in a barn. Altercations and insults degenerated into violence perpetrated by both sides. The Protestants threw rocks at the duke of Guise's troops. Seized by an extreme anger, Guise ordered an assault on the barn by his troops. Between thirty and fifty Protestants were run through with swords, including several women and a child. The duke's immoderate response touched off an explosion, and massacres of Protestants multiplied throughout the kingdom.

FIGURE 4. *The Massacre at Vassy*, March 1, 1562. Engraving by Jacques Tortorel. Image courtesy of the University of Chicago.

The first War of Religion began with an uprising of the Protestant cities. In Bordeaux, it was feared that the city would fall into the hands of the Huguenots, whose influence in the parlement was presented as proof of immediate danger. Montaigne did not allow himself to be carried away by this logic of violence, but his political position was clear. The lieutenant general in Guyenne, Charles de Coucy, lord of Burie, seconded by Monluc, saved Bordeaux in extremis: on October 15, 1562, he defeated the insurgents under the orders of Symphorien de Durfort, lord of Duras, at the Battle of Vergt. Guyenne was temporarily brought back under royal control. Montaigne had not flinched. Between the massacre at Vassy, the point of departure for the first War of Religion, and the battles of Jarnac (March 13, 1569), La-Roche-l'Abeille (June 25, 1569), and Moncontour (October 3, 1569), Montaigne leaned toward the Catholic side without for all that evincing proof of fanaticism or accepting the usual violence that accompanied these shows of force. However, we know practically nothing about what he did in the parlement during the deliberations bearing on religion, in which he took little part. But he was not unaware that some councillors and even presidents of the chambers showed a scarcely veiled sympathy with the ideas of the reformed religion. Soon overwhelmed by an unprecedented increase in violence, he preferred to take refuge behind a more serene conception of the Church and the Christian faith, an expression of custom and tradition.

The first three Wars of Religion were punctuated by massacres committed on both sides in Guyenne, and Montaigne certainly felt the difficulty of putting things in perspective. The events and battles led to hasty judgments that would have deserved more reflection, but it was no longer a time for debates. By 1569, the situation had become worrisome. Montaigne blamed both sides. For example, hundreds of peasants had been massacred by Protestants at La Roche-l'Abeille in the Limousin and at La Chapelle-Faucher in Périgord, in reprisal for the death of Condé at Jarnac. The region had succumbed to the reign of terror. Despite this headlong rush into barbarity, Montaigne tried to retain an overall viewpoint from which he could look down on these extreme acts. He wrote the following commentary on the massacres at La Roche-l'Abeille, Moncontour, and Jarnac:

> It is enough for a Christian to believe that all things come from God, to receive them with acknowledgement of his divine and inscrutable wisdom, and therefore to take them in good part, in whatever form they may be sent to him. But I disapprove of the practice I see of trying to strengthen and support our religion by referring to the good fortune and prosperity of our enterprises. Our belief has enough other foundations; it does not need events to authorize it. For when the people are accustomed to these arguments, which are plausible and suited to their taste, there is a danger that when in turn contrary and disadvantageous events come, this will shake their faith. Thus in the wars we are engaged in for the sake of religion, those who had the advantage in the encounter at La Roche-l'Abeille make much ado about this incident and use their good fortune as showing sure approbation of their party; but when they later come to excuse their misfortunes at Moncontour and Jarnac as being fatherly scourges and chastisements, unless they have their following completely at their mercy, they make the people sense readily enough that this is getting two grinding fees for one sack, and blowing hot and cold with the same mouth. It would be better to tell them the true foundations of the truth.[142]

Montaigne does not explain, however, what the truth in matters of religion would look like. People should have taken time for reflection, avoided rushing into violent acts, shown moderation, and perhaps negotiated. But religion cannot be negotiated; it escapes the usual rules of politics, because it is situated beyond all historical temporality. Montaigne was not prepared to meddle in theology and was forced to approach religion as a custom. This expedient had at least the advantage of calming people's minds. He was born a Catholic and was determined to remain one, not by personal choice but by customary obligation and respect for traditions.

The religious conflict was punctuated by violent actions that were supposed to reveal God's true elect. Ephemeral victories strengthened the parties in their respective beliefs and defeats were perceived as supplementary proofs of the adversary's cruelty and monstrosity. Each camp stuck to its position with the feeling of being engaged in a fight to the death between the kingdom of light and the kingdom of darkness. Montaigne's criticism in the passage cited above is addressed above all to the Protestants who were seeking on the battlefield the proof that their religion was the sole true religion of France. He gives as an example the English who had long occupied Guyenne and with whom he had "such intimate acquaintance."[143] He tells how he saw those laws of the English change three or four times. According to Montaigne, changing religion does no good. He confesses that he is "shamed and vexed" by these reversals that undermine civil peace.[144] Religion is a source of social stability, and the religious conflicts of the 1560s were for Montaigne a confirmation of the correctness of his judgment.

The chapters "Of freedom of conscience" (II: 19) and "Of prayers" (I: 56) allowed Montaigne to participate in his own way in the theological debate of his time. But these were outmoded issues when he published his *Essais* in 1580. Freedom of conscience had been granted the Protestants and confirmed by various edicts. As for prayer, he considered it a false problem, because he was convinced that "it is always the same substance and the same thing,"[145] whatever the religion. In his view, freedom of conscience is based on a good intention, but it leads to "very vicious acts."[146] The chapter on this subject was not revised in 1588, and only one sentence—a reference to Marcus Brutus and to the Nazarenes—was added in the Bordeaux Copy, as if nothing had changed since the 1560s. For Montaigne, the maintenance of the old religion was the only option, because the *religionnaires*[xxvi] ("religionists") confused politics with belief. For Montaigne, religion was not a matter of dogma, but of morals and customs. "We pray out of habit and custom,"[147] he asserts, cutting short any theological debate. Montaigne's position regarding freedom of religion also remained ambiguous; it was a subject he preferred not to discuss.

[xxvi] Another term used to designate Huguenots. In Montaigne's time, people did not speak of Protestants but of partisans of the *religion prétendue réformée* ("the so-called reformed religion").

Royal policy had hesitated to define a clear line, and the edicts promulgated by Catherine de Medici and the chancellor, Michel de L'Hospital, long oscillated between the carrot and the stick. In the end, Montaigne thought that these constant shifts in policy were harmful to the public welfare, because they undermined the people's confidence in their monarch. He wonders whether political compromise was not a sign of weakness that would only incite unrest and increase religious dissensions, or whether, on the contrary, a policy of conciliation would not be able to mollify his enemies and "dull the point"[148] of their demands. For Montaigne, this remained an open question; from the 1560s on he hesitated to take an overt position and remained skeptical regarding any resolution of the religious conflict in the near future. Unlike La Boétie, he proposed no solution and made no predictions, obeying the twenty-sixth article of the order of 1560 forbidding the printing or sale of almanacs and "prognostications," precisely in order to avoid gratuitous overstatements. At the beginning of the Wars of Religion, imagining the future was a seditious business, and Montaigne preferred to stick to Antiquity. However, he was certain of one thing: political actors only reacted to situations that overtook them and tried to cope with them by issuing edicts, decrees, and orders that were mere responses or adjustments after the fact. Princes no longer did what they wished but only what they could: "having been unable to do what they would, they have pretended to will what they could."[149]

The time for negotiations and dialogue was over, and now only battles spoke. Actions in the field had become the only possible language. Peace was defined by the relationship to the war that had preceded it, and the terms of that peace were valid only until the next conflict. Montaigne experienced three wars during his years as a member of parlement, followed by four more between 1570 and the publication of his first essays in 1580. We can understand the pessimistic vision that emerges from his writings. All the edicts that had been promulgated had changed nothing in the political and religious situation, which had grown steadily worse. The peace treaties signed in Amboise (March 19, 1563), Longjumeau (March 23, 1568), Saint-Germain (August 8, 1570), La Rochelle (July 11, 1573), and Beaulieu (May 6, 1576) produced only respites. In 1572, the Saint Bartholomew's Day massacre reaffirmed in an abrupt and definitive way an operational mode to which people had slowly become accustomed. From one massacre to the next, this event only confirmed Protestants in the belief that any negotiation was doomed to fail and would end up turning against them. The Protestant propaganda machine was fired up and pamphleteers took over to recount the story of what Catholics still called, using an outmoded, negationist euphemism, the "troubles." In 1576, Henry III thought he had made a decisive gesture of conciliation by promulgating the edict of Beaulieu to satisfy the demands of the party of the *Malcontents* (the dissatisfied).[xxvii] It granted the Protestants freedom of worship and several secure areas in the kingdom. A counterpower was now institutionalized in France. In the parlements, chambers were created in which Protestants and Catholics had equal representation, as if equality and parity could calm people down.

[xxvii] Led by Henry III's own brother, the duke of Alençon, the Malcontents represented a party of Catholic and Protestant aristocrats who jointly opposed the absolutist ambitions of the king.

CHAPTER 3

La Boétie and Montaigne: Discourse
on Servitude and Essay of Allegiance

La Boétie's name is forever linked to that of Montaigne. The famous and chaste definition of their friendship, "because it was he, because it was I,"[1] made the two men inseparable in posterity's eyes. It is the image of perfect friendship that Montaigne proposes. However, this ineffable friendship also reflected professional and publishing ambitions. Political intentions sometimes merged with the literary expression of a friendship erected into a model. La Boétie played an important role in shaping Montaigne's politics and literary development. Two years and four months older than Montaigne, La Boétie had begun a rapidly advancing and promising career in the parlement, and his *Discourse on Voluntary Servitude* is now considered one of the fundamental texts of modern political philosophy. This political treatise was originally supposed to constitute the core of Montaigne's book, but at the last minute it was omitted from the first edition of the *Essais* in 1580. In fact, the place of La Boétie's writings in Montaigne's work has always been problematic, and the friendship idealized by the author of the *Essais* is not free from personal calculations.

Estienne de La Boétie was born in 1530 in Sarlat, in the province of Périgord. Descended from a family of magistrates, he studied law at the University of Orléans, whose faculty included Anne du Bourg, one of the Reformation's first martyrs who, after being condemned as a heretic, was tortured and put to death in 1559. La Boétie obtained his diploma in law on September 23, 1553, with a royal dispensation because he was not yet twenty-five years old. He began his career as a magistrate in the présidial court of Sarlat and the following year succeeded Guillaume de Lur Longa in the office of councillor in the parlement of Bordeaux. He married Marguerite de Carle, the niece of Pierre de Carle, president of the Bordeaux parlement. With her first husband, Jehan d'Arsac, who had died in 1552, she had had two children: Gaston, who in 1563 married Louise de La Chassaigne, the daughter of the president Geoffroy de La Chassaigne and aunt of Montaigne's future wife, and Jacquette, who in 1566 married Michel de Montaigne's brother Thomas de Montaigne, lord of Beauregard. La Boétie's mother's brother was Jean de Calvimont, a former ambassador extraordinary to Spain and Portugal who had become president of the parlement of Bordeaux and judge of a special chamber where Protestants were tried. The La Boétie, Calvimont, Montaigne, and La Chassaigne families were closely tied by these intermarriages; as we have seen, this was common in the milieu of the Bordeaux parlement. These arranged marriages allowed members of the families to attain the most desired offices in both the jurade and the parlement. The friendship between La Boétie and Montaigne thus included significant family ramifications and was situated in a network of relationships that was foreseeable for *robins* sharing the same social ambitions.

In his edition of La Boétie's literary works, published in Paris in 1571, Montaigne reveals that his "acquaintance [with La Boétie] began only about six years before his death,"[2] that is, in 1557. In the chapter "Of friendship," (I: 28) Montaigne initially wrote that he had known La Boétie for "four or five years" before his death on August 18, 1563, but later corrected this to read "four years," that is, since 1559. This "reduction" by two years of the length of his friendship with La Boétie allows Montaigne to avoid mentioning an earlier meeting while he was holding his first office at the Cour des Aides in Périgueux. It was thus in Bordeaux in 1559, during a municipal reception, that the friends found each other: "At our first meeting, which by chance came at a great feast and gathering in the city, we found ourselves so taken with each other, so well acquainted, so bound together, that from that time on nothing was so close to us as each other."[3] This first encounter was like love at first sight, even if there is no doubt that Montaigne already knew La Boétie by reputation, mainly through his *Discourse on Voluntary Servitude*, which was circulating in manuscript form.

During the first half of 1559, La Boétie was very active in the Bordeaux parlement, where he quickly made a place for himself. We know of ten rulings for which he was the reporter between March 29, 1559, and August 17, 1560,[4] and with the help of his reputation, he did many more between May and August 1561.[5] He was soon entrusted with administrative and political responsibilities. That same year he was assigned to a mission in the Agenais to help Burie, the lieutenant general in Guyenne, punish agitators who were trying to foment a popular uprising against royal authority. La Boétie's religious positions at this time were, like Montaigne's, unambiguous, and he was categorically opposed to any negotiation with the Protestants. A ruling dated April 1562, bears, for the first time, Montaigne's and La Boétie's names side by side. On this document, Montaigne is presented as the *relator*, that is, the reporter, the president of the court being François de La Guyonnie and the councillors, Estienne de La Boétie, Antoine Beringuier, Jean de Massey, Henri de La Taste, Jean Rignac, Bertrand de Makanam, François Fayard, and Pierre de Saint-Angel. This document marks the beginning of a judicial cooperation that lasted for a little over three years.

The friendship between La Boétie and Montaigne was relatively short, and their professional exchanges took place primarily in the parlement. Four years is not a long time to establish an exemplary relationship, but Montaigne explains that their social interactions were intense between 1560 and 1563. We can easily imagine that their conversations at that time bore chiefly on religious questions. In a parlement that was politically divided and exposed to all sorts of machinations, the two companions' political views were quite close. At the beginning of the civil wars, they openly defended the Catholic cause and proved little receptive to the idea of making religious concessions to the Protestants. They also shared the same vision of a parlement that was independent but respected royal authority.

The *Discourse of Voluntary Servitude*, written by La Boétie at the age of eighteen, and the *Memorandum* on the edict of January 1562 were crucial for Montaigne's political development. Through these works, which circulated sub rosa or in a semiprivate way, La Boétie had shown a rare aptitude for commenting on the political and religious decisions of his time. For that reason, the story of the bond of friendship and publication between the two men—before and after La Boétie's death—had undeniable repercussions on the writing and publication of the *Essais*. From the outset, books and manuscripts were central to the relationship between the two men. For example, Montaigne's first library was composed of books inherited from La Boétie, the "close brother and inviolable friend"[6] who had bequeathed to him as a "token of friendship," the Greek and Latin books he had in Bordeaux,[7] with the exception of a few volumes on law that belonged to his cousin, the legitimate son and heir of the president Calvimont. La Boétie's death in 1563 marked the beginning of a *bookish relationship* (*relation livresque*) that arose from their common profession and shared convictions.

In Montaigne's account (written almost twenty years later), this friendship dated from 1559, when the future author of the *Essais* (in contrast, La Boétie never published anything during his lifetime) left his office as councillor at the Cour des Aides de Périgueux and joined the parlement of Bordeaux. Montaigne made the acquaintance of La Boétie during his first career as a magistrate, from 1559 to 1563. After 1588, that is, twenty-five years later, Montaigne relates in detail, in a late addition to the chapter "Of friendship," his feeling of divine inspiration when they met: "We sought each other before we met because of the reports we heard of each other, which had more effect on our affection than such reports would reasonably have; I think it was by some ordinance from heaven. We embraced each other by our names."[8]

This fortuitous encounter between La Boétie and Montaigne was thus, according to him, the result of Divine Providence. The text of the *Discourse on Voluntary Servitude* had to be embodied in a physical form that could carry it through the Wars of Religion. Montaigne had heard about La Boétie through his political writings, but this "bookish" acquaintance was not reciprocal because Montaigne had not yet conceived the work that would one day make him famous. When the two men met, their respective careers and reputations had nothing in common. La Boétie was certainly more mature and career oriented than the young Montaigne, who seemed more interested in worldly pleasures. This substantial difference between the two men is made clear in a Latin poem left by La Boétie and addressed to Montaigne.[9] In this neo-Latin satire, Montaigne is depicted as a young man of promise who, in spite of his qualities, seems mostly driven by pleasure and even debauchery. La Boétie retells Xenophon's fable known as "Hercules's Choice" between Virtue and Happiness. Each one attempts to persuade the young Hercules to enjoy different rewards such as honor and fame or idleness and sexual pleasure. In this poem La Boétie transforms Happiness into *Voluptas* and substitutes Hercules for Montaigne. This poem can be read as a warning against the dangerous charms of hedonism:

> To you [Montaigne], who in your father's footsteps are struggling
> To climb the arduous paths to virtue,
> Shall I, who am burning with youth and who would look
> Ridiculous as a preceptor, give counsel and advice?
> . . .
> On the lewd whore. But, youth,
> While you have the strength flee the treacherous
> Favors with which she now enchants your ears, for soon
> The poison will penetrate your mind.
> . . .
> What good is life to someone who is slothful
> If, living, he differs little from the dead?
> He who lazily sleeps away the year and moves
> Silently through life is more dead than alive.[10]

The neo-Latin poems written by La Boétie offer a very different image of the young councillor to the parlement of Bordeaux. Montaigne is depicted as a lost soul who chases women in brothels. More interested in sexual prowess followed by long periods of laziness, the young Montaigne represents a very different kind of friendship for La Boétie. Some scholars have even alluded to a possible homosexual relationship between the two men.[11]

In 1559, Montaigne certainly had more to hope from his friendship with La Boétie than La Boétie did from his friendship with Montaigne. Although we can understand why Montaigne would approach La Boétie, we can doubt whether La Boétie felt the same emotion when he first met a councillor who had just entered the parlement by the back door, from the Cour des Aides in Périgueux. What did he have to gain, on a strictly professional level, from this friendship? What was the exact nature of the "obligation" that Montaigne considers to be reciprocal? We know nothing about this, because Montaigne confuses the humanist topos of friendship with the social and professional reality of the parlementary milieu in Bordeaux at the beginning of the 1560s.

It would be an exaggeration to claim that Montaigne was about to embark upon a brilliant parlementary career, because his work as a councillor did not really allow him to distinguish himself from his colleagues. The closeness between Montaigne and La Boétie, which was, according to Montaigne, recognized by both of them, is more likely to have corresponded to a choice related to politics and clienteles about which he later kept silent. Although it was surprising, this sudden friendship is presented as inevitable, as if La Boétie had divined the role that Montaigne was to play for him after his death or had sensed in him the author that he would become twenty years later. Montaigne may have taken his desires for realities, because the a posteriori writing of this friendship deliberately compresses time in order to create the premises of an enhanced friendship that was to find its expression only much later, long after the friend had died, and mainly through the *Essais*.

The story of a friendship recounted by Montaigne calls for commentary. Without the manuscript of the *Discourse on Voluntary Servitude*, the friendship between the two men would never have existed. It was a paper friendship before it became a human friendship. We can note first that according to Montaigne La Boétie was, like the Ancients whom he claimed to be following, consubstantial with his work. But his work is known to us only through an "interpreter" (*truchement*), a "necessary intermediary"; Montaigne reinvents La Boétie just as Plato reinvents Socrates. Socrates and La Boétie share many common points; their words are known to us only thanks to go-betweens. Another similarity pointed out by Montaigne: Socrates and La Boétie both had ugly bodies but beautiful souls. Plato created a place for Socrates in the history of philosophy; Montaigne tried to find a place for La Boétie in the history of political philosophy, even if the political and religious events of the late Renaissance forced him to abandon this project. This renunciation was a liberation that made it easier for him to obliterate the "seam" that usually defines friendship between two human beings. It could not be quantified, either, because it consisted in a project that had hardly begun, a preliminary sketch for a friendship. In the *Essais*, Montaigne describes a friendship that remained at an initial stage. The famous "because it was he, because it was I"—a reformulation of the consubstantiality theorized by Montaigne—allowed the author of the *Essais* to get along without La Boétie. In speaking of himself, he was also speaking about his friend. Can we, after all, imagine Plato without Socrates or Montaigne without La Boétie? No, because their respective stories and writings are closely connected and merge with each other. Everything we know about La Boétie is given us by Montaigne.

The Letter about La Boétie's Death

La Boétie died in 1563, at the age of thirty-three, from an illness—probably dysentery—that carried him off in less than ten days. Montaigne witnessed his last moments and reported his friend's death in a letter written to his father. This famous letter is a key document for biographers of these two authors, not only because it is Montaigne's first "literary" text, but also because this relatively short piece defines the terms of a friendship that is supposed to have led to the conception of the *Essais*. Perhaps not as original as initially thought, this letter has even been read as a paraphrase of a letter from Lancelot de Carle on the death of the duke of Guise in 1563.[12] During his slow agony, La Boétie placed Montaigne before a series of responsibilities that were later to haunt him. Whether it was by bequeathing his library to him or by begging him to see in his friend a "brother" and to continue a work originally conceived to be written together, La Boétie assigned to Montaigne a political mission with far-reaching implications.

It has often been suggested that the letter about La Boétie's death was written with great care, and that this text anticipates the *Essais*. But it is important to take this document for what it is and nothing more. At the time when he wrote this letter, or at least when he revised it for publication, Montaigne had just resigned his position as a councillor at the Bordeaux parlement—if we accept the possibility that this text (despite the fact that it is addressed to Montaigne's father) was written not in 1563 but long after the death of Pierre Eyquem in 1568, and on the occasion of the publication of La Boétie's works in 1571. The precise date of the composition of this text is still in doubt. The extract from the *privilège* for the collection published by Federic Morel is dated October 18, 1570, that is, less than six months after Montaigne ceded his office as councillor to Florimond de Raemond and more than seven years after La Boétie's death. Internal contradictions in this text—notably the date of La Boétie's testament as reported by Montaigne—force us to question the actual proximity of the events Montaigne recounts. Whatever date we assign to the composition of this letter, Montaigne was not yet an essayist. He was then only a translator who had just published, one year before, a French version of Raymond Sebond's *Theologia naturalis*.

Montaigne's letter on La Boétie's death is supposed to put the seal on an inimitable friendship that presents itself as *ouï-dire* (hearsay), that is, as a testimony of which Montaigne is only the objective and disinterested *relator*. We note that the beginning of this "extract from a letter" is lacking, as if the document had been found incomplete or had been censored by Montaigne himself before its publication in Paris in 1571. This lack makes even more ambiguous his attitude with regard to the death of a man who had been considered one of the best orators at the parlement of Bordeaux. This letter without a beginning reminds us of Montaigne's "travel journal," which also begins "underway." As texts without introductions that would make it easier to understand the exact terms of the writing, these "Montaignian fragments" do not claim to be finished objects; they are presented as unstable, incomplete testimonies. On that point, let us note that the title page of the edition printed by Morel announces a "Discourse on the death of the aforesaid Seigneur de la Boëtie by M. de Montaigne," whereas Montaigne's "letter," which appears at the end of the volume, is titled "Extract from a letter that Monsieur the Councillor de Montaigne wrote to Monseigneur de Montaigne his father, concerning certain particularities that he observed in the illness and death of the late Monsieur de la Boëtie." We may note in particular the use of the word "discourse" (*discours*), insofar as this extract from the letter is constituted above all by a series of discourses, not by Montaigne, but by La Boëtie—Montaigne playing the role that he learned with La Boëtie, that of reporter.

A rapid first reading of the letter on La Boëtie's death reveals that Montaigne ultimately had very little to say about his friend. The clerk that he was simply records what he saw and heard of the councillor La Boëtie during the last hours of his life. This was in no way a new role for him, but he was less used to playing it than his friend was. Montaigne is trying his hand at a somewhat different kind of "discourse." He sets himself the task of describing the "particularities" of this death that he wants to be exceptional but which in the end appears rather ordinary. What then are these particularities that moved Montaigne? From the outset, the reader has to concentrate his attention on La Boëtie's last words. We cannot yet speak of friendship; that tie is not even mentioned. The first words of the letter allow us to suppose that other points have already been explained in the introduction that has disappeared or been eliminated. The reader discovers this letter when it is already "underway," and the end of a narrative that omits La Boëtie's upbringing and career. Everything is not presented to us. For example, the history of his illness, and the history of the friendship that is revealed only in the *Essais* in 1580, are lacking. La Boëtie is described only on his deathbed: "As for his last words" is an unusual first sentence to find at the beginning of an exemplary narrative. This locution puts the accent on the discourse, that is, on an oratorical performance presented as essential. But in this letter, Montaigne is interested solely in a dying man's speech. The author of the "Discourse" gives way to the litigant in the parlement. Rather than inquiring into his friend's attitude as he faces death, Montaigne concentrates entirely on the flow of words La Boétie expresses.

Montaigne tells us that La Boétie was exceptionally voluble in his last moments and that "throughout his illness he spoke more willingly to me than to anyone else."[13] Among those who attended to La Boétie during his illness, Montaigne considers himself privileged. It was to him that La Boétie mainly addressed himself. His family occupied only the second rank and faded into the background in the presence of his friend. Montaigne informs his father that in view of La Boétie's very elevated and virtuous life, one could only hope for words of the same kind. This anticipation, and the fact that Montaigne was in a way preparing his reader for the remarks to follow, offers a striking contrast with the slow deterioration of La Boétie's rhetorical aptitudes during the nine days of his death agony. From the very beginning of his letter, Montaigne asserts unhesitatingly that his friend had an art of discourse unequaled at the time and that he was a better orator than an author: "though when in former years he spoke on serious and important matters, he did so in such a way that it was hard to express them as well in writing, yet at the last his ideas and his words seemed to be competing with each other to render him their final service."[14] The oratorical performance is opposed to writing: two kinds of competence that Montaigne distinguishes at the outset. In other words, while Montaigne lacks La Boétie's loquacity, he has pretensions as a writer that he succeeds in realizing.

Then begins the account of the vicissitudes of La Boétie's interminable death. When Montaigne returned from the Palais on Monday, October 9, 1563, he sent one of his servants to invite La Boétie to dine with him. At that time, Montaigne was one of the busiest people in Bordeaux. He was working on two appeal cases. Not being able to get about because he was slightly ill, La Boétie asked Montaigne to come visit him that afternoon to spend some time with him before he left for Médoc. Soon after dinner (that is, in the middle of the afternoon), Montaigne went to the Rue Rostaing, where La Boétie had leased a house from Dominique Du Rochier's heirs. Fearing the plague, since the building was "very close to houses infected with plague, which he was rather afraid of,"[15] Montaigne advised La Boétie to leave Bordeaux as soon as possible, but only to go to Germignan, where Richard de Lestonnac, Montaigne's brother-in-law, owned a country house. This house was two leagues, or about eleven kilometers, from Bordeaux.

Following Montaigne's recommendation, La Boétie left Bordeaux with his wife and his uncle, Monsieur de Bouillhonas. He had hardly arrived in Germignan when his condition rapidly deteriorated. That is the point at which Montaigne begins the chronicle of his friend's slow death. Early on the morning of August 10, a valet sent by La Boétie's wife urged him to go to Germignan as soon as possible because La Boétie was very ill. Montaigne went to see La Boétie, who was "delighted to see [him]," but he had planned to return to Bordeaux that same evening and prepared to take leave of his friend. La Boétie begged Montaigne, "with more affection and insistence than he had ever done anything else, to be with him as much as I could." Not knowing how much his friend was suffering, Montaigne nonetheless decided to go back to Bordeaux. He returned to Germignan on Thursday. La Boétie was dying, and "his flow of blood and his abdominal cramps, which weakened him still further, were growing from hour to hour." This time, Montaigne spent the night at Germignan but left for Bordeaux the next morning. He returned to Germignan on Saturday. La Boétie then told Montaigne that his illness was probably contagious and suggested that he "be with him only now and then, but as often as I could." Ignoring this recommendation, Montaigne decided to stay by him, and the two friends spent Sunday talking about one thing and another: "and we spoke only about particular occurrences connected with his illness, and what the physicians of antiquity had said about it. [We spoke] very little about public affairs; for I found him completely uninterested [in them] from the first day." No public affairs, no political discourse were ever mentioned by Montaigne. La Boétie was reduced to talking about his health. There were actually two La Boéties: the one reported by Montaigne, who talked about things that were ultimately trivial, and the one who in his writings commented on the political affairs of his time or theorized about freedom and servitude. This second La Boétie, all on paper, existed only through Montaigne. In this letter, Montaigne chose to show only the La Boétie who spoke of relatively ordinary things.

La Boétie's condition worsened on Sunday, and Montaigne tells us that he fell "into a state in which everything was confused."[16] A "dense mist and dark fog" overcame his reason. La Boétie ceased to be himself and lost forever the eloquence that differentiated him from his colleagues. "Everything was pell-mell and without order," Montaigne writes. Incoherent in his remarks, he feared he would surprise those around him: "And then he asked me if the weaknesses he had suffered had not somewhat astonished us."[17] Montaigne reassured him. Then La Boétie began his first "great" discourses to his uncle, his wife, and Montaigne. In contrast to Montaigne's silence, La Boétie's exuberant loquacity sheds light on the friendly relationship between the two men. We witness a scene in which the roles have been reversed. La Boétie spoke, Montaigne transcribed and edited. The division of labor Montaigne wanted thus already finds its logic in the first text written by the author of the *Essais*.

On Sunday evening, according to the chronology reported by Montaigne, the notary finally showed up. Montaigne helped La Boétie put in writing his last wishes and urged his friend to sign his will. La Boétie hesitated; was it because a testament had already been drawn up the day before, in Montaigne's absence? In any case, La Boétie asked for more time: "My brother, I would like to be given a little leisure; for I find myself extremely tired and so weak that I can hardly go on."[18] Montaigne called in the notary again, and that Sunday evening, August 15 according to Montaigne, La Boétie dictated his will so quickly that it was very difficult to follow him. Montaigne gives the impression that he was present when La Boétie prepared his will with his notary, Jean Raymont. La Boétie is said to have asked Montaigne to read the text to make sure that it was in conformity with his last wishes. This will is, however, dated Saturday, August 14, and was signed by La Boétie; Thomas de Montaigne, lord of Beauregard; Nicolas Brodeau, his doctor; Charles Bastier, a pharmacist from Bordeaux; François Gailhand; Sardon Viault; Raymond Dumas; and Pothon Chayret. Montaigne is not even mentioned as a witness. Is that because he was not present when the will was written and signed? In fact, he spent most of Saturday in Bordeaux, arriving in Germignan only late in the evening.

Montaigne's letter on his friend's death nears its end. There were many people in La Boétie's bedchamber. His uncle Estienne; his wife; his daughter-in-law; his niece, Mademoiselle de Saint-Quentin; Thomas, lord of Beauregard; and Montaigne were at his bedside. Accustomed to declaiming in a court of justice, La Boétie thought he was before the chamber of the parlement—rather than in a sickroom. We are rather far from a Stoic death and are witnessing instead a relatively noisy and confused melodrama. La Boétie constantly groaned and Montaigne seemed submerged by such a flow of words. The passage from one chamber (parlement) to the other (bedchamber) changed nothing; to his last breath, La Boétie remained a gifted speaker. That may be the idea Montaigne is suggesting. The discourses followed one another, on and on. La Boétie made a speech to Mademoiselle de Saint-Quentin, then to Jacquette d'Arsac, his daughter-in-law. Impassive, Montaigne remained a silent witness. La Boétie was such a good orator that he bowled his listeners over: "The whole chamber was filled with cries and tears, which did not, however, interrupt in the slightest the series of his speeches, which were rather long."[19] One by one, more than a dozen friends and relatives crowded into the bedchamber of the dying councillor, in a procession that resembled those at a fair.

Montaigne remained in the background, continuing to be the master pleader's clerk and keeping his distance. His brother Thomas was then called in by La Boétie, who made a speech to him that quickly turned into a sermon. La Boétie reproached him for his Protestant positions and urged him not to associate himself with the Protestant party—and not to divide his family. Thomas, who had recently converted to Protestantism, was the widower of Serène Estève de Langon, from whom he had had no child, and he was getting ready to marry Jacquette d'Arsac. Still another marriage between the Montaignes and the La Boéties, but one that risked throwing the family into the Protestant camp.

Montaigne reports this conversation which, at the time it was published, might have been dangerous—or at least compromising—for his brother Thomas. Confronted by La Boétie's outpourings, in the end Montaigne found very little to say. Detached from the scenes he was describing, he seems ill at ease at La Boétie's bedside and amid the mixed feelings that are supposed to have secretly gnawed at him as he walked through the halls of the parlement with his friend: "the jealousy I always felt regarding his glory and his honor."[20] In the language of the sixteenth century, the word "jealousy" (*jalousie*) refers to a form of extreme attachment that can go as far as covetousness and envy.

The state of La Boétie's health further deteriorated on Monday, August 16. He found it harder and harder to express himself. As death approached, he fainted, and everyone thought for a moment that he was no longer of this world, but he regained consciousness and began another speech. First he addressed a reproach to Montaigne: "And you, too, my brother, so you don't want me to be at peace? O, what repose you cause me to lose!"[21] Faced with this strange remark, Montaigne did not know what to reply. He was on the hot seat before this friend who was admonishing him. The reporter listened but remained silent, once again.

On Tuesday, La Boétie asked to see a priest. After throwing a bit of Cicero in Montaigne's face, he fell asleep and awoke with a start: "Well, well, let it come when it wishes, I am waiting for it, with fortitude and calm."[22] Montaigne tells us that La Boétie repeated these words several times during his illness. Seeing that his friend was delirious, he asked him what were the visions he was talking about as if it was important for him to understand these hallucinations provoked by the fever. La Boétie became a medical case; ordinarily so eloquent, he could no longer explain himself clearly. Shortly before he died, his voice became more strident. At this point in Montaigne's account comes the famous passage in which La Boétie asks Montaigne for a "place." Montaigne is concerned by such remarks because "these words were not those of a man in his right mind," that is, in complete possession of his reason. A remark that amplifies the importance of the word: "To the point that he forced me to convince him by reason, and to tell him that since he breathed and spoke, and had a body, he consequently had his place."[23] So long as La Boétie spoke, he incontestably occupied the "place" he asked Montaigne for. La Boétie could exist only through the mediation of the word, the mediation that Montaigne gave him in the printed text of the letter on his friend's death. On August 18, La Boétie finally fell silent.

Three days later, the parlement's *Registres secrets* reported a speech by Montaigne during a session that paid homage to La Boétie: "The aforesaid day Me Michel Eyquem de Montaigne, royal councillor at the Court, stated, being in the assembled chamber, that Bouilhonnas de Fartas, the uncle of the late Maître Etienne de la Boetie, during his lifetime royal councillor in the Court, very humbly begs the Court to be allowed to honor by his presence the body of the said De La Boetie tomorrow morning, which was approved to be done."[24] After this last public farewell, La Boétie was rapidly forgotten. The members of the parlement had other concerns, and La Boétie, though he had been a councillor with a promising future, had ultimately left nothing in writing that could justify the admiration of his peers. Only Montaigne brought him out of this silence to which he seemed forever relegated. Paradoxically, it was on Huguenot terrain that La Boétie recovered his voice, thanks to Geneva's appropriation of the *Discourse on Voluntary Servitude*, a short extract from which was published in *Le Réveille-Matin des François et de leurs voisins* in 1574.[25] The warning addressed to Thomas de Montaigne had been transformed into a prophecy. Montaigne was henceforth confronted by the subversive reception of a friend who was escaping him.

La Boétie's Political Treatises: The *Memorandum* and the *Discourse*

The encounter between Montaigne and La Boétie took place at the beginning of the Wars of Religion. Both of them operated within the machinery of the parlement of Bordeaux.[26] According to Montaigne, La Boétie wrote the *Discourse on Voluntary Servitude* "as a kind of trial [*essai*]" when he was very young. On the Bordeaux Copy, Montaigne makes La Boétie two years younger: "eighteen" is struck out and replaced by "sixteen," which makes the first composition of the *Discourse* date from around 1548. Montaigne takes care to de-historicize this treatise, and presents it as a "general" text "in honor of liberty against tyrants."[27] At the outset, the use of the French word *essai* to define the *Discourse* allows Montaigne to establish a link with his own work, but it also makes more precise the political goal of his friend's reflection. Thus we can ask whether the *Discourse* was not conceived specifically to respond to a precise historical event. Jacques-Auguste de Thou maintains that La Boétie wanted to react against the brutal repression that had followed the salt-tax revolt of 1548 in Bordeaux, thus overtly criticizing Constable de Monmorency's ferocious repression.[28]

Bordeaux had been particularly affected by the new tax levies, and in 1542 the city had been forced to lend the king 20,500 *livres* and in 1543 to contribute to the maintenance of 50,000 soldiers. The modification of the system of salt storage depots had served as a trigger for the popular uprising. The current mayor, Guy Chabot, was absent when the revolt broke out in 1548. Overwhelmed, the jurats did not react, and in a few hours more than twenty thousand armed men were in the streets. On August 21, the king's lieutenant general, Tristan de Moneins, was killed by the rioters. Montaigne, who was then fifteen years old, might have witnessed this murder.[29] There is an allusion to this bloody episode in the *Essais*. As we have seen, the parlement and the jurats were held responsible for not having been able to prevent the outburst of "popular fury."

Despite the political importance of this popular uprising, it is hard to see in this event the sole origin of La Boétie's treatise. The *Discourse* was revised several times by its author—notably in 1554, during the battle over the edict of the Semester[i] at the time of La Boétie's nomination to the Bordeaux parlement and Lur Longa's appointment to the Paris parlement—and we know that it circulated in manuscript form during La Boétie's lifetime as well as after his death in 1563.[ii] The text was modified later, as is indicated by the eulogies of Ronsard, Baïf, and Du Bellay, which are posterior to 1550. In fact, the history of the reception of the *Discourse* far exceeds its author's initial intention, whatever it may have been.[30]

Montaigne decided not to include the *Discourse* when he had his friend's works published in 1571. La Boétie's diatribe against voluntary servitude was more appropriate in the *Essais*, which were intended—at least in the first version of 1580—as a personal reflection on political, diplomatic, military, and moral questions. On the other hand, the *Memorandum* on the January edict was too limited to its time and not in tune with the political situation after the Saint Bartholomew's Day massacre. Besides, Montaigne does not dwell on the *Memorandum*, which often contradicts the liberal and humanistic ideas of the *Discourse*. The two texts are so different in nature that most critics still refuse to consider La Boétie the author of the *Memorandum* and prefer to keep Montaigne at a distance from a much less open-minded La Boétie. However, several references in the text, and especially Montaigne's mention of it, allow us to conclude that La Boétie is the author of the *Memorandum* on the edict of January 1562.[31] From a purely stylistic and lexical point of view, the two texts present significant similarities.[32]

The apparent impression of continuity between the *Memorandum* and the *Discourse on Voluntary Servitude* is strengthened when the two texts are read one after the other. That is why it is important to situate them in their respective historical and political contexts. They are separated by fifteen years. If we believe Montaigne, the *Discourse* dates from 1546–48—that is, before he entered the Cour des Aides in Périgueux—whereas the *Memorandum* was written to-

---

[i] An edict issued in Fontainebleau in 1554 (or 1555) establishing an Inquisition, which two successive *semestres* of the Parlement refused to register. [Trans.]

[ii] The *Discourse* had circulated in several European countries. A copy (of English provenance) was recently discovered in the Folger Shakespeare Library in Washington, DC, another in the Ambrosiana Library in Milan, and a third one in London. Other manuscript copies of the *Discourse* are held by French libraries (notably Chambéry and Bordeaux), including one at the BNF in the Dupuy collection.

ward the end of 1561. La Boétie's political career had developed between those two dates, and the role that he played within the parlement of Bordeaux had greatly changed him. The Protestant Reformation had also spread widely in Guyenne between the end of the 1540s and the beginning of the 1560s. In the course of 1561, seditious insurgents acted openly in Bordeaux and Guyenne, and recourse to violence quickly became the best way of expressing oneself, in the camp of the Catholics as well as in that of the Protestants. In this infernal logic of terror, La Boétie recommended an intransigent political position in response to an ordinance of October 1561 issued by the king of Navarre's lieutenant governor in Guyenne, Charles de Coucy, lord of Burie. One of the propositions considered intolerable by Catholics involved reserving a church for Protestant worship in the main cities of Guyenne. This concession was judged unacceptable by Montaigne and La Boétie because in their view it opened the door to other concessions that would ultimately weaken the Catholic Church and, in the meantime, disturb the civil peace.

The *Discourse* and the *Memorandum* are distinct texts whose statements contradict each other. The divergences can be explained by the fact that the *Memorandum* anticipates and seeks to forestall a precise political and historical event, namely, the edict of tolerance promulgated at Saint-Germain (January 17, 1562), which granted Protestants public places of worship, whereas the *Discourse* is more theoretical and refers to an ideal conception of liberty, making servitude a natural inclination in humans that was already present in Antiquity. The audiences to which these two political texts are addressed are also very different. For example, the *Discourse* has a rhetorical dimension that corresponds quite well with the erudite practices of jurisconsults and magistrates with a keen interest in history and ancient models, without it being possible to reduce it to a pure exercise in *declamatio*.[33] Far from being a diatribe against the Constable's tyranny and barbarity—La Boétie never names any name or makes the slightest clear allusion to a contemporary—the *Discourse* was conceived rather as a professional practice, the *habitus* of a *robin* beginning his career as a young councillor. On this point, Montaigne is right to say that it constitutes a youthful exercise. Conversely, the *Memorandum* is a politically engaged text that was made moot by the beginning of the Wars of Religion in 1563. Montaigne's position with regard to this text changed over the years between 1560 and 1570. By 1580, the *Memorandum* was completely out of date and out of phase with the political and religious reality of the time, whereas the *Discourse* remained relevant, precisely because it had been conceived as a theoretical exercise and was less anchored in history.

For November 26, 1561, the Bordeaux parlement's registers mention a mission that involved Montaigne "going to the Court for other affairs."[34] From this it has been inferred that he took the *Memorandum* to Paris. This is pure speculation; the object of his mission is not known. As we have seen, Montaigne often served as a courier for the parlement. He was a good horseman—he was still young—and he could make the 550-kilometer trip between Bordeaux and Paris in less than seven days. The parlement was concerned in particular about the political bipolarization in the southwest, and lost no opportunity to address a report to the king when Protestants seized churches, destroyed crosses and altars, or burned the ornaments of places of worship. Let us recall that at this time, faced with the rise in the Huguenots' military power, the Constable de Montmorency had joined with François de Guise and the Marshal de Saint-André to form the triumvirate supported by the king of Spain. France was henceforth divided into two parties: that of the triumvirs with the Catholics and that of the "conspirators" (*conjurateurs*)[iii] with the Protestants. Burie tried in vain to reestablish order in Bordeaux and in Guyenne. That was the immediate context of La Boétie's *Memorandum*.

In the hope of putting an end to the hostilities and pacifying seditious Huguenots, Burie had decreed that in cities that had several churches, one would be reserved for the use of the Protestants. This was a courageous decision, but it was controversial. The edict of July 1561 had forbidden Protestants to assemble in groups, but it had ultimately been counterproductive, because the number of their assemblies increased and they also seized the Catholic churches, which they used for their own services after driving out the priests. In November, a royal edict ordered the Protestants to return the churches on pain of death. As De Thou put it in his *Histoire universelle*, "the July edict, instead of calming, only embittered people."[35] The colloquy at Poissy was of no use. An assembly was convoked at Saint-Germain in January 1562, where representatives from all the kingdom's parlements gathered to write a more conciliatory edict. La Boétie's *Memorandum* is conceived as a document preparatory to this edict. His goal was to present recommendations for this new text aimed at pacification. Other memoranda, both Protestant and Catholic, were also prepared for the Saint-Germain colloquy. After the publication of the edict, Michel de L'Hospital tried to reassure the extremist Catholics while at the same time implementing the concessions granted the Protestants. Catherine de Medici sought to be perceived as conciliating and ready to give the Huguenots even more rights. However, this policy of tolerance failed, because the Catholics saw it as a betrayal.

In his *Memorandum*, La Boétie envisaged only three possible ways of resolving the religious dilemma: retaining the old doctrine in matters of religion, introducing the new one, or else maintaining an equilibrium between the two

---

[iii] The term refers to the "Amboise conspiracy" (*conjuration d'Amboise*), a failed attempt in 1560 by the Protestants to gain power in France by abducting the young king Francis II and arresting the duke of Guise and his brother, the Cardinal of Lorraine.

religions "under the care and guidance of the magistrates."[36] This last solution was neither political nor religious, but judicial. It corresponded to the position of the parlements, which saw in it a political recognition of their function and attributed to them a central importance in the resolution of the conflict. Montaigne also supported the judicial solution. After 1570, his position was obviously quite different, and the propositions made in the *Memorandum* no longer corresponded to his conception of the parlement. According to La Boétie, it was incumbent upon the parlements to see to it that the negotiated solutions were respected by both sides. But there was no question of having two religions within the same kingdom. In fact, between two such contrary doctrines, "there can be only one true one,"[37] writes La Boétie. The concessions had limits.

La Boétie defends the idea of a compromise during a determinate period: the two religions were to coexist until an ecumenical council ironed out the theological differences. Moderation and compromise could be conceived only as provisional. It was not a matter of changing religions, but of reforming questionable practices. La Boétie defended this transitional phase in the name of the only remedy that could be envisioned, a future peace. This was not a perfect solution, but for him it was the only one possible. Without this "tolerated interim," nothing could be discussed. This notion of a temporary tolerance is strange coming from the author of the *Discourse on Voluntary Servitude*. Montaigne distanced himself from such a practical definition of tolerance, and after 1572 he understood that the word "tolerance" could not be modified by any adjective indicating a restriction. Tolerance cannot be conceived for a definite time. The January edict went much further than the *Memorandum* in making Protestantism legitimate. Freedom of conscience and worship could not be conceived as limited to a specific period of time, and that is why the *Memorandum* was doomed to fail. La Boétie muddled things somewhat by arguing that "the dissimulation of private and secret assemblies is the starting point of the problem: the tolerance of public [assemblies] increased our calamities."[38]

Granting rights for a time and then taking them away makes no sense from a political point of view. The concessions the king accorded led the Protestants to believe that they had been right to disobey him. Some maintained, like La Boétie, that compromises made it possible to win one's enemies' indulgence and to appease them for a time, but in the long term any accommodation would inevitably be seen as an irrevocable privilege. La Boétie was categorical on this point: "People are deceiving themselves,"[39] he declared, because according to him France would then be filled with impiety and irreligion. Moreover, he seems really not to have believed that an ecumenical council could resolve the differences. After many hesitations, he recommended beginning with "the punishment of the insolent acts that have been committed because of religion."[40] Those who love well chastise well. After the dogmatic and intransigent positions, the time for compromise seems to have come at the end of the *Memorandum*, whose key word is "reform": "But let us reform the latter [the Church] in such a way that it seems wholly new, and let all others die, and in so doing, make use of such moderation that everything be granted the Protestants that Church doctrine can allow, in order to bring them all together in a flock."[41] Specific proposals regarding offerings and relics follow, as if the question could be settled by agreement on details. La Boétie imagines what might offend the Protestants and suggests "omitting everything that serves no purpose" in Catholic churches. By doing away with images, people would be prevented from falling into idolatry, and the Protestants would no longer have any reason to complain, since "they would no longer have any reason to find paintings in public places worse than those in private homes, and the matter would be restored to its first and natural state."[42]

The attenuation of visible signs of the Roman Catholic religion was supposed to substitute for a temporary solution. For La Boétie, it was all a matter of patience; he did not doubt that "with time people will recognize that it is a good and holy tradition of the universal church."[43] When it is a question of grieving for the dead, La Boétie prefers to give each person the right to express his pain as he wishes. Wars are a storm that will necessarily pass. The goal of the *Memorandum* is to "divert this tempest"[44] that has fallen on France. His message is essentially to gain time. The laity had a duty to intervene when the theologians could not agree or find a compromise. This secularization of politics is no doubt the lesson Montaigne learned; he saw in the mediator that he aspired to become a man who respects both religions, even if, he says, the question of religion had never really come up for him. Protected from possible criticisms of Christian dogma, Montaigne could not be influenced on religion. Tradition was untouchable. No one could ever maintain that he leaned, at a certain point in his life, toward the Protestant cause, even if many of his ethical and moral positions were not incompatible with the idea of freedom that was at the heart of the Huguenots' demands. La Boétie and the *Memorandum* probably taught Montaigne to avoid theological debates. In his *Essais*, Montaigne set himself above the storm La Boétie referred to. In this sense, he may not have been wrong to see in the Wars of Religion one episode among others in the long history of humanity. Paradoxically, the *Essais* based themselves on history the better to reject it.

Since the reformation of the Church could proceed only from a member of the clergy, to present the ideas defended in his *Memorandum* La Boétie turned, naturally enough, to the bishop of Orléans, Jean de Morvilliers, who was known for his moderation and equity.[45] Morvilliers, who was also praised by Montaigne, sought a reconciliation between the two religions. As a state minister, he attended the Council of Trent but did not succeed in imposing his views regarding the reformation of Roman institutions. The reform La Boétie desired led to nothing that made it possible to satisfy the Protestants. The foundations of his *Memorandum* no longer rested on anything more than good intentions, and did not make it possible to imagine a genuine political participation for the Protestants. The claim that the partisans of the reformed religion no longer had any reason to persist in their error and would naturally return to the bosom of the Roman faith once the Catholic Church's practices had been reformed had no validity in practice. La Boétie's wish "to reform the old Church quickly and promptly, to break the order and establishment of the new [church],"[46] remained a pious and chimerical wish.

In the *Discourse on Voluntary Servitude*, it was the humanistic *robin* who was addressing the intelligentsia of his time, whereas in the *Memorandum* it was the political agent of the king's government who, asked to set forth arguments to refute the Protestants' positions, contested any compromise and drew up a list of proposals to reform the only conceivable church. La Boétie's role was to present the points that could be used by the representatives of the royal party ("your company") during the parleys at Saint-Germain-en-Laye. It is risky to read this *Memorandum* from a later perspective (for instance, in the light of the Saint Bartholomew's Day massacre), because in the very early 1560s the current relevance of La Boétie's exhortations made his arguments still legitimate. At that precise stage in the conflict (before the massacre at Vassy), La Boétie's repressive justifications (which were based on a practical line of argument that rejected any compromise with the Huguenots in the name of the maintenance of royal authority) proved to be a genuine political option for Charles IX. Seen in retrospect, this position was, of course, doomed to fail, but in late 1561 there was no reason to foresee the armed conflicts that were to come. In the *Memorandum* La Boétie presents arguments that were judged to be acceptable and recommendations that were perceived as necessary by many people, including Montaigne. The historical arguments set forth in the *Memorandum* are not found in the *Discourse on Voluntary Servitude*. Politics is also the art of adapting one's discourse to reality, and at that time it was not as rare to find such contradictions between theory and practice as it is today. Naturally, we think of Montaigne, who also advocates freedom in the name of a conceptual humanism, but rejects any real political change in the name of custom.

At the end of the chapter "Of friendship"—and separated by means of three asterisks (usually not reproduced in modern editions) the better to isolate it—Montaigne offers an explanation of his decision not to publish the *Discourse*:

> Because I have found that this work has since been brought to light, and with evil intent, by those who seek to disturb and change the state of our government without worrying whether they will improve it, and because they have mixed his work up with some of their own concoctions, I have

changed my mind about putting it in here. And so that the memory of the author may not be damaged in the eyes of those who could not know his opinions and actions at close hand, I beg to advise them that this subject was treated by him in his boyhood, only by way of an exercise, as a common theme hashed over in a thousand places in books. I have no doubt that he believed what he wrote, for he was so conscientious as not to lie even in jest. And I know further that if he had had the choice, he would rather have been born in Venice than in Sarlat, and with reason. But he had another maxim sovereignly imprinted in his soul, to obey and submit most religiously to the laws under which he was born. There never was a better citizen, or one more devoted to the tranquility of his country, or more hostile to the commotions and innovations of his time. He would much rather have used his ability to suppress them than to give them material that would excite them further. His mind was molded in the pattern of other ages than this.[47]

In this passage, Montaigne provides several keys to the reading of the *Discourse on Voluntary Servitude*. First of all, he underlines the speculative and abstract aspect of this text, which, according to him, cannot be confused with other, more time-bound writings that refer to political events since 1572, even though they seem at first to be of the same kind. Montaigne hastens to add that this "subject" does not represent a simple exercise because the young La Boétie believed in the ideas he proposed. He explains that it was his friend's principle always to obey and to submit "most religiously" to the laws of his country. In clear contradiction to the theses advanced by La Boétie, this maxim disqualifies any political usage of the *Discourse* and raises the question of allegiance in its relation to servitude. Can one compose an apology for freedom and at the same time submit to the "unjust" laws of the country—Montaigne prefers the word "fatherland" (*patrie*)—in which one was born? Is it possible to develop a discourse on freedom and the emancipation of man while at the same time accepting what Descartes called a "provisional morality" (*une morale par provision*), that is, a morality that is presented as a universal in a determinate cultural space and that cannot be challenged on the political, cultural, and social level? The regulative principle Montaigne advanced is that of a balance to be found between custom and freedom. According to the author of the *Essais*, religious practices do not depend on human understanding: "Our faith is not of our own acquiring, it is a pure present of another's liberality. It is not by reasoning or by our understanding that we have received our religion; it is by external authority and command."[48]

La Boétie was a fervent defender of the parlement's power and opposed the military and political power of the governors. For example, in December 1561 his name appeared on a list of twelve councillors assigned to take various police measures, notably disarming believers in the new religion. The Bordeaux parlement was encouraged by the military successes of the governor of Guyenne, Monluc, who had replaced the duke of Montpensier and who was rightly regarded as a redoubtable military man who was always ready to do battle with the seditious elements.[49] The *Memorandum* was written at this time, and La Boétie still believed that the Protestants could be brought into line. At the end of this year, 1561, Montaigne was sojourning in the capital. In June 1562, on his own initiative, he affirmed his Catholic faith before the parlement of Paris. He fully shared the views of the members of the Bordeaux parlement who were supporting the Catholic repression of the Protestants. For instance, like La Boétie, he was opposed to any kind of religious tolerance, because he had a hard time understanding how two religions could coexist in the same country. This position reflected the point of view of most of the members of the Bordeaux parlement. Montaigne and La Boétie were defending an ideological position that was related to a form of *robin* corporatism. We find this rather uncompromising—even dogmatic—vision of the political and religious order in the chapter "It is folly to measure the true and false by our own capacity" (I: 27):

> Now what seems to me to bring as much disorder into our consciences as anything, in these religious troubles that we are in, is this partial surrender of their beliefs by Catholics. It seems to them that they are being very moderate and understanding when they yield to their opponents some of the articles in dispute. But, besides the fact that they do not see what an advantage it is to a man charging you for you to begin to give ground and withdraw, and how much that encourages him to pursue his point, those articles which they select as the most trivial are sometimes very important. We must either submit completely to the authority of our ecclesiastical government or do without it completely. It is not for us to decide what portion of obedience we owe it.[50]

For Montaigne, there was no intermediary position. La Boétie recommended moderation in 1561, but not concession. In chapter I: 27 of the *Essais* we see a clarification, and even a rectification intended to show Montaigne's difference from La Boétie.[51] Obviously, in 1580 the civil wars had taught Montaigne that the January edict—and any policy of moderation in general—had changed nothing at all in the troubles that were raging in France. Montaigne never had any intention of publishing this *Memorandum*, which he considered not only outmoded but also counterproductive when it was a question of leading such a divided country. History had shown that La Boétie was wrong, and it was better for Montaigne to distinguish himself from a friend whose past choices were now difficult to explain. Montaigne had the advantage of having *experienced* the civil wars, and in 1580 he was encouraged to transform into a law what had been only an idea in 1561. When Montaigne, sure of himself, declares that compromise merely invigorates adversaries who are encouraged by this show of weakness to redouble their demands in order to obtain even more concessions, he knows what he is talking about. In retrospect, it is easy for him to judge the errors committed by those who believed in appeasement. It is possible to be right on the level of ideas and wrong on the level of action.

At first, Montaigne declared that he wanted to publish this *Memorandum* someday. Thus in 1580 he writes that La Boétie's "memoranda" "will find their place elsewhere." However, after 1588 he adds a circumstantial "perhaps" that says a great deal about his disappointment. The more Montaigne progressed in his own political career, the more he doubted the interest of the *Memorandum*. La Boétie's political thought slowly disappeared from the *Essais*, which became, from one edition to the next, much more personal. It is hard to see how the *Discourse*, and still less the *Memorandum*, could have found their place in the *Essais*. To include them would have been to expose himself to reproaches for a burdensome friendship with La Boétie, who had earlier advocated positions that were so contradictory with regard to tolerance and freedom that it had become complicated to explain them in view of recent political developments. The Protestant appropriation of the *Discourse* opened Montaigne's eyes; he ended up worrying, rightly, about the interpretation that might be given to this text.

If he had doubts about the utility of publishing the *Discourse*, a rereading of the *Memorandum* almost twenty years later made Montaigne aware of the fragility of the arguments given. La Boétie's proposals were, moreover, of very short duration because Catholic theologians refused to prejudge the decisions of the Council of Trent. The conciliatory policy of L'Hospital and the concessions proposed by La Boétie were all rejected by the Catholic Church. In the *Memorandum*, La Boétie sets himself up as a theologian, which might have shocked Montaigne, who was very careful not to fall into this trap himself. The decrees of the Council of Trent having rejected the compromises presented in the *Memorandum*, Montaigne had to leave himself a way out as he prepared for a journey to Rome that might make this text even more explosive. He therefore chose to clarify at least his position, while at the same time attributing the existence and paternity of the *Memorandum* to La Boétie. It was not a philosophical text like the *Discourse*, and he had reason to fear that the echo of this now politically outmoded memorandum might harm his own political ambitions. In politics, to deal with a problem it is often better to confront it directly. Praising these juvenilia was not the same thing as publishing them, and it was in deciding not to publish the *Discourse on Voluntary Servitude* that Montaigne showed his political aspirations and began to distance himself from a friendship that had become awkward. In 1580, he was no longer able to hush up a friendship regarding which he had left many written traces thanks to his publication of La Boétie's works eight years earlier.

Voluntary Servitude and Allegiance

In the *Discourse*, La Boétie analyzes the paradox of voluntary servitude. In his view, servitude and allegiance illustrate the two sides of political obligation and obedience. Although *servitude* was widely used in the Renaissance, *allégeance* appeared in French only at the end of the seventeenth century (in 1669, to be precise) with the strengthening of monarchical power during the reign of Louis XIV. The French term comes from the English "allegiance," which was popularized after the restoration of the monarchy in England at the time of the civil wars (1642–51). If allegiance is always voluntary, since it is based on an oath or vow, servitude, at least as La Boétie defines it, can be conceived only as an authoritarian imposition. The expression "voluntary servitude" is thus paradoxical in the context of the late sixteenth century. Montaigne frequently uses the word "obedience" (*obéissance*) to testify to this obligation of the lord or the public servant toward the monarch or toward the government in general. He refers to "obedience to the public reason"[52] and reminds the reader on several occasions that royal authority demands fidelity and obedience. He was never to change his mind about this fundamental principle, making mistakes in his political itinerary without departing from this rule that he had imposed on himself during his parlementary period.

It is useful to see how the idea of voluntary servitude is theorized with respect to allegiance on the basis of La Boétie's text in the *Essais*.[53] It is through this comparison—which is far from being an idiosyncrasy peculiar to Montaigne—that the two notions are defined in a structural opposition. The theoretical articulation between allegiance (obedience) and voluntary servitude encourages us to make an essential distinction between the idea of liberty and "the practices of liberty" in the liberal ideology of the late sixteenth and early seventeenth centuries. This liberal ideology, which separates the ideal of liberty from the acceptable practices of that liberty in the light of a political necessity, later found its best theoretician and spokesman in John Locke. In 1580, Montaigne, as a noble, conceived his political existence only in a relationship of allegiance, which he dissociates from the *robin* ideal by advocating individual freedom in a universal and atemporal way, an ideal that he had shared with La Boétie when he was a member of the parlement. After 1588, that is, after he had abandoned any political ambitions, he returned to this freedom of thought, which for posterity made him an archetype of modernity.

Allegiance constitutes the "other maxim sovereignly imprinted on his soul" that Montaigne mentions in connection with La Boétie. This deep structure does not need to be defined, because it is part of a natural form that is itself determined by custom and religion. According to La Boétie, servitude is of a different nature, because it results from a political accident: "What evil chance has so denatured man that he, the only creature really born to be free, lacks the memory of his original condition and the desire to return to it?"[54] The "evil chance" designates a social accident whose effects are steadily amplified, to the point that man has forgotten the founding event and the history of his submission. La Boétie proposes to recall what has been forgotten and reintegrate it into the collective political memory.[55] Here we could refer to Pierre Clastres's analyses of silent peoples or societies without a history,[56] or establish a link between the institution of a false consciousness and the ideological development of voluntary servitude. As La Boétie emphasizes, the love of servitude was gradually substituted for the desire for liberty, and obedience was then transformed into custom. Law itself can be considered a reification and codification of customs over time.[57]

As in La Boétie's writings, the notion of *people* remains rather vague in Montaigne's *Essais*. This word is often linked to custom and used to designate cultures as different as the Native Americans of the New World, the Athenian or Roman people, or the French society of the sixteenth century. On the whole, it can be said that Montaigne—like almost all his contemporaries—distrusted the common people, who were often associated with social disorder, and even with arbitrary power and tyranny.[58] The masses constituted an unpredictable, violent, irrational, and credulous force. Thus Montaigne speaks of "the common run of men today, ignorant, stupid and asleep, base, servile, full of fever and fear, unstable, and continually tossed about by the tempest of the diverse passions that drive them to and fro."[59] Montaigne attenuated this description by eliminating on the Bordeaux Copy the adjectives "ignorant," "asleep," and "full of fever and fear." He had a less negative conception of the people after 1588— when he had abandoned all pretense to participate in the public life of his time—but he did not really change his views. Whether he is referring to the danger of "the people, unable to bear such varied changes of fortune,"[60] "the hatred of the people,"[61] the "license and sedition of the people,"[62] or simply the naïveté of "the people, stunned and dazed,"[63] Montaigne's idea of the people is usually negative, with the exception of the Roman people, who, in his view, always showed good sense when faced with the corruption and abuses of Rome's emperors.

The salt-tax revolt in Bordeaux in 1548 did not help produce a positive image of these uncontrollable popular uprisings. Montaigne found it difficult to imagine a form of government that would give even limited power to the populace. According to him "Nations brought up to liberty and to ruling themselves consider any other form of government monstrous and contrary to nature."[64] By nature, "popular opinion is wrong"[65] most of the time, and we must be wary of those who try to seduce a populace that Montaigne considers childish and unreasonable. It is easy to manipulate the people, and Montaigne reports that in his time he has "seen wonder in the undiscerning and prodigious ease with which peoples let their belief and hope be led and manipulated in whatever way has pleased and served their leaders, passing over a hundred mistakes one on top of the other, passing over phantasms and dreams."[66] The simple observation of the practices of power—Huguenot or Catholic—showed him that religious leaders made use of the populace to advance their personal political ambitions. Populism leads to anarchy; and Montaigne was always in favor of order. The turmoil and disorder of civil wars put in question the social bond between people; on this point, Montaigne remains intransigent.

The populace exists in order to obey those who command: "Happy the people who do what they are commanded better than those who command, without tormenting themselves about the reasons, who let themselves roll relaxedly with the rolling of the heavens. Obedience is not pure or tranquil in a man who reasons and argues."[67] The Wars of Religion generated in Montaigne a genuine fear of popular excesses: "The murders in victories are usually done by the mob and the baggage officers. And what causes so many unheard-of cruelties is wars in which the people take part is that that beastly rabble tries to be warlike and brave by ripping up a body at their feet and bloodying themselves up to their elbows, having no sense of any other kind of valor."[68] The civil wars allowed him to see on a daily basis the abuses committed by a populace left to its own devices, the same populace that La Boétie had already pointed to in his *Memorandum* on the January edict, because it "is becoming accustomed to irreverence toward the magistrate, and with time learns to willingly disobey and allow itself to be led to the bait of liberty, or rather license, which is the sweetest and most delicious poison in the world."[69] The common people's demands often lack good sense. In the same spirit, Montaigne observes that "peoples are apt to assume about kings, as we do about our servants, that they should take care to prepare for us in abundance all we need, but that they should not touch it all for their own part.[70] And yet, on several occasions in the *Essais*, he declares that he has "felt compassion for the poor people who were taken in by these follies."[71] In fact, in this case he speaks mainly of peasants, for whom he feels a profound respect that is essentially connected to the land and to tradition. Montaigne's conception of the people hardly changed between 1560 and 1590. These multiple declarations that deny the common people any possibility of action have led some to tax Montaigne for being conservative, but it would be anachronistic to accuse him of being a reactionary when we know that the great majority of political theorists of the Renaissance shared this very negative view of a populace left to itself.[iv]

The discourse on custom replaces the discourse on liberty and transforms it into an ineluctable law. We note that in the 1580 edition of the *Essais* Montaigne comes back to this conception of custom in the service of a servitude to which we become accustomed: "She [custom] establishes in us, little by little, stealthily, the foothold of her authority; but having by this mild and humble beginning settled and planted it with the help of time, she soon uncovers to us a furious and tyrannical face against which we no longer have the liberty of even raising our eyes."[72] Servitude is merely a logical consequence of the clientele system in which Montaigne is deeply involved. But after 1585, he no longer sees himself in this implacable social logic and declares that he is "mortally avoiding servitude and obligation."[73] He wonders about his past state of dependency and describes his youth this way: "I was, I think, better fitted to live on another man's fortune, if that could be done without obligation and servitude."[74] He notes elsewhere that on the political and sociological level, "This was a very useful way of attracting men to obedience by honor and ambition."[75] This reflec

---

[iv] Hobbes removed the ambiguities present in La Boétie, Montaigne, Bodin, and Duplessis-Mornay as to the possibility of the people becoming a political actor. For Hobbes, "when a man receiveth any thing from the authority of the people, he receiveth it not from the people his subjects, but from the people his sovereign." Thomas Hobbes, *The Elements of Law Natural and Politic* (1640; first printed edition London, 1650), chap. 21, sect. 9. In a famous distinction, Hobbes explains the twofold meaning of the word "people": an aggregate of persons in a defined space, a simple "multitude of particular persons," but also a "person civil" (chap. 21, sect. 11), what the theorists of the late sixteenth century were beginning to call a "citizen." Those who do not distinguish between these two meanings attribute to "a dissolved multitude" rights that "belong only to the people virtually contained in the body of the commonwealth or sovereignty" (chap. 21, sect. 7). It is on the basis of this argument that Hobbes explains the role of the people in public action: "though any one man may be said to demand or have right to something, yet the heap, or multitude, cannot he said to demand or have right to any thing. For where every man hath his right distinct, there is nothing left for the multitude to have right unto; and when the particulars say: this is mine, this is thine, and this is his, and have shared all amongst them, there can be nothing whereof the multitude can say: this is mine" (chap. 21, sect. 11). Thus for Hobbes the people has no existence other than civil, once it has been subjected to the authority of the body politic; this form of voluntary servitude theoretically restores to it the right to act on the basis of the body politic that it constitutes. To be sure, La Boétie and Montaigne did not yet conceive the individual as a simple part of an aggregate constituted as a body politic, but we already find in their writings numerous references to what the author of the *Essais* calls "the crowd" (*la foule*).

tion on voluntary servitude examined in the light of his own political experience led to his distancing himself from the *Discourse on Voluntary Servitude* and to the virtual disappearance of La Boétie in the posthumous edition of the *Essais* published in 1595.

Montaigne's political dependence on the monarch and the influential lords of Guyenne and Gascony—particularly the Foix-Gurson family—dated from the early 1570s and lasted until 1588, that is, until after his second term as mayor of Bordeaux (1583–85) and his imprisonment in Paris in July 1588. Montaigne was not always "free" with regard to the established government. He does not deny the principle of allegiance to royal authority, but after 1588 he draws an important distinction between the king's function and his person: "We owe subjection and obedience equally to all kings, for that concerns their office: but we do not owe esteem, any more than affection, except to their virtue."[76] Here a slight difference is discerned between social allegiance and political allegiance—which is in part founded on custom—and individual freedom. Montaigne understands servitude as a political necessity indispensable for the proper functioning of society, but at the same time he demands the right to freely exercise his judgment. He got out of this problematic distinction by separating the public from the private and by transferring to the monarch or to any other recognized authority his freedom of action for everything having to do with the public sphere while preserving his personal judgment in the private domain.[v] After 1585, the *Essais* put the spotlight more and more on the private man and remained silent about the mayor and the governor of Bordeaux, or about the negotiator between Henry III and Henry of Navarre. Montaigne distanced himself from the royal government and separated in his own way the king's two bodies. Having withdrawn from any political action, he adopted the analyses of

---

[v] We find the same idea in Hobbes's *The Elements of Law Natural and Politic* (op. cit.), written in the late 1630s, circulated in manuscript in 1640, but printed only in 1650. Hobbes writes that, "When a man divesteth and putteth from himself his right, he either simply relinquisheth it, or transferreth the same to another man" (chap. 15, sect. 3). This form of voluntary servitude, a relinquishment of one's rights, is for Hobbes a "transfer": "To TRANSFER right to another, is by sufficient signs to declare to that other accepting thereof, that it is his will not to resist, or hinder him, according to that right he had thereto before he transferred it" (ibid.). For Hobbes, this transfer is a "FREE GIFT" (chap. 15, sect. 7). We already find in Montaigne this form of political gift, which he also sees in his relationship to La Boétie, the source of his own political positions in the early 1560s. This gift is understood solely outside any contractual consideration; instead, it is a natural inclination. Moreover, this gift of freedom creates an obligation for the person who receives it: "For where liberty ceaseth, there beginneth obligation," Hobbes writes (chap. 15, sect. 9), adding that such conventions are always "de voluntaris." According to Hobbes, "particular men enter into subjection, by transferring their rights" (chap. 21, sect. 12). Voluntary servitude constitutes them as a body politic that allows them to act through an intermediary authority, that of the sovereign.

Duplessis-Mornay and the "Monarchomachs"[vi] on the difference between a legitimate monarch and the tyrant he could become in the concrete exercise of power.

Influenced by the reflections of the Monarchomachs on royal absolutism, Montaigne also inquired into the bond between the king and his subjects. Likewise, La Boétie had tried to imagine the role of the emancipated people in this redistribution of power: the common people allows itself to be enslaved by the simple fact that it does not choose to be free. Wanting to be free would already represent a kind of freedom. This conception of liberty resembles more freedom of conscience (a term redefined by the religious practices of the time) than genuine freedom of action, and we can understand how the *Discourse on Voluntary Servitude* could logically be appropriated by the Huguenots, who needed first of all to establish this abstract form of freedom before they could move on to the following stage of individual resistance and political action. As people had been fond of pointing out since the 1570s, what was the use of freedom of thought without its expression and concrete application on the political level? In *The Discourse on Voluntary Servitude*, La Boétie does not adopt the Monarchomachs' argument that freedom of conscience cannot exist without freedom of worship. However, that is what allowed his treatise to come down to posterity. This precise question of religious practices was what had caused the political failure of the *Memorandum*.

We see looming in La Boétie—and consequently in Montaigne—the cornerstone of modern liberalism: individual freedom detached from any political or social action. La Boétie never recommends action (an uprising, for instance) against servitude, and on this essential point he agrees with Luther's position in his famous text on Christian freedom and still more in his response to the peasants who were demanding that this "freedom in people's heads" be given a concrete application in everyday life.[77] La Boétie is categorical on this issue: for the common people it is a question "not of freeing [itself] but only wanting to do it."[78] Freedom amounts to a question of will. That is a rather extraordinary distinction, because it dissociates theory from practice. La Boétie explains what he means by liberty and defines the limits of any action against the master or the tyrant: "I do not ask that you place hands upon the tyrant to topple him over, but simply that you support him no longer; then you will behold him, like a great Colossus whose pedestal has been pulled away, fall of his own weight and break in pieces."[79] The apology for inaction raises a moral problem: should one keep silent or revolt—with words, but also with weapons—against tyranny? Does taking this position put in question the oath of allegiance advocated by

---

[vi] The Monarchomachs ("those who fight against monarchs") were Huguenot political theorists who were notorious for having justified tyrannicide. [Trans.]

Montaigne between 1570 and 1588? These are questions that complicated Montaigne's reflections on servitude and kept him from publishing La Boétie's text after 1572.

Montaigne reflects on the bond between patron and client, master and slave. He could have recalled the beginning of the *Discourse on Voluntary Servitude*, where La Boétie excludes any enduring social relationship between two beings: "it is a great misfortune to be at the beck and call of one master, for it is impossible to be sure that he is going to be kind, since it is always in his power to be cruel whenever he pleases."[80] Does allegiance have to be independent of the kindness of the master or the king when the prince's magnanimity is essentially contractual (insofar as each party benefits from the allegiance and the servitude)? To tell the truth, such a remark on the consequences of servitude is of little use for understanding what leads people to give up part of their freedom to attain a stable material position within a social and political network where corruption and exploitation can never be excluded. Allegiance presupposes an expectation and an anticipated profit, but nothing is ever certain. On this point, the first part of the *Discourse on Voluntary Servitude* is imbued with a disconcerting idealism. However, the farther we advance in this text, the more La Boétie's observations evince a political realism that greatly influenced Montaigne.

It was precisely the problematic relation between servitude (a term that is too abstract and idealized) and allegiance (a term that implies a structure of reciprocal obligations and mutual benefits) that led Montaigne to distinguish two forms of liberty: one theoretical (which he often expressed *qua* private individual—Michel de Montaigne—master of his judgment), and the other more practical, which corresponds to the public man (the mayor or the negotiator) in a larger framework defined by power relationships, obligations, and allegiances that allow the subject to exist socially. All people have their individual freedom in the private sphere; this remark proceeds from a qualitative approach. But political or public liberty depends on the quantitative nature of the exchange between two beings. These two notions of liberty seem incompatible in Montaigne.

The solution recommended by La Boétie to emancipate people from their "voluntary servitude" is not to call for the organization or assembly of individuals within a group or a class; it does not lead to the formation of a rebellious collectivity. On the contrary, he gives priority to the development of a form of friendship between the master and the subordinate. This idea of a coalescent friendship was taken up again by Montaigne; it proceeds by the mutual absorption of one friend into the other, not by a union or a regrouping of one with the other. The distinction is subtle, but because this liberty "has revealed in every possible manner her intention, not so much to associate us as to make us one organic whole," La Boétie writes, "there can be no further doubt that we are all naturally free, inasmuch as we are all comrades. Accordingly it should not enter the mind of anyone that nature has placed some of us in slavery, since she has actually created us all in one likeness."[81]

La Boétie rapidly perceived that he had ventured onto the abstract terrain of philosophical discourse and sophisms. From that point on, his *Discourse* takes on a historical dimension and is more anchored in the political reality of his time: "Therefore it is fruitless to argue whether or not liberty is natural, since none can be held in slavery without being wronged."[82] Then he takes an interest in the problem of false consciousness of oneself and of the world, that is, ideology. Montaigne accepts this major contribution of the *Discourse* and the essential difference between the desire for freedom and the necessity of political allegiance thanks to respect for laws that are always conceived, as Montaigne often reminds us, by those who exercise power. Being conscious of abuses of the judicial system does not, however, authorize one to take up arms. This logical contradiction between political theory and political practice—an opposition inherent in Montaigne's text—has often troubled the reception of the *Essais* and caused many commentators to say that Montaigne's political ideas were too conformist.

The empire of custom is opposed to the growing role given to reason. This foundation of Montaigne's thought is already clearly expressed by La Boétie, who claims that "form defines content and that the human being retains the form given him by his upbringing."[83] In a profoundly Montaigne-like passage, La Boétie even goes so far as to assert that custom alone is responsible for political organization (and thus for the voluntary servitude he has just described) in human societies: "All those things to which he is trained and accustomed seem natural to man. . . . Thus custom becomes the first reason for voluntary servitude."[84] Montaigne appropriated this argument by asserting that one cannot rid oneself of custom in order to conceive new political or religious systems, and that it is impossible to live outside the culture we have inherited. Given that custom is the main cause of servitude, La Boétie's "misfortune" is logically transformed into a necessity, because custom, far from being a simple accident of history, is on the contrary a sign of continuity.

Should we infer from this that servitude, like ideology, is inevitable? Because humans are social animals, the solution Montaigne proposes consists in being aware—and only aware, without wishing for all that to change society or the world—of his human condition. It is not yet a question of proposing a social contract, in Rousseau's sense of the term, but simply of recognizing the material and historical situation of humans through the obligatory acceptance of a morality, for lack of something better. One is born Catholic and French, as Montaigne reminds his reader; that is a form of voluntary servitude that is obligatory and inevitable, insofar as religion and politics result from custom. Custom is necessarily voluntary because it is imposed on everyone in the same way. We can only embrace it. We might as well dissociate freedom of thought from submission to the rules and laws that make us social beings. Thus it is logical that freedom is a form of voluntary servitude for La Boétie and Montaigne. It does not result from a metaphysics, but from a sociology, since its basis is political and goes beyond personal choices. That is why allegiance to rules established by others is not incompatible with freedom in principle. To be free is to retain the possibility of emancipation, while at the same time conforming to the laws that force us into servitude. For La Boétie, this "possible freedom" takes the place of freedom, as it does for Montaigne, and it anticipates in many ways John Locke's theses on individual freedom.

For La Boétie, the consequence of voluntary servitude is not so much the giving up of each individual's free choice as it is the possible manifestation of tyranny. After all, voluntary servitude does not prevent society from functioning; tyranny, on the contrary, represents the unacceptable degree of a necessary evil. For La Boétie, it is the limit that must not be passed in the practice of power. Once this threshold has been crossed, the contract that binds the prince to the people is necessarily broken. Tyranny transforms the power of a single person over all others insofar as the individual can no longer draw any benefit from his subjection; it challenges the very idea of voluntary servitude (or, more precisely, of allegiance). This observation raises the question of armed uprising in the Protestant texts of the 1570s, notably in Duplessis-Mornay's *Vindiciae contra tyrannos*. In 1548, the probable date of the composition of the *Discourse on Voluntary Servitude*—at least in its first version—La Boétie could not imagine the bloody events of the first civil wars. But twenty years later, when he was thinking about publishing La Boétie's text, Montaigne was no longer able to ignore the different reading that could be given the text in the light of the recent history of the religious conflict in France.

Those who had recuperated La Boétie's *Discourse* in the 1570s emphasized a theory of political representation based on magistrates—limited in number—whose function was supposed to have been to serve as a counterpower to the sovereign. These elect of God are in a way the guarantors of human freedom, and their role consists in opposing any form of submission. La Boétie remarks that "there are always a few, better endowed than others, who feel the weight of the yoke and cannot restrain themselves from attempting to shake it off: these are the men who never become tamed under subjection."[85] We understand how Simon Goulart, Duplessis-Mornay, and other thinkers close to the Huguenots were able to see in these "few," the magistrates "possessed of clear minds and far-sighted spirit," the elect of God who are not satisfied, "like the brutish mass," to follow those who lead them into a state of voluntary servitude. These chosen individuals not only have (and we find here one of Montaigne's favorite expressions) "a well-made head," but one that is "also well-polished by study."[86] According to La Boétie, there are individuals who are born to lead others. Montaigne was strongly influenced by this analysis of the political elite, although he took care to separate the private from the public and to offer a theory of political power based on obligatory allegiance. This new political authority, which is associated with a form of conservatism, is no longer completely equivalent to voluntary servitude as defined by La Boétie, because servitude exists through a false consciousness of oneself, which is no longer the case in Montaigne—at least after 1588. Montaigne emphasizes the necessity of government and establishes a difference with allegiance, the particular form of servitude based on the principle of unconditional respect for authority and the laws—even if they run counter to one's personal beliefs.

La Boétie had understood that political power is not founded solely on the prince or the tyrant, but also on a structural organization in the form of a pyramid composed of intermediaries who serve to implement the policies of those who are at the apex. As he writes, there are always four or five men who allow the tyrant to assert his authority, and then five or six hundred others who keep the four or five in place, and six thousand more who perpetuate the power of the six hundred, "upon whom they confer the government of provinces or the direction of finances."[87] This analysis of tyranny was not likely, of course, to be adopted by his Protestant readers, perhaps because it reminded them a little too much of the form of government that their leaders were advocating at that time. It could be claimed that the "magistrates" imagined by Duplessis-Mornay and other Huguenot theorists correspond exactly to this intermediate stratum of power whose function is to apply tyrannically the prince's policy. For La Boétie, the structure of government greatly exceeds the question of tyranny; it applies to every form of government. If this fundamental organization of power is accepted, whether it is tyrannical or not, the distinction between servitude and allegiance no longer functions very well. Montaigne seems to have understood the difficulty involved in such a generalization of power and preferred to dissociate his judgment regarding the particular forms of government from his critical reflection on power in general.

In any event, servitude and obedience cannot be confused. On several occasions in the *Discourse* La Boétie draws a distinction between these two terms: "What an unfortunate vice it is to see an endless multitude of people not merely obeying, but driven to servility, not ruled, but tyrannized."[88] Obeying is a matter of choice—one obeys the laws of his country—and results from an allegiance, whereas serving testifies to a false consciousness, a situation perceived as a matter of fact. It is this consciousness that Montaigne was later to explore in his *Essais*, in an introspection that allowed him to reinterpret La Boétie's text in the light of his own political experiences, both positive and negative. In a fundamental passage in the *Essais*, he associates consciousness and education and even seems to suggest that (internal) study leads to a better evaluation of one's own status in a political system: "what it is to know and not to know, and what must be the aim of study; what are valor, temperance, and justice; what the difference is between ambition and avarice, servitude and submission, license and liberty."[89] How should the distinction between servitude and subjection be understood? Is there a genuine difference on the practical level between serving and obeying? This consciousness may be only the product of a bourgeois mentality that locates liberty at the individual and not the collective level.

Montaigne never separates the aspiration to liberty from the obligation to obey, which must be, according to him, "simple and naive": "We are so eager to get out from under command, under some pretext, and to usurp mastery; each man aspires so naturally to liberty and authority, that to a superior no useful quality in those who serve him should be so dear as their natural and simple obedience."[90] This natural subjection is unavoidable for those who have made a vow of allegiance. But the question that remains is whether the duty of allegiance is applicable to all subjects. Toward the end of his life Montaigne pondered this fundamental point regarding submission to political authority: "On the other hand, however, one might also consider that such constrained obedience belongs only to precise and stated commands,"[91] mentioning in this connection a servitude whose framework has been set in advance, through a contract, a promise that has to be respected by both parties. If the contract is broken, the individual can put an end to his subjection and thus reclaim a kind of liberty.

The Politics of a Friendship

The friendship between La Boétie and Montaigne expresses the humanist ideal and sublimates the bond that connected the author of the *Essais* to his late friend. This poetic vision of the friendship between Montaigne and La Boétie has too often been presented as a model of fraternity and altruism.[92] This forgets that, in the Renaissance, friendship remained above all a topos. Therefore we have to avoid idealizing the feeling of affection and closeness that then had a precise literary function and well-defined rules of expression.[93] The point of departure for the discourse on friendship is the tripartite distinction presented in Aristotle's *Nicomachean Ethics*, that is, friendship in relation to utility, pleasure, and virtue. For Aristotle, only friendship in relation to perfect virtue is a true friendship. Utility is relegated to a form of false friendship. On the basis of this Aristotelian distinction, there was a codified language of friendship in the sixteenth century. As a discourse, friendship does not need to be concretely embodied in reality; it is shaped and related in accord with the rules of rhetoric and on the basis of the ethical premises elaborated by Aristotle. It is an exercise for men of letters that leads to a rapprochement with Antiquity and its universal values. In the Renaissance, friendship was often more ideal than lived, at least in its literary representation.

Friendship fortifies the individual by the properties that are attributed to it: transcendence of history and reference to a common fund of humanity and universal harmony, as if friendship defined man's essence. Humanism puts friendship on a pedestal, because it symbolizes the most human of feelings. That said, every rule has its exceptions that are so many counterexamples reminding us that man is above all a political animal. Friendship also refers to more futile and worldly concerns that are connected with career expectations or other, more material, benefits. Its utility rapidly spread to all domains of discourse in the Renaissance. This was the hidden side of friendship. Montaigne begins the third book of the *Essais* with the theme of denatured and corrupted values. In the chapter "Of the useful and the honorable," (III: 1) he notes the decline of noble values marked by honorability and the rise of a bourgeois, mercantile ideology symbolized by utility. In short, friendship gradually leaves the domain of ethics and is transformed into sociability, which then confers political implications on it.

In Montaigne, the bond of friendship (here we put "bond" in the singular) corresponds to a particular, unique experience that structures the writing of the *Essais* by its presence or its absence. A man (La Boétie) and a text (the *Discourse on Voluntary Servitude*) define friendship. The two parts (the individual and the book) are inseparable. Friendship always has a face corresponding to a unique experience during a period of social and religious turmoil. That is why it has a political significance that cannot be reduced to a simple topos. The bond of friendship can be conceived only in its sociological and historical context. The break with the Aristotelian model of friendship as well as the transformation—certainly unconscious—of utility into a productive value make the discourse on friendship more functional in Montaigne's work. In this sense the bond of friendship moves away from ethical discourse and approaches political discourse. Its temporality is irremediably modified.

In the *Essais*, Montaigne presents several judgments and commentaries on friendship. Let us begin with the essential distinction between friendship and friendships: "For the rest, what we ordinarily call friends and friendships are nothing but acquaintanceships and familiarities formed by some chance or convenience, by means of which our souls are bound to each other. In the friendship I speak of, our souls mingle and blend with each other so completely that they efface the seam that joined them, and cannot find it again."[94] The bond of friendship Montaigne is talking about is invisible; it unites and welds together two beings in order to fuse them and leaves no remaining joint that would be the trace of a division between them. The two beings, united in a single discourse, become indissociable; two particular existences are transformed into a universal category. The very name of the friend no longer needs to be mentioned, because it finds its continuation in the name of the author who makes it live or relive in him. That is how Estienne de La Boétie is revived in the *Essais*. The deceased friend recovers a social and political existence thanks to Montaigne, who declares on two occasions—after seven years (1570) and seventeen years (1580)—that he wants to restore and disseminate his forgotten or deformed political message.

Friendship is also the expression of a sociability. To make friends, one must be convivial, affable, and *practiqueur*, in the sense that this word was given in Montaigne's time. *Practique* ("practice") implies artifice, manipulation, intrigue, the deformation of discourse, and the betrayal of promises.[95] In the name of political efficacy, *practique* brings Machiavellian considerations into personal decisions. These under-the-counter political schemes became the norm in the late Renaissance, and they force us to take them into account, even when we are talking about friendship. The particular circumstances of the meeting between Montaigne and La Boétie prove this. Montaigne was a public man used to deliberations with the crowd. Friendship sometimes results from a form of worldliness and, as he himself says, "public business" does not displease someone who, like him, readily allows himself to be "led by the general way of the world."[96] Montaigne was clearly ill at ease in drawing rooms, but he nonetheless always found a way to the court and adjusted perfectly to the company of men who occupied powerful positions. However, we must not confuse the public roles he played with his private being. On this point, the *Essais* claim to be a book different from the others, because its author dreams of painting himself and stripping himself naked, showing himself to his readers in all transparency.

In the *Essais*, Montaigne sketches a not very flattering picture of his aptitude for sociability and draws up an inventory of his faults: "Idle. Cool in the duties of friendship and kinship, and in public duties. Too self-centered."[97] This distressing observation that makes him a bad friend, a bad father, a bad husband, and a bad mayor of Bordeaux is, of course, a late posture whose goal is to foreground an egoism and detachment—a sort of literary dilettantism or nonchalance—that are transformed into a virtue in the course of the editions of the *Essais*. His friendship with La Boétie is all the more remarkable because this feeling is almost foreign to him. It is a bond that goes *against his nature*. How can he have experienced such a perfect friendship when his character is so little inclined to social and familial obligations? It is not easy to count Montaigne among one's friends; that, at least, is the message that the author of the *Essais* likes to convey after 1588. It is also the image of him that has come down to us:

an individual retired to his château who, reaching the supreme stage of wisdom, is supposed to have isolated himself in his tower in order to distance himself the better to think about man, society, and the world. Without a friend, friendship could belong only to the past of a life of which only a book remained, consubstantial with its author. So what had La Boétie become? Was he still in Montaigne, without the seam being visible? What tangible traces of this friendship, ordinarily so absent in the *Essais*, are to be found in the Bordeaux Copy?

According to Montaigne, friendship—in the materiality of the book—is above all an empty space surrounded by "grotesques," the fantastic decorations that frame a central theme. The association between painting and friendship is revealing because it symbolizes the other side of the self-portrait, that is, the depiction of the absent other who, thanks to the consubstantiality between author and book advocated by Montaigne, is systematically associated with the *Essais*. Friendship is also the writing (and the writings) of the other constructing the space of a self that remains at the stage of a project and is conceived only as in progress. This self in permanent construction on the basis of elements taken from something else (the *Discourse on Voluntary Servitude*, for instance) also bears the indelible marks of a past that is visible in the earlier editions (1580, 1582, 1588) and establishes itself as the only material proof of the friendship. The friendship represents a past without memory at the moment of the rewriting, and whose "grotesques" (the book of the *Essais*) figure the only possible recollection. In Montaigne, friendship constitutes a frame, a series of rather vague contours that delimit the boundary of a writing that exists only as a preliminary sketch and, like every preliminary sketch, is destined to disappear. Imitating Montaigne's book, friendship is being tried out. The form has become substance: it is the definition Montaigne gives of both the *Essais* and friendship.

Friendship constitutes a fabric that is constantly being woven, but also, inevitably, unraveled. The writing of friendship thus carries out an undermining work in the *Essais*. The beginning of the chapter "Of friendship" (I: 28) describes the technique used by painters that consists in first putting a composition in the center of a wall before filling the empty parts with "grotesques":

> As I was considering the way a painter I employ went about his work, I had a mind to imitate him. He chooses the best spot, the middle of each wall, to put a picture labored over with all his skill, and the empty space all around it he fills with grotesques, which are fantastic paintings whose only charm lies in their variety and strangeness. And what are these things of mine, in truth, but grotesques and monstrous bodies, pieced together of divers members, without definite shape, having no order, sequence, or proportion other than accidental?[98]

Filling up the void takes the measure of the subject represented and defines it. In the case of the picture of La Boétie, one wonders, however, where the center is, because there remain only the "grotesques" of the painter Montaigne. The announced central composition is fragmented and relegated to the periphery of the book. The *Discourse on Voluntary Servitude* has been removed from its frame. The monstrous, deceased body Montaigne presented has been dismembered and scattered; there remain only vague allusions and obscure references to La Boétie and to the works of his youth. In the *Essais* we find very strange traces of a vanished friendship.

Similarly, the introduction to what was supposed to be the *Discourse on Voluntary Servitude* now gives way to lines directly and impudently addressed to a woman. The beginning of the chapter titled "Twenty-nine sonnets of Etienne de la Boétie" (I: 29) and dedicated "To Madame de Grammont, Comtesse de Guissen," accords an important place to this woman, better known as "la Belle Corisande." The chapter as a whole, reworked to approach this friend—political patroness—announces the new stake of a redefined friendship. Montaigne says he will one day whisper in her ear licentious verses by a La Boétie "in his greenest youth, when he was inflamed by a fine and noble ardor."[99] For La Boétie, marital coolness, for Montaigne, the warmth of lusty whispers in the ear and playful, irregular poetry: "The others were written later, for his wife, when he was suing for her hand, and they already smack of a certain marital coolness. And I am one of those who hold that poetry is never so blithe as in a wanton and irregular subject."[100] La Boétie gives Montaigne the opportunity to rediscover his first relations with women,[vii] which he had declared were over: the friend allows him not only to approach high state officials such as Lansac, Mesmes, and Foix, but also the women that are so present in the *Essais*.[101]

The history of the friendship between La Boétie and Montaigne is unverifiable, and we do not know the exact circumstances or the motives for the redac-

---

[vii] Women have a much more important part in Montaigne's work than has been thought. Several chapters of the *Essais* are dedicated to them, and the positive reception of the *Essais* by women readers of the time has been demonstrated. We can even say that Montaigne accords a special place to women in his book. Thus the chapter "Of the affection of fathers for their children" (II: 8) is dedicated to Louise d'Estissac; "Of the education of children" (I: 26) is dedicated to Diane de Foix, who was expecting her first child; the "Twenty-nine sonnets of Etienne de La Boétie" (I: 29) evicts the friend to make room for another woman, Madame de Gramont; and finally, the chapter "Of the resemblance of children to fathers" (II: 37) is dedicated to Madame de Duras. But it is especially in the chapter "On some verses of Virgil" (III: 5) that Montaigne speaks at greatest length regarding his relations with women. Behind this deceptive title—this essay could just as well have been entitled "Of love" or "Of sexuality"—Montaigne offers a long reflection on the relations between men and women.

tion of the *Discourse*, but that did not prevent Montaigne from disseminating La Boétie's words without worrying about the interpretations that might hand him over to a different political camp. Montaigne wants to be his friend's *apostle*. The term "apostle" corresponds quite well to the position he adopts, for he is La Boétie's first and only messenger, the only one who disseminated his speech and his writings. We can imagine Montaigne's surprise when he discovered that the *Discourse on Voluntary Servitude* was serving the cause of Protestantism, that false religion with its false prophets. The presentation of the *prophet La Boétie* (the visionary of the *Discourse on Voluntary Servitude*) is strengthened by an impressive number of Christian references in the "story of La Boétie" recounted in the chapter "Of friendship," and in the famous letter on his death. Montaigne thus takes up in La Boétie's writings, which he sees as veritable "relics,"[102] a political question that is discussed in the *Discourse* as well.

When La Boétie asked Montaigne to "play the same role" and insisted on being given a "place," Montaigne appeared rather reserved, even haughty. He did not seem to understand the importance of this place and remained almost indifferent to his friend's injunctions. We recall that La Boétie begged Montaigne in vain: "My brother, my brother, are you refusing me a place, then?"[103] Montaigne took care not to reply to this awkward question that foreshadowed the difficulties he felt later on in granting a place in the *Essais* to La Boétie, whose political writings were ultimately never of any use to him. As we have seen, the problem of the place of friendship in the *Essais* is presented clearly in Montaigne's first literary document, namely, the famous letter on La Boétie's death. It is characteristic in this regard that what was supposed to constitute the heart of the first book of the *Essais* (chapter 29 presenting La Boétie's *Discourse* or his *Sonnets*) does not exist as such in the first edition printed by Simon Millanges in 1580, since the chapter titled "Twenty-nine sonnets of Etienne de La Boétie, To Madame de Grammont comtesse de Guissen" is incorrectly numbered. This chapter is actually the twenty-eighth and not the twenty-ninth. We might think this is a printing error, but the disappearance of La Boétie at the heart of the first book of the *Essais* was systematically repeated in the editions of 1582 and 1588 as well as in the Bordeaux Copy, without Montaigne noticing it—or perhaps he knew it. On the material level of the book, it is thus impossible to say that La Boétie occupies the physical heart of the first book of the *Essais*.[104]

Why was Montaigne so ill at ease with regard to this friend who wanted to become his brother? Friendship is chosen, whereas blood ties are transmitted. Can a brother be a friend? Montaigne's family does not offer the best example of this. We know about the religious dissensions between Montaigne and his brother, Thomas de Beauregard, and his sister, Jeanne de Lestonnac, both of whom had adhered to Protestantism. We also recall Montaigne's commentary on blood ties, which he distinguishes from perfect friendship. He carefully avoids answering the awkward question La Boétie asks and finds it difficult to grant a place to the friend (but not to friendship) in the *Essais*. He does not understand this vehement desire to find a place to give form to the friendship. As he sees it, the bond of friendship remains diffuse and scattered, because friendship always exists elsewhere, outside all space. A chimerical desire, it is transformed into a mental object that no longer claims a fixed place and does not occupy the center of Montaigne's thought. Friendship henceforth escapes any kind of commerce (friendship is one of the three "commerces" defined by Montaigne); to refuse a place for the intercourse of friendship is in a way to give it the possibility of existing ideally. Desire is enjoyment, but the materialization of this desire—the need to carry out an exchange and to engage in this commerce—would be the beginning of the end of the friendship. A distance between oneself and the friend must always be maintained; that is the secret of perfect friendship, and on this point Montaigne often recommends that a physical distance be established between oneself and the object of desire. He himself practiced this art of separation and distancing in the domain of politics, both in the parlement and, later on, as the mayor of Bordeaux. Montaigne definitely found it difficult to speak about friendship in his *Essais*—just as he did not succeed in finding a stable place for La Boétie. The explanation may have to do with the fact that a place devoted to the commerce of friendship does not really exist in the *Essais*. Even in the chapter titled "Of friendship," Montaigne does not succeed in "establishing a firmer and more lasting pact,"[105] and seems to accept the inevitable truth: "in friendship there are no dealings or business except with itself."[106] The essayist seems to resign himself to the idea of a *nonplace* for friendship, or at least to accept the fact that friendship will always correspond to an impossible commerce, without a space of its own. In the chapter "Of three kinds of association" ("De trois commerces"), Montaigne admits that "the object of this association [*commerce*] is simply intimacy, fellowship, and conversation."[107] To give is to please oneself, in accord with the logic of "the loser wins." By borrowing La Boétie's texts and sending them to the great figures of the kingdom, Montaigne sought to create his own space. Like an intermediary or interpreter, the messenger rises to the level of the message, the apostle of the loftiness of the Word. The role that Montaigne gives himself in the diffusion of La Boétie's works in 1571 prepared him for his future *Essais*, because his friend's works were supposed to occupy a central place in the first edition of the *Essais* in 1580. That is at least the idea that emerges from the publication of the *Mesnagerie de Xenophon*, to which we shall return. We find here again the method of "grotesques" that serves as a preamble to the chapter "Of friendship." Montaigne had interfered in La Boétie's work in the name of the principle of "because it was he, because it was I"; it was logical that La Boétie should enter into the *Essais* in the same way. The fusion of the two beings demanded similar writing strategies.

Montaigne describes the exemplary nature of his friendship with La Boétie as "so entire and so perfect," "fostered, as long as God willed."[108] As we have said, this friendship lasted less than four years, which, it has to be admitted, is not long. The parlementary archives record only a few examples in which Montaigne and La Boétie worked together on the same cases in the parlement of Bordeaux—from February 1562 to June 1563—La Boétie always playing the primary role and Montaigne playing, during these years (1562–63), only a secondary or even tertiary role. At that time, Montaigne was far from having a remarkable career. In contrast, La Boétie was considered the parlement's child prodigy and had won a reputation as an orator. In the world of the magistracy, intellectual recognition necessarily involved the publication of a treatise on law, history, or political theory. The opportunity had not yet presented itself, and despite the circulation of manuscript copies of the *Discourse on Voluntary Servitude* and the *Memorandum*, the recognition on which La Boétie could pride himself was still rather limited. It was Montaigne who won for him a posthumous fame that he was far from enjoying during his lifetime. However, Montaigne's friendship with La Boétie claimed to escape any political logic: "it is a lot if fortune can do it once in three centuries," he tells us. But the motives of this perfect communion between two souls are never explained.

The friendship between Montaigne and La Boétie was based on a common view of politics and religion in the early 1560s, when the civil wars had not yet begun. In the late 1550s, Montaigne still hoped to have a brilliant career as a member of the parlement and sought the company of colleagues capable of helping him in his projects and ambitions. Meeting an influential figure who had a well-established position in the parlement represented a non-negligible advantage in a system in which alliances and the patronage of influential persons were necessary to succeed.

For Montaigne, friendship is founded on an equality between persons who are socially unequal. This is an essential point for his friendship with La Boétie. The family did not allow such an equality:

> From children toward fathers, it is rather respect. Friendship feeds on communication, which cannot exist between them because of their too great inequality, and might perhaps interfere with the duties of nature. For neither can all the secret thoughts of fathers be communicated to children, lest this beget an unbecoming intimacy, nor could the admonitions and corrections, which are one of the chief duties of friendship, be administered by children to fathers.[109]

For Montaigne, the bond of friendship is the complete contrary of the bond of blood. The author of the *Essais* draws an important distinction between the friendship of children for their fathers or that of husbands for their wives, and "perfect" friendship, which is always chosen. Thus he contrasts "that common affection of fathers toward their children"[110] with the singular and unique friendship he felt for La Boétie, a "single perfect friendship":[111] "Common friendships can be divided up: one may love in one man his beauty, in another his easygoing ways, in another liberality, in one paternal love, in another brotherly love, and so forth; but this friendship that possesses the soul and rules it with absolute sovereignty cannot possibly be double."[112] Far from this exemplary friendship are found the "numerous and imperfect friendships."[113]

Friendship cannot be quantified, and it does not follow the rules of commerce; Montaigne conceives it solely as a gift, without the slightest hint of profit. Its singularity constitutes its quality. It is supposed to be the expression of a relationship that is atypical and does not respect familial and social rules. Rejecting authority and decorum, it establishes an equality between men by elevating the inferior one on the social scale to the level of the one who is socially—or professionally—superior to him. That is how the friendship with La Boétie authorizes Montaigne to converse directly with the great men of the kingdom. This careerist use of friendship also reminds us of the paternal filiation Marie de Gournay claimed after the death of her "adopted father" (*père d'alliance*); this established link made it easier for her to get Abel L'Angelier to publish her *Proumenoir de Monsieur de Montaigne*. Friendship was also included in the social and political *practiques* that might promote a literary career. In this case, the tie of friendship served as a pretext—in the literal sense of the term—for social ambitions.

The best proofs of friendship are rarely found among people of the same rank or social status, and Montaigne recounts singular friendships between a king and a slave or between a prince and his servant. Social inequality favors the expression of friendship by reaffirming the equality of men when the friend sets aside his power and authority in order to lower himself to the level of his friend. Thus friendship is supposed to be the expression of a voluntary servitude in which the master consents to put himself at the slave's level. Then we understand why the chapter "Of friendship" could have served as an introduction to La Boétie's treatise. It is also a practice that Montaigne uses again in the chapter that provides an apology for Raymond Sebond—which could be read as a prologue to a deconstruction of Sebond and of La Boétie—in order to explain his work as translator and editor of texts that had become compromising, each in its own way, in the political and religious context that prevailed between 1560 and 1570.

In practice, friendship is resolutely situated on the side of the middle of the road, the general, the moderate. In fact, for Montaigne, it expresses a balance that allows one person to rise and the other to lower himself to the latter's level. This is also a political attitude that consists in putting oneself in the place of the other and seeking the golden mean. The manifestations of friendship reflect the moderation and leveling of the affects. Free of passion, this relationship, which is often unequal, requires a certain effort; it is not natural and at first sight there is nothing remarkable about it. It results from a calculated choice, from a new form of sociability: "In friendship, it is a general and universal warmth, moderate and even, besides, a constant and settled warmth, all gentleness and smoothness, with nothing bitter and stinging about it."[114] What more is there to say? Friendship dispenses with words because it offers nothing sensational, and that is exactly what happens in the *Essais*. The more Montaigne discovered his talents as a writer, that is, the more he asserted himself as an author, the more friendship was "settled" (*rassize*): "Father and son may be of entirely different dispositions, and brothers also. He is my son, he is my kinsman, but he is an unsociable man, a knave, or a fool. And then, the more they are friendships which law and natural obligation impose on us, the less of our choice and free will there is in them. And our free will has no product more properly its own than affection and friendship."[115]

Montaigne twice puts the accent on voluntary freedom in this often-cited passage from the chapter "Of friendship." This term is primordial for understanding friendship in his work. While La Boétie wrote a treatise on voluntary servitude, in "Of friendship" Montaigne composed a treatise of voluntary freedom. Moreover, there is a rather vague difference between these two terms. Insofar as the friend gives himself entirely to the other, the freedom of one of them is inevitably transformed into servitude for the other. Politics then functions in a power relationship established on the basis of a zero-point, as Montaigne reminds us in a short but important chapter, "One man's profit is another man's harm" (I: 22). How can we act so that only the profit is taken into account? Simply by doing without the other. That may be why the absence of the friend is presented to us salutary in Montaigne's work, because it avoids the servitude inherent in friendship. The bond of friendship—in its phase of servitude—no longer exists in the *Essais* because it refers to a time that is over and done. Since it testifies to a singular and unique experience, this bond is presented to us as opposed to Montaigne's two other kinds of commerce, namely, commerce with women and commerce with books, which are always the expression of experiences that are repeated and dependent on a quantitative logic.

It is customary to suggest that the chapter "Of friendship" symbolizes the space necessary for putting friendship "into commerce." I would like to suggest just the reverse. The theme of friendship appears in the background in many chapters, but never really finds its own place. Although amorous commerce refers to the boudoir ("On some verses of Virgil") and the tower forms the privileged space of reading and writing ("Of books"), the space of friendship is always lacking in the *Essais*. Germignan (the village where La Boétie died) was that space for a time, and we know how hard it was for La Boétie to keep Montaigne in his bedchamber. After 1571, this space has only a literary existence and shapes the quest of Montaigne's writing. The writing of friendship is the search for the place of friendship, but it is also a project that is supposed to lead Montaigne to find his place in society. The fusion between La Boétie and Montaigne required a single space that could be shared, no matter who the author of the work was. Friendship retains an ideal form that Montaigne could not reproduce; that is perhaps why the form of friendship almost never corresponds to the content of the chapters whose main function is to talk about this bond. In the course of the writing, far from finding its definitive place in a single chapter, friendship traverses the *Essais* without being able to settle itself where we expect it to be.

We cannot ignore this bond of friendship that marks and influences Montaigne's writing but that also denotes his desire to separate himself from his friend. The more Montaigne becomes an author, the weaker and more fragile this bond becomes. Friendship is not realizable in its practice—that is, as a series of encounters or continuous relationships over time. It is a pure ideal, like equality among men: "Friendship, on the contrary, is enjoyed according as it is desired."[116] The desire of friendship, like the quest for equality among men, merges with the idea of an idealized friendship that dispenses with any practice. For Montaigne, friendship refers to a primitive economy in which the very idea of commerce is absent; it frees itself from any materiality in order to exist solely as an unrealizable fantasy. Montaigne refers to friendship as a "noble commerce."[117] Even though at that time the word "commerce" (*commerce*) also had the sense of "intercourse" or "association," Montaigne cannot have been unaware that it was also part of the discourse of economics. This expression is an oxymoron because in the Renaissance there could be no noble commerce. The noble ideal condemned work and advocated idleness. Commerce was an activity necessary for the proper functioning of society, but there was nothing elevated about it. Many treatises of the time are explicit on this question. The inherent contradiction between this particular quality of friendship gives rise to a noneconomic conception of what is ultimately becoming a literary relationship in Montaigne. Since it constitutes a gift, friendship no longer has a value. Montaigne explains that friendship "receives no increase."[118] Friendship is a dispossession of oneself: "For this perfect friendship I speak of is indivisible: each one gives himself so wholly to his friend that he has nothing left to distribute elsewhere."[119] The rules of this particular commerce run counter to any utilitarian logic: "If, in the friendship I speak of, one could give to the other, it would be the one who received the benefit who would oblige his friend."[120] The primitive economy of friendship escapes the usual commercial rules; it is situated in an ideal relationship that reminds us of potlatches and other ritual exchanges practiced by the Indians of the New World.

After 1588, the rejection of politics in the *Essais* led inevitably to the disgrace and disappearance of La Boétie. Perfect friendship became an absence:

> In true friendship, in which I am expert, I give myself to my friend more than I draw him to me. I not only like doing him good better than having him do me good, but also would rather have him do good to himself than to me; he does me most good when he does himself good. And if absence is pleasant or useful to him, it is much sweeter to me than his presence; and it is not really absence when we have means of communication. In other days I made use and advantage of our separation.[121]

A friend in difficult times, La Boétie had to disappear from the *Essais*, more than twenty years after his death. His presence was then transformed into an absence and his retreat was the best proof of the perfection of a friendship about which Montaigne no longer could or wanted to speak.

It could be said that La Boétie represented a "salutary friendship" for the author that Montaigne was becoming. The more absence is noted, the more the bond is idealized. The representation of friendship cancels all future practice of friendship. This voluntary servitude has no obligation, it is freedom. The other to whom we had wholly given ourselves lives in us without our feeling the need to talk about him. The wheel had turned full circle and Montaigne finally rediscovered the state of voluntary freedom in which the subject is self-sufficient. From that moment on, friendship became a past that Montaigne no longer really needed, and on which it was preferable not to dwell. A generic reader without name or history replaced the friend, and a new consubstantiality between Montaigne and his book was substituted for the one originally produced by friendship. La Boétie henceforth incarnated the past of the *Essais*, and the generic reader, their future.

CHAPTER 4

"Witness My Cannibals": The Encounter with the Indians of the New World

Montaigne was twenty-two years old and the religious conflict between Protestants and Catholics in France had not yet broken out when, in 1555, the Knight Hospitaller Nicolas de Villegaignon sailed into the bay of Rio de Janeiro and took possession of Guanabara, a small island situated at the entrance to the bay.[1] This colonial expedition to "Antarctic France"—the name given it by Villegaignon and popularized by the cosmographer André Thevet—strongly marked the imagination of Renaissance France. French territories in America were even described as a "second earthly paradise,"[2] despite the lack of potable water. With this exotic space of the New World, people soon associated the image of the Indian of Brazil: the Cannibal. Although the French occupation of this part of the world was short-lived, the writings of André Thevet and Jean de Léry immortalized the French and Protestant encounter with the natives of Brazil.

André Thevet was a major figure in the construction of the image of the inhabitants of the New World. His experience among the Cannibals, though very brief—hardly ten weeks—nonetheless allowed him to write a copious description of the manners and customs of the Tupinamba Indians. It was first in his *Singularitez de la France antarctique, autrement nommée Amerique: et de plusieurs Terres et Isles descouvertes de nostre temps* (1558), and then in his *Cosmographie universelle* (1575), that this rope maker turned cosmographer described the everyday life of the Cannibals. His idealized depiction of the Indians of Brazil influenced the writing of the famous chapter "Of cannibals" (I: 31), which appeared in the first edition of the *Essais* in 1580. Montaigne made many references to the Cannibals in the third book of his *Essais* published in 1588, especially in the chapter "Of coaches" (III: 6). Each time, the inhabitants of Brazil lead him to wonder about the morality of his time and to relativize customs that have their own cultural logic.

A long passage in the chapter "Of custom, and not easily changing an accepted law" (I: 23) provides the foundation for a cultural critique proceeding on the basis of the notions of custom and variety. The idea of custom is an essential theme for Montaigne; it appears in the titles of three chapters in the *Essais*: "Of custom, and not easily changing an accepted law" (I: 23), "Of ancient customs" (I: 49), and "A custom of the island of Cea" (II: 3), or even four if we consider that the word *usage*, "Of the custom [*usage*] of wearing clothes" (I: 36), is frequently used as a synonym of *coutume*. The discovery of the New World, through the accounts given by Spanish, Portuguese, and French travelers in various cosmographical and topographical works, as well as by eyewitnesses (chiefly French sailors who had returned from expeditions to Brazil), allowed Montaigne to acquire a considerable knowledge of the peoples recently "discovered" on the other side of the Atlantic.

Montaigne was enchanted by the customs of the Indians of the New World. What caught his attention was the diversity of habits and manners, and their difference from European practices. He does not discuss social or political divergences in detail; on the other hand, bodily habits strike him, particularly the Indians' sexuality. The writer who would like to show himself "wholly naked" ("To the Reader") describes at length the naked bodies of the inhabitants of the New World. While the body—with the pleasures and suffering it produces—had occupied a preponderant place in ancient philosophy (in Stoicism and Epicureanism, for example), the way of using the body in the New World was marked by a difference so great that it could not be theorized or reconciled within a Western vision of man. The customs of the Cannibals could be described only in the infinity of their variations and in accord with an essentially anthropological procedure. Habits and customs are inseparable from societies and are always determined by local experiences. By definition, customs are relative with regard to the foreign observer's conventions and morality. Comparing cultures would be a waste of time, because it would consist of establishing an order of cultures on the basis of the principle of civilization, whose points of reference are exclusively Western. As Montaigne understands, barbarity is always the other, in a definition perfectly suited to the time of the civil wars. The author of the *Essais* offers a critique of modernity via the practices of Cannibals.

Cannibalism takes different forms and has multiple faces. It is best to describe it as exhaustively as possible, using an approach that always seeks to avoid the traps of moral prescriptiveness, chiefly Christian. Montaigne thus limits himself to a depiction that is itself "savage," that is, outside human rationality and outside any religious considerations. Freed from the constraints imposed by reason, the imagination follows its course and naturally flourishes. In this sense, the New World—on the basis of the materiality of the examples reported—produced an image that was liberating with respect to the social and moral constraints of the Old World's own civilization. To describe the other in its culture is also to imagine oneself virtually in the other's society. The inversion is salutary, because it elicits an *analytical astonishment*. Montaigne was struck dumb on reading travelers' accounts of their experiences among the Indians of Brazil, Peru, and Mexico. In turn, he imagined himself among the Cannibals the better to observe them from within. Divesting himself of his judicial robes, Montaigne transformed himself into a Cannibal.

A logic emerges from the examples he chooses when he discusses the New World. Since 1580, Montaigne had taken an interest in the Indians' sexual practices and in the role of women in the domestic life of Cannibal societies. Lineage, filiation, and kinship in general occupy an important place in his remarks. Thus family ties and the institution of marriage among the Indian tribes interest him, especially in the chapters "Of the affection of fathers for their children" (II: 8) and "Of the resemblance of children to fathers" (II: 37), where these themes are taken up again to illustrate cultural variations. Although the Cannibals have many of the qualities of nobility, they seem little concerned with their genealogy. Food is also a constant preoccupation in Montaigne's observations. For example, in the first edition of the *Essais*, Cannibal customs are defined this way: "Here they live on human flesh."[3] Montaigne and his contemporaries were fascinated by the idea that humans could live on the bodies of humans. While anthropophagy always represents a necessity, cannibalism refers to a ritual comparable to Christian rites, and particularly to the sacrament of the Eucharist offered during the mass,[4] as if the cultural practices of the most remote societies had necessarily to be interpreted in the light of Christian rites.

Montaigne read more and more about the Indians of the New World and rapidly accumulated a long list of their peculiar customs that were completely opposite to Western practices. The testimonies (derived from books or from direct experience) regarding the New World were precious because they expressed differences in attitudes and social behaviors that served Montaigne as a mirror to shed light on Western customs that were too often perceived as universal. The observations reported by travelers naturally generated reflections on his time, because the New World led him to question the conventions and traditions of the Old World.

The New World became a phantasmal space where everything was possible, an oneiric land that allowed the most daring and improbable comparisons to be made. This liberation of the mind led to a critical examination of the Old World, which was tearing itself apart over obscure points of religious doctrine. However, there was no question of overidealizing the image of the "noble savage"; on this point, Montaigne does not challenge the political functioning of his own society. Cultural criticism and "public government" must not be confused with each other. For him, the New World remains an *outside world*, the expression of cultures that are worthy of esteem, but so distant from Western practices that it would be absurd to take them as a model. Montaigne could not be clearer about the theoretical and physical separation of these two worlds:

> And indeed all those imaginary, artificial descriptions of a government prove ridiculous and unfit to put into practice. These great, lengthy altercations about the best form of society and the rules most suitable to bind us, are altercations fit only for the exercise of our minds; as in the liberal arts there are several subjects whose essence is controversy and dispute, and which have no life apart from that. Such a description of a government would be applicable in a new world, but we take men already bound and formed to certain customs.[5]

A new world is not the equivalent of the New World, even if this world provides extraordinary wealth for the human spirit. A "description of government" would be welcome, but this description can be no more than decorative on bodies already shaped by custom. One cannot make oneself a Cannibal so easily, and the outside observer can only give his *impressions* of these societies. Montaigne maintains the critical distance that relativizes his assessments of these peoples. Description is ephemeral, an exercise—or an "essay"—that has to be constantly repeated when talking about others. "There are peoples where . . ." remains an unfinished painting, always waiting for another brushstroke, another touch, a new example. The Cannibal is permanently under construction.

The New World symbolizes a model of the political that contradicts the practices of Montaigne's time. The Indians' government is adapted to the political situation and translates a pragmatic vision of power. Montaigne notes this lesson in the margins of the Bordeaux Copy (that is, after his own experience in politics); there are places where "they depose the king when it seems good, and rely on elders to hold the tiller of the state, and also sometimes leave it in the hands of the people."[6] When the leaders of the Brazilian tribe first disembarked at Rouen in 1550, Montaigne himself had no political competence. However, in the *Essais* he recounts his meeting with the Cannibals, even affirming that he asked them several questions of a political and military order. As a detractor of purely bookish knowledge, he accords great importance to direct testimonies that he can relate to his own readings about the New World. Nevertheless, there remain several obscure points in this famous encounter between Montaigne and the Cannibals.

Tupinambas and Tabajaras

On Wednesday the first and Thursday the second of October 1550—that is, five years before the French established themselves in "Antarctic France"—in the framework of Henry II's royal entry into Rouen with his wife Catherine de Medici, fifty Brazilian natives who had recently disembarked, accompanied by some two hundred naked sailors, their faces and bodies painted so that they, too, could pass for inhabitants of the New World, undertook a reconstitution of everyday life in America, including a simulated battle between neighboring tribes. For the occasion, a Tupinamba village was reconstructed.[7] Everything was done to make this staging of the Cannibals in their "natural" habitat as verisimilar as possible. Tiered seating was set up to accommodate the Court and high-ranking visitors. The highlight of Henry II's royal entry into Rouen, this Cannibal tableau had been conceived to be striking and strengthen the image of a benevolent king who had inherited the throne only three years before.

The king, his gentlemen, ambassadors from all over Europe, the clergy, and a significant number of humanists and magistrates occupied the best seats to witness this extraordinary spectacle worthy of the world expositions of the nineteenth and twentieth centuries. To reproduce Brazilian exoticism, a strip of land along the Seine river had been planted with several species of trees and bushes, such as "broom, juniper, and box," to create a dense copse. The organizers of this event—mainly rich ship owners in Rouen—went so far as to paint the trunks of the trees, to whose tops box branches had been fastened, "representing fairly closely the natural appearance of the leaves of trees in Brazil."[8] Other bushes were loaded with fruits of various colors, imitating almost perfectly the "natural appearance" of South American forests. A bit of wild nature had been reconstructed on the banks of the Seine.

Huts had been built at each end of this area, their roofs covered with reeds and leaves, "fortified with a surrounding palisade instead of a rampart, or *boulenerd*, in the form and manner of the *mortuables* and habitations of the Brazilians."[9] An engraving from the same period depicts quite faithfully the setting built for the Cannibal festival in Rouen. Released to create the illusion of a three-dimensional space, exotic birds flew over the heads of the astonished spectators. They included parrots, aras, conures, toucans, and other brightly colored birds from America. Marmots, tamarins, and various other animals that were unknown in Europe and had been brought back in the holds of Rouen's merchant vessels populated this strip of Brazilian land along a French river. A veritable colonial transposition from one continent to the other was presented to spectators delighted by this unexpected change of scene. Whereas French camps had been constructed on the banks of the rivers of the New World, one could now witness (for a few hours) the everyday life of a Brazilian colony transplanted to the heart of the kingdom. All this had been conceived so that spectators might have the feeling of having been transported to Brazil. They had become actors.

The general idea of this staging was to recreate a world in which the abundance of nature allowed 250 "Indians" to cohabit peacefully with one another and with Westerners as their neighbors, at least during the first act of this idyllic tableau recounted by the citizens of Rouen for the king and his Court. It was, in fact, the beginning of the story. Everything begins with peace, quiet, and civility in what we might describe as the "Rousseauist moment" of an irenic and tranquil world. Nature was in harmony with man, and Indians and European sailors merged:

> Here and there, throughout the area, as many as three hundred men, completely naked, tanned and bristling, were rushing about. Without covering at all the parts that nature commands [us to cover], they were made up and equipped in the manner of the savages of America whom the Brazilian forest supports, [and] among their number were about fifty natural savages just brought from the country, having in addition to the other simulations, decorated their faces by piercing their cheeks, lips, and ears, and inserting into them longish stones, the size of a finger, polished and rounded, enamel white and emerald green in color.[10]

On the banks of the Seine, Catherine de Medici went into raptures over the savages' "playing and simulated battles." Everything seemed peaceful in early October 1550. The civil wars had not yet begun in France, and this pleasant tableau of conviviality and brotherhood transcended the political and religious troubles that were already brewing. It was then noted that the sailors from Rouen imitated the language and gestures of the Indians so well that it was impossible to tell the true from the false savages. The Western sailors had completely "cannibalized" themselves for the occasion. Humanity merged with the state of nature. Men hunted with bows and blowguns, a few savages ran after monkeys, while others swung in hammocks suspended from trees or simply lay on the ground, in the shade of a bush, resting. A few Indians were cutting wood, and a group was busy constructing a kind of fort along the river. From the banks of the Yguarassu to those of the Seine, the reduced space along the river served as a microcosm of the European (Portuguese and French) conquest. It authorized the most daring comparisons.

But these marvelous and paradisiacal scenes were only a prelude to the violence that was soon to break out like a thunderclap. Interrupting this initial bucolic tableau, a savage tribe appeared: "And at that point, here came a troop of savages who called themselves, in their language, Tabagerres, according to their parties, and who squatted on their heels around their king, whom they called Morbicha."[11] The chief of the Tabajaras suddenly began to harangue the Indians who had assembled around him. He started gesticulating and waving his arms in a "passionate gesture" and in a Brazilian language. The Tabajaras abruptly abandoned the civility that had hitherto prevailed. At some point, the essential activity of the Cannibals that had been reported by Western visitors and idealized by Montaigne had to be represented. According to the description given at the time, the assembly reacted promptly and obediently, and the Tabajaras "came to attack violently another troop of savages who called themselves, in their language, Toupinabaulx." Thereupon followed a merciless battle of an extreme ferocity, in which arrows and blows with war clubs were exchanged. The battle between the Tupinambas and the Tabajaras was clearly the theme of this Cannibal second act theatricalized in the extreme. Peace naturally followed the war.

The abrupt battle that took place before the king and the members of his Court was won by the Tupinambas, who valiantly resisted the Tabajaras' sneak attack, forcing them to flee. The aggressors had lost the war in a moment. Order could be reestablished. The camp of those who had fled was burned, as if to remind others of the consequences of an unjust aggression. The Tupinambas (most of whom were sailors from Rouen) emerged victorious from this confrontation between the good Cannibals (the Tupinambas) and the cruel Cannibals (the Tabajaras). The commentator on this rather successful staging (successful, at least, for the assembly that witnessed it) gave this description of it:

> The aforementioned simulated battle was performed so close to the truth, as much by the natural savages who had mixed among them, as by the sailors who in the course of several voyages had trafficked with the savages and lived for a long time with them, that it seemed true, and not simulated, and the proof of this is that several people of this kingdom of France, in sufficient number, having long frequented the country of Brazil and the Cannibals, sincerely attested that the effect of the preceding figuration was a certain simulacrum of the truth.[12]

This "simulacrum of the truth" or true psychomachia, naturally reminds us of the passages in which Montaigne describes the two highlights that regulate Cannibal life: repose and war. This rhythm of life soon came to mark France during the eight civil wars that devastated it and gave Montaigne reason to inquire into these simulacra of peace punctuated by truces and reconciliations that were impossible to respect.

The representation of Cannibal life in Rouen in 1550 was the object of numerous descriptions and was widely commented upon during the years following the event. An engraving from the period put its stamp on people's minds and established the image of the Cannibal that was quickly transformed into a cultural infatuation. It was all there: scenes of hunting and fishing, men climbing trees, dancing in the middle of a superabundant nature, or relaxing in hammocks. Not to mention the battle between opposing tribes that was raging in the foreground. These moments of war and peace are inseparable (figure 5). The West was able to capture in a single image what was to form the essence of its fantasy regarding the New World. Montaigne did not witness this reconstitution of a Cannibal day. He may have been in Paris at that time. We can imagine his amazement and wonder had he been present. In the *Essais*, he tells us that it was at the same place, in Rouen, that he met the Cannibals twelve years later, on the occasion of the siege of that city by the royal armies of Charles IX, at the very beginning of the Wars of Religion. He even had the good luck—still according to him—to be able, thanks to an interpreter, to question some of the Brazilian "captains."

The Cannibal festival of 1550 shows us that if one cannot have a Cannibal at home, it will always be possible to find a sailor who can be confused with one of them. The sailors who went to Brazil knew the natives so well that they could imitate them perfectly. That was the lesson learned from the reconstitution carried out in 1550. Montaigne noted that he had such a man in his service: "I had with me for a long time a man who had lived for ten or twelve years in that other world which has been discovered in our century, in the place where Villegaignon landed, and which he called Antarctic France."[13] Twelve years spent in Brazil is no meager experience, though one may doubt this figure, which is twice that of the very short existence of Antarctic France (November 15, 1555–March 15, 1560). Montaigne probably exaggerated the length of his servant's stay among the Indians. Nonetheless, he needed the authority of a direct witness to validate his knowledge of the cultural practices of the Indians of the New World.[14] His readings on the subject could not suffice for a person who gave spontaneous speech priority over academic erudition. His encounter with the Cannibals is situated in the logic of a narrative authority that allows the author of the *Essais* to report direct experiences. As has been suggested, Montaigne's interview with the Cannibals is mainly part of the topos.[15]

Let us consider the sources on the New World and the Cannibals that were available to Montaigne. In addition to Thevet's and Léry's "testimonies," we must add the secondhand accounts produced by professional writers like Sébastien Munster; Urbain Chauveton, the translator of Benzoni; and François de Belleforest, a prolific author whose *Cosmographie universelle* (1575) enjoyed a resounding success in Montaigne's time. The author of the *Essais* preferred to-

Figure des Briſilians.

FIGURE 5. Engraving representing the Cannibals in Rouen in 1550. *It is the Narrative of the sumptuous order of pleasing spectacles and magnificent theatres set up and exhibited by the citizens of Rouen . . .* Rouen: R. Le Hoy, 1551 (private collection).

pographers to cosmographers; he liked descriptions of things observed in the field, even in the form of simulacra, insofar as they corresponded to a reality close to lived experience, such as the ones provided by his servant who had resided in the New World, or, better yet, a conversation with the Cannibals themselves. The conversation with the Cannibals thus acquires an entirely essential importance in his discourse on the New World. Montaigne's face-to-face meeting with the Indians symbolizes a necessity that, just like the testimony of the sailor who worked for him, had to be reported. But this time Montaigne experienced the cannibals at first hand, without intermediaries.

At the end of the chapter "Of cannibals," when he has already commented at length on Cannibal culture, Montaigne buttresses the authority of his personal judgment by describing a personal meeting with the Brazilians. He begins by declaring that he has met "three of them" before witnessing a long discussion between the king and these three Indians: "The king talked to them for a long time"; then another interlocutor addressed them: "After that, someone asked their opinion"; finally, Montaigne's turn comes: "I had a very long talk with one of them, but I had an interpreter who followed my meaning so badly, and who was so hindered by his stupidity in taking in my ideas, that I could get hardly any satisfaction from the man."[16] Several remarks need to be made regarding this series of conversations reported by Montaigne. First, while the king talked with the Indians "for a long time," Montaigne had a "very long talk with one of them." We may, however, have doubts about the quality of this exchange. For Montaigne, the point was not to obtain precise information—he already had that, thanks to Jean de Léry, André Thevet, and Urbain Chauveton, who remained by far his most important sources—but rather to prolong a moment that validated his *own experience of the Cannibals*. The Indians of the New World are often called upon in the *Essais*. They serve as witnesses for the prosecution in all kinds of criticisms and accusations: "witness my Cannibals,"[17] Montaigne writes—without, however, developing what he means by that.

Montaigne's interview with an Indian chief is one of the highlights of the *Essais*. It authorizes him to play the topographer in his turn. Rouen is assumed to be the port closest to the New World in the sixteenth century, a colonial transposition that validates the objectivity of the information gleaned in this second land of the Cannibals. Montaigne deliberately places his conversation with the Cannibals on the level of orality and proximity. He introduces this meeting with the help of a remark on the language of the Indians, which he perceives as "a soft language, with an agreeable sound, somewhat like Greek in its endings."[18] Only a direct witness could make such a remark. Moreover, this association of the Brazilian language with an ancient language (Greek) creates a link of community between civilizations that, had they coexisted in history, would have been able to understand each other. If the Athenians are the founders of Western civilization and modern forms of government, the Cannibals also have a language with the same humanistic and political potentialities. Montaigne's ear is worth more than all the eyewitnesses who were able to accompany Villegaignon to Brazil. The tonality of the cannibal language makes these people the equivalent of the Greek citizens of Antiquity.

Although we can agree that there was an interview between Montaigne and some Cannibals, we still need to be sure as to when it might have taken place. The author of the *Essais* admits on several occasions that his memory often fails him. When he reports his "cannibal conversation," we are in 1579, seventeen years after his interview in 1562, the date critics usually give for this famous face-to-face encounter with the Indian chiefs. Montaigne's interview with the Cannibals has been associated with his possible sojourn in Rouen during the siege of that city. The king, who had recently turned thirteen, accompanied his mother, Catherine de Medici, to witness the taking of the city, which was in the hands of Protestants commanded by Count Montgomery. The rebel city was sacked by the royal troops, and the event was not accompanied by any ceremony likely to include a parade of the Indians of the New World. For that reason, it is possible to wonder exactly where this interview, which is capital for Montaigne, actually took place. In fact, we have no other testimony to such an encounter between him and Cannibals at the end of October 1562. The siege of the city makes a royal audience and a parade of Cannibals implausible; no text attests to such events after the siege of Rouen, despite the declarations made by Montaigne, who describes, seventeen years later and in considerable detail, his conversation with Indian "captains" who had recently arrived from Brazil—even though he acknowledges that he forgot the third remark the Cannibals made to him.

Montaigne declares that he met the Cannibals in Rouen while Charles IX was in that city. If he did, it could only have been in his capacity as a member of a parlement. A mission had already been entrusted to him by the parlement of Bordeaux on November 26, 1561, because in the parlement's records he is described "going to the Court for other affairs." According to these same records, Montaigne was back in Bordeaux in February 1562. He returned to Paris on June 12. This second mission for the parlement might thus have allowed him to go to Rouen in late October, but only as a private individual, since it is hard to imagine a member of parlement witnessing a military operation. Montaigne's two careers must not be confused. An amalgam is often made between the Montaigne of the parlementary period and the Montaigne-gentleman after his admission to the Order of Saint Michael in 1571. In 1562, Montaigne was not in a position to be part of the king's entourage and even less to participate in one way or another in the siege of the city in his capacity as a councillor at the parlement of Bordeaux. Thus we have to consider other scenarios for this meeting with the Cannibals.

Following the pacification edict of Amboise, Charles IX went back to Rouen in August 1563 after witnessing the fall of Le Havre, which had been held by Ambrose Dudley, third Earl of Warwick. Brantôme wrote that the city had recovered part of its former prosperity after being sacked the preceding year and had undertaken great expense in preparation for the royal entry. Did Montaigne witness Charles IX's entry into Rouen on Thursday, August 12, 1563? Did he represent the parlement of Bordeaux five days later, on August 17, during the *lit de justice* held at the parlement of Rouen, where the king's majority was proclaimed—he had just celebrated his thirteenth birthday—and thus his accession to the throne? In conflict with the Paris parlement, the chancellor, Michel de L'Hospital, and the queen mother had chosen Rouen "to spite the parlement of Paris, and to reduce its authority and preeminence."[19] To put the final touch on the provocation for that parlement's members, Charles IX took advantage of his stay in Rouen to confirm the edict of Amboise with a second edict of pacification. Michel de L'Hospital sharply criticized the parlements and accused them of interpreting royal edicts as they pleased, an old rebuke that had often been repeated by a royal government that was not happy about the growing political autonomy of the regional parlements and its courts of justice. Since the advent of Charles IX in 1560, most of the king's and the queen mother's initiatives had been systematically blocked by the Paris parlement, which considered itself the sole legal tutor of the minor king. The 1563 *lit de justice* constituted revenge taken on the parlement of Paris after three years of mutual suspicion. In the eyes of the members of the Paris parlement, the convocation of the *lit de justice* in a provincial parlement and not in Paris was an additional affront, and they contested its legality. However, they lost the battle, and their parlementary supremacy was greatly diminished. Charles IX took advantage of the precedent set in Rouen to hold two other *lits de justice*, in Toulouse in 1564 and in Bordeaux in 1565.[20] If Montaigne had been present in Rouen in 1563, we may wonder how he would have felt about these admonishments directed against the members of his profession while he was laboring to make a place for himself in the hierarchy of a parlement that was soon to be, in its turn, the object of the chancellor's wrath.

We have detailed knowledge of Charles IX's entrance into Rouen in 1563 because every ceremony, procession, and public event was meticulously recorded and described.[21] We also have all the speeches that were made there.[22] However, nothing attests to any presence of Cannibals on August 12. Moreover, if we look attentively at the dates of Charles IX's travel to Rouen and Montaigne's schedule in Bordeaux, we see that Montaigne could not have been present in Rouen during the summer of 1563, either.

In his letter on the death of La Boétie published in the *Mesnagerie de Xenophon* in 1571, Montaigne gives a detailed chronology of his presence in Germignan, a village near Bordeaux, where Richard de Lestonac, his brother-in-law, owned a house. We have already recounted these extraordinary days, which Montaigne reported in great detail. We learn that Montaigne returned from the Palais de Justice on August 9, when he found his friend ill and advised him to leave Bordeaux and go to Germignan. He then made several visits to La Boétie's bedside until August 18, the date of his friend's death. Thus Montaigne could not have been present when Charles IX made his entrance into Rouen, or attended the *lit de justice* held in the same city on August 17. Charles IX left Rouen on August 19, the day after La Boétie's death. Furthermore, documents in the archives prove that during most of July, Montaigne was working with La Boétie on several cases being appealed to the parlement. In fact, we have a ruling of the parlement, signed by Montaigne and dated July 24, concerning Jean Vernet and Pierre Viaut, appellants before the judges of the présidial court in Saintes, on the one hand, and Matthieu Salesse, a merchant from Hiers, in his own name and as assignee of Christophe de Vignoles, the appellee, on the other hand.[23] Thus it is impossible that Montaigne attended the accession of Charles IX in Rouen or the *lit de justice* that followed it in August 1563. He spent the whole summer in Bordeaux, and also made visits to Germignan and a few stays in his château.

From Rouen to Bordeaux

The description of the royal entry into Rouen in 1550 and the staging of the New World on the occasion of this event made it possible to establish the image of the Cannibal, but Montaigne probably did not meet the Indians in that city, as he implies he did. On the other hand, the presence of Cannibals in Bordeaux in 1565 is attested. Everything suggests that Montaigne's meeting with them actually took place in Bordeaux. In fact, Indians from Brazil paraded in Bordeaux in 1565 on the occasion of Charles IX's entrance into that city. Abel Jouan, Charles IX's servant, wrote an account of the royal tour through France.[24] Let us follow his itinerary in southwest France.

On Sunday, April 1, 1565, the king sailed down the Garonne to spend the night in Bordeaux. On April 2 he arrived at the little château of Thouars, one league from the city, where he stayed for six days, long enough to prepare his royal entry. On the occasion of his entrance into Bordeaux on April 9, 1565,[25] three hundred men-at-arms paraded, leading twelve foreign captives, including Greeks, Turks, Arabs, Indians, Canarians, and "American and Brazilian savages," who were harangued by their chiefs. Interpreters translated the king's speeches when the Cannibals passed in front of him as a sign of submission.

This other way of representing Cannibals, more servile than in Rouen—the subjection and allegiance of the Indians to the king of France—was chosen for the reception of Charles IX in Bordeaux. It corresponded more to the political climate of the royal visit during the grand tour of France carried out between January 24, 1564, and May 1, 1566. The sovereign and the Chancellor of France wanted to reassert their authority during this stop in Bordeaux and had the Cannibals and the magistrates march in the same procession, perhaps in a spirit of concord and obedience. Militarily the year 1564 had been fairly peaceful, and a relative calm prevailed in Guyenne. The winter of 1564 had been among the harshest in a generation, and the rivers had frozen, as well as the grapevines and the wheat. In the spring, the king wanted to take advantage of the thaw and the lull in the religious conflict to get to know his kingdom and listen to his people's grievances. Obedience and submission were the two key words of his passage through Bordeaux. The similarity between the experience Montaigne describes in Rouen and the account Theodore Godefroy gives of the speeches delivered by the Brazilian chiefs three years later in Bordeaux[26] is striking.

Montaigne was definitely in Bordeaux at that time, and he participated in the festivities organized by the municipal authorities and the parlement, which had begun in mid-January 1565 to prepare for a reception of Charles IX with great pomp. Their preparations were the object of bitter and turbulent discussions within the parlement and the jurade. The king's formal entrance into the city required the councillors of the parlement to be present at the various official ceremonies; like other members of the parlement, Montaigne was personally involved, even down to small details, in the organization of this event that was to effect a rapprochement with the chancellor, who did not spare his criticisms of the kingdom's parlements. It was also an opportunity to pledge allegiance before the supreme representative of the kingdom's judicial system. In the course of a session orchestrated by the parlement's first president, Montaigne spoke along with twelve of his colleagues:

> Wednesday January 24 . . . the aforementioned Eyquem said that in speaking to the king, he had to be made to see, by means of convincing reasons, how fitting it was for a good King to make frequent visits to the lands of his subjects, and how that benefited the affairs of his domain; that the low esteem and disorder of the judicial system came from the infinite number of officers of justice that are involved in it; from the bad order in which they are chosen and from the fact that everything is venal; that it is necessary to request that all these defects be rectified and eliminated from our justice system; that no request must be made that tends to increase or augment the profit that we derive from our offices.[27]

We seem to be listening to the chancellor himself. We can imagine the unpleasant surprise of the members of parlement, who must have wondered what side Montaigne was on. All of them were subject to the king's orders, but between that and denouncing the corruption of a venal parlement, there was, of course, a limit that could not be transgressed. Montaigne paid the price for this moment of bravery as a righter of wrongs.

Five weeks later, on Sunday, April 1, 1565, the king dined at the home of the Foix-Candales in Cadillac. He spent Monday in Bordeaux; on Tuesday he went to Thouars, where he stayed from April 3 to April 8 because of the rainy, windy weather that was raging in Bordeaux. Finally, on April 9, 1565, Charles IX made his entrance into Bordeaux in a ceremony that had been rehearsed at length. Many members of the parlement openly opposed royal authority and wanted to use the king's passage through their city to show their discontent. Some had even prepared "remonstrances," but it was deemed inappropriate to antagonize once again the chancellor, who was making this visit a personal matter. The members of the Bordeaux parlement—like many of their colleagues in the kingdom's other courts—demanded loudly and clearly their independence and tried to free themselves from the power of the parlement of Paris. Although it was in the hands of the Catholics, the parlement of Bordeaux demanded its autonomy with regard to the capital's interference in its functioning. The members of the parlement balked at registering the letters patent relating to the edicts of pacification, not necessarily because they disapproved of them, but because they did not like having to ratify what had been decided elsewhere.

In 1565, the religious conflict was gathering force in the region, and a group of moderate members of the parlement—including Montaigne—recommended doing everything possible to avoid displeasing the sovereign. For Montaigne, the arrival of Charles IX in Bordeaux was to be an opportunity to reaffirm the parlement's submission to royal authority. It was to be one of the highlights of his career as a councillor. Nevertheless, his colleagues were far from unanimous in supporting this position.

The parlement's *Registres secrets* report at length several debates on what would be said in the king's presence. On January 17, there was a debate regarding what "remonstrances" should be made to the king "for his service, the good of his domain, and the relief of his subjects."[28] A week later, several councillors proposed "diverse things" while others declared that "they wished to say nothing." Finally, it was agreed to reaffirm that the parlement had always been submissive to the monarch's authority and fully intended to keep the city of Bordeaux obedient to the king. That was Montaigne's position.

Nonetheless, on March 21, following another debate, the court assigned the presidents La Chassaigne and Roffignac, assisted by councillors Vergoing, Malvyn, Gaultier, and Guilheragues, along with the presidents at the Chambres des Enquêtes Alesme and La Vergue, "to look into and consider other things." The officers were unable to agree on the words to be used to reaffirm the parlement's submission, and a revolt was organized with a few recalcitrant members. It was finally decided to send representatives of the parlement to meet the king before he entered the city, and each councillor was advised to "promptly" buy himself a "scarlet robe" if he did not already have one. It was also decided that during the king's sojourn in the city, "the Presidents and Councillors entering the Palais shall wear suitable robes with tippets, and not chamber robes, nor large trousers and garters, small, pointed hats, low-cut shoes, nor slippers and shoes of velvet."[29] The councillors decided to wear their red robes and a fur-lined hat. The parlement got dressed up to receive the monarch and to display the signs of its privileges.

To please the young king—he was then fifteen years old—and to conform to the ritual of the sovereign's authority over foreign territories (including Antarctic France) another "Cannibal exposition" had been arranged in the form of a procession through the streets of Bordeaux. It was chosen to exhibit prisoners.

In the public procession, which brought together all the notables of the city and the parlement, and following the Cannibals and other captive people, the municipal officials paraded in front of the king. The members of parlement—including Montaigne—rode through the center of the city on horseback and in ceremonial garb, wearing red robes with hoods for the councillors who had earlier dined at the Palais at the king's expense.[30] Montaigne, in the same way as the Cannibals, was part of the cortege that passed in front of the king in Bordeaux on this April 9, 1565. He was richly dressed; the Cannibals were naked. After the distinction drawn in 1550 between the Tupinambas (Indians allied with the French against the Portuguese) and the Tabajaras (enemies of the Tupinambas and thus of the French), we can conclude that because they were captives, the Indians who marched through the streets of Bordeaux were Tabajaras—at least in the rather confused image of the representation of Indian nations in Brazil. Montaigne chose to remain silent about these Cannibals who had been defeated and enslaved by the French and their allies the Tupinambas. His conception of Cannibal wars without either victors or vanquished was perhaps not in conformity with his encounter with Cannibals in Bordeaux.

La Popelinière reports that during Charles IX's ceremonial entrance into Bordeaux, spectators saw "three hundred men at arms leading twelve captive foreign Nations, such as Greeks, Turks, Arabs, Egyptians, Taptobanians, Indians, Canarians, Moors, Ethiopians, savages, Americans and Brazilians; whose captains spoke before the King each in his own tongue, understood by the translator who interpreted for his Majesty."[31] Thomas Richard, the printer of one of the descriptions of the royal entry into Bordeaux, regrets not having been able to reproduce the speeches that were delivered to the king by the twelve foreign nations, each in its own language, "which diversity of language is very familiar to Bordeaux sailors."[32] In his *Histoire universelle*, Agrippa d'Aubigné also recounts the presence of Brazilians in Bordeaux. He speaks of "twelve bands" of foreigners, including "Cannibals, Margajats, and Thaupinambous; who were represented by their chiefs."[33] His description (of the presence of the king, the interpreter, the speech) is not very different from Montaigne's in the *Essais*. Thus we can consider that Montaigne probably met the Cannibals in Bordeaux. If he had already talked with them in Rouen in 1562, it would be surprising that he did not mention his second interview with the Indians of the New World in Bordeaux, three years later. Must this be considered a vagueness of his memory or is there a political explanation of this omission or confusion?

In both cases—Rouen and Bordeaux—it would have been impossible for Montaigne to hear the translation given by the interpreter. This is a matter of the physical distance between Montaigne, on the one hand, and the king and the interpreter, on the other hand. His rank as a simple councillor in the parlement did not allow him to be near the king or the numerous other nobles, ambassadors, prelates, and high state officials. The protocol of these meetings (conceived in the specific ceremonial of royal entries) is set forth in precise and detailed sixteenth-century descriptions.[34] Protocol was always followed to the letter, and a simple councillor in the parlement obeyed the rules that governed the formation of corteges and interviews. Montaigne could not have been close enough to the Cannibals to hear them when they addressed the king. His private conversation with them could certainly have taken place both in Rouen and in Bordeaux, but in that case the chronology given in the *Essais* poses a problem. It could not have occurred between 1560 and 1563.

The royal entry into Bordeaux was also an occasion for the members of parlement to parade before the inhabitants in order to show them that they represented the only royal justice, a justice that the jurats and the city also claimed the right to dispense in numerous cases. Their cortege was led by Louis de Pontac, a comptroller at the chancellery.[35] The clergy conducted the procession before the king, followed by a large number of soldiers, royal sergeants, members of the présidial courts, of the university faculty, and representatives of the parlement with its councillors in red robes who paraded "with great gravity," on horseback or on mules.[36] Little children on horses, dressed in white and holding small flags painted with the arms of France, passed in front of the platform where the king sat. At the end of the procession, the jurats and the master of the mint preceded three hundred soldiers leading the twelve foreign nations, each dressed "in its way": the "Taprobains in the Taprobain way; Americans in the American way; Indians in the Indian way; Canarians in the Canarian way; savages in the savage way; Brazilians in the Brazilian way . . ."[37]

The parade lasted four hours. Each captain of these nations made a speech in his language "which was translated by an interpreter." The presidents and councillors marched two by two. The presidents wore their mantles, with mortars "on their heads"; behind them came the councillors and four bailiffs, then thirty lawyers with their fur-lined hats, and finally twenty prosecutors wearing their hoods with bourrelets. Montaigne remained standing during the speech addressed to the king, who was sitting across from him on a red velvet chair placed on a platform erected for the occasion; the monarch was surrounded by the prince of Navarre, the Cardinal of Bourbon, the lords of Lansac and Nemours, the Cardinal of Guise, and several foreign ambassadors.

The four presidents of the parlement, the clerk, and a bailiff knelt on the ground in front of the king, their heads bared. Benoît Lagebaston, first president of the parlement, spoke first, giving a long speech. Seeking to please both the king and the members of the parlement, who had expressed the sharpest criticisms of the presence of the royal Court in Bordeaux, he delivered a discourse that went round in circles and lacked substance. The king, annoyed, got angry and brusquely interrupted him to show his displeasure. Godefroy relates this incident:

> The King was irritated by the speech given by Maistre Jacques Benoist, First President, and cut him off, and without waiting until he had finished said to him: I praise my Justice for the good duty it has done, and if there is someone who still has arms in his hands, I shall render such a Justice that it will be an example to the others; and after he rose from his seat, the aforesaid Presidents, the Clerk, and the Bailiff all lined up on the platform waiting to see the Companies of the City pass before them.[38]

The protocol that had been elaborated over more than two months was suddenly suspended. The young king's ill humor, displayed before members of parlement who were a little too sure of themselves, had spoiled the celebration. We can imagine the coolness that followed. The king rose and the members of parlement, paralyzed by the situation, did not budge. The procession continued and it was the turn of the representatives of "each foreign Nation," Greeks, Turks, Egyptians, Moors, Tartars, Indians, and Savages "dressed in accord with the aforesaid Nations" to express themselves. At 6:00 p.m., everything was over and the king went off to sup after everyone else had silently gone away.[39] The royal entry was far from a success.

The king reprimanded the members of the parlement, through the intermediary of the chancellor, Michel de L'Hospital, during a *lit de justice* held on April 12. The councillors of the Great Council were associated with the councillors of the court of the parlement of Bordeaux. The chancellor reminded the members of parlement that justice did not belong to them and that it emanated from the king, in accord with his legitimate orders. He admonished them, emphasizing the fact that their personal judgments remained closely bound to the laws (*astricta legibus*).

Displeased with the magistrates' behavior, the king found many faults in his parlement of Bordeaux, going so far as to accuse its members of an "infinity of murders, plunderings, and instances of public violence that have been committed in your jurisdiction."[40] L'Hospital reported that he himself had "received many complaints about your seditious people and public quarrels."[41] The parlement was compared to an "ill-regulated" household in which great disobedience to the king prevailed. Royal orders were often ignored or even rejected.

In Bordeaux, the members of the parlement had to grin and bear it, and the councillors were more "split up into diverse factions" than in any other parlement. The youngest councillors at the bottom of the hierarchy—including Montaigne—had to choose their camp in order to have any hope of advancing their careers and someday being promoted according to their political alignment. After consulting the registers, the chancellor told the members of the parlement that they too often succumbed to insults and did not hesitate to "resort to violence without having respect for either yourselves or the place where you are."[42] Not mincing words, he urged them to keep their "hands clean" and to rise to a higher level to recover some of their dignity. While the chancellor considered the councillors of the parlement of Paris too "serious," he considered those of the parlement of Bordeaux too "familiar," and a national shame for this lofty profession.

The chancellor then accused them of numerous judicial dysfunctions: they were slow in registering royal orders, and too many protests emanated from this rebellious parlement. He chastised the parlement for its excessive resistance to the execution of royal orders and said that he was dismayed that justice had not been administered with as much exactitude and impartiality as it ought to have been. The members of the Bordeaux parlement too often put their personal interests before the king's, he said. Justice was for sale, particularly to the Bordeaux bourgeoisie, which distributed generous bribes to the councillors. L'Hospital also questioned their competence and accused them of being fainéant and dishonest, even liars: "In this body there are some who are lazy and serve only a few times a year, and yet always sign their *debentur* and certify that they have served."[43] L'Hospital expressed his indignation at the avarice of magistrates who took "gifts to give audiences" and thus became "great thieves"[44] of the court. The chancellor's public admonishments marked people's minds, at least for a time. This warning shot was taken as a slap in the face.

We can imagine Montaigne, silently savoring his victory; he could be satisfied to have committed himself against his colleagues and to have denounced the trafficking in influence and the financial malversations that were corrupting from within a system closed in on itself. Michel de L'Hospital's speech before the Bordeaux parlement was unchallengeable on that point, since it pertained to political and financial collusion between the *robins* and the bourgeoisie: "there is something else that I have been told, that there are, in this chamber, those who lend their money to merchants at interest, and they should take off their robes and become merchants: perhaps they would do better; for today there is nothing that spoils commerce so much as too great communication with the people of the long robe: because as soon as a merchant has something, he has to make his son a lawyer or a councillor."[45] On May 18 of the same year, the chancellor reprimanded the parlement once again, castigating the councillors for their excessive familiarity and their tendency to "communicate too much with the parties." He accused the members of the parlement of being too "dissolute in their lives, conversation, and dress."[46]

Montaigne witnessed these calls to order in due form; and we can imagine his reaction, given that he was counting on pursuing a career in the Bordeaux parlement. He could have spoken out—and perhaps he did in private conversation with the chancellor—but he must also have thought about his future. Once the king had returned to Paris, things would resume their usual course in the parlement, and it was better to treat one's enemies carefully. Since La Boétie's death, the network of Montaigne's allies had considerably diminished, and to be able to envisage a promotion, he had to make friends. Fifteen years later, when the first edition of the *Essais* was published, Montaigne preferred not to recount his participation in Charles IX's royal entry into Bordeaux in 1565. His memory of it might have been too painful, and an encounter with the Cannibals in Rouen—rather than in Bordeaux—on the occasion of the reconquest of the city from the Protestants sounded a much more appropriate note.

In the early 1560s, the intransigent Catholics found Charles IX's concessions to the Protestants outrageous, and the edicts of pacification were no longer applied in Bordeaux. The Huguenots missed no occasion to complain to the king.[47] At first, Charles IX replied favorably to the Protestants' demands and granted them letters patent that authorized them, for example, to sing psalms in their homes or to sell the Bible in French. Protestants—including members of the parlement—were also to be allowed to hold public offices in the city—a well-intentioned but inapplicable rule. For example, the parlement of Bordeaux had refused to register the letters patent sent by the chancellery. Finally, these letters were confirmed not by the parlement but directly by the seneschal of Guyenne, an unusual formality that weakened the application of their content and made it possible to revoke several articles favorable to the Protestants. Montaigne's position with regard to the edicts of pacification in the early 1560s is not very clear. A fervent Catholic and not much inclined to conciliation, he nonetheless considered himself a representative of the royal power and was not prepared to join the rebellion that was shaking the unity of the Bordeaux parlement.

The significant fact about Charles IX's stay in Bordeaux was precisely this call to order issued to the parlement at the *lit de justice* that followed the king's entrance into the city and the procession of the captive peoples. In 1580, when the *Essais* were first published, and while Henry III was still having the same problems with the parlement of Bordeaux, this reminder of Charles IX's visit to Bordeaux could have been misinterpreted. For Montaigne, it was a matter of recognizing an embarrassing incident that it was better to keep silent about. In 1565, Montaigne was still a member of the parlement of Bordeaux, and to make reference to the king's irritation before the members of parlement was also to refer to the fact that, in the 1560s, he belonged to the world of the *robins*. Charles IX's displeasure and Michel de L'Hospital's reprimands were addressed to Montaigne as well, as a member of parlement, even if he was not necessarily as rebellious as some of his colleagues. Esprit de corps among people in the same profession prevailed at that time, and Montaigne assuredly preferred to avoid mentioning Charles IX's not very memorable visit to Bordeaux. It seemed to him far better to refer to the young king's presence in Rouen for the siege and the conquest of that city by the Catholics, which became a bastion of the Catholic League after 1584.[48]

After the king's departure on April 20, 1565, the prince of Navarre, accompanied by his uncles, the Cardinal of Bourbon (1523–1590) and Charles of Bourbon (1515–1565), prince of La Roche-sur-Yon, appeared in turn before the parlement to take possession of his government of Guyenne. All the councillors were summoned for the occasion. A document from the period informs us that on May 2, "Eyquem de Montaigne" received instructions to go to Saintonge.[49] Montaigne was definitely in Bordeaux in April 1565. That is where he met the Cannibals.

"Their Warfare Is Wholly Noble and Generous"

The word Montaigne chose to describe the exchanges between the New World and Europe is "corruption"—a term that cannot fail to remind us of the discourse the chancellor Michel de L'Hospital delivered before the members of the Bordeaux parlement in the very year in which Montaigne encountered Indians from the New World—an irreversible contamination that led the three "Cannibals" he met to their ruin. They had "let themselves be tricked by the desire for new things,"[50] Montaigne writes. Here we find a theme that was to be repeated by Rousseau in the eighteenth century: the harmful influence of civilization. The Cannibals were shown Western customs, which Montaigne calls "our way," such as the pomp of the king's court—but to make this point, the royal entry into Bordeaux would be a much better example than the more private encounter in Rouen in 1562. For Montaigne, the Indians' contact with Europe initiated an irreversible process. The Brazilian natives did not yet know the price they were going to pay for having traveled to the old continent. Their nudity made them simpler, more naive, and thus less corrupted, the exact opposite of the members of the Bordeaux parlement scolded by Michel de L'Hospital.

Montaigne also liked to strip himself naked and paint himself in a very particular way, with a certain "original naturalness,"[51] or a "naturalness so pure and simple."[52] As for his "public acts," they are supposed to be unpremeditated, and claim to follow the natural movement of the unspoiled body associated with the Cannibal. Reproducing the battle staged between the two Cannibal tribes in Rouen in 1550, the Wars of Religion—especially after 1572—also defy any rational explanation. In the Western world, conflicts were henceforth based on constant political bargaining that deprived them of any nobility. On the other hand, the nobility of the Cannibals was founded on the feudal organization of their society. The tribal chieftainship led Montaigne to draw a parallel with the role of the feudal lord and to demonstrate the superiority of a society dominated by virtue. He agreed with Pierre d'Origny, an ardent defender of the nobility, when he declared that "to be truly noble is to follow virtue."[53] The principal duty of the chief consists first of all in teaching virtue and then in ensuring his people's material life, and he is responsible for the accumulation of foodstuffs and their distribution. War represents the moment when virtue becomes visible. Glory and honor are the two essential qualities in battle: "Their warfare is wholly noble and generous,"[54] Montaigne writes. From their enemies, the Cannibals want to derive nothing but honor and virtue.

Fourteen years later, in 1579, Montaigne tried to recall this encounter, which clearly marked him, but which he seems not to remember very well. He recalls having heard the Brazilian captains make only three judgments concerning his own society, but he is incapable of recollecting the third one. We have to inquire more fully into this faulty memory, which affects the factual truth of the experience reported. Montaigne's memory flags, but he tells us the essential point: the fact that tall, strong, bearded men (the Swiss guards) submitted to obey a child (Charles IX). The Cannibals were also astonished by the great social differences prevailing in France, with, on the one hand, "men full and gorged with all sorts of good things," and, on the other hand, "beggars at their doors, emaciated by hunger and poverty."[55] In fact, they did not understand a political and social system founded on inequalities accepted by a large part the population that neither rebelled nor took "the others by the throat or set fire to their houses."[56] This last remark is luminous and has numerous political implications at the end of the sixteenth century. Without exaggerating the political import of the cannibal chiefs' observations, and despite Montaigne's opinion regarding the mediocre performance of the interpreter put at his disposal, we have to recognize that the *truchement* was able to express a social problem that is not so easy to understand (in another language) and still less to translate (so economically).

We may also examine two other examples Montaigne reports. He declares that he was able to question a Cannibal directly concerning the number of warriors he commanded in Brazil. The Cannibal is supposed to have replied by pointing to "a piece of ground, to signify as many as such a space could hold."[57] This image seems to be taken directly from the speech given by Michel de L'Hospital on April 25, 1565, before the parlement of Bordeaux. L'Hospital reported how the kings of Macedonia and Epirus sent two explorers who, perched "high on a hill," were able to evaluate the size of the Roman armies by the space they occupied. Similarly, at the beginning of the chapter "Of cannibals" Montaigne repeats almost verbatim a remark made by L'Hospital and drawn from Livy and Plutarch, to the effect that, "That army was not at all a barbarous army but a Greek [army]."[58] Strange similarities. It is as if Montaigne had not wished to reveal the fact that it was actually in Bordeaux and not in Rouen that he had encountered the Cannibals. L'Hospital's speech before the Bordeaux parlement might also have allowed Montaigne to apply the chancellor's examples to the Cannibals.

The sociological analysis made by the Cannibals, who had just arrived from the New World, refers us to a question that is not only relevant today but also permits us to look into the political foundations of the society that Montaigne knew. This relationship of dependency between the poor (beggars) and the wealthy is not based solely on a power relationship or on fear and repression, but also has to do with what La Boétie calls voluntary servitude. This bold sense of the term "servitude" is reflected upon in the chapter "Of cannibals," though it claims to be simply repeating a commentary made by the Indians in Montaigne's presence. The reference to La Boétie in a parenthesis introduced by the author of the *Essais* reveals a political reflection that goes beyond Montaigne and the Wars of Religion: "(they have a way in their language of speaking of men as halves of one another)."[59] Here we find again the definition that Montaigne later gave to his exceptional friendship with La Boétie. Is that a simple coincidence? The Indians extend this definition to society as a whole, believing that private interest must yield to the common good. Both the needy and the privileged are "halves" of each other in a mutual and necessary interdependence that reflects a model of society. One of the most important political lessons offered by Montaigne in this real or imagined exchange with the Indians of the New World is the importance of not cutting oneself off from one's other half.

The Cannibals' statements and Montaigne's commentary on the social organization of the Old World have to be placed in the political and religious context of the time. The royal edict of January 17, 1562, gave Protestants the right to assemble. In response to that concession, the Paris parlement decided, on June 6, that its members had to make a public profession of their Catholic faith. In Guyenne, the disturbances were becoming more intense; Catholics and Protestants were waging a veritable war of propaganda—before that war became a very real one. In July, Monluc challenged the Protestant troops in Targon. In Bordeaux, Catholic reaction was organized in the parlement while the jurats promised an equal fidelity to the king and to the "old religion." Montaigne, who was in Paris at that time, spontaneously presented himself at the parlement on June 12, asking that he also be asked to make an oath of Catholic faith.

The parlement's clerk, Du Tillet, reports Montaigne's action in terms that suggest his astonishment:

On that day, Maistre Michel de Montaigne, councillor at the parlement of Bordeaux, paid his respects to the Court and asked, so that he might have a vote in the court's audience, to be allowed to make a profession of faith, in accord with what he had been informed had been ordered by a ruling of this same court on the sixth of this month, which he did.[60]

This supplication is difficult to understand, since this profession of faith was in no way required of members of the parlement of Bordeaux. It is true that as a member of parlement, that is, an official in the service of the king and the Christian religion, Montaigne might have felt concerned. But this hasty step tells us a great deal about his political convictions in the early 1560s. Montaigne deliberately chose to side with the king and thus distinguished himself from the great majority of his Bordeaux colleagues, who were more inclined not to obey what might be decided in Paris. But what did he have to gain from this gratuitous demonstration? This spontaneous proof of allegiance to the Catholic religion and the king is all the more remarkable because Montaigne was absolutely not obliged to present himself before the Paris parlement, or to submit to its injunctions, even though he was subject to it administratively, like every other member of a parlement in the kingdom. This unaccustomed zeal on his part expressed a personal choice.

If he decided to make a public profession of his Catholic faith in 1562, it could only be as a result of a personal political conviction or a career choice—the two not being incompatible, moreover—that is, in order to situate his commitment in a well-defined ideological framework. Paris could count on him, even if he belonged to a rebellious parlement. This impulsive profession of faith has been seen as a fanatical act motivated by a desire to win the king's favor.[61] That interpretation no doubt goes too far, but it is true that the Catholics' religious intransigence was far stronger in 1562 than it was to be two or three years later. It was not a time for compromises, and it is in that context that we must understand the political position taken by Montaigne, who on this point shared the views developed by La Boétie in his *Memorandum* on the January edict.

This manifestation of allegiance to the Catholic religion expresses a clear political choice, and that is why Rouen (and the meeting with the Cannibals) acquires an important symbolic meaning in the opposition between Catholics and Protestants. Montaigne took care to situate the Cannibals in a heroic culture that had disappeared in his age.[62] That culture had to be protected, just as the Roman church had to be defended. It was an ancestral custom that had to be preserved at any price. Montaigne notes that in his time religious commitment accorded disproportionate importance to political efficacy, to the detriment of the noble values incarnated in the faith. After 1572, he was confronted with a new political reality that would force him to modify his views on the religious question. The political response to Machiavellianism—given by Innocent Gentillet soon after the Saint Bartholomew's Day massacre and the first civil wars—criticized precisely the corruption of the ancestral values of the government in their most honorable and heroic form.

The imaginary journey to Rouen at the time of the siege of the city in 1562 was a notable political act that expressed a clear commitment (in 1562, but it was recounted in 1580) to the Catholic side, at a time when it was not yet fashionable to make concessions to the Protestants. If Montaigne preferred to have seen the Cannibals in Rouen, it was perhaps because his presence alongside Charles IX on that occasion is the manifest sign of his adherence to the Catholic religion at the very beginning of the denominational conflict. The Wars of Religion had not yet officially begun at the time of his supposed sojourn in Rouen in 1562; the siege of that city could be interpreted as an important victory won by the Catholic party at that time. Montaigne's political attitude is in reality rather close to, if not identical with, the one La Boétie had expressed at the end of 1561. By 1580, speaking retrospectively of the 1560s had become rather delicate. In 1580 Montaigne might have seen in this early commitment to the side that he repeatedly calls "our religion" a considerable advantage in the political career that was opening up to him.

Whether he wished it or not, because of his office as councillor, Montaigne was associated de facto with the recalcitrant parlement of Bordeaux. Thus it is in this context that we must understand Montaigne's hesitation to refer to his interview with the Cannibals in Bordeaux—and consequently to remind the reader of his presence in Bordeaux at the time of the famous *lit de justice* held there. In his *Essais*, he says relatively little about his first career as a *robin*. Following the king to Rouen situated him in another social order to which he was proud to belong after 1580; no longer that of the *robins*, but that of gentlemen. The king's presence in Rouen in 1562 was essentially military and thus much more appropriate for situating the lord of Montaigne's experience with the Cannibals, which he reported in writing in 1579. It is probable that, in 1579–80, Montaigne preferred to forget his first career as a member of the parlement and hence to mention only his presence alongside the king, in the restricted circle of the members of the nobility, and within earshot of the Cannibals and their interpreter in a context that celebrated a Catholic victory over the Protestants, far from Bordeaux. In a way, Montaigne ennobled his encounter with the Cannibals.

A "Simulacrum of the Truth"

During the extravagant staging of Cannibal life in 1550, the sailors had two choices: they could be Tabajaras or Tupinambas. Their war was a civil war, a violent confrontation between incomprehensible beliefs leading to barbarous acts.

The victims of aggression (the Tupinambas) ultimately emerged victorious from the conflict that had suddenly broken out before the king and his Court. One could, like Montaigne, compare this Cannibal conflict with the Wars of Religion. In an effort to make peace between the denominations, the edict of January 1562 and Michel de L'Hospital had wanted to propose realistic solutions that were adapted to the situation on the ground. Catholic zealots could not accept what they saw as a first step toward the establishment of the reformed religion in France. The *Memorandum* on the January edict looked like a response to the compromise proposed by the French chancellor. It also reflected Montaigne's political position in the early 1560s. As we have seen, the massacre at Vassy, provoked by extremists to demonstrate the nullity of the edict, marked a decisive political turning point. The Protestants called for a popular uprising. They seized Rouen and Dreux, cities that at that time incarnated the people's revolt. However, the Catholic party quickly regained control of the situation after the siege of Rouen on October 26, 1562, and that of Dreux on December 19, 1562. These two cities have an important place in the *Essais*, not only through the encounter with the Cannibals in Rouen but also through a short chapter titled "Of the battle of Dreux" (I: 45).

We see that the dates of these possible meetings (imaginary or real) with the Cannibals are closely linked to Montaigne's political career and religious commitment between 1560 and 1565. Without being an intransigent Catholic, Montaigne shared with La Boétie a conception of religion rigid enough to reject compromises that in his opinion weakened sovereignty and threatened to plunge the country into social and political chaos. He became much more conciliatory in the late 1570s. His memory of the Cannibal parades contrasted two cities that were opposed politically and religiously: Rouen, which had been in the hands of the Protestants, and Bordeaux, which had remained faithful to the king in matters of religion, but whose parlement was administratively rebellious. The lesson of the Cannibals has to be understood in this complex relationship, which is both spatial (Rouen and Bordeaux) and temporal (1550, 1562, 1563, 1565, 1575–80). Montaigne had not allowed himself to be "deceived" by the sirens of religious "novelties" at a time when many of his neighbors and even members of his family had chosen the reformed religion, often simply out of political opportunism. Whereas the Cannibals had fallen into the Old World's gilded traps, Montaigne had resolutely opted for tradition, from the very beginning of the religious conflict. For him it was better to be a gentleman among the Cannibals than to be a simple councillor before the gentlemen of the court and the parlement. That is why his encounter with the Cannibals had to be private and outside any ceremony, whether it was in Rouen or in Bordeaux.

It is clear that in his account of his encounter with the Cannibals, Montaigne also projected his bookish knowledge onto the New World. These two experiences of the New World—a minimal direct testimony and detailed bookish knowledge—complemented each other, somewhat as in the Brazilian festival of 1550, where it was very difficult to distinguish the real Indians from the sailors disguised as Cannibals. The simulacrum was so perfect that the distinction between the savage and the Westerner was almost entirely effaced. In 1580, Montaigne played the Cannibal in his turn, after having so thoroughly come to know them through texts and through the stories he had been told about them, and when he was capable of understanding them and conversing with them. He almost spoke their language. He too, had traveled to the other side of the Atlantic, at least in his head. If we accept the fact that Montaigne's communication with the Cannibals was extremely brief—but long enough, Montaigne adds— we have to recognize that it could not have taught him much that he did not already know through his readings or the stories transmitted by his house employee, the sailor who had traveled around Antarctic France.

The quality of the information provided by this former sailor who had lived "in that other world," and who might have participated in the festival at Rouen in 1550, was certainly superior to that provided by the interpreter who officiated during the brief encounter with the Cannibals and who no doubt lacked imagination. But that is not the key point. The conversation with the Cannibals involved an experience that was mainly political, and not only cultural. Memory is often selective and depends in part on the dominant ideology of the moment. Confronted by memories that were not very glorious on the level of his new career projects, Montaigne displayed a duty to forget that may have conveniently forced him to prefer, consciously or unconsciously, a new political space (Rouen instead of Bordeaux) the better to explain his affinities with the inhabitants of the New World and thus to highlight a social and political system that he considered closer to the noble ideal.

Montaigne emphasizes the fact that his knowledge of the Cannibals' way of life was transmitted to him at first hand by "a simple, crude fellow" who had formerly lived in Brazil. This companion of Villegaignon's was worth more than all the narratives of Thevet and Léry, because he was less tempted to deform the truth. "A simple, crude fellow—a character fit to bear true witness,"[63] the former sailor in Montaigne's service also played the role of a Cannibal in a perfect simulacrum. Speaking of his eyewitness, Montaigne adds: "Such was my man, and besides this, he at various times brought sailors and merchants, whom he had known on that trip, to see me. So I content myself with his information, without inquiring what the cosmographers say about it."[64] These travelers—the sailors and merchants who had gone to Brazil—allowed Montaigne to enter a group of privileged witnesses who lent credence to his own descriptions of the Cannibals and his judgments concerning them.

Montaigne almost always bases his authority on the physical proximity of his sources: "from what I have been told,"[65] "according to my witnesses,"[66] "I had a very long talk with one of them."[67] The truth results from a legal judgment after an oral hearing of the witnesses. That is what judicial experience had taught him during more than ten years at the Bordeaux parlement.[68] In 1565, he saw his Cannibals as witnesses, just like those who had been heard during investigations in the law court. His office as councillor amounted precisely to verifying and "extracting" the testimonies of the appellants and appellees during an appeal in the parlement's first investigative chamber. He had learned his trade as a reporter in Guyenne and was just applying it to the New World. Used to writing "briefs" that were supposed to sum up oral testimonies, Montaigne had to remain as close as possible to the experiences naively reported by "simple, crude" witnesses. Travelers who had become servants were ultimately not so unlike Cannibals. Despite their cultural differences, a sailor imitated a Cannibal so well—in his gestures and his language—that the two merged. The same was true for Montaigne in 1580: to pass for a Cannibal, all he had to do was make the necessary gestures, strip himself naked, and cover himself with paint. While this simulacrum necessary for the comprehension of the New World and its social organization was rather delicate in 1562 or 1565, it was fully conceivable and accepted in 1580.

Could the *Essais* be the particular expression of a sciamachy, a battle against an imaginary enemy? At the beginning of the chapter "Of liars" (I: 9), Montaigne admits that he has a very bad memory: "There is no man who has less business talking about memory. For I recognize almost no trace of it in me, and I do not think there is another one in the world so monstrously deficient."[69] Should we see this as a confession? For Montaigne, there is a difference between lying (*mentir*) and "telling a lie" (*dire mensonge*). This truer truth or "simulacrum" does not go "against his conscience" and cannot be described as a lie. The Cannibals are above all the result of a labor of imagination, and for Montaigne their existence is certainly more symbolic than real. It is important to report a real encounter, but the time and the place count for little. The word "sciamachy," which is derived from Greek, represents a kind of exercise or test. In Antiquity, this kind of combat against oneself served as training for a fight to come. In this sense, the *Essais* are a "simulacrum of the truth" in which the gentleman and the Cannibal merge. One takes the place of the other: no longer "a Cannibal in breeches" but a gentleman as a Cannibal.

CHAPTER 5

The Making of a Gentleman (1570–1580)

In the course of the 1560s, the Bordeaux parlement was affected by political and religious dissensions that made it difficult for a judicial system that was supposed to be serene and equitable to function properly. Montaigne found it hard to insert himself into an institution in which cabals were daily occurrences at the Palais de l'Ombrière. The internal quarrels of the years between 1559 and 1562 had given way to much more dangerous religious conflicts, whose end result was no doubt the witch-hunt that began in early 1569. The second War of Religion had accentuated the cleavage between the moderates and the smaller but much more activist group opposing the Reformation. The first group included First President Benoît Lagebaston, who favored dialogue and tried to maintain peaceful ways of operating in the four chambers of the parlement (even though he did not believe in a reconciliation of Catholics and Protestants). The second group, the "faithful papists," was led by Christophe de Roffignac; they rejected any compromise with the supporters of the new religion and sought to bring proceedings against any form of heresy or "false religion" within the parlement. Unconditional zeal had led, as we have seen, to the suspension of ten councillors and a president between January 1569 and September 1570.

Montaigne's position with regard to these two parties had slowly evolved. In the early 1560s, he had felt an intellectual and political sympathy with those who wanted to rid themselves of any Protestant influence in Bordeaux. Like La Boétie, he had not been able to conceive the possibility of a peaceful coexistence of the two religions and saw in the advance of the Reformation's ideas a serious problem that might lead to insecurity and chaos. The 1560s did not entirely disconfirm this view, but that feverish decade made Montaigne understand that the Reformation was not going to disappear from one day to the next. The Wars of Religion would be ended only over the long haul.[i] Gradually, and perhaps also for personal reasons, his relatively intransigent position at the beginning of

---

[i] In actuality, the Wars of Religion ended only in 1610—that is, almost half a century after the massacre in Vassy.

the 1560s changed after a series of negative experiences in which he discovered that his political allies were not necessarily of the same religious persuasion as he. Rather than a sudden political conversion, it was a matter of a slow ideological evolution toward the center.

This political drift toward positions that favored understanding and compromise resulted primarily from his negative experience in the parlementary milieu. Montaigne became much more pragmatic than most of his contemporaries and developed a realist conception of politics and of power in general. In 1568, a Huguenot *Memorandum* described these moderates as "*politiques*, because they strive to maintain peace and are opposed to disturbances."[1] Montaigne was opposed to disturbances, and thus became a *politique* after having long thought that the initial religious disorders had been resolved with firmness. He had never been a fighting man, and confrontation was alien to his temperament; for lack of a better solution, tolerance was imperative for the sake of a necessary civil peace.

Political alliances are often determined by time-specific career choices and do not always reflect personal ideological convictions. Over ten years, Montaigne had been subjected to professional arrangements and accommodations more than he had shaped them. The parlement was naturally a site of political confrontation, but it had also recently become an arena of "combat" where competing clienteles did battle and where each camp counted its supporters and soldiers, who did not always join their camp because they agreed with its political or religious views. In the parlement, one had to have a professional alignment, because internal promotions depended on a pronounced clientele system. Montaigne had been marginalized at the time of his transfer from the Cour des Aides in Périgueux, and it took him several years to get accepted as a councillor. He had come into the magistracy by the back door and had never really succeeded in entering a clan in a clear and distinct way, at least in the eyes of the other members of the parlement. Montaigne's failure to fully commit himself ended up leaving the impression that he lacked convictions, at a time when religious incidents were increasing in Guyenne at an alarming rate. Montaigne also had few effective supporters in either the Great Chamber or among the presidents of the two Chambres des Enquêtes or of the Tournelle. This reality suddenly became obvious in 1569, when an opportunity to enter the Great Chamber arose, thanks to his seniority. This was a necessary stage for anyone hoping to someday be president of one of the parlement's chambers.

The atmosphere was not really propitious for rational decisions in 1569 and 1570. The parlement's usual operating rules had been replaced by considerations that were more political than professional, and relations between the diverse factions had deteriorated to the point that its sessions were regularly the scene of exceptionally violent verbal exchanges. Recusal had remained the weapon of choice for keeping one's enemies at a distance, and it was invoked during almost every deliberation of the assembled chambers. The parlement's sessions turned into family quarrels with insinuations, insults, and accusations exchanged in private and in public. It was in this context, which was not very favorable for career advancement, and following important changes that had taken place in his private life—notably the death of his father, taking up residence in the château of Montaigne, and the birth of his daughter Léonor—that Montaigne had an opportunity to be promoted to the Great Chamber. The Bordeaux parlement's *Registres secrets* report the debate that took place on this occasion and give the names of the four councillors of the Chambre des Enquêtes who were supposed to benefit from this career advancement.[2]

The Break with the Parlement

Montaigne's family name had allowed him to join the magistracy, but he quickly discovered that this name could turn against him and prevent him from entering the Great Chamber or becoming president of one of the two Chambres des Enquêtes. In fact, in 1569, when he had just made an administrative request to his peers to join one of the two upper chambers (the Tournelle and the Great Chamber), he suffered an unexpected and categorical refusal, on the ground that members of his family were already part of these chambers: the lord of La Chassaigne, his brother-in-law, presided over the first Chambre des Enquêtes, while Richard de Lestonnac, his sister's husband, served in the second. He was asked to obtain a dispensation from the king. In the eyes of a majority of the members of the parlement, there were already too many Montaignes in key posts at the Palais de l'Ombrière. This was a technical problem that could usually be worked around without too much difficulty, but Montaigne had powerful enemies. This refusal was a real thunderbolt for him, but it was also a revelation that forced him to reconsider his future within that honorable institution. The author of the *Essais* tells us nothing about this humiliating episode, and the exact circumstances of the abandonment of his judicial career remain rather vague.[3] However, it is possible to reconstitute what triggered this first withdrawal from public life.

At the precise moment when it was finally Montaigne's turn to accede to the Great Chamber, after a long stay in the first Chambre des Enquêtes, he gave up his career as a member of the parlement. Perhaps he found it incompatible with his dignity to request a dispensation, even though it was generally granted in such cases. In any event, he chose not to comply with this bureaucratic procedure. This refusal was more a symptom than the cause of his break with the parlement, because it was the logical outcome of several years of marginalization in a milieu full of intrigues and machinations. His decision was certainly motivated by the disapproval of which he had been the object, but this incident in his career was only the straw that broke the camel's back. Montaigne was accused of having too many relatives in the parlement, but he was not the only one, far from it, who had family ties to other magistrates. In this squabble he rightly saw a personal attack. A royal dispensation would have led to a debate in the parlement, and on that point nothing could be taken for granted in this time of political schemes and negotiations.

To realize how isolated Montaigne was at the Bordeaux parlement in 1569, all we have to do is consider the farcical circumstances of this incident. Since his father's death, he had not been very assiduous in the first Chambre des Enquêtes, and his friends had distanced themselves from him. His usual supports (all members of his family) were also the targets of political attacks mounted by zealous Catholics who had adopted a policy of religious cleansing of the parlement's four chambers. The moment of his promotion was therefore rather badly chosen. Nevertheless, according to tradition, Montaigne's seniority should have allowed him to enter the Great Chamber. His turn had finally come when he found himself at the center of internal struggles that overwhelmed him. It is almost ludicrous to report these two days in detail, as they are related in the parlement of Bordeaux's *Registres secrets* according to Savignac's transcription. The session of Monday, November 14, 1569, inventories the episodes of a serious procedural conflict.

To form the new chambers in the customary manner, the chambers had assembled under the presidencies of Christophe de Roffignac, Antoine de Belcier, Louis Goyet de La Ferrière, and Joseph de La Chassaigne. The parlement's clerk, Jacques de Pontac, reported the deliberations of this stormy session. Despite his absence, Lagebaston was named first president, but not without difficulty. As a precaution, he had decided not to attend the session, because he had been denounced as a heretic, and, despite the support of the king's men, he feared being arrested. Several councillors declared that they had information that made him ineligible "because he is with the rebels, enemies of the king."[4] These were not new accusations; Lagebaston had long been seen as a sympathizer with the Protestant cause whose policy of conciliation did not enjoy unanimous support. The attacks on him were also motivated by personal career considerations. President Roffignac wanted to get rid of him and spared no effort to have him recognized as an enemy of the king and of the parlement. Several members of the parlement coveted a nomination to the Great Chamber, and for them this first plenary session of the parlement was an opportunity to count their supporters and their enemies.

Montaigne did not attend this assembly; that was assuredly a mistake on his part. Was he ill? It is possible that the fall from a horse that he recounts in the

Essais dates from this period, which would explain his absence. He devotes almost three pages to this serious accident, which occurred in late 1569 or early 1570, and as a result of which he was unconscious for several hours. After a terrible collision with another horseman, Montaigne was thrown to the ground, unconscious. His friends even thought for a time that he was dead, and they had a hard time getting him back on his feet. Badly bruised both in body and in soul, Montaigne felt that his life was escaping him: "I closed my eyes in order, it seemed to me, to help push it out, and took pleasure in growing languid and letting myself go."[5] However, if this accident had prevented him from going to Bordeaux, we would find his request to be excused, but the *Registres secrets* mention no such request. Those who had reported sick were always announced at the beginning of the session. We know that Montaigne was also not on a mission at the Court. Was he perhaps busy with private affairs on his lands, or did he simply anticipate the agitation that was going to reign during this first session of the parlement? Not attending the usual negotiations could only be disadvantageous for him, because those who are absent often lose out. This absence was, moreover, badly interpreted, because President Lagebaston, who had only minority support and was being harassed about his religion, had also decided to stay away from this first assembly. From this it could be inferred that they had been in cahoots, and subsequent events lend some support to that hypothesis.

Charles Dusault, one of the attorneys general, replied that he had long ago presented to the court the evidence requested regarding First President Lagebaston, and that he was still waiting for a decree to be issued to deprive Lagebaston of his office. Despite his political supports, Lagebaston was in the minority again. Montaigne was known for being on good terms with him and had not called for his suspension. The attorney general repeated his demand that an end be put to the suspicions of heresy against the first president, but that did not take into account the plot that had been brewing in the Palais de l'Ombrière ever since the summer.

President Belcier intervened to explain that even though the required evidence against Lagebaston had been reported, it would still take ten or twelve days for it to be validated by the parlement. Belcier asked that this evidence be presented again so that the court could form an opinion about it. He recused himself, but insisted that the king's men themselves should assemble as a chamber at the Tournelle in order to debate this question, adding that he would gladly serve in that chamber to observe the deliberations.

Councillor Jean du Duc answered that he had studied for a long time the charges brought against Lagebaston, and had even prepared a report that he could present immediately to the court. He admitted, however, that he had left this report in his office and proposed that, if it pleased the court, the discussion be put off until the following day. He argued that since Lagebaston still presided over the Great Chamber, there was no reason not to inform the chambers before the presentation of the report concerning him. He suggested to his colleagues that during their next session they proceed to the reading of the evidence collected on Lagebaston. Everyone who was absent (including Montaigne) was counted as present; "if in the interim they write to have a longer extension," their personal excuses connected with this absence would be discussed later. We see that Montaigne's absence was probably considered political rather than medical.

After a few points of order and procedure, the promotions were nonetheless made. Councillor Richard de Lestonnac—Montaigne's brother-in-law—was designated to sit at the Tournelle, but he refused to serve under Belcier's presidency. He complained that Belcier had insulted him when he was presiding over the Great Chamber. Lestonnac supported First President Lagebaston, and Belcier was in the camp of the Catholics led by Roffignac. Thus for Lestonnac it was inconceivable that he would serve at the Tournelle under Belcier's presidency. This quarrel between Belcier and Lestonnac was nothing new; for several years there had been a deep animosity between the two men. Lestonnac begged the court to excuse him from serving at the Tournelle and adduced several precedents based on personality incompatibilities among the members of the parlement. For the time being it was decided to remove him from the Tournelle to avoid a probable confrontation. In his turn, Belcier took the floor to explain that it was he who had been insulted by Lestonnac, and not the other way around, and that, as a question of honor, he had decided not to make public his dispute with Lestonnac, and had therefore not talked to the presidents. He deplored the cabal mounted against him by Lestonnac and his friends, insinuating that Montaigne belonged to this clan.

Montaigne was indirectly implicated in both the discussion regarding Lagebaston and the quarrel between Belcier and Lestonnac. When the agenda finally made it possible to move on to the question of promotions to the Great Chamber, the climate was no longer very favorable to Montaigne. After deliberating, and in accord with the strict rule of seniority, it was decided that four councillors from the Enquêtes would rise to the Great Chamber: the names of François de Nort, Hugues Casaulx, Antoine de Poynet, and Michel Eyquem de Montaigne were initially mentioned. However, several councillors denounced Montaigne's promotion, arguing that "the aforementioned de Montaigne was incompatible in the Great Chamber with the aforementioned councillor Lestonnac, because he is his brother-in-law, and in the Tournelle because President de Lachassaigne is his father-in-law, so that it would be wise to reconsider."[6] Joseph de La Chassaigne had been named president on October 1, 1568, and was received into his new office on July 18, 1569. The family ties between the La Chassaignes and the Montaignes now worked against the two families.

After deliberation, it was ruled that Montaigne would remain in the first Chambre des Enquêtes and that his seat in the Great Chamber would be given to François Fayard, who like Montaigne had been a councillor since 1561 and also originally came from the Cour des Aides in Périgueux.[ii] All the same, a commitment was made to reexamine the deliberations regarding his promotion "when the aforementioned de Montaigne shall have obtained a dispensation from the king."[7] Absent on that day, Montaigne could not defend himself. His colleagues had just denounced once again the overrepresentation and excessive power (perceived as such by at least some people) of the Montaigne clan within the parlement. All this was, of course, a pretext for forcing Montaigne to make political choices. The demand for a dispensation to which he had to submit was a rather effective way of exercising political pressure that would allow his opponents to bring him into the group of intransigent Catholics. Even though such a dispensation was not very difficult to obtain, it would nonetheless oblige Montaigne to yield and join a clan if he was to have any hope of pursuing his career.

The situation created in November 1569 testifies to the difficulty in which Montaigne found himself at that time, isolated and without genuine support in the parlement. Without knowing it, he was perceived as being politically aligned with the sympathizers with the Reformation; a rather paradoxical situation and contrary to his own religious convictions. Anyway, nothing was firmly settled, since the court had to consider his promotion on the basis of the arguments presented in his defense. The court would have to deliberate again once the royal dispensation had been granted. The same day, it was also ruled that Lestonnac would serve at the Tournelle "as being in his rank," despite his request seeking not to sit in the same chamber as Belcier. This decision in favor of Belcier and Roffignac could be perceived as a defeat for the Montaigne clan. After considering several procedural points, the assembly finally moved on to the formation of the chambers.[iii] Adding insult to injury, Montaigne was for the first

---

[ii] François Fayard, lord of Chasseloup, died suddenly on September 4, 1570. His son, Pierre, took over his father's office as councillor at the parlement of Bordeaux in December 1570.

[iii] The composition of the chambers for the year 1569–70 was the following: the Great Chamber had two presidents, Christophe de Roffignac and Louis Goyet de La Ferrière; eighteen councillors: Charles de Malvyn, Denis de Baulon, Jean de Gascq, Jean de Mabrun, Jean d'Auzaneau, Louis de Gentils, Laurent de Lagear, Jacques Massiot, Pierre de Pomiés, Joseph Eymar, Pierre du Duc, Pierre Ducasse, Estienne de Beaunom, Jean Rignac, Florent de Nort, Hugues Casaulx, Antoine de Poynet, and François Fayard. La Tournelle also had two presidents: Antoine de Belcier and Joseph de La Chassaigne; and eleven councillors: Jean de Monenh, Richard de Lestonnac, Joseph d'Alis, Jean Mérignac, Jean de Massey, Jean de Lange, Gabriel de Cruseau, Mathurin Gilibert, François d'Alesme, Joseph d'Andrault, and Geoffroy de Malvyn. The presidents named to the first

time relegated to the second Chambre des Enquêtes, where several of his ene-mies sat.[iv]

The next day, Tuesday, November 15, 1569, the court assembled again under the aegis of First President Christophe de Roffignac, a declared enemy of Lage-baston in the parlement, in order to hear Louis de Lansac, a representative of the king and a member of his Privy Council, explain what had led him to in-tervene directly before the court. He reminded his audience that as a sign of goodwill his Majesty had made an exception and authorized the nomination of a sixth president in the Bordeaux court. Up to that time, the members of the parlement had not been able to agree on a name, and the king was beginning to become impatient. Lansac reprimanded the councillors for their incessant disputes and proposed that the new president be received as soon as possible. He also reported that a complaint had been made against the councillor Ber-trand de Camain, lord of La Tour-Carnet, because his wife belonged to "the new sect." After examining this complaint, Lansac rejected it and encouraged the court to proceed rapidly to nominate Camain as a councillor. The Ca-mains were close to the Montaignes, since Thibaud de Camain, a brother of the councillor Bertrand de Camain, was to marry Montaigne's sister, Léonor, in 1581. Montaigne recalled Lansac's political support when the following year he dedicated part of La Boétie's writings to him. In this quarrel between four or five parlementary families, we see emerging the political lines that had been created in relation to the religious sympathies of the members of the par-lement—religion serving, of course, as a pretext for dissimulating the real stakes, which were political and thus less respectable. Montaigne's lack of com-mitment alongside the zealous Catholics and his good relations with Lagebas-ton, Lestonnac, and Camain reinforced his image as a *politique* and worked against him when the time came to accede to a position of power within the parlement.

Chambre des Enquêtes were Léonard d'Alesme and François de La Guyonnie; ten in number, the councillors of the first chamber included François de Merle, Bertrand Duplessis, Mathurin Gilibert, Raymond de Pontac, Antoine de Castera, Christophe Babiault, Pierre de Cruseau, Geoffroy de La Martonie, and Jean de Gascq. The second Chambre des Enquêtes was presided over by Jacques Robert de Lignerac and had eight councillors: Pierre Blanchier, Jean du Faure, Sarran de Lalanne, François de Merle, Mi-chel Eyquem de Montaigne, François Gaultier, Romain de Mullet, Bernard Pichon, and Guillaume de La Chassaigne. François de La Roche and Charles du Saulx were advocates general; Jean de Lahet was the general prosecutor.

[iv] On this point, the different transcriptions of the *Registres secrets* diverge. The Savignac version (Bibliothèque municipale de Bordeaux) gives Montaigne's name in the second Chambre des Enquêtes, while Verthamon d'Ambloy's version (Archives munici-pales de Bordeaux) lists Montaignac, not Montaigne, in the second chamber (without giving the name "Montaigne" in any of the chambers).

Roffignac reminded Lansac that several councillors—including the Montaigne clan—had been recused in what had become "the affair of the sixth president," but he thought that those who had not been recused could deliberate in all serenity. Hoping to make inevitable the choice of a president favorable to the party of the Catholic zealots, he suggested hearing a report by the councillor François Gaultier on the situation in Bazas and La Réole. The Protestants had approached Bazas and had seized the Franciscan convent, thereby arousing the indignation of the people of Bordeaux. This regrettable episode led Roffignac to say that the Huguenots were the declared enemies of the kingdom. The *politiques* were offended by this conclusion, and after the report had been read, Charles de Malvyn—an old friend of Montaigne's—asked to be recused as a sign of protest and giving as a pretext the fact that his wife and that of the general prosecutor were relatives in the fourth degree.

Faced with the Catholics' power play, a great many councillors recused themselves and left the court to express their displeasure. Gilibert was the first to go, on the pretext that he had formerly done business with Roffignac, and that this prevented him from delivering any objective judgment. For him, this was a way of distancing himself from Roffignac and signaling his membership in Lagebaston's camp. He was followed by La Martonie and Castera, who invoked reasons just as extravagant, claiming that they had once refused to accept the king's general prosecutor as a judge in a proceeding that he had brought against a certain Pichon, the city hall clerk. The most preposterous excuses were presented to allow the councillors opposed to Roffignac to recuse themselves. As a mark of their displeasure with Roffignac's maneuver, about ten councillors chose to express their support for Lagebaston in this way. But they had lost the battle of the nominations and found themselves in the minority again during this first plenary session.

La Ferrière, the second president of the Great Chamber, also left, saying that he had been recused a few days earlier by the general prosecutor on the ground of a dispute he had had with Charles de Montferrand, the lieutenant governor of Bordeaux. But the recusal was not judged acceptable, and the court forced him to attend the deliberations. In their turn, Baulon, father and son, Monenh, Gaultier, Mullet, and Mabrun all asked to be recused on account of a disagreement they were supposed to have had with Roffignac over an earlier trial. Finally, two presidents of the Great Chamber and ten councillors of the first Chambre des Enquêtes were recused or recognized as absent. Confronted by the problem of attaining a quorum, Alesme, the president of the first Chambre des Enquêtes, proposed bringing the two investigative chambers together to judge the case and render the necessary rulings: "this having been done, all the aforementioned who had left because they were recused, returned to the chamber. The said Alesme, president [of the investigative chamber] recalled the said court to consider whether, given that of the first investigative chamber there were only 8 councillors and a president, and of the second 7 councillors, it would be good that they assemble [together] and make only one common chamber . . . in order to obtain a sufficient number to pass judgment."[8]

After deliberations, it was ruled that the two investigative chambers would remain as they were; that Guillaume de La Chassaigne, a councillor in the second Chambre des Enquêtes, would serve in the first, while President La Chassaigne would go to preside over the aforementioned second chamber and would serve at the same time as a councillor until a sufficient number of councillors could sign the rulings. Gascq, a councillor in the first chamber, was also temporarily transferred to the second to replace Guillaume de La Chassaigne. It was probably in this way that Montaigne was transferred to the second chamber. On the whole, it could be said that Roffignac won and that Lagebaston's days were numbered. He was suspended in June 1570. More than ever, the parlement was divided into two camps, and Montaigne was on the side of the defeated. His promotion to the Great Chamber had taken a political turn, and it was henceforth impossible for him to envision his parlementary career in a strictly professional perspective.

On November 16, the king's attorneys general, La Roche and Dusault, confirmed that the evidence concerning Lagebaston had been registered. Roffignac repeated his complaint, according to which he had been insulted by Lagebaston and that his honor had been besmirched. The preceding day's scenario was played out again. To show his exasperation with the plenary powers Roffignac was seizing, Alesme left after declaring that he too had exchanged unfortunate words with the general prosecutor, Lahet, regarding the brotherhood of the Saint-Sacrement, and that this constituted grounds for recusing him. Then Joseph de La Chassaigne left, stating that Roffignac had addressed insulting words to him, "because La Chassaigne would not want to be Roffignac's judge here."[9] Out of solidarity, the councillor Guillaume de La Chassaigne also left the chamber after recusing himself because of the dispute between Roffignac and Joseph Eymar.

The clan of the La Chassaignes and the Montaignes was the big loser in this final confrontation. Montaigne had preferred to keep his distance and not participate in these jousts at the parlement. It is true that Montaigne's presence would not have changed much. He was paying the price for stakes that went far beyond him, and it is hard to see how, in the charged climate of the parlement, a dispensation, even if granted by the king, could have been well received by his peers. Only one option remained available to him: leaving with his head held high a parlement that had been transformed into a shop where everything was for sale and could be haggled over. From that moment on, the name Montaigne no longer appears in the parlement's *Registres secrets*. The refusal he suffered was a regular slap in the face, and this ultimate insult marked a complete break for him. Fayard began serving in the Great Chamber the following day. This final setback led Montaigne to leave the Palais de l'Ombrière forever and to take temporary refuge on his seigneurial lands.

The situation in the region was rapidly deteriorating, and in early January 1570, President La Chassaigne and several councillors at the parlement were arrested and detained in Blaye, a town situated on the right bank of the Gironde that had been controlled by the Protestants since October 1568. Captain Piles, Count Montgomery, and a few horsemen had crossed the Dordogne at Castillon, not far from Montaigne's château, and seized several noblemen's houses between Castillon and Saint-Émilion.[10] It was becoming difficult for Montaigne to move around, and his membership in the parlement made him an easy target and potential hostage. His journeys to Bordeaux were no longer safe, and he had to protect his château from hostile intrusions. The usual ideological and political landmarks had been overthrown and the enemy (whoever it was) was at his door. For him, the preservation of his family heritage was a priority that had suddenly taken precedence over his preoccupations as a member of the parlement.

After a first career in the parlement that his father had imposed on him in the 1550s, Montaigne decided to leave the magistracy and to turn over a new leaf. Three months later, on April 10, 1570, he sold his councillor's office to Florimond de Raemond[11] for 8,400 *livres tournois*, a significant sum that was, however, about average in his time. For instance, in 1585 Robert Bochard sold his office as a councillor in the Paris parlement to Francis III Miron for 6,000 *livres*.[12] Montaigne's annual remuneration had not changed for almost ten years, and did not exceed 400 *livres* in 1570.[13] The councillors who served at the Tournelle received a supplement of 50 *livres* a year, but salaries were depressed by the multiplication of the number of officials. We cannot say that the professional investment made between 1563 and 1569 had brought Montaigne much. To complete his frustration, his colleague at the Cour des Aides in Périgueux, François Fayard, had taken his place in the Great Chamber, even though he had served as reporter on only sixteen occasions between 1562 and 1567, while Montaigne had done so thirty-seven times during the same period, not to mention the numerous missions and journeys he had undertaken. Fayard was the very image of a rather self-effacing official little inclined to draw attention to himself. But in the politics of the parlement, he was the one who had played his cards right and taken Montaigne's seat in the Great Chamber.

Giving up his office as a member of the parlement was not an easy decision to make, because it involved running the risk of losing his title of nobility—which had been acquired on the basis of his membership in the parlement—but Montaigne was fairly confident. Since the death of his father, he had been living nobly on his lands, and the hundred-year period of the prescription of nobility (true nobility) was almost up. It was a question of a few years, because the Eyquems had purchased the noble house of Montaigne in 1477. Since the parlement had ceased to offer him a career equal to his ambitions, Montaigne would henceforth be a full-time gentleman. He could not be accused of activity not befitting a noble, since he had deliberately kept his distance from the commercial world.[v] In particular, he had been careful not to engage in commerce,[14] and following in his father's lineage, he would have no difficulty being perceived as a lord and a gentleman by his neighbors. This clear separation from the third estate (bourgeois or *robin*) was soon transformed into an ethos in the *Essais*; noble ambitions rapidly replaced judicial pretensions.[15]

The nomination of Florimond de Raemond to the office of councillor at the parlement of Bordeaux left vacant by Montaigne's resignation took place on July 23, 1571.[16] On September 7 of the same year, Montaigne's sale of his office to Florimond de Raemond was ratified for the sénéchaussée of the Agenais by Me Robert Raymond, councillor at the présidial court.[17] Montaigne thus recovered the investment made in his office as a councillor. The availability of his office allowed his cousin Geoffroy Montaigne de Bussaguet to become a councillor in his turn and to follow in the footsteps of the Eyquems in the parlement. Montaigne lent him 2,000 *livres* to purchase this office, and Geoffroy was received on January 22, 1571. He had a long career in the parlement of Bordeaux, where he sat until 1613.

Montaigne's personal life, and more particularly his relationship with his wife, could also have played a role in his decision to give up his office in the parlement and to spend more time in his château and on his lands. A receipt given by Antoinette de Louppes to Michel de Montaigne in May 1569, for "a gold chain" that Michel had found in one of his wife's coffers, where Arnaud de Montaigne, his recently deceased younger brother, had left it, but which Antoinette claimed as her property, makes us wonder how much significance to attribute to this enigmatic and incredible episode in his private life:

Today, the 23rd day of May, 1569, in the château of Montaigne in Périgord, the noble Michel de Montaigne, lord of the said place, speaking to Lady Antoinette de Louppes, his mother, declared to her that he had found in the chests of his wife a gold chain that the late noble Arnaud de Montaigne, lord of Saint-Martin, his brother had left there; which the aforementioned damoiselle de Louppes said appertains and belongs to her and requires it to be given back to her. And the lord of Montaigne, in the

---

[v] In 1560, an ordinance of Orléans (article 258) forbade any noble from engaging in commerce.

presence and with the consent of the nobles Thomas de Montaigne, lord of Beauregard, and Pierre de Montaigne, lord of La Brousse, brothers of the aforesaid Saint-Martin, has presently given and delivered this gold chain to the aforesaid de Louppes, which she has received.[18]

This strange document has been interpreted in different ways. Some have wondered whether Montaigne's wife had a romantic relationship with Montaigne's youngest brother, Arnaud, before the latter's death in 1569.[19] The suspicion of an adulterous affair between Captain Saint-Martin and Françoise de Montaigne, while her husband was spending most of his time away from the château, on mission or at the parlement in Bordeaux, gives a domestic twist to this episode. Since he had presided over the distribution of his brother's property after his sudden death, Montaigne might have been astonished not to find the gold chain that had belonged to his brother in inventory of his goods. Suspicious, he might have searched his wife's coffers, where he found the infamous chain. Montaigne's mother then came to the aid of her daughter-in-law by claiming that this chain belonged to her and that she had first lent it to her youngest son before giving it to her daughter-in-law. We will never know the real story behind this family dispute, because the accusations that might be made against Françoise depend on pure conjecture. However, it has to be recognized that this incident had taken on enough importance for Montaigne to have it recorded before a notary and in the presence of his brothers. He wanted to leave a legal paper trail of this testamentary imbroglio. It has been suggested that the austere conception of marriage Montaigne developed predisposed him be a cuckold.[20] However, economic considerations are always to be taken into account in this kind of family problem. In view of the value of this chain, we understand that the dispute had to be settled in an official manner before a notary.

This family episode could also explain Montaigne's views on marriage: "We do not marry for ourselves, whatever we say; we marry just as much or more for our posterity, for our family. The practice and benefit of marriage concerns our race very far beyond us."[21] Thus, for Montaigne, marriage's function is to provide descendants, preferably male if one wants to transmit the name of the family and ensure its posterity. Montaigne's marriage was a failure. The remarkable absence of Françoise de La Chassaigne from the *Essais* is revelatory of a misfortune; after 1580, the name of the La Chassaignes was more an obstacle than an advantage on the social level. Not only had Françoise failed to give Montaigne a male heir, but she also constantly reminded her husband of an alliance that had turned out badly. In his *Essais*, Montaigne chose not to expatiate on the parlementary milieu that he had left behind and remained silent on his wife's antecedents.

For the nobility, having children was primarily a social activity; Montaigne irrevocably separates marriage from the pleasures of the body and from feelings: "Those who think to honor marriage by joining love to it act, it seems to me, the same as those who, to favor virtue, hold that nobility is nothing else but virtue."[22] He even feels a certain shame for wanting to reconcile the two: "I have seen in my time, in high place, love shamefully and dishonorably cured by marriage."[23] The pleasures of marriage are related to those of monastic life, regulated and ordered: "Marriage is a religious and holy bond. That is why the pleasure we derive from it should be a restrained pleasure, serious, and mixed with some austerity."[24] A successful marriage is also based on a subtle mixture of blindness and deafness: "That man knew what it was all about, it seems to me, who said that a good marriage was one made between a blind wife and a deaf husband."[25] Montaigne could have applied this quip to his personal situation. Françoise opted to close her eyes, and he seems never to have heard his wife's reproaches.

In the *Essais*, the conception of marriage is similar to that of friendship. Thus, like friendship, marriage has its own contradictions. It is based on a desire that cannot be satisfied because it denies a woman's sexuality and transforms her into a kind of friend. Montaigne explicitly formulates a parallel between these two states: "A good marriage, if such there be, rejects the company and conditions of love. It tries to reproduce those of friendship."[26] The idealization of marriage moves this institution closer to perfect friendship. The author of the *Essais* declares that the sole merit he grants the Platonists on this subject is to have declared that love inevitably evolves into friendship. When he was sojourning in Paris in September 1570, he sent his wife La Boétie's French translation of Plutarch's "Consolation to his wife," to remind her that his absence was a proof of friendship, because "It does not befit a gallant man, according to the rules of this time, to continue to court and caress you."[27] The deceased friend—La Boétie—reminds him, it seems, of another desire that has long since vanished. He harshly reproaches his wife who, after four years of marriage, has still succeeded only in giving him a daughter: "Having no child other than a long-awaited daughter, at the end of four years of our marriage, you had to suffer her loss in the second year of her life."[28] Here Montaigne confuses months with years (Thoinette died two months after her birth), as if he had already lost the memory of this death. "My wife, let us live, you and I, in the old French way," Montaigne goes on, drawing a parallel between his relationship of friendship with his wife and the noble tradition. He also recalls chivalric values, as if they had been transmitted to him by his father and his ancestors.

Montaigne's views on marriage are in perfect accord with the noble ideal that considers the wife a "perfect friend" (*parfaite amye*). The woman's role is to renew the race and to produce male descendants. In this regard, Montaigne's mother had done her duty, and Pierre Eyquem could be proud of having ensured the transmission to his first-born son not only of his name (Eyquem), but also of his seigneury. We shall see later that Montaigne was to develop this conception of marriage at length after 1585, notably in the chapter "On some verses of Virgil" (III: 5) in the third book of the *Essais*.

A period of hesitation, falsely presented as a definitive withdrawal from the affairs of the world, followed the permanent agitation of the Palais de l'Ombrière. Montaigne henceforth resided as a lord on his lands, deliberately keeping his distance from the storm raging in Bordeaux. During the winter of 1571, he had a tower built on one corner of his home. The ground floor had a chapel; the second floor a bedroom; and the third a study, which he transformed into a *librerie* that was "a handsome one among country libraries."[29] In the margins of the Bordeaux Copy Montaigne specifies the location of his library: "It is on the third floor of a tower; the first is my chapel, the second a bedroom and a dressing room where I often sleep in order to be alone. Above it is a great wardrobe. In the past it was the most useless place in my house."[30] He provided himself with the means to begin a new career by having maxims painted on the beams and joists of his library, having shelves installed to hold the books he had inherited from La Boétie, and having mottos and bucolic scenes painted on some of the walls of his tower. In a word, he prepared a studious framework to house his new activity. This founding moment is literally inscribed on one wall of the tower, at the threshold of his library:

> In the year of our Lord 1571, aged thirty-eight, on the day before the calends of March, the anniversary of his birth, Michel de Montaigne, long weary of the court [and of] the servitude of the Parlement and public offices, still in the prime of life, retired to the bosom of the learned Virgins, where, in peace and security, he shall spend the days that remain to him to live. May destiny allow him to complete this habitation, this sweet retreat of his ancestors, which he has devoted to his liberty, his tranquility, and his leisure.[31]

Montaigne thus decided to live nobly on his lands. We are told the motive for this "whim": he had long been exasperated by the servitude of the parlement and public offices, which can be understood. Peace and security had become a priority for him, even if a vain hope. Giving up his career in the magistracy was a decisive turning point. Far from being the outcome of mature reflection, this decision probably resulted from less respectable motives: as ambitious as all of his colleagues in the parlement, Montaigne had seen himself refused an advancement that he nonetheless deserved according to his seniority. This period of transition, which was supposed to mark his "retreat" from the world and to express his weariness—more certainly his disappointment—and his desire to spend the rest of his life studying the Ancients, led him to set new priorities, both familial and political. Perhaps he foresaw a favorable destiny that would allow him to make a place for himself in politics. As if to make his own destiny, he had carved a very suggestive—though sufficiently ambiguous, which must have pleased him—maxim on the seventh joist of his *librerie*. When he raised his eyes, he henceforth saw a Greek epigram by Palladas translated into Latin by George Buchanan, his former teacher at the College of Guyenne: "If the fates carry you, put up with the fates, and let yourself be carried. Those who put up with them, are carried along by the fates, but if you do not put up with them, they will carry you away."[32] That is a whole program. On September 9 of the same year, Montaigne's daughter Léonor was born; she was his only child who survived him. We can also imagine a period of intense social activity that brought him closer to his powerful neighbors, the Foix-Gursons.

Once he had broken with the world of the magistracy, Montaigne showed his aristocratic ambitions more and more conspicuously all through the 1570s. If he had been a *robin* in the 1560s, he was a gentleman in the 1570s, moving from the magistracy to the country nobility just as his ancestors had moved from the bourgeoisie to a seminobility by purchasing the noble land of Montaigne. The making of the lord of Montaigne dates from the 1570s. However, the sword worn by his father was not for him, and he replaced it with the pen. Writing would leave a trace of this noble life. The society of the Renaissance was structured in accord with two modes of organization. It was divided into orders that had historically raised rigid barriers between them, even if in practice there were many gateways linking them, for instance, between the third estate and the nobility.[33] The traditional gap between a political power that has long taken refuge behind the defense of its prerogatives and an emerging economic power that is still kept from participating in political decisions, but has nonetheless succeeded in finding other ways of creating for itself a sphere of power at the regional level—of which the parlements were the privileged expression—was greatly reduced during the second half of the sixteenth century. Montaigne is a characteristic example of the *robin* who suddenly moved in the direction of the true nobility and in very short order constructed a gentleman's life for himself.

But as we shall see, he could not have achieved this social ascent without major support from the high nobility, which saw in him an intermediary capable of serving their own ambitions. Renaissance society was also based on clientele relationships.[34] Montaigne made a place for himself in a clientele system and put himself under the protection of a few families of the high nobility of Guyenne. Although during his years in the parlement he had always refused to be affiliated with a clan of *robins*, now he did not hesitate to seek the sponsorship of powerful lords to realize his ambitions. This system of socialization was based on an "exchange" between a patron and a client: the patron provides protection for the client, who puts himself at the former's disposition, subjecting himself to him. This allegiance constitutes a kind of voluntary servitude, but it is never contractual, because the relationship of dependency can be broken at any time by one of the parties. Its efficacy is generally gauged over the long term and is based on bonds that are loose enough to keep the patron and the client from feeling any precise obligation to each other.

On October 18, 1571, eighteen months after ending his career as a magistrate, Montaigne received a letter from Charles IX informing him that he had just been named a knight of the Order of Saint Michael, a rather extraordinary reward if we consider that at that time he had not yet accomplished anything, that in addition he did not belong to the high or the middle nobility, and that he was far from being considered an important figure of his time. On the professional level, his career in the Bordeaux parlement might even be considered a failure.[35] Thus there is a genuine mystery that demands reflection. How was Montaigne able to be so suddenly introduced into the milieu of the middle nobility and to receive what was at that time considered to be the kingdom's highest distinction? We shall return to these honorific rewards that Montaigne was granted shortly after his unfortunate experience in the parlement.

In a first stage—the arrangement of his tower was part of this—Montaigne desired to resume an intellectual activity that had been lacking during his years at the parlement in Bordeaux. His library became a privileged site, and it was in this space of erudition that he sought the less burdensome company of the Greek and Roman thinkers. This was certainly a liberation in comparison to the parlementary milieu. Reading texts from Antiquity led him to rediscover, not without nostalgia, the Greek and Latin authors he had studied at the College of Guyenne. The legacy of La Boétie's library marked this learned period's point of departure. Montaigne felt that he was obligated to this friend whose religious and political ideas he had shared in the early 1560s. The time had come for him to pay homage to him by working in accord with the humanist values and ideals of his time. After having been Raymond Sebond's translator, Montaigne would be La Boétie's editor.

Montaigne as Editor of La Boétie's Works

The publication of La Boétie's works came logically after Montaigne's break with the Bordeaux parlement; it settled a dispute with the world he was leaving behind. Now he turned toward a new, exclusively princely audience. Montaigne understood that La Boétie could give him access to a social milieu with which he was still little acquainted. After the publication of his translation of Raymond Sebond's *Theologia naturalis* in 1569, having some of Estienne de La Boétie's works printed by Federic Morel[36] in 1571 was the second highlight of Montaigne's career as a man of letters. He had gone to Paris in 1570 to have La Boétie's manuscripts printed there; they appeared the following year.[37] This editorial work was a tryout for a future career as an author.

The choice of Morel as the printer was not arbitrary. He had printed Chancellor Michel de L'Hospital's works in 1558 and begun by specializing in short books on contemporary history, such as the *Chant sur la prise de Calais et de Guines*, the *Chant sur la prise de Thionville*, a poem on the marriage of Crown Prince Francis to Mary Stuart, an epistle addressed to Margaret of Savoy, Henry II's sister, and anonymous letters to the duke of Guise and the Cardinal of Lorraine. Printer to the king since October 1570, Morel's commitment to the cause of the extremist Catholics never flagged. In 1573, Morel attracted attention by printing a defense of the Saint Bartholomew's Day massacre, whose author was none other than Guy du Faur de Pibrac. In 1577, the most important work Morel printed was a justificatory history of the Guise family, including portraits of the two brothers, François and Charles of Lorraine.[vi] Similarly, in 1562 Morel had printed several booklets openly criticizing the edicts of tolerance as well as a Catholic version of the massacre at Vassy. In the same vein, the following year (1563) Morel published *Des Differens et troubles advenans entre les hommes par la diversité des opinions en la Religion*, by Loys Le Roy, who was an ardent defender of the political status quo.[38]

Montaigne had given up any ambitions in the parlement without having as yet officially thrown himself into a political career. He preferred to publish two short volumes in which he had collected his dead friend's incomplete drafts of what remained of his speeches, since no political text was included in the *Mesnagerie de Xenophon* or in *Vers françois de feu M. de La Boétie*. He had to finish this editorial undertaking before setting out to write *around* a more political La Boétie. At least that was his plan at the end of 1570. He had to finish publishing La Boétie before writing the *Essais*; perhaps it was a promise made to his friend as he lay on his deathbed. Because it contains not only a series of reported discourses and La Boétie's translations and poems, carefully edited by Montaigne, but also Montaigne's letter on his companion's death, the *Mesnagerie* plays a double role. These intertwined texts mark both the end of La Boétie's discourses and the beginning of the "tryouts" (*essais*) of Montaigne's

---

[vi] *Caroli Lotharingi cardinalis et Francisci ducis Guysii, literae et arma, in funebri oratione habita Nanij à N. Bocherio, theologo et ab eodem posteà latinè plenius explicata.*

discourse; they served as a bridge and allowed Montaigne to abandon his role as clerk and reporter and finally become an author. The construction of the *Essais* on the fragments and vestiges of La Boétie's texts is asserted as a project, and the publication of selected works by him marks an indispensable point of departure for the man who was forming political ambitions, no longer in the parlement, but at the royal Court.

In his preface to the reader, Montaigne recalls that, without him, La Boétie would simply not exist: "Reader, you owe to me everything that you enjoy of the late M. Estienne de la Boëtie: for I inform you that as for him, there is nothing here that he would ever have hoped to show you, or even that he would have thought worthy of bearing his name in public. But I, who am not so proud, having found nothing else in his library that he bequeathed to me by his testament, have not wished that it be lost."[39] As for La Boétie's political tracts, Montaigne declares that he has no intention of publishing them, because he "finds their fashioning too delicate and fair to leave them to the crude and heavy air of such an unpleasant season."[40] The Wars of Religion had been shaking France for eight years, and the *Discourse on Voluntary Servitude* and the *Memorandum* on the edict of January 1562, though they were mentioned by Montaigne in his preface to the reader of the *Mesnagerie*, were reserved for a later publication. However, in 1571, one year before the Saint Bartholomew's Day massacre and its deadly sequels in many of the kingdom's cities, including Bordeaux, Montaigne could still hope to publish the *Discourse* as a text on political theory detached from contemporary events. The "monarchomachs" had not yet entered the political landscape, and tirades against tyranny had not yet become the cornerstone of the Protestants' theological-political rhetoric.

After having been a translator, Montaigne made his way into the domain of letters by trying his hand as an editor. He grouped together a few scattered works by his dead friend to put together a volume in his memory. His contemporaries were grateful to him for undertaking this task. De Thou noted: "We are obliged to Michel de Montaigne, his close friend, for the fact that [La Boétie] is not entirely dead," adding that had he not died so young, La Boétie "would have been capable of the greatest things."[41] It fell to Montaigne to carry out these great political projects. The publication of La Boétie's works in *La Mesnagerie de Xenophon. Les Regles de mariage, de Plutarque. Lettre de consolation, de Plutarque à sa femme. Le tout traduict de Grec en François par feu M. Estienne de la Boetie Conseiller du Roy en sa court de Parlement à Bordeaux. Ensemble quelques Vers Latins et François, de son invention. Item, un Discours sur la mort dudit Seigneur De la Boëtie, par M. de Montaigne* (figure 6), represents the first stage in this transformation of Montaigne into his friend's political heir.

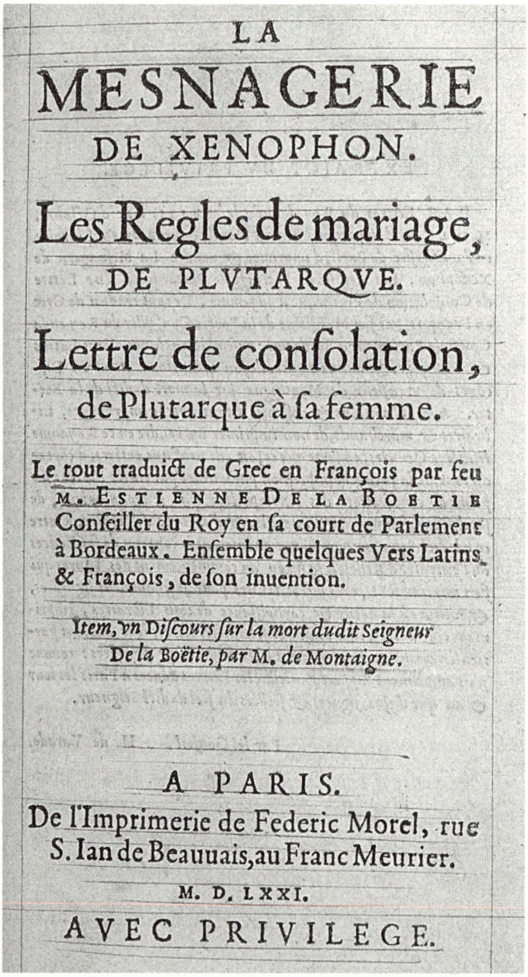

FIGURE 6. Title page of La Boétie's works edited by Montaigne (private collection).

The work Montaigne had published bore a "privilege"[vii] dated October 18, 1570, and its printing was completed on November 24, 1570. Montaigne had thus conceived this editorial project after resigning his position as a councillor. This publication symbolizes a genuine commemoration of La Boétie, whose memory was beginning to fade. Some have seen in it a *tombeau littéraire* celebrating La Boétie.[42] A second fascicle, printed at the same time and titled *Vers françois de feu Estienne de la Boetie Conseiller du Roy en sa Cour de Parlement*,

[vii] A privilege, or printing privilege, is an exclusive authorization to print a book. It is granted by royal or ecclesiastic authorities to a printer or bookseller for a limited time—usually between five and nine years. It is the precursor of modern copyrights.

was published by the same printer (a few copies bear the date 1572). This small octavo booklet had only nineteen numbered pages, but Montaigne insisted on printing it separately. He did in fact edit two works by La Boétie. This second booklet includes an epistle to Paul de Foix, La Boétie's translation of the twenty-second canto of Ariosto's *Orlando furioso* ("Bradamante's complaints"), as well as twenty-five sonnets by La Boétie. The letter to Paul de Foix, which serves as an introduction to this little volume, is dated September 1, 1570. Montaigne decided to bring together in the form of fragments the few pieces by La Boétie that were found after his death, in order to increase the impact of publishing them. This patchwork of texts that seem at first glance disjointed is governed by an editorial logic that is not without political intentions.

For Montaigne, the publication of La Boétie's "incomplete works"—because all of his political writings are lacking—represented his first entrance into the world of letters. In his "library" he had filled his bookshelves with volumes inherited from La Boétie seven years earlier. He had marked these works—mainly in Greek or in Greek and Latin—with the letter "b" followed by a period in the upper right corner of the title page, thus making it possible to distinguish his friend's books from his own.[43] His chief concern was to show his admiration for his late friend by publishing his translations as well as various poetic works, temporarily keeping aside his political texts, which he had the vague plan of reserving for his *Essais* or which he hoped to publish later. In late 1570, the political situation was relatively calm in France; the edict of Saint-Germain (August 8, 1570) led to a truce that it was thought would last, and that offered a brief respite favorable to this publication.

With that expectation, the void left by La Boétie was filled by the two disparate fascicles bringing together various short pieces. These works published by Montaigne in 1571 make us think of "patchworks" (*bigarrures*), that is, of a "curious mixture" composed of "fleeting pieces." They collect diverse texts without a precise theme or definite unity—the poems are mixed with the translations—except in the last part, which is a letter from Montaigne to his father, a document that is supposed to immortalize La Boétie's last moments. As we have seen, this letter of Montaigne's symbolizes the paradox of a friendship that could be expressed only by the other. La Boétie's friendship for Montaigne, recounted by Montaigne, is located in the parlementary milieu of the early 1560s, in a period of broad political reflection on the government of the kingdom and the limits of absolute monarchy. Through the intermediary of La Boétie, Montaigne soon associated himself (in 1580) with a debate that had marked the preceding generation. That was even what led him to publish his first text under his own name, while reserving La Boétie's political writings for another volume. According to Montaigne, there are several La Boéties. The first was political: the La Boétie of the *Discourse on Voluntary Servitude* and the *Memorandum* on the January edict. That La Boétie was soon stolen from Montaigne, appropriated by Simon Goulart and the Protestant pamphleteers. The second La Boétie, the one Montaigne offered the public in 1571, limited himself to the role of a poet.

For political reasons, but also for editorial reasons that were to benefit Montaigne, who reserved the *Discourse* for another occasion, La Boétie's posterity was henceforth based on a second-rate literary corpus in which he appeared chiefly as a poet (the La Boétie of the "twenty-nine sonnets" that replaced the *Discourse* in the 1580 edition of the *Essais*) in remarkable continuity with the La Boétie published in 1571. Montaigne erased La Boétie's political dimension and gave him a posthumous life diametrically opposite to what had made his reputation in the parlement of Bordeaux. The author of the *Essais* also had ambitions that were more political than literary in the 1570s, and that forced him to be careful with his contemporaries if he hoped to give form to his nascent public and diplomatic aspirations. The friendship could not be allowed to harm this new career Montaigne envisaged, and for the time being he preferred to keep La Boétie's political writings to himself.

Among the works of La Boétie that Montaigne published in 1571, we find translations, poems in French and Latin, a potpourri of writings without the two major political pieces, the *Discourse on Voluntary Servitude* and the *Memorandum* on the January edict, which Montaigne later alluded to vaguely when he recounted the history of an exceptional friendship:

> It has occurred to me to borrow one from Etienne de la Boétie, which will do honor to all the rest of this work. It is a discourse to which he gave the name *La Servitude Volontaire*; but those who did not know this have since very fitly rebaptized it *Le Contre Un*. He wrote it by way of essay in his early youth, in honor of liberty against tyrants. It has long been circulating in the hands of men of understanding, not without great and well-merited commendation; for it is a fine thing, and as full as can be. Still, it is far from being the best he could do; and if at the more mature age when I knew him, he had adopted a plan such as mine, of putting his ideas in writing, we should see many rare things which would bring us very close to the glory of antiquity; for particularly in the matter of natural gifts, I know no one who can be compared with him. But nothing of his has remained except this treatise—and that by chance, and I think he never saw it after it left his hands—and some observations on the Edict of January, made famous by our civil wars, which will perhaps yet find their place elsewhere. That was all I could recover of what he left—I, to whom in his will, with such loving recommendation, with death in his throat, he bequeathed his library and his papers—except for the little volume of his works which I

have had published. And yet I am particularly obliged to this work, since it served as the medium of our first acquaintance. For it was shown to me long before I had seen him, and gave me my first knowledge of his name, thus starting on its way this friendship which together we fostered as long as God willed, so entire and so perfect that certainly you will hardly read of the like, and among men of today you see no trace of it in practice.[44]

On the strength of La Boétie's deathbed recommendations, Montaigne set to work on a project that at first might seem uninspiring, since he sliced up his friend's work, so to speak. This fragmentation cannot fail to remind us of the Cannibals' practice of cutting their defeated enemies into pieces (*lopins*), which Montaigne reports in his chapter on them. In his preface to the reader—dated August 10, 1570 (that is, two days after the edict of Saint-Germain)—Montaigne begins by claiming that everything by La Boétie that had been printed had passed through his hands. The brilliant councillor at the parlement of Bordeaux had not thought it necessary to have his writings published. The legacy of La Boétie's library allowed Montaigne to separate the wheat from the chaff among his friend's papers, not without difficulty, because he admits that he does not know what had happened to most of the La Boétie's French and Latin verses: "But I do not know what happened to all that, any more than what happened to his Greek poems."[45] La Boétie lacked organization and wrote on the first piece of paper that came into his hands, "without any care to preserve it." Montaigne explains that his editorial role was reduced to "dividing [La Boétie] into as many pieces as I could,"[46] in order to send fragments to various famous persons (Louis de Lansac, Henri de Mesmes, Michel de L'Hospital, and Paul de Foix), adding to each of them a dedicatory piece under his own name—comments embedded in the discourse of his late friend.

In a letter dated September 1, 1570,[viii] Montaigne depicted La Boétie, presenting him as one of the great orators of his time, but he also took advantage of the opportunity to draw attention to himself. He used La Boétie's name, which was known in the parlementary milieu not only of Bordeaux but also of Paris, to spread his own name and make himself more widely known, not concealing the fact that he was thereby "killing two birds with one stone."[47] In the dedicatory epistles accompanying La Boétie's fragmented writings, Montaigne seems to be training himself. It is in that spirit that the letter to Paul de Foix to accompany the *Vers françois de feu Estienne de La Boétie* points out Montaigne's lack of oratorical skill compared to La Boétie. One's strong points are the weaknesses of the other. But Montaigne had other qualities that he was able to emphasize when the time came. He drew an important distinction between a

---

[viii] This letter was sent along with the *Poemata*.

truth that results from a "simple testimony" and one that is produced by "the tools of persuasion" and eloquence:

> For the nature of things having, I know not how, made it so that the truth, no matter how beautiful and acceptable it may be in itself, is nonetheless embraced by us only infused and insinuated into our belief by the tools of persuasion, I find myself so deprived of credit to authorize my simple testimony, and of eloquence to enrich it and assert it, that I would nearly have given up all this effort, had only there not remained to me something of his through which I could worthily present to the world at least his mind and his knowledge.[48]

In 1570, Montaigne unequivocally accepted what he was later to call *perspicuité de langage* ("lucidity of speech").[49] Far from grandiloquence, his language scorns the high-flown, superfluous turns of phrase commonly found among the magistrates of his time: "My language has no ease or polish; it is harsh and disdainful."[50] This clarification made him distance himself from La Boétie. His language (close to that of the Indians of the New World) is more natural and thus less inclined to the dissimulation and pretense characteristic of the magistrates' discourse. Such a language, stripped of all ornamentation—and that is precisely what criticism, over the centuries, has learned to appreciate in the *Essais*—is opposed to the eloquence of the parlements. Montaigne defends another type of discourse—the opposite of La Boétie's—in the letter he wrote to his father (but also to those to whom he dedicated his edition of La Boétie's works) in order to reproduce the last words of this friend who was both so similar to and so different from him.

How could Montaigne make himself known when he had no powerful contacts at the Court? He sought first of all to get his name into circulation by using that of La Boétie. In the same spirit, Montaigne did not neglect opportunities to mix with courtiers and made several trips to Paris in the course of 1571. Perhaps he wanted to enter the king's Privy Council, where the men to whom La Boétie's works were dedicated sat; we have to now turn to them if we want to understand what led Montaigne to have his friend's papers printed. The publication of the *Mesnagerie de Xenophon* was part of a strategy whose goal was chiefly political. More than La Boétie's texts, it was the dedications and the letter on La Boétie's death that are fundamental in these two volumes printed in Paris: each piece was separately dedicated to influential politicians.[ix] Who

---

[ix] In *Ma bibliothèque poétique*, vol. II, *Contemporains et successeurs de Ronsard. De Desportes à La Boétie* (Geneva: Droz, 2001, 278), Jean-Paul Barbier notes that the dates of the various dedications of the *Mesnagerie de Xénophon* are inconsistent. The foreword

were they, exactly? And why did Montaigne address La Boétie's "selected works" to them?

Dedicatees Influential at the Court

Louis de Lusignan de Saint-Gelais, lord of Lansac (1513–1589), was the first dedicatee of the works by La Boétie edited by Montaigne, who addressed to him *La Mesnagerie de Xenophon*, whose title is also that of the volume. We can consider Lansac the most important dedicatee of the work conceived in 1570. According to Montaigne, the lord of Lansac's titles and qualities (counselor to the king, member of the king's Privy Council, superintendent of the royal finances, and captain of a hundred gentlemen of the king's house), duly enumerated at the beginning of the dedicatory epistle, make La Boétie's translation "a present that seemed to me to be suitable for you."[51] In his epistle, Montaigne engages in hyperbolic praise of his deceased friend[52] before he reveals his current preoccupations to his illustrious dedicatee. Lansac was pertinently aware that Montaigne had just given up his career as a magistrate. The two men shared the same ideas and had always shown a mutual respect for each other. It will be recalled that the preceding year Lansac had defended Montaigne before the assembled members of the Bordeaux parlement when he had been put in a difficult position at the time of his promotion to the Great Chamber. In his epistle, Montaigne situates himself in a system of clientele-style dependency and suggests to Lansac that he can count on him to continue to serve his name and his household, reiterating his fidelity and submission to a family of the high nobility.

The Lansacs and the Montaignes had been connected for several generations, and the editor of La Boétie had every intention of perpetuating this reciprocal attachment, though no obligation of any kind is mentioned in the epistle. Favors are never clearly defined and are based solely on the goodwill of each party. The Montaignes and the Lansacs were also two Bordeaux families who provided administrators for the city, since Louis de Lansac had formerly served as its mayor after the term of Pierre Eyquem, and his son, Guy de Lansac, completed two terms as mayor between 1567 and 1571. Montaigne reminds his interlocutor of the friendship that united the two houses: "I would just as willingly give you something of my own, in recognition of the obligations I have to you, and of the long-standing favor and friendship that you have had for those

---

is dated August 10, 1570, the dedication to Henri de Mesmes April 30, 1570, the epistle to his wife September 10, 1570, the dedicatory epistle to Michel de L'Hospital April 30, and the printing date November 24, 1570. The dedication of the *Vers françois* bears the date September 1, 1570.

of our house."[53] Montaigne's letter to Lansac ends with a scarcely veiled offer of service: "But, Monsieur, lacking any better currency, I offer you in payment a very heart-felt desire to do you humble service."[54] Montaigne stresses his availability and puts himself at the disposal of this high-ranking figure in the government. Why did he choose Lansac as one of the dedicatees of La Boétie's works?

Louis de Lansac was twenty years older than Montaigne. His first military experience was under the reign of Francis I, in the war against Charles V and the kingdom of Spain.[55] At the apogee of his career as a soldier, he commanded six thousand men. Named captain of the city and of the château of Bourg in 1536, at the age of twenty-five, he had made himself noticed and esteemed by Henry II during the popular revolt against the salt tax in Guyenne. As governor of Bourg, he put down the rioters with an iron hand, which slowed for a time the propagation of Protestant ideas in Guyenne. Later on, his main political responsibility was to keep the cities of Bourg and Blaye, as well as the surrounding country, in the bosom of the Roman Catholic Church. An inflexible Catholic from the outset, Lansac had joined the Guises' clientele very early on. He returned to the Court after the revolts in Guyenne and served the king as plenipotentiary ambassador. More skilled in bargaining than in military strategy, Lansac excelled as a diplomat. Henry II employed him in a series of delicate negotiations with foreign powers; we find him again serving as a special ambassador in England to resolve the dispute between the Scots and the English.

In 1552 Lansac had been assigned to carry conciliatory messages to the pope and specifically to solicit a cardinal's hat for Louis of Guise. It was in the Eternal City that he made a reputation as a subtle diplomat and became the point man for the most delicate missions. Next we find him in Siena, Venice, and Florence. Italy became his chief political terrain, and he distinguished himself as a negotiator in the service of the king of France. Each time, he was praised for having "nimbly and prudently governed and led."[56] He attracted Catherine de Medici's good graces at a time when she was trying to move closer to the Guises. Thus Lansac was sent as a special ambassador to Duke Maurice de Saxe and the other princes of the German Empire. Back in France in 1554, he was appointed one of the sixty-two gentlemen of the king's chamber, receiving an annual salary of 1,200 *livres*.

For a time, Lansac seemed to be a providential man for Bordeaux, which was still struggling to recover from the trauma of the 1548 revolt, and where Protestant ideas were beginning to penetrate the administration as well as the parlement.[57] Elected mayor of the city in 1556, Lansac served only one term, during which he was hardly present in Bordeaux at all. However, this election allowed the city to regain a little credit with Catherine de Medici. It was probably at that time that Montaigne noticed the soldier and the experienced diplomat who had won a reputation for flawless loyalty to the kings he served without hesitation. At the age of twenty-three, Montaigne was already, thanks to his father's networks, part of the city's "gentry," and he was certainly impressed by this gentleman who had been granted special authorization to wear a sword during the parlement's sessions. Faced with the rise of Protestant ideas, Lansac presented himself as a man of good sense and pragmatic nature. He guaranteed the security of the châteaus of Trompette and Le Hâ, undertook to strengthen the guard at the city's gates, and even ordered the repair of the fortifications destroyed after the 1548 revolt. In 1560, shortly after his two years as mayor of Bordeaux, his good and loyal services won him promotion to the Order of Saint Michael, along with seventeen other knights. He then sat on the king's Privy Council. At that time, Montaigne had just joined the parlement of Bordeaux.

It was probably Lansac's service as a special ambassador that attracted Montaigne. Henry II had become accustomed to sending Lansac on urgent missions, a practice that had become increasingly common since the reign of Charles IX. The last Valois had established a diplomatic model based less on ordinary ambassadors than on special envoys and well-informed negotiators who enjoyed the confidence of the king and the queen mother, and who could rapidly move back and forth all over Europe. Lansac belonged to this category of men. Brantôme confirms that he was sent "at least thirty times to various places and embassies during his lifetime,"[58] thus testifying to his influence at the Court in matters of foreign affairs. Lansac's correspondence displays the breadth of his networks. He was in contact with most of the princes of Europe, especially in Italy. In 1557, we find him on a mission to Rome, which he had reached in less than three weeks by riding at full speed, after making a detour via Ferrara.[59]

This image of a negotiator who was also a good horseman was sure to please Montaigne, who considered himself an excellent horseman, as he suggests in the chapter "Of war horses": "I do not like to dismount when I am on horseback, for that is the position in which I feel best, healthy or sick."[60] Lansac's role was to report directly the king's words, at a time when the roads were unsafe and messages, even coded, were easily intercepted. Rather than rely on the usual couriers and diplomatic mail, Lansac delivered the king's instructions directly to Paul IV and the other princes of Italy, Spain, and England. He did this during his missions to Spain, where he served as special ambassador after the Treaty of Cateau-Cambrésis. It was again he who had accompanied Elisabeth of France (Isabelle of Valois) to Spain for her marriage to Philip II. He had passed through Bordeaux on his way and had attended the various festivals, receptions, and spectacles on the occasion of the visit of the king of Navarre, Antoine de Bourbon, to that city.[61] The members of the parlement were part of the cortege that passed in front of the royal party, and Montaigne, as a councillor, probably participated in these festivities.

Back in France after a triumphal stay in Spain, Lansac became one of Catherine de Medici's favorites and was named her knight of honor. In February 1561, we find him in Bordeaux again, where he was assigned to come to an agreement with Burie and Duras regarding the military precautions to be taken to ensure the city's protection on a long-term basis. But as always, his sojourn in Bordeaux was rather brief, and he soon set out for Rome in order to solicit a loan from the pope to raise an army against the Protestants. Highly esteemed and greatly respected by the pope, he joined the delegation composed of Arnaud du Ferrier and Guy du Faur de Pibrac—both known for their sympathy for the reformed religion—at the Council of Trent. Lansac was by far the most Catholic of the three ambassadors delegated by the king of France. But he was caught up in a religious controversy and had to defend himself against accusations that he was a Huguenot in disguise. Annoyed by the endless disputes over questions of precedence and protocol, he repeatedly asked Catherine de Medici to relieve him of his functions, without success.

In the late 1560s, when he had attained the high point of his career as an ambassador and right-hand man, Lansac incarnated the type of the plenipotentiary ambassador par excellence; he was a model for Montaigne, who also had some pretensions in matters of diplomacy and ambassadorship. Lansac was involved in almost all the important events of his time. Close to Catherine de Medici and to Charles IX, in 1570 he had had printed in Angoulême, by Jean de Minieres, a *Copie des lettres du Roy & du sieur de Lansac, au seigneur de Pardaillan gouverneur de Blaye, avec la responce par luy faicte à Sa Majesté et audict sieur de Lansac*. He symbolized an unprecedented kind of diplomacy, more reactive to events and always loyal to the king and the queen mother. The same cannot be said for his son, Guy de Lansac, who became an informer for the Spanish crown and gave Montaigne a lot of trouble during his two terms as mayor of Bordeaux; a political deviation that led Lansac to foment the assassination of the duke of Épernon.[62]

Dedicating the first text of La Boétie's works to Louis de Lansac allowed Montaigne to show his interest in this new way of serving the prince and to insert himself into a political and ideological system with which he felt strong affinities. Montaigne also knew that La Boétie's political positions were particularly close to those of Lansac. La Boétie—whom Lansac had known personally—created an additional connection and offered Montaigne an opportunity to display clearly, without any possible ambiguity, his own political positions.

The second dedicatee of La Boétie's works also sat on the king's Privy Council and was one of the most prominent men in the kingdom in the early 1570s. Henri de Mesmes (1531–1596), lord of Roissy and Malassise, belonged to Montaigne's generation; he was only one year his elder. At the end of 1569, Lansac and Mesmes—along with Morvilliers, Pellevé, L'Aubespine, and Birague—had been appointed to the king's Privy Council (*conseil étroit*), a very restricted group of six men responsible for the royal finances.

Henri de Mesmes's career path has several things in common with Montaigne's. After eighteen months' study (in the third-year class) at the College of Burgundy in 1542, Henri de Mesmes received a humanistic education comparable to the one that made the reputation of the College of Guyenne. Like Montaigne, Mesmes later complained about the time wasted learning classical authors by heart and commented ironically on the fact that at the end of the *cursus* he was capable of reciting Homer's poems from beginning to end. When he was fourteen, his father sent him to Toulouse to study civil and canon law. He studied with the greatest jurists for three years, beginning his days at five in the morning and listening to various lectures until ten o'clock. Like Montaigne, he spent his afternoons reading Sophocles, Aristophanes, Euripides, Demosthenes, Cicero, and Virgil. In the evening, he met Adrianus Turnebus, Denis Lambin, and Honoré Châtelain, the physician to the king and the queen mother, to exchange with them his opinions regarding questions of philology. He was also accustomed to meet Pibrac and Paul de Foix during erudite parties at which they talked about France's affairs.

At the age of twenty, Henri de Mesmes was presented to the king by his father and obtained employment in the service of Cardinal Bertrandy (Pierre Bertrand), and was soon after appointed councillor at the Cour des Aides. Admitted to the Great Council with an age dispensation and without examination, he inherited the office of *maître des requêtes* from his father, and he exercised this function for four years. Shortly afterward, he was named to lead a mission to Siena, Italy. He went first to Rome as plenipotentiary ambassador to transmit to the pope certain proposals made by the king, who was worried about the dispute between Charles V and the sovereign pontiff. Mesmes's mission was to assure the pope of the imminent arrival of an army corps commanded by François de Lorraine, duke of Guise, and intended to provide military support for the interests of the papacy. The pope had been very concerned since the duke of Alba, governor of Naples, had gone on the march with his army and established his camp near Tivoli. Mesmes acquitted himself with skill on this first mission. Destined for a brilliant career as a diplomat, at the age of twenty-four Mesmes nonetheless refused an embassy. He, too, had a different conception of public service and saw himself rather as a plenipotentiary ambassador assigned to specific missions. He rapidly became renowned for his abilities as a negotiator who always preferred conciliation to confrontation. Challenged by the legendary harshness of governors, he proposed a model of arbitration based on dialogue. Less rigid than his predecessors, he considered negotiations to be crucial for arriving at a stable accord. For him, everything was negotiable, without religious or political exclusions.

The negotiation of the treaty of Saint-Germain gave Henri de Mesmes an opportunity to put into practice his conciliatory approach to the Protestants. He made major concessions to them—including freedom of conscience—in return for a lasting peace, and he worked to have the Protestants allowed to worship in the large cities. In principle, they could even aspire to the highest offices in the state. The Peace of Saint-Germain was a sign of the evolution in the king's policy toward the new religion, and it had sealed the disgrace of the chancellor, Michel de L'Hospital, though his policy of moderation was not abandoned. The architect of a political opening to the Protestants, Mesmes was nonetheless exposed to the most virulent criticism by the intransigent Catholics. His treaty was called "*mal assise*," to cite a famous epigram of the period that targeted him directly and mocked one of his titles.[x] Montaigne seems to have approved of Memes's way of proceeding, seeing in him a man with new ideas who always made carefully weighed decisions. In Montaigne's eyes, Mesmes's attempt to bring the French people together through the Peace of Saint-Germain remained one of the best examples of political moderation in his time. It was assuredly this model of the temperate, reflective negotiator that he emphasized in the first *Essais* of 1580.

Henri de Mesmes may have allowed Montaigne to foresee having a career as a special negotiator, outside the bounds of the classical service of ordinary embassies and traditional diplomacy. Mesmes's career, which was marked by a succession of retirements to private life and returns to politics and to the service of the kingdom, offered an atypical course that Montaigne sensed might be right for himself. Like Montaigne, Mesmes finally gave up servitude to the Court and retired to his library. Abandoning the public stage was not an easy decision. In 1570, Montaigne found himself in a similar position and certainly felt sympathy for Mesmes.[63] This separation between public and private life and the return to books after periods of "consulates" at the Courts of the princes of Europe represented, at that time, a model of intellectual independence rather unusual for a powerful man. Whereas Montaigne had just retired temporarily from the world after a disappointing experience as a magistrate, he found in Mesmes a certain freedom of mind that he could put into practice in turn. Mesmes's learned entourage could also have fascinated Montaigne. In fact, a group of men of letters such as Buchanan and Grouchy maintained close links to Mesmes. By dedicating part of La Boétie's works to Mesmes, Montaigne was at the same time at-

---

[x] One of Henri de Mesme's titles was "lord of Malassise"; *mal assise* means "poorly based," "unstable." [Trans.]

testing to his membership in this group of men of letters. Hadn't he also known these same men at the College of Guyenne?

In his *Traité des nobles et des vertus dont ils sont formés* (1577), François de L'Alouëte blames nobles who "have abandoned the sciences and disciplines, and have filled themselves and garbed themselves with ignorance: and have made themselves unworthy of the offices, dignities, and honorable titles that were so loftily granted them."[64] Henri de Mesmes also criticized the uncultivated nobility on several occasions, presenting it in a caricatural form as ignorant and illiterate; he maintained that in France, "those who have weapons hardly use quills except in their hats."[65] In his view, the nobles' ignorance was responsible for their decline. In addition, they had abandoned functions and offices and no longer kept their place within the parlements. At a time when it was fashionable in the nobility to scorn literature, Mesmes allowed Montaigne to aspire to a form of learned nobility. Mesmes also confirmed for him that it was possible for a noble to be called to the highest offices of the state if he had the necessary competencies. The *Essais* show that Montaigne by far preferred study to idleness, even if he did not entirely share the concern for erudition that was found among the most famous jurisconsults of his time. For example, for him there was no question of remaining idle in his château or living sluggishly without ambitions. The publication of La Boétie's works continued a tradition in which humanist gentlemen devoted part of their lives to translation and editing. Mesmes himself had frequented the most esteemed humanists and poets of his time, such as Jean Dorat, Denis Lambin, François Hotman, and Claude Fauchet.[66] His library was famous, and a literary group was accustomed to gather at this home in Paris in the 1550s. Even though we have no proof that Montaigne participated in this humanist salon, he certainly would have heard about it.

But there were also more private reasons for the choice of Henri de Mesmes as the dedicatee of the *Règles de mariage de Plutarque*. Montaigne knew him personally, since he had spent part of the summer of 1565 at his side. In early May 1565, Mesmes had been assigned to establish two extraordinary courts to judge the trials in Saintes.[67] Concerned to keep control of a parlement that refused to register his edicts and that regularly opposed his policies, Charles IX had sent to Saintes a president of his choice from Paris. Henri de Mesmes was the one who had to be certain that the councillors of the parlement of Bordeaux served the king's interests as best they could. During the years 1564–65—after La Boétie's death—Montaigne had thrown himself completely into his career as a magistrate and still expected to be promptly appointed to the Great Chamber. It was in that state of mind that he left for Saintes, accompanied by Léonard d'Alesme, the president of the first Chambre des Enquêtes, and the councillors Joseph Eymar, Antoine de Belcier, Antoine de Poynet, and Léon de Merle. For six weeks he and Mesmes held hearings in Saintes. The two men shared the same inn and had plenty of time to get to know and esteem each other. They were even able to talk about La Boétie and his famous *Discourse on Voluntary Servitude*. We know that Mesmes had a manuscript copy[68] of this work, and that he had also written notes with a view to refuting this treatise, whose arguments he considered to be the "slight and empty fantasies of dreamers who do not understand the state."[69] Mesmes also had some of La Boétie's Latin poems, which he had perhaps received from Montaigne during the summer of 1565.

Five years later, Montaigne called Mesmes's attention to this, once again through the intermediary of La Boétie, whose works he was currently publishing. He addressed himself to Mesmes in all complicity, reminding him that they shared the same vision of a politics aimed more at transparency than at dissimulation: "For my part, I prefer to be more at my ease, and less clever; happier, and less heard."[70] This personal consideration gives way to a "we" (*nous*) that explicitly associates the two men in a common approach to public affairs: "That is why, Monsieur, although clever people make fun of the care that we have for what will happen here after we are gone." Montaigne thinks that one's posterity is not to be judged by reputation or immediate fame alone. The unsettled judgments of public opinion matter little; Montaigne and Henri de Mesmes are located in a different temporality, because they share the same conception of politics. The dedicatory epistle to Henri de Mesmes ends in the same spirit and with the same intention as the one that we find in the letter to Lansac: "For me, it will always be an honor to be able to do something that will give pleasure to you or your people, because of the obligation I have to serve you."[71]

Paul de Foix (1528–1584), the count of Carmaing, a churchman and diplomat who was at that time ambassador to Venice, also enjoyed favor at the Court in the early 1570s. Five years older than Montaigne, he held the office of almoner to Catherine de Medici and councillor-clerk in the parlement of Paris. He was also a politician famous for his magnanimity; he was one of the chief architects of the measures of tolerance advocated by the edict of 1562, which led him to be suspected of sympathies with the Protestants. He was even arrested in 1559 at the time of the Mercuriale.[xi] Set free after having retracted, in the eyes of the pope and zealous Catholics, he remained suspect for the rest of his life. Protected by Catherine de Medici, between 1562 and 1566 he obtained missions to Scotland and England before entering the king's Privy Council. He replaced Arnaud du Ferrier as ambassador to Venice from 1567 to 1570. In early 1571, Catherine de Medici had offered him the office of Keeper of the Seals, but Foix declined the offer, preferring to serve the king as a special ambassador. He was

---

[xi] A plenary session of the parlement of Paris, at which Foix had made a speech for which he was imprisoned for seven months. [Trans.]

considered one of the most cultivated minds of his time, knew both Greek and Latin, and had served his country at the highest level. De Thou left us a laudatory portrait of Foix in which he praises his virtue and zeal in the service of the state and the public welfare. Famed for his aversion to vice and seditious uprisings, Foix had unlimited confidence in his friends. Admired by many people, he was, along with Henri de Mesmes and Michel de L'Hospital, one of the modern models of great servants of the state.

Montaigne decided to dedicate to Paul de Foix a separately published book of La Boétie's works. This choice could have borne fruit, because Foix was certainly the one of the three dedicatees who was in the best position to confirm Montaigne in his diplomatic ambitions. Thus he had separately printed—but at the same time as the *Mesnagerie de Xenophon*—the *Vers françois de feu Estienne de la Boétie*. This strategy of multiplying dedications addressed to great political figures of the late sixteenth century may explain why Montaigne chose to have La Boétie's works printed independently, even if that may seem artificial. We might wonder about the necessity of printing the *Vers françois de feu Estienne de La Boétie* separately; Montaigne mentions vaguely the reservations that had been expressed regarding the quality of his friend's poems. At first, the French verses were considered too delicate. But people were soon reassured; Montaigne had changed his mind after being persuaded that "these poems . . . are worthy of being presented on the market."[72]

The dedication to Paul de Foix is longer than the other introductory pieces, as if Montaigne wanted to compensate for the brevity of the volume by the length of the introduction. This text, dated September 1, 1570, must be placed in the context of the new political career envisioned by Montaigne, who was sponsored by another branch of the Foix family—the Foix-Gursons[xii]—in the early 1570s. In this introductory piece, Montaigne praises the merits of this old Gascon family, with which he associates himself by his lively and unapologetic way of speaking. He reminds Paul de Foix of the roots in the land that unite them "with the rank of the first house of Guyenne, received from your ancestors, [to which] you have added by yourself the first rank in every kind of ability."[73] In his turn, Montaigne could serve the interests of his patron and of his

---

[xii] The Foix family had four branches: (1) the Foix-Lautrecs, represented by Thomas de Foix, lord of Lescun; (2) the Foix-Candales, represented by Gaston III de Foix and François de Foix-Candale, a councillor at the Bordeaux parlement until 1570, before becoming bishop of Aire and capital of Buch from 1572 to 1587 (he devoted himself chiefly to alchemical research, translated Euclid's *Elements*, and in 1579 had a translation of the *Pimandre de Mercure Trismesgiste* printed by Simon Millanges, which he dedicated to Margaret of Valois); (3) the Foix-Gursons, represented by Germain-Gaston de Foix, Montaigne's neighbor, the marquis of Trans, count of Gurson and of Fleix; and (4) the Foix-Carmaing, represented by Paul de Foix.

region. Foix's prestigious diplomatic career added further to Montaigne's admiration for this influential man who was capable of helping him realize his own political ambitions. We shall see that he had an opportunity to spend time with Foix during his stay in Rome in 1581, while the two men were waiting for an appointment as the king's representatives to the Holy See.

Louis de Lansac, Henri de Mesmes, and Paul de Foix shared one characteristic: all three had had successful careers as special ambassadors—two of them in Rome—and had served as negotiators for the king. They also had the rare gift for dialogue and compromise, and incarnated, each in his own way, an avant-garde conception of politics in the time of the last Valois. These three high-ranking servants of the state symbolized a new era in diplomacy. They did not have bellicose temperaments and accorded capital importance to negotiation and political arbitration. Ready to take over politically for a family devoted to the king, and on the strength of his publication of the works of La Boétie, Michel de Montaigne drew attention to his availability and identified himself with his three dedicatees with whom he shared a humanist education, a passion for ancient models and literature, and also a modern and original vision of royal service: frankness replaced dissimulation and honor recovered its initial noble meaning. Finally, Montaigne expressed his familial and political allegiance to a region and to a king, which can be discerned in his letter addressed to Henri de Mesmes: "For me, it will always be an honor to be able to do something that will give pleasure to you or your people, because of the obligation I have to serve you."[74] It is possible that Montaigne also wished to join the king's Privy Council, on which sat all the men to whom La Boétie's works were dedicated.[75]

Michel de L'Hospital (1507–1573), the last dedicatee of La Boétie's works, is a special case. As we have seen, Montaigne had met the chancellor in Bordeaux during a *lit de justice* in 1565, and he admired in him the neo-Latin humanist poet who had held the highest offices in the state.[76] When Montaigne offered him La Boétie's *Poemata*, the former Chancellor of France had just published his *Mémoire sur la nécessité de mettre un terme à la guerre civile* (1570), in which he expressed his dreams of religious tolerance and concord. His failure to work out a national council, and the anger aroused by the Peace of Longjumeau signed on March 23, 1568, hastened his departure from the government. Montaigne dedicated to him La Boétie's Latin poem at a moment when the chancellor had just fallen into disgrace after returning the royal seals during the course of 1568.[77] It was only in 1585, twelve years after his death, that *Michaelis Hospitalii epistolarum seu sermonum libri sex* appeared. Montaigne had perhaps already sensed that the chancellor would someday be admired for his poetic compositions and not only as Chancellor of France. But he could also hope that Michel de L'Hospital would make a political comeback, because he was now convinced that compromise was the only way of putting an end to the Wars of

Religion. Should the chancellor return to grace, Montaigne would thus have shown his loyalty in the most difficult times. He was beginning, moreover, to see the value in political lives studded with successes, disgraces, and returns to the limelight. In his introduction to the *Poemata*, he openly offered his services and presented "this slight gift, to kill two birds with one stone, [which will] serve to testify to the honor and reverence that I have for your excellency, and to the exceptional qualities that you possess."[78] The offices disappear, the human qualities remain.

With these dedications to influential men at the Court, Montaigne uses the space of the prefaces to La Boétie's pieces to place himself in the lineage of his father and his ancestors who were all good servants of the political power in Guyenne and formerly occupied municipal and parlementary offices in Bordeaux. This historical reminder was motivated by the professional expectations that were to facilitate Montaigne's entrance into politics.

An Inconvenient Publication

La Boétie served as an intermediary for Montaigne by affording him an opportunity to present himself to those who could help him realize his ambitions. Of course, La Boétie's memory was preserved by this editorial enterprise, but the name of Montaigne—which appears on the title page—also benefited from these publications. How else can we interpret these dedications to counselors of the king who were influential at the Court, as well as to the Chancellor of France? These men were in a position to incorporate Montaigne into their clienteles. Thus at a time when he was trying to "break into" the political milieu of the Court, Montaigne used La Boétie's writings for professional purposes. Never has the expression "editorial politics" better designated these ulterior motives of the future author of the *Essais*, who at the beginning of the 1570s was suffering from a lack of recognition. La Boétie allowed him to cope with this problem and make himself better known. Mindful of the recommendations La Boétie made on his deathbed (which had up to that point been known only to Montaigne, but were now made public), the future author of the *Essais* set out to disseminate the memory of his friend while at the same time ensure that he would always be associated with this brilliant man who had died too soon, and who was oriented toward the "public good" and the king's cause. The association of Montaigne's name with that of La Boétie allowed him to expect certain benefits, but these did not turn out to be as great as he had hoped.

The publication of La Boétie's works in 1571 might be interpreted as an error on Montaigne's part, given the Protestants' political highjacking of La Boétie after 1574, when they began to use the *Discourse on Voluntary Servitude* as a pamphlet for their cause. In the 1550s, and then again in the early 1560s, the *Discourse* (in its unpublished form) had been seen as a universal reflection on liberty, a meditation free of any dogma or political constraint. Many books written by the greatest jurisconsults of that period, notably Jean Bodin's first reflections on universal law, also offer material for a "universal reflection on the human condition."[79] The manuscript circulation of the *Discourse on Voluntary Servitude* in the parlementary milieu could be understood in the context of a culture of the nobility of the robe. However, a distinction must be drawn between the reception of the *Discourse* in the 1560s and its appropriation by the Protestants in the 1570s; we are dealing, on the one hand, with a text that fits into the magistrates' critical tradition and advocates freedom in its most idealized form, and on the other hand, with a text that took on a completely different dimension after the Saint Bartholomew's Day massacre in 1572. The *Reveille-Matin des François* (1574)—which consisted of dialogues attributed to Nicolas Barnaud—was the first political appropriation of the *Discourse* in print: a Protestant diatribe denouncing Charles IX's political tyranny. A few selected passages, which had been reworked and truncated, were extracted from La Boétie's text and interpreted in the context of contemporary events. The *Discourse* had now become a pamphlet in the service of the Huguenots.[xiii]

At first, the appearance of a few pages of the *Discourse*—without the name of their author—in a publication with a rather limited circulation seems not to have bothered Montaigne; in fact, we might even wonder whether he had looked into the Protestant use of part of this text in 1574. At that time, he did not foresee any problem with publishing the *Discourse* in a work that would take up political and diplomatic questions in a rather general way and principally on the basis of examples drawn from Antiquity. There was no obstacle to a more fully worked-out discussion of man and his natural liberty, which, according to Montaigne, transcended the particular situations of states and governments. Despite this assurance, his initial project, which consisted of inserting the *Discourse* into the corpus of his own writings, rapidly became untenable after 1578, not so much because of the partial publication of the discourse in 1574, and then again in 1577 and 1578 in a more widely disseminated work—the *Mémoires de l'Estat de France*[xiv] edited by Simon Goulart[80]—but because of its

---

[xiii] The second dialogue (p. 178 and pp. 180–90) reproduces two passages from the *Discourse on Voluntary Servitude*, which are integrated into the declarations of the "Politique" in his conversation with the "French historiographer," while the two of them are on their way to "an inn in Fribourg."

[xiv] The complete title is *Mémoires de l'estat de France sous Charles IX, contenans les choses plus notables, faites & publiees tant par les Catholiques que par ceux de la Religion, depuis le troisieme Edit de pacification fait au mois d'Aoust 1570 jusques au regne de Henry Troisiesme, & réduite en trois volumes, chacun desquels a un indice des principales matières*

local political implications. The *Mémoires de l'Estat de France* was burned in front of the parlement of Bordeaux, on the Place de l'Ombrière, on May 7, 1579,[81] two days before the privilege granted Simon Millanges for the *Essais* and other "new things" was obtained.[82]

At the last minute, in an editorial panic, and when the pages of the *Discourse* had already been set up in Millanges's print shop, Montaigne substituted twenty-nine sonnets by La Boétie for the *Discourse*, which now looked for all the world like a Huguenot polemic. As an irreprochable Catholic, he had to explain his friendship with La Boétie. The public burning of the *Mémoires de l'Estat de France* in Bordeaux, at the very moment when the *Essais* was being printed, did not allow Montaigne to associate the *Discourse* with his own writings, when his ambition was to serve a Catholic king. It was not simply a matter of defusing an explosive situation, but also of reminding people that this text could be read in several different ways.[83] Montaigne had also been forced to change the book's organization as it was being made, after having planned to publish the *Discourse on Voluntary Servitude* at the heart of his *Essais* and thus to pay homage to a friendship that was not as simple as has been thought. The *Discourse* could have favored the political tone that Montaigne considered giving his books, but now it was necessary to repudiate it. The last-minute replacement of this text by La Boétie's twenty-nine sonnets accentuated the rather careless and somewhat disorganized aspect of the book. But evidently it was necessary to act quickly.[xv] Montaigne was learning his first political lessons in matters of publishing. The last-minute withdrawal of the *Discourse* and its "provisional" replacement by the twenty-nine sonnets reveal another trait of his character: always aware of the political stakes in his time, Montaigne took no risks. One sometimes gets trapped by hasty publications with politically delicate content.

In the 1560s, the *Discourse on Voluntary Servitude* had not yet been loaded with the polemical ballast it received ten years later. At that time the Huguenots had not yet instrumentalized it.[84] The *Réveille-Matin* had not lent this text much visibility. Likewise, a pirated edition of the *Discourse*—also printed in

---

y contenues. Meidelbourg [Geneva]: Henry Wolf, 1577, 1578. La Boétie's *Discourse* fills 46 pages (f. 116v–139v) of the second, expanded edition published in 1578. The table of contents at the end of the volume presents it under the title "Discourse, on Voluntary Servitude."

[xv] George Hoffmann has noted that in 1582 Montaigne corrected a few verses in La Boétie's sonnets that make up the twenty-ninth chapter of the *Essais*, which proves that he read them more attentively in 1582 than when he substituted them for the *Discourse on Voluntary Servitude* in the first edition. This haste may explain why Montaigne speaks of his book as a "bundle of so many disparate pieces" (*Essais* 80, II, 37, p. 595; Frame, p. 574).

1574—allegedly published in Reims by Jean Mouchar under the title *Vive description de la Tyrannie et des Tyrans, avec les moyens de se garantir de leur joug* remained rather confidential. To this date, only five copies of this edition have been located in libraries and private collections.[85] Erroneously attributed to Odet de La Noue, this little volume in 16° represents the first separate publication of the *Discourse*. In an annotation written with a pen in a sixteenth-century hand, a copy recently put on the rare books market identifies the author of this text, which is in every respect identical with that published the same year by Simon Goulart, as "le sieur de La Boétie, Conseiller au Parlement de Bordeaux." On the other hand, the publication of La Boétie's text in 1577 and 1578, in the third volume of the *Mémoires de l'Estat de France, sous Charles Neufiesme*, edited by Simon Goulart, seriously compromised Montaigne's plan to publish the *Discourse* in his *Essais*. The *Mémoires de l'Estat de France* had given the *Discourse* a sufficiently wide distribution to make La Boétie's name suddenly associated with the Huguenot camp.

Montaigne's good editorial intentions had caused him to forget that in the late sixteenth century, editing and publishing a philosophical or literary text was also a political enterprise. Once again, he fell into an editorial trap. He now had to defend La Boétie's writings. It was enough to make it seem that his *Essais* would have no function other than to justify his editorial aberrations and to defend his political and religious affinities, which were considered suspect. Texts often escape the control of their authors. How could Montaigne have been the friend of a Huguenot pamphleteer? In fact, we have to read the history of his friendship with La Boétie—as it is reported in the *Essais* of 1580—in the light of his role as the editor of the works of the councillor from Sarlat. A material trace of this friendship already existed in the books edited by Montaigne that preceded the *Essais* by more than a decade, a considerable interval in the turbulent history of that period. The edition of La Boétie's works in 1571 took on a whole new dimension after the *Discourse* was included in Simon Goulart's collection. Montaigne could no longer ignore the political dimension of his friendship with La Boétie, and he had to explain it. He had left the parlement ten years earlier, after giving the impression that he was on the side of Lagebaston and the sympathizers with the Reformation. His desire to reaffirm his Catholic faith and his allegiance to the sovereign was once again compromised by the publication of the works of La Boétie, who was considered a political theorist who had been won over to Protestant theses.

One of Montaigne's first tasks in the *Essais* was to reassure his readers about La Boétie's religion, as he had about Sebond's true theological convictions. He explains that La Boétie's political texts are "in honor of liberty" and have no practical consequences. Montaigne claims that his friend accorded them only a relative interest, as he did for the *Memorandum* on the Edict of January, which had become famous during the civil wars and which might "perhaps" (the adverb was added later by Montaigne) find a place elsewhere. Montaigne had become a specialist in the *elsewhere*. Reacting to events and taking into account the development of the situation, politics redefines intellectual spaces and proposes a new way of raising questions. The Protestant reading of La Boétie after the Saint Bartholomew's Day massacre had changed the situation and forbade Montaigne to discuss La Boétie's political writings in the same way. For him, there could no longer be any question of associating himself with these "juvenilia"; he had his own card to play and could not allow himself to be accused of consorting with unsavory characters. Montaigne found it all the more difficult to distance himself from these texts because he had praised them so highly in 1571. However, one thing was in his favor, and he decided to exploit it: in his initial plan of publishing La Boétie, he had limited himself to the poetry and a few fragmentary translations. He decided to emphasize this poetic and apolitical vein in La Boétie by replacing the *Discourse on Voluntary Servitude* with the "Twenty-nine Sonnets," deliberately leaving his political writings aside.

There no longer remained any trace of the political La Boétie in the *Essais*, and his texts on the subject, withdrawn or left unmentioned, were never published by Montaigne. The friendship did not survive the political and religious situation of the 1570s. The La Boétie the Protestants printed—that of the *Discourse on Voluntary Servitude*—had become too dangerous and embarrassing for Montaigne, who had always proclaimed to be a loyal servant of the king and the Catholic religion. What remained to him to save this friendship? Buried among La Boétie's papers, he found a few new poems that looked like offshoots of La Boétie's political writings. For lack of something better, La Boétie would be a poet and a translator, since he could not be a political thinker. The political proximity that had allowed the two friends to find each other was replaced by poetic and aesthetic considerations. History had redefined the nature of the friendship between Montaigne and La Boétie.

In 1580, Montaigne was seeking political and diplomatic responsibilities within the state apparatus. He also flaunted his membership in the nobility of the sword and distanced himself from the world of the *robins*, wanting to forget his unfortunate experience in the parlement of Bordeaux. His competence as a councillor was an asset for entering politics, but he had never really shared in the rebellious spirit of the Bordeaux magistrates. His political position in the 1570s had evolved considerably since the 1560s, and the *Discourse on Voluntary Servitude* suddenly appeared as an inconvenient work that he saluted on the theoretical level—in the name of an unshakeable friendship with La Boétie—but repudiated on the practical level of realpolitik. His political future depended on his fidelity with regard to a clientele system, and he feared blurring the image of a moderate Catholic and *politique* that he was forging. In his *Essais* of 1580, Montaigne repeatedly emphasizes his role as a loyal servant, determined to follow his patrons unconditionally: "Thus I am fit only to follow, and I let myself be carried away easily by the crowd. I do not trust my own powers enough to command, or to guide; I am very glad to find my steps traced out by others."[86] Montaigne was a good soldier, ready to assume the responsibilities that might be entrusted to him, perhaps even someday in the service of the state.[87]

The *Essais* were initially conceived as a work that would contribute to its author's entrance into politics, because at first Montaigne had viewed his work as a simple commentary of La Boétie's political writings, and more particularly on the *Discourse on Voluntary Servitude*. Then La Boétie was reduced to his poetry by the editorial work done by his friend, who erased the political man. After 1588, Montaigne abandoned politics in his turn, in favor of philosophical introspection. In a parallel but paradoxical way, these merged trajectories then bent back on themselves in an internal subjectivity (poetic or philosophical) that set aside history and politics for posterity. That was at least the choice (conscious or unconscious) Montaigne made when he deleted the political La Boétie and kept only the poet La Boétie in the 1570s, and then his *Essais* of 1580. Montaigne transformed the friend into a poet, whereas La Boétie's career and reputation were essentially political. This editorial tour de force testifies to Montaigne's ability to react rapidly to the vicissitudes of politics. This form of adaptation to present events was to stay with him throughout his life, and it allowed him to survive a number of delicate political situations.

An Influential Neighbor: The Marquis of Trans

Montaigne received no favorable response from the four powerful dedicatees to whom he had addressed "pieces" of La Boétie, accompanied by a presentation written by himself. On the other hand, he found local support that allowed him to envisage new political responsibilities. His neighbors the Foix-Gursons sponsored him in his aspirations.[88] A former special ambassador to England, Germain-Gaston de Foix (1511–1591), marquis of Trans, count of Gurson and of Fleix, viscount of Meilles, was a member of the Guyenne high nobility. In his youth, he had been a soldier and had followed Francis I to Italy, where he was taken prisoner at Pavia. Sent on a diplomatic mission to England in 1559, he proved to be a skilled negotiator. Also a member of the king's Privy Council and captain of fifty lancers, he quickly established himself as one of the leaders of the Catholic extremists in the southwest. At the beginning of the Wars of Religion, he had reacted violently to the Calvinists' maneuvers, and then, after Charles IX's death, he considerably tempered his activities as a member of the Catholic League and ended up close to Henry of Navarre. He maintained various châteaus, including those of Gurson and Fleix, which served as his usual residences.

In 1561, Gaston de Foix denounced "those who belong to the churches they call reformed, [who] continue the invasions and destructions of the temples that they have already almost all ruined in my diocese, [and] still increase more and more their violences and furies, despite the fact that they have their own temples in every city."[89] The historian Mézeray presented him as one of the main instigators of the League in Guyenne, whereas D'Aubigné refers to a "league formed in Cadillac between the Count of Candale, the Marquis of Trans, Montluc, Bishop of Ayre," and a few other gentlemen of the region.[90] In March 1563, Frédéric de Foix-Candale had founded a league devoted to the service of God and complete obedience to the king. Montaigne and La Boétie had shown themselves to be favorable to this first league at a time when many people still thought the Reformation would be nipped in the bud. In 1565, despite the edicts of pacification, this league, better known under the name of "league of the treaty of Cadillac," equipped itself with the means of waging an all-out war against the Huguenots in Guyenne and Périgord. The bishop of Aire, Christophe de Foix-Candale,[91] the marquis of Trans's cousin, had told the queen mother about the crimes committed by Huguenot bands on his lands, and then organized a Catholic militia to purge the region of Protestant influence. After La Boétie's death, Montaigne distanced himself from this private army, which was committing as many abuses in the region as the Huguenots were.

In the early 1570s, the marquis of Trans had withdrawn from politics and was seeking to soften the position as an intractable Catholic that he had taken at the beginning of the Wars of Religion. Looking for liege men sufficiently informed about regional and national affairs, he saw in Montaigne a way of preserving his influence in the region and at the Court. He may have dangled some political or diplomatic responsibility before Montaigne's eyes after introducing him at the Court. The marquis of Trans was well placed to favor the political careers of those who swore allegiance to him, and the proximity of Montaigne's château and that of Fleix allowed Gaston de Foix to have direct and almost immediate access to his client. The Foix-Gursons had shown a Catholic fervor that prevented them from playing a direct political role with regard to the Protestants in the 1570s. They now acted in the background and made use of intermediaries to advance their interests.[92] The marquis had known Montaigne for a long time, and Montaigne's friendship with the La Boétie of the *Memorandum* on the Edict of January could reassure him regarding his political and religious convictions. For example, in December 1562, the name of La Boétie appeared on a list of twelve councillors assigned to implement various repressive measures against the Huguenots. From 1561 to 1563, Montaigne and La Boétie had moved much closer to the Foix-Gursons and their political activity. On the strength of these early positions, Gaston de Foix eased Montaigne's social and political ascension by introducing him at the Court. However, beforehand he had to improve his pedigree in the nobility.

In October 1571, a little more than a year after ending his career as a *robin* and while he was conceiving the project of writing essays to frame a few of La Boétie's political discourses, Montaigne received a letter from Charles IX informing him that he had just been made a knight of the Order of Saint Michael. In this rather exceptional title that had just been conferred on him we must see the sign of a political will on the part of his patrons—the marquis of Trans and the Foix family—who were counting on this Gascon gentleman to win back a political space that had been redefined by ten years of religious conflict in a region that had become supremely strategic for both the royal party and the Protestants. The Foix-Gursons and the Foix-Candales now sought to be more conciliating than they had been early in the reign of Charles IX, and Montaigne could help them in their policy of rapprochement with the Huguenot lords of Périgord and Guyenne.

The history of this event that marked Montaigne's political career began on October 25, 1571, when the new client of the marquis de Trans received a royal message sent from Blois and dated October 18:

> Monsieur de Montaigne, for your virtues and merits, I have chosen and elected you to be one of the knights of my Order, so that you might be associated with them; to notify of you of this election and give you the necklace of the aforesaid order, I am presently writing to my cousin the marquis of Trans, to whom you shall go to receive from him the necklace of this order, which he will give you on my behalf in order to increase ever more the affection and good will I have for you and to encourage you to persevere in your devotion to my service.[93]

At the same time, his neighbor, Gaston de Foix, received instructions to deliver to Montaigne in person the insignia of the order. A meeting was rapidly arranged, and on October 28 Montaigne received the much-desired necklace that introduced him into the political elite and confirmed his nobility. He recounts this ceremony in an entry in his almanac dated October 28: "In the year 1571, in accord with the King's command and the dispatch that His Majesty sent me, I was made a knight of the Order of St. Michael by the hands of Gaston de Foix, marquis of Trans."[94] There could be no better proof of nobility than such an honorific reward conferred by the king.

From that day on, Montaigne could embrace his new political career with greater serenity. Thanks to his illustrious neighbor, he now had access to the political elite. Although lacking the military valor formerly required for entry into this order, he met the criteria connected with his qualities as a man of judgment, and even as a diplomat: "There is another kind of valor, true, perfect, and philosophical . . . much greater than ours and fuller, a valor that is a strength and assurance of the soul, equally despising all sorts of adverse accidents, equable, uniform, and constant, a valor of which ours is only a very feeble ray."[95] This says a great deal about a second nobility that had to resign itself to seeking elsewhere the origins of princely rewards.

Montaigne also mentions this high distinction in the "Apology for Raymond Sebond," where he expresses, not without vanity, his satisfaction in belonging to the "French nobility": "I asked of Fortune when I was young, as much as anything else, the Order of Saint Michael; for it was then the utmost mark of honor of the French nobility, and very rare. She granted it to me ironically. Instead of raising and lifting me from my place to attain it, she treated me much more graciously: she debased it and lowered it to the level of my shoulders, and below."[96] Thanks to the Foix family, Montaigne could foresee a political career that had been difficult to imagine earlier. The distinction he received from the marquis of Trans also allowed him to be presented to influential political figures in the region, and the ceremony at which the necklace was awarded undoubtedly further strengthened the close tie that already bound him to his "political sponsor."

For some time, the insignia had no longer been conferred by the king in person, but rather by officers of the order. This relatively recent ritual offered the provincial nobility an opportunity to play a more important political role: because they officially represented the king, they benefited from a relocated authority that enhanced their regional power. In his "Additions aux Mémoires de Castelnau," the abbé Le Laboureur explains this recent practice:

> Under the last three kings of the Valois line there were never so many great people at the Court, and especially so many knights of the king's Order; under Charles IX it was necessary to put an end to the pomp of the chapters in which the king participated with the members, and to allow the ceremony to be carried out in the provinces by the commanders of the Order, to whom the task was delegated because the king would have been busy every day making new knights in greater numbers than the sick whom he touched on festive occasions.[97]

However, Le Laboureur confuses the two orders—Saint Michael and the Holy Spirit—because the Order of Saint Michael had no commanders. Nonetheless, the pomp described by Le Laboureur certainly did not displease Montaigne who remained found of such ceremonies his entire life.

Montaigne's publishing choices during the 1570s—including composing the first *Essais*—were profoundly influenced by the title he received in 1571. This introduction into the Order of Saint Michael marked the beginning of a series of honors that brought the Gascon gentleman closer to the Court and made him a political figure on the regional and even national scale. In 1571, the Order of Saint Michael was still the supreme honorific distinction awarded by the king. This mark of honor was dethroned only in 1578, with the creation of the Order of the Holy Spirit.

The Order of Saint Michael was used extensively by Charles IX and Henry II to dispense favors and attract lords who might have been tempted by the Reformation. During Charles IX's youth, it was chiefly Catherine de Medici and the Guises who had the power to name knights to this order. This was an excellent way of attracting the loyalty of provincial gentlemen and gaining their devotion by distributing the necklace to those who wanted it out of vanity. Originally limited to thirty-six gentlemen but soon expanded to a hundred, the number increased exponentially as soon as the king began to award the necklace to captains of the second rank and to minor lords of the middle-level nobility, and even to the mayors of cities. The figures speak for themselves. In the time of Henry II, only about twenty names were added to the order each year;[98] twenty-three necklaces were awarded in 1559 and 1560. At the beginning of Charles IX's reign, the rewards remained at a stable level of fifteen or twenty necklaces a year until 1569, which marks an important turning point, because 151 lords were granted entry into the order in that year. Subsequent years followed the same trend toward a considerable increase in the number of knights named to the order. Thus there were seventy-one in 1570, 103 in 1571—the year that Montaigne received his necklace—and ninety in 1572. Starting in 1573, the average decreased considerably, to only half a dozen knights per year; two in 1574, six in 1576, three in 1577, eight in 1578, and three in 1579, the year that the Order of the Holy Spirit was created. Montaigne benefited from this exceptional prodigality in the attribution of necklaces between 1569 and 1572. Many of these knights were already members of the king's chamber, and it was logical that shortly afterward Montaigne might be awarded in his turn this second mark of honor, which was, however, accompanied by no salary. Thus out of the 151 people admitted to the order in 1569, fifty-eight were already ordinary gentlemen of the king's chamber.

Among the recipients of the Order of Saint Michael, we find regimental commanders, captains of companies of harquebusiers, governors of small and middle-sized cities (Péronne, Saintes, Mantes, Samets, Quirieu, Forcalquier, Bigorre, Montélimar, and so on), the commander of a Swiss regiment in Piedmont, the lieutenant of a company, two captains of the king's galleys, and a valet and grand master of the king's wardrobe. The distribution of the group inducted with Montaigne in 1571 was quite similar. We find a large number of gentlemen of the king's chamber, principally minor provincial lords. Most of the people inducted during these four boom years are now completely unknown, and only about ten of them went down in history. What can we say, after all, about Mathurin Broc, baron of Saint-Mars; Guillaume Tuffin, lord of La Roirie; Claude Molette, lord of Morangies; Jean de Beauxoncles, lord of Sigoignes; or Nicolas du Peloux, seigneur de Gourdon, all of whom entered the order in the same year as Montaigne?

The Order of Saint Michael had become a political tool like any other for attracting allies, and especially for producing liege men. Montaigne did not escape the logic of honorific rewards, which are never disinterested, whatever the author of the *Essais* says about them. Montaigne adapted to his recent title of nobility;[99] the patronymic "Eyquem" was now definitely behind him, and he had an additional argument for asserting that he was "well born." He wore the necklace, the mark of nobility par excellence, even if his contemporaries gossiped about these "paper nobles" who sported a sword without ever having set foot on a battlefield. In his eulogy of the marshal of Tavannes, Brantôme targets Montaigne by name when he explains the abuses that affected that honor in the late sixteenth century:

> We have seen councillors leave the courts of Parlement, abandon the robe and mortarboard, and begin sporting a sword, and [be] immediately granted this collar without having waged war in any way; as did the lord of Montaigne, who would have done better to continue to use his pen to write his *Essays*, than to exchange it for a sword that did not befit him as well. The marquis of Tran [*sic*] easily obtained from the king an order for one of his neighbors; mentally mocking it, because he was a great scoffer. He also had his maître d'hôtel, called Paumier, made a knight.[100]

And Brantôme goes on to cite an epigram of the time that corresponds rather well to Montaigne's case:

> If you think I'm too small
> For such noble neckware,
> Take a straw man withal
> To make a knight as fair.[101]

This was not far off the mark: Montaigne had become a straw man in the service of his political patrons, the Foix-Gursons. Another quatrain, written on the occasion of the king's decoration of nineteen knights in 1567, emphasizes the results expected from this mark of distinction:

> Since each man lists his merits
> To attain this honor and reward,
> I can do the practical bits
> For love of some great lord.[102]

Montaigne became a *practiqueur*,[103] in the sense that he learned to negotiate his political support in the mode of "I'll scratch your back, you scratch mine," or *troque pour troq*, as Ronsard would have put it. He was henceforth obligated to his patron as a loyal servant who did rather well what was expected of him. The Order of Saint Michael was an "advance on performance," so to speak. The Constable de Montmorency's remark that "the order was thrown into disorder because it was granted to several people against its original intention"[104] mattered little. Despite the proliferation of insignia and the discredit into which the order had fallen, which was equally criticized by the Huguenots, the necklace of Saint Michael still remained a distinctive sign of nobility, and that was what counted for Montaigne. In 1577, François de L'Alouëte noted that the order was "beginning to perish and decline sharply, being disdained by the greatest men: because it is no longer given to the Noble and virtuous, but indifferently to all those who have more sway and credit, commoners or others."[105] Again, the expression is apt: Montaigne had the wind at his back, and his entry into politics had to be reckoned on. He had succeeded in playing his cards well in receiving these distinctions, and thanks to the marquis of Trans he suddenly enjoyed much more credit. Later on, he was to be able to mock in his turn the vanity associated with such marks of honor, but during the 1570s he attached great importance to this distinction. His father would have been proud to see him accede so publicly to the nobility to which the family had aspired for several generations.

Montaigne's elevation in late 1571 to the rank of knight of the Order of Saint Michael followed shortly after the publication of the *Mesnagerie de Xenophon* and the *Vers françois de feu Estienne de la Boétie*. Was that a coincidence, or were these works already part of a deliberate strategy? One thing is certain: the year 1571 mattered in Montaigne's life. The marquis of Trans had made him a member of the middle-level nobility to which he did not belong when he left the parlement. Montaigne did not need to be ennobled, because his father already had considered himself to be a noble (as early as 1540), and his claim was confirmed by his membership in the province's military reserve forces. However, in Michel de Montaigne we see a case of the passage from a simple nobility connected with the way of life and the possession of a fief, to a "mid-level" nobility, which could play a political role and receive honors. In less than eight years, Montaigne acquired all the titles necessary for entering in a dignified way the Courts of Henry III and Henry of Navarre. The role he was asked to play testifies to his meteoric rise in politics, since the responsibilities he was asked to assume could be entrusted only to a high-ranking gentleman. His *Essais* leave a very visible trace of the confirmation of his titles of nobility and of these honorific rewards. Montaigne insisted on having them appear on the title page of his book in 1580 and 1582.

Belonging to an order of the king implied obligations, notably that of wearing the necklace at all times.[106] There were two different necklaces: the heavy, ceremonial necklace of gold that was worn on special occasions, and a lighter, everyday necklace to be worn daily or while traveling. However, the knights were supposed never to take off their insignia for any reason. Article III of the statutes stipulates that the knights "shall be expected to wear every day around their necks, and showing, on pain of having a mass said and giving for God, the whole up to the sum of 7 *sols* 6 *deniers tournois.*" When they were traveling, the knights of the order were required only to wear "the said image of St. Michael, suspended from a small gold chain or silk ribbon."[107] The large gold necklace was reserved for official ceremonies.[xvi] The knight had to conform to the way of life defined in detail in the order's statutes. He could not leave the kingdom or enter the service of any other prince without having first taken leave of his sovereign. This helps us understand why Montaigne felt compelled to obtain such a permission from the king before he left for Germany and Italy in 1580.

In the event of war, all the knights were to come to the aid of the king and rally behind his flag. This rule was applied in 1560, when Charles IX ordered the knights of Saint Michael who were younger than sixty and not already in the armies to join immediately the troops of his brother, the duke of Anjou, who was fighting insurgent Protestants. The knight swore an oath of loyalty to the person of the king, a commitment that Montaigne observed throughout his life. In addition, the knight had obligations toward the other members of his order. On this point, Montaigne remained dutiful, even if conciliation seemed to him necessary to cope with the abuses customarily associated with the exer-

---

[xvi] The necklace could not be sold; at the knight's death, it had to be returned to the king. The weight in gold of this large necklace was considerable. Article III of the order's statutes specifies that the necklace had to contain 200 *écus* worth of gold and consist of clam shells connected with one another by a chain with gold links. For instance, the necklace of Saint Michael that was made in 1526 to replace the one that Francis I had lost at Pavia weighed 933 grams. In 1560, another necklace weighed 826 grams. In 1701, the only necklace of Saint Michael that was part of the order's treasury, and which had belonged to Henry III, weighed 877 grams. In 1578, a goldsmith in Paris received from a knight's widow a necklace estimated to be worth 274 *écus.*

cise of power.[108] The knights were also supposed to work to "glorify the Holy Church" and defend the Catholic faith. New rules added in the early 1550s obliged knights to attend mass as often as possible wearing the order's necklace, dress, mantle, and hat, and "this collar and dress shall be scented with incense after the priest has censed the altar."[109] After 1550, the oath sworn by the knights mentioned "the glorification of our Catholic faith." The chapel that Montaigne had installed on the ground floor of his tower, where he could hear the mass, dates precisely from the time when he was received into the order. This place of worship was intended to allow him to respect the order's statutes regarding the sacraments. Rather than a proof of faith, attending mass was an obligation for the knight.

In his *Mémoires*, Cheverny tells us that in September 1574 Henry III sought to assemble all the knights of the Order of Saint Michael to "decide with them what was necessary for its reformation."[110] The order, which had "then fallen somewhat in esteem because of the excessive number of people of mediocre quality and valor who had been appointed to it," needed reorganizing. Upon returning from Poland, Henry III called the knights together in the church of Saint-Jean of Lyon on Saint Michael's feast day. Cheverny was elected chancellor to replace Cardinal Crequy, who had died shortly after the demise of Charles IX. The ceremony, which was to mark a new departure for the order, took place in the great church in Lyon, where Montaigne was certainly present, as it was his duty to be. A few days later, the king ordered that the state secretaries henceforth send out only summons that were "granted and signed with his own hand."[111] The count of Cheverny, in his capacity as chancellor of the order, had as his main function to receive recommendations and nominations so as to have them directly approved by the king. Further assemblies of the order took place in Poitiers in September 1577 and in the royal chapel in Fontainebleau in 1578. Montaigne may have attended these ceremonies, but he does not mention them.[xvii] In 1579, the king held a chapter of the order in the church of the Augustins. Belonging to this order was very important to Montaigne, who constantly wore the small necklace, as he was supposed to. Many portraits show him wearing this insignia, or at least part of the ribbon from which the medal hung, sometimes held by a simple cord, sometimes attached to a necklace made from one or two slender chains interlaced with scallop shells.

After 1572, the Saint Bartholomew's Day massacre had destroyed any possibility of a lasting peace between Catholics and Protestants, and Montaigne remained silent about the massacre, as if he could not find the words to condemn

---

[xvii] The order's festival, which the knights were supposed to celebrate by a solemn assembly, was set for May 8, the anniversary of the archangel's appearance at Mont-Saint-Michel.

this action.[112] His membership in the Order of Saint Michael also required him to be reserved, and perhaps that is how we must interpret his reticence, which still shocks Montaigne specialists today. The news of the massacre traveled like wildfire throughout France, and the bloodbath was reproduced in many of the kingdom's cities. In Bordeaux, a Catholic priest, Edmond Auger, urged the residents of the city to imitate the Parisians.[113] He was determined to exterminate the heretics, and his repeated sermons forced the governor of Bordeaux, Charles de Montferrand, to act. The executions, on which Montaigne also fails to comment, took place on October 3, 4, and 5, and resulted in about 250 deaths. Montaigne was living in his château during these bloody days. In the presence of the jurats, the governor of Bordeaux had forty notables belonging to the reformed religion executed. The president of the parlement, Benoît Lagebaston, reports on the massacre in terms that leave no ambiguity regarding the responsibility of its instigators.[114] Three parlement councillors were killed. Their murderers belonged to the bourgeoisie and even included members of parlement who had settled personal accounts under the authority of the prosecutor La Brousse, assisted by a few other members of the parlement of Bordeaux.

Prudence was necessary in these troubled times; Montaigne had several friends who had made the mistake of committing themselves too much to one camp or the other. The example of Guy du Faur de Pibrac illustrates the political danger run by those who applauded the Saint Bartholomew's Day massacre. Here we must remember that the Cardinal of Lorraine prided himself on being the instigator of that massacre, even if he seems not to have participated directly in the decision to launch it. As we have seen, in 1573, Pibrac had published—anonymously—an *Ornatissimi Cujusdam Viri, de rebus Gallicis ad Stanislaum Elvidium Epistola*, translated into French shortly afterward and printed by Federic Morel, the publisher of La Boétie's works.[115] This text enjoyed a certain success under the title *Apologie de la Saint-Barthélemy*.

A friend of Henri de Mesmes and Paul de Foix, Pibrac had pursued a career as a diplomat.[116] In the early 1560s, when he was distinguishing himself as Charles IX's ambassador to the Council of Trent, he defended the same positions as La Boétie and Montaigne. At that time, along with Lansac and Arnaud du Ferrier, the future ambassador to Venice, he had argued that a new ecumenical council was necessary. For that reason, he had been accused of being in the pay of the Huguenots. However, Pibrac was a fervent Catholic and soon became a high-ranking servant of the state. In the wake of the Saint Bartholomew's Day massacre, he had felt it imperative to defend Catherine de Medici, pushing a little further his role as an advocate for the government. His justification of the massacre put an end to his political pretensions, and this publication was the great misstep in his political career. Although he remained Catherine de Medici's protégé—he became her chancellor—Pibrac performed no official function after 1574. This was a lesson for Montaigne, who did not make the same mistake.

Condemning or approving a political act amounted to the same thing: confronted by such events, it was wiser to remain silent if one wanted to retain some hope of pursuing a career. That is how we should interpret Montaigne's silence after Saint Bartholomew's Day, which has led people to read between the lines; some have even seen a hidden reference to this event in the defense of Seneca and Plutarch in chapter II: 32, which was probably written in 1579.[117] In reality, things are much simpler. Between 1570 and 1580, Montaigne was a conformist; that was the only way to realize his political ambitions.

In 1574, in response to the recent political configuration in Guyenne, the marquis of Trans put an end to his activity as a member of the Catholic League. He remained loyal to the king of France, even though he was also bound by the feudal ties that connected him with the king of Navarre.[118] Montaigne was a key figure in this political and religious opening. The power of the Foix-Gursons in the region was thereby increased, because the marquis of Trans had succeeded in his political reconversion. In 1576 he was elected to represent Périgord at the Estates General held in Blois. His sons converted to the Protestant religion and the marquis of Trans subsequently became a moderate. He moved closer to Henry of Navarre and saw in Montaigne an ideal intermediary who was clearly a Catholic, but also a man of dialogue.

A trip made by Margaret of Valois and Catherine de Medici to Guyenne in 1577 provided an opportunity to organize several meetings in Coutras, Fleix, and Sainte-Foy. The marquis of Trans took advantage of these meetings to introduce Montaigne to the Catholic and Protestant leaders. It was actually starting at this time that Montaigne belonged to the regional political elite and acquired a certain visibility at the national level. The political situation in Guyenne had changed. Charles IX had just died and Henry III was already imagining his cousin, Henry of Navarre, succeeding him on the throne of France. Henry III was able to use the mediation of clear-sighted and dedicated men who knew all about the special functioning of regional clienteles to gain the support of the high nobility in the provinces. Gaston de Foix's extroverted, passionate temperament made him one of those men whom it was better to treat considerately and have on one's side.

Honorific Rewards and Clientelism

The beginning of Montaigne's political career must be situated in a local framework, that is, in immediate proximity to his château. Built less than twenty kilometers from Montaigne's château, the château of Fleix, the marquis de Trans's residence, was a regional political center and military capital where many decisions were made and the greatest figures met to discuss the religious situation in France. In 1577, Catherine de Medici and her daughter, Queen Margot, stayed there; the peace treaty that put an end to the seventh War of Religion was signed there in 1580. On horseback, it took Montaigne about two hours to ride to Fleix to see the Foix-Gursons. His remarkable political ascension can be explained by the relationship, both clientelist and affective, that he developed with Gaston de Foix and his family.

After his difficulties in the Bordeaux parlement, Montaigne was certainly satisfied to keep his distance from the forms of power based on filiation and kinship ties. He had experienced the alliances and quarrels that resulted from an obscure and distant consanguinity transformed into a mode of social organization. His career as a member of parlement had been too dependent on genealogy; for his political career, he chose clientelism. The clientele relationship assumes a reciprocal exchange of favors between two individuals on an equal footing, in a system of asymmetrical assistance that has nothing contractual about it, but depends instead on each party's goodwill. On this point, the relation between a patron and his client involves no economy of favors comparable to the rules and mutual duties of the relation between a noble and his vassal.[119] As a system of exchange, clientelism remains informal and has no precise code or mode of functioning. Relationships are cultivated over time; each of the two parties has his own resources and expends them as he wishes in the form of gifts.

In the late 1560s, Montaigne was a virtual member of the nobility, but he was not yet well enough recognized to be propelled to the royal Court. The marquis of Trans had great hopes for him; counting on him, he accelerated his transformation into a gentleman by allowing him to obtain rapidly the necessary titles and qualities. We can speak of the *making of a gentleman* in the sense that, in less than three years, the marquis of Trans made it possible for Montaigne to be received at Court and to frequent the most influential people of the kingdom. What Louis de Lansac, Henri de Mesmes, Michel de L'Hospital, and Paul de Foix had not been able to give him was now happening, thanks to Gaston de Foix. Montaigne had found a patron who helped him enter power groups to which his minor nobility would not previously have given him access. The clientele relationship made it possible to cross barriers that would have been impenetrable without a patron's permission. This peculiar relation between patron and client includes three aspects that are intrinsically linked to the point of merging.

First, the relation between the patron and his client is personal, reciprocal, and dependent. This moral bond reflects a chosen and intentional obligation, a form of voluntary servitude. The patron has a duty to help his client, but solely in the form of a gift, the expected reciprocity never being explicitly or clearly expressed. This "expectation" may never be perceived as a relationship of dependency or allegiance on the part of the client;[120] sometimes it substitutes for kinship ties.

Second, the clientele system, which is based on personal loyalty, is not for all that egalitarian on the social level. It gets around the rigid structure of the orders by facilitating the creation of political networks that escape the Old Régime's traditional social organization. Historically, clientele systems are strongly developed in societies in which the state is weak, as it was France during the Wars of Religion. Never expressed as such, the relationship between patron and client is generally based on "probable" expectations of mutual favors that are never quantified and always remain vaguely defined. Each party gives and receives in accord with his means and opportunities in a system of vertical relations in which equality is not a determining relational criterion. Thus clientelism does away with hierarchy to level out human relationships on the basis of a relative reciprocity conceived over the long term.

Finally, the relationship between patron and client presupposes that the client has direct access to the patron, without protocol or ceremony. When Montaigne went to Fleix, the château's doors were always open to him, whereas other people had to obey the rules of protocol or arrange for ceremonious introductions. Clientelism is particularly effective when there is a visible disproportion and inequality, experienced as such, between the two parties in what is called the political order of the clientele system. This order is governed by the mutual dependence between two individuals who come from different milieus and do not move in the same spheres of power. Clientelism facilitates access to worlds that are socially closed and ordinarily inaccessible. In this redefined order, the client never seeks to rise to the level of his patron, but simply to benefit from a unique and privileged relation conceived as a *friendship*. Patron and client participate in a generalized exchange in the form of reciprocal gifts and favors exchanged without any accounting. These gifts might be material or symbolic, and they might include information, which in the sixteenth century was also considered an object of exchange. Since it was a matter of reciprocal gifts, no one thought about the exchange value of the goods involved; people limited themselves to projecting their own needs and desires for reciprocity onto the object *freely* transmitted.

The political use of what is given serves as the basic principle of the exchange and determines the utility of the clientele system. Disinterestedness and the rejection of commercial logic corresponds rather well to Montaigne's conception of human relationships.[121] As we have suggested, clientelism is based on a form of reciprocity, on the basis of "gifts" that do not, however, have the same value. In this unbalanced exchange, the patron can offer more or less immediate rewards to his client, who generally returns them later on because they always represent a social or political investment over the middle or the long term. If on the one hand Montaigne received honorific rewards thanks to his patron's rather rapid intervention, on the other it took more than ten years before the marquis of Trans benefited from a "return on his investment" delivered by Montaigne. This temporal imbalance in the services rendered is an integral part of the clientele system. In every case, the exchange is advantageous, and ultimately each party gets something out of it. An honorific reward like the necklace of the Order of Saint Michael can be envisaged only on the recommendation of a patron. It is a gift, but also an obligation that makes a commitment over time, an obligation for the client, for example, to provide his patron with information—certainly of less value, but nonetheless important—regarding the latest negotiations or events at the city hall, the parlement, or the Court.

The servitude inherent in the status of client implies a false self-consciousness that normalizes relationships and transforms the instrumentalization of the client into an affective relationship. The benefits demanded from the client do not have to be expressed because they are a matter of affect. Thus Montaigne might inform his patron of the latest rumors at the Court and tell him about part of his negotiations without feeling that he was betraying confidences. His correspondence teems with references to trips made to Fleix to transmit information to Gaston de Foix, but also to inform Matignon of his conversations with his patron: "Then they tell me about Fleix."[122] Or: "Right now, I've got boots on my legs to go to Fleix,"[123] or "I have just arrived from Fleix."[124]

Over the years, Montaigne became expert at playing the role that his patrons expected of him. He had become an informer who went back and forth between the king's men (Matignon), the local high nobility (Gaston de Foix), and the Protestant camp (Henry of Navarre). He had played his cards right by distributing different political information to the three parties involved. In Montaigne's case, it is sometimes very difficult to make the fine distinction between a negotiator for the king and Henry of Navarre, on the one hand, and a double agent in the service of a third political force (the Foix-Gurson), on the other hand.

This form of clientelism requires respect and loyalty to one's patron as well as a certain autonomy, because the client is not formally attached to his house and receives no salary for his service. Nor does he have any explicit duty, and that is why friendship is indispensable in any clientele relationship. Montaigne adapted to this extremely well. It suffices to read the chapter "Of three kinds of association" (III: 3) to see how much he idealizes the possibility of giving oneself entirely to one's friend in a disinterested way. This gift of oneself allows the individual to preserve a certain independence and to feel free in his relationship with his patron. Clientelism also authorizes private relationships that set aside the order or the social status of the parties involved; it authorizes a frankness and a more direct style of speech that Montaigne was soon to transform into a literary genre. Rather than an exchange—in the commercial sense of the term—the clientelist economy is based on freely consented reciprocal contributions. On several occasions in the *Essais*, Montaigne makes the gift the ideal mode of interaction between two friends.

At a time when a commercial logic was gradually being established in people's ways of thinking and when the new capitalist economic order was overturning and replacing the feudal order, Montaigne rediscovered in the clientele relationship a bygone noble ideal. These contradictory mentalities—bourgeois and noble—are found in the *Essais* in the form of two series of values that have become incompatible: the "gain" (*gaing*) and the "knowledge" (*sçavoir*) of the new commercial class are opposed to the "honor" (*honneur*) and "virtue" (*vertu*) of the true nobility. The clientelism whose rules he accepts allowed Montaigne to retain a vaguely feudal mode of life while increasing his freedom and independence with regard to the social constraints of his time. Not extensively developed during the Middle Ages, clientelism made its appearance in a society in which the individual was demanding a certain autonomy and creating around himself a private space, access to which he reserved for a limited number of individuals. Thus the gift leads to a redefinition of the terms of exchange while at the same time preserving the illusion of a coded structure in which what was left unsaid and allusions counted as much as promises. We can say that clientelism is based on a tacit code of honor that governs relations between two people but is never formulated; it is a kind of nobility to which Montaigne learned to adapt.

For example, clientelism proposes to recreate family ties outside the family, drawing on the proximity of residence or the family's ancestral knowledge of its patron or its client. It is not rare to find a patron serving as a godfather to a client's child, or, inversely, to find a client serving as a witness at the wedding or the baptism of a member of his patron's family. It was in this spirit that Montaigne was present as the proxy of Louis de Foix's father and mother. He also attended the nuptial celebrations at Gurson from March 30 to April 18, 1579, when one of the marquis de Trans's sons, the Count of Gurson, married Diane de Foix, to whom Montaigne dedicated a chapter of his *Essais*, "On the education of children." He considered the Foix-Gursons to be full-fledged members of his family.

The clientele relations between members of the high nobility and those of the middle nobility, who came from the third estate but occupied posts with economic or administrative responsibilities, are particularly interesting because they elevated the social position of clients by associating them with patrons who belonged to the nobility of the sword. However, these relations also gave lords, who were still relatively isolated on their lands, access to the new centers of power in the cities.

In Montaigne's case, belonging to the clientele of a member of the high nobility was a sign of full-fledged nobility, and also gave him access to networks that could help him realize his professional ambitions. In his *Essais*, he emphasizes this form of voluntary servitude (the gift of oneself to the other), but he also disparages this tie if it is based on an immediate gain. This contrast in the discourse is present in many chapters of the *Essais*. In "Of custom" (I: 23) Montaigne clearly articulates these two opposed systems of values: "One should have charge of peace, the other of war; one should have gain as its share, the other honor; one knowledge, the other virtue; one words, the other action; one justice, the other valor; one reason, the other force; one the long robe, the other the short."[125] Language betrays these oppositions; the confrontation of two antagonistic systems of value provokes a series of paradoxes and heteroglossias that denote the ideological ambiguity of Montaigne's discourse on economics, for example. The long robe is behind him; make way for the short robe in a system of social exchanges whose cornerstone is regional clientelism.

Thus, confronting the growing influence of commercialism in human relationships, friendship with the patron expresses nonexchange in the *Essais*; it symbolizes the fulfillment of a primitive economy based on the gift. However, the situation in which it is uttered allows us to discern a contradiction in the way this ideal is expressed. In the society in which Montaigne lived, this system founded on seigneurial estates and the exchange of favors was historically obsolete. In a situation in which contractual relations were increasingly dominated by the bourgeois (the market) and the *robin* (the parlement), clientelism was anachronistic.

Fidelity and loyalty are the only constraints on the clientele relationship. No other form of pressure can be exercised by the client, who can always withdraw from this connection. That often happens when a client finds himself in a power relationship or a new political group that leads him to detach himself from his patron and associate himself with a new one. It is not rare to see clients change patrons to join a power group that will bring them closer to the Court. The perception of power is more important than power itself. Then obligations and duties are created in relation to mutual expectations that often remain at the stage of desires or projects. The patron possesses a symbolic capital that has not yet been perceived as essential or that has not yet been exploited, and the client hopes to benefit, if possible, from the future effects of this capital. It is up to him to exploit it. To do so, he is prepared to declare his allegiance and to wait patiently to be called, someday, to serve his patron to the extent of his means and in the hope of receiving a reward that is disproportionate with respect to what he himself is able to offer.

As we have suggested, clientelism functions most effectively in a limited space. A personal relationship developed between the marquis of Trans, a member of the high nobility, and Montaigne, who belonged to the minor provincial nobility, because their châteaus were near each other. The client's availability and his ability to go rapidly to his patron's home facilitated the development of friendly relations over time. Moreover, the marquis of Trans offered Montaigne access to a more elevated group of members of the nobility in Guyenne, thus allowing him to be recognized as one of them. This promotion was possible only after a reminder of his titles of nobility. After he obtained the necklace of the Order of Saint Michael, the next step in the making of the gentleman Montaigne was his presentation at the Court. In 1573, shortly after he had entered the nobility, Montaigne was named an ordinary gentleman of the chamber of King Charles IX. This title represented more an honorific reward than a real function; as an inferior office, it imposed no obligation of residence or any particular constraint. Simply named and not accompanied by letters patent, minor officials replaced *valets de chambre*, an old-fashioned and "very base" title, as Charles Loyseau remarked in his treatise *Du droict des offices*.[126]

Loyseau describes the title and function of these minor royal officials this way: "The proliferation of almoners under Henry II and of ordinary gentlemen of the chamber under Charles IX had as their goal to win the service of nobles." Loyseau denounces the growing multitude of these officers who "were suddenly found in enormous numbers, especially under the late King Henry III."[127] They were so numerous (more than a 150) that they no longer received any salary and were considered to be honorary officers. This was the case for Montaigne, who boasts about not being paid for his services. Several cases of officers who bore the title of "ordinary gentlemen" but were not descended from noble families are reported at this time. They were ritually denounced by nobles of the sword, who were indignant to see so many minor provincial lords entering the king's chamber. These recriminations against the non-noble origin of gentlemen of the king's chamber led to several complaints during the 1570s. In 1579, article 259 of the order promulgated at Blois stipulated, for example, that "no one will be received into the condition of gentlemen of our chamber unless he is a noble of the sword; and if there are some who are not of the aforesaid quality, his Majesty will provide others to replace them."[128] Montaigne had once again come in at just the right time. He prominently publicized these two honorific rewards—the knighthood in the Order of Saint Michael and the status of ordinary gentleman of the king's chamber—on the title pages of the first editions of the *Essais* to indicate that he belonged to a respectable nobility, if not to the nobility of the sword.

Considered a loyal and moderate man, Montaigne had the qualities necessary to play a political role in his region. But before he could be propelled into the Bordeaux political milieu, he first had to acquire recognition in Paris, that is, he had to be admitted, considered, and esteemed at the Court. The Foix-Gurson family intervened to accelerate the beginning of his political career, which had necessarily to take him to Paris. Grateful to his "sponsors," Montaigne always showed a special affection for the members of this family that had helped him make a name for himself in politics. In his almanac, Montaigne sees the sons of the marquis of Trans as true "lords and friends,"[129] and throughout his life he maintained a privileged relationship with his protector, even if he ended up distancing himself from him after 1585. Thanks to this family, Montaigne succeeded in rising as far as the king's first circle. He admitted that he owed this to the Foix-Gursons and acknowledged his dependency and the obligations that accompanied any form of political submission to his patrons between 1570 and 1585. However, for him this form of servitude was far preferable to the administrative and familial straitjacket he had experienced at the parlement of Bordeaux.

Montaigne openly refers to his servitude in the chapter "Of the education of children," which is dedicated to Diane de Foix, the countess of Gurson: "For having had so great a part in bringing about your marriage, I have a certain rightful interest in the greatness and prosperity of whatever comes out of it; besides that, the ancient claim that you have on my servitude is enough to oblige me to wish honor, good, and advantage to all that concerns you."[130] However, let us note that the word "servitude," which implies political advantage, has no negative connotation in this passage written shortly before the first publication of the *Essais* in 1580. But the perception of this servitude evolved over time. Its coming to consciousness—which at first seems contradictory if we do not compare the different editions of the *Essais*—was gradual and was clearly acknowledged only after 1585, and especially after 1588, when Montaigne had detached himself from his political ambitions of the 1570s and early 1580s. After 1585, he was overcome by irony when he thought about his vassalage and dependency on his protectors: "As things stand, I live more than half by others' favor, which is a harsh obligation."[131]

The marquis of Trans offered Montaigne, as we have said, all the honorific rewards (with the exception of his Roman citizenship) that allowed him to consolidate a nobility that his ancestors had roughed out a century before. Montaigne never forgot this friend, with his frankness of speech and his legendary fits of rage, even if he did not always approve of him when he behaved like a Gascon soldier. "He strikes, he bites, he swears," Montaigne says, explaining that "All that is just a farce."[132] In the same passage of the *Essais*, Montaigne added, after 1588, that in his view, Gaston de Foix was "the most impetuous master in France." Thanks to the marquis of Trans, the Montaignes were henceforth perceived as the equals of the prestigious lineages of the Foix-Candales, the Foix-Gursons, and the Foix-Carmaings. Montaigne's nobility was largely consolidated by the clientele relationship that bound him to the Foix. Without this relationship developed in the 1570s, it is probable that Montaigne would never have had access to royal Courts, and we can hypothesize that his book would not have been conceived in the same way or with the same intentions. Moreover, it is not clear that the *Essais* could have been imagined outside of his new political career conducted thanks to this clientele relationship with the Foix-Gursons.

After 1577, Montaigne could consider himself a noble without worrying about being challenged. Hurault de L'Hospital, in his *Discours sur l'état de France* (1591), asserts that France had between twenty and thirty thousand nobles at the end of the sixteenth century.[133] At that time the kingdom counted about sixteen million inhabitants. It is not easy to define nobility,[134] but from a strictly legal point of view, the criteria were relatively simple. Nobles were divided into two groups: the first were called *nobles de race*, to use the expression of the time, because they could prove their origin and their noble lineage and show that they had been living nobly on their own lands, without paying the *taille*, for at least a century. The second group of nobles were born commoners, but had been ennobled by the king.[135] They might have received letters of ennoblement confirmed in the court of the parlement.

The problem with these definitions is that they do not take into account the temporal aspect of the quality of nobility. In the sixteenth century, members of the minor nobility, or the second nobility, exercised a political power that was increasingly visible in the French provinces, but their origins were more problematic.[136] For example, what did it mean to have "always lived nobly"? Recourse to the collective memory, or on the contrary to its forgetfulness, served to transform commoners into nobles without their necessarily needing to have been officially ennobled by a royal act. The confusion grew when one acquired a seigneurial property. It goes without saying that fiefs and noble lands did not ennoble the men who bought them,[137] but often it sufficed that they take up residence on these lands and live there in obscurity for two or three generations in order then to proclaim themselves to be nobles without arousing much protest. If after several generations a commoner who owned an ancient noble land was known to have lived nobly on it, that is, without engaging in any activity incompatible with nobility, he became a noble, at least at the local level. Over time, these commoners who had become nobles often succeeded in liberating themselves from the *taille* and then left their commoner status behind. It was they who increased the numbers of the minor provincial nobility at the end of the sixteenth century.

In the early 1570s, Michel de Montaigne belonged to the minor nobility, that of the *arrière-ban*.[xviii] In 1594, the roll of the nobles and others who held a noble fief subject to the *ban et arrière-ban* included no less than 220 names in the region where Montaigne lived.[138] These nobles were classified by their place of residence: Bordeaux (twenty-seven names); the "Gasque" land (twenty-two); Médoc (fifty-seven); Entre-deux-Mers (fifty-four); the countries of Castillon, Saint-Émilion, and Libourne (nineteen); Blayais (seventeen); the seigneury of Puynormand (seven); Cubzagais and Bourgeais (twenty); and Fronsadois (seventeen).[xix] As we have said, Montaigne's domain was not one of the most imposing in the region, and his residence looked more like a big house than a genuine château, but his lands nonetheless constituted a fief, and thus he was subject to the *arrière-ban*. As a gentleman, Montaigne was obligated to do military duty whenever the sovereign called upon him. On May 11, 1574, in his capacity as a gentleman of the king, he joined the royal army in Poitou. However, the obligation to provide military service was not very pressing under the last Valois, even during the Wars of Religion, because fewer than 15 percent of French gentlemen were militarily involved during the second half of the sixteenth century.[139] So far as Périgord is concerned, about 30 percent of the gentlemen took up arms during these same civil wars.[140] The military expenditures that normally accompanied membership in the order of nobility were small or even nonexistent in certain cases like that of Montaigne, who never had to lodge men at arms.

Among the members of the *ban et arrière-ban*, Jean-Louis de Nogaret de La Valette, the duke of Épernon, was considered the leader of this first nobility in Guyenne. Épernon had also developed a sizable clientele in the southwest, and had been able to surround himself with loyal Gascons. He never traveled without an escort of a hundred gentlemen[141] and intervened directly in the election of jurats. The king used him to reduce the Guises' influence in Aquitaine. The roll of nobles holding fiefs in the Bordeaux region mentions Bertrand de Montferrand; Jean de Lur; Jacques de Duras; René de Lansac; Thomas de Pontac; Joseph de La Chassaigne; Pierre de Brach; the baron of Vaillac; the lord of Pressac; and Thomas de Montaigne, lord of Beauregard and Montaigne's brother, among others.[142] Most of these lords formed the first circle of Montaigne, who, despite his common ancestry, belonged to a large group of minor lords who en-

---

[xviii] The *ban et arrière-ban* consisted of king's vassals who could be called up for military duty. [Trans.]

[xix] This list is problematic insofar as it gives indiscriminately feudal lords' names, titles, and qualities. Persons are sometimes designated by their family name, sometimes by the name of their fief. That is precisely the ambiguity played upon by this new nobility, whose origins are often not clear.

joyed the right of franc-fief and a noble title within a relatively limited geographical space.

Concerned to legitimate his membership in the middle-level nobility, Montaigne multiplied "proofs of nobility" in his *Essais*, one of his acknowledged goals being to leave a written trace of his noble way of life: "Now, we ... are trying on the contrary to make not a grammarian or a logician, but a gentleman."[143] L'Alouëte mentions a "sickness in the nobility" (*mal de la noblesse*)[144] and scolds the nobles who have abandoned noble values such as loyalty, magnanimity, constancy, patience, modesty, and all the other chivalric virtues valued in the Middle Ages. Likewise, Montaigne criticizes the pernicious transformations of the noble ideal that had come about over less than two generations and alludes to the profound changes that were warping the old nobility: "How many gentlemen have we in France who are of royal blood by their account?"[145] In this way he defends his own path for attaining this "modern" nobility which, without being a *noblesse de race*, nonetheless incarnated the noble values that had been compromised by the rise of a utilitarianism that corrupts society and human relationships. Montaigne was proud to display the coat of arms that he had painted in his château, engraved on a token, and even hung in a chapel at Our Lady of Loretto in Italy: "I bear azure powdered with trefoils or, with a lion's paw of the same, armed gules in fesse."[146] He comments ironically on the fact that after his death his son-in-law will transport his coat of arms into another family, forgetting, however, that this same coat of arms was in the family for less than a hundred years and that it had been acquired from another family of nobles who had gone bankrupt. One may therefore wonder with him whether "some paltry buyer will make of it his first coat of arms."[147]

The years between 1570 and 1574 were marked by the making of the gentleman Montaigne, who was also concerned to live in a civil way, that is, in accord with the precepts of the perfect courtier. In the *Essais* we find two passages borrowed from Castiglione's *Book of the Courtier*. The man of letters and diplomat of the Court of Urbino allowed Montaigne to redefine civility in accord with the values of the nobility.[148] At this time, frequenting great lords occupied a large part of Montaigne's time, and in less than four years, he had made his way into the political milieu of his region. Having made himself somebody and projected himself into the forefront of politics in Guyenne, he acquired a public fame he had never had as a member of parlement. He began to be entrusted with missions. In May 1574 the governor of Bordeaux, Montferrand, asked him to go see Louis II of Bourbon (1519–1582), duke of Montpensier and commander in chief of the royal army for the southwest, to tell him about the unrest and divisions provoked by the rivalry between the lord of Limeuil and lord of Bourdeille (Brantôme's brother). Soon afterward, Montaigne was sent to the camp of Saint-Hermine in the Vendée by the duke of Montpensier, who was assigned to wage war in Poitou against La Noue, and who was waiting there for an opportunity to attack. Montaigne was chosen to transmit a message to the parlement of Bordeaux, and he rode hard to get there as soon as possible and read out Montpensier's instructions in the Great Chamber.[149] His arrival at the Palais de l'Ombrière is reported in the parlement's *Registres secrets*, which even reports his speech:

> May 11, 1574. When it was reported that the lord of Montaigne, knight of the king's order and formerly a royal councillor at the court, was in the hearing room and had asked to speak to that court, it was ruled that he should be seated and placed in the middle of the Great Chamber's table, which he was among the other councillors of that chamber, and the aforesaid Montaigne having entered, he presented the letters from the lord of Montpensier addressed to the court, which were read out, and afterward the aforesaid Montaigne gave a long speech.[150]

This description of Montaigne's presence in the Great Chamber must be compared with the one he gives in his almanac:

> In the year 1574, Monsieur de Montpensier having sent me hither to the camp of Sainte-Hermine on business, and being assigned to communicate on his behalf with the court of the parlement of Bordeaux, the court agreed to hear me in the Council Chamber, seated at the table and above the king's men.[151]

The same event is perceived rather differently. It was one of Montaigne's first official missions (perhaps *the* first) as a plenipotentiary envoy in the service of the king, and he considered this assignment sufficiently important to record it in his almanac. We can imagine the pleasure he took in appearing before his former colleagues as a gentleman and a representative of the king. He had never been able to take a seat in the Great Chamber during his stay at the parlement, and he must have felt a deep satisfaction—if not a feeling of revenge—in upsetting the usual protocol when he took the floor. Obviously, Montaigne did not mention the fact that he had been prevented from speaking until he took his seat among the councillors, as the parlement's rules required. He also had to present the order entrusting him with a mission before he was allowed to speak, and then forced the members of the parlement to listen to "a long speech." Unfortunately, the parlement's registers do not tell us what he said, but it is nonetheless possible to imagine his tone and his vehemence.

The following year, Montaigne was in Poitiers on another mission;[152] some scholars have suggested that he fought against the Protestants at the siege of Fontenay,[153] but on the whole these first years in the king's service and in the Foix-Gursons' clientele remain rather poorly documented and do not allow us to know all his movements. However, Montaigne seems to have been on the look-out for every opportunity to transmit orders and instructions through the region. He considered himself a representative, almost a plenipotentiary ambassador within the kingdom. His titles as knight of the king's order and ordinary gentleman of the king's chamber gave him political legitimacy and access to great figures that he quickly learned to exploit. Always ready to set out on horseback to travel the roads of France, he avidly sought these missions that might be transmitted to him by his neighbors in the château of Fleix, in the hope of making himself better known to the high nobility that he was beginning to frequent.

The death of Charles IX on May 30, 1574, raised a serious problem for Montaigne and his protectors. After the king's demise, everything had to be redone. Montaigne had received his honorific rewards from Charles IX; thus he had to make himself noticed by the young Henry III and the queen mother, and prove his allegiance to the new king. He developed a strategy for approaching the Court that was not unusual in his time; perhaps it was the marquis of Trans and the Foix family that suggested he make himself known at the Court by publishing a book that might help him introduce himself there. In the meantime, the marquis of Trans did all he could to bring his client closer to the Court. We can assume that the Foix family once again intervened directly in the nomination of Montaigne as a gentleman of the chamber of the king of Navarre in November 1577. Henry of Navarre had a certificate of gentleman of his chamber sent to Montaigne while Montaigne was away.[154] Once again, Montaigne recorded this notable event in his almanac: "1577, Henry of Bourbon, king of Navarre, without my knowledge and in my absence had letters patent as gentleman of his chamber sent to me in Leitoure [Lectoure]."[155] This appointment alludes to "other recommendations" probably made in person by the marquis de Trans, who had established closer relations with the king of Navarre and was now working to reconcile the two Henrys and to bring peace between the two religions:

> For the good and praiseworthy report that we have received regarding the person of our dear and beloved Michel de Montaigne, knight of the order of the king my lord, and regarding his good sense, ample learning, virtue, valor, and commendable merits, we have named the aforesaid, moved by these reasons and other considerations, to the condition and office of ordinary gentleman of our chamber.[156]

It is clear that Montaigne's protectors were promoting his career without consulting him, on both the Catholic and the Protestant sides. From a political point of view, making Montaigne a gentleman of the Court of the king of Navarre allowed the Protestant leader to enlarge his clientele among the Catholic gentlemen. He was seeking a legitimacy that did not depend solely on the usual religious cleavages, and he needed the support of the middle-level nobility of Aquitaine. It was beginning at this time that Montaigne's political career took on a national dimension, because he could henceforth play the role of an ideal mediator while at the same time guaranteeing the king that he was a "good Catholic." There was no doubt about his religion, and neither could he be blamed for being too close to the party of the *politiques*, who were perceived as dangerous because they openly advocated negotiation with the Protestants. Montaigne stuck strictly to his role as mediator, without giving the impression of taking sides; he constantly reaffirmed that he belonged to the Catholic religion, but he was nonetheless capable of maintaining his convictions outside the religious debate that divided his time, preferring to justify them by culture and by tradition. The *Essais* allowed him to repeatedly reassert this singular position.

Although Montaigne had earlier appeared to be, all considered, a very average figure of limited scope, when he was confirmed as a gentleman by Henry III and Henry of Navarre he suddenly became much more interesting to his entourage. As a member of the middle-level nobility, his critical judgment was remarkable and uncommon for a lord of that time. The ignorance of the gentlemen of Henry III's time was notorious and has been commented upon at length.[157] Passing from the condition of a *robin* to that of a gentleman, Montaigne found himself a member of the intellectual elite of the nobility of his time, especially in the provinces. A mediocre member of parlement, he became a brilliant gentleman who was an exception amid a nobility that still preferred the sword to the pen.[158] His education now turned out to be a significant advantage that many nobles of the sword did not enjoy. He chose to write in a new style that reflected his status as a gentleman, opting for a genre that contrasted with the writing of the *robins*. His *Essais* are a mixture of, on the one hand, erudition and a knowledge of ancient culture, particularly historical and legal culture—the prerogative of an elite consisting of jurisconsults and members of parlement—and, on the other hand, especially in the first edition of the *Essais* in 1580, the presence of a significant number of reflections on war, horsemanship, dueling, and other desiderata peculiar to a gentleman.[159] The genre and style of the *Essais* of 1580 seem to have led Montaigne to distinguish himself from a group and an order that he rejected while at the same time giving priority to the values of the nobility, without for all that being completely associated with it. As a form, the essay is not the product of a political experience, but a new genre that takes into account what is most essential and determinative about politics in the formation and expression of experiences that are perceived as personal and singular.

Montaigne at Work

During these years, when he was at home and intermittently, Montaigne dictated his reflections to a secretary. The shaping of the *Essais* leading to the first edition of 1580 occupied him from 1571 to 1579. Eight years might suggest meticulous preparation, but it was not a full-time activity, because writing was not Montaigne's chief occupation during these years; it was a secondary labor that he conceived as a complement to his main political activity. Montaigne declares that "It was only just two weeks ago that I passed the age of thirty-nine years"[160] when he began to write one of his first chapters. Thus the commencement of his work as an author can be dated to the end of 1571 or the beginning of 1572, at the time of a first and short-lived "retirement from the world," but he was also putting his energy into making his name known and agreed to numerous political encounters to which his protectors invited him. His return to professional life required his physical presence at meetings organized by Gaston de Foix. Montaigne rapidly became involved in a system of "sociability" that was rather demanding for someone who still suffered from a lack of recognition. His increased presence in the networks developed by his patrons was incompatible with retirement from the world. This transition from the world of the *Palace of Justice* (where he frequented the *robins*) to that of the *princely palaces* (where he played the role of a courtier among members of the high nobility) marked a necessary stage in his transformation into a public figure.

Like some of his contemporaries, Montaigne had the ambition of becoming a historian of his time. It was perhaps in view of that goal that he attempted writing contemporary history and considered composing a commentary on the election of Henry of Anjou to the throne of Poland.[161] A seventeenth-century text refers to this project of becoming a historian that was "abandoned by Michel de Montaigne, who had undertaken to write about this whole expedition."[162] However, he is supposed to have given up this plan after the sovereign's return to France. The death of Charles IX in May 1574 had suddenly transformed Henry of Anjou into the king of France. His flight from Poland without the permission of the Diet left a bitter memory in Poland, and from that moment on, writing the history of that country became a delicate exercise.

After the coronation of the duke of Anjou as Henry III in early 1575, it is likely that Montaigne decided to change tactics. Toward the end of 1574 he was considering a very different project in which history was also supposed to have a place. However, he had to distance himself a bit from events. The king who had decorated him with the necklace of the Order of Saint Michael had just died, and Montaigne had to reckon with a court that had been thrown into turmoil by the arrival of a new monarch. Under the pressure of events, Montaigne abandoned his projects involving the writing of contemporary history, but without apparent regret. This ability to understand political reality and to respond to it in a pragmatic way was to accompany him throughout his political career, because the fiery actuality of the Wars of Religion and of international scheming were more the area of pamphleteers, who practiced a kind of writing Montaigne did not much esteem. For that reason, in the *Essais* he remains relatively silent regarding the years 1572–75. This period, which was pivotal on the social and political level, nonetheless allowed him to conceive an authorial strategy that was intended to bring him closer to the royal Court and to diverse centers of power, on both the regional and the national levels.

Very early on, Montaigne seems to have made efforts to find a publisher for his writings. Since he had obtained the necklace of the Order of Saint Michael, he had forged, thanks to the Foix-Gursons, an image of himself as a Gascon gentleman, and it seemed to him preferable to look for a publisher not too far from his home in order to ensure that his writings would be diffused among those who knew him. In 1572, a new printer, Simon Millanges, had just established himself in Bordeaux, near the College of Guyenne and the Jesuit college, and very close to the Palais de l'Ombrière. In early 1573, the city's jurats had signed a contract with Millanges to establish a printshop there. At that time, Millanges was a regent at the College of Guyenne. It has been claimed, wrongly, that he was the first printer in Bordeaux, but it is true that he was the first "big" printer in the city. He had bought from Pierre Haultin, a printer in La Rochelle, two printing presses as well as all the equipment necessary to set himself up as a printer. To establish himself in Bordeaux, he asked the jurats for 200 écus and a dwelling on the Rue Saint-James; he also wanted to be received as a citizen of Bordeaux and exempted, along with his descendants, from all the fees and taxes levied on citizens. The city agreed to his demands and offered him 400 *livres* "to help him find lodging and purchase provisions and other things he needs." In exchange, Millanges promised not to print any "prohibited or scandalous" book "against the edicts of the king."[163]

Looking for a printer, Montaigne made Millanges's acquaintance through François de Foix-Candale, whose translation of the *Pimandre de Mercure Tris-megiste*[xx] was published by Millanges in 1574, and then again in 1579, the year in which Laurent Joubert's *Erreurs populaires* appeared. A mathematician, alchemist, and savant with a great reputation, François de Foix-Candale had also served as a councillor in the parlement of Bordeaux until 1570, before becoming bishop of Aire-sur-Adour. The remarkably fine folio volume that Millanges printed for Foix-Candale probably persuaded Montaigne to do business with this printer. As one of Foix-Candale's neighbors, Montaigne met him fre-

---

[xx] The *Pimandre* is a chapter in the *Corpus Hermeticum*, a famed wisdom text attributed to Hermes Trismegistus. [Trans.]

quently, and it is very likely that his considerations on the reform of the Gregorian calendar in 1582 were inspired by his conversations with this savant, who had counseled the pope on this subject.[164] The publication of the *Pimandre* lent a humanist veneer and respectability to Millanges, who was already accepted in learned groups in Bordeaux. It is likely that Montaigne met him as early as 1574 or 1575, but his book may have taken him longer to finish than he had anticipated. Whether they came from the Foix-Candales or the Foix-Gursons, Montaigne listened to the counsels of these high-ranking figures who could open doors for him. Before he could hope to serve the king at a higher level, he had to reaffirm his membership in the nobility of the sword and publish a book associated with a new genre that would allow him not only to demonstrate his judgment in matters of politics and diplomacy, but also to sketch a portrait of himself that could win the confidence of princes.

It may have been in order to help him think or feel himself confirmed in his nobility that Montaigne had a token cast marked with his arms surrounded by the necklace of the Order of Saint Michael, on which was inscribed "Michel Seigneur de Montaigne."[165] On the reverse side was depicted a scale with horizontal pans surrounded by the formula "ΕΠΕΧΩ. 43. 1576" ("I abstain," Montaigne's first motto, accompanied by his age—forty-three in 1576).[xxi] At that time, he had a single political principle: he could judge personally, but he relied entirely on the authority of those who were above him in the hierarchy. He had understood that his political future would consist in serving as an intermediary, a negotiator or diplomat for a patron or a king. As a counselor or a representative of the government, his personal role was limited to faithfully and loyally transmitting and "reporting"—here his training as a councillor in the parlement came in handy— the views and opinions of others. A form of skepticism already defined his view of received truths. However, Montaigne did not yet see himself as a judge, simply as a reporter. The device "I abstain" was later to be replaced by the famous "Que sçais-je?" ("What do I know?"), which expressed a less political and more philosophical position. Montaigne's first motto sounds like a political slogan that he tried to put into practice in his role as a public man and an administrator.

The credo "I abstain" engraved on his token was a device particularly well chosen on the part of an intermediary between two parties that were fighting each other or on that of an ambassador whose role was to recount conversations

---

[xxi] The mold for this token was first described in 1856 by Dr. Payen (*Recherches sur Montaigne: Documents inédits*) and presented as Montaigne's "seal." In fact, it is a "*coin*" that served to strike a medal with a raised legend. This mold used to make the token was found among the rubble at Montaigne's château and was recently on the private art and antiquities market. A single token made of copper, measuring 27 mm in diameter and 1 mm in thickness, has been preserved and was until recently on display at Montaigne's château.

without taking sides. The balance-scale is doubly symbolic: first of all, it symbolizes justice, and Montaigne thus highlights his past as a member of the parlement, now emphasizing his expertise; second, it symbolizes the political equilibrium between two camps, each of which was trying to make the scale tip in its favor. Montaigne conceives his position as respectful of this delicate balance that makes it possible to maintain the political aplomb and stability of the kingdom. This transformation of a judicial symbol into a political allegory corresponds to Montaigne's idea of his role in the service of the princes. Maintaining a balance between the parties concerned, showing moderation in his own judgments, and abstaining from taking a position are the political principles that Montaigne emphasizes in his first *Essais*. The token—probably held in his hand or set before him on his worktable—could have made him think of all that when he was dictating his first reflections for the 1580 edition. This suspension of judgment also reflected a just reserve in a member of the nobility (of which the other side of the token reminds us). Montaigne tried to project the image of a devoted servant who was capable of determining what was essential in a statement in order to report it as accurately as possible. He obeyed the orders that were given him by the princes and applied the directives received. This is another Montaigne, quite different from the one to whom we are accustomed, who emerges in the 1570s. This other Montaigne puts himself entirely in the service of his patrons and sees himself first of all as a servant of princes and kings. We shall see that this attitude of submission and allegiance to the power that employs him is omnipresent in the first *Essais* of 1580.

From 1571 to 1579, the *Essais* were conceived as actual work; we have to imagine Montaigne laboring away in his library, surrounded by books that enabled him to pursue his enterprise of assembling texts to arrive at something that might resemble a book. His first chapters are short, as if he felt some difficulty in developing the titles chosen for his essays. He thought big because the first book consisted of fifty-seven chapters, most of them less than six pages long when printed in the octavo format of the first edition. At that time, Montaigne worked by accumulation; he added text to his "essay-drawers," which he filled as he read *randomly* in his library. But he had a few major themes, mainly political and diplomatic, which led him to organize his commentaries.

The order of the writing of the chapters in the first two books remains largely unknown, despite several efforts to retrace the evolution and organization of his first works.[166] Montaigne seems to have proceeded from core of ideas representing groups of chapters. The initial organizing scheme nevertheless remains rather vague, and the order of composition (which is impossible to determine precisely) must not be confused with the order Montaigne intended (the place of the chapters in the first edition of the *Essais*). Several chapters may even be considered to be couples, the line between which remains relatively porous. This is the case for the chapters "Of the inequality that is between us" (I: 42) and "On sumptuary laws" (I: 43), which might well have been separated after initially being written as a single unit. In a similar way, the theme of the uncertainty of battles is found in "Of the battle of Dreux" (I: 45), "Of the uncertainty of our judgment" (I: 47), and "Of ancient customs" (I: 49). Montaigne was not indifferent to the connection between his chapters, since in the first printings of the *Essais* their physical separation was minimal—to save paper.

The creation of a book involves a stage of across-the-board accumulation, that is, an accumulation without apparent order. The order and organization come afterward, once the book has begun to take shape. This quantitative stage is necessary and determined the form of the *Essais* at the time of the publication. Their author's work can be quantified, and statistical data concerning the material aspects of the fabrication of the *Essais* offer a few keys to the interpretation of the work as a whole. Very early on, Montaigne denounced the illusion that consists in seeing in his book a coherent whole, possessing a unity, because the text often contradicts itself, sometimes on a single page. Publishing a work several times under the same title necessarily produces contradictions and digressions in the course of the years and the editions—indeed, even from one chapter to the next, where the same themes are sometimes taken up. The author eludes this problem and fully accepts his book's incoherencies; he replies to the reproaches that might be made by emphasizing the "ambitious subtleties" that might escape the eyes of his reader.

The iconography of Montaigne is rich in representations of the author at work, holding the work of an ancient writer in his left hand and a quill in his right, putting down on paper critical commentaries on his readings. This conventional image is founded on an anachronism. In fact, the discovery of the Bordeaux Copy in the eighteenth century led to an overestimation of the work of writing and correction that Montaigne did on his own works after 1588. This manuscript is the origin of the myth according to which the author devoted every day to writing as his essential concern, as if only his book mattered in his life. The truth of the matter, however, is that the writing of the *Essais* actually occupied a very small part of Montaigne's life; he was engaged in many other domestic and political activities, both between 1570 and 1580 and afterward. Thus we have to limit our estimate of the time spent dictating and writing the *Essais*, which must have been written more intermittently than continuously.

It has been asked whether Montaigne wrote or dictated his *Essais*. The answer to this question depends on the period concerned, and on the role Montaigne gave himself when he was writing his *Essais*. From 1575 to 1580, it was mainly the gentleman who was asserting himself. Every lord of the middle and high nobility had a secretary (Montaigne dismissed one when he was in Rome). Between 1570 and 1580, he still did not imagine himself in the role of a writer, in the modern sense of the term. This professional activity would not be really valorized until after 1588. Montaigne was preoccupied instead by the making of a book, and he amassed remarks to put together a volume of reflections on politics, warfare, and diplomacy that mixed points of view and led him to distinguish himself from other authors of similar works.

The *Essais* of 1580 are situated in the tradition of memoirs, minus the political experience. Montaigne had not yet theorized the work of writing, and he probably dictated the first edition of his *Essais*,[167] whose content was certainly more important than its form or the act of writing itself. Montaigne tells us, for example, that after 1588 he abandoned the practice of *brouillars*—the making of a clean text on loose sheets of paper. A passage deleted from the Bordeaux Copy allows us to verify the way he worked up to 1585:

> Because it seems to me very like our own, I have decided to take this passage from its author, having earlier taken the trouble to say at length what I knew about the comparison of our arms with Roman arms: but this piece of my *brouillars* having been stolen along with several others by a man who was my servant, I shall not deprive him of the profit that he hopes to make from it: it would also be very difficult for me to chew the same meat twice.[168]

This anecdote reveals the drawbacks of dictating to a secretary. After 1588, Montaigne no longer trusted his house servants and preferred to do his own writing directly on copies of his *Essais* printed in Paris, but his relation to his text had evolved. His work on the text—thanks to the generous margins in the 1588 edition, and also to the simple fact that he henceforth did without the services of a secretary—was changed forever. He took a greater interest in the process of writing and rewriting and went so far as to correct, often in a meticulous way, the punctuation and capital letters in his earlier texts.

In this first labor whose goal was to *make* a book—no easy task, since it took Montaigne ninety-four chapters—he still did not see himself as the writer who systematically painted his *persona* after 1588. He describes his work this way: "I leaf through books, I do not study them,"[169] and "I leaf through now one book, now another, without order and without plan, by disconnected fragments. One moment I muse, another moment I set down or dictate, walking back and forth, these fancies of mine that you see here."[170] Montaigne fabricated his book as he read; he amassed texts until a book took physical form. The second description of "leafing through" stresses his dilettantish method of reading and writing. This way of writing may seem identical over time, but after 1588 it emphasizes above all the reveries of a walker who has become solitary,[xxii] whereas between

---

[xxii] An allusion to Jean-Jacques Rousseau's *Reveries of a Solitary Walker* (1782). [Trans.]

1571 and 1579 the book was more connected with the social and political reality of its time. The mental "walk" asserted itself rather late in Montaigne's work; it came after his terms as mayor of Bordeaux, a period of intense political activity that was followed by a second withdrawal from public life. Thus it was only after 1585 that he created a veritable ritual of writing in his library that critics have been too quick to generalize to all the periods of his life.

Montaigne organized his workroom in a special way; this space devoted to writing reflected the different possiblilities of consulting books. There were what we might call the "nearby books" and the "peripheral books," depending on how he maneuvered around his library. Montaigne also had manuscripts in his library. For example, a manuscript bearing Montaigne's ex libris was recently rediscovered in the Herzog August Bibliothek in Wolfenbüttel. This manuscript is a clean copy of extracts from the course taught by the jurist and humanist François Bauduin in Paris in 1561. Although this document is not in his hand and there is no reason to think that he attended this course in person, Montaigne did copy his name—in Latin—on the first page of the manuscript: "Michaël montanus." Let us add that the ex libris indicates possession, and is not the mark of the author or the copyist.[171] We must therefore imagine a library composed of books, manuscripts, documents, and notes taken on loose sheets of paper.

Montaigne's work with the volumes he kept close at hand (his reference books) took two rather distinct forms: the first was connected with a single reading of a work that he summed up and commented upon in a few lines. Nothing prevented this book from being consulted again several years later. The notes left in the books then took on all their importance. Montaigne explains the principle of rereading that he applied, not only to the writings of the Ancients and of his contemporaries, but also to his own writings, after an interval of a few years: "I have adopted the habit for some time now of adding at the end of each book (I mean of those that I intend to use only once) the time I finished reading it and the judgment I have derived of it as a whole, so that this may represent to me at least the sense and general idea I had conceived of the author in reading it."[172] We can see how much the rereading of the *Essais* after 1580 must have made Montaigne feel that he was reading a book by a different man, a text that had to be reworked to make it more intelligible to the reader (whom Montaigne imagined differently), and also to make it part of a publishing project that had evolved. These attempts to update the text were influenced by various experiences he had had in his public life and by the development of his political ambitions. Far from being isolated from the world, Montaigne's library was related to civil society. No one ever reads without preconceptions, and Montaigne's lack of memory was often a convenient excuse. In this sense, reverie is the result of forgetting or at least of a retreat from the social and political world. In any case, there is no authorial work without an authorial project.

Between 1572 and 1580, Montaigne's reading of the books in his library was primarily political, whereas after 1588—starting at the time when he himself wrote the last "extension" (*allongeail*) of his *Essais*—they tended to become more reflective and might even be described as introspective and philosophical. When he first began to write as an author, Montaigne dwelt on a passage, which he dictated to his secretary. His goal was not to formulate synthesizing reading notes. He was interested in particular passages, recording quotations or commentaries that would help him illustrate his own reflections in the chapters of the first two books of the *Essais*. The subjects chosen seem not to have been supplied in the same way, which tends to explain the imbalances between chapters. Montaigne borrowed from others' books to construct his own. The Ancients continued to nourish his own text until the point at which it became possible to speak of a book in its own right, after eight years of laborious accumulation. The first *Essais* represented the end result of a text that had been worked over, probed, and filled with elaborate erudition, but it was envisioned only in the context of a noble's relation to writing. These eight years of work— punctuated by interruptions and intermissions—finally gave birth to the lord of Montaigne's book, which was conceived to consolidate and serve political aspirations.

Beyond his political activities and the book to which he devoted part of his time, in the 1570s Montaigne also had children, five of them in seven years, all girls,[xxiii] only one of whom survived him. He recorded in his almanac the names of those who died in infancy;[173] without a son, he had to find a way to perpetuate his name. The name "Montaigne" begins and ends with Montaigne! What a paradox for a man who constantly demonstrated that he had a noble spirit and sought to construct a renown for posterity, without any concern for his descendants. Ultimately, his marriage to the muses produced his sole male child—the *Essais*—which bore his name and allowed him to foresee a new kind of posterity. It might even be argued that the success of his first *Essais* of 1580 allowed Montaigne to glimpse the possibility of an illustrious fame without putting him at the mercy of hypothetical descendants or the unforeseeable vicissitudes of the battlefield.

[xxiii] Montaigne's wife bore six daughters: Toinette, born June 28, 1570, died two months later; Léonor, born September 9, 1571, the only one who provided her parents with descendants; Anne, born July 5, 1573, lived seven weeks; N., born December 27, 1574, lived three months; N., born May 16, 1577, lived one month; Marie, born February 21, 1583, lived only a few days.

CHAPTER 6

The *Essais* of 1580: Moral, Political, and Military Discourses

In 1579, the Huguenot leaders met with their Catholic counterparts at Nérac. In accord with the latest edict of pacification, the king decided to grant the Protestants several strongholds. This step did not produce the hoped-for results; instead of calming people down, political and religious recognition actually increased the hostility between the two camps. The Catholic extremists had no intention of accepting the slightest compromise, and Henry III found himself more isolated than ever. Faced with the failure of this meeting, the king of Navarre had a declaration in the form of a protest published, in which he explained the necessity of taking up arms to defend Protestant churches in France.[1] The Protestants claimed that Henry III's edict had not been fully executed, notably in Bordeaux, where violent acts aimed at Protestants had increased in number. Thus in Langon, six leagues away,

> after the king of Navarre had caused the meeting to take place, evacuated all the foreigners, and that the lord of Saint-Oreux had resumed his functions as seneschal, the inhabitants, trusting in the public faith, were attacked at night by armed men using ladders . . . , as many as two or three hundred of them, the most conspicuous being from Bordeaux; fifteen or sixteen people were killed, women were raped, and all the goods were pillaged; without any compensation being received.[2]

The southwest was prey to this kind of settling of accounts in an infernal atmosphere of unrest and terror. Fighting had just begun again in Guyenne, and the lieutenant governor advised the king to reply with military force. He insisted that the men at arms be paid, "and not engage in robbery and extortion . . . without imposing any further trafficking on the great crowd of the poor."[3] Too much ravaging and pillaging had thrown the population into a state of near famine, and the region was being reduced to a disaster zone where insecurity prevailed. In this context of human suffering and deep hatred between

Protestants and Catholics, Montaigne published his first *Essais* in Bordeaux in 1580.

In February 1580, the king received contradictory reports on the political situation and the unrest in Guyenne. A memorandum written on February 26 by Armand de Gontaut, baron of Biron and marshal of France, insinuated that the monarch had been deceived by the reports from the Court of Nérac, and that the situation was much more worrisome than they suggested. Looting and murder were becoming more frequent in the region, and a number of cities were in imminent danger of falling into the hands of the Huguenots.[4] We have to resituate the first edition of the *Essais* in the local context of Bordeaux and Guyenne to grasp the work's political dimension. On April 21, 1580, Catherine de Medici wrote to Henry of Navarre: "My son, I cannot believe that it is possible that you desire the destruction of this kingdom, as will occur, along with yours, if war begins; and I beg you to consider what you are and what good you could derive from the ruin of this state."[5] On this same date, Henry of Navarre addressed a manifesto "To the gentlemen of the Nobility," in which he gave the reasons that had led him to take up arms on April 15.

In early 1580, things were moving toward an inevitable confrontation between the two Henrys, and Guyenne had suddenly become the center of this conflict between the royal party and the Huguenots. The first *Essais* printed in Bordeaux appeared in a climate of religious hostility and political maneuvering. It could even be suggested that the 1580 edition is an occasional work that was necessarily read in the context of the Wars of Religion. It was supposed to serve as a springboard for a career that Montaigne envisaged—a career not in writing, but in politics. He could believe that his book offered a new approach to post-Machiavellian politics, and many of the chapters in the first two books stressed their political, diplomatic, and military orientation.

Montaigne's geographical situation placed him at the heart of the religious discords of his time. We must never lose sight of the deep anchoring of the *Essais* in the episodes that punctuated the Wars of Religion in southwest France. The *Essais* have rightly been called a mirror and a critique of their time,[6] but the book also shows—at least in its first version—Montaigne's *participation* in the political debate and in political life. Far from being detached from the events of his time, Montaigne contributed to them in his own way. The particular circumstances of a private life were transformed into advantages on the public chessboard, not only in Guyenne and Gascony, but also, more generally, in Aquitaine. Montaigne may have been approached as an ideal mediator between Henry III and Henry of Navarre. His political conceptions made him a faithful servant of the king, and he was irreproachable on the religious level, but he was also welcome at the Court of Nérac and had succeeded in winning the esteem of the Gascon gentlemen who had rallied to the cause of Henry of Navarre.

His trips to Paris between 1575 and 1578 allowed Montaigne to remain close to the center of political power. His nobility had recently been confirmed, but he was not considered a courtier or a royal favorite. Moreover, unlike most of his contemporaries, Montaigne did not display religious ardor. He soon joined the camp of the *centristes* and *politiques*, even if he always proved independent and refused to be associated with any pressure group. He listened, reported, and seldom took sides. He created the persona of a moderate, simple man who was always frank; in short, his behavior contrasted with the political practices of the late sixteenth century. Imbued with a rusticity that made him more credible, he used his first *Essais* as a mirror reflecting the essential qualities of a confidant in the service of the king. He took his role seriously and considered pursuing a career in diplomacy, where his political perspicacity could best serve the royal cause. His models in the early 1570s continued to guide him.

"A Discourse on My Life and Actions"

The first edition of the *Essais* was printed with haste in Simon Millanges's shop, and the result shows it. The two volumes have print of different sizes, there are numerous misprints, the pagination is faulty, and the general presentation is uneven because the sizing was imprecise and the page format was changed in the course of the printing.[7] The typographical composition by plates required a meticulous assessment of the manuscript copy provided by the author to determine with precision the number of pages that were to appear on each of the printer's sheets. This imposition method was necessary to make it possible to fold the printed sheet in accord with the format chosen. This way of printing demanded rigorous sizing. However, we know that the work done by the compositor was faulty and that the printer had to modify the justification (the length of the lines) repeatedly as the book was being printed. Montaigne—who always accorded great importance to the book as an object—could not have been satisfied with the visual aspect of his work.

It has been suggested that the 1580 edition of the *Essais* was not intended to be distributed solely in the Bordeaux area, since the books Millanges printed were sold nationally, or at least in Paris, which amounted to the same thing.[8] In my view, this suggestion is anachronistic, because it presupposes Montaigne's later literary career. We might, for example, be surprised that he chose Millanges as his printer had he truly thought that his book would be distributed nationally. As early as the 1570s, he had several contacts in the milieu of Paris booksellers, and he could easily have sought out a Parisian publisher for his *Essais*. For instance, he had used printers in the capital for his translation of Sebond's *Theologia naturalis* and his edition of La Boétie's works.[i] It is certainly possible that it was Montaigne's father who found the printer for the *Theologia naturalis*, but Montaigne seems to have known enough about the Parisian publishing world to be capable, in 1580, of getting himself published in Paris—especially at his own expense! For his book, he deliberately chose a local printer, no doubt in order to root his reflections in their regional context and thus to show that he belonged to a tradition of learned Gascons. I have already indicated that François Foix-Candale may have encouraged him to proceed in this way. Furthermore, the decision to publish his book in Bordeaux had nothing to do with the fact that Montaigne became mayor of that city, because when he began to write the first chapters of his book, or even when he set out to find a printer for it after 1575, he could not have known that he would later hold that office.

Montaigne may have chosen Simon Millanges simply to accelerate the production of his book, and also the better to supervise the foremen and compositors in the print shop. Publishing in Bordeaux had many advantages.[9] The proximity of the printshop would save time for someone who accorded great importance to the presentation of his book, and who had set a publication date that he intended to respect. A volume corresponding to the material and graphic requirements the author imposed had to be produced rather quickly, even if the abrupt omission of the *Discours de la servitude volontaire* gave rise to unexpected problems.

It is likely that the bookseller's activity, in which Millanges also engaged, was secondary in Montaigne's view. Let us not underestimate, either, the fact that Millanges had specialized in publishing books that were new and "on trial" (*à l'essai*), such as those of Pierre de Brach and Guillaume du Bartas. The privilege accorded the *Essais* of 1580 (kept in the 1582 edition) authorized him, for example, to print "all new books," provided that they had been approved by the archbishop of Bordeaux, Antoine Prévost de Sansac, or his vicar, as well as by one or two doctors of theology.[10] Montaigne's friendship with the bishop of Aire, Christophe de Foix-Candale, naturally made it easier for the printer, who also worked for the city's civil and religious institutions, to obtain the required privilege. In addition to his eclectic publications, Millanges had specialized in works that deviated from the beaten paths and did not fit into the usual categories of publishing.

In 1580 Montaigne was preoccupied with publishing a book, but he had little interest in the distribution of his work; only the printing itself seems to have

---

[i] Michel Sonnius, Gilles Gourbin, and Guillaume Chaudière for the *Theologia naturalis*, and Federic Morel for La Boétie's *Mesnagerie de Xenophon* and *Vers françois*.

really concerned him. We shall see that he probably knew his reader in advance—at least, that is what he hoped—and did not yet foresee the possibility that his book would be a "literary success." In accord with the principle of personalization, such a work necessarily had to include its author's name in its title: *Essais de Messire Michel seigneur de Montaigne.*[ii] Moreover, in the 1580 and 1582 editions, the emphasis is put on the word "MESSIRE," printed in capital letters far larger than the rest of the title. This honorific denomination reserved for great lords (notably the knights in the Order of Saint Michael) sheds light on this first edition's literary project: it was without doubt a noble gentleman's book (figure 7).

In their octavo format with the two books bound in a single volume, the *Essais* of 1580 consisted of about 180,000 words.[11] It was only in 1588 that Montaigne added a third book composed of thirteen chapters. We note a major imbalance between the two books of the princeps edition (fifty-seven and thirty-seven chapters, respectively), a disparity that is, however, hardly visible because the font used for the second book is smaller in size and the printed page has fewer lines per page. The two books were printed on different presses, the sign of hasty production that resulted in a lack of consistency between the two volumes. One chapter stands out from the others by reason of its length: the "Apology for Raymond Sebond" (44,300 words). Montaigne composed the great majority of this chapter *before* 1580, that is, for the edition published by Simon Millanges in Bordeaux. The "Apology for Raymond Sebond" contains only 8,000 additional words in the 1588 edition, whereas Montaigne was to add nearly 13,000 new words to it after 1588. The first version of 1580 thus constitutes 68 percent of the final text of II: 12, whereas the additions of 1588 constitute only 12 percent of the final text and the additions made between 1588 and 1592, 22 percent. If we set aside this important chapter of the second book, we see that the two books are of about the same size—70,000 and 72,000 words respectively. The chapter devoted to the defense of Raymond Sebond thus represents a book within a book; modern editors have often published this chapter as a separate text. The first edition of the *Essais* was far from being in a noble format; its principal function was to get into print the *first book* published by Montaigne as an author.

In 1580, Montaigne believed in political action. His book is a collection of observations not only on his life but also on his actions. It bears on questions of

---

[ii] The noun "*Essais*" was preceded by a definite article (*Les Essais*) only after Montaigne's death. The posthumous edition of the *Essais* produced by Marie de Gournay in 1595 included this article for the first time; it is found in all the later editions throughout the seventeenth century. The edition published in Lyon by Gabriel La Grange (1593) uses the title *Livre des Essais*. The pirated edition published "in Lyon" (Geneva) in 1595 by François Le Febvre also introduces the definite article (*Les Essais*).

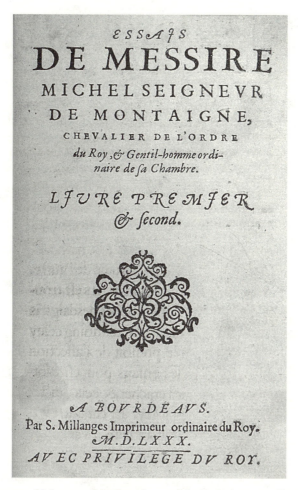

ESSA JS
DE MESSIRE
MICHEL SEIGNEVR
DE MONTAIGNE,
CHEVALIER DE L'ORDRE
*du Roy, & Gentil-homme ordi-
naire de sa Chambre.*

*LJVRE PREMJER
& second.*

A BOVRDEAVS.
Par S. Millanges Imprimeur ordinaire du Roy.
M.D.LXXX.
AVEC PRIVILEGE DV ROY.

FIGURE 7. Title page of the first edition of the *Essais* (private collection).

politics and diplomacy. Montaigne's first translators into Italian and English were clear about this, since they chose to render the title of his book by a longer description that corresponded better to the content they considered essential in the first edition of the *Essais* in 1580. Thus in 1590, when the author of the *Essais* was still alive, Girolamo Naselli gave his Italian translation the following title: *Discorsi morali, politici e militari* (figure 8).[12] We owe this very fragmentary translation, made on the basis of the first Paris edition of the *Essais* published in 1587, to a gentleman in the service of the duke of Ferrara. During a trip to France—between March and May 1589—Naselli discovered the *Essais* and undertook the translation of a few selected passages as soon as he returned to Italy. He had greatly admired the work of the French gentleman for its moral,

DISCORSI
MORALI, POLITICI,
ET MILITARI;
DEL MOLTO ILLVSTRE SIG.
Michiel di Montagna Caualiere dell'ordine del
Re Chriſtianiſſimo; Gentil'huomo ordinario
della ſua Camera, primo Magiſtrato
& Gouernatore di Bordeos.

TRADOTTI DAL SIG. GIROLAMO
Naſelli dalla lingua Franceſe nell'Italiana.

Con vn Diſcorſo ſe il foraſtiero ſi deue admettere alla
adminiſtratione della Republica.

All'Illuſtriſs. & Eccell. Sig. Don Ceſare d'Eſte.

IN FERRARA, Per Benedetto Mamarello.

Con Licenza de' Superiori.   M D X C.

FIGURE 8. Title page of the first Italian edition of the *Essais* (private collection).

political, and military reflections on Antiquity and the sixteenth century. Dedicated to Cesare d'Este, Naselli's translation of the *Essais* includes only half the chapters, and numerous passages were omitted or regrouped in other chapters.[13] A few years later, in 1603, the first translator of Montaigne into English, John Florio, also considered it necessary to explain what was meant by the word "essais." The title he gave his translation retains "Essayes," but he clarifies the term: *Essayes or Morall, Politike, and Millitarie Discourses.*[iii] These titles connected

[iii] It was at the request of Sir Edward Wotton that John Florio undertook, in 1595, the translation of a single chapter of the *Essais,* "Of the education of children," on the basis of the 1588 edition published by Abel L'Angelier, which implies that Florio had not

with the first reception of the *Essais* emphasize the political character of Montaigne's book.[14] In its thematic presentation—especially if we consider the first twenty chapters of Book I—the *Essais* accords considerable importance to political and moral questions rather distant from introspection and Montaigne's later preoccupations regarding the form of his book.

The initial reception of the *Essais* was largely associated with the genre of moral, political, and diplomatic discourses, which corresponded to the spirit of the time and was concerned chiefly with problems of governance, the art of war, embassies, and civic morals. In her preface to the 1595 edition of the *Essais*, Marie de Gournay defines Montaigne's book as a "record" of his actions, comparing him to Blaise de Monluc[iv] and François de La Noue:[v] "After all, have not Messieurs Montluc and La Noue in our own time described and represented themselves also by the record of their actions, which they have presented to their country? They are worthy to be thanked twice for this: once, for their effort; secondly, for having applied it to this subject; for they would not have been able to write anything more true."[15]

Montaigne had made himself familiar with the tradition of these political "discourses," but he decided not to use the term in his title, though he did consider it for a time.[16] Many other chapters in the 1580 edition can also be explained by reference to the interests of Henry III, as seen in the subjects debated and the speeches delivered at the Académie du Palais between February 1576 and September 1579.[17] Among the themes of moral and intellectual virtues and the nature of the emotions Montaigne took up, he also considered "Of sadness," "Of idleness," "Of constancy," "Of fear," "Of virtue," and "Of anger."[18] Numerous other chapters in the first two books of the *Essais* may have been intended to engage and participate in the philosophical and moral debates that enlivened the Académie created by Henry III.

The book finally emerged from Simon Millanges's presses in April or May 1580, later than planned. The same year, Millanges published eleven works (compared to nine in 1579). Among the books printed in 1580 in his shop, let us

---

yet received the posthumous edition of the *Essais* when he conceived the project of putting Montaigne into English. He completed his first draft while he was residing at the home of the Countess of Bedford, who encouraged him to continue his translation of the *Essais*.

[iv] Blaise de Monluc (1502–1577) fought through all the wars of Francis I. During the religious wars, he held Guyenne for the king and against the Protestants. He became marshal of France in 1574. His *Commentaires* were first published in 1592. Montaigne met several times with the marshal and evokes him in his *Essais*.

[v] François de La Noue (1531–1591) embraced the Protestant cause and fought alongside Henry of Navarre. Montaigne speaks eloquently of La Noue in his *Essais* and probably read his *Discours politiques et militaires* (1587).

mention the following authors and titles: Élie Vinet, *Eutropii Breviarium historia Romana* . . . ; Renoul, *La Mort aux vers ou traité nécessaire, utile, et salutaire au corps humain contre les vers*; Virgil, *Georgicorum liber I*; Arnaud de Pontac, *Constitutiones promulgatae a reverendissimo D. Arnaldo de Pontac*; Andrea Palladio, *Liber de Architectura*; Ausonius, *Burdigalensis, viri consularis* . . . . He also printed two works on Greek grammar and the Greek alphabet, as well as two books of ordinances and "remonstrances" addressed to Henry III.

The omission of the *Discourse on Voluntary Servitude* from the first book of the *Essais* might have led Montaigne to seek a new title (*Essais*) if he had originally the intention of giving an even more political connotation to his book (*Political Discourses*). Since the *Discourse* no longer was part of the *Essais*, it was better to find a title that avoided all controversy. The emphasis could now be put on the author's classical erudition and on his judgments in the form of essays. Moreover, the word "essai" ("try-out," "attempt") corresponded rather well to Montaigne's conception of the politician as an intermediary who *tried* to bring together parties divided on questions of belief and governance.

In 1584, in his *Bibliothèque françoise*, La Croix du Maine presented Montaigne's work as "so sufficient to testify to his great learning and marvelous judgment, and also to his diverse lesson, or the variety of authors he has read, that there is no need to speak further about it here."[19] The first *Essais* of 1580 displays a knowledge of Antiquity and ancient authors, but it also shows a good understanding of the political events connected with the Wars of Religion. However, Montaigne chose to distance himself from the genre of the discourse to stress a form better adapted to a more modest goal. La Croix du Maine offers this commentary on the title Montaigne chose: "In the first place, this title or inscription is very modest, because if one wants to take this word Essais to mean try-out or apprenticeship, that is very humble and unassuming, and has nothing proud or arrogant about it."[20] Paradoxically, the author of the *Essais* presents with competence and candor his expertise and "learning" on various political questions, but he is also able to reserve his own judgment and avoid falling into the didactic and pretentious flaws of the discourse. Whereas the discourse is by definition peremptory and allows no maneuvering room for negotiation, the essay requires a certain respect for the different positions set forth. Here we come back to the motto engraved on Montaigne's token: "I abstain." Unlike the discourse, the essay seeks to present the ideas concerned and compare them; it retains a form of instability of judgment that is inherent in it.

In 1580, Simon Millanges obtained a privilege for "innovations" (*nouvelletés*) and undertook to sell Montaigne's work and to present it as an exceptional book, unprecedented in the history of publishing. Montaigne must have known about this choice his publisher made. Moreover, it is surprising that a work famous for being "consubstantial" with its author was presented as an "innovation," whereas Montaigne repeatedly claims that he detests innovations: "I am disgusted with innovations, in whatever guise."[21] This is a political assertion par excellence, because it certainly bears on the historical situation. Montaigne is no rebel; he is satisfied with what tradition offers him: "For whatever appearance of truth there may be in novelty, I do not change easily, for fear of losing in the change. And since I am not capable of choosing, I accept other people's choice and stay in the position where God put me. Otherwise I could not keep myself from rolling about incessantly."[22]

In 1588, Montaigne indicates that this fashion of novelties goes back "twenty-five or thirty years," that is, to between 1558 and 1563, precisely at the beginning of the religious conflict in France. He maintains that it is useless to "shake up a state," because ultimately one arrives at the same point. The first chapter of the *Essais* stresses the paradox of innovation: "By diverse means we arrive at the same end." An emblematic threshold to the *Essais* that sets the tone for the book, this chapter also serves as a profession of loyalty to the established regime. It praises political inaction and an acceptance of the status quo that is to remain, despite the new religion and its political opposition, a guideline throughout the book.

As if he wanted to define the political field of his discourse, Montaigne takes a local example as the first historical reference point of the *Essais*, the case of Edward, Prince of Wales and regent of Guyenne. After taking Limoges, Edward halted the massacre of the city's women and children only when he witnessed the incredible boldness of three French gentlemen who were continuing to resist his victorious army. Consideration and respect for their military virtue aroused his mercy, not only for the three brave combatants, but also for all the residents of the city.[23] This spontaneous act of clemency, which was contrary to the military practices of the period, shows that in politics it is difficult to argue on the basis of examples grouped together as models. The exceptional, anachronistic, and anecdotal are also important when making political decisions. In 1580, Montaigne already had a relativist conception of human beings and their judgments: "Truly man is a marvelously vain, diverse, and undulating object. It is hard to found any constant and uniform judgment on him."[24] Of course, this observation applies to kings and princes as well.

The essay situates itself in a perspective seeking to redefine political and diplomatic service; Montaigne offers a writing style better adapted to his period, one that takes into account political practices after the Saint Bartholomew's Day massacre in light of the endless religious conflicts. The first chapters of the 1580 edition of the *Essais*, all of which are very concise, are part of a paean to *brevitas*, a virtue emphasized by Erasmus and humanism at the beginning of the Renaissance, but they are no longer adages, aphorisms, or apophthegms, strictly speaking. Far more than the expression of a particular style, the *Essais* are a

guarantee of proximity and truth. Speech being naturally direct and disconnected, the form Montaigne chose was bound to imitate the open and fluid way
of saying things plainly, as they are seen. Rather than a rhetorical procedure, it
was a matter of effectiveness. The first essays have often been seen as *centons*,[vi]
with elements taken from other works and rearranged to form a new object.
Although Montaigne was fond of patchworks and things that were pieced together, his project was not initially literary, but instead sought to present a concise form of political expression very different from the long discourses typical
of the parlement. Far from being stylistic experiments, the first essays are more
like the constitutive elements of a political project that remains to be more fully
defined. The short chapters in the 1580 edition do not herald the form subsequently taken by the *Essais*; instead, they simply denote another Montaigne
who is quite different from the later image of the essayist as a master of introspection and the depiction of the self.

The Montaigne of 1580 participates in a political conversation whose principal objects are the governance of a country torn apart by civil wars and the representation of royal power in foreign Courts. In his first *Essais*, Montaigne adopted, like most of his contemporaries, an anti-Machiavellian moral position,[25]
without however sharing the anti-Italian feeling that prevailed in France at that
time. Innocent Gentillet's *Discours sur les moyens de bien gouverner et maintenir
en bonne paix un royaume ou autre principauté* (1576) had greatly contributed to
a negative perception of Machiavelli in France.[26] Montaigne's denunciation of
Machiavelli was not as radical, and he found Gentillet's followers just as dangerous: "Machiavelli's arguments, for example, were solid enough for the subject,
yet it was very easy to combat them; and those who did so left it no less easy to
combat theirs."[27] In the course of a generation, Machiavelli had become one of
the symbols of "Romanism,"[vii] whereas before he had been considered an ally of
the Gallican party. Machiavelli's success among Protestants as a theorist of political science had to do with the fact that he gave history a certain autonomy
with regard to theology and to conventional moral judgments. It was not only
the absence of a theology, but more precisely the absence of a *Catholic* theology,
in Machiavelli's work that initially attracted French Protestant historians.[28]

Of course, the Wars of Religion, and the bloody night of Saint Bartholomew's
Day, were to reverse this perception forever and put the Italian author on the
side of the Catholic extremists and of Catherine de Medici, who was accused of
being an avid reader of Machiavelli. The best example of this turnaround in the
opinion of Machiavelli is found in Jean Bodin. In 1566, referring to the governance of states in his *Methodus ad facilem historiarum*, Bodin declared that Ma-

---

[vi] A collection of poems or adages; a miscellany. [Trans.]

[vii] A pejorative term the Protestants used to describe the religious doctrine of the
Roman Catholic Church.

chiavelli was "the first, in our opinion, who has written on this subject after about twelve hundred years of universal barbarism."[29] Ten years later, in his *Six Livres de la République* (1576), Bodin has apparently changed his mind about Machiavelli, since he now held him responsible for all of France's ills—including syphilis—with a tone and vehemence that leave no doubt regarding his anti-Machiavellianism. Soon it was rumored that the queen mother, Catherine de Medici, had made *The Prince* her Bible, and that she had had the idea of the Saint Bartholomew's Day massacre while reading Machiavelli during one of her walks. Henry III was also said to keep a copy of Machiavelli's works in his pocket. In his *Contre-Machiavel*, Gentillet accused Machiavelli of teaching the French "Atheism, Sodomy, perfidy, cruelty, usury, and other similar vices."[30] Machiavelli was given a diabolical mask and his name was systematically connected with all kinds of political intrigues.

In this context, around 1575, the neologism *machiavélique* became a common expression. The precise meaning of this term was defined by Agrippa d'Aubigné, whose phrase "Our Kings who have learned to machiavelize"[31] reflects a redefinition of politics and of the way of governing states. Despite the scathing criticism of Machiavelli among Protestants, a certain fascination with his work prevailed in France all through the sixteenth century. Although he had many detractors, he also had defenders, among whom Jean de La Taille is certainly the best known. La Taille published *Le Prince nécessaire* (1573), which he dedicated to Henry de Bourbon, the future Henry IV.[32] Between 1572 and 1580, a political polarization occurred that put Machiavelli and his detractors at the center of all political reflection. Montaigne's conception of politics in the 1570s was more nuanced, because it did not make Machiavelli's thought incompatible with the exercise of power. Thus, in a way that is certainly exaggerated, people have spoken of Montaigne's "Machiavellianism,"[33] but Montaigne did not participate in the polemic and prudently made few references to Machiavelli in his *Essais*. He could have exploited this fashion of discourses for and against Machiavelli, but he chose a very different approach to the subject of politics, preferring to pave the way for a veritable ethos of political prudence.[34]

Imitating the motto of Rabelais's Abbey of Thélème, the *Essais* begin with an inscription that guides the reading of the work: "This book was written in good faith, reader. It warns you from the outset that in it I have set myself no goal but a domestic and private one. I have had no thought of serving either you or my own glory."[35] This makes it clear: Montaigne will resolutely keep public considerations out of his book. Neither servant nor master, without ambitions for his fame or glory—at least that is what he claims—Montaigne has written the *Essais* to leave a private portrait for his family and friends. It is as if his experience and the image that others may have of him in everyday life are not enough or do not correspond to reality. Did Montaigne really think that his family and friends knew him so little that they needed a book to discover another man, different from the one alongside whom they lived? And if he did not, then what was the purpose of this work? A portrait amplifies the memory of great men and writers, but this remark also has to be understood in the context of the first edition of the *Essais* in 1580. Posterity means little to Montaigne in 1580; when he began to write his *Essais*, he had not yet accomplished anything. He had given up his office in the parlement and had not yet acquired the public and political dimension that would allow him to write memoirs retracing the path of a rich and remarkable career. The genre of the *Essais* as it was worked out in 1580 offers few hints that would allow us to understand Montaigne's future reputation, at least on the basis of literary criteria. However, the book may have been conceived as a means to other ends.

So we must inquire into what this book represented in 1580. It contains a total of ninety-four chapters (a considerable number), most of which deal with commonplaces and subjects connected with contemporary political and moral concerns. These political topoi developed in the first edition of the *Essais* contrast with the personal motivations the author invokes in his preface to the reader. To give a few examples: "Whether the governor of a besieged place should go out to parley" (I: 5); "Parley time is dangerous" (I: 6); "Ceremony of interviews between kings" (I: 13); "A trait of certain ambassadors" (I: 17); "Of custom, and not easily changing an accepted law" (I: 23); "Of a lack in our administrations" (I: 35); "Of sumptuary laws" (I: 43); "Of the battle of Dreux" (I: 45); and many other chapters that are far from the depiction of the self Montaigne announces. Even a chapter like "Of liars" (I: 9), placed near the beginning of the *Essais*, has to be understood as a reflection on the fundamental difference between lying and not telling the truth, a subtle difference investigated at length in the *Essais*. It is difficult to see in this semantic variant a simply private concern. However, the linguistic distinction Montaigne draws is more pertinent on the political and diplomatic level, and it is necessary for a representative of the king on assignment abroad. This chapter on liars is followed by another key chapter in this first version of the *Essais*: "Of constancy" (I: 12), which praises a quality indispensable in a servant of the king who wants to rise at the Court.[36] We could, for example, relate constancy to etiquette and see in this quality a way of controlling the behaviors necessary for the formation of a Court society. Examples of this kind are numerous in the first edition of 1580.

In his preface to the reader, Montaigne creates the illusion of a disengagement and clear separation between public life and private life, whereas a significant number of chapters in this first edition put the accent on the governance of states, military strategies, diplomatic interviews, and the moral values of the nobility of the sword. It is therefore not toward private life that we should turn, but rather toward public life and political action.

In 1580, Montaigne's goal was to please the king and his high-ranking servants by highlighting his personal qualities (moderation, candor, affability, fidelity, honesty), all of them applicable to public service and political action. But he did not conceal his defects, as he emphasizes in the preface to the reader: "My defects will here be read to the life, and also my natural form." Nevertheless, this concern for transparency encountered the limits of decorum and formal propriety: "as far as respect for the public has allowed," Montaigne adds. Such a judgment on social limitations is also a quality required in the exercise of public offices. Montaigne's book is indeed a private portrait, not so much for his friends or relatives as for the great people who, by reading his book—especially the first chapters—will gain a good idea of the man who seems to be offering them his services. The author of the *Essais* sketches the portrait of a devoted, loyal man, one who shows both discernment (in public) and naturalness (for his reader) in military and diplomatic matters. Under the last Valois, ambassadors were essentially recruited for their loyalty and allegiance in a relationship (a form of friendship) of absolute confidence. For Montaigne, it was a question of exhibiting certain particularities of his private life in order that the man might be associated with his book. The king could form an idea of the character of his potential servant far better than during a brief royal audience; thus the book did have as its goal to reveal the man in depth, not for himself, but rather in a way preparatory to public service.

In the first edition of the *Essais*, Montaigne foregrounds his concise, direct style, appropriate to the straightforward and laconic speech of the "briefs" dictated or written by ambassadors. He seeks to demonstrate that he would be capable of transmitting reports that would get to the heart of the matter, without beating around the bush or rhetorical effects. Montaigne thinks he has mastered this simple, frank way of writing and is convinced that his *Essais* demonstrate this. His writing has an efficacy equal to that of the letter. As a matter of fact, the essay is supposed to represent a logical evolution of the letter, combining description and judgment in a single document. The short form of his first chapters corresponds to the synthetic turn of mind expected of ambassadors, whose main work consists in extracting the essence of their interviews with the princes and high officials with whom they meet.[viii] His experience as a councillor in the first Chambre des Enquêtes can even be considered an advantage. We recall that Montaigne made many extracts in studying cases for which he was responsible as reporter. He not only served for ten years as a councillor at the

---

[viii] Deborah Losse (*Montaigne and Brief Narrative Form: Shaping the Essay*. London: Palgrave Macmillan, 2013) has shown how the growing political disturbances during the Wars of Religion led Montaigne to distinguish himself from the conventional forms of exemplary narratives to develop a style in which detailed ethnographic observations and the contingent occupied a primordial place.

parlement of Bordeaux, but also succeeded in distancing himself from lawyerly language to develop a style that corresponded better to the career he had in mind. This distinction inevitably involved the depiction of his character and temperament.

Montaigne's intention of presenting himself to Henry III as a man in whom he could have confidence to defend the interests of the kingdom and the crown explains the presence in the *Essais* of 1580 of these two levels (private and public) that are apparently contradictory but are in fact complementary. The depiction of private life could help him land a public office because such decisions were based above all on a sound knowledge of the servant. In Montaigne's case—that is, in view of the new career he desired—the knowledge of a future ambassador's private life was an essential condition for his nomination by the king. The first version of the preface to the reader in 1580 could not, however, directly identify its (royal) audience, and Montaigne preferred to remain in the background, concealing himself behind the presentation of a "book written in good faith." The emphasis on the fact that this book's intention was in no way to "seek the world's favor" is rather revealing of a constant posture that consists of stressing his interests while at the same time seeming to neglect them. It was not the world's favor that concerned Montaigne in 1580, but rather the king's favor.

We could ask whether the essay as a form is really based on a separation between the public and the private. Can the mayor and Montaigne—and especially Montaigne *after* his terms as mayor (1581–85)—really have been two different men? In several passages of the *Essais* Montaigne ponders the pleasures of private life: "I love a private life because it is by my own choice that I love it, not because of unfitness for public life, which is perhaps just as well suited to my nature. I serve my prince the more gaily because I do so by the free choice of my judgment and my reason."[37] This passage refuses to establish an exclusive distinction between private life and public life. Serving the prince would thus be a choice, rather than an obligation. This declaration allows Montaigne to make room for both his private life and his public life. He does not really commit himself to one side or the other.

This affirmation must however be taken with a grain of salt, because it appeared only after a period of political disillusionment that followed his service as mayor of Bordeaux. The celebration of private life came later and does not correspond to the character or the content of the *Essais* of 1580. It should be noted that the addition "without personal obligation" at the end of this sentence on the Bordeaux Copy marks a definitive break with public life, which was, in the Renaissance, based on the principle of obligation, indeed, of servitude. This a posteriori clarification regarding public life reveals a change in attitude with regard to Montaigne's expectations after 1588. Serving one's king by the "free choice" of one's judgment, as if a friend were concerned, is a strange notion. Such an idealization of public life (exactly as if it were a continuation of private life) is far from corresponding to reality, and Montaigne could not have been unaware of that. Once again, his discourse is based on the model of friendship (incarnated by La Boétie), but it became untenable over the years and in the course of his own experiences in politics. The prince's exercise of power is not a choice, but a requirement, indeed, a constraint. The same goes for a person who counsels the prince. Politics involves obligations that must be assumed, and serving the king amounts to obeying him, without ulterior motives. This duty of obedience and allegiance is constantly present in the *Essais* of 1580, that is, at a time when Montaigne fully assumed the responsibilities that might be incumbent upon him. As we see, the author is playing on two levels at once: he is an essentially private man who would be capable of assuming a public office were he asked to do so.

The First Reader of the *Essais*

A book presupposes readers, and the *Essais* does not escape that rule. Although the reader of the first edition of the *Essais* is presented as one of Montaigne's familiars, the social instability and political reversals that took place during the twenty years of writing and publication of the *Essais* led to several redefinitions of the reader and new conceptions of the notice to the reader that serves as a preface. Montaigne had given much thought—in the course of the various editions—to an ideal reader, and he always tried to predict the ideal reader's reactions. The notion of a reader had been an integral part of his thought ever since the first edition of the *Essais* in 1580. The famous preface "To the Reader," placed at the beginning of the first book and dated March 1, 1580, reflects an awareness of the very indeterminate nature of the reading audience at that time. The ambiguities and contradictions of this short text have to be interpreted in the context of the first publication of the *Essais*. An a posteriori reading of this preface would lead us to all sorts of conjectures, notably that of a Montaigne who was in perfect control of his text and was playing ironically with his reader. The author's insecurity with regard to a hypothetical audience is in no way ironical, since in 1580 it is likely that the book was addressed to a small number of individuals: relatives and friends, but also, perhaps, an unidentified person who was more capable of helping him pursue his political ambitions.

Préface, avis, avertissement, introduction: Montaigne's short text that serves as a discourse preliminary to the *Essais* has been called by various names. Marie de Gournay opted for the term *préface*, which she also used for her own introduction to her "adopted father's" book, published after his death in 1595. Montaigne himself made no decision about this, because his foreword refers to a single, generic dedicatee: simply "Au lecteur" ("To the Reader"). This form of address is assuredly a topos, which is also found, for example, in Ronsard, but in Montaigne it also expresses a certain ambivalence toward an ideal or real reader who changes over time. It is an introduction by the author (Montaigne) for a reader (both nameless and particular because of the choice of the singular), which he has judged necessary to explain how to approach the following text. It is not addressed to just any reader, nor is it a mere editorial convention, since Montaigne speaks elsewhere of an "able reader,"[38] and also of a "candid reader."[39] These two qualities—intelligence and candor—are also foregrounded in the preface to his book.

The reader capable of understanding Montaigne's way of proceeding in the *Essais* must not be confused with the common reader. In fact, Montaigne puts the common reader in a category that is more general and, shall we say, uncritical, which he later calls "most readers."[40] Several references to the bad reader can be found in the *Essais*. Montaigne defends himself against such readers who fail to follow him: "It is the inattentive reader who loses my subject, not I."[41] In the heavy seas of the *Essais*, Montaigne needs a reader who is a good swimmer: "To which may be joined what a certain Crates said of the writings of Heraclitus, that they needed a good swimmer for a reader, so that the depth and weight of Heraclitus's learning should not sink him and drown him."[42] It is no coincidence that we find the image of the swimmer painted on one of the walls of the tower of Montaigne's château where he wrote part of his *Essais*. This later allegory of the reader-swimmer inscribed in the margins of the Bordeaux Copy represents the end result of a long journey in search of the ideal reader. It is not easy to navigate among the chapters. The reader is in danger of drowning on every page of this profound text full of hazards.

We should take literally what Montaigne wrote in 1580. It was difficult to foresee the reception and success or failure of a book that lay outside booksellers' conventional channels in the period concerned. Montaigne's *coup d'essay* (which Cotgrave's contemporary French-English dictionary defined as "a tryall-peece, or maister-peece") sought chiefly to leave a trace of himself at a time when the absence of a male descendant, and thus of the continuity of his lineage and the transmission of the name "Montaigne," began to be perceived by the author as a real problem. It was equally difficult to speak about his own experiences before 1580. Although he had a few titles, they were all recent. So why did he publish this work, and consequently this generic but singular foreword to the reader?

The *Au lecteur* is constructed in accord with the most familiar rules of classical rhetoric,[43] but the effect sought went far beyond mere literary conventions. Montaigne wrote for a reader imagined on the basis of ancient models, but he also refers to more specific readers connected with the publishing history of the *Essais* and their hoped-for first reception. The question is therefore exactly what reader he was addressing in 1580. This foreword to the reader was not reworked in the course of the following editions, although Montaigne did reread it attentively, going so far as to change the date. This prologue to the *Essais* is supposed to provide keys for reading and to set the reader on the right path, while at the same time Montaigne is well aware that any advice is doomed to fail, because it is contrary to the very nature of the essay: open, full of digressions, and constantly changing direction. Montaigne repeatedly declares that he has gotten lost in his own text, and after 1588 he is rather proud of this. The message is both simple and unusual: look out, reader, you too are in danger of getting lost and wasting your time. This exordium was, however, normal for an author who was still unknown. Outside the chapters, which are all numbered, this foreword serves in 1580 as a *warning*, and indicates for everyone the way to proceed.

The first sentence of the preface to the reader reveals the three essential elements of the essay as a genre: the book, the author, and the reader. The author disappears behind his book, which addresses itself directly to the reader: "This book was written in good faith, reader." The book rapidly becomes an autonomous, independent object. Everything begins (in the second sentence) with the use of the familiar *tu* form of address, not by Montaigne, but by the book, which speaks about itself. Montaigne's familiar way of approaching his reader — through the book—presupposes a proximity, but once again it is not the proximity of the author, but that of the reader, as if the book were expressing itself independently of its author. Montaigne later underlined, in the third book, the *Essais'* self-sufficiency: "Reader, let this essay of myself run on, and this third extension of the other parts of my painting."[44] He has been able to create a distance between himself and his reader, who can no longer demand anything from him: "Do not blame me, reader."[45] This is a matter between a book and its reader, in which Montaigne puts himself out of play. At least, that is what he clearly announces in his foreword in 1580.

Critics almost always approach the *Au lecteur* as if the meaning of this text did not change over time. I am not referring to the text itself—that is, its minimal reworkings—but rather to what it necessarily expressed for the reader in 1580, 1582, 1588, and 1595. In reality, this foreword's meaning could not be interpreted in the same way by either Montaigne or his reader at the time of the three editions of the *Essais* published during Montaigne's lifetime, not to mention the Paris edition of 1587, which he did not review, or the missing edition, called as the "fifth edition," or the posthumous edition of 1595. The Montaigne of the first *Essais*, who held no political office, had not yet made the journey to Germany and Italy and was on the verge of publishing, at his own expense, a book whose title distanced it from existing literary categories. In 1580, Montaigne imagines a hypothetical reader who still escapes him. And yet he addresses him (in the singular) and seems to know him. This reader could verify in person not only the author's good faith but also that of the book.

Good faith is located on the side of the printed object; it is dissociated from the subject and objectified in the book. The threshold of the book is thus truly a *warning*:[ix] "It warns you from the outset . . ." that this singular, innovative work founds a genre that minimizes the place of the author, at the price of making him the object of the book. People do speak of the *"Essays of Michel, lord of Montaigne."* Just as the noble name of Montaigne cannot exist without the land that is attached to it, the proper name undergoes an objectification by the book that incarnates the space in which the author will move in his turn, like a lord on his lands. The *Essais* are a fief. By publishing his book, Montaigne makes a noble land his own. We are moving in a private and noble space (associated with the château), and this is reaffirmed at the beginning of the foreword: "I have set myself no goal but a domestic and private one." The *Essais'* original discourse certainly has a strong aristocratic connotation, that of a noble family whose name has been known for several generations. In Guyenne, people knew that Montaigne's ancestors had held administrative offices in Bordeaux and in the region. The *Essais* reaffirmed a name and a lineage that had enjoyed social and political recognition for more than a century.

In a relatively unexpected way, Montaigne then amuses himself by making the reader whom he had addressed disappear. This reversal of the situation may seem surprising. In fact, Montaigne suddenly declares that he has had "no thought of serving either you or my own glory." Here the generic aspect of the reader is canceled because the author returns to a more traditional model of the noble and familial dedication: "I have dedicated it to the private convenience of my relatives and friends." The reason Montaigne mentions "for not seeking a broader public" is supposed to have to do with his mental or physical condition: "My powers are inadequate for such a purpose." There is no apparent calculation in this text that claims to be a portrait in which people will be able to "recover" after his death, "when they have lost me (as soon they must)," "some features of my habits and temperament." Montaigne claims to have written his book without ulterior motives, without truly expecting a "return on his investment." This work for posterity is a sort of "memory" of a new kind, which is not a memory of events or of a period, but the memory of Montaigne in the history of a great family: "and by this means [they may] keep the knowledge they have had of me more complete and alive." The generic reader fades away, and the fam-

---

[ix] *Avertissement.* The French word means "notice" or "foreword" and "warning." [Trans.]

ily occupies the foreground. But all this is clearly stage setting, and it is very probable that by means of these effects that tend to detach the book from himself, the author is giving himself something to fall back on in the event that the book is poorly received by the reader with whom he is concerned at this point.

Montaigne emphasizes that there is no other way to read his text: the reader has to be in the private and proximate world of the author. However, this may be doubted. The precedent set by the publication of La Boétie's works in 1571 clearly demonstrates that Montaigne knew how to use a book to approach the great men and women of the kingdom. In the Renaissance, when a book was given, it had a precise social function that implied duties and obligations. Giving a book made it possible to envisage a benefit in return in the form of a favor.[46] It was on the basis of this logic of "you scratch my back, I'll scratch yours" that Montaigne presented a copy of his translation of Raymond Sebond's *Theologia naturalis* to his neighbor, Germain-Gaston de Foix, marquis of Trans.[47] But maybe we need to look higher. When Montaigne offers his book to an anonymous reader, we can imagine another very real reader whose name does not need to be mentioned and raises the essential question of the *Essais'* horizon of expectation in 1580. Is Montaigne's potential reader a friend or relative, or is he a public person? The author anticipated the question and responded to the reproaches that would not fail to be directed against him: "If I had written to seek the world's favor, I should have bedecked myself better, and should present myself in a studied posture." To what do these verbs in the pluperfect subjunctive correspond?[x] They express a condition that is not realized and an effect that is not sought. What assertions to distinguish oneself from ordinary petitioners!

By publishing the *Essais*, Montaigne's goal was no longer to occupy a place among the intelligentsia of the *robins*, because such a book did not have a sufficiently elevated level of erudition to make a reputation as a learned savant. His audience was quite different. Similarly, although his goal was to be recognized by the nobility, the essay is not the best of genres, either, because it accords genealogy only a secondary place. Many aristocratic values are certainly represented in Montaigne's book, but the priority given to *present* experience at the expense of tradition and custom runs counter to an aristocratic conception of politics. On the other hand, if it is a question of creating a strong image of himself and promoting that of a man who offers an innovative analysis of politics and public service in an unprecedented language, but who nonetheless abides by the conventions of the world, then Montaigne's book has a definite interest for

---

[x] In the 1580 edition, this reads: "Je me fusse paré de beautez empruntées, ou me fusse tendu et bandé en ma meilleure démarche." [Trans.]

a privileged reader who is able to recognize the author's talents and reward him. The private portrait drawn in the foreword thus has a primordial importance that seeks to make him better known and possibly to obtain a political favor, perhaps even a post as advisor or a diplomat. The *Essais* of 1580 can be read as a kind of curriculum vitae, in which Montaigne displays his knowledge of history and politics while breaking with the traditional image of the counselor or diplomat.

In the *Au lecteur*, Montaigne distances himself from the established genres, but immediately takes the measure of this personal and idiosyncratic introduction by indicating its limits: "I want to be seen here in my simple, natural, ordinary fashion, without straining or artifice." Here he is praising a form of truth, the truth of the ordinary man, with a dose of deliberate and well-considered naïveté, beyond overrated forms of knowledge. Montaigne is a man of good sense who takes responsibility for his exhibitionism insofar as he can. The *Au lecteur* serves him, so to speak, as a kind of calling card. This transparency— which is still not equivalent to the consubstantiality developed later on—is reinforced by the famous "it is myself that I portray." The portrayal of the self follows the rules of the schools and manners of the time. However, it must not be confused with exhibitionism and ostentation: "My defects will here be read to the life, and also my natural form, as far as respect for the public has allowed." Montaigne introduces for the first time a public and social component into the presentation of his personality. His book attains another dimension: he underlines that the author pays attention to his time; he knows how it works and what its decorum is, and that is necessary at the Court and in embassies. Montaigne's naïveté is not for everyone, but solely for a small circle of close friends, and it is thanks to this clarification that we understand that it is reserved for a limited entourage, not private—in the strict sense of family and intimate friends—but public.

In his foreword addressed to a reader who will have the privilege of knowing him in his innermost nature, Montaigne clarifies several points. He is not an idealist and in no way seeks to transgress cultural rules, because he is aware that the established power is always conservative. His role is to innovate while at the same time to recognize immutable values: that is more or less the task Montaigne set himself in the *Essais* of 1580. Montaigne was born French; he is a citizen of the Old World and cannot paint himself entirely naked, because social conventions do not allow him to do that: "Had I been placed among those nations which are said to live still in the sweet freedom of nature's first laws, I assure you that I should very gladly have portrayed myself here entire and wholly naked." Montaigne respected this interdiction in the name of a civil modesty. Here he shows that reason, and particularly public reason, frequently takes priority over personal considerations. In this preface we note two contradictory forces that oppose each other: a procedure that consists in distinguishing himself from others and exhibiting his difference, on the one hand, and on the other an attitude that reminds the reader that this difference has limits the author will not violate.

Although at the beginning of the foreword the author disappeared behind the book, Montaigne soon recovers his grip on his book: "Thus, reader, I am myself the matter of my book." This is indeed the lord of Montaigne, gentleman of the king's chamber, who finally reveals himself. Consubstantiality replaces transparency; the book and the man coincide to the point of becoming indistinguishable. Anyone who loves one loves the other. One is not judged without the other, the book *is* Montaigne and Montaigne is summed up in his book. At the end of the foreword the game is over. The author has retaken possession of his discourse and the *Essais* henceforth serve as a professional calling card, a way of presenting the future royal servant.

Thus we are confronted with an equivocal warning. Although Montaigne has accepted the idea of a generic reader, he declares that the generic reader should not read his book: "you would be unreasonable to spend your leisure on so frivolous and vain a subject." Unless, of course, reading is a form of leisure. The reader of Montaigne has other things to do. The author knows that his reader has little time for him, and that it would be importunate to impose on him the reading of such a peculiar book. Therefore, he has to go straight to the heart of the matter and reveal in the first chapters the spirit of the book and the project it symbolizes. Montaigne's book, in its first version of 1580, serves to distinguish its author by presenting his judgment of situations which are mainly military and diplomatic. This first Montaigne is presented in a kind of teaser that foregrounds not only his knowledge of the Ancients, but also his competence in matters that concern the functioning of the state and its government. The reader, even if he is not explicitly named, would then be an individual known to everyone, to whom Montaigne offers his services by giving him an advance sample of his competencies; this reader being in a position to judge the book and thus the man.

The 1580 edition was conceived by Montaigne to be given rather than sold. This in no way prevented Millanges from selling as many copies as possible if the opportunity presented itself. The risks were lower for the publisher, because the author paid part of the expenses, Montaigne having provided the paper. Millanges had revenues guaranteed by his publications for the colleges as well as for the local religious and political authorities. Thus the first publication of the *Essais* was not bound by commercial logic. Several elements support such an interpretation. The first known forms of the title page show that Montaigne insisted that his titles as *seigneur, chevalier,* and *gentilhomme* (lord, knight, and gentleman) appear prominently.[xi] The goal of such attention was to produce an *effet de cour* (courtly effect) to which Henry III and his entourage could not remain indifferent. The title page plays a considerable role in the reader's first assessment of a book; Montaigne's titles, which are duly reported, speak for themselves and lend credibility to the following foreword addressed to the reader. Montaigne's "courteous"—and personal—presentation of his book to an important figure was certainly intended to favor his access to the royal Court; the *Essais* served him literally as *letters of nobility.* This interpretation allows us to understand better the clarification in the *Au lecteur.* Isn't it possible to think that this short preface was written at the last minute to express the author's reservations concerning the bookseller's commercial initiatives? It was considered in good taste for a gentleman to take his distance from the world of "commerce" (what the author of the *Essais* calls *mercadence*). The discomfort Montaigne expresses concerning a random and uncertain reader would then also be a warning against the commercial operation envisaged by the publisher.

When Montaigne published his first *Essais* in 1580, he did not yet enjoy the fame that was soon to make him one of the best-known authors of the French Renaissance. In the first days of 1580, Montaigne had delivered to Simon Millanges a very unusual manuscript, and the time had come to give it to its addressee. The religious and military schisms in southwest France led Montaigne to emphasize that he was not dogmatic and fanatical like many of his neighbors. In February 1580, the king had received contradictory reports concerning the political situation and the unrest in Guyenne. Henry III was looking for solutions. The 1580 edition of the *Essais* was supposed to offer Montaigne a chance to introduce himself at the Court and to make himself better known to members of the king's inner circle than he had been able to do in 1571 with the edition of the La Boétie's works.

All the ambiguity maintained with respect to the reader rests on an unacknowledged expectation. Montaigne was not a beggar, and the contradictions in the *Au lecteur* served to shelter him from the accusations—especially of being arrogant and ambitious—that might be made against him in the event of failure. When Montaigne refers to his relatives and friends, we should perhaps un-

---

[xi] The place occupied by Montaigne's various titles on the title page did not allow Millanges to put his printer's mark on it, and that is why it appeared only on the title page of the second book of the *Essais.* The mark was replaced by a smaller fleuron with arabesques. We find the same fleuron in several works published by Millanges as early as 1573 (in the *Epigrammata* of Martial Monier [1573] and the *De rheumatismo* of Pierre Pichot [1577], for example). This fleuron was used again in the 1582 edition of the *Essais.*

derstand this as the Court, that restricted group of gentlemen united by bonds of blood, members of the high nobility who liked to call each other "friends" and "cousins" when they were at the Court. Finally, the *Essais* of 1580 were no doubt intended less for a genuine audience—the genre hardly lent itself to that—than for individualized presentation to a prince or great lord. We have two examples of these private presentations of the first edition of the *Essais* in sumptuous bindings: one is De Thou's copy in a gilt vellum binding with its first owner's coat of arms, and the other that of Queen Elizabeth I of England. The binding of the copy presented to Queen Elizabeth includes her sign and heraldic emblem. This binding was doubtless made in England, but its exact origin remains unknown. It has been suggested that this book might have been given to the Queen of England by the duke of Anjou, the king's brother and the heir to the throne of France.[48] The idea of a book dedicated to a prince also corresponded better to Montaigne's aristocratic conception of writing, at least so far as the first edition of his book is concerned. With his *Essais*, Montaigne was targeting a single reader, Henry III, whom he must have impressed in 1580 and who received his book in the form of a gift in early July 1580, at Saint-Maur-des-Fossés. We will return to this royal presentation later.

"Of the Battle of Gods"

The table of contents in the first book of the *Essais* published in 1580 shows a typographical error, a lapsus that reflects the turmoil of the Wars of Religion. The title of the chapter, "Of the battle of Dreux" (I: 45), was transformed into "Of the battle of Gods" (*De la bataille de Dieux* [sic]). This slip-up, which can be blamed on the compositor who set type for the table of contents, tells us much about the political unconscious of the last quarter of the sixteenth century. If we put ourselves back at the end of the 1570s, the printer's error seems extremely appropriate when we consider more closely the content of this short chapter, which was left almost unchanged later on. The Battle of Dreux was one of the most frequently discussed episodes of the civil wars. We find descriptions and analyses of this famous battle in Théodore de Bèze, François de Lorraine, in Coligny's *Mémoires*, La Noue's *Discours*, Condé's *Mémoires*, Brulart's *Journal*, Michel de Castelnau's *Mémoires*, Mézeray's *Histoire de France*, and many other authors of the sixteenth and seventeenth centuries. The iconography of this battle is also very rich, because we have several series of engravings that illustrate the successive phases of the day, December 19, 1562. These images have immortalized the charges carried out by the Catholic and Protestant forces. The series of six engravings by Tortorel and Perrissin, published in 1570, gave the battle a spatial dimension and allowed it to leave a lasting impression on people's minds. These prints divided the battle into distinct phases that were the object of numerous commentaries and military analyses.[49]

As almost always when discussing events of his own time, Montaigne was very discreet regarding this battle, and we have to recognize that his analysis of it is very thin. He does not mention the chief actors, with the exception of the duke of Guise. The initial commentary on this battle that prefigured the carnage of the civil wars remains on the whole rather technical and never leads to reflection on the nature of the Wars of Religion, or even on the religious questions that were, however, the principal crux of the conflict between the Huguenots and the Catholics. A short addition made to the 1588 edition, offering a comparison with a battle that occurred in Greek Antiquity, even allowed Montaigne to distract the reader's attention by diluting this battle in a broader historical system that now included ancient history. The Battle of Dreux—one of the best documented and most discussed events of the Wars of Religion—remained, all through the various editions of the *Essais*, a kind of textual embryo and was even, through its lack of development, dissolved in a military topos that caused it to lose its historical specificity. We wonder why Montaigne conceived such a chapter without really developing it in the course of the three editions published during his lifetime, or in the Bordeaux Copy.

When Montaigne set out to write a book in the early 1570s, less than ten years after the Battle of Dreux, analyses of this episode in the Wars of Religion were a subject of conversation in salons. Naturally, the analysis made of the Battle of Dreux depends on the ideological and political position of the commentator. But none of this appears in the first draft offered by Montaigne. For him, the Battle of Dreux was an unavoidable commonplace that could be reduced to a technical discussion of the art of war. It is, in a way, a textbook case. When he finally settled on a book divided into fifty or sixty rather brief chapters, it was completely logical that the battle should occupy one of these chapters, because this clash between two armies was still very present in people's minds. The chapter dates from 1572–73, that is, from the beginning of the writing of the *Essais*. We can imagine Montaigne intending to comment on this battle in a work that initially had more to do with military and diplomatic discourses than with the genre of the essay, with which we are now familiar and which created his literary persona. Thus this chapter probably occupied an important place in the notion of the book he had conceived before he began writing it. Like "Parley time is dangerous," (I: 6), "Ceremony of interviews between kings" (I: 17), "Of a lack in our administrations" (I: 36), and "Of sumptuary laws" (I: 53), this chapter is firmly anchored in its time and gives a political dimension to Montaigne's writings. It could be affirmed therefore that in 1580 Montaigne took up questions involving current affairs, but he did so obliquely.

However, it proved difficult to speak of this battle without taking sides, and this chapter helps us understand how Montaigne deals with the Wars of Religion in his *Essais*.

A first observation: "Of the battle of Dreux" is an important chapter in the 1580 edition, not by its size, but by the fact that it refers to a current subject. Before seeing how Montaigne approaches this battle, let us briefly summarize its high points and reversals. All the commentators, whether Protestants or Catholics, agree in minimizing the role played by chance and in underlining the tactical aspect of the combat: strategy and the value of military decisions, not chance, led to François de Lorraine's final victory. It is also a battle in which appearances were deceiving, because the victory, initially attributed to the Catholics, then, in an incredible reversal on the field, to the Huguenots, was soon transformed into a defeat for the Protestants, thus lending a psychological dimension to the belated but decisive charge ordered by the duke of Guise.

The battle took place near the city of Dreux, between the villages of L'Épinay, Nuisement, Blainville, and the Maumusset valley with its windmill.[50] The Catholic forces were commanded by Constable Montmorency, Marshal Saint-André, and François de Lorraine. The Protestants were led by the Prince of Condé, Louis I of Bourbon, the king of Navarre's brother; Admiral Coligny; and Théodore de Bèze. It is difficult to imagine a better cast. We find here all the great military leaders of the first Wars of Religion. The Protestant forces consisted of 9,000 foot soldiers (4,000 German mercenaries and 5,000 French) and 4,500 cavalrymen (3,000 Germans and about 1,500 French). They had five cannons. The forces of the Catholic Triumvirate were composed of 16,000 foot soldiers and only 2,000 cavalrymen, but they had 22 cannons. The vanguard was led by Marshal Saint-André, but the duke of Guise was the overall leader of the troops without, however, assuming official command over them. On the Protestant side, the vanguard was led by Admiral Coligny. Coligny was the subject of controversy, and the Catholic pamphleteers raged against him, because the German mercenaries, these "Goths, Ostrogoths, Vizigoths, and Huguenots,"[51] as Ronsard called them, were seen as invaders of the kingdom and barbarians to boot.

After a brief period during which the two camps observed each other, the Protestant forces moved out on December 19, and the leaders of the royal forces decided to attack them immediately in order to block their access to Dreux. Marshal Biron was sent as a scout. After a short preliminary engagement, the Prince of Condé, sensing that he was too close to the Catholic battalions to escape them, decided to throw himself fully into the battle. He recalled Admiral Coligny to aid him. Thus the admiral was in the first line, with 500 horsemen, supported by two squadrons of German mercenaries. The Prince of Condé was on the admiral's left, flanked on the left by 800 German mercenaries. On the right wing, the Protestant troops were in position near the windmill. The Protestants' charge began around 11:00 a.m., and the Catholic regiments were overwhelmed. The Catholics' cannons were all taken at once. The first phase of the battle quickly turned into a disaster for the Catholics, and their defeat seemed inevitable. Many Catholic soldiers were run through with swords. The royal army's horsemen and infantry fled. Then the constable tried to rally his troops, but his horse was shot out from under him. He was seriously wounded in the face and taken prisoner. This first episode of the battle is known under the name of "the first charge." Its significant element was the Protestants' capture of the constable. The defeat was turning into a debacle.

The dukes of Damville and Aumale attempted a countercharge to help the constable, but they were also put to flight by the German mercenaries. During this second charge, the constable's fourth son, Gabriel de Montmorency, lord of Montbiron, was killed, and the duke of Aumale, thrown off his horse, was taken prisoner. During all this time, the duke of Guise made no sign; prudently and patiently, he was waiting to see what was going to happen on the field. The mercenaries, who thought the victory was final, began pillaging the baggage abandoned by the Catholic forces. Marshal Saint-André and the duke of Guise remained impassive. Before he was wounded and taken prisoner, the constable had asked the duke of Guise for help, but the duke of Guise had not moved. This not very chivalric attitude—which was, however, perfectly adapted to a war that was more strategic than heroic—was noted in most of the commentaries on the battle.

Louis I of Bourbon, Prince of Condé, led the Protestant companies on the third charge (figure 9), but he in turn fell into the hands of the royal troops. Gaspard de Coligny then took command of the Huguenot forces. But the 2,000 German mercenaries quickly abandoned their position. The duke of Guise finally decided to direct operations for the Catholics and launched a charge that scattered the mercenaries. There remained no more than a thousand horsemen under the command of Saint-André and the duke of Guise, which was very little to cope with 4,000 Protestant horsemen. The Prince of Condé and the admiral were unable to regroup their regiments, which were disorganized after having thought they had won. Coligny rallied the mercenaries who had taken refuge and brought them back to the field, while the Prince of Condé sought to do the same. But his horse was also wounded, and he was taken prisoner by Admiral Damville. Each camp had its high-ranking prisoner: Constable Montmorency was in the hands of the Huguenots and the Prince of Condé in those of the Catholics. The battle had recovered a certain equilibrium.

Near the village of Blainville, after the flight of the Protestants, the duke of Guise succeeded in disarming 2,000 German mercenaries who agreed to cease

La troisieme charge de la bataille de Dreux, ou M. le prince de Condé fut prins le 19. Decembre 1562.

A. L'auangarde encore entiere, conduicte par M. de Guise & M. le Ma-
reschal S. André.
B. Bataillons des Suisses rompus & poursuyuis par ceux du Prince de
Condé.
C. Bataillons de François de M, le Prince de Condé rompus & pour-
suyuis par ceux de M. de Guyse.

D. Bataillons des Lansquenets de m. le Prince de Condé, suyans sans
auoir combatu, se retirans dedans le village.
E. Reytres se retirans en trouppe pour se rallier de là le bois.
F. Caualerie de m. le Prince de Condé se venans s'allier aussi.
G. La prinse de m. le Prince de Condé dedans le bois par m. d'Annille.
H. Caualerie de m. le Prince de Condé s'allicepar m. l'Amiral.

FIGURE 9. *Third Charge at the Battle of Dreux*, a print by Tortorel and Perrissin, 1570. Image courtesy of the University of Chicago.

fighting and go home. At this point a squadron with 1,500 horses emerged from the forest and rode toward him. Admiral Coligny was leading the charge. Everything seemed about to be reversed again. François de Guise mounted a fresh horse and Marshal Saint-André tried to do the same, but could not find his page. Then he leaped onto a tired horse that abruptly collapsed. Not being able to get away in time, he was on the verge of being taken when a horseman, Baubigny-Mézière, shot him in the head with a pistol. Left alone, Guise had to withdraw. Harquebusiers placed in the rear finally spotted Admiral Coligny's cavalry and forced Coligny to give up his pursuit of Guise. The battle was reaching a decisive turning point. After assembling his troops, François de Guise launched a last charge against Admiral Coligny, who finally gave the signal to retreat. In the end, the Battle of Dreux was won by the Catholics after a long day full of reversals. The following day, negotiations began between the two camps to arrange for an exchange of prisoners.[52]

The battle's outcome had long remained uncertain, though it was not confused. It was even waged in the old style, that is, frontally and without skirmishes. The four successive charges and the final retreat produced an impressive number of episodes that were fairly distinct chronologically. Agrippa d'Aubigné summed up this uncommon battle in six points: an old-style combat; the extreme valor of the Swiss soldiers explaining the final victory of the Catholic troops; the duke of Guise's patience, which made a major contribution to the legend that viewed him as a remarkable strategist; the long duration of the fighting (more than four hours); the capture of the two leaders; the retreat of both armies on the same day.[53] D'Aubigné estimated the casualties at eight thousand men, while other authors set the figure at six thousand. Tortorel's, Perissin's, and Hogenberg's engravings testify to the complexity of the troop movements and the magnitude of the successive charges.

Concerning this battle, Montaigne notes only Guise's patience and does not mention the battle's different phases or the role played by its various actors, on either the Protestant or the Catholic side. He makes no comment on the multiple charges or the strategies adopted by the adversaries. What are we to think, for example, about the impassiveness of François de Guise while his army was being trounced? Montaigne needs to make only a simple remark to evoke a hot topic of conversation: "those who do not strongly favor the reputation of Monsieur de Guise are fond of averring that he cannot be excused for having halted and temporized with the forces under his command while the Constable, the commander-in-chief of the army, was being smashed by the artillery."[54] Against this accusation, Montaigne mentions only the result of the battle and offers a meager commentary, referring merely to "what the outcome proved," as if the outcome of the battle guaranteed the integrity of the decisions that Guise made. Montaigne seems to place himself on the side of the Machiavellian logic that gives priority to the end at the expense of the means. The victors are always right because they won.

Montaigne takes the side of the duke of Guise because he was able to aim at "victory as a whole" and foresee the result of the battle. Thus he refuses to divide the battle into *charges*, because then he would have to comment on François de Guise's decisions in their direct relationship to the particular events that took place on the battlefield. For Montaigne, the Battle of Dreux is an indivisible whole with a victory, the only one that counts: that of the duke and the Protestants' retreat. His commentary emphasizes the sense of duty. It is in the name of a lofty idea of the state that the duke of Guise is supposed to have chosen not to intervene to help his companions in arms. Only the final victory matters; it is therefore pointless to discuss the development of this battle in detail.

Here we are in the "post-Machiavelli" period, and Montaigne is defending a fundamental principle of a new conception of politics. Because they are ultimately effective, the *raison d'état* authorizes actions that are not very glorious or heroic. The soldier is only an instrument of the state, and in this sense, only the duke of Guise incarnated the state on December 19, 1562. On that day, Constable Montmorency and Marshal Saint-André were only soldiers in the service of a cause that transcended them and of which they never had an overall vision. François de Guise apparently better incarnated the ineluctable character of history and destiny.

Is the military man in the service of politics (as Montaigne seems to imply) or, on the contrary, do the chivalric ideal and the values it represents constitute the main stake in battles? It seems to me that Montaigne, over the years—and especially after 1585—defends precisely the latter position, which should have led the duke of Guise to rush (like the Chevalier Bayard, for example) to the aid of the constable. This aristocratic ideal that Montaigne finds in the Cannibals is in complete contradiction with the behavior of the duke of Guise, who acts here in a Machiavellian way. In the first edition of the *Essais* published in 1580, Montaigne repeatedly justifies politics and thus a strong state that acts against the very principles of humanism. In this way he understands that one can kill people in the name of a higher conception of politics. However, after 1585, and after his own failures in politics, he seems no longer to want to follow this path and prefers on the contrary to defend a noble and chivalric idea of politics. That is probably why this short text on the Battle of Dreux was not developed—at least as a particular battle—in the 1588 edition or in the margins of the Bordeaux Copy.

Then comes the "second charge in the chapter," that is, its incorporation into a system of exemplarity in which Greek Antiquity and France at the end of the Renaissance are included. Montaigne was not able to offer an extensive commentary on the Battle of Dreux, and over time, this chapter became mute. The Guises succeeded in taking Paris in 1588, and Montaigne was even their prisoner at the Bastille for one afternoon—although he was set free by the duke of Guise himself. Depending on the side chosen, the commentator was free to make François de Guise a remarkable strategist or a dark calculator. Montaigne defends Guise without offering a single incriminating argument, other than his victory. Did Guise allow the constable to be defeated in order to get rid of him? Was it simply military genius? Everything depends, of course, on what was to follow. In the end, the Battle of Dreux occupies only a third of the chapter that bears its name, since two examples drawn from Antiquity permit Montaigne to generalize his remarks—one example is present in the 1580 edition, in direct association with the duke of Guise, and the other was added in the 1588 edition. From the *bataille de Dieux* (a lapsus that gives a pagan connotation to the Wars of Religion) to the *bataille de Dreux*, there is only a minimal gap in the construction of the chapter. In it, Montaigne defends an idea that was later to disappear from his repertory when he asserts that "there was more craft than valor in it."

The richness of the description of the battle and the small amount that Montaigne draws from it, while at the same time choosing to devote a chapter to it in his *Essais* in 1580, has not failed to astonish his readers. In my opinion, this contradiction between Montaigne's original intention and his inability to comment in detail on the duke of Guise's actions can be explained by the absence of political calculation and the value attributed to gratuitous acts and ideals in his work after 1585. Moreover, his relation with the Guises changed considerably after 1585 and until the assassination of the third duke of Guise in 1588. Montaigne remained silent regarding the fact that the kings he served (Henry III and then Henry IV) had been driven out of Paris by the League and the Guises. Commenting on the actions of François de Guise, the father of the third duke, was rather delicate at a time when the League was gaining ascendancy over the kingdom and defying the sovereign's authority.

Moreover, twenty years after the Battle of Dreux, the Catholic cause was no longer the same. As we have seen, at the beginning of the Wars of Religion, Montaigne proved rather intransigent and little inclined toward negotiation with the Huguenots. We recall, for instance, that he had spontaneously presented himself before the parlement of Paris in 1562 to profess his Catholic faith. At that time François de Guise could still claim to be uniting the kingdom behind the king by presenting himself as an indispensable intermediary between God and Charles IX.[55] However, after 1580, his son, Henry de Guise, defied the monarch's power. It had become difficult for Montaigne to criticize one without alienating the other. Henry de Guise had founded the Catholic League with which Montaigne had never had any political affinity. He chose to be faithful and loyal to Henry III, but he also developed ties of friendship with Henry of Navarre, while at the same time rejecting any possibility of a parallel government: "We may wish for different magistrates, but we must nevertheless obey those that are here."[56] On the other hand, his relation with the Guises changed over the years, in inverse proportion to the exacerbation of their religious extremism. From one edition to the next, this chapter is not a defense of the duke of Guise but instead bears the mark of a criticism that became even more important after the beginnings of the League and Henry de Guise's defiance of Henry III and Henry of Navarre.

After 1588, Montaigne preferred to keep silent on this subject, though he did not eliminate this chapter, which henceforth occupied a relatively small place in a book whose size increased from one edition to the next. Finally, "Of the battle of Dreux" is a rather misleading title. Although Montaigne is discreet regarding religious questions, in this chapter he shows that he is not a historian, either, at least not so far as his own period is concerned. Faced by the profusion of his contemporaries' commentaries on this battle, Montaigne displayed restraint, or perhaps he simply found nothing more to say. He could not have been unaware that readers might have expected a little more from him in a chapter that remained skeletal. His critical parsimony on the battle certainly astonished his contemporaries more than it does us today. This battle is no longer relevant to our concerns and has been largely forgotten. However, if we put this chapter abandoned by Montaigne back in the historical context of a generation (from 1563 to 1585, for example), the perspective is quite different. Montaigne's judgment of François de Guise—and consequently of Henry de Guise—is more equivocal than it seems. Praised at several points in the *Essais* for his character and political presence, in the chapter "Of the battle of Dreux" François de Guise appears as a man of practical judgment, more political than human. History suggested to Montaigne that this might be a family trait on which it was better not to comment.

Although Montaigne still considered historians as coming "right to [his] forehand"[57] and gave them pride of place in his library, contemporary history—as he admits on more than one occasion—was not really his favorite reading, and that is probably why he decided, in the final analysis, not to title his book *Mémoires*, *Journal*, or *Discours*. Montaigne did not like labels, whatever they might be. In an addition to the chapter "Of husbanding your will" (III: 10) inscribed on the Bordeaux Copy, he proclaimed his political independence and his individual judgment:

> I adhere firmly to the healthiest of the parties, but I do not seek to be noted as especially hostile to the others and beyond the bounds of the general reason. I condemn extraordinarily this bad form of arguing: "He is of the League, for he admires the grace of Monsieur de Guise." "The activity of the king of Navarre amazes him: he is a Huguenot." "He finds this to criticize in the king's morals; he is seditious in his heart."[58]

Montaigne cannot be accused of having opined in one way or another in "Of the battle of Dreux." He summed up the battle in a single remark: "There were plenty of unusual incidents in our battle of Dreux." He leaves it to the reader to inform himself elsewhere if he wants to know more about this crucial event in the Wars of Religion.

An Apology for Sebond or a Justification of Montaigne?

The first book of the *Essais* of 1580 gave a preponderant place to political reflections, but in the second book, theological questions are more prominent because of the space occupied by chapter 12, which is supposed to be a defense of Raymond Sebond's *Theologia naturalis*. Since the end of the fifteenth century, the *Theologia naturalis* had enjoyed great success in Europe, first in Germany and Holland and then in France in the early sixteenth century. In it, Sebond demonstrated the truths of Christianity through the testimony of the Creation. The first chapter clearly states the method, which could have appealed to Montaigne: "because they are reasonable, they [human beings] also have intelligence, discretion, judgment, and the power to reason: [they] are capable of conceiving by experience and by art: [they] are capable of knowledge and doctrine, which other animals are not."[59] Thus human beings can arrive at knowledge by themselves, thanks to reason and experience. This program involves a previous knowledge of oneself, and for that reason the book was worth the trouble to translate and defend. It had paved the way for Montaigne's method of proceeding; without being a theologian, he tested his judgment on humans and other creatures. The "Apology for Raymond Sebond" is a chapter monstrous in its size and in its content. Further elaborated in successive editions, as we have seen, it already occupied a major part of the 1580 edition. Why did Montaigne accord so much importance to Sebond, and why did he spend so much time on this famous defense that is an apology only in name? To answer this question, we have to examine this chapter, remembering the translation Montaigne had made of it twenty years earlier, and once again place the publication of the 1580 *Essais* in the context of its author's personal ambitions, without neglecting the political and religious situation in which he acted.

In her *Mémoires* written during her sequestration in Paris by her brother Henry III in 1576, Margaret of Valois[xii] wrote that she found comfort in "reading in this beautiful universal book of nature so many marvels of its Creator."[60] She was referring to Raymond Sebond's book, *Theologia naturalis, sive liber creaturarum* (1436), Montaigne's translation of which had appeared in Paris in 1569 under the title *Théologie naturelle*.[xiii] She and her younger brother, the duke of Anjou, had been kept at the Court against their will, and one night in January they tried to escape. Francis of Anjou managed to deceive the guards at the Louvre and rejoin his army in Flanders. Left alone in Paris, Margaret was subjected to the gossip of the Court favorites regarding her love affairs. Her former affair with Henry de Guise as well as her more recent adventures were the object of malicious rumors at a time when the Prince of Joinville was pre-

---

[xii] Usually known in English as Margaret of France, or as "Queen Margot." She was the daughter of Henry II and Catherine de Medici and the wife of Henry of Navarre. [Trans.]

[xiii] A French translation of Sebond's *Liber creaturarum* had already been published in 1519. Montaigne seems not to have known this work. However, it is less certain that he was unaware of the abridged translation of Sebond's book, better known under the title of *Viola animae*, made by Jean Martin in 1551 and republished by Vascosan in 1565 and 1566.

senting himself as the natural leader of the Catholic League. Margaret set out to convince the king and the queen mother to let her join her husband in Guyenne. She was finally allowed to leave her gilded cage and travel to Pau with her mother, where she rejoined Henry of Navarre in July 1578.

At the Court of Nérac, Margaret was able to surround herself with the local intelligentsia, and she used her title as queen to try to maintain a fragile peace between the moderate Catholics supported by Henry III and the Protestants under her husband's command. Her mother, Catherine de Medici, remained in Guyenne to try to negotiate a lasting peace. The meeting held at Nérac, the fruit of eighteen months of talks, produced the illusion of a lull in the religious conflicts in the southwest. Montaigne, as an ordinary gentleman of the king of Navarre's chamber, frequented the Court of Nérac. The Court of the queen of Navarre rapidly became a major locus of power for the Gascon nobility. It was in this intellectual sphere of influence that Montaigne had the idea of devoting a whole chapter of his *Essais* to Raymond Sebond, a Catalan theologian of whom Margaret had a favorable opinion. Montaigne had earlier become acquainted with Sebond's work when he translated it into French at his father's request. He set out to write a defense of the theologian, but a rather complicated one, as we shall see. In addition, this long chapter might serve as an introduction (placed at the heart of the second book of the *Essais*) to the reprinting of his translation of Sebond, of which Margaret of Valois thought highly, and which Montaigne intended to have reprinted at the same time as his *Essais*.

To accompany his slightly revised translation, and writing a long chapter, "contrary to [his] custom," Montaigne nonetheless undertook to defend "your Sebond" (he is addressing Margaret). He chose to give a central place to this chapter which, along with that on La Boétie, displays the name of a "near-contemporary" in its title.[xiv] Obviously, the queen of Navarre's "Sebond" was also his, because he had translated him in the early 1550s. Montaigne explains the reasons for his choice. He says that he likes Sebond's "peculiar (*ordinaire*) form of argument," by leaps and gambols, which he associates with his own way of writing. However, Sebond was a controversial author, and Montaigne is careful to distance himself from arguments based on reason. He reminds Margaret of Valois that "our mind is an erratic, dangerous, and heedless tool: it is hard to impose order and moderation upon it."[61] Reason shows itself under "a varying and formless body," because it inevitably communicates through language; ultimately, it is fully a form of rhetoric. This remark, which has the authority of a political precept, together with the veiled counsel Montaigne gives Margaret, sets the limits of Sebond's procedure.

[xiv] All the other names mentioned in a chapter title belong to Greek or Roman Antiquity: Cato, Cicero, Democritus, Heraclitus, Julius Caesar, Virgil, Seneca, Plutarch, and Spurina.

Montaigne is making sure he has something to fall back on; he declares his agreement with the queen—without naming her—and explains in turn the pleasure he took in translating the Spanish theologian's book. He nonetheless distances himself from it by warning the queen against the thinkers of his time who have the unfortunate habit of being "nearly all, we see, incontinent in the license of their opinions and conduct." Montaigne assuredly encourages Margaret to defend Sebond—after all, the new edition of his translations was, so to speak, in press—but solely for his "peculiar" way of arguing, "in which you are instructed every day, and in that you will exercise your mind and your learning."[62] It is a matter of making Sebond more flexible and less didactic, that is, of taking an interest in the form of his argumentation rather than in its content. Montaigne seems to admire the theologian's style. We can understand the interest he took in the 1550s in translating this text into French while preserving the allegedly "ordinary" form of the author. On this view, Montaigne's translation was a stylistic exercise, and he would never have translated Sebond for his ideas. A youthful exercise, just like La Boétie's *Discourse on Voluntary Servitude*, Montaigne's translation of the *Theologia naturalis* also needed to be clarified at the beginning of the 1580s.

The "Apology for Raymond Sebond" occupies a disproportionate space in the second book of the *Essais*. It is a book within the book. This chapter deals more than any other with theology and religion. Montaigne admits that he is hardly well versed in theology, and declares elsewhere, not without emphasis, and after 1588, that he is not a philosopher. This undermining of his own competency clearly shows the ambiguous position taken by the author of the *Essais* with regard to religious questions. This ambivalence is part of a strategy of distancing and confirms Montaigne's ability to understand the thorniest arguments on precise points of theology. Such a stratagem allowed him to detach himself "theoretically" from Sebond in case the analyses proposed by the theologian were judged contrary to Catholic dogma. Montaigne was sufficiently familiar with Patristic writings and religious rites to know when he was deviating from Roman apostolic doctrine. Although he cannot be accused of not being a practicing Catholic,[63] we must question the foundation of his faith, which appears at several points in the *Essais* to be more the result of a cultural heritage than of a conviction drawn from the teaching of the Gospels. For example, we may be surprised that Montaigne does not apply to Catholic doctrine the same principles that allow him to form an opinion of almost every subject. Apparently theology does not lend itself to "judging" (*contreroller*) and remains a dogma that he does not question, except perhaps in a veiled way and with many precautions. In the chapter "We should meddle soberly with judging divine ordinances" (I: 32), Montaigne "dares" to criticize those who claim to interpret and judge divine matters: "To whom I would be prone to add, if I dared, a whole pile of people, interpreters and controllers-in-ordinary of God's designs, claiming to find the causes of every incident and to see in the secrets of the divine will the incomprehensible motives of his works."[64]

Who is targeted here, if not the Protestants? Or at least those who systematically saw the hand of God behind natural phenomena or human actions. Obviously, a Christian must believe that everything emanates from God, but that is an affirmation in principle and not a way of operating or an excuse for acting in accord with one's own convictions. We must not see in human actions the proof of a divine will: "I think that the practice I see is bad, of trying to strengthen and support our religion by the good fortune and prosperity of our enterprises."[65] Montaigne puts things in perspective: "Our belief has enough other foundations; it does not need events to authorize it."[66] Wouldn't it be preferable to accept religion as one submits to the laws of one's country? Montaigne respects the authority of theology, but nothing prevents him from offering a commentary, without claiming to be an expert. He is not a theologian, but he nonetheless discusses religious questions. For example, it is possible to criticize the laws of a country while at the same time obeying them. Montaigne endorses the dogmas of the Roman Catholic Church because he thinks humans are incapable of producing better ones without upsetting the social balance. If he was not tempted by the Protestants' ideas—some of which were, however, in accord with many of his own convictions—that is certainly because he was horrified of change, as he admits on several occasions in the *Essais*. This conservatism, which he associated with tradition, in no way prevented him from making anthropological comparisons between various "religious customs," as if religion were itself part of habits and customs. It is possible to observe them and describe these customs, but rarely to change them.

Nonetheless, we are allowed to interpret divine matters, and that is precisely the theologian's task; but the common man—which Montaigne claims to be— has to take a few precautions before venturing onto a terrain that he does not know well, because, "In short, it is difficult to bring down divine things to our scale."[67] The fact that it is not easy to judge religious beliefs does not mean that it is impossible to form an opinion. Thus in 1580 Montaigne does not completely exclude theological considerations from his reflections. If the *Essais* claims to offer a political commentary on its time, it has to discuss all the subjects that were then upsetting people. Montaigne is "hardly" a theologian, but he is nonetheless enough of one to devote several chapters to the religious problems that were dividing his contemporaries: "We should meddle soberly with judging divine ordinances" (I: 32), "Of prayers" (I: 56), "Of freedom of conscience" (II: 19), and especially "Apology for Raymond Sebond" move in this direction and allow him to participate in the debate on tolerance and pacification between the churches. However, in an important addition made after 1588,

Montaigne noted "human reason's" failure to explain divine phenomena. Henceforth theology represented "a conflict that is decided by the weapons of memory more than by those of reason."[68] But as we shall see, Montaigne had not always held that view. In 1580, he still believed it was possible to read Sebond in a productive way.

To be a theologian is to defend a dogma. In this sense, Montaigne could not be a theologian. However, in the late 1570s everyone was talking about religious issues, and taking sides was obligatory. One could not escape the grip of the religious question. Thus it was normal, in this social and political context, and especially in Aquitaine, that Montaigne should take an interest in the freedom of religion, in prayer, and in religious tolerance. In his own way, he meddled in theology in 1580. He had no other choice, because his translation of Raymond Sebond was interpreted in a way he could not have foreseen thirty years earlier.

We must return to 1552–54, the time when Montaigne probably undertook his translation of Sebond's *Theologia naturalis*. But the date of the translation must not be confused with that of its first publication (1569), even if Montaigne declares that he translated Sebond into French more or less around the time of his father's death on June 18, 1568. It is likely that he made a few revisions to his translation to prepare it for publication, but the bulk of the work had been done long before the latter date. Montaigne's statements regarding theology and theologians in the 1580 edition of the *Essais* have to be read in relation to his translation of Sebond. In 1569, the *Théologie naturelle* marked Montaigne's entrance into the world of letters, when he was already more than thirty-five years old. According to Montaigne's account, it was his father, as we have said, who "ordered" him to translate into French the Catalan theologian's text, which was written in an incomprehensible (*baragouiné*) Latin. He presents this work as the result of pure filial respect, without offering the slightest judgment on this considerable task imposed on him by an overbearing father.

While he was pursuing a career in the parlement in the 1560s and could still hope to rise in the hierarchy of the nobility of the robe in Guyenne, Montaigne remembered this schoolboy exercise, which could allow him to display a learned erudition and show a solid knowledge of the Latin language, which was still considered essential for an ambitious magistrate. In the 1560s, Montaigne was not yet expressing the pretensions to nobility that obsessed him after 1570, that is, after his father's demise, his resignation from his office in the Bordeaux parlement, and his nomination to the Order of Saint Michael. When Pierre Eyquem died in 1568, his son was not yet a writer and he did not even plan to be one, nor did he foresee a career as a negotiator, diplomat, or ambassador. At that time, he still wore the long robe and was fully engaged in his first career as a councillor at the parlement of Bordeaux. Several of his colleagues had published learned works, and Montaigne's good knowledge of Latin had allowed his father—and Montaigne himself—to anticipate a brilliant career in the parlementary milieu. We have already emphasized the professional logic in which this translation of Raymond Sebond was situated.

It is obvious that this work was not a learned one. It was a schoolboy assignment that took on a quite different connotation after the beginning of the Wars of Religion. The relative autonomy of the members of the parlement with regard to the ecclesiastical world justified Montaigne's choice to see in this translation a career asset in 1569, independently of the disputed theological points Sebond made. However, after 1572, when Montaigne had already embarked upon a political career, Sebond's book no longer had the same meaning, and it had to be admitted that it was indeed a theological book. Montaigne's translation was now seen as a contribution to the theological debate and not simply as an exercise in style. In 1580, not able to remain silent about this reality, Montaigne recognized openly that Sebond was a "great Spanish theologian and philosopher." If prior to 1569 he had approached this text as a simple translation from Latin into French, the *Théologie naturelle* had in the meantime become a book whose ideas now had to be discussed, and whose content had to be "defended." In 1569, the *Théologie* could be seen as a "memorial," or at least a conversation with his father. It was normal for Montaigne to publish his first scholarly work of translation as the outcome of the insistence of a father concerned about his son's education.[69] In 1569, Montaigne took little interest in the religious controversies contained in Sebond's book. However, the reprinting of his translation published in Paris in 1581 played a very different role: revising or cleaning up the translation allowed Montaigne to interpret and rephrase several questionable passages in Sebond's work to produce a rather free reading that is sometimes quite distant from the original text.[70] The "Apology for Raymond Sebond" served to salvage and justify a project carried out in his youth (1552–54) and an awkward publication (1569) that might have harmed Montaigne's political aspirations.

The Wars of Religion officially began in 1563, and translating a text like the *Theologia naturalis* immediately after the first armed conflicts between Catholics and Protestants showed a certain independence of mind with regard to the two camps that were battling each other. However, nothing allows us to say that Montaigne knew exactly what he was translating in 1552 or 1553. Quite the contrary: in his "Apology for Raymond Sebond" he clearly explains that this translation was imposed on him by his father. He nonetheless took care to attenuate certain emphatic passages in Sebond's prologue. The translation of this work, in which the qualities of judgment and reason are emphasized, which "appeals to no authority,"[71] and which was prepared for publication soon after Montaigne's father's death, was perfectly suited to advance a career as a jurisconsult and a member of the parlement. The fact that the book was written by a theologian hardly mattered, and in 1552 Montaigne could not have known that the *Theologia naturalis* would be put on the *Index* in 1559—seventeen years after it was given to his father by Pierre Bunel, in April or May 1542, during a brief stay at the family château.

After 1559, it obviously became difficult to publish this book, and that was probably why Montaigne's translation remained in a drawer. Here we have to distinguish between the *Auctores quorum libri & scripta omnia prohibentur* (that is, a list of authors all of whose writings were prohibited) and the *Certorum auctorum libri prohibiti* (a list of certain prohibited books). Sebond's *Theologia naturalis* was put on the latter list in the *Index* of 1559.[xv] Thus Montaigne began his translation long before Sebond's book was put on the *Index*. However, five years later, *only* the "Prologue" to the *Theologia naturalis* was censured and put on the Tridentine *Index* published in 1564, immediately after the conclusion of the Council of Trent. From that time on, Montaigne's translation became salvageable. Moreover, the authors and texts put on the Tridentine *Index* were not really monitored by the Inquisition—for example, regarding the entrance of books into Rome—until June 1569.[72] Only Sebond's introduction was forbidden, and nothing any longer stood in the way of the publication of Montaigne's translation. His father's death was an opportunity for Montaigne to pay homage to him, but also to demonstrate his ability to translate and "edit" a text in Latin. As a member of parlement, he was running no great risk in 1569.

In 1580, when he was about to become an author, Montaigne preferred to forestall the accusations that might be made against him. In that event, he could always count on Margaret of Valois to protect him. Without giving her name or putting her in any pointless danger, he nonetheless acted in such a way that there was no possible doubt as to this chapter's true dedicatee. In the first pages of the "Apology for Raymond Sebond" the translator explains the circumstances that led him to translate the Catalan theologian. The account Montaigne gave was written almost thirty years after the translation. Pierre Eyquem had been dead for more than a decade when his son explained the circumstances of his translation. He completely changed his strategy. A declared gentleman and lord, he had left the long robe behind and was now part of the royal entourage of Henry III and the Court of Navarre. Having achieved a regional career

---

[xv] *Index Auctorum et Librorum, qui ab officio S. Rom. & uniuersalis inquisitionis caueri ab omnibus & singulis in uniuersa Christiana Republica mandantur, sub censuris contra legentes, vel tenentes libros prohibitos in bulla, quae lecta est in coena Domini, expressis & sub aliis poenis in de creto eiusdem sacri officii contentis.* Rome: ex officina Salviana, XV. Mens. Feb. 1559. As we will see, in 1581, the Roman censors notified Montaigne that Sebond's prologue had been condemned. An expurgated Latin version of the prologue was published without difficulty in Venice in 1581. Sebond's "Prologue" was removed from the *Index* only in the nineteenth century.

in the magistracy, he was now seeking a post at the national, even international, level. His youthful translation might be misinterpreted, because the religious situation had changed for the worse in the late 1570s. The case of the *Discourse on Voluntary Servitude*, withdrawn from the *Essais* at the last minute, must have made him worry that he might be accused of deviating from the Roman church's dogma, of excessive indulgence toward the Protestant cause, or even of heresy. Montaigne had already had an opportunity to see how a text could be diverted from its original meaning and transformed into a tool for propaganda in the service of a political cause.

For someone who was hoping to serve the king, this youthful translation might come back to haunt him and compromise his political ambitions. Religious questions were obviously at the very heart of the conflicts, and for that reason theology had to be kept out of any political negotiation. Montaigne no longer desired to take sides and had resigned himself to pursuing a career as a "centrist," though one who continued to respect royal authority. In 1569 he had considerably attenuated the prologue by tempering almost all the passages that put the emphasis on natural reason.[73] Thus when Sebond writes "the foundation of all the knowledge that is necessary for man," Montaigne translates this as "the little foundations of the doctrine pertaining to man for his salvation" ("les petits fondements de la doctrine appartenante à l'homme pour son salut"). He changes "all the truth necessary for man" into "truth, so far as it is possible for natural reason" (vérité, autant qu'il est possible à la raison naturelle); "[the reader] will learn more in less than a month from this knowledge than from the study of learned doctors for a hundred years" is rendered by "in a few months he will make himself more knowledgeable and versed in several subjects, to know which it would be required to spend a long time reading several books" ("il se rendra par cette doctrine en peu de mois savant et versé en plusieurs choses, pour lesquelles savoir il conviendrait employer longtemps à la lecture de plusieurs livres").[74] These sensible deviations from the original text still needed further explanation.

Now Montaigne had to explain this text and distance himself from it without too much damaging his image as an independent thinker, while at the same time reaffirming his unconditional intention to serve the king faithfully. This translation could be seen as a "career error" that might compromise his political ambitions. Although such a translation was acceptable in the parlementary milieu, it certainly became more problematic after he had resigned his office and entered politics. There was also the problem of the text and its partisan interpretation. Giving the impression of being concerned with theology would expose Montaigne to political commentaries seeing him as taking sides in the religious situation, which would in turn make him a committed man. Declaring oneself too strongly for one religious camp was risky for a man who proclaimed himself a servant of the king and sufficiently independent and open to listen to the grievances of the Protestant party.

In the first edition of his *Essais*, Montaigne tried to keep a foot in both camps. He owed obedience to the king, but he also criticized the Catholics. He had learned to put political commitments drawn from events into perspective. Politics must be seen in the middle and long term, and never considered as a simple reaction to the crises that arise every day:

> I can say this for having tried it. In other days I exercised this freedom of personal choice and selection, regarding with negligence certain points in the observance of our Church which seem more vain and strange than others; until, coming to discuss them with learned men, I found that these things have a massive and very solid foundation, and that it is only stupidity and ignorance that make us receive them with less reverence than the rest. Why do we not remember how much contradiction we sense even in our own judgment? How many things were articles of faith to us yesterday, which are fables to us today? Vainglory and curiosity are the two scourges of our soul. The latter leads us to thrust our noses into everything, and the former forbids us to leave anything unresolved and undecided.[75]

Montaigne proposed a line of political conduct that he will later try to apply during his two terms as mayor of Bordeaux. Theology had to be approached as a necessary and inevitable discourse for the gentleman that he now was. It was not a matter of fleeing responsibilities that would force him to take sides, but rather of clarifying certain points that might seem equivocal. Moreover, could theological discourse be separated from the social and political practices of the Renaissance? Montaigne situates religious practices—notably, prayer—in the context of the Wars of Religion and regrets that his contemporaries did not hesitate to "call God to our company and society."[76] That is a fact, and no one can be unaware that in the early 1580s politics was closely linked to the religious, which was then transformed into ideology in the service of the parties that were battling in the political arena. Montaigne pondered the true theological foundations of systems of belief and noted that our mind is itself not exempt from vengeance and resentment. Religion performs particular functions depending on the period, and that is why it is essential to distinguish the motivations that mark the translation done in 1552–54, the publication of the *Théologie naturelle* in 1569, and its republication in 1581.[xvi]

[xvi] When the *Théologie naturelle* was reprinted, Montaigne was already in Italy. It is dated September 22, 1581. Montaigne had just left the baths at Villa to go to Rome.

The enthusiastic judgments that see in the republication of the *Théologie naturelle* in 1581 a significant work on Montaigne's part must be qualified. Without having compared the texts of the 1569 and 1581 editions, most critics assure us that Montaigne engaged in a task equivalent to what we can observe in the Bordeaux Copy. That is not true. The 1581 version does not substantially modify Montaigne's original translation. He merely corrected misprints in the 1569 text, which are not very numerous in comparison to those in the 1580 edition of the *Essais*.

A revised copy of the 1569 *Théologie naturelle*[xvii] that belonged to Montaigne and that was presented by Alain Brieux in 1958[77] illustrates well the way Montaigne corrected his text, mainly by changing the punctuation or a single character in a word in the framework of the printed page. According to Brieux's count, out of the 229 words or "groups of letters" corrected, no passage was the object of a genuine rewriting. It was a matter of simply cleaning up the text. Moreover, we must be wary regarding the nature of these corrections. Thus in the 1569 prologue, the text gives "convaincu fause," which becomes "convaincuë faulse" in 1581. Is this correction attributable to Montaigne or the foreman in the printshop? It is hard to decide so long as the copy of the *Théologie* corrected in Montaigne's own hand and mentioned by Brieux has not yet resurfaced. Similarly, "d'avantaige" (1569) becomes "d'avantage" in 1581, and "maistre d'ecole" (1569) becomes "Maistre d'ecole." The punctuation is often increased in 1581, and allows the text to breathe more easily. Where in 1569 we have "d'avantage ils sont privez de mouvement de lieu à autre," in 1581 we read "d'avantage, ils sont . . .", or again "Ceux de la seconde à cause de leur memoire, ont mouvement" has another comma in 1581: "Ceux de la seconde, à cause de la memoire, ont mouvement."[78] On the same page, twenty lines farther on, we read "ny reng auquel l'homme puisse monter par de là" in 1569, and "ny reng auquel l'homme puisse monter au delà" in 1581: a set of minor stylistic corrections.

What should we say about the errors attributable to the printer? A methodical comparison between a 1569 copy (Sonnius) and two copies of the 1581 edition (Sonnius and Chaudière) does not allow us to validate what Montaigne says when he claims that his translation was printed "with the nonchalance that is seen in the infinite number of errors that the printer, who carried out the work alone, left in it."[79] This criticism of the printer has more to do with a commonplace than with reality, and Montaigne justifies the reprinting of a controversial work for purely philological reasons, namely, the simple correction of errors in the first printing. I have found only corrections bearing on spelling

---

[xvii] This copy is now in the hands of a private collector.

and punctuation; in short, changes that affect the text itself very little. It is often errors in reading made by the compositors that have been rectified. How long exactly did it take Montaigne to change the spelling of a few words and modify the punctuation on the 1569 copy? A week at most. What is more, it was a task that could easily be carried out while traveling. Montaigne might very well have made these corrections between Bordeaux and Saint-Maur-des-Fossés during the summer of 1580. Finally, a very large number of pages (more that 95 percent), even though all recomposed, end up with the same guide words, which proves that the compositors were able to keep the same references when putting together the 1581 edition. The number of pages is the same in the two editions, and only the additions in the margins differ in their fonts: in Roman letters for those in 1581 and in italics for those in the 1569 edition. Thus it is an exaggeration to claim that the *Théologie naturelle* of 1581 constituted an entirely reworked edition; rather, it was a reprinting with a few corrections.

Montaigne explains the absence of François d'Amboise's encomiastic sonnet in the 1581 edition of the *Théologie naturelle*. For him, the omission of these verses is a matter of fashion, nothing more. He accuses the printer, Gilles Gourbin, of having succumbed to the lure of the "commissioned and borrowed prefaces"[80] that were in vogue at the time of the first edition.

Must we be satisfied with this explanation of the publishing practices of the 1560s? Let us note first that in the last years of the sixteenth century, far from having disappeared, preliminary pieces were becoming even more fashionable. It is more likely that in 1581 Montaigne demanded an authorial independence that was less obvious in 1569. Was François d'Amboise competent in theology, as has been suggested?[81] From 1568 to 1572, d'Amboise did teach philosophy as regent of the second class at the College of Navarre, where he had a fellowship as an "Écolier du roi."[82] At the time, d'Amboise was proud of his poetry and had managed to place his verse in numerous collections. In 1569, he also published a *Tombeau de A. Sorhin* with Guillaume Chaudière, the copublisher of Montaigne's translation of the *Theologia naturalis*. It was probably through this connection with Chaudière that d'Amboise was able to convince the publisher that a sonnet placed at the head of Montaigne's translation would embellish this work done by an unknown. Inserting the poem was not without interest for the bookseller because the young d'Amboise was then openly aligned with the party of the Catholic extremists. It was perhaps thanks to the contacts with d'Amboise that a privilege was rapidly obtained, apparently without difficulty, whereas Sebond's *Theologia* was on the *Index*. The publication of this sonnet could be seen as Chaudière's way of thanking d'Amboise for services rendered. The name of François d'Amboise clearly situated the work in the camp of the Catholics and probably explains why Chaudière agreed to place his verses at the head of the *Théologie naturelle* of 1569.

In 1581, François d'Amboise's status had changed. He had accompanied Henry III to Poland, but after his return to France, he had given up all pretension to be a poet in order to study law in Paris. He became a *robin* and followed a career path the inverse of that followed by Montaigne, who had abandoned his office in the parlement. Received by the parlement of Paris as a *novus advocatus*, François d'Amboise was named prosecutor in 1575 and rapidly rose through the parlementary hierarchy. He was successively magistrate at the parlement of Paris and Brittany, *maître des requêtes*, and councillor of the king in his Great Council.

If François d'Amboise's poem had helped the publisher obtain a privilege and thus to make the printing of Montaigne's translation possible in 1569, his name meant something quite different in 1581, at a time when Montaigne was trying precisely to keep his translation at a distance from theology and theologians. In 1569, François d'Amboise's last verses unhesitatingly presented Sebond's book as a theological work:

That is why Nature with its theology,
Better than art marks on us the true effigy
Of God, of his essence, and his high power.

This is a reminder that Montaigne wanted to avoid in 1581. Similarly, this poem by a member of parlement threatened to be misinterpreted,[xviii] even if François d'Amboise remained a militant Catholic. In the end, he represented another generation (he was seventeen years younger than Montaigne), and the author of the *Essais* was annoyed by the fact that this sonnet made no reference to his work as translator. In 1581, the name of François d'Amboise would have served only to complicate the reception of this new edition of the *Théologie naturelle* by reminding readers that questions of theology were the principal subject matter of this book, which Montaigne now wanted to present as a work that was stimulating for its thought and a style that pleased by its simple and peculiar form of argumentation.

As we have seen, rather than the text itself, it is the prologue to the *Theologia naturalis* that had been a problem for the Roman censors and had caused the entire book to be put on the *Index* in 1559, while the prologue was put on the *Index tridentum* in 1564. In 1580, it was again the prologue that Montaigne had to explain or at least interpret in his own way in the "Apology for Raymond Sebond"; this was a rather difficult task, considering the number of Sebond's propositions repeated in one form or another in the *Essais*. For example, what are we to think of the passage in which Sebond maintains that man is "illumi-

[xviii] At the end of the 1570s, François d'Amboise signed his poems using the title "Advocate at the Court." See for example his poem in Pierre de Larivey's book, *L'Institution morale du Seigneur Alexandre Piccolomini*, published in Paris by Abel L'Angelier in 1581.

nated to know himself"? This Socratic principle expresses one of the foundations of the *Essais*. This turn inward, without passing through an ecclesiastical mediator, was, as we might expect, the main reproach addressed to Sebond by the censors. If Sebond's recommendations are taken literally, it can be deduced that man can attain truth by his own means and through reason.

We understand why Sebond was read with interest by the Protestants, who regarded favorably this ability of man to base knowledge on reason, and thus outside the doctrine and institutions of the Roman Catholic Church.[xix] However, it has to be added—and Montaigne did not fail to do so—that Sebond's book was written before the "innovations" of Luther and Calvin. The very special knowledge that appeals to personal judgment, outside of disciplines, became one of the *Essais'* credos after 1585. The truth, Sebond writes in Montaigne's translation, "presupposes neither grammar, nor logic, nor any other liberal art, nor physics, nor metaphysics." This passage reminds us of what Montaigne says in "Of the education of children," where he states that it is only after having regulated the child's "behavior and his sense, that will teach him to know himself,"[83] and "after the tutor has told his pupil what will help make him wiser and better," that he can be instructed in "the meaning of logic, physics, geometry, rhetoric."[84] In fact, we find in Sebond a few of the great principles of the *Essais*, notably the will not to be content with bookish knowledge and to argue "only from things that are clear and known to everyone through experience."[85]

It is equally disturbing to find in Montaigne's translation of the prologue to the *Theologia naturalis* the title of what was to become a literary genre. Sebond recommends that "everyone [has] tried out (*essayé*) in himself" the method he advocates, because it "has need of no witness other than man."[86] This exhortation of Sebond's might have been recalled—unconsciously—by Montaigne and used again twenty years later to explain man and to recycle—in the title of his book—an expression that he had initially chosen when translating Sebond's critical work from Latin into French. Similarly, in a way unexpected in a theologian—and this was probably what alarmed the censors—Sebond says that he adduces "no authority, not even that of the Bible." Montaigne made this axiom one of the pillars of his own critical approach; this was acceptable for a *robin* in 1569, but not for a gentleman in 1581. Whence the necessity of a defense of the

---

[xix] In *The Protestant Ethic and the Spirit of Capitalism*, Max Weber argues that Protestantism represents the triumph of reason over the irrationality of Catholic dogma. Lamennais did not hesitate to assert that "Protestantism is ultimately only a kind of spiritual idolatry in which man, after having made a god of his reason, consecrates and adores all his thoughts just as the pagan consecrated and adored his passions" (*Essai sur l'indifférence en matière de religion*, in *Œuvres complètes*. Paris: 1836–37, vol. III, p. 124).

translation of Sebond's book, which must not be confused with a defense of Raymond Sebond.

A Skeleton in the Closet

An attentive reading of the opening pages of the "Apology for Raymond Sebond" in the text of the first edition of the *Essais* in 1580 produces a rather strange feeling in the reader, as if the author were trying to distance himself from a youthful exercise imposed by a despotic father, which he had to accept without hesitation. Why this later detachment? Eleven years after the first edition of the *Théologie naturelle*, Montaigne might be harried for translating this work whose prologue was still on the *Index*. However, we must not overdramatize the situation. After all, Montaigne was "hardly" a theologian, and endorsing certain of Sebond's ideas did not give rise to genuine persecution, especially if it is recalled that the main quality he attributes to Sebond is his peculiar way of arguing. For an intelligent man who was demanding a certain independence with regard to the political and religious elites, such an exercise was not necessarily a mistake. We have to distinguish between Montaigne's motivations in 1569 and his expectations and ambitions in 1580.

If one wanted to put oneself at the disposal of the king's policy, on Catholic territory—Rome, for instance—this translation could lead the ecclesiastical authorities to wonder about the translator's religious convictions. For Montaigne it was preferable to approach the problem head-on, and offer a new edition of this work done at another time, openly emphasizing his simple role as a translator whose name did not even appear on the title page of the first edition of 1569. The revised 1581 edition could provide an opportunity to explain the circumstances under which he did the translation. Why not accompany it by a prologue, an apology for Raymond Sebond that could at the same time serve as a self-justification? Better yet, why not propose an apology *outside* Sebond's text, thus creating an additional distance between this youthful exercise and the theologian's book? It was pointless to make too much of it or to deny the translator's interest in some of Sebond's ideas and the way they are defended. So these ideas had to be situated in their historical context in order to show that they could now serve the Catholic cause against the atheists or the heretics. Sebond might even have been a visionary: "In this he was very well advised, rightly foreseeing by rational inference that this incipient malady would easily degenerate into an execrable atheism."[87]

After recognizing the utility of knowledge at the beginning of his apology for Sebond, Montaigne admits that he does not accord it disproportionate importance. Knowledge is not the mother of all virtue. He recounts his everyday family life in his father's time, and describes the château as open to learned men of all denominations, "inflamed with that new ardor with which King Francis I embraced letters and brought them into credit." Therefore, it was natural for a lord to follow the humanist fashion of celebrating arts and letters. However, Montaigne adds that his father was not well read, and that his judgment was sometimes faulty, making him incapable of telling good books from bad ones, "collecting their sayings and discourses like oracles, and with all the more reverence and religion as he was less qualified to judge them, for he had no knowledge of letters."[88] Then Montaigne recounts the circumstances under which his father hosted Pierre Bunel, "a man of great reputation for learning in his time," at the château for a few days, probably in 1542 or 1543.[xx]

In his *Mémoires*, Henri de Mesmes reports that when he was studying in Toulouse he often saw the famous humanists Pierre Bunel and Guy du Faur de Pibrac.[89] Montaigne tells us that his father liked to surround himself with learned men and received them "like holy persons." Receiving "oracles" was part of a country gentleman's way of life. As he was saying farewell to his host, Bunel gave Pierre Eyquem a book titled *Liber naturae sive creaturarum*. However, it was long after Bunel's visit that Montaigne's father "ordered" him to translate into French a "very useful book and suited to the time in which he [Bunel] gave it to him."[90] The Wars of Religion had not yet begun, and Montaigne's father could not be accused of having given his son a controversial book. Nonetheless, we know that in his time Pierre Bunel had been forbidden to live in Toulouse and was accused of "false religion." It was only thanks to the protection of Arnaud du Faur that Bunel had been able to return to his native city. Pierre Eyquem did not know about this incident and had not seen the urgency or interest of having Sebond's book translated; it remained in a chest in the château for about ten years.

When a career in the judiciary loomed on the horizon, Michel, like the good son he was, carried out this work that was *imposed* on him to prevent him from forgetting his Latin. In the dedication of his translation, addressed to this father, Montaigne explains that he had "shaped and trained the manner of Raymond Sebond, that great Spanish theologian and philosopher, [giving him] a French dress and divesting him, so far as I was able, of the savage bearing and barbarous demeanor you first saw in him: so that in my opinion, he now has enough good behavior and civility to be presented in any good company."[91] It is as if Montaigne were still too young—in 1581 he was forty-eight years old—to form his own opinion regarding religious dogmas. We emphasize this obligation because that was how he presented this *pensum* of his youth.

[xx] Pierre Bunel died in Turin in 1546.

The accent is put on the book as a present rather than on its author. This present is also explained by the fact that it was "written in an obscure Spanish with Latin endings." Bunel thought he would please Montaigne's father, who knew a little Spanish and Italian because he had fought in those countries. This "very useful book and suited to the time in which he gave it to him"—it was in fact the time when Protestant ideas were beginning to take root in Aquitaine—allowed Montaigne to pay homage to Sebond for having promoted before its time a new form of theological discourse that was capable of being used to fight the heretics. Montaigne explains that the "common herd" cannot judge what is reported to it, and that reason is a dangerous tool if it is not put in good hands. He hastens to condemn the qualities that he was soon to claim as his own: the ability to "judge opinions" and to put "beliefs in doubt and upon the balance."[92] According to him, the turmoil engendered by the theological debates injured the principle of civil peace necessary for any society. The authority of the laws was seriously compromised by the new ideas. Montaigne defends the Catholic religion unreservedly, less on the basis of a theological analysis than simply in the name of the proper functioning of political institutions. Weak minds, the "vulgar"—and Montaigne adds that "(almost everyone belongs to this category)," a parenthesis struck out on the Bordeaux Copy—have to be kept out of decisions based on reason. The "common herd" is not capable of putting things in perspective or choosing among good and bad beliefs. Theology is, without any doubt, a matter for specialists. Montaigne situates himself between these extremes and limits himself to commenting on Sebond's text, describing himself as an "ordinary man," his political leitmotif in the following years.

After this clarification, Montaigne explains how, by a simple coincidence, "some days before his death" his father came across this book, which had been forgotten "under a pile of other abandoned papers," and "commanded" him to put it into French. We have to examine the chronology of this episode a little more closely here. Pierre Eyquem died on June 18, 1568. If we believe Montaigne, who tells us that his father gave him this work to translate a few days before his death, it is hard to see how, in "a few days" the book could have been translated and sent to a printer, because Montaigne claims that it was not he, but rather his father, who took the initiative for this publication. Still, according to the account given by Montaigne in the "Apology for Raymond Sebond," translating was for him a "very strange and new occupation," because he considered this work to be a schoolboy exercise, but he was "unable to disobey any command of the best father that there ever was."[93] Twice, in a few lines, Montaigne refers to his father's *command*. He carried out this assignment as best he could and his father "ordered it to be printed."

In the short dedication preceding his translation, Montaigne also refers to "the task you [Pierre Eyquem] assigned me last year at your home at Montaigne," thus during the year 1567. The printing of the book was completed on December 30, 1568, and the title page bears the date 1569. The letters patent for the authorization of the printing were given on October 27, 1568. Six months separate the death of Montaigne's father and the appearance of the translation of Raymond Sebond's book (in all, 496 printed sheets—that is, nearly a thousand pages—in the 1569 edition). Could Montaigne have translated this thick volume in a few days, or even in a few weeks? That seems highly unlikely.[94] He ends his dedication this way: "My lord, I pray to God that he may give you a very long and happy life," as if the notice had been written in the morning, whereas Montaigne's father had died in the afternoon. The dates are a problem here. Oddly, this dedication claims to have been written "from Paris," which is probable if Montaigne had made the trip to Paris to have his translation printed. However, if the date were correct (and it cannot be), Montaigne would not have been present at the château of Montaigne, at his father's side, at the time of his death. We must, of course, take this (symbolic) date for what it is: a decisive turning point in his life and in his career.

Another contradiction must also be noted. Montaigne writes that he had "once inquired of Adrianus Turnebus, who knew everything, what could be the truth about this book. He replied that he thought it was some quintessence extracted from St. Thomas Aquinas."[95] But Turnebus died on June 12, 1565, which proves that this book was not "rediscovered" a few days before Pierre Eyquem's death and that Montaigne probably began to translate Raymond Sebond long before, and not just before his father's death. Montaigne does not tell the whole truth about his intellectual encounter with the *Theologia naturalis* and plays down his work as a translator, going so far as to suggest that it was a schoolboy exercise quickly dashed off.

Questions have also been asked about the omission of any reference to Sebond's title—"theologian"—in the "Apology for Raymond Sebond" of 1580. Montaigne states that Sebond "was a Spaniard, teaching medicine in Toulouse." However, he did not omit to mention his title of theologian in the dedication of his translation to his father in 1569.[96] The narrator who reports the history of the *Théologie naturelle* in the "Apology for Raymond Sebond" presents himself as a popularizer, giving Sebond's text a civil aspect in order to make it accessible "in any good company," including women: "many people are reading it, and especially the ladies."[97] That allowed him to show that Sebond's book is not really a work on theology, because, as he remarks in "Of prayers," women are "hardly fit to treat theological matters."[98] The adverb "hardly" (*guiere*) recalls—and strengthens—Montaigne's admission that he is "hardly well-versed" in theology. He puts himself on the same level as his ideal female reader: Margaret of Valois. We find the same interest in the stylistic composition of Sebond's text at the expense of its theological import.

The question is not whether Montaigne betrayed Sebond, but rather how to understand the reception of Sebond from the time Montaigne translated the book in 1552–54—that is, for the first publication of it in 1569—and the reprinting of this text in 1581, accompanied by the first edition of the *Essais* (published a year earlier) in which the "Apology for Raimond Sebond" is dominant. Sebond's thesis surely did not displease Montaigne; otherwise, how could we explain the reprinting and the major place given this author in the second book of the *Essais*? In any case, Montaigne had to explain this translation done in his youth. That is the primary function of the "Apology for Raymond Sebond," which is so long that one has the feeling that Montaigne is trying to cloud the issue. Wasn't the chief goal of the 1580 edition of the *Essais* to offer a political explanation—under the veil of a pseudo-philosophical discussion—of this first publication, which could rub the political and religious authorities the wrong way? Things had greatly changed in ten years, and suddenly Sebond's book had acquired a contemporary relevance that it had lacked in 1569, and even more in 1552–54.

Now, after the beginning of the armed conflicts between Protestants and Catholics, this work could serve as a foil to Luther's "innovations," which "were beginning to gain favor and to shake our old belief in many places."[99] This was a hijacking of Sebond that proceeded from a good political feeling. In 1580, all Montaigne had to do through the mediation of his father was to ensure that this translation appeared to be relevant on the political level, without going too far in order to avoid upsetting any party. He had to deconstruct Sebond within an apology (which was an apology for his translation and not an apology for Sebond) that sometimes looks like a condemnation. From this chapter it emerges that Montaigne seems not to have understood Sebond all that well. But is that really a bad thing? Pretending to be naive in matters of religion was a political strategy that made sense at that time. Moreover, Montaigne has told us many times that he is not a theologian and took an interest in Sebond's text only for his free style and way of arguing.[100] To hear him tell it, Sebond might even have been the first essayist!

Montaigne finds Sebond's argumentation "so solid" that he thinks it difficult to do better at making "that argument," but he does not judge Sebond's approach itself. Then he lists the accusations made against Sebond's book. He tries to analyze Sebond's arguments but takes the precaution of reaffirming, once again, that he is not a theologian: "This would be rather the task for a man versed in theology than for myself, who know nothing about it." Here we have moved from "hardly" to "nothing." Montaigne adds: "It is faith alone that embraces vividly and surely the high mysteries of our religion."[101] This is final. A specialist in reversals, Montaigne nonetheless continues with a "But . . ." He praises Sebond's enterprise while politicizing his theses. For him, the more the existence of God is proven, the better, especially in times of heresy and atheism. Montaigne transforms the author of the *Theologia naturalis* into a prophet of the ills that were soon to divide France. Thus it is with the help of the text of the "Apology" that we must understand the reprinting of Montaigne's translation in 1581. Montaigne transforms Sebond's book into a political discourse on his own time. There is Religion and religion: the general sense of the term contrasts with a practical meaning that arose from the civil wars. Unfortunately, politics and theology became confused. Montaigne chose politics, sheltering himself from theological quarrels. He explains that he had to explain several passages that had been misunderstood and to defend Sebond's text against "two principal objections that are made to it,"[102] and he concludes that Sebond is both bold and courageous in his confirmation of the articles of Christian faith against the atheists. On this point, Montaigne cites Turnebus, whose opinion he says he asked regarding Sebond's book.

The apology for Sebond is situated outside theology—at least in 1580, at the time of the publication of the *Essais*. Montaigne argues that reason must be put in the service of religion without, however, seeking to perfect "a knowledge so supernatural and divine." Moreover, if faith sufficed, man would not waver and would not doubt. The arguments reason offers may have their interest from a strategic point of view—in the name of the Catholic religion, of course. Montaigne proposes to "accommodate to the service of our faith the natural and human tools that God has given us."[103] Reason's purpose is to "embellish, extend, and amplify the truth of [our] belief"; we must not "think that it is on us that faith depends." Montaigne offers a new prologue to the *Théologie naturelle* that is more moderate than Sebond's censured one and is intended to replace it. Faced with a theological problem that he nonetheless thinks he can resolve, the author of the *Essais* begins by praising Sebond's enterprise and then deems it absurd to think that one can base faith on reason. This contradiction does not frighten the amateur theologian that Montaigne is.

The publication of the *Essais* of 1580 exonerated Montaigne of a "youthful error." He recognizes "Sebond's errors" but nevertheless approves his approach in a period in which disbelief was spreading in France, and particularly in the southwest. Sebond's aberrations with regard to the dogma of the Catholic Church might be excusable if their author was not represented as a theologian. Thus we can understand why Montaigne preferred not to mention Sebond's title in his apology. He also takes care to display a flawless faith, but follows Sebond in lines of reasoning that go around in circles and are sometimes completely contradictory. Montaigne notes that "God owes his extraordinary help to faith and religion, not to our passions,"[104] but immediately passes on to considerations more sociological than theological in nature. For example, he states—in accord with the views he was to develop later—that "All this is a very evident sign that we receive our religion only in our own way and with our own hands, and not otherwise than as other religions are received."[105] This relativist vision of religious belief considerably weakens the argument of the preceding pages, and the author of the *Essais* is venturing onto a slippery slope. The reader loses his way, because this long apology for Sebond looks like a labyrinth from which one cannot emerge.

Didn't Montaigne misunderstand, or at least misread, Sebond's work? Perhaps not. On the contrary, we see in these contradictions the a posteriori necessity of transforming Sebond's text into a currently relevant document that could be used politically. Montaigne pretends to be a skeptic the better to assert the necessity of a rational, durable foundation for any power, either political or religious. As we have seen, his political conservatism has to be situated in the practices of his time. Montaigne often defends the status quo, even though he constantly makes—frequently in a contradictory way—skeptical judgments regarding any form of authority acquired through tradition or custom. To those who reproached the theologian for the weakness of his demonstrations, Montaigne replies that it is impossible to acquire and prove universal truths. This historicization of the arguments presented by Sebond corresponds to an updating of Sebond's book in the context of the Wars of Religion. The beginning of the "Apology" designates a constant oscillation between the orthodox positions of the Catholic Church and a systematic questioning of the foundation for truths that are supposed to be truer than those of other religions. Montaigne inclines more toward an explanation that makes religion the result of "human ties." What are we to think, for example, of this statement: "Another region, other witnesses, similar promises and threats, might imprint upon us in the same way a contrary belief"?[106] Here Montaigne deconstructs his preceding statements. Then begins a veritable miscellany of remarks that move further and further away from the original intention of the "Apology." The apologist allows himself to be taken over by his writing, but he can still refer critics to the first pages of the chapter, which offer a glimpse of the possibility of a human interpretation far removed from theological discourse.

In the "Apology," Montaigne covers his tracks by turning around once again the arguments given against Sebond. He sees faith as the backdrop for the proofs produced by reason and argues that it is very difficult to dissociate the two: "Faith, coming to color and illumine Sebond's arguments, makes them firm and solid."[107] And Montaigne concludes: "And even if we strip them of this ornament and of the help and approbation of faith, and take them as purely human fancies, to combat those who are precipitated into the frightful and horrible darkness of irreligion, they will still be found as solid and as firm as any others of the same type that may be opposed to them."[108]

Montaigne engages in an updating of the *Theologia naturalis*. Whereas before Luther and Calvin it was possible to consider such arguments dangerous to the Roman church, the same analyses could now be useful in combating the new beliefs. Montaigne puts one more author in the service of the Catholic cause. Only sixteen pages later, Montaigne moves on to the second objection against Sebond: his arguments are "weak and unfit to prove what he proposes."[109] Montaigne maintains that reading Sebond is not for people whose religious belief is strong, like his, but for weak minds. Sebond is useful for bringing back to the bosom of the Catholic Church those who have strayed from it: "Let us consider for the moment man alone, without outside assistance, armed solely with his own weapons, and deprived of divine grace and knowledge."[110] This line of reasoning can be interpreted as a variant of Pascal's wager. Let us take up our enemies' weapons the better to combat them, Montaigne says. But he knows that he is on dangerous terrain and emphasizes that those who lack faith are "ridiculous," "miserable and puny creatures."[111] Why not use the weapons we have received from God the better to defeat those who are in error?

The first edition of the *Théologie naturelle* published in 1569 could now be seen as a skeleton in the closet. However, in 1581 Montaigne published it again, at the precise time when he was seeking political and diplomatic responsibilities. We can interpret this "recidivism" as strategic and believe that he had reflected at length on the accusations that might be made against him, and that he rejected them on the basis of many reasoned considerations. By republishing his translation of the *Theologia naturalis* at a time when he had just published his *Essais*, Montaigne persisted and took responsibility for the work, thus cutting the ground out from under those who might disapprove of an author who had been put on the *Index* and who was read by Protestants. This political and publishing strategy proved successful, since Montaigne was never reproached for this venture. The Roman censors had pointed out to him that the prologue to the *Theologia* was a prohibited text, but Montaigne's translation was not even mentioned in the verbal remonstrances that the *Maestro del Sacro Palazzo* addressed to him during his stay in Rome. Montaigne could have seen in them a kind of exoneration. However, one question remained. Why didn't he join to his translation of Sebond (in the 1581 edition) a preface in which he could have replied directly to the objections that he lists in his *Essais*? Why didn't he add his "Apology" to the revised edition of the *Théologie naturelle* published in 1581? A political interpretation is necessary and allows us to offer an answer to these questions. Although Montaigne could not have known that the *Theologia naturalis* would soon be placed on the *Index* when he made his translation in 1552–54, he could no longer have been unaware of this when the second edition was published in 1581. The desire to accede to political responsibilities required a clarification separate from the controversial text, or at least that is how the author of the *Essais* seemed to see the matter in 1580.

Montaigne cleared the air before launching into his new political career. We can understand why he republished (without major change) his translation of the *Theologia naturalis* almost at the same time as the first edition of his *Essais*. The two texts complement each other: the *Essais* served as a political justification for this youthful incursion into the domain of theology, and the *Théologie naturelle* of 1581 enabled Montaigne to take refuge behind the more political understanding of the "Apology," which minimizes Sebond's theological design. In his *Bibliothèque françoise* (1584), La Croix du Maine mentions this translation of the *Theologia naturalis*. He does so in terms that distinguish the translation work done by the young Montaigne from the taking of any theological position. Thus La Croix du Maine notes that it was "at the command of his father" that Montaigne undertook to translate Sebond. Montaigne's strategy had paid off, and this explanation was henceforth part of his biography. His father was also excused at the same time. La Croix du Maine explains that Pierre Eyquem "did this expressly, as much to instruct him in the fear of God as to teach him more and more to learn good literature and to exercise himself in languages."[112] On this point, the remark (which may have been suggested by Montaigne) is very true.

The best way to get rid of a skeleton in one's closet is to bring it out into the daylight where everyone can see it. Montaigne does not conceal his "youthful mistake" (a lack of judgment with regard to the request made by an "unlettered" father), but he explains that it was a choice for which he takes responsibility. In the reprinting of the *Théologie naturelle* in 1581 we have to see a desire to limit the damage that might be done to a political career by a potentially dangerous book. If Montaigne succeeded in getting past the Roman censors on this point, then the battle would be won and his future in the service of the king assured. The author of the *Essais* acted as an amateur theologian in giving a political dimension to his apology. This famous chapter 12 of the second book of the *Essais* of 1580 must be considered an exercise in diplomacy. If it reassures Montaigne's reader (here he was in no way thinking of a common reader, but rather of the political and religious authorities), he also reaffirms his own religious convictions and confirms his talent as a negotiator. Unlike in theology, in diplomacy nothing is ever achieved by being dogmatic.

A Royal Audience and a Military Siege

Montaigne's book was brought out by Millanges in May 1580. According to modern estimates, the print run was limited to three or four hundred copies, of which the author could receive fifty copies gratis because he had provided the paper, that is, he had met the most important expense involved in producing a book.[xxi] Montaigne had planned to go to Paris, where he intended to deposit with a printer a slightly reworked and "corrected" version of his translation of Sebond. But the main goal of this trip to the capital was to present a copy of his *Essais* to the king. This meeting was probably arranged by the marquis of Trans. An audience with the king could not be improvised, and Montaigne had to respect the date set a certain time in advance. We can understand his desire to see the *Essais* emerge from Millanges's printshop without delay. With his book hot off the presses, he prepared to travel to the Court.

Since June 2, an epidemic of "coqueluche" (whooping cough) had been raging in Paris; actually, it was a kind of influenza, since the reported symptoms were severe pains in the head, stomach, back, and aches all over the body. According to Pierre de L'Estoile, ten thousand people fell ill with this form of "cold or catarrh."[113] The king, the duke of Mercœur, and the duke of Guise also caught this flu. As soon as he recovered, the king left Paris, on June 18. This sudden manifestation of the flu was immediately followed by a much more serious epidemic, because the plague spread suddenly and violently in Paris around the middle of June. No one wanted to go to the capital, and Pierre de L'Estoile reports that on June 12 the duke of Nevers, informed that the duke of Montpensier was at the gates of Paris with five hundred horsemen ready to do battle with him, avoided the capital by pretending to go to Plombières. The plague scared people more than battles.

Rapidly overwhelmed by this scourge that threw Paris into chaos, the provosts did not know how to stop this contagion, whose last outbreak in the city, in 1562, had caused 25,000 deaths. Everything suggested that this record would be broken. Plague victims were rounded up in every quarter of the city and transported to the Hôtel-Dieu hospital. A genuine panic had seized the city's residents. L'Estoile reports that 30,000 people died in this epidemic during the summer of 1580. The terror was so great that most of those who could leave the

---

[xxi] A contract signed by Simon Millanges and Pierre Charron, dated May 10, 1601, allows us to form an idea of the Bordeaux publisher's commercial practices with regard to his authors: "in addition, it was agreed that for each printing and new edition of the said works the said Millanges will be expected to provide the following to the said lord of Charron: for the first printing, fifty copies, and, for each of the others, thirty, part of the whole bound and part unbound" (see J. N. Dast Le Vacher de Boisville, "Simon Millanges, imprimeur à Bordeaux de 1572 à 1623." *Bulletin historique et philologique du comité des travaux historiques et scientifiques*, 1896, 792–93). It was not unusual for an author to receive a number of copies that he could then distribute to his friends and to people who could help him professionally. The first edition of the *Essais* in 1580 was thus supposed to permit Montaigne himself to see to the distribution of his book to readers selected in relation to precise expectations.

city did so. Outsiders did not return for six months, and the capital was deserted by foreigners. Paris was so empty that people played skittles on the Notre-Dame bridge and in several other streets in the capital.[114]

Montaigne, like many others, preferred to remain outside the walls of the capital. His attitude with regard to the plague is well known. Five years later, when he was within a few days of the end of his term as mayor of Bordeaux, he refused to go into city, which was infected by the contagion, and transferred powers to jurats outside the city. He cannot be blamed for this decision. For the same reasons, he certainly preferred to present himself at the Court at Saint-Maur-des-Fossés and avoid Paris. His meeting with the king therefore took place at Saint-Maur, where Henry III and Catherine de Medici were accustomed to spend a few weeks every summer since the queen mother had bought the château built by the architect Philibert Delorme in 1541. The château of Saint-Maur had belonged to Cardinal Jean du Bellay, who had been obliged to sell it in 1563 after falling into disfavor. It was there that in 1568 Charles IX signed the edict of Saint-Maur prohibiting Protestant worship.[115]

On June 22 or 23, Catherine de Medici arrived at her château in Saint-Maur with the king.[xxii] On June 24, she wrote to Louis Chasteigner, lord of La Rochepozay and Abain, the ordinary ambassador in Rome, to inform him that Jehan de Pilles, the abbé d'Orbays and the secretary ordinary of the king's chamber, had just left for the Eternal City in order to transmit to him more ample instructions regarding financial negotiations to be carried out with the Holy See. In this same letter, Catherine asked her ambassador to intercede on her behalf with the pontiff, requesting that he confirm the abbeys of Corbie and Ourcamp, whose commendatory abbé was Charles I of Bourbon, cardinal of Vendôme and archbishop of Rouen.[116] On July 20, the king sent a missive to Pope Gregory XIII to ask him to attribute the bishopric of Saluzzo to Horatio Blanco. He strongly opposed another candidate who enjoyed the pope's favor. Relations between the Vatican and Henry III were extremely tense, and the pope openly accused the king of France of allowing himself to be manipulated by Henry of Navarre and the Huguenots. In 1580, Rome was a major concern for Catherine and the king, who were looking for a replacement for Chasteigner. After rejecting his increasingly pressing appeals, they now had to grant

---

[xxii] Since 1564, Catherine de Medici had usually spent part of the summer at the château of Saint-Maur. Thus in 1566 she resided there from May 10 to May 31, from June 18 to June 30, and from November 8 to November 27; in 1567 from May 11 to May 21; in 1568, from September 2 to September 30; in 1580, from June 19 to June 24, and then from July 1 to July 30 and from August 2 to August 29; in 1581, she resided there from June 23 to June 29, and from July 11 to July 31; in 1582, from June 12 to June 18 and from September 4 to September 30. Thus her stay at Saint-Maur in 1580 was by far the longest (more than two and a half months).

the wish of their ambassador, who for several months had been repeatedly requesting permission to return to France. The pope was not unaware that Chasteigner was expecting his recall to France any day now, and this made negotiations with the Holy See even more delicate for the king. During the month of July 1580, Montaigne presented himself at Saint-Maur to present his book to the king in person. He had left his château on June 22, perhaps in the company of his young brother Bertrand, lord of Mattecoulon, twenty-seven years his junior; and Bertrand de Cazalis, lord of Frayche, who had recently lost his wife, Montaigne's sister Marie. Although it is also quite possible the two Bertrands only joined him later, as we will see.

The gift of his book to the king had been prepared with care, and we can suppose that Montaigne expected much from this meeting. After all, it was not every day that a lord from a small house in Guyenne—even if he was a knight of the Order of Saint Michael and an ordinary gentleman of the king's chamber—could expect a private audience with the monarch. We can imagine that Montaigne rehearsed this interview in his head and gave special thought to what he was going to ask of the king. The book he had had delivered to the king a few days earlier was supposed to allow him to show himself in the best light and to produce a positive, unusual image of himself, one that might impress Henry III. His book was the best possible career résumé. Things went as planned. The only extant account of this meeting was written by La Croix du Maine, who reports it briefly in his *Bibliothèque françoise*.

According to La Croix du Maine, the king complimented Montaigne on his work. Montaigne replied: "Sire, . . . I must necessarily please your Majesty because my book pleases you, for it contains nothing but a discourse on my life and my actions."[117] Who could have been La Croix du Maine's source for this remark except Montaigne himself? Or at least one of his close relatives. We see again here the project of the *Essais* as it is presented in the *Au lecteur*, which makes the king a privileged reader, if not the first reader. The wager Montaigne made in this short introductory text would thus have been completely won. We understand better this literary strategy that consisted in establishing a consubstantiality between the book and its author. If the book pleased the king, the man would please him. And if one pleases the king, one can expect some largess. The gift of the book entailed obligations in the symbolic economy of the Renaissance. Montaigne was ready to serve his king, and his book was an extension of himself that made an exchange of services possible. It can be argued that in 1580 the book served Montaigne as an introduction into a career that was not in any way literary, but rather political. His ideal reader (the king) was less fond of literature than he was looking for a good servant capable of representing him. Montaigne's book realized an offer of service based on the fidelity and personal friendship that could develop between a king and one of his counselors.[118]

Unfortunately, apart from Montaigne's remarks to the king reported by La Croix du Maine, we know nothing about the exact nature of their conversation, which, if we take into account the protocol of such royal audiences, lasted no longer than ten or fifteen minutes. In fact, the general protocol in August 1578 forbade courtiers to approach the king directly and to speak to him. Meetings were set for precise times and the list of visitors was drawn up in advance.[119] The information La Croix du Maine provides does, however, allow us to make a few hypotheses. We have seen that the king was thinking about a possible successor to replace—even temporarily—Chasteigner in Rome. In the first chapters of his book, Montaigne had highlighted not only examples of embassies but had also shown that he could make judgments compatible with and desirable in diplomatic service. Still more important, the king was very preoccupied with the political situation in Bordeaux and the southwest. Montaigne could be useful on both these fronts even though he far preferred to pursue a career in diplomacy, which corresponded better to the models with which he had identified himself since his publication of La Boétie's works. He believed that he was completely capable of following the path laid out by the Foixs, the Lansacs, and the Mesmeses. We could imagine that the king suggested that Montaigne should go to Rome, where he could serve him as an extraordinary ambassador until a replacement for Chasteigner could be found. Henry III was also considering sending Charles d'Estissac on a mission to deliver documents in Italy, and may have proposed that d'Estissac and Montaigne travel together. However, there was no hurry, and the first priority was to deal with the military matter of the siege of La Fère, the king's other major concern during the summer of 1580. Indebted to the king and as if to prove his fidelity, Montaigne went to La Fère long enough to prepare his journey with the young d'Estissac.[120] We shall return to this scenario, which gave the trip to Italy—generally seen as a pleasure trip on the model of such tours in the eighteenth and nineteenth centuries—a quite different meaning, not touristic but political. But let us first return to the question that was most pressing, at least for the king: the siege of La Fère.

On June 15, shortly before his departure for Saint-Maur, the king had declared his intention to besiege the stronghold of La Fère in Picardy, near the cities of Saint-Quentin and Laon. He expected the Catholic nobles of his kingdom to go to La Fère to fight alongside his army. For him it was an occasion to make a show of force with the French nobility behind him. The siege was being conducted by his best marshal, Jacques II de Goyon de Matignon, a "wily and capable Norman" who was soon to be governor of Guyenne and mayor of Bordeaux. Matignon was on a roll and was considered one of the best military strategists. He had been made a marshal of France on July 14, 1579, and was received the same year into the Order of the Holy Spirit (December 31, 1579). After having pacified Normandy, he restored order in Picardy before leaving for Guyenne to replace Biron, who had become undesirable in the region. Did Montaigne know about the call to the nobility sent out by the king? If he did, we could understand the obligation he felt to attend this siege to show his allegiance to the king of France whom he had just met at Saint-Maur. After obtaining some favor—in the form of a vague promise—from his audience with the king, he felt obliged to demonstrate his fidelity and specifically to reaffirm his membership in the nobility. As a gentleman and the lord of Montaigne, he had military duties.

The king's correspondence shows that the political situation concerned him a great deal during his summer sojourn at Saint-Maur. In early July 1580, everything was going badly. Pillaging had taken place in the churches in Senlis, Compiègne, and Reims. The king wanted to regain the upper hand over the duke of Anjou and Henry of Navarre. Marshal Biron, the mayor of Bordeaux and governor of Guyenne, was ordered to begin a military campaign to dispossess Henry of Navarre of the cities he controlled in the southwest. The situation was rapidly degenerating, despite Biron's optimism and the assurances he had given the king regarding his reconciliation with Henry of Navarre. At the end of the summer 1580, La Fère was a point of tension between Catholics and Protestants, and the taking of this stronghold was supposed to demonstrate the king's military domination. The time had come for a showdown. Highly symbolic, the conquest of La Fère was supposed to send a strong message from the king to Henry of Navarre and put a stop to his military ambitions in Aquitaine.

Condé (Henry I of Bourbon-Condé, the second prince of Condé) had entrenched himself at La Fère in the spring of 1580, and despite his repeated efforts since the "Peace of Monsieur" to avoid military conflict with the Protestants, the king had no option other than to confront Condé directly. This peace had been short-lived, and the intransigent attitude adopted by Biron (who was actually faithfully following the king's orders) in Bordeaux and Guyenne had inflamed people's minds and was beginning to cause serious problems for the king. In addition, Henry III's correspondence shows that Biron still enjoyed the king's full confidence and was repeatedly praised by him. For example, on May 15, 1579, Henry III wrote to his lieutenant general: "I esteem your virtue and entrust myself to your prudence and loyalty."[121] Loyalty is one thing, and prudence another; the least one can say is that Biron was singularly deprived of the latter. It was in this voluntarist and bellicose context that he had proposed to serve the king in a "Bironian" way,[122] that is, without gloves. He had already used artillery against Margaret of Valois and had won a reputation as a warmonger. In his defense, it has to be admitted that the king secretly encouraged Biron to resume the war against the Protestants. These constant hesitations between peace and all-out war reveal the dilemma of royal policy, which ceaselessly oscillated between repression and negotiation, without a happy medium. The royal army's soldiers, paid only irregularly, deserted by the hundreds, and Biron found it harder and harder to recruit new ones. The king did not have the means to pursue his policy.

The siege of La Fère began on July 7, 1580, and lasted nine weeks, until September 12. The Catholic nobility had been convoked to help reconquer the stronghold from the Huguenots, and they responded to the call in great numbers. During the summer of 1580 it was better to be at the siege of La Fère than in Paris, where the plague epidemic had caused a large part of the population to flee. The Court was at La Fère, where festivities, merry-making, and sumptuous dinners alternated with cannon fire. The duke of Épernon, Joyeuse, and the king's minions hastened there to put in an appearance, dressed in luxurious clothing as if they were at the Court. A mocking sonnet was published on this occasion:

> These engraved corsets and celestial headdresses
> Of the heedless band, and these fanciful heads,
> Traveled the roads to lay waste to La Fère.
> What think you, Sibillot? They'll have much to do!
> These ruffled dandies, both active and passive,
> Will they join the assault? Will they do it in earnest?
> Will they take it soon? What will be the outcome?
> In the end they'll be beaten, if not worse.
>
> Then the plague, which carries off the big and small,
> Will cause the kingdom to remain quite naked,
> And a surviving third party, which had no thought of it,
> Seeing God far too offended everywhere
> By our impieties, abhorring our life,
> Will soon establish a new colony there.[123]

As a gentleman and a soldier, Montaigne was also obliged to make an appearance at La Fère. He went there after his audience with the king and it is likely that Henry III urged him to participate in the siege, where he had an opportunity to make the acquaintance of Matignon. Although this siege was nicknamed the "velvet siege," no less than four thousand men lost their lives on the side of the assailants and eight hundred on that of the besieged.[124] Even if Matignon had shown a great patience that contributed to his reputation, the royal party nonetheless suffered major losses. La Valette, a minion of the king, was wounded on July 18. On August 2, Philibert of Gramont, governor of Bayonne and seneschal of Béarn, a friend of Montaigne and the husband of Madame de Gramont to whom Montaigne had dedicated the chapter "Twenty-nine sonnets of Estienne de la Boétie" (I: 29), was mortally wounded by a cannon ball that tore off his arm. He died of his wound four days later, on August 6. Philibert had abjured his Protestant faith the day after the Saint Bartholomew's Day massacre, and like Montaigne he was an ordinary gentleman of the king's chamber, and he was the mayor and governor of Bayonne. His brother-in-law, the viscount of Duras, also followed the royal party led by Marshal Biron against Henry of Navarre, and was "a great friend"[125] of Montaigne; he had joined him in Picardy with "several other friends of his." Madame de Gramont, Henry of Navarre's future mistress, suddenly found herself a widow and soon played an important role in Montaigne's new career as a negotiator. Along with the Foix-Candales, the Foix-Gursons, and Duras, the Gramonts were one of the leading houses of Guyenne and Gascony. Montaigne had just dedicated "Of the resemblance of children to fathers" (II: 37) to Marguerite de Gramont (also known as Madame de Duras) after she had visited him in his château, along with other ladies, during the winter of 1579. Montaigne recounts the death of Philibert de Gramont in his *Essais* and in his almanac.[126]

Montaigne left La Fère to escort the body of his friend to Soissons: "I was one of several friends of Monsieur de Gramont who escorted his body from the siege of La Fère, where he was killed, to Soissons."[127] On the way, he was astonished by the tears and lamentations of the people caused by the mere sight of the funeral cortege, even though these people knew nothing about the identity of the deceased. Soissons is thirty-five kilometers from La Fère. From Soissons, Montaigne went to Beaumont-sur-Oise by way of Villers-Cotterêts, Crépy-en-Valois, Senlis, and Chantilly, traveling a total of ninety-five kilometers, probably with an overnight stop between the two cities. In Beaumont he joined Charles d'Estissac, who "had with him a gentleman, a valet-de-chambre, two lackeys, a muleteer and a mule."[128] The expenses of the trip were to be shared "by halves." On September 5, 1580, the caravan was formed and the journey to Italy could then begin. The first stage took the group from Beaumont-sur-Oise to Meaux, about sixty kilometers (twelve leagues, the secretary tells us). The travelers went around Paris without entering it and headed for eastern France. Montaigne did not return to La Fère and did not witness the end of the siege. Accompanied by the lord of Mattecoulon (his younger brother), the lord of Cazalis (his brother-in-law), Charles d'Estissac,[xxiii] and a friend of the latter, Count Du Hautoy, who seems to have joined the group later, Montaigne began his journey to Rome.

[xxiii] Charles d'Estissac died tragically in a duel in March 1586. Six young gentlemen (the eldest was only twenty-five) had met at dawn to settle "a very slight quarrel"—as Pierre de L'Étoile put it—that had occurred the preceding day. Charles de Gontaut-Biron, the marshal's son, had brought with him François de Montpezat, lord of Laugnac, and Bertrand de Pierre-Buffière, baron of Génissac, as witnesses. In the other party, Claude de Peyrusse d'Escars, prince of Carency, had d'Estissac and La Bastie as his sec-

La Fère fell ten days later, in mid-September. We do not know exactly where Montaigne was between August 10 and September 5, the date on which we find him in Beaumont-sur-Oise. Did he stop in Paris during the second half of August to visit Gilles Gourbin—the bookseller who had obtained the privilege for the printing of the 1569 edition of the *Théologie naturelle*—and who was to print the new edition of Sebond's book in 1581[xxiv]—and to take care of a few matters before traveling on to Germany and Italy? We can suppose that during a brief stay in Paris, Montaigne deposited with the Paris printer a corrected and slightly revised version of his translation of Sebond. His name appears prominently on the title page with all his titles "messire Michel, Seigneur de Montaigne, Chevalier de l'ordre du Roy, et Gentil-homme ordinaire de sa chambre." We note that the order of his titles is identical to that on the title page of the 1580 edition of the *Essais*, which allows us to infer that Gourbin copied the title from a copy of the 1580 *Essais* received from the author during the summer of the same year. Montaigne thus doubled his bet: his titles were now disseminated on two different works.

If he did stop off in Paris, Montaigne took the risk of being exposed to the epidemic that left 120,000 people dead, according to François de Syrueilh.[129] No doubt he chose another way of transmitting his books without having to stay in the capital. His travel journal tells us nothing about this, because the secretary, probably hired in Paris, wrote nothing before Beaumont-sur-Oise, to which Montaigne made a detour to visit before leaving to rejoin the party of Charles d'Estissac. Charles d'Estissac was the son of the late Louis de Madaillan d'Estissac,[130] a powerful lord in Guyenne who had been the Dauphin's *panetier* (an official responsible for distributing bread) before becoming the governor of La Rochelle and then lieutenant general in Poitou.[xxv]

---

onds. The six duelists threw themselves on each other and d'Estissac, La Bastie, and Carency ended up losing their lives. This story was widely discussed at the time and we find several accounts of this tragic day, notably in Brantôme's *Discours sur les duels*, vol. VI, 315–16. In his turn, Montaigne had to get his youngest brother out of a jam (and out of prison) during a duel in Italy that was just as absurd. In his *Essais*, he remains very critical of the way in which duels were decimating the youth in the nobility of the sword.

[xxiv] Although the 1569 edition of the translation had gone almost unnoticed, Montaigne hoped to give more visibility to this new printing in Paris. It has been suggested that he made corrections on a copy of the 1569 edition that he took with him on his journey to Italy. This hypothesis is, however, not very plausible. The printing of the 1581 *Théologie naturelle* is dated September 22. If we assume that it took at least five months to produce the book, printing could not have begun before spring 1581. It is hard to imagine Montaigne sending a corrected copy from Italy without having previously come to an agreement with the publisher regarding the details of the printing (including the new title page).

[xxv] At the assembly of the nobility of the Agen region in March 1557, the contribution to be made by the lord d'Estissac was set at seven light horse. In a notice issued by

The Madaillan d'Estissacs were among the oldest families in Guyenne. Montaigne had dedicated to Madame d'Estissac[xxvi] the chapter of his *Essais* titled "Of the affection of fathers for their children" (II: 8).[131] His family origins gave the young d'Estissac precedence over Montaigne. He carried with him letters of recommendation from Henry III and Catherine de Medici that he was to deliver to Alfonso d'Este, the second of that name, duke of Ferrara, of Modena, and of Reggio since 1558.[132] The content of these letters shows that the young d'Estissac's trip was not an ordinary one. Henry III presents him as "worthy of continuing the service" that his predecessors "have always formerly performed for this kingdom"; Catherine speaks of the reciprocity of good procedures. These two letters were written in Saint-Maur-des-Fossés on August 27 and 29. Although he was still very young, it is likely that d'Estissac had been entrusted with delivering letters of instruction. The fact that he traveled with Montaigne shows that these two men were probably on a mission.

Montaigne's secretary does not mention Cazalis at first, but he names him in his account of an excursion to Lake Garda on October 30. The husband of Montaigne's sister Marie, Bertrand de Cazalis, lord of Frayche, was a widower. There remain, however, certain doubts regarding the identity of this Cazalis who accompanied Montaigne as far as Padua, where he stayed to study at the university. Some have argued that he might be Bernard de Cazalis, the husband of Margaret Blanc de Séguin, rather than Bertrand de Cazalis.[133] However, several bits of evidence connect Bertrand de Cazalis with Montaigne's party, especially when Montaigne rented three horses for Cazalis, Mattecoulon, and himself, while d'Estissac rented two horses for himself and the lord du Hautoy. If it had been Bernard de Cazalis, Montaigne probably would not have rented a horse for him. As for Du Hautoy, he seems to have joined the travelers already en route to Italy. He will also be received by the pope during the French travelers' audience in Rome. Between Bar-le-Duc and Neufchâteau, the group passed close to Du Hautoy's lands,[134] perhaps to allow him to make a quick stop there. Montaigne was leaving France to go to Rome.

Henry of Navarre to maintain order in Paris in 1560, we find the name of d'Estissac among the signatures, along with those of the Cardinal of Bourbon, the Cardinal of Guise, Montmorency, Saint-André, and Chavigny.

[xxvi] Madame d'Estissac (Louise de La Béraudière) has often been confused with one of her cousins, also named Louise de La Béraudière, but better known as "La Belle Rouet."

PART TWO

Practices

CHAPTER 7

The Call of Rome, or How Montaigne Never Became an Ambassador (1580–1581)

The Treaty of Cateau-Cambrésis signed in 1559 had put an end to French ambitions in Italy. In fact, it led to a veritable reversal of alliances. A common enemy, Lutheranism, was about to define a common policy, and for a time bring a large number of European countries closer to the Roman church. This peace treaty opened a new era in European diplomatic relations. Consular representation and the sending of ambassadors both ordinary and extraordinary made it possible to reevaluate what was expected of these representatives of the king. Rather than membership in the high nobility, royal agents were required to have negotiating abilities, a proximity and indefectible loyalty to the king's person—and not to the state or to France—a talent for psychological analysis, and an adequate knowledge of the political culture of the country of residence. The men who made up the diplomatic corps under Charles IX and Henry III were recruited mainly from the middle-level nobility and retained, thanks to their family affiliations, important connections with the regions from which they had come.[1] Most of the ambassadors of that time were part of the king's immediate entourage and held the title of gentleman ordinary of the king's chamber or another office in the royal household. Like Montaigne, many of them were members of the Order of Saint Michael, the highest distinction conferred by the king before 1579. Since the reign of Charles IX, an increasing number of ambassadors also had experience in negotiation acquired in the judicial world. *Maîtres des requêtes*, royal counselors, or simple councillors in a regional parlement, they were prepared to go abroad to represent the king, even on a short-term assignment.

The missions entrusted to ambassadors implied a more or less lengthy residence abroad. Diplomacy was a form of provisional exile. In fact, there were different kinds of exile. Embassies and diplomatic missions took the men named to them away from the Court, and thus from royal favors. To be absent from the Court was to risk being forgotten. An appointment was an honorable reward and a pledge of fidelity, but it was also the beginning of an estrangement from national and regional political networks. Although exile is generally seen as a banishment or expulsion from one's country of origin, this absence can sometimes be voluntary and, in that case, part of a political strategy. For the ambassadors of the last Valois, exile even represented a long-term investment. Montaigne's stay in Germany, Switzerland, and Italy can be seen as a voluntary exile, an obligatory sojourn abroad that kept him in a position of waiting, away from his region, where the political climate was deteriorating from one day to the next. Taking a distance from the political chaos that then prevailed in Guyenne and Bordeaux allowed him to be in the situation of an exile to whom political or diplomatic responsibilities could be entrusted, particularly when the desired post consisted in serving the king abroad. When we discuss Montaigne's sojourn in Italy, we will have to ask whether Montaigne intended to remain longer in that country. Thus we need to reexamine the nature of this journey.

In early 1580, a storm was brewing in Guyenne. Aquitaine as a whole was on the point of sinking into terror, and the *président à mortier*,[i] Sarran de Lalanne, baron of Uzeste, wrote to the queen mother: "the storm and unrest still subsist and threaten us with a shipwreck if you, Madame, who are at the helm of this kingdom, do not pacify, by your prudence and singular dexterity, this turmoil, and especially this province and duchy of Guyenne, which has been troubled so long."[2] The Protestants had taken up arms again and violence was spreading in the neighborhood of Montaigne's château. At the end of May, Henry of Navarre and his Protestant troops took the cities of Montségur and Cahors, both of which were pillaged and sacked.[3] Montaigne's departure, first to Paris and then abroad, was logical and prepared. His voluntary exile was to distance him from a region that had become dangerous and allow him to take the initiative and observe more closely the Holy See's political practices. He intended to take up residence for a time in Rome, once the king had named him to a post as ambassador—probably interim or plenipotentiary—or diplomat, that is, for a particular mission that had been verbally proposed to him during his meeting with the king at Saint-Maur-des-Fossés. Diplomacy was not unknown territory for Montaigne. As we have seen, the first *Essais* of 1580 accord considerable importance to ambassadorial problems. If the king had read or perused, even cursorily, the first chapters of the *Essais* of 1580, he certainly must have gained the impression that Montaigne had reflected at length on the role of ambassadors.[4] Many chapters in the first two books of the *Essais* strengthen the work's political and diplomatic orientation.

To understand what led Montaigne to envision a trip abroad while his region was sinking into chaos, we have to look into his political ambitions between

---

[i] Under the Old Régime, a *président à mortier* was the principal magistrate of a parlement. [Trans.]

1575 and 1580. Let us note first that the endpoint of this voluntary exile was Rome, and not the other cities he visited, which were only stages on the way to the capital of Christianity. Montaigne's journey to Rome must not be confused with his movements through other Italian cities before arriving there or after his first stay in the Eternal City, that is, between November 30, 1580, and April 19, 1581. The author of the *Essais* knew from the outset that his travels would take him to Rome, the end of his journey. At a time when he was seeking to attract the attention of the great to the services he could render them, and when he was sufficiently well regarded at the Court to hope for a favor that would help him realize his diplomatic ambitions, Montaigne chose to go to Rome to be at Henry III's disposal. This was not a tourist trip, but a political trip on behalf of the king. Montaigne considered himself to be on a mission.

This stay abroad was governed by a career plan that he henceforth conceived as the outcome of a long political preparation. His exemplars of the early 1570s had also passed through this necessary stage of exile in the service of their king. Moreover, Montaigne had an idea of exile rather different from the usual one. He did not feel homesick. Contrary to what has been claimed, especially during the Romantic period in the nineteenth century, he never longed for his region or his home. He was a man who liked travel and was prepared to accept a post abroad. He did not see being away for more than a year as a pleasure trip, but neither did he see it as a constraint. The reader should be forewarned: the "journey to Italy" does not at all correspond to the sense that this term acquired in the eighteenth century, when the travel notes Montaigne and his secretary made were rediscovered.[5]

In the sixteenth century, representatives were exiles in the service of their king. On this point, Montaigne remarks that even the banished can live happily in a foreign land: "Those who are in pressing fear of losing their property, of being exiled, of being subjugated, live in constant anguish, losing even the capacity to drink, eat, and rest; whereas the poor, the exiles, and the slaves often live as joyfully as other men."[6] For Montaigne, exile is a kind of liberty,[7] but a liberty in the service of the prince. His sojourn in Italy also symbolizes a distancing from the clientelist choices that polarized political life in his region. It allowed Montaigne to wait for new responsibilities that he hoped to receive in Rome, far from turmoil that reigned in Bordeaux and Guyenne.

On Territory "Subject to the Emperor"

Montaigne and the group accompanying him did not take the fastest route to Rome. Instead of going through Lyon, they first went to eastern France and then crossed Germany, Austria, and Switzerland before finally reaching Italy.

Apparently they were not in a hurry. At the beginning of their journey, Montaigne and the gentlemen with him went to visit the "famous abbey of religious women";[ii] he told the nuns that their travels would take them to Rome: "Early on the morrow we set forth, and after we had mounted, the doyenne sent a gentleman to M. de Montaigne begging him to go to her. He went, and this visit cost us an hour's delay. This society of ladies gave him power of attorney to deal with their affairs at Rome."[8] Since the death of the former abbess, Renée de Dinteville, the abbey's doyenne had tried to accelerate her succession and told her guests of her intention to expedite this matter.[9] Montaigne already knew the goal and the reasons for his journey to Rome and shared them—at least their main terms—with his hosts. The canonesses entrusted Montaigne with documents for the Holy See.[iii] Montaigne gives no commentary on the outcome of this mission, but while he was still in France, his eyes and thoughts were already turned toward Rome.

Montaigne and his group entered Germany at Thann, "the first [city] over the German border, subject to the Emperor,"[10] as his secretary wrote. Contrary to what one might think, Montaigne was as much interested in the cities of the Catholic Church on Protestant territory (controlled by Philip II) as he was in commenting on the rites and practices of the sects of Luther, Zwingli, and Calvin. Germany seemed the perfect example of a country in which two religions had learned to coexist without engaging in constant fighting.

The route had at first led the travelers to Mulhouse, an imperial city allied with the Swiss cantons. Montaigne took the trouble to go to see the Protestant church and found it "in good condition," that is, not very different from Catholic churches, "except with regard to the altars and images,"[11] of course. The tone is set and the remarks that abound in the *Journal* often result from a comparative reading of Catholic and Protestant rituals. This work is primarily descriptive, because the secretary—who wrote the journal at the beginning of the trip—almost never indulges in judgments that would openly reflect his own beliefs. Anthropological in genre, these descriptions highlight the differences between the religions. Not everything can be reduced to faith. For example, we learn that the Swiss mercenaries sell their services to both the king of France and the Huguenots, regardless of their own religious convictions. This observation leads Montaigne to show that the religious conflicts also depend on economic and political concerns and are not solely the result of denominational choices.

[ii] The ancient Abbey of Saint-Mont at Remiremont, in the Vosges, founded circa 620. [Trans.]

[iii] Jean Balsamo has establishesd a link between a certain Georges du Hautoy and his aunt, Philippe, the future grand almoner of the chapter. This family tie could explain the detour the group of travelers made to visit the abbey of Remiremont.

In Basel, Montaigne and d'Estissac were received in accord with their ranks and went to see the rather unusual house—which "was painted and decorated in delicate French fashion"[12]—of the famous physician Félix Platter.[13] At dinner, they joined the Platters, Johan Grynaeus, a professor at the university and a follower of the Zwinglians, and François Hotman, who had taken refuge in Basel, where he taught law. After his conversation with Hotman—with whom he later corresponded—Montaigne judged the diversity of religions problematic insofar as it did not favor a strong conception of the city or the citizen, and was too dependent on local beliefs. According to Montaigne, Calvinists, Lutherans, and Zwinglians were quarreling about points of detail whereas he realized that many of them still "had in their hearts a liking for the Roman religion."[14]

This was certainly more a desire than a reality, but the meeting nonetheless allowed Montaigne to formulate a judgment that only experience could validate. That was the goal of this detour through the territories controlled by the Protestant churches. Montaigne considered these encounters instructive; they prepared him for his stay in Rome, because they authorized him to speak his mind with a full knowledge of the facts. His experience of the Reformation in Bordeaux had not permitted him to take enough distance on it to discuss questions of theology. His journey to Germany, Austria, and Switzerland gave him a greater political legitimacy thanks to the distance taken from his own culture. Obviously, we do not know what directives he gave his secretary. Perhaps to please him, the secretary engaged in a genuinely anthropological description of the Protestant rites. As if to assure himself that he understood well the political government of the cities through which he passed, Montaigne regularly visited the burgomasters of the ones where he stopped. Each time, he received, along with d'Estissac, the honors of the city and talked with the political authorities. We sometimes have the feeling that we are accompanying Montaigne and his group on a study trip. He may also have been following the recommendations made by Pierre Danès, who in his *Conseils à un ambassadeur* (1561) suggests to ambassadors that they should "learn the nature of the country, its fertility, its sterility, the people's industry, their commerce, their inclination to arms or to letters."[15]

But Germany was also a Catholic country. Thus Constance was controlled by the archduke of Austria after the Lutherans were driven out of it by Charles V in 1548. Montaigne's secretary adds that "many Lutherans" nonetheless still lived in the city, without there being any conflict between the religions. Similarly, the small Catholic cities of Markdorf, Friedrichshafen, Wangen, Isny, Pfronten, and Füssen gave Montaigne the impression of a country where the Catholic and Protestant religions coexisted. Could this model of peaceful harmony be applied to France? The secretary tells us that on this point "there was mixed up with his judgments a certain asperity and want of regard for his own country, against which for other reasons he harboured dislike and discontent."[16] But we should not draw hasty conclusions from this, because these explorers on Protestant terrain observed that too much freedom of religion can lead to cultural and economic isolation insofar as cities live in a religious and cultural autarky and keep their distance from one another according to their beliefs and the rites that are associated with them.

Montaigne's secretary notes that, "All the imperial towns have liberty in the matter of the two religions, Catholic and Lutheran, according to the leanings of the people, and they devote themselves more or less to that form which they prefer."[17] Some towns that had opted for the Reformation occasionally had a handful of Catholics who lived on good terms and peacefully with the rest of the community. In Landsberg, Montaigne visited the college of the Jesuits, who "were finely housed in quite a new building,"[18] and discovered islands of Catholic dogma in a Protestant sea that was roiled by numerous sectarian divisions. In Schongau, Montaigne was almost astonished to find believers who were "exactly Catholic[s]" and saw that there reigned in Germany a religious diversity that had established rather strong boundaries between cities. This land of religious experimentation was not exempt from bitter quarrels. Thus in Lindau, when he talked with a Protestant minister, Montaigne discovered the deep hatreds that divided the different Lutheran churches. His secretary reported his master's conclusion: "almost every separate place holds for its belief some particular view."[19]

Diversity has its limits, and it weakens states politically. Whereas freedom of religion might at first have seemed ideal in a divided country, it was soon realized that the divisions led to interminable disputes regarding the interpretation of Luther's texts. In Basel, Baden, Isny, Lindau, Kempten, and Augsburg, Montaigne always visited the Protestant churches and engaged in numerous exchanges regarding points of theology with the Protestants he encountered. He rapidly developed a comparative view of the numerous Protestant religious services and was surprised by the many conflicts among the different sects. Montaigne's experience of religions in Germany inevitably led him to think that a single religion had to be preserved. In his *Essais*, he confirms having "observed in Germany that Luther has left as many divisions and altercations over the uncertainty of his opinions, and more, as he raised regarding the Holy Scriptures."[20] Starting from a simple religious observation, Montaigne ends up drawing sociological conclusions. No, this model of the diversity of dogmas would definitely not benefit his own country in any way, because civil concord would be still more disturbed by it.

In Augsburg, Montaigne drew up an inventory of the city's very numerous churches. His secretary reports that there were six Lutheran churches and no less than sixteen ministers in this city. Two of these churches had been "usurped"

from the Catholics and were now sites of Protestant worship. Despite these social changes, Montaigne found the Catholic service very well done and noted
that marriages between Catholics and Lutherans were "common, and the one
most keenly set on marriage commonly conforms to the faith of the other."[21]
More concretely, Montaigne talked with the Protestant ministers and questioned them regarding their incomes. One thing also caught his attention: "in
the case of the men it is a hard matter to say who is noble and who is not, foras-
much as all sorts of men wear bonnets of velvet and carry swords by the side."[22]
In the Lutheran religion the external signs of nobility appear to be erased, and
Montaigne could only regret this lack of social distinction among men. The
author of the *Essais*—like his secretary, moreover—rarely takes up questions of
theology; he discusses only practices. For example, he offers the beginning of a
theological analysis only regarding the Eucharist, but soon abandons a discussion he deems risky. Montaigne seems more interested in the details of the ceremonies and in their visible, external aspects, which allow him to broaden his
knowledge of behaviors. Religious diversity, often from one city to the next, as-
tonishes him, but he never suggests that this model might be applied to his own
country. On the contrary, the farther the travelers penetrated into Protestant
territory, the more they detached themselves from the rites they reported. Montaigne's role in his crossing of Germany and Switzerland was not to linger over
theological debates, but rather to observe, in order to have the best possible
information that would later authorize him to judge on the basis of real
knowledge.

After leaving Augsburg, the group went to Bruck and Munich, noting that
the latter was "strongly Catholic, and it is populous, finely built, and busy,"[23]
but unfortunately Montaigne could not enter Zurich, where the plague was raging. These stops were not without a few disappointments. For instance, while he
was in Innsbruck, Montaigne was not able to meet with Archduke Ferdinand.
The Archduke refused to see him on the pretext that the French were enemies
to the House of Austria. On the whole, it can be said that his German experience was rapid but sufficient. It gave Montaigne the authority of a human geog-
rapher, of someone who sees places, meets with people, experiences cultures,
and describes them.

This journey was profitable because Montaigne used this experience to keep
himself informed of the latest political and religious developments in the cities
he passed through.[24] The first part of his travel journal highlights this political
preoccupation. For example, his encounter with Maldonat in Épernay,[25] his
dinner with Hotman in Basel, and his conversation with Zwinger in the same
city[26] are situated in this logic of collating information concerning religion that
would allow him to gain a certain credibility in any theological-political conversations he might have in the course of a future diplomatic career, in which reli-

gious questions would necessarily be of considerable importance. Montaigne's detour via Switzerland and Germany before his sojourn in Rome reinforced the same image of himself that he was forging, that of a man who listened to the Reformers' theses, but who nonetheless reaffirmed his solid anchorage in the bosom of the Roman church.[27] The road taken to Rome was not the shortest, but the experience with Protestants gained on the way was worth the trouble. Germany and Switzerland were unavoidable political stops for someone who was envisaging a career as an extraordinary ambassador in Rome or in another Italian city that supported the Roman Apostolic Church. Venice, one of the last stops on the journey to Rome, offered Montaigne a different view of the city and its political possibilities.[28] Once again, it was the diversity of political systems—within a single religious denomination and a single culture—that drew his attention.

It has been rightly emphasized that the first part of Montaigne's travel journal, the one that deals with Alsace, southern Germany, Alemanic Switzerland, and Austria, is presented as a series of "impressions of a journey in the land of the Eucharist,"[29] that is to say, a laboratory to confront the different theses that were tearing apart Protestants and Catholics in France. Without going so far as to compare this journey with an excursion in Cannibal territory or in the New World, it remains true that Montaigne discovered political models fundamentally different from those that the Reformation had caused him to experience in France. His visits with the members of the various sects allowed him to discover a diversity of beliefs unknown in France. The great contribution made by this trip through Germany, Austria, and Switzerland was surely a perception of religion that was more anthropological and more political than it was theological;[30] it promoted the development of experience in the field before he reached Rome.

The Ambassador's Trade

In Montaigne's time, ambassadors were not part of any established body and were completely dependent on personal appointment by the king. The designation of an ordinary or extraordinary ambassador required no presentation before the Council or any political or juridical authority. After being proposed by the king, the new ambassador simply went to the appointed place and presented his credentials to the local prince. His predecessor and the princes or kings were informed by letters. These direct nominations allowed the king to keep control over his foreign policy and above all assured him of the fidelity of his diplomats in a system in which rewards given for services rendered allowed servants of the king to hope for some favor when they returned to France. Specialists in diplomatic history insist that the crucial criterion in choosing an ambassador was his fidelity.[31] The dedicated execution of the instructions received was an absolute necessity for ambassadors at that time. Diplomats were also expected to have a good general knowledge of the political and religious situation in Europe.[32] Jacques-Auguste de Thou confirms that the first concern of an ambassador passing through a city in a foreign country was to visit the scholars and men of letters who lived there.[33] Montaigne had just shown that he had the kind of political curiosity that makes a good ambassador.

French diplomacy was subjected to a major reorganization at the beginning of Charles IX's reign. The king replaced a large proportion of his ambassadors, whose chief mission was henceforth to seek peace through negotiation;[34] Henry III continued this policy of pacification during his reign. The agents Catherine de Medici recruited to defend her interests during the third period of the Council of Trent were often presented as men receptive to new ideas. Henry III tried to avoid offending the gentlemen who had opted for the Reformation. The Roman Curia and the Spanish envoys opposed these new-style ambassadors, going so far as to accuse the head of the French delegation, Louis de Saint-Gelais, lord of Lansac, of being in the pay of the Huguenots. The two other members of this delegation, Arnaud du Ferrier and Guy du Faur de Pibrac, both friends of Montaigne, were also subjected to the pope's criticism. However, this model of diplomatic representation was rather well suited to the extremely explosive situation in France, because the king wanted to give the impression of treating the Huguenots with consideration, in contrast to Rome's intransigent position. Here we must note that despite the pope's allegations of heresy, for the author of the *Essais*, Lansac, Pibrac, Henri de Mesmes, and Paul de Foix remained the best models of the ambassador. These men had not come from the high clergy and belonged to the rising "class" of nobles who had also served as members of the parlements.

Under the last Valois, French diplomacy was weakly institutionalized and the diplomatic network was a kind of extension of the Court.[35] An embassy was neither a commission nor an office, it was an honor. Its duration was almost never defined, although in theory it was limited to three years. However, this ideal duration was not often respected because of the difficulty of finding a replacement. Even though the designation of an ordinary ambassador required a letter of credentials (a memorandum countersigned and registered by a state secretary, then signed by the king), the nomination might in practice be formulated during a royal audience. The extraordinary or interim ambassador then received oral instructions, which he was to transmit in person by going as quickly as possible to the site of his mission or residence.[36] This was probably the case for Montaigne, whom the king presumably asked to go to Rome and await his instructions: an ambassador could be nominated in writing at the site of his embassy. All that was required was a letter from the king or from Catherine de

Medici to confirm his service. Several ambassadors were already on site when they received their credentials. That was the case for Pierre de Séguson, lord of Longlée, who was residing in Spain when he replaced Jean de Vivonne in 1582. Neither was any practical or legal distinction made between an ordinary and an extraordinary ambassador, both of them receiving essentially identical credentials, which often led to difficulties in differentiating temporary missions from permanent missions.

The recruitment of ambassadors under Charles IX and Henry III was carried out according not only to the competence but also to the fidelity of the men selected. For example, the king chose Lansac as ambassador to the Council of Trent because he was a "knight of his order, his councillor and chamberlain, being one of those closest to his person."[37] Similarly, when it was a question of sending a French envoy to Poland in July 1572, there was a long negotiation between the king and the queen mother. The king preferred to send "a notable person who has both the intelligence and the experience to conduct such a great enterprise in accordance with his wishes."[38] He considered closeness and personal friendship more important than competence. Four gentlemen were in competition for this post. The king and the queen mother agreed that this ambassador must be "a man of the long robe who knew, as people say, how to go and speak," that is, a man that could be trusted, affable, capable of negotiation, not dogmatic—in short, a *politique*. The envoys were expected to present the royal position "by public orations and other discourses . . . and in a known language," because the king gave transparency priority over intrigue. Pibrac and Jean Truchon, first president of the parlement of Grenoble, were mentioned. But the king had Pibrac in mind for other missions and Truchon was in poor health. Catherine de Medici decided on Lansac, who accepted the post after having chosen as his trusted collaborator Pierre-Gilbert Malloc, a councillor at the parlement of Grenoble and a "man of letters." A good education and judicial and oratorical competence were considered an advantage. The ideal training was that of the parlementary councillor. If one was in addition a gentleman of the king's chamber, or even a knight of the Order of Saint Michael, then one had the supreme qualifications to be named an ordinary or extraordinary ambassador. In addition to these qualifications, closeness and "friendship" with the king remained by far the most important criteria for being appointed to an ambassadorial post. Finally, the term "ambassador" designated both permanent residents and temporary envoys.

Ambassadors were frequently royal counselors, but exceptions to this rule were possible. Sometimes men were chosen on the basis of their place of residence. Certain technical abilities might also be taken into account depending on the country where the ambassadors were to be posted. For instance, Claude Blatier—who presented himself as the lord of Belloy but in fact belonged to the

Paris commercial bourgeoisie—was named ambassador to the Low Countries from 1580 to 1585 on the ground of his competence in economics. Let us also mention Raymond of Pavia, baron of Fourquevaux, who was ambassador to Spain from 1565 to 1572. Born in Toulouse in 1508, Fourquevaux studied law there. In 1548 he wrote his *Instructions sur le faict de la guerre*, became an ordinary gentleman of the king's chamber in 1551, and then knight of the Order of Saint Michael in 1563, shortly before being named ambassador. It is true that he had already carried out a few missions in Scotland and Ireland, and then in Bohemia, Parma, and Ferrara, but this was a classic itinerary before becoming an ordinary ambassador. Extraordinary missions often served as preparations for a nomination as ordinary ambassador. Upon his return from Spain, Fourquevaux was named superintendent of Henry of Navarre's household, but he never performed this office.[39]

We note the resemblance to Montaigne's career: these two men had received the same education, moved in the judicial milieu, were named gentlemen of the king's chamber and knights of the Order of Saint Michael, and carried out special missions before being offered more important diplomatic responsibilities. Fourquevaux's book on the *Instructions sur le faict de la guerre*, translated into Italian in 1550 and into English in 1589, gave him a reputation as a military theorist. Thus he used a book to compensate for what was lacking in his pedigree. Montaigne's political trajectory is quite similar to Fourquevaux's, and the *Essais* have certain points in common with the *Instructions*.

Fourquevaux exemplified the new kind of ambassador, whose career was a model for many aspiring diplomats. The years between 1560 and 1570 were marked by the establishment of what has been called a "ministerial class" based on diplomats' negotiating ability—on this point their parlementary experience was a non-negligible advantage—and their membership in the king's household.[40] At the beginning of the 1560s, twenty-two families related to one another, often in a local and regional network, shared the high offices of the state. This state bureaucracy produced a large number of delegates, emissaries, negotiators, and other diplomatic officers. Similarly, forty-seven ambassadors appointed under the last Valois were also domestic officers of the king's household—most of them gentlemen of his chamber. Thus we understand better the importance attached to the distinction Montaigne received in 1573. This honorific title, even though it was not accompanied by any remuneration, increased his chances of being named to a diplomatic post. Of course, one had to belong to the nobility, but an increasing number of royal agents did not come from the high nobility. This policy of recruiting ambassadors was followed by Henry III, who retained the diplomats appointed by Charles IX. When the time came, he replaced them with gentleman who were more used to parlementary work and, moreover, were among his close advisors.[41]

Under Henry III, extraordinary ambassadors came mainly from the nobility. Thus we find 44 percent of the missions carried out by nobles as compared to 18 percent by *robins* and 16 percent by ecclesiastics. Seventy-eight percent of the nobles who had held the post of ordinary or extraordinary ambassador were also members of the king's household or held the office of gentleman of his chamber; 85 percent of these were also knights of the Order of Saint Michael.[42] Montaigne could offer both of these guarantees.

Nor was it unusual for a serving ambassador to propose a close relative as his successor: a brother, child, nephew, or cousin. For example, in 1586 André Hurault, lord of Maisse, was seeking a position for his nephew, and wrote to Villeroy to recommend him. Of course, before a replacement could be proposed he had to be known to the king; a meeting was essential if one hoped to be named to an extraordinary or temporary post. Making a good impression during a private audience was part of the process of nomination. On July 31, 1572, François de Noailles, the bishop of Dax, suggested as a replacement Légier de Montaignac, one of Noailles's relatives and collaborators, in the event that his brother decided not to make the journey to the Levant: "I have here a relative who is a gentleman from a good family, a fine man, with knowledge and intelligence, a councillor in your parlement of Bordeaux, named s^r de Montaignac, to whom I have always talked freely about my office, and it would be take a newcomer a long time to learn as much about your affairs and the humor of the people here, as he knows about them, and in addition your finances would be spared by at least half."[43] Légier de Montaignac had joined the parlement of Bordeaux on June 21, 1553, as a clerk, shortly before Montaigne. He gave up his career in late 1569. He continued to draw his councillor's salary until the beginning of November, but his name no longer appeared in the formation of the new chambers on November 14, 1569.[44] He seems to have abruptly withdrawn from the parlement at almost the same time as Montaigne.

Two years later we find Montaignac in another career: in September 1572 he was sent to the Court to deliver a treaty with the sultan that the ambassador had just signed in the king's name. On February 7, 1573, Catherine de Medici replied favorably to the bishop of Dax and thanked him: "the Sr de Montaignac has informed us of the great affection and sense of duty with which you have conducted yourself in the negotiations over there."[45] On March 13, 1573, François de Noailles announced in a letter to the bishop of Valence that he had just sent Montaignac, "whom you know well," to report on the negotiations begun for the election of the king of Poland. This letter was sent from Constantinople. Montaignac had apparently returned to Paris in early summer 1573. On July 24, he was sent on another mission to Noailles, the king "having informed him in detail of his [the king's] intention, which I am sure he will faithfully report to you, with the instruction that has been given him for you."[46] He left for Constantinople with new instructions and arrived in the Levant on October 12.[47]

Montaignac was then on a special mission to Constantinople, where the current ambassador tried to get have designated as his successor. As we shall see, everything suggests that Montaigne found himself in a similar situation. Moreover, Montaigne knew Montaignac personally because he had practiced the same trade at the parlement of Bordeaux. In the 1560s, Montaignac had held the office of councillor in the second Chambre des Enquêtes,[iv] while Montaigne was serving in the first chamber, but the two men had also worked together on several cases. For example, the parlement's archives reveal that Jehan d'Alesme—who worked on a large number of appeals with Montaigne—and Montaignac examined together a sale of goods authorized by signature in the case of a disputed succession that was before the parlement's court.[48] The suit opposed Gelaine de Fayolles and Jean del Peyron. The court refused to hear the appeal and ruled that there was no new relevant evidence. Montaigne himself had voted on this affair and thus knew Montaignac well. A ruling of the parlement dated May 17, 1566, mentions their names in the same document: a suit between Estienne Soulard and Jane Rigauld, in which the issues are not clear. The appeal had been made possible by the introduction of new evidence, but the court ended up deciding that it was not relevant (figure 10).[49] Between April and August 1566, Montaignac dealt with nine appeals in collaboration with d'Alesme, mainly involving inheritances. The passage from the parlement of Bordeaux to a post as extraordinary ambassador was not rare. However, despite the recommendation of the serving ambassador in Constantinople, Montaignac in turn failed to become an ordinary ambassador. The king preferred to entrust him with a mission to Poland and he died not long afterward, in 1574, while he was crossing Transylvania. It seems that at this time Montaigne himself showed a certain interest in Poland and the election of Henry of Anjou to the throne of that country.[50] Montaignac's career path, which was completely contemporary with Montaigne's, shows how a member of the parlement belonging to the middle-level nobility could hope for a post as extraordinary ambassador if he had the recommendation of a high-ranking figure or of a currently serving ambassador who was looking for a successor.

From 1559 to 1589, of 251 diplomats inventoried about 40 percent obtained their posts thanks to family connections or to a connection with an extraordinary or resident ambassador.[51] Clientelism was the determining factor and nominations were almost always made on the basis of personal considerations. The king sometimes granted favors to other gentlemen in his service while mak-

---

[iv] He was received as a councillor clerk at the court in March 1564 after an inquiry to verify that he had reached the age of twenty-five years.

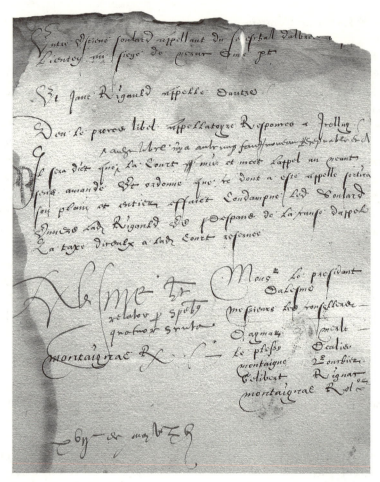

FIGURE 10. Ruling of May 17, 1566. Image courtesy of Archives départementales de la Gironde.

ing sure that his ambassadors had the titles and qualifications required to represent him faithfully and honorably. This form of patronage was particularly common when it was a matter of covering periods of transition between two ordinary ambassadors or of finding replacements who were to occupy temporary posts. Ordinary lords—as opposed to princes of the blood—were broadly represented in these interim appointments, and 17 percent of them are unfamiliar to historians, for we know nothing about them other than their names or the names of their lands. The numbers of these minor lords named to extraordinary or interim posts grew significantly in the ranks of ambassadors under Henry III and finally reached almost 30 percent of the appointments. The king made use of minor lords to represent him abroad—gentlemen who were often members of his chamber, but without great family lineages—as well as members of the mid-level nobility with deep provincial roots.[52] He preferred to choose gentlemen of the mid-level nobility who would remain loyal to him rather than princes or barons on whom it was not always easy to rely. Members of the high nobility moved in a milieu more permeable to conspiracies, treacheries, and schemes. The clientelism involved in winning an ambassadorship worked better thanks to these minor lords recently raised in the aristocratic hierarchy through nominations to the king's chamber and by the awarding of the honorific distinction represented by the necklace of the Order of Saint Michael. These honorific rewards created obligations and ensured attachment to the king and allegiance to his person.

Petitions for appointments as interim or extraordinary ambassadors were frequent at the Court, and Henry III started handing out such posts without consulting his advisors. Thus in 1579–80 the king began to choose his diplomats and negotiators by himself. He developed a network of faithful representatives and gradually emancipated himself from the decisions that, in the past, had generally been made by his mother. In matters of diplomacy, Catherine de Medici was now "only a counselor, not always listened to."[53] Toadying and intriguing were part of the game, and reminders of the commitments made with regard to them were common on the part of gentlemen waiting for a nomination. It was in this climate of promises not kept that André Hurault wrote to Villequier in February 1585: "It is enough for me that you do me the honor of loving me and keeping me in your protection while I am in this place [on assignment abroad], as it has pleased you to promise me."[54] Ambassadors saw being far away from the Court, the site of power par excellence, as a kind of exile, and one of their objectives was to keep the king from forgetting them while they were in residence abroad. No longer having access to the Court was a considerable risk if an ambassador hoped for some advancement in his career.

In his *Mémoires*, Philippe Hurault, lord of Cheverny and cousin of the current ambassador to Venice, Jean Hurault, lord of Boistaillé, explains in detail how he almost obtained a post as ambassador. In 1565, after winning the esteem of princes, and even though he was still only a simple *maître des requêtes*, he offered himself as a candidate for two embassies: Venice and London. But the queen mother had other plans for him and promoted him to chancellor of her household.[55] In Montaigne's time, the criteria for selection had changed, and the king was looking for younger men, all of them members of his chamber and knights of the Order of Saint Michael. Generally speaking, at least in the domain of ambassadorial nominations, Catherine de Medici's political ascendancy over Henry III weakened after 1580. The king imposed his preferences in the choice of the members of his Council, and also of an increasing number of the members of diplomatic delegations. These missions were of two types: negotiation and representation. The task of ambassadors on extraordinary missions was to transmit instructions orally abroad and to report orally the responses during secret negotiations, or simply to represent the king in important events or ceremonies. At a time when dispatches could easily be intercepted by spies, these secret missions were increasingly frequent.

Ambassadorial appointments were not all governed by the same system of recruitment. Representations in the countries of the north required economic knowledge and a religious sensitivity that favored men more receptive to Protestant ideas. Rome and Spain were, of course, special cases, particularly Rome. For example, in Rome it was very difficult for the king of France and the queen mother to impose their first choice, who the pope often rejected. Thus the replacement of Louis Chasteigner, who wanted to return to France as soon as possible, proved to be extremely delicate for the sovereign; it explains Montaigne's first stay in Rome, waiting for the nomination of a new ordinary ambassador. Like his colleague Montaignac, Montaigne might have made himself available there, hoping not only for a royal confirmation but also the pope's approval. That would have been his first entrance into the diplomatic profession, and the Foix family had shown him the path. However, Montaigne found himself in a particularly difficult position; Paul de Foix, one of the dedicatees of Montaigne's edition of La Boétie's works, was also a candidate for a nomination as ordinary ambassador in Rome to replace Chasteigner. But this nomination had almost no chance of succeeding, because the pope was strongly opposed to it. Montaigne was well aware that Paul de Foix was expecting to be named, but the latter was likely to wait a long time, because his appointment had already been repeatedly rejected by Pope Gregory XIII. Weary of a service made difficult by the political and religious situation in France and by the expenses involved in maintaining his rank, Chasteigner had informed the queen mother that he would not wait much longer for a replacement.

The financial difficulties of resident ambassadors were frequent and gave rise to interminable complaints. Being a diplomat for too long led to ruin. The best example is probably Charles de Danzay, ambassador to Denmark. Born in 1515, the son of notables, he pursued a career in the magistracy and arrived in Copenhagen in 1547 at the age of thirty-three. Initially a representative, he was kept there as an ordinary ambassador. Alternating stays in France with stays in Denmark, he nonetheless was proud of representing the interests of his country as best he could.[56] In 1575, he wrote to the king of France to tell him that he was living in a state of absolute indigence, and begged him to see to it that the payment he was justly due was made. He sent a letter to the queen mother to inform her of his desperate financial situation: "When I arrived in Denmark I had no debts. At present, Madame, I swear to you that I am in such need and so pressed to pay those to whom I owe money [that] it is not possible for me to leave here without perpetual ignominy."[57] In fact, his situation only got worse, and his creditors soon put Danzay under house arrest. The king and the queen mother repeatedly reassured him, but the money never came. Desperate, Danzay had to resign himself to selling all his furniture and domains to pay part of his debts.

On August 19, 1579, the king wrote to him to assure him that he had asked "the people who handled [his] finances" to remedy the situation. Then followed excuses based on the extraordinary expenses caused by the wars. The king dangled before him the prospect of employing him in the royal household with the same wages as received by other members of his household, that is to say "in the state of [his] domestic affairs and at the same wages that they have."[58] Habitual but empty promises. In the course of 1581, Danzay was once again incarcerated in Copenhagen because he could not pay his creditors. He begged the king to send him only half the amount he was due, but the king's financial officials never loosened their purse strings. Riddled with debts, all of which were connected with his service as ambassador, Danzay was held prisoner by his creditors and plunged into personal bankruptcy. His embassy had been transformed into a nightmare. Still imprisoned in late 1583, he never received from the king's majordomo the salary for his office, which had gone unpaid for twenty-two years. Moreover, in April 1586 he lost his office after the queen mother informed him that the king had been obliged to dismiss several officers of his household. In 1588, Danzay was informed that he would finally receive what he was owed. It was a little late in his long career as an ambassador, and Danzay died insolvent on October 12, 1589. The royal treasury owed him 20,000 crowns.

Jean de Vivonne, lord of Saint-Gouard, had the same experience when he arrived in Madrid in 1572. From the beginning of his embassy, he was bitterly short of money. After only six months in Spain, he was already begging the king to recall him to France, because, he said, he missed life in the camps; the real reason was the extravagant expenses connected with his residency. He complained to the duke of Anjou that "leaving here, I shall have nothing in the world that I can live on."[59] On the brink of ruin, he constantly lamented his fate and regretted every day having accepted this embassy. He was sent no money. Faced with his repeated complaints, the king replied that his office was one of the most useful and pleasant, one way of telling him that he should draw on his own fortune. We almost always find the same petitions in connection with the condition of ambassadors at this time: the threat of resignation and despair, with the permanent hope of a future reward in the form of a nomination to a title of counselor of the king or inclusion in the Order of the Holy Spirit created by Henry III on December 31, 1578. Catherine de Medici even suggested to Vivonne the possibility of replacing the Cardinal d'Este when the prelate died. Bitter in what he now considered an "exile," the word chosen by Vivonne to describe his situation in 1581,[60] he wrote to Villeroy that he hoped God would preserve him from being "so vile in my avarice that I desire the death of such a person." Villeroy hinted at long-term gains, for example, the abbey of Sablonceaux, which he had also been promised, but which was finally given to Biron. Vivonne could groan and beg the king all he wanted, going as far as to invoke his war wounds, reminding him that he was "crippled in the arm and in the leg"; nothing worked. At that time, an embassy sometimes turned into a genuine banishment, far from the favors of the Court.

In Venice, the situation was no more enviable. Arnaud du Ferrier also complains on several occasions that his salary has not been paid.[61] Scévole de Sainte-Marthe explains how Du Ferrier was long frustrated not to receive fair compensation for his services. He nonetheless maintained his rank "with as much dignity as largess."[62] When the king passed through Venice in July 1574, Du Ferrier spent 43,804 crowns on presents. This was a considerable sum. He was obliged to borrow 35,714 "écus pistolets" from the bankers Strozzi, Guadagni, and Carnesecchi, and then again 12,000 crowns from Strozzi and Balbiani, a sum that the king had commanded him to borrow against a bill of exchange. With this loan, Du Ferrier covered the various expenses, including a note for 1,125 crowns paid to the perfumer du Lys in Venice; he spent 1,400 crowns on presents for ambassadors: a diamond of a value of 1,050 crowns for the prince of Venice; the rental of seventeen gondolas for 228 crowns; 2,400 crowns for those who had accompanied the king during his stay "from the time that he entered the lands of these Lords to the time that he left them,"[63] along with a gold chain that cost 500 crowns. Such expenses were frequent.

The thirty-nine Venetian gentlemen who accompanied the king received the total sum of 3,900 crowns, accompanied by a chain worth 100 crowns for each of them. Twenty-five crowns were paid to the six wine stewards, thirteen cooks, and Pietro Vinantino "who presented the thirty-nine miniature and gilded sugar figures." Two men assigned to handle the sails on the boats and thirty-eight musicians (drummers and trumpeters) were paid 190 crowns. The servants employed to prepare the royal lodgings, Marthe Thudesque "and her husband, who have been brought in twice to sing and play the lute and viol," received 40 crowns; the chaplain who performed the mass was given 100 crowns. A large number of gold chains—recurring gifts at the time—were also distributed to the various lords who had participated in the royal festivities.

This detailed list of the expenses made on credit tells us much about the work of an ambassador, who was also a manager and spent a good part of his time borrowing money. The expenses incurred by Du Ferrier for this royal visit were considerable when we consider that in Venice, in 1586, André Hurault, lord of Maisse, was supposed to receive 5,000 crowns a year to maintain a garrison at La Mirandola. In 1579, Du Ferrier demanded 40,000 livres from the royal treasury for salary unpaid over the preceding five years.[64] Deprived of the honoraria for his office, like many other ambassadors, and riddled with debts, Du Ferrier had to use his own funds before asking that he be recalled to France. Once he had returned, the king promised to pay the debts he had accumulated in Venice.

In this kind of situation, the king often promised posts and the payment of debts that had been contracted: "When you have returned from over there, I will have your debts paid and will recognize, on all occasions, toward you and your family, your former and continued services."[65] Under the last Valois, ordinary ambassadors were commonly in debt. They had to have a personal fortune if they wanted to maintain their rank over several years. Their salaries were seldom paid, and they often had to borrow from local bankers or from friends. In 1560, Jean Nicot, the French ambassador in Portugal, complained that he had been "forced to take money at interest, which causes me great extraordinary expenses." His pension was no longer paid to him and the *maître des requêtes* had not paid his salary—400 *livres* per annum—for almost four years. He even proposed that he be paid in kind, asking that "a load of a thousand barrels of wheat" be sent to him, "because in that way I could make an agreement with the aforesaid merchant and pay my debts while waiting until it pleases you to intervene with the king."[66]

In 1574, Bertrand de Salignac, a gentleman from Périgord who was posted in England, wrote to Catherine de Medici to complain about his meager income: "It pleases him [the king] to remember that no gentleman of all those who are in my service, has been asked to work as long as I have, and that at this time many needs press on me that can no longer wait. Among other things, I can assure you, Madame, that prices are extremely high here, that over the last year the cost of all provisions has risen by half, and a few have more than doubled, so that the ordinary salary of an ambassador can hardly suffice to pay for them."[67] Ambassadors' salaries were rarely adjusted to cover the rampant inflation in certain countries. After a few years of service—often less than three—their financial situation worsened and most of them asked to be brought home. In Rome, salaries were paid more regularly, but expenses there were far greater than those in other European cities.

Keeping up a way of life worthy of a royal officer was an obligation for an ambassador. But one had to have the means to do so. Lords of the mid-level nobility regarded ambassadorships as a short-term investment and hoped that they would rapidly be recalled—after a service of eighteen to twenty-four months, on average—to avoid bankruptcy. Nonetheless, requests for ambassadorships remained constant, because diplomacy was often considered a necessary stage on the way to other offices in the higher administration of the state. Did Montaigne have the means to occupy such an office without counting on regular honoraria? Probably. In 1570, he had received 8,400 *livres* from the sale of his office in the *parlement* of Bordeaux, and his lands had yielded substantial profits during the 1570s. A stay in Rome for eighteen to twenty-four months, even at his own expense, was certainly possible and reasonable for him in view of his assets. Of course, he could not count on revenues from his status as a gentleman of the king's chamber, because this distinction was no longer remunerated—earlier, it had been remunerated at the rate of 1,200 *livres* per annum, but most gentlemen never received any payment for their offices. In 1568 Fourquevaux wrote to Catherine de Medici that the salary associated with his title as ordinary gentleman of the king's chamber had not been paid for sixteen years.[68]

The litanies of complaint about the expenses incurred by ambassadors and the lack of funds to maintain an appropriate way of life were constant between 1570 and 1585. Bertrand de Salignac, the ambassador to England, Arnaud du Ferrier, on duty in Venice, and Sébastien de L'Aubespine, the ambassador in Madrid, confronted the same financial difficulties; their correspondence with the king and the queen mother is full of supplications and lamentations on this subject. After a few years in residence, seeing their personal fortunes melting away month after month, their first concern was sometimes to find a replacement for themselves as soon as possible. Their requests were often ignored, and the "triennial" rule, which consisted in not leaving an ambassador on duty for more than three years, was already no longer respected under Henry III. An increasing number of ambassadors were impatiently waiting to be relieved and fretted about it in their correspondence.

The direct consequence of the catastrophic financial situation in which ambassadors found themselves during the reigns of Charles IX and Henry III was that it became far more difficult to recruit them. In general, one needed a minimum of 4,000 *écus* (12,000 *livres*) per annum to cope with the day-to-day expenses of an embassy. However, extraordinary expenditures were not rare and could significantly increase this budget. It has been estimated that ambassadors' average expenses varied between 27,000 and 37,000 *livres* per annum between 1566 and 1580.[69] It is difficult to compare these expenditures in view of the variations in the official exchange rate of the *livre tournois*. Nonetheless, lords of the high nobility saw no advantage in being named to a post abroad, and soon only second-tier gentlemen and recently ennobled *robins* could hope to receive some benefit from these offices. They alone had sufficient fortunes to envisage making a financial sacrifice for two or three years. Despite the exorbitant expenses connected with the title of ambassador, this position represented a sure way of acceding to honors and of ensuring that one's name would be transmitted to posterity. Regardless of the economic difficulties linked with the office of ambassador and the relatively slim compensations, few men refused this prestigious nomination, which was considered an investment.

Sometimes the remunerations were set on a case-by-case basis or resulted from a power relationship between the ambassador in question and the state secretaries responsible for the royal finances.[70] For example, in Rome, Henri Clutin, lord of l'Oisel, received 12,000 *livres* per annum; in Madrid, Jean de Vivonne received 18,000 *livres*; but others, such as Raymond de Fourquevaux, received only 7,200, or even, as in the case of Charles de Danzay in Denmark, less than 5,000 *livres*. An ambassador who was a member of the second-tier nobility thus had to be sure that he could maintain an adequate way of life for a year, or even two.

It must be said that in the candidates' calculations the considerable expenses connected with the office of ambassador were compensated by favors whose value was always difficult to quantify. After their return to France, ambassadors could hope to receive a reward commensurate with their sacrifice and thus get their money back. In his *Bibliothèque ou thrésor du droit françois*, Laurent Bouchel admonishes those who have accepted an assignment in the hope of making their fortune and recommends that they abandon their mercantile ambitions. He reminds them that "this office consists entirely in honor and was formerly given to honor those who had performed a good service for the republic. So that it must be neither competed for nor too ardently sought, to avoid incurring the suspicion of avarice."[71] The quest for these positions was based on the hope of a political reward and future benefits. An ambassadorship—extraordinary or ordinary—symbolized the second-tier regional nobility's preferred entry point into national politics. That was the illusion that Montaigne might have had regarding this profession.

Most candidates had a more optimistic view of diplomatic assignments. The post of ambassador implied a temporary financial sacrifice, but in the long run the majority of agents obtained what they wanted. Once they were back in France, they could hope for a few favors from the prince, and some ambassadors could hardly complain on this count. For instance, upon his return from Spain, Sébastien de L'Aubespine was named superintendent of finances and became counselor to Charles IX and Catherine de Medici. Similarly, ambassadors who belonged to the clergy often received major ecclesiastical benefices. Jean Ebrard, lord of Saint-Sulpice, who had replaced L'Aubespine in Spain, was made knight of the Order of Saint Michael in 1563 and was later called to the king's Privy Council.[72] Henry III compensated Jean de Vivonne in the same way for his ten years of good and loyal service in Spain by making him enter the Council of State in 1576 and then naming him knight of the Order of the Holy Spirit in 1583.[73] Many ambassadors were compensated in the same way, with honorific rewards in place of salaries. Promotions to the Council of State, to the king's Privy Council, and to all the other offices of the households of the king and the queen mother were particularly prized.

During the second half of the sixteenth century, nearly fifty ambassadors acceded to the very coveted dignity of member of the Council of State.[74] Diplomats who had occupied less prestigious posts or served as extraordinary or interim ambassadors were generally rewarded with the title of *maître des requêtes*. The ambassadors' jeremiads were part of a strategy that allowed them to put their discontent in quantitative terms while waiting for a position in the king's household once they had returned to France. These complaints often ended up paying off. The case of Louis Chasteigner, the ambassador in Rome when Montaigne went there, provides a good example, since the lord of La Rochepozay became a state councillor in 1576, while he was still in residence in the Eternal City. Similarly, Jean de Vivonne, baron of Saint-Gouard; Jacques de Germigny, baron of Germoles; Nicolas de Harlay, lord of Sancy; and Henri Clausse, lord of Fleury, were named state councillors in 1577, 1581, 1581, and 1584, respectively, to recompense their fidelity as ordinary ambassadors.

The last Valois had always more easily compensated and recognized those who represented them at the Holy See. For example, François Rougier, baron of Ferrals and lord of Malras, had served the king as ordinary ambassador in the Low Countries from 1568 to 1571, before being named to Rome, where he served from 1571 to his death in 1575. He held the honorific titles of the king's ordinary majordomo from 1564 to 1569 and then Catherine de Medici's majordomo, eventually becoming a knight of the Order of Saint Michael and a member of the Privy Council. The same titles were conferred on Just de Tournon, viscount of Polignac and nephew of Cardinal François de Tournon, who had also been made ordinary gentleman of the king's chamber before being received into the Order of Saint Michael in 1567, at the time when he was the French representative to the Holy See, from October 1566 to July 1568. The same goes for Henri Clutin, seigneur d'Oisel et de Villeparisis, who was named gentleman of the king's chamber in 1546 and knight of the Order of Saint Michael in 1560, just before he served as ambassador to Rome from 1564 to 1566.[75] Being a gentleman of the king's chamber and belonging to the Order of Saint Michael appears to have been indispensable for becoming an ordinary, extraordinary, or interim ambassador to Rome.

Montaigne's experience of the political milieu in Bordeaux and Aquitaine confirmed his ability to understand the parties opposing each other on the religious terrain in the late 1570s. It could not be said that he had been influenced by the humanist manuals on embassies; on the contrary, he prided himself on having a pragmatic approach to government that was more compatible with the political logic of his time. As for the eloquence required of ambassadors, his lack of it was compensated by other qualities. The author of the *Essais* was aware that he did not have the gift of eloquence that humanist treatises so often considered essential for the perfect diplomat. He had a shaky grip on rhetorical effects (at least, that is what he tells us) and could not begin to rival La Boétie when it came to giving speeches. To make up for these defects, he came up with a new quality, ingenuousness, which replaced eloquence. The queen mother liked this frankness, which she considered a crucial advantage in diplomats. It was a quality that she had noted, for example, in François de Barbezières, lord of La Roche-Chémerault, who by his free way of talking had won the esteem of politicians, which he could not have won by his eloquence alone: "I think that the lord Chémereau appeased the Holy Spirit, that he spoke to the king more freely than anyone else, for his fidelity and affection and the long time that he had had the honor of serving him very faithfully: that made me speak to him more freely . . . because he will tell me everything more freely, and the king will also speak to him more openly."[76] Montaigne repeatedly emphasizes this free way of speaking without ceremony or grandiloquence. His *Essais* of 1580 were systematically associated with a form of orality, because as he says about his mind, "its speech is better than its writings."[77] Montaigne proposes to speak first to himself before putting his remarks into the public domain. His very materialist conception of hearing seems diametrically opposite to introspection, at least in the first printing of the *Essais* of 1580: "what we speak we must first speak to ourselves, and make it ring on our own ears inwardly, before we send it to other ears."[78]

Fidelity is a necessity in diplomacy, and this quality is an essential attribute of the ambassador. Montaigne repeatedly emphasizes this aspect of his character. His loyalty is legible on his face, and his sincerity is one of the themes often developed in his *Essais* of 1580. Montaigne never claims to be associated with the humanists of his time; he depreciates writing (according to him, there are too many books about books) to the benefit of direct presence and the voice. He also praises improvisation and his ability to grasp what is essential in a conversation or a speech. His functions as a reporter at the Cour des Aides in Périgueux and as a councillor in the parlement of Bordeaux allowed him to attach great importance to his ability to synthesize when it was a question of reporting political discourses. Religious questions were just as important in a period when doctrinaire invectives were being launched in large numbers. Wasn't Montaigne himself something of a "theologian" in his youth, when he translated Raymond Sebond's works? Having a certain amount of theological baggage was an advantage for an ambassador, especially if he resided in Spain or was assigned to the Holy See.

In his *Essais* of 1580, Montaigne also proved that he gave priority to personal conversations—as with the Cannibals in Bordeaux—in order to forge his own opinions and create the general framework in which he could present his king's official positions. A sense for dialogue, even if brief or imaginary, was indispensable for the ambassador, who had to consult the largest possible number of people before reporting on a situation. Then the agent delegated by the king had to show good judgment. Jean Hotman, in his treatise *L'Ambassadeur* (1603), asserts that the main quality required of an ambassador is "native good sense."[79] A representative to the Holy See had to have an excellent knowledge of Latin, and so did several other representatives of the king serving abroad. Thus Henri de Mesmes speaks in his *Mémoires* of his journey "to the Emperor and the Princes of Germany, where it was necessary to speak Latin," whereas the king had offered him an embassy in Vienna that he refused for reasons of health.[80] Montaigne was astonished to find so many people speaking French in Rome, a city where he was expecting to use his Latin.

In the chapter titled "A trait of certain ambassadors" (I: 17), Montaigne relates an anecdote that was well known at the time and that led him to reexamine the qualities expected of an ambassador. This anecdote offered him an opportunity to distinguish himself from the ambassador whose story he recounts: the bishop of Mâcon, the lord de Velly. The events involved occurred in Rome in 1536. While meeting with the French ambassadors, Charles V, in a moment of rage, challenged Francis I to "fight him in his shirt with sword and dagger in a boat."[81] The ambassadors were stunned by this extravagant reaction, and even pretended not to have understood the emperor, who had supposedly spoken in German. Seeking to hush up the affair, the pope asked the ambassadors to attenuate Charles V's remarks in the report that they were to send to Paris.

Montaigne condemns the ambassadors and finds it "very strange that it should be in the power of an ambassador to make his choice of the information that he should give his master, especially in material of such consequence, coming from such a personage, and spoken in so great an assembly. It seems to me that the function of a servant is to represent things faithfully in their entirety just as they happened, leaving to his master the liberty to arrange, judge, and choose."[82] According to him, the final decision is for "the master," that is, the king, to make, and the ambassadors had clearly gone beyond their mission. Montaigne offers this comment on their decision to mask the truth from the king: "For to alter the truth or hide it from another for fear that he might take it otherwise than he should and that it might push him into some bad course, and meanwhile to leave him ignorant of his affairs—such conduct seems to me proper for him who gives the law, not for the man who ought to think himself inferior in prudence and good counsel as well as in authority. However this may be, I should not like to be served in this way, in my little doings."[83] This diplomatic incident, which was widely commented upon at the time, allowed Montaigne to express his judgment and show the king that he could count on him in any situation. Without deforming the words of others, he reports them directly and simply and presents himself as a trustworthy man who chooses not to hide anything. Truth cannot be altered by an ambassador worthy of the name, and transparency is necessary in diplomacy. Montaigne would have acted differently, with more frankness, and his *Essais* are the proof of this. He depicts himself as naked as possible, without transgressing the rules of good manners and Court decorum.

The personal judgment of the ambassador, who is not a councillor, can even turn against him. In "Of liars" (I: 9), Montaigne recounts an anecdote that marks the gap between an ambassador's private convictions and the role he should play:

> Pope Julius II sent an ambassador to the king of England to incite him against the French king. When the ambassador had had his audience, and the king of England had dwelt in his reply on the difficulties he found in making the preparations that would be needed to combat so powerful a king, and stated some of the reasons for those difficulties, the ambassador inappropriately replied that he for his part had also considered them and indeed had mentioned them to the Pope. From this speech, so far removed from his mission, which was to urge him headlong into war, the king of England got the first inkling of what he later actually found out, that this ambassador in his private intent leaned toward the side of France. And when the man's master had been informed of this, the man's goods were confiscated and he barely avoided losing his life.[84]

The desire for freedom (one of the *Essais'* important themes) seems out of place in an ambassador, who must apply strictly the instructions he has received. Here Montaigne puts the accent on ambassadors' allegiance and fidelity and declares that he would never stray from the command he had been given. Such is, for example, the conclusion of the chapter "A trait of certain ambassadors" in 1580, though an addition on the Bordeaux Copy nonetheless sounds a discordant note. After 1588, Montaigne continues to criticize those who "are so eager to get out from under command" and want to usurp mastery, but he henceforth emphasizes the freedom of judgment and authority that is "so naturally" inherent in us. The blind obedience demanded of representatives of the king is no longer suitable, and Montaigne now seems to prefer ambassadors who have a "freer" office and do not simply execute orders they have received: "On the other hand, however, one might also consider that such constrained obedience belongs only to precise and stated commands. Ambassadors have a freer commission, which in many areas depends in the last resort on their judgment; they do not simply carry out, but also by their counsel form and direct their master's will."[85] How can we explain this turnabout with regard to orders that are supposed to be executed without hesitation? In fact, this late addition corresponds to a disabused view of public offices and royal missions. But this belated awareness became possible only after his disappointment in Rome.

In his *Conseils à un ambassadeur* (1561), Pierre Danès lists the fundamental principles that must be inculcated in an ambassador before he takes up his post abroad.[86] Étienne Dolet also took an interest in ambassadors in his *De officio legati*. The two humanists put the accent on the honesty that is expected of ambassadors. This humanist ideal that advocates frankness and loyalty was, however, far from being put into practice at the time of the Wars of Religion. Henry Wotton, the English ambassador in Venice, offers a realistic and opportunistic definition of the ambassador at the beginning of the seventeenth century: "An ambassador is an honest man sent to lie abroad for the good of his country."[87] Fewer and fewer military men were named ambassadors, and in the second half of the sixteenth century, honesty was no longer any more than the vestige of an aristocratic ideal until it was put back on the agenda in seventeenth-century salon culture. Brantôme saw the use of military men as a necessity to resist the pressures exercised on the king's representatives in foreign countries.

Brantôme was certainly right, but he was also on the defensive and resisting the trend of diplomatic and political practices in the late Renaissance. In reality, the people of the long robe and the second-tier nobility were acceding to these posts thanks to their financial situation. Brantôme emphasizes that these new ambassadors lacked authority and were incapable of "arousing the slightest terror" in their foreign interlocutors, but he does not grasp the fact that the mission of the "modern" ambassador is oriented toward peace at any price rather than toward war. The civil wars that were shaking France had redefined political priorities and put ambassadors in the service of national religious interests. Brantôme had difficulty accepting the new image of the ambassador, who was less soldierly and more pragmatic in his conception of international relations. The diplomatic corps included fewer and fewer captains and nobles of the sword. Of course, it was still preferable to belong to the nobility—that was Montaigne's case—but the bravado of the battlefields was no longer appropriate during negotiations. A generation of sons of magistrates had taken over the posts previously occupied by military men. We can mention Antoine Séguier, the son of a magistrate, who represented Henry IV in Venice at the end of the century.

In his *Vie des hommes illustres et grands capitaines français*, Brantôme raises the question of the social origin of ambassadors and diplomats in general.[88] The number of prelates was rapidly diminishing in European embassies, even though it remained relatively high. Thus, of the 114 sixteenth-century ambassadors identified by Fleury Vindry, one-third are ecclesiastics. However, at the end of Henry III's reign, they no longer constituted more than 13 percent of the total number of ambassadors.[89] We register a constant evolution that goes from the clergy toward the nobility (but not necessarily toward military men), a second-tier nobility that had succeeded in rising socially thanks to its *robin* antecedents. Sébastien de L'Aubespine, the ambassador to Spain from the end of Henry II's reign until 1562, is representative of this recent orientation of the diplomatic corps. The L'Aubespines descended from merchants who had become members of parlements in the Loire valley and La Beauce. They chose to serve the king and provided four state secretaries. Catherine de Medici made the diplomatic career of Sébastien, in whom she always had confidence. In the following generation, Claude III de L'Aubespine became a state secretary in 1567. Claude IV, lord of Verderonne, better known under the name of L'Aubespine the younger, was also named ambassador to Spain in 1567, then secretary of Finances, and finally personal secretary to Catherine de Medici.

In Montaigne's time, among extraordinary diplomats, 44 percent were gentlemen; only 18 percent were *robins*, and 35 percent were clerics. Among ordinary diplomats, the figures are 23 percent gentlemen, 40 percent *robins*, and 20 percent clerics. In Rome, the proportion of diplomats belonging to the Church was not more elevated than in other European residences. Ecclesiastics represented 33 percent between 1559 and 1589: 20 percent in London, 38 percent in Venice, and 25 percent in Constantinople. Logically, *robins* are underrepresented in French diplomacy at the Holy See, only 22 percent as compared with 63 percent in Venice, 29 percent in London, and 75 percent in Brussels.[90] Under the last Valois, there was no profession of negotiator or ambassador because the choice of the ambassadors named in Italy was made on the basis of personal considerations and in a relationship of absolute confidence during the Wars of Religion. Under Henry III, we often find modest origins among diplomats and ambassadors. On this point, Étienne Dolet remarks that high nobility and lineage should not be taken into consideration in attributing ambassadorial offices; the sole desiderata should be the man's character and qualifications. He recommends that only men of letters be named and pays special attention to their external appearance, particularly their size and their faces. According to him, men with agreeable physiques compel the admiration of their interlocutors. In his funeral oration on the death of Paul de Foix, Marc-Antoine Muret also relates Paul de Foix's appearance to his ability to become a famous ambassador: "His exterior was handsome, and all the parts of his body so well formed that no one looked at him who did not seem to see in him the true portrait of honesty and virtue."[91]

In addition to closeness and loyalty, Montaigne emphasizes sincerity and transparency, at least insofar as appearances are concerned.[92] Diplomats and negotiators owe their positions to the private relationship they entertain with the king. Catherine de Medici also favors men who are close to the king. She wants less experts than people who are close to the party with whom they have to negotiate. Being a member of the king's chamber or of his Privy Council is a necessity, because these titles guarantee attachment. Montaigne reflects on this transparency and closeness in the *Au lecteur* in the *Essais*. He confirms elsewhere that he has "a thrifty and somewhat deceptive honesty."[93] He is not a liar and devotes a chapter ("Of liars") of his first *Essais* to this problem. In its first version, this chapter is based almost entirely on examples of ambassadors who falsify the truth. He elaborates on the distinction drawn by grammarians between lying and "telling a lie." From the outset, he asserts that he does not have this defect and is in this respect "singular and very rare, and thereby worthy of gaining a name and reputation."[94] This chapter was fundamentally reworked after 1587, and then again in the margins of the Bordeaux Copy. However, the statement generally cited, in which Montaigne recognizes that "in truth lying is an accursed vice. We are men, and hold together, only by our word,"[95] is not present in the first edition of the *Essais*; at first, Montaigne defended the possibility of "telling a lie" in the service of his king, but he was careful to refrain from lying to his "patrons."

Among the competencies required of an ambassador at the end of the sixteenth century, great importance was accorded to education and the ability to write reports, the ambassador's principal task. Montaigne spent several years writing reports when he was a member of the parlement of Bordeaux. In particular, these reports made it possible to judge the admissibility of an appeal to the law court of Bordeaux. Listening to his interlocutors and reporting the gist in the form of a letter pretty much sums up the ambassador's work. In his *Legatus*, published in 1598, Charles Paschal—the annotator of translations of Tacitus—emphasizes these intellectual qualities. According to him, the ambassador must show an ability to synthesize and master the art of epistolary exchange. Montaigne thought he had these two virtues. In 1580, his *Essais* were part of a project of demonstrating synthetic knowledge. Extracting the essence of a case and reporting it while at the same time comparing it with other cases that are similar but different in time and space—that is what is peculiar to his book.

In his treatise *L'Ambassadeur*—dedicated to Villeroy, a state councillor and first secretary—Jean Hotman de Villiers, the son of François Hotman, insists on the general knowledge required of a good ambassador, who cannot perform his task "if he does not have some reading, and especially a knowledge of history, which I find to be more necessary for him than any other study."[96] Another characteristic of the modern ambassador is his general culture, which is no longer solely religious and humanist, but also political. Montaigne thinks he has sufficiently demonstrated his knowledge of ancient societies to be able to propose comparative models, a little as Machiavelli had done in his *Prince*. In the funeral oration for Paul de Foix, Muret offers the recipe for a "good ambassador": he must have studied the works of Plato, Aristotle, Plutarch, "and other similar authors who seek chiefly to shape people's lives"; occupy himself "greatly with reading history, knowing well that the examples serve infinitely to confirm the truth of the precepts"; and also know geography, law, and the public government of states, "the manners and the diversity of the spirits of peoples." Only then does one become "very capable of being employed in Embassies."[97] Montaigne had been well trained, having studied with Muret at the College of Guyenne.

But the presentation of royal instructions changed in the late sixteenth century, and Montaigne bet on an unprecedented form of diplomatic rhetoric. The time for long harangues was over; as Hotman emphasized, they displeased the king, who, "now annoyed by the long discourses of a lord who had recently returned from Italy, said to him: Please be brief, I'm well aware that you are coming from the country of fine words." Hotman recommends a more French mode of expression, "a concise and subtle way of speaking."[98] He notes that ambassadors' dispatches should be "sober, short, pithy, containing much in a few words, couched in common terms rather than studied ones: sometimes mixed with witticisms and sententious remarks."[99] He also suggests diversifying one's style in order to distinguish oneself from what Hotman calls "the protocol of Notaries." Here we are far from the rhetorical rules taught at the College of Guyenne. Henceforth writing must have a kind of effectiveness, not in a Ciceronian style, but on the contrary all in witticisms. Montaigne considers his inclination toward the Senecan style a definite advantage, both for diplomatic writing and—later—for the genre of the essay. Length was out of fashion and now short forms had to be given priority.

The writing of dispatches constituted a large part of the ambassador's work. In Rome, it was even his main activity. Chasteigner frequently wrote to the king and to Catherine de Medici to keep them informed of the latest rumors. On this point, Montaigne was convinced he was suitable, and his friends confirmed him in this opinion: "On the subject of letter writing, I want to say this: that it is a kind of work in which my friends think I have some ability."[100] In a way, the *Essais* are a compilation of letters, and the last chapter of the second book ends, significantly, with an epistle addressed "To Madame de Duras," a singular way of concluding this work with a new title. Montaigne's style seeks to be direct and unceremonious; no doubt he hoped that its brevity, which relates it to the report genre, would help him in his work as an ambassador. He calls things as he sees them, with a frankness that could only please the sovereign or Catherine de Medici: "Now for my part, I would rather be troublesome and indiscreet than flattering and dissembling."[101] This approach to diplomacy led him to distance himself from practices of which he disapproved and that he repeatedly criticized in the first chapters of the *Essais* of 1580.

Montaigne counted on his "frankness" (*franc-parler*) to establish a privileged relationship with the king. His freedom of expression had limits, however, and, as he reassured his readers, he always respected the rules of decorum. The *Au lecteur* was intended to remind the sovereign that language imposes constraints that he will obey. Once fidelity had been established and trust won, Montaigne avoided the usual formulas of courtesy and went straight to the crux of the matter. He practiced the epistolary genre on several occasions during his life, for instance in the dedicatory epistles he addressed to great servants of the state when he published La Boétie's works in 1571. As we have suggested, his entry into "letters" was marked by the composition of an epistle on the death of La Boétie. However, we must not confuse the humanist letter with the diplomatic letter, which was more anchored in the political reality of his time.[102] Moreover, Montaigne was fond of letter collections: "The Italians are great printers of letters. I think I have a hundred different volumes of them."[103] Whereas many of his contemporaries were still strongly influenced by medieval treatises on the style of secretaries and ambassadors, or by the epistolary elocution suggested by Danès or Erasmus, Montaigne offered a direct, concise way of writing that went straight to people's hearts. He ignored the principles of the *dispositio* laid out in chancellery manuals.[104] Understanding people rather than their writings is the general rule Montaigne set for himself; it was also an essential rule for anyone who wanted to pursue a career in diplomacy. Style comes afterward; in any case, it is inseparable from its author.

The ambassador's task was to write regularly to the king or to the queen mother to inform them of what was happening in the country where he resided. For that reason, the embassy style sought to be familiar and personal. That said, in these missives that related all kinds of rumors and gossip, ambassadors often found it difficult to convey only the essential. In long messages they reported a jumble of stories without gauging their relative importance for the prince they served. Many ambassadors also simply lacked the ability to analyze their foreign counterparts psychologically. Montaigne once again avoided these pitfalls. His style seeks to be direct and uncluttered with diplomatic formulas: "I cannot close a letter the right way, nor could I ever cut a pen."[105] He explains that he prefers to write his own letters rather than dictate them to a secretary:

> I always write my letters posthaste, and so precipitously that although my handwriting is intolerably bad, I prefer to write with my own hand rather than employ another, for I find no one who can follow me, and I never have them copied. I have accustomed high personages who know me to

put up with scratchings and crossings-out, and a paper without fold or margin. The letters that cost me the most are those that are worth least; as soon as I begin to drag them out, it is a sign that I am not there. I am prone to begin without a plan; the first remark brings on the second. The letters of this age consist more in embroideries and preambles than in substance. Just as I would rather compose two letters than close and fold one, and always resign that job to someone else, when the substance is finished.[106]

After 1588, Montaigne intercalated the following passage:

And I would have preferred to adopt this form to publish my sallies, if I had had someone to talk to. I needed what I once had, a certain relationship to lead me on, sustain me, and raise me up. For to talk to the winds, as others do, is beyond me except in dreams; nor could I fabricate fictitious names to talk with on a serious matter, being a sworn enemy of any falsification. I would have been more attentive and confident, with a strong friend to address, than I am now, when I consider the various tastes of a whole public. And if I am not mistaken, I would have been more successful.[107]

Thus it was for lack of opportunity that Montaigne did not become a letter writer. In the *Essais* Montaigne turns back on himself, for in the end he "talked to the winds." Not having succeeded in conversing with itself about serious matters, the ambassador's epistolary writing was transformed into a self-sufficient text, a correspondence with the author. This late approach is a wager, a bet on the *desocialization* of the essays and the definitive abandonment of the epistolary genre. However, as we have noted, ambassadors' letters often drew no distinction between the frivolous and the essential, and the psychological dimension in these messages always remained problematic.[108] It was on this point that Montaigne declared his difference.

Frivolous details are effective when it is a matter of sketching a man's portrait. Montaigne's strategy is not very different from that of the rising class of *robins* trained in the parlements and experienced in debate. We encounter more and more former magistrates among ordinary and extraordinary ambassadors. On the whole, their letters sought to be more synthetic, because they "reported" without lingering long over details, or at least if they put the accent on anecdotes that at first seem frivolous, it was the better to sketch the portrait of a prince. Ambassadors increasingly showed discernment and pointed out differences more easily. Less interested in truth than their predecessors, they put public declarations in perspective the better to analyze political postures and the psychology of the historical actors.

A last necessity for an ambassador: he had to have the services of a competent secretary. In the *Trésor politique*, the author urges ambassadorial secretaries to "write at length, without abbreviations, to punctuate and review diligently everything that one writes, not to scrape the paper, but to strike it out and write over it."[109] These conventions of writing addressed to secretaries recall Montaigne's practices. The unknown secretary of Montaigne's *Journal de voyage* might have performed a function of this importance, and, as we have suggested elsewhere,[110] it is even possible to approach the journal of the trip through Germany and Italy as a kind of "training in writing" (for the secretary) with which Montaigne may not have been entirely satisfied. The role of the secretary being to "relieve the ambassador of the burden of his office," he had to faithfully record the minutes of his master's conversations. His main work consisted in taking notes for his employer, on a daily basis. He kept a kind of diary that could later serve as the basis for the ambassador's reports.

In his treatise on the *Desseins des professions nobles et publiques*, one of Montaigne's contemporaries, Antoine de Laval, proposed a definition of the good secretary as one "whose duty and office is to declare in writing, etc. It is he who must write his Master's will."[111] The secretary has to "divine [the will] of others." As Laval notes, everyone is capable of writing what he feels, but the secretary must "play the role of another person"[112] and sense his master's reactions. Laval recommends, for example, that the secretary speak little and listen much in order to put himself in the skin of the man he serves. Silence and discretion are the two qualities essential in a good secretary.[113] This rather surprising position that consists in thinking as close as possible to one's master makes it possible to understand Montaigne's reaction when he read the journal kept by his secretary while he was traveling to Rome. The secretary may not have been able to "imagine" his master's thoughts well enough. Recording a dictated text is one thing, and having the qualities of a secretary as defined by Laval is another. Montaigne's secretary in Italy was assigned to take notes on the anecdotes or meetings that could subsequently be used by Montaigne. He seems to have been given precise instructions regarding the kind of journal he was to keep. Thus until the first stay in Rome we note a predilection for observations of a political nature, an exercise that was certainly imposed on him. However, it is probable that this secretary did not meet his master's expectations and for that reason lost his job.

Montaigne thus envisioned a second career as an ambassador that might lead him to be named a temporary, interim, or even ordinary resident. He had before him two examples: Jean de Vivonne, ambassador to Spain in 1572, who performed his functions until December 1582,[114] and also Paul de Foix, a veteran of European embassies, who had been unsuccessfully seeking the post at the Holy See for more than a decade. The author of the *Essais* did not want an ambassadorship in order to get rich; he was convinced that this profession was right up his alley and corresponded to the idea of public service he had at that time. As an ordinary gentleman of the chambers of the kings of France and Navarre, he tried to remain outside purely economic questions and never complained about the financial insecurity these titles generated. Instead, he saw the absence of remuneration for assignments and royal offices as a guarantee of freedom and was rather proud of having received no payment for the missions that had been entrusted to him. The first edition of the *Essais* can even be considered the exposition of a model of diplomatic representation in which the author constantly stresses the transparency of his character and his fidelity to the master he serves.

A Montaigne in Spain

We have seen how, starting in 1572, Montaigne had officiated as an envoy or plenipotentiary ambassador in the context of various missions in the service of the king. A "Montaigne" appears in the royal correspondence during the summer of 1572 in connection with an extraordinary mission to Spain. In fact, in a letter dated August 29, 1572, and addressed to Jean de Vivonne, the ordinary ambassador in Madrid, Catherine de Medici declares that in order to take messages to her two granddaughters, Isabelle, born in 1566, and Catherine-Michèle, born in 1567, she "would have sent Montaigne, without what happened, but I fear that he would not be safe on the roads. For that reason I want Viscount Horte to accompany the person whom we send as far as Bordeaux and Montferrand and do the same [on the return trip] as far as Poitiers, where I shall give the order that he shall be taken and led safely to me."[115]

This "Montaigne" personally delivered a letter to Vivonne on September 12 and left to return to France seven days later with the ambassador's reply. Sent to Madrid in September 1572, this same "Montaigne" had instructions to carry the official news of the events of Saint Bartholomew's Day, even though Spanish spies residing in Paris had conveyed the information to Philip II almost a week earlier by fast courier dispatched by the Spanish ambassador in Paris, Juan de Olaegui. With this extraordinary mission, Catherine de Medici killed two birds with one stone: she inquired about her family in Spain and reassured Philip II regarding Charles IX's very Catholic intentions. Moreover, Charles had recently decided—on August 28—to suppress the Protestant religion, which was undoubtedly good news for the king of Spain.

On September 12, Vivonne wrote to Charles IX to confirm that the news of the events of Saint Bartholomew's Day had been delivered on Saturday, September 7 by a courier sent by Don Diego de Zúniga.[116] In October of the same year, following "Montaigne's" probable journey as plenipotentiary envoy to Spain,

Don Antonio de Guzmán was sent in turn to Paris to compliment Charles IX on the blow struck on Saint Bartholomew's Day. On October 2, 1572, Catherine de Medici wrote to Charles IX that she had "sent Montaigne to visit the children."[117] On October 5, chancellery letters from Bordeaux were delivered for "Messire Michel de Montaigne, lord of that place, knight of the order of the king, ordinary gentleman of his chamber." This is the first mention of his titles in an official document. On December 5, the queen mother informed Vivonne that "Montaigne has returned, and I was very happy to hear news of my granddaughters."[118] This six- to eight-week journey to Spain made by someone named "Montaigne" remains unexplained. However, let us note that the chronology of the Montaigne whom we know does not contain, between Saint Bartholomew's Day and December 1572, any trace of his presence in Bordeaux or elsewhere—not even at his château. We know only that he began to work on the chapter "That to philosophize is to learn to die" in March 1572 and that he read Guicciardini, Plutarch, Seneca, and Josephus early in the same year. Now that he could be presented as a knight of his order, a journey of several weeks to Spain could make him an accredited plenipotentiary ambassador. Such a diplomatic mission was not out of the question.

It was certainly the same Montaigne who was sent to the duke of Savoy, Emmanuel Philibert, in August 1573, a personage of whom Catherine de Medici speaks once again: "My brother, the king is sending you Montegne [*sic*], and because he will not travel with great haste, I am not writing you a long letter. . . . And for my part, I do not think I will be fully pleased until I have this boon, and because the aforesaid Montegne, though he is little, will notwithstanding not fail to render you a good account of what is going on here, I shall rely on him, and make an end."[119] His quality as a gentleman could make Montaigne a royal representative. Is our Montaigne the "little Montaigne" to whom Catherine alludes in this letter? Our Montaigne may have been short—as the queen mother seems to indicate—in comparison to another Montaigne who was taller but bore the same name. It has been suggested that François de Montaigne, who is listed on the roll of the domestic officers of Catherine de Medici's household (he was her secretary in 1573 and was paid a salary of 400 *livres* per annum[120]), could have made these trips to Spain and Savoy. However, it is unlikely that a simple secretary served as an ambassador to princes. No one had yet heard about this "little Montaigne" in 1573, and it is not clear why all of a sudden the queen mother would have described her secretary as "little Montaigne." He was thus a newcomer in the domain of diplomacy. It has also been suggested that the envoy might have been the son or nephew of Catherine's secretary—in the sense that "little" could mean "son of" or "nephew of"; however, no other Montaigne—except for François—appears on the queen mother's registers between 1570 and

1580. I have found no mention of a son or a relative of the same name who was in the service of Catherine de Medici's household.[121]

On the other hand, our Montaigne—Michel—had sufficient titles to serve as an extraordinary ambassador. In the early 1570s, he belonged to the network and the clientele of François de Foix-Candale, a fierce defender of the Roman church and one of the organizers of a Catholic League in southwestern France. Montaigne was a good horseman, and we know that he was always ready to travel to represent the parlement in Paris. Long rides on horseback did not frighten him, and as early as the end of 1572 it was possible for him to picture a career—intermittent, to be sure—as an emissary or diplomat mandated for specific missions. Montaigne had been the object of an extremely rapid political "construction." Catherine was not unaware that he came from the minor nobility and that his titles had propelled him to the front of the stage in record time. Recommended by the Foix-Gursons and the Foix-Candales, who were close to the queen mother in the wake of Saint Bartholomew's Day, Montaigne could become an interesting candidate for missions on which the person delegated had to have sufficient titles to be received by princes, but whose name gave him no true power of his own. In sum, he was a man worthy of trust and sufficiently unknown not to arouse suspicions.

The expression "little Montaigne" was therefore in no way abnormal as late as 1579: before his appointment as mayor of Bordeaux and before the publication of the *Essais*, this expression certainly referred more to his height than to his social status or his family connection with a social superior. Moreover, this qualification takes on meaning if it makes it possible precisely to distinguish our Montaigne from Catherine's secretary, who was taller. We know that Montaigne considered himself short: "on pavement, since my early youth, I have not liked to go except on horseback. On foot I get muddy right up to my buttocks; and in our streets small men are subject to being jostled and elbowed for want of presence."[122] He also complains about his small stature that represents, according to him, a disadvantage in the political and diplomatic milieu.

We find the name "Montaigne" in Spain in 1579, during another extraordinary mission. In fact, in March 1579 Catherine sent a "Montaigne" once again to Spain as a diplomatic courier. In a letter addressed to the king and dated January 4, 1579, she refers once more to this "little Montaigne": "since I still cannot use my hand, I have had little Montaigne write for me my expressed opinion which I am sending you."[123] Seven years after the first reference to a "little Montaigne," we have the feeling that the adjective "little" (*petit*) refers to the height rather than the age of the person in question. However, it is hard to imagine Montaigne serving as secretary to Catherine de Medici, and it is therefore not impossible that she is referring to another Montaigne—perhaps the son or nephew of her secretary. That said, it would once again have been rather un-usual to send a simple secretary to the Court of Philip II. Was it rather Michel de Montaigne who was sent there in 1572 and 1579?

Our knowledge of Montaigne's various activities around these dates makes these missions entirely possible. In the spring of 1579, he was at home and was busy turning his lands to good account. He had attended Diane de Foix's wed-ding in Bordeaux and had even served, on March 8, as the proxy for Louis de Foix's father and mother. Then he attended the nuptial festivities given at Gur-son. In January 1579, Montaigne was also putting the finishing touches on the *Essais*, for which a privilege was granted on May 9. For a good rider, traveling by horseback to Madrid took about twenty days round trip. It might have been too much for the time limits he had to observe, but this mission might also be able to explain the delay in the printing of his book and the subsequent haste that marred it. On September 17 of the same year, Catherine wrote to Bellièvre to tell him that she had received "from Montaigne the letter you wrote me."[124] She clearly refers to an envoy and not to a secretary. We have to admit that here there is a Montaigne mystery, because Montaigne's biographers have still not succeeded in distinguishing in a convincing way among these multiple "Mon-taignes," and because historians have often confused them.

For example, we have to determine whether this "little Montaigne" is Ber-trand de Mattecoulon, Montaigne's youngest brother, who was only nineteen years old in 1579—but in that case it could not have been he in 1572, because he would have been only twelve. Or was it simply François Montaigne, Catherine de Medici' secretary, who held the office of ordinary secretary of the king's chamber and of Catherine de Medici until 1579? In her correspondence, Cath-erine refers to her secretary as "Montaigne," "Monsieur Montaigne" (1563), "François Montaigne our secretary" (1574), and "Montegne" (1579).[125] In 1584, in a letter addressed to Villeroy and sent from Monceaux, Catherine writes: "I am sending you a letter from Monteyne to his wife; look at it and then show it to the King, and have it delivered to his wife."[126] This Montaigne is no longer "little," but we are in 1584 and in the meantime Montaigne had had important responsibilities, such as serving as mayor and governor of Bordeaux. The publi-cation of the *Essais* had also allowed him to make himself known on the na-tional level. Was it once again the "little Montaigne" who was now called simply "Montaigne"?

This last letter addressed to Raoul Féron is of a very different kind from those in which the first references to a "Montaigne" appear. In fact, as we will see later, it is not easy to see how a letter from a secretary to his wife would be worthy of being shown to the king. On the other hand, if Catherine's message to Villeroy refers to our Montaigne—which is more likely at this time—it is possible to infer that it was also he who was referred to in 1572. There is a troubling coincidence here that needs to be investigated. At this point, we have no convincing proof, no document that would allow us to assert that Montaigne was employed as a plenipotentiary ambassador in Spain and in Italy between 1572 and 1579. Nevertheless, several bits of circumstantial evidence—which remain, of course, suppositions—suggest that he might have been employed in an irregular way for specific diplomatic missions in France and in Spain and Italy in the 1570s.

If we search the *Essais* for traces of a trip to Spain made by Montaigne, we find a few interesting remarks that have not received all the attention they deserve. For example, Montaigne makes a number of comments on the Spanish Court and clothing fashions in that country. In the chapter "That the taste of good and evil depends in large part on the opinion we have of them" (I: 14), Montaigne reports the way women force their bodies into corsets: "to get a slim body, Spanish style, what torture do they not endure, tight-laced and braced, until they suffer great gashes in the sides, right to the live flesh—yes, and sometimes even until they die of it?"[127] In several passages of the *Essais*, he seems to show direct knowledge of the habits of the Spanish Court. We could, of course, imagine that Montaigne had occasion to make the acquaintance of Spanish gentlemen in Paris and Rome, but it was rarer to meet "very Hispanicized" women outside the Court of Spain. In spite of all this, there is no tangible proof, only a bundle of circumstantial evidence suggesting that Montaigne might actually have made one or two trips to Spain in the 1570s.

But if he had, why would he never speak of these missions carried out before 1580? First, we must note that this silence is not the only one, and that Montaigne keeps silent about a large number of experiences that were nonetheless very important in the development of his various careers. If we consider the first possible trip to Spain to announce the events of Saint Bartholomew's Day, it goes without saying that Montaigne had no desire to talk about that mission. So far as the "Montaigne" of 1572 goes, the almanac kept by the author of the *Essais* does not enlighten us on this point, because the page corresponding to the date of the Saint Bartholomew's Day massacre has nothing written on it in Montaigne's hand. The page for the subsequent massacre in Bordeaux (October 3, 1572) is missing; it could have been torn out. Later on, Montaigne had every interest in not mentioning that bloody episode of the Wars of Religion when he was serving as an intermediary between Protestants and Catholics. A journey to Spain under the circumstances outlined above—to announce the events of Saint Bartholomew's Day to the king of Spain—even though he was on a mission for the king of France, had no place in the *Essais*. In 1580, Montaigne did not want to give anyone the feeling that he was associated with the extremist Catholics, and such a journey to the Iberian Peninsula could have damaged his political ambitions in the southwest. But once again, the mystery remains, and for the time being it is impossible to arrive at a certain, well-founded opinion regarding the reality of this trip to Spain.

Montaigne changed his point of view concerning embassies when he published the *Essais* for the third time in 1588. To understand the disillusioned development of his judgment, we have to go back to the circumstances of his stay in Italy, and particularly in Rome. At the beginning of September 1580, after presenting his book to the king at Saint-Maur-des-Fossés in July and briefly attending the siege of La Fère, Montaigne set out for Rome. Italy was then the main destination of diplomatic missions, with more than a third of the 413 extraordinary missions carried out by 269 ambassadors (ordinary, extraordinary, or interim) recorded between 1569 and 1589, including fifty missions to Rome alone.[128] These missions to the Holy See almost always had to do with France's internal situation, with the Wars of Religion, and with the distribution of emoluments and other ecclesiastical benefices to the king's protégés. Montaigne's mission must not have been an exception to that rule. When he left for Italy in the autumn of 1580, it does seem that the king had dangled an ambassadorship or an extraordinary diplomatic post before his eyes.

The situation in Aquitaine was in no way reassuring for the king, because the Huguenots were in a state of virtual insurrection. Marshal Biron was no longer making progress, and he was now considered an obstacle to royal policy in the southwest. Even the most committed Catholics wanted to get rid of him. In a letter addressed to the duke of Anjou in late October 1580, Henry III expressed his astonishment that his brother-in-law wanted to deprive Biron of his offices. He added that Biron had always scrupulously executed his orders in Guyenne and suggested that the return to peace made forgetting necessary.[129] Shortly afterward, in November 1580, faced with the alarming political situation, Henry III contemplated for the first time dismissing Biron as mayor and governor of Bordeaux. All at once, the office of mayor of Bordeaux acquired a considerable political importance, because a Huguenot takeover of the city had to be prevented. In addition, it was necessary to calm people's minds and find a man who could be accepted by both religions, and who was, above all, capable of running the city with tact and restraint.

Henry III's correspondence confirms that on May 27, 1581, he had still not considered replacing Biron as governor of Guyenne.[130] At that time, the king was preoccupied with being informed, practically on a daily basis, of what was going on in Guyenne. During the summer of 1581, Matignon was chosen to govern the region in Biron's stead, because the situation could wait no longer. A faithful servant of Catherine de Medici, Matignon was not much liked by Margaret of Valois, who saw him as "a dangerous and wily Norman."[131] According to her, Matignon had a fierce hatred for François d'Alençon, the duke of Anjou.

But Matignon had won a solid reputation in Normandy and had learned to handle his enemies with care. He quickly became the man for the job.

Abandoning Biron to the many criticisms that were raised against him, the king was forced to calm people while at the same time reasserting his authority. He had logically chosen Marshal Matignon, a faithful servant and defender of the royal cause in Normandy, who had arrived in Bordeaux around October 20, 1581. The situation was worrisome. Faced with a rebellion by members of the parlement who refused to register the royal edicts, on October 12, 1581, Henry III had sent, for the fourth time, letters ordering the parlement to register his edicts, but its members continued to refuse to confirm the edict creating twelve councillors in that court (edict of August 1580), thus establishing a new Chambre des Requêtes in Bordeaux. The members of parlement still would not agree to share their revenues with councillors coming from outside. It was once again a matter of money, because the king hoped, as always, to draw a profit from these offices. He made no secret of that fact. On October 12, 1581, he wrote to Matignon to tell him that he urgently needed money and that if the Bordeaux parlement persisted in its disobedience, it would incur "[his] wrath and indignation."[132] Henry III had already chosen among the members of the Paris parlement the presidents and councillors of the new chamber of justice in Guyenne.[133] We can imagine the reaction of the Bordeaux *robins* when they learned that this royal prerogative defied tradition and their autonomy.

Montaigne in Rome

The French embassy in Rome had a turbulent history in the sixteenth century. Under the last Valois, French ambassadors remained there a short time: less than three years for Philibert Babou, Baron of La Bourdaisière, bishop of Angoulême (May 1558–February 1561); only eighteen months for André Guillart, lord of l'Isle (June 1561–March 1563); Just de Tournon was then designated, but was not appointed until 1566; François de Noailles, bishop of Dax, nominated in September 1563, preferred to remain in Venice because Pius IV wanted to have him arrested by the Inquisition—Philibert Babou took over in the interim; only sixteen months for Henri Clutin (February 1564–June 1566), who died while still in office. Cardinal La Bourdaisière served as ambassador during the transition, because Paul de Foix, who had been been proposed, was rejected for suspicion of heresy; fifteen months for Just de Tournon (October 1566–July 1568); thirty-six months for Charles d'Angennes (July 1568–December 1571); less than four years for François Rougier (December 1571–March 1575), who died while in office. Paul de Foix was nominated a second time, but the pope refused to receive him; in the interim, Jean d'Angennes served for a little more than a year (May 1575–June 1576), but without having the title of ambassador, and was a representative *ad interim*.

First, we may note that since 1550, the kings of France had had to resign themselves to naming several interim ambassadors to cope with various hasty departures, deaths, or rejections of the persons proposed. The last ambassador to be appointed, Louis Chasteigner de La Rochepozay, who had been in residence for almost five years (since June 1576), was the only one who had lasted that long since the beginning of the religious conflict between Catholics and Protestants in France. Chasteigner had accompanied the duke of Anjou to Poland, and Catherine de Medici considered him trustworthy. The duke of Anjou's hasty return after the death of Charles IX left the Polish throne vacant, and Stephen Báthory was elected king of Poland in his place. On Henry III's instructions, Chasteigner's principal task in Rome was to prevent the pope from receiving the ambassador sent by the new Polish sovereign. The son of Jean, baron of Peuilly in Poitou, and knight of the Order of Saint Michael, Louis Chasteigner had been born in 1535[v] and was almost the same age as Montaigne.[134] A personal friend of Montaigne long before Montaigne's stay in Rome, Chasteigner came from a family that had held the offices of both majordomo and gentleman of the king's chamber.[135] The Chasteigners were allies of the Clutin d'Oisel and of Villeparisis and close to the Schombergs and other great families represented in the king's household.

In addition, there were close ties between the La Rochepozays and the La Chassaignes. Thus in 1586 Françoise de La Chassaigne's brother, Geoffroy II de La Chassaigne, *soudan* of Pressac, married Jeanne de Gamaches, the niece of Louis Chasteigner de La Rochepozay.[136] In 1587, Louis Chasteigner wrote to François de Foix-Candale, bishop of Aire-sur-l'Adour, to ask him to employ his nephew Pressac.[137] In his travel journal, Montaigne speaks of Chasteigner as "a long-standing friend."[138] We can reasonably infer from this that Montaigne knew that Chasteigner, who was weary of his work at the Holy See, intended to give up his post as ordinary ambassador in March 1580. Fidelities and clienteles played a determinative role in the king's and the queen mother's choices of ambassadors and state secretaries,[139] and Montaigne could consider himself an ideal replacement for Chasteigner and imagine himself interim ambassador in Rome. The case of Montaignac in Constantinople made this calculation plausible, and Montaigne could have asked Chasteigner to recommend him directly to the king. In any case, Montaigne already knew what he was going to ask of the king at their meeting in July 1580.

---

[v] Chasteigner died on September 29, 1595.

This audience with the king having gone very well, Montaigne felt that he could travel on to Rome and wait there for a nomination. There was no lack of precedents, since Chasteigner had also begun his career as an ambassador by serving as a plenipotentiary envoy; during his first trip to Italy as an extraordinary ambassador he negotiated the marriage of Princess Christine of Lorraine to Ferdinand de Medici, the grand duke of Tuscany. At that time, he was close to the party of the *politiques*. Denouncing the League's excesses after Saint Bartholomew's Day, Chasteigner had recognized the king of Navarre as a legitimate king, despite his religion. Montaigne could play on the continuity, because in 1580 he considered himself to be following the same political line as Chasteigner and shared humanist values with him. Named ordinary ambassador to replace François Rougier—whose embassy Henry III, who had just succeeded Charles IX, considered a failure, notably because of a disastrous financial negotiation with Florence[140]—Chasteigner remained on duty in Rome for five years, from June 8, 1576, to March 17, 1581.

When Montaigne arrived in Rome on Wednesday, November 30, 1580, his first order of business was to meet with the ordinary ambassador in residence there. Very soon, with Chasteigner, he was received by the pope in a private audience. This meeting with Gregory XIII, as soon as he arrived in Rome, indicates that a mission had probably been entrusted to him; such an audience with the pontiff was part of a well-established protocol that allowed the ambassador leaving his post to introduce his successor, whether he was ordinary, extraordinary, or simply interim, and whatever the duration of the interim assignment. As a candidate for an ambassadorial post, Montaigne probably had letters of recommendation—though no credentials—that authorized him to visit the pope. It was certainly not a simple matter of courtesy on the part of an ordinary foreign visitor. Montaigne felt relatively confident in taking this step because he was immediately received by the pope. That had not been the case for François de Noailles in 1563. Papal audiences were never improvised and followed very strict rules of etiquette and decorum.

Montaigne's ceremonious presentation to the pope by Chasteigner allows us to suppose that our traveler was expecting to replace the ambassador, probably on an interim basis. The first audience with the pope was extremely formal, as was traditional. Despite the absence of credentials that would allow him to officially replace Chasteigner, Montaigne could interpret the pope's conversation with him as a public recognition of his status. His secretary reports this interview in accord with protocol: "The pope, with courteous expression of face, admonished M. d'Estissac to cultivate learning and virtue, and M. de Montaigne to maintain the devotion he had always exhibited towards the Church and the interests of the most Christian King."[141] Thus it was as a loyal servant and trustworthy representative of Henry III that Chasteigner introduced Montaigne to

Gregory XIII. Moreover, the pope's remarks on his devotion to the Roman church were certainly received with pleasure by Montaigne, because the pontiff was always wary of the men Henry III recommended to him. This time, he had expressed no hesitations regarding the candidate. The reference to the "service of the king" confirms that this interview was in no way a private audience. As soon as he arrived in Rome, Montaigne had been eager to be received by the pontifical authorities in the company of the ambassador in residence who was leaving. Everything began well for Montaigne, who could consider his interview with the pope as an initial success before the king's confirmation of his diplomatic service.

Montaigne intended to stay in Rome for several months, far longer than a traveler merely passing through the city. He had just taken up residence in the city, with his secretary, as he was expected to. On this subject, Antoine de Laval mentions that "among us there is no Gentleman with a hundred crowns of income who does not have his [secretary]."[142] Montaigne had engaged this secretary specifically for his stay in Rome. It would have been very odd to travel with a secretary to keep a simple "travel journal." The expenses incurred for taking notes on places visited were high, and we know that Montaigne was quite capable of keeping his own diary. Thus we cannot see this secretary as simply accompanying Montaigne on his journey. His role consisted of residing in Rome with his master, and the "travel journal"—as we know it today—was only a preparatory work in which the secretary learned his trade before beginning his real work in Rome in the service of an interim ambassador. Diplomats in residence in Rome had illustrious secretaries. Before leaving for Italy, Paul de Foix had chosen to accompany him a secretary "taken from the bar."[143] Arnaud d'Ossat was so well trained in the art of negotiation that he later became a cardinal, following in the footsteps of his master. Montaigne's secretary was supposed to help him in the burdensome task of the writing associated with the ambassador's trade. Every potential ambassador engaged the services of a competent secretary, and Montaigne was no exception.

Moreover, Montaigne's careful study of Roman geography reported, not without astonishment, by his secretary, might thus be meaningful. Perhaps Montaigne made use of the little popular guide written by Lucio Mauro, *Le antichita de la città di Roma*, published in Venice in 1556. Studying the map of Rome was not very common among travelers simply passing through the city. On the other hand, if Montaigne was expecting to spend several months in Rome, he had to become familiar with the place. A passage in the travel journal explains this: "At this time he [Montaigne] diverted himself entirely in studying Rome. He had at first engaged a Frenchman as guide, but this fellow took himself off in some ridiculous humour, whereupon M. de Montaigne prided himself on mastering by his own efforts the art of a guide. In the evening he would study certain books and maps, and next day repair to the spot and put in practice his apprenticeship, so that in a few days he could have shown his guide the way."[144] Becoming familiar in this manner with the layout of the city's streets and monuments presupposed a prolonged stay.

In 1580, Rome had hardly 75,000 inhabitants. The jubilee of 1575 had certainly brought more than 100,000 pilgrims to the city, but despite this influx of foreign visitors, the Eternal City retained an almost rural aspect. For instance, one might see cattle grazing among the ruins of the ancient monuments. Archaeological excavations were beginning to reveal the history and splendor of the city of the popes, but in 1581 Rome was reduced to a narrow perimeter in which there were many vacant places.[145] Montaigne remarks that the space inside the city's walls was two-thirds empty, and that Rome "would fall short of Paris by one-third"[146] in grandeur. As for the numerous monuments encountered in the city, he seems hardly to have noticed them, and offers only a few remarks on Rome's artistic heritage (paintings, statues, bas-reliefs), finding even its churches less beautiful than those in other cities of Italy, Germany, or France. While we know of Montaigne's interest in everything that had to do with the Order of Saint Michael, he seems not to have seen the statue of that saint sculpted by a student of Michelangelo's, Raffaello da Montelupo, nor even Pellegrino Tibaldi's fresco (1545), which also depicts the archangel Michael. These two works could nonetheless be seen at the Castel Sant'Angelo dedicated to Saint Michael; the statue towered over the castle's dome, and the fresco decorated one of the walls of a reception room frequently used to receive ambassadors or other important personages. On his first stay in Rome, Montaigne did not act like a tourist, admitting, for example, that he had "only gathered acquaintance with the public aspect of the city."[147] The author of the *Essais* had obviously not made this trip to "get to know Rome more intimately."[148]

During his stay in Rome, Montaigne lodged at "The Bear," the city's most respected inn, after having first stayed at the "Vaso d'Oro," an inn "furnished with silk and cloth of gold such as kings use,"[149] as his secretary informs us. Montaigne found this "magnificence" useless and preferred to rent a large apartment worthy of a gentleman of his status. His new lodgings comprised "three fine chambers, a living room, a larder, a stable, and a kitchen, for twenty crowns a month."[150] This rent was considerable, since it was equivalent to 588 grams of fine silver, whereas at that time a nice room in Rome went for two crowns per month, or 58 grams of fine silver.[151] Montaigne knew that ambassadors inevitably had to draw on their personal resources to maintain their households. He was prepared for this eventuality and was not without funds that would enable him to contemplate a long stay in Rome under comfortable conditions. The size of these Roman lodgings foretold a stay of middle or greater length, because a traveler who was just passing through would have limited himself to renting a room in an inn by the day or week. Montaigne was probably expecting to stay in Rome for several months, perhaps even a year. Everything depended on the king's pleasure and the local situation. During this time, Montaigne's secretary continued to keep a record of his master's encounters with a view to what was supposed to become a long-term position.

Montaigne showed a veritable "diplomatic fever" during the first months of his stay in Rome. On March 6, 1581, he went to see the holdings of the papal library and was proud to have been given access to all the books, even the rarest ones, and "taken to every part thereof by a gentleman, who invited me to make use of it as often as I might desire."[152] He was impressed by the free access to the library that he had been granted, even though the French ambassador, Chasteigner, had not even been able to consult its famous Seneca, because, as Montaigne's secretary tells us, he had not courted Cardinal Guglielmo Sirleto, the library's curator. Muret had also been denied access to a manuscript considered impious. The secretary remarks: "Thus it seems all things come easily to men of a certain temper, and are unattainable by others. Right occasion and opportunity have their privileges, and often hold out to ordinary folk what they deny to kings."[153] Montaigne was one of those most esteemed by the pontifical authorities. This "political bias" that he claims to have is transformed into a quality indispensable in every serving diplomat. Clearly, Montaigne enjoyed a state of grace during the first weeks of his first stay in Rome, and he was patiently awaiting the royal favor that would have allowed him to replace Chasteigner. He met other diplomats in residence in Rome and now felt well introduced into the city's diplomatic milieu.

In the expectation of a nomination that he counted on receiving while he was in Rome, Montaigne could hope to take Chasteigner's place in April. Determined to go back to France as soon as possible, Chasteigner had repeatedly asserted his desire to return to his country and his family. On January 19, 1580, Catherine de Medici had asked the sieur d'Abain—Chasteigner—to serve the king one more year, and had assured him that all his expenses would be covered during the end of his term: "And with regard to what you are owed, he [the king] will also make a fair decision on that, once he has seen state of the finances for this year."[154] Fourteen months had gone by since this message from Catherine, and Chasteigner was still hoping for a favor that was agonizingly slow in coming.[vi] He did not succeed in getting his expenses in connection with his stay in Rome reimbursed. According to a certificate issued on November 6, 1576, his ambassador's allocation amounted to 6,000 *livres*, but like all the others, he had great difficulty in receiving his emoluments. Like many other ambas-

---

[vi] Upon his return to France, Chasteigner will eventually be made a knight in the Order of the Holy Spirit in his own château.

sadors, he had to draw on his personal fortune to pay secretaries and servants. For several months he had been growing impatient with his endless exile and was counting on the king's generosity to accord him a post as *maître des requêtes* or as royal counselor. Despite his pressing insistence, Catherine de Medici and Henry III still needed his services in Rome, notably to settle once and for all the interminable "Paul de Foix affair."

For fifteen years, Paul de Foix had wanted to be named ordinary ambassador to Rome, and Catherine de Medici was more determined than ever to secure this post for him. Gregory XIII wanted to hear nothing of it, and repeatedly refused to receive Foix. Making a final effort, Catherine asked Chasteigner to do everything he could to help her protégé.[155] It was then planned that Chasteigner would return to France early in 1581. That at least was what the king thought when Montaigne made his visit to Saint-Maur-des-Fossés during the summer of 1580. As we have suggested, he probably asked Montaigne to put himself at his disposal, possibly to serve as interim ambassador in Chasteigner's place until Paul de Foix's nomination was finally accepted by the Holy See.

The uncertainty of this nomination might have led Montaigne to plan for a stay in Rome lasting several months, or even a year or two. Montaigne knew Foix personally—he was one of the dedicatees of Montaigne's edition of La Boétie's works—and Foix could count on the friendship of the Gascon gentleman, who would withdraw when the affair was settled. There was no competition between them, because Montaigne knew his place in the hierarchy of the new profession to which he aspired. An experienced diplomat, Foix incarnated the queen mother's choice as ordinary ambassador, and Montaigne expected only to provide the transition between Chasteigner and the man whom it was not even known that the pope would finally accept. During this transition, Montaigne would be the interim ambassador. This was to be a first step in a career that at that time almost always began with a nomination as extraordinary or interim ambassador.

Being recommended by a serving ambassador was an excellent way to succeed him. Family ties had their importance in this kind of patronage, and considerations of fidelity and clientelism often determined professional prospects in the social and political structure of the time.[156] In a letter dated May 7, 1580, Henry III had told Chasteigner that he had not forgotten his request to designate a successor for him by the end of the following August. Unfortunately, we do not have Chasteigner's letter that perhaps recommended a successor. As we have seen, we can assume that Montaigne knew that this post was soon to be vacant. Had Henry III promised or suggested this post to Montaigne a few weeks later at Saint-Maur? In order to give his *Essais* to the king in person, Montaigne had presented himself in his role as ordinary gentleman of the king's chamber and knight of the Order of Saint Michael, distinctions that Chasteigner also possessed. He had all the titles necessary to hope for a royal favor in diplomacy, and an opportunity had opened up in Rome. Since he was well aware that Paul de Foix had been a candidate for this post for a very long time, it might even be thought that Montaigne could do a better job than Chasteigner—of whom the pope was wary—of convincing the pontiff to accept Foix as ordinary ambassador. That would, of course, take time, but Montaigne felt himself close enough to Foix to be considered the right man in this situation. While waiting he would make an excellent interim ambassador, which would allow him then to hope for other rewards in a career as an extraordinary diplomat. His Latin was useful for conversing with representatives of the Holy See, and his Italian was serviceable and certainly sufficient to follow a conversation in that language. In addition, numerous treatises and writings on the function of the ambassador celebrated moderation, an essential quality in diplomacy. Montaigne would certainly have sung its praises; it is one of the great themes of the first *Essais* that he presented to the king. "Of moderation," the twenty-ninth of the fifty-seven chapters, occupies the physical center of the first book of the 1580 edition.[vii]

Rome was following very closely the negotiations between the king of France, the king of Navarre, and the duke of Anjou. A letter dated November 28, 1578, shows that these negotiations were encountering difficulty. The king presented to Chasteigner the complex political situation with which he was confronted in order to prepare him for the pope's questions and criticisms:

> Monsieur Dabain [Chasteigner], although it has been only two days since the sr. de Lancosme left to go there [Rome], and by whom you will have been amply informed about everything that is happening and the state of my kingdom's affairs, nevertheless having received your dispatch of October 5 that you gave to Laubespine's secretary . . . I have not wished to delay warning you about this . . . . And particularly since I have previously ordered that you had to oppose on my behalf, along with all my servants who are there, the said profession of obedience or any other act that might have an impact on the right that I claim to the said kingdom, I am sure that you have not allowed the opportunity to pass and that you will have formed the oppositions, about which I expect to be informed by return letter. Moreover, the queen mother is presently engaged in communication with my brother the king of Navarre and those of his faction, the outcome of which I hope will please people of good will for the establishment of pub-

---

[vii] In this edition there is an error in the numbering of the chapters of the first book. The chapter "Vingt neuf sonnetz d'Estienne de la Boëtie a Madame de Grammont contesse de Guisen" bears the number 28 and "De la modération" the number 29.

lic peace in my kingdom. . . . As for my brother the duke of Anjou, he is still in the city of Mons, from which I desire no less his return to my kingdom than I regret his going to the Low Countries. Every day I do what I can to dissuade him from going there, and I shall not be very content until I see him completely outside it, as you may assure His Holiness.[157]

In another letter to Chasteigner, Henry III admits his helplessness when faced with a pope who, according to him, does not truly want peace in his kingdom:

Monsieur Dabain, although I have some reason to doubt the affection and good will of our Holy Father because of the small regard he has shown for the supplications and prayers that I have made to him concerning the approval of the order of the Holy Spirit, nonetheless I have been very happy to learn by your letter of the 7th of this month that His Holiness has shown you his happiness about the return to me of my brother the duke of Anjou and the good and fortunate outcome of the meeting held at Nérac to establish public peace in my kingdom.[158]

In this letter, we can sense the king's concern when he asks Chasteigner to remain vigilant and to inform him of everything that might be being plotted in Rome, where the ambassador was in his view one of the most important servants for convincing the Holy See of the wisdom of his policy. He not only needed a trustworthy man—and on this point his correspondence with Chasteigner shows a deep intimacy and complicity with his ambassador—but also to find someone who would be sufficiently esteemed and respected by the pope.

Disagreements between Henry III and Gregory XIII were increasingly frequent in the late 1570s. Let us give the example of Stephen Báthory, the "Voivode of Transylvania,"[viii] who proposed with a certain success nominations to the pope for benefices in Poland. The Holy See was plotting with Báthory against France.[159] Henry III complained on several occasions about the allocation of these benefices, which, according to him, belonged to his crown, and asked Chasteigner to remind the pope of this fact.[160] Chasteigner faithfully represented the king in Rome, but he found it increasingly difficult to make himself heard by the pope's immediate entourage. He was, for example, unable to succeed in persuading the pope of the necessity of a truce with the Huguenots. Formerly presented as a zealous Catholic, he was now the object of numerous criticisms at the Holy See, which considered him a *politique*. A letter from Henry III dated 1576 and sent to Jacomo Boncompagno, Castellan of Rome

---

[viii] From the twelfth to the sixteenth centuries, the Voivode was the highest-ranking official in Transylvania. [Trans.]

and governor general of the pope's men-at-arms, announced the nomination of his new ambassador to Rome "for the good information and knowledge that I have of the praiseworthy qualities that are in him, his integrity and zeal in the Catholic religion." After all, in contrast to Montaigne, Chasteigner had been refused access to certain precious books in the papal library,[161] a sign that his credit had been significantly damaged and that the author of the *Essais* enjoyed a better image. Between 1576 and 1581, the king of France's "Catholic religion" was the object of doubts openly expressed in Rome. The king of France had necessarily to raise the bar, because the French ambassador in Rome could only be a Catholic who was above reproach. Could that be said of Montaigne? The author of the *Essais* thought it could; in a region in which the Reformation was solidly implanted, he constantly played the card of the loyal Catholic while at the same time listening to the other parties.

Chasteigner faithfully and conscientiously informed the king regarding the plots of the supporters of the League in Rome, and he maintained a regular correspondence with Catherine de Medici, to whom he reported the slightest actions of the crown's enemies. The ambassador also had chosen to develop connections with Italian bankers. Chasteigner's biographer, André de Chesne, tells us that one of his activities was to

> deal and negotiate with every private person he found who was disposed to grant us a loan of such sums as their means might allow . . . take and receive the aforesaid money, promise in his name to return and repay it on the agreed terms, and, to do so, the king pledged all his goods both moveable and immoveable, and to come, together with those of his heirs having rights, and for greater security the aforesaid ambassador could put into the hands of the lenders our rings and gems that we had entrusted him with for that purpose until the debt was paid.[162]

Faced with the royal expenses, which were constantly increasing, a man with experience in negotiations on economic matters was needed.[163] On that point Montaigne might have lacked experience. In fact, if "tender" negotiation is an advantage in politics, it indicates weakness when it is a matter of negotiating loans. It is not clear that Montaigne's conception of the given word was a good thing in a world of bargaining and contracts that were constantly being canceled and renegotiated. It is true that he was rather proud of having made his estate prosper after he received it from his father in 1568.

In Montaigne's case, the term "ambassador" has to be understood in the broad sense of the term, because it covers activities as well as representation and negotiation. "Ordinary, extraordinary, and interim diplomat" are terms that are not precisely delimited. These formal distinctions were far from clear at the end of the sixteenth century, and especially in Rome. The siege of La Fère marked the beginning of an intense political activity on the part of Henry III. The queen mother encouraged the king to change the little circle of his faithful servants and made several recommendations to that end. For example, she praised as royal agents the young François d'Espinay de Saint-Luc and Jean-Louis de Nogaret de La Valette, who had been promoted to duke of Épernon in 1581. In this regard, scholars have spoken of a "genuine nobility of service" in the years of 1580 and 1581.[164] Twenty years younger than Montaigne, Épernon took part in the negotiations with Henry of Navarre, and like Montaigne, tried to get him to abjure his Huguenot faith. A native Gascon, he was chosen for his close ties with Henry of Navarre's immediate entourage from 1575 to 1576. Montaigne also had the same enormous advantage of being a gentleman of the chambers of both the king of France and the king of Navarre.

In the 1560s and 1570s, Montaigne reaffirmed on several occasions his faith in the Roman Catholic religion. His privileged situation in Henry of Navarre's milieu, his desire to confront events over the short term, and his taste for the philosophy of chance made him a serious candidate for an embassy in Rome.[165] Montaigne considered it very important to seize a good opportunity and presented himself as a very flexible man who could quickly size up a situation. Adapting to the constant turns of fortune was seen as an advantage at a time when nothing seemed stable. A good ambassador must not prove dogmatic but adjust to what happens. Montaigne also appeared to be a convinced Catholic who regarded religion as the sole source of stability for political systems. His strength and success consisted of knowing how to adapt to the circumstances of time and place. Diplomacy amounts to an encounter between people who are by nature different and changing. As Montaigne puts it in the very first pages of the 1580 edition of the *Essais*, "Truly man is a marvelously vain, diverse, and undulating object. It is hard to found any constant and uniform judgment on him."[166] The perfect ambassador is one who makes up his own mind on the basis of situations directly experienced.

Montaigne had presented himself as an ideal mediator (*truchement*) between the two Henrys and the duke of Guise.[167] There could be no doubt about his Catholic faith. The selection criteria for the post of ambassador in Rome were slightly different from those for other European cities. A good knowledge of religious dogmas and their respective political arguments was necessary for evaluating the positions taken by the Holy See on the complex French chessboard. Montaigne was well acquainted with the political and religious situation in Aquitaine in the early 1580s. His firsthand knowledge was a definite advantage for defending the crown's interests against a pope who was astonished by the Protestants' growing power in cities like Bordeaux and Toulouse. The French ambassador in Rome had to be sufficiently well informed about recent developments in the kingdom on both the Catholic and the Protestant sides. Henry III's correspondence with Chasteigner frequently sums up the state of the negotiations with Henry of Navarre. By choosing a man like Montaigne, Henry III could count on the general political education of his representative, who was perfectly capable of grasping the specific religious context of France in general and of the southwest in particular.

Once again, on February 20, 1581, while Montaigne was in Rome, Chasteigner informed the king of his intention to put an end to his service as ambassador. He was homesick and languishing more and more in a foreign land. Moreover, his purse was emptier than ever. Henry III had replied positively a year earlier, but had not yet named a replacement. Confronted by Chasteigner's pressing requests, the king soon had to make up his mind to let him go without revealing the name of his successor: "Monsieur d'Abain, I think that shortly after the last dispatch that you sent me on February 20 of the past year, you should have received the one in which I gave you leave to depart Rome whenever you wish." No decision had been made regarding his replacement. In March 1581, Catherine de Medici asked Cardinal d'Este to serve for a short time as interim ambassador: "The king my son has been forced to allow sr. Dabin to come back here because of the regular prayers and requests that he made to him, and also he has many private affairs here that greatly require his presence. However, because he has not yet been able to decide on the one whom he must send to Rome as ambassador, he desires that you shall embrace his affairs and take charge of them."[168] Chasteigner had finally obtained the authorization to return to France. As for Montaigne, he was still on the sideline, and Cardinal d'Este was the one who had been asked to handle the ongoing affairs. The king and the queen mother were still hesitating to choose a replacement for Chasteigner.

In fact, two days later, on March 15, Catherine de Medici decided to deal the cards anew. Everything seems to have been overturned very rapidly, and the name of Paul de Foix reappeared again. Catherine had been fighting with Gregory XIII for ten years to impose her faithful confessor on him. After repeatedly urging the pope to accept him, Catherine de Medici and Henry III had finally decided to have Foix named archbishop of Toulouse. In early 1581, this was a compromise, but the queen mother still had in mind an embassy in Rome, though she understood the difficulties and shifted her attention to the archbishopric of Toulouse. This was not a new idea, but this time the pope seemed inclined to accept a compromise. In 1574 the king had already tried to name Foix ambassador to Rome to replace the baron de Ferrals, but the Holy See had rejected this choice. On September 14, 1575, after several months of negotiations, the nuncio Salviati finally announced the appointment of Chasteigner after having duly remarked that "this coming puts an end, in large measure, to the affair of M. de Foix, which has lasted so long."[169] For the pope, the case was closed and there was no longer any question of an ambassadorship in Rome for Paul de Foix. Catherine de Medici was still officially waiting for the nomination of Foix as archbishop of Toulouse, but she no longer seemed to believe in it. She resumed her effort to impose Foix as ambassador. On March 15, the die was cast and Chasteigner's replacement was not Montaigne!

On the same day, March 15, 1581, Catherine de Medici suggested to her son that he replace Biron with Matignon, who found himself governor of Guyenne. Biron had written the queen mother to tell her about his weariness and the fact that for the past four years he had not been able to live in his house for more than four months. He said he was ill and incapable of taking care of his personal affairs. Biron had just had a moment of political lucidity and informed the queen mother that "he saw clearly that peace would never come in Guyenne so long as he was there." Whatever he did would meet with suspicion and mistrust on the part of the king of Navarre. Catherine de Medici then proposed to separate herself from the faithful Biron: "All that, communicated with his letter, made me wonder whether this wouldn't be an opportunity we could take to withdraw Marshal Biron from the country of Guyenne and to assign command there to my cousin the duke of Montpensier and to Marshal Matignon."[170] Catherine de Medici and Henry III now had another idea of the service that Montaigne could provide for them.

In early March, Montaigne still had every chance of becoming an interim ambassador, because Catherine and the king still had the archbishopric of Toulouse in mind for Paul de Foix. But faced with the difficulties they had encountered, one name appeared at the beginning of March 1581: Anet de Maugiron, who was supported by Catherine de Medici. In a letter to the cardinal of Como (dated April 21, 1581, and sent from Blois), Dandino reports that Maugiron had been approached about serving as ambassador to Rome, although the queen mother still preferred Paul de Foix for this post.[171] The Maugirons belonged to the Guises' party, and Anet would have no difficulty being accepted by the pope. So Henry III proposed to name the younger brother of Laurent de Maugiron, Anet, lord of Lessins and lieutenant in the company of the duke of Nevers since 1572, even though he clearly had no diplomatic experience.[172] This was obviously a reward for services rendered, because Laurent de Maugiron, as the governor general of the Dauphiné since 1578, had played a major role in the battle against the Protestants who had established themselves in that region. Thus he had obtained his governorship from the king, against Catherine de Medici's advice, and thanks to the influence of his son, François de Maugiron, one of Henry III's favorites.

The king preferred a man of the sword for the post of ambassador, and the queen mother, a man of the church. Montaigne could have been the man of compromise—as the king might have hinted to him during the summer of 1580—but his voluntary exile for more than six months—far from the Court—seems to have worked against him. Henry III would have liked to wait a bit longer before replacing Chasteigner, but the situation was becoming untenable, with the sudden withdrawal of Biron and Paul de Foix's case, which had to be settled once and for all. However, Maugiron's nomination soon collapsed and the king found himself without a clear successor for Chasteigner. When he had just arrived in Paris, the nuncio Anselmo Dandino recounted how the king seemed to harbor some resentment against Chasteigner for the conditions under which he hastily departed Rome.[173]

It might be thought that the king still felt he owed something to Montaigne, but no longer in the same way. The impossibility of getting Foix confirmed as archbishop of Toulouse, the replacement of Biron by Matignon, and the political situation in Guyenne all helped change his plans. Once Chasteigner had left Rome, it was necessary to act swiftly, and Foix was a necessary choice, because Gregory XIII now showed himself more opposed to seeing him archbishop of Toulouse than ordinary ambassador in Rome. Obligated to do something for Montaigne, and perhaps a little ill at ease for having gone back on a promise, the king then logically thought that the office of mayor of Bordeaux would suit him better, since he had already named Matignon lieutenant governor of Guyenne. Initially approached for a post as interim ambassador, Montaigne suddenly had an appreciable advantage in the context of recent political developments in the southwest. The king hesitated a long time to replace Chasteigner in Rome, because he had to avoid the problems associated with Arnaud du Ferrier's embassy in Venice; Ferrier had acquired a reputation as a clandestine Protestant[ix] and

---

[ix] Arnaud du Ferrier embraced the Protestant cause toward the end of his life, without, however, formally converting. But his "conversion" is reported by Duplessis-Mornay in his handwritten notes on Jacques-Auguste de Thou's *Commentaire de sa vie*, in the third book of De Thou's *Histoires* (BNF, ms., coll. Dupuy 409: *Advis, censures, et Lettres sur l'Histoire de Mr Le Président de Thou*, 1634). Duplessis-Mornay had exhorted du Ferrier to publicly declare his Protestant faith when he returned from his embassy in Venice in 1582. In fact, just like Montaigne in the 1570s and 1580s, Du Ferrier never considered himself an enemy of one of the two denominations, Catholic or Protestant. In the wake of the Saint Bartholomew's Day massacre, Du Ferrier had distanced himself from the policy of the queen mother and the duke of Anjou, writing to her from Venice that even in Italy, this act "so greatly aroused and changed the mood of those who are otherwise very attached to your crown, even though they are all Catholics, they cannot be satisfied with any excuse" (Du Ferrier to Catherine de Medici, September 16, 1572. Imperial Library, Saint Petersburg, French documents, vol. XCVIII, item no. 35, p. 41, encoded letter). A diplomat and the politician, Du Ferrier advocated dialogue between the denominations and avoided sectarian conflicts throughout his life. Montaigne praises Du Ferrier in his *Essais*: "A personage great in years, in name, in dignity, and in learning, boasted to me that he had been led to a certain very important change in his faith by an

was considered too tolerant with regard to the Huguenots.[174] Was it, moreover, judicious to name an ambassador who came from a region disturbed by religious troubles that were among the most serious in the kingdom? A promise made in July 1580 no longer had exactly the same value a year later.

Paul de Foix and the Suspicion of Heresy

The difficult situation in which Paul de Foix found himself in early 1581 was also one of the reasons that Henry III changed his mind. For the past eight years the king and Catherine de Medici had been vainly seeking to get Foix confirmed as archbishop of Toulouse, at the same time they had been trying to have him named ambassador to the Holy See. His nomination to this post and to that of ambassador to Rome had been repeatedly rejected by Gregory XIII.[175] The pope refused to hear of a major benefice, that is, of an archbishopric, for Foix, and he had also strongly opposed his nomination as ambassador to Rome in 1573. Foix had been only an extraordinary ambassador—that is, he had not been confirmed by the Holy See.

The pope's disapproval was due to an episode that went back to 1559, when Foix had been arrested and condemned by a parlementary commission for his unorthodox opinions regarding the application of the edict of Compiègne on the punishment of heretics. In the *mercuriale*[x] for 1559, Foix had expressed excessively liberal ideas, notably proposing to establish distinctions among heretics. He suggested, for example, not to condemn "sacramentalists," that is, Lutherans who denied the form of the Sacrament but not its substance (the real Presence). This technical differentiation accepted by Foix was contrary to the merciless battle being waged by the Holy See against sectarians. Foix was accused of having shown too much clemency, indeed, even sympathy, for the heretics. Gregory XIII was never to pardon him this weakness with regard to the Protestants. Foix even went so far as to advise granting freedom of religion to the Huguenots, a position the pope considered untenable and reprehensible. At Foix's request, this proposition had been included in the edict of January 1562 but was rejected by the parlement of Paris. He was put on trial and condemned to retract before the combined chambers; he was also forbidden access to the parlement for a year.[176]

---

external impulsion that was just as bizarre, and moreover so inconclusive that I thought it a stronger argument in the opposite direction. He called it a miracle, and so did I, in a different sense." (*Essais* EB, II, 29, f. 302r. Frame, p. 537.)

[x] An assembly of the Parlement of Paris held on the first Wednesday after Easter, during which the first president denounced abuses committed in the administration of justice.

As a result of his statements at the *mercuriale* of 1559, Foix was arrested on June 10 and had to publicly renounce the offending view and ask to be pardoned for it. This affair dogged him for twenty years and aroused the Holy See's suspicion. At that time, many Protestant refugees lived in England, and Foix had remained in contact with them. He served as Catherine de Medici's almoner in 1552, then as a councillor in the parlement of Paris from 1555 to 1562. In 1562 Foix was named resident ambassador at the English Court, where he remained for four years. After 1564, he joined the *politiques* for a time and served as a negotiator with the Protestants. Charles IX then tried to name him ambassador to Rome, but Pius V categorically opposed the appointment. At that time, Arnaud du Ferrier—who had also been compromised in the affair of the *mercuriale*—asked the king to be replaced in Venice, and in June 1567, Foix took up his functions as ambassador in Venice for three years. In 1571, he was once again sent to the Court of England on a mission to negotiate the marriage of the duke of Anjou to Queen Elizabeth. His stay in "liberal Venice" and his return to London made him even more suspect in the eyes of Gregory XIII, who proved to be just as intransigent as his predecessor. Foix's turbulent diplomatic career was nonetheless considered exemplary by Montaigne. Foix was more a man for missions than an ambassador; that was perhaps what Montaigne had learned from his career as a diplomat. He was sent to Savoy, Mantua, Florence, Rome, Genoa, and then back to Rome, in 1579, as an extraordinary ambassador. Without any doubt, Paul de Foix was a model, if not a sponsor, for Montaigne.

In 1573, Foix was arrested in Ferrara as he was on his way to Rome to take up the post as ordinary ambassador. After Charles IX's death, Henry III tried to name Foix permanent ambassador in Rome, but he failed in his turn. The nuncio Salviati recounted this incident in his correspondence, and Chasteigner was finally named in Foix's place. Disappointed by these repeated setbacks, in 1573 Foix changed strategies and decided to pursue a religious career that should have led him to become a cardinal. But that did not take into account the resentment felt by Gregory XIII, who repeatedly rejected his nomination as archbishop of Narbonne in 1573 and then, shortly afterward, as archbishop of Lyon. Even though on several occasions the king had named Foix to ecclesiastical positions, in the case of the archbishopric of Lyon the pope preferred to send the bulls of confirmation to Pierre d'Épinac, the nephew of the archbishop who had just given up his archbishopric in the same city. Such incidents occurred throughout the 1570s.

Paul de Foix's problem was also that he had too well served the king in the south of France, where he had acquired a reputation as a conciliator with the Protestants. When the duke of Alençon fled the Court, and Henry of Navarre also escaped Paris to lead the Protestants in Guyenne, it was Foix whom Henry III called upon in July 1576 to negotiate with the king of Navarre. His closeness with the king of Navarre was used as a proof of his Protestant ideas. Considered a heretic, Foix was prevented for a time from entering Rome. A few years later, when Cardinal Armagnac gave up the archbishopric of Toulouse in 1578, Foix was a candidate for this post once again, but after the reverses suffered during his abortive nominations as archbishop of Narbonne and as ambassador to Rome, he decided to proceed with caution and diplomacy. In March 1578 he tried to reconcile himself with the pope and proposed to the nuncio Dandino, who had recently arrived in Paris, to retake the fortress of Ménerbes, which had been under Protestant control. On this occasion, Catherine de Medici wrote directly to Gregory XIII to renew her support for Paul de Foix.[177]

The king sent Foix to Rome to justify himself directly before Gregory XIII. He arrived in Rome on November 29, 1579,[178] that is, a year before Montaigne. Suspected of heresy and of doing political favors for the Protestants, Foix went before a commission of three cardinals (*compurgatores*), where he was finally absolved and authorized to receive the papal blessing. In spite of this gesture of goodwill, the pope made Henry III wait again, and Foix was not for all that confirmed in Toulouse, the pope's excuse being that he had not yet officially accepted Armagnac's resignation in that city. In fact, the pontiff simply did not trust Foix. The archbishopric of Toulouse was a benefice with a large income, and in the pope's eyes Foix was too close to the king of France, who, according to him, would not fail to receive indirectly the dividends of this benefice. Henry III and Gregory XIII also disagreed concerning the granting of benefices vacant in the Court of Rome. The pope insisted on enjoying his prerogatives and naming the recipients of benefices himself, whereas his predecessor had promised the king of France the privilege of assigning these benefices. The pope's argument was not without foundation, because Henry III could very well make use of Foix to increase his kingdom's revenues. If we consider, for example, the church of Narbonne, we see that Foix had promised to pay back to the crown half the pensions and benefices produced by that prebend. But this benefice became vacant *in curia*, and the pope reserved the right to name a successor of his choice, or at least to approve him with the necessary bulls. After Narbonne, the archbishopric of Lyon eluded Foix for similar reasons. It was a question of money, but with official motives of a political and religious order.

Confronted by these interminable obstacles, Foix showed his frustration and communicated it to the queen mother. The royal entourage then recommended that he return to France and patiently await his confirmation as archbishop of Toulouse. It was during these negotiations that Montaigne was considered as an interim ambassador to replace Chasteigner. It was a question of finding a man who could provide a transition while Paul de Foix withdrew. In fact, the nuncio Dandino secretly thought that once Foix was in France it would be possible to offer him a benefice of lesser importance. During the winter of 1580, Foix fell ill

and informed his entourage that he would not be able to leave Rome. He preferred to await his nomination as archbishop of Toulouse in Rome, under the
eyes of Gregory XIII. Without success, Henry III repeatedly tried to have his
ambassador in Rome, Chasteigner, intervene to get Foix confirmed. Henry III's
correspondence with the pope and with Chasteigner in early 1581 shows the
king's repeated efforts to obtain the archbishopric of Toulouse for Paul de Foix.
Gregory XIII did not yield to the pressure, and his obstinacy ultimately worked
to the disadvantage of Montaigne.

A short time later, in early April 1581, not long before he left for Paris, where
he had just been named, the nuncio Giovanni Battista Castelli received the following instructions from the cardinal of Como:

> Your lordship must be informed about the affair concerning M. de Foix in order
> to make a suitable response in the event that Their Majesties speak to you on this
> question. You must know that this gentleman was examined by the Inquisition
> several years ago because he was suspected of heresy. It is true that he was cleared
> of these suspicions here in Rome; he was exonerated and the case is closed. But it
> emerges that the King would like Our Lord [the pope] to name him at the head of
> the archbishopric of Toulouse, and His Holiness thinks that, because of these sus-
> picions that have fallen on him, suspicions that were not without importance,
> there can be no question of sending him to a diocese that is so distinguished and
> perhaps the most Catholic in all of France. Moreover, His Holiness has been asked
> by certain notable persons in that place not to give his accord. For that reason, the
> King, and especially his Mother, have sometimes complained about this exclusion,
> and have done all they could to obtain the appointment. Our Lord [the pope] has
> suggested that if the King wanted to name him in a diocese in the region around
> Paris, he would very willingly consent. Thus the negotiations are suspended while
> M. de Foix remains in Rome. You could show all this information to Monsignor
> Dandino, and ask him, who is a person very well-informed about these events,
> advice concerning the questions you will have to deal with.
>
> May God Our Lord protect you during your journey and give you all prosperity.
> ROME, AT THE APOSTOLIC PALACE, APRIL 1, 1581.
> *The Cardinal of Como.*[179]

Another letter from Dandino to the Cardinal of Como, dated March 27,
1581, relates why Cardinal Birague—a fierce opponent of the Protestants—
thought the replacement of Chasteigner in Rome inopportune.[180] Two days
later, still according to Dandino,[181] the queen mother once again begged Gregory XIII to send the bulls for Toulouse to Paul de Foix. Faced with this increased pressure, and against the advice of several of his cardinals, the pope fi-

nally agreed to accept Foix as the French ambassador in Rome. It was assuredly a compromise, and a lesser evil in his eyes. During this time, Montaigne and Chasteigner were patiently waiting in Rome. Henry III and Catherine de Medici did not agree on Chasteigner's successor, the king favoring Montaigne (and later Maugiron), the queen mother, Foix.[xi]

At the beginning of April, the king and the queen mother changed their strategy and decided to concentrate their efforts on the nomination of Paul de Foix as ambassador. They finally authorized Chasteigner to return immediately to France, thus forcing the hand of the pontiff, who now had to choose between giving Foix the archbishopric of Toulouse or accepting him as the ambassador to the Holy See. The pope decided to that it would be easier and wiser to keep an enemy close to him. Montaigne was probably informed of these developments around April 10, at the time of Chasteigner's departure. Chasteigner did not have to be coaxed, and he left Rome almost immediately for France.

On April 21, 1581, the king wrote to the pontiff to inform him that Chasteigner had returned to France and that he could now designate his successor: "We have deemed it very appropriate for our service to give this title and office to our Cousin the Sieur de Foix, who is already there, so that the aforesaid office, the most worthy and honorable of all, may not remain empty."[182] Henry III then implored the pope to accept this nomination. The same day, a letter with almost exactly the same content was sent by Catherine de Medici. In this letter, Paul de Foix is presented as a "personage very commendable for the notable virtues and great experience he has in handling the greatest and most important affairs."[183] A regular courier could cover the 1,100 kilometers separating Paris from Rome in twelve to fifteen days,[xii] but a rapid messenger could make the trip in about nine or ten days.[184] Urgent royal messages took between ten and twelve days to reach Rome. The pope was officially informed of this decision between May 3 and May 6, 1581. Paul de Foix received his nomination on May 11 and obtained his credentials two days later. On May 15, 1581, he thanked Henry III: "Sire, I received on Thursday morning, the eleventh day of this month, the dispatch by which it has pleased Your Majesty to honor me with the title and office of ordinary Ambassador in Rome."[185]

An audience with the pope was immediately requested, and on Friday evening Foix was received, together with the French cardinals. He was officially introduced to His Holiness by the cardinal of Sens and "received by [him] as honorably and graciously as could be desired, and as befits the grandeur and dignity of Your Majesty."[186] Without any preamble, the pope told Foix that he

[xi] See his letter of April 12, 1581.

[xii] Paul de Foix says for example that he received on July 6, "by ordinary post," a letter that the king had sent him on June 19.

"had already understood the mission [his] Majesty had given [him]." The matter was therefore settled. The king had a new ambassador in Rome, but Foix was still waiting for his confirmation as archbishop of Toulouse. The pope took advantage of the opportunity to clarify his position regarding the new ambassador. Accepting Foix as the representative of French interests at the Holy See, he asked Dandino to transmit to the queen mother the "very important" reasons that prevented him from granting the archbishopric of Toulouse to Paul de Foix.[187] Foix had become an ambassador for lack of being archbishop of Toulouse. It was only after the nuncio Castelli's recommendation, in 1582, that the pope finally yielded and confirmed Foix as archbishop of Toulouse on November 5, 1582. In fact, Foix never set foot in Toulouse, because he died in Rome on May 12, 1584, eighteen months after having received his archbishopric and more than ten years after Charles IX first requested this benefice of the pope.

We can imagine Montaigne's reaction and his disappointment when he learned in early April that his stay in Rome—almost five months—had led to no employment. Sensing that Foix's nomination as ambassador was imminent, he chose to leave Rome. On March 22, 1581, he had visited with Foix "the seven pilgrim churches"[xiii] in Rome: a last look at Rome with the man who had been chosen at his expense. Whereas the guides of the time recommended taking three days to visit Rome and its seven churches,[188] Montaigne and Foix completed the tour in a little more than five hours. What did they say to each other? Did Foix already know that he was going to be named ordinary ambassador? Since March 17, Chasteigner had no longer been the official ambassador, and their conversation must have centered on the nomination of the next ordinary or interim ambassador. We can imagine this meeting of two men who were bitter for different reasons: Foix, because he had never been confirmed as archbishop of Toulouse (whereas he had been hoping to become a cardinal), and Montaigne, because this ambassadorship he had so much desired since the summer of 1580 had escaped him.

Nothing more keeping him in Rome, Montaigne decided to leave the city on April 19 and make a pilgrimage to Our Lady of Loreto.[189] He stayed there from April 23 to April 26, 1581, performing his devotions and depositing an ex-voto—this was a veritable local industry—in the Santa Casa, as was then the custom. The walls of this place of worship were covered with offerings, and Montaigne had to use his fame (he says)—and a significant sum of money—to have an ex-voto hung on it.

[xiii] At that time, visiting the "seven pilgrim churches" was (as it still is today) a traditional urban tour in Rome. It includes four major basilicas: Saint John Lateran, Saint Peter's, Saint Paul Outside the Walls, and Santa Maria Maggiore, and three minor basilicas: San Lorenzo fuori le mura, Santa Croce in Gerusalemme, and San Sebastiano fuori le mura.

In Guyenne, the situation had changed considerably—for the worse—between February and May 1581, and Montaigne apparently had no intention of returning too quickly to his lands or to Bordeaux. The letters from the ambassadors testified to the political concerns that followed the war waged by the Prince of Condé in Languedoc and Guyenne. For instance, on February 17, 1581, Du Ferrier gave a pessimistic assessment of the military situation: "For a few days, we had great hopes that the peace declared in France would put an end to the misfortunes here: but this last message bore contrary news, and [informed us] that the Prince of Condé was fighting in Languedoc and Guyenne."[190] Military conflicts were spreading.

Following the loss of the ambassadorship, Montaigne received two consolation prizes: letters patent granting him Roman citizenship and the office of mayor of Bordeaux. Rome and Paris were making a gesture. In early April, he had little more to expect from his stay in the Eternal City. The call of Rome had been transformed into a professional fiasco. When he heard talk about Maugiron, he wondered if the king had changed his mind. Shortly afterward, he understood that Paul de Foix was again a contender for the ambassadorship in Rome. Ten months outside Guyenne had caused him to be forgotten by the inner circles of power, and his name had ended up being discarded. It was not easy to remain close to the princes and the pinnacle of the hierarchy of the political elites.[191] To leave the royal entourage and the Court was to risk falling into oblivion. Confronted by increasingly numerous and pressing demands, promises not kept were common at the Court, where Henry III had a reputation for changing his mind. Paul de Foix was an old friend, and the Foix family had more than once favored Montaigne's political career. Montaigne chose to quietly withdraw, frustrated by his unfortunate experience in Rome. Did he have any other choice?

What Montaigne was to remember about Rome was that its chief grandeur lay in its "appearance of devotion" or "show of religion."[192] The religious ardor of the common people, or least their fascination with the perfectly orchestrated ceremonies and processions, made him aware that the inclination toward rites and religious fervor must not be confused with faith. Montaigne shared this view with Maldonat, who, like him and contrary to appearances, thought that the common people were more devout in France than in Rome.

Roman Citizen

When he left Rome on April 19, Montaigne had not yet been elected mayor of Bordeaux (the election took place on August 1). On the other hand, five weeks earlier, on March 13, a papal bull granted him the title of Roman citizenship.[xiv] He remained in Rome until he had officially received these patent letters, which were "delivered to him" on April 5.[193] It was only on that date that he learned of the bull conferring Roman citizenship on him.[194] Instead of being an ambassador, he had to be content with an honorable mention as a citizen of a civilization that had long since disappeared; his political victory referred to another time, another Rome.

This mark of recognition, avidly sought by Montaigne, was perhaps the only positive aspect of his sojourn in Rome. It was he who had petitioned the Roman Senate to grant it to him:

> Most Illustrious Lords—Petitioning your Most Illustrious Lordships of this illustrious People to be admitted among you as a Citizen, I come to beg you to count me, along with my children, among your fellow Citizens, and to grant me the privileges connected with that title, knowing that I shall pay the full price, with singular gratitude, by offering Your Most Illustrious Lordships and this illustrious People to devote my own life to their service. From my domicile, March 11, 1581.—Of your Most Illustrious Lordships the Servant, Michel de Montaigne, knight of the order of the Most Christian King and ordinary gentleman of his Chamber.[195]

This *supplica* (figure 11) had been prepared in advance, following a well-established procedure, and Montaigne had engaged in the appropriate lobbying to obtain this distinguished honor. The petition to the Roman Senate was a mere formality and followed a short, banal formula without offering any details regarding the beneficiary's competencies or accomplishments—except for his status as a gentleman and his title of knight of the Order of Saint Michael—but

---

[xiv] In the library of the Arsenal in Paris (ms. 2152) there is a copy of this bull, translated on parchment, but this must not be confused with the original. It is simply a translation made a century later—more precisely, in 1664 (or 1669?)—certainly at the behest of someone who was or claimed to be Montaigne's descendant. In fact, the original (reproduced by Montaigne in his *Essais*) gives "*ipsum posterosque in Romanam Civitatem adscribi*," whereas the French version paraphrases this, reading "together with all his children, nephews, descendants, and successors in perpetuity and eternally." The names of the Roman officials at the bottom of the translation are different from those found on the bull of 1581. A descendant of Montaigne who wanted to appropriate the benefit in perpetuity of Roman citizenship probably had the original translated and authenticated by the Roman authorities. To complicate a little further the enigma of this document, the copy in the Arsenal is certified by Matthias Van der Spict, the burgomaster-alderman of Brussels. The coat of arms reproduced at the beginning of this document bears the same elements as Montaigne's, but they are arranged differently. The original of this certificate of citizenship is preserved in Rome: *Registro di Privilegi di Cittadini Romani Creati*, Archivio Storico Capitolino, cred. VI, vol. 115, f. 189r–v.

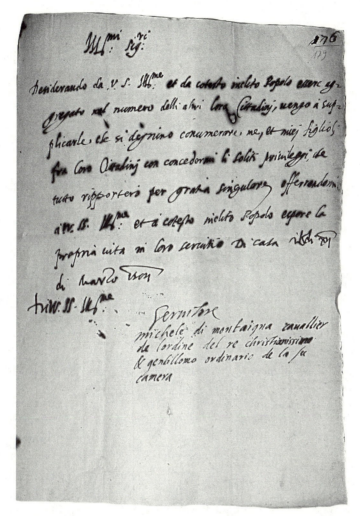

FIGURE 11. Citizenship *supplica*. Image courtesy of Archivio Storico Capitolino, Rome.

the decision was not made on that basis. If Montaigne did not elaborate on the reasons that might allow him to hope that his request would be favorably considered, that is certainly because he had already received assurances, not from the municipal oligarchy but from the Roman *curia*. We know that Montaigne expected to "serve" the city for a time in the service of the king of France. His sojourn in Rome was to be of moderate length, far beyond that of an ordinary tourist. Montaigne was a French gentleman on a mission, and it was on that basis that he hoped to receive this honorific reward.

Thanks to a skillful campaign that he reported, Montaigne obtained what he hoped, because on the recommendation of Orazio Massimi, Marzio Ceccio, and Alessandro Muti, conservators of the city of Rome with respect to citizenship, the author of the *Essais* succeeded in adding another title to his recent collection of certificates of nobility and various honors. Throughout his life, he was to retain for Rome an affection that he considered even equal to that he had for Paris: "the Rome and Paris that I have in my soul."[196] He does not conceal that he schemed to obtain Roman citizenship: "However, I sought in every way and used all my five natural senses to win for myself the title of Roman citizen,"[197] and admits that it was not easy: "I found the task a difficult one."[198] This was a rather extraordinary honor for a foreigner. Moreover, Montaigne did not necessarily meet all the criteria for this kind of recognition. But the fact that he had overcome the administrative complications was also proof of his political influence and reputation, which was beginning to spread in the best Roman circles. In the past, this rare privilege had been accorded to only a few foreign visitors. Montaigne boasts of not having had any acquaintance of his or any French authority to intervene on his behalf, because it was solely thanks to the direct intervention of the pope's majordomo, Alessandro Musotti,[xv] who was also prefect of the Apostolic Palaces and "who had always been extraordinarily kind to me,"[199] that Montaigne received this outmoded but highly symbolic title, which was reserved for a small number of gentlemen, artists, and persons of great reputation.

What did obtaining such a title mean? How many individuals received the same favor in the early 1580s? The answers to these questions will allow us to evaluate the symbolic importance to be accorded to this event reported by Montaigne. From a historical point of view, the records in the municipal archives of Rome[200] reveal that at the beginning of the fourteenth century Pope Benedict XI issued bulls of banishment from the city of Rome on grounds of schism and heresy. Thus one could lose one's Roman citizenship for purely dogmatic reasons or even for having harmed the welfare of the Roman people. For example, a decree issued by the Public Council and dated December 11, 1565, proclaims that Count Ippolito da Sessa, the "inventor" of a monopoly on grain mills (*monopolio delle mole*) in the city—a regulation relating to the possession of a mill—who was "for that reason hated by the Roman people" is sentenced, along with his family and his heirs, to be deprived of the title of Roman citizen, and to "perpetual dishonor." The decree also stipulated that his effigy was to be painted throughout the city with "his feet in the air and a millstone around his neck."[201] Roman citizenship was therefore not a title to be taken lightly.

[xv] Montaigne gives the name of "Filippo Musotti"—the former secretary of Cardinal Seripando, and then the secretary of the cardinal of Lorraine—but he is certainly referring to Filippo's brother, Alessandro Musotti, Pope Gregory XIII's majordomo, who had been named bishop of Imola on December 9, 1579.

The criteria for granting Roman citizenship changed over the centuries.[202] In the fifteenth century, most of the requests were strictly administrative, because they concerned individuals who, although they lived in other cities, claimed Roman citizenship by arguing that they had been born in the Eternal City. Many requests were refused because the documents submitted did not establish past residence in Rome. At the very beginning of the sixteenth century, the rules for obtaining Roman citizenship changed significantly, and the title became more symbolic than based on true residence. Starting in the 1540s, it was considered a purely honorific reward. A large number of Italian gentlemen took advantage of this new interpretation of the status of Roman citizen to receive this distinction. A decree issued by the Secret Council, dated April 30, 1579, prohibited members of the clergy to become Roman citizens. Confirmed by the Public Council, this decree reserved the honorific title for members of the civil and lay society.[203] As if to remind people of his jurisdiction in Rome, the pope nonetheless continued to reward a small number of prelates by granting them Roman citizenship.

It also became increasingly common to grant citizenship to artists, chiefly poets, humanists, painters, and architects—for instance, the historian Paulo Giovio in 1524, the painters Michelangelo in 1537 and Titian in 1545, the architect and sculptor Guglielmo Della Porta in 1546, and also the poet and Latinist Fabio Spoletano and the historian Carlo Sigonio, who, along with other scholars, had contributed to Rome's fame. The largest contingent of new citizens remained, however, nobles, including the foreign ambassadors in residence in Rome. In this category we can note several diplomats and ambassadors, such as Ambroise de Gumpenberg, who represented Bavaria's interests at the Court of Rome in the late 1540s, Lourenço Pires de Távora, Portugal's ambassador to the Holy See in 1561, and André Guillart, lord of L'Isle, who was France's ambassador in Rome from June 1561 to March 1563. In 1576, it was the turn of Bartolomé d'Olalla, representing the king of Spain in Rome, to have this honor conferred on him. At the pope's request, and without going through the city's Public Council, Roman citizenship was sometimes accorded to the emissaries of foreign powers who resided in Rome.

Apparently well informed about this tradition, which since the beginning of the century had allowed a limited number of diplomats to request Roman citizenship, in early 1581 Montaigne had high hopes of benefiting in his turn from this purely symbolic sign of recognition. He could adduce his membership in the nobility thanks to his titles of knight of the king's order and gentleman of his chamber. That is how Montaigne's request should be interpreted, because he planned to spend several months, or even one or two years, in Rome. Foreigners had in particular to prove that they were residing in Rome for at least three-quarters of the year, that they were engaged in a professional activity, and that they were completely integrated into the life of the city. This requirement of residence or of property ownership was not, however, made for honorary citizens like Montaigne. His petition must be understood instead in a tradition of famous humanists who sought this privilege that would bring them closer to ancient Rome.

On this point the case of Hubert Goltzius (1526–1583), a humanist scholar, painter, engraver, historian, editor, and numismatist is revealing. Fourteen years before Montaigne, on May 9, 1567, Goltzius had been made a Roman citizen[204] as a reward for his history of the Roman emperors based on their coins: *Fastos magistratvvm et trivmphorvm Romanorvm ab vrbe condita ad Avgvsti obitvm ex antiqvis tam nvmismatvm qvam marmorvm monvmentis restitvtos* (1566).[xvi] Like Montaigne, he reproduced the complete text of his certificate of citizenship in his work *Sicilia et Magna Graecia* (1576) and again in his *Thesaurus huberrimus* (1579).[205] Learning of this practice that consisted in honoring those who had contributed to the fame of the ancient city, Montaigne could have thought that his own publications, though far from being in the humanist tradition of a Goltzius, might perhaps help him obtain this title.

Starting in the 1520s, the Roman Senate accorded between twenty and thirty citizenships per year. This figure remained more or less stable between 1530 and 1580. The records reveal that 1,104 Roman citizenships were granted between 1560 and 1608, for an average of twenty-three a year, though some years there were more.[206] Among the fortunate elect, we find mainly Italian nobles; foreigners represent a very small minority. For instance, we find forty-three Roman citizenships awarded for the year 1579, and thirty-eight in 1580, including only two foreigners, who were apparently diplomats. In 1581, the year in which Montaigne was made a Roman citizen, forty-five citizenships were granted. That was a good year. For that year, a bull dated January 13 typically awards citizenship to three noble Italians: a Bolognese (Ridolfo Bonfiglioli), a Piedmontese from Turin (Ercole Arcatori), and a Venetian (Antonio Stella). In March, Montaigne received this honor in his turn. The Roman Senate's report for the grant of citizenship to Montaigne has been preserved in Rome's municipal archives.[207] On the same date, the city's Public Council conferred this same reward on eight Italian gentlemen. Again, on April 24 another document issued by the Public Council confirmed citizenship for six more Italians.

Finally, Montaigne was the only Frenchman to receive this title between 1577 and 1585. Several Spaniards and Portuguese obtained Roman citizenship

---

[xvi] Montaigne might have had a book by Goltzius in his library: *C. Ivlivs Caesar sive historiae imperatorum caesarumque romanorum ex antiqvis nvmismatibvs restitutae liber primvs* (Bruges, 1567). This copy, presented in a rare bookseller's catalog in 2011, includes Montaigne's ex libris above the engraved title. However, doubts persist regarding the authenticity of Montaigne's signature.

in the 1570s and 1580s, but very few French did. After Montaigne, we must wait until 1585 to see two more Frenchmen rewarded in this way: first a certain "Helias Magnoli Gallus" (January 1585), whom we have not been able to identify, and then Nicolas de Pellevé—"Nicolaus Pervue Gallus" (December 1585)—a creature of the cardinal of Lorraine who was one of the heads of the League; he was named archbishop of Sens in 1563 and had been a cardinal since 1570. During his stay in Rome, Montaigne had met Pellevé and had even dined at his home along with the young d'Estissac. He had gone to visit the Jesuits in his company. The cardinal was highly esteemed by the pope for his ultramontanism favoring the spiritual and jurisdictional primacy of the pope over the political power of kings and princes. With this Catholic zeal—at least for the Holy See—Montaigne was in good company. We can then understand why his sojourn in Rome might have seemed desirable to the pontiff's delegates, because Montaigne was considered an irreproachable Catholic. In a way, obtaining this honorific reward could seem to be proof of his accreditation by the pontiff and the Roman *curia*. The author of the *Essais* is justified in describing this event as completely remarkable and extraordinary for a person of his status and rank.

The title of honorary citizen of Rome was generally granted to persons universally recognized for their artistic or cultural contribution, to artists, scholars, or diplomats esteemed for their virtue and irreproachable probity, and it was granted with the goal of increasing the prestige of the city of Rome. We can understand Montaigne's pride; he rightly saw this decision made by the Roman Senate as exceptional and an extreme mark of a great privilege received by a Frenchman sojourning in Rome. His noble origins and numerous honorific titles had been invoked during the Roman Senate's deliberations, because it was principally as a representative of the king of France that Roman citizenship was awarded to him. Contrary to the case of Goltzius, we find in the privilege issued by the Roman Senate no mention of his writings or of any scholarly contribution. If Goltzius symbolized the republican model of humanist erudition in the service of the city and the Roman people, Montaigne received a strictly political recognition. We have noted that the privilege accorded Montaigne is more grandiloquent than usual, even repetitive, imprecise, and generic. Whereas the record of Goltzius's privilege occupies more than a page and is relatively detailed, praising his merits as a humanist and his contribution to the fame of the Eternal City, the record of Montaigne's privilege consists of less than six lines and expatiates hardly at all on the gentleman's competencies. His competence has to do strictly with his nobility. There is, for instance, no mention of his rights as a Roman citizen, as if the civilian government of the city wanted to express its disagreement with a reward imposed from above, that is, by the religious authority. Montaigne's case brings out a tension between the Church and the municipal administration, which did not have the same conception of this honorific title. We know that Montaigne had gone through the pope's major-domo, but he had nonetheless insisted on addressing his request to the representatives of the city's civilian government.

Originally distinct from the religious authority, in Rome the *civitas* gradually came to fall under the competence of the *curia* which, in Montaigne's time, was increasingly using its influence to reward members of the Italian nobility and a few foreigners who met the same aristocratic and political requirements.[208] Gregory XIII's interference in the city Council's deliberations was frequent, and in this case it indicates that Montaigne was "in favor" with the pontiff. For example, the pope granted him several private audiences and showed a certain indulgence with regard to the reproaches made by the "censors" who had glanced through his book. The pope may even have intervened directly in this grant of citizenship to a foreigner who was to represent the king of France's interests in Rome. Gregory XIII accorded great importance to these attributions of citizenship. Thus in 1582 he attended in person several ceremonies awarding Roman citizenship. It is likely that without the pope's intervention Montaigne would never have received this title of Roman citizen. The record of the privilege written by the Public Council shows—in a veiled way, of course—a disagreement with the pope's interference and his policy of attributing Roman citizenship to gentlemen whose cultural contribution to the city of Rome was far from clear.

Despite the intermediaries Montaigne called upon and the political choices he made to obtain Roman citizenship, it remains that he did receive what he hoped. He had just demonstrated his good reputation with the pontiff and the *curia*, even if he had annoyed the civil authorities who had accorded him this honor without praising his literary or cultural accomplishments. Our French traveler's modesty was set aside for the occasion. Not exempt from a vanity that he nonetheless repeatedly denounced, Montaigne was more than a little proud of being a citizen of a city that represented in his view the best that Antiquity had achieved in matters of letters and culture: "Among [Fortune's] empty favors there is none that so pleases that silly humor in me which feeds upon it, as an authentic bull of Roman citizenship, which was granted to me lately when I was there, pompous in seals and gilt letters, and granted with all gracious liberality."[209] Montaigne was a noble in France and a bourgeois in Italy: "Being a citizen of no city, I am very pleased to be one of the noblest city that ever was or ever will be."[210] Recognized by a monarchy and by a republic, he could pride himself on being above simple questions of governance or political regime. Lucid regarding the reproaches that might be made against him on this subject, he notes in his *Journal*: "This title is now altogether a vain one, nevertheless I felt much pleasure from the possession of the same."[211] However, this judgment is belied by the energy he expended to receive this proof of honor for a man who was intending to take up residence in Rome to serve his king and his country. We can imagine that this argument might even have been able to help him convince Alessandro Musotti. Montaigne took refuge in Antiquity after seeing himself shoved aside by the political actors of his time. In a way, the Roman bull expressed a redemptive return to an outdated political ideal.[212]

Well aware of this excess of vanity, and like Goltzius before him, Montaigne reproduced the Roman bull in his chapter "Of vanity" (III: 9) in the *Essais* of 1588:

> Considering that, by ancient custom and practice, those men have ever been adopted among us with ardor and eagerness, who, distinguished in virtue and nobility, have been greatly useful and ornamental to our Republic, or might be so in the future; We, deeply moved the example and authority of our ancestors, resolve that we should imitate and follow this noble custom. Wherefore, since the most illustrious Michel de Montaigne, Knight of the Order of Saint Michael, and Gentleman of the Chamber in ordinary to the Most Christian King, is most zealous for the Roman name, and, by the honor and distinction of his family and his own virtuous merits, most worthy to be admitted to Roman citizenship by the supreme judgment and will of the Senate and People of Rome: it has pleased the Senate and People of Rome that the most illustrious Michel de Montaigne, adorned with all qualities and very dear to this noble people, should be inscribed as a Roman citizen, himself and his posterity, and invested with all the advantages and honors enjoyed by those who were born Citizens and Patricians of Rome, or who have been made such by the best of rights. Wherein the Senate and People of Rome consider that they do not so much confer the Rights of Citizenship on him as a gift, as pay them as debt, nor do him more benefit than they receive from him, who, in accepting this Citizenship, gives a singular ornament and honor to the City itself. Which Senatus-Consultus these Conservators have caused to be transcribed by the secretaries of the Roman Senate and People and deposited in the archives of the Capitol, and have had this act drawn up and sealed with the common seal of the City. In the year 2331 since the foundation of Rome, A.D. 1581, 13th of March.[213]

We should finally note that the Latin text given by Montaigne is in fact the same as the one granted Cosimo de Medici ("*Cosmus Francesci de Medicis in nobilissima Florentia civitate ortus*"), with one significant omission: "*cuius studio Reipub. Nostrae adiuta in dies augeatur.*" Cosimo de Medici had been made a Roman citizen on the same date as Montaigne, along with Giorgio and Giuseppe Giustiniani, Giuseppe Ferri, Giovanni Rocchieri, Giacomo Ausazza, Angelo Rainieri, Ermete Cavalletti and Bonifazio Forlai.[214]

We see here that the *Essais* are also the chronicle of a public life. Anachronistically, Montaigne obtained an honorable mention worthy of another time. The "most illustrious Michel de Montaigne" was destined to enjoy all the honors and advantages reserved for the patricians of Rome, but the city would not see him represent the interests of his king in a foreign land.

The *Essais* "Castigated and Brought into Harmony with the Opinions of the Monkish Doctors"

Montaigne writes that when he first entered Rome on November 30, 1580, his book was "taken" by the customs authorities. Much has been written about the seizure of his book and the "censure" that followed. On these points, a few false ideas have to be rectified. It is true that since 1569 the inspection of books brought into Rome had been much stricter, and more power had been given to the Inquisition, which had agents to perform these inspections. Nonetheless, a significant number of forbidden books coming from Germany and Switzerland were available in Italian bookshops,[215] and the pontifical authorities had great difficulty keeping prohibited books out of Rome. Once they had been seized, the books were usually destroyed at the customs office. The agents examined travelers' baggage and compared the titles of the books they found in it with a list of prohibited books, to ensure that no forbidden book entered the city of seven hills. The *Essais* were obviously not on this list, and it is therefore improbable that it was seized when Montaigne entered Rome.

This episode, reported by his secretary, has to be analyzed in detail. Denying that there was as much freedom in Rome as in Venice, Montaigne noted that

> his own boxes had been searched [*visités*] by the tax-officers on entering the city and turned over even to the smallest articles of apparel, while in the other towns of Italy the officers had been satisfied by the presentation of the boxes for search; that in addition they had seized all the books they found there with the view of inspecting them, over which task they spent so much time that anyone in different case might well have given up the books as lost. Again the regulations were so extraordinary that one of these books, the "Hours of our Lady," having been printed at Paris and not in Rome, was looked at with suspicion, as were certain books against heretics by German doctors who, in argument, happened to make mention of the errors of their opponents. At this juncture he congratulated himself

over his good fortune in that, having no premonition of the search which awaited him, and having passed through Germany where forbidden books abound, he had not brought away with him a single one these, notwithstanding the curious interest which often possessed him with regard to divers of them. Certain gentlemen from Germany informed him that had any such volume been found, he would have paid the penalty by losing all his books.[216]

Montaigne's books were examined, but not seized (perhaps with the exception of Simler's *République des Suisses*). In the worst-case scenario, the compromising books would simply have been seized (and destroyed).

Critics have emphasized that the *Essais* was seized, whereas the secretary himself tells us that the book was returned to its author. In fact, if his *Essais* was "returned" *later*, that was probably because Montaigne himself had submitted it for the approval of the religious authorities in Rome. He wanted to have his book validated by the competent authorities as soon as he arrived in Rome and took the initiative to ensure that he would not have troubles later on for having published it. He had learned the lesson of his translation of Raymond Sebond's *Theologia naturalis* and of the edition of La Boétie's works, and had no intention of seeing his diplomatic career compromised by a book that had not completely triumphed over Roman censorship. On that subject, more than four months after his arrival in Rome, it is no longer the secretary but Montaigne himself who says on March 20: "This evening they brought back to me the volume of my *Essais*, castigated and brought into harmony with the opinions of the monkish doctors."[217] Montaigne mentions Josias Simler's *République des Suisses* (in Innocent Gentillet's translation): "They kept back my copy of 'The History of the Swiss,' translated into French, simply because they had found out that the translator was a heretic, though his name did not appear anywhere in the volume. It is wonderful what a wide knowledge they have of men and foreign lands."[218] In the same sentence, Montaigne also mentions Sebond in association with Simler's book, which seems to have been "held" *against him* rather than confiscated or seized. This passage is rather ambiguous and contradictory when it is compared to the statements made by the secretary, who says nothing about any book being seized and even emphasizes that "not a single" forbidden book was found in Montaigne's baggage.

It is probable that Montaigne himself sought the pontifical administration's approval of his book. In addition, contrary to what has been written on this subject,[219] it was not the *Congregatio pro Sancta Inquisitione* that carried out the first "censure" (it was more a reader's report than censorship in the modern sense of the term), but rather the *Congregatio pro indice librorum prohibitorum* (the Congregation of the Index),[xvii] which apparently was not in the habit of providing reports on books belonging to foreigners passing through Rome.[220] Planning on staying in Rome for a relatively long time, Montaigne deemed it preferable to have his book accepted by the competent authorities. He was prepared to respond to possible objections. Taking the initiative and anticipating potential problems was now part of his activity as a writer and editor.

On Montaigne's recommendation, his *Essais* were therefore read by a *consultor*, in this case a French *frater*, because neither the master of the Apostolic Palace, Sisto Fabri, nor the other members of the Congregation of the Index were sufficiently versed in Montaigne's language to be able to provide a report on the book.[221] The texts (the reading reports) of this first *censura* were recently discovered in the Vatican archives by Peter Godman. Montaigne was confronted with the first censure on March 20, 1581, by the master of the Apostolic Palace, probably in the presence of the secretary of the Index, Giovanni Battista Lanci.[222] Eighteen points (objections) were communicated to him in the first stage (first "censure") by these two "monkish doctors." The remarks made by the first *consultor* were all based on specific passages in the *Essais*, because on each occasion the page number of the first edition is given alongside the objections made. The *consultor* criticized Montaigne's profane language, his references to the philosopher's stone and to Machiavelli's *Discorsi*, and his mention of the names of Théodore de Bèze, Buchanan, and the "buon Marot," all of them heretics. More seriously, the *consultor* noted (point no. 16 on this list of objections): "And in the first book, on p. 180: he says that theology teaches us neither to act well nor to think well."[223]

When the censure was presented to him verbally, Montaigne considered these objections arbitrary and unfounded. It was a matter of incompetence on the part of the ecclesiastical authorities. He accused the French monk who had "corrected" his *Essais* of not having understood many ironic passages in his book. His arguments were apparently well received by the master of the Apostolic Palace, since the master, probably at Montaigne's request, ordered a second reading of the *Essais*, giving the new *consultor* precise instructions, notably concerning the *Essais'* irony.

Three weeks later, Montaigne was called back to the Apostolic Palace, and Sisto Fabri informed him regarding the second reading (second "censure") of his book. The second *consultor* had reexamined point by point the text of the first censure and confirmed the presence of ironic passages not detected by the first reader. Thus the fourth objection (concerning a passage on p. 30 in the 1580 edition) was the object of a clarification that adopts the arguments Montaigne

---

[xvii] The Congrégation of the Index did not meet for more than a year, from February 28, 1581, to April 5, 1582.

had advanced: "The author will perhaps reply that it is with irony that he mocks Parisians, but even if that were so, this passage is very dangerous, because of this ugly question that is so ugly and this irony that is so hidden."[224] We see that Montaigne had defended himself on this point by arguing that he had deliberately chosen irony to express the contrary of what was written.

After a second reading requested by Montaigne, the second *consultor*, though he confirmed some of the first censor's objections, nonetheless admitted that irony was indeed present in many passages in the *Essais*. For example, in the chapter on "A custom of the island of Cea" (II: 3), Montaigne writes, regarding women who committed suicide to avoid being raped and dishonored: "In truth, these cruelties are not worthy of the gentle ways of France; and so, thank God, our atmosphere has been thoroughly purged of them by that man's good advice. Enough for them to say 'no' while doing it, following the rule of our good Marot."[225] The first *consultor* had been incapable of grasping the irony of this passage and had simply concluded that Montaigne approved of Marot, a heretical poet: "And page 32: he approves a motto of the good Marot and calls it good, granting that he is a heretic—These authors are either heretics or not very good."[226] Montaigne complained to Sisto Fabri about this abusive interpretation whereas the passage mentioned was obviously ironic and could not be read otherwise. The second *consultor* partly confirmed Montaigne's objection, moderating it somewhat: "I have already said that this passage can be considered as irony, but perhaps not everyone would do the same."[227] The passage in question could be interpreted ironically, but as the censor remarks, it is also true that all readers would not read it in that way, and that is why it becomes reprehensible. The second *consultor* raises here the essential question of irony and satire in Montaigne's work.[228] This incident shows at least that the author of the *Essais* was fully aware of his stylistic effects and that he had to explain them to the censors that he himself had convoked.

As for the "Apology for Raymond Sebond," the first *consultor* made a single, very general objection that refers only to the title Montaigne gave to this chapter: "And chapter 12: he defends Raymond Sebond."[229] We can imagine Montaigne's response; he justified himself to the master of the Apostolic Palace by reminding him that Sebond was not on the *Index* and that only the preface to the *Theologia naturalis* was now condemned. Moreover, wasn't that why he had proposed to explain this preface in his apology for Sebond? Once again, the second *consultor* confirmed Montaigne's view: "It is true that he defends Raymond Sebond, but in this author only the preface is prohibited."[230] Montaigne showed himself to be better versed in theology than this poor French monk who had read his *Essais* incompetently, without grasping the text's rhetorical effects or its ironic import, and being unaware of the changes made to the *Index* between 1559 and 1564. Sure of his defense, Montaigne waved away all the objections that could be made to him regarding this chapter in the second book. On the whole, the strategy that consisted in anticipating the possible censorship of his book had worked relatively well.

Before leaving Rome, Montaigne made a last visit to Sisto Fabri. Paul de Foix had just been named ambassador, and the translator of Sebond wanted to present his greetings to the master of the Apostolic Palace before setting out on the roads of Italy. In the course of this second visit, Fabri told him about the second *consultor*'s report, and reproached him for making numerous references to Fortune in the *Essais*—an objection the first *consultor* had not made. In this subsequent audience with the Holy See's theologians, Montaigne pretended to be naive when Sebond's name came up: "they told me the preface of the aforesaid books was condemned,"[231] he reports in his journal. This attitude contrasts with the energy he had displayed in countering the criticisms made by the first *consultor*. Montaigne no longer felt like defending himself, because he now knew that he would not be staying in Rome very long. The post of ambassador had just escaped him, and he was about to leave the city. In his travel journal, he distinguished between the two "censures" of his *Essais*. The second audience (there may have been another one before this last session) in the Apostolic Palace is presented as a farewell visit, nothing more. On this occasion, he was assured that his book would not ultimately deserve any censure worthy of the name.

Montaigne even reports that he was asked to simply ignore the first *consultor*'s report:

> On the 15th of April I went to take leave of the Maestro del Sacro Palazzo and his associate. They begged me to pay no regard to the censures which had been passed upon my book; censures which, as certain Frenchmen had informed them, contained many ignorant statements; they declared that they honoured my purpose, my affection towards the Church, and my ability: that they rated my good breeding and conscientiousness highly enough to allow me at my own discretion to cut out of my book with my own hand, at the next reprinting of the same, any passages that might seem too plain spoken, and amongst others those remarks about Fortune.[232]

Montaigne was reassured: no severe reprimand had been officially expressed. He comments on this favorable outcome in his travel journal:

> It seemed to me that they were not ill pleased with me: moreover, to justify their careful examination of my book and their condemnation of the same in divers particulars, they instanced several contemporary books, written by cardinals and ecclesiastical personages of high repute, which had been

censured for blots of a like character, the good name of the author and the book itself having been left quite scatheless thereby.[233]

Excuses, points of detail; in short, Montaigne had not been subjected to any serious admonishment, and we must speak of a "warning" rather than a genuine censure of his *Essais*.[234] Now we can easily understand why he felt no obligation to delete or modify anything. This decision, he tells us, was left to his own discretion.

The "Apology for Raymond Sebond" had disturbed the theologians of the Congregation of the Index hardly at all, and Montaigne was in no danger of being officially condemned for his translation of the *Theologia naturalis*. In his view, all this was without great importance. A happy outcome for a somewhat risky venture onto the terrain of theology. Montaigne had recounted in a convincing way the "family history" of this translation and had amply justified his youthful work in the "Apology for Raymond Sebond." Apparently, his explanations and clarifications had been deemed sufficient. He had succeeded in convincing the Catholic theologians that through the mediation of Sebond he was fighting the Protestants' schism in his own way, and was using the Catalan theologian's text—and that of the *Essais*—against the atheists and heretics. Irony was his preferred weapon. He had benefited from the support of the pontiff, who had shown great benevolence toward him while he was in Rome.[235] His devotion to the Catholic Church had been recognized by those close to the pope and had allowed him to avoid having his book censured.

On April 15, 1581, Montaigne took leave of the master of the Apostolic Palace. He had refuted the eighteen points counted against him during his first interview with the master of the Apostolic Palace on March 20, 1581. During this second meeting, the pontifical administration recognized that the first *consultor*, a "French *frater*," had misread the *Essais* and lacked the theological competencies necessary to condemn the book. Our traveler had succeeded in demonstrating his good faith and even a certain skill in matters of theology. Sisto Fabri reassured Montaigne, who reported his interview in a positive way. In the end, the reproaches amounted to little. According to Montaigne, Fabri almost presented his excuses. Four days later, on April 19, Montaigne left Rome for Loreto, holding his head high. He traveled around Italy for three and a half months. Disappointed by his political setback, and even though his career as a diplomat was quite compromised, he transformed this Italian journey into a pleasure trip: he went to the baths at La Villa, did some sightseeing, and began to write his journal in Italian—though he had earlier complained that everyone he'd met in Rome spoke nothing but French. He had also gotten rid of his secretary, who may not have met his expectations. In any case, he no longer needed to have someone else write down his experiences in Italy. He was amused to find he was capable of continuing this journal himself in Italian. Exile then took on another dimension and Montaigne soon discovered a saving sociability at the baths.

The Sociability of the Baths

The second part of the travel journal, which Montaigne composed in Italian, is very different in nature from the first part, which was written by the secretary. Rome is no longer the most important place, the endpoint and goal of the journey. Now begins the period of taking the waters and the return to the body. The author of the *Essais* suffered from renal colic and at that time "taking the waters" was a highly recommended therapy for this disease. Taking the waters could only do him good because, as he aged, kidney stones were becoming an increasingly serious problem.[236] Montaigne tells us that he visited "almost all the famous baths of Christendom."[237] He saw no improvement in his health, no miraculous or extraordinary effect, but neither had he met anyone whose condition had grown worse after taking the waters. In the late Middle Ages, balneotherapy became far more widely practiced in Italy and in the Germanic world, where at the beginning of the fifteenth century the spa at Baden had already acquired a reputation for being a place of sociability.[238] Spas provided much more than therapeutic treatments; they also offered opportunities to meet people. Thus in Plombières, Montaigne made friends with and became close to the lord d'Andelot, a brigadier in John of Austria's army, whose father was grand equerry of Charles V the emperor. Montaigne stayed at L'Ange, the best inn at the spa. Other more carnal meetings may also have taken place at the baths. In the early fifteenth century Poggio Bracciolini had already praised the prostitutes there, and worldly life at the baths continued to develop throughout the Renaissance. The freedom of behavior at the baths was advertised by the spa towns, which attracted visitors, certainly less for their therapeutic benefits than for the pleasures to be had there—for a certain price. Parties, entertainments, balls, musical events, and amorous encounters were the pleasant counterparts of the physical ailments that were the original reason for visiting spas. People of all kinds mixed there—noble lords and rich bourgeois, but also scholars. There was no better place to combine the pleasures of conversation with erotic adventures.

Although he was not indifferent to the medical benefits of taking the waters, Montaigne also mentions the more "social" motivation of his stays at the baths. "Anyone who does not bring to them enough cheerfulness to be able to enjoy the pleasure of the company that is found there, . . . will doubtless lose the best and surest part of their effect."[239] Numerous treatises praise the therapeutic qualities of the German and Italian spas, the most famous of which is no doubt Andrea Bacci's *De thermis*.[240] The account given in Montaigne's travel journal accords great importance to the baths in Plombières, Baden, Spa, and of course Italy. He met, for instance, Maldonat, who was returning from taking the waters at Spa. Montaigne spent eleven days at Plombières, where he became accustomed to drink as many as nine glasses of mineral water in the course of a morning. Since Antiquity, and still in the Middle Ages, the baths had always been meeting places, as frivolous as they were serious.[241] All sorts of private and public activities were carried on. Spas became fashionable in the Renaissance, and they were full of establishments where travelers liked to stay for several days or even several weeks. Montaigne probably used the baths as "ambassadorial spaces," that is, as places that favored conversation and encounters with people who differed in their culture, politics, and religion.

In the sixteenth century, Italian spas were places where not only the local aristocracy but also gentlemen from all over Europe met and spent holidays. That was why they were frequented by courtesans who sold their favors to the rich visitors passing through. People went to spas to make interesting encounters, whether erotic or social. These interpersonal relations also facilitated the development of networks and the multiplication of acquaintances, but the baths remained chiefly a site of frivolity, not to say debauchery. Numerous sermons from the time allude to the prostitution that was very widespread at the spas. In Plombières, a series of "rules" concerning behavior was intended to curb the increasing numbers of "loose women" who, on the pretext of taking the waters, took advantage of the situation to sell their charms. The indiscriminate mixture of bodies is frequently depicted in engravings from the period that show men and women sharing the same baths.

Early in his journey to Italy, Montaigne had stopped at the spa of Plombières. In that city, the baths were carefully supervised, and Montaigne's secretary, for whom this was probably his first visit to one of these very special places, had been impressed to the point that he reproduced the regulations of the baths in the journal that he was keeping for his master. A local ordinance posted before the entrance to the baths denounced the immorality of the place. "Prostitutes and shameless women" were required to remain at least 500 paces from the baths, and it was expressly forbidden to "make any lascivious or shameless remarks . . . to ladies, maidens, and other women and girls." The prohibition was not limited to lewd remarks, since any indecent touching[242] was also forbidden. However, these rules of conduct between men and women point to a widespread practice that attracted visitors. A woodcut from 1553 shows unclothed bathers of both sexes sharing a big pool around which several gentlemen are walking (figure 12). Latin verses by Conrad Gessner accompany this engraving: "We see bathing, pell-mell in the warm water, women, men, children, girls; the

FIGURE 12. Woodcut, *Balneum Plummers*, 1553 (private collection).

poor, the noble; the learned and the ignorant; the old, the young." The baths also promoted social mixing, because the waters and the nakedness made it possible to encounter people from other milieus or social orders whom one could not meet elsewhere.

Aware that the baths made it easier to meet influential figures in the cities where he stopped off, Montaigne sent out multiple invitations when he stayed in a spa. During his first visit to the baths at La Villa, near Lucca, he explained how he organized his evenings: "on the day previous I sent special invitations to all the gentle-folk then sojourning at either of the baths. I bade them come to the ball, and to the supper afterwards, and sent to Lucca for the presents, which are usually pretty numerous, so as to avoid the appearance of favouring one lady above all the rest."[243] The local practice consisted in awarding prizes during these balls—eight or ten, we are told by Montaigne, who willingly conformed to this custom and ordered gifts to win his guests' goodwill:

> Many ventured to jog my memory, one begging me not to forget herself, another her niece, another her daughter. On the day previous Messer Giovanni da Vincenzo Saminiati, a good friend of mine, brought me from Lucca, according to my written instructions, a leathern belt and a black cloth cap as presents for the men. For the ladies I provided two aprons of taffetas, one green and the other purple (for it must be known that it is always meet to have certain presents better than the bulk, so as to show special favour where favour seems to be due), two aprons of bombazine, four papers of pins, four pairs of shoes—one pair of which I gave to a pretty girl who did not come to the ball.[244]

Here Montaigne talks about the price of bodies in commercial terms.

The precision of Montaigne's description tells us a great deal about the social interest of the baths, and we can easily understand why they had cultural rules that attracted him. The gifts promoted sociability and access to women. This form of rapid seduction, thanks to the presents given, allowed courtesans to maintain a status more elevated than they had in the cities. The staging of balls as a new space of erotic conquest had a kind of decency, of nobility, even of chivalry, and got around the social taboos separating people of such different origins and ranks. However, the presents given women were not considered a way of purchasing their services—at least, that was the appearance that the baths tried to preserve by functioning in accord with their own human and social codes.

The spa culture made it possible for Montaigne to join a system of sociability that he says he quickly mastered. This sociability of the waters was in perfect harmony with an aristocratic practice of conversation. The baths promoted an art of intercourse, communication, and company, or what was then called the knowledge of *l'entregent*.[245] Montaigne made use of the baths not only to perfect this knowledge but also to meet women. The balls and the distribution of prizes that he mentions served as an excuse for a more specific trade in which the value of the objects handed out was supposed to find an equivalent in the carnal pleasure that he counted on receiving. Montaigne acknowledges having distributed nineteen prizes during a ball at the baths of La Villa, for a total cost of six crowns. Such generous giving helped him create for himself a reputation as a well-off gentleman. The prizes were "hung on a loop, richly ornamented, and visible to all the company."[246] Montaigne's social status was confirmed by this public generosity displayed by the number of presents distributed.

Montaigne's strategy also consisted in attracting the attention of the powerful lords who resided for a time at the spas: "We began the dance on the plaza with the people of the place, and at first feared we should lack company, but after a little we were joined by a great number of people of all parties, and notably of the gentle-folk of the land, whom I received and entertained to the best of my powers; and I succeeded so far that they all seemed well content."[247] In this passage we see that Montaigne saw little interest in the entertainments and was chiefly concerned to attract the attention of the men and women who participated in the political life of the region. Establishing contacts with people of a rank equal to his own was also his objective when he organized these balls. Showing himself in good company and entering into conversation with his peers was a social and political priority that far transcended his therapeutic concerns. As soon as he arrived in a spa, Montaigne sought to meet its major "customers." He quickly succeeded in making himself part of these transitory networks which, by their fluctuating character, favored links between gentlemen. We can imagine the conversations that went on in these places. Thus at the baths in La Villa, Montaigne notes that "this same morning I received a visit from the deputy-judge and the other chief personages of the State, an attention equivalent to that which had been paid to me in other baths where I had sojourned."[248]

The lord of Montaigne spent his days in conversations and took advantage of his stay to fill out his address book. Eloquence was not his strong point, but casual, free-wheeling conversation was. It was certainly the informal aspect of the baths that attracted him and pleased the "diplomat of the antechamber" who had just failed in his first attempt to become an ambassador. Moreover, the environment of the baths did not lend itself to the decorum of the court, and conversations there sought to be more direct and frank. In a way, the political space suggested by the *Essais* of 1580 found its realization in the spas. His reputation, Montaigne tells us, was too great and far exceeded his true abilities as a diplomat. But political successes were of little importance; in diplomacy, all that mattered was appearances, and the spas were essentially theaters where everyone played the role that had escaped him in society. The spas were a microcosm of social experimentation without any real political stakes. Montaigne played with appearances when he passed through the spas. Ironically, the baths were a substitute for the diplomatic activity that he had proposed to the king the preceding year.

Montaigne left the mark of his coat of arms at every stop. He wanted there to be a trace of his passage through the Italian spas where he stayed and told a judge in La Villa that "I was minded to begin here a custom prevalent in all the famous baths of Europe, to wit, that all persons of a certain position should leave behind a copy of their coat-of-arms as a testimony of the efficacy of the waters. In the name of the government he thanked me for this suggestion."[249] On various occasions in the course of his journey, for example in Plombières, Augsburg, Pisa, and Loreto, Montaigne ordered his secretary to hire artists to paint his coat of arms on badges that he had hung on the walls of the various inns where he stayed. Montaigne explains how in Pisa he had his coat of arms painted in bright colors and gilded "for the cost of a French crown and a half," had them framed at the baths, and then had the picture "carefully nailed to the wall of the chamber I had occupied."[250] His coat of arms literally marked his stops along the way and enabled him to leave a trace of his passage for those who would follow him.

The "efficacy of the waters" is one of the constitutive elements of his interest in spas: it was the whole body that was politicized via illness. Recently ennobled, Montaigne felt flattered by the tradition of the baths that immortalized his presence in a semipublic space. The baths symbolized a privileged place where it was easy to display his rank and his ideas without there being any political consequences. Long after the traveler's departure, the name of Montaigne remained alongside those of the other great European families. These places of sociability were like portrait galleries, because the baths had the ability to classify people according to their social status: their clothing, the kinds of inns they chose, the number of their servants, and such, were so many signs of nobility in a highly symbolic economy.

The references to spas in Montaigne's travel journal reveal that these places had a social complexity with their own codes and rules of behavior.[251] However, Montaigne chose to begin his account—and thus his "advertisement" for the baths—with a glorification of the body. In a famous passage in the *Essais*, he explains what he learned from his stays at spas: "In general, I consider bathing healthful and believe that we incur no slight disadvantages to our health for having lost this custom, which was in times past generally observed in almost all nations and still is in many, of washing our body every day. And I cannot imagine that we are not much the worse for thus keeping our limbs encrusted and our pores stopped up with dirt."[252] Montaigne was preoccupied with hygiene, and this was far from the norm in his time. But the baths remained above all a convenient place for meeting "the infinite number of people of all sorts and constitutions who assemble there."[253]

This comment on the social and cultural variety of the spas explicitly situates this place outside any particular religious belief. This may well be why miracles did not take place there: "I have perceived no extraordinary and miraculous effect there, but rather, on investigating a little more carefully than is usual, I have found false and ill-founded all the rumors of such effects that are spread in those places and believed (since people easily fool themselves about what they desire)."[254] Here we recognize Montaigne's ability to judge phenomena that might seem extraordinary or prodigious. The spas designate a space of contradiction—or at least an opposition—between words and things: on the one hand, the discourse on the benefits of the waters; on the other, the phenomena that are observable—or not observable, if we are speaking of miracles. Montaigne wants to be pragmatic; so long as taking the waters does no harm, it can only do good. Let people believe in miracles so long as these miracles serve political or economic ends.

For Montaigne, the baths incarnate a place of convenience. Compared with the insecurity of the highways and the extraordinary variety of comfort level and security in inns, the spas are safe and clean, as well as a place where the company of others can be enjoyed and the quality of the lodging is guaranteed by the gentlemen who stay there. The accent has to be put on what Montaigne calls "the amenity of the place, the fitness of the lodging, the living, and the company," because these are the essential points that persuade him to stop at baths on his way to the great cities, which are his destination. Moreover, a number of spas were conveniently located not far from large cities, as is the case of Battaglia. Politics is not experienced there in the same way. The baths mix gentlemen who don't know exactly the place others' have in the city where they reside. In fact, spas were utopias of a sort that allowed Montaigne to approach all sorts of bodies without worrying about ethical or political implications. The concentration and availability of bodies was combined with the leveling and social standardization that make possible a practice of politics in a form freed of social constraints. The spas are the space where Montaigne crossed the famous limit that he had imposed on himself in the *Au lecteur* of the *Essais*: "as far as respect for the public has allowed." We might say that, in the baths, Montaigne literally stripped himself naked. Spas symbolize, in a way, a Cannibal land where exhibitionism is in good taste.

Spas denote an ideal place for understanding human diversity, what Montaigne calls "the infinite number of people of all sorts and constitutions"[255]—a meeting place where numerous points of view can be found and where it is possible to compare cultures, perhaps better than in the large cities of the Renaissance. Spas had a certain advantage over Italian cities, which with their particular political systems were considered to be more homogeneous. The baths, because they are a place one passes through, mix together and aggregate different people. Within a limited space, wealthy merchants, princes from distant lands, and local gentlemen mix. Spas represent miniature worlds that spare Montaigne the anthropologist the need to move around. At a glance, within an enclosed space, the observer can engage in a political and social decoding that goes far beyond the space in which he finds himself. Thus one could compare spas to gardens, concentrations of nature that fascinated Montaigne during his journey to Italy. Spas also facilitate direct and immediate comparison without calling upon the memory. One has before one's eyes a palette of men and women that it would have been impossible to bring together elsewhere. Spas are indeed like a garden, which, by its concentrated form, facilitates the presentation of the whole of the variations present in nature—in the case of spas, the variations of human nature.[256]

For Montaigne, the garden is never the equivalent of nature; it represents a displaced piece of nature, rearranged the better to bring out the variety encountered in larger spaces. Like the baths, the garden is a concentrated form of nature. In this respect the garden responds to the spatial constraints connected with the urban world. The garden makes possible an economy of displacement by transporting nature into the heart of cities. It corresponds to an arrangement that is hardly different from the pictorial landscape, since neither ever claims to be the equivalent of a nature in infinite space. Whether in painting or in cities, the frame of the landscape, like the wall of the garden, marks the limits of a reappropriated nature. For that reason, in Montaigne's travel journal the garden also designates a place of sociability, both at the villa of Castello, not far from Florence, and at Fossombrune.

Finally, spas provide a kind of reification of various societies that can be instantaneously compared. They favor conversations that would otherwise be impossible. By gathering people around the same glass of water or in a single pool, they create a social proximity that delighted Montaigne. The baths at Battaglia, like those at La Villa, marked an important step in the process of elaborating a particular knowledge, and Montaigne soon claimed to be an expert on balneotherapy.[257] Like Rovigo, Ferrara, and Bologna, Battaglia allowed him to engage in a "learned" and expert discourse, perhaps the only learned discourse in the *Essais*. We must draw a distinction between the kind of philosophical reflections present in the *Essais* and the more scientific discourse Montaigne delivers on the baths. For example, he reproaches himself for not having taken more notes on the different characteristics of the baths during his numerous sojourns in Europe's spas: "Seeing that I have often repented that I did not more particularly note down details of other baths I have used, I am now minded to enlarge somewhat on this subject and to gather together certain rules for the benefit of my successors."[258] Montaigne is clearly aware that this kind of knowledge can be valuable, and he is rather proud of the experience he has gained in the field. This acquaintance with the baths even became a favorite subject of conversation and thus useful when he met other gentlemen of his rank.

At this period baths were in fashion, and spa towns competed with one another. Each spa differed from the others by some specialty that attracted travelers. Montaigne knew the baths and their respective reputations, and he could talk at length about the therapeutic qualities of this one and that one. At Bern-abò [xviii] it was, of course, the curative nature of the waters that was highlighted. A single cure had sufficed to revive activity at this watering place after it had fallen behind more fashionable ones. On this point, Montaigne recounts an anecdote that reveals his own experimental impression of the spas. A leper named Barnaby had benefited from this spring's "less digestible" and "violent" waters, and this led Montaigne to evaluate its curative qualities, which differed from those of other springs in the area. According to him, a strong, heavy, violent water was necessary to cure leprosy. Montaigne explains Barnaby's recovery in this way, attributing to it a scientific value based on the empirical observation of the waters peculiar to these baths. His expertise seeks to put the idea of a miracle into perspective and goes beyond the simple narrative that normally accompanied the choice of Bernabò. Montaigne offers a rational explanation that is conveyed in an expert's discourse. He qualifies his claim by noting that "of those who used these baths, more died than were cured."[259] But these doubts regarding the medicinal benefits did not put in question the social advantage of sojourns at spas.

What should we conclude from the "thermal discourse" in the *Essais* and in the travel journal? A conversation Montaigne had with an old man who lived near the baths at La Villa, shortly before his return to France, sounds the death knell for an ideal view of the baths and announces the return to the reality that would have to be faced once he was back in France:

> I inquired of a very old man whether the baths were much used by the inhabitants, whereupon he answered that the people about Lucca were like those living near the Madonna of Loreto, who very rarely go on pilgrimages to the shrine there; in like fashion the baths of Lucca enjoyed little favour, except from foreigners and people coming from afar. Moreover, there was one matter which gave him disquiet, to wit, that for some years past there had appeared manifest signs that the baths had done more harm than good to those who used them. He declared the cause of this to be that, whereas in former days there was no apothecary in the whole district, and physicians were rarely seen, these gentry now swarmed.[260]

The emphasis on the therapeutic value of the baths should be interpreted as a deconstruction of the medical discourse of the period concerning their supposed benefits. In the end, the baths did good only to foreigners. This astonishing conclusion led Montaigne to become aware of the limited value of his

---

[xviii] A bath at Lucca. The English equivalent of Bernabò is "Barnaby." [Trans.]

knowledge of the baths and of his own observations in the field. How could the baths be harmful to the natives and beneficial for outsiders? That was a question of perception whose consequence was to relativize the curative powers of taking the waters. The investment in travel created expectations more difficult to disappoint and put visitors to spas in a particular situation. Coming from far away, they fabricated stories regarding the power of the waters and found what they were looking for. At this point Montaigne recognized the social and political aspect of the baths while at the same time commenting ironically on the acknowledged purpose of his own stays in spas. The specific knowledge of the waters is abandoned and replaced by a social discourse that allows everyone to express deeper needs and less frivolous concerns. To be cured is to believe in the principle of curing, apart from any medical knowledge. The miracles of the baths must be resituated in the framework of a belief that transcends the chemical and hydrological contributions of the hot springs.

Montaigne believed in the power of the imagination and noted the relative nature of all knowledge. We may wonder about the "knowledge of the waters" that he acquired during his repeated visits to European spas. Didn't this knowledge have a political dimension, since it provided an opportunity to base authority on direct experience that could later serve as substance for conversations of a more social or religious nature? For that reason, the baths represented a space of sociability. At first, Montaigne had perhaps considered this knowledge of the baths from the point of view of simple salon conversation, as a subject that facilitated interesting encounters and authorized him to establish initial contact with gentlemen, pretty courtesans, and interesting persons staying at the baths. His various reflections on the practice of taking the waters—as opposed to medicine—might then have been made part of a general and relative perception of the baths based on experience.[261]

The Travel Journal and the Secretary

It is difficult to speak of Montaigne in Italy without looking into the status of the *Journal de voyage* in his works. At the outset, we must note that this text is not a "travel journal" in the sense the term has today, or at least that such a title does not, in my opinion, apply to the whole of the text.[xix] Today, we still read

[xix] One has only to consider the first words of Joseph Prunis's preface to his plan for an edition of the *Journal de voyage* (1772) to realize to what point the eighteenth century was incapable of conceiving the manuscript of the journal of Montaigne's journey to Italy outside the genre of travel narratives: "The taste for journeys has been, in every age, the favorite passion of men of letters" (*Journal de voyage*, 301).

too often that the goal of Montaigne's journey was to visit Europe, as if he owed it to himself to get to know the world, or to take a vacation. Praiseworthy intentions for a humanist, but nonetheless very distant from reality. The title *Journal* was given only in the eighteenth century, at the time of the publication in 1774 of the original manuscript, which Canon Joseph Prunis had found in a coffer at Montaigne's château in 1770. Moreover, as we have seen, the first part of this journal was written by a secretary and not by Montaigne. The secretary had spoken in his own voice, often in a personal way, and this was not contrary to his function as secretary as it was understood in the Renaissance. For that reason scholars have spoken of a journal "with two voices."[262] This famous "journal" was thus initially a notebook kept by another person, even if this secretary was writing under Montaigne's orders; later it was written in Montaigne's own hand—in both French and Italian.[263] The first part written by the secretary is informative and political, whereas the second part seems more dilettantish.

Montaigne's travel to Italy, Switzerland, Germany, and Austria represents a journey of 5,100 kilometers that stretched almost fifteen months—from September 4, 1580, to November 30, 1581. One should not confuse the departure from the château with the beginning of the journey to Italy. In fact, even if Montaigne left his château on June 22, 1580, the trip to Paris is not part of the *Journal de voyage*. Montaigne went to Paris to give the king a copy of his *Essais* that had just come out of Simon Millanges's presses in April of the same year. It is only after meeting Henry III in Saint-Maur-des-Fossés, and after his brief stay at the siege of La Fère, that he undertook his journey to Rome. In total, Montaigne was absent 525 days from his château, but the *Journal de voyage* only covers 450 days.

Wrongly, critics have assumed that the château of Montaigne represents the starting point of his travel to Italy.[264] However, this first part of the journey—between June 22 and September 4, 1580—must be considered differently. The *Journal du voyage de Michel de Montaigne en Italie, par la Suisse & l'Allemagne en 1580 & 1581*—here we speak of the manuscript discovered by Prunis and published by Meunier de Querlon—begins on September 4, 1580, in Mours (Mors), a small village situated less than two kilometers from Beaumont-sur-Oise and thirty-five kilometers north of Paris, and ends on November 30, 1581, at the château de Montaigne. Contrary to what modern editions of the *Journal de voyage* (all based on the Leydet Copy[xx]) tell us, the first stage of the journey to Rome cannot be Niort, a town situated 400 kilometers southwest of Paris. Identifying the first city of the *Journal* as Niort is the result of an error of transcrip-

---

[xx] Guillaume-Vivien Leydet gave a partial transcription (known as the Leydet Copy) of the original manuscript of the *Journal* in 1771. This copy was discovered in the early 1980s.

tion by Leydet who confused Niort and Mours.[xxi] He mistook the capital *M* for a capital *N* followed by an *i*.

In the original edition of the *Journal* published in 1774, Meunier de Querlon had wisely decided to ignore the name of this village he could not decipher. Since the first sheet of the manuscript was missing when the journal was discovered, we do not know the cities that precede Beaumont-sur-Oise, the first town clearly identified in the journal. However, logically we can infer that the lack of a single sheet suggests that the document was started in the Paris region and not around Bordeaux. Indeed, 540 kilometers separate the château of Montaigne and Beaumont. For a traveler of this time, such a distance represents between ten and twelve stages of about fifty to fifty-five kilometers per day. For comparison, while in Germany and Italy, Montaigne and his company rarely exceeded fifty kilometers per day. If the secretary had begun to write in the journal at the château of Montaigne or in the region of Bordeaux, and without taking into account the information he might give about himself or the purpose of this journey to Rome, or even circumstances of his hiring, we easily see that it would require more than a sheet of paper to record the dozen of stages that preceded the arrival in Beaumont, not to mention the eight weeks that separate the meeting with the king and the official departure for Rome.

Of the 450 days of travel between Mours and his return to the château of Montaigne, 126 days were spent on horseback and 324 days represent various stays in European cities and sojourns at different baths, including 152 days spent in Rome. During his trip to Italy, Montaigne therefore spent more than a quarter (28 percent) of his time on horseback.[265] This figure confirms that he was an excellent rider who could stay in the saddle for ten hours a day: "I stay on horseback, though I have the colic, without dismounting and without pain, for eight or ten hours."[266]

Linguistically, the journal can be divided into four parts, according to the writers and languages used: (1) a first part written by the first secretary in French, which extends from September 5, 1580, to February 15, 1581 (164 days); (2) a second part also in French, written in part by a second secretary and partly

---

[xxi] For more than two centuries specialists on Montaigne have attempted to identify the count that Montaigne's young brother, Bertrand de Mattecoulon, had visited at the request of Montaigne just before starting their journey to Rome. Following up on the wrong identification made by Leydet, scholars looked around Niort, but Mours (and not Niort) offers an easy answer to this puzzle. The count mentioned at the beginning of the journal is Charles du Plessis-Liancourt, Lord of Liancourt, Count of Beaumont-sur-Oise and Marquis of Guercheville who resided at the time in Mors (Mours). He was wounded in the siege of La Fère and was recovering in Mours. He died in 1620 at the age of sixty-nine. Today, his effigy can be found in the Saint Martin church, in the village of Liancourt, thirty-five kilometers from Mours.

by Montaigne, which extends from February 16, 1581, to May 12, 1581 (87 days); (3) a third part written in Italian by Montaigne, and sometimes with the help of another scriptor (the second or third secretary), but probably dictated by Montaigne, which runs from May 13, 1581, to November 1, 1581 (172 days); and (4) a fourth part in the hand of Montaigne and written in French on the way back to his château, between Mont Cenis and the château of Montaigne, from November 1, 1581, to November 30, 1581 (30 days).

Should this text be attributed to Montaigne, as is customary? If we take into account the fact that the first two pages have been lost, we realize that Montaigne's secretary wrote half (49 percent) of the travel journal as we know it today. Montaigne himself wrote one-fourth (25 percent) of the journal in Italian, with the help of several other hands, and only one-fourth (26 percent) in French. If we examine the part in Italian, it proves very difficult to get an idea of the content and form of the text, because it was extensively corrected and put into an eighteenth-century Italian when the work was published by Le Jay in 1774. In fact, as Meunier de Querlon wrote in his "Preliminary Discourse" to the journey, "the part of this journal that must have cost the most effort was undoubtedly Montaigne's Italian, which was even more difficult to read than the French text, as much because of its bad spelling as because it is full of licenses, various dialects, and gallicisms."[267] Putting the text into modern Italian was entrusted to Giuseppe Bartoli, the king of Sardinia's antique dealer, who had recently been elected a "foreign associate" of the Académie royale des inscriptions et belles-lettres in Paris.[268] Bartoli's effort to make Montaigne's Italian more legible—indeed, comprehensible—was surely substantial and now makes difficult, if not impossible, any evaluation of Montaigne's Italian. Montaigne himself acknowledges the limits of his Italian: "in Italy I said whatever I pleased in ordinary talk, but for serious discourse I would not have dared trust myself to an idiom that I could neither bend nor turn out of its ordinary course. I want to be able to do something of my own with it."[269] Commentary on the Italian part of Montaigne's journal is thus particularly specious, at least so long as we have not rediscovered the original manuscript.[xxii] The secretary's identity also remains unknown, even though half of the text was written by him.

Montaigne's "journal" actually corresponds to two projects that differ not only in time but also in intention. The first part, written by the secretary, is rich in political remarks and has a "professional" function; the second part, written by Montaigne, is both a linguistic exercise (in the Italian part) and a looser text that exists only as a continuation of an enterprise begun by someone else. This

---

[xxii] Either deposited in the Royal Library or given back to Charles-Joseph Ségur, the owner of the château of Montaigne in 1774, the manuscript of the *Journal de voyage*, which comprised 139 folios, disappeared shortly after it was discovered, and has not yet been found again.

second part seems to be the work of a "dilettante" who is trying his hand at a language that he is beginning to like and prides himself on continuing the work of the secretary he had dismissed. While waiting to be named as an extraordinary or interim ambassador, Montaigne had used a secretary to write accounts of his various private and official meetings connected with his residence abroad. The Roman part of the journal occupies an important place in the conception of the journey: it was both the culmination of a learning process begun in France and developed in Switzerland, Austria, and Italy, and the beginning of a way of serving the king of France. After the dismissal of the secretary and the departure from Rome, the journal became something quite different.

On the chronological level, the journal was initially "abandoned" for two months. After February 9, 1581 (the date of the secretary's last entry in the journal), Montaigne wrote in it only twice between February 16 and March 13. He had fired his secretary on February 8, 1581, for what reason we do not know, but we can formulate a few hypotheses. Let us consider first of all the incompatibility of humors and styles. We discern a certain independence in Montaigne's secretary, who expressed his own opinions.[270] In numerous passages of the journal he offers judgments that sometimes differ from those of his master. He is also critical regarding persons met and recounts several anecdotes with a touch of irony that is not necessarily compatible with that of his employer. Was that why he was dismissed? It is hard to say. We can also imagine that Montaigne knew as early as February that his nomination as ambassador was going badly and that he considered it prudent to rid himself of a secretary who caused him expenses that had become useless. Whatever the reasons that forced Montaigne to fire his secretary might be, one thing is certain: he had no intention of publishing an expanded version of his *Essais* when he was in Rome, and he seems to have devoted himself entirely to his vocation as an ambassador.

Montaigne resumed writing the journal only after giving up any illusions regarding the desired ambassadorship. *Then* he wrote the journal in Italian, starting with his stay at the baths of La Villa (late May 1581). From that moment on, we note an important change in the nature of his remarks and commentaries: the political allusions fade away and the tone of the journal is very different, more detached from the political reality. As we have said, Montaigne went to Loreto to make a vow.[271] Was this the sign of a disappointment or a new resolve? Then he went to the baths and did some sightseeing. By continuing to write his journal, he undertook a task he had never foreseen, because he had many other priorities during his first stay in Rome. We can conclude that the first part of the journal was a kind of inconclusive learning process. The secretary's role was to "keep a record," that is, to write down Montaigne's doings, to keep track of potential relationships, and to select the essence of his master's everyday life.

In his turn, Montaigne began writing the journal every day (or at least he gave the impression of a continuous record). The *Essais* may have undergone an unconscious influence of this practice of recording—as another form of journal, what Montaigne later defined as a "record of the essays of my life."[272] That is how we must understand the part of the journal he wrote: as a preparation of the essays to come. Montaigne took pleasure in playing the role of his secretary once he had seen that, from a professional point of view, he really didn't need such a man at his side. The work given up by the secretary allowed him to put himself in another's place, a procedure that was to become essential to his writing project. Montaigne transformed this career incident into a literary advantage. According to Gabriel Chappuys, the translator of Francesco Sansovino's treatise *Del secretario* (1564), there is a French "way of writing" without "ceremony and formal preambles."[273] Montaigne identified with this way of writing and seems to have wanted to continue this French style on the model left by the secretary.

Let us propose a final possible motive for firing the secretary. The man chosen for that job had to "be discreet, and avoid divulging things, because being, as it were, the main member of the prince's Advisory Council, he must have his ears and his mind, but not his tongue, outside the Council."[274] Montaigne had difficult relations with his secretaries, who were not always worthy of his confidence. For example, when we read the journal it is difficult to tell whether the secretary overstepped his function, and we may wonder whether during the first part of the journey he was not too much "tongue" and not enough "ears." A valet had also stolen several chapters of the *Essais*, and Montaigne may not have had complete confidence in this secretary who was sometimes too eager to draw attention to himself. Similarly, other "hands" appear in the travel journal, though we do not know what happened to these various secretaries.

It was only after 1588, that is, after having used Marie de Gournay as a secretary during a brief stay at Gournay-sur-Aronde, that Montaigne made up his mind to write his *Essais* alone. Thus the journal may have allowed him to consider the possibility of writing his book himself, doing without secretaries for the first time. This was, moreover, a wise decision, because although it was easy to find a good secretary in Paris, the reverse was true in Guyenne. In the Renaissance, secretaries were learned men in their own right who had ambitions that were often justified. It was in this sprit that Chappuys advised them to be savants, an uncommon characteristic in Montaigne's time, especially in the provinces. The secretary, Chappuys tells us, must be "learned and know literature, be loyal, and faithful, with a gentle spirit, and pleasant, industrious, and prudent,"[275] and above all faithful, that is, he had to have the essential quality that Chappuys calls "loyal silence." The secretary who wrote the first part of Montaigne's travel journal seems not to have followed this advice, and Montaigne may have objected to his inappropriate chatter.

Over the centuries, critics erased Montaigne's secretary. The first editor of the *Journal de voyage*, Meunier de Querlon, even spoke of Montaigne's marginal additions to the first part of the journal written by the secretary, as "prolongations" (*allongeails*) comparable to what we find in the Bordeaux Copy, which was discovered at almost the same time. It is as if Montaigne had reread his travel journal, whereas it is clearly established that the first part was definitely written by a secretary who displayed a certain freedom of mind and judgment. It has even been claimed that the secretary wrote at his master's dictation. Thus a large number of the secretary's remarks have been erroneously attributed to Montaigne, and confusion of the two men still prevails among specialists.

Finally, let us mention a final, troubling bit of evidence. The first two pages of the journal are lacking. Its first editor, Meunier de Querlon, explains that it "seems to have been torn out at some time in the past." It has been said that it was eaten by mice, but the journal lay in an old coffer in the château, so that this explanation is difficult to believe, and we can imagine that the first two pages of the manuscript might have been omitted by Montaigne himself. The secretary might have given certain details regarding Montaigne's mission in Italy and the particular circumstances of a journey undertaken in the framework of an embassy. He could also have revealed his identity on the first page. Montaigne's failure in Rome would have been even more flagrant with this reminder of the motive for his stay in Italy. Montaigne might have thought it better to suppress the first writer's identity when he decided to make this journal his own after he dismissed the secretary. Let us note that the *Essais* never mention the travel journal. After March 1581, the first remarks made by Montaigne in his journal simply no longer corresponded to the original project of a diary kept by the secretary. Nonetheless, the journal changed authors after March 1581. At that time, its reason for being was profoundly altered. Back in his château, Montaigne put the manuscript in a chest and never thought about it again. The call of Rome had ended in failure, and Montaigne never became an ambassador. The journal might have reminded him of painful memories.

CHAPTER 8

"Messieurs of Bordeaux Elected Me
Mayor of Their City" (1581–1585)

While he was still in Italy—on August 1, 1581—Montaigne was elected mayor of Bordeaux, apparently against his will: "Messieurs of Bordeaux elected me mayor of their city when I was far from France and still farther from such a thought. I excused myself, but I was informed that I was wrong, since the king's command also figured in the matter."[1] He received the news on September 7, while he was staying at the baths of La Villa: "This same morning there came to hand, by way of Rome, a letter from M. de Tausin, written from Bordeaux on August 2nd, in which he informed me that, on the preceding day, I had been chosen to be mayor of that city by public choice, and begged me that, out of my goodwill for the city, I would take up this burden."[2] Montaigne had been expecting a quite different kind of appointment. On September 1, he had written in his journal: "if I had received from France the news for which I had been waiting—indeed for four months I had heard nothing at all—I should have set forth at once."[3] It was therefore not for pleasure that he spent several months traveling in Italy and sojourning at different baths. In fact, he had been waiting for news from the royal Court since April, when he learned that he would not be ambassador in Rome. Had the king hinted at the possibility of another diplomatic post for him in Italy? Probably. That would explain Montaigne's decision to remain in the country after his departure from Rome. He did not leave the baths at La Villa until five days later, on September 12, when he went to Lucca, where he attended the Sainte-Croix festival and the ceremony of the changing of the city's *gonfalonieri* (high magistrates) before leaving for Rome a week later. He dawdled along the way, and it was only on October 1, when he finally arrived in Rome, that he learned of the letter from the jurats of Bordeaux informing him of his election and urging him to return as soon as possible.[4]

Montaigne's election as mayor of Bordeaux must be seen as a political compromise that was made at his expense. The possibility of serving the city was probably never mentioned to him. The political situation had developed in an unfavorable direction and Biron was no longer desirable in the city. He had become estranged from Henry of Navarre and no longer enjoyed Catherine de Medici's support. The king had decided to get rid of him, and it was more urgent than ever to replace him with a strongman. Montaigne did not have the political weight necessary to govern Guyenne and had no military experience. On the other hand, over the generations the Eyquems had retained a good reputation as managers of the city. In the view of various local powers and the Bordeaux élites, the mayor could not come from another region, and the king already had enough problems with the parlement of Bordeaux without proposing such a choice. He balked at the idea of appointing a man who had not lived in Bordeaux, at least for a time, and decided to divide the two functions normally performed by the mayor: the mayor of Bordeaux and the governor of Guyenne. These two titles would be separated and the functions associated with them performed by two different men.

The king was opposed to the nomination of a mayor who came from the milieu of the *robins*. In a letter to the parlement of Bordeaux dated July 2, 1577, he had asked the councillors to overcome their differences so that "without anyone of the long robe being able to intervene, an honorable gentleman of the short robe[i] might be elected mayor of this city of Bordeaux."[5] Here we can see Henry III's problem in early 1581. If the governor could come from another province—and that was the case for Marshal Matignon—there was no question of choosing a mayor who would not be familiar with the political networks that had developed among the great Bordeaux families. Confronted by the overt resistance of the *robins* in the parlement of Bordeaux, the king was determined to remove them from the administration of the city, but he had to find a man who could stand up to them. The city's statutes did not explicitly stipulate that the mayor had to be a member of the nobility, but the king had already expressed this wish on July 11, 1577, when in a letter to the Bordeaux parlement he asked that the person elected mayor of Bordeaux not be, "nor ever again hereafter, anyone of the long robe."[6] In late summer 1581, after a short hesitation and a preliminary agreement with the queen mother, the king finally made up his mind: the governor would be Matignon and the mayor Montaigne. The mayor's political power was thus weakened and Henry III would rely chiefly on Matignon to reestablish order in Aquitaine.

Far from being enthusiastic about this news, Montaigne did not hasten to return to France. He preferred to visit the baths of Diocletian at Monte Cavallo, and two days later, at the invitation of Paul de Foix, who was now the French ambassador to Rome, he went to see, in the suburbs of Rome, the furniture and other objects of interest that had belonged to Cardinal Ursino. Montaigne admired a bed covering made of taffeta and stuffed with swan feathers,

---

[i] That is, a nobleman. [Trans.]

and described an ostrich egg that was carved and painted with great skill. On his way back, at Marignan, he went fifteen kilometers out of his way in order to visit Pavia. Service to his city seemed far from his immediate concerns.

He finally left for Bordeaux on October 15. A good horseman—and Montaigne was one—even with baggage, could travel as far as ninety kilometers a day; fast couriers managed to ride as many as 170 or even 200 kilometers a day. In the chapter "Of coaches," Montaigne says he had learned to ride all day "in the Spanish fashion," that is, without stopping. The distance from Rome to Bordeaux being about 1,500 kilometers, the journey should have taken him about twenty-five days—at an average of sixty kilometers a day with trunks and baggage. Montaigne took forty-five days to get home, that is twice as long as an average horseman.[7] The itinerary he chose for returning to Bordeaux was not the shortest: he crossed the Mont Cénis pass and arrived in Chambéry, but instead of proceeding directly to Lyon—the most direct route and the normal itinerary, which passed through Pont-en-Beauvoisin—Montaigne made another detour via the Lac du Bourget. He may have chosen this route, which took him across the Rhône near Yenne, to meet Francesco Cenami,[8] a banker in Lyon who had retired to this small village, and who made him "several very generous compliments" during his passage through the region.[9] He also bought new horses in Lyon and a mule in Limoges.

Montaigne had left his young brother, the lord of Mattecoulon, in Italy. Mattecoulon planned to study fencing with famous teachers and had decided to remain in Rome a little longer. Montaigne had left him forty-three crowns to cover his expenses. Being quarrelsome in temperament and carried away by his youthful ardor, Mattecoulon had the bad idea of putting his fencing lessons into practice. He was arrested for having fought a duel and spent some time in a Roman jail for serving as a second to Esparezat, a Gascon gentleman, in a duel with Louis de Saligny, baron of Rousset, seconded by La Villate. During this duel, Rousset and La Villate were killed, and Montaigne's brother was once again in serious trouble. After several efforts were made, Mattecoulon was finally freed after the king intervened directly, surely at Montaigne's request.[10]

As Montaigne indicates in his almanac, it was only on November 30 that he arrived at his château, after an absence of seventeen months and eight days. The new mayor was in no hurry to take up his functions, and he was reminded of his obligations. A threatening letter from Henry III, dated November 25, was waiting for Montaigne when he arrived home. Quite irritated by this delay, the king openly scolded him and ordered him to assume his municipal functions "without delay or excuse":

> Monsieur de Montaigne, because I have great esteem for your fidelity and zealous devotion to my service, I was pleased to hear of your election as

mayor of my city of Bordeaux, having found very pleasant and having confirmed the aforesaid election and all the more willingly because it was made without intrigue and when you were far away. On the occasion of which it is my intention, and I order and enjoin you very expressly, that you return, without delay or excuse, as soon as the present letter is delivered to you, to do the duty and service of the office to which you have so legitimately been called. And you shall do something that will be very pleasing to me, and the contrary would displease me greatly.[11]

It is always smart to play hard to get, and at this time it was not rare for a politician to refuse an office offered him by the king. For example, Henri de Mesmes was quite proud of having had to be ordered twice to join the king's Council.[12] Montaigne could not refuse to serve Henry III, because this letter was an order, but he did express his reluctance—and probably his displeasure at not being named ambassador—by dragging his feet and making the king wait.

At odds with the parlement, the king was counting on Matignon to establish his authority in Guyenne. Montaigne was part of this strategy of moving closer to the municipal authorities, but the parlement continued to meddle in the city's affairs. Thus, on November 21, the parlement had designated Richard de Lestonnac and Florimond de Raemond to attend the deliberations of the jurats at the city hall[13] regarding the implementation of the royal edicts. Montaigne had not yet taken up his functions, and the king was impatient to see him defend his point of view and represent his interests. On December 4, the king's general prosecutor tried to get the parlement to register the letters patent concerning Matignon's power "in order to complete the edict of pacification in this country of Guyenne, begging the Court to decide that it will register its Registers in accord with the king's will."[14] In no hurry to recognize Matignon as governor of Guyenne, the members of the parlement once again delayed the registration of his letters patent, claiming that the letters patent could not be presented by the king's prosecutor, but only by Matignon himself. These quibbles served chiefly to assert the parlement's autonomy and to remind the king that nothing would happen in Bordeaux without prior consultation with the members of parlement, who retained the right of inspection concerning the city's affairs and were constantly preoccupied with their honor and their authority. Montaigne thus began his first term in a climate of mutual distrust.

Four months late, the "elected" mayor finally took the oath of office in the church of Saint André in Bordeaux. In the presence of the people, Montaigne swore on the Bible and relics that he would "uphold the customs, ways, statutes, privileges, and liberties of the aforesaid city and its commune."[15] He had hardly taken up his office before he returned to his estate. He continued to take his task lightly and seemed in no hurry to get to work in early 1582. Putting the finishing touches on a new edition of the *Essais*, he spent most of his time in his château and seldom appeared in Bordeaux. He did the minimum, and the jurats of the city reproached him for his repeated absences and dilettantism. To respond to the critics who were already making themselves heard, Montaigne addressed these remarks to the jurats: "I beg you to excuse a little longer my absence, which I shall no doubt abbreviate as much as the burden of my affairs may permit. I hope that it will be short. However, you will keep me, please, in your good graces and command me, should the occasion present itself, to act on behalf of the public welfare."[16] The tone of this letter is sufficiently explicit. Montaigne was courteous and reverential, but he had other priorities. He claimed to be dealing with a few private and family matters, but perhaps he was also already thinking about his reelection at the end of July 1583.

Montaigne's public career in Aquitaine officially began in 1581, but his civic service had unfortunately put an end to other ambitions that were just as political and corresponded more to his aspirations. His election as mayor of Bordeaux in 1581 did not match his expectations at the time; instead, it was the result of particular circumstances and a political strategy worked out by those who had facilitated his rapid ascension in the entourage of Henry III and at the king's Court. Moreover, Montaigne had not even been consulted in the matter. The decision to have him "elected" mayor of Bordeaux was made during meetings at Fleix, that is, in his neighbor's château, in November 1580, almost three months after his departure for Italy. Montaigne seems not to have been informed of this political choice before he was elected. It is probable that he owed his election to the marquis of Trans, who had sponsored him and presented him at the Court.

Back on his estate, Montaigne became aware of the role that he was being asked to play on the regional political chessboard. Flattered, but not enthusiastic, he entered public life hesitantly, initially invoking the necessity of settling his private affairs. Of course, such a long stay abroad required particular attention to the economy of his household, but after the slow return from Italy, this absence of six months (from December 1581 to late May 1582) at the beginning of his first term as mayor of Bordeaux is explained mainly by the preparation of the second edition of the *Essais* for printing by his publisher, Simon Millanges.

The Mayor's Book

Montaigne's election as mayor of Bordeaux suddenly thrust him onto the political stage where Henry III was opposed by the king of Navarre in Aquitaine. In this context the first *Essais* of 1580 took on a public dimension, because their author was now mayor of Bordeaux. Simon Millanges saw in this development an opportunity at a time (early 1582) when he seems not to have been swamped with work, contrary to what was the case in late 1579 and early 1580. In 1582, Millanges printed mainly leaflets. In addition to the *Essais*, the inventory of his publications for that year is the following: a new edition of Pierre de Brach's poems; *Decreta Concilii provincialis Burdigalae*; *Edicts du Roy* (12 f.); *Edict du Roy sur la reformation du calendrier ecclésiastique* (4 f.); *Lettres du Roy pour l'Establissement de la Cour de la Justice en ses pays et duché de Guyenne* (4 f.), *Pomponii Melae de situ orbis libri tres* (61 p. and 13 f.); and *Hieracasophioy sive de verratione per accipitres libri duo* de Jacques-Auguste de Thou (published anonymously)[17] (less than 60 f.). When we add up the pages Millanges printed in 1582—with the exception of Montaigne's *Essais*—we arrive at a very low number. He had very few books in the pipeline and the reprinting of the *Essais* was the only important project he had for 1582. That is why it is likely that Millanges suggested, or at least encouraged, the publication of the 1582 text. The plan for a corrected edition of the *Essais* was conceived *after* Montaigne's return to Bordeaux. This scenario allows us to explain several particularities relative to this edition of 1582. If in fact Montaigne had made corrections and additions during his trip to Italy, we would have more remarks concerning his experiences on the other side of the Alps. For instance, the travel journal testifies to the richness of his encounters and his observations during his absence of seventeen months. If he took notes—in particular after his first sojourn in Rome—Montaigne included very few of them in the 1582 edition. This latest version of the *Essais* was prepared with a rapidity that is explained by the jurats' repeated urging that he assume his functions as soon as possible. Montaigne hastily produced a new edition on the cheap by correcting typographical errors in the text of 1580 and sprinkling it with a few Italianizing references.

If the 1580 edition was addressed to a royal audience and must be considered a *private edition* whose goal was to make its author known to a small group of influential people (which is not so different from the medieval model, in which the only thing that mattered was the personalized presentation of the book to the king, a prince or a patron), the 1582 edition was governed by a very different logic. The reprinting of the *Essais* during Montaigne's term as mayor served the publisher as much as it did the author, and for that reason it must be related to Montaigne's entrance into politics. Even enlarged, his audience nonetheless remained local or regional, and the publication sought mainly to confirm Montaigne's political power while at the same time stressing his membership in the nobility. In 1582 Montaigne had become a public man.[18] The reprinting of the *Essais* in 1582 is an excellent example of the political use to which his book could be put. In fact, it is not certain that in 1581, when he had just returned from Italy to take up his functions as mayor of Bordeaux, Montaigne intended to publish a new edition of his *Essais* so rapidly. What did he have to add, after all? In fact, very little. He did not have time to expand significantly the book he had published just before his departure, but his election as mayor of Bordeaux now made him a public man who had suddenly been projected onto the regional political scene. Simon Millanges was well aware of how he could make use of the notoriety acquired by one of his authors.

In 1582, François Grudé, lord of La Croix du Maine, had conceived the project of a dictionary of contemporary authors; it was a general catalog of all sorts of authors (those are the words used in the title: *toutes sortes d'auteurs*) who had written in the French language over the past five centuries. According a privileged place to the authors of his own time, La Croix du Maine drew up brief biobibliographies of more than three thousand writers in French in order to produce a general catalog of authors who had published books of their own or translations. After spending fourteen years in researching and compiling all kinds of biographical information, he had moved to Paris in May 1582 in order to receive authors at his home there. He acknowledged having obtained "notices or memoranda" from numerous authors who transmitted information about their lives to him directly. We can imagine that Montaigne was one of them, since the entry for "Montaigne" in the dictionary gives details that only the author or a member of his family could know.[19]

The article on Montaigne in La Croix du Maine's *Bibliothèque française* allows us to see how Montaigne presented himself to the public in the 1580s. The biographical part of the article begins with the author's titles, which are identical to those presented on the title page of the 1582 edition of the *Essais*. Then we learn that Montaigne was "initially" a councillor at the parlement of Bordeaux, and then, after the death of his elder brother, he "abandoned that estate in order to follow [that of] arms." However, so far as we know, Montaigne had no elder brother. According to this first biography, Montaigne is supposed to have left the parlement for a simple family reason, to concern himself with the noble lands of his ancestors. This invented brother of Montaigne's allowed him to explain easily his resignation as a member of parlement and to find a more honorable justification for his failure in that profession. Such an ideal biography made necessary his condition as a gentleman *replacing* an elder brother who had died prematurely. The expression "to follow arms" (*suyvre les armes*) used by La Croix du Maine (or by Montaigne) is clearly an exaggeration, since Montaigne did not participate in any battle, the siege of La Fère being the only time he was close to a battlefield. From a literary point of view, La Croix du Maine noted in Montaigne "his great learning and marvelous judgment" as well as the number and diversity of the authors he had read. According to La Croix du Maine (or more probably his source), "this work has been well received by all men of letters," but he also mentions that he had heard that there are some who "do not sufficiently praise this book of Essais, and do not attach as much importance to it as it deserves." However, this book is "very recommendable" for the education of anyone, because of "other very remarkable things that are included in it," though La Croix du Maine does not provide any further details.

La Croix du Maine associated the *Essais* with a kind of biography, "because this book contains nothing other than an ample statement of the life of the said lord of Montaigne, and each chapter contains a part of it." The confusion of the man and the work was deliberately maintained by the printers who anticipated—as early as the beginning of the seventeenth century—the public's taste for particular biographies. The silly project of portraying oneself, to adopt Pascal's formula, corresponded to an expectation on the part of readers at a time when portraits of famous men constituted a fashionable genre.[20] The title of the book includes its author's name: *Essais de Michel, seigneur de Montaigne*. How can a book on Michel, lord of Montaigne be read without learning when he was born, what education he received, what his occupation was, and under what circumstances he died? The life of Montaigne established itself very early on as a tool that could help the reader forge an opinion regarding the commentaries and judgments presented in each chapter of the *Essais*.

The second edition of the *Essais* was undoubtedly a commercial operation cooked up by Millanges. The author made very few changes to the text and only a few Italian quotations were added. The *Au lecteur* was recomposed by the printer for the occasion, but it remained fundamentally unchanged. We note only a few spelling corrections, probably made in the printer's workshop: *entrée* replaces *antrée*, *ils* replaces *ilz*, *moyen* replaces *moien*, and *connoissance* replaces *coignoissance*. The most notable difference is the capital letter on the word *Lecteur* (Reader), which was to be retained in the 1588 and 1595 editions. Montaigne's reader had changed, and he was aware of that fact. He had not received the diplomatic post he had been counting on, and he now had a political responsibility in Bordeaux. Having arrived very belatedly to take up his functions, he had hardly had time to revise his text. Nonetheless, the *Au lecteur* remains as equivocal as it was in 1580, despite a completely different context of publication. This probably did not displease Montaigne. What did he have to add? He had not received the desired post and a consolation prize had been proposed to him—or rather, imposed on him—as compensation. Montaigne was mayor because he had not been named ambassador. Keeping the same *Au lecteur* could then be considered (by him) as a reminder of a promise that had not been kept. Not changing the preface to his book offered him an opportunity to reassert an unsatisfied political ambition that acquiring a municipal office had not impaired. Montaigne projected the image of an editorial coherence that the vicissitudes of politics could not shake.

The preface to the reader (who in 1582 was no longer necessarily the king) could remain as it was. Montaigne's election as mayor of Bordeaux made him a political man who had suddenly been propelled into the heart of the religious

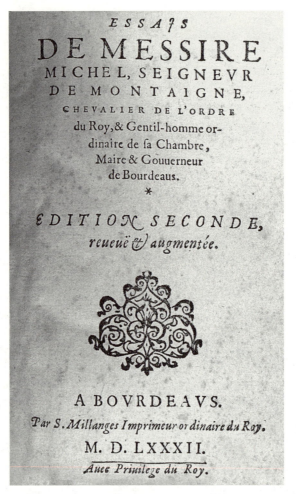

ESSAIS
DE MESSIRE
MICHEL, SEIGNEVR
DE MONTAIGNE,
CHEVALIER DE L'ORDRE
du Roy, & Gentil-homme or-
dinaire de sa Chambre,
Maire & Gouverneur
de Bourdeaus.

*

EDITION SECONDE,
reueuë & augmentée.

A BOVRDEAVS.
Par S. Millanges Imprimeur ordinaire du Roy.
M. D. LXXXII.
Auec Priuilege du Roy.

FIGURE 13. Second edition of the *Essais*, 1582 (private collection).

conflict dividing France. His publisher understood the advantage to be derived from the recent notoriety of one of his authors. He could count on an audience that was better defined than it was in 1580 and present his author as "Mayor and governor of Bordeaux" (figure 13). The *Essais* belonged to him by privilege, and it could reach a public unhoped for two years earlier. The minimal additions to the 1582 edition served to create the illusion of an "augmented" or "corrected" edition, but they did not result from any true work on Montaigne's part;[21] the additions from 1582 included only eight Italian quotations, eight Latin quotations, one Latin quotation translated into Italian, and thirty-four new passages of at least two lines each. On the whole, few changes. It is impossible to assert with certainty that Montaigne made these additions on a 1580

416

copy of the *Essais* that he had carried along with him to Italy. It seems more likely that he made these few additions after his return from Italy and at Millanges's request. They are very few for a stay abroad that lasted almost fifteen months.[ii]

The 1580 and 1582 editions of the *Essais* were thus addressed to different readers. The first was addressed to a *familial* and *royal* audience, while the second was addressed to a more *local* audience in the area of Bordeaux and Périgord. Although it had not succeeded in launching its author's career in diplomacy, the *Essais* of 1580 had still made it easier to obtain an important political office (as mayor), whereas the 1582 edition was conceived with a twofold objective: first as a commercial operation for Millanges but also as a way of making Montaigne's name better and more widely known in the region. This objective was connected with political propaganda. Millanges hoped to capitalize on his closeness to the mayor and benefit from his situation as a bookseller in Bordeaux. He had the necessary support in the city to publicize the mayor's book, and also to assert a claim to receive new printing contracts from the city. He enjoyed a monopoly on the books of ordinances, customs, and other texts relating to the administration of the city, and he also printed a large number of school textbooks for the College of Guyenne, which was also under the control of the mayor and the jurats. For example, in June 1582 the Chamber of Justice of Guyenne ordered that Simon Millanges be paid "cinq escus d'or sol deux tiers d'escus trois sols tournois" for having provided the court with two volumes of *Ordinances* along with the *Coustumes de Guyenne* and the *Edicts de pacification*.[22] Montaigne's election as mayor of Bordeaux was a genuine windfall for Millanges, who had one of his authors as leader of the city. By reprinting the mayor's book, he almost did the city and the region a favor, and publicly reaffirmed his friendship with one of his authors. It is useful to be well acquainted with the people who govern you; that could have been the printer-bookseller's motto. The name of Montaigne, along with his titles and functions printed on the title page, made it possible to increase the number of readers of a book that portrayed the mayor.

However, we must not exaggerate the success of this second edition, which seems to have had a relatively limited print run. It has been claimed that Montaigne's book had a national distribution as early as 1580 and 1582, but this view seems exaggerated, even if a catalog of booksellers in Augsburg—Hans Georg Portenbach and Tobias Lutzen—shows that the *Essais* was for sale at the Frankfurt Book Fair in the autumn of 1581.[23] It seems more likely that the 1582 edition was aimed at a local audience and that it was mainly in Guyenne that Mil-

---

[ii] Here we are only counting the months spent abroad, and not his stay in the Paris region before he left for Rome.

langes hoped to sell copies of the second edition of the *Essais*. After seventeen months outside of Bordeaux and Guyenne—fifteen of them outside France—the name of Montaigne was far from being on everyone's lips at the time of his return from Italy.

We must also consider the way in which the reprinting of the *Essais* in 1582 might have played an important role in the presentation of the mayor, not only to those he administered but also to the Bordeaux nobility. In fact, in the context of the election to the mayor's office in Bordeaux, the *Essais* of 1582 might have allowed Montaigne to shape his political image and confirm his independence of mind. Theological questions were now relegated to the background; the book had suddenly recovered a more secular and civil flavor, that it had in fact always had.

Driven by down-to-earth considerations, Montaigne did not take into account the oral "censure" and the reproaches that had been addressed to him regarding his book during his stay in Rome. He did not delete any reference to Fortune in the 1582 edition, even though we have proof that he reread attentively the passages found objectionable. At the end of the fourth chapter of Book I ("How the soul discharges its passions on false objects when the true are wanting"), he changed "d'autant que l'impieté y est jointe, qui s'en adressent a Dieu mesmes a belles injures, ou la fortune, comme si elle avoit des oreilles sujectes a nostre batterie" (1580) to read "ou à la fortune," adding the preposition *à* before *fortune*, thus correcting what he saw as a syntactical error, but he did not eliminate the reference to Fortune. The same thing happens at the end of chapter 12: "et est bien plus aisé a croire que la fortune ait ja favorisé" (1580). Here, Montaigne changes the tense of the verb that accompanies the word "Fortune": "a croire que la fortune favorisa." These examples show that Montaigne reread the passages in which the pagan goddess is mentioned but did not eliminate or modify them. So let us take literally what he says when he refrains from following the recommendations of others: "I flee command, obligation, and constraint. What I do easily and naturally, I can no longer do if I order myself to do it by strict and express command."[24] Attentive to others, Montaigne was nonetheless determined to act in accord with his own interests and convictions, often rejecting any pragmatic consideration connected with specific situations or events.

Montaigne resolutely situated himself in the humanist tradition and found it difficult to put up with the practical political questions that arose in his everyday work as mayor. In this sense, his term as mayor of Bordeaux permitted him to test the limits of politics when it amounts to simple governance. By repeating his attachment to the humanist tradition (with its obligatory dose of ancient paganism), the author of the *Essais* does not, however, distance himself from the Catholic religion. He simply dissociates literary license and religious faith.[25] In many another passage of the *Essais*, Montaigne insists on this essential distinction. But as we have suggested, the "noncorrections" in the 1582 edition of the *Essais* may also indicate that he did not have time to undertake major textual revisions. The most flagrant example of these rapid clarifications occurs at the beginning of the chapter "Of prayers," whose title was likely to attract his contemporaries' attention, as is shown by the suggestions and reproaches made by the Roman censors. Montaigne decided to take the initiative by cleaning up the somewhat controversial content of this chapter with as little loss as possible. Adding a clarification in the form of a preamble, he attenuated passages that might be judged philosophical or didactic by presenting his ideas as personal, unresolved "notions":

> I put forward formless and unresolved notions, as do those who publish doubtful questions to debate in the schools, not to establish the truth but to seek it. And I submit them to the judgment of those whose concern it is to regulate not only my actions and my writings, but even my thoughts. Equally acceptable and useful to me will be condemnation or approval. And therefore, always submitting to the authority of their censure, which has absolute power over me, I meddle rashly with every sort of subject, as I do here.[26]

This passage, added as an introduction to the chapter "Of prayers" in 1582, expresses an attempt at temporization and submission, but it also allows us to glimpse a "bolder" kind of writing. At the risk of overinterpretation, modern readers, at least, might nonetheless see in it a mark of literary temerity. Montaigne distances himself from the debates that were raging in his time and chooses to rise above the battle—or at least that is what he hopes to do. But it is not clear that this kind of temerity was intentional on Montaigne's part. On the other hand, the clarification carried out in these few lines does considerably attenuate the rest of the chapter, which it qualifies and defangs. With this addition, Montaigne seeks to reassert the instability of his judgment and especially his political and religious submission to those who "regulate" his actions, his writings, and even his thoughts. Thus we see appear a first trace of distancing between his ideas on political and religious questions and their shaping in the *Essais*. The two are not necessarily identical.

The preliminary discourse in the chapter "Of prayers" also sheds light on the corrective work he did in early 1582. Rather than revise a whole chapter in order to attenuate its import, Montaigne decided to defuse the explosive content that follows these lines, which are more literary than political. In this literary "paratext," Montaigne distances himself from the events of his time. His "formless and unresolved notions" are nothing more than that and must not be confused with a mark of commitment to a particular denomination. Montaigne submits to the authority of the Church, but did not have time to modify his text in detail to follow the recommendations of the censors. He repeats on several occasions that he is a good Catholic and reasserts elsewhere that he adheres to "the ancient beliefs of our religion, in the midst of so many sects and divisions that our century has produced."[27] These amplified passages allow the 1582 edition of the *Essais* to appear more Catholic than that of 1580.[28]

The political context of Montaigne's appointment as the mayor of Bordeaux also required him to tone down the political passages that might attract attention in this time of religious troubles. Montaigne was now a public figure, and his *Essais* were inevitably going to be subjected to an examination that he could not have foreseen for the 1580 edition. His audience had escaped him by the simple fact of the religious divisions, and Montaigne needed to warn it against drawing any abusive conclusions. That is how the opening of the chapter "Of prayers" must be read. Montaigne was not yet operating in the logic of "extensions" that we find later on; he had to move quickly to reprint his *Essais* as soon as possible. Everything suggests that the "Catholic reframing" of the chapter "Of prayers" was carried out rapidly when the 1582 edition was being prepared, that is, between December 1581 and March 1582. Montaigne's book had become a public work and was liable to be read by potential political or religious detractors.

The corrected edition of the *Essais* supplanted the preceding edition, because Montaigne kept the same title for his work. The *Essais* of the period when Montaigne was mayor is thus a revised edition rather than a new work. This kind of amendment of the 1580 text had a considerable political function, because Montaigne could no longer be attacked for an earlier text. The 1582 printing brought his thought up to date, or at least gave that impression. The rapid clarifications in the 1582 edition must therefore be interpreted in the light of his election as mayor of Bordeaux. Montaigne accepted a few remarks that had been addressed to him, cites a few Italian authors, and recalls various specific events of his sojourn in Italy.[29] The quotations drawn from Dante, Stefano Guazzo's *La Civil Conversatione*, and Benedetto Varchi's *Ercolano* make it possible to speak of a new book. The same goes for the quotations from Petrarch and an Italian translation of Propertius that seems to come from Guazzo. So far as the quotations from Tasso are concerned, though there is no trace of them in the travel journal, Montaigne was marked by his meeting with the Italian poet in Ferrara, which he describes in an addition in the 1582 edition: "I felt even more vexation than compassion to see him in Ferrara in so piteous a state, surviving himself, not recognizing himself or his works, which, without his knowledge and yet before his eyes, have been brought out uncorrected and shapeless."[30] Montaigne uses the same technique of briefly reported impressions to describe the statues of Suetonius he saw in Rome; and we find it again in an anecdote about Henry III that tells us that the king never wore gloves and did not wear different clothes in the winter.

These additions give an Italian flavor to his book without for all that representing a major rewriting. Montaigne's impressions of Italy were all drawn from a memory still fresh, and he had no need to refer to his travel journal to remember anecdotes from it. He also took advantage of the opportunity to revise his text to standardize the spelling and systematically correct (in rather distant passages) words written in different ways, such as *arondes*, corrected to read *arondeles* (modern French *hirondelle*, "swallow"). This hasty correction did not prevent the author from rereading his whole text to add a few details regarding Italian customs. The Turks customarily kiss on greeting one another, and in the 1582 edition Montaigne adds: "as the Venetians do."[31] Similarly, he comments on the rigor with which the common people are sometimes treated, and tells of having witnessed in Rome the execution by strangling of the famous thief Catena. The allusions to Italy are almost always based on personal experiences and refer to recent memories, but these "Italian commentaries" are not numerous and are always brief.[32]

The second edition of the *Essais* published in 1582 should still be considered a political document rather than a literary work. Few changes were made in the text, and Montaigne limited himself to moderating certain questionable passages and sprinkling his book with Italian anecdotes and examples. However, he omitted one important event that occurred during his stay in Italy, because his acquisition of Roman citizenship is not reported. Not until the 1588 edition of the *Essais* did he reproduce the text of the bull according him this privilege. This remarkable absence testifies to Montaigne's lack of time, between returning from Italy and taking up his functions as mayor of Bordeaux, to put together a new edition with major additions. It is likely that his election inspired Millanges, who was eager to print an enlarged edition of the *Essais* as soon as possible, to ask his author to provide one. Whatever one says about Montaigne's corrections and additions, these alterations did not require strenuous work, and it was possible to make them in less than three months. Nonetheless, they allowed Millanges to specify that this edition had been "revised and enlarged" (*revuë et augmentée*), an effective bookseller's trick.

Unfortunately, we know nothing about how many copies of the 1580 and 1582 editions were printed. In a list of 220 inventories of private libraries in Paris in the sixteenth century made after their owners' deaths, we find Montaigne's *Essais* in only six of them: those of Pierre Cabat, a bookseller (1598); Claude Cousin, the wife of Nicolas Millot, doctor-regent of the Paris faculty of medicine (1597); Jean Labas, a councillor (1585); Pierre Le Sannoys, a bookseller and bookbinder (1583); Pierre de Sayvre, a magistrate (1589); Charlotte Teste,

the wife of J. Chevalier, a prosecutor at the Châtelet (1586). It is however difficult to compare this list with that for other authors of the Renaissance. For example, we find thirteen occurrences for Rabelais's books, twenty-three for
Rondard, and ten for Du Bellay.[33]

The market for rare books (based on an inventory of sales catalogs over the
past century and a half) may tell us more than the holdings of public collections,[34] and leads us to think that the print run for the 1582 edition of the *Essais*
was about the same as that for the 1580 edition, maybe slightly more. This edition of a revised text ultimately shows the interest for Millanges, as much as for
Montaigne, of a less inaccurate publication. It was likely to help Millanges obtain further contracts with the city, and it displayed the author's titles of mayor
and governor of Bordeaux. Although Millanges had probably seen only a moderate interest in publishing the *Essais* in 1580, he now felt much more involved
in what represented a commercial operation of an entirely different scope because of the recent public notoriety of his author.

Finally, if Montaigne did not change the title of his book, it was probably
because this second edition was too close to the first. The *Essais* of 1582 is a *reprinting*, and Montaigne did not think it necessary to change the date of the
preface *Au lecteur*. Despite the handful of additions written in 1582, after the
return from Italy, neither the author nor the publisher considered the book sufficiently distinct from the 1580 edition to give it a different title. The objective
of making Montaigne's name better known in Bordeaux and in the surrounding region had been realized. The author of the *Essais* did not yet see himself as
a full-fledged writer and launched into a career as a municipal administrator
without even imagining that his book would one day appear in a third edition.
Keeping the same title for his book of 1582 was not yet part of a literary strategy
that was not clearly conceived until after 1585, when the Paris publisher Abel
L'Angelier was to play an essential role in transforming Montaigne's *persona* as
an author. In 1582 Montaigne's book was still profoundly marked by the political content of the first edition. However, without even thinking about it, Millanges and Montaigne had established—starting with the 1582 edition—a literary precedent that the author of the *Essais* would later turn to his advantage
when changing his publisher. What was at first a publishing expedient later
became an authorial strategy.

Bordeaux and Its Administration

It was only after the publication of the *Essais* of 1582, toward the end of the
summer, that Montaigne finally familiarized himself with the issues facing the
city of Bordeaux.[35] He was already halfway through his term, which at that

time was only two years. Without managerial experience—even though he had succeeded in increasing his family's patrimony since the death of his father—he was about to confront various interest groups that were fighting tooth and nail for control of the city and its economic resources. Unfortunately, Bordeaux's municipal archives no longer contain enough documents to evaluate with precision Montaigne's work as mayor, and the registers of the jurade are lacking for this period. Thus it is difficult to form an exact idea of the mayor's governance for the years 1581–85. However, other printed sources allow us to assess Montaigne's work at the head of one of the largest cities in France. As mayor, he probably preferred to live in the home made available to him in the Rue des Ayres. During his stays in Bordeaux, Montaigne had the use of this house, the *mairerie*, which had served as the official residence of the mayor of Bordeaux and his family since the Middle Ages.[36] Montaigne's own house in the Rue de la Rousselle reminded his critics that his family belonged to the world of commerce, and the mayor had to display a way of life more appropriate to a member of the nobility. He had no difficulty in covering in a single day the forty-three kilometers that separated his château from the City Hall. It took him approximately four hours on horseback.

Montaigne received his political instructions directly from the king and from Matignon, the king's lieutenant governor in Guyenne. His principal role—at least for the king who had had him "elected"—was to inform Matignon of what was going on in Bordeaux, a city that was still suspect in the eyes of the king's government.[37] He fully assumed his responsibility as a political observer. As mayor of Bordeaux, he was in permanent contact with Matignon.[38] On October 30, 1582, Montaigne wrote to Matignon that nothing "new" had happened in the city. Two years later, when the end of his second term as mayor was approaching, he continued faithfully to submit his reports to Matignon: "The rest of the country remains quiet and there is nothing on the move."[39] His correspondence with Matignon shows clearly that the mayor was following the orders of the lieutenant governor who was his superior.

Promoted to Marshal of France in 1579, Matignon had been sent to Guyenne after the peace of Fleix to replace Biron, who no longer enjoyed unanimous support in the region. Brantôme later said about Matignon that he "was as cold as the other [Biron] was hot."[40] Famed for his abilities as a negotiator (not Biron's strong point), Matignon had also succeeded in halting the Protestants' establishment in Normandy, his own ancestral area. To the king and the queen mother, he seemed to be the man of the hour to bring Guyenne into line. Although he was appointed by Henry III to represent his interests in Guyenne, Matignon also had to answer to Henry of Navarre and keep on his good side. It was on this point that Biron had failed. Matignon excelled in maintaining an equilibrium between the king and the Huguenot leader in Aquitaine. He could not be elected mayor of Bordeaux immediately (he was elected in 1585) because he had first to make people forget his reputation as a Norman and then make himself accepted by the Guyenne aristocracy. It was inconceivable to elect a "foreigner" to lead a city proud of its political past and aware of its cultural specificity.

The king and his counselors had decided that the offices of mayor and governor of the region—titles that had historically been given to the mayor of Bordeaux—would be temporarily separated. Montaigne was mayor and "governor" of the city—a title that did not mean much—whereas Matignon, as lieutenant governor of Guyenne, had been given the real political and military powers and served as a de facto governor of the region. Since the edict of Beaulieu issued in 1576, the king of Navarre had recovered his title of governor of Guyenne, but the gates of the city of Bordeaux remained closed to him because of his religion. The lieutenant governor designated by Henry III was responsible for ensuring the city's military security and for seeing to it that the Protestants neither exercised too much influence there nor took power. The former mayor of Bordeaux, Biron, had assumed these functions of lieutenant governor of Guyenne and mayor of Bordeaux with a certain success before he came to be seen as a man of another time—a time when it was still possible to ignore the Huguenots' demands and reply to them with gunpowder. This policy was no longer relevant, and it had been replaced by an approach based on compromise and negotiation. Montaigne had not yet returned from Italy when Matignon arrived in Bordeaux to take up his military command, on October 15, 1581, around eight in the morning.[41]

About 40,000 people lived in Bordeaux when Montaigne was mayor (figure 14).[42] It was the fifth-largest city in the kingdom after Paris (300,000), Rouen (75,000), Lyon (65,000), and Toulouse (60,000).[43] According to Théodore de Bèze, 7,000 Protestants lived in Bordeaux. Although this figure may appear to be exaggerated, it is confirmed by a document from the period that estimates the number of Huguenot households in the city at the time of the Saint Bartholomew's Day massacre in Bordeaux[44] to have been 1,200, or nearly 6,000 Protestants. Protestants represented more than 15 percent of the city's population, a figure far above the national average (less than 10 percent). This high proportion of Protestants eager to have political representation had to be pacified and controlled. The king feared that the city would be seized by a Huguenot coup, and he needed to be informed about the political situation and troop movements in the region. It was essential that communications between Matignon and Montaigne be frequent and swift in order to forestall any military operation within the city walls. For four years, Montaigne was first of all a faithful servant of the king in Bordeaux and only secondarily an administrator in the service of the city. His relations with Matignon remained constant and

FIGURE 14. Joris Hoefnagel, *Civitatis Burdegalensis in Aquitanea genuina descrip*, 1554 (private collection).

predictable, and he fully performed his role as an informer. In addition to this political responsibility to represent royal authority in Bordeaux, Montaigne also had to arbitrate the constant frictions between the parlement and the jurade, and prevent the deplorable political and religious climate—which was exacerbated by personal quarrels—from affecting the proper functioning of the city's economic and commercial activity.

The parlement was increasingly meddling in the city's affairs and had infiltrated the jurade. The administrative jurisdiction of this municipal council was sometimes contested, notably in matters of policing and regulating the transportation of merchandise within the city walls. For example, a memorandum written by Biron in April 1580 proposed to the king that the election of the jurats in Bordeaux take place without the parlement's intervention, and that the English who came to Bordeaux to buy wine should be forced, as they had earlier, to ask the jurats' permission to do so. Thus Biron tried to reduce the growing power of the parlement in the city's affairs.[45] Three months later, he warned the king that there was a great danger that the Protestants might seize the city.

The city walls had large breaches in several places, and the jurats could not repair them for lack of public funds. Annoyed by the members of parlement who
meddled increasingly in the city's affairs, the jurats constantly complained
about the diminishing power of the jurade and the mayor's office. It was to win
back their administrative powers that they wrote to the king, explaining that
the parlement's councillors were not formerly accustomed to attend general assemblies or the election of the jurats. The municipal administration was trying
to free itself from the power of the parlement, and Montaigne found himself
directly involved in this political battle.

The way in which the mayor was elected had been changed after the 1548
revolt. Since 1550, the mayor had no longer been chosen for life; instead, he was
now elected every two years. According to the chronicler Jean Darnal, the
mayor of Bordeaux "had always been chosen and elected from the most noble,
valiant, and capable lords of the country."[46] This change allowed the king to
control the city's administrative and political apparatus more easily. The requirement that he reside in the city was not very restrictive. For example, the
mayor's presence was not required for the election of jurats, since the city's statutes stipulated that "the aforesaid mayors [must] attend and preside over elections, if they are in town."[47] The office of deputy mayor was eliminated after
1550 in order to concentrate power in the hands of a single man, whose main
task consisted in "defending the privileges, statutes, and liberties of the aforesaid city." Confronted by the steady growth of the population in the course of
the second half of the sixteenth century, the city had to considerably enlarge its
police force. We see, for example, a great increase in the number of officers of
the guard between 1550 and 1580. There were twenty of them during Montaigne's term as mayor. The salaries of municipal officials were increased just
before his election. In 1579 the wages of the captain, the lieutenant, and the officers of the guard were raised to a thousand *livres* per annum. The development
of the municipal administration led, of course, to higher taxes.

By virtue of the city's ancient titles, the mayor and the jurats were also called
"governors of Bordeaux," since in the absence of the king's lieutenant governor
they held the "password" and kept the keys to the city's gates and towers. Montaigne considered himself to be technically a governor of Bordeaux, and did all
he could to restore the reputation of an administration that the king had mistreated since the revolt of 1548. In June 1556, the king had returned to the
mayor and the jurats all the honors they had enjoyed before the troubles of
1548.[48] Despite the restoration of the city's privileges, Montaigne had to cross
swords repeatedly with the military authority of the captain of the guard and
the governors of the two strongholds situated within the city, the castles of
Trompette and Le Hâ, in order to impose his municipal authority. Although at
first the captain of the guard rejected the jurisdiction of the jurats and the

mayor, new letters patent relating to the mayor's powers ordered him, along with his lieutenant and officers, "paid and salaried from the aforesaid city's coffers," to obey the command of the mayor and the jurats.[49] This slow reconquest of the authority of the mayor and the jurats was completed only at the time when Montaigne became mayor in 1581. Thus it was with an increased political power and a control that was greater than ever over the city's police that Montaigne entered office to defend in Bordeaux the interests not only of Henry III but also those of the jurats who were counting on him to make their city prosper.

Initially, Montaigne had to put up with jurats who had more local ambitions and responsibilities. Moreover, he was expected to be their spokesman in dealing with Matignon and the king of Navarre. When Montaigne was mayor, the jurade of the city of Bordeaux was composed of six jurats (instead of twelve before 1550)—on the model of the Paris aldermen (*échevins*)—half of who came up for election every two years. Two jurats were elected from the nobility, two from the bourgeoisie, and two from the magistracy. A jurat elected for two years could run for office again only five years after the end of his term. The electorate also consisted of twenty-four (originally, thirty) notables recruited in equal numbers from the gentlemen, merchants, and magistrates of the city. These notables (all of whom were members of the Council of Thirty) were elected each year and had as their function to advise the jurats in matters concerning management and the municipal police. The mayor had to belong to the nobility of the sword, and the people of Bordeaux would not have accepted a foreigner at the head of their city. Thus we can understand why it was important for the author of the *Essais* to emphasize his noble titles (*Messire, gentilhomme, seigneur*) placed prominently on the title page of his *Essais* in 1582. From the administrative point of view, the role of the mayor consisted primarily in supervising the jurade and serving as an arbiter in the event of a conflict.

Montaigne had a hard time managing the often contradictory interests of the nobility, the bourgeoisie, and the parlement. During her visit to Bordeaux in September 1578, Catherine de Medici had been warmly received by the jurats, who had given her an eight-foot-long dolphin caught the same morning, as well as a "golden pentagon weighing two marcs,"[iii] but on the other hand she was poorly received by the parlement. Annoyed by these members of parlement too insistent on their independence, she "caused to be drawn up a regulation regarding the government of the city and the nomination of intendants to the jurades."[50] On this occasion, she addressed copious remonstrances to the court, which she had harangued by M. de Foix before leaving Bordeaux, very unhappy,

[iii] A unit of weight used by jewelers, equivalent to approximately half a pound. [Trans.]

on October 1. Like other great cities of the Renaissance, Bordeaux had several interest groups competing with one another, and the mayor found himself in the middle of these rival pressure groups, tugged at by each of them. His arbitration was often perceived as treachery by the losing party. Tensions were frequent among representatives of the nobility and those of the bourgeoisie, the parlement, and the jurats, Matignon, and the king of Navarre.

During his first term, Montaigne's strategy consisted in not openly taking sides and remaining outside local political scheming. As he said after 1585, he preferred to keep to himself: "Outside the knot of controversy I have maintained my equanimity and pure indifference."[51] He presented himself as a moderate man, a centrist, who used his humanist erudition to adopt a more universal perspective. Gabriel de Lurbe, the author of a *Chronique bordeloise* and a prosecutor-syndic in 1581–82, speaks of Montaigne, mayor of Bordeaux, in very laudatory terms and describes him as endowed with a "singular erudition,"[52] thus emphasizing his qualities as a humanist more than his political or administrative competencies. Montaigne's book had helped present him as a man in the service of the *civitas* (in conformity with the antique ideal) and not of the *urbs* (in its present concrete form), and this constituted a considerable advantage when particularly difficult decisions had to be made. His knowledge of the Ancients and the numerous Greek and Latin quotations scattered throughout his book won him a certain intellectual respect. The city had at its head a humanist, an image that was unlikely to displease Montaigne. What a difference from the preceding mayor, Biron, who took a more "soldierly" approach to his office and did not hesitate to fire cannon shots to resolve the slightest problem!

From the outset, Montaigne had announced his intentions to the jurats. If he was mayor, that was not because of his experience as a manager, but because of his political innocence, which placed him above the usual municipal cabals: "On my arrival I deciphered myself to them faithfully and conscientiously, exactly such as I feel myself to be: without memory, without vigilance, without experience, and without violence."[53] He presented himself as a political model out of the ordinary for a city subject to high tensions. Far from the usual political struggles and personal quarrels, he offered an independence of judgment that could be verified in his *Essais*, which had been reprinted in Bordeaux that year. The famous consubstantiality of the man and the book, defended before the king a little more than two years earlier, served him once again to define the political framework of his municipal function. We can easily see how he could consider as strategic the decision to reprint his book before taking up his position in Bordeaux. Simon Millanges might even have been able to convince him to indicate his administrative responsibilities on the title page—"mayor and governor of Bordeaux"; a book in the service of an office.

As we have said, the mayor entered upon his functions more than ten months after his election. How can we explain a humanist's lack of interest in serving his city and his king? His election—rather a nomination—was a disappointment for Montaigne, who had not even campaigned to obtain a municipal office. For him, his election as mayor came as a surprise, because he was expecting different favors. A diplomat's title would have been better suited to his inclination and temperament. Being well acquainted with the world of Greek and Roman antiquity, Montaigne may have thought that the politics of Bordeaux was at the antipodes of the conception he had formed of the city and its administration. On the other hand, the choice of Montaigne as mayor of Bordeaux had a considerable advantage on the level of local and municipal politics. The descendant of a family of notables that had been living nobly for more than a hundred years (since the purchase of the noble house of Montaigne dated from 1477), and that had served the city in its time, he was well acquainted with the functioning of the parlement to which he had belonged in an earlier career that was not so far in the past. The name of Eyquem had long been associated with the administration of the city, and Montaigne had the advantage of continuity. His grandfather, Grimon Eyquem, had been a jurat in 1485 and provost in 1503. His father, Pierre, was also a jurat and provost of the city in 1530, before being chosen as deputy mayor in 1536, and then elected mayor in 1554. Even if he had not imagined this responsibility, Montaigne was definitely situated in the lineage of great municipal servants. In principle, his family history should also have made it easy for him to be accepted by the Guyenne nobility.

His name had not encountered any opposition when it was mentioned during the discussions at Fleix. This proposal was endorsed by the marquis of Trans. In 1581, Montaigne could count on the support of members of the jurade who belonged to the nobility and who saw in him an ardent defender of their values. After all, they had been seduced by the ideas put forward by this gentleman in his book: glory, heroism, bravery, and virtue occupied a considerable place in it. Logically, the nobility thus saw in him an ally. Similarly, the bourgeois on the jurade did not oppose his election, because Montaigne had already presented himself as a man full of pragmatism and common sense. This situation is rather paradoxical when one knows Montaigne's scorn for anything that had to do with business and the world of commerce in general. He was thus officially "elected" mayor of Bordeaux at the king's will, but also after he had been unanimously approved by the jurats Pierre Dupérier, Gabriel de Lurbe, François Treihes, Guillaume de Cursol, Jehan Turnmet, and Mathelin Fort.

The social origin of the members of the jurade had changed since the first half of the sixteenth century, a period during which the jurats who came from the nobility represented almost half the members of the administration of the city,[54] while bourgeois represented only 15 percent and magistrates 40 percent.

On the other hand, during the second half of the century there was a steady increase in the number of bourgeois and merchants (40 percent) elected to the jurade, to the detriment of the nobility, which now represented only 30 percent, about the same as the *robins*.[55] Against his nature, and for strictly political reasons, Montaigne saw himself obliged to support the demands of the bourgeoisie, often to the disadvantage of the interests of the nobles and the *robins*. Despite the uncontested political domination of the bourgeois on the jurade, it has nonetheless been observed that during Montaigne's term of office, the bar retained much of its power.[56] We shall see that the parlement gave Montaigne a great deal of trouble and forced him to confront directly his former colleagues at the Palais de l'Ombrière.

The bourgeois, whose prosperity came essentially from their economic and commercial activity, were not entirely satisfied to see a noble at the head of the city. Since 1550, the law provided that "the institution and deposition by the treasurer of the public funds of the aforesaid city belongs forever to the mayor and jurats of that city,"[57] but the bourgeois and powerful merchants intended to have a right to inspect the city's accounts, being well aware that they were mainly responsible for the wealth that made Bordeaux a flourishing city. They wanted to be sure that the money they paid to the city through various taxes would be returned to them in the form of municipal investments intended to promote the transportation and storage of merchandise in the city. Consequently, it was only fair to complain to the mayor and to accuse him of defending the nobility's prerogatives. By means of this constant pressure, the bourgeois sought to ensure that the city's administration was indeed on their side and responded to their demands. They were particularly intent on influencing the supervision of the treasury. However, a decision of March 7, 1583, reaffirmed the mayor's privilege with regard to what concerned the treasury.[58] Montaigne had no intention of yielding to the bourgeois's pressure, even if he often made concessions to them for political reasons. Against all expectations, he had understood that the bourgeois could become his best allies.

In 1561, the king had authorized the people of Bordeaux to hold, by virtue of their ancient privileges, two free fairs per year, each lasting thirty days, the first starting on October 15 and the second on February 15. These free fairs permitted the merchants who went to them to enjoy the same privileges as those who went to the fairs in Paris, Lyon, and Rouen, or those of Brie, Champagne, and Poitou. Their merchandise—with the exception of woad—was exempt from all the taxes usually levied by the king.[59] Letters patent issued by Charles IX and dated March 27, 1571, granted these two free fairs for an indefinite time. To avoid cheating, a declaration made by Henry III limited the freedom of fairs in 1576, establishing a distinction between merchandise brought into the sénéchaussée of Guyenne before the opening of the fairs—commodities that would be sold during the fairs but outside their area of freedom—and the merchandise that would merely pass through the city during these fairs without having been unloaded inside it.[60] During his two terms as mayor, Montaigne had to cope with numerous cases regarding foreign merchants navigating on the Garonne River who had unpacked their wares at the port, thus exposing themselves to a fine of three hundred Bordeaux *sols*, since the city's statutes stipulated that it was "also forbidden to all sorts of people, merchants and others bringing and conveying any merchandise into the city, to sell it in any way without having first acquired a ticket."[61] This kind of incident happened almost every day and demanded immediate action on the part of the mayor and the jurats.

On the administrative front, the parlement continued more than ever to meddle in the current affairs of the city. In 1556, Charles IX had decided that two councillors of the parlement would attend the general assemblies at the City Hall the better to supervise what was debated there. This parlementary surveillance was criticized by the jurats coming from the nobility and the bourgeoisie, who sought to separate the powers of the parlement and those of the city. In the sixteenth century, Bordeaux was considered a nonconformist, even rebellious city. During the first half of the century, the sovereign's authority became increasingly unpopular and contested in Bordeaux, in Saintonge, and in Guyenne as a result of the repeated levies and new taxes. The parlement was supposed to be a tool of royal power, but it was in permanent conflict with the jurats and the municipal government. At the center of the disagreement was the parlement's police power over the city and its almost daily interference in the city's affairs. However, on December 21, 1556, eight years after the tax revolt of 1548, the king had restored to the mayor and the jurats their police powers in the city. The city's privileges were confirmed in 1573 by royal letters patent[62] that also ordered the parlement of Bordeaux to maintain the mayors and jurats in the possession of the honors that had been returned to them by letters patent in June 1556. In 1557, just after the end of Pierre Eyquem's term as mayor, the people of Bordeaux were once again authorized to carry arms. The same year, the mayor and the jurats were able to resume their places in ceremonies and public processions. They were once again authorized to precede presidial judges and the city's provost. The city hall bell, which was a symbol of Bordeaux's power and had been removed after the disturbances in 1548, was put back in place on September 21, 1561.

While Pierre Eyquem was mayor, the city of Bordeaux recovered most of its privileges. The jurats regained their authority in matters of criminal justice in the city and its suburbs, and civil justice was entrusted to the seneschal, who could issue judgments in the first instance. The Bordeaux parlement essentially handed down decisions regarding appeals, whereas the seneschal decided présidial cases in first and last instance, and all other cases in the first instance, though these could be appealed before the parlement. In Montaigne's time, this distinction between the legal jurisdictions was a constant source of conflict, and the judgments rendered at the level of the city were sometimes invalidated on appeal by the parlement after a report from one of the Chambres des Enquêtes. It had taken the city twenty-five years to recover its privileges in matters of municipal policing. Thus the Edict of Amboise, issued in January 1572, proposed the creation of a chamber of police composed of a jurat (bourgeois) and a councillor in the parlement. The jurade and the mayor defended tooth and nail their judicial authority, and almost always saw interventions by members of parlement as inappropriate interference.

We can imagine the political alliances that were formed on both sides to influence judicial decisions relating to the proper functioning of the city. For example, on May 7, 1572, the parlement sent an emissary to the king to inform him of remonstrances affecting his "judicial authority."[63] The parlement argued that the chamber of police infringed on the royal authority represented by the parlement. For their part, after the Saint Bartholomew's Day massacre, the mayor and jurats of Bordeaux wrote in turn to Charles IX, congratulating themselves on the "public tranquility" prevailing in the city, "in accord with Your Majesty's intention that thanks to God no turmoil occurred there."[64] Municipal officials even mentioned a great number of conversions among the Protestants. That was what better police could produce. In the early 1580s, both the parlement and the jurats made every effort to make it known that they were the only ones who were resolutely on the side of the royal authority when it was a matter of policing the city. As mayor of Bordeaux, Montaigne found himself thrust into the heart of an open war punctuated by scathing judicial skirmishes.

In order to clarify the question of justice and political jurisdiction in Bordeaux, a ruling of the Council stated that the Edict of Amboise did not in any way abolish the authority of the mayor and the jurats. Indeed, it even reconfirmed the mayor and the jurats in "the justice and political jurisdiction belonging to them in the aforesaid city and suburbs," and also did not "intend that the court of parlement of Bordeaux alter or diminish their jurisdictions; nor that the nomination of jurats and bourgeois who are to assist the police, in accord with the aforesaid edict, appertain to the court of parlement."[65] It was clear that in matters of political jurisdiction the parlement was supposed to follow and respect the jurisdictions of the municipal officials. After 1550, "the mayor and the jurats of the city of Bordeaux will all have the justice and political jurisdiction of the city of Bordeaux and its suburbs."[66] These privileges were confirmed in 1573. Judicial practice was an entirely different story, however. Since the creation of the parlement of Bordeaux, the authority of the jurats in matters of justice had significantly diminished. All the decisions made by the mayor, the seneschal, and the jurats could be appealed to the parlement.

The new powers granted to the mayor and the jurats were very quickly reduced by rulings issued by the parlement. For example, in 1551 the parlement ordered that the appeal of sentences handed down by mayors and jurats in police matters had to be presented to the seneschal of Guyenne before moving on to the parlement. Similarly, a ruling stipulated that the seneschal of Guyenne would attend the elections of mayors and jurats.[67] A war over administrative and judicial jurisdiction had been declared among these three axes of power in the city: the city and its administrators; the parlement; and the seneschal, the king's military representative in Guyenne.

The mayor and the jurats opposed the jurisdiction of the lieutenant governor of Guyenne, and the king, in an order issued in 1553, changed his mind for a time. The presence of royal soldiers garrisoned in the Trompette castle and the fort of Le Hâ also created tensions with the municipal officials, who did not like having these garrisons escape their control. They issued several municipal edicts to make the life of the royal troops more difficult. For example, the people of the city were not required to provide them with wood, candles, "or other utensils, unless paid for."[68] The Trompette castle was under the command of Louis Ricard Gourdon de Genouillac, baron of Vaillac, who was later devoted to the Catholic League but was above all a hot-headed detractor of Montaigne and the most redoubtable opponent to his reelection as mayor in 1583. Matignon and Montaigne had to constantly temper the Catholic ardor of a faction that was in the minority but was among the most active, and that they could not confront openly because doing so would expose them to accusations of being in the pay of the Protestants. Montaigne was also expected to maintain good relations with the king of Navarre. The League was gradually gaining a hold over Henry III, who was being overwhelmed by the extremist Catholic party. It was only after many hesitations that Matignon and Montaigne finally succeeded in impressing Vaillac in the spring of 1585 and forced him to hand over the stronghold that was supposed to be controlled by Henry III but was in reality under the influence of Guise's followers. This political development also pleased the king of Navarre, who did not like Vaillac.

The power of the king's lieutenant governor was rather limited in matters affecting the city alone. However, the religious aspect of current affairs soon exceeded by far any administrative consideration, and it was through the maintenance of the right religion (the Catholic) that he was authorized to intervene. Henry III's letter patent relating to the attributions of military authorities stipulated that the king's governor and the lieutenant governor would not have their own jurisdiction, but only the right to repress uprisings, the municipal magistrates and the ordinary tribunes being the only ones in charge of the police in the cities. The captains of the two castles could therefore not officially hinder the execution of decisions made by the judiciary.

This ongoing struggle between the parlement and the city in matters of legal jurisdiction was still continuing when Montaigne became mayor. As a result of the obligations of his office, he was often in disagreement with the parlement of which he had once been a member. Not only had he abandoned this milieu ten years earlier, but also his office had transformed him into the unwilling head of the opposition. He took advantage of this to settle a dispute that went back to the beginning of the 1560s. As soon as he was elected mayor, Montaigne found himself in a particularly ambiguous situation and made decisions that were often contrary to his personal convictions. The complexity of the judicial relations between the city and the parlement did not make the mayor's task any easier when it came to arbitrating conflicts connected with commerce and merchandise. However, Montaigne could not allow himself to confront openly the parlement, which was the official representative of royal authority. The jurats and the mayor of Bordeaux were regularly in conflict with the parlement to ensure that the city's privileges were respected, and Montaigne was always negotiating compromises. The parlement demanded superior authority and played on the political weakness (real or perceived) of the city to force the king to increase its judicial purview. Caught between these different pressure groups, the author of the *Essais* was aware of the "little power he ha[d] in this city," and complained overtly about it in a letter to Matignon in October 1582.[69]

One of Montaigne's functions—and not the least important one—was to arbitrate legal disputes between merchants and to review the statutes of the various professions. Almost all the statutes of the artisanal professions were reviewed and amended during his two terms as head of the municipal administration. Thus the creation in 1563 of a consular jurisdiction in Bordeaux had made it possible to deal with quarrels between merchants in order to resolve "all the suits and disputes that would afterward arise between merchants with regard to merchandise alone."[70] The consuls' jurisdiction was however strictly limited, because they were to concern themselves only with sales, purchases, and promises of sales, or the purchase of merchandise by wholesale or retail businessmen. This consular jurisdiction concerned only conflicts between merchants regarding merchandise. Because it was responsible for the regulation of the police, the city ratified the statutes of the crafts and the guilds. Between 1582 and 1585, the mayor intervened regularly to arbitrate disputes between trade associations whose areas of authority overlapped, thus giving rise to conflicts.

As mayor, Montaigne was surrounded by a large number of officials and municipal employees. At that time, the administration of the city included a city clerk, a tax inspector, twenty-four sergeants, a wine marker for the wines of the "haut pays,"[iv] two heralds, two collectors of the tax on fish, a porter at City Hall, a bread inspector, a bread weigher, an executioner, a river guard, a wheat clerk, two river inspectors, two salt fish inspectors, an attorney and a prosecutor at the parlement, a guest of the city, a city solicitor, two prosecutors in the county of Ornon and the barony of Veyrines, an almoner, a cleaner of the grating on the River Devise, and a cleaner of the public wash house. All these officials received wages that varied between 100 *livres* for the prosecutor, the syndic, and the clerk, and four *livres* for the cleaner of the grating and the cleaner of the public wash house. Other employees were supposed to clear away rubbish and keep the streets free of obstacles. The College of Guyenne, which operated under the authority of the city, was a considerable expense. The principal of the college received a salary of 1,000 *livres* per year, and each professor received 600 *livres*. Barbers, priests, and sergeants were also remunerated by the city, as was the superintendent of the city workers. Just after Montaigne was named mayor, letters patent issued by Henry III ordered the continuation of the payment of 3,000 *livres* allocated for various municipal expenses. These discretionary funds were under the control of the mayor and the jurats. The amount was payable on presentation of the receipt of the two *coutumes*[v] for the needs of the city and without any explanation of the sums expended being required.[71]

In Montaigne's time, the municipal administration constituted a workforce that varied between sixty and seventy persons placed directly under the authority of the mayor. The list of municipal employees makes clear the activities that allowed the city to raise the majority of its revenues, chiefly the wine trade, which was the subject of a disproportionate part of the city's ordinances and regulations, but also the sale and exportation of salt fish and the trade in wheat. The bourgeois thus made a major contribution to the city's wealth and for that reason benefited from significant political and economic advantages. The privileges Henry III granted to the city of Bordeaux stipulated that "the aforesaid bourgeois of our city of Bordeaux, even though they are not nobles but commoners, will nonetheless be able to acquire fief and noble lands."[72] This dispensation, which had far-reaching consequences, was perceived as a veritable affront by a nobility that was no longer able to impose its prerogatives. Considered as a representative of the nobility at the beginning of his term, Montaigne soon came to be seen as a spokesman for the bourgeoisie. The city's wealthy merchants were accumulating dispensations and were increasingly able to escape taxation. For example, they were exempt from the *taille*, and a growing number of them were also exempted from paying other taxes. Adding insult to injury,

---

[iv] *Les vins du haut pays* were those produced inland from Bordeaux, as far away as Cahors and Gaillac, but "marked" and shipped through Bordeaux. [Trans.]

[v] The *coutume* was a sales tax. [Trans.]

the bourgeois could even acquire dignities. And Montaigne let them do it—not that he could have halted this historical tendency, but he was accused of not having sufficiently defended the interests of his order.

The Public Welfare

In 1581, Montaigne was not yet fifty years old, and he still had ahead of him a political career of which the mayor's office was far from being the conclusion. At least, that was how he saw it after 1583. He was planning to use his experience as mayor of Bordeaux as a political stepping stone to move on to other offices more compatible with his ambitions. The marquis of Trans continued to serve as his advisor in all matters concerning public affairs, and Montaigne remained more faithful than ever to his sponsor in politics. Until the end of his second term as mayor of Bordeaux, he often made the trip to Fleix to consult his protector. For example, on February 9, 1585, he wrote that he had his "boots on his legs to go to Fleix."[73] As he acknowledged, the visits to Fleix to consult Gaston de Foix were an integral part of his service, just as were his written reports to Matignon.

Montaigne was well aware that one cannot succeed in politics without support in high places, and that it was essential to maintain political networks. He also knew that it was dangerous to put all his eggs in the same basket. Royal favors disappeared as quickly as they appeared, and he therefore constantly had to broaden the company he kept. This was the logic of the politician and the courtier. Montaigne could not forget that one of those whose support he had formerly sought at the time of the publication of La Boétie's works in 1571, Henri de Mesmes, had fallen into disgrace in early January 1582, at the same time that Montaigne was taking up his functions in Bordeaux. It was Catherine de Medici who had caused Mesmes to lose Henry III's favor.

The king frequently changed his mind and did not always keep his promises—Montaigne was well placed to testify to that after his disappointments in Rome. Immediately after his arrival at the mayor's office, on December 13, 1581, Henry III had dissolved the tripartite chamber (one-third of which was composed of Protestant magistrates) by letters patent addressed to the parlement of Bordeaux. This tripartite chamber had been established in Agen in July 1578 in conformity with article 22 of the Edict of Bergerac, but it had not fulfilled the king's expectations.

Two and a half years later, the Fleix accords between the duke of Anjou and the king of Navarre had foreseen several measures relating to secure places, the burial places of the Protestants, and especially the creation of an exceptional chamber in Guyenne. Article 11 of this accord stipulated that the king would send two presidents and fourteen councillors to Guyenne to judge "all causes, trials, and disputes and contraventions of the Edict of pacification."[74] This chamber, composed of members of the Privy Council and councillors of the parlement of Paris, was supposed to receive the approval of the king of Navarre "so that if any of them were suspect, it would be permissible to make this known to his Majesty, who would elect others to take their places."

On November 26, 1581, a new edict changed the situation once again, decreeing that "on the advice and deliberation of the queen our mother . . . we establish a Chamber of Justice in our country of Guyenne, which is in the jurisdiction solely of our court of parlement of Bordeaux," and granting it "the knowledge and sovereign jurisdiction of all matters both civil and criminal as well as any others of whatever kind."[75] This chamber of justice had as its first president Pierre Séguier, the sixth president of the Paris parlement and a member of the Council of State; it comprised thirteen Parisian councillors, including Jacques-Auguste de Thou, Claude du Puy, Antoine Loisel, and Pierre Pithou, who held the post of royal prosecutor.[vi] They were all Catholics.[76] On January 8, 1582, when Montaigne had just taken up his duties as mayor, the members of the chamber sent from Paris arrived in Bordeaux to see to it that the royal edicts were implemented and to restore order in the city. The chamber held its first meeting in the Jacobin fathers' school, that is to say in the Dominican convent. It was probably on that occasion that Montaigne made the acquaintance of Loisel and De Thou, who left a laudatory portrait of the mayor: "He [De Thou] also learned . . . a great deal from Michel de Montaigne, a man of independent mind and foreign to all factions who was then performing the extremely honorable functions of the mayor of Bordeaux: he knew in depth the affairs of France and in particular those of his Guyenne."[77]

The elected officials in Bordeaux and the parlement had no choice but to accept the new chamber of justice. Feeling wronged and furious at having lost their right of representation in the tripartite chamber, the Protestants plotted to seize several cities in the region. Thus on January 17, 1582, the mayor and the jurats of Bordeaux warned their counterparts in Saint-Émilion that a surprise attack on their city was planned. They recommended that an eye be kept out for seditious Huguenots.[78] It was a time for prudence.

[vi] The complete list of this chamber is as follows: Jean Séguier (*maître des requêtes*), Jehan de Lavau, Estienne Fleury, Jérosme Angenoust Jérosme de Montholon, Jehan Scarron, Guillaume Bernard, Adrien du Drac, Pierre Séguier (first president), Lazare Coquilley, Jehan de Thumery, Claude du Puy, Jacques-Auguste de Thou, Michel Hurault de L'Hospital, Antoine Loisel (king's advocate), Pierre Pithou (king's prosecutor), Charles Poussemothe (notary, king's secretary and clerk), Loys Perrot (king's secretary and comptroller), Maître Truejan (clerk for the civil party), Rolland Neufbourg (huissier), and Jacques Le Maistre (bailiff).

Faithful to his idea of politics, Montaigne tried to calm the waters and was already beginning to see himself as a negotiator between Henry III and Henry of Navarre. He kept a low profile during his first term as mayor, but he fully accepted the responsibility incumbent on him to make the Fleix accords respected. Article 45 of these accords stipulated that the mayor and other royal officers "will be responsible in their own and private names for offenses that may be made against the aforesaid edict, if they fail to punish and chastise the offenders, both civilly and corporally, if the case arises."[79] In his *Essais* Montaigne provides an analysis of his attitude, which consisted in taking a distance on the obligations of his public office: "Not all important offices are difficult. I was prepared to work myself a bit more roughly if there had been any great need of it. For it is in my power to do something more than I do or than I like to do. I did not leave undone, so far as I know, any action that duty genuinely required of me. I easily forgot those that ambition mixes up with duty and covers with its name."[80]

The chamber of justice sent from Paris performed its functions until June 1584, when it finally returned to Paris. It held its first session on January 26, 1582, and reaffirmed the close connection between the Catholic Church and royal justice. The councillors began their work only "after having all heard the mass in red robes."[81] After the religious service, they held a public session that was attended by Matignon and "a great crowd of people." The parlement quickly showed an unprecedented severity, and Montaigne could only witness the spectacle of this justice ordered from the capital by the king. Perhaps he was also flattered to find himself once again in the company of such eminent scholars. De Thou reports in his *Mémoires* the warm welcome he was given by the mayor when he arrived in Bordeaux. The main function of the chamber consisted as much in representing monarchical power with all its pomp and ceremony as in debating the cases it had to decide.

Although the initial reception by the Bordeaux parlement had been positive, conflicts between the parlement and the chamber of justice soon made themselves felt because their respective functions were too similar. It was on procedural points and jurisdiction that the parlement fought back, denouncing serious infringements of its prerogatives. The jurats were absent during the first session, and it is not certain that Montaigne was there to welcome them. It is likely that he remained in his château to reread his corrections to the edition of the *Essais* that he was preparing at the time that the royal authority was being reestablished in such a manifest way in Bordeaux. However, he heard the praise of Bordeaux and of its learned men: Ausonius, Buchanan, Muret, Vinet, and the "les Boities, Mallevins, Pontac, Montaignes" pronounced by Antoine Loisel in January 1582 at the convent of the Jacobins in Bordeaux. On the other hand, Montaigne was not present to hear Loisel's famous harangue that concluded the chamber's session on August 22, 1582,[vii] and it was only eight years later that he addressed his compliments to Loisel, thanking him "for the fine presents you gave me" in a short dedicatory epistle that accompanied a copy of the 1588 edition of the *Essais* published by Abel L'Angelier in Paris.[82] Nevertheless, on February 8, 1582, Montaigne had thought it important to go to Cadillac with the jurats to welcome the king and queen of Navarre. He was accompanied by the president of the parlement, Jean de Villeneuve, and the councillors Richard de Lestonnac and Joseph d'Andrault. In Cadillac he attended the baptism of a daughter of Louis de Foix who was held at the baptismal font by her godmother, Queen Margot.[83] This proof of Montaigne's goodwill, while he was mayor of Bordeaux, toward the king of Navarre contrasted symbolically with the attitude of his predecessor, Biron.

When Montaigne assumed his functions at the end of May 1582, he was immediately faced with a demand sent from Paris for the collection of funds. Letters from the king asked that the jurats and the mayor allocate 8,000 *livres* to repair the tower of Cordouan, another 8,000 *livres* in unspecified levies, and finally 4,000 *livres* for the chamber of justice he had sent to Bordeaux. Needless to say, these demands were badly received. The jurats convoked the assembly of the Cent-Treize to deliberate on this request and composed remonstrances to the king to explain to him that the city could not pay these sums, because its residents had been ruined by the uprisings and wanted only to "beg the king to consider their present and past woes."[84] The chamber of justice even supported the municipal administration on this point and expressed its astonishment at these letters from the king, because article 14 of the Fleix accord specified that the cost of maintaining the new chamber would be borne by the sovereign. A promise not kept by the king, whose reversals people feared.

Despite his hesitation to criticize Henry III overtly, the mayor of Bordeaux, as the city's spokesman, had to become involved in this affair and uphold the jurats' remonstrances. But this step did not succeed, and in 1583 the jurats repeated their complaint, and this time they sought to gain the support of the king of Navarre. In the remonstrances addressed to him, Montaigne and the jurats Geoffroy d'Alesme and Gabriel de Lurbe begged Henry of Navarre to intervene with Henry III so that "the wages of the lords of the high chamber of

---

[vii] In November 1582 Loisel thanked and warmly praised the mayor for his work at the head of the city: "You will find there more particularities of your city and lands of the Bordeaux area. As in fact I don't know to whom I could better address this conclusion than to the man who, having been mayor and one of the first magistrates of Bordeaux, and is also one of the main ornaments not only of Guyenne, but also of France as a whole." *La Continuation a Monsieur de Harlay*, a speech given in January 1582 at the Jacobin convent in Bordeaux, was published only in 1595, in *De l'œil des rois et de la justice* (Paris: Abel L'Angelier), 78.

justice, presently in Périgueux, might not now be levied on the poor people, which has borne alone this mass of surcharges over the past two years." In his response dated December 17, 1583,[85] the king of Navarre ignored this request made by Montaigne. One more frustration for a mayor who had to provide more and more funds for a king short of resources and pay the legal costs normally borne by the state budget. Montaigne was testing the limits of a friendship that was less simple than he had imagined.[86]

The funds flowing into the city's coffers were steadily diminishing. The mayor and the jurats were responsible for levying the *coutumes*, a tax on all the merchandise sold within the city walls. For example, merchants were prohibited to go "ahead" of merchandise to buy it or sell it outside the city or on ships and barges to avoid paying the *coutume*. This kind of cheating was, however, frequent at the time. Since 1548, there had been two kinds of taxes: the small and the great *coutume*. The small *coutume* consisted of a levy of two and a half *deniers* per *livre*. For the people of the region and their own consumption, no tax was levied. On the other hand, if they engaged in local commerce, then they were subject to the small *coutume*, and if they sold merchandise they had not produced, they had to pay both the great and the small *coutume*, that is, eight *deniers* per *livre*. If they transported merchandise outside the region, they were taxed at the rate of six *deniers* per *livre*. Merchants who resided "above the Saint Martin Brook" paid no *coutume* to bring in merchandise they had produced themselves, but if they sold their products outside this space, then they had to pay eight *deniers* in taxes.[87] There were countless ways of avoiding the rules regarding taxes.

Exceeding its authority, the chamber of justice imposed on Bordeaux by Henry III sometimes went astray, making zealous, partisan decisions that caused an uproar in the region and shocked humanistic minds. For instance, on June 2, 1582, the lord of Rostaing, the son of the marquis Tristan de Rostaing, a gentleman and declared Huguenot, but also a pillager who spread terror in the region under the pretext of his religious commitment, was sentenced to death for the crime of rebellion by the chamber of justice, and was decapitated on a scaffold erected in front of the city hall.[88] About this sentence, De Thou tells us that "such a great example of severity against a gentleman had not been seen for more than thirty years."[89] A few days later, the son of Captain Cornet, a native of Bordeaux, was sentenced to death by this same court. On June 28, convicted of murders, rebellion, violence, and other unspecified crimes, Philippe de Saint-Georges, lord of Le Fraisse and Meyrignac, was also executed, his property was confiscated, and his house razed. Like the others, he was put to death on the public square, in front of the Bordeaux city hall. Henry of Navarre protested to Henry III, who replied brusquely that there was only one justice in the kingdom and that it was applied in the same way to all his subjects, Catholic or Protestant, "without distinction of religion."[90]

During this time, behind the windows of the city hall, Montaigne was witnessing with resignation the bloody repression of the Huguenots. He seems not to have flinched, and we understand the famous passage in the *Essais* in which he defends the notion that "the public welfare requires that a man betray and lie; let us resign this commission to more obedient and suppler people."[91] And after 1588 he adds: "and massacre," thus expressing his consternation with regard to public service. This a posteriori reflection may have been inspired by his personal experience during the first months of his term as mayor. The public office indirectly involved him in these partisan decisions, and he put up a good show when faced by a partial and repressive justice.

At the king's request, a provincial council under the auspices of Antoine Prévost de Sansac, the archbishop of Bordeaux, was held in the city from July to November 1582. According to the decrees issued after the Estates General held at Blois, the provincial council, which had not met for a very long time, was henceforth to assemble every three years. The bishops of Poitiers, Saintes, Périgueux, Angoulême, Sarlat, and Maillezais were convoked for the occasion. Montaigne and the jurats attended the opening ceremony of the council. The litanies, the *Veni Creator* and the *Te Deum laudamus*, were sung during the high mass, which was attended by the mayor wearing his official robe. Apparently Pierre Charron, "schoolmaster," was present during this council, and it was probably on this occasion that he made Montaigne's acquaintance.[92]

The council's agenda proposed to raise the question of the residence of members of the clergy, of seminars, and of the church service according to the order of the Council of Trent. On November 6, toward the end of the Council, Pierre de Villars, archbishop of Bienne and state councillor; Louis Angennes, lord of Maintenon, state councillor, and captain of fifty men-at-arms; Jehan Forget, private councillor to the king and president "es enquestes" of the Paris parlement; and Denis Barthélemy, councillor to the king and ordinary master of the Chambre des Comptes of the Paris parlement, arrived, all of them "commissioned, ordered, and delegated by the king to travel to the provinces of Guyenne and Languedoc to inform themselves of the state of both the clergy and all others."[93] The mayor and the jurats had to give these representatives a warm welcome in their city. The king was multiplying occasions of this kind to manifest his authority through the intermediary of the chamber of justice and the council that he controlled, thinking in this way to cut the ground from under the feet of the extremist Catholics, who were increasingly active in Bordeaux and who reproached the king for his soft Catholicism. The clergy and the members of parlement marched together to prove the sovereign's omnipotence. Official processions took place one after the other in the streets of Bordeaux, and the city was rapidly transformed into a symbolic place of the unchallenged exercise of royal power. For the occasion, Montaigne reaffirmed his loyalty to Henry III and the Catholic faith.

Apart from the political and religious considerations often mentioned, the mayor's responsibilities were mainly practical. The office required a manager capable of dealing with the pressing needs of a city in full expansion. One of the mayor's chief concerns was, for instance, to "keep the city clean." While Montaigne was directing municipal affairs, two rulings, on September 10, 1584, and March 1, 1585, regulated the dumping of rubbish on the city's streets.[94] The growth of the city's population had led to a problem of sanitation and odor. At that time, unsanitary conditions in cities were associated with epidemics of plague. Sewage, manure, mud holes, and garbage piled up on the street and created a public sanitation problem. During his first term, a municipal ordinance forbade throwing anything out of windows on pain of having to pay a fine. The decision stipulated that refuse would henceforth be collected twice a week, on Tuesdays and Fridays. A great project of standardizing paving stones was also launched during Montaigne's second term. Similarly, draining by the middle of the streets was made obligatory and manure was removed from the main arteries.

Another municipal responsibility: we find Montaigne supervising boat traffic on the Garonne. In early 1582 the congestion caused by boats on which merchandise was stored was so great that it became almost impossible to navigate on the Garonne. On March 24, Montaigne and the jurats published a decision forbidding the storage of merchandise on boats and ships moored in the city.[95] Unhappy about this decision, the merchants felt wronged and considered it to be a hindrance to the free circulation of merchandise. They blamed the mayor and expressed their dissatisfaction with an administration they found too repressive and that they felt was slowing the expansion of commerce in the city. A few months later, Montaigne was busy reforming the statutes of the parchment makers to stop the influx of people who were pursuing that craft without being "certified in the aforesaid trade." The recent statutes limited access to the guild by requiring those practicing the trade to be trained and certified, thus forbidding the exercise of the craft by those who were neither "masters, nor journeymen, nor apprentices in it . . . on pain of being fined a sum to be determined."[96] These statutes were decided upon and published in the jurade on May 2, 1582. This way of proceeding was followed by many crafts in Bordeaux; with the encouragement of the mayor and the jurats, they reformed their statutes to protect themselves better from the influx of outside craftsmen who sought to sell their products in the city.

During the summer of 1582, the mayor of Bordeaux was trying to settle a disagreement between master hose makers and dressmakers. The decision required a technical and industrial knowledge with the steps in the fabrication and distribution of the commodities associated with each guild. Montaigne commissioned an expert report on the trades and, after municipal deliberation, the dressmakers were forbidden to make "any hose, whether of cloth, velvet, silk, or any other material at all" on pain of paying a fine of 50 crowns per infraction, except for "wide or high hose for use on boats, which we have allowed them and will continue to allow them to make."[97] On September 19, 1582, the jurats convicted the dressmakers of having contravened the articles of their statutes, and the parlement confirmed this sentence by a ruling issued on August 1, 1583. Still determined to reorganize the craft professions in the city, in 1583 the municipal administration sought to revise the statutes of shoemakers, hat makers, and glove makers.

We do not know exactly how much Montaigne involved himself in the study and reform of these statutes, but he must have become acquainted with the municipal decisions that were issued from these statutory reforms. All these examples confirm that the mayor's duties were quite distant from the philosophical or philological concerns of a humanist with a bookish culture that allowed him to immerse himself in Antiquity. Dealing with the problems of glove makers, doublet makers, and pin sellers could not have corresponded to Montaigne's idea of public service and the government of the city. For someone who liked to read the rhetoricians of Athens and Rome, the everyday worries of a city like Bordeaux must have seemed very insignificant. It was certainly a time when great questions of society and religion were being discussed, but it was also, at least for Montaigne as mayor of Bordeaux, a time for the most concrete and prosaic management of the guilds and professions operating within the city walls. On certain occasions, the mayor and Montaigne had to be quite distinct, and the humanist had to find a place to which he could withdraw: "We must reserve a back shop all our own, entirely free, in which to establish our real liberty and our principal retreat and solitude."[98] This salutary retreat from the everyday work of the mayor's office and its bureaucracy was of course his château, far from the obligations of the city. Although Montaigne continued to devote himself to reading books, it is nonetheless unlikely that he envisaged a third volume for his *Essais* during his two terms as mayor of Bordeaux.

At the end of 1582, the mayor and the jurats had to apply the reform of the calendar desired by Pope Gregory XIII. Ten days were removed from the month of December, and Christmas was celebrated on the fifteenth. In 1582, the month of December had only twenty-one days, which led to several trials and disputes, as Darnal tells us in his supplement to the *Chronique de Bordeaux*.[99]

We can imagine that Montaigne discussed this matter with François de Foix-Candale, an eminent mathematician, alchemist, and savant who had served as an advisor to the pope on this reform. The author of the *Essais* offers his own considerations on this reform, of which he did not approve and which he found it difficult to put up with: "I want to mention this as an example: that the recent eclipsing of ten days by the Pope has so taken me aback that I cannot feel comfortable with it,"[100] and suggests elsewhere that this reform might have been "carried out in a less inconvenient fashion."[101] The role of a mayor also consisted in implementing reforms and decrees, even if he personally disapproved of them.

The end of Montaigne's first term as mayor of Bordeaux provoked a political stir. His repeated absences and his detachment from the city's current concerns had made people think he might not run for a second term. Some accused him of having paid too much attention to the interests of the bourgeoisie and not enough to the demands of the nobility. His political enemies openly campaigned in favor of a mayor who was more Catholic and less conciliatory toward Henry of Navarre. Others went so far as to denounce Montaigne's suspect friendship for Henry of Navarre. By adopting a wait-and-see attitude, Montaigne came to be seen as a politician without firm judgment, and in the end he attracted the criticism of both camps. Sympathizers with the League were annoyed by the cordial relationship between Henry of Navarre and Matignon and accused the mayor of having a large part in this unnatural rapprochement. It was an election year and people were becoming hot-headed. The nobles and Catholic extremists saw in Jacques d'Escars, lord of Merville, grand seneschal of Guyenne since 1566, and captain and governor of Le Hâ castle, an ideal candidate who would allow them to get rid of Montaigne. Although at first Montaigne may have considered not running, the disagreeable turn of events and the accusations made against him made him change his mind. Wounded in his vanity, he decided to seek a second term.

A Contested Reelection

In his role as arbitrator and conciliator between the various political and ideological interests represented in the jurade, Montaigne occupied a rather delicate and ambiguous position in 1583. He looked like a typical *politique* at the time when all-out commitment was in fashion. The municipal ordinances and decrees of the past two years made it possible to think—at least for his detractors—that in matters of municipal administration Montaigne usually was on the side of the merchants and bourgeois of the city. The nobles ended up aligning themselves with the *robins* and members of parlement to form an opposition group determined to prevent Montaigne's reelection. This policy of rapprochement, the result of personal animosities between Montaigne and a significant number of councillors in the parlement, bore fruit at the time of his reelection, because the nobility's candidate (a notorious member of the Catholic League) allied himself with the president of the parlement, Jean de Villeneuve, and also with the highest representative of the clergy in Bordeaux, Archbishop Antoine Prévost de Sansac. The *robins* found a sufficient ideological affinity between the milieu from which most of them came (the bourgeoisie) and from which they were trying to free themselves, and an order to which they aspired (the nobility). They represented a force influential enough to tip an election their way. This particular, decisive position of the *robins* explains why the seneschal Merville and the baron of Vaillac did everything they could to win their votes to prevent Montaigne's reelection.[102] Documents in the archives show us that they came very close to winning this political battle. We note in particular a major defection of magistrates who joined Merville's clan and overtly campaigned for him during the summer of 1583. In his *Essais*, Montaigne preferred to keep silent about these intrigues and the difficulty he had in getting reelected, simply congratulating himself on the confidence in him shown by the people of Bordeaux, "who did everything in their power to gratify me both before they knew me and after."[103] A declaration that is as political as it could be, but is nonetheless far from reality.

In Montaigne's time, the castles of Le Hâ and Trompette were royal enclaves within the city. These strongholds played an important role in the military control of the city. However, many conflicts regarding jurisdiction, precedence, and more specific problems connected with the establishment of a military garrison made it difficult for the city administrators and the captains commanding these strongholds to coexist. Brawls, quarrels, and various kinds of conflicts between soldiers and city dwellers were frequent. Between September and December 1582, Montaigne and the jurats had presented a memorandum to Matignon to demand the right to place guards near the castles and fortifications. The governors prevented sentinels "for guarding the city" from being stationed near their strongholds.[104] Having this zone forbidden to sentinels but controlled by the city was an intolerable situation for the mayor and the jurats.

Montaigne had repeatedly complained about the abuses committed by the governors of the castles of Le Hâ and Trompette, who hindered the free passage of city patrols around their strongholds and delivered, in exchange for payment, certificates of indulgence to the residents, even going so far as to exempt them from serving as guards and paying taxes. The true conflict actually had to do with the space situated near the castles that the soldiers occupied. There, for example, they maintained vegetable gardens. Housewives even had to pay a fee to spread their laundry to dry on the grass of the prairies that surrounded the strongholds. The captains also levied a tax on all the merchandise stored at the foot these two forts. Vaillac, the captain of the Trompette castle, forbade carts to pass over the fausse-braye[viii] bridge, which forced residents and merchants who wanted to bring their wares into the city to make a long detour. The jurats and the mayor firmly pointed out that passage over this bridge was supposed to be controlled by the city authorities, in particular in order to facilitate bringing carts into the city at the time of the wine harvests. It was always useful to use arguments bearing on the wine industry in a city that depended chiefly on the trade in wine.

According to the jurats, the esplanade that extended between the first houses in the Chartreux quarter and the Trompette castle belonged to the city, but Merville and Vaillac thought differently. In response to the numerous remonstrances made by the mayor and the jurats, the governors wrote in turn and in common a long memorandum in which they discussed various points regarding the control of the area adjacent to the king's military sites.[105] In reality, they were above all attacking Montaigne, who had wanted to build a storage depot on an empty site that he owned near the Trompette castle. It was a piece of land he had inherited from his father, Pierre Eyquem. In an initial will dated February 4, 1561, we find mentioned "one of the wine storage depots I have at the site of the Chartreux lès Bourdeaulx, nearest the Trompète castle. . . . Also the place adjacent to the aforesaid storage depot toward the Trompète castle, containing the aforesaid place, which is to be built upon, fifty feet from the river as far as the vineyards." The purchase went back to 1527–28, a period for which we have ninety-seven notarized documents drawn up by the notary Pierre Perreau for the "nobleman Pierre Eyquem, squire, lord of Montaigne and of Belveyou." These property acquisitions had allowed Pierre Eyquem to considerably enlarge his lands and increase his real estate holdings in the region and in Bordeaux.[106] Merville and Vaillac's complaint was therefore directed against the mayor personally.

Montaigne had apparently obtained special permission from the king (requested and granted during one of his visits to the Court) to build on this land, but Vaillac vehemently opposed this, invoking a security problem. Vaillac denounced a conflict of interests between Montaigne, the mayor of Bordeaux, and Montaigne, the private person. Montaigne defended himself: "As for the place of the aforesaid castle, outside the city, on which the lord Montaigne, currently mayor of the city, claims to have some right to build, which Vaillac . . . prevented him from doing, which gave the mayor and the jurats reason to complain about him."[107] The captain of the Trompette castle warned the king that because of the disturbances it was dangerous to construct houses and depots against the

---

viii A secondary defensive wall outside the main rampart. [Trans.]

walls of the castle or near the garrison posts; he noted that it had recently been decided to tear down homes in the area that were too close to the castle's ramparts. He accused Montaigne of profiting personally from his term as mayor and of using his office to obtain special privileges.

This was a supreme insult for Montaigne, who prided himself precisely on not deriving any advantage from his office. He responded to Merville and Vaillac's memorandum with another memorandum addressed to Matignon, in which he refuted the grievances filed against him and accused in turn the captains of having it in for him personally because of the dark affair of his reelection. He explained the matter of the building site this way: "And regarding the place that is outside the city, between the Trompette castle and the Chasteaulx [Chartreux], it is not only now that this complaint has been made by the mayor and the jurats, but their predecessors have often filed a grievance about it."[108] His memorandum ends with a defense of the freedom of the citizens and of their privileges. In their turn, the mayor and the jurats accused the baron of Vaillac of having helped fraudulently to bring wine from the Haut Pays into Bordeaux, to the great detriment of the bourgeois of the city. That was an argument that did not fail, as one can imagine, to rally the merchants behind Montaigne's cause. In politics, it is sometimes necessary to find allies where one does not necessarily expect them. Throughout his life, Montaigne was able to attract the support necessary to advance his personal interests. Thus in May 1588, Montaigne demanded a dispensation (in the form of a request) from the parlement in order to bring into Bordeaux "fifty barrels of wine produced by his house of Montaigne." Contrary to the city's customs, and certainly after the intervention of well-placed persons, the parlement authorized him to bring this wine into the city on the condition of having it conveyed "by Catholic people and sailors" and after presenting a certificate proving that the grapes had been harvested on his land.[109]

In the matter of the storage depot, Montaigne's defense insisted that this was an old affair that they had to put behind them. But Vaillac brought the matter directly to the attention of Henry III during one of his sojourns to the Court in April 1583. The king seems to have allowed himself to be convinced that there was a conflict of interests and that Montaigne had indeed used his office to obtain personal advantages. In response to Vaillac's accusations against Montaigne, the king wrote to Matignon, asking him for a clarification of this affair:

> However much the permission that was sent to the mayor of Bordeaux to build on the site that he claims belongs to him near my castle of Trompette may have been made as a result of the earlier ones, still, having seen the memorandum presented to me by the baron of Vaillac regarding this case, and considering also what he told me orally, I have deemed it necessary, for

the good of my service and the security of the aforesaid castle, on which depends that of my city of Bordeaux, to defer the execution of the aforesaid permission until I have been further informed in greater detail and truthfully about its consequences. By which means you shall forbid, on my behalf, the mayor to make use of it until I have ordered otherwise, and you shall send me a true map of the castle and the site, on which the distance between the two shall be specified; and you shall also tell me what you think should be done about it, and if the content of the memorandum presented by the baron of Vaillac is true and if you consider that it was appropriate to revoke the aforesaid permission to build on the aforesaid site. I shall be happy to buy it from the mayor, so that he might have no reason to complain, because I do not desire to do him any wrong; consequently, you can discuss it with him, and if you think it needful, send me his response.[110]

After investigating, Matignon finally decided in favor of Montaigne, but he was certainly also biased. Another year had been lost in quarrels that cost Montaigne dearly. He finally obtained his revenge on Vaillac when Matignon disarmed Vaillac and deprived him of his command of the castle of Trompette in April 1585.

Lord Merville, captain and governor of the castle of Le Hâ, had decided to be a candidate in the municipal election of 1583. This was not the first time he had tried to seize the mayor's office. Eight years earlier he had already campaigned to replace Charles de Montferrand, but had not succeeded in defeating the president Joseph Eymar, a man of the long robe. At that time, he had already tried to have the election nullified by arguing that Eymar did not come from the nobility. However, the king had reminded him that "this election was approved by His Majesty for this one time, without having any consequences, this office being reserved for gentlemen pursuing the profession of arms."[111] Letters of ennoblement were conferred on Eymar in order to resolve the problem. In his *Traité de la noblesse*, Laroque explains that "the office of mayor of Bordeaux has always been so considerable that the people of Bordeaux, instead of seeking a noble origin in the mayor's office, have had nobles of high rank as mayors."[112] However, this remark is far from corresponding to reality, since at the time of Montaigne the "nobility" of several mayors of Bordeaux had been contested. Well informed about these disputes, the author of the *Essais* had no intention of allowing himself to be put on trial for false claims to nobility. Merville had numerous influential supporters, notably a large contingent of members of the parlement led by the second president of the parlement, Jean de Villeneuve (in reality, he was the true head of the parlement, because the first president, Benoît de Lagebaston, was very old and no longer exercised his office) and his wife, Marie Potier, who served as campaign directors for Merville. This Villeneuve was a first cousin of Montaigne's mother, and we know the difficult relations that Montaigne had with her.

The Merville clan also included the archbishop of Bordeaux, Antoine Prévost de Sansac; a general prosecutor (not named); the councillors Léon de Merle, lord of Montsalut, and his son-in-law, Pierre de Termes; the councillors Jean de Lange, Pierre Dunoyer, and Bertrand Duplessis; and the clerk Jehan de Pontac. In all, more than fifty councillors overtly sided against Montaigne— more than two-thirds of the parlement. At this time, the parlement was largely dominated by intransigent Catholics who had all rallied behind Merville. It is likely that they disliked this former colleague who supported a policy of conciliation with the king of Navarre. In addition, Montaigne had not left a memorable trace of his service in the parlement, and many people were surprised that this gentleman raised to the office of mayor of Bordeaux had been able to form so quickly political alliances prejudicial to their interests as members of parlement.

During Montaigne's reelection, we see emerging resentments that are not strictly speaking political but are also rooted in personal animosities within the Montaigne family. Among the opponents of Montaigne's reelection were Montaigne's own brother-in-law, Richard de Lestonnac, and also a "lord of Montaigne" who was a councillor, both of whom were very active in support of Merville and did all they could to get him elected. The "lord of Montaigne" was none other than Geoffroy de Montaigne, lord of Bussaguet and of Gaujac, a cousin of Michel de Montaigne who had become a councillor in the parlement in 1571. We will recall that when Montaigne retired from the parlement he had lent Geoffroy 2,000 *livres* to buy his office. The cousins did not get along, and this was not their first disagreement. The most serious of these occurred in 1575, during the settlement of the heritage of their uncle, the canon Pierre de Gaujac. Family relations were extremely tense, and the author of the *Essais* aroused a jealousy disguised behind religious dissensions. His brother, Thomas de Beauregard, and his sister, Jeanne de Lestonnac, had adhered to the Reformation and thus created a religious cleavage within the family. For almost three months, Geoffroy de Montaigne put pressure on his colleagues in the parlement to get Merville elected. We must also mention the repeated squabbles between Montaigne and his mother, especially at the time when Pierre Eyquem's will was executed, which continued to feed resentments between members of the family. These divisions within a single phratry are in no way astonishing in a city like Bordeaux, where power had historically been held by a small number of great families that had exploded politically and were prepared to tear each other apart at any time.

The nobility, the members of parlement, and the clergy thus tended to lean toward Merville, but Montaigne retained the support of the bourgeoisie, which was on the whole rather satisfied with his first term as mayor. By manipulating the method of election Montaigne succeeded in short-circuiting Merville and his supporters. The role of the Council of Thirty (now reduced to twenty-four electors designated by the jurats) was to elect and to advise the jurats. This was the level at which the deck was stacked, since Montaigne and his friends nominated notables favorable to his reelection. In their turn, the notables named by the municipal administration elected three jurats aligned with the political program Montaigne had proposed. They were supposed to respect the secrecy of the deliberations, but leaks were inevitable. It was precisely this question of the nomination of the notables and the overrepresentation of the bourgeoisie among them that provided the grounds for the accusation of electoral "fraud" made by Montaigne's enemies.

As was traditional, on August 1, 1583, the twenty-four electors forming the Council of Thirty met and reelected Montaigne to a second term of two years. They also elected three new jurats favorable to Montaigne. Merville and his friends contested this election. They found a technical legal problem in Montaigne's election to the mayor's office, and also considered the election of the three jurats irregular because it had not made sufficient appeal to the representation of the nobility. Their argument was based primarily on a point of interpretation regarding the election of the mayor and the jurats as it was described in the city's statutes in the ordinance of 1550: the text says that "instead of the mayor who used to be elected for life, and received thirteen hundred eight-three *livres* and fifteen *sols* in wages per annum, henceforth one [mayor] will be elected every two years and will have no wages other than two robes a year, in the colors of the aforesaid city."[113] The election of a mayor "every two years" (*de deux ans en deux ans*) is subject to interpretation. Does the text say that a new and different mayor must be elected every two years, or that the election simply takes place every two years? In any case, Montaigne did not take the precaution of requesting a royal dispensation before running for a second term.

So far as the jurats were concerned, the city's privileges did not specify more explicitly the former customary representation that consisted in electing two representatives for the nobility, two for the bourgeoisie, and two among the magistrates. The nobility's consultation to name its representatives was also normally carried out on good terms, a practice that seems to have been forgotten in this election. After Merville's complaint, a legal proceeding was instituted by the seneschal's lieutenant, Thomas de Ram, who had the indictment introduced before the parlement. Montaigne replied to this attack by trying to have recused more than fifty councillors who had overtly sided with Merville during the campaign. Merville and President Villeneuve simply demanded the annulment of the election of the mayor and the three jurats, Raymond Budos, Jean de Lapeyre, and Jean Claveau. Meeting at first with no opposition, they won a semivictory, because while Montaigne's reelection was upheld, the election of the three new jurats was declared invalid, and they were forbidden to take office until the Council of State had ruled on the matter. The jurats were suspended pending the completion of a complementary inquiry and the king's decision. In fact, this suspension went into effect officially only after notification of the Council of State's ruling in February 1584. The records of the Council's deliberations have been preserved. They confirm Montaigne's reelection but declare "null and abusive" the election of the jurats. Montaigne had barely avoided a political rout, probably thanks to Matignon's direct intervention with the king.

Thus it was on technical points that Montaigne's reelection was contested, but the true reason was obviously political. Since the publication of the city's new statutes, it was not unusual for a mayor to be elected for a second term. In his *Essais*, Montaigne remarks that "the term is two years; but it can be extended by a second election, which happens very rarely. This was done in my case, and had been done only twice before: some years earlier to Monsieur de Lansac, and recently to Monsieur de Biron, Marshal of France, to whose place I succeeded."[114] But it is also true that an election or reelection required the consent of the king, who apparently was not consulted when Montaigne was reelected in 1583. Montaigne was accused of getting elected in secret, thanks to his "bourgeois friends" who had probably manipulated the notables to ensure that they had the necessary number of votes to defeat Merville. The claim that the election of the jurats had been rigged was not without foundation, and the king himself was troubled by this not very honorable stratagem used by a member of the nobility.

This incident directly implicating Montaigne at the time of his reelection allows us to assess the vague borders that existed between private interests and public offices. Unhappy about having been lectured by the Council of State, Montaigne and the jurats went on the offensive and denounced in turn the suspicious agreements between President Villeneuve and Lord Merville, the governor of the castle of Le Hâ. The petition filed by the jurats who had been recused by certain members of the parlement lists the links of family and friendship between Villeneuve and Merville:

> They [the jurats] consider President Villeneuve very suspect . . . , because he is a great and close friend of Lord Merville, with whom he drinks and eats, and because of the great and close friendship existing between Merville and the president [Villeneuve] and his wife, Dame de la Terrasse, who insistently sought to cause Lord Merville to seek election as mayor of the city in the last election and to have Lord Merville preferred in that office over Messire Michel de Montaigne, knight of the king's order and lord of the aforesaid place, a close relative of the aforesaid lord president

[Villeneuve], this latter president having greater friendship for Lord Merville than for Montaigne his relative, and the president has conceived a great enmity against the aforesaid lord of Montaigne, petitioning because they could not have Lord Merville elected mayor, having pretended on several occasions, in their hatred for him [Montaigne], that he would make them and the city see his power and that they would pay a high price for the displeasure that [they] caused him in this place, which is so notorious that the aforesaid petitioners beg the court not to require more ample proof.[115]

The jurats' petition contests the first inquiry conducted by Thomas de Ram, royal councillor and lieutenant general, who is said to have also organized a cabal to get Merville elected. Faced with the failure of this machination, Ram "is said to have had interjected the appellation . . . that would have been pleaded in court." The jurats then accused Ram of being a difficult fellow who had quarreled with their "predecessors and conceived a mortal and capital enmity for them and is even supposed to have said that, in hatred of the fact that Lord Merville had not been elected mayor, he would now be a governor, referring, as might be expected, to the aforesaid lord." The mayor and jurats also denounced Jehan de Pontac, the clerk, because he had married a close relative of Merville and was consequently one of his close friends and "insistently sought to get him elected mayor of the city in the last election and because the latter Lord Merville was not [elected] he conceived a great enmity against the petitioners." One would think we had returned to the early 1560s, when the councillors in the parlement mutually challenged and recused each other. Montaigne had clearly left one nest of vipers only to find himself in another just as execrable.

It was not in the king's interest to openly take sides in what was above all a petty squabble. Henry III tried to straddle the dispute, not wanting to alienate Montaigne, who, alongside Matignon, had always conducted himself as a loyal servant. But he also had to mollify the governors of his two strongholds in Bordeaux, especially because they had powerful supporters not only in the parlement but also among the religious authorities. For that reason, the Council of State's document sought to split the difference, concluding that the nobles had to have equal representation in the jurade and that "those of the nobility of the city must be called upon to have a voice and give their votes, and be admitted and elected to the aforesaid offices like other residents." The Council of State settled the argument with an arbitration in the form of a conciliation, hoping in that way to forestall an open war between the city's administration and the parlement. Montaigne could "just this time" (*pour cette fois*) "be re-elected," but his political practices were nonetheless condemned:

considering that for some good reasons it would be good that the election of the aforesaid Montaigne remain confirmed just this time, and that he be continued in the office of mayor for the two years that are extended for him without this having any consequence, prohibiting the residents of Bordeaux ever again to use such prorogations in the election of the mayor beyond and above the two years that were set by the order of the late King Henry in the year 1550, unless they are allowed to act in this way by the express concession of His Majesty.[116]

Two contradictory documents, dated February 4, 1584, simultaneously confirmed and invalidated the mayor's tenure of his office but decided against the jurats Budos, Lapeyre, and Claveau. One of them charges Montaigne:

Regarding the petition that His Majesty referred to his Council of State and which the nobility and the more worthy part of the native bourgeois and citizens of the city of Bordeaux presented to him, requesting that the election carried out on the first day of August of the Lord of Montaigne to be the mayor of that city be continued for the next two years after having been mayor the two preceding years, and the election also carried out on the same day of messieurs Budos, Lapeyre, and Claveau to be new jurats of the city, both [elections] will be declared null and abusive and as such cancelled and annulled and thus proceed to hold new elections of a different mayor and jurats of the city.

We do not know exactly how Montaigne survived the invalidation of his election. Once more, Matignon probably appealed directly to the king. We have no further documentation of this reelection battle. Montaigne seems to have once again emerged victorious from this situation, because in the end his term of office was renewed.

Since the jurats remained suspended, the jurade now had only three active members. Deprived of half of its officials, the jurade moved slowly and could no longer serve as an intermediary with the king to restore the three jurats to their offices. Montaigne and the jurats let Matignon know they were unhappy about this, and they asked him once again to serve as an intermediary between them and the king to ensure the reinstatement of the jurats. To this end they sent Henry III a long petition—dated March 5, 1584—in which they replied point by point to the accusations that had been made against them. They presented a direct appeal to the king, referring to the "particular passions" of their enemies, and at the same time stressing that they had acted in accord with all the rules. Montaigne personally denounced the suspension of the three jurats, which resulted in slower public service (*service publicq retardé*) and hindered the proper functioning of the municipal administration:

> Some residents of this city of yours having, out of particular passions, appealed the election and continuation of the mayor in the person of Lord Montaigne, and the election of three new jurats carried out last August, and pursued their appeal in your court of parlement, they abandoned their initial suit without having summoned us, and presented to Your Majesty a petition seeking new ends, full of false facts, and in our absence obtained a ruling from your Council of State by which, among other things, the aforesaid new jurats have been forbidden the exercise of their offices until they have been heard in your Council;
>
> Sire,
>
> Had we been so fortunate as to have been allowed to present our reasons we would have hoped to show Your Majesty that all the forms included in our statutes and privileges have been carefully and religiously observed in this election, and that it was a choice made by twenty-four wise men, notable and reliable citizens who all together duly carried out the election of these jurats, good, honorable men, as we have seen through experience with their conduct in their offices. The prohibition has since been made known to them, but without their being summoned to your Council, so that of six jurats there remain to us only three in office, who are by that much overloaded, and public service is slowed, something that requires prompt amendment and settlement which we very humbly beg Your Majesty to order for the preservation of our honor in the aforesaid election, and of the rights and privileges of the aforesaid city, in which we have been maintained by the kings who preceded you whom God absolve, and by Your Majesty up to the present, and not allow that such divisions be tolerated in the future, which can only engender disorder, confusion, and disrespect of our offices, as well as the decisions made by the rulings of your court of parlement, rendered in similar matters and confirmed by Your Majesty, the prosecutor and syndic of your city to cause you to hear more amply our complaints and grievances regarding this fact and others, had it not been that Monsieur the Marshal de Matignon, in his prudence, esteemed it not expedient for the present that any of us give up the service of your city.[117]

The petition was communicated to Matignon, who sent a report on the situation to Villeroy, a secretary of state. We can logically imagine that Matignon supported the three jurats who had been attacked and demanded their reinstatement. In any case, the affair came to an end in late April 1584, not without having created a profound resentment between Montaigne and a major fringe of the nobility and the parlement of Bordeaux. We do not know the exact outcome of this judicial challenge, but a few months later we find the names of the three jurats on several of the city's administrative documents. It seems that they recovered the right to exercise their offices and that the affair was finally settled at the highest level.

Very much against his wishes, and perhaps because the political forces at play had already decided to which camp he was going to belong in order to get himself reelected mayor, Montaigne was unable to avoid forming political alliances that might have been unnatural and regarding which he preferred to remain silent in his *Essais*. We can understand that. Make no mistake, Montaigne was a political animal who must have taken into account the political situation, what Machiavelli had called "the conditions of the times."[118] The circumstances were such that Montaigne was obliged to defend the merchants' cause to retain his power in Bordeaux and be reelected mayor. Practically, he chose a camp that he nonetheless rejected on ideological grounds. If we consider only these two incidents opposing Montaigne to the Bordeaux nobility, he seems to have been an ardent defender of the bourgeoisie and a sworn enemy of the two gentlemen who claimed to be the only true representatives of the king's interests in Bordeaux. But one swallow does not make a spring, because the requirements of political governance do not always go hand in hand with personal affinities.

Manager of the City and "Tender Negotiator"

Although Montaigne was not "elected" (in the modern sense of the word) for his first term, he had acquired an incontestable political legitimacy when he was elected to a second term. He had gotten hooked on the play of alliances and political intrigues and henceforth took the measure of his responsibilities as the city's leader. He was, moreover, very proud of his reelection, which he described as rare. He had been reelected thanks to the support of the bourgeoisie, and the time had come to keep his electoral promises. The beginning of a term in office is generally considered a propitious time to announce a political agenda for the coming years. It was in that spirit that, in early August 1583, Montaigne already undertook a revision of the *Coutumier de Guyenne* (*Common Law of Guyenne*).[119] Similarly, shortly after his reelection, he cosigned with the jurats a letter of grievances that strongly resembled a list of political commitments he might have made during his reelection campaign. Here we find a Montaigne attentive to the people's demands, especially those of the poor, who in a city like Bordeaux constituted around 20 percent of the population. The accelerated socioeconomic development of cities in France during the second half of the sixteenth century resulted in a decrease of population in the countryside. "Wanderers" came to take refuge in the cities and municipal administrations were sometimes confronted by serious problems of overpopulation and indigence.

Elected officials deplored the growing mendicancy in the city, and blamed it on the Wars of Religion that had led to an increase of poverty in the southwest. The jurats reaffirmed each parish's responsibility to feed the poor and declared that "in addition the priors and administrators of the hospices, most of which were founded by the king and are dedicated to feeding pilgrims going to St. James and other religious sites, are obligated, on pain of having their temporal goods seized, to feed and house these pilgrims for the time stipulated by the aforesaid foundation, to prevent them from being forced to go begging through the city, as happens every day, to the great dismay of everyone."[120] This list of grievances, dated August 31, 1583, was an opportunity to remind the king that "the great mass of people has had to cope with new circumstances and calamities." The mayor and the jurade expressed the wish that "all levies might be imposed equally on everyone, the strong carrying the poor, and suggest that it is very reasonable that those who have greater resources feel the burden more than those who survive only by chance and the sweat of their brows."[121] In the view of the jurats and the mayor, this social justice was supposed to make it possible to combat the increase in criminal activity inside the city walls. According to them, the fresh outbreak of thefts and attacks resulted from the impoverishment of the common people, who were being crushed by taxes. The city had paid a high tribute during the past two years, especially in the form of taxes levied to pay the wages of the members of the présidial courts, but also battling a deficit caused by the suppression of the tax during the fairs, the repair of the Cordouan tower, and the salaries of the chamber of justice, not to mention the contribution the king obliged it to make to the expenses of the Portuguese army.

Montaigne had hardly been reelected before he turned on the members of the parlement and denounced abuses related to tax evasion. Too many officers of the court were exempted from taxes, too many children of presidents and councillors had been declared noble and not subject to taxation, so that "now when it is necessary to levy some tax, it must be borne by the smallest and poorest part of the residents of the cities, which is completely impossible."[122] The mayor and the jurats complained about the fact that the richest and most opulent families of the city would have been exempt from these taxes "because of the privilege claimed by all the officers of the court and their widows, the officials handling your finances and elections, vice-seneschals, lieutenants, domestic officials in the service of Your Majesty and of the king and queen of Navarre, officials of the chancellery, of the mint, of the artillery, and soldiers garrisoned in castles and those who supply them."[123]

All these officials were considered nobles and escaped taxation. This was an astonishing reversal on Montaigne's part, and it might be asked whether, in these attacks on the *robins*, he was not simply trying to get back at the group of members of the parlement who had actively opposed him during his campaign for reelection as mayor. His animosity toward the magistracy was not new, because he had suffered enough affronts in the course of the 1560s to retain a strong resentment against that profession. His *Essais* teem with barbs and mockeries aimed at the world of the magistracy. The time had come for him to express himself openly and take his revenge. In the course of the year 1583, Montaigne spoke out firmly regarding social justice and openly denounced the ennoblement of members of parlement and their families. At present, he spoke as a noble and seems to have forgotten his own family's rise in society in another time when the Eyquems themselves benefited from the advantages and privileges he now denounced.

In the early 1580s, the city had a serious liquidity problem and showed an alarming deficit. Less and less money was flowing into the public coffers. Along with the jurats, Montaigne criticized the excessively large number of exemptions, and the city officials blamed a particularly extravagant ruling of the parlement solemnly proclaimed on April 6, 1583, that declared noble, and thus not subject to taxes, all the children of the presidents and councillors of the court. The king was increasing his largess to members of the parlement and their families, but the city saw in these political gifts a considerable loss of revenue. It was only fair that Montaigne should remember that the members of the parlement had recently actively sought to prevent his reelection. These fiscal exemptions, granted for purely political reasons, were opposed to the very principle of good governance of a city like Bordeaux, whose merchants and craftsmen paid an ever larger portion of the taxes. To be sure, the richest families had countless ways of escaping taxes, because the city's bourgeois were also "free," that is, exempt from taxation. Faced by the exemptions granted by the king to members of the parlement and to the bourgeois, the city had to impose still heavier taxes on those who did not enjoy these titles.

The mayor and the jurats reminded the king that by the privileges accorded by the king, "the knowledge and provision of certificates to all craftsmen, and the enforcement of the aforesaid statutes that are registered in the city belongs to the mayor and the jurats."[124] Their area of authority included, for instance, the regulation of keepers of taverns and cabarets, certified and erected into an "estate" to sell wine in the city. The jurats worried more particularly about a recent practice that allowed keepers of taverns and cabarets who sold wine in Bordeaux to be directly certified by royal officials. The former had thus "found a way to obtain edicts to make these certifications venal, together with the freedom to sell wine, by erecting new estates of tavern and cabaret keepers, which is a direct violation of the terms of these privileges" confirmed on December 21, 1556, and verified in the court of the parlement. The wine merchants were constantly trying to get around the tax by obtaining royal edicts authorizing them to sell wine without the approval of the municipal authorities and by writing themselves new statutes for their profession. Montaigne reminded the king that these professions fell within the purview of the jurats and the mayor and that the city would be driven into bankruptcy "if by your generosity it is not provided for, and if the aforesaid edicts obtained by circumvention and great pressure, as may be presumed, are not revoked and nullified, as the mayors and jurats and residents very humbly request and beg of you."[125] Soon another reform regarding the sale of wine was undertaken by municipal officials. This modification of the statutes concerned "the knowledge and provision of certificates to all craftsmen, and the enforcement of the aforesaid statutes that are registered in the city." On this point, Montaigne and the jurats reasserted their authority in administrative matters.

Several other professions circumvented the city's privileges and had succeeded in obtaining royal edicts that gave them greater freedom. The tax burden had been significantly decreased, and the city was no longer able to tax its craftsmen. In this context, a "great alteration of the public welfare" prevailed in Bordeaux, and the city could no longer meet its obligations, for lack of money. Because of its high cost, the judicial system had ceased to be accessible to the disadvantaged; what had earlier cost one *sol* now cost two: "and for one clerk who had to be paid, three [now] had to be paid, namely: the court clerk, an ordinary clerk, and the clerk's clerk."[126] The poorest people were forced to give up defending their rights. This all-out attack on the cost of justice in Bordeaux seems to have been Montaigne's preferred hobbyhorse during the second half of 1583. We wonder about the personal motivations of the mayor, who intended to make life difficult for his former colleagues in the parlement.

The last grievance filed by the jurats in August 1583 addressed specifically the sale of offices. Montaigne reminded Henry III that the king's justice had to be administered free of charge and "to the smallest number of the mass of people as possible." The sale of judicial offices was officially prohibited. However, in practice, and "through the injure of time," the multiplication of officials was greater than ever, "with the result that the poor people suffers greatly, at the same time that in the last year the court clerks in the city and sénéchaussée have been elevated in office and their salary increased." The judicial bureaucracy increased excessively in size, and officials' salaries were directly paid by those who used the judicial system, "so that the poor, not having the means to meet so many expenses, are usually forced to abandon the pursuit of their rights and what should be used to support their families or to pay for public necessities is in this way spent to satisfy the ambition of certain individuals to the detriment of the public."[127] The jurats asked the king to reaffirm their authority in this still-undecided matter and to remind everyone of the authority and competence of each person. They requested that offices, functions, and responsibilities be clearly defined.

During Montaigne's first term, the city had levied a large sum to pay for the repair of the Cordouan lighthouse. However, nothing had been done. Already in the hands of the tax collector, the money raised had been "used elsewhere to the great detriment of the public," since no repairs or even preparations for the work had yet been made in August 1583. Montaigne and the jurats urged the king to order this money to be put back in the city's coffers in order to cover current expenses. To that end, Montaigne proposed to supervise personally, together with one of the presidents of the parlement and one of the treasurers, the expenses necessary for the restoration of the Cordouan lighthouse and to see to it that the money already paid out would be used to repair as soon as possible this light, which was considered crucial for navigation and commerce on the river. For example, on December 10, 1583, the mayor had signed a letter of remonstrance to Henry of Navarre in order to defend freedom of commerce on the Garonne. In 1584, Montaigne participated in the drawing up of a contract between Louis de Foix, the king's official architect, and the city of Bordeaux, represented by Matignon, François de Nesmond, and Ogier de Gourgues, the secretary general of finances in Guyenne. The subject of this contract was the reconstruction of the Cordouan tower that stood at the mouth of the Gironde estuary.[128] On May 2, 1584, an agreement was finally reached for the repair of the lighthouse and was initialed by Matignon and Montaigne.[129]

The mayor's everyday activity sometimes consisted of arbitrations and unusual problems that divided public opinion. Thus the first important matter in Montaigne's second term had to do with a criminal case that is reported in an order issued by the mayor and the jurats and dated August 15, 1583.[130] The mayor of Blaye, Pierre Duboys, had been murdered in Bordeaux a few years earlier in the course of an altercation on a city street. This crime dated from the time when Biron was mayor. A certain Gailhard Baudet, known as La Reballerye, was found guilty. The mayor and the jurats of Bordeaux sentenced him in absentia, but the matter was brought before the parlement of Toulouse, which asked that the relevant documents be sent to it. This amounted to an attack on the authority of the mayor and the jurats in a criminal case, and Montaigne decided to file an appeal to preserve the city's privileges. The jurats Geoffroy d'Alesme, Jean Gallopin, Pierre Régnier, Jean de Lapeyre, and Jean Claveau supported the mayor. After being reelected to a second term, Montaigne ordered that the copies of the interrogation and the verification of the witnesses be retained, but he lost his appeal and had to yield to judicial decisions made in

Toulouse. He was even forced to pay a fine for having slowed the transfer of the documents. The recent problems with the governors of the castles in Bordeaux at least allowed the municipal team to emerge more united than ever from this difficult moment.

The poverty that afflicted a growing part of the population of Bordeaux also raised the problem of supplying bread inside the city walls. The jurats reformed the regulation of bakers to facilitate the distribution of bread. The bakers henceforth had to have a three-month reserve of wheat. If the city experienced a bread shortage, the bakers had to pay a fine of hundred Bordeaux *livres*. The mayor's office set up an agency to supervise the flour supply. But it was commerce, the sale and serving of wine, that most occupied the municipal administration and was the subject of most of the city's regulations. On the wine question, Montaigne played a prominent role and was directly involved in the drafting and revision of decrees protecting Bordeaux wines.[131] The number of tavern keepers authorized to sell wine retail rose from 75 in 1548 to 120 in 1556. They had to receive letters from the city, a kind of license to serve drinks. They were placed under the authority of the mayor and the jurats and had to swear before the city's officials that they would not "defame or sell at low prices, or fraudulently, the wine of the bourgeois and residents of the city."[132] Those who sold or served wine had to pay a tax at the rate of six jars of wine from each barrel sold retail in a tavern, a hostelry, or a cabaret.

During Montaigne's second term as mayor, the protection of Bordeaux's wines was strengthened. A ruling of June 26, 1584, stipulated that "bourgeois wine[ix] shall be sold before any other."[133] Montaigne was once again going along with the bourgeois who wanted to retain their commercial advantages and prohibit the entrance into the city of wines from the Haut Pays. The wines of Castillon, Montravel, Saint Antoine, Sainte-Foy, Saint Pey, Sainte Radegonde, Duras, Gensac, Rauzan, Pujols, Cyvrac, Blaignac, and the Côtes de Blaye had to be "clearly labeled on both ends of every barrel" and, once labeled, had to remain in the suburbs (Les Chartreux) of the city, "and not inside it." Every barrel of wine so labeled was taxed two *sols* and six *deniers*. The sale of bourgeois wines within the city had to be protected. This protectionism for Bordeaux wines was, of course, exactly what the local bourgeoisie wanted, and Montaigne repeatedly found himself involved in drafting these increasingly strict regulations that sought to promote and sell bourgeois wines. For example, selling wines from the Haut Pays in the city's taverns was forbidden. The bourgeois were not allowed to buy wines from the Haut Pays or any other region on pain of losing their status as citizens of Bordeaux. To avoid fraud, it was also forbidden to sell wine on the Grave along the river.

[ix] Wine produced by residents of Bordeaux. [Trans.]

Other professions also succeeded in benefiting from Montaigne's election and were able to take advantage of a mayor receptive to their concerns. Thus *courretiers*, brokers "living in the city, solid people of good character and decent conversation" who stored barrels of wine until a deal was made between the buyer and the seller, saw their salary double after public discussion before the city's General Council in 1584. Their number grew to forty-six while Montaigne was mayor. Their revenues rose from the earlier six *sols* per barrel of wine to twelve *sols*. *Courretiers* were forbidden to lodge foreign merchants in their homes, to store their merchandise in their houses, or to engage in "any traffic for them." These rulings had recently been confirmed by rulings of January 31 and March 30, 1579. While Montaigne was serving as mayor, a ruling dated September 6, 1584, forbade anyone to harvest grapes without the express permission of the jurats of the cities, officials, and the local judges. On August 11, 1584, he undertook the revision of the statutes of pin makers, and on August 22, 1584, he and the jurats of Bordeaux signed a contract with Jacques Gaultier to teach painting in the city.[134] The mayor of Bordeaux intervened personally in the many municipal initiatives that sought to moralize public life and transform a city that was chiefly oriented toward commerce into a haven of culture propitious to the development of the arts and letters.

During his second term, Montaigne devoted himself fully to the service of the city and denounced the abuses committed by royal representatives who, with the parlement's help, were succeeding in getting around the authority of the jurats and the mayor. This kind of dispute regarding the sale of wine in Bordeaux was certainly not new, but the liberalization of the wine trade through the sale of "new statutes" to cabaret or tavern owners made it possible to escape the old statutes of these professions and thus considerably decrease the city's revenues. Another municipal ruling of October 23, 1584, forced hotel keepers and cabaret owners to pay for objects "lost" in their establishments or stolen by their servants or household staff.[135] At the beginning of his second term, Montaigne seems to have been much more interested in the management of the city. Although at first he had adopted an aloof attitude, by 1584 he was completely invested in what made Bordeaux an economically prosperous city, namely, the wine trade. In a letter to the jurats, he expresses his satisfaction with the favorable result of a deputation to the king seeking the repression of fraud concerning wines in Bordeaux.[136] Montaigne had become, so to speak, the herald of the local bourgeoisie and had found more allies among the rich wine merchants than among the nobility of the sword. Let us not forget that Montaigne was a wine producer. He had gradually transformed himself into a manager.

In 1584, Montaigne's political career changed drastically. Although his first term had been relatively calm, his second began with turmoil before it settled back into administrative routine. In the middle of his second term, things took a radically different turn and gave Montaigne the status of a national political figure by allowing him to take advantage of his office as mayor to negotiate a peace agreement between Henry III and Henry of Navarre, while at the same time being well aware that he remained subordinate to Matignon. The sudden death of Francis of Anjou, the duke of Alençon, on June 10, 1584, significantly changed the political map. The last Valois prince, Francis of Anjou had died without an heir, and Henry of Bourbon, king of Navarre, found himself the presumptive heir to the French throne. Confronted by this intolerable possibility, the Catholic princes hastened to organize a counterstroke by creating a Paris branch of the League in late 1584. From that moment on, Montaigne began to frequent people of a different caliber, for instance, Philippe Duplessis-Mornay.

Expelled from the Court by her brother, Margaret of Valois was at that point on her way to join her husband at the Court of Nérac, humiliated after being very badly treated at Bourg-la-Reine. Margaret complained to her husband, who wrote a harangue delivered to the king by Pibrac, who was at that time serving as Margaret's chancellor. Henry of Navarre protested vehemently. Duplessis-Mornay, Bellièvre, and finally Pibrac demanded that amends be made for the insults inflicted on the queen. What was at first simply a sister's indignation against her brother quickly took a political turn. Pibrac had to defend himself against suspicions that he had been the queen of Navarre's lover. Henry of Navarre was himself put in a difficult situation by the arrival of his wife in the southwest; during the preceding summer, he had fallen in love with Diane d'Andoins, who had since become his mistress. Montaigne found himself in the middle of all these political and amorous turpitudes.

In the autumn of 1584—that is, halfway through his second term—Montaigne seems to have spent more time in his château than in Bordeaux. In December 1584, the jurats demanded that he be present in Bordeaux, but Montaigne begged off on the pretext that he had "the whole Sainte-Foy Court . . . to deal with."[137] He was preparing for the arrival of Henry of Navarre and his Court at his château, and suddenly attending the deliberations of the jurade had ceased to be a priority. He had moved closer to Henry of Navarre and now had, in the person of Diane d'Andoins, a faithful ally in his entourage.[138] Montaigne had known the Countess of Guiche in the 1570s. She was the widow of Philibert de Guiche, Count of Gramont, who had been killed at the siege of La Fère, which Montaigne has witnessed. Montaigne had dedicated La Boétie's twenty-nine sonnets to this woman famed for her beauty, going so far as to make suggestive remarks to her, "inflamed by a fine and noble ardor whose details, Madame, I shall one of these days whisper in your ear."[139] That day had come. The Countess of Guiche had been Henry of Navarre's mistress since May 1582,[140] and Montaigne could count on his friendship with the widow of one of his close friends to have access to Henry of Navarre. Whereas Épernon's mission during the first months of the year 1584 had failed, Montaigne thought that his friendship with the Countess of Guiche and Henry of Navarre could help him bring Henry of Navarre back to bosom of the Catholic Church. At least that was the idea he broached with the king and Catherine de Medici, or perhaps it was the Marquis of Trans who had suggested this approach to him, in order to make himself a necessary intermediary.

Henry of Navarre and his entourage reached Montaigne's château on December 19. Urged by the Marquis of Trans to play the role of a political intermediary, Montaigne suddenly recovered national political ambitions that the everyday work of the mayor's office had caused him to forget for a time. Henry of Navarre's stay at Montaigne's château led to a new political awareness on the part of Montaigne, who began to think he could play a role as a negotiator between the two Henrys. He reported this meeting in his almanac, stressing the importance of the event:

> 1584, the King of Navarre came to see me at Montaigne, where he had never been, and stayed there for two days, served by my people, without any of his officers. He would neither have his food tasted nor utensils provided, and slept in my bed. He had with him Messieurs the Prince of Condé, de Rohan, de Turenne, de Rieus, de Béthune et son frère, de La Boulaye, d'Esternay, de Haraucourt, de Montmartin, de Montataire, de Lesdiguières, de Poe, de Blacon, de Lusignan, de Clervan, Savignac, Ruat, Sallebeuf, la Rocque, La Roche, de Rous, d'Aucourt, de Luns, Frontenac, de Fabas, de Vivas and his son, la Burte, Forget, Bissouse, de Saint Sevrin, d'Auberville. The lieutenant of Monsieur the Prince's company, his squire, and about ten other lords slept here, along with the valets de chambre, pages, and the soldiers of his guard. About the same number were lodged in the villages. From here, I had a stag released in my forest, which led him a chase for 2 days.[141]

Henry of Navarre's stay at Montaigne's château represented one of the highpoints of Montaigne's second term as mayor of Bordeaux. However, it was the master of the château and not the mayor who received the king and about thirty gentlemen. Montaigne was not unhappy to have resumed for the occasion his titles of lord and knight of the king's order, which allowed him to distance himself from usual quarrels of the mayor's office. Henry of Navarre's visit to Montaigne restored the image of the author of the *Essais*, who glimpsed the possibility of serving his country in a different way. Thus it was as a gentleman of Guyenne and not as the mayor of Bordeaux that he entertained Henry of Navarre.[142] It occurred just before the official birth of the Catholic League created by the Guises and supported by the king of Spain to prevent the accession of a

Protestant—Henry of Navarre—to the French throne. This visit's goal was probably to test the waters and to see if an entente between the two Henrys against the Guises might be possible.

The end of the year 1584 was thus marked by a rapprochement between Montaigne and Henry of Navarre, very certainly through the mediation of the Marquis of Trans. Three successive meetings with Henry of Navarre reoriented Montaigne's political ambitions and offered him an opportunity to serve the king in the role of negotiator. These consultations made him a privileged interlocutor: first, at Mont-de-Marsan in December 1583, then at Bergerac in April 1584, and finally the visit to his château in December 1584. Montaigne's reelection as mayor and his victory over the commanders of the castles of Le Hâ and Trompette had given him an appreciable political weight by demonstrating that he had a firm hand and that his calculations could be redoubtable. From this time on we sense in Montaigne a renewal of interest in high political missions and the role he could play in a rapprochement between the two Henrys, and consequently between the two religions. The meeting between Henry of Navarre and Matignon that Montaigne organized for June 12, 1585, marks the apogee of his role as a negotiator, at a time when his second term as mayor was coming to an end. In fact, for the past six months he had practically ceased to perform his duties as administrator of the city in order to devote himself almost exclusively to his role as intermediary. The greater volume of correspondence with Matignon shows that Montaigne considered himself a central figure in the negotiations that were being conducted between Navarre and Henry III.

Montaigne thought he had an advantage in his position as negotiator. The expression "a tender and green negotiator"—that is, a neophyte, but also one who is flexible—that he uses to describe his superiority over others in matters of diplomacy refers to a form of candor and spontaneity overrated in the service of the political:

> In what little negotiation I have had to do between our princes, in these divisions and subdivisions that tear our nation apart today, I have studiously avoided letting them be mistaken about me and deceived by my outward appearance. Professional negotiators make every effort within their power to conceal their thoughts and to feign a moderate and conciliatory attitude. As for me, I reveal myself by my most vigorous opinions, presented in my most personal manner—a tender and green negotiator, who would rather fail in my mission than fail to be true to myself.[143]

Montaigne's pretense of naïveté allowed him to keep his distance from partisan commitments, just as his direct style allowed him to present the points to be negotiated without worrying about the status of his interlocutors. He returned to the message he had tried to send the king in 1580 and had finally found a political interest in his novice's attitude. Monopolized by his mission as negotiator, Montaigne neglected the business of the mayor's office. He now had other, much more pressing priorities.

In early February 1585, Montaigne once again excused himself to the jurats for his absence and congratulated them on having begun the new year so well, "hoping to enjoy it with you at the first opportunity."[144] Despite his assurances, he seemed more concerned with Matignon. Since March, fighting had flared up again in Guyenne, and everything suggested that the king was going to come to an agreement with Navarre to oppose the League. In the southwest, most of the large cities were experiencing serious grain shortages, and the people were starving. Montaigne and Duplessis-Mornay thought that whatever entente between Henry III and Guise might emerge, "they will never be united in will."[145] Montaigne had found a new center of interest that allowed him to consider himself a key figure in the negotiation between the royal party and the Huguenots. The geographical location of his château made him an ideal mediator, because he was able to make numerous rapid round trips between the Court of Navarre and Bordeaux, where he received his orders from Matignon. His château was near both Bergerac and Sainte-Foy, which were Protestant strongholds. Thus it was as much the geographical situation of his noble estate as his acquaintances in Catholic and Protestant circles that made him indispensable.

Montaigne had just learned of the reconciliation of Henry of Navarre and Margaret of Valois and hastened to tell Matignon about his discussions with the Protestants. He was delighted with the confidence Turenne showed in him, despite the fact that he "does not much rely on courtly words."[146] Montaigne was extremely active in early 1585. He made several trips to the Fleix château, met Arnaud du Ferrier, the former ambassador to Venice who had recently converted to Protestantism, and met with emissaries from Henry of Navarre. One of Margaret's couriers was arrested three leagues from Nérac while he was carrying a message from Catherine de Medici. As a loyal servant of the king, Montaigne informed Matignon of this episode and its possible consequences. Everything passed through him and he was in on all the secrets. He knew things that could not be written down. Matignon urged him to return to Bordeaux, but in a rare moment of independence from his superior's orders, Montaigne refused, and suggested to the lieutenant governor that everything take place on his estate, or at least at Fleix. Montaigne was at the summit of his career as a negotiator and wrote to Matignon that "I shall never withdraw so deeply into solitude nor leave public affairs so far behind that I shall not retain a singular devotion to your service."[147]

However, Montaigne was not a member of Catherine de Medici's diplomatic corps. Among the queen mother's negotiators were Jean de Monluc (the brother of Blaise de Monluc[x]); Cardinal Charles of Bourbon; Guy du Faur de Pibrac; Louis de Saint-Gelais, lord of Lansac; Pomponne de Bellièvre; Louis II of Bourbon, duke of Montpensier; Paul de Foix; the brothers Nicolas d'Angennes and Louis d'Angennes; and Méry de Barbezières de La Roche-Chémerault.[148]

But all these men, most of whom came from famous lineages, were too involved in the religious conflict that divided France. New men who were less aligned with one side had to be found, men on whom Protestants and Catholics could agree. A second tier of negotiators proposed by these experienced diplomats had the advantage of operating more freely and more secretly. When they traveled, they were not accompanied by an entourage as large as the one that accompanied first-tier negotiators. Confronted by the inflexible positions taken by the members of the League, it was also necessary to find men who were moderate while remaining loyal to the sovereign. There were not many such, because they ran the risk of being denounced as covert Gallicans.[xi] This was the case for Paul de Foix, who had formerly advocated tolerance and had barely escaped being killed during the Saint Bartholomew's Day massacres. It was also the case for Lansac, who had been accused in 1556 of not having observed Lent. Most of these men knew Montaigne and proposed his name to Catherine de Medici, who had been informed of the twists and turns of Montaigne's reelection as mayor of Bordeaux. As we have seen, she had known him since the early 1570s and certainly recalled the Roman episode of 1581. Indeed, four years earlier, Montaigne had almost obtained an ambassadorship, and thanks to Matignon's recommendations, he had since acquired a reputation as a loyal servant of the king. He was to be among these less famous negotiators who brought the two Henrys together so that they could agree to oppose the Guises.

At this point, Montaigne began to correspond with Duplessis-Mornay, nicknamed "the Huguenots' pope."[149] Let us note that the exchange of messages between the two men was limited in time and was perhaps less amicable than has been said. Only six letters written in Duplessis-Mornay's hand have been preserved. Since we cannot know for certain what Montaigne's point of view was, we are reduced to imagining an essentially political dialogue that took place between November 25, 1583, and January 25, 1584.[150] These two months testify to an intense, remarkable political activity on Montaigne's part. In a letter dated December 9, 1583, Duplessis-Mornay describes his exchanges with Montaigne as "profitable," if not "pleasing": "Monsieur, if my letters please you, yours profit me; and you know how much more valuable profit is than pleasure."[151] Duplessis-Mornay warns Montaigne and explains that the king's ac-

---

[x] Marshal of France since 1574 and later the author of the famous *Commentaires de Messire Blaise de Montluc* (1592), which Henry IV called "the soldier's Bible." [Trans.]

[xi] Members of the French Catholic clergy who advocated limiting the pope's control over governments and churches. [Trans.]

tions against the Protestants have limits that will have to be respected. The reasons for this epistolary exchange have to do with the rise of Henry of Navarre, who, on the night of November 21/22, 1583, had retaken the town of Mont-de-Marsan, which had been in the hands of the Catholics since 1580. For Duplessis-Mornay, this was a legitimate operation, and he asked Montaigne to report it as such. The Fleix accords provided for the restitution of the Protestant cities, but this agreement had never been respected, and Navarre, who was furious with Matignon, had taken advantage of his military strength in the region.

For the Protestants in the southwest, the time for action had come. It is probable that Duplessis-Mornay saw in Montaigne an ideal go-between to present the king of Navarre's point of view to Henry III. Duplessis-Mornay and the Protestants thought that Henry III was ill-informed about the situation in the region and saw in Montaigne a way of making their proposals heard. They had the wind at their backs, and someone like Montaigne was likely to understand better than anyone the true political stakes in the southwest. His character was far from being quick-tempered and this personal trait was considered an advantage. The Protestants also trusted his objectivity:

> We are writing to you who are, in this tranquility of mind, neither moving nor moved by minor matters, for a different reason, not to assure you of our intention, which is well known to you and cannot be hidden from you, either because of your frankness, or because of the wit of your mind, but rather to pledge and testify to it for you, if need be, with regard to those who judge us ill, because they do not see us, and because they see instead through the eyes of others rather than through their own.[152]

These lines describe rather well the reputation Montaigne enjoyed at this time—that of a calm, peaceful, frank man independent of the conflicting parties. He was trusted to report objectively the reality on the ground. Duplessis-Mornay also seems to warn Montaigne that wit and frankness are one thing, but the Protestants have deep beliefs that will not be weakened by court gesticulation or diplomatic posturing.

Montaigne was now perceived as an ideal intermediary for the Huguenots, who were counting on him to open a dialogue between the two sovereigns and thus avoid an alliance between Henry III and the Guises. Montaigne responded favorably to this request to serve as intermediary between the two Henrys. From one day to the next, he abandoned his responsibilities at the mayor's office and withdrew to his estate to be closer to the Court of Navarre. This was also a sign of independence. He considered this situation the logical continuation of his service to the king, and he wrote more and more reports to Matignon. Duplessis-Mornay explained Navarre's new policy to Montaigne. His patience had been interpreted as weakness, and he was now obliged to make war to respond to the Catholics' intransigence: "Our goal has been only to show that our peaceful behavior proceeded not from necessity, but from goodwill. This prince has realized that his patience was seen as the result of a lack of means. He wants it henceforth to have the name of patience, moderation, and virtue."[153] After the duke of Alençon's death early in the summer, Henry of Navarre had to act as the future sovereign of the kingdom. Duplessis-Mornay trusted in Montaigne to convey the Protestants' opinion: "I know that you are doing it as well as you can." Although he was in the service of Matignon and Henry III, Montaigne considered himself to be working for Henry of Navarre as well. The political initiative had come from the Protestant camp, and Montaigne now felt himself to be above the usual ideological and religious lines. This situation as a privileged political actor did not last long.

The ephemeral correspondence between Duplessis-Mornay and Montaigne abruptly halted. Was that a sign of failure? Could Montaigne succeed, after all, in convincing the Catholic extremists that the Protestant demands were well founded? Certainly not. The last letter of January 25, 1584, alludes to the queen of Navarre's mistreatment by her brother, which had more to do "with vinegar than with oil, and ill-suited to such a painful wound." After having scoffed at the king of Navarre's honor, the intransigent Catholics were no longer believed to be sincere, "and now quibble over trivialities."[154] Duplessis-Mornay soon began to doubt that the negotiations would produce results. Montaigne tried to calm people down, at first with a certain success, but his policy of openness was doomed to fail. A letter from Turenne, undated but probably written at the end of the year 1584, attests to Montaigne's influence at Navarre's Court:

> When he returned, the king of Navarre decided to see Marshal Matignon; I beg you to keep your hand in this, because we are well aware here that with your persuasion and depending on how you push, this can be done for the good of the service, for the king, for the peace of the government, and to the contentment of all good people. . . . I beg you to believe that I greatly cherish your friendship, and thus you can make use of me as a humble and sure friend who will obey you.[155]

The League appeared as a third party and urged the king to fight Navarre. The Navarre's conversion to the Catholic faith seemed the only compromise hoped for by Henry III, who sent the duke of Épernon to Navarre to convince him to convert. The Protestants put pressure on Navarre not to yield on any point and forced him to remain faithful to Protestantism.

In September 1584, Montaigne was able to ask Duplessis-Mornay to intercede on behalf of his youngest brother, Bertrand de Mattecoulon, to help him obtain the title of ordinary gentleman of the chamber of the king of Navarre, and, as if to recall his family's ties with the regional aristocracy, he thus put his brother in the highest rank of the nobility of Guyenne. Montaigne carried the letter of receipt written from Montauban by Duplessis-Mornay to Macé Duperray, Navarre's treasurer general, so that his brother might receive the wages of his office, which came to 500 *livres* per annum.[156] This letter emphasizes that it concerns the "brother of M. de Montagne [*sic*], mayor of Bordeaux." Montaigne's recent political visibility allowed him to obtain a few favors for his family.

Montaigne felt close enough to Navarre to be able to hope that his mission as a negotiator might be successful. A letter addressed to Matignon, dated January 18, 1585, allows us to divine Montaigne's strategy, particularly the pressure he put on Diane d'Andoins to convince Navarre to come to an agreement with Henry III to oppose the League. This was an intermediate avenue that still seemed to him possible:

> My lord, according to several accounts given me by M. de Bissonse, on behalf of M. de Turenne, regarding the judgment that he makes of you and of the trust that this prince [the king of Navarre] has in my views, even though I do not much rely on courtly words, it occurred to me, at dinner, to write to M. de Turenne: that I bid him farewell by letter; that I had received the letter from the king of Navarre, who seemed to me to take good advice in trusting in the affection that you offer him to do him service; that I had written to Mme de Guissen to make use of his boat for convenience, this while I would work with you, and that I had advised him to display his passions only for this prince's interest and fortune, and, since she had so much influence over him, to attend more to his utility than to his particular humors.[157]

In this letter, Montaigne informs Matignon that he could hope to manipulate the Countess of Guiche and to use her to advance the king's plans. This was a major advantage for him, and in the name of an old friendship, he was still counting on Diane d'Andoins to get the king of Navarre to convert.[158]

On March 30, 1585, the League proclaimed, in a manifesto, its leaders' decision to oppose the enemies of the Catholic religion and designated the Cardinal of Bourbon as the presumptive heir to the throne. Their man in Bordeaux was Louis Ricard Bourdon de Genouillac, baron of Vaillac and commander of the Trompette castle. The city was swarming with members of the League, and they were happy to cause Montaigne's negotiations to fail. Facing the danger of seeing the city in the hands of supporters of the Guises, Matignon intervened with the authority given him by his title as lieutenant governor of Guyenne. The commanders of the castles of Le Hâ and Trompette had been a constant source of concern for the past two years, and Matignon feared that they might set up a counterauthority too favorable to the League.

In late April, Matignon summoned the presidents of the parlement, the mayor, the jurats, the main city officials, and Vaillac. During this meeting, he set forth the schemes of the members of the League who were fomenting a revolt against the sovereign and thus disturbing the peace in Bordeaux. He publicly accused Vaillac of disloyalty to the king and told him that the king wanted him to put Trompette castle back in his (Matignon's) hands. Despite Vaillac's protests, Matignon ordered the commander disarmed. Matignon's determination took Vaillac by surprise. Turning to Montaigne, Matignon ordered him "to make the king's intentions and his own known throughout the city, to dispose the bourgeois, truly faithful servants of His Majesty, to join his troops to subdue the soldiers in the garrison in the event that Vaillac's punishment did not force them to surrender." After a little hesitation, Vaillac agreed to surrender. Brantôme lauds Matignon's skill in this affair. The disarming of Vaillac and his public humiliation was a kind of revenge for Montaigne as well.

Thus it was toward the end of his second term that the mayor acquired a national stature that made him think he might have a political career as a negotiator. However, this window quickly closed. In late July 1585, the Treaty of Nemours forced Henry III to accept the League's demands and canceled the treaties of tolerance, the better to prepare for a test of strength with the Protestants. The policy of negotiation had fizzled out. Starting in July, 1585, Henry III chose rapprochement with the League, because no other military option was available to him. There was no longer any question of Henry of Navarre abjuring his Protestant faith. The whole policy of negotiation had been based on this sole possibility, which evaporated once again. Montaigne's career as a negotiator had lasted only a few months, and his second term as mayor was drawing to a close. In this climate of bitterness and consternation, Montaigne briefly returned to the city's current affairs.

In May 1585, a general review of the troops in Bordeaux had been the occasion for a political reflection on Montaigne's part. Faced with the rise of the League's power in Bordeaux, it was feared that there might be attempted assassinations of members of the city government, perhaps even including the mayor, who was perceived as close to the Protestants. Matignon was not in Bordeaux at this time, and the mayor's office discussed the attitude to adopt and the precautions to take during this military review. In the chapter "Various outcomes of the same plan" (I: 24) Montaigne explains his decision:

Once it was planned to have a general review of various troops under arms. That is an excellent occasion for secret vengeances; never can they be executed with greater security. There were public and notorious evidences that things would go badly for some who had the principal and necessary responsibility for the reviewing. Various plans were proposed, since the matter was difficult and had much weight and consequence. Mine was that they should above all avoid giving any sign of fear, and should show up and mingle in the ranks, head high and countenance open, and that instead of cutting out anything (as other opinions mostly aimed to do), they should on the contrary urge the captains to instruct their soldiers to make their volleys fine and lusty in honor of the spectators, and not spare their powder. This served to gratify the suspected troops, and engendered from then on a useful mutual confidence.[159]

In this passage we find once again Montaigne's favored strategy that consisted in putting himself above political agitations while at the same time displaying a certain naïveté that he erected into a means of political activity.

A few weeks later, Montaigne wrote to Matignon to inform him of the movements of the League armies commanded by Mayenne and Charles I of Lorraine. Bordeaux feared an armed intervention, and the mayor spent "every night either in the city in arms, or outside the city at the port."[160] In particular, he kept an eye on Trompette castle and distrusted Vaillac and the king's garrisons, which had been infiltrated by supporters of the duke of Guise.

As if the point was to remind Montaigne of the everyday duties of the mayor of a large city in France, from March to June 1585, when Montaigne was almost at the end of his second term, the city once again took up the recurrent problem of the refuse that had piled up on the streets, and, more generally, the pervasive unsanitary conditions.[161] It was a public health question, and the mayor's office set out to combat "the infection and stench of sewage, manure, refuse, and other filth" that was strewn on the streets, leading to "serious illnesses and deaths." Once again, it was forbidden to throw garbage out the windows, including water in which cod, herring, and other fish had been soaked. The city forced business owners to replace broken or missing paving stones in front of their shops. It even went so far as to forbid flowerpots on windowsills, because they could fall and wound or kill passersby. In the *Essais*, Montaigne dedicated a short chapter on odors in cities, "Of smells" (I: 55), in which he expressed his annoyance with this problem created by the too rapid expansion of cities during the Renaissance.[162] The Bordeaux mayor's office had left a bad smell! Several contemporary testimonies indicate that despite disappointments that were in no way unusual for such an administrative responsibility, Montaigne took his role as mayor seriously, especially at the beginning of his second term, and that he was liked by the majority of the members of the jurade. His task had not been easy. He had tried to show consideration for the three political forces represented in the jurade, but he alienated the nobility and the *robins*.

In June 1585, Montaigne was back in his château. At that point, plague broke out in Bordeaux. The contagion was to last until November, and according to the chronicler Gabriel de Lurbe, it killed more than 14,000 persons. Coming from Libourne, a traditional refuge for the notables, where he had been along with Matignon, Montaigne went as far as the city's suburbs in order to transfer his powers to the jurats. His last meeting with municipal officials did not go as planned. It occurred at the end of his term, and Montaigne had spent a large part of his time defying his enemies in a divided city. He felt that he had done his duty and considered himself no longer obligated to his fellow citizens, thinking he had performed his function as best he could. It was dangerous to stay in a city still affected by an epidemic, and a few years earlier Montaigne had avoided Paris for the same reason. His contemporaries, like his biographers, reproached him for his lack of courage. However, this accusation is unfair to a man who had concerned himself on several occasions with problems of public sanitation and health. It was a matter of good sense, and besides, he was mayor for only a few more days. He refused to go to Bordeaux to preside over the election of his successor and three new jurats, and proposed to meet the jurats outside the city.

Some people took offense at the cowardice of a lame-duck mayor who no longer had any political influence. They criticized Montaigne who, according to them, was abandoning his post and his responsibilities faced with the peril of the plague. Montaigne's term was almost over; he had only two days to go, and the game was not worth the candle. He decided not to go and presented his excuses to the jurats, admitting that he was refusing to "take the chance of going into the city, in view of the bad condition it is in, especially for people who come from such good air, as I do."[163] He preferred to remain on his estate, which was not yet affected by the contagion. Who could blame him? The city had not yet adopted regulations for times of plague, and it was only in June 1588 that the responsibilities of each elected official in the event of an epidemic were clearly defined.

Moreover, the religious troubles had led to a new outbreak of pillaging by armed bands, and Montaigne had to protect his home from the *picoreurs*—marauders and brigands—who were operating in the region. After an initial refusal, he finally agreed to meet with the jurats in the little village of Feuillas to convey to them Matignon's latest instructions as lieutenant governor of Guyenne. It was a question of electing a new administrator for the city. The elections took place and Matignon, now considered a Gascon, was named mayor of Bordeaux and remained in that office for twelve years, until his death in 1597. Although Montaigne's term as mayor had begun with his absence, it ended with what his biographers have often described as a flight.

An "Administration . . . without a Mark or a Trace"?

A brief glance at Montaigne's everyday routine as mayor of Bordeaux has allowed us to see the diversity of his activities and the amplitude of his ambitions during the years 1581–85. Although he had begun his term with an open political affinity that placed him resolutely on the side of the nobility to which he belonged, political reality on the ground quickly led him to adopt a pragmatic politics that often contradicted his own convictions and aristocratic aspirations. It was only after 1585 that his political career was considerably compromised, though not entirely halted. The failure of the negotiations between Henry III and Henry of Navarre pushed Montaigne to the sidelines. His subdued passage through the mayor's office in Bordeaux led him to glimpse a new orientation for his literary activity. Thus the third book of the *Essais*—written *after* this experience as mayor of Bordeaux—offers us several testimonies to his recent disillusion with offices and honorific rewards.

Montaigne shows an attitude that is critical of but no less grateful to the "duties of honor" and "civil restraint," because he had entered politics as a result of a favor or reward. On this point, the addition of the word *recompense* (reward) in the Bordeaux Copy is revealing:

> Now I hold that we should live by right and authority, not by [Bordeaux Copy: *recompense* or by] favor. How many gallant men have chosen rather to lose their lives than to owe them! I avoid subjecting myself to any sort of obligation, but especially any that binds me by a debt of honor. I find nothing so expensive as that which is given me and for which my will remains mortgaged by the claim of gratitude, and I more willingly accept services that are for sale. Rightly so, I think: for the latter I give only money, for the others I give myself. The tie that binds me by the law of honesty seems to me much tighter and more oppressive than is that of legal constraint.[164]

What conclusion can we draw from Montaigne's two terms as mayor of Bordeaux? The economic situation at the time of the Wars of Religion greatly influenced his contemporaries' judgment. In October 1585, Gabriel de Lurbe sketched a rather critical picture of the city's economic activity. According to him, the city and the region were in a wretched state, but he admits that the religious conflicts were largely responsible for this crisis.

A few people spoke out to reproach Montaigne for his political weakness and lack of involvement in the everyday affairs of the mayor's office. He was a decent manager, but no one ever saw him as a visionary. Some read the *Essais* in the light of Montaigne's administrative functions. For example, in his *Entretiens*, Guez de Balzac recounts the following anecdote:

> Our man still tried to persuade us that the selfsame Montaigne had not had much success as mayor of Bordeaux. This news did not surprise Monsieur De La Thibaudiere, and he remembered well that in my presence he had one day told Monsieur De Plassac-Méré, an admirer of Montaigne who praised him that day to the disadvantage of Cicero: you can esteem your Montaigne more than our Cicero all you want; I could not imagine that a man who knew how to govern the whole earth was not worth at least as much as a man who did not know how to govern Bordeaux.[165]

The question raised is whether Montaigne's supposed failures as mayor of Bordeaux should influence our reading of the *Essais*. Can we give a theoretical account of the works without taking an interest in their author's social existence?

The author of the *Essais* did not contradict his critics: "Some say that my administration passed without a mark or a trace. That's a good one! They accuse me of inactivity in a time when almost everyone was convicted of doing too much."[166] Montaigne could have done more, but the political price would have been even higher. The acceleration of public life resulted in the multiplication of negative judgments after Montaigne's two terms as mayor, but most of these reproaches ignored the necessity of social stability in times of political and religious troubles—this constant preoccupation for social stability was perhaps less visible for his critics but no less essential for Montaigne. In politics, Montaigne never felt at ease with quantifiable results. He always defended the qualitative to the disadvantage of the quantitative, even if it made him seem nonchalant and indolent: "Some say about this municipal service of mine (and I am glad to say a word about it, not that it is worth it, but to serve as an example of my conduct in such things) that I went about it like a man who exerts himself too weakly and with a languishing zeal; and they are not at all far from having a case."[167] Haste was never his strong point, and he almost always favored reflection and the status quo.

Obviously, Montaigne's role was more that of an intermediary than that of a leader. He was expected to promote dialogue between Navarre and the king, under Matignon's supervision, nothing more. From the outset, he had been chosen as mayor of Bordeaux to calm people down and slow somewhat the rhythm of political actions in the region. And on this point Montaigne had succeeded in calming things. A letter he sent Matignon makes his role perfectly clear: "My lord, I have just now received your [letter] of July 6, and very humbly thank you for indicating that you do not find my assistance disagreeable, by commanding me to get back to you. That is the greatest good I hope to receive from this public service of mine, and I hope to go meet you as soon as possible."[168] We must not forget that, as a "Protestant," Henry of Navarre was forbidden to sojourn within the city walls. Nonetheless, he was the uncontested political and military leader in the southwest because he had succeeded in gaining the support of an appreciable number of members of the middle-level nobility.

Montaigne considered the mayor's office a privileged space that could have positive repercussions on the national scale, and on this point he was not wrong.[169] Aware of the reproaches being made against him, he nevertheless said that his conscience was clear and that he felt he had done his duty: "I did not leave undone, as far as I know, any action that duty genuinely required of me."[170] However, this claim—made shortly after the fact, since Montaigne expresses it in the edition of the *Essais* published in 1588—still shows a trace of bitterness. As had already been the case fifteen years earlier at the parlement of Bordeaux, Montaigne was unable to avoid personal conflicts. The mayor's office had never been a goal in itself, because managing the city had remained rather distant from his conception of public life. On the other hand, from the moment that his administrative function allowed him to acquire visibility on the national level, he distanced himself from the jurats to play in the big leagues and to try to influence politics on the national scale. He took up his duties as mayor almost a year late, and we see that he detached himself from activities related to that office before the end of his second term. Montaigne was engaged full time in the work of this office a little more than two years out of the four that he held it. Thus as we might expect for a mayor of the fifth-largest city in France who managed to be absent half the time, his record of achievement is rather slim. The political situation in Guyenne might have required greater attention, but Montaigne—in the course of 1585—had finally ceased to believe that he could influence a state of affairs that was constantly being redefined by the various episodes of a merciless war between Catholics and Protestants.

During the summer of 1585, a single lesson could be learned: Montaigne's service as mayor was a failure so far as the reconciliation between Henry III and Henry of Navarre was concerned. The duke of Guise and his supporters in Bordeaux had not made this rapprochement any easier. The edict of Nemours issued on July 7, 1585, made Navarre an outlaw. When Montaigne left the mayor's office, nothing remained of the compromises envisaged a few months earlier. Like many *politiques*, and in view of recent developments, Montaigne shared the feeling that the League had become the kingdom's true enemy. In this sense, the end of Montaigne's term as mayor marked the beginning of a new chapter in the Wars of Religion. The division between Catholics and Protestants was greatly surpassed by the rise in power of the duke of Guise, who was now acting on his own. The house of Lorraine was gaining the ascendant among the people, and particularly among the bourgeoisie in the large cities. In his role as negotiator between the two Henrys, Montaigne was sidelined by the omnipresence of the Catholic extremists. His political experience in Guyenne had legitimately given him an opportunity to hope for responsibilities on the national level, but the rise of a third party upstaged him and complicated his plans.

In the third book of his *Essais*, Montaigne inserted a chapter devoted almost entirely to his experience in the public sphere. "On husbanding your will" (III: 10) answers many of the questions and reproaches that were addressed to him by his friends and contemporaries regarding his management of the city or his style of governance. Montaigne explains himself, presenting an image that is distinguished from the realpolitik often formulated at the time, first of all by Machiavelli. This chapter was for the most part written immediately after his service as mayor, when he returned to his château after having been on the road for almost six months, keeping far away from the plague that was raging in Guyenne. It was during this second withdrawal from the world that Montaigne wrote the third book of the *Essais*, from March 1587 to January 1588, in a period of political inactivity that led to a redefinition of his literary project.

Montaigne admits that he could sometimes seem detached from the responsibilities incumbent on him: "I do not engage myself easily. As much as I can, I employ myself entirely upon myself."[171] He develops an individualist position with regard to social relationships: "My opinion is that we must lend ourselves to others and give ourselves only to ourselves,"[172] or again: "The main responsibility of each of us is his own conduct."[173] This judgment after the fact is an understandable reaction. Montaigne's setbacks in politics forced him to work out a theory of turning inward on himself. That was when what modern criticism learned to appreciate in him was born: an introspection that allows the subject to judge and "taste" himself. The isolation provided by writing confirms a forced distancing from public life; literary introspection results from a political failure. It might even be suggested that the form of the essay is the product of a political reality that forced Montaigne to withdraw to his estate, because he had failed to have a career in the service of the state and the king. Not being able to list or comment on his successes as an administrator and politician, Montaigne began to talk about himself, for lack of a better subject. His political defects thus naturally became human qualities. For example, he confesses his lack of commitment, which he transforms into a positive attribute: "I do not know how to involve myself so deeply and so entirely. When my will gives me over to one party, it is not with so violent an obligation that my understanding is infected by it. In the present broils of this state, my own interest has not made me blind to either the laudable qualities in our adversaries or those that are re-proachable in the men I have followed."[174]

Montaigne failed in politics because he was "too human"; that, at least, is the idea that he would like to spread after his two terms as mayor of Bordeaux. His unconditional confidence in people is supposed to have caused him to be de-ceived. In the same way, his alleged difficulty in conceiving of people as aggre-gates or groups sharing a single ideology is supposed to be revealed as a disad-vantage for someone who felt at ease only in individual relationships. He was never a party man, and his personal judgment was ill adapted to political plat-forms or positions based on unnatural alliances. Ultimately, Montaigne was a lone wolf in his political behavior. The *Essais* allowed him to invert his experi-ences and to emphasize the positive flipside of a coin that had been considerably tarnished by his experience as a public man.

Montaigne's humanism, as it was conceptualized starting in 1585, implies a renunciation of politics. His book, which was first published in 1580 as an es-sentially political book, was gradually transformed into a humanist book that testifies to an individual experience presented as universal. The 1588 edition marks a decisive turning point, that of reflection on and evaluation of earlier experiences. He had done his work seriously, but without ever confusing private and public life: "If people have sometimes pushed me into the management of other men's affairs, I have promised to take them in hand, not in lungs and liver; to take them on my shoulders, not incorporate them into me; to be concerned over them, yes; to be impassioned over them, never. I look at them, but I do not brood over them."[175] This is more an observation than a philosophy. Montaigne notes that by nature, people like to serve, continuing in the voluntary servitude that had fascinated him in La Boétie. "Men give themselves for hire,"[176] he writes. In serving others, people lose their judgment and their freedom, Mon-taigne seems to say, as if by drawing this distinction he was situating himself outside the social and the political. For example, we might wonder about his election to a second term. Did he not owe it to the temporary alliances he was able to form—in a purely political way—with the bourgeoisie? Did he really think that chance alone made it possible for him to be elected? That is what he claimed immediately after his experience as mayor of Bordeaux: "Fortune willed to have a hand in my promotion."[177] However, this remark is contra-dicted by reality. Even if politics always involves an element of chance, since Machiavelli we know that the essence of politics consists in minimizing the role played by fortune in order to increase the role played by free will. Whatever he says, Montaigne knew Machiavelli well enough to be aware of this fundamental rule of politics.

Montaigne engaged in a literary exercise that consisted in producing a theory of detachment when faced with the proximity of events: "We never conduct well the thing that possesses and conducts us."[178] For Montaigne, when a politician is called upon to serve, he must become a technician or a technocrat:

> He who employs in it only his judgment and skill proceeds more gaily. He feints, he bends, he postpones entirely at his ease according to the need of the occasions; he misses the target without torment or affliction, and remains intact and ready for a new undertaking; he always walks bridle in hand. In the man who is intoxicated with a violent and tyrannical intensity of purpose we see of necessity much imprudence and injustice; the impetuosity of his desire carries him away. These are reckless movements, and, unless fortune lends them a great hand, of little fruit.[179]

Montaigne justifies his service as mayor by explaining that his detachment was the only way to properly manage the city's affairs. Moving things along without becoming too involved is in a way the good manager's modus operandi. What was perhaps only a character trait thus becomes a political philosophy.

The mayor had not proposed any great reforms—apart from those desired by the bourgeois representatives in the *jurade*, particularly the revision of the statutes of the artisanal professions—but faced with the urgency of the national situation, he could hardly be blamed for that. Politics too often amounted to a series of hasty reactions, and Montaigne wanted to preserve his image as a reflective man. For him, the time of politics, like the time of the *Essais*, was not linear, and it is in this sense that his perspective on the events of his age constantly forced him to compare the present situation with examples from the distant past. Thus being reproached for inaction became a mark of honor for Montaigne, who criticizes those who act without having weighed the consequences of their actions. The author of the *Essais* thinks that "most of our occupations are low comedy,"[180] scenes independent of one another and of limited value in the tragedy of the Wars of Religion.

Politics comes down to a question of the roles that we play at a given moment and in relation to the circumstances in which we find ourselves: "We must play our part duly, but as the part of a borrowed character. Of the mask and appearance we must not make a real essence, nor of what is foreign what is our very own."[181] After 1588, Montaigne added the following observation to this passage: "It is enough to make up our face, without making up our heart."[182] He had learned to play roles in his scholarly curriculum at the College of Guyenne, but he always remained aware of this very clear difference between appearances and reality. The mayor was a borrowed role, or rather a series of roles that had been able to disconcert those who believed they could situate him politically. With a certain success, Montaigne covered the whole of the religious and political spectrum of his period, even giving the impression that he occupied no stable place in it. He had the qualities of a chameleon, at least in the eyes of others. However, he had never fallen into the Machiavellian trap of confusing means with ends. His judgments, Montaigne tells us in "Of husbanding your will," bore on persons rather than on what they represented. Appearances had never impressed him, and he had learned to sound out people to discover what they really were deep within themselves. After 1588, Montaigne developed further this position that consists in emptying out the social part of life and relating it to a universal model or a human condition.

In the early 1580s, politics looked very much like the form of the essay. Everything was in movement and contested: "Notably in political matters, there is a fine field open for vacillation and dispute."[183] But politics also had its uses, and it was an honorable profession that our author was proud to have practiced: "Political philosophy may condemn, for all I care, the meanness and sterility of my occupation, if I can once acquire a taste for it. . . . I am of the opinion that the most honorable occupation is to serve the public and to be useful to many."[184] Montaigne had made a different choice: "For my part, I stay out of it; partly out of conscience (for in the same way that I see the weight attached to such employments, I see also what little qualification I have for them; partly out of laziness [*poltronerie*].[xii] I am content to enjoy the world without being all wrapped up in it, to live a merely excusable life, which will merely be no·burden to myself or others."[185] *Poltronerie* is not a word associated with our usual image of Montaigne. But "living his life" was a new priority, and this life no longer gave politics and public service a major place.

After 1588, Montaigne even claimed to have always been motivated by the search to discover the character of the men he had met in the course of his public service. The political realism prevailing at that time was based on the Machiavellian principle that gave priority to appearances over reality. Montaigne very early opposed this modern paradigm of politics and defended the possibility of judging human actions in a general way, apart from particular actions and words. This idealism with regard to politics was nonetheless contrary to his experiences as mayor of Bordeaux, four years during which he had to show realism and political pragmatism. Despite this Machiavellian apprenticeship, Montaigne persisted in believing in a form of sincerity that transcended history and its events, leaving to others what he called "the chicanery of the Palace of Justice": "You must not consider whether your action or your word may have another interpretation; it is your true and sincere interpretation that you must henceforth maintain, whatever it costs you. Your virtue and our conscience are addressed; these are not parts to be put behind a mask.

[xii] *Poltronerie*. Frame translates this word as "laziness," but it could also mean "cowardice"; both meanings are given in contemporary dictionaries. [Trans.]

Let us leave these vile means and expedients to the chicanery of the Palace of Justice."[186]

Montaigne knew what he was talking about: his first career as a member of parlement had led him to be a better judge of the true stakes involved in family or clan quarrels; his second career as a public servant had revealed to him another logic of interests that were often petty and partisan. In both cases, these political experiences reinforced in him the desire for an ethics separated from any social practice. The de-historicized, de-politicized, and de-socialized individual was gradually becoming his subject of study. After 1585, Montaigne made more and more declarations intended to distance him from the events of his time, even going so far as to state that a century later, no one would remember the Wars of Religion. Renown itself was changed by this: "Renown does not prostitute itself at so cheap a rate. The rare and exemplary actions to which it is due would not endure the company of that innumerable crowd of petty everyday actions."[187] From that time on, Montaigne repeated to anyone who would listen that he never confused his private being with his public life: "I have been able to take part in public office without departing one nail's breadth from myself," and he adds after 1588, "and to give myself to other without taking myself from myself."[188] His political attitude is thus supposed to be modeled on his temperament: "In short, the occasions in my term of office were suited to my disposition, for which I am very grateful to them."[189]

The military operations that were breaking out in the region led to an increasing lack of security. In the chapter "Of physiognomy" (III: 12), Montaigne reports that marauders were at the gates of his château and were threatening his family: "I was writing this about the time when a mighty load of our disturbances settled down for several months with all its weight right on me. I had on the one hand the enemy at my door, on the other hand the freebooters, worse enemies."[190] The civil wars had caused people to lose their moral compasses and had become a fatal disease. Good and evil were inseparable and the final judgment remained in suspense. Politics had been transformed into an illness whose advanced state made it impossible to distinguish the limbs affected: "In these epidemics one can distinguish at the beginning the well from the sick, but when they come to last, like ours, the whole body is affected, head and heels alike; no part is free from corruption."[191] All the usual ethical reference points had disappeared. Montaigne expresses, for example, his shame at seeing these armies composed mainly of foreigners with corrupt commanders leading them. He mentions Roman models, in which war was honorable and armies disciplined. To this "monstrous war" he opposes the noble war of the Cannibals, which corresponded more to a chivalric ritual than to the liquidation of one's enemies. Although he preferred to keep silent about the Wars of Religion, he took pleasure in describing the warlike customs of the inhabitants of the New World, which confirmed him in his idea of the political.

After a first year as mayor in which he was rather proud to have been a "nonmayor," Montaigne rapidly got caught up in the political game, hoping to make use of his position to seek further responsibilities on the national level. He had done his best to administer a city that could serve him as a springboard toward public offices closer to his ambitions in the service of princes. Confronted by the rising power of regional parlements, the mayor's office was supposed to serve as a counterauthority to provide a firmer basis for royal power and to emphasize Montaigne's competence as a proven negotiator. His mission was to be Matignon's eyes and Henry III's herald in a city that had a long tradition of administrative and political independence, indeed even of uprising against royal authority. The Wars of Religion had only poisoned a situation that had been tense for several generations, and Montaigne had not succeeded in imposing his conception of politics. He did not regret any of his decisions, and ended up attributing success—and his failure—in politics to chance. In the chapter "Of repentance" (III: 2), he claims that he had always "proceeded wisely":

In business matters, several good opportunities have escaped me for want of successful management. However, my counsels have been good, according to the circumstances they were faced with; their way is always to take the easiest and surest course. I find that in my past deliberations, according to my rule, I have proceeded wisely considering the state of the matter proposed to me, and I should do the same a thousand years from now in similar situations. I am not considering what it is at this moment, but what it was when I was deliberating about it.[192]

Leaving office after two terms as mayor of Bordeaux, Montaigne felt that he had performed his function well. If he had been able to do it over again, he would have made exactly the same decisions. A good administrator judges things on the spot, while a good humanist puts things in a universal perspective. The two positions were thus irreconcilable, and that is perhaps why Montaigne's municipal service can be considered a failure. Too humanist to become a good manager, and too concerned with resolving current problems to leave a mark on the political history of his time, Montaigne did not succeed in establishing his way of seeing politics during his term as mayor of a municipality riven into pressure groups defending irreconcilable interests and ideologies. The practice of politics led him to discover what he called his "natural disposition,"[193] and the self could then be constructed on the ruins of politics.

CHAPTER 9

"Benignity of the Great" and
"Public Ruin" (1585–1588)

While the king, cheerful and careless, was playing at cup-and-ball in the streets of Paris, with the dukes of Épernon and Joyeuse imitating him, surrounded by young people in colorful costumes, the "great and furious"[1] plague was raging in Lyon, Dijon, Senlis, and Bordeaux. We are in August 1585. Montaigne had just completed his second term as mayor. He had refused to go to Bordeaux for fear of the contagion and had holed up on his estate before setting out to wander the roads of the region to escape the epidemic. On the religious level, the situation was deteriorating from day to day, and any hope of a political solution between the two Henrys was indefinitely deferred. In September, Henry of Navarre and Condé were excommunicated by the "private bull" issued by Pope Sixtus V. Supported by the Guises, Charles of Bourbon appeared as the pretender to the crown. Henry III had once again yielded to the pressure of his entourage and had not been able to carry to success the negotiations begun at the end of 1584. His "not warlike, but timid and fearful, temperament was the object of caustic criticism on the part of those whom he thought could do him a disservice."[2] His mother's influence reinforced his image as a poor decision maker, and people denounced the duplicity he was said to have learned from her. For Montaigne, dissimulation and deceit were not recommendable qualities in a sovereign.

In this climate of uncertainty and contempt for the king, Montaigne withdrew from the Court. He had not been able to understand the logic of Henry III's political decisions. In an addition to the Bordeaux Copy he offers this not very flattering portrait of the last Valois king, without naming him: "No middle position, always being carried away from one extreme to the other by causes impossible to guess; no kind of course without tacking and changing direction amazingly; no quality unmixed, so that the most likely portrait of him that men will be able to make some day, will be that he affected and studied to make himself known by being unknowable."[3] Henry III was a true mystery,[4] and

Montaigne, like many of his contemporaries, more than once paid the price for an unpredictable royal politics that was punctuated by abrupt reversals and often conducted in accord with the caprice of the moment.

Despite his character weaknesses, the king had an elevated conception of his responsibilities. For example, he had an excessive confidence in the judicial system and the law, which Montaigne admired in him. Against the views of the Catholics who wanted war, Henry III continued tirelessly to seek religious reconciliation and tried to find a compromise between the extreme policies that were polarizing public opinion. The last Valois was often forced to yield to those who wanted to settle matters by force. He did all he could to avoid the country's ruin and the danger toward which it was irremediably heading. A man of ideas who preferred dialogue to violence, Henry III was not able to create a political sphere that would allow the *politiques* to exert a decisive influence on his decisions. After 1585, prudence was no longer fashionable, and the king applied his mother's teachings to governmental matters, going so far as to legitimate violence to preserve royal authority. Fifteen years after the Saint Bartholomew's Day massacres, he was now confronted by a power relationship that favored his opponents.[5] In early 1585, he still wanted to avoid resorting to force, even though the League had taken up arms. There followed a short period of hesitations. Many gentlemen still had a few scruples about siding with the princes of Lorraine, whose audacity fascinated them, however.[6] Montaigne no longer shared the Guises' point of view, as he had at the beginning of the first civil war. Certainly, he respected their unconditional commitment to the service of the Catholic religion, but he was opposed to "seditions" and "troubles" that brought "disorder into our consciences."[7] "Public sedition" was always to be avoided, according to Montaigne, who considered himself, in the course of the civil wars and his own experiences, to be a man of compromise and dialogue.

Henry III had just given in to the Catholic extremists. The Treaty of Nemours in July 1585 was an abdication of royal power in favor of the League. The edicts of toleration were canceled, and the situation returned to what it had been several years before. All that had been achieved by Montaigne's diplomatic efforts to reconcile Henry III and Henry of Navarre was destroyed in an instant. Southwestern France was transformed into a battlefield, and religious tensions between Protestants and Catholics were exacerbated more than ever by the increase in military maneuvers in Guyenne. Religious divisions within a single village, or even a single family, were frequent, and Montaigne's family did not escape this religious and ideological explosion. Thus one of his brothers—Thomas, lord of Beauregard—and his three sisters embraced the Protestant cause. His youngest brother—Bertrand, lord of Mattecoulon—retained his Catholic faith, but now was a gentleman of the king of Navarre's chamber, as was Montaigne himself. The relations between Montaigne and his siblings were difficult, both because of religious divergences and for reasons connected with Pierre Eyquem's legacy. Let us also recall that Thomas's second wife was Marguerite de Carle, La Boétie's daughter-in-law. La Boétie's heirs' drift toward Protestantism certainly awakened bad memories in him. These conversions to the new religion within his family also made Montaigne himself suspect. Located in Huguenot territory, his château was "situated at the very hub of all the turmoil of the civil wars of France."[8] He was surrounded by neighbors who had opted for the Reformation, and he lived on high alert in a zone of permanent insecurity.

In a context of military preparations and at the king's order, Matignon convoked the nobility of Guyenne in the autumn of 1585. Questions remain regarding Montaigne's actions and movements in late 1585. Some think he joined the army of noble volunteers Matignon had raised in Guyenne,[9] but this hypothesis is improbable. It is true that as a Catholic gentleman Montaigne had an obligation to join the royal army. However, he did not respond to this call and did not fight alongside Matignon. For him, the only wars worthy of being waged were those that took place abroad, or at least outside his region: he took part in a war "most willingly when it is most distant from my neighborhood."[10] Matignon seems not to have reproached him at this time. In the eyes of the lieutenant governor of Guyenne and new mayor of Bordeaux, Montaigne's status as a *politique* was worth preserving for the time being.

Chosen by Catherine de Medici "to subjugate the Huguenots there as he had done in Normandy,"[11] Matignon favored a political solution between Henry III and Henry of Navarre. Famed for his patience and his prudence—he was later to be accused of having "a very slow humor"[12]—Matignon spared Henry of Navarre, but he was forced to respond to his military operations. He tried to make everyone happy, serving Henry III while at the same time maintaining cordial relations with Henry of Navarre. Matignon wanted to avoid the mistakes made by his predecessor, Marshal Biron. Moreover, once the storm had passed, Montaigne's noninvolvement in the royal army might be transformed into a diplomatic asset. At that point, the League army led by the duke of Mayenne reached Matignon's garrisons. The troops in the service of the Guises wanted to come to grips as soon as possible with the leaders of the "so-called new religion."[13] Under Huguenot control, Bergerac, Castillon, and Sainte-Foy suddenly became highly symbolic military stakes. Matignon slowed Mayenne's advances as much as he could, while continuing to communicate with Henry of Navarre. However, this balanced policy was not to last long faced by the League's growing demands.

Toward the end of 1585 a political polarization was emerging. The Catholic

Union, better known under the name of the League, rallied around Henry of Lorraine, duke of Guise, who presented himself as the defender of the Roman Church and opposed both Henry III, whom he accused of weakness toward the heretics, and the presumptive heir to the French throne, Henry of Navarre. This religious confrontation was aggravated by personal conflicts and individual desires arising from the political realignment. René de Lucinge speaks of the "religious zeal"[14] that was a handy excuse justifying choices and decisions that were essentially matters of clienteles. On both sides, lists of supporters and enemies were drawn up. For example, a report written by an Italian observer in 1589 lists fifty-three lords who had gone over to the League and fifty-nine who remained loyal to Henry III.[15] One had to choose sides. The *politiques* were accused of waiting passively on the sidelines, whereas, according to the zealous leaders of both the Huguenot and the League parties, the religious conflict required more than ever that commitments be made and strong and resolute actions taken. Montaigne's noncommitment—trying to maintain a position between Henry III and Henry of Navarre—soon turned against him. It was a time for polemical pamphleteers, and the inconclusive essays of a Gascon gentleman seemed a little anachronistic confronted by the ideological assurance that marked most people's minds at this time. Montaigne engaged in a kind of subtle propaganda that advocated political and religious immobility: "As long as the image of the ancient and accepted laws of this monarchy shines in some corner, there will I be planted."[16]

This "wait-and-see" posture adopted by those that were then called the "laughers" (*rieurs*) was, of course, not peculiar to Montaigne. In fact, more than 60 percent of the nobles in Languedoc, Guyenne, and Gascony played the neutrality card.[17] The great majority of the knights of the Order of Saint Michael remained loyal to Henry III. Of seventy-eight members of the order in Guyenne and Gascony, 32 percent embraced the royal cause, 10 percent fought for Henry of Navarre, and only 1 percent sided with the League, the rest preferring to remain neutral.[18] This nonalignment reflects sympathetic goodwill toward Henry of Navarre, no doubt more out of tradition than a genuine religious choice. Montaigne's neutralist attitude was thus in no way exceptional and followed a regional tradition well established in Guyenne. The Gascons liked to display their difference with Paris. Moreover, Henry of Navarre was a neighbor, while the Guises were foreigners in the southwest. The nobility of Aquitaine joined the Huguenot army in far greater numbers than did the nobility of other parts of France, and also gave the least support to the League—so little as to be negligible. In Gascony, 40 percent of the nobles were Protestants, a figure three times higher than the national average.[19] On several occasions, Montaigne reaffirmed his adherence to the Catholic religion, but he was never prepared to fight against Henry of Navarre to defend his religious convictions. That kind of involvement would have alienated many of his neighbors.

In light of the events that were occurring on the military front, the author of the *Essais* admitted that after 1585 his political convictions had considerably evolved:

> In truth, and I am not afraid to confess it, I would easily carry, in case of need, one candle to Saint Michael and one to the dragon, according to the old woman's plan. I will follow the good side right to the fire, but not into it if I can help it. Let Montaigne be engulfed in the public ruin, if need be; but if not, I shall be grateful to fortune if it is saved; and as much rope as my duty gives me, I use for its preservation.[20]

Serving the king so far as possible, without prejudicing the security of his home or his reputation in the region: that is the foundation of Montaigne's political position in late 1585. This attitude is based on a realistic and practical conception of power. Evasion when faced by "public ruin" seemed to Montaigne an inevitable choice.

René de Lucinge comments with realism and perspicacity on the political situation in early 1586. According to him, the duke of Guise was well aware that the pope considered him one of the pillars of the Roman Church in France, and knew that in the event of Henry III's death, the king of Navarre, even if "Catholicized," could still influence the forms of government and destroy "the foundations of the Catholic Church in France."[21] Faced with this apocalyptic analysis, people spoke less of the Huguenot leader's conversion than of his destruction. Every compromise was viewed as a breach that would cause the ship of the Roman Catholic Church to sink. The clock had been turned back twenty years and only the military solution was on the agenda. In December 1584, the Guises had signed with the Spanish the Treaty of Joinville, which made the Cardinal of Bourbon Henry III's legitimate successor. They had no intention of considering the possible accession to the throne of a prince who sympathized with the heretics. A plan of action was rapidly put in place, and many cities were retaken by the League.

Weakened politically, Henry III issued several edicts intended to satisfy his new political partners. The kingdom's future was henceforth to be contested among three men: Henry III, Henry of Navarre, and the duke of Guise. The intransigence of the princes of Lorraine gave the king little room for maneuver, and he was easily influenced by the events of the moment. The problem with Henry III was that he was a modern prince, more pragmatic than his adversaries and totally out of step with the dogmas expressed by the Huguenot and

Catholic extremists. The League was gaining ascendancy, and for Henry III the Guises were beginning to be a more immediate danger than Henry of Navarre. For a time, he considered adopting a solution based on the interim agreement signed in Augsburg in 1548, a political turning point when Charles V found himself forced to allow states and cities within the Empire to follow the Augsburg Confession.[i] But this solution fizzled out and any compromise soon became impossible. The eighth War of Religion began in the spring of 1585, that is, at the end of Montaigne's second term as mayor of Bordeaux.

For all that, Montaigne did not blame Henry III for this rush into armed conflict. On principle, military leaders always called for war, and the sovereign's duty was to remain as dignified as possible amid the confrontations: "The toughest and most difficult occupation in the world, in my opinion, is to play the part of a king worthily. I excuse more of their faults than people commonly do, in consideration of the dreadful weight of their burden, which dazes me."[22] According to Montaigne, it is difficult to "observe moderation"[23] and not become enraged in dangerous situations. In this passage, and in several others written around the same time, Montaigne shows that he has not only a sense of civic duty but also a profound respect for the sovereign's authority, as opposed to other forms of authority. He places royal decisions above any moral consideration, and never allows himself to challenge the policies of his king. For him, it is not easy to act as a head of state, because adversaries often do not see the political necessity of decisions and almost always direct their criticisms to the person of the sovereign, preferring to blame the actors rather than the actions. This reflection on the relation between the individual and government was to occupy an important place in the *Essais* after 1588.

"Through an Extraordinarily Ticklish Part of the Country"

Military operations in Guyenne were resumed at the end of 1585. Montaigne chose to distance himself from current political and religious events. Holed up in his château, he spent most of his time in his library, reading and writing part of the third book of the *Essais*. As we see from the notes that he wrote at the end of the books in his possession, he did a good deal of reading at this time. Thus in early 1586, Montaigne was consulting especially history books. Very early in his life, he had already thought of historians as coming "right to [his] forehand."[24] In February, he read Herburt de Fulstin's *Histoire des rois et princes de Pologne* (Paris: Pierre L'Huillier, 1573), translated by François Bauduin; in March,

---

[i] The primary confession of the Lutheran Church (1530). [Trans.]

he plunged into Denis Sauvage's *Chronique de Flandres* (Lyon: Guillaume Ro-
ville, 1562) and commented on Olivier de La Marche's *Mémoires*. On March 6,
he wrote the following commentary on a flyleaf of the *Chronique de Flandres*:

> Finished reading on March 6, 1586/52 [at the age of fifty-two], at Mon-
> taigne. L'Histoire de Flandres commonly known and is presented better
> elsewhere. The boring introduction of speeches and prefaces. The *Mé-
> moires* is a pleasant book, and useful, especially for understanding the laws
> of combats and jousts, a subject peculiar to this author, and [he] says he
> wrote about it in detail. His narrative is exact in every way and conscien-
> tious. He mentions Philippe de Commynes, as Philippe de Commynes
> mentions him.[25]

Montaigne preferred the military stratagems of earlier ages, which he evalu-
ates and comments on, to the history that was being made with cannon balls at
the gates of his home. One might be surprised by this detachment with regard
to events that were taking place around him. The southwest was on fire, it was
becoming a war zone, and Montaigne returned to his books.[26] He began a second retirement and took pleasure in being idle while at the same time denouncing the immorality of public life: "The corruption of the age is produced by the
individual contribution of each one of us; some contribute treachery, others
injustice, irreligion, tyranny, avarice, cruelty, in accordance with their greater
power; the weaker ones bring stupidity, vanity, idleness, and I am one of them."[27]
This salutary withdrawal represented more a necessity than a genuine career
choice. The château was once again transformed into a refuge.

The author of the *Essais* recounts this difficult and perilous period of his life
in "Of physiognomy" (III: 12). Despite his silence and recent retirement from
political life, Montaigne was suspected by both sides. Supporters of the League
reproached him for having friends too close to Henry of Navarre and for not
displaying his Catholic faith more openly. The Protestants suspected him of
being in the pay of the Catholic princes and of not having been an impartial
negotiator. In short, Montaigne was isolated: "I incurred all the disadvantages
that moderation brings in such maladies."[28] Without political support, he gave
the impression of an ambiguous indifference at a time when it was practically
impossible to separate the public and the private: "The situation of my house,
and my acquaintance with men in my neighborhood, presented me in one aspect, my life and my actions in another." Montaigne continues the description
of his difficult situation and explains why he feels torn between the opposing
political parties: "I was belabored from every quarter; to the Ghibelline I was
a Guelph, to the Guelph a Ghibelline,"[29] identifying in this passage the
Guelphs with the League and the Ghibellines with the Huguenots. The his-

torical comparison Montaigne makes here is appropriate to describe the delicate situation he faced in 1586. The Guelphs and the Ghibellines were two factions that opposed each other in thirteenth- and fourteenth-century Italy.[ii] These two clans supported different dynasties that were fighting over the throne of the Holy Roman German Empire. It has often been suggested that Dante, who experienced this conflict because he sat in various Florentine political assemblies, was himself a white Guelph,[iii] even though he argued, in his treatise *De monarchia*, in favor of a Ghibelline emperor reigning with the pope's blessing. The comparison with Dante no doubt pleased Montaigne, who saw himself as also forced to ally himself with several parties because his place of residence put him at the heart of the conflict. As he puts it in the *Essais*: "It was mute suspicions that were current secretly, for which there is never a lack of apparent grounds in such a mixed-up confusion, any more than there is of envious or inept minds."[30]

In this climate of mutual distrust, Montaigne traveled little in the period immediately following his two terms as mayor. There was still plague in Bordeaux, and it was too dangerous to roam roads that had been taken over by deserters, foreign mercenaries, and highway robbers. For greater security, and for lack of political prospects, he chose to remain in the relative calm of his château from August 1585 to July 1586. Montaigne was waiting, holding back. This was an opportunity to return to his *Essais*, which he expanded considerably in light of his experience as mayor of Bordeaux. Some of the chapters of the third book were written during 1586. However, it would be a mistake to see this period as uniquely a time of writing. It was, of course, difficult to ignore the military situation that was taking on a menacing form all around him. Troop movements, skirmishes, sieges, and all kinds of discussions and negotiations were brewing just outside the gates of his château and did not allow him to insulate himself from the intense military and political activity prevalent in the region.

Confronted with the growing insecurity, Montaigne developed a strategy that consisted of keeping the gates of his château wide open. He reports two incidents in which he claims to have avoided great peril and even saved his life thanks to a naïveté feigned for the occasion. A "certain person" whom he knew, who was probably motivated by the weakened political situation in which Mon-

---

[ii] The term "Guelph" (Italian *Guelfo*) derives from the name of the Welf dynasty—of the family of Otto IV—and designates the faction that supported the papacy. The term "Ghibelline" refers to the *Ghibello*, a diminutive of *Guibertus*, an Italian form of "Waiblingen" in Baden-Württemburg, the name of a Swabian castle with which the supporters of the Hohenstaufen identified. The poet from whom Montaigne borrowed the expression has never been identified.

[iii] A "white" Guelph was one who was aligned more with the rising merchant class than with the old aristocracy. [Trans.]

taigne found himself at that time and who was "to some extent a relative of mine," showed up alone at the gate of the château. Montaigne let him enter. The man told him that he was being pursued by an "enemy" whom Montaigne also knew, thanked his host for having saved his life, and asked that his men might also be allowed to take refuge inside the walls of the château. Montaigne understood that a trap was being laid for him, and that this man, whose intentions were hostile, was trying to take control of his château by means of a ruse. Not having men-at-arms to oppose this invasion of his lands, he decided to play along with his adversary: "I tried quite naïvely to comfort, reassure, and refresh him."[31] Four or five armed men quickly appeared, followed by several other soldiers. A small group of about thirty armed men, "pretending to have the enemy at their heels," was soon in his courtyard. Then Montaigne saw how much he was envied by some of his neighbors, and that the age favored such attacks on those who showed weakness.

This kind of misadventure was common in the region, and several nearby châteaus had been assaulted on religious pretexts. Caught in this delicate situation, from which he could hardly imagine a peaceful escape, Montaigne made use of a technique he had earlier practiced to display his qualities as a negotiator and diplomat. His character, which was little inclined to either effusiveness or anger, allowed him to keep cool despite the immediate danger. Confronted by this threat, he remained calm and imperturbable. His adversaries took his impassiveness for naïveté. The effect Montaigne sought was, of course, to destabilize this armed group and make it believe that it was welcomed. Still astride their horses in the château's courtyard, the soldiers waited in vain for their leader to order them to act and seize Montaigne's château. Disconcerted by the friendly reception he had received from the master of the house, the would-be brigand gave up his sinister scheme and departed with his men as he had come. Montaigne adds that, "He has often said since, for he was not afraid to tell this story, that my face and my frankness had disarmed him of his treachery. He remounted his horse, his men constantly keeping their eyes on him to see what signal he would give them, very astonished to see him go away and abandon his advantage."[32] The frankness Montaigne showed for the occasion was, however, equivalent to dissimulation, since he had immediately recognized his visitor's hostile intentions. In this anecdote we find a quality—false naïveté—that Montaigne associates with success in politics. The sincerity and candor shown on Montaigne's face were a considerable advantage for a man who did not have the means to demonstrate by force his political or military power. Without any guarantee other than his own face, Montaigne thus explains his sincerity and straight talking: "If my face did not answer for me, if people did not read in my eyes and my voice the innocence of my intentions, I would not have lasted so long without quarrel and without harm, considering my indiscreet freedom in saying, right or wrong, whatever comes into my head, and in judging things rashly."[33]

In the chapter "Of physiognomy," Montaigne relates a second episode in which his face once again saved his life. Reassured by the announcement of several truces between Protestants and Catholics, Montaigne was traveling "through an extraordinarily ticklish part of the country"[34] when he was caught by twenty masked gentlemen after a furious chase. Taken prisoner, he was led into a forest and robbed. His "money box," his chests, his horses, and his equipment were taken. This band of Huguenots (or League supporters?) began to negotiate with him a high ransom for his liberation. Once again, Montaigne was in great danger. After two or three hours of intense discussion, surrounded by some fifteen harquebusiers, separated from those who were accompanying him, and as his captors were getting ready to take him off to a secure place to await the payment of ransom, a rather astonishing reversal occurred. Montaigne recounts it: "Behold, a sudden and very unexpected change came over them. I saw the leader return to me with gentler words, taking pains to search for my belongings scattered among the troop, and having them returned to me as far as they could be recovered, even including my money box."[35] As if by a miracle, Montaigne was freed and his goods were returned. Clearly Montaigne could have lost his life that day, but chance was on his side. He concludes the narrative of this incident with an important realization about his own existence: "The best present they made me was finally my freedom; the rest did not concern me much at that time."[36]

However, it is difficult to believe in such a reversal of the situation without imagining other, more prosaic and far more plausible causes. Had his captors realized who he was? The fact that he was on a mission and was negotiating on behalf of Henry of Navarre may have produced the happy outcome of this affair. We can reasonably say that Montaigne explained to his captors that he was personally acquainted with the king of Navarre and other Protestant leaders. Otherwise it would be difficult to explain why these masked soldiers suddenly changed their minds. Naturally, Montaigne tells us nothing about the arguments he gave for his release, except that he "kept standing on [his] rights under the truce."[37] He prefers to make us think that his face alone sufficed to deliver him from a perilous situation. What could be interpreted as the success of a political negotiation is for him the result of a personality trait, a kind of political disposition opposed to rhetorical effects or other kinds of byzantine quibbles.

Such incidents logically led Montaigne to stay home. He received several visitors at his château and traveled little during the summer of 1586. On July 2, he received Pierre Charron "in suo castello"[iv] and gave him a copy of Bernardino Ochino's *Catechismo*.[v] Montaigne lived in the countryside and took care to avoid attracting the attention of the hostile soldiers, Huguenots, or supporters of the League, who were roaming around the region. The summer was marked by a military event fateful for Montaigne and his family. On July 10, 1586, Mayenne and Matignon set siege to Castillon, only a short distance from Montaigne's estate. The royal army was camped less than a league from his château. It was one of the longest and bloodiest sieges of this military campaign conducted by the League in the southwest. To feed themselves, 25,000 soldiers (according to D'Aubigné), poorly supplied, resorted to pillaging the nearby lands, including Montaigne's. The Huguenot garrisons led by Turenne infiltrated the royal army's lines to harass the soldiers. There was fighting on the border of Montaigne's land and looters plundered the region. An undisciplined army of 15,000 to 20,000 soldiers—including 5,000 Swiss—threatened Montaigne's château and his people every day. The siege going on and on; the soldiers were no longer paid and deserted in large numbers. That meant even more armed men on the roads in Guyenne. The long encirclement of Castillon spelled economic ruin for many gentlemen who could no longer cultivate their lands and who saw their harvests pillaged by starving soldiers.

The region was full of soldiers who came from other countries. Montaigne was scandalized by the recruitment of foreign mercenaries by both the Protestant and the Catholic forces: "Our armies are no longer bound and held together except by foreign cement; of Frenchmen one can no longer form a steadfast and disciplined army corps. How shameful! There is only so much discipline as borrowed soldiers show us; as for ourselves, we follow our own lead and not our leader's, every man his own way."[38] He deplored the internationalization of the conflict, regretting that religious disputes could not be settled among Frenchmen, and above all was annoyed by the inefficiency of these armies and their leaders' lack of authority. Conflicts had changed, and Montaigne by far preferred the noble war of the "time of our fathers" or of the Cannibals of the New World, a distraction from his own military disillusions. Recourse to force is never excluded in politics. It is a final but necessary resort in the event that negotiations fail. The political conservatism of which Montaigne has been accused expresses more a survival reaction than a genuine ideological position. According to him, civil wars make no sense politically because they are fought between people from the same country, the same culture. A good war is an honorable war fought between people of different countries and cultures. The reli-

---

[iv] Italian; "in his castle." [Trans.]

[v] This copy, which is in the BNF, includes this *ex dono*: "*Charron, ex dono dicti domini de Montaigne, in suo castello, 2 julii, anno 1586.*"

gious conflict marks the failure of diplomacy and compromise, because the opposing parties are culturally too close to one another to be able to make any concessions to an "enemy" who speaks the same language and dresses in the same way. It is often easier to understand foreigners from distant lands than to imagine what happens in the heads of one's neighbors. For example, Montaigne is astonished by the associations formed for denominational reasons and deplores the "disturbances in the neighborhood"[39] that were reorganizing the society of his time: "I see from our example that human society holds and is knit together at any cost whatever. Whatever position you set men in, they pile up and arrange themselves by moving and crowding together."[40]

Despite the royal army's victory, the siege of Castillon resulted in a slowing of the League's initial momentum. However, their revenge was bloody and shocked Montaigne. The day after Castillon fell, the duke of Mayenne had a large number of the city's inhabitants ruthlessly hanged. It was becoming increasingly difficult to commit oneself as a Catholic or a Protestant in Guyenne without being caught up in the infernal system of political reprisals. A declared advocate of moderation, Montaigne tried in his turn to put into practice his convictions in favor of a "golden mean." Compared with the extreme positions taken by the League and some Huguenot leaders, the king's party established itself as a lesser evil, as a "political necessity" to safeguard the state.[41] Despite his veiled critiques of the king's government, Montaigne saw no option other than a quick agreement between Henry III and Henry of Navarre. Now it was the League that determined events and set the political agenda. It could be said that after the siege of Castillon Montaigne realized that Mayenne, the military man, had prevailed over Matignon, the political man.[42] The middle way and compromise had suddenly disappeared, and in the future it would be necessary to deal with the new forces in the arena.

For Montaigne, the siege of Castillon made it even harder to be both a Gascon and a Frenchman. The national stakes involved upset the regional political balance, and he felt himself caught between the principles of being a good neighbor and his desire to serve his king. A red line had been crossed, and he was witnessing, from a front-row seat, a distressing spectacle that was setting the kingdom ablaze in the name of a more correct faith. Mutinies were rife, and the royal army was falling apart as the siege went on. Commanders spent more time cultivating good relations with their soldiers and calming them down than they did setting up military strategies. Montaigne commented on the paradoxes of this siege: "The leader has more trouble within than without. It is for the commander to follow, court, and bend, for him alone to obey; all the rest is free and dissolute."[43] In a disconcerting confusion, the parties to the conflict stuck to their positions but were unable to impose them militarily. At the end of August, nothing had been decided. It was then that an epidemic of plague struck the region. Montaigne testifies: "Both outside and inside my house I was greeted by a plague of the utmost virulence."[44] Was this the same epidemic that had raged in Bordeaux the preceding year and that had now reached Montaigne's lands? Scholarly opinion is divided on this point. In any case, the unsanitary conditions of the siege of Castillon and the high density of soldiers in the region allowed the plague to spread like wildfire. The preceding summer, Montaigne had fled Bordeaux to hole up in his house. Now his château itself was no longer the safe refuge to which he had retired after handing his powers over to Bordeaux's jurats. The epidemic that was ravaging his region was now becoming an immediate threat to him. Moreover, his land was no longer being cultivated, and he did not have sufficient income to maintain his usual way of life.

Montaigne decided to "escape" from his château. Frightened by the contagion, he hastily put a few possessions in a cart and departed his estate with his wife and a few servants:

> I had an absurd situation to put up with: the sight of my house was frightful to me. All that was in it was unguarded and abandoned to anyone who wanted it. I, who am so hospitable, had a great deal of trouble finding a retreat for my family: a family astray, a source of fear to their friends and themselves, and of horror when they sought to settle, having to shift their abode as soon as one of the group began to feel pain in the end of his finger.[45]

From August 1586 to February 15, 1587, Montaigne wandered the highways with his family serving "for six months of misery as guide to this caravan."[46] The danger was too great to go south, and it is likely that Montaigne and his family headed for Poitou. Great poverty prevailed in the kingdom. Pierre de L'Estoile writes about the indigence in which he found France at that time: "Almost all over France, the poor in the countryside, dying of hunger, went to the fields in groups to cut kernels of wheat and eat them on the spot, so desperate was their hunger."[47] Montaigne was then at an important turning point in his life. He had suddenly become a gentleman vagabond, dependent on his acquaintances for lodging: "As things stand, I live more than half by others' favor, which is a harsh obligation. I do not want to owe my safety either to the kindness and benignity of the great, who approve of my obedience to the laws and my independence, or to the affable ways of my predecessors and myself."[48]

Abandoned by those close to him and by his political acquaintances, Montaigne experienced some of the darkest moments of his life. He had to rely on his friends' kindness and his neighbors' protection: "A thousand different kinds of troubles assailed me in single file; I would have suffered them more cheerfully in a single pile. I was already considering to whom among my friends I could commit a needy and unfortunate old age; after letting my eyes wander all over, I found myself stripped to my shirt."[49] Even his political protector, the marquis of Trans, seems to have abandoned him. His mentor may not have understood his withdrawal or his apparent indifference with regard to recent military developments. The tyrannical old man was known for his unbridled rages and may have been annoyed by the passivity, or even the cowardice, of the man whose political career he had made. In a long passage handwritten on the Bordeaux Copy, Montaigne sketches a not very flattering portrait of his patron, presenting him as "the most tempestuous master in France."[50] Florimond de Raemond identified this man about whom Montaigne spoke in a rare moment of exasperation as the marquis of Trans.[51]

It is improbable that Montaigne was able to write his *Essais* during this forced peregrination. He still nourished a few political ambitions and kept an eye out for any opportunity that might present itself. Although discouraged by his failure as a negotiator at the end of his second term as mayor, he still hoped to be able to serve his king. An opportunity came up late in 1586. Confronted by the mounting power of the Guises, Henry III and Catherine de Medici tried once more to relaunch negotiations with Henry of Navarre. More than ever, they wanted to convince Henry of Navarre to abjure his religion and to return to the Court. The League was firmly established in Paris, and the king felt that his position in the capital had grown weaker. It was in this context that Catherine de Medici undertook her trip in Poitou to negotiate with the presumptive sovereign. A meeting between Navarre and Catherine took place in the château of Saint-Brice, near Cognac, on October 18, 1586. The queen mother was rather poorly received and was not able to convince Navarre to convert to the Catholic religion.[52]

The negotiations conducted at Saint-Brice were described in the "letter from a French gentleman" published in the *Mémoires de la Ligue* (book VIII) printed in Paris in 1631. In this conversation, Navarre tells the queen mother that he has not obeyed the king for the past eighteen months and complains about the League's hostilities. Catherine is said to have thereupon grown angry, having replied that the members of the League were all good French Catholics who feared being oppressed by the Huguenots. This confrontation made her realize that the negotiations with Navarre would take more time than she had anticipated. Some have doubted her intention of arriving at a rapprochement with Navarre. For example, the duchess of Uzès, one of the queen mother's ladies-in-waiting, reported to Sully that during these discussions Catherine's goal was to amuse Henry of Navarre "so that he would undertake no further operations, and that he would slow the advance of the foreign army."[53] Despite this testimony that treats Catherine as a perpetual conspirator, the situation was alarming enough that her effort at conciliation can be taken seriously.

On December 3, Catherine informed her son that she had assembled princes and lords at Cognac to decide with them how she should proceed with Navarre to avoid a break with him. The discussions at Saint-Brice did not advance the royal cause because Navarre, banking on his military successes in the southwest, was not about to abjure his religion. His commanders had convinced him that they now had an army that would allow them to stand up to the Catholic troops. Navarre was evasive, declaring that he would have to confer with the Reformed churches. He was no longer inclined to negotiate with a king whose authority was challenged by the duke of Guise. On December 16, after three meetings, the parties finally agreed on a fragile truce of two and a half months. In fact, this negotiation had failed, and Navarre was already recruiting German mercenaries. This was a dead end, and Catherine de Medici tried to conceive bold political solutions to bring the two Henrys together. As is often the case, diplomacy was a matter of individuals more than one of ideas or programs. Tired of having failed in his negotiation with Navarre during the ceremony of the Knights of the Holy Spirit, Henry III announced that he would accept only the Catholic religion in his kingdom. He made ready to go to war, with the help of 8,000 Swiss soldiers.

Catherine did not want to give up her efforts and was prepared to receive new suggestions. Montaigne's name arose on this occasion. His good relations with Henry of Navarre were an advantage. The queen mother was also aware that the Gascon gentleman was loyal to Henry III, and that the failure of the 1585 negotiations had resulted from external circumstances over which Montaigne had no control. Thus he could once again appear to be an ideal intermediary figure. Catherine had to find men who were experienced in political negotiation, who belonged to the Huguenot leader's inner circle, and who could gradually push the idea of an abjuration in the name of national reconciliation. She told Turenne about her plan, "whom I also persuaded to do the right thing in this matter; I found him well-disposed to do so, it seems to me, and I believe that he will do what he can with regard to the king of Navarre and also the sister of Montmorency, his uncle."[54] On December 17, she appealed to several gentlemen in Guyenne to join Matignon's army. But Montaigne was not in a position to join the royal cause; he was wandering around Poitou without sufficient funds to maintain men-at-arms. In 1586 and 1587, famine struck the Paris region, Normandy, the Loire valley, and the area around Lyon. This context was unfavorable to a diplomatic mission and so Catherine came up with a better way for Montaigne to serve the king. He was not expected to bear arms, because he had other qualities that were more useful to the royal cause. Perhaps that is how, on several occasions, Montaigne's military nonengagement with Matignon should also be interpreted.

The political setback at Saint-Brice notwithstanding, Catherine de Medici obtained a short truce. It was precisely at that time that Montaigne reappeared in politics. The queen mother imagined a role as an "interpreter" (*truchement*) for this Gascon gentleman who belonged to both Henry III's chamber and Henry of Navarre's, an appreciable advantage that could facilitate an accord between the two monarchs and thus contribute to a lasting peace. On December 31, 1586, Catherine de Medici dictated the following letter to her treasurer:

> M[c] Raoul Feron, my treasurer and general tax collector, because I am writing to Montaigne to tell him and his wife to come to see me, I wish and command you to provide, in addition to the one hundred crowns that you already gave him a few days ago, another hundred and fifty crowns, partly to replace one of the horses of his carriage, and partly to cover the extraordinary expense of traveling overland and also to purchase a few clothes that they need; and when you have receipts from Montaigne for the sum of a hundred and fifty crowns, it will be paid [to] you and credited to your account without difficulty.[55]

Some scholars have expressed reservations concerning the identification of the author of the *Essais* with the Montaigne mentioned in this letter, suggesting that he might instead be one of the queen mother's secretaries, François Montaigne. However, this secretary was no longer employed by Catherine in late 1586. The list of the domestic officers of the queen mother's household,[56] from 1547 to 1585, confirms that François Montaigne served as her secretary, but only between 1571 and 1578.[57] We have a letter from him written later, but it is a private document that has nothing to do with his service to Catherine, which had ended eight years earlier. Moreover, the amount of the travel costs proposed by Catherine (250 crowns, that is, 750 *livres*) was significantly higher than the annual salary of a secretary, which was set at 400 *livres* per year.[58] On the other hand, this sum would not be extravagant if it was to be paid to a gentleman.[59] It is true that Catherine does not use the title "lord" (*sieur* or *Monsieur*), which was always appropriate in correspondence with a gentleman—a practice required by etiquette—but the details of this letter nonetheless make it possible to identify Montaigne as its addressee. He had fled his château and had been roaming the roads with his family since September. He declared that he was short of money at this time, and complained about being dependent on others' favors. Without resources and in great distress, the author of the *Essais* did not cut a fine figure. There is nothing surprising in the fact that he had to replace one of his horses and dress properly in order to present himself before the queen mother. Montaigne's wife was also asked to come (which would be unusual in the case of a secretary's wife) because she was accompanying him. If we decide that it was Montaigne, we can then infer that the goal of this meeting Catherine desired was to entrust him with a mission as an intermediary seeking a rapprochement with Henry of Navarre.[60] Montaigne had no fresh horses, and though he was not in rags, we can understand why he might have asked Catherine for money to travel to the meeting he had just been ordered to attend.

The letter addressed to Raoul Féron, the queen mother's tax collector, is part of a series of missives sent by Catherine on the same day. These messages show the extensive diplomatic activity the queen mother deployed to persuade Henry of Navarre to give up the Protestant faith. On December 31, 1586, she sent a messenger named Verac to inform Matignon of "the state that we are in here with respect to my negotiation in favor of peace."[61] Catherine's letter was intended to ask for instructions from her son to authorize her to send new emissaries to Henry III, Montaigne probably being one of them. Thanks to his past experience as a negotiator, Montaigne might have been chosen by Catherine to restart a dialogue with Navarre after the semifailure of the discussions at Sainte-Foy. She had persuaded herself that an entente between the king of Navarre and her son was desirable to pull the rug from under the feet of the dukes of Lorraine. The name "Montaigne" is mentioned in another letter sent to Henry III, dated January 18: "In accord with your intention I have told and commanded the lord of Malicorne what you want done with Montaigne; I will also assist in this endeavor and in any other matter concerning your service, in accord with your intention, in this province."[62] The phrase "in this province" (*es province de deçà*) refers to Guyenne, which worried the king, and a secretary could not have played the role of negotiator.

At first, Henry III seems to have accepted Montaigne's mediation, but in the end Catherine preferred to make use of Jean de Chourses, lord of Malicorne. When the queen mother presented her plan to Henry III in greater detail, the king forbade her, in a letter written in late January 1587, to reestablish contact with the Huguenots through "persons who were their confidants."[63] Among these "confidants" we must count Montaigne, who was well acquainted with the king of Navarre because he had lodged him at his home. Henry III mistrusted Gascon gentlemen, whom he thought too close to Henry of Navarre. Montaigne was certainly disappointed by the king's decision, and when the reply was received, he went back to his château. The mission was compromised and the name "Montaigne" disappeared from Catherine de Medici's correspondence. The plague epidemic had abated, and Montaigne could go home safely. The queen mother headed back to Paris at the same time, that is, in March 1587, not without having informed Montaigne of Henry III's reluctance to negotiate with Navarre through intermediaries: another disappointment for Montaigne and another setback for Catherine de Medici.

After roaming the roads of France for six months—from September 1586 to March 1587—Montaigne returned home and resumed composing the third book of the *Essais*. He made many additions to the first two books—about 13 percent of the whole text. Between 1582 and 1588, he spent at most two years "working" on his *Essais*. After an initial period of writing, from August 1585 to July 1586, Montaigne put the final touches on the thirteen chapters of the third book and the additions he had made to the first two books between February 1587 and December 1587. The year 1587 had given the *Essais* an unexpected re-orientation, and Montaigne was now planning to have his book printed in Paris. His *Essais* were going to allow him to join a select and limited group of European humanists. It was in this perspective that at the beginning of 1588 Montaigne began a correspondence with Justus Lipsius, who was then residing in the Low Countries. We have two letters from the famous humanist addressed to Montaigne and dated April 15 and August 30, 1588. In May 1587 Montaigne bought a Bible and, in early summer, read and annotated Quintus Curtius.

In a letter written in June 1587, Montaigne reminded Matignon of his existence by asking him to grant a safe-conduct to Madame de Brigueux, the wife of the governor of Beaugency. He ended his letter by asking the mayor of Bordeaux and lieutenant governor of Guyenne if he could do anything for him: "If not, at least this letter will have served to bring me back to your memory, from which I may have been dislodged by my small merit and the long time that I have not had the honor of seeing you."[64] On July 29, 1587, Montaigne noted in his almanac the loss of his neighbors and patrons, the three sons of the marquis of Trans—Louis, count of Gurson; Gaston, viscount of Meilles; and François-Phoebus, knight—all of whom died at the battle of Moncrabeau.[vi] Although they were Catholics, they had fought alongside the king of Navarre. Montaigne was deeply marked by these deaths, which reminded him of the horror of the Wars of Religion.

The League was more active than ever, and had the advantage militarily. The Huguenots had obtained the support of 40,000 German mercenaries recruited in the Empire and paid by the queen of England and the king of Denmark. This "Huguenot league" comprised chiefly of German soldiers had been created to provide aid to the Huguenots in Aquitaine. Strengthened by this foreign support, Henry of Navarre won at Coutras, on October 20, 1587, his first great victory in the eighth War of Religion.[65] The royal army was routed, and more than 2,000 soldiers lost their lives, including 300 nobles. The duke of Joyeuse and his brother, Claude, baron of Saint-Sauveur, were killed in this battle,

---

[vi] A fourth son, Gaston, count of Fleix, who was also devoted to Henry of Navarre, died in 1591 as a result of a wound received during the siege of Chartres.

which had a great effect on people in the southwest. As a courtesy, Navarre sent a letter of condolences to Matignon, who was a distant relative of Joyeuse. In this letter, Navarre declares that he makes no distinction between "good, native-born Frenchmen" and "the supporters and adherents of the League," adding that "at least those who have remained in my hands will testify to the courtesy they have found in me and in my servants who have taken them."[66]

The Battle of Coutras rebalanced the forces involved and gave Montaigne's political career a new breath of air, because it was more necessary than ever to negotiate with Henry of Navarre, who now had gained the military advantage. But ironically, the initiative for the negotiations now fell to Navarre. Although Henry III did not want to negotiate through third parties, the Battle of Coutras had changed the power relationship between Protestants and Catholics. The Huguenots' military victory aroused serious concern in the capital, where the people feared the arrival of the German mercenaries. The king appealed to the princes of Lorraine to defend the capital and protect him. Henry III no longer inspired confidence, and only the duke of Guise looked like a liberator. He was summoned in the spring of 1588 and made his entrance into Paris in broad daylight, acclaimed by the people. Hurt and worried, Henry III took refuge in the Louvre palace. Loyal to his king, Montaigne then thought an agreement between the king and Navarre could keep the League from seizing power. Henry of Navarre's second visit to Montaigne's château, three years after the first, restored a political role to Montaigne, who now appeared to be an inevitable negotiator. We can suppose that in dealing with Henry III and Catherine de Medici Montaigne emphasized his friendship with Navarre's mistress, Diane d'Andoins, countess of Guiche, who offered him direct access to the king of Navarre.

On October 23, 1587, three days after his victory at Coutras, Henry of Navarre dined and slept at Montaigne's château while he was crossing the region to carry the twenty-two banners taken at Coutras to his mistress, who was living in Béarn. Montaigne did not mention this second visit in his almanac, but we can sense the importance of this meeting. It was probably during this encounter, when he was still intoxicated by his recent victory, that Navarre decided to call upon Montaigne to propose a negotiated peace to the king. Now it was Navarre's turn to take the initiative in the negotiations with Henry III, and he asked Montaigne to be his envoy and intermediary. This request was advantageous for Montaigne, because it suddenly made him indispensable. If the king had not thought it useful to retain his services after Catherine de Medici's proposal, the Protestants now saw in him an ideal negotiator. Resurfacing in politics thanks to the Protestant leaders was hardly an unpleasant prospect for Montaigne. What neither Henry III nor Catherine de Medici had been able to give him—an ambassadorship in Rome in 1580 or a role as an official negotiator ten months earlier—now suddenly became possible through the opposite party. Montaigne's wait-and-see strategy, which had been so heavily criticized in the preceding period, now finally bore fruit.

Secret Mission

Catherine de Medici failed to make Montaigne an intermediary between Henry III and the Huguenots, so now it was Henry of Navarre's turn to make use of Montaigne's services. Matignon approved of Navarre's initiative, because he had a good opinion of the presumptive sovereign and still believed in an agreement between the two Henrys as a way to stop the League. This proposal of mediation was also encouraged by Diane d'Andoins, who was fond of Montaigne. A descendant of a very old family that had been connected since 1444 with the house of the Foix—through the marriage of Bernard of Cauna and Isabelle of Béarn, the daughter of Jean I—Diane d'Andoins, known as Corisande, had been flattered by the attention Montaigne gave her in his dedication of one of the chapters of his *Essais* in 1580. A combination of circumstances in Henry of Navarre's love life thus allowed Montaigne to make a political comeback. To this must be added the more political calculation of one of the Belle Corisande's friends, Cyprien de Poiferré, lord of Varène, who protected Diane d'Andoins's interests and who had transmitted La Boétie's sonnets to Montaigne in the early 1570s.[67]

In 1587, Diane d'Andoins had a considerable influence on Henry of Navarre, and through her Montaigne enjoyed privileged access to him. Montaigne had previously seen the Belle Corisande on the occasion of a meeting with Navarre between May 5 and May 10, 1584. Shortly before, he had expressed concern about her health. We recall that, after so much attention to her, Diane d'Andoins had not failed to propose Montaigne's name to present her lover's point of view and political proposals at the Court of Henry III. In 1587 she continued to enjoy a notable influence on Henry of Navarre. The foreign diplomats posted in Paris were not taken in and rapidly understood that the Belle Corisande was a woman of great ambition who "governeth the king of Navarre as she listeth."[68] The English ambassador in Paris, Sir Edward Stafford, considered Montaigne himself "a great favorite" of the countess of Guiche.

In order to thwart the League's ambitions, a proposal for a reconciliation—or at least a political agreement—between Henry of Navarre and Henry III was worked out in October 1587. This required Navarre to agree to "Catholicize" himself, as Lucinge put it. Montaigne had a role to play in these difficult negotiations, and the task pleased him. In early 1588, the conflict between Henry III and Henry of Navarre was no longer religious in nature—at least in the sense of the Huguenots/Catholics opposition of the early Wars of Religion. The League was now considered a common enemy and represented a still more pressing danger for the king and Catherine de Medici. Navarre was delighted by the political orientation that could only benefit him in the meantime. In a letter to his mistress, he observes that "the League is very active. This is so much leisure for us."[69] Montaigne's trip to the capital in early 1588 is situated in this political context favorable to Henry of Navarre. Montaigne was playing the key role, and that is how he was perceived by foreign observers and the Protestant leaders.

Thus Montaigne set out for Paris in January 1588. His château was about 550 kilometers from the capital, or about eight to ten days' travel on horseback with baggage. He expected to be busy with his affairs, but this stay in Paris was also to give him an opportunity to deposit a greatly expanded edition of his *Essais* with a printer of the palace, Abel L'Angelier. During this trip, Montaigne was accompanied by Commander Odet de Thorigny, Matignon's son, who was supposed to introduce him more easily at the Court and also to ensure his security between Bordeaux and the capital. There is no reason to think that Pierre de Brach traveled with them, as has been claimed. We know that the poet from Bordeaux went to Paris at the same time, but he probably arrived in the capital a few days or weeks after Montaigne. No mention is made of him in the account of an incident that occurred while Montaigne and his group were approaching Paris. It is true that in one of his books, Brach dedicated a poem to Thorigny—which led some specialists on Montaigne to think that he might have made his acquaintance during this trip—but Brach could just as well have met Thorigny in Bordeaux under other circumstances. As for Montaigne, he was "on a mission," assigned to transmit Navarre's latest proposals to the king. He was once again playing the role of an extraordinary ambassador—this time for the king of Navarre—a diplomatic function that had escaped him seven years earlier during his stay in Rome. His visit to the Court was in no way a pleasure trip and did not go unnoticed.

In a letter dated January 24, 1588, Duplessis-Mornay, one of the king of Navarre's counselors, informed his wife that "Monsieur de Montaigne has gone to the Court. We are told that we will soon be sought out in peace by neutral persons."[70] This "neutral person" was none other than Montaigne, who succeeded in projecting the image of an impartial, honest intermediary. The description of him as a dispassionate negotiator marks a major reversal of the situation in relation to the orders Henry III gave his mother a year earlier, during the discussions at Sainte-Foy. Montaigne could once again begin to imagine a "nameless office"[71] conceived specially for him, in the long tradition of extraordinary ambassadorships that he had dreamed about in the 1570s.

In reality, Montaigne had more talent for "interpreting" than for negotiating. He did not mince words and was famous for his frankness. For example, he declares that, "In Paris, I speak a language somewhat different than at Montaigne."[72] Estienne Pasquier described a man "who took pleasure in being pleasantly unpleasant,"[73] an unusual style for a negotiator, it has to be admitted. But it was a style he had been able to construct for himself over the years. His "frank speech" (*libre parole*) might have repelled some people, and it remains to be seen whether frankness is really an asset for a man who has political pretensions. Despite this real or imaginary quality, Montaigne had all the attributes required to be a valuable advisor to Henry of Navarre. He was sufficiently familiar with the political situation in Guyenne to be able to convey Navarre's proposals in the capricious context of the political pressures the Huguenot leaders put on their pretender to the French throne. A significant number of nobles in the southwest felt caught between their obligation to be loyal to the king and the desire to see their interests better represented on the national level. The political network the Protestants had set up in the region over the past few years had revealed to Navarre new opportunities—both political and economic—that led him to think on the regional scale more than on the national scale. Montaigne was well acquainted with this frame of mind characteristic of Guyenne and Aquitaine.

A week later, on February 1, 1588, Stafford reported to his superior, the principal secretary Sir Francis Walsingham, the imminent arrival at the Court of a gentleman on a secret mission: "The news arrived today that the son of the Marshal de Matignon is coming here, and is expected at any moment; that he is bringing with him a certain Montigny [*sic*], a very wise man of the King of Navarre, to whom he has given his word to present to the King. I have never in my life heard anyone speak of this man."[74] Stafford clearly associates Montaigne with Navarre's entourage and considers him his envoy. Stafford was an occasional secret agent of Spain and an informer for the duke of Guise, from whom he received 3,000 crowns in recompense for the information provided. Montaigne's arrival in Paris was seen as bad news for the Spanish party, and people distrusted this Gascon gentleman little known at the Court. The Catholic extremists disapproved of an agreement between the king and Navarre, fearing that an abjuration of the Protestant faith might be merely temporary and part of a strategy that would allow the Huguenots to accede to the French throne. To prevent any such entente between the two princes, the League had strengthened its presence in the capital and succeeded in putting the bourgeoisie and common people of Paris on their side.

At two days' ride from the capital, Montaigne and Thorigny were stopped and robbed in the forest of Villebois, not far from Orléans, by a band of "villainous murdering soldiers of these days,"[75] masked men whose leader, "a certain Matois," called "le Lignou"[76]—and not "le Ligueur," as many commentators have thought—is associated with a Huguenot in the correspondence between

Lucinge and the lawyer Mondragon: "In Poitou the Huguenots stole the baggage of Count Toriginy, the Marshal de Matignon's son, and took prisoner a few gentlemen among those who were accompanying the body of the late Mr de Joieuse, which was being taken to this city to bury him in the superb and sumptuous tomb that the King has had made for him."[77] In fact, the infamous Captain Lignou was not in the pay of any party. A text from that period describes him as a bandit, "neither for one [Henry III] nor the other [Henry of Navarre], but for himself alone."[78] Montaigne was captured by the same brigand who had already taken Barrault and La Rochefoucauld prisoner. His safe-conduct had hardly helped him travel in safety. This Lignou had the annoying habit of roaming the region with his band of robbers and taking hostages, with the goal of holding them at ransom, gentlemen who were traveling the main roads between Tours and Paris. Montaigne adds that he was more affected than the others, because he was carrying all his money on him. Although his "papers and belongings" were not returned to him, we can imagine that he managed to keep the manuscript of the *Essais* from his aggressors. The count of Thorigny lost fifty crowns and various objects and articles of clothing.

Montaigne was sequestered by the bandits for several days, and he reported this disagreeable event in a letter to Matignon:

> My lord, you will have been told that our baggage was taken from us in the forest of Villebois, before our eyes, and then, after much confusion and delay, the capture was deemed unjust by Monsieur the Prince [Condé]. However, we did not dare to reveal our intentions, because of our uncertainty regarding the safety of our persons, which should have been guaranteed by our safe-conducts. It was Le Lignou who captured us, the same who took Monsieur de Barrault and de La Rochefoucauld. The storm hid me hardest, because I had my money in my box. I recovered nothing, and most of my papers and belongings remained in their hands. We did not see Monsieur the Prince. Monsieur the Count of Thorigny lost some fifty crowns, a silver ewer (*aiguière*), and a few minor articles.[79]

In the same letter, Montaigne informs Matignon of the latest political developments: "The trip to Normandy has been postponed. The king [Henry III] has sent Messieurs De Bellièvre and La Guiche [Diane d'Andoins] to Monsieur de Guise to summon them to the Court. We will be there Thursday."[80] Montaigne was confident and had resumed his duties, considering himself to have Navarre's mandate for a mission of the greatest importance. He was finally released when the brigands learned that Thorigny and Montaigne were on a mission to negotiate an agreement between Henry III and Henry of Navarre. The prey the brigands had captured was a little too big for their nets, and they decided to let them go without demanding ransom. This incident seems to be different from the one reported in the chapter "Of physiognomy."

After an extraordinary journey, Navarre's envoys and Matignon finally arrived in Paris on February 18. Montaigne had stayed in the capital on many occasions, and in his *Essais* he declares that he is French only through this great city. For a gentleman, Paris, which already had a population of almost 300,000 at that date, meant mainly the Court, a world of intrigues where rumors flew around. Spies in the service of the English and Spanish were numerous there.

Thus on February 20, Stafford sent a report to his protector, William Cecil, Lord Treasurer of England:

> I have spoken with milord the Secretary (Walsingham) in a coded message—I cannot know whether he will show it—about the arrival here of a certain Montaigne on behalf of the King of Navarre, sent with Matignon's son; and how all the servants of the King of Navarre here are jealous of his arrival, because on the one hand he does not have to address them, and on the other hand they do not know anything at all about the reasons for his trip; and moreover (I can write this to your Lordship), because I know that it will not be spoken of, I beg you, they suspect all the more that he is a great favorite of the countess of Bishe [Guiche], who governs, it is said, the King of Navarre as she wishes; and who is a very dangerous woman; and who is spoiling the King of Navarre's reputation throughout the world; for he is completely mad about her, as people say. They fear, and so do I, that he [Montaigne] has come to discuss some special matter with the King, without the religious knowing about it; for certainly no one knows anything, and it is believed that neither Du Plessis [Mornay] nor Viscount Turenne, nor any one else of that religion knows anything about it. Besides, the man in question is a Catholic, a very capable man; he was once mayor of Bordeaux, and is not a man to accept the assignment to bring the King something that does not please him. And the Marshal de Matignon would not have undertaken to have him escorted by his son if he had not been very sure that his message would please, and not displease, the King. I have not written without some purpose in my long letter delivered by M. Hacklytt that I feared that the King of Navarre might find himself forced, whether he will or not, to satisfy the King; which I would not willingly see happen without the Queen's knowledge, and without her having had, as it were, her part in the affair.[81]

Montaigne and his traveling companions arrived in Paris in the greatest secrecy. Thorigny and Montaigne were quickly received by the king. On February 25, a letter from Lucinge confirms that "the King continues to prepare his trip to

Poitou and Guyenne for this spring, and on the other hand because the Bis-cayne [Henry of Navarre] is holding his assembly in Montauban to decide what he should do, and while waiting to see what he decides, the King has delayed La Guiche's [Diane d'Andoins] and Bellièvre's missions; they will not leave to find the Guisard until it is clearer what Navarre wants to do for his religion."[82]

We begin to understand better what the king was asking of Navarre: if he agreed to convert, Henry III was prepared to visit him in Guyenne. This gesture would make it possible to send a strong message concerning the legitimate heir to the French throne. However, in light of the events that followed over the coming weeks, this plan was quickly abandoned. Montaigne's extraordinary embassy was doomed to failure because Navarre had no intention of abandon-ing his faith, despite his mistress's recommendations.

To the spies and foreign diplomats Montaigne seemed to be a pawn on a complex chessboard. He was thought to be manipulated by or in the pay of Navarre. In reality, he escaped the control of Navarre's Court because, as Staf-ford stresses, this "capable" man was not one to defend positions of which he did not personally approve. The Spanish ambassador in Paris, Bernardino de Men-doza, was not deceived either, and on February 25 he also hastened to recount a Gascon gentleman's suspicious visit to the Court: "And here, they say, has ar-rived Monsieur de Montaigne, who is a Catholic gentleman and a follower of the man from Béarn under the direction of Matignon; and because those who handle the affairs of the man from Béarn do not know the reason why he has come, they suspect that he is on some secret mission."[83] Thus Montaigne really was on a *secret mission*, and those close to Navarre new nothing about the exact content of the message he was conveying to the king. Mendoza moved in the hushed milieu of spies, diplomats, and other official or unofficial negotiators in Paris. He had served as ambassador to London in 1578 before being expelled for lacking in respect toward the queen of England. Having long experience with political subtleties and diplomatic negotiations, Mendoza arrived in Paris as the Spanish king's ambassador in mid-October 1584. His task was to avoid at all cost a reconciliation between the Guises and Henry III.[84] And on this point, every day brought news that made an entente between Navarre and the king less likely. On February 18, Mary Stuart, François II's widow, was executed by Queen Elizabeth of England after eighteen years in captivity. This news, which was spreading among members of the League at the time Montaigne arrived in Paris to present what was then considered a Protestant plot, increased the ani-mosity against Henry III, who was called an "Englishman of the Garter"[vii] and a tyrant.[85]

[vii] Apparently an allusion to the Order of the Garter, England's highest order of chiv-alry. [Trans.]

On February 28, after obtaining additional information, Mendoza provided new details regarding Montaigne:

Monsieur de Montaigne, about whom I wrote to your Majesty in one of my letters of the 25th, is considered to be a man of understanding, though somewhat addlepated. They tell me that he controls the countess of La Guisa [Diane d'Andoins], who is a very beautiful lady and lives with the sister of the man from Béarn, since she is the brother's lady. They say that the man from Béarn has dealings with him, and therefore they judge that he [Montaigne] is entrusted with some commission and that the King wants to make use of Montaigne so that he [Montaigne] may intercede with the said countess of La Guisa, that she may persuade the man from Béarn to come to what the King desires.[86]

Henry III's counterproposals were transmitted to Navarre by François de Montesquiou, lord of Sainte Colombe, who was sent to the Court of Nérac. Henry III, under pressure from the Guises, once again urged Navarre to immediately abjure his faith. In a letter to his mistress, Navarre discusses the difficult situation in which he found himself: "The Devil is on the loose. I am to be pitied, and [it] is a miracle that I am not succumbing to the burden. If I weren't a Huguenot, I'd become a Turk! Ah! The violent trials by which my brain is sounded! I cannot fail soon to be either a mad man or a clever one. . . . All the torments to which a mind can be subjected are constantly inflicted upon mine."[87] Although Navarre proposed to Henry III that they make a common front against the League, he was not ready for any compromise in matters of religion, not being able to "silence his conscience," as he put it.

Montaigne's arrival in Paris came at a critical time in the relations among France, England, and Spain. After his initial career in local and regional politics, Montaigne now found himself literally propelled onto the international scene. A series of particular, more personal circumstances, such as the growth of the duke of Guise's power and the new power relationship favorable to Navarre, made the author of the *Essais* an inevitable intermediary in 1588. Because he knew the two Henrys personally without ever having openly sided with either of them against the other, Montaigne was able to serve as a relatively neutral intermediary. The king was greatly weakened, because his position was considered ambivalent. He had almost no room for maneuver with respect to the Guises, but he still persisted in trying to satisfy both sides. Starting in March 1588, a test of strength between the duke of Guise and Henry III began. Lucinge tells us that henceforth neither the duke of Guise nor Mayenne was willing to disarm. The negotiations were once more at an impasse, and the king emerged from this situation even weaker than before. The people were concerned to see foreign troops entering the kingdom. On the point of rioting, Paris finally fell under the control of the League. Montaigne had few options and decided once again to remain faithful to his king. Little inclined to take conflictual positions, he had long since acquired the habit of siding with the established government. A passage in the 1580 edition of the *Essais* comments on his natural inclination to be a "follower": "Thus I am fit only to follow, and I let myself be carried away easily by the crowd. I do not trust my own powers enough to undertake to command, to guide, or even to counsel; I am very glad to find my steps traced out by others. If I must run the risk of an uncertain choice, I would rather it should be under some man who is more sure of his opinions and wedded to them than I am to mine."[88] On the Bordeaux Copy, Montaigne crossed out "or even to counsel," thus removing all trace of his experience in this matter. He was going to put into practice, once again, this character trait that made of him a loyal and devoted servant of the king, whom he followed not by political choice, but simply because it was the duty of a man of his rank and status.

"I Buy Printers in Guienne, Elsewhere They Buy Me"

In early 1588, Montaigne and Pierre de Brach planned to go to Paris to work on their literary and publishing projects. Montaigne was to see to the publication of his *Essais*, augmented by a third book (thirteen chapters) and "six hundred additions to the first two books," while Brach was thinking about collecting verses by Paris poets for the *Tombeau d'Aymée*, a volume paying homage to his wife, who had died shortly before. In the middle of the excitement of his diplomatic and political activity, while he was an active participant at the heart of complex negotiations, Montaigne was therefore also busy having a new edition of his book published by Abel L'Angelier, one of the most famous publisher-booksellers of the Palace. However, as we have suggested, everything indicates that Brach did not accompany Montaigne in February 1588, but rather arrived in Paris shortly before. The two men had ambitions as authors, and the capital had attracted them to carry out their respective publishing plans.

Pierre de Brach might have suggested to Montaigne that a move from Bordeaux to Paris, to find a new publisher, would ensure greater visibility and better distribution for his book. Longtime friends, Montaigne and Pierre de Brach both came from the *robin* milieu, and both loved poetry. Brach had once dedicated a poem to Montaigne and probably suggested that he talk to the publisher who had brought out his *Poèmes* in 1576. The common publishing route the two writers followed has already been mentioned, and although to date no publishing contract between Montaigne and L'Angelier has been found, the author of the *Essais* mentions that his relations with publishers had changed since 1588.[89]

Whereas in 1580 he had bought the paper on which his *Essais* were printed, in 1588 he was offered much more favorable conditions. Like many authors of this period, he was not paid, but he did receive a few free copies of the book that he could distribute by himself to make his book known or to offer to his friends—a very widespread practice. Several extant copies of this 1588 edition bear the mark of having been sent or given to friends or acquaintances.

Simon Millanges and Abel L'Angelier had commercial agreements. Thus Brach had his *Imitations*—translations of Tasso's *Aminta* and the Olympia episode from Ariosto's *Orlando furioso*—published by Millanges in 1584, and L'Angelier republished the book under the title *Aminte, l'Olimpe* in 1584–85.[90] The title page stipulated: "In Bordeaux, by S. Millanges. Ordinary printer of the King. They are sold in Paris by Abel L'Angelier." Similarly, a contract signed on October 19, 1579, between François de Foix-Candale and Simon Millanges indicates that of the 150 copies printed in Millanges's workshop in Bordeaux, 140 were to be sold in Paris and Lyon. In 1574, Foix-Candale had published with Millanges a French translation of fragments of Hermes Trismegistus. He had a second, revised and expanded, edition printed by the same printer in 1579, before it was brought out again by L'Angelier on the Paris market in 1587. Millanges had been working with his Paris colleague since 1584, and several titles published by Millanges thus passed to L'Angelier in accord with a distribution agreement between the two publishers. Montaigne's *Essais* were probably ceded to L'Angelier in the framework of this arrangement.

After the relatively local publication of the first edition of the *Essais* in 1580 and their republication in 1582 by Simon Millanges in Bordeaux, Montaigne decided to have his book printed in Paris by Abel L'Angelier. His political ambitions required a broader readership. L'Angelier allowed Montaigne to acquire greater fame and to move closer to the Court and to political power. Located at the "first pillar of the great hall of the Palace," L'Angelier had become a university-certified bookseller in 1581. He had good contacts in Aquitaine and counted among his authors several scholars and poets from the Bordeaux region: Pierre de Brach, François de Foix-Candale, Florimond de Raemond, Blaise de Monluc, and Jean de Sponde. L'Angelier's privilege (authorization to print) for the publication of the *Essais* of 1588 was valid for nine years, a longer-than-average period at the time.

The edition L'Angelier printed in 1588 should logically be the fourth, and not the fifth, as the title page indicates. Much has been written about the famous "missing" edition of the *Essais*. A third edition, with a title page bearing the name of Jean Richer, had been published in Paris a year earlier. Composed on the basis of the 1582 text, it does not contain the third book. This Paris edition of 1587 is the least known of those that appeared during Montaigne's lifetime. Some have wondered what role the author played in its production and whether it was authorized by him or by Simon Millanges, who still held the first printing privilege granted in May 1579 for a period of eight years starting from the date of publication. The 1587 edition was printed without a privilege, just after the expiration of Millanges's privilege. No mention is made of a possible transfer or sharing of the *Essais* between Millanges and Richer—also a university-certified bookseller from 1572 to 1599 who was considered a partisan of the royal cause. It is probable that Richer took over, with Millanges's agreement, the remainder of a pirated Rouen edition (which may be the missing edition) that had been seized by the authorities. Richer is then supposed to have put this counterfeit edition on sale after adding a new title page, as was often done at the time.

Most of the known copies of this 1587 edition of the *Essais* have modern bindings, and all the copies with sixteenth-century bindings (three in number) have the peculiarity of having a title page that has been replaced or is a facsimile, or is even handwritten. It has been suggested[91] that Richer had planned to reissue the 1587 edition with an intermediate title, a plan he abandoned when the L'Angelier edition of 1588 was announced. There is another possible explanation, which takes into account the replaced title pages: the 1587 edition might have been instead a reissue of an earlier edition in which, in accord with a practice common at the time, the original title page was replaced by a title page bearing the new date when it was put on sale, in this case 1587. The "rejuvenated" earlier edition would be none other than the so-called missing edition, the one that was probably printed in Rouen, around 1583–84, and which La Croix du Maine mentions in his *Bibliothèque françoise*.[92] At that time printers in Rouen had the unfortunate habit of publishing pirated editions that they sold in France, the Low Countries, Belgium, and Switzerland. It would therefore be logical to connect this fourth edition of the *Essais* published in Rouen with the Paris edition of 1587. This hypothesis explains why Montaigne considered the L'Angelier edition of 1588 the "fifth" edition of his *Essais*. In that case, the 1587 edition, traditionally seen as the fourth edition, would constitute the missing link between the "second edition" published in Bordeaux in 1582, the pirated edition printed in Rouen in 1583 or 1584, and the Paris edition of 1588.

In 1588, Montaigne had a different idea of his reader and his book. The presence of a third book and numerous additions had practically doubled the size of the *Essais*, which could no longer be contained in a single octavo volume. The growing prestige of Montaigne's book now required that it be printed in the quarto format usually reserved for "more academic" books. In addition, the ample margins of L'Angelier's edition—at a time when paper was the main cost involved in producing a book—made it look like a semiluxury volume. For the occasion, Montaigne reread attentively his preface to the reader. However, he made no major change and altered only one word: "aucune" replaced "nulle."

The most important correction changed the date from March 1, 1580, to June 12, 1588. Thus Montaigne updated his introductory text to make it correspond to the new publication date, but giving up the first date also marks a disillusionment with regard to the reader he had envisaged in 1580. Montaigne chose not to modify his preface to the reader, knowing full well that the 1588 edition was something very different from the book Millanges had published for him eight years earlier. Thus he deliberately opted for continuity, despite the development of his situation and the four years he had spent as mayor of Bordeaux. On the political level, Montaigne found himself almost back where he had started. Nonetheless, his hope for a diplomatic career had resurfaced since his secret mission to Paris, and for that reason the king remained his privileged reader, even if the additions written between the summer of 1585 and December 1587 demonstrate a certain distance taken from politics and public service. In the brief window of professional opportunity that presented itself in the spring of 1588, Montaigne once again had the feeling of being able to serve his king and play a political role at the highest level. Even though it had a new date, the *Au lecteur* remained valid and thus did not need to be changed.

The form and content of Montaigne's book had been revamped, and after 1588 it no longer had anything to do with the *Essais* of 1580. Following his service as mayor of Bordeaux and the failure of his first negotiation between Henry III and Navarre, Montaigne had not thought it best to pursue the military and diplomatic developments in his first chapters. On the contrary, he had written much more about himself, his experiences, his personal judgments, even his eating habits and other details of his private life. After a negative experience in politics, the third book of the *Essais* reinforced what Montaigne had already announced in the preface to the reader of 1580: the *Essais* were now a more personal book (the book of Michel de Montaigne) and reflected political and literary itineraries that intersected but could not be superimposed.

On the material level, thirteen chapters in the first book of the *Essais* have been slightly modified with respect to the 1580 edition. However, several chapters include more substantial additions that make them longer than they were in 1580. Many chapters remain unchanged and are still relatively short—for example, "Of prompt or slow speech" (I: 10), "Ceremony of interviews between kings" (I: 13), "We should meddle soberly with judging divine ordinances" (I: 32), "Fortune is often met in the path of reason" (I: 34), "Of sumptuary laws" (I: 43), and "Of smells" (I: 55). These little-developed or slightly modified chapters, which number twenty, are drowned in the mass of the 107 chapters composing the three books of the *Essais* and are dominated by the *big chapters*, such as "Of the education of children" (I: 26), "Of friendship" (I: 28), "Of cannibals" (I: 31), "Of books" (II: 10), "Apology for Raymond Sebond" (II: 12), "Of presumption" (II: 17), "Of repentance" (III: 2), "Of three kinds of association" (III: 3), "On some verses of Virgil" (III: 5), "Of coaches" (III: 6), "Of vanity" (III: 9), "Of physiognomy" (III: 12) or "Of experience" (III: 13).[viii]

On the other hand, a small number of chapters, even though very short in the 1580 edition, have been greatly expanded in this new edition of the *Essais*. For example, "We taste nothing pure" (II: 20), which covered less than a page in 1580, is considerably longer in L'Angelier's 1588 edition. The same goes for "Of the greatness of Rome" (II: 24), which was very short in 1580; it was revised for the 1588 edition, which includes a new quotation and two short additions, but a development that doubles the length of the chapter was added after 1588, in the margins of Bordeaux Copy. Other chapters, such as "Of evil means employed to a good end" (II: 23), were enriched with Latin quotations, but no new commentaries or developments were added to them in 1588. Apart from the "Apology for Raymond Sebond," which Montaigne continued to expand to a lesser degree, with respect to the appearance of the third book, the remaining ninety-four chapters in the first two books were on the whole left as they were. What should we think about this rather surprising "evolution" of the already existing chapters between 1580 and 1588?

After 1580, the work done on the chapters in the first book was far from even, and Montaigne "forgot" or even gave up on several chapters. And yet these short chapters that were present in the 1580 edition and were very little revised in 1588 have a considerable political significance. Their simple existence (with names that reveal Montaigne's main interests between 1572 and 1580) allow us to better define the publishing goal of the first edition of the *Essais* and the way in which this goal changed considerably in the course of the following years and

---

[viii] The list of the chapters Montaigne "forgot" or neglected in the edition of the *Essais* published by Abel L'Angelier in 1588 is the following: "Of idleness" (I: 8)—two Latin quotations are added; "One is punished for defending a place obstinately without reason" (I: 15)—a sentence is added; "Of the punishment of cowardice" (I: 16); "One man's profit is another man's harm" (I: 22)—a single word is corrected; "It is folly to measure the true and false by our own capacity" (I: 27)—two Latin quotations are added; "Twenty-nine sonnets of Etienne de La Boétie" (I: 29); "To flee from sensual pleasures at the price of life" (I: 33)—no addition; "Of sleep" (I: 44); "Of the battle of Dreux" (I: 45)—one example taken from Antiquity added at the end of the chapter; "Of ancient customs" (I: 49)—two Latin quotations and two lines added at the end of the chapter; "Of the parsimony of the ancients" (I: 52)—one line added; "Of a saying of Caesar's" (I: 53)—three Latin quotations added without commentary; "Of age" (I: 57)—one Latin quotation and two lines added; "Let business wait till tomorrow" (II: 4)—three lines added; "Of honorary awards" (II: 7)—one sentence added; "How our mind hinders itself"(II: 14)—no change; "Of freedom of conscien" (II: 19)—no change; "Of evil means employed to a good end" (II: 23)—six Latin quotations added but no other addition except for a few words to introduce the quotations; "Of thumbs" (II: 26)—a brief final sentence added. I have given the titles in English to be consistent with other titles of chapters given throughout the text.

the successive editions. We might wonder why Montaigne neglected certain chapters after 1580. These forgotten chapters call for explanation. This neglect is generally associated with a lapse in memory—and Montaigne likes to remind the reader that he has a bad memory. Several chapters are little revised from one edition to the next (1588 and the Bordeaux Copy), as if Montaigne had given up on them without going so far as to omit them from his book. They are, in a way, orphans needing attention, but that fell into oblivion. It does not mean, of course, that the author did not glance at them from time to time, changing a word or modifying the punctuation, adding a sentence or a Latin quotation, but as a rule these interventions are minimal, and these chapters never really grew with time. These essays are the traces left behind by a different publishing project, by another Montaigne. It is in this sense that the edition that appeared in Paris in 1588 testifies to publishing choices.

The "forgotten" chapters in the *Essais* received little attention after 1580. However, it is difficult to present a qualitative argument and to offer any kind of generalization regarding the essays as a whole. Of course, a changed sentence or a spelling correction testifies to Montaigne's continual work on *all* his essays. But we have to note that all the chapters are not equal in the eyes of posterity. The modern age has given priority to the chapters in which Montaigne portrays himself openly and exhibits the traits of his personality, more particularly in the last two chapters of the third book, "Of physiognomy" and "Of experience." The expression of his subjectivity and his private self has become an end in itself, and the reader takes pleasure in picking out the contradictory judgments in a work associated with a modern form of impressionism. The short chapters are more rigid and do not display the "leaps and gambols"[93] that delight a modern reader. They present themselves as fortuitous impressions, as if Montaigne had mistaken the value that had to be accorded them in his book or had wandered away from the themes originally chosen. These chapters arrest our attention as vestiges of neglected projects, discourses to be completed by new examples taken from contemporary history and quotations drawn from the Ancients. They are the traces of past preoccupations and appear as admissions of past expectations and hopes. Their subjects have to be understood in the context of the years between 1572 and 1580, because they represent an initial version of the *Essais* that was soon to become outmoded as a result of Montaigne's direct experience with politics.

The work done by Montaigne for the 1588 edition thus consisted chiefly in the addition of a third book, and the changes he made to the first two books after 1580 are relatively modest. Thus, so far as the 1588 edition is concerned, we see that Montaigne did not change eight chapters and that fourteen other chapters in the first two books were expanded by less than 5 percent. Twenty-two of the fifty-seven chapters of the first book were left practically unchanged for the 1588 edition. In the second book, nine chapters out of twenty-seven have additions amounting to less than 5 percent of their length. Thus the first book was expanded by only 21 percent in 1588 and the second by 19 percent. Consequently, we can state that the goal of the 1588 edition was to introduce a third book of a kind rather different from the first two books of the *Essais*. Although most chapters of the third book were written after his second term as mayor, chapter 2 ("Of repentance") and chapter 6 ("Of coaches") seem to have been conceived at the end of 1584, at least in part.[94] After 1585, Montaigne developed his initial text very little and gave priority to the thirteen new chapters, which are on the whole much longer. Thus the work done on the 1588 edition of the *Essais* distanced Montaigne from his original plan. The *Essais* became a different book that was based on a different project.[ix] Montaigne very quickly acquired the habit of concentrating his work on some chapters and neglecting others. An analysis of the content of the additions he made also allows us to state that after 1585, and especially after 1588, Montaigne talks more about himself and his experiences than he did in the 1580 edition. We can say that the 1580 edition gave priority to a "political Montaigne," whereas starting with the 1588 edition, and a fortiori in the additions to the Bordeaux Copy, it was on the contrary the author's private self that gained superiority over social, religious, and political reflections.

The time of publication and the time of politics coexisted, but they were not simultaneous. In this sense, the *Au lecteur* of 1588, even though it was very little revised, is *truer* than that of 1580. Montaigne strips and exposes himself to his reader more than ever; he returns to the initial intention announced eight years earlier, despite the fact that he now had a very different reader. On rereading his preface, Montaigne discovered that the ambiguity present in the 1580 edition now worked to his advantage. Whereas in 1580 the *Au lecteur* was clearly addressed to the Court and the king, in 1588 it could be taken literally, while at the same time sufficiently retaining the appearance of a curriculum vitae to still serve his professional and political ambitions, especially at a time when he was beginning to be known for his frankness and independence of mind. It was clear that this book still had an unexploited potential.

Montaigne's readership had grown larger, and he was now confronted by an uncontrolled reception of his book, which led him to ask himself how the *Essais* might be read and interpreted by an audience he did not know. Although Mil-

---

[ix] In 1588, three chapters in the third book stand out in contrast to the others by their length: "On some verses of Virgil" (16,300 words, to which 5,000 words were added in the Bordeaux Copy); "Of vanity" (17,000 words in 1588, increased by 5,000 words after 1588); and "Of experience" (also 17,000 words in 1588, with 4,800 additional words in the Bordeaux Copy). Most of the other chapters in the third book run to between 4,000 and 6,000 words, with additions of as much as 1,000 to 2,000 words in the Bordeaux Copy. Rounded numbers are given here.

langes had foreseen a mainly local distribution for the book in a region in which Montaigne was beginning to be known, the Paris printing of 1588 created a new distance between the author and his readers. The consubstantiality of the subject and the object of writing was compromised, because the author was now separated from a text whose interpretation he could no longer control. Moreover, since Montaigne had gained more visibility during his two terms as mayor of Bordeaux, and then during the negotiations he conducted between Henry III and Navarre, his *Essais* were beginning to attract the attention of unscrupulous printers who were always on the lookout for a work that might allow them to make a quick profit.

In order to produce pirated books more rapidly, at lower cost, and under a false address, in the hope of making a quick killing, these counterfeiters were accustomed to ignore the publishing privileges granted to printers. However, doing so was not without dangers, because the counterfeiters were running the risk of having the unsold copies of the pirated book seized by the authorities, being subjected to a substantial fine, and even having their printing equipment confiscated. Many counterfeiters set up their operations abroad in order to escape the French authorities. Others, despite the risks they ran, chose to remain on French territory to sell their unauthorized printed materials more rapidly. Such illicit practices were particularly found among a small number of printers in Rouen. The publishing history of the *Essais* thus includes several counterfeit editions produced in Rouen, even though the place of publication was generally claimed to be Antwerp or Leiden, and which were to be distributed throughout Europe by the beginning of the seventeenth century. As we have already noted, it is likely that a pirated printing of the *Essais* was planned in Rouen in 1584, before the first edition published by L'Angelier in 1588. However, far from being seen as a problem, this counterfeit edition showed Montaigne the extent of his growing success as an author while he was still displaying some political pretensions and was trying to acquire even more visibility. After all, the more books that were printed that bore his name on the title page, the more his fame grew.

The pirated edition printed in Rouen shows the increasing success of Montaigne's book after 1582. He now had a sufficient readership to allow an unscrupulous printer to invest money to reprint a relatively long book and publish it under a false imprint. Counterfeits are generally a good indication of the market for a book. Without being a best seller, the *Essais*—in Millanges's editions or in its counterfeit edition produced in Rouen—were gradually coming to be read by a broader public than Montaigne had at first imagined. For example, Marie de Gournay declared that she read the *Essais* "toward the end of the period of two or three years that passed between her first view of the book and the first time she saw its author,"[95] that is, between 1585 and 1586. The rare book market has made it possible to identify several of Montaigne's "first readers" and to infer a certain sales success.[96] Montaigne's book was a "novelty" and as such put its stamp on the minds of its first readers. Its success was measured not so much by the number of copies sold as by the number of conversations generated by a relatively limited number of readers, because it was the difference between the content and form of the *Essais* and those of all other genres that made the reputation of the book and its author. The Paris edition of 1588 was to confirm Montaigne's success as an author.

In 1588 Abel L'Angelier made sure that the reader knew what he was buying by stating on the title page that it was a "Fifth edition augmented by a third book and six hundred additions to the first two." The six hundred additions listed by the publisher for the Paris edition of the *Essais* were very differently distributed.[x] The introduction of numerous elaborations, in addition to the third book, was apparently necessary to enable L'Angelier to obtain a new privilege for the same title. He had to make it clear that he was publishing a book different from the *Essais* of 1580 or of 1582. This imposing quarto volume of 508 folios with broad margins in no way resembles the first two editions, which economized on paper and had been printed hastily. The engraved frontispiece is unique among the books produced by L'Angelier and other Paris printers of the time. An etching made with little skill, an oversize frame with relation to the printed page, it gives the book a baroque look. The ornamental plate is rather elaborate and executed in a style that contrasts with the simplicity of the 1580 title page. Frontispiece title pages, which were expensive, were not frequent, and this engraving (or at least its frame) was probably provided by Montaigne, who had miscalculated the volume's size. L'Angelier was very active as a publisher in 1588, since he published twenty-two titles. The high number of extant copies of this edition (almost sixty in public libraries and more than 120 in private collections) indicates a larger print run than for the editions of 1580 and 1582, even though this difference in the number of copies inventoried is partly explained by the more imposing format that favored better preservation of the copies over the centuries. In accord with the practices of the time, copies of the book were sold in signatures or with a temporary binding—often simply a cardboard cover—and it was up to the buyer to have his copy bound at his own cost.

In 1588, Montaigne did not participate actively in the material production of the book. That was the disadvantage of having his book published in Paris. Furthermore, the very special circumstances of his stay in the capital during his secret mission on behalf of Henry of Navarre probably did not allow him to supervise the production of his book as he would have wished. Dissatisfied with the printing and the general presentation of the book, he wrote on the flyleaf of

---

[x] The L'Angelier edition of 1588 runs to 312,978 words, which represents an increase of 132,416 words, or 73 percent, over the first edition of 1580.

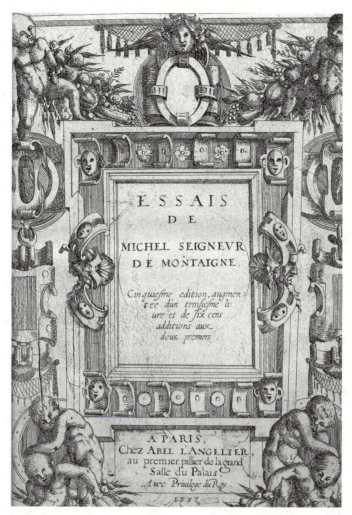

FIGURE 15. "Fifth" edition of the *Essais*, but the third edition revised by Montaigne, 1588 (private collection).

the Bordeaux Copy precise instructions for the printer of a future edition. He drew up a list of corrections to be made on points of language (Old French, for example), punctuation, the use of capital letters, and running heads on the printed page—all points of detail that he had not been able to check and correct during his stay in Paris in 1588. He gave particular attention to the general presentation of the book. Montaigne now called his writings a "record of the essays of my life"[97] and had mention of his public offices removed from the title page. The 1588 *Essais* seemed a more personal book. Since he was no longer mayor, references to his municipal offices were logically omitted and replaced by a concise presentation: "Essais de Michel seigneur de Montaigne" (figure 15). What is more surprising is that Montaigne also deleted his titles as knight of the king's order and ordinary gentleman of the king's chamber, as if these qualities were no longer essential for his book. Was this an early sign of the sharp separation that was soon to be effected between his public and private life? Montaigne began to situate his book clearly on the side of the private. It was thus logical that the traces of a work that was originally conceived as a collection of reflections on public life were removed in this first more private edition. The retention of the *Au lecteur* was in accord with this new conception of the book, and the recent call to serve the king as a negotiator once again had come too late to change the book's orientation, which Montaigne had decided on after 1585. The *Essais* now existed outside politics, or at least it was no longer dependent on its author's expectations in the service of the king or his patrons.

The edition published by L'Angelier in Paris was completed, according to its "achevé d'imprimer," on June 12, 1588. The printer had taken about four months to produce this "fifth" edition. The work was probably done in the shop of Pierre Chevillot,[98] who had been working for L'Angelier since 1578. The privilege granted L'Angelier for nine years is dated June 4, 1588, and Montaigne's preface "To the Reader" is dated June 12. We must add that L'Angelier was not a printer but a publisher and bookseller. As the first Paris printing partly supervised by the author—he gave instructions regarding the format, choice of an ornamental plate for the title page, printing with large margins—Abel L'Angelier's edition gave Montaigne a national scope. Like Millanges, L'Angelier emphasized the work's "novelty" and explained in a prominent place on the title page that this was an edition enlarged by more than a third. Montaigne was rather proud of having reversed the terms of his relationship with the printer: "I buy printers in Guienne, elsewhere they buy me,"[99] he notes with delight. After having had the first edition printed at his own cost, he now received his book's dividends. Through their length and content, the thirteen chapters of the third book gave a new direction to the *Essais*. The body occupied a much more important place in it, and over the subsequent centuries, chapters like "Of physiognomy" and "Of experience" succeeded in making Montaigne seen as one of the first "modern" authors. Whereas in 1580 his discourse consisted in promoting himself with a view to a possible public office and was based above all on essentially bookish experiences, in the third book published in 1588 the remarks on politics were based on real experiences gained in the field.

Thus the third book was written in a climate of retirement with respect to politics, during a difficult period (fighting on his doorstep, plague, flight on the roads of the region) that led the author of the *Essais* to distance himself from events and emphasize a more personal and autobiographical side. We also find less historical and more moral or ideological reflection in this third version of the *Essais*. This is best illustrated by the first chapter of the third book, "Of the useful and the honorable." At a time when polemical pamphlets were being produced in large numbers and aggressive words and discourses were proliferating, Montaigne began his third book with an appropriate incipit: "No one is exempt from saying silly things. The misfortune is to say them with earnest effort."[100] The first sentence of the third book of the 1588 *Essais* sets the tone for the rest of the book. The whole work bears on the representation of man and the world, on the way of saying things rather than on reality. For the first time, Montaigne acknowledged a form of political indifference for which he had been reproached when he was mayor. What he had at first considered his political strength others saw as a form of naïveté that could lead to failure. Montaigne now chose to recapture these traits of his personality in a more general form and chose to "speak to [his] paper": "I speak to my paper as I speak to the first man I meet."[101] For him, this was an unprecedented way of associating with his reader, and the chapter "Of three kinds of association" makes official this new de-historicized, de-socialized activity. Conversing with his book also offered him an opportunity to feel more independent.

For the occasion, Montaigne undertook to draw up an initial balance sheet of a life in which luck had not always been on his side. In a passage written after his experience in the mayor's office, he divides his life into three distinct periods, and it is interesting that he does so in relation to money. Thus he speaks of a first period in which, having "none but casual means," he depended on others. Montaigne considers this early youth to be the best part of his life, because he was "dependent on the authority and help of others, without rule or fixed revenue." During this first part of his life, his "spending was done the more joyously and carelessly for being all at the hazard of fortune."[102] The insouciance connected with dependency procured a kind of happiness. And Montaigne concludes: "I was never better off." This economic irresponsibility allowed the young man to escape any pecuniary worries and thus to avoid the "malady" of avarice, a constant preoccupation in the *Essais*.[103] Avarice leads to a very special state of imaginary satisfaction, because the desired objects remain accessible (through gifts made by others for example) without it being necessary to separate oneself from one's money in order to acquire them. Sixteenth-century society and its commercial mentality had become very good at acquiring services and goods at little expense. In a perpetual state of accounting, the name of the game consisted in receiving more than was expended, at both the material and symbolic levels. Thus avarice was judged harmful to the proper functioning of society.

Montaigne goes on to explain his evolution with regard to money. His "second situation was to have money."[104] During this period, Montaigne put aside a little nest egg and grew corrupt in the vile process of accumulating capital, which led him to hoarding, another form of avarice. It has been estimated that

Montaigne saved more than 20,000 *livres* between 1570 and 1577.[105] This immoral state led him to speak of his money only to lie, and his life was governed solely by his "strongbox":

> Was I going on a journey, I never thought I was sufficiently provided. And the bigger my load of money, the bigger my load of fear: now about the safety of the roads, now about the fidelity of those who had charge of my baggage, of which, like some others I know, I was never sure enough unless I had it before my eyes. Did I leave my strongbox at home, how many suspicions, how many thorny and, what is worse, incommunicable thoughts![106]

From Montaigne's "strongbox" to Harpagon's money box it is only a short step. This passage in the *Essais* should be compared with Marx's analysis of the transformation of money into the universal commodity and the alienation of the subject with respect to this universal commodity. Montaigne himself admits that his relationships to society were redefined by his financial situation and the material goods he possessed. His sociability decreased in inverse proportion to the number of gold coins in his coffer. For this reason, at the end of the sixteenth century avarice was often associated with misanthropy. However, Montaigne had a kind of revelation that allowed him to change his relation to money, but the result of this belated realization was to make him spend with too great liberality. He refers more particularly to "the pleasure of a certain trip at great expense having overthrown this stupid fancy."[107] Should this be seen as a direct reference to his stay in Rome and his ambassadorial ambitions? Probably. After 1577, he drew heavily on his coffer to cover the new expenses arising from his offices as gentleman of the chamber of the kings of France and Navarre.

Henceforth, that is, after 1585, in this third period of his life that followed his two terms as mayor of Bordeaux, Montaigne was determined to live in the moment: "I live from day to day, and content myself with having enough to meet my present and ordinary needs."[108] Avarice and excessive spending are countered by an economic equilibrium that consists in "regulating" profits and expenses: "I make my expense run abreast with my receipts; now one is ahead, now the other, but they are never far apart."[109] However, this balance of receipts and expenses creates a new dependency: the individual conceives himself only as an economic subject whose leitmotiv (or even philosophy) is moderation erected into the supreme value.

We must nonetheless be wary of drawing hasty conclusions regarding this parallel Montaigne makes between money and his life's trajectory. In the *Essais*, there are relatively few extended and reasoned commentaries directly connected with money, and our knowledge of the domestic economy of Montaigne's estate is rather limited. It is impossible to make Montaigne a skinflint—even a miser who hoarded during a large part of his life—or a convinced mercantilist who sold his office as a magistrate in order to increase his savings.[110] But we know—and he's the one who says it—that Montaigne succeeded in getting away from this unhealthy and dangerous path of money (whether hoarding or spending) that would assuredly have brought him closer to the "other nobility," that of the *robins*. Moderation logically appears to be the remedy for avarice and is transformed into a virtue in the *Essais*. Thus Montaigne devoted a chapter to moderation (I: 30), an essay that doubled in length after 1585, and was again greatly expanded after 1588.[111] Starting in 1585, moderation plays the role of a liberating force opposed to the servitude of avarice and extravagant expenses. Montaigne's disappointments as mayor of Bordeaux and the period of hesitation that followed it enabled him to take a distance on the political and economic requirements of power, at all levels.

The third book draws up a balance sheet of a life and offers a direction unanticipated in 1580. Montaigne's preface to the reader suddenly rediscovered a truth that was hidden in 1580. Of course, Montaigne pictured the possibility that his book might be a genuine best seller. He looked with confidence on the form of the essay becoming a genre of its own. He claimed to be close to the genre of memoirs, minus the history, and recounted his political experiences on the same level as his private experiences. He notes that professional politicians remain covert and masked, never showing their hands. On the contrary, he explains that he has always chosen to be transparent. The project he had of depicting himself naked now took on a more personal dimension. When one knows his style of "leaps and gambols," he can justifiably be considered disorganized or, as the Spanish ambassador in Paris put it, "somewhat addlepated."

Montaigne admits that he lacks flexibility, and he explains his mitigated political success by saying that he is too frank. Frankness can be perceived as a form of incivility, but it is more likely to be a kind of nonchalance or *sprezzatura*—to adopt the term used by Castiglione in his *Book of the Courtier*—but a nonchalance that is not feigned and does not make use of dissimulation. Often associated with a kind of "softness" (*mollesse*),[112] Montaigne's nonchalance claims to be natural, and is for that reason not ideal in society—contrary to what the author of the *Essais* might have believed in his diplomatic experiences—because it represents an end more than a means. Despite this disadvantage of being really what he appears to be in the eyes of others, Montaigne took pleasure in seeing a continuity in his instinctive naïveté, which can be perceived as a defect in politics, but was a revelation for an author whose remarks are always located between discourtesy and candor:

When I display to great men the same extreme freedom of tongue and bearing that I exercise in my own house, I feel how much it inclines toward indiscretion and incivility. But besides the fact that I am made that way, I have not a supple enough mind to sidestep a sudden question and escape it by some dodge, or to invent a truth, or a good enough memory to retain something thus invented, and certainly not enough assurance to maintain it; and I put on a bold face because of weakness. Therefore I give myself up to being candid and always saying what I think, by inclination and by reason, leaving it to Fortune to guide the outcome.[113]

However, we have to recognize that stripping oneself naked is far from corresponding to the political or diplomatic practices then current. We have the feeling that in the third book, Montaigne also engages in an analysis of his political experiences, whose failure he tries to explain. Nonetheless, this political bankruptcy is quickly transformed into an asset for the essayist. That may be how we should read the chapter titled "Of experience," at least in what could be considered the first draft of the 1588 edition, since this chapter was to be amply developed in the margins of the Bordeaux Copy between 1588 and 1592.

Starting in 1588, Montaigne made an increasing number of changes regarding the form of the *Essais* to the detriment of its content. People were beginning to praise his stripped-down prose and simplicity, and on this point, he was prepared to reply favorably to his critics. For instance, in 1588 the poet Tabourot des Accords praised the *Essais* and their "immaculate purity":

Whoever sees the immaculate purity
Of your writings, reads them with such a heart
As if it were some gentle work
He had himself once meditated:
Then, delighted by its simplicity,
Recognizing your inimitable style,
Adores you as were you a divinity
Since you are like no one but yourself.[114]

Everything suggests that, at first, Montaigne had not properly assessed the reception of his book. He might have addressed the wrong audience, and the form of the *Essais* seemed to many people to be superior to its content. Then Montaigne greatly increased his reflections on the form of his writing, going so far as to confess that he had never been made for negotiations. In short, his discourse was more in tune with the reactions to his book, which was lauded less for its political contribution in the public domain and the context of the Wars of Religion than for its private style:

I have naturally a humorous and familiar style, but of a form all my own, inept for public negotiations, as my language is in every way, being too compact, disorderly, abrupt, individual; and I have no gift for letters of ceremony that have no other substance than a fine string of courteous words. I have neither the faculty nor the taste for those lengthy offers of affection and service. I do not really believe all that, and I dislike saying much of anything beyond what I believe.[115]

This passage, added in 1588, allowed Montaigne to conclude that his style was "a far cry from present practice." From that time on, this became his principal claim. He felt that he had found a vein that had not been mined. After having known doubt and uncertainty, ignorance was soon to become his "ruling form" (*forme maistresse*). The author of the 1580 text now "smelled a bit foreign,"[116] and Montaigne struggled to recognize himself in his book: "How often and perhaps how stupidly I have extended my book to make it speak of itself!"[117]—as if he were gradually detaching himself from the book conceived in the 1570s. In 1588, Montaigne was already beginning to work up a theory of the transformation of the moral and political content of his *Essais* in a form that would be self-sufficient: "by long usage this form of mine has turned into substance."[118]

Imprisoned in the Bastille

In early May 1588, the printing of Montaigne's book was almost completed. During this time in Paris public rumor announced the arrival of Swiss garrisons. The confrontation between the duke of Guise and Henry III was inevitable. In a last attempt to assert his authority, the king forbade the duke of Guise to enter the city, but he also wanted to avoid armed conflict. Public opinion was not on his side, and the king understood that on the military level the Catholic extremists could also count on the support of the Spanish. Lucinge confirms that Henry III lived "in continual alarm regarding the Spanish army."[119] A test of strength with the duke of Guise had begun. Despite the orders given by the king, Guise disobeyed the monarch to show his own authority. Citizen militias united with the League troops, and the common people of Paris daily defied royal authority. Guise was presented as the savior, the "new Moses" or the "second Gideon." Accompanied by only seven gentlemen, he made his entrance into the capital on May 9 and was acclaimed as a liberator, "as if by a miracle,"[120] by the people won over to the League's cause. Fearing he would be assassinated, Henry III had holed up in the Tuileries palace. Montaigne was wary of the common people, whom he considered manipulated by political men seeking popular support for their personal ambitions: "I have in my time seen wonders in the undiscerning and prodigious ease with which peoples let their belief and hope be led and manipulated in whatever way has pleased and served their leaders."[121] Events would prove him right.

Henry III found himself with his back to the wall, and he had no solution but to harden his position. He no longer had the option of negotiating, and finally decided to show determination in the face of the League. This decision was a turning point in a policy that, up to this point, he had wanted to be conciliatory toward the princes of Lorraine. The dissidents were plotting with the duke of Guise to seize the sovereign during Lent. Henry III was secretly planning to take Paris, but the public rumor led to a rebellion of League supporters and a popular uprising against the sovereign, who had ordered a garrison of Swiss soldiers to enter the capital. These movements of foreign troops into the capital threw the people into a great terror. In a few hours, on May 12, 1588, barricades were erected against the Swiss garrisons, which had entered the capital at three o'clock that morning. The alarm bell was rung, and the bourgeois of the city, who considered their privileges to have been violated, organized themselves to resist the king and his mercenaries. After a brief political hesitation in which Henry III and the duke of Guise tried by turns to seize the advantage by means of intimidating maneuvers, it was the king who yielded first, and fearing for his life, secretly left the capital. The die was cast, and Montaigne once again found himself at the mercy of events.

As a loyalist among loyalists, and perhaps at the request of the queen mother, Montaigne accompanied the king in his flight. He had hardly any other political option. If it was difficult for him to choose between the king and Navarre, he had no scruples about opting for the royal party faced with the revolt in Paris, which, as we have said, was less an overthrow by the League than an uprising of the bourgeois of Paris who had revolted against the lack of respect for their privileges. Before the famous Council of Sixteen set up in January 1589,[122] the city of Paris was administered by forty or fifty bourgeois representing the sixteen quarters of the city. The bourgeois had expressed their resentment toward the royal government that had extorted considerable sums from them under cover of forced loans and greater and greater special tax levies (April 1576, September 1582, December 1583, January 1584), as well as a series of "free gifts," as in March 1577 and March 1584.[123] The "honorable men" (rich merchants) who constituted the "people of Paris" had rebelled against a king "thirsting for money,"[124] to use Pierre de L'Estoile's expression. By "people" we must thus understand the notables of the capital, chiefly the bourgeois who paid the municipal taxes and served in the militia. These men had their own idea of power, based on a sociability stitched together with common interests. They were not all rich (yet), but most of them were about to become rich. Their commitment on the side of the League was based on considerations that were more economic than religious, and they took hardly any interest in the political manipulations carried out by the zealous Catholics of the Guises' party.

Following the famous day of the barricades, the public coffers had been closed with the seal of the Guises, and the Louvre, the Arsenal, and other strategic places in the capital fell under their command. Jacques Carorguy summed up the situation rather well in his journal: "People are angry at the government."[125] This revolt created a grave crisis for the state, whose legitimate power was being challenged. The printing of the *Essais* was nearing completion when Montaigne made a fateful decision. After the day of the barricades, he hurriedly left Paris with the king, who had yielded to panic and projected a poor image of his authority. Sully tells us that when he fled, Henry III was accompanied by sixteen gentlemen and twelve valets, including Montpensier, Longueville, the count of Saint-Paul, the cardinal of Lenoncourt, the marshals Biron and Aumont, and the lord of La Guiche.[126] Was Montaigne part of this little group of loyalists? It is likely that he was, because that would explain the reprisals taken against him when he returned to Paris two months later. Catherine de Medici had remained in Paris to negotiate with the Guises. Lucinge writes that this flight "was so stunning that most of His Majesty's servants did not have time to take their boots, and worst fellows around him were the least confident. The King, with a very small entourage, went to sleep in a house owned by the lord of Rambouillet, and the next day slept in Chartres."[127] The king, accompanied by Cheverny and "a few other"[128] gentlemen, including Montaigne, arrived in Chartres on May 14. We do not know with certainty whether Montaigne then followed the king to Mantes and on to Rouen, but it is probable. This rather extraordinary episode put him back at the center of the political scene; following the king was a real wager.

On May 24, the duke of Guise demanded that the Estates General be immediately convoked. The same day, Mendoza, the Spanish king's ambassador, told the queen mother that the Armada had departed. The Spanish fleet had left Lisbon on May 9. The negotiations were going very badly for the king, whose image had been greatly tarnished by his flight. For a long time, his political and administrative decisions had seemed quite debatable, and this last incident didn't help. He tried to react by stripping Épernon of the offices he had obtained after Joyeuse's death.

Then began a period in which the Catholic extremists perceived each statement, each act as a provocation. The war was no longer between Navarre and Henry III but between the king the League. The king considered Navarre more than ever a potential ally to brake the League's aspirations. Forced to explain his desertion and to move closer to a people who no longer understood royal policy, on May 29 the king accepted all the Parisians' grievances and recognized that he had overburdened them with taxes; he regretted the disorders and admitted that he was in immense financial distress. According to him, all that was the fault of the heretics. After spending several weeks in Chartres, Henry III went to Rouen, where he made a solemn entry on June 13. During his stay in that city that had formerly been won over to the Protestant cause, he decided to convoke the Estates General to meet in Blois on September 15. In the Renaissance, the government usually traveled with the king. However, after his flight the Court ceremonial no longer had the same symbolic impact in the cities of the provinces, and in general the monarch's image was suffering from the delocalization of government. When Henry III established his capital at Tours in March 1589, he distanced himself still further from the people of Paris, who were quite satisfied to have driven him out of the city the preceding year. Moving the Court and the parlement away from the capital amounted to cutting himself off from a place that was highly symbolic for royal authority and thus to weakening the legitimacy of his power. More than any other city, Paris represented the kingdom's general interest, because historically it had enjoyed the privilege of speaking in the name of the other "good cities" of France.[129]

By the end of June, the king was ready to accept almost all the demands made by the princes of Lorraine: the formal renewal of the Edict of Union, a public declaration depriving the king of Navarre of his hereditary right, the appointment of Guise as constable, and the creation of secure places. These measures signified complete submission to the League, which thus put the king under its supervision. During this time, the religious purge had begun. In Paris, two sisters were hanged and then burned as "obstinate Huguenots."[130] The Guises had once again managed to polarize the conflict and to lump Henry III and Henry of Navarre together as enemies of the kingdom. Since July, bourgeois, royal officers, and *robins*, all suspect, had been arrested in the capital. A "bunch of League rascals"—the expression is Pierre de L'Étoile's—seized the reins of the city. Repression was rife. In this witch-hunt atmosphere, Montaigne decided to return to Paris. He chose a bad time, because the city was in a state of aggravated excitement. Several of the king's officers were expelled from the city and a few were imprisoned.

Meanwhile, Navarre had allowed himself to be convinced that the explosive situation prevailing between Henry III and the duke of Guise favored the Huguenot party. He informed Queen Elizabeth of England of the latest political developments in France and told her: "It is time . . . to make use of the occasions that present themselves, and the opportunity has never been greater."[131] Henry of Navarre was aware that the French crown was faltering. Concerned about the Spanish fleet, Henry III had no option other than to make peace with the princes of Lorraine, to whom he granted eight cities out of the twelve they had demanded. But this peace forced on Henry III could only lead to the continuation of the war. Lucinge's analysis is once again very accurate: "This peace will be the entry into a war, because the king promises everything and will not want to keep his promise, and the others [the League partisans] will be prepared to steal and carry off the prize at the slightest opportunity."[132] The people of Paris were backing the Guises more than ever, and the king was not about to set foot in the Louvre. Paris held financial power over the rest of the kingdom, and in the provinces the bourgeois in the capital were particularly detested, but they held the state's purse strings.

Montaigne was not in Paris when his book appeared. He was probably in Rouen, where he had followed the king with a few of his faithful servants. While the book was being printed, he had left Paris for Chartres, and then Rouen, where the king stayed until the beginning of July.[133] Pierre de Brach, who also seems to have joined the Court in Rouen, was still in that city on July 8, the anniversary of his wife's death, when he sent a letter to Justus Lipsius (who was living in Leiden), along with his portrait, which he had had engraved in Paris shortly before he fled.[134] We know that on May 10 or 11, 1588, Brach had his portrait drawn and then engraved for use as the frontispiece to his book.[xi] He may have taken Montaigne with him to an artist's studio.[135] Publishing history then coincides with history in general. Did Montaigne hesitate between two careers that suddenly appeared to open up to him? He was at the intersection of two distinct paths: author and political actor. He had to establish his priorities. On the one hand, he was concerned to oversee the printing of his book by one of the greatest Parisian booksellers, and on the other, he was tempted to follow a king in peril. He chose the second option. It was probably a poor choice, but he cannot be reproached for his loyalty during this decisive episode in the reign of Henry III. This man who was not inclined to rush into things found himself, for once, with no alternative. He had no liking for the

---

[xi] This engraved portrait was published only in 1596, on the occasion of his translation of *Quatre chants de la Hierusalemme de Torquato Tasso*, published by Abel L'Angelier. The custom was to have one's portrait made first, in order to provide the engraver with a design. This portrait of Pierre de Brach was sketched shortly before the day of the barricades and was ready in its engraved form in June 1588. We can conclude that Montaigne's famous portrait was made around the same time. The sketch of Montaigne, probably made by François Quesnel, was not engraved then, but rather taken back to Bordeaux to serve later on (after Montaigne's death) as a model for the engraving made by Thomas de Leu. This portrait of Montaigne might have been preserved by Pierre de Brach and found after his death in 1605; that would explain why it appeared so tardily to be used in the Paris edition of the *Essais* published in 1608. This hypothesis allows us to understand why Pierre de Brach did not keep Montaigne's engraving but rather an original drawing, probably made during their sojourn in Paris in 1588. It would then have been on the basis of this drawing that De Leu engraved—much later, between 1605 and 1608, after the death of Pierre de Brach—Montaigne's portrait.

Guises' aggressive practices, and his decision to follow the king had to do with both his unshakeable fidelity to the established government and his well-known aversion to sudden attacks and other methods of intimidation in matters of politics or diplomacy.

Montaigne's flight along with Henry III was the culmination of a political commitment that could have cost him his life. When he returned to Paris at the beginning of July, he took lodging in the Faubourg Saint-Germain, where an attack of gout forced him to stay in bed for three days. Officially, peace prevailed between the king and the duke of Guise, but reprisals were frequent. This violence was highly symbolic, and its function was to solidify the League's hold on the capital. On July 7, the king sent Alphonse d'Ornano to confirm to the Guises that the peace agreement was "resolved." On July 9, Lucinge stated that "yesterday, at the queen mother's apartments, the peace agreement was assured and the arrival of Mr de Villeroy alone confirmed that opinion."[136] On July 10, between three and four o'clock, in this climate of "apparent peace," Montaigne was taken prisoner. He was immediately incarcerated in the Bastille, on the order of the duke of Elbeuf, Charles I of Lorraine, "by right of reprisal" against the king of France, who had had a gentleman of the League imprisoned in Rouen.[137]

Villeroy, who was a state secretary, hurried to inform the Court and burst into a session of the Council with the result that the duke of Guise immediately signed an order releasing the prisoner and ending his incarceration. However, Montaigne was apparently not freed right away. On the evening of the same day, Catherine de Medici finally had Montaigne released as an "unprecedented favor." Montaigne had been detained only a few hours, but he nonetheless reported this traumatic incident in his almanac:

> 1588, between two and three in the afternoon, being lodged in the Faubourg S. Germain in Paris and sick with a kind of gout that had first set in three days before, I was taken prisoner by the captains and people of Paris. This was at the time when the king had been driven out by Monsieur de Guise. Taken to the Bastille, and I was told that it was at the behest of the duke of Elbeuf, by right of reprisal and as a counterpart of a gentleman relative of his whom the king was holding prisoner in Rouen. The queen mother of the king, informed of my imprisonment by Mr Pinard, state secretary, obtained from Monsieur de Guise, who happened to be with her, and from the provost of the merchants to whom she sent (Mr de Villeroy, state secretary, taking great care in my favor) to see to it that at eight in the evening of the same day one of Her Majesty's butlers came to free me by means of rescripts issued by the lord duke provost addressing the clerk then commanding the Bastille.[138]

Montaigne was freed thanks to Catherine de Medici and Michel Marteau, lord of La Chapelle, city councillor, *Seize*[xii] of the Saint-Innocents quarter and provost of the merchants since May 20. Marteau had been head of the League in Paris since 1587 and, according to Pierre L'Éstoile, he could be considered a "creature of the duke of Guise." Described as an "arch-Leaguer," Marteau had met Montaigne a few years earlier—in April 1581—at Loretto in Italy. The two men had sympathized, and Marteau had been able to ascertain that Montaigne was a good Catholic who had left in the church of Our Lady of Loretto, in "a little house, very old and mean," that had been transformed into a place of worship, an ex-voto that had cost nearly fifty crowns.[139] Recalling this mark of Catholic faith, Marteau facilitated Montaigne's liberation.[140] Not long afterward, Marteau was investigated because he had been accused of embezzlement. Set free that evening, Montaigne was able to pick up copies of his *Essais* that had been printed a few weeks earlier.

This imprisonment left its mark and for that reason was a crucial moment in Montaigne's political career. He offers a detailed account of this incident that contrasts with the brevity of other entries in his almanac. The circumstances of his arrest in Paris, a city controlled by the League, shook his confidence in a new approach to politics. His wager had turned into a fiasco, and once again, politics had not been good to him. Paris was a dangerous city that had been won over to the Guises' extremism, and Montaigne may have been in greater danger then than at any other time. A Gascon could be there only at the risk of his life. He understood this fact while he was weakened by a high fever that had struck him a few days earlier. Pierre de Brach described the state in which he found his friend the day after this misadventure. Even the doctors gave him up for lost. In addition to his health problems there were partisan hassles, and Montaigne had just been caught up in politics that went far beyond his worst expectations. His mission for the king of Navarre had achieved nothing, and it was another gentleman, François de Montesquiou, lord of Sainte Colombe, who continued the talks between Henry III and Navarre.

Exhausted and disillusioned by this Parisian misfortune, Montaigne left the capital and its political turmoil. In July–August or perhaps August–September he undertook the "two or three journeys" of several weeks to Gournay-sur-Aronde, in Picardy, not far from Compiègne, in the company of Marie de Gournay, to her family home. On July 15, five days after Montaigne's imprisonment, a peace treaty was signed, and the king finally resolved to publish, on July 21, the Edict of Union that sealed the reconciliation between Henry III and the League. He swore "never to make any peace agreement or truce with the heretics, or any edict in their favor."[141] Navarre was the great loser in this affair, and

---

[xii] The "Seize" (sixteen) was a council of bourgeois League supporters in Paris.

Montaigne could no longer expect anything from a situation that put an end to his ambitions as a negotiator. The Guises could savor their victory. Doubtless this was a defeat for the king and for Montaigne, and it is hard to imagine that Montaigne did not feel it to be such. In early September, Henry III dismissed all his ministers, abruptly separating himself from those who had counseled him for several years. Montaigne gave up on the past, accepted the invitation of the young Marie de Gournay, and accompanied her to her family's estate. It was in Picardy, far from the capital, that he recovered from his psychological wounds and decided to become a full-time author.

"A Girl in Picardy"

Seriously affected by this political setback that could have cost him his life, Montaigne almost immediately left the capital and its intrigues. He later recalled this trial, offering the following analysis of his experience in Paris in one of the margins of the Bordeaux Copy: "I ordinarily assist the unfair presumptions against me that fortune sows about by a way I have always had of avoiding justifying, excusing, and interpreting myself, thinking that it is compromising my conscience to plead for it."[142] It was better to forget this incident. Montaigne's imprisonment (at least as he relates it) likely caused him to become aware of the dangers of any political commitment, whatever it might be. His arrest led him to question his service to one party or another. After this failure, Montaigne visibly detached himself from the political affairs of his time. The "public ruin" anticipated a few years earlier, when he was entering politics on the national level, had just caught up with him and affected him personally. Public occupations were beginning to weigh on his physical and mental health. It was at this time that he met Marie de Gournay: a new chapter began for him and for his posterity.

Marie de Gournay was born in Paris on October 6, 1565, the first child of Guillaume Le Jars, the king's treasurer since 1563, and Jeanne de Hacqueville. In 1568, the Le Jars de Gournay family moved into the manor of Gournay-sur-Aronde in Picardy.[143] Self-taught, Marie discovered Montaigne's *Essais* in 1583–84, at the age of nineteen. She was bowled over by it, and fell in love with the book and its author. Marie de Gournay occupies a crucial place in the publishing history of the *Essais*. During the first half of the seventeenth century she worked tirelessly to have the work of her "adopted father" (*père d'alliance*) reprinted and accompanied throughout her life this "orphan entrusted to her," as she called the text of the *Essais* in the preface she addressed to Cardinal Richelieu in 1635. Learning that Montaigne was residing in Paris in 1588, she sent her greetings to the man whose works she admired, to "declare her esteem for his person and his book."[144] In a short autobiography written in the third person, Marie de Gournay says that at the age of "about eighteen or nineteen, this girl read the *Essais* by chance: and although they were still new and enjoyed no reputation that could guide her judgment, she not only assessed them at their true value, which was very difficult to do at such an age and in a century so little likely to bear such fruit, but conceived a desire to make the acquaintance of their author, more than anything else in the world."[145]

Flattered by the young woman's affectionate zeal, Montaigne came to visit her the following day. Thus began the relationship with the woman who became his "adopted daughter" (*fille d'alliance*) and who devoted herself body and soul to the publication of her "father's" writings until her death in 1645 at the age of eighty. In a letter to Monsieur de Pellejay, Estienne Pasquier recounts their first encounter:

> Demoiselle de Jars, who is related to several great and noble families in Paris; who never sought to have any husband other than her honor, enriched by the reading of good books; and above all others the *Essais* of the Lord of Montaigne; in the course of a long sojourn in the city of Paris in the year 1588, went expressly to visit him, to become acquainted with him personally. The Demoiselle de Gournay and her mother even took him to their house of Gournay, where he resided for three months in two or three trips, and was received with all the honor that could be desired.[146]

Gournay tells us that she received the Gascon gentleman "with all the more joy" because despite the great difference in their ages she had felt "in her heart such a connection with him since the first time she looked into his book: and that [was true] regarding the proportion of their ages, and the intention of their minds and manners."[147] It was truly love at first sight.

An impromptu, intense friendship formed between a man of fifty-five and his new admirer of twenty-three. More than ever resolved to get a change of air, Montaigne accepted the young woman's invitation and followed her to Gournay-sur-Aronde where, far from the tumult in Paris, he began to write further additions in the margins of a copy of the new edition of the *Essais* that had just been printed in Paris. Perhaps it was after having told her about the ups and downs of his secret mission to the king that Montaigne opened his book at the place where he had sketched a portrait of Navarre, without directly naming him:

> I know a man [here Montaigne adds on the Bordeaux Copy: "of a very martial courage by nature, and enterprising"] whose fine career is being corrupted every day by such persuasions: that he should hear of no reconciliation with his former enemies, should keep apart and not trust himself

to hands stronger than his own, whatever promise may be made him, whatever advantage he may see in it.[148]

In the margin of this text, Montaigne had Marie de Gournay write:

I know another who has advanced his fortune beyond all expectations by following a wholly opposite plan. Boldness, the glory of which they [princes] seek so avidly, displays itself, when necessary, as magnificently in a doublet as in armor, in a room as in a camp, with arm hanging as with arm raised.[149]

In what is probably the first addition in the margins of what was to become the Bordeaux Copy, Gournay expresses a political observation through another person, as if Montaigne were no longer capable of making this political commentary himself (figure 16). He took pleasure in his role as author and commentator, and the young Marie was delighted to serve as his secretary.[150] Writing in the margins had just been born in him. At that precise instant, Montaigne found a new career: he would be a writer, period. An audience—other than the king and high government officials, and even his friends and relatives—existed for his book, and it was young Marie who made him aware of that.

At Gournay-sur-Aronde, Montaigne had plenty of time to discuss his experiences as a skillful negotiator and familiar of princes. Full of bitterness and still exhausted by his recent difficulties in the capital, he sketched portraits of the king and of Navarre that were not very flattering. In the first part of the passage quoted above, an allusion to Henry III and Henry IV has been seen in the description of the second prince added later on the Bordeaux Copy. However, one of Florimond de Raemond's annotations suggests a different identification that corresponds better to the political reality of the moment and to Montaigne's state of mind after his brief incarceration at the Bastille. Without hesitation, Raemond recognizes Navarre in the description of the first prince: "He is referring to King Henry IV, to whom he was very close when he was Henry of Navarre." In the other prince, Raemond sees not Henry III but rather Henry of Guise: "He is referring to M. de Guise: but he is mistaken, since good fortune abandoned him [Guise] at Blois, where he was killed."[151] The first prince, more martial and enterprising, rational in nature but badly counseled by Huguenot warmongers, corresponds to Montaigne's conception of Henry of Navarre in 1588. The passage about his martial courage and his enterprising character, added after 1588, could serve to ensure that the first prince mentioned would not be confused with Henry III. Since in that case the second description could not refer to Henry III, Raemond's interpretation seems completely justified, because the person mainly responsible for France's ills in 1588 was the duke of

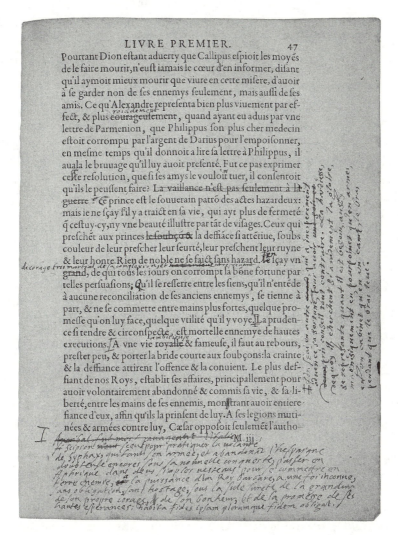

FIGURE 16. Manuscript addition by Marie de Gournay, Bordeaux Copy of the *Essais*, f. 474. Image courtesy of Bibliothèque municipale de Bordeaux.

Guise. This contrasting, off-the-cuff political description of the second prince, made before the assassination of the duke of Guise in Blois on December 23, 1588, might have been written by Montaigne after his return to Bordeaux in November. Another passage in the *Essais* speaks in the same way of Catherine de Medici as if she were still alive, whereas she died only thirteen days after Henry of Guise. Montaigne accuses Henry of Navarre of having made the wrong choice, but it is Henry of Guise who is the object of Montaigne's wrath. Without the duke of Guise's implacable political rigidity, Montaigne might have been able to carry out his mission successfully. In the autumn of 1588, he no longer had any hope of playing a political role. Nevertheless, he had met a young woman determined to devote the rest of her life to spreading the fame of her "adoptive father." Although he had not yet realized the consequences of this meeting, Montaigne had just found the ideal literary agent who was to allow him soon to be recognized as a major author of the French Renaissance.

Without knowing it, Montaigne was going to go down in history thanks to Marie de Gournay. He claimed to be completely detached from the political world, and the separation between public and private life was clearer than ever. The famous Bordeaux Copy was born at Gournay, and Montaigne conceived at that time the possibility of an expanded edition. At Gournay, Montaigne guided the hand of his unconditional admirer to help her intervene directly in what was to become, seven years later, the first posthumous edition of the *Essais*. At least two manuscript additions on the Bordeaux Copy are in the hand of Marie de Gournay, including at least one that dates from this time.[152] Montaigne's first stay in Picardy, between mid-July and October 16—the date of the opening of the Estates General in Blois, which he attended as a simple spectator—influenced the orientation of the *Essais*, which was henceforth literary and personal.

Marie de Gournay's temperament was demonstrative, indeed almost exuberant. Her lavish affection apparently did not displease Montaigne, who sojourned at Gournay two or three times during the autumn of 1588. He was warmly received at the Gournay's family home in Picardy, about one day's journey from the capital. In the dedicatory epistle of her *Proumenoir de Monsieur de Montaigne*, dated November 26, 1588, Marie de Gournay reports that Montaigne had left Gournay-sur-Aronde three days earlier, that is, on November 23. One passage—different on the Bordeaux Copy and in the *Exemplar*[xiii]—emphasizes that Montaigne saw Marie de Gournay *before* he went to the Estates General at Blois: "[1595: When I came from these famous Estates of Blois] I have seen [1595: I had just seen, in Picardy], a girl, to show the ardor of her promises, and also her constancy, strike herself, with the bodkin she wore in her hair, four or five lusty stabs in the arm, which broke the skin and made her bleed in good earnest."[153] In the Bordeaux Copy, this passage includes no reference to the Estates General and does not identify the region where Marie de Gournay

---

[xiii] The *Exemplar* is the name given to another copy of the 1588 edition with marginalia and corrections in the hand of Montaigne that served to produce the posthumous edition of the *Essais* in 1595. Destroyed during the fabrication of the 1595 edition (as it was usual at that time), the *Exemplar* was a cleaner copy than the Bordeaux Copy. The Bordeaux Copy remained at the château. Since the two copies were not identical, slight variations exist today between the 1595 edition of the *Essais* and editions based on the Bordeaux Copy.

resided. On the other hand, the *Exemplar* that was used to compose the posthumous edition of the *Essais*, published in 1595, gives us this information. We can imagine that it was perhaps added by Marie de Gournay. Similarly, a long passage in the 1595 edition is also absent from Montaigne's manuscript, but an *X* marks the placement of an addition that might have been written on a separate piece of paper (*brouillar*). However, Montaigne was not in the habit of writing on separate sheets and he had plenty of space to add this passage in the margin of the Bordeaux Copy. Doubts remain regarding the veracity of the information given by Marie de Gournay in the 1595 edition. In this passage in the posthumous edition of the *Essais*, Marie de Gournay is named, whereas her name does not appear in the Bordeaux Copy. She might have revised Montaigne's text to give herself a more important role. We know that she had a tendency to take certain liberties in her work as an editor. For example, her rewriting of half the verses of Ronsard's "Harangue du Duc de Guise aux Soldats de Metz" in 1624 deprives her of part of her editorial credibility. By trying to restore the prestige of the poets of the Pléiade in the time of Malherbe, she produced a counterfeit, claiming to have discovered a later version of Ronsard's poem.[154] It is thus permissible to have certain reservations about Gournay's account.

In reality, Montaigne probably made three trips to Gournay-sur-Aronde: two during his sojourn in Paris and a final one after a brief stay in Blois. Long walks with her adoptive father led Marie de Gournay to write a book titled *Proumenoir de Monsieur de Montaigne* (Walk with Monsieur de Montaigne). They read ancient authors together. Montaigne was fond of learned conversations. It was in the course of a walk on the grounds of the château, after reading Plutarch together, that Marie is supposed to have told him the story that she had put down in writing in 1584 and that she renamed *Proumenoir de Monsieur de Montaigne*. This story was inspired by a work of Claude de Taillemont, *Les Discours des Champs Faëz*. We imagine the romantic scene, and it is probable that Montaigne and Marie had an amorous relationship. In a passage that she later omitted, Marie de Gournay admits that Montaigne "loved her much more than paternally." In another passage in the *Exemplar* that was used to compose the posthumous edition of 1595—but which, suspiciously, does not appear in the Bordeaux Copy—we find the following reference to Marie de Gournay: "She is now the only one I see in the world." Montaigne describes an affection for the young woman that is "more than superabundant." He then lauds this young prodigy's intellectual feats and gives her, in book II, chapter 17, the title of "adoptive daughter" (*fille d'alliance*). The compliments go far beyond simple marks of friendship and suggest a more romantic adventure: "Her judgment of the first *Essays*, as a woman, and in this century, and so young, and alone in her region, and the extraordinary vehemence with which she loved and long desired me on the sole basis of the esteem she had for me, before she had seen me, is a circumstance very worthy of consideration."[155] Critics have often maintained that this passage could not have been written by Montaigne, and accused Gournay of having invented and imagined a relationship that she never had with the author of the *Essais*. Even if these words might have been added by Marie de Gournay, nothing allows us to assert that they are the result of fantasizing.

To forestall the gossips who might be astonished by her relation with Montaigne, Marie de Gournay explains that "if someone is shocked by the fact that we were father and daughter only in name . . . we shall say to him that nature holds the scepter among animals, but among men reason must hold it."[156] We can rightly speak of Marie's fascination with Montaigne. At that time, she had not yet written anything, and it is not impossible that Montaigne found in her something other than an opportunity for erudite conversations about Plutarch and other philosophers. It has also been suggested that Marie de Gournay made use of him to advance her own career. That may not be entirely false, but Montaigne had done the same with La Boétie twenty years earlier. Hadn't he given Marie to understand that he could help her in this domain? During his stay at Gournay, he even gave her a diamond: "the diamond bodkin he gave me bears the symbol of a double 'm m' in a circle."[157] This gift was very costly for a simple friendship, and may have had a more sentimental value. Marie decided to return the jewel to Montaigne's daughter after meeting her during her stay at the château after the death of her "adoptive father" in 1592. Marie Le Jars de Gournay's will, drawn up in 1596, stipulates that if she happened to die in Gascony (one wonders why, since at that time she was living in Paris), she wished to be buried—like Montaigne—in the church of the Feuillants in Bordeaux, and she gave the convent a hundred crowns for her burial.[xiv] But she was never buried there.

After a very hectic summer, Montaigne spent several months in Picardy, with Marie, and far from the political turmoil of the Court. This retreat "in two or three journeys" of several weeks each in the company of the demoiselle de Gournay helped him distance himself from the events of his time.[158] The 1588 edition of the *Essais* had transformed him into an author capable of independent judgment and detached from the affairs of the world. Ultimately, Montaigne was not a man who reacted hastily to events, or at least that was the image of himself that he sought to project between 1588 and 1592. The famous

---

[xiv] Marie de Gournay also returned to Léonor de Montaigne the receipt she had received from her for the furniture that she had left in the château before returning to Picardy in July 1595, after having prepared the posthumous edition of the *Essais*. She eventually made her a present of this furniture "both for the good offices and friendship received from her, for which I feel very obliged, and for being descended from an adoptive father and for offices which I can never return."

portrayal of the self—in its movement, but also in its atemporality—established itself as a goal. In the meantime, he could concentrate on the pleasures of a body that was returning to life. Was he seduced by the young woman's grandiloquence, or did he see in her instead an opportunity for a more carnal than intellectual relationship? Today, Montaigne's sexuality is dealt with prudishly; it is a taboo question, hidden behind his literary and philosophical renown. In contrast, Florimond de Raemond, who was close to the author of the *Essais*, sketches a portrait of a "wanton and debauched" man:

> I have often heard the author say that he had married his very beautiful and pleasant wife while he was still full of love, ardor, and youth, and yet he had never played with her except with respect for the honor that the marital bed requires, without ever having seen uncovered more than her hand and her face, not even her breast, although with other women he was extremely wanton and debauched. I leave the truth of what I say about this on his conscience.[159]

La Boétie had made similar reproach to Montaigne in the early 1560s. As we have noted, Montaigne's wife, Françoise de La Chassaigne, is one of the major absences in the *Essais*. Montaigne never confounds love and marriage, women and *his* woman. For him a married woman (his wife) lacks any feminine attribute, he transforms her into an asexual object. Marriage is a dead end that can give rise only to a series of banal comments; it is a fixed point that is not very compatible with Montaigne's way of writing, which is all movement, freedom, and development. That may be why his wife has no place in his book. Only the entrance into marriage is free; the rest is only constraint; it is a contract that has goals other than love, because there are "a thousand foreign tangles to unravel, enough to break the thread and trouble the course of a lively affection."[160]

For example, in the chapter "On some verses of Virgil," Montaigne reproaches Virgil for having depicted "a marital Venus," "a little too passionate," in terms too sensual.[161] This contradicts his idea of sexuality in marriage. For "In this sober contract [marriage] the appetites are not so wanton [Bordeaux Copy: *follastres*]; they are dull and more blunted."[162] Sleeping alone seems to him the ideal way to spend one's nights: "I like to sleep hard and alone, even without a woman, in the royal style."[163] It was outside marriage that Montaigne gave birth to his only male progeny: the *Essais* long remained a bastard child, and Marie de Gournay first its nurse, and then its tutor. After 1588, Montaigne was more concerned than ever to ensure the transmission of his name through his book, which was born of the muses but was raised after his death by Marie de Gournay, who strove ceaselessly to make better known this "orphan" for which she felt responsible.

Like her adoptive father, Marie de Gournay became hooked on literature and published her first work, *Le Proumenoir de Monsieur de Montaigne*, in 1594, which she says she sent to Montaigne in manuscript form in 1588. In 1589, after introducing herself as one of his close friends, she entered into regular correspondence with Justus Lipsius. This epistolary relationship lasted a decade before it began to deteriorate in 1601. In a letter in French addressed to Moretus and dated December 27, 1601, Justus Lipsius writes: "I once praised this French lady, and am not very happy about the judgment I made of her, and (perhaps) others are not, either. It is a deceiving sex, and it has more luster than substance."[164] Justus Lipsius was not the only one who quarreled with Marie, who was the object of the gibes and jeers of many of her contemporaries. The intellectual class gave her a hard time, going so far as to call her an "old maid," a "bluestocking," "witch," "counterfeiter," "old madwoman" or "old virgin" (she never married). She was the laughingstock of her time, and her "incestuous" relations (was she not his adoptive daughter?) with Montaigne were often stressed to prove her bad faith. She was violently attacked in an *Anti-Gournay ou Remerciement des Buerrières de Paris*, and was ridiculed in a *Comédie des Académistes*. Despite these sexist prejudices, Marie de Gournay took part in the intellectual life of her time and frequented the salons of libertine thinkers such as La Mothe Le Vayer and Théophile de Viau.

Although it is undoubtedly true that she was not very diplomatic, Marie de Gournay's main misfortune was to be a learned woman in a period dominated by men of letters. She was one of the first to defend the cause of women, and after 1607 she reworked, for instance, a long passage of the *Proumenoir* in order to publish it under the title *Égalité des hommes et des femmes* (1622). Along with the "Grief des Dames" published in the first edition of her works in 1626, this text now gives her a justified reputation as a feminist. Her long walks at Gournay in Montaigne's company were far more beneficial to her than has been thought, and like Montaigne, she never ceased revising her works to transform them and adapt them to the expectations of her period. Thus in 1634 a new edition of her works originally published in 1626 appeared under the title *Les Advis, ou, les Presens de la demoiselle de Gournay*, completely reorganized and enriched by previously unpublished pieces. In 1641, she published a final edition of her *Advis*, again rearranged. Montaigne had at least produced a follower in the way of conceiving a text in perpetual movement.

The encounter between Marie de Gournay and Montaigne allowed the *Essais* to be "transported" from the sixteenth to the seventeenth century.[xv] Mon-

---

[xv] Numerous reprintings of the *Essais* revised by Marie de Gournay appeared in the early seventeenth century, up to the famous 1635 edition with its dedicatory epistle to Cardinal Richelieu. This was the last edition overseen by Gournay, and it marks the end

taigne's editorial work served as a model for the young woman who was in her turn driven to deal with editorial minutiae. She went over with a fine-toothed comb every printed copy of her "adoptive father's" writings, correcting by hand the smallest typographical error and the defective punctuation or spelling on the copies she had in her possession. She was reproached for this excess of zeal, and the battle between the Bordeaux Copy and the 1595 edition that she prepared for Abel L'Angelier was a battle for the right to Montaigne's text. What is its precise legitimacy? It can be justifiably argued that the practice of the margins resulted from Montaigne's sojourn at Gournay-sur-Aronde, and that Marie de Gournay was a revelation that led to Montaigne's distancing from politics and allowed him to recover the essence of life, namely, the body and its affects. The meeting—we might call it an adventure—between Montaigne and Gournay was short. In November 1588, he left the young woman and never saw her again. She seems also to have forgotten him for almost four years, because we have no correspondence between them. She learned of Montaigne's death indirectly, and then she devoted herself entirely to her role as the editor of his *Essais*.

Observer at the Estates General of Blois

Under the constraint of the princes of Lorraine, Henry III convoked the Estates General in Blois for September 15, 1588, twelve years after the last session of this assembly in the same city. Since the death of the duke of Anjou in 1584, the League had benefited from considerable favor among the people, and a large number of cities and provinces had joined the ranks of the Union. On September 6, the king had dismissed all his state ministers. Bellièvre, Pinard, and Brulard had been sidelined in the hope of breaking with the royal policies of the preceding two years, thus marking an opening. He named Montholon, Ruzé, and Revol to replace them and kept at his side only his most faithful supporters, all of them devoted to his interests. The work of the Estates General began on September 16, the day after the king arrived in Blois. On October 2, all the deputies had not yet arrived. The meeting places were distributed and rooms were allotted to the representatives of the three orders: the clergy was lodged at the convent of the Jacobins, the nobility in the palace, and the third estate in the city hall.[165] The nobility of the duchy of Guyenne and the sénéchaussée of Bordeaux were represented by Jacques d'Escars, lord of Merville, grand seneschal of Guyenne, governor of the château of Le Hâ—and Montaigne's enemy.

---

of a journey in twenty stages: twenty editions of the *Essais* since Montaigne's death in 1592, eleven of them under her direction.

The third estate of Guyenne was represented by Thomas de Pontac, a councillor of the king on the Great Council and clerk of the parlement of Bordeaux; Fronton du Verger, a lawyer at the parlement of Bordeaux and a jurat of the city; and Pierre de Métivier, also a lawyer at the parlement. Mathurin Bertin, canon, archdeacon, and vicar general of the archbishopric of Bordeaux, represented the clergy. Publicly, the reconciliation the king sought started out well, but secretly the die was already cast. Out of the 191 deputies of the third estate, more than 150 were overt supporters of the League. Obviously, the clergy was almost entirely won over to the Guises' cause. Only the nobility, with 180 representatives, was divided; nonetheless, it mostly supported Henry III.

After the usual protests and quarrels regarding questions of protocol and precedence between the deputies of the various provinces, the 505 members representing the three orders constituted themselves as a deputation. The kingdom's nine governments still had to agree on the terms of the remonstrances that would be addressed to the king, the representatives of the third estate fearing for their security if they gave the impression of being won over to the clergy (controlled by the Guises) even before they had officially assembled. La Chapelle Marteau, the provost of Paris, was elected president of the third estate. This was the same Marteau whom Montaigne had met in Italy and who had helped get him released from the Bastille. Cardinal Guise and Charles I of Cossé, count of Brissac, presided over the clergy and the nobility respectively. The grand master of the Estates remained Henry of Guise, who made use of the Estates General to establish his power over the three orders. On October 5, while awaiting the opening of the *cahiers*,[xvi] debate began regarding how the complaints and remonstrances of the provinces and bailiwicks about the subsidies, tax levies, and past edicts would be reported. These preparations, which were customary on such occasions, in no way suggested the extreme violence that was to mark this assembly convoked by Henry III.

The official session opening the Estates General took place on October 16; it began with a speech given by the king "in which he did not forget to express his complaints, in covert words, concerning past things and the contempt and bypassing to which he was subjected."[166] As agreed, in his inaugural discourse Henry III asked for the renewal of the Edict of Union, the defense of the Roman Catholic faith, and the abolition of the Protestant heresy, but he could not refrain from criticizing "all the other leagues [that] ought not to exist under my authority." This remark was, obviously, badly received by the supporters of the League. Two days later, while the king's speech was being printed, the duke of Guise insisted that this reference to the League be omitted. The queen

---

[xvi] The "Cahiers de doléance" were lists of grievances drawn up by each of the three estates. [Trans.]

mother advised her son to compromise, and the passage was finally suppressed. This new insult to royal authority set the tone for the rest of the assemblies' work. After he swore to drive out the heretics, Henry III thought he had finally succeeded in rallying a majority of the representatives behind him. Étienne Bernard, a lawyer at the parlement of Dijon and a deputy for the third estate of that city, shared the king's illusion and reported that all the princes went away satisfied, "accompanied by the common consent and the general voice of the whole people, crying *vive le roi* and displaying an extreme joy and delight."[167] On October 21, the king commanded the aldermen of Paris to set off fireworks, have the *Te Deum* sung, and fire a cannonade to thank God for the confirmation of the Union. The deputies of the three estates committed themselves to the firm intention to expel and exterminate the kingdom's heretics. This joy was ephemeral, because the political and religious cleavages remained untouched.

During this time, Montaigne was still in Gournay-sur-Aronde. In his heart, he still believed in an entente that would make it possible to avoid the precipice that awaited the principal political actors of his age. Constantly seeking balance and moderation, over the past decade he had developed a new conception of politics, independent of simple conjunctural analyses and the bellicose reactions that almost always followed them. That was why the Estates General represented for Montaigne a true hope of reconciliation. Curious about the latest developments and the final negotiations, and to see a few friends who were attending as spectators or participating as representatives to these Estates General, Montaigne abandoned Marie de Gournay to go to Blois, where he met Antoine de Laval, Estienne Pasquier, and Jacques-Auguste de Thou, whom he advised to agree to replace André Hurault de Maisse as ambassador to Venice.[168]

In his *Mémoires*, De Thou reports in great detail the remarks Montaigne made concerning his role as a negotiator:

Michel de Montaigne . . . had, before and after the sedition in Paris, accompanied the Court to Chartres and to Rouen, and he was then also present in Blois; he was a great friend of Jacques, and urged him every day to seriously consider the ambassadorship to Venice that had been offered him. . . . Montaigne was thinking of going to Venice himself, and said he was ready to keep Jacques company as long as he stayed in that city. Now, reasoning on the causes of these troubles, he said—for he had once served as an intermediary between Navarre and Guise when they were both at the Court—that Guise had tried to win Navarre's friendship by means of all the good offices and all the zeal possible; but when, deceived and hypocritically rejected by the man whose friendship he had sought and whose favor he thought he had won, he understood that in him he had an enemy of the most implacable kind, and he had been obliged to take up arms as the ultimate resort to defend his person and the honor of his house; this enmity that had begun to oppose them to one another had flared up in the conflagration of this war, whose end he foresaw only with the death of one or the other. All this because Guise believed that as long as Navarre lived, and as long as he himself remained alive, neither of them could defend his right to succeed to the throne. As for religion, which they both emphasized, it was a good pretext for their followers, but neither of them cared about it. Navarre, had he not feared being abandoned by his people, would have been quite ready to return to the religion of his ancestors; and Guise, if he could have done so without risk, would not have hesitated to accept the Augsburg Confession, of which his uncle Charles, the cardinal, had once given him a foretaste. That was the state of mind in which Montaigne found them both at the time when he served as their intermediary.[169]

This conversation attributed to Montaigne makes him a passive actor at the Estates General, an observer who seems to have put the history of the civil wars behind him. It was as a spectator, and with a certain distance, that he met the representatives in private. Disillusioned, he broadened his analysis to religion, which he saw as accessory to politics. He did not imagine that he was in the eye of the storm.

The negotiations to which De Thou refers necessarily preceded the death of the duke of Anjou, and thus took place toward the end of the 1570s.[170] However, there is reason to doubt the remarks De Thou reported. Hasn't he mixed up the nature of the missions entrusted to Montaigne? It is improbable that Montaigne was able to negotiate directly between the duke of Guise and Henry of Navarre, or to serve Henry III as a messenger, as he had done on several occasions in the early 1570s. De Thou seems to have confused Guise with Henry III.

One thing seems certain: in Blois, Montaigne did not get involved in such matters. He was more interested in the psychology of the historical actors. De Thou tells us that he even considered going to Venice to serve him as a guide. Disappointed by his own failures as a negotiator, Montaigne was convinced that religion had become a pretext, and that the true stakes involved were mainly political: "both of them are pretending [to be concerned about religion],"[171] he said of Henry of Guise and Henry of Navarre. Estienne Pasquier also met Montaigne in Blois. Their discussion bore solely on the language of the *Essais*, and Pasquier offered the following comment on Montaigne's book: "And as we were walking in the courtyard of the château [of Blois], I happened to say to him that he had somewhat forgotten that he had not communicated his work to a few of his friends before publishing it."[172] Thus we can say that Montaigne was in Blois more to promote his book and present himself as an author than truly to participate in the three orders' debates. He certainly claimed to be an "expert," because he had also been close to power, but his book now sufficed to make him a recognized and respected man.

On November 1, the nobility had compiled its *cahier*, but the third estate was behind schedule. Distressed to see the king's authority ridiculed and "debased by his excessive patience,"[173] De Thou thought of leaving Blois. On November 4, the clergy invited the third estate to join in the recommendations it planned to make to the king to send an army to Guyenne, "which was the most desolate and ravaged by the heretics."[174] In line with the League's positions, most of the deputies wanted to ensure that no heretical pretender could accede to the throne. The clergy was determined "not to accept as king, or swear obedience to any prince who is a heretic or an abettor of heresy" (article 3). Proposed by the clergy, the term "abettor of heresy" (*fauteur d'hérésie*) sought to exclude the possibility of a conversion on the part of Henry of Navarre. Étienne Bernard wrote in his journal that the clergy even proposed to declare Navarre "guilty of lèse-majesté divine and human."[175] Three-quarters of the clergy's deputies being League supporters, they constantly presented proposals offensive to the sovereign, who nonetheless saw himself forced to remain impassive.[176] On November 5, 6, and 7, the situation in Guyenne was discussed. The three orders declared themselves resolved to "no longer seek the king of Navarre; that he was a rotten limb, and that being excommunicated, he could in no way be recognized by them."[177] The representatives of the third estate passed a resolution asking the king to give the government of Guyenne to a Catholic prince and not to a heretic.

A proposal was made to exclude from the crown all those who had been heretics since the age of fourteen and those who, since 1585, had shown themselves to be heretical. This proposal aimed at Henry of Navarre without naming him was finally omitted, and it was decided to be satisfied with the Edict of Union. After these deliberations, each more absurd than the last, Montaigne understood that there was no longer anything to be expected from the Estates General and decided to leave for Gournay-sur-Aronde. In the course of October, he left Blois to visit Marie de Gournay one last time. The spectacle of a weakened king was sad, and the situation in Guyenne was more explosive than ever. After a brief stay at Gournay, Montaigne set out (without going through Blois again) for his château on November 23.[xvii] He was back in Guyenne by the beginning of December, before Guise's assassination.

The assemblies' political work ended in late October, and the month of November was devoted primarily to economic questions. The third estate had be-

[xvii] In her dedicatory epistle in the *Proumenoir de Monsieur de Montaigne*, dated November 26, 1588, Marie de Gournay states that Montaigne had left Gournay-sur-Aronde three days earlier.

come involved in a series of considerations regarding the analysis of the baili-wicks' *cahiers*, the auditing of accounts, and various discussions on taxes and finances. On November 24, an agreement was reached among the three orders for the reduction of the *tailles* to the rate in force in 1576. The king promised to cut expenditures, requiring only three million crowns for "the maintenance of his royal dignity" and two million for his armies in Guyenne and the Dauphiné, out of a total state revenue of nine million crowns. However, these concessions made by the king were untenable on the financial level, but that was no longer what was at stake for a king who was now concerned only with his political survival. It was in accord with the same logic that, on December 3, the king granted all the third estate's requests without worrying about their applicabil-ity. These unexpected concessions, which were more political than realistic, were followed by applause.

Henry III was gaining time, and he was prepared to make the boldest and most completely unrealizable compromises. The discussions got lost in endless negotiations. The question of the chamber of justice was one of the most labori-ous points to be settled. The king yielded to all the demands, and every day his humiliation became a little more evident. On December 16, the king decided to avenge himself for all these affronts. After three months of hesitations, one thing was clear: the majority of the representatives of the Estates General sup-ported the princes of Lorraine. Henry III now believed that all his problems could be solved by the duke of Guise's death. He could no longer bear the con-stant hostility during the endless mediations and he put together the conspiracy that hastened his end a few months later.

On December 23, during a general session of the assemblies, Henry of Guise fell into a trap. Brought in on the pretext of a private meeting in the king's cabi-net, he was stabbed to death. His brother Louis, Cardinal Guise, his son Charles, the archbishop of Lyon, Pierre d'Espinac, Cardinal Bourbon, and the chief supporters of the duke of Guise were all arrested. The following day, Car-dinal Guise was assassinated in prison. The representatives of the Estates Gen-eral were stupefied to learn of the assassination of the duke of Guise and his brother. Panic spread through the city. The representatives of the third estate slept in a single room because they were afraid to be alone. It was decided to close the *cahiers* as soon as possible. Several deputies of the third estate were held prisoner. Henry III tried to insert several articles relating to the crime of lèse-majesté, but the deputies refused to follow him in this and did not want to meet in conference. Threatened and fearful, they continued their work. The king had certainly regained his authority, but at what cost?

Thinking that he had the representatives of the three orders under his con-trol again, the king ordered them to choose four deputies to deliberate on the *cahiers*, but he was met with a stinging refusal by the third estate. On January 4,

1589, the *cahiers* were finally submitted to the king. The deputies, fearing for their lives, now had only one thing on their minds: leaving Blois as soon as possible. The king took advantage of the situation to demand new subsidies, but again met with refusal. The closing session of the Estates General was held on January 15, and two days later all the sessions ended. By resorting to terror, the king had lost his prestige, or at least what remained of it. The results of this policy based on terror were obviously short-lived. Henry III had not obtained the subsidies he was counting on, and the *cahiers* presented to him did not lead to any true reform. Sully expressed rather well the state of mind that prevailed when the Estates General closed: "Every deputy returned to his province, his heart sick with hatred and vengeance."[178]

"Actum est de Gallia"

The Estates General of 1588 singly effected a deepening of the already existing political cleavages. They were more an occasion for a theatrical political confrontation than for genuine negotiation among the constituted orders and the sovereign. When he learned of the assassination of the duke of Guise, the lieutenant of Blois turned to Étienne Bernard and said: "Actum est de Gallia." "France is done for!" Reconciled, Henry III and Henry of Navarre besieged Paris in May 1589. The two kings were opposed militarily to the Catholic extremists and indirectly to the pope's authority over the Roman Apostolic Church. A deep hatred for what was perceived as a betrayal was concentrated on the person of Henry III. In the people's eyes, the king had become a tyrant. On August 1, 1589, seven months after the closure of the Estates General, Navarre abandoned the siege, more out of impotence than as a result of a strategic choice. The following day, on August 2, as the king was preparing a new attack on Paris, a young Dominican friar by the name of Jacques Clément, under the pretense of delivering documents to the monarch, plunged a knife in the abdomen of Henry, who passed away a few hours later. Before his death, Henry III had time to exhort those present to pledge allegiance to the new king: Henry of Navarre. This reconciliation was achieved at the expense of the League. Navarre had sought without success to retake Paris while at the same time showing consideration for the Catholics. Once he became Henry IV, he tried again to enter the capital, but without success. He had to wait until 1594 to set foot in Paris, and even then only after having publicly abjured his Protestant faith in Saint-Denis on July 25, 1593, almost a year after Montaigne's death.

After the Estates General and the wave of assassinations that had decimated a great part of the political class, the time had come for Montaigne to note the failure of political talks to pacify Bordeaux, Guyenne, and France:

I once tried to employ in the service of public dealings ideas and rules for living as crude, green, and unpolished—or unpolluted—as they were born in me or derived from my education, and which I use, [Bordeaux Copy: if not] conveniently [Bordeaux Copy: at least surely], in private matters: a scholastic and novice virtue. I found them [Bordeaux Copy: inept and] dangerous for such matters. He who walks in the crowd must step aside, keep his elbows in, step back or advance, or even leave the straight way, according to what he encounters.[179]

This passage, written before 1588, but reworked after the dramatic events that took place after his return to his estate, serves as a political balance sheet. On rereading it, Montaigne was able to realize to what extent his analysis made him a visionary. He said he was disgusted with his experience of public life, but he retained all the same a little ambition deep within him. However, nobody seemed to attach much importance to him. Bitter at having been manipulated by Navarre and questioning Henry III's political will, Montaigne attributed his failure mainly to the League, which was incapable of the slightest compromise. Although little inclined to criticize royal authority directly, he proved more discreet regarding Henry III's political decisions and the tragic consequences of his multiple flip-flops.

Montaigne's Parisian misadventure, which was ultimately connected with a bad choice, cannot be understood solely as the outcome of a turbulent political trajectory whose limits, and especially whose redoubtable consequences, he was beginning to perceive. He continued to write his essays, but they could no longer have the same goal or the same audience. The episode of his imprisonment in the Bastille in July 1588 had marked a decisive turning point for him. This ordeal hastened once and for all the end of his political ambitions. In the impassioned, violent context leading to "public ruin" between 1585 and 1588, his dependency on the "favors of others" led him to give up politics to begin a career as an author, the only career that could allow him to transmit his name down through history.

Rejecting the history outside his book, Montaigne chose to keep silent about the events that took place between 1588 and 1592. In his *Essais*, he mentions neither the duke of Guise's assassination nor that of Henry III; on the other hand, in his almanac he reports the murder of Henry of Guise in a relatively neutral way, though finding the act regrettable: "Henry, duke of Guise, in truth one of the first men of his age [his generation], was killed in the king's chamber."[180] In one year, politics had taken a sinister turn. The "ruin" anticipated by Catherine de Medici when Montaigne was having his first *Essais* printed and making his entrance into politics had become a reality. Montaigne was subjected to politics more than he influenced it in his region. We can reasonably speak of a disappointment on his part when faced with the political setbacks that followed his journey to Paris in 1588. Thus we must consider his withdrawal in late November to be the only choice he had. Montaigne could now concentrate on a book that he had conceived in other times for other objectives. He took refuge in writing, in writing in the margins of a copy of his *Essais* of 1588 that he had shown to the young woman from Picardy after his imprisonment and before he attended as a witness—in October and November—the tragedy that was brewing in Blois. He was already back in Bordeaux when the test of strength between Henry III and the princes of Lorraine reached its bloody climax, and it was in his château that he learned the news of the assassinations of the Guises. The sovereign had won a battle, but the state could only suffer from this criminal expedient. Soon after, it was again in his château that he heard of the tragic death of his king. Montaigne voluntarily put himself on the margins of politics.

If Montaigne had at first been able to believe that the innocence displayed on his face could serve him in pubic offices like ambassadorships, after 1585 he recognized that his "private" style was ultimately not suited to public negotiations. We understand why on rereading the preface to the reader when the *Essais* of 1588 was published in Paris Montaigne identified himself—certainly in a somewhat different way—with the new practice of a much more private writing. Not without irony, the preface to the reader no longer corresponded to a desire, but rather to a reality that wounded. The prospect of a public career was behind him, and Montaigne had ended up convincing himself that he had to live a private life, for lack of something better. That was all that remained to him, and he thus wrote of individual experience and introspection in the chapters of the third book. In a long development, Montaigne recounts the history of his complicated relationship to public offices and public life. According to him, public life never represented a choice, but rather a milieu in which he had been immersed since he was a child:

> This whole procedure of mine is just a bit dissonant from our ways. It would not be fit to produce great results or to endure. Innocence itself could neither negotiate among us without dissimulation nor bargain without lying. And so public occupations are by no means my quarry; what my profession requires, I perform in the most private manner that I can. As a boy I was plunged into them up to the ears. and it worked; yet I disengaged myself in good time. Since then I have often avoided becoming involved in them, rarely accepted them, never asked for them, keeping my back turned on ambition; but, if not like rowers who thus advance backward, yet in such a way that I am less obliged to my resolution than to my good fortune for not having embarked in them. For there are ways less

hostile to my taste and more suited to my capacity, by which, if fortune had formerly called me to public service and to my advancement toward worldly prestige, I know I would have passed over the arguments of my reason to follow it.[181]

Montaigne is said to have been thrown into public life by force. We think here, obviously, of the influence of his father. When it was necessary to explain the translation of Raymond Sebond's *Theologia naturalis* at the beginning of "Apology for Raymond Sebond," Montaigne exculpated himself by blaming an authoritarian father. Michel practiced what he calls politics "backward," trying to model public life on his private life. Starting in 1585, and especially after 1588, Montaigne finally succeeded in separating private life and public life. The study of Montaigne's experiments in politics nonetheless proves that this de-sired and stated "very clear separation" is more a literary invention than a bio-graphical reality. Created rather late, during his last career as a writer, the arti-ficial dichotomy between private and public life finally led Montaigne to present himself as a moralist and to judge politics from outside. His renunciation of public life marginalized him and no longer allowed him to influence the great political actors, but it also made it possible for him to avoid being associated with practices he deplored. He retained his privilege of expressing himself on all subjects without claiming to be an expert.

Montaigne might have chosen to write works in which the history of his time had a more important place. It has even been suggested that he engaged in that exercise, which was very fashionable in his time.[182] It is incontestable that Montaigne was always interested in history and in the writing of it. In "Of the power of the imagination" (I: 21), he suggests what that might have produced: "Some urge me to write the events of my time, believing that I see them with a view less distorted by passion than another man's, and from closer, because of the access that fortune has given me to the heads of different parties."[183] Mon-taigne the author of memoirs! This admission tells us a great deal about what the *Essais* might have become. Significantly, Montaigne also admits the exis-tence of a busy political life, a public life based on a model of allegiance (ambas-sador, negotiator, intermediary, a man behind the scenes) in which the spoken word plays a more important role than the written word. From 1588 on, Mon-taigne's conception of politics gave priority to spoken communication rather than to pamphlets or treatises. This was a different idea of public life. Mon-taigne was not a Monluc or a D'Aubigné; his public life left few documents for historians. But does that mean that private life finally won out, allowing him to pass into posterity?

CHAPTER 10

The Marginalization of Montaigne (1588–1592)

Toward the end of his life Montaigne wrote in a margin of the Bordeaux Copy: "My world is done for, my form is emptied; I belong entirely to the past."[1] That is a political observation, without any doubt. Montaigne's political supports had disappeared one by one, and he felt more isolated and marginalized than ever. Since August 1589, France had a new king. But like his predecessor, Henry IV had not succeeded in making himself accepted by his people and was still not allowed to reside in Paris, which was in the hands of the League. Montaigne had retired to his château, for the fourth time. This time, his reclusion was final. As before, retirement was not the result of choice but of necessity. Fifty-five years old, Montaigne was having difficulty getting around, because he was suffering more than ever from kidney stones. He had long since learned to live with this problem he had inherited from his father: "I am at grips with the worst of all maladies, the most sudden, the most painful, the most mortal, and the most irremediable."[2] As he grew older, the attacks came more frequently and their intensity no longer allowed Montaigne to consider long journeys. His tower had become a refuge, a place of exile *by necessity*. He was aware that he had little to hope for on the political level, and the time had come for him to think about the memory that he could bequeath to posterity. Montaigne commented on his situation: "It seems reasonable, when a man talks of retiring from the world, that he should set his gaze outside of it."[3] Looking outside the tower, outside the château, outside Bordeaux, Paris, the world—that was to give man a universal dimension, to grant him an imaginary space transcending the cultures and customs that shape him. Montaigne made his book an antiworld that helped him put his mind "in motion" (*en bransle*) the better to understand the world around him.

Lacking a male descendant who could perpetuate the name of the Montaignes, he had at least one sure asset: his book. This was no longer the same work it had been in 1580, and flattered by the favorable comments that had been addressed to him when his *Essais* appeared in 1588 expanded by a third book, Montaigne felt detached from current politics. He accepted the consequences and chose to emphasize his moral discourse and to increase the number of general reflections on man and the world. His experiences were no longer an end in themselves, but rather a means of universalizing his remarks and giving them the status of philosophical essays. The additions on the Bordeaux Copy are very different in nature from the first essays of 1580. Montaigne henceforth unapologetically dared to put himself at the center of all his reflections, and he took responsibility for the preponderance of his being in a particular form—the essay—that favored exhibitionism and that he transformed into a literary genre. This allowed Éstienne Pasquier to say that anyone who "deleted all the passages he used to speak about himself, and about his family, would have shortened his work by a quarter, at least, especially in his third book, which seems to be a history of his manners and actions."[4]

This display of the self and the body even becomes Montaigne's leitmotif. This "last" Montaigne is the one we treasure most today, because he is self-sufficient and accepts his subjectivity as an end. Montaigne also conceives his book in a completely novel way by putting the accent on the act of writing rather than on the content. He found this literary space literally in the margins of the book he published in 1588. The modern reader takes pleasure in discovering the multiple facets of a subjectivity that changes in accord with constantly renewed experiences. Montaigne sums up his new project this way: "I dare not only to speak of myself, but to speak only of myself; I go astray when I write of anything else, and get away from my subject."[5] Montaigne belatedly understood that his *Essais* was a book very different from others, and that this unique object would allow him to go down in history—*literary history*. He fully accepted the difference between private discourse and public language, and even developed a language and a style of his own always adapted to the situation and milieu—Paris, Rome, or his château—he found himself in.[6]

Whatever the author of the *Essais* tells us, there is indeed a difference between Paris (a public space par excellence) and Montaigne (the ultimate private sanctuary). He now judges people apart from the events that mark their time, in an ahistorical way. Montaigne is more interested than ever in the character and psychology of people and authors rather than in their actions or writings:

> I adhere firmly to the healthiest of the parties, but I do not seek to be noted as especially hostile to the others and beyond the bounds of the general reason. I condemn extraordinarily this bad form of arguing: "He is of the League, for he admires the grace of Monsieur de Guise." "The activity of the king of Navarre amazes him: he is a Huguenot." "He finds this to criticize in the king's morals: he is seditious in his heart."[7]

In this addition on the Bordeaux Copy, Montaigne reproaches the people of his time for drawing political conclusions from the affective or moral judgments that their contemporaries formulate regarding human beings. He now claims the right to speak of people outside their historicity, and thus without being harassed. To last, one has to jettison history. From this time on, his discourse tends to examine only the private character of individuals and to seek in them the universal form of the human condition. That is the only niche that remained to him.

A Tranquil Life

"All the glory that I aspire to in my life is to have lived it tranquilly—tranquilly not according to Metrodorus or Arcesilaus or Aristippus, but according to me. Since philosophy has not been able to find a way to tranquility that is suitable for all, let everyone seek it individually."[8] Montaigne had not won glory on battlefields or in embassies; in the future, he saw his existence as that of a mild-mannered, apolitical fellow. Until recently a supporter of moderation in politics, he now advocated a settled way of life. His *Essais* were transformed into a haven of peace where he found quietude and tranquility. To do this, between 1588 and 1592 Montaigne pursued a literary perspective that he had not previously envisioned. The preface to the reader now expresses less a wish and an opening onto society and the world than a coming to awareness of the political reality that forced him to turn inward on himself: introspection for lack of something better, one might say. However, one cannot convey disillusionment without preserving the traces of disavowed practices that make it possible to grasp the career path that led Montaigne *outside politics*.

The time had come to assess a public life that was far from having met Montaigne's expectations. Henry III had not kept all the promises he made in 1580, and Montaigne had been sidelined. Margaret of Valois spoke of her brother in these terms: "the king was of such a humor that he was offended not only by effects but also by ideas, and being resolved in his opinions he carried out everything that came into his mind without considering advice from either her or anyone else."[9] Montaigne left us a qualified judgment of Henry III, who he found lacking a "middle position, always being carried away from one extreme to the other by causes impossible to guess; no kind of course without tacking and changing directions amazingly; no quality unmixed; so that the most likely portrait of him that men will be able to make some day, will be that he affected and studied to make himself known by being unknowable."[10] Often yielding to the pressures of the moment, Henry III changed his mind easily and had acquired the reputation of being as unpredictable as the weather. Navarre also seemed to practice this politics of perpetual hesitation; before his conversion at Saint-Denis, he had already changed his religion five times. His title as presumptive heir to the throne implied new duties and a faith in accord with the religious tradition of his country. The very notion of freedom of religion, which was so central to the Protestants' demands, was deliberately relegated to the background of a political necessity that he deemed more important.[11]

The hope of acceding to the throne had required Navarre to abandon regional interests that had up to that point allowed him to base his political power on a local clientele. The next king of France had to unite a divided country and lead a weakened state with an iron hand. His conversion must not be seen as a religious decision, but rather as the obligatory transition from a regional power to a national responsibility. The reason of state prevailed. Montaigne had been a disillusioned witness to these religious reversals provoked by the political situation of the moment, and he had also been led to develop an essentially political view of religion, because, as he remarked after 1588, in these civil wars "religion serves as a pretext,"[12] and is often put in the service of political ends. Whereas all his neighbors were armed to protect themselves, Montaigne had chosen to cloister himself on his land, sheltered from military hostilities: "It is my retreat to rest myself from the wears. I try to withdraw this corner from the public tempest, as I do another corner in my soul. Our war may change forms all it will, and multiply and diversify itself into new factions; as for me, I do not budge. Amid so many fortified houses, I alone of my rank in France, as far as I know, have entrusted purely to heaven the protection of mine."[13]

Like many of his contemporaries, Montaigne endured, powerless, events that rushed ever more rapidly toward his door. He turned inward on himself because he could not act. Introspection was simply one way of escaping politics. Adopting the ostrich's strategy, Montaigne decided to close his eyes to the events of his time. His home offered him a relatively safe refuge, and he devoted himself to rereading his *Essais* with a view to a new edition. Many of the remarks and developments written during the years 1572–79 now seemed to him outdated, and he sought to find a clear separation between public life and private life. This reorientation had been begun in the essays written after 1585, but it became even more crucial after 1588. For this reason, the final "extension" (*allongeail*) of the *Essais* sought to transform a mainly political text into a new object that was essentially literary and philosophical. The generous margins of the Bordeaux Copy offered Montaigne an opportunity to invent a new private space in order to deliberately marginalize himself.

The political marginalization of Montaigne corresponds, grosso modo, to the "marginalization"—writing in the margins—of the *Essais*. Whereas he had formerly tried to impose his natural inclination toward justice and honor by demonstrating their compatibility with political practices, Montaigne now dissociated himself from politics, which he no longer considered as the "control of oneself."[14] Montaigne retained a deep respect for the great military leaders of

Antiquity, particularly Epaminondas,[15] but he formulated a more nuanced judgment of the princes of his own time. The *Essais* were no longer compatible with political practice, especially in light of the events that followed the assassination of the Guises at the Estates General in Blois. But it was once again on the regional scale that Montaigne felt the greatest bitterness. The military situation in Guyenne explains Montaigne's failures in politics. Moved by a sense of honor, he had never ceased to make himself available to serve his king in his region, but his efforts were rather ludicrous in a context little suited to personal initiatives. Bordeaux and its region were more than ever given over to intrigues and machinations, and were subject to the growing influence of the League.

In March 1589, Bordeaux revolted, but Matignon more or less succeeded in maintaining order and locked down the city. The supporters of the League and the Protestants were fighting each other openly in Guyenne, and Matignon was in an uncomfortable situation, trying to prevent excesses on both sides. He attempted to renew the dialogue between the local factions. The supporters of the League were not fooled and denounced these illusory negotiations, in which Montaigne had not so long ago participated. Aware that he had been manipulated in the past, the author of the *Essais* no longer believed that politics and diplomacy could be defined by a strong soul filled with praiseworthy convictions. Far from thinking that he could impose a new practice of politics, Montaigne was then drinking the bitter cup to the dregs. More than ever, he became conscious that he had alienated both the supporters of the League and the Protestants.

Between 1588 and 1592, Montaigne was reduced to imagining himself as a simple author. That was the only activity he wanted to emphasize, and he was able to find arguments to convince himself: "The world is swarming with commentaries; of authors there is a great scarcity."[16] According to Montaigne, an author does not offer commentaries on his own time, he situates himself above the melee and speaks of man in the absolute. Did he have to erase this disagreeable past and do away with his old political conceptions or, on the contrary, did he have to put his youthful aspirations in perspective and transform them into positive experiences that led him to become an author? For Montaigne, the realization of his failure took a long time, but the ruins of politics could serve as a foundation for the literary edifice he intended to construct.

After 1588, Montaigne revisited the chapter "Of solitude" (I: 39) to add a commentary that looks like a confession: "[1588]: The greatest thing in the world is to know how to belong to oneself. [Bordeaux Copy]: It is time to untie ourselves from society, since we can contribute nothing to it."[17] Knowing how "to belong to oneself" is less a choice than an observation, since the failures in politics led him to an inevitable realization. His book now had to emphasize the self without erasing his numerous judgments on public life. Besides, what would his book look like if he suddenly deviated from his initial intention? He would have to begin everything all over again. Montaigne was over fifty-five years old and lacked time. Doing away with half the text would certainly have made the position of the "last Montaigne" more coherent, but the mistakes one makes are an integral part of writing and have just as great a share in the form of the essay. After 1588, Montaigne found a solution to these problems. As he admits, "[He] produces Essays, who cannot produce results" ("faict des Essais qui ne sauroit faire des effaicts").[18] The pun on "essai" and "effet" is revealing.

Thus Montaigne decided to remain silent regarding the events that plunged Guyenne into chaos. He was now preoccupied with finding an ideal reader outside history. Aware of the contradictions between his first essays and the additions to the Bordeaux Copy that were beginning to fill the margins of what was becoming his working manuscript, Montaigne developed a theory of reading and writing: "It is the inattentive reader who loses my subject, not I. Some word about it will always be found off in a corner, which will not fail to be sufficient, though it takes little room. . . . My style and my mind alike go roaming."[19] After 1588 Montaigne had his political career *behind him*; he no longer looked back and had given up his pretensions and aspirations of the early 1580s. He still recognized that "We corrupt the function of command when we obey through discretion, not subjection,"[20] but he offered a conclusion very different from that drawn in the first version of this chapter:

> On the other hand, however, one might also consider that such constrained obedience belongs only to precise and stated commands. Ambassadors have a freer commission, which in many areas depends in the last resort on their judgment; they do not simply carry out, but also by their counsel form and direct their master's will. I have in my time known people in command to be reprimanded for having obeyed the words of the king's letters rather than the demands of the situation they were in.[21]

This discordant view of the ambassador's function is in complete disagreement with Montaigne's initial judgments regarding this profession. The statement also contradicts the example reported concerning Pope Jules II's ambassador to the king of England. Similarly, after 1588, Montaigne had a very different view of public office. Thus he was soon to relate this knowledge to himself and no longer to a state or a king: "Moreover, it is a very useful knowledge, this knowledge of social dexterity. Like grace and beauty, it acts as a moderator at the first approaches of sociability and familiarity, and consequently opens the door for us to learning by the examples of others, and to bringing forth and displaying our own example, if it has anything instructive and communicable about it."[22]

On January 5, 1589, Catherine de Medici had died in the château of Blois at the age of seventy-two. Her death marked a genuine eclipse of the political practices of the 1570s and 1580s, because for more than twenty years she had managed to cope with the extremist Catholics and had succeeded in establishing a minimum of respect for the person of the king. A page in history had been turned. The supporters of the League were demanding total war against the Protestants. In the spring of 1589, the political situation was deteriorating from one day to the next in Guyenne and Languedoc. Bordeaux was threatening to go over to the League. Matignon took advantage of the revolt in Bordeaux to expel the Jesuits, who had been accused of fomenting rebellion. A few years before, Montaigne had accused them of not paying enough attention to the education of their pupils, but that may have been a pretext for more political reproaches connected with their meddling in the city's affairs.[23] There was a rumor that they had hidden weapons meant for the League supporters in an underground passage between their college and the church of Saint James. The king sent Matignon letters patent to expel the Jesuits from the city. The parlement of Bordeaux hesitated to follow the parlement of Toulouse, which had overtly declared its solidarity with the League and was trying to raise other cities against the king. The members of the Toulouse parlement distributed articles that they had the people swear to.[24] In their turn, Auch, Fleurance, and Moissac declared for the League, and the residents of Cahors expelled their bishop, who wanted to remain loyal to the king. On May 30, it was Périgueux's turn to side with the Union. Agen joined the League in June. In Bordeaux, League supporters had tried to seize the city under the direction of a member of Pontac family, Thomas, lord of Escassefort, who had opened the Saint-Julien gate to let in the rebels, but Matignon succeeded in putting down the insurrection by going out into the street "with his sword in his hand and his head lowered."[25] The leaders of the group of rebels, a barrel maker and a sergeant, were sentenced to death by the parlement on April 3, but the people really responsible for this sudden attack were not punished. On April 24 a formal session of the parlement of Bordeaux was held, at which Matignon, surrounded by his guards and a large contingent of the nobility, tried to reassert royal authority against the supporters of the League. To calm people down, from April 24 to April 30 a conference was held at Plessis-lès-Tours that resulted in a short-lived accord between Henry III and Henry of Navarre.

On August 1, 1589, Henry III was assassinated. Just before he died, he recognized Henry of Bourbon, king of Navarre, as his successor, in accord with the Salic law. France now had a Protestant king. Henry IV swore the oath at Saint-Cloud on August 4, surrounded by princes of the blood, dukes and peers, officers of the Crown and other officers loyal to the late king.[26] The news reached Matignon around August 8. It was brought by a messenger who urged Matignon to return to Bordeaux to prevent the city from falling under the control of the parlement or into the hands of the League. On August 18, after three stressful days during which Matignon tried to out-fox the parlement, which refused to hear of a heretical king, the lieutenant general and mayor of Bordeaux wrote to Henry IV to assure him of his loyalty. Upon learning of the death of Henry III, the Bordeaux parlement had entered into open conflict with Matignon. An envoy of Henry IV found "things very confused"[27] in Bordeaux. A loyal servant of kings, Matignon supported the new sovereign, but in Bordeaux the sympathizers of the League caused him many difficulties. In the name of their neutrality, the members of parlement refused to recognize the king so long as he had not abjured his Protestant faith. Henry IV understood that it was nonetheless possible to buy them off, and he wrote to Matignon to tell him that "their wills are for sale."[28] In the worst case, the king was prepared to imprison recalcitrant members of the parlement or simply to expel them from Bordeaux.

This crisis in the parlement lasted until early 1590. The members of the parlement finally yielded under Matignon's pressure, saving face by sending a deputation petitioning the king to hasten his conversion to the Catholic religion. After many reversals, Henry IV was finally recognized in Bordeaux as the legitimate heir to the throne. From that moment on, the chronicler Estienne de Cruseau no longer calls the sovereign "the king of Navarre" but Henry IV. To reward the members of the Bordeaux parlement, the new king created a special tax designed to increase their salaries[29] and went even further by revoking Henry III's edict providing for the establishment of a Chambre des Comptes in Bordeaux. The parlement had always refused to register this chamber and received the new king's decision favorably. Henry IV could not afford to have cities like Bordeaux and Toulouse against him, and he was prepared to make concessions to bring the parlements onto his side.

What did Montaigne have to say about these developments in Bordeaux? In the course of 1589, just before Henry III's death, De Thou and Schomberg had visited him in his château. They were received by his wife, because Montaigne was in Bordeaux, certainly to deal with private matters. Matignon was no longer consulting him, and he was not part of the group of the lieutenant governor's advisors. It is clear that Montaigne did not approve of the concessions made to the members of the parlement, who had always put a spoke in his wheel. Similarly, the expulsion of the Jesuits seems not to have surprised him, because he, too, had had problems with them during his two terms as mayor. In Bordeaux, the new order of the Feuillants had taken their place and was propagating a message more respectful of the king's person. The founder of this order, Jean de La Barrière, had taken refuge in Bordeaux after fleeing the revolt in Toulouse. The Feuillants had established themselves in the church of Saint Anthony, which the city had made available to them. They preached service to Henry III, and after the his death, La Barrière had even given a funeral oration in which he openly praised Matignon and advocated respect for royal authority.[30] The Feuillants offered an alternative less political than the Jesuits, and for that reason they were well received by Matignon and Montaigne, the latter having especially appreciated the abbot of the Feuillants' political mediation between Henry III and the League in 1588–89.[31] Several witnesses even claimed that, thanks to the Feuillants' sermons, Bordeaux had experienced an unusual calm for several days after the death of Henry III.[32] This political moderation fully corresponded to Montaigne's conception of religion, and that is probably why he decided to have himself interred in their church.[33] Not long afterward, Montaigne's wife took La Barrière as her spiritual advisor.[i]

In the second half of 1589, after preaching Lent in Angers, Pierre Charron came to Bordeaux, where he formed a friendship with Montaigne, whom he had already met in the Montaigne's château two years earlier. We do not know much about this friendship, but Montaigne's retirement attracted visitors of all kinds, eager to converse with the author of the *Essais*. The friendship between the two men has certainly been exaggerated, and Bayle provides no proof in support of his assertion that Montaigne allowed Charron to bear "after his death the full coat of arms of his noble family, because he left no male children."[34] Charron's outspokenness probably did not displease Montaigne. Their respective careers as members of parlements surely created a kind of complicity between the two men, because Charron had also worked for six years as a lawyer in the parlement (of Paris) before giving up this profession. There he had developed an ease of speaking and had proven to be a peerless orator. It was entirely natural that Charron later turned toward theology—a career choice rather than a true vocation—and entered orders. His first biographer, Gabriel de La Rochemaillet, tells us that Charron "had a ready tongue" and rapidly acquired great fame for his sermons. His facility as an orator was such that his reputation reached as far as the Court of the king of Navarre. Margaret of Valois had taken him as her ordinary preacher, and although he was a Protestant, Henry of Navarre liked to listen to the sermons of this eloquent Catholic monk. Charron's outspokenness and his populist style made him a demagogue, but his independent judgment made him likeable.

The year 1588 had been turbulent for Montaigne and Charron alike. On his way to Paris, Charron made the error of stopping off in Angers, where events caught up with him. The League was gaining ground every day, and the king had decided to convoke the Estates General. In Angers, the elections were clearly favorable to the League. Charron preached on this occasion, in the church of Saint Peter, "a sermon full of great doctrine."[35] Things took a very bad

---

[i] In 1614, Françoise de La Chassaigne sent the Bordeaux Copy to the Feuillants without her daughter's agreement. She was probably trying to make people forget the "misunderstanding" (legal suit) that made the Feuillants oppose her during the construction of the new chapel.

turn when the king suddenly decided to have the Guises assassinated before the assembled estates. Passions and hatred inflamed the residents of Angers, who had already been very agitated by Charron's incendiary words. Charron gave sermon after sermon favorable to the League, more out of opportunism than real religious conviction, and he was partly responsible for the uprising of the people of Angers.[36] In March 1589, when the duke of Aumont finally regained control of the rebel city in the name of Henry III, he hastened to punish the guilty parties. Charron was among the most prominent, and he was "forbidden to preach and arrested by the city,"[37] as he himself tells us in his correspondence. On May 12, 1589, he wrote to La Rochemaillet: "I now have permission to preach and yesterday I was restored to the pulpit on the day of the Ascension; but the arrest continues; I have not been able to obtain permission to leave."[38] Between these two dates—October 1588 and April 1589—Charron had simply submitted by recognizing his errors. He made amends publicly on Easter— April 2, 1589—in the church of Saint Maurice, before the duke of Aumont and his officers, and publicly retracted his statements by beginning his sermon with the famous phrase: "I told you so, messieurs of Angers." Charron had just saved his skin, but the members of the League interpreted his recantation as a betrayal. The lesson had cost him dearly, and Charron kept out of politics after taking this disastrous stand. In a letter written in April 1589 to a doctor at the Sorbonne, he concluded that it is not permissible for a subject, for any cause or reason whatever, "to league, band together, and rebel against his king." He desperately tried to explain his actions: "There was a time when I was thinking about joining the League, and I put a foot in it. For in truth, I was never entirely in it, or resolutely; indeed, I was terribly offended by their actions."[39] Thus in 1589, Charron was, like Montaigne, in retirement after an unfortunate political engagement that had almost cost him his life. As we see, the two men had things to talk about in the château. Their common trajectory outside politics had several similarities.

On September 17, 1589, Justus Lipsius sent a copy of his *Politica* to Montaigne. He enclosed a letter in which he asked for Montaigne's judgment, considering that he had some expertise in the matter. An edition of the *Politica* printed in 1584 was already on the market, and Montaigne might have bought it earlier. It has been suggested that Lipsius's *Politica* was an important source for the revised version of the *Essais* published in 1588.[40] Both the subject of the book and its illustrious author must have received the attention of Montaigne, who thought that politics needed to regain elevation and thus to be dealt with in a humanist discourse. However, Montaigne never embraced Lipsius's conception of politics, and the third book of the *Essais* might even be seen as a refutation of Justus Lipsius.

Montaigne nonetheless felt obliged to praise Lipsius, who the preceding year had sent him dithyrambic letters about the *Essais*.[ii] Published during Montaigne's lifetime, Lipsius's letters to Montaigne testify to his admiration for the man whom he had called, as early as 1583, the French Thales.[41] They also attest to Montaigne's fame after 1588 and put him on the same level as Turnebus, Scaliger, De Thou, and Michel de L'Hospital, who were also members of Lipsius's pantheon. Montaigne now had a reputation as an author that largely eclipsed his political notoriety. He was beginning to be considered a man of solid and upright judgment. Thus Lipsius placed Montaigne "among the Seven Sages, or a group still wiser than they, if it existed," and praised "the rectitude of his judgment," even implying that he had "not found in Europe anyone [except Montaigne] who on such subjects had sentiments that were in agreement with his."[42] Montaigne returned the compliment in his *Essais*, referring to those "who stand out in this sort of writing as well as in other kinds, as does Lipsius in the learned and laborious web of his *Politics*."[43] He benefited considerably from his reading of the Flemish humanist after 1588, since a substantial number of the quotations in the margins of the Bordeaux Copy are copied from Justus Lipsius. Montaigne seems in particular to have read and used the *Justi Lipsi adversus dialogistam liber de una religione*, published in 1590. That said, the author of the *Essais* kept his distance from Lipsius, perhaps declining to enter into his game of honeyed praise and mutual back-scratching that corresponded so little to his temperament.[44] Pedantry has limits. Moreover, the ease with which Justus Lipsius converted from Protestantism to Catholicism—leaving Leiden for Leuven—might have seemed to be a form of opportunism contrary to his principles and certainly in contradiction with Lipsius's famous treatise *De constancia*, which had made his reputation. The idols were losing their luster, and Montaigne was beginning to have a writer's ideas and see himself as the equal of the best humanists of his time.

Whereas Montaigne had resigned himself to corresponding and conversing only with the great figures of humanism, the arrival of Henry of Navarre on the throne gave him new hopes. It is not so easy to rid oneself of the demon of politics. At that time, the easy-going king was not much loved by his people, and, as we have seen, he was still forbidden to enter Paris. The majority of the French did not recognize him as their king. Montaigne may have had advice to offer Henry IV. He wrote to him on several occasions to congratulate him on his succession to the throne and to offer him his services. However, this last effort to relaunch a political career that had come to a halt lacked determination. Besides, Henry IV may have needed him more than he needed the king at this

---

[ii] These letters are dated April 15 and August 30, 1588.

point in his life. A reply from Henry in early January 1590 gave Montaigne an opportunity to write a fine letter in which he shows his joy at being read by the king who had "deigned to consider my letters and command a response."[45] Montaigne reminded him of the mutual trust that had long existed between the two men, and he took advantage of the occasion to show Henry IV that he was keeping up with political developments in Guyenne. After praising Matignon's "sincere zeal and marvelous prudence," he hinted that he would still be capable of working for the governor of Guyenne. Pretending to be well informed about the latest negotiations in Bordeaux, he declared that he knew that Matignon was sending good reports every day, as if he himself knew the content of the missives sent by the lieutenant governor and mayor of Bordeaux.

The letter from Henry IV to Montaigne brought out the demon of politics that still lived in Montaigne, but it was assuredly more an instinctual reaction than a genuine project. Montaigne would have liked to go to Paris or any other city where the king was residing, but that was a pious wish: too many factors prevented him from realizing it. The rapid deterioration of his health did not allow him to undertake a sojourn at the Court, and the times were not favorable to his conception of public occupations. He had resigned himself to pursuing a career as an author, and found it hard to imagine resuming political service. Negotiating with Henry III was one thing, but coming to an agreement with members of the League, the same people who had imprisoned him in Paris, was quite another. In the old days, Charles IX, thanks to the marquis of Trans, had allowed him to make his entrance into politics; Henry III had then promised him a diplomatic career before putting him at the head of a city on the edge of revolt; what could the heir to the throne of France promise him that he had not already experienced? Although he was flattered by the idea of serving a third monarch, Montaigne had nonetheless become realistic in matters of politics. He could still imagine himself in the role of a wise counselor, offering advice drawn from ancient examples and his personal experiences, but he no longer had the ability to be the king's man on the ground. In another letter dated January 18, 1590, Montaigne made one last desperate attempt, without having much faith in it:

> Sire, your letter of the last day of November reached me only just now, and beyond the period that it pleased you to set for me, of your sojourn in Tours. I receive as a singular grace that your majesty deigned to make me feel that you would be glad to see me, a person so useless, but yours, even more out of affection than duty. You have very laudably adjusted your external forms to the lofty height of your new fortune, but the calm and ease of your internal humors, you have just as laudably not changed. It has pleased you to have respect not only for my age, but also for my desire, to

call me to a place [Tours] where you were somewhat in repose from your laborious activities. Will it soon be in Paris, Sire? And I will spare no means or health to go there.[46]

This question remained unanswered, because Henry IV was authorized to enter Paris only after having converted to the Catholic faith, nearly a year after Montaigne's death. Despite his disillusionments, Montaigne assured the king once again of his unshakeable friendship and, despite his resolute choice of the Catholic religion, reminded him that he was always close to his political ideas: "Even when I had to confess to my priest, I did not fail to look to some extent favorably on your successes. Now [that you are king of France], with more reason and liberty, I embrace them with full affection."[47] Just as if the king had Montaigne's qualities, including the "sincere zeal" and "marvelous prudence" of the Marshal de Matignon, who also followed the model left by his predecessor as mayor of Bordeaux: "from whom I do not suppose that you receive every day so many good and signal services without recalling my assurances and hopes." In short, Montaigne had prepared the ground for Matignon, and Henry IV was obliged to recognize the political and diplomatic qualities of a servant who was still putting himself at his king's disposal. Montaigne shared with the king what he called a "common tranquility," the theme he had decided to emphasize in his last essays.

On March 31, 1590, the parlement of Bordeaux sent a delegation to the king composed of Guillaume Daffis, *président à mortier*, and the councillors François d'Alesme, Gabriel de Tarneau, and Geoffroy de Bussaguet Montaigne—Montaigne's cousin—to assure the king of their loyalty and obedience.[48] On Saturday, May 26, 1590, Montaigne's daughter, Léonor, nineteen years old, married François de La Tour, who was thirty-one. Léonor's dowry amounted to 20,000 *livres tournois*, two-thirds of which (6,000 *écus* from Montaigne, and 666 *écus* from Françoise de La Chassaigne) were payable after the respective deaths of the parents, who made their daughter their universal heir. This sum was considerable for the time and shows that the noble land of Montaigne and other possessions had allowed Montaigne to exploit his holdings and grow rich during the 1580s.

Montaigne took advantage of this family event to put his affairs in order and plan the future of his seigneury. He was fifty-seven years old and his wife was forty-six. Married for twenty-five years, they would not have any more children, and thus had to resign themselves to conveying their property to their sole daughter. In the marriage contract between François de La Tour and Léonor de Montaigne, Montaigne had included several clauses and provisions concerning the transmission of his house's name and coat of arms.[49] He openly envisaged his own death and that of his wife, and the time had come to ensure that the seigneury of Montaigne would survive him. He bequeathed to his wife half the usufruct of the seigneury so long as she lived; Françoise de La Chassaigne did the same by granting to her husband a similar usufruct of her property. One provision in the marriage contract stipulated that if one of the parties involved refused to bear as the head of the family the name and coat of arms of Montaigne, the house would go to Léonor's closest male descendent. However, Montaigne reserved the right, during his lifetime, to change this clause and to substitute anyone he pleased to bear the coat of arms of his house. This very detailed document allows us to sense the anxiety Montaigne felt with regard to the survival of his name, his coat of arms, and his seigneury. Nevertheless, he had to resign himself to foreseeing all the possible outcomes. Four weeks later, on June 23, Léonor left the family château to go with her husband to Saintonge.[iii] Montaigne found himself alone with his wife in his château.

On July 20, from his camp at Saint-Denis, Henry IV wrote another letter to Montaigne, asking him to come and occupy a position in his service. Two days before, the king had written a letter addressed to the mayor and the jurats of Bordeaux to reassure them concerning what he called the restoration of his authority. He told them that he was expecting to "recover within a few days our city of Paris or to win a battle," and asked for their political support. As a reward for their fidelity, he revealed to them his intention to reduce the taxes on the entrance of merchandise into the city as soon as his affairs were going better. The terms of the contract with the city were sufficiently clear: "However, we desire that this [tax] now be paid, and without grumbling or opposition, if possible."[50] This promise was tempered by another missive addressed to Matignon and dated July 20. Henry IV congratulated his governor—and not the mayor of Bordeaux—on his prudence (repeating Montaigne's praise) and gave him instructions concerning the levy of a new tax of 40,000 crowns on the region for "the maintenance of the army."[51] The king also intended to bring the sénéchaussées of Armagnac, Quercy, and Rouergue into the parlement of Bordeaux and planned to nominate six new councillors, thus making it possible to establish a third Chambre des Enquêtes in the parlement. This was a way of foreseeing additional revenues for the crown. Aware that this would not be well received by the current members of the parlement, the king left it to Matignon to decide regarding this project of integrating the sénéchaussées into the par-

---

[iii] On March 31, 1591, thus during Montaigne's lifetime, Léonor gave birth to a daughter, Françoise de La Tour. Her husband died in 1594. With her second husband, Charles de Gamaches, Léonor had another daughter, Marie, in 1610. Marie de Gamaches (1610–1782) married Louis de Lur Saluces in 1627. Since she had no direct descendants, it was Louis de Lur Saluces's nephew, Jean de Ségur, lord of Montazeau, the son of Madeleine de Lur, who ensured Montaigne's heritage down to 1811, the date at which the château and the land of Montaigne were sold to a third party outside the family.

lement. He wanted to avoid alienating the members of the parlement, and he needed the political support of cities like Bordeaux and Toulouse. In this letter to Matignon, Henry IV also complains about having been deceived and poorly informed regarding the political situation in Gascony. Was he thinking about asking Montaigne to inform him about troop movements and political negotiations in the southwest? Matignon could have used an "assistant" who would serve as a liaison with the king. Henry IV was looking for an intermediary who could work with Matignon, and logically he thought that Montaigne had already occupied such a position with a certain success during the reign of Henry III. We can imagine that the job Henry IV offered Montaigne that same day— July 20, 1590—was connected with this.

Six weeks later, on September 2, 1590, Montaigne replied to the king:

Sire, the one [the letter] it pleased Your Majesty to write me on July 20 was delivered to me only this morning, and found me in the grip of a very violent tertian fever widespread in this area for the past month. Sire, I deem it a very great honor to receive your commands and I did not fail to write to M' the Marshal de Matignon, very expressly three times, about my deliberations and the obligation I was under to go to see him, to the point of telling him the route I would take to safely meet him if he agreed. Having received no reply, I think he considered how long and dangerous the roads to be taken would be for me. Sire, Your Majesty, I beg you to do me the grace of believing that I shall never spare my purse on the occasions when I would not seek to spare my life. I have never received any boon from the liberality of kings, any more than I have asked for or merited [such a boon], and I have received no payment for the steps I have taken in their service, which Your Majesty knows in part. What I have done for your predecessors [Charles IX and Henry III] I will do even more willingly for you. I am, Sire, as wealthy as I wish to be. When I have exhausted my purse for Your Majesty, in Paris, I shall be bold enough to tell you, and then, if you deem me worthy of continuing to be part of your entourage, you will get a better bargain than from the least of your officers.[52]

Henry IV had probably asked him to put himself at Matignon's disposal and allowed him to foresee a meeting in Paris or in Tours. Montaigne did not expect any remuneration for the services he could render to the king, declaring that he was rich enough to pay the expenses associated with his travel. However, his health did not permit him to realize his new political projects, and Montaigne did not set foot in Paris after 1588. Neither was he to meet with Henry IV.[53] This letter to Henry IV is Montaigne's last political document. Matignon paid no attention to his offers of service, probably believing him incapable of serving as a negotiator between Charles I of Lorraine, the recognized leader of the League after his father's assassination, and Henry IV. Moreover, Henry IV had little to negotiate, other than the renunciation of his Protestant faith. Only a conversion could allow him to enter Paris, but he was still reluctant to take this step. In the meantime, Tours served him as a provisional capital, and the king had resigned himself to establishing the seat of his government there, because in the autumn of 1590 Paris remained his main political problem. Henry IV had begun the siege of the capital on July 30, 1589, had repeatedly lifted it, and then resumed the blockade of the city between May and August 1590, without success. He had considered every means of seizing the capital, including having gentlemen and soldiers disguised as flour merchants enter through the Saint-Honoré gate.[54] He did not take control of Paris until March 1594, but Montaigne was never to experience that moment.

At the end of 1590, the king's authority was no longer respected in Guyenne, and the League had seized several strongholds. The parlement of Bordeaux sent a letter to the king concerning the disastrous condition of the province. In this letter the members of the parlement lamented the "ruin and subversion" that currently prevailed in Guyenne. On November 15 a further letter expressing the same fears was sent to the king. After the League forces took Rions and then Ayre de Mezin and Villandrault, the parlement considered Bordeaux "already under siege" and war imminent.[55] Royal edicts no longer had much effect, and most of the time they were not even applied. The confusion reached its apex, and the members of parlement considered the political situation anarchical. The League had infiltrated the city's administrative apparatus and enjoyed an unprecedented influence in Bordeaux, including in the parlement, which endlessly debated the question of whether it should recognize the king of Navarre as the king of France. A motion presented during the "interregnum" proposed to declare Navarre "incapable of being king of France."[56] The motion was made and debated from September 22 to September 26 before it was rejected, because the court judged that ultimately it had "few means . . . of making Henry of Bourbon, king of Navarre, recognized as king of France in Guyenne."[57] At the end of October, the parlement still had not decided whether it should use the word "king," or simply refer to his "Majesty" in addressing Henry IV. A vote followed "and approved, twenty-five to twenty, the use in memoranda of the word 'majesty' in order to put an end to the interrupted deliberation and still honor him with the title."[58] Polarized more than ever, the parlement persisted in its rebellion against royal power. After many delays, and thanks to Matignon's skill, the parlement of Bordeaux finally recognized officially, on December 26, Henry IV as king of France. However, on the same date, the supporters of the League proclaimed Cardinal Bourbon king, under the name of Charles X.

In March 1591, Montaigne attended as a witness, along with Geoffroy de Bussaguet Montaigne, his cousin, and Caumont de La Force, a Protestant, the drawing up, before a notary, of the last will and testament of the marquis of Trans, Germain-Gaston de Foix.[59] The marquis died four months later, on August 7, 1591. Deeply distressed by the heroic death of three of his children during the battle of Moncrabeau, Montaigne's protector had fallen into senility. He was over eighty years old. With him a major political force in the region disappeared. The marquis of Trans had asked Montaigne to accept the responsibility of serving as "honorary tutor" of his children and grandchildren. The political patron of the 1570s had made his client the executor of his will, forbidding his daughters to "contract marriage with anyone without the consent of the aforementioned [Montaigne, Geoffroy de Bussaguet, and Caumont de La Force]."[60] However, on account of his declining health, Montaigne no longer had the ability to play the role of tutor and protector for Germain-Gaston de Foix's grandson, the young Frédéric, age eleven, because he found it increasingly difficult to go to Fleix on horseback. After twenty years of good and loyal service to his sponsor in politics, Montaigne was no longer capable of responding to this last request made by his neighbor and friend.

On March 31, 1591, Montaigne mentioned in his *Éphéméride* the birth of his granddaughter, Françoise de La Tour. This was the last entry in his almanac and the last known document from the last eighteen months of his life. The same year, Geoffroy Bussaguet Montaigne—who had usurped the name of Eyquem de Montaigne—obtained letters patent to have his son Raymond, lord of Saint-Genest,[61] received as a councillor at the parlement of Bordeaux and to reestablish the office of Raymond Eyquem, Geoffroy's father, who had been dead for twenty-nine years. Geoffroy de Bussaguet-Montaigne was the parlement's deputy to Henry IV and used his acquaintances to get his son into the parlement. Anticipating difficulties in having the letters patent registered, Raymond de Bussaguet had Gabriel de Cruseau, president of the Cour des Enquêtes, and Geoffroy de Malvyn, who were able to hinder his election, recused in the parlement. A quarrel ensued in which thirteen councillors were recused, in accord with the usual mode of confrontation between clientelist cliques. The councillor Joseph d'Andrault proved to be particularly virulent in his speech against the Montaigne family and curtly opposed the appointment of Raymond de Bussaguet in order to nominate another candidate for the vacant post of councillor in one of the Chambres des Enquêtes.

This was the starting point for a series of increasingly extravagant denunciations and accusations. The "lord Aiquem de Montaigne" (Bussaguet) rose to denounce Antoine de Belcier, who, according to him, had tried to assassinate him in his house of Rignac. He now demanded reparations, if not vengeance against Belcier's friends, who, still according to him, were forming a conspiracy against his family. The animosity between the members of parlement was such that insults were made on both sides. Finally, Geoffroy de Bussaguet Montaigne and Joseph d'Andrault were expelled for a time "from courts and trials" for fear that they might come to blows. This incident is reported by Estienne de Cruseau in his chronicle[62] and shows that the parlement was still functioning in the same way, and that nothing had changed since the time when Montaigne had also had to battle every day against rival families that were trying to impose their relatives as councillors. There is no doubt that Montaigne heard about this quarrel that was tarnishing the Montaignes' name. On May 15, 1591, the letters patent reestablishing the office of the late Raymond Eyquem were finally confirmed in favor of his nephew, Raymond de Bussaguet, the son of Geoffroy de Bussaguet Montaigne, "called Montaigne." In 1595, three years after the death of Michel de Montaigne, by a ruling of the parlement, Raymond de Bussaguet officially obtained the right to bear the name "Montaigne." On Friday, November 22, 1596, Raymond de Bussaguet Montaigne joined the Great Chamber under the name of "Bussaguet, *sive* Aiquem." Finally, one year later, in 1598, Geoffroy appears under the name "De Montagne," and his son Raymond under the name of "De Montagne fils." Once again there were two Montaignes in the parlement of Bordeaux.

"The Only Book in the World of Its Kind"

Far from expressing the essence of the *Essais*, the separation between public life and private life Montaigne made after 1588—in the third book of the *Essais* and especially in the additions on the Bordeaux Copy—came late in his reflection and only after a series of political disappointments. After 1588, Montaigne no longer had any choice but to theorize about what has to be seen as a political failure. His preface to the reader did not need to be modified, because it also reflected an observation. That is the whole irony of this text that the author of the *Essais* left practically unchanged from one edition to the next. Montaigne always weighed his words, and the *Essais* certainly remain the antithesis of the pamphlet or any form of politically engaged literature, but the *Essais* were now loaded with a disapproving commentary and a hardly concealed, second-level critical appreciation. His book became, over the years and editions, the manifestation of his political disenchantment and his forced disengagement from public life. The goal of Montaigne's book had never been to participate in or to settle the disputes and conflicts of his time, but rather to propose a countermodel for a different way of practicing diplomacy and politics. Similarly, current events had never occupied a central place in his reflections and judgments, but they were nonetheless present as a background. Montaigne drew most of his examples from Antiquity, but like Machiavelli, he had also found historical or political similarities to his own century. The absence of an immediate history now allowed him to reorient his book without the successive projects seeming too contradictory. It was simply a question of establishing an even greater distance from public life and of separating the private from the public, of theorizing this distance and emphasizing the form of the *Essais* rather than their content. It was from that moment on that Montaigne resolutely and consciously opted for form.[63] He could also settle accounts with a public life that had more or less disappointed him. For this reason, the critique of this public life (across the ages and places) occupies a more important place in the work of the last Montaigne (1588–92); it is determined and influenced by his personal experience of diplomatic and political functions.

After 1588 Montaigne redefined the ideal reader that he had initially imagined as capable and candid. Confronted by a text that is paradoxical[64] and often contradictory, the reader is henceforth conceived as an active participant in what Montaigne was beginning to conceive as a unique genre of literature, "the only book in the world of its kind."[65] Read in an essentially linear way in 1580, the text now includes multiple points of entry and subjects itself to the aleatory laws of the capable reader. The additions are only "overweights" that challenge the chronology of narratives and confuse the time of experiences in order to accentuate a more universal conception of human beings:

> My book is always one. Except that at each new edition, so that the buyer may not come off completely empty-handed, I allow myself to add, since it is only an ill-fitted patchwork, some extra ornaments. These are only overweights, which do not condemn the original form, but give some special value to each of the subsequent ones, by a bit of ambitious subtlety. Thence, however, it will easily happen that some transposition of chronology may slip in, for my stories take their place according to their timeliness, not always according to their age.[66]

The goal of this late addition is to create the illusion of a harmony among chapters that are, however, very different in form and content. From this moment on, Montaigne asks his new reader to read differently, that, is to lend himself in his turn to the practice of *feuilletage*.[iv] Reading has to adapt to the writing the better to blur the history of the text and its editions. However, the author also asks for greater concentration on the reader's part; he requires a sustained reading that demands more attention. He conceives longer chapters to keep his reader captive. His *Essais* have slipped over to the side of leisure activities and

---

[iv] Roughly, "leafing through." [Trans.]

entertainment: "Because such frequent breaks into chapters as I used at the beginning seemed to me to disrupt and dissolve attention before it was aroused, making it disdain to settle and collect for so little, I have begun making them longer, requiring fixed purpose and assigned leisure. In such an occupation, if you will not give a man a single hour, you will not give him anything."[67]

These successive transformations of the reader—or at least of Montaigne's conception of the reader—were influenced by the different conceptions of a text that is henceforth envisaged as an indissociable whole. We can say that, after 1588, Montaigne claims that his book has a coherence, but it is a formal rather than a conceptual coherence. The logic of this homogeneity escapes understanding, but that matters little because Montaigne is offering an unprecedented book. The reader will have to let himself be persuaded to read in a different way the text he is given. The coherence of the text has to do solely with the fact that it emanates from an individual who assures us of the well-foundedness of his project and who presents himself as a model for the reader. The famous "strata" of the *Essais*, generally indicated in modern editions, must necessarily disappear in Montaigne's conception of his book after 1588. It is no longer a didactic or evolving text, but simply a mirror in which the author's self becomes an other in the construction of the reader's self.

Between 1588, the beginning of a definitive retirement to his château, and September 13, 1592, the date of his death, Montaigne acquired the habit of working in the margins of several printed copies of the 1588 edition of the *Essais*. Printed on large sheets of paper with wide margins, these working copies allowed him to add new commentaries and reflections, and also to correct his text for a printing that unfortunately did not take place during his lifetime. In the Bordeaux Copy, Montaigne modified the *Au lecteur* one last time, going so far as to delete and then to rewrite one sentence, cross out two words, and change the punctuation. The *Essais* were no longer seen as a way of gaining access to coveted careers; instead, they now represented a career in themselves. Writing was no longer a means but an end in itself. We can finally speak of retirement, but a retirement that must not be confused with an exile because from this time on the tower became the place of creation, the seat of a new career.

Whereas earlier Montaigne had to leave his château to reach the sites of power he dreamed about (the parlement, embassies, the Court), going to Rome, Bordeaux, and Paris, he now fashioned an image of a recluse that better served his final career. The tower is worth visiting, because in it one finds the famous library where the author now spent most of his time:

> It is on the third floor of a tower; the first is my chapel, the second a bedroom and dressing room, where I often sleep in order to be alone. Above it is a great wardrobe. In the past it was the most useless space in my house.

> In my library I spend most of the days of my life, and most of the hours of
> the day. I am never there at night. Adjoining it is a rather elegant little
> room, in which a fire may be laid in winter, very pleasantly lighted by a
> window. And if I feared the trouble no more than the expense, the trouble
> that drives me from all business, I could easily add on to each side a gallery
> a hundred paces long and twelve wide, on the same level, having found all
> the walls raised, for another purpose, to the necessary height.[68]

This late description of his workroom locates Montaigne in his château. The
travel that went hand in hand with political or diplomatic careers gives way to
another sort of movement, this time in books. Montaigne no longer moves
through the world, the world comes to him. Whereas the first essays responded
to a centrifugal movement, pushing Montaigne outside his book toward active
and public life, now, inversely, the additions to the Bordeaux Copy form a cen-
tripetal force that directs Montaigne toward the interior, into his book, the only
place of his existence as an author.

We have several texts testifying to visits to Montaigne, where the author of
the *Essais* lived, between 1588 and 1592. It was fashionable to visit the writer
closed up in his tower; that had already become a kind of pilgrimage for scholars in the region. Montaigne was in the process of acquiring a high opinion of
himself and of his career as an author. Marie de Gournay attests to Montaigne's
fame in her preface to the posthumous edition of the *Essais* published in 1595,
but was he really aware of the true nature of these visits? Marie de Gournay
seems clear-sighted when she reports an anecdote that reveals this gap between
Montaigne's conception of himself after 1588 and the perception that his guests
had of him:

> My father [Montaigne], wanting to displease me one day, told me that he
> thought there were thirty men in our great city [Paris], where he then was,
> who were as smart as he was. One of my arguments to refute him was that
> had there been someone, he would certainly have come to greet him, and,
> it pleased me to add, to idolize him; and that so many people received him
> as a man from a good house, a man of renown and rank: none of them as
> Montaigne.[69]

Did people come to visit Montaigne for his reputation as an author or simply
because he was a gentleman? Gournay answers this question when she comments on Montaigne's attitude toward his book and his new career: "I shall tell
you [the reader] that the public favor he talks about is not the one he believed he
was owed, but rather the one he thought all the less about obtaining because a
fuller and more perfect one was due him."[70] This surprising declaration on the

part of Marie de Gournay reveals a wide gap between Montaigne's perception of his own work from 1588 on and the reality of the reception of the *Essais*. On the one hand, Montaigne declares that he enjoys the public's favor, and on the other hand Gournay tells us that Montaigne was short-sighted when he imagined his audience and took his desires for realities. In a letter, Estienne Pasquier confirms that Montaigne had a high opinion of himself: "while he pretends to disdain himself, I never read an author who esteemed himself more than he."[71]

Whereas he had formerly tried to make his inclination toward justice and honor jibe with the political practices of his time, Montaigne now detached himself from politics and from public service to devote himself to his "back room," the curiosity cabinet that his book had become. Freedom and idleness are reconciled in a model that recovers its title to nobility: "Freedom and laziness, which are my ruling qualities, are qualities diametrically opposite to that trade [public service]."[72] The tower was no longer a refuge that allowed him to let the crises that inevitably punctuated political life pass him by, but rather an experimental laboratory where a new literary genre was taking form. After 1588, the *Essais* were constructed in opposition to the first *Essais* based on a strong conviction that politics and diplomacy could be improved. After having erased (or rather "drowned") the references to the political events that punctuated his first *Essais*, Montaigne now took an interest in the human condition in its universality and atemporality.

Let us consider Montaigne in his library after 1588. He had accumulated on his shelves several editions of his *Essais* as objects *independent* of each other, all bearing witness to publishing projects that had evolved over time. These objects/books reminded him of his different intentions. This observation offers us an opportunity to look into the relation that Montaigne might have had with the books in his library (including those that had his name on the title page). The author of the *Essais* provided a remarkable number of details regarding the arrangement of his books and his way of consulting them. As we have seen, historians "came right to his forehead" and certainly occupied a privileged place in the layout of his library. The fitting out of the second floor of his tower corresponded to an organizational logic derived not only from his reading habits but also from his own work as an author after 1588. We can imagine a deliberate organization of the shelves allowing rapid and repeated access to the books he used most often. Montaigne then took his own book as the starting point for new textual developments. From one year to the next, the author "Montaigne" occupied more and more space—as new editions of the *Essais* came out—on the shelves of his library. The production of the *Essais* was based not only on the consultation of other people's books but also on the recasting of his own works.

After 1588, the author "Montaigne" occupied one shelf, or even a whole bookcase, because he kept several copies of each edition of the *Essais* that were reserved for the work of correction, constituting proofs, as well as others that were intended as presents to be given to visitors passing through. From a simple Montaigne shelf, we have passed to a Montaigne bookcase. In fact, we have to add to this list the "Montaignes" (*Essais* of 1580, 1582, and 1588), the two editions of Sebond's *Théologie naturelle* (1569 and 1581), the edition of La Boéties' works (1571), and the manuscript of the journal of his travels in Germany, Switzerland, and Italy. These objects must have occupied a place of choice in his library. They represented singular objects, but they were also separate texts, each of which had a different goal and a different audience. For that reason, we must lay to rest the myth perpetuated since the nineteenth century, according to which Montaigne was the author of a single book. The *Essais* existed in their plurality and their variety, and they never had the unity that is assigned to them today. How, for example, can we understand the long chapter "Apology for Raymond Sebond" (a book within a book) without the editions of Montaigne's translation of the *Theologia naturalis* by this same Raymond Sebond?

As Montaigne acknowledges, books that he seldom looked at were also in his library. These are the ones that occupied a place on the periphery of his shelves. Montaigne took care to inscribe a few notes and brief commentaries at the end of these works in order to refresh his memory in the event that he decided to consult them again. Among these peripheral volumes, Montaigne placed "his Guicciardini" (*La Historia d'Italia*) and "his Philippe de Comines" (*Mémoires*). Over time, these books disappeared from his memory and fell into oblivion. Thus Montaigne more than once happened "to pick up again, as recent and unknown to me, books which I had read carefully a few years before and scribbled over with my notes."[73] However, we must be wary of the importance assigned to the books annotated in Montaigne's hand that have been found. The fact that they are extant today does not mean that they had a central place in Montaigne's library. The hundred or so books that belonged to Montaigne and that have been accounted for are naturally more revered than the ones that have been lost. However, the tree hides the forest. In Montaigne's case, one book bearing his signature may mask many more. We must therefore question the relative importance of the few books containing "reading notes" that have been put on sale over the past two centuries and that are too often presented as if they played a determining role in the development of his thought. It is not a matter of minimizing the importance of these works, but only of putting into perspective the significance of these notes in Montaigne's hand in relation to the totality of a collection of books of which we now have only about one-tenth.[74]

In 1588, the *Essais* were already established as the book of books, a library in itself; they became the antithesis of the *Discourse on Voluntary Servitude* the moment Montaigne denied his text any possibility of being used for political purposes. It was in accord with this logic of distancing from history that Montaigne claimed that he presented only opinions produced by "a tumultuous and vacillating mind."[75] Whereas for La Boétie the *Discourse* was a work of his "boyhood" written "only by way of an exercise,"[76] after 1585—and especially after 1588—the *Essais* was a text that expressed Montaigne's maturity, his political resignation, and his sense of a history that he no longer made and that was behind him. La Boétie could now disappear from the *Essais*. The few traces of him that remained in the first editions of the *Essais* gradually faded away. La Boétie's twenty-nine sonnets had remained like a wart on Montaigne's face, and we can imagine his relief when he discovered that these verses had been published "elsewhere"—perhaps in the famous description of the Médoc area that has now been lost.[v] It had become pointless to reproduce these verses any longer, and Montaigne crossed them out. After all, La Boétie was known as an orator, not as a poet. Each person has his abilities: La Boétie became a politician again and Montaigne now erected himself into a literary man. Deleting these sonnets full of "originality and beauty"[77] was an obvious move, but once again, instead of omitting the whole chapter, Montaigne cut only the verses. The title—"Twenty-nine sonnets of Etienne de la Boétie"—remained as a remnant of another time, another conception of the *Essais*. The sonnets had initially replaced a treatise on political philosophy, and the time had come to do away with this "false space" that might leave the impression that La Boétie still had a place in the book. Paradoxically, this La Boétie, who existed "outside the *Essais*," had become a herald of the Protestant cause, and Montaigne no longer saw any reason to keep him in his own writings. Since politics had been relegated to the space outside the book, La Boétie obviously had to pay the price for this disappearance and could be eclipsed in his turn.

The Bordeaux Copy marks a decisive turning point toward the *practice of the margins* that now defines Montaigne. But it would be wrong to see in the editions of 1580, 1582, and 1588 the origin of a *literary* and *philosophical* tendency that asserted itself only after 1588, following the disastrous, traumatizing experience of his brief imprisonment and his failure as a negotiator between Navarre and Henry III. When Montaigne wrote or dictated his first essays, he did so under the weight of history and the events of his time. Later on, in his library, Montaigne was able to create an independent work space, sheltered from the troubles outside. His past works reminded him of past publishing intentions; they constituted the memory of a social and political itinerary that went back

---

[v] In the eighteenth century, in *Bibliothèque historique de la France* (1768) by P. Lelong, published by Févret de Fontette, we find under no. 2230 the following item: "*Historique description du solitaire et sauvage pays de Médoc (dans le Bordelois), par feu M. De La Boétie*, Millanges, 1593, *in-12°*." In a note, we read: "A few verses by the same author have been added to this description, which are not found in the edition of his works Michel de Montaigne published."

more than twenty years. Each edition of the *Essais* offered itself to the public as a singular object that replaced the preceding editions. In Montaigne's case, and by way of his library, all the editions of the *Essais* had their own lives that corresponded to distinct and often contradictory stages; we have only to compare the work repeatedly done on the 1580 text with the addition of new chapters in 1588 and the addition of copious manuscript developments on the Bordeaux Copy. Montaigne slowly became aware of the political failure of the years between 1588 and 1592.

Montaigne evolved into an author by accident, at least that is what he says. But let us be wary of legends. According to him, he cared little about his audience and wrote only to live on after his demise, in the memory of his relatives and close friends. Moreover, he was not really an author: "Authors communicate with the people by some special extrinsic mark; I am the first to do so by my entire being, as Michel de Montaigne, not as a grammarian or a poet or a jurist."[78] This universality of being corresponds to a late construction and reflects an observation rather than a choice, because Montaigne had tried hard to assert himself by some "special extrinsic mark." We might even say that his book is the precise opposite of a writing that is "unpremeditated and accidental."[79] Thus we must take with a grain of salt Montaigne's repeated statements concerning his private and particular publications—for his father in the case of the *Théologie naturelle*, for his deceased friend in the case of the *Mesnagerie de Xenophon*, or simply "dedicated to the private convenience of [his] relatives and friends"[80] in the case of the *Essais*. Montaigne's book naturally grew over time, but it developed in divergent directions. For that reason, the maturity of the text coincides with its monstrosity, because the *Essais* are pieced together and do not necessarily form a harmonious whole. But the manuscript additions of the last four years, written in the margins of the Bordeaux Copy, gave the book a more personal character that transformed forever our judgment of the book and allowed it to become a canonical work. The Virgilian epigraph, *Viresque acquirit eundo* ("As it goes on, it gathers strength") is written by hand on the title page of the Bordeaux Copy and henceforth served as a motto for the *Essais*, because Montaigne had understood that his text had arrived at maturity.[vi] The quotation Montaigne chose to introduce and summarize his *Essais* comes from the *Aeneid*, where it refers to the propagation of rumor. Montaigne gives this Virgilian fragment a new meaning by associating this phrase with the growth of his book as a result of his successive additions; the *Essais*, like

---

[vi] This motto was not added on the *Exemplar* used for the printing of the posthumous edition of 1595. On the other hand, Marie de Gournay added this quotation on the copy she sent to Justus Lipsius (known as the "Antwerp Copy"). It was only starting in 1535 that this inscription gave way to the motto "Que sçay-je?" ("What do I know?") on the title page of the *Essais*.

rumor, progresses and becomes stronger thanks to the additions Montaigne made to his text.

The different editions of the *Essais* correspond to *distinct* moments, but not to the stages of some kind of coordinated evolution. While the 1580 edition was addressed to a limited audience and can be considered a *private edition* published to make himself known to a small circle of influential men (which is not very different from the model prevalent in the Middle Ages, in which the only thing that mattered was the personalized presentation of the book to the prince), the 1582 edition responded to a very different logic and benefited Millanges as much as it did Montaigne in the context of his election as mayor of Bordeaux. These first two editions nonetheless remained firmly anchored locally or regionally, and their printing had as its principal goal to establish the author's political role while at the same time asserting his membership in the nobility. After 1585, Montaigne's political pretensions were significantly compromised, though his career had not come to a complete end. The difficulties he experienced as mayor of Bordeaux led him to consider a different orientation of his activity as an author. The third book of the *Essais* offered several testimonies to this disillusionment with public office, but Montaigne nonetheless retained the hope of a political career in the service of princes. The year 1588 brought a rupture and revealed a new attitude toward the "duties of honor" and "civil constraint." Far from considering this last Montaigne as the outcome of the years from 1570 to 1588, we must see in his work on the *Essais* after 1588 a form of resignation and the expression of a realization of a political misfortune that is explained by the author's political biography.

This failure led to a late revelation. In fact, after 1588 the positive reception—on the qualitative and not the quantitative level—of the *Essais* allowed Montaigne to glimpse the possibility of a career as an author. From this time on the staging of Montaigne as a *daily author*, a practician and theoretician of the "textual extension," began. The 1588 edition certainly marks an important moment in the construction of this image to which we are now accustomed, but it has the defect of obscuring the independent projects of 1580 and 1582 without having yet fully accepted the writing of the self as its main object. The tumultuous events in Paris at the time of the barricades and Montaigne's imprisonment in 1588 put an end to any political pretensions. The myth of the lord retired to his estate and to his tower could then take on substance. Once and for all, the private was given precedence over the public.

The writing in the margins of the Bordeaux Copy marks the beginning of a new project, and it is this work that defines Montaigne today. But it would be a mistake to seek in the publication of the editions of 1580 and 1582 the origins of a tendency that truly asserted itself only starting in the period between 1585 and 1588. That is why the *Essais* of 1580, 1582, 1588, and the text of 1595 form very different political and literary projects and must be understood in relation to the political and religious climate in which Montaigne lived before and after his return from Italy and his two terms as mayor of Bordeaux. One of the last additions to the Bordeaux Copy offers a disappointed, a posteriori commentary on his political commitment to Henry III his allegiance to Henry IV, the new king of France. It was now with a greater *concern for himself* and a certain detachment that the author of the *Essais* judged these two kings and, more generally, politics: "I look upon our kings simply with a loyal and civic affection, which is neither moved nor removed by private interest. For this I congratulate myself."[81] A salutary, but belated distance for someone who had earlier boasted of having developed a privileged friendship with the two Henrys.

Montaigne's different publishing projects were determined by different political logics and must be studied sociologically. These projects may seem cumulative, but they respond to strategies that varied over time. It is here that Montaigne's biography allows us to distinguish precisely what the successive stages of writing and publishing the *Essais* from 1570 to 1592 represent. Montaigne's books have an undeniable presence and temporality, because they testify to the materiality of a text subject to publishing operations determined in space and time. Montaigne was always aware of the materiality of his *Essais*, going so far as to change the form of their presentation—I refer to the development of the formats (octavo, quarto, and folio for the printings of 1580–82, 1588, and 1595, respectively). Earlier publishing choices no longer corresponded to Montaigne's idea of his book and his reader.

Generally speaking, we can also say that the first two books of the *Essais* are now placed under the preeminence of the third, which is associated with the "last Montaigne." The thirteen chapters of the third book, almost five times less numerous than those in the first book, provide the overwhelming majority of the passages cited by critics over the past fifty years. In particular, this "qualitative" and selective practice of Montaigne gives special priority to the additions to the Bordeaux Copy, that is, to the manuscript part of the *Essais* that arrogantly dominates the short chapters in the 1580 edition. We note, for example, that after 1588 Montaigne is more inclined to make additions to the third book, almost all of whose chapters include rather copious additions made in the margins of the Bordeaux Copy. A single chapter in this book stands out as an exception: "Of the disadvantage of greatness" (III: 7), which is not as long as the others and appears to be the third book's poor relation.

Montaigne's work on the Bordeaux Copy tends to unite the three books in a vision of the writing of the self. Contradictions and digressions abound, but they are now the proof of a self in movement and a kind of writing that gives priority to intuition at the expense of reasoning. The chapter "Against do-nothingness" (II: 21), which is very short in its first version in the 1580 edition, is significantly expanded in the margins of the Bordeaux Copy in order to make it more personal and allow Montaigne to offer a few more philosophical reflections on the subject. Similarly, the chapter "Of riding post" (II: 22), although very short in the editions of 1580 and 1588, undergoes a new development that establishes a certain balance among the three strata of the text (approximately equal in length). Montaigne now puts the accent on the private character of his reflections and displays himself as "nakedly" as possible, often showing a kind of exhibitionism. Thus the chapter in the third book most extensively reworked after 1588 (in terms of the percentage of words added) is "Of physiognomy," with about two-thirds of the final text appearing in the 1588 edition and one-third written after 1588, whereas in the case of the other chapters in the third book only between 20 and 25 percent of the text was added after 1588.

Very early on, Montaigne perceived and commented on the *foreign character* of his first writings. Thus in 1588 he noted that "of my first essays, some smell a bit foreign."[82] In the Bordeaux Copy, he returns to this observation, which can now no longer escape the reader, as if to reassure us regarding the unity of his project after 1588. The neglected chapters we have already discussed now raise the question by their simple presence, even if they continue to be ignored. Montaigne accepts in a way their difference and considers them an integral part of the *Essais*. They testify to what Montaigne called, toward the end of his life, an "ill-fitted patchwork."[83] Publishing the same text under the same title, on several occasions and with extensive revisions of the chapters, calls for a clarification that is not always obvious for the reader. The *Essais* are a model of the genre insofar as recycling text is concerned, and Montaigne ends up bringing the contradictions and digressions of his book together in a general theory of the essay. He has an overall view of his book and labors to explain it.

Insofar as the Bordeaux Copy is concerned, only five chapters of the first book and four of the second include no additions to the 1588 text, while nine chapters are left unchanged (as compared with twenty-two in the 1588 edition in its relation to the 1580 edition). The posthumous edition of the *Essais* published by Marie de Gournay in 1595 reveals the extent of the work done by Montaigne after 1588. Generally speaking, we can say that starting in 1588 Montaigne accorded equal attention to his three books.

In the posthumous 1595 edition (whose text is not very different from the Bordeaux Copy), the *Essais* have 408,790 words distributed in the following way: 45 percent in the 1580 text, 33 percent added in 1588, and 22 percent added by hand on the Bordeaux Copy, most of them incorporated in the 1595 edition. In the latter, the first book includes 26 percent additions, the second 20 percent, and the third 22 percent. These figures testify to the homogeneous work done by the author, who modified the three books in an almost uniform manner during the last four years of his life. Thus after 1588, Montaigne reread and added as much to his first two books: 30,783 words added to the first book, 33,251 to the second and 28,318 to the third.

These additions are distributed relatively equally among the three books and make it possible to conclude that by this point Montaigne had fully accepted the major differences in content between his first two books and the third published in 1588. After 1588, his work consisted primarily in harmonizing the whole of his text while at the same time respecting its contradictions as an integral part of the form of the essay as he understood it toward the end of his life. Montaigne now sought to establish transitions that were not obvious in the 1588 edition. The *Essais* acquired a greater coherence, and the self, placed at strategic places in the first two books, represents a kind of leading thread running through the three books. The highlighting of the self and the writing of Montaigne's experiences serve as a common denominator and make it possible to connect editions that were conceived in different ways over time.

After 1588, Montaigne reread his book with a new conception of writing that tended to highlight personal judgment and minimize the political discourse that was overrepresented in the *Essais* of 1580. He deconstructed his original political discourse in order to resituate it in a private perspective in which the subject is freed from social constraints. He de-historicized his first essays and transformed them into an enduring discourse on himself and systematically eliminated politics and history from his remarks. His own experiences are presented as universal and now pertain to the human condition. Thus between 1588 and 1592 Montaigne engaged in a systematic work of rereading (and rewriting), with the goal of making his book more homogeneous and coherent.

If the *Essais* of 1580 and 1588 were, at least for the most part, certainly dictated to a secretary, the Bordeaux Copy perpetuated the idea of a "manual labor" that, for purely material reasons, could not be carried out on the *Essais* before 1588. To illustrate the constant contemporaneity of his various publishing enterprises, we have only to cite the instructions Montaigne gave the printer on one of the flyleaves of the Bordeaux Copy: "Put my name all along on each page Essays of Michel de Montaigne liv. I"[84] (figures 17 and 18). Montaigne did not like it that his name had been truncated in the running heads at the top of each page and asked the master printer to restore his full name in the planned new edition of his *Essais*. He also advised the compositors to use capital letters only for proper names and to see to it that the same word did not appear sometimes with a capital letter and sometimes without one. He also insisted on the quotations in Latin or Greek prose being made more visible and more clearly distinguished from his own text by using italics. Similarly, verses were to begin

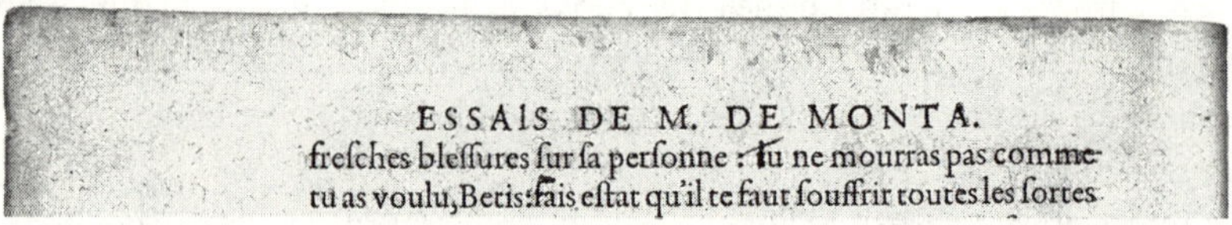

ESSAIS DE M. DE MONTA.
fresches bleſſures ſur ſa perſonne : tu ne mourras pas comme
tu as voulu, Betis: fais eſtat qu'il te faut ſouffrir toutes les ſortes

FIGURE 17. Running head, Bordeaux Copy of the *Essais*. Image courtesy of Bibliothèque municipale de Bordeaux.

on separate lines and thus be differentiated from prose. He also made recommendations regarding spelling and the use of parentheses, and he left the printer little discretion, reminding him that the presentation he had chosen for his book was of great importance: "In addition to the corrections that are on this copy there are countless others to be made of which the printer may become aware, but pay close attention to the points that are of great importance to the style."[85] Montaigne was more concerned than ever with the physical and visual aspect of his book. He addressed the printer directly and gave him a series of precise instructions regarding the format and physical presentation of his book. The title page also included additions in Montaigne's hand that designated the Bordeaux Copy as the manuscript to be used for the printing of a future "sixth" edition.

The manuscript part of the Bordeaux Copy represents almost a quarter of the whole text of the *Essais*.[vii] These additions made during the last four years of Montaigne's life are now predominant when passages are cited from the *Essais*. We can see why, since this last "stratum"[86] of the *Essais* is generally considered the final stage of a supposedly premeditated and coherent route, a Montaigne who is both personal and wise, who emphasizes his subjectivity and is a precursor of modernity. This image of the last Montaigne is quite distant from the first Montaigne, who was more attentive to his period and prepared to participate in political life. Montaigne's work on the Bordeaux Copy is important, because it allows us to reconstruct the practices of writing (which were limited periods of writing often separated by several years) that testify not only to Montaigne's personality but also, more generally, to the relationship authors of the late Renaissance had to their books. For a little more than four years, Montaigne continued to add, delete, and correct passages in the Bordeaux Copy, because the 1588 edition was not supposed to be the last.

The Bordeaux Copy is a writer's manuscript with all the problems of legibility that this kind of text implies.[87] It is not easy to decipher the additions and pentimenti Montaigne formulated. All Montaigne's editors, from the sixteenth

---

[vii] The manuscript additions on the Bordeaux Copy run to 91,552 words, or 22 percent of the total text of the *Essais*.

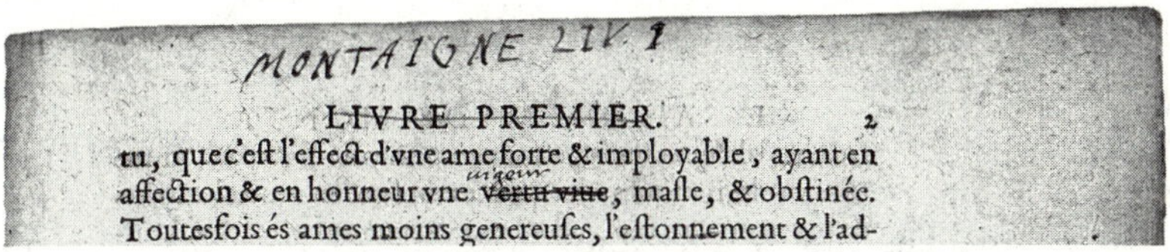
MONTAIGNE LIV 1

LIVRE PREMIER. 2

tu, quec'eſt l'effect d'vne ame forte & imployable, ayant en affection & en honneur vne ~~vertu viue~~, maſle, & obſtinée. Toutesfois és ames moins genereuſes, l'eſtonnement & l'ad-

FIGURE 18. Manuscript correction by Montaigne. Bordeaux Copy of the *Essais*. Image courtesy of Bibliothèque municipale de Bordeaux.

century to the present day, have faced insurmountable editorial obstacles in trying to establish the text of the *Essais* on the basis of the Bordeaux Copy. A quick glance at this document makes it easy to judge and gauge the difficulty.[viii] Moreover, for more than two centuries Montaigne specialists have been debating the final state of the text of the *Essais* and thus the editorial status of the Bordeaux Copy. Today we can be certain that when Montaigne died there were two copies of the *Essais* of 1588 that included additions written in his hand. The Bordeaux Copy has the particularity of having been two distinct things at two different moments: first the copy that was to be used for the printing of a new edition (which explains the instructions to the printer), and then a copy abandoned by Montaigne in favor of another copy—the *Exemplar*—on which he made a clean copy of his changes to the 1588 edition.

First, Montaigne wrote on the Bordeaux Copy precise, scrupulous annotations addressed to the compositors. For example, he marked in the margins of the first folios of the Bordeaux Copy the corrections to be made by the compositors, and these are still followed today. He noted changes of characters, deleting a large number of capital letters for titles and institutions: "seigneur" instead of "Seigneur," "comte" for "Comte," "parlement" for "Parlement." At one point Montaigne gave up the systematic rereading of what he had formerly considered the equivalent of printer's proofs. From then on, the Bordeaux Copy was transformed into a rough draft manuscript that would allow Montaigne to transfer his additions in more legible form to another copy of the 1588 *Essais*. This explains why this second copy was sent to Marie de Gournay to be used for the composition of the posthumous edition of 1595. Initially,

[viii] The problem of the reproduction of the manuscript additions and pentimenti contained in the Bordeaux Copy was already raised in 1862, when Reinhold Dezeimeris and Jules Delpit approached the Bordeaux printer Gounouilhou concerning a possible printing of the Bordeaux Copy in his workshop. In a letter to Dr. Payen, Dezeimeris wrote: "M. Delpit must have written to you about Montaigne. The sight of the copy that bears his copy preparation for the printer literally floored Gounouilhou's compositor. He saw it as an inextricable typographical labor, and felt sorry for the typographer who would be forced to reproduce this text." Reinhold Dezeimeris, letter to Dr. Payen, BNF, Fonds Payen, dossier Z Payen 656 (correspondence).

Montaigne considered the Bordeaux Copy the basis for printing a new edition. But when he decided to postpone this printing, he continued to write directly in the margins of the Bordeaux Copy, often in a less legible hand no longer meant for a third party but only for himself. In order to register his text on a second copy, and because he wanted to provide more legible corrections and additions for the printer, Montaigne later made a clean copy of the "textual extension" of the Bordeaux Copy in another copy (the *Exemplar*), which, after being checked by Pierre de Brach (whose task was to ensure that the two copies were "practically" identical), was sent to Marie de Gournay. During the making of this clean copy, Montaigne corrected himself, giving special attention to the punctuation and segmentation of the printed text,[88] even though in disparate ways in the two copies available to him—the Bordeaux Copy and the *Exemplar*.

From History to the Essay: Commynes and Tacitus

We have argued that the author of the *Essais* of 1580 was situated in a tradition of memoir-writers more than he was already a true essayist. Montaigne conceived his book and his career in direct relation to current history. Thus the reading of historians was essential in preparing Montaigne for the political and diplomatic responsibilities he envisioned. It was during this period of reflection on the subject matter of history and on historical thought that Montaigne wrote many passages in which he asserts that "History is more my quarry,"[89] or again "the historians are the true quarry of my study."[90] The inventory of Montaigne's library shows a pronounced taste for historical works. The first Montaigne had a very broad conception of history: "the reading of history . . . is everybody's business,"[91] because in the category of history he included all kinds of cultural or anthropological writings. Montaigne literally fed on others' stories to arrive at the essay, which, thanks to a universalization of the self, ends up leaving history behind in order to propose a new form of narrative, that of a life sufficient unto itself.

The reading of Commynes's *Memoirs* contributed to this disintegration of traditional history to the advantage of a "better history."[92] For that, Montaigne followed with interest Commynes's career in the service of kings, and he was able to evaluate the way the chronicler had slowly inserted himself into the history of those about whom he was supposed to be writing. In the fifth book of his *Memoirs*, Commynes clearly differentiates his enterprise from the chronicles of his predecessors: "Those who write Chronicles, frame their stile commonly to their commendation of whom they speake, omitting divers points, sometimes because they know not the truth of them. But as touching myself, I minde to write nothing but that is true, and which I my selfe either have seen or learned of such parties as are woorthie of credite, not regarding any mans commendation."[93]

There can be no doubt that initially it was this sincerity that Montaigne liked in Commynes's work, ten years before he entered politics. However, Montaigne's "good faith" slipped away in the course of his political experiences, and he became aware that deception and Commynes's banishment prefigured his own political career. At first, Commynes's concern to preserve his independence with regard to the established government lent a certain credit to this distancing from the clientelism associated with historical writing. Montaigne believed he had finally found an example in which the subject inscribed his place in history, or even in spite of history. The tormented and often unpredictable course of a life greatly influences the theories that authors may construct to explain—after the fact—a literary practice that is basically connected with the demands of a career. Commynes and Montaigne resemble each other to a certain extent, because both had political ambitions and developed new literary genres.

Commynes and Montaigne both claimed, each in his own way, to have broken with earlier political practices. Certainly they operated at the Court and, with different degrees of success, they belonged to the inner circle of government before experiencing setbacks and finally finding a new space (both political and literary) where they could assert themselves in a different way. But what links the two authors is that after a long practice of the memoir or essay, they realized that their true subject was their experience of themselves. The prince's counselor had things to say about himself, and so did the mayor of Bordeaux. What matters is the transformation that takes place over the years in genres that can be conceived only in a long-term perspective and bear on a life consisting of highs and lows. It is impossible to provide a stylistic analysis of Commynes's *Memoirs* and Montaigne's *Essais* without understanding these authors' individual situations in their immediate political context. The genre of the memoir, like the genre of the essay, as developed by Commynes and Montaigne, are intrinsically connected with their political experience.

Commynes and Montaigne explored literary genres different enough to account for their relations with their princes. Commynes's *Memoirs*—though written between 1489 and 1491, and then between 1497 and 1498—cover a historical period of thirty-five years (from 1464 to 1498), while Montaigne's *Essais* bear on more than twenty years of religious conflict (from 1570 to 1592). It is hard to maintain ideological and political unity over such long stretches of time. For that reason, the two men needed to include political points of view that were sometimes contradictory and—without really admitting it, but perhaps more importantly—career concerns that accompanied their paths toward becoming authors. In both cases, the lack of unity is more an obvious fact than a preference. For Commynes and Montaigne, the goal was to explain contradictory positions in light of a different conception of the individual, a being in movement who assumes in response positions regarding which we will, moreover, never know the whole truth. The coherence of the analyses made within a particular situation in which the author is supposed to present himself as a sage fades to make way for a self that occupies a growing place in a text that is slowly dispossessed of its initial function, depicting (or discussing) history or politics. In the work of both Commynes and Montaigne, the history of princes is transformed, through good times and bad, into a history of the self. The events that were the commentary's point of departure are relegated to the background the better to show that history results from a series of situations that can be understood only in their immediate context and on the basis of an analysis that is more psychological than truly historical.

The chronology of princes is secondary, and only the temporality of the counselor or the mayor transformed into a narrator lends a simultaneously punctual and universal dimension to these "great men": Louis XI, Charles the Bold, Henry III, Henry of Navarre, and the dukes of Guise, who are presented with their peculiar character traits. Digression and narrative disorder then make it possible to cover the tracks of an impossible coherence. Repetitions have a paradoxical historical value, because they discredit the chronological narrative. Contradictions, repetitions, and digressions serve to establish the basis for a new form of writing in which the subject is self-sufficient. The commentary on government and society has value only because it serves as a starting point for the interpreter, who presents his judgment as the only possible history. To serve princes is to be capable of putting things in perspective, to place oneself above the historical object while constantly asserting that one's own authority is based only on a particular, subjective experience. Personal opinion serves history because, thanks to a general leveling of humanity, the prince, the memoirist[ix] and the essayist are all on the same footing. Memoirs and the essay lower kings in order to raise the interpreter who plumbs the depths of his unconscious; the historian and the essayist become psychologists in the name of a principle that makes each individual, no matter what his rank, the essential reference point for understanding human beings in their universality. This human dimension of historical actors implies a fragility inherent in man, and this fragility explains failures, even those of Commynes and Montaigne. They cannot be superior to those whose decisions and actions they relate. Instability of judgment is not

---

[ix] I use the term *memoirist* instead of *memorialist* since I want to emphasize the genre of *mémoire* writing, not to be confused with the genre of *memorial* writing. In French such a distinction does not exist and the noun *mémorialiste* applies to both genres.

uniquely an attribute of princes; it defines human beings in general. Thus nothing must be excluded from history, because everything is meaningful and can illuminate situations to come.

Following Commynes, Montaigne made a deliberate choice to get lost in digressions, with the same will not to hide anything. This logic of *saying everything* merges the history of others with one's own experiences. The self transforms history into stories, because stories play a fundamental role in putting the self and its writing in movement, and they are indispensable for voicing opinions. Commynes had exploited history by transforming it in accord with his own needs: history became at once topos and example. It is the repetition of experiences that explains what is essential in human actions. Montaigne seems to have adopted Commynes's lesson, which he made into a principle in his *Essais* after 1585. It is not the quality of the information, but the quantity of information that makes it possible to select, classify, and rank events with the necessary distance. Commynes's *Memoirs* and Montaigne's *Essais* offer us the best examples of this phenomenon of reinterpretation and rewriting bearing on events that had already been commented upon by the memoirist or essayist at a time when they occupied a different position with respect to political power. If Commynes did not reject points of view that were now in contradiction with a different reality on the ground, he did depart from them in order to offer an object of analysis that demanded its own autonomy. In his turn, Montaigne came to discover the fundamental role of the interpreter; it is the interpreter's point of view or the impression made on him that gives meaning to political acts and historical events. Without the memoirist or the essayist, no history or politics would be possible. Commynes's *Memoirs* had been to history what Montaigne's *Essais* were becoming for politics.

In both cases, the reader is faced with a fundamental opposition between the form (memoir or essay), which refers to stylistics, and content (history), which has to do with politics and ideology. The two genres, even though they claim to acquire a certain autonomy with regard to this content, are fundamentally connected with it. Form asserts itself at the expense of content without, however, renouncing or rejecting it. Here we must not confuse Commynes's *Memoirs* with the memoirs written in the second half of the sixteenth century and in the seventeenth century.[94] What unifies the memoir genre created by Commynes is the instability of the status of history—the instability of particular and rather negative experiences concerning the history he is interpreting, but in which he was not able to be a genuine actor. Seventeenth-century memoirs reconnected with a certain stability of history and had a very different partisan function. In this sense, the memoir genre, after Commynes and Montaigne, acquired a positive conception of history in which the interpreter felt himself to be fully engaged. It is no longer content that makes history; on the contrary, history is made by the interaction between the historical object (the example invoked) and the work done on the historical material by the reader-author, who espouses a form and denies the authority of these histories to claim a univocal view and understanding.

The distance necessary to report a "truer" history consists in the reification in the present moment of all past historical experiences. At the opposite pole, the confrontation between the event and the self of the narrator provokes a reaction that is simultaneously ideological and stylistic. This reaction to the history of the other (the prince and the king) and its inscription in the self was already present in Commynes, but it became crucial in the genre of the essay. To this distancing with regard to history, Montaigne added an abandonment of politics and an extreme theory of the separation between public and private. The transition from memoirs to essays thus implies a disenchantment with regard to history and a saving turn toward personal opinion. For Montaigne, relating his past experiences raised a series of questions both conjunctural (ideological) and universal (stylistic). Conjunctural, first of all, because every discourse needs a reference point that is essentially historical, that is, an object that is identifiable and accepted by all. No expression of an opinion, whatever it might be, can escape its historicity. And stylistic, because Montaigne transformed the political content into a particular form that was supposed to express the point of view of a singular, private individual.

The composition of the *Memoirs* required an active participation on the part of the author that might be seen as a kind of historical investment. He needed the other (the prince) to make his self appear. This transformation of an earlier self into another form is an essential component of the *Essais*. Montaigne crossed swords with the alterity of his former self; he could enter into conflict with it and thus produce new "essays" (attempts to write the self) that remained incomplete. Time was an obstacle to the form of the essay, and the author always exceeded his writing, which was constantly transcended by the present moment, the moment that puts in question past experiences and objectifies them as the history of another person, which is most often verifiable (usually a topos) and thus becomes "historical." History, which is necessary to put the self in motion, is at the center of the genre of the memoir, and it could not be otherwise for Montaigne. In the essay, this history occupies an increasingly central place, but only the better to be ultimately denied. It is this negation of history and the posture of retirement adopted by the historical actor that distinguishes the form of the essay and that of the memoir. Commynes's *Memoirs* lead to a questioning of the event-logic of the great figures, while the *Essais* bear witness to its failure; in both cases, the outcome is a new literary form and reflects a personal itinerary *in* history. Feeling essential in history while at the same time feeling marginalized (for different reasons, to be sure: treachery or a bad political choice) by this same history marks and structures the writing of both Commynes and Montaigne.

Two tendencies with regard to objectivity and history emerge from the *Memoirs*: first, a certain detachment with respect to the verification and veracity of the stories that Commynes uses. This was amply theorized by Montaigne in 1580: "I refer the stories that I borrow to the conscience of those from whom I take them."[95] Commynes uses history to find in it the topoi that authorize him to speak. The examples of the great military commanders found in various historical writings give him an opportunity to begin a dialogue with an other in himself, but this dialogue transcends the territory defined by the historian. Each time, Commynes moves outside the framework of the story he has in front of him in order to make of it an object that he ultimately relates to himself. Montaigne proceeds in a similar way by using chapter titles that are only pretexts for talking about something else. The memoirist, perhaps like the essayist—but without the explicit awareness we find in Montaigne—had understood that history did not exist as an immobile object; it begins to exist only when it passes through the work of memory. In Montaigne's work, one of the meanings of the word "essay" (*essai*) refers precisely to the idea of examining and testing, because history takes form only when it is put to the test of memory by the essayist.

By denying the history of the other, the essay universalizes the self and proposes a history that reduces the experience of the other to the advantage of the experience of the self. In his *Memoirs*, Commynes had opted for a "better history," truer and resolving the contradictions inherent in the expression of particular points of view. But this "better history" (which starts after Commynes had rejoined Louis XI) was possible only because he had had the experience of writing a less accurate history (the one he had written in the service of Charles the Bold). The experience of the self served to select, group, sift, and organize the historical material within a form that gave priority to repetitions and digressions and rid itself of chronology in the name of a rediscovered unity of historical truth, of which the universalized self was the only guarantor. The image of the counselor in the service of two princes (Louis XI and Charles the Bold) who were opposites in every way had not failed to catch Montaigne's attention before 1580. Montaigne also imagined that he could serve two princes at once, not one after the other, as Commynes had done, but at the same time. After the break with politics in 1588, Montaigne no longer had anything to accomplish, and his professional situation was compromised. It was at that moment that Montaigne seems to have changed his mind about Commynes, who according to him had betrayed one prince to rejoin another. Montaigne had never betrayed his king.

A specialist in covert operations, Commynes had perhaps gone too far; his book could even be seen as a traitor's confession. After abandoning his first patron, Charles the Bold, he had joined Louis XI, apparently without hesitation. Montaigne had not betrayed anyone, and he was proud of not having sunk into treachery. Commynes's *Memoirs* represented two moments of power. The fact that he combined them in a single work initially pleased Montaigne, but this conglomeration later seemed problematic to him. He had, in a way, gone beyond Commynes, and after 1588 he preferred to ignore that fact. For him, the historian was no longer a model, even if the form of the *Memoirs* had strongly influenced his writing and allowed him to conceive the genre of the essay. Montaigne's conception of politics was now at the antipode of Commynes's idea of public life. He questioned Commynes's good faith, even thinking he had found an instance of plagiarism in the historian's work: "When some years ago I read Philippe de Commines, certainly a very good author, I noted this remark as uncommon: that we must be very careful not to serve our master so well that we keep him from finding a fair reward for our service. I should have praised the idea, not him; I came across it in Tacitus not long ago."[96] Although it is undeniable, Commynes's influence on Montaigne has more to do with the memoir form than with the political lessons Montaigne learned from his reading of the *Memoirs*. Commynes ceased to be a model for Montaigne at the moment when Montaigne's own political career was beginning to slip away. Tacitus thus logically replaced Commynes after 1588. Each in his own way, the two historians and counselors of princes had shown great political prudence, a quality Montaigne valued.[97] Montaigne had long believed in Commynes's good faith, but he had recently found an even more elevated expression in Tacitus. After the belated discovery of Tacitus, Commynes was no longer a political model.

Nevertheless, the absence of references to Commynes after 1588 merits reflection. Montaigne took his political models chiefly from Antiquity. Among the historians, Tacitus occupies a privileged place, even though Montaigne read him rather late in his life. After 1588, he came to regard the historian and Roman senator as the best example of the separation of private life from public life, a separation that he now emphasized in his *Essais*. Tacitus perfectly embodies the figure of the politician who has withdrawn from society, a salutary attitude when faced with the events of his time.[98] The Roman history of which Tacitus gives a lively and colorful account spoke directly to Montaigne. Just as in ancient Rome, tyrants, dictators, assassins, poisoners, rebels, and agitators abounded in late sixteenth-century France, and Montaigne had no difficulty in drawing a parallel between the two periods. The massacres and delusions of power were in no way exceptional and were part of the same political logic. On this point, Tacitus's writings were a revelation for Montaigne. The suggestion that he read the Roman historian had been made by "a gentleman whom France esteems highly,"[99] during a dinner with Antoine de Laval and Charles Paschal at the time of the Estates General at Blois in 1588. Paschal had just published a political commentary on Tacitus's *Histories*. The guests at this dinner may have seen in this book a form of therapy for the affliction Montaigne was suffering from in the wake of his misadventure as a negotiator between the Catholic and Protestant parties.

Descended from a great patrician family, Tacitus was the historian par excellence of troubled times. After beginning his public career as a lawyer, he had become a member of the "Council of 26" under Vespasian, a quaestor under Titus, legate to Belgian Gaul, consul under the emperor Nerva, senator, and finally governor of the province of Asia, before retiring from politics to devote himself to writing history. Today, he is criticized for being more a writer than a historian, but after a rich political career, writing had become for him the last refuge from an unsettled history and represented the logical outcome of a series of negative political experiences. The parallel with Montaigne's political career is striking, or at least it was for Montaigne, who identified with Tacitus. This relationship to a text constructed on the ruins of a calamitous history pleased Montaigne after 1588, a time when the author of the *Essais* was also in a situation of exile or political retirement. He recognized himself in Tacitus and saw in his critical, concise style a model of writing.

The *Histories* of the Empire—the dynasty of the Flavians—cover a period of almost thirty years, between 69 and 96 CE. Tacitus had been able to combine private discourse and public discourse, whereas Montaigne advocated a sharp separation of the two. Tacitus criticized the regimes in which he had participated and was pessimistic about politics after having lived through the time of the plebs and the tyrants. Even Tacitus's name (in Latin "tacitus" means "he who has kept silent"; it is the past participle of *tacere*, "to keep silent") caught the attention of Montaigne, who accorded great importance to proper names and observes, in the chapter "Of names" (I: 46), how convenient it is to have a handsome name that is easy to remember. Montaigne was attracted by Tacitus, and he liked the way the Roman writer skillfully combined a description of the manners of his time with more personal reflections: "I know of no author who introduces into a register of public events so much consideration of private behavior and inclinations."[100] Tacitus became a model for Montaigne, whereas Commynes had disappointed him. Tacitus had found his voice as an author when his political career was behind him, and Montaigne was about to do the same.

Furthermore, in contrast to Commynes, Tacitus had not committed treason and had been able to make a wise withdrawal from political practices of which he no longer approved. The Catholic Church of the sixteenth century considered him suspect. For example, the humanist Marc-Antoine Muret was severely reprimanded by the cardinals when he announced, in 1572, his intention to introduce the reading of Tacitus into the courses he taught.[101] A few years later, however, things had settled down and the first books of the *Annals* were the subject of lectures Muret gave in Rome in 1580 and 1581.

Muret had his commentaries on Tacitus printed in the form of opuscules, but it was Charles Paschal who published the first political commentary on Tacitus, in 1581. A few years earlier, Abel L'Angelier had published a French translation of the *Annals*, soon followed by Tacitus's *Works*. A short time before, Justus Lipsius's first edition of Tacitus's *Histories* had been published by Plantin.[102] This body of Tacitus's works, published by the greatest European printers, had made him known to sixteenth-century readers. He spoke to their concerns because his political history offered numerous points that could be compared with the political situation in France at that time. For these reasons, Tacitus enjoyed enormous success in the 1580s. The publisher Abel L'Angelier wrote that "France was eager to read such a historian, and showed that his study pleased many people."[103] The historian of Tiberius offered a critical model for analyzing events and actions that were distant in time but that were also analogous to current ones through the universal aspect of human behavior. The notion of tyranny was central to the debates, because the tyrants' acts could not be separated from their biographies. Montaigne saw in this a way of writing a commentary on the events of his time via a general portrayal of the human being.

Whereas after the Saint Bartholomew's Day massacre Machiavelli quickly came to be considered a rather unsavory author, the interest in Tacitus gave new credit to many of the subjects taken up by the Florentine historian. The author of the *Annals* provided material for understanding, in a broader framework, political and religious developments in France. Montaigne wrote:

> This form of history is by far the most useful. Public movements depend more upon the guidance of fortune, private ones on our own. This is rather a judgment of history than a recital of it; there are more precepts than stories. It is not a book to read, it is a book to study and learn; it is so full of maxims that you find every sort, both right and wrong; it is a nursery of ethical and political reflections for the provision and adornment of those who hold a place in the management of the world.[104]

A book to be studied rather than read, a book full of *sententiae* and moral precepts for those who hold public office. We have the feeling of finding in Tacitus the very form of the essay as Montaigne conceived it. It was Tacitus's judgments, rather than his long narratives, that held Montaigne's attention. The Bordeaux Copy offers the following commentary on the passage quoted earlier:

And it seems to me, in contrast to how it seems to him, that having specially to trace the lives of the emperors of his time, so strange and extreme in every way, and the many notable actions that their cruelty in particular produced in their subjects, he had a stronger and more attractive matter to treat and narrate than if he had had to tell of battles and universal commotions. So that I often find him sterile, skimming over these noble deaths as if he were afraid to bore us with their number and length.[105]

This criticism of the military narrative produced at the expense of human psychology led Montaigne to better understand the originality of his *Essais*. What he values in Tacitus is above all his ability to judge people, whatever their rank might be, and to sketch a psychological portrait that leads to an explanation of their motivations and acts. Nonetheless, he finds fault with him for his reticence to speak of himself, "For not to dare to speak roundly of oneself shows some lack of heart."[106] Montaigne did not hesitate to speak of himself in his *Essais*, and neither did Commynes in his *Memoirs*. After 1588, for reasons mainly connected with these authors' respective biographies, Tacitus replaced the historian Commynes, in whose work Montaigne had formerly appreciated the originality of the genre of the memoir, but whom he now reproached for not having been able to distance himself from the kings he had served. Tacitus's attitude with regard to his former patrons corresponded better to Montaigne's own situation, because his sharp breaks with politics led Montaigne to formulate an independent judgment and to distance himself with respect to history. However, we must recognize that Montaigne's political disillusionment after 1588 considerably reduced his interest in history, and that, in the end, he preferred Plutarch—Tacitus's contemporary—and his particular taste for the private lives of the great figures of Antiquity.

Socrates or Political Suicide

One of the essential aspects of the "political knowledge" in the *Essais* is connected with what Montaigne calls "the knowledge of opposing" (*la science de s'opposer*, knowing how to oppose or contradict) without ending up in a confrontation. Opposing requires skills, cleverness, and diplomacy. On this point, Socrates served Montaigne as a model, at least at first. But the capacity for political opposition can also produce blatant defeats if it is not restrained by a form of moderation or compromise. This observation allowed Montaigne to interpret the trial of Socrates in the light of his own political experience. In the first edition of the *Essais*, Socrates is mentioned seventeen times, almost always positively. In 1588, the name of Socrates appears forty-eight times, or almost three times more often. After 1588, the text of the *Essais* includes a hundred and fifteen references to the Greek philosopher. The references to Socrates were thus multiplied by seven between the 1580 edition and Montaigne's last text with his handwritten additions. There are several sources for his knowledge of Socrates—notably Plutarch and Diogenes Laertius—but the two principal ones are doubtless Xenophon's *Memorabilia* and of course the various dialogues of Plato, in Marsilio Ficino's Latin translation. Montaigne seems to have studied first the Socrates of Xenophon, whom he read very early on, before later discovering Plato's Socrates after 1588, when he was looking for historical details regarding the Greek philosopher, and more particularly regarding his death.[107] How can this growing interest in the inventor of moral and political philosophy be explained? Socrates's constant questioning of preconceived ideas offers an initial answer. After 1588 Montaigne recognized that Socrates, "always asking questions and stirring up discussion, never concluding, never satisfying . . . says he has no other knowledge than that of opposing."[108] Socrates, a philosopher who had the spirit of contradiction, understood "argument" as a goal in itself, always revisiting established wisdom: "I shall question him and examine him and test him,"[109] he exclaims in Plato's *Apology*. We understand Montaigne's interest in this kind of permanent questioning of knowledge, but is there really a "knowledge of opposing" in politics? And would Socrates be the best example of that knowledge? There again, Montaigne's political experience and the historical events of his time somewhat complicate the perception of the ancient philosopher.

Montaigne often associates individual experience with the ability to discuss things in general, and Socrates provides him with the ideal example for exploring the relation between what might at first seem to be an idiosyncratic discourse and universal truths expressed in the philosopher's dialogues: "What does Socrates treat of more fully than himself? To what does he lead his disciples' conversation more often than to talk about themselves, not about the lesson of their book, but about the essence and movement of their soul?"[110] We find here a theme often taken up in the *Essais*, namely, the lessons to be learned from an individual life, and their influence on the principles worthy of being made into a morality that transcends their simple subjective expression, to the advantage of civil society. Systematic opposition to every truth expressed by another person is then transformed into knowledge in the service of all. Knowledge is a permanent questioning that allows Montaigne to formulate his famous "What do I know?" ("Que sçay-je?"). The repeated expression of a disagreement that seems at first individual consequently leads to a model beneficial to the whole of human society. Thus it suffices to speak of oneself to speak about human beings in general. Here we arrive at the fundamental principle endorsed by Montaigne, the consubstantiality of the writer's body and his book, a consubstantiality that the author of the *Essais* thinks he discerns in Socrates in the passage quoted above. Sixteenth-century readers of the *Essais* had for this reason no difficulty imagining Montaigne as a "French Socrates."[x]

Very early in the writing of the *Essais*, notably in a passage of the chapter "Of cruelty" (II: 11) that was written for the most part between 1578 and 1580, Montaigne drew a parallel between the form of the essay and Socrates's way of proceeding: "Socrates, it seems to me, tested himself still more roughly, keeping for his exercise the malignity of his wife, which is a test with the naked blade [that is, without mercy]."[111] We recognize the style Montaigne advocated—straightforward, without ceremony or decorum; a direct style that contrasts with the diplomatic practices that Montaigne was intent on overthrowing. Was this opposition the result of an apprenticeship, of a modus vivendi, of an interpretive procedure, of a rhetorical effect, or was it the product of a personal intuition? Socrates said he was inhabited by a *daimon* who whispered in his ear all his principles in the domain of both philosophy and his private life. His confidence in this prophetic inspiration allowed him to show, in his intercourse with others, a flawless self-assurance and what we have to see as a kind of arrogance. Socrates claimed to communicate directly with the gods, who, through the medium of his *daimon*, conveyed truths to him, making him a sage. His conversations with the youth of Athens could be considered prophecies, or at least they far transcended the expression of particular opinions. That was precisely what his judges accused him of at his trial.

Socrates's daimon can be perceived as the expression of an insolent and impertinent character. If the evocation of the daimon turns out to be a considerable advantage in an exchange between one individual and another (and for Socrates, this is by far the privileged mode of interaction), the daimon's spell is more problematic when Socrates is expressing himself before a large audience. Here we are referring to Socrates pleading before his judges during his trial. In this case, he was addressing an audience of about five hundred people. The tried-and-true strategies of opposition he used when questioning a single individual, in a relationship that Socrates always conceives as one between equals, are no longer the same when one is addressing a larger audience that is, moreover, the legal representative of the city of Athens. However, Socrates refuses to change registers and claims to have only one language, that of the public square: "One thing, however, I do most earnestly beg and entreat of you. If you hear me de-

---

[x] A manuscript (Codex Vaticanus 9693) from the Vatican Apostolic Library presents Montaigne as a "Socrates from France." This document was written on the occasion of Montaigne's Roman citizenship, while he resided in the Eternal City. It is mentioned by Ferdinand Gregorovius in *Alcuni cenni storici sulla cittadinanza romana* (1877, p. 30) and by Alessandro D'Ancona in his edition of Montaigne's *Journal de voyage* (1889, p. 321). I have not been able to consult this manuscript.

fending myself in the same language which it has been my habit to use, both in the open spaces of this city—where many of you have heard me—and elsewhere, do not be surprised, and do not interrupt. Let me remind you of my position. This is my first appearance in a court of law, at the age of seventy, and so I am a complete stranger to the language of this place."[112]

Socrates does not separate the language of his private conversations from that of his public defense. He explains himself before the Athenian authorities as if he were talking to a young man met in the street: it is difficult to distinguish the private man from the public philosopher. Montaigne distinguishes on the one hand, the "diligent reader" (in his singularity), and on the other hand, what might be called "the man being represented," that is, the reader (or the judge) in his social dimension. It is the citizen of Athens in his public incarnation, and not the person in his individuality, that must be considered here. Montaigne seems to be aware of this nuance. When Socrates expresses himself before his judges, he should have understood this essential distinction between private and particular assessment and public judgment. However, he denies that he ever established a difference between his private relations and public affairs: "You will find that throughout my life I have been consistent in any public duties that I have performed, and the same also in my personal dealings."[113] By rejecting such a separation, Socrates left his judges no choice; they were obliged to consider the public Socrates. In fact, for the Athenians, Socrates existed chiefly as a philosopher and not simply as an individual. The philosopher and Socrates are always one, contrary to Montaigne, who created a distance (artificial, of course) between himself and his various public functions.

Ultimately, and since every person is intrinsically social in the eyes of others, the famous consubstantiality Socrates claimed could never be more than an inconsequential rhetorical effect in a defense that sought to merge the man and his work. In his turn, Montaigne claimed this consubstantiality between the man and his public writings (because they were printed), but in flagrant contradiction with this principle, he also articulated a sharp distinction between the public and the private. This kind of friction is visible, for example, in the preface to the reader, where Montaigne declares that his *Essais* are dedicated to the small number of his friends and relatives, but nonetheless conceives the possibility of a much broader audience and an anonymous reader whom he addresses in generic way. These fundamental and sometimes contradictory aspects of Montaigne's Socratism (the duality of the private man and the public man that is opposed to the consubstantiality of the man with his words), considered in the light of the trial of Socrates and in the social and political context of the period in which Montaigne wrote, allow us to understand better how we should understand *la science de s'opposer*. Opposition has its limits, above all in politics.

Although Montaigne had no trouble revealing himself to an idealized reader, he nonetheless found it difficult to express his feelings and opinions—through a text that inevitably transcended him—to the same reader reified and objectified in relation to his religious and political beliefs. On this precise point, the author of the *Essais* theorizes that "Montaigne" and "the mayor of Bordeaux" are indeed two distinct entities—a practical separation when it was a matter of reaching a politically and religiously unstable audience. Unlike Montaigne, Socrates seems not to have understood this essential distinction when he was on trial. The least one can say is that on that day his daimon failed him, perhaps because he mistook his audience. Montaigne was interested in this failure—a lack of political judgment—that led to a death sentence for the philosopher. Socrates's demise was directly connected with his conception of his daimon, a daimon that turned against him and made his case worse.

For Montaigne, this observation is drawn from the *Apology of Socrates*, a text he must have known well, because he refers to it on many occasions in the *Essais*, including four references to Socrates's daimon. The question is whether this daimon, when it is connected with what Montaigne calls "the knowledge of opposing" (without, however, distinguishing the levels on which this opposition occurs), does not constitute an uncertain and equivocal authority. Montaigne offers several reflections on this subject. All these analyses derive from his own conception of politics and his experience in public offices. Montaigne's Socratism would thus be limited to a dialogue between peers, between the author and the reader, but have no possible application or anything to teach us from the moment that the author (Montaigne) is considered a political or religious agent. The knowledge of opposing—frontally and directly, without gloves, we might say—seems to be an absurdity. Opposition requires moderation and taking the political into account. That is why "Montaigne" and "the mayor" had to be separated. In diplomacy and politics, the knowledge of opposing inevitably involves prior negotiation and compromise, terms that Socrates found indecent.

The first book of the *Essais* shows a marked affinity for Socrates's ideas, which Montaigne describes as "vivid," in other words, impromptu thoughts inspired by the daimon. Following Socrates, Montaigne believed, even before he entered diplomacy and politics (from 1572 to 1588), that he too was inhabited by a guardian spirit that allowed him to get himself out of delicate situations. However, what is striking is that the situations Montaigne describes are always based on a personal relationship established between two persons in an almost complete equality (initially symbolized by his friendship with Estienne de La Boétie). In such a case, the exchange is based on a form of innocence visible in a person's face. Two anecdotes Montaigne reports, and which we have already commented on, illustrate this quality of candor and human simplicity. During an armed group's abortive attempt to take over his château, Montaigne used his "natural innocence" to force the brigand to give up his original intentions. During a second, rather similar incident, after being robbed of his property in a forest, Montaigne also believed that his innocent, naive face had saved his life a second time.

Like Socrates, Montaigne thought at first that his "imagination" could help him in his judgment and actions: "For my part I hold that whoever has a vivid and clear idea in his mind will express it, if necessary in the Bergamask dialect, of, if he is dumb, by signs: 'Master the stuff, and words will freely follow.' "[114] On the Bordeaux Copy, after "I hold," Montaigne added "and Socrates makes it a rule." His natural inclination (in the *Essais* of 1580) was later associated (in the Bordeaux Copy) with Socrates's attitude. This conduct that left room for intuition and imagination, even in the most delicate episodes of a life, is *historically* situated in the lineage of Socrates. Plato's *Apology* demonstrates a rather similar acceptance of intuitions, without premeditation or consistent development. However, this kind of naïveté proved fatal to Socrates. Montaigne had the advantage of being able to learn the lessons of Socrates's mode of behavior. Although up to the beginning of the 1580s the author of the *Essais* expressed an ideal vision of the "knowledge of opposing," his political and diplomatic experience soon caused him to discover a quite different reality after 1588. This quotation is rather typical of the position Montaigne defended in the 1580 edition, at a time when he seemed still to believe that his frank, direct language was a definite advantage in politics and in any diplomatic relationship. However, over the years this self-assurance with regard to a language that is non-premeditated and that develops by itself in all sorts of situations, accompanied by a blind faith in his power of persuasion, without recourse to reason or to rhetoric, was transformed into a disappointment. Montaigne's initial absolute Socratism needed to be seriously moderated.

A connection can be made between Socrates's daimon and Montaigne's "imagination." However, imagination encounters limits that proceed from the domain of authority in the end. Regardless of one's wishes, the knowledge of opposing can be expressed solely in a power relationship:

> My thinking [*mon imagination*] so often contradicts and condemns itself that it is all one to me if another does the job, especially seeing that I give to his criticism only as much authority as I wish. But I break off with a man who bears himself as high-handedly as one man I know, who regrets having given advice if it is not accepted, and is affronted if you balk at following it. That Socrates always smilingly welcomed the contradictions offered to his arguments might be said to be due to his strength and to the fact

that, since the advantage was certain to fall on his side, he accepted them as matter for new glory. But we see on the contrary that there is nothing which makes us so sensitive to contradictions as the idea of our superiority and the disdain for our adversary and that in reason it is rather for the weaker to accept with good grace the criticisms that correct him and set him right.[115]

This addition on the Bordeaux Copy expresses a disappointment, a new recognition that, in the end, might is right. The weak have no choice in this relationship of authority Montaigne describes so well. Let us also be wary of these "contradictory ideas" to which the author alludes. Contradiction is hardly tolerated in the public domain, even if it is a natural aptitude worthy of being reported when it is a question of describing humans in their instability and transience.

Political or religious truth is located on the side of the person who can impose it on others. This strategy, which consists in combining the discourse on human beings and a critique of it within a precise social and religious system (in this case, Athens or the period following the assassinations of the duke of Guise and Henry III) seems to have worked well for Socrates so long as he limited himself to dialogue with young people, but the latter were also members of the polis. Facing the Athenians gathered together in an administrative and juridical body—his judges—Socrates discovered in a rather dramatic way the essential distinction made by the representatives of civil society, that is, by the political power. Montaigne went through a similar experience—which of course turned out better—and his disenchantment with politics after 1588 led him to recognize that giving free rein to his imagination, which he associated for a time with Socrates's daimon, could end up being dangerous: "I once tried to employ in the service of public dealings ideas and rules for living as crude, green, unpolished—or unpolluted—as they were born in me or derived from my education, and which I use [Bordeaux Copy: if not]: conveniently, [Bordeaux Copy: at least] surely, in private matters: a scholastic and novice virtue."[116] The new way of practicing politics and conducting negotiations at the highest level had proven to be a clear failure. The subtle reinterpretation in the Bordeaux Copy shows to what point Montaigne now distinguished between public affairs and private affairs.

Although Montaigne did not believe in an external force (his imagination depended on him and his experiences alone) that could inspire him in difficult moments, he nevertheless repeatedly adopted an unconventional attitude that made the most experienced diplomats uncomfortable. By his own admission, his remarks are jerky and sometimes contradict one another. This natural impulse of the way he spoke could look like a kind of frankness. For example, Montaigne acknowledges Socrates's impetuousness: "The daemon of Socrates was perhaps a certain impulse of the will that came to him without [Bordeaux Copy: waiting for] the advice of his reason,"[117] but was this "impulse of the will" really a sign of frankness or wisdom? Impetuousness, repartee, and systematic questioning are hardly appropriate in public life. It is not even certain that such attitudes are in conformity with the work of the judge or member of a parlement, and that might explain Montaigne's limited success in that profession. To La Boétie's eloquence, Montaigne opposed his outspokenness as an expression of a gentleman's freedom, because in contrast to the grandiloquence of the tribunes and other public officials, his language displayed no high-flown or superfluous turns of phrase.

However, the prince and all those who hold public offices are urged to heed the "advice of reason." Thus we find here a contradiction inherent in the *Essais*. For example, Montaigne had a very special idea of himself, and of what he could accomplish thanks to his disjointed, straightforward style, which he associated with Seneca's. However, this image does not seem to correspond completely to the opinions that others had of him. Although he quickly came to be considered an excellent painter of himself and of humanity, in the sixteenth century he was sometimes seen as no more than a mediocre mayor of Bordeaux. His contemporaries' judgments on this point are not all flattering. There were offices in which eloquence still had a place, especially if the office consisted in representation. In politics, there is often a greater need to bring together than to oppose. Besides, what is the outcome of that famous "knowledge of opposing" Montaigne alludes to in speaking of Socrates? Is it a question of convincing one's adversary or of shaping public opinion? Is this knowledge directed toward an end, or is it rather a means? What would be the point of that kind of knowledge if it did not lead to tangible advances recognized by a part of society or a political group? Finally, what is the *function* of this knowledge of opposing? The answers offered by Montaigne and by Socrates diverge increasingly as the writing of the *Essais* advances. Socrates's daimon was still the guarantor of a universal truth; it implies certainty regarding what is said. But in Montaigne the opposition so necessary to the form of the essay is more a principle than a certitude. For example, we know the difficulty Montaigne had in conceiving of universal truths. His relativism was not expressed in a method of discourse (dialogue, for instance), but he did move beyond the superficiality of rhetorical effects.

The paradox of this knowledge of opposing—at least for someone who is writing *after* Socrates's death—consists in recognizing that it cost the philosopher his life, unless we believe that Socrates himself was fully aware of his failure and had anticipated it. That is one of the possible readings of Plato's *Apology*, but I do not think it was Montaigne's after 1588. Montaigne returned to this text at several points in his life and in his political career. The possibility that this knowledge of opposing might lead to a dramatic failure is thus expressed in the *Essais* on several occasions after 1588. In a passage reworked in the Bordeaux Copy, Montaigne comments on Socrates's natural inclination and his knowledge of opposing:

> In a well-purified soul such as his, prepared by a continual exercise of wisdom and virtue, it is likely that these inclinations, [Bordeaux Copy: although instinctive and undigested], were always good [Bordeaux copy: important] and worth following. Everyone has [Bordeaux Copy: felt] within himself some likeness of such stirrings [Bordeaux Copy: of a prompt, vehement and accidental opinion. It is my business to give them some authority, since I give so little to our wisdom]. And I have had some [Bordeaux Copy: as weak in reason as violent in persuasiveness—or in dissuasiveness, as was more ordinary in Socrates—] by which I let myself be carried away so usefully and fortunately that they might be judged to have in them something of divine inspiration.[118]

This passage that Montaigne extensively rewrote stresses the moments of vehement agitation emanating from a divine inspiration. These violent opinions are certainly desirable when one seeks to express a point of view fully without censuring it, but are they really effective when it is a question of convincing parties who are opposed to these "instinctive and undigested" views? Quick temper and impetuosity rarely produce the results sought. Montaigne's personal experience since 1581 had led him to recognize this evident political fact, and to qualify his initial declarations regarding what could henceforth be seen as Socrates's naïveté.

On the basis of this passage, which dates from 1585, Montaigne offered the following commentary in the Bordeaux Copy: "It is my business to give them some authority." This addition allows us to clarify a few crucial points: first, the recognition of the fortuitous aspect of thought—the emphasis on the famous portrayal of change; then the obvious fact that this kind of intuitive writing reaches its limits when an effort is made to express political or social ideas that always have to be "put in authority" (*mises en autorité*). Letting oneself be carried away by passions has nothing to do with divine authority. After 1588, Montaigne draws a clear distinction between private speech and public speech—the first *Essais* were governed by a completely different logic. He underlines the particular and private aspect of his writings while at the same time recognizing the importance of decorum and the rules of discourse so far as the public sphere is concerned. It is here that Socrates's daimon—or Montaigne's—can be considered a disadvantage.

Besides, for Montaigne, wisdom and virtue have little meaning when the subject is situated in a social or political framework. This observation was already present when Montaigne first began writing his *Essais*, that is, between 1570 and 1580. At that time, he anticipated the impossibility of applying Socratism in the domain of public service. To succeed in politics, one has to have a dose of "vicious appetite";[119] in 1580, Montaigne thought he had found this in Socrates. In the "Apology for Raymond Sebond" Montaigne pursued his analysis of Socrates's virtue and concluded that it was above all a personal quest detached from political reality. Socrates's "imaginations" (ideas) are formless and thus impossible to convey: "Just as the virtuous actions of Socrates and Cato remain vain and useless because they did not direct them toward the end of loving and obeying the true creator of all things, and because they did not know God; so it is with our ideas and reasonings: they have a certain body, but it is a shapeless mass, without form or light, if faith and divine grace are not added to it."[120] The same goes for Montaigne's "imaginations." The author of the *Essais* distinguishes between the private character of his "imaginations," which are only tryouts (*essais*) or intuitions, on the one hand, and their transformation into a more didactic discourse, on the other hand. For example, Montaigne refers to La Boétie's text as if it were a discourse, whereas his own writings are only essays. By becoming a public figure, Socrates is supposed to have committed the error of transforming his "imaginations" into moral precepts for the youth of Athens.

But perhaps Montaigne had gone a little too far in this first apology. After 1585, he had less political ambitions on the national or international scale. He had just ceased to be the mayor of Bordeaux and expressed himself freely regarding the excesses of theology. The apology for Sebond remained, but it took a very different turn. The text of the *Essais* of 1588 directs more criticism at theology and at the Christian religion in general: "Compare our morals with a Mohammedan's, or a pagan's; we always fall short of them. Whereas, in view of the advantage of our religion, we should shine with excellence at an extreme and incomparable distance, and people ought to say: 'Are they so just, so charitable, so good? Then they are Christians.'"[121] After 1588, Montaigne went further: "All other signs are common to all religions: hope, trust, events, ceremonies, penitence, martyrs. The peculiar mark of our truth should be our virtue, as it is also the most heavenly and difficult mark, and the worthiest product of truth."[122] Religion can even lead to lying: "Some make the world believe that they believe what they do not believe. Others, in greater number, make themselves believe it, being unable to penetrate what it means to believe."[123] Montaigne was hardly a theologian in 1580, but we see that after 1588 he was no longer a theologian at all; for him, theology had become a "science of guzzling"[124] like any other; his truths are only appearances and believing comes down to making people believe. Like the theologians of his time, Montaigne could give free rein to this "imaginations" in his turn: "'If God is, he is animal;

if he is animal, he is sentient; and if he is sentient, he is subject to corruption. If he is without body, he is without soul, and consequently without action; and if he has a body, he is perishable.' Isn't that a triumph?"[125] Ironically, Montaigne's theology had moved on, far beyond Sebond.

While at first Montaigne had been interested in Socrates's daimon, going so far as to justify it when he reported his personal experiences, he was soon forced to wonder whether inspiration was suitable for the arguments that sought essentially to convince others, not individually, but as a group, a class, or an order. In contrast to classical rhetoric, the discourse *en pointe* (straightforward), as Montaigne defines it, is far from being compatible with a discourse of the political or diplomatic type. Socrates's daimon had simply forgotten this important dimension of human beings, who live in society and must sooner or later explain in public their private positions. Finally, can the knowledge of opposing be transmitted to others, to the youth of Athens, for example. Can it be taught? Socrates defends himself by stating that he addressed only individuals and never the people: "It may seem curious that I should go round giving advice like this and busying myself in people's private affairs, and yet never venture publicly to address you as a whole and advise on matters of state."[126] He distinguishes the individual opinion from public expression and does not understand how the two might be linked in the eyes of his judges. He also declared that he had never busied himself with public affairs: "You may be quite sure, gentlemen, that if I had tried long ago to engage in politics, I should long ago have lost my life, without doing any good either to you or to myself."[127] The idea that the public and the private are inseparable completely escapes him, and his principal defense consisted in reasserting a division that he alone was defending. Montaigne did the same thing toward the end of his life. However, Montaigne could not deny that he had engaged in public business, and he decided simply not to mention it.

Can Socrates—or any individual—be sacrificed in the name of the maintenance of the social order? The same question arises when it is a matter of finding out whether Montaigne's *Essais* represent solely the expression of a particular life. Do they have didactic value or are they dedicated only to "a domestic and private" end? Socrates's trial—as it is described by Plato—hardly offers a good example of a kind of knowledge that would be worth transmitting. Montaigne accepts the possibility of a negative judgment of the daimon that inspired Socrates and holds against the philosopher his supposedly natural mode of argumentation:

> Besides, isn't the method of arguing that Socrates uses here equally admirable in its simplicity and its vigor? Truly it is much easier to talk like Aristotle and live like Caesar than it is to talk and live like Socrates. There lies the extreme degree of perfection and difficulty; art cannot reach it. Now

our faculties are not so trained. We neither essay them nor know them. We invest ourselves with those of others, and let our own lie idle. Even so someone might say of me that I have here only made a bunch of other people's flowers, having furnished nothing but the thread to tie them.[128]

Montaigne draws a distinction between what Socrates and he tried to accomplish, on the one hand, and on the other the reception others gave to these "essays," which might in certain situations be considered failures. We are always judged by others in relation to a result that is often unpredictable, and despite our good intentions; Socrates found that out only too soon. By definition, our natural faculties do not allow us to put things in perspective; the truth arises from an interpretation inscribed in time, because in this world straddling two systems—the Aristotelian and the Cartesian—"fabulous testimonies, provided they are possible, serve like true ones. Whether they have happened or no, in Paris or Rome, to John or Peter, they exemplify, at all events, some human potentiality, and thus their telling imparts useful information to me."[129] Montaigne did not set out to say what happened in his time, as a historian or chronicler might have done, but rather "what could happen," in the manner of a Machiavelli who considers politics to be a science oriented toward the future rather than toward the past. It is also the science of diplomacy, which consists in predicting reactions and anticipating the effects of political actions.

Direct, simple, and vehement opposition (to adopt Montaigne's expression) is not always the best way to proceed in the domain of politics. Either Socrates was pertinently aware that he was losing his case when he addressed his judges, or he was sure of himself and underestimated his opponents' strength. Frankness is not sufficient and appearances often override reality: these two observations put a deep mark on the late Renaissance. Socrates's appearance turned out to be decisive during his trial. On this subject, Montaigne notes: "About Socrates, who was a perfect model in all great qualities, it vexes me that he hit on a body and face so ugly as they say he had, and so incongruous with the beauty of his soul."[130] Only appearances matter when one is being judged by others, and it is better to have a "fine face" than an "ugly mug." In this sense, Socrates's and Montaigne's experiences are diametrically opposed. This sharp break between reality and appearances had been commented upon and theorized at length by Machiavelli, and Montaigne must have known that. Moreover, he was aware of the power of appearances in juridical matters. Reality passes through language and produces a truth that can no longer be anything but social. The exception Socrates represented, neglecting the importance of appearances, was no longer tenable in Montaigne's time. The feeling the Greek philosopher inspired in him was limited to the strictly personal.

By experience, Montaigne was less idealistic than Socrates; that is why he was a little better at politics. Between death and exile, one must choose exile, and on this point Socrates was wrong right to the end: "What Socrates did near the end of his life, in considering a sentence of exile against him worse than a sentence of death, I shall never, I think, be so broken or so strictly attached to my own country as to do,"[131] Montaigne wrote in "Of vanity" after 1588. Times had changed, and Socrates's haughty, noble attitude was now incompatible with the realpolitik that marked the end of the Renaissance. In the age of the Wars of Religion, the Saint Bartholomew's Day massacre, the assassination of the duke of Guise and Henry III, Montaigne drew the practical conclusions: "The version of the sayings of Socrates that his friends have left us we approve only out of respect for the universal approval these sayings enjoy, not by our own knowledge. They are beyond our experience. If anything of the kind were brought froth at this time, there are few men who would prize it."[132] Socrates and Socratism belonged to the history of philosophy; they were anachronisms in the period when Montaigne was writing. Montaigne's own political experience simply no longer allowed him to preserve this idealized aspect of Socratism. Thus one critic has spoken of a "strategy of self-preservation" in Montaigne.[133] Socrates is supposed to have paid the price for having been incapable of grasping the political stake involved in his philosophical teaching.

The references to Socrates's daimon acquired a different connotation after 1585. Montaigne certainly continued to emphasize his points in common with the philosopher, notably with regard to his imagination, sometimes associated with a mild form of madness: "A man must be a little mad if he does not want to be even more stupid," a sentence before which Montaigne added after 1588: "My style and my mind alike go roaming."[134] A little dose of madness is a good thing if it applies only to the individual alone and does not extend to the public and political domain: that is perhaps the lesson Montaigne learned. If one wants to play a role in society, one must recognize that "fantasy" and imagination conflict with the common good. At least that is what Montaigne seems to have understood after 1585, and especially after 1588. Now that politics was behind him, Montaigne accorded a very different place to imagination in his *Essais*.

In the *Essais* there are two very different conceptions of the imagination and of Socrates's daimon. These two conceptions correspond to different periods: from 1570 to 1585, Montaigne was relatively sure that his imagination and his casual, unpremeditated style would be an advantage in all sorts of situations, both individual and political, but after 1585 his own political experience proved to him that this conviction was an illusion. From that time on he gave a different dimension to Socrates's death, which he no longer perceived as a willful choice or a conscious, unconditional strategy for defending a universal truth expressed by the daimon. Montaigne now considered Socrates's death a failure or, worse yet, a suicide. The Greek philosopher had put too much trust in his daimon and was simply mistaken, not understanding that the dynamics of persuasion must necessarily be different when one is facing a constituted group or even individuals who refuse to accept a logic of dialogue based on a relationship of authority (the sage confronting the people or the reader).

Montaigne adopted another of Socrates's mottos: "'According to one's power,' that was the refrain and favorite saying of Socrates, a saying of great substance. We must direct and fix our desires on the easiest and nearest things."[135] The author of the *Essais* chose this middle way. His political experiences modified his initial Socratism, which over the years became more practical because he had learned to adapt to the philosophical demands of his time. A significantly reworked passage in "Of physiognomy" tells the story of the reception of Socrates's death.

After 1585, Montaigne argues that Socrates, before being a philosopher, was first of all an Athenian. After 1588, the author of the *Essais* takes his analysis still further, emphasizing that Socrates owed his life "to the world as an example," and that his defense was of an "unstudied and artless boldness and a childlike assurance," showing even an "ignorance" with regard to the political reality of the polis:

> [Bordeaux Copy: he owed his life not to himself but to the world as an example. Would it not be a public loss if he had finished it in an idle and obscure fashion?] Assuredly, such a nonchalant and mild way of considering his death deserved to have posterity consider it all the more on his behalf; which it did. And there is nothing in justice as just as what fortune ordained for his glory. For the Athenians held those who had been the cause of his death in such abomination that they shunned them like excommunicated persons; they considered everything they had touched as polluted; no one would wash with them at the baths; no one greeted them or said hello to them. So that finally, no longer able to bear this public hatred, they hanged themselves. If anyone thinks that among the many examples of the sayings of Socrates that I might have chosen to serve my purpose I selected this one badly, and if he judges that this speech is elevated above common ideas—I chose it deliberately. For I judge otherwise, and hold that it is a speech which in its naturalness ranks far behind and below common opinions. [Bordeaux Copy: In an unstudied and artless boldness and a childlike assurance] it represents the pure and primary impression [Bordeaux Copy: and ignorance] of

Nature. For it may be believed that we are naturally afraid of pain, but not of death for its own sake; it is a part of our being no less essential than life.[136]

Montaigne had learned to adapt, to pretend to be simple and to conceal his thoughts if he found himself in a politically unfavorable situation. Knowing how to oppose has its limits, and questioning depends on the power relationship in which one finds oneself. A distinction has to be drawn between private "imaginations" and public discourses. These two levels could no longer be confused. The example of Socrates, reassessed in the light of particular experiences, allowed Montaigne to resolve the problems inherent in the consubstantiality he had initially claimed—the man and his work are always one: whoever touches one, touches the other—by distinguishing in practice the public from the private in his *Essais*, while at the same time preserving the ideal principle of this consubstantiality. By reaffirming the subjective and private nature of his writings, Montaigne solidified Socrates's vain defense before his judges: "I have never promised or imparted any teaching to anybody, and if anyone asserts that he has ever learned or heard from me privately anything which was not open to everyone else, you may be quite sure that he is not telling the truth."[137] This defense Socrates offered could also serve as an apology for Montaigne, if not as his defense.

Montaigne's Death

In the chapter "That to philosophize is to learn to die" (I: 20), Montaigne suggests that if he had been a "maker of books" he would have written a register of deaths worthy of being reported, for the good reason that anyone who "would teach men to die would teach them to live."[138] The deaths of philosophers, like those of great men, must necessarily match the level of their lives, insofar as they determine their last image for posterity. If Socrates's death can be considered a failure of philosophy confronted by politics, Montaigne's death gave a different dimension to the consubstantiality he so ardently sought. Montaigne had earlier declared that he would write "as long as there is ink and paper in the world";[139] he had finally run out of ink and paper. His life ended on September 13, 1592, at a time when his future renown was uncertain. His death concluded his *Essais* forever, but they were given a new breath of life by Marie de Gournay's limitless devotion.

The death of philosophers is hardly different from that of ordinary people, at least so far as the medical causes are concerned. In Montaigne's case, kidney stones were mentioned, but it does not seem that Montaigne died from this hereditary disorder that had caused him pain for more than a decade. A letter from Estienne Pasquier to Claude de Pellejay, a royal counselor and master of the king's Chambre des Comptes, provides us with a few details concerning Montaigne's last three days. Probably written in 1605—that is, thirteen years after Montaigne's demise—this letter was first published in 1619 in *Les Lettres d'Estienne Pasquier* (Paris: Laurent Sonnius and Jean Petit-Pas). Pasquier refers to a "quincy[xi] on the tongue that for three days made Montaigne unable to speak, though he remained fully conscious."[140] This sudden loss of the capacity for speech that left him able to communicate only in writing—"to resort to the pen," as Pasquier puts it—reminds us of La Boétie's long death agony. Each had received the death that suited him: La Boétie as an orator, and Montaigne as an author.

In 1996, a group of physicians met to determine the causes of Montaigne's death. After finding a few symptoms in the *Essais* and in the travel journal, and considering several diagnoses, they concluded that Montaigne probably died of a stroke followed by aphasia.[141] Montaigne had in fact had other attacks of this kind that indicated vascular impairments. While he was in Italy, on Sunday, June 18, 1581, he had been "seized with cramp in the calf of the right leg. The pain was sharp, intermittent, and not continuous, and lasted about half-an-hour."[142] This transitory ischemic event presaged others to come. That was probably what happened to him again on September 10, 1592, when he lost part of his ability to express himself verbally. Then came a second stroke, which proved fatal on September 13. So much for Montaigne's medical-legal death.

The question is not, however, what caused Montaigne's death but how he died. The finest deaths must be represented as in a painting. On this point Montaigne's death was a success. The very Christian death described by Pasquier allowed Montaigne's first biographers to make him a model of saintliness and, in the wake of the Wars of Religion, to anchor him once and for all in the Catholic camp:

> He was forced to resort to his pen to make his desires understood. And when he felt his end approaching, he asked his wife, by means of a little note, to summon a few gentlemen who were his neighbors, so that he might bid them farewell. When they arrived, he had the mass celebrated in his bed chamber; and when the priest was about to elevate the *Corpus Domini*, the poor gentleman lurched up as best he could, headlong, on his bed, his hands clasped: and in this last act rendered up his spirit to God. This was a fine mirror of the interior of his Soul.[143]

[xi] A peritonsillar abscess. [Trans.]

This silent death contrasts with the exuberant death of La Boétie, an eloquent speaker who had talked right up to his last breath.[144] Montaigne had "tried" (*essayé*) to speak, but without success, and had finally resigned himself to writing "little notes" meant for his relatives and friends. These late "notices to the reader" (*avis au lecteur*) permitted him to continue to his last breath his habit of "speaking to the paper." Montaigne could be said to have died with his pen in his hand. In the early seventeenth century, Bernard Automne even chose the image of a Montaigne-manager, concerned primarily with questions of legacy in his last moments: "The late Montaigne, the author of the *Essais*, feeling the end of his life approaching, rose from the bed in his shirt, put on his chamber robe, opened his strongbox, called in all his valets and other legatees, and paid them the legacies he had left them in his will, foreseeing the objections his heirs would have to paying his legacies."[145] This portrait did not correspond to what people wanted to hear about Montaigne. In 1635, Marie de Gournay preferred to speak of a "very constant and philosophical death."[146] The Romantic painters and illustrators of the nineteenth century loved it.

Alexis Joseph Pérignon (1806–1882), a painter of history, religious subjects, and battle scenes, a student of Gros, by whom he was influenced, left us a representation of this death that completes the picture of the young Montaigne in the company of kings at Saint Denis that his teacher had painted twenty-four years earlier. Gros had chosen to represent Montaigne's political birth, and it is striking that his pupil left us a painting of his historical death. This picture, painted in 1836, shows Montaigne with a priest at his side.[xii] In the center of a large room in the château, where we can make out a monumental fireplace at the right of a canopied bed, Montaigne lies in that bed; he has raised himself slightly on his left elbow, his hands clasped, waiting to receive the last sacraments. His wife, kneeling, is already wearing mourning clothes and reinforces the moral and religious composition of this scene. Her daughter, Léonor, is to the right of her mother, her face turned backward in a kind of contortion, showing her grief and despair. On the left, gentlemen (relatives and friends) present their last respects. The priest is elevating the host: this is the moment when Montaigne returns his soul to God. This painting was interpreted and reproduced several times throughout the nineteenth century.[147]

Nothing marked people's minds like cheap illustrations and engravings. A lithograph published in *L'Illustration* in 1854 was to immortalize Montaigne's last moments and make the essayist's death exemplary (figure 19). Jules Laurens (1825–1901), an illustrator, lithographer, watercolorist, and painter, a pupil of Paul Delaroche, created this interpretation of Pérignon's painting, dramatizing

---

[xii] This painting (oil on canvas, 128 x 193 cm) is now in the Museum of Cambrai (inventory no. 324 P).

still further the scene of Montaigne's death by depicting a kind of chaos in Montaigne's bedchamber.[xiii] Laurens added well-stocked bookshelves the better to emphasize the bookish setting of Montaigne's last moments. He considerably reduced the size of the room to give more intimacy to this historic event. The room (is it in the tower?) is too small to accommodate all the visitors, and in the doorway we can make out a crowd waiting to render a last homage to the philosopher. This time, Françoise de La Chassaigne stands, her hands clasped, while her daughter is absent and it is the men who are prostrate. Most of them wear a ruffled collar, a sign that they are gentlemen. The political elite of Guyenne—twelve gentlemen, if we count those who cannot get into the room—is present to witness Montaigne's death, for as Pasquier puts it so well in the conclusion of his letter to Pellejay, "the life of this Gentleman could not have ended with a final act more beautiful than this one."[148] But who did people come to see? The public man or the private man? Is Montaigne surrounded by his friends, family, and neighbors alone? Maybe not. The artist has deliberately chosen to represent a public death in harmony with Montaigne's youth as depicted in Baron Gros's painting of 1812. These two scenes chosen by the artist form a diptych of Montaigne's public life—his political birth and historical death—and they are characteristic of the ambivalent reception of Montaigne's work over the centuries.

Montaigne's legacy was estimated at 60,000 *livres* in land and 30,000 *livres* in receivables, producing an annual revenue of 6,000 *livres*. According to the preface to the posthumous edition of the *Essais* published in 1595, Montaigne had asked his brother, Pierre de La Brousse, to write in his place a farewell to Marie de Gournay. It was up to his wife to find a burial site suited to his status as a noble lord. His heart was placed in the Saint-Michel-de-Montaigne church, and his body went to the convent of the Feuillants, in accord with the desires of Françoise de La Chassaigne, who ordered for the occasion a funeral monument that was supposed to be built in the Saint-André cathedral. However, this initial project was not realized, perhaps in order to respect one of the Council of Trent's rulings that prohibited burials in places of worship. Montaigne's tomb was finally erected in the convent of the Feuillants, in 1593. A contract dated January 27, 1593, between Jean-Jacques Bertin and the lord of La Brousse, acting for Françoise de La Chassaigne, stipulates that the monks authorized Montaigne's wife to "have built in front of the main altar of the church of the said monastery a crypt, and to place in it the body of the said lord of Montaigne, of the said lady, and of their posterity, and to place and erect thereupon a sepulcher."[149] In exchange for this authorization to construct a sepulcher with an ef-

---

[xiii] Laurens's lithograph reproduces another painting of Montaigne's death by Joseph-Robert Fleury, which was exhibited at the Salon of 1853.

FIGURE 19. *The Death of Montaigne*. Lithograph by Jules Laurens, 1854, based on the painting by Joseph Robert-Fleury (private collection).

figy, Madame de Montaigne promised to pay the monks a certain sum annually and to have the inside of the church of the Feuillants whitewashed. The Feuillants agreed "to say . . . two high masses . . . and two low masses, namely one every thirteenth day of each September, which is the same day that the said lord of Montaigne died, and the other on the selfsame day that the body of this late lord shall be placed in the aforesaid crypt."[xiv]

Montaigne's body was therefore interred on May 1, 1593, in a crypt constructed in front of the church's main altar. We do not know whether the tomb was ready for this occasion or was constructed shortly afterward. When the church was enlarged in 1614, the tomb was moved to a chapel dedicated to Saint Bernard. In January 1616, the body of Montaigne's daughter Léonor was buried in this same tomb, and in 1627, Françoise de La Chassaigne joined her husband and her daughter. In 1871, a fire in the church of the Feuillants (which had become the Lycée de Bordeaux) somewhat damaged the cenotaph, which was rebuilt in 1886 in the vestibule of the Faculty of Sciences and Letters. Today, Montaigne's cenotaph resides in the Museum of Aquitaine in Bordeaux. This cenotaph in the form of an altar supports a recumbent sculpture representing Montaigne as a man-at-arms. The monument itself is made of Taillebourg mar-

[xiv] The original of this document has now been lost, but a copy is found in one of the Feuillants' registers. Archives départementales de la Gironde, fonds des Feuillants, H. 620, f. 8v–10v.

ble and is rectangular in shape; it rests on a base that supports the recumbent sculpture of Montaigne wearing a coat of mail and his knight's armor; a lion lies at his feet. Montaigne's coat of arms is engraved on both sides of the cenotaph, and above them we see two epitaphs, one in Greek couplets, the other in Latin prose.[150] Today, there are still a few doubts regarding the sculptor of this monument, because the contract between the artist and Montaigne's family has never been found. The names of the Bordeaux master masons and sculptors, Jacques Guillermain and Pierre Prieur, have been proposed, but this tomb was very probably made by Louis Baradier.[xv]

The face of the sculpture is quite similar to those in other known portraits of Montaigne, especially Thomas de Leu's engraving and François Quesnel's drawing. Montaigne is represented wearing his necklace of the Order of Saint Michael, his hands are clasped for a prayer, and he has all the attributes of a noble knight. Nobility and Christianity are the two themes emphasized. Montaigne's coat of arms is inscribed in a medieval composition surrounded by laurels, and the necklace of the Order of Saint Michael frames the coat of arms of Montaigne's family. It is indisputably a baroque work made by talented ornament makers who received precise instructions as to what should appear on the monument. This image of the Lord Montaigne is also in accord with the ideal that the essayist had set for himself, and that his close friends and relatives thought it desirable to hand down to posterity. However, this kind of cenotaph is fairly unusual for a member of the minor nobility. Montaigne had probably never worn armor during his life, at least not on a battlefield. The recumbent figure must therefore be seen as a final homage rendered to his father, the only member of the Eyquem family who had actually waged war. The transformation of Montaigne into a noble gentleman was completed only after his death.

The Latin epitaph engraved on the monument gives Montaigne's chronology and lists his titles and offices. It also lauds his moral values, notably his affability and broad-mindedness:

> To Michel de Montaigne, born in Périgord, son of Pierre, grandson of Grimond, great-grandson of Raymond, knight of the order of St. Michael, Roman citizen, former mayor of Bordeaux. Destined to be the glory of the human race by the gentleness of his manners, the penetration of his mind, his lively eloquence, and an incomparable judgment. Although he had as friends not only great princes and the most distinguished figures in France, but also the leaders of a party that had formed there, he was nonetheless attached to the laws of his country and to the religion of his forefathers;

[xv] Born in the sixteenth century, Louis Baradier died in Bordeaux in 1608. He was the king's project supervisor and official master mason of Bordeaux. We know that he worked for Feuillants of Bordeaux on several occasions in the late sixteenth century.

and without flattering or annoying anyone, he was able to make himself likable to everyone. As during his life, he constantly professed, in speech and in writing, a philosophy that had fortified him against all troubles, when his end approached, after having courageously struggled against the attacks of a lengthy and cruel illness, and conforming his actions to his principles, he finally concluded, when it pleased God, a fine life and a fine death. He lived fifty-nine years, seven months, and eleven days, and died on September 13, in the year of our Lord 1592. Françoise de La Chassaigne, mourning the death of this faithful and constantly cherished husband, devoted this monument to him as an eternal testimony to her attachment and her regrets.[151]

Montaigne, the friend of princes, lived a beautiful life. The Greek epitaph, whose author is unknown,[152] concludes without any possible ambiguity that Montaigne has entered posterity and joined the immortals: "I have gone to take my place among the immortals, where my homeland is."[xvi]

[xvi] This Greek epitaph was translated into Latin by Bernard de La Monnoye for the edition of the *Essais* published by Pierre Coste in 1725.

PART THREE

Post Mortem

CHAPTER 11

Montaigne's Political Posterity

In an addition to the Bordeaux Copy, Montaigne imagines the usefulness of his book for future generations: "perhaps I shall keep some pat of butter from melting in the marketplace."[1] In the sixteenth century, butter merchants wrapped butter in the pages of worthless books. The reader will savor this quip that transforms the book into a recyclable, utilitarian object. Of course, the *Essais* never served as wrapping, and butter merchants had to find other books to package their products in. Rather quickly, Montaigne acquired a reputation as a remarkable author, and his book, without becoming a best seller, was nonetheless found in the libraries of a respectable number of cultivated people.

The public man and the servant of the state were not ignored. As early as 1584, in his *Bibliothèque françoise*, La Croix du Maine presented Montaigne as a man in the service of princes and the republic: "He flourished in Bordeaux that year 1584, at the age of fifty, and continued to benefit the republic in all sorts of praiseworthy ways."[2] There is no doubt that Montaigne's public life influenced the publication of his *Essais* and shaped his literary awareness. In this sense, there is no Renaissance writer who is not as much and first of all a political author. That said, the reputation of an author or of a politician is never exempt from manipulations. And on this point Montaigne is no exception.

After Montaigne's death in 1592, the question of the political reading of the *Essais* and how they could be used ideologically was raised. The book was separated from its author, consubstantiality set aside, and in the end all that remained was a text rather dangerous for weak minds. For a time, Montaigne's body was replaced by that of Marie de Gournay, who for almost half a century literally carried this child that had been entrusted to her. She died in 1640, and her last great editorial revision of the *Essais* dates from 1635. The success of the 1595 edition of the *Essais* allowed Montaigne's name to become better known and increased his fame not only as a literary man but also as a moderate politician in a century marked by religious fanaticism. Once the Wars of Religion were over, it became easier to insert Montaigne into his history and to make him a visionary who had rejected political maneuvering in order to speak of human beings in their universality. Even if people were particularly interested in the author's private life, the reception of Montaigne in the seventeenth century did not ignore his public life.[3] The goal was to reconcile public life and private life, or at least to see a logical progression between these two aspects of an uncommon life. Then the question arose as to whether such an innovative book would make it possible to understand the decline of the Renaissance and the crisis of humanism. For some, Montaigne was an opportunity to rediscover a moral grandeur in a corrupt age; for others, he appeared to be the precursor of a skeptical movement that was soon to sweep across Europe. In any case, the text of the *Essais* was subjected to the most audacious appropriations and made the object of partisan interpretations, including among the Protestants.

Political Appropriations

Hardly two years after his death, and while Abel L'Angelier was printing in Paris the posthumous edition of the *Essais* prepared by Marie de Gournay, Montaigne was politically appropriated by Protestants in Geneva. The *Essais* underwent the same fate as the *Discourse on Voluntary Servitude*, which had first been published twenty years earlier in *Le Reveille-Matin des François et de leurs voisins*. It was Simon Goulart who had inserted the *Discourse* into the *Mémoires de l'Estat de France sous Charles IX*, thus transforming La Boétie's text into a Huguenot pamphlet and forcing Montaigne to remove it from the first edition of his *Essais* in 1580. It was again Simon Goulart who broadened the reception of Montaigne to make him a writer compatible with Protestant ideas. While we can understand how the *Discourse* could be made to serve the Huguenot cause in the 1570s, it is harder to conceive a Protestant reading of the *Essais* in 1595. Montaigne had never wavered in his Catholic faith and had seen to it that his book could not be easily highjacked by any political party, but that was perhaps also its weakness. In the early 1590s, when a large portion of the population had not yet recognized Henry IV as king of France, it was in Geneva, under Goulart's guidance, that Montaigne was adapted for Protestant readers. It was enough to make Montaigne spin in his tomb.

What had to be done to adapt the *Essais* to allow them to be read in Protestant circles? First of all, passages that might offend the religious authorities had to be deleted, and then the form and style of the writing had to be emphasized; in short, the content had to be played down to the benefit of the form. The individualism and intellectual independence of the author of the *Essais* was relatively compatible with the new ideology that was slowly establishing itself not only in Geneva but also in several cities in the Low Countries[4] and in England. Without adopting Max Weber's thesis regarding the connection between the Protestant ethic and the spirit of capitalism,[5] we can suggest that it is possible to see Montaigne as one of the best representatives of a bourgeois ethic in which the individual advocates his independence of judgment with regard to political or religious authorities. By the end of the sixteenth century, Montaigne had become an author entirely acceptable to Protestants, and we can wonder whether his repeatedly affirmed decision to remain in the bosom of Catholicism, which was certainly made more on the basis of tradition than of ideological choice, did not contradict many of the positions defended in his *Essais* after 1585.[6] Doctrines set aside, and strictly on the level of institutions, Montaigne had been sufficiently critical of the Roman Catholic Church's rites to appear to be a Protestant author. An advocate of doubt and almost always skeptical with regard to dogmas, whatever they might be, the friend and editor of an author (La Boétie) who had been highjacked by the Protestants, suspect in the eyes of the League, close to the Court of Henry of Navarre—Montaigne, the unconditional dissident, could rather easily be appropriated as a critical author in the service of the Protestant cause.

We must approach the edition of the *Essais* published in Geneva in 1595 under Simon Goulart's supervision in this spirit of ideological appropriation.[7] Montaigne's book was not incompatible with Protestant thought. A circumstantial cleanup in no way diminished the overall feeling that made the *Essais* a machine for deconstructing authority. The satirical dimension might also have pleased the first Protestant readers, who were adept at and versed in that literary genre.[8] Montaigne had, moreover, spent his life surrounded by Protestants, both in his own family and among his neighbors. His education at the College of Guyenne had exposed him to Protestant values when he was still very young, and it was in a way logical that he should finally be appropriated by a Protestant ideology. He could even have gone over to the Protestant side, because on the intellectual level his *Essais* abound in criticisms of religious practices and often present judgments contrary to the Roman Catholic Church's official positions. Of course, Montaigne never converted to the Calvinist faith, because for him religion was an integral part of culture. Faith was for him a custom, so to speak. He adopted a critical distance by means of satire and irony,[9] but he never chose Protestantism. Even if it has been suggested that the chapter "Of cannibals" was a coded criticism of the Saint Bartholomew's Day massacres,[10] Montaigne preferred to remain outside religious controversies. However, it is true that this chapter represents one of the key points in a Protestant political reading of the *Essais*, but that does not mean that the author's intention should be confused with the reception of his work.

The form of the essay may have been even more popular with readers in England than in France in the early seventeenth century. We may mention, for instance, Francis Bacon, who published his first *Essays* in 1597, only five years after Montaigne's death. This initial edition included only ten essays, but the

1612 edition had thirty-eight essays and the 1625 edition had fifty-eight. William Cornwallis also published *Essays* in 1600 and 1617. In the same vein, Abraham Cowley wrote *Several Discourses by Way of Essays.* The beginning of the seventeenth century was rich in translations of French texts into English. At the time when John Florio, an Italian Protestant who had taken refuge in England, was beginning his translation of Montaigne's *Essais*, Thomas Danett was translating Commynes (1596) and Arthur Golding was translating Jacques Hurault (*Politicke, Moral and Martiall Discourses*, 1595). For Florio, the first translator of Montaigne into English, the *Essays* belonged to the genre of political discourses. In the same tradition of political discourses, François de La Noue, Pierre de La Primaudaye, and Henri Estienne were also translated into English around the turn of the century. The period from 1595 to 1600 saw a revival of attempts to translate Montaigne's *Essais*, or at least of intentions to translate them, in England.[11] Today, in public and private collections, a great number of copies of the *Essais* in Florio's translation contain copious annotations by contemporaries of Florio and Shakespeare,[12] and testify to Montaigne's success in England in the first years of the seventeenth century.[i]

In her various prefaces to the *Essais*, Marie de Gournay tried to control erroneous interpretations of this book "of a new kind."[13] Montaigne's adopted daughter thus embarked upon an all-out defense of her father's book, going so far as to regret the text's difficulties and imprecisions: "I wish that they [the *Essais*] might be made clearer in a few places and that in others they did not say so rashly things that may be interpreted dangerously if they are not fully clarified."[14] In the letter just cited (which she sent to Justus Lipsius when she did not yet know of Montaigne's death and thus had not yet begun her editorial work that resulted in the posthumous edition of 1595 published by Abel L'Angelier),[ii] Marie de Gournay leaves no doubt regarding the dangerous and controversial aspect of the *Essais*. She concludes that "this book is not a conversation for apprentices; it is a lesson for masters. It is the breviary of demigods, the antidote for error, the emancipator of souls, the resurrection of truth, the hellebore[iii] of the human mind and the spirit of reason."[15] Nothing more than that! The remark may be exaggerated, but Marie de Gournay was not wrong to emphasize

---

[i] In the eighteenth century, the essay established itself in Britain, especially in the domain of philosophical discourse. We need mention only Locke's *Essay on Human Understanding*, Pope's *Essay on Man*, or Addison and Steele's *Tatler* and *Spectator* essays to realize that Montaigne's *Essays* had a positive, important reception in English-speaking countries.

[ii] Justus Lipsius had been informed of Montaigne's death three months earlier by a letter from Pierre de Brach (dated February 4, 1593). It was through Justus Lipsius (letter dated May 24, 1593) that Gournay learned, belatedly, of Montaigne's death.

[iii] Hellebore was thought to be a remedy for madness. [Trans.]

the problematic character of the *Essais*. They are a book that is disconcerting for the average reader, because it escapes its author's stated intentions and easily lends itself to political and ideological misappropriations.[16]

Very early on, the editors of the *Essais* tried to reconcile the text's statements and analyses with the author's life, as if Montaigne's biography made it possible to sort out the most tangled developments. Written by a Protestant publisher and printer, Pyramus de Candolle (Jean Doreau), the first biography of Montaigne, "extracted from his book," was published in 1602 as an appendix to a pirated edition of the *Essais* printed in Geneva. Placed at the end of an index of the "rarest remarks" in his book, the life of Montaigne had as its goal to provide supplementary information to promote a better reading of the *Essais*: "Plus the life of the Author by principal and valuable remarks on his own book, the whole in the form of commonplaces." This compilation of commonplaces regarding the "life of the Author" consists of a rather heterogeneous list of "private" information and covers only five pages. This life is still not presented narratively, but rather in the form of a table related to Montaigne's text. We find entries on his youth, informing us about the fact that "he ordinarily carried a stick in his hand" and that he had a "weak memory," about "his voice" and "from what illness he died," about "the plague near his house," his "illnesses," and so on.

In 1608, five Parisian booksellers had the idea of adding to the text of the *Essais* a "Short Discourse on the life of Michel, Lord of Montaigne" by systematically collecting the personal details dispersed in the *Essais*.[17] At the beginning of the volume, the publishers also inserted, for the first time, a portrait of Montaigne engraved by Thomas de Leu.[iv] The "Short discourse" on the author's life contains only information given in the *Essais*, but it includes nearly all the events and episodes that were to be taken up again during the Romantic period, notably the infant Michel's being put out to a nurse in a village, Latin as his first language, his German tutor, being awakened by music, his studies at the College of Guyenne, the journey to Italy, his elevation to the Order of Saint Michael, the bull granting him Roman citizenship, and his election as mayor of Bordeaux. It also gleans information regarding his height, his weight, his physiognomy, his kidney stones, and his temperament. Montaigne now had a face, and the reader could rapidly find the anecdotes and events of his public and private life. The consubstantiality of the man and his book was in a phase of reconstruction. Despite its defects, this "first biography" of Montaigne has the advantage of not dissociating public life and private life. However, we have to wait until the end of the seventeenth century for information external to the

---

[iv] Probably based on a drawing by François Quesnel. As we have discussed, it was presumably during his sojourn in Paris with Pierre de Brach in 1588 that Montaigne had himself sketched in Quesnel's studio. The portrait of Montaigne was not engraved at that time, but later, as was then the practice in engravers' workshops.

Essais to make its appearance in biographies of Montaigne. Its summary aspect notwithstanding, this life of Montaigne set the tone for the biographies to come.

Marie de Gournay refused to draw a distinction between the private and public life of her adoptive father, yet she preferred to minimize the political aspect of the *Essais* in order to bring out their philosophical content. She quickly understood that contemporary history could damage Montaigne's future reputation. Similarly, the seventeenth century neglected the diverse public functions Montaigne performed during his lifetime, thus accepting Montaigne's own recommendation that public life and private life be separated. His first career as a member of the parlement and his two terms as mayor of Bordeaux were recognized, but he was not considered—as were D'Aubigné or La Noue, for example—a major historical figure. In general, he was reproached for having spoken too much about himself and not enough about his time. But this criticism had the effect of transforming Montaigne into a man of letters and a philosopher. However, there are a few curious exceptions to this dominant first impression. Paradoxically, two seventeenth-century engravings present the author of the *Essais* as a *politician*. In these engravings, the epigraphs placed in cartouches might appear strange, because they put the accent solely on Montaigne as an "Aquitanian politician" (*Politicus Aquitanicus*), leaving almost completely aside the author of the *Essais*. Moreover, one of the inscriptions that accompanies the line engraving does not mention the author of the *Essais*, and the other refers to him in a completely accessory way. These iconographic oddities that consider Montaigne only as a political actor are accentuated by the fact that engraving plates came from Germany, thus giving Montaigne a political dimension far exceeding his usual regional and national framework.

The first of these portraits strongly resembles Thomas de Leu's famous engraving that apparently served as its model. This portrait is anonymous and dates from between 1630 and 1635 (figure 20). Montaigne wears an official garment generally identified as his robe as mayor of Bordeaux. The great necklace of the Order of Saint Michael hangs on his chest, and he sports a ruff such as was fashionable during the reign of Henry III. Thus the accent is put on the public figure. The interest of this engraving can be seen in the legend offered below the portrait:

> Michel de Montaigne, Périgordian, French Knight, Senator [member of the parlement] and Consul of Aquitaine, then gave up the magistracy of his own free will. Having been honored with the insignia of the Order of the King, he devoted the rest of his life and his leisure to the muses. Author of the book of the *Essais*, for which he was later received among the number of Roman citizens. Born in 1533, died in 1592.

FIGURE 20. Portrait of Montaigne based on Thomas de Leu, circa 1635 (private collection).

Taken from Scévole de Sainte-Marthe's eulogy of Montaigne,[18] this short biography in Latin traces the great dates of Montaigne's life, lists his different titles and offices, and describes him as a French knight. The engraving was supposed to be part of a series of portraits of European "great men"—perhaps published abroad—that never appeared. The text emphasizes the public offices Montaigne held, before he gave them up "of his own free will."

The second portrait was printed in Nuremberg in 1688 in a book by Paulus Freher, a German physician and biographer, *Theatrum virorum eruditione clarorum cum eorumdam iconibus* (figure 21). This representation of Montaigne was distributed in Freher's great biographical work published after his death by his nephew, Charles Joachim Freher. This book contains 2,850 biographical notices and 1,312 portraits on eighty-four plates. Most of these portraits are imaginary, and a good many of them are virtually identical. The loss of the copper plates made it impossible to bring out a second edition. The article on Montaigne is

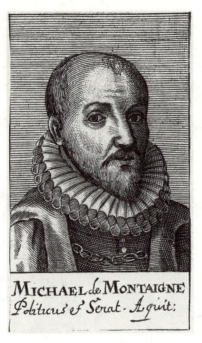

FIGURE 21. Portrait of Montaigne, in Paulus Freher, *Theatrum vivorum . . .*, 1688 (private collection).

also extracted from Sainte-Marthe's eulogy. Small in size, this portrait appears on the same page as those of Plantin and Baïf.[19] No medal hangs from the chain the figure wears around his neck. The letter of this engraving, *"Politicus & Senat. Aquit."* ("Aquitanian politician and member of the parlement") presents solely Montaigne's public life and does not mention his career as a writer. This was a rather surprising choice at the end of the seventeenth century, which was, on the whole, beginning to see in Montaigne a moralist and a philosopher.

For more than two centuries, the iconographic history of the representations of Montaigne has hesitated between the political portrait of a Montaigne wearing the official robe of the mayor of Bordeaux and the more private one of a "Montaigne wearing a hat" invented at the end of the eighteenth century. After the French Revolution, Montaigne lost the nobiliary particle in his name, and his membership in the nobility of the sword was quickly forgotten; in the republican fervor following the Revolution, he became simply Michel Montaigne, or Michel Montagne, and after the discovery of his travel journal at the end of the eighteenth century, he was transformed into a traveler, even a cultural tourist. However, contrary to a good number of his contemporaries who were rather proud of their public service and did not hesitate to pose for posterity, the author of the *Essais* did not deem it necessary to have his portrait printed at the beginning of his book. This omission was quickly rectified after his death, and the face of the public man appeared prominently in most of the editions of the *Essais* published in the seventeenth and eighteenth centuries. Paradoxically, the two portraits mentioned above lend disproportionate importance to a political Montaigne. They allow us to imagine how the author of the *Essais* could acquire a reputation as a regional political actor (in Périgord or Aquitaine) at the time of the civil wars.

Censure and Morality

Although the reprimand the pontifical authorities gave Montaigne in 1581 had been friendly, in 1676 the *Essais* were subjected to a genuine censure that led to their prohibition. This Roman censure formulated two objections: first, to a certain casualness on Montaigne's part regarding ecclesiastical history; second (and this is perhaps more important for what concerns us here), to the large number of obscenities present in the *Essais* that made them an immoral book. It repeated the feeling already hinted at by La Croix du Maine in 1582, though of course it was anachronistic regarding a period in which vulgar language was far more common than in the seventeenth century. In particular, the censors condemned the *Essais* for a passage in which Montaigne mentions Diogenes masturbating in public, and for his quotation of obscene epigrams by Martial. The consultant who was entrusted with examining the *Essais* in 1676, Father Antoine Gilles,[20] a French Minim monk at the monastery of La Trinité-des-Monts and a protégé of pope Innocent XI, concluded his report for the Holy Office[v] by recommending the prohibition of the *Essais* not only because they contained several passages suspected of being heretical, but also because they were "on the whole" contrary to the good morals of the time.[21] This censure was more moral than theological in nature, and bore mainly on the chapter "On some verses of Virgil" (III: 5). As if to confirm this affront to public morals, it is not unusual to find on the rare books market copies of the *Essais* in their seventeenth-century vellum binding but with this chapter torn out, a proof that the reaction of some readers of the time could be violent with regard to this chapter in which sexuality plays a prominent role. The age of Rabelais was definitely over. The condemnation of 1676 ignores, for example, the complaints registered in 1581; now it was Montaigne's "licentiousness" (*libertinage*) that was judged offensive, for Augustinian thinkers and the milieu of Port-Royal. Putting the *Essais* on the *Index* had a major impact on the publication of Mon-

---

[v] Formally known as the Congregation for the Doctrine of the Faith (*Congregatio pro Doctrina Fidei*). [Trans.]

taigne's works, and from 1676 on, the *Essais* simply changed their name and were presented in selected passages after being heavily expurgated.[vi]

Then began the period of books titled "The Spirit of Montaigne" and "Montaigne's Thoughts." While it was forbidden to publish the *Essais* under their original title, it was still possible to extract the pious and moral passages and bring them out under a different title. In short, Montaigne's book had to be run through the sieve of public morality and cleansed of its linguistic excesses. *L'Esprit des Essais de Montaigne*, published in Paris in 1677 by Charles de Sercy, offers a Montaigne transformed into a moralist. The *Essais*, rearranged and cut up into themes respectful of decorum, offered countless selected passages presented in the form of moral precepts. Extensively censored, Montaigne's text was organized into a series of moral maxims on the right way of leading a Christian life. Sercy offered a manual for the *honnête homme*, a decorous work full of examples that could be imitated. The editor remarks that Montaigne's thoughts will delight decent people and enable them to educate the young.

The age lent itself to such ambitions because gentlemen's breviaries and handbooks for men of the world abounded. Let us recall that Cardinal Du Perron had defined Montaigne's *Essais* as a *bréviaire des honnêtes gens*. After Nicolas Faret's *L'Honneste homme*, François de Grenaille published *L'Honneste fille* (1640) and *L'Honneste garçon* (1642), works in which he considers Plutarch and Montaigne the best models for the decency that leads to the "accomplished man" (*homme achevé*): "The *Essais* of Monsieur de Montagne, and chiefly the two treatises he wrote against pedantry and in favor of the education of children, can make an accomplished man."[22] After the *Essais* were put on the *Index*, Sercy and others tried to extract this "accomplished man" to give him a more moral appearance. To do so they eliminated all the daring passages that spoke about the body, but they also did away with Montaigne's public life and engaged in a reconfiguration of the *Essais* in which the politician gave way to a charitable, altruistic, generous, and fraternal Montaigne. However, these Christian values were deemed incompatible with the political context of the Wars of Religion, and for that reason Montaigne was stripped of everything that had to do with his public life.

This ideological appropriation of the *Essais* was continued a quarter century later by the bookseller Anisson, who published another Montaigne in "thoughts" (*Pensées de Montaigne, propres à former l'esprit et les mœurs*, Paris, 1700) that reduced the *Essais* to a series of aphorisms that could be used to edu-

[vi] The *Essais* remained on the *Index librorum prohibitorum* until it was done away with in 1966. A personal authorization to read it had been granted to an individual by the bishop of Périgueux, Mgr. George, on May 27, 1854. This permission to read a prohibited book has often been misinterpreted; it in no way represented a "suspension" of Montaigne's placement on the *Index*.

cate the young. The end of this work includes an "Approbation" by a censor, assuring the reader that this new "moralized Montaigne" was in no danger of being censured: "At the behest of Monsignor the Chancellor, I have read the Book entitled *Pensées de Montaigne propres à former l'esprit et les mœurs*, in which I found nothing that might prevent its printing." Compiled by Artaud, these thoughts were preceded by a notice that made it possible to include the *Essais'* immorality in a broader view of literature in which good and evil coexist. At the dawn of the eighteenth century, Artaud had reduced the *Essais* to a compilation of witticisms and moral maxims detached from one another: "The thoughts that we have gathered in this collection are for the most part not only independent of one another, but also very short and very diversified. There are moral ones, cheerful ones, serious ones, and amusing ones; each in its own kind, very solid, and all of them in general very suitable for revealing the heart of man, and shaping a taste for good things."[23] Since the *Essais* are a disorganized book par excellence, the learned editor had set himself the task of untangling the text and listing the themes that could be used for the moral education of young people:

> There are few books so bad that something good cannot be found in them; and few so good that something bad cannot be found in them. It is on this principle that we have worked to make the collection that we give to the public. Montaigne did not lack for censors, and we can hardly fail to be aware that he is a very ambiguous and very muddled author; the true and the false, the good and the evil are found by turns equally distributed in his work.[24]

Artaud explains his procedure this way:

> Thus we have thought it good to draw and pluck many good things from a work in which these good things are spoiled by the bad, and almost always, at least, suffocated, as it were, by a great deal of jumble. In this way, in addition to the current taste for detached thoughts, every reader will find, without effort on his part, all ready and all chosen, what we have thought might either please or instruct him.[25]

All that was required to restore a moral veneer to the *Essais* was to get rid of the "spoiled" passages. Excusing Montaigne for his licentious remarks in the name of a lofty idea of literature, Artaud was not without detractors. It was even believed that the editor of this "Montaigne en pensées" was no other than Father Bouhours.[vii] The Jesuits hastened to deny the rumor in the *Mémoires de*

[vii] Dominique Bouhours (1628–1702) was a French Jesuit priest, essayist, grammarian, and neoclassical critic. [Trans.]

Trévoux[viii] and vehemently contested this attribution. But once cleansed of his impurities, Montaigne had nonetheless succeeded in being taken for a moralist. It was, moreover, unthinkable to publish Montaigne "in bulk"; the reader would have gotten lost in it. For this reason, the work of moralizing the *Essais* done by Artaud consisted in isolating the "good" moral thoughts and eliminating thoughts that might contaminate them. In any case, historical events were systematically removed from the *Essais*, because they contributed nothing to the ethical discourse and limited the universality of the moral principles.

In the eighteenth century, Pierre Coste, a Protestant refugee in London, transformed the *Essais* into a kind of "encyclopedic summa" of man in general. During his lifetime, Coste produced five editions of Montaigne's works: in 1724, 1725, 1727, 1739, and 1745. His editorial enterprise went far beyond the text of the *Essais* to offer the public what can be deemed the first edition of Montaigne's complete works. For example, Coste was the first to include the writings of La Boétie in his edition of the *Essais*. He also added a considerable number of documentary items regarding the reception of the *Essais* in the wake of his editions. He did not really like Montaigne's style, and he explained its rambling character this way:

> Montaigne's style, as it appeared in the first editions, and as it is in the last after having been spoiled by these additions, might be compared to a pearl necklace that was initially composed of pearls that were perfectly round and of equal size, and between which were inserted others of an equally perfect roundness, but much larger. These last pearls, while increasing the value of the necklace, would make it lose a good part of its beauty. The same goes for most of the thoughts that Montaigne inserted from time to time into his book. We would be sad to lose them: but they disfigure it in several places, by the way in which they are set into it.[26]

Coste was convinced that at the beginning of his literary career Montaigne wrote relatively well. But following his bad habit of making abundant additions in the margins, he is supposed to have completely lost his train of thought through this practice and gotten lost in endless digressions. The century of the *philosophes* found it difficult to bring the author's subjectivity into the philosophical systems it was trying to elaborate. People strove to find and inventory Montaigne's "great ideas" without looking into the way in which these ideas had been influenced by the period in which they had been produced. As for the political aspect of his work, it seems not to have attracted any particular atten-

---

[viii] An influential academic journal that began publication in 1701; most of its authors were Jesuits. [Trans.]

tion. To reinvent Montaigne as a *philosophe*, history had to be done away with and his thoughts had to be regrouped within the framework defined by reason.

Although in the eighteenth century the *Essais* were still officially on the *Index*, condemned for their attack on Christian morality, French society seemed to have arrived at *l'âge de raison* (maturity), and Montaigne was beginning to be admired by educated people, despite the Church's condemnation. His instinctive skepticism made him a genuine *philosophe*. Thus the century of the Enlightenment gradually brought the *Essais* back into the history of skepticism by making Montaigne a precursor of a philosophical trend in which rationalism and pyrrhonism could coexist. Nonetheless, when Montaigne was proposed as the subject for the *concours des éloges* in Bordeaux in 1769, the result was disappointing, because only two eulogies were submitted to the Academy. He was proposed again in 1774, but this second attempt also inspired only two authors. However, the eulogy submitted by Abbé Talbert (1728–1803) was judged sufficiently meritorious to award him the prize, for lack of a better alternative. Talbert reinforced the image of Montaigne as a genius who was ahead of his time, a light amid barbarism. In his view, Montaigne had helped reestablish philosophy's honor, "under those stormy reigns in which superstition, plunging everything in its shadows, blinded peoples in order to sacrifice them, in which people believed in astrology, magic, and divination; in which minds, the playthings of all errors, were still in a state of infancy."[27] Talbert respected the philosophical orientation of the author of the *Essais*, celebrating the *Essais* as a "summary of all philosophy,"[28] without neglecting the Christian apology. The biographical part is rather slim, because according to Talbert it contributes little to philosophy. However, he notes the influence of Christian religion on Montaigne's education and concedes that the author's biography explains in part the thinker's development and maturity.

In the end, Talbert presents Montaigne as a model of life that supports the *philosophes* of the eighteenth century; it was as a philosopher that he had examined "the strange variety of manners" and adopted a "wise pyrrhonism . . . in order to move toward truth through doubt."[29] Talbert's conclusion is a call for Montaigne to be included in the French philosophical pantheon: "Philosophers, learn from him to deserve the august title that honors you; let your actions instruct the world as do your writings, and philosophy will no longer have enemies other than those of society, reason, and virtue."[30] What Descartes was to be to the knowledge of nature, and Montesquieu to politics, Montaigne was to morality.

In contrast to the relative failure of the *Essais* in the eighteenth century, Montaigne's works enjoyed a real publishing triumph in the nineteenth century. For the first time, Montaigne became a writer. This incontestable success on the book market was in part due to the French Academy's having put Montaigne on the list for the *concours des éloges* in 1810. Between 1769 and 1810, France had experienced the Revolution, the Terror, and the seizure of Church property. Although Christian morality had remained strong, an antireligious and materialist trend—associated with the reign of Napoleon I—had developed enough to make it possible to include Montaigne in the canon of French literature. The genre of eulogies was highly esteemed at the beginning of the nineteenth century and made a major contribution to the rediscovery of authors who had been forgotten or little studied during the preceding century. Contrary to the *concours des éloges* the Academy of Bordeaux held in 1769, the one the French Academy held in 1810 changed forever the way literary history saw Montaigne and his place in the educational curriculum. The second class of the French Institute (which replaced the French Academy under the Empire) set the *Éloge de Montaigne* for the competition in 1810, the prize to be awarded in 1812. Eleven eulogies were submitted, and eight chosen by the jury. Following this competition, twelve texts were published, two coming from Bordeaux and ten from Paris.[ix] Several of these texts were recycled in the various editions of the *Essais* all through the century—notably the eulogy by Joseph-Victor Le Clerc, which served as an introduction to his famous edition of the *Essais*; this edition was often reprinted until the beginning of the twentieth century, and was long considered the vulgate. Suddenly, Montaigne acquired an unprecedented fame and was more than ever read as a moralist.[31]

Readers very early took an interest in the morality of the *Essais*, making Montaigne a moralist on the same level as La Bruyère, La Fontaine, Nicole, or La Rochefoucauld. From the end of the seventeenth century on, the author of the *Essais* was labeled a *moraliste*. We find several editions of the *Essais* published at the end of the seventeenth century and during the eighteenth century that present this text as a book on morals. The famous portrait of Montaigne engraved in 1772 by Étienne Ficquet shows the essayist before a large folio volume on which is written: "Essays on morals by Michel de Montaigne" (*Essais de morale par Michel de Montaigne*), thus establishing a direct link between morals and the essayist's enterprise. It is relatively easy to extract from the *Essais* moral

---

[ix] These biographical and literary eulogies were signed by Jean-Baptiste Biot, Joseph Droz (gold medal of the Institut impérial de France), the marquis Du Roure (honorable mention), Antoine Jay, Joseph-Victor Le Clerc (not honored by the Academy, but the eulogy appeared in revised form under the title "Discours sur la vie et les ouvrages de Montaigne" in the edition of the *Essais* Le Clerc published in 1826), Marie Jean-Jacques Victorin-Fabre, Abel-François Villemain (who won the prize for eloquence awarded by the Institut's class of French language and literature at its session on March 23, 1812), Émile Vincens (whose eulogy did not arrive in time to participate in the competition), F.-A.-J. Mazure (honorable mention), and Joseph-Michel Dutens (also honorable mention).

maxims that can then be regrouped as thoughts.[32] But such a practice runs counter to the form of the essay Montaigne invented. Let us not forget that Montaigne constantly plays with contradictions and always refuses to objectify and imprison his self in maxims or aphorisms. Far from depicting things, the author of the *Essais* is more interested in the passage of time over the different objects he writes about. The world acquires meaning only through the way the subject looks at it: a way that is always particular (and hence subjective) and situated in time and space. It is difficult to transform the *Essais* into a moralizing text.

Among all these editions of the *Essais*, the one that transmogrified Montaigne into a moralist was produced by Amaury Duval and appeared in the "Moralistes français" series. The text was based on the Bordeaux Copy and it was first published by Naigeon[x] in 1802.[33] In his preface, Duval presents Montaigne as the greatest of the French moralists, and places him at the head of the "Pléiade" or gallery of moralists, surrounded by Charron, Pascal, La Rochefoucauld, La Bruyère, Vauvenargues, and Duclos, authors whose works he also published in his series. The author of the *Essais* is presented both as the precursor of and the best example of the French moralist. A few explanations were necessary to get around the religious censure. In particular, Montaigne had to be defended against the accusations of immoralism made during the preceding centuries, but it was with a certain confidence that the *Essais* were then approached as the foundation of an exclusively French moral science. In 1829 Pierre-Sébastien Laurentie took a stand against those who made Montaigne an immoralist: "Montaigne is one of the most misjudged writers. The philosophers wanted to make him a skeptic; the authority of doubt is great for these minds whose reason lead to believing nothing and knowing nothing. After that, unreflective Christians thought themselves obliged to take the philosophers at their word, and Montaigne was considered impious, no more nor less than if he had spent his life insulting Christianity, like Voltaire, or engaging in cynicism, like Jean-Jacques [Rousseau]."[34]

Laurentie's *L'Esprit de Montaigne* represents rather well this tendency that, at the beginning of the nineteenth century, made the *Essais* a moralized text. Laurentie published a new edition of *L'Esprit de Montaigne* in his *Bibliothèque choisie* (morality section), but this work is only a pale reproduction of the *Pensées de Montaigne* edited by Charles-Étienne Pesselier. As had been the rule for more than a century, the scholarly editor made a number of deletions to ensure

---

[x] A close associate of Diderot, Jacques-André Naigeon remained throughout his life a great admirer of the philosopher whose ideas he embraced as a whole. A good soldier in the service of the *Encyclopédie*, to which he contributed several articles, Naigeon was the first to publish an edition of the Bordeaux Copy of the *Essais* that François de Neufchateau discovered in 1777.

that Montaigne would be properly seen as a thinker both Christian and French: "In this collection we have retained what must have been inspired solely by Christianity; the Greek of the Stoa has disappeared. This book contains, not the Montaigne who escaped from the schools of Athens, but the French, Christian Montaigne."[35] It sufficed to delete any reference to Greek or Roman Antiquity to moralize Montaigne and make him a French moralist. In fact, the nineteenth century often presented Montaigne as Descartes's *alter ego*, or at least as his precursor. The author of the *Essais* embodies the moment of imagination and intuition, philosophical stages that have to precede reasoning and method. At the beginning of the nineteenth century these two sides of French thought were reconciled in republican educational programs. The *concours des éloges* brought Montaigne out of his moral censure and emphasized a thought that proceeds "by leaps and gambols," a source of imagination for the young people of France.

Laurentie admits that Montaigne's problem is his way of speaking off the cuff, or again his rambling imagination "that lets escape all his thoughts, the ones that are right and the ones that are wrong."[36] Montaigne ran after countless contrary things, finding along the way errors that he mixed with truths. He was reproached for his lack of critical judgment, but on the other hand the creative diversity of his judgments in a period when historicism was beginning to be fashionable was acknowledged. Then Montaigne was slowly transformed into the representative of a specifically French critical tradition, going so far as to make him the first intellectual. His inventive spirit and the importance of imagination in his work gave him a place of choice in the republican educational system that was developed during the second half of the nineteenth century. Little by little, Montaigne's immorality disappeared and people began to see in him the proof of a critical tradition that had facilitated the birth of a typically French intellectualism. He had become a model—one among others—for the young. His transformation into a skeptic challenging any form of dogmatic thought contrasted sharply, once and for all, with the first readings by his contemporaries who doubted his "honesty" (*honnêteté*). It also made it possible to forget the censures issued in the sixteenth, seventeenth, and eighteenth centuries, by both Catholics and Protestants who tended to see in the *Essais* a profoundly immoral text.

The twentieth century has been largely preoccupied with determining what made Montaigne a modern and fundamentally secular author. Why are the *Essais* considered the first great text of modern philosophy, a work foreshadowing the arrival of Descartes on the scene of metaphysics? This question seems more interesting than ever.[37] In fact, the idea of Montaigne's modernity is not a recent one; every century has commented on it and explained it in its own way. It refers to our ability ceaselessly to reinterpret works from the past and to reappropriate these objects so that they can be adapted to our current concerns. To do that, we accommodate the texts to our present human condition, which is perceptible in our everyday life, on the moral level and in our cultural and scientific practices. Determining Montaigne's modernity is supposed to consist in locating in the *Essais* what we have become today. As if the questions that the author of the *Essais* asked were also our questions. There is no need to say that such a procedure can be gratifying, because it offers proof of a development or an implacable evolution toward progress and wisdom. Montaigne has finally been appropriated by philosophy.

The message is simple: the individual triumphs and always liberates himself from systems of thought that prevent him from expressing his most personal convictions. Montaigne is supposed to be the best proof of this unconditional freedom of the subject and of the victory of private judgment over systems or schools of thought. The birth of philosophy is supposed to coincide with a certain conception of individual liberty and its expression. Modern liberal thought discerns in Montaigne the starting point of its history. This is notably the case for readings that see in the *Essais* a quest for freedom, that is, an intellectual posture that gives priority to freedom of thought and freedom of expression to the detriment of political action, which is deemed to be inessential and is thus relegated to the background. But let us make no mistake: most of the strictly philosophical readings of Montaigne are the expression of a form of (unconscious) ideological appropriation that aims to place the universal subject on a pedestal, to the detriment of its purely historical and political dimension. The risk has always been that a philosophical Montaigne would be universalized at the expense of a political Montaigne whose writing situates him in his period and demands to be read in its immediate historical context. This kind of philosophical appropriation serves principally to reassure us by giving us the illusion of an irresistible progress toward a better life in which the individual blossoms and finally asserts himself in all the complexity of his subjectivity. Confronted by this utopia of a Montaigne father of universal thought, it is essential to warn the reader against the dangers of a strictly philosophical approach that would reinforce the myth of a universal subject.

Before becoming a modern author, Montaigne was necessarily an author of his own time. Historicizing his thought is hardly fashionable in a time when everything is supposed to converge toward the present moment—as if history, since Antiquity, had been nothing more than a long phase preparatory to our period in which everything suddenly takes place. The ahistorical view of human thought lets us glimpse an ideology that conceives history as only a *state of the present* and systematically de-historicizes the thought of earlier centuries. Economic liberalism has forced systems of thought to adapt in order to relate them to the only possible view of its own notion of universal progress, of which modernity is supposed to be the outcome. The best texts of the past would be the ones that include germs that prefigure our present human condition. This idea of an evolution of thought is in itself a problem of which Montaigne seems to have been fully aware: his interpretation of today—the moment when he was writing—never surpasses the one he had offered the day before. Still in the spirit of this liberal appropriation of Montaigne, he has even been seen as the first blogger, as if it were impossible to read Montaigne without relating him to our present activities, even the most insignificant ones. Montaigne's modernity is said to be his anticipation of Twitter or Facebook, and even the invention of the "selfie." The question that arises is how one is supposed to read Montaigne outside his history. Is it really necessary to reify Montaigne in our social networks and universalize the *Essais* as a blog of modernity?

There is no doubt that what appeals to us in Montaigne is his hypersubjectivity with regard to a world that is increasingly objectified and globalized. For this reason, in the last ten years, Montaigne has become a truly "global" author, bringing him sudden, worldwide celebrity. He is no longer regarded as a specifically French or European writer and his thought has become internationalized and universalized. His readership has expanded world-wide and the *Essais* are now accessible in more than thirty-five languages.[38] Most often, the freedom of judgment, outside schools, is emphasized in order to prove that the subject can always understand the world by himself. This self-sufficiency of the subject, removed from his historical reality, is the trap par excellence of many contemporary commentaries on the *Essais*. We might say that in Montaigne the reader finds few actions, but too many reflections. We like to see in him the moment of introspection, of withdrawal and self-sufficiency. The possibility of a theoretical truth of the world confirms the dominant ideology, because it isolates the subject from his social and political environment. Montaigne, in retirement in his tower, anticipates Descartes closed up in his stove. Each in his own way, Montaigne and Descartes are said to have left the world to give us philosophy. This idea, which seeks to essentialize human experiences, expresses an abandonment of politics, because it transforms all reflection into a meditation in which action is relegated to the crowds or the masses who agitate outside good sense, and usually without apparent reason. By doing away with time, philosophy has separated itself from its history in order to produce the illusion that human beings are stable. Montaigne's universality is supposed to save us from modernity's insecurity. That is how Montaigne has been emptied of his political dimension, in the name of a modernity without history that refers us to a view of man as powerless to affect the events that surround him and as having no solution other than to take refuge in his inwardness (his *for intérieur*), or, in Montaigne's case, in his tower, his inner fortress (*fort intérieur*).

EPILOGUE

Montaigne always claimed that he was consubstantial with his book: "I have no more made my book than my book has made me—a book consubstantial with its author, concerned with my own self, an integral part of my life; not concerned with some third-hand, extraneous purpose, like all other books."[1] In the chapter "Of experience" (III: 13), he even hints that the form of the essay is heavily dependent on a life's "practices" (*usages*): "I have lived long enough to give an account of the practice that has guided me so far. For anyone who wants to try it I have tasted it like his cupbearer."[2] The events of Montaigne's life exercise an incontestable influence on the composition of the *Essais*. On the basis of that obvious fact, I have undertaken to trace the practices, rules, decorum, rituals, etiquettes, conventions, habits, and customs that governed the milieus Montaigne frequented.

Where it was not possible to verify particular attitudes and actions, I have appealed to the *habitus* of orders, clans, families, clienteles, and constituted bodies; social and political practices that emerged from the rivalry between the different social orders in the Renaissance: clerics, nobles, *robins*, bourgeois. In this way, I hope to have brought out the importance of corporatist and clientelist behaviors, notably in the parlementary, diplomatic, and administrative milieus in Bordeaux, without forgetting Montaigne's accession to the middle-level nobility of Guyenne, the outcome of the Eyquem family's long social ascent. As an ambassador extraordinaire, representative, mayor and governor of Bordeaux, negotiator between Henry III and Henry of Navarre, and a man the League had imprisoned "as a reprisal," Montaigne constantly saw himself as a political actor and navigated between different pressure groups, sometimes abandoning his natural allies to join his former enemies.

To evaluate the social, political, and religious context in which Montaigne lived, I have turned to other texts and other actors who, at some point in their own professional or political careers, shared with him the same convictions and political positions. Of course, it is always difficult to generalize political behaviors and to extrapolate on the basis of particular observations. Despite these reservations, I am nonetheless able to affirm that the case of Montaigne is not an isolated one, and that his public conduct frequently corresponded to the reactions typical of political groups or parties. His aspirations, as they appear in his public life and in his *Essais*, indicate a qualitative change in the ideological reconfiguration that operated in his time. For example, the opposition between honor and utility, the main theme of the first chapter of the third book of the

Essais, raises the problem of the decline of aristocratic ideals and the rise of mercantile values in the society of the late sixteenth century. All these elements, which could be defined as a sociology of the *Essais*, seem to me indispensable for understanding Montaigne's relation to his writings; they must consequently be taken into account before undertaking any reification of the text into a literary or philosophical object. The *sociological* and the *political* are the presuppositions of the *philosophical* and the *literary*. My approach does not seek to make Montaigne's singular consciousness disappear, but rather to emphasize that Montaigne has to be understood on the basis of the social and political facts that led him to write and act. Historical time—that of the Wars of Religion and Montaigne's successive careers—literally structures the *Essais*.

In what way does the conception of a "political Montaigne" affect our reading of the *Essais*? To answer this question, we must first recall that in the Renaissance, literature and politics were intrinsically linked. If today Montaigne is viewed primarily as a man of letters, and secondarily as a philosopher, in the sixteenth century he was simply an author, just like all those who published a book. The boundaries separating literature, philosophy, religion, and politics were extremely porous. Montaigne dabbled in everything, and in this sense he was an author before he became a writer. In his work the essay is not solely a literary form, it is also the expression of the judgment or the critical mark of the mind. More a way of thought than a form of thought, the new genre of the essay, as it was invented and practiced by Montaigne, includes the author's political and social beliefs as subjects of reflection, because reading and writing are essentially social.

Having one's work printed is also an activity governed by motivations that go far beyond the simple assertion of an individuality. In the Renaissance, the book market was an integral part of a symbolic economy in which publications served as means of approaching the Court and made it easier to obtain favors. Montaigne's works express professional expectations—in the form of a return on investment—even if these expectations are often not mentioned. Montaigne was constantly concerned with realizing his political ambitions, and the publication—or nonpublication—of the various works he undertook (the translation of Raymond Sebond, the edition of La Boétie's works, the writing of the *Essais*, and the composition of the travel journal) was situated in the context of careers (in the plural) that he considered primarily political.

Seeking to grasp the variety of the points of view Montaigne expressed in his *Essais* has led critics to regroup and reduce the different printings of this book to a single text, a single edition, thanks to the representation on the same page of the famous strata of the text (A, B, and C) that refer to the 1580 and 1588 editions and to the manuscript additions on the Bordeaux Copy. However, when Montaigne published his first *Essais* in 1580, he did not yet enjoy the fame that was to make him one of the most celebrated authors of the French Renaissance. He had submitted to the Bordeaux publisher Simon Millanges the manuscript of a book that lay outside the publishing categories of the time. Eight years later, in Paris this time, he had his book published again, but the horizon of his expectations had changed considerably. For that reason, the *Essais* of 1580 are in no way comparable to what Montaigne's project became starting in the years between 1585 and 1588.

The biographical approach has allowed us to bring out the way in which Montaigne accumulated text between 1572 and 1592, and to see how his relationship to writing was motivated by expectations that developed in relation to his political experiences. When he added a third book to the *Essais* in 1588 and revised most of the chapters in the first two books, Montaigne was fully aware that he was giving an unprecedented shape to his project, which was transformed forever by a withdrawal from public life. From that point on, it is impossible to generalize practices of reading and writing that changed in response to what was happening in the author's life, from the first chapters—which were probably dictated to a secretary—to the last additions written in Montaigne's hand in the margins of a printed copy of the *Essais* of 1588.

These philological and editorial observations help us understand better the reasons that encouraged Montaigne to publish his *Essais* in 1580, 1582, and 1588, and to prepare the new edition that he was working on when he died in 1592. Montaigne's different enterprises in the literary domain, first as translator, then as editor, and finally as author, accompanied and promoted his political ambitions. These activities were ways of attaining his goals and are part of career strategies. However, late in life, Montaigne became a writer and a philosopher, and that is how he has been viewed by his posterity. This transformation of the text of the *Essais* followed a path marked by political successes and setbacks that led Montaigne to gauge the extent of his failure in public life and to withdraw into writing, for lack of a better alternative. Nonetheless, and no matter what the author of the *Essais* says about it, his public life remains inseparable from his private life, because after many trials and tribulations during the civil wars, it was his political efforts (*essais en politique*) that enabled him to find the right tone for a literary and philosophical genre that prefigured modernity.

Today, readers are still struck by the differences in content that radically oppose the *Essais* printed in 1580 and the last manuscript additions of the Bordeaux Copy. These variations, which concern both the form and the content of the text, reflect aims that changed over time. It has been necessary to "decompress" the text that we read in modern editions to restore a temporality that has disappeared from it. The object of this biography of Montaigne consists in recovering the time of writing the *Essais* and superimposing it on the time of history. Montaigne's work on his *Essais* was far from homogeneous between

1572 and 1592; it almost always corresponded to successive intentions that were antithetical. As I have suggested, for that reason it is preferable to speak of "campaigns of writing" whose publishing history can be traced in the light of historical events and Montaigne's political experiences. Montaigne found time to write during short periods of political inactivity, especially just after his second term as mayor of Bordeaux and again after his imprisonment in 1588. The first *Essais* of 1580 were a completely different kind of work; conceived in an aristocratic logic, they were presented as an activity very suitable for a country gentleman who had recently retired to his estate. Montaigne had not yet held public office, but he was already seeking to satisfy political ambitions that remained ill-defined and completely dependent on the goodwill of his patrons and the king. The relationship to writing changed in the course of the different editions and the author's experiences; it was marked by career disappointments and successes whose ups and downs this study has described.

Approaching the *Essais* on the basis of Montaigne's social and political motivations gives a new and often unexpected dimension to the text. This biography of Montaigne has led me to inquire into the process of the mutation of the publishing project of the *Essais* over time. It is in the relationship between public life and private life—which was already complex between 1570 and 1580, and became paradoxical after 1588—that we can find the keys to interpret a text that had distinct objectives for its author at different points in his life.

ABBREVIATIONS

Montaigne's *Essais* is quoted from the original editions published in 1580, 1582, and 1588, and from the manuscript additions and corrections he made on the copy of the *Essais* (known as the *Exemplaire de Bordeaux* (EB) or "Bordeaux Copy") found in his château after his death in 1592. The notes give the year of publication, the book number, chapter, and page or folio of the edition quoted. All these editions, and also the *Journal de voyage*, are accessible on the *Montaigne Studies* Internet site, both in image mode and in text mode: http://montaignestudies.uchicago.edu.

Essais 80: *Michel Eyquem de Montaigne, Essais. Reproduction photographique de l'édition originale de 1580 avec une introduction et des notes sur les modifications apportées ultérieurement au texte en 1582, 1587, 1588 et sur l'Exemplaire de Bordeaux*, ed. Daniel Martin. 2 vols. Geneva; Paris: Slatkine; H. Champion, 1976.

Essais 82: *Michel de Montaigne, Essais. Reproduction photographique de la deuxième édition (Bordeaux 1582)*, ed. Philippe Desan. Paris: Société des textes français Modernes & *Montaigne Studies*, 2005.

Essais 88: *Reproduction en quadrichromie de l'Exemplaire de Bordeaux des Essais de Montaigne*, ed. Philippe Desan. Fasano; Chicago: Schena Editore; *Montaigne Studies*, 2002. The edition of the *Essais* published by Abel L'Angelier in 1588 is identical with the printed text of the Bordeaux Copy.

Essais EB: *Reproduction en quadrichromie de l'Exemplaire de Bordeaux des Essais de Montaigne*, ed. Philippe Desan. Fasano; Chicago: Schena Editore; *Montaigne Studies*, 2002.

Essais 95: *Montaigne, Les Essais*, ed. Jean Balsamo, Michel Magnien, and Catherine Magnien-Simonin. Paris: Gallimard, coll. "Bibliothèque de la Pléiade," 2007.

Journal de voyage: *Journal de voyage de Michel de Montaigne*, ed. François Rigolot. Paris: Presses Universitaires de France, 1992.

Théologie naturelle: *La Theologie naturelle de Raymond Sebon, traduicte nouvellement en François par messire Michel, Seigneur de Montaigne, Chevalier de l'ordre du Roy, & Gentil-homme ordinaire de sa chambre*. Paris: Gilles Gourbin [Guillaume Chaudière, Michel Sonnius], 1581.

Lettres de Montaigne: "Lettres missives de Monsieur de Montaigne." In Alain Legros, ed., *Montaigne manuscrit*. Paris: Classiques Garnier, 2010.

Éphéméride: "Éphéméride du Seigneur de Montaigne." In Alain Legros, ed., *Montaigne manuscrit*. Paris: Classiques Garnier, 2010.

Mesnagerie de Xénophon: *Œuvres complètes d'Estienne de La Boétie*, ed. Paul Bonnefon. Bordeaux; Paris: G. Gounouilhou; J. Rouam, 1892.

Vers françois: *Œuvres complètes d'Estienne de La Boétie*, ed. Paul Bonnefon. Bordeaux; Paris: G. Gounouilhou; J. Rouam, 1892.

Discours de la servitude volontaire: *Œuvres complètes d'Estienne de La Boétie*, ed. Paul
  Bonnefon. Bordeaux; Paris: G. Gounouilhou; J. Rouam, 1892.

Mémoire sur l'édit de Janvier: Estienne de La Boétie, *Mémoire sur la pacification des troubles*, ed. Malcolm Smith. Geneva: Droz, 1983.

Quotations from Montaigne's works given in English translation cite the following editions:

The Complete Essays of Montaigne, trans. Donald M. Frame. Stanford, CA: Stanford
  University Press, 1958, rpt. 1965.

The Journal of Montaigne's Travels in Italy by Way of Switzerland and Germany, trans.
  W. G. Waters. 3 vols. London: John Murray, 1903. Online: https://archive.org/de-
  tails/journalofmontaigo1montuoft.

Discourse on Voluntary Servitude, trans. Harry Kurz. New York: Columbia University
  Press, 1942. Online: http://www.constitution.org/la_boetie/serv_vol.htm.

NOTES

Prologue

1. See Philippe Desan, *Portraits à l'essai: Iconographie de Montaigne.* Paris: H. Champion, 2007, 98n35.
2. G. Dargenty, *Le Baron Gros.* Paris: Librairie de l'Art, 1887, 48.
3. *Essais* 88, III, 1, f. 345r. Frame, p. 600.

Introduction

1. *Essais* 88, III, 10, f. 447v. Frame, p. 774.
2. *Essais* 88, III, 2, f. 350v–351r. Frame, p. 611.
3. *Essais* 88, III, 10, f. 447r. Frame, p. 773.
4. *Essais* 80, I, 20, p. 117. Frame, pp. 65–66.
5. See Philippe Desan, "Montaigne et la théâtralité du politique." In Concetta Cavallini and Philippe Desan, eds., *Le Texte en scène: Littérature, théâtre et théâtralité à la Renaissance.* Paris: Classiques Garnier, 2016, 131–49.
6. On the importance of the theater in Montaigne's education and, more generally, on his actor's dispositon and his predilection for role-playing, both in the *Essais* and in his public life, see George Hoffmann, "Self-assurance and acting in the *Essais.*" *Montaigne Studies,* vol. XXVI, 2014, 55–78.
7. *Essais* 88, III, 1, f. 348r. Frame, p. 605.
8. Émile Durkheim, *The Rules of Sociological Method,* trans. W. D. Halls. 2nd ed. Houndmills: Palgrave Macmillan, 2013, 24.
9. Ibid., 26.
10. Stephen Greenblatt, *Renaissance Self-Fashioning: From More to Shakespeare.* Chicago: University of Chicago Press, 2005; and, more recently, Marie-Clarté Lagrée, *"C'est moy que je peins": Figures de soi à l'automne de la Renaissance.* Paris: Presses de l'université Paris-Sorbonne, 2011.
11. Michel Simonin, "Poétique(s) du politique: Montaigne et Ronsard prosopographes de François de Guise." In Michel Dassonville, ed., *Ronsard et Montaigne écrivains engagés?* Lexington, KY: French Forum, 1989, 83–101.
12. Norbert Elias, *The Court Society,* trans. Edmund Jephcott. New York: Pantheon, 1983.
13. For an example of this approach, which makes it possible to reconcile the heterogeneity and ambiguity of private behaviors within organizations that are nonetheless well-regulated, see the classic study by John F. Padget and Christopher K. Ansell, "Robust action and the rise of the Medici, 1400–1434." *American Journal of Sociology,* vol. 98, no. 6, 1993, 1259–319.

14. See the recent studies by Biancamaria Fontana, *Montaigne's Politics: Authority and Governance in the* Essais. Princeton, NJ: Princeton University Press, 2007; Paolo Slongo, *Governo della vita e ordine politico in Montaigne*. Milan: Franco Angeli, 2010; Dominik A. Eberl, *Michel de Montaigne und das Politische in den Essais*. Würzburg: Ergon Verlag, 2009; Nicola Panichi, *Les Liens à renouer: Scepticisme, possibilité, imagination politique chez Montaigne*, trans. Jean-Pierre Fauquier. Paris: H. Champion, 2008; Frédéric Brahami, "Montaigne et la politique." *Bulletin de la Société des amis de Montaigne*, no. 33–34, 2004, 15–37; id., "'Être à soi': La place du politique dans les *Essais*." In Philippe Desan, ed., *Montaigne politique*. Paris: H. Champion, 2006, 39–56; and David Quint, *Montaigne and the Quality of Mercy: Ethical and Political Themes in the* Essais. Princeton, NJ: Princeton University Press, 1998.

15. *Essais* 80, II, 10, p. 113. Frame, p. 303.

16. BNF, Fonds Payen, Z. 649, f. 17v.

17. For example, Martin Lowenthal, *The Autobiography of Michel de Montaigne*. London: Routledge and Sons, 1935.

18. Pierre Villey, *Les Sources et l'évolution des* Essais *de Montaigne*. 2 vols. Paris: Hachette, 1933.

19. Hugo Friedrich, *Montaigne* [1949], ed. Philippe Desan, trans. Dawn Eng. Berkeley: University of California Press, 1991.

20. Alphonse Grün, *La Vie publique de Michel Montaigne: Étude biographique*. Paris: Librairie d'Amyot, 1855.

21. Bayle Saint John, *Montaigne the Essayist*. 2 vols. London: Chapman and Hall, 1858.

22. Théophile Malvezin, *Michel de Montaigne, son origine, sa famille*. Bordeaux: Charles Lefebvre, 1875.

23. Donald Frame, *Montaigne: A Biography*. New York: Harcourt, Brace and World, 1965.

24. For an overview of the biographies of Montaigne, see George Hoffmann, ed., *The New Biographical Criticism*. Charlottesville, VA: Rookwood Press, 2004; and the issue of *Montaigne Studies* (*Biographies of Montaigne*, vol. XX, 2008), also edited by George Hoffmann.

25. *Essais* EB, III, 13, f. 490r. Frame, p. 845.

26. That was the choice made by Lucien Goldmann in *Le Dieu caché, étude sur la vision tragique dans les* Pensées *de Pascal et dans le théâtre de Racine*. Paris: Gallimard, 1955.

27. Jean Starobinski, *Montaigne in Motion* [1982], trans. Arthur Goldhammer. Chicago: University of Chicago Press, 1985.

28. *Essais* EB, III, 9, f. 425r. Frame, p. 736.

29. Pierre Bourdieu, *The Logic of Practice*, trans. Richard Nice. Stanford, CA: Stanford University Press, 1990, 55.

30. On the constant tension between private life and public life, see Jean Balsamo, "'Le plus grand bien que j'atande de cete miene charge publique': Montaigne entre

vie publique et vie privée." *Nouveau bulletin de la Société internationale des amis de Montaigne*, no. IV, 2008, 359–75.

31. *Essais* 80, II, 16, p. 424. Frame, p. 476.

32. *Essais* 80, 82, 88, EB, "Au lecteur." Frame, p. 2.

33. *Essais* 80, I, 31, p. 330. Frame, p. 159.

34. *Mémoire de Henri de Mesmes, seigneur de Roissy et de Malassise*, ed. Édouard Frémy. Paris: E. Leroux, 1886, 42.

35. Ibid., 43.

Chapter 1. The Eyquems' Social Ascension

1. *Essais* 88, II, 17, f. 278v. Frame, p. 494.

2. *Coutumes générales de la ville de Bordeaux sénéchaussée de Guienne et pays Bourdelois* [1520]. In Alexis and Delphin de Lamothe, *Coutumes du ressort du Parlement de Guyenne*, Bordeaux: Chez les Frères Labottiere, 1769, p. 183.

3. *Essais* 80, II, 11, p. 135. Frame, p. 311.

4. *Essais* 88, III, 11, f. 441v. Frame, p. 764.

5. Étienne Dravasa, " 'Vivre noblement': Recherches sur la dérogeance de noblesse du XIVᵉ au XVIᵉ siècle." *Revue juridique et économique du Sud-Ouest, série juridique*, vol. 16, no. 3–4, 1965, 135–93; vol. 17, no. 1–2, 1966, 23–129.

6. François de L'Alouëte, *Traité des nobles et des vertus dont ils sont formés*. Paris: Guillaume de La Noue, 1577, f. 32v–33r.

7. Robert Descimon, "*Nobles* de lignage et *noblesse* de service: Sociogenèses comparées de l'épée et de la robe (XVᵉ–XVIIIᵉ siècle)." In Robert Descimon and Élie Haddad, eds., *Épreuves de noblesse: Les expériences nobiliaires de la haute robe parisienne (XVIᵉ–XVIIIᵉ siècle)*. Paris: Les Belles Lettres, 2010, 277–302; Albert Cremer, "La genèse de la notion de noblesse de robe." *Revue d'histoire moderne et contemporaine*, vol. 46, no. 1, 1999, 22–38.

8. Jean Balsamo, "Montaigne, le style (du) cavalier, et ses modèles italiens." *Nouvelle revue du seizième siècle*, vol. 17, no. 2, 1999, 253–67.

9. Sandrine Lavaud, "Les marchands et le vin à Bordeaux (XIIIᵉ–début XVIᵉ siècle): Des destins liés." *Nouveau bulletin de la Société internationale des amis de Montaigne*, no. 4, 2008, 209–27.

10. *Archives historiques du département de la Gironde*, vol. VIII, 1866, no. CCVII, 550–51.

11. Ibid., no. CCLII, 547–53.

12. Ibid., no. XC, 174.

13. Agnès Marcetteau-Paul, *Montaigne propriétaire foncier*. Paris: H. Champion, 1995.

14. Théophile Malvezin, *Note sur la maison d'habitation de Michel de Montaigne à Bordeaux*. Bordeaux: Feret et fils, 1889; René Forton, *La Maison familiale de Montaigne à Bordeaux*. Bordeaux: J. Brière, 1935; Laura Willett, "Rue de la Rousselle:

Domicile conjugal." *Nouveau bulletin de la Société internationale des amis de Montaigne*, no. IV, 2008, 19–40; Jessica Fèvres, "À propos de la maison de Montaigne." *Revue archéologique de Bordeaux*, vol. XCV, 2004, 131–42.

15. *Archives historiques du département de la Gironde*, vol. X, 1868, no. CCVII, 508–9.

16. Ibid.

17. Jean-Marie Constant, *La Noblesse en liberté (XVIᵉ–XVIIᵉ siècles)*. Rennes: Presses Universitaires de Rennes, 2004, 75.

18. George Huppert, *Les Bourgeois Gentilhommes: An Essay on the Definition of Elites in Renaissance France*. Chicago: University of Chicago Press, 1977. Huppert quotes the jurist Charles Loyseau who, in his treatise *Des ordres* published in 1613, speaks of this urban nobility in the following terms: "decent Bourgeois living on their investments, notably those who have the right to bear the status of nobleman."

19. *Essais* 80, I, 35, p. 343. Frame, p. 165.

20. Roger Trinquet, *La Jeunesse de Montaigne: Ses origines familiales, son enfance et ses études*. Paris, A.-G. Nizet, 1972, 79.

21. *Essais* EB, II, 2, f. 141v. Frame, p. 248.

22. *Archives historiques du département de la Gironde*, vol. XV, 1874, no. LXXV, 278.

23. Théophile Malvezin, *Michel de Montaigne, son origine, sa famille*. Bordeaux: Charles Lefebvre, 1875, 92.

24. Ibid., 257.

25. Ibid., 111–14.

26. See Raymond Corraze, "Les Lopez, ancêtres maternels de Michel de Montaigne." *Bulletin philologique et historique du comité des travaux historiques et scientifiques*, 1932–33, 283–98. Montaigne's Judaism and "marranism" are foregrounded by Sophie Jama in *L'Histoire juive de Montaigne*. Paris: Flammarion, 2001; see also Géralde Nakam, *Le Dernier Montaigne*. Paris: H. Champion, 2002, chap. IV. Scholars who emphasize Montaigne's Judaism see in the form of the essay a sort of Talmudic exercise in accord with the rabbinical tradition.

27. *Archives historiques du département de la Gironde*, vol. X, 1868, no. XCI, November 9, 1530, 174–75.

28. See Jean Marchand, "Documents originaux relatifs à Montaigne et à sa famille." *Bulletin de la Société des amis de Montaigne*, no. 19, 1969, 9–42.

29. Arlette Jouanna, "Perception et appréciation de l'anoblissement dans la France du XVIᵉ et du début du XVIIᵉ siècle." In *L'Anoblissement en France, XVᵉ–XVIIIᵉ siècles: Théories et réalités*. Bordeaux: Publications de la Maison des sciences de l'homme d'Aquitaine, 1985, 1–37.

30. John Durkan, "John Rutherford and Montaigne: An early influence." *Bibliothèque d'Humanisme et Renaissance*, vol. XLI, 1979, 115–22.

31. *Ephéméride*, 78.

32. Ibid., 80.

33. *Essais* 88, III, 13, f. 489r. Frame, p. 844.

34. *Essais* 88, III, 12, f. 468r. Frame, p. 811.

35. *Essais* 80, II, 17, p. 446. Frame, p. 487.

36. In an essay that has not yet been published, George Hoffmann makes a subtle distinction between nature (blood) and nurture (milk) and suggests that Montaigne's "nature honnête" might have resulted more from his nurse's milk than from his father's blood.

37. Bibliothèque municipale de Bordeaux, ms. 738 (3), f. 20r.

38. *Archives historiques du département de la Gironde*, vol. IV, 1863, no. CXVI, 163.

39. Ibid., 167.

40. *Essais* 88, III, 9, f. 427v. Frame, p. 741.

41. *Essais* EB, I, 35, f. 94v. Frame, p. 166.

42. Bibliothèque municipale de Bordeaux, ms. 738, f. 107r.

43. *Essais* EB, I, 35, f. 94v. Frame, p. 166.

44. Loys Ernaud, *Discours de la noblesse, et des justes moyens d'y parvenir*. Caen: Benedic Macé, 1584, preface.

45. Jehan Bacquet, *Quatriesme traicté . . . des droicts des domaines de la couronne de France. Concernant les Francs Fiefs, Nouveaux Acquests, Anoblissements & Amortissements*. Paris: Sébastien Nivelle, 1582, f. 2v.

46. Ellery Schalk, *From Valor to Pedigree: Ideas of Nobility in France in the Sixteenth and Seventeenth Centuries*. Princeton, NJ: Princeton University Press, 1986.

47. Marc Bloch, *Les Caractères originaux de l'histoire rurale française*. Paris, A. Colin, 1952.

48. Jehan Bacquet, *Trois premiers traictez . . . des droicts du domaine de la couronne de France. Avec l'establissement et jurisdiction de la Chambre du Tresor*. Paris: Sebastien Nivelle, 1580, f. 62v–63r.

49. Laurent Bourquin, *La Noblesse dans la France moderne (XVIᵉ–XVIIIᵉ siècles)*. Paris: Belin, 2002.

50. Jehan Bacquet, *Trois premiers traictez . . . des droicts du domaine de la couronne de France*, op. cit., f. 65r.

51. François de L'Alouëte, *Traité des nobles et des vertus dont ils sont formés*, op. cit., f. 27r.

52. "To justify nobility of blood, it must be shown that the father and grandfather lived nobly." Cardin Le Bret, *Recueil d'aucuns plaidoyez faicts en la cour des Aydes. Par. M. C. le Bret seigneur de Vely Conseiller du Roy & Avocat general en ladicte Cour: Avec les Arrests & reglements advenuz sur iceux*. Paris: Abel L'Angelier, 1602, f. 32v.

53. Ibid., f. 26r.

54. Henri de Bastard d'Estang, *Les Parlements de France: Essai historique sur leurs usages, leur organisation et leur autorité*. 2 vols. Paris: Didier, 1857, vol. I, 260.

55. Jehan Bacquet, *Trois premiers traictez . . . des droicts du domaine de la couronne de France*, op. cit., f. 72v.

56. Etienne Dravasa, " 'Vivre noblement': Recherches sur la dérogeance de noblesse du XIVᵉ au XVIᵉ siècle," art. cit.; and Gaston Zeller, "Une notion de caractère historico-social, la dérogeance." *Cahiers internationaux de sociologie*, no. XXII, 1957, 40–74.

57. Jean Papon, *Recueil d'arrests notables des cours souveraines de France: Ordonnez par titres en vingt-quatre livres, par Jean Papon, conseiller du Roy, & lieutenant general au Bailliage des Forests*. 4th ed. Paris: Robert Foüet, 1621, 254.

58. Jean-Richard Bloch, *L'Anoblissement en France au temps de François Iᵉʳ*. Paris: Félix Alcan, 1934, 26.

59. *Essais* 88, III, 9, f. 441v. Frame, p. 764.

60. On this subject, Roger Trinquet cites the *Nouvelle Coutume de Bretagne* (1580), which took as its point of reference "un partage noble avant les Cent ans." In *La Jeunesse de Montaigne*, op. cit., 54.

61. François de L'Alouëte, *Traité des nobles et des vertus dont ils sont formés*, op. cit., f. 30v.

62. François Lebrun, *La Vie conjugale sous l'Ancien Régime*. Paris: Armand Colin, 1975.

63. *Essais* 88, III, 1, f. 350v. Frame, p. 610.

64. Henri Gabriel O'Gilvy, *Nobiliaire de Guienne et de Gascogne*. 4 vols. Paris: Éditions du Palais Royal, 1973, vol. I, 393–404.

65. *Essais* 80, I, 26, p. 234. Frame, p. 128.

66. Ibid.

67. Ibid.

68. Ernest Gaullieur, *Histoire du Collège de Guyenne*. Paris: Sandoz et Fiscbacher, 1874; and George Huppert, *Public Schools in Renaissance France*. Urbana: University of Illinois Press, 1984.

69. See François-Martial de Verthamon d'Ambloy, *Registre secret du Parlement de Bordeaux, recueilli et mis en ordre par les soins de François-Martial de Verthamon d'Ambloy commençant le 28 février 1555 et finissant le 14 février 1557*, 1770. Archives municipales de Bordeaux, ms. 764, f. 25r.

70. Archives départementales de la Gironde, E, notaires, minutes de Mathieu Contat, nos. 111–8.

71. Jules Quicherat, *Histoire de Sainte-Barbe*. Paris: Hachette, 1860.

72. *Essais* 80, I, 26, p. 235. Frame, p. 128.

73. On Buchanan in Bordeaux, see Philip Ford, "George Buchanan et Montaigne." *Montaigne Studies*, vol. XIII, 2001, 45–63; H. de La Ville de Mirmont, "George Buchanan à Bordeaux," *Revue philomatique de Bordeaux et du Sud-Ouest*, 1906, 289–312.

74. *Essais* 88, I, 26, f. 66v. Frame, p. 131.

75. *Essais* 80, I, 26, p. 238. Frame, p. 130.

76. Letter from Gelida to La Taste (Epist. XV, *pridie calendas Septembris*). Quoted by R. Trinquet, *La Jeunesse de Montaigne*, op. cit., 533.

77. Quoted by Trinquet, ibid., 534.

78. Élie Vinet, *Schola Aquitanica*. Bordeaux: Simon Millanges, 1583. In Louis Massebieau, ed., *Schola Aquitanica: Programme d'études du Collège de Guyenne au XVIᵉ siècle*. Paris: C. Delagrave, 1886, 7.

79. Élie Vinet, *Schola Aquitanica*, op. cit., 41.

80. On the teaching of rhetoric at this period and its inclusion in the school curricu-

lum, see Peter Mack, *A History of Renaissance Rhetoric, 1380–1620*. Oxford: Oxford University Press, 2011.

81. Élie Vinet, *Schola Aquitanica*, op. cit., 25.

82. Montaigne says that he played several roles in the Latin tragedies staged at the College of Guyenne: "I played the leading parts in the Latin tragedies of Buchanan, Guerente, and Muretm which were performed with dignity in our College of Guyenne." *Essais* 88, I, 26, f. 66v; Frame, p. 131.

83. Ian D. McFarlane, "George Buchanan and France." In J. C. Ireson, Ian D. McFarlane, and Garnet Rees, eds., *Studies in French Renaissance presented to H. W. Lawton*. Manchester: Manchester University Press; New York: Barnes and Noble, 1968, 225.

84. Jean Dupèbe, "Un poète néolatin: Jean Binet de Beauvais." In *Mélanges sur la littérature à la mémoire de V.-L. Saulnier*. Geneva: Droz, 1984, 613–28.

85. *Essais* 80, I, 26, p. 235–36. Frame, p. 129.

86. *Essais* EB, I, 26, f. 65r. Frame, p. 129.

87. *Essais* 80, I, 26, p. 236. Frame, p. 129.

88. See Philip Ford, "La bibliothèque grecque de Montaigne." In Philip Ford and Neil Kenney, eds., *La Librairie de Montaigne*. Cambridge: Cambridge French Colloquia, 2012, 25–38.

89. Élie Vinet, *Schola Aquitanica*, op. cit.

90. Quoted by Marcel Rouxel, *La Compétence de la cour des jurats de Bordeaux*. Bordeaux: Bière, 1949, 86.

91. This judgment was transcribed by Guillaume Paradin in his *Histoire de notre temps*. See *La Révolte de la Gabelle en Guienne l'an mil cinq cens quarante huit, tirée de l'Histoire de notre temps de maître Guillaume Paradin, doyen de Beaujeu*. Bordeaux: Atelier Aldo Manuzio, 1981, 56–57.

92. Camille Jullian, *Histoire de Bordeaux depuis les origines jusqu'en 1895*. Bordeaux: Feret et fils, 1895, 343.

93. George Hoffmann, "Montaigne's lost years." *Bulletin de la Société internationale des amis de Montaigne*, no. 55, 2012, 121–41.

94. On Montaigne and the trial of Martin Guerre, see Émile Telle, "Montaigne et le procès Martin Guerre." *Bibliothèque d'Humanisme et Renaissance*, vol. XXXVII, no. 3, 1975, 387–419; and John O'Brien, "Suspended sentences." In Keith Cameron and Laura Willett, eds., *Le Visage changeant de Montaigne / The Changing Face of Montaigne*. Paris: H. Champion, 2003, 195–206.

95. These two possibilities are proposed respectively by Philip Ford, "George Buchanan et Montaigne," art. cit.; and Michel Simonin, "Montaigne et ses frères: Un poème inédit de George Buchanan conservé par Henri de Mesmes." In Philippe Desan, ed., *"Sans autre guide": Mélanges de littérature française de la Renaissance offerts à Marcel Tetel*. Paris: Klincksieck, 1999, 97–115.

96. I. D. McFarlane, "George Buchanan and France," art. cit., 239n20.

97. See Guy Demerson, "Les *exempla* dans le *Discours de la servitude volontaire*: Une rhétorique datée?" In Marcel Tetel, ed., *Étienne de la Boétie: Sage révolutionnaire et poète périgourdin*. Paris: H. Champion, 2004, p. 195–224. On the edict of the

Semester, see Michel Magnien, "Sur un échange poétique méconnu entre Dorat et La Boétie autour de l'Édit du semestre (1554)." In Christine de Buzon and Jean-Eudes Girot, eds., *Jean Dorat: Poète humaniste de la Renaissance.* Geneva, Droz, 2007, 369–92.

98. On dialectic and method, see my book *Naissance de la méthode (Machiavel, La Ramée, Bodin, Montaigne, Descartes).* Paris: A.-G. Nizet, 1987.

99. *Essais* 80, I, 26, p. 186. Frame, pp. 106–7.

100. *Essais* EB, II, 17, f. 282r. Frame, p. 498.

101. *Essais* EB, II, 12, f. 212v. Frame, p. 376.

102. *Essais* 80, II, 12, p. 296. Frame, p. 403.

103. *Essais* EB, II, 12, f. 212v. Frame, p. 376.

104. *Essais* EB, II, 12, f. 215r. Frame, p. 383.

105. Alexandre Koyré, *From the Closed World to the Infinite Universe.* Baltimore: Johns Hopkins University Press, 1957.

106. *Essais* 80, II, 12, pp. 348–49. Frame, p. 430.

107. Ernst Cassirer, *The Individual and the Cosmos in Renaissance Philosophy*, trans. Mario Domandi. New York: Harper and Row, 1964, 110.

108. *Essais* 80, II, 12, p. 389. Frame, p. 455.

109. Alexandre Koyré, *Études d'histoire de la pensée scientifique.* Paris: Gallimard, 1985, 52.

110. *Essais* 80, II, 12, p. 345. Frame, p. 429.

111. Jan Miernowski, *L'Ontologie de la contradiction sceptique: Pour l'étude de la métaphysique des Essais.* Paris: H. Champion, 1998.

112. *Essais* EB, III, 12, f, 467r. Frame, p. 809.

113. *Essais* 80, I, 14, p. 74. Frame, p. 47.

114. *Essais* 80, II, 12, p. 338. Frame, p. 425.

115. *Essais*, 80, I, 26, pp. 194–95. Frame, p. 110.

116. *Essais* 88, III, 3, f. 362r–v. Frame, p. 629.

Chapter 2. A First Career as a Magistrate (1556–1570)

1. *Archives historiques du département de la Gironde*, vol. XIX, 1879, no. CLXXXII, 468–75.

2. M. Peyrecave, *Arnauld Le Ferron conseiller au Parlement de Guyenne.* Bordeaux: G. Gounouilhou, 1877.

3. Jean de Métivier, *Chronique du Parlement de Bordeaux*, ed. Arthur de Brezetz and Jules Delpit. 2 vols. Bordeaux: G. Gounouilhou, 1886–87, vol. II, 335.

4. François-Martial de Verthamon d'Ambloy, *Registre secret du Parlement de Bordeaux, recueilli et mis en ordre par les soins de François-Martial de Verthamon d'Ambloy commençant le 12 novembre 1561 et finissant le 22 avril 1562*, 1770. Archives municipales de Bordeaux, ms. 768, f. 26r.

5. Olivier Loussouarn, "Les Milieux parlementaires bordelais: 1520–1550." T.E.R., Université de Bordeaux-3, 1996, 70–73.

6. *Archives historiques du département de la Gironde*, vol. XXX, 1895, no. XVIII, 40–41.

7. Olivier Loussouarn, "Les Milieux parlementaires bordelais," op. cit., 71.

8. Pierre Meller, *Les Anciennes familles dans la Gironde*. Bordeaux: E. Grugy, 1895, vol. I, 99.

9. On the Pontacs and the wine trade in Bordeaux at the beginning of the sixteenth century, see Clive Coates, *Grands Vins: The Finest Châteaux of Bordeaux and Their Wines*. Berkeley: University of California Press, 1995, 311–12.

10. Pierre Meller, *Notes pour servir à l'histoire de la famille de Pontac*. Tarbes: Imprimerie Croharé, 1910, 5.

11. Roland Mousnier, *La Vénalité des offices sous Henri IV et Louis XIII*. Paris: Presses Universitaires de France, 1971; Barbara B. Diefendorf, *Paris City Councillors in the Sixteenth Century: The Politics of Patrimony*. Princeton, NJ: Princeton University Press, 1983; Robert Descimon, "Modernité et archaïsme de l'État monarchique: Le Parlement de Paris saisi par la vénalité (XVIᵉ siècle)." In Jean-Philippe Genet, ed., *L'État moderne, genèse: Bilan et perspectives*. Paris: Éditions du CNRS, 1990, 147–61; id., "La vénalité des offices et la construction de l'État dans la France moderne: Des problèmes de la représentation symbolique aux problèmes du coût social du pouvoir." In Robert Descimon, Jean-Frédéric Schaub, and Bernard Vincent, eds., *Les Figures de l'administrateur: Institutions, réseaux, pouvoirs en Espagne, en France et au Portugal, XVIᵉ–XIXᵉ siècle*. Paris: Éditions de l'EHESS, 1997, 78–93; Jean Nagle, *Un orgueil français: La vénalité des offices sous l'Ancien Régime*. Paris: Odile Jacob, 2008.

12. Jean Savaron, *Traicté de l'annuel et vénalité des offices*. Paris: Pierre Chevalier, 1615, 16.

13. Camille Jullian, *Histoire de Bordeaux depuis les origines jusqu'en 1895*. Bordeaux: Feret et fils, 1895, 427.

14. Jean de Gaufreteau, *Chronique bordelaise*. 2 vols. Bordeaux: Société des bibliophiles de Guyenne, 1876–78, vol. I, 321.

15. Jean Savaron, *Traicté de l'annuel et vénalité des offices*, op. cit., 14.

16. Natalie Zemon Davis, *The Gift in Sixteenth Century France*. Madison: University of Wisconsin Press, 2000, 163.

17. Anne-Marie Cocula, "Formation et affirmation d'un patriciat: Le parlement de Bordeaux au XVIᵉ siècle." In Claude Petitfrère, ed., *Construction, reproduction et représentation des patriciats urbains de l'Antiquité au XXᵉ siècle*. Tours: CEHVI, 1999, 283–97.

18. Pierre Bourdieu, *The Logic of Practice*. Trans. Richard Nice. Stanford, CA: Stanford University Press, 1990, 64.

19. Donald R. Kelley, "*Jurisconsultus perfectus*: The Lawyer as Renaissance Man." *Journal of the Warburg Courtauld Institutes*, vol. 51, 1998, 84–102.

20. Robert Descimon, "Les De Thou au miroir des archives notariales du XVIᵉ siècle: Les chemins de la haute robe." In *Jacques-Auguste de Thou: Écriture et condition robine*. Paris: Presses de l'université Paris-Sorbonne, 2007, 13–35. On De Thou's exceptional career, see Samuel Kinser, *The Works of Jacques-Auguste de Thou*. The

Hague: M. Nijhoff, 1966; and Ingrid De Smet, *Thuanus: The Making of Jacques-Auguste de Thou (1553–1617)*. Geneva: Droz, 2006.

21. Sylvie Daubresse, "Christophe de Thou et Charles IX: Recherche sur les rapports entre le parlement de Paris et le Prince (1560–1574)." *Histoire, économie & société*, vol. 17, no. 3, 1998, 389–422.

22. Bernard de La Roche Flavin, *Treize livres des parlemens de France, esquels est amplement traicté de leur origine et institution, et des présidens, conseillers, gens du roy, greffiers, secrétaires, huissiers et autres officiers....* Bordeaux: Simon Millanges, 1617, 30.

23. Maïté Etchechoury, *Les Maîtres des requêtes sous les derniers Valois (1553–1589)*. Paris: H. Champion, 1991.

24. Édouard Maugis, *Histoire du parlement de Paris de l'avènement des rois Valois à la mort d'Henri IV*. 3 vols. Paris: Picard, 1913, vol. III, 184.

25. Camille Trani, "Le Grand Conseil de Henri II à Henri IV (1547–1610)." Thesis in the faculty of law. Paris: 1969; id., "Les magistrats du Grand Conseil au XVIᵉ siècle (1547–1610)." In *Mémoires publiés par la fédération des sociétés archéologiques de Paris et de l'Île-de-France*, vol. 42, 1991, 61–218; Jean-Louis Thireau, "Le Conseil du roi au XVIᵉ siècle." *Revue administrative*, no. 3, 1999, 10–19.

26. Olivier Loussouarn, "Les Milieux parlementaires bordelais," op. cit., 48.

27. *Mémoires de Messire Philippe Hurault, comte de Cheverny*. In *Collection universelle des Mémoires particuliers relatifs à l'histoire de France*. London: 1789, vol. L, 54.

28. Ibid., 56.

29. Ibid., 59

30. Jehan Bacquet, *Quatriesme traicté... des droicts des domaines de la couronne de France. Concernant les Francs Fiefs, Nouveaux Acquests, Anoblissements & Amortissements*. Paris: Sébastien Nivelle, 1582, f. 56v.

31. Ibid., f. 61v.

32. Ibid.

33. Ibid., f. 63r.

34. Jonathan Powis, "Aristocratie et bureaucratie dans la France du XVIᵉ siècle." In Philippe Contamine, ed., *L'État et les aristocraties XIIᵉ–XVIIᵉ siècle: France, Angleterre, Écosse*. Paris: Presses de l'ENS, 1989, 230–43; and Sharon Kettering, *Patrons, Brokers and Clients*. Oxford: Oxford University Press, 1986.

35. Jehan Bacquet, *Quatriesme traicté... des droicts des domaines de la couronne de France*, op. cit., f. 63v.

36. Robert Descimon, "La haute noblesse parlementaire parisienne: La production d'une aristocratie d'État aux XVIᵉ et XVIIᵉ siècles." In Philippe Contamine, ed., *L'État et les aristocraties*, op. cit., 357–84.

37. Olivier Loussouarn, "Les Milieux parlementaires bordelais," op. cit., 54–57.

38. Bernard de La Roche Flavin, *Treize livres des parlemens de France*, op. cit., 48.

39. James Russell-Major, *The Deputies to the Estates General in Renaissance France*. Madison: University of Wisconsin Press, 1960, 29.

40. George Duby, *Les Trois Ordres ou l'imaginaire du féodalisme*. Paris: Gallimard, 1978.

41. Yves Lemoine, *La Grande Robe, le Mariage et l'Argent. Histoire d'une grande famille parlementaire*. Paris: Michel de Maule, 2000.

42. Michel Cassan, "Pour une enquête sur les officiers 'moyens' de la France moderne." *Annales du Midi*, vol. 108, no. 213, 1996, 89–112.

43. George Huppert, *Les bourgeois gentilshommes: An Essay on the Definition of Elites in Renaissance France*. Chicago: University of Chicago Press, 1977.

44. Jonathan Dewald, *The Formation of a Provincial Nobility: The Magistrates of the Parlement of Rouen (1499–1610)*. Princeton, NJ: Princeton University Press, 1980.

45. M. Peyrecave, *Arnauld Le Ferron conseiller au Parlement de Guyenne*, op. cit., 22.

46. For a list of works written by members of the parlement of Bordeaux during the first half of the sixteenth century, see Olivier Loussouarn, "Les Milieux parlementaires bordelais," op. cit., appendix I: "Les parlementaires et leurs écrits."

47. Ernest Gaullieur, *Histoire du Collège de Guyenne d'après un grand nombre de documents inédits*. Paris: Sandoz et Fischbacher, 1874, 132–33.

48. This practice has been studied by Stéphan Geonget, "L'arrêt notable entre droit et littérature, les choix de Jean Papon." In Laurence Giavarini, ed., *L'Écriture des juristes (XVᵉ–XVIIIᵉ siècles)*. Paris: Classiques Garnier, 2010, 206–22.

49. Jean-Marie Hippolyte Aymard Saint-Saud, *Magistrats des sénéchaussées, présidiaux et élections, fonctionnaires des vices-sénéchaussées du Périgord*. Bergerac: Imprimerie générale du Sud-Ouest, 1931.

50. Denise Bège-Seurin, "La Cour des aides de Périgueux (1553–1561)." In *Sarlat et le Périgord*. Périgueux: Société historique et archéologique de Périgueux, 1987, 321–30; Géraud Lavergne, "Les conflits de la Cour des aides de Périgueux avec les Cours des aides de Paris et de Montpellier (1554–1557)." *Bulletin philomatique et historique*, 1936–37, 37–45; Simone Quet, "La Cour des aides de Guyenne, ses rapports avec le Parlement de Bordeaux." *Revue historique de Bordeaux*, 1939, 97–111 and 167–82.

51. The receipt is reproduced in Théophile Malvezin, *Michel de Montaigne, son origine, sa famille*. Bordeaux: Charles Lefebvre, 1875, 263.

52. *Mémoire sur la constitution politique de la ville et cité de Périgueux, où l'on développe l'origine, le caractère & les droits de la seigneurie qui lui appartient, & dont tous ses citoyens & bourgeois sont propriétaires par indivis*. Paris: Imprimerie de Quillau, 1775, 545.

53. Jean de Métivier, *Chronique du Parlement de Bordeaux*, op. cit., vol. II, 175; and Anatole de Rouméjoux, "Essai sur les guerres de religion en Périgord." *Bulletin de la Société historique et archéologique du Périgord*, vol. XXIX, 1902, 111–64, 221–56, 336–99, 428–71, 543–51.

54. The letters of dispensation regarding his age granted La Boétie on October 13, 1553, are held in the archives of the department of the Gironde: *Archives historiques du département de la Gironde*, vol. XXV, 1887, no. CLXIV, p. 337.

55. *Mémoire de Henri de Mesmes, seigneur de Roissy et de Malassise*, ed. Edouard Frémy. Paris: E. Leroux, 1886, 147.

56. Olivier Loussouarn, "Les Milieux parlementaires bordelais," op. cit., 7.

57. Jean de Métivier, *Chronique du Parlement de Bordeaux*, op. cit., vol. II, 69.

58. Ibid., vol. II, 65.

59. Ibid., vol. II, 157.

60. Ibid., vol. II, 145–46.

61. On Montaigne's interest in fortune, luck, and the fortuitious in general, see the chapter "Hasard" in Philippe Desan, *Montaigne: Les formes du monde et de l'esprit*. Paris: Presses de l'université Paris-Sorbonne, 2008, 107–20.

62. Olivier Loussouarn, "Les Milieux parlementaires bordelais," op. cit., 6.

63. Bernard de La Roche Flavin, *Treize livres des parlemens de France*, op. cit., 36.

64. See the transcript by François-Martial de Verthamon d'Ambloy, *Registre secret du Parlement de Bordeaux, recueilli et mis en ordre par les soins de François-Martial de Verthamon d'Ambloy*. Bordeaux, 1770, Archives municipales de Bordeaux, ms. 767.

65. Jean de Métivier, *Chronique du Parlement de Bordeaux*, op. cit., vol. II, 159.

66. See Henri de Bastard d'Estang, *Les Parlements de France: Essai historique sur leurs usages, leur organisation et leur autorité*. 2 vols. Paris: Didier, 1857; C.B.F. Boscheron des Portes, *Histoire du Parlement de Bordeaux*. Bordeaux: C. Lefèvre, 1878; Eugène de Brezetz, *Essais historiques sur le parlement de Bordeaux*. Bordeaux: Crugy, 1856.

67. Paul Guilhiermoz, *Enquêtes et procès: Étude sur la procédure et le fonctionnement du Parlement au XIVe siècle, suivie du style de la Chambre des enquêtes, du style des commissaires du Parlement et de plusieurs autres textes et documents*. Paris: A. Picard, 1892, 7.

68. Katherine Almquist has described this work in several articles. See in particular "Montaigne et la politique du Parlement de Bordeaux." In Philippe Desan, ed., *Montaigne politique*. Paris: H. Champion, 127–138; id., "Examining the Evidence: Montaigne in the *Registres secrets du Parlement de Bordeaux*." *Montaigne Studies*, vol. XVI, 2004, 45–74.

69. Roland Mousnier, *Les Institutions de la France sous la monarchie absolue* [1974]. Paris: Presses Universitaires de France, 2005, 960.

70. Jean Tarneau, *Stile et usage observé au parlement de Bourdeaux, touchant l'exercice de la justice. Avec la forme de ses entrées, sceances, et audiances. Et une table des jours des roolles ordinaires de châque seneschaussée du ressort*. Bordeaux: C. de la Court, s.d.

71. The judicial procedure followed in the Chambres des Enquêtes in investigations as well as the work of the reporers and *compartiteurs* (judges expressing views contrary to those of the reporter) in trials under the Old Regime are described and explained in Henri de Bastard-d'Estang, *Les Parlements de France. Essai historique sur leurs usages, leur organisation et leur autorité*. 2 vols. Paris: Didier, 1857, vol. I, 204–33.

72. Nussy Saint-Saens, "Montaigne au Parlement de Bordeaux." *Revue historique de Bordeaux*, 1953, 119–35.

73. *Archives historiques du département de la Gironde*, vol. VI, 1864, no. VI, November 14, 1561, 7–8.

74. Labat de Savignac, *Registres secrets du Parlement*, 1734. Bibliothèque municipale de Bordeaux, Fonds patrimoniaux, ms. 369 (2), f. 86r.

75. Jean de Métivier, *Chronique du Parlement de Bordeaux*, op. cit., vol. II, 162.

76. Roland Mousnier, *Les Institutions de la France sous la monarchie absolue*, [1947]. Paris: Presses Universitaires de France, 2005, 871.

77. These figures are given by Fontainemarie, *Recueil*, 2 vols. Vol. 1: "Livre noir de l'Hôtel de Périgueux." Bibliothèque municipale de Bordeaux, ms. 380, p. 1–6. Quoted by Denise Bège-Seurin, "La Cour des aides de Périgueux (1553–1561)," art. cit., p. 6.

78. Bernard de La Roche Flavin, *Treize livres des parlemens de France*, op. cit., 349.

79. *Archives historiques du département de la Gironde*, vol. XII, 1864, no. CXVII, 129.

80. Ibid., no. CXVIII.

81. *Inventaire sommaire des registres de la jurade 1520–1783*. Bordeaux, Archives municipales de Bordeaux, vol. IX, 1909, 274.

82. For additional figures regarding the revenues of the magistrates in the Bordeaux parlement, see the (unpublished) thesis by Jonathan Powis, "The Magistrates of the Parlement of Bordeaux c. 1500–1563." Doctoral thesis, Oxford University, 1975.

83. Jean de Coras, *Arrest memorable du Parlement de Tolose. Contenant une Histoire prodigieuse d'un supposé mari advenue de nostre temps: enrichie de cent et onze belles et doctes annotations.* Lyon: Antoine Vincent, 1561; Guillaume Le Sueur, *Histoire admirable d'un faux et supposé mary, advenue en Languedoc, l'an mil cinq cens soixante.* Paris: Vincent Sertenas, 1561. On this case, see Natalie Zemon Davis, *The Return of Martin Guerre.* Cambridge, MA: Harvard University Press, 1984; John O'Brien, "Comment estre un bon juge?" *Bulletin de la Société des amis de Montaigne*, no. 21–22, 2001, 185–92; id., "Suspended sentences." In K. Cameron and Laura Willett, eds., *Le Visage changeant de Montaigne / The Changing Faces of Montaigne.* Paris: H. Champion, 2003, 91–102; Nicola Panichi, "La boiterie de la raison: Le cas Martin Guerre." *Bulletin de la Société des amis de Montaigne*, no. 21–22, 2001, 171–83.

84. *Essais* 88, III, 11, f. 456r. Frame, p. 788.

85. Stéphan Geonget, "L'humanisme littéraire de Jean de Coras: Un juriste lecteur de Budé et de Rabelais." In Nathalie Dauvois-Lavialle, ed., *L'Humanisme à Toulouse (1480–1580)*. Paris: H. Champion, 2006, 271–87.

86. *Essais* 80, I, 28, p. 259. Frame, p. 137.

87. Ingrid A. R. De Smet and Alain Legros, "Un manuscrit de François Baudouin dans la 'librairie' de Montaigne." *Bibliothèque d'Humanisme et Renaissance*, vol. LXXV, no. 1, 2013, 105–11.

88. Eugène Voizard, "Les relations de Montaigne avec la cour." *Revue d'histoire littéraire de la France*, 1894, 446–50.

89. *Essais* 80, I, 46, p. 422. Frame, p. 201.

90. *Archives historiques du département de la Gironde*, vol. XIII, 1872, no. XLIV, 120–21.

91. Jean de Métivier, *Chronique du Parlement de Bordeaux*, op. cit., vol. II, 272. The Savignac version of the *Registres secrets* presents Montaigne as "being most senior according to the complete number of those who are supposed to perform such

tasks" ("estant le plus ancien apres le nombre parfait de ceux qui doibvent servir esdites vacations"). BNF, ms. Fonds français 22.372.

92. L. Braye, "Le premier voyage de Montaigne à Bar-le-Duc en 1559." *Bulletin de la Société des lettres de Bar-le-Duc*, 1938–39, 184–86.

93. *Registres secrets du Parlement de Bordeaux, recueilli et mis en ordre par les soins de François-Martial de Verthamon d'Ambloy*, ed. François-Martial de Verthamon d'Ambloy. Archives de la ville de Bordeaux, ms. 768, f. 190–94.

94. Ibid., f. 192–93.

95. Katherine Almquist, "Montaigne et la politique du Parlement de Bordeaux," art. cit., 127–38; id., "Writing Pluralist Biography of Montaigne's Legal Career." In George Hoffmann, ed., *The New Biographical Criticism.* Charlottesville, VA: Rookwood Press, 2004, 58–76.

96. Alexandre Nicolaï, "Les grandes dates de la vie de Michel de Montaigne." *Bulletin de la Société des amis de Montaigne*, nos. 13–14, 1948–49, 24–27.

97. *Archives historiques du département de la Gironde*, vol. XXVIII, 1893, no. XXXVI–LV, 123–143.

98. Ibid., no. LVI, 144.

99. Ibid., no. LVII.

100. Ibid., no. LVIII, 145; see also no. LX, 147.

101. Until recently, we had only five rulings bearing the name of Montaigne. These rulings were published by Paul Bonnefon, "Cinq arrêts du Parlement de Bordeaux rendus au rapport de Michel de Montaigne." *Archives historiques du département de la Gironde*, vol. XXVIII, 1893, 121–47. Katherine Almquist showed that Montaigne dictated some fifty rulings, signed as reporter or commissioner, and voted on more than 350 other cases in the first Chambre des Enquêtes. Four recently discovered rulings have been published: Katherine Almquist, "Quatre arrêts du Parlement de Bordeaux, autographes inédits de Montaigne (mai 1566–août 1567)." *Bulletin de la Société des amis de Montaigne*, no. 9–10, 1998, 13–38.

102. Quoted by Jean-François Payen, *Recherches sur Montaigne: Documents inédits.* Paris: Techener, 1856, no. 4, 20.

103. Quoted by Donald Frame, *Montaigne: A Biography.* New York: Harcourt, Brace & World, 1965, 54.

104. Document discovered by Mathurin Dréano and quoted by Fortunat Strowski, *Montaigne.* Paris: Éditions de la Nouvelle Revue critique, 1938, 64.

105. On the difficulty of interpreting the edicts of tolerance, see Mario Turchetti, "Une question mal posée: La 'tolérance' dans les édits de Janvier (1562) et d'Amboise (1563); les premiers commentaires et interprétations: Jean Bégat." In Henry Méchoulan et al., eds., *La Formazione storica dell'alterita: Studi di storia della tolleranza nell'età moderna offerti a Antonio Rotondò.* 3 vols. Florence: Leo S. Olschki, 2001, vol. I, 245–94.

106. *Archives historiques du département de la Gironde*, vol. X, 1868, nos. LXXXVII and LXXXVIII, 163–71. There are two versions of this contract, both dated the same day, as is the rest of the guarantee provided by Joseph de La Chassaigne for his daughter's dowry. Ibid., no. LXXXIX, 171–73.

107. *Archives historiques du département de la Gironde*, vol. X, 1868, no. LXXXVII, September 22, 1565, 163–67.

108. Michel Simonin, "Françoise (de La Chassaigne) et (son ?) Michel." In François Lecercle and Simone Perrier, eds., *La Poétique des passions à la Renaissance: Mélanges offerts à Françoise Charpentier*. Paris: H. Champion, 2001, 155–70.

109. Katherine Almquist, "Montaigne Judging with Henri de Mesmes (May–June 1565)." *Montaigne Studies*, vol. XVI, 2004, 37–40.

110. *Archives historiques du département de la Gironde*, vol. X, 1868, no. CVI, August 22, 1568, 252–56.

111. Bibliothèque municipale de Bordeaux, ms. 738 (3), f. 100–104. This is all that remains of a dossier of which we now have only a single signature in an old cover: "1568. Mémorial des affaires de feu Messire Michel de Montaigne, après le décès de monsieur son père, no. 255, coté V." Bibliothèque municipale de Bordeaux, ms. 738 (3), f. 107.

112. *Archives historiques du département de la Gironde*, vol. XIII, 1872, no. CXLI, 399–441.

113. Ibid., ruling of April 6, 1569, no. CXLI, 399–420.

114. Ibid., ruling of February 1, 1570, no. CXLIV, 427–429.

115. François de Syrueilh, *Journal* [1568–1585]. In *Archives historiques du département de la Gironde*, vol. XIII, 1871–72, no. CIII, 270.

116. See Henry III's letters relating to the administration of the city of Bordeaux's finances in *Livre des Privilèges*. Bordeaux: Imprimerie G. Gounouilhou, 1878, vol. II, appendix, 313–14, no. XXVIII.

117. *Essais* 88, III, 13, f. 472r. Frame, p. 817.

118. *Essais* 88, III, 10, f. 451v. Frame, p. 780.

119. *Essais* 80, II, 17, p. 460. Frame, p. 497.

120. *Essais* 80, II, 8, p. 574. Frame, p. 505.

121. *Essais* EB, I, 3, f. 4v. Frame, p. 9.

122. *Essais* 80, II, 12, p. 353. Frame, p. 437.

123. *Essais* EB, II, 12, f. 245r. Frame, p. 436.

124. On these categories of the nobility of the robe, see Robert Descimon, "La haute noblesse parlementaire parisienne: la production d'une aristocratie d'État aux XVIe et XVIIe siècles," art. cit.

125. Alain Dufour, "Le colloque de Poissy." In *Mélanges d'histoire du XVIe siècle offerts à Henri Meylan*. Geneva: Droz, 1970, 127–37.

126. Philippe Desan, "Une autre histoire: Les droits de la conscience." In *Penser l'histoire à la Renaissance*. Caen: Paradigme, 1993, 221–42.

127. On Montaigne's attitude toward the Wars of Religion, see Marcel Françon, "Les guerres de religion et Montaigne." *Bulletin de la Société des amis de Montaigne*, no. 20, 1970, 39–47; id., "Montaigne, J.-A. de Thou et les guerres de religion." *Bulletin de la Société des amis de Montaigne*, no. 18, 1969, 33–42; Isida Cremona, "La pensée politique de Montaigne et les guerres civiles." *Studi Francesi*, vol. 23, 1979, 432–48; James Coleman, "Montaigne and the Wars of Religion." In Keith Cameron, ed., *Montaigne and His Age*. Exeter: University of Exeter Press, 1981, 107–

19; and especially Géralde Nakam, *Montaigne et son temps: Les événements et les Essais*. Paris: A.-G. Nizet, 1982, 87–111.

128. *Essais* 88, III, 12, f. 462v–463r. Frame, p. 800.

129. *Essais* 80, II, 6, p. 49. Frame, p. 268.

130. On this point, see Géralde Nakam, op. cit., 104.

131. Denis Crouzet, *Les Guerriers de Dieu: La violence au temps des troubles de religion (v. 1525–v. 1610)*. Seyssel: Champ Vallon, 2005.

132. *Essais* 88, I, 23, f. 42v. Frame, p. 87.

133. *Essais* 80, I, 5, p. 21. Frame, p. 17.

134. *Essais* 80, II, 5, p. 39. Frame, p. 264.

135. *Essais* 88, III, 9, f. 427v. Frame, pp. 741–42.

136. Frieda Brown, *Religious and Political Conservatism in the* Essais *of Montaigne*. Geneva: Droz, 1963; Jean Starobinski, " 'To Preserve and to Continue': Remarks on Montaigne's Conservatism." *Diogenes*, no. 118, 1982, 103–20; and Timothy Reiss, "Montaigne et le sujet politique." *Œuvres et critiques*, vol. 8, no. 1–2, 1983, 127–52.

137. *Essais* 80, II, 19, p. 507. Frame, p. 506.

138. Ibid.

139. Anatole de Rouméjoux, "Essai sur les guerres de Religion en Périgord." *Bulletin de la Société historique et archéologique du Périgord*, vol. XXIX, 1902, 111–64, 221–56, 336–99, 428–71, 543–51.

140. *Discours au vray et en abbregé, de ce qui est dernierement advenu à Vassi, y passant Monseigneur le Duc de Guise*. Paris: Guillaume Morel, 1562; *Discours entier de la persecution et cruauté exercée en la ville de Vaissy, par le Duc de Guyse, le 1 de Mars 1562*, 1563; and *Histoire de la cruauté exercee par Françoys de Lorraine, Duc de Guyse, et les siens en la ville de Vassy, le premier jour de Mars*, 1562.

141. On the iconography of the Wars of Religion, see Philip Benedict, *Graphic History: The Wars, Massacres and Troubles of Tortorel and Perrissin*. Geneva: Droz, 2007.

142. *Essais* 80, I, 32, pp. 331–33. Frame, p. 160.

143. *Essais* 80, II, 12, p. 353. Frame, p. 436.

144. Ibid.

145. *Essais* 80, I, 56, p. 482. Frame, p. 230.

146. Essais 80, II, 19, p. 513. Frame, p. 506

147. Essais 80, I, 56, p. 482. Frame, p. 230.

148. *Essais* 80, II, 19, p. 515. Frame, p. 509.

149. Ibid.

Chapter 3. La Boétie and Montaigne:
Discourse on Servitude and Essay of Allegiance

───────

1. *Essais* EB, I, 28, f. 71v. Frame, p. 139.

2. "Avertissement au lecteur par M. de Montaigne," *Mesnagerie de Xénophon*, 61.

3. *Essais* EB, I, 28, f. 71v. Frame, p. 139.

4. Rulings of March 29, 1559; May 2, 8, 14, and 24, June 18, July 16, August 3, 14, and 17, 1560. *Archives historiques du département de la Gironde*, vol. XXVIII, 1893, 121–32. These rulings were all issued under the presidencies of Jehan d'Alesme and François de La Guyonnie.

5. Rulings of January 23, February 21, May 13, July 12 and 31, August 20, 1561; April 6 and September 7, 1562; May 7 and 21, 1563. Ibid., p. 123–31.

6. Last will and testament of La Boétie, August 14, 1563. *Archives historiques du département de la Gironde*, vol. XVII, 1877, no. XIV, 161–62; vol. XXVIII, 1893, nos. XLV–LII, 134–39.

7. On the books La Boétie left to Montaigne, see Alain Legros, "Dix-huit volumes de la bibliothèque de La Boétie légués à Montaigne et signalés par lui comme tels." *Montaigne Studies*, vol. XXV, 2013, 177–87.

8. *Essais* EB, I, 28, f. 71v. Frame, p. 139.

9. See Robert Cottrell, "An Introduction to La Boétie's Three Latin Poems Dedicated to Montaigne." *Montaigne Studies*, vol. III, no. 1, 1991, 3–14.

10. La Boétie, *Poemata*, "Ad Michaelem Montanum." In James S. Hirstein, ed., and Robert D. Cottrell, trans., *Montaigne Studies*, vol. III, no. 1, 1991, 21–25: "An te paternis passibus arduos / luctantem honesti vincere tramites, / et ipse fervidus iuventa, / ridiculus monitor, docebo? / . . . / obscena paelex. At, puer, effuge, / dum fas valenti, perfida munera / quis illa nunc demulcet aures, / mox animo expositura virus. / . . . / Quo vitam inerti, si minimum interest / vivus sepultis? Occupat is mori / qui desides edormit annos / et tacitum innumeratus aevum."

11. See, for example, Gary Ferguson, "Montaigne's Itchy Ears: Friendship, Marriage, (Homo)sexuality, and Scepticism." In his *Queer (Re)readings in the French Renaissance: Homosexuality, Gender, Culture*. Hampshire: Ashgate, 2008, 191–243.

12. See Roger Trinquet, "La lettre sur la mort de La Boétie ou Lancelot de Carle inspirateur de Montaigne." In *Mélanges d'histoire littéraire (XVIᵉ–XVIIᵉ siècles) offerts à Raymond Lebègue par ses collègues, ses élèves et ses amis*. Paris: A.-G. Nizet, 1969, 115–25.

13. *Mesnagerie de Xénophon*, 307.

14. Ibid., 308.

15. Ibid.

16. Ibid., 309.

17. Ibid., 310.

18. Ibid., 315.

19. Ibid., 317.

20. Ibid., 314.

21. Ibid., 318.

22. Ibid., 319.

23. Ibid., 321.

24. Bibliothèque municipale de Bordeaux, Fonds patrimoniaux, ms. 369 (2), f. 133r.

25. On the paradoxical reception of the *Discourse on Voluntary Servitude* in the Protestant milieu, see Philippe Desan, "Le *Discours de la servitude volontaire* et la cause

protestante: les paradoxes de la réception de La Boétie." *Studi Francesi,* vol. 180, no. 3, 2016.

26. Francis Hauchecorne, "Le parlement de Bordeaux pendant la première guerre civile (décembre 1560–mars 1563)." *Annales du Midi,* vol. LXII, 1950, 329–40.

27. *Essais* 80, I, 28, p. 252. Frame, p. 135.

28. Stéphane Claude Gigon, *Contribution à l'histoire de l'impôt sous l'Ancien Régime: La révolte de la Gabelle en Guyenne (1548–1549).* Paris: H. Champion, 1906. Also see Guillaume Paradin, *La Révolte de la Gabelle en Guienne l'an mil cinq cens quarante-huit, tirée de l'Histoire de notre tems de maitre Guillaume Paradin.* Lyon: Pierre Michel, 1558; and Jean Bouchet, *Histoire de la révolte de la Gabelle en Guyenne et à Bordeaux... tirée des Annales d'Aquitaine.* Poitiers: Enguilbert de Marnef, 1557. Texts reproduced in *La Révolte de la Gabelle en Guyenne et à Bordeaux en 1548.* Bordeaux: Atelier Aldo Manuzio, 1981.

29. Anne-Marie Cocula, " 'Je vis en mon enfance un Gentilhomme commandant à une grande ville...': Montaigne et la révolte bordelaise de 1548." In *Pouvoir, contestations et comportements dans l'Europe moderne: Mélanges en l'honneur du professeur Yves-Marie Bercé.* Paris: Presses de l'Université Paris-Sorbonne, 2005, 531–47.

30. See John O'Brien, ed., *Pour une réévaluation de la diffusion manuscrite et imprimée du Discours de la servitude volontaire.* Paris: H. Champion, 2017; Marc Schachter, "Presentation of a newly discovered manuscript of La Boétie's *Discours de la servitude volontaire* and hypotheses on the datation of the BNF manuscripts." *Montaigne Studies,* vol. XX, 2008, 185–206; and Jean-Eudes Girot, "Une version inconnue du *Discours de la servitude volontaire* de La Boétie." *Bibliothèque d'Humanisme et Renaissance,* vol. LXIII, no. 3, 2001, 551–65. Among the numerous studies tracing the history of the *Discourse on Voluntary Servitude,* see in particular Renzo Ragghianti, "*Discours de la servitude volontaire* et Étienne de La Boétie: D'une énigme à l'autre." *Rinascimento,* vol. XLIII, 2003, 507–52; id., *Rétablir un texte. Le* Discours de la servitude volontaire *d'Étienne de La Boétie.* Florence: Leo Olschki, 2010. For a bibliography (up to 1997) of works on La Boétie and the *Discourse,* see Michel Magnien, *Étienne de La Boétie.* Paris; Rome: Memini, 1997.

31. Michel Magnien, "Pour une attribution définitive du Mémoire de l'édit de Janvier à Estienne de La Boétie." In *Cité des hommes, cité de Dieu: Travaux sur la littérature de la Renaissance en l'honneur de Daniel Ménager.* Geneva: Droz, 2003, 123–32.

32. Michel Magnien, *Mémoire d'habilitation,* 369–72.

33. That is the thesis proposed by Jean Lafond in "Le *Discours de la Servitude volontaire* de La Boétie et la rhétorique de la déclamation." *Mélanges sur la littérature de la Renaissance à la mémoire de V. L. Saulnier.* Geneva: Droz, 1984, 735–45.

34. Bibliothèque municipale de Bordeaux, Fonds patrimoniaux, ms. 369 (2), f. 117r.

35. De Thou, *Histoire universelle.* London, 1734, vol. IV, 128.

36. *Mémoire sur l'édit de Janvier,* 45.

37. Ibid., 46.

38. Ibid., 52.

39. Ibid., 54.

40. Ibid., 62.

41. Ibid.

42. Ibid., 66–67.

43. Ibid., 75.

44. Ibid., 80.

45. Gustave Baguenault de Puchesse, *Jean de Morvillier, évêque d'Orléans, garde des Sceaux de France, 1506–1577: Étude sur la politique française au XVIe siècle, d'après des documents inédits.* Paris: Didier, 1869.

46. *Mémoire sur l'édit de Janvier*, 91.

47. *Essais* 80, I, 28, pp. 273–74. Frame, p. 144.

48. *Essais* 80, II, 12, p. 257. Frame, p. 369.

49. C.-B.-F. Boscheron des Portes, *Histoire du parlement de Bordeaux.* Bordeaux: Charles Lefebvre, 1878, 166.

50. *Essais* 80, I, 27, pp. 249–50. Frame, p. 134.

51. Malcolm Smith, *Estienne de La Boëtie: Mémoire sur la pacification des troubles.* Geneva: Droz, 1983, 22.

52. *Essais* 88, III, 11, f. 457v. Frame, p. 790.

53. François Rigolot, "Friendship and voluntary servitude: Plato, Ficino, and Montaigne." *Texas Studies in Literature and Language*, vol. 47, no. 4, 2005, 326–44.

54. *Discours de la servitude volontaire*, 19. *Discourse on Voluntary Servitude*, trans. Harry Kurz. New York: Columbia University Press, 1942.

55. John O'Brien, "L'oubli comme mémoire: À propos de l'amitié politique." In Stéphan Geonget and Laurent Gerbier, eds., *Amitié & Compagnie: Autour du* Discours de la servitude volontaire *de La Boétie*. Paris: Classiques Garnier, 2012, 95–111.

56. Pierre Clastres, "Liberté, malencontre, innommable." In Étienne de La Boétie, *Le Discours de la servitude volontaire*, ed. P. Léonard, preceded by "La Boétie et la question du politique," texts by F. de Lamennais, P. Leroux, A. Vermorel, G. Landauer, S. Weil, P. Clastres, and C. Lefort. Paris: Payot, 1976, 229–46.

57. Ullrich Langer, "Montaigne's customs." *Montaigne Studies*, vol. IV, 1992, 81–96.

58. Arthur J. Gionet, "Les idées de Montaigne sur la capacité de raisonner du peuple." *Kentucky Foreign Language Quarterly*, vol. 10, no. 1, 1963, 140–44.

59. *Essais* 80, I, 42, p. 397. Frame, p. 191.

60. *Essais* 80, I, 14, p. 59. Frame, p. 35.

61. *Essais* 88, III, 6, f. 396r. Frame, p. 689.

62. *Essais* EB, III, 9, f. 422r. Frame, p. 733.

63. *Essais* 88, III, 6, f. 400v. Frame, p. 696.

64. *Essais* EB, I, 23, f. 40v. Frame, p. 83.

65. *Essais* EB, III, 13, f. 493v. Frame, p. 852.

66. *Essais* EB, III, 10, f. 447v. Frame, p. 775.

67. *Essais* EB, II, 17, f. 281v. Frame, p. 498.

68. *Essais* 80, II, 27, pp. 503–4. Frame, p. 524.

69. *Mémoire sur l'édit de Janvier*, 36.

70. *Essais* 88, III, 6, f. 395v. Frame, p. 688.

71. *Essais* 80, I, 27, p. 243. Frame, p. 132.

72. *Essais* 80, I, 23, pp. 134–35. Frame, p. 77.

73. *Essais* 88, III, 3, f. 359r. Frame, p. 625.

74. *Essais* 88, III, 9, f. 420r. Frame, p. 728.

75. *Essais* 88, I, 43, f. 112v. Frame, p. 269.

76. *Essais* EB, I, 3, f. 4v. Frame, p. 9.

77. See Philippe Desan, "Le *Discours de la servitude volontaire* et la cause protestante: Les paradoxes de la réception de La Boétie," art. cit.

78. *Discourse on Voluntary Servitude*, Trans. Kurz, 14.

79. Ibid.

80. Ibid., 2.

81. Ibid., 16–17.

82. Ibid., 17.

83. Ibid., 29. [Trans. modified.]

84. Ibid.

85. Ibid., 30.

86. Ibid. [Trans. modified.]

87. Ibid., 46.

88. Ibid., 5. [Trans. modified.]

89. *Essais* 80, I, 26, p. 209. Frame, p. 117.

90. *Essais* EB, I, 17, f. 25v. Frame, p. 51.

91. Ibid.

92. See for example Gérard Defaux, *Montaigne et le travail de l'amitié*. Orléans: Éditions Paradigme, 2001.

93. Ullrich Langer, *Perfect Friendship: Studies in Literature and Moral Philosophy from Boccaccio to Corneille*. Geneva: Droz, 1994.

94. *Essais* 80, I, 28, pp. 260–61. Frame, p. 139.

95. Xavier Le Person, *"Practiques" et "practiqueurs": La vie politique à la fin du règne de Henri III (1584–1589)*. Geneva: Droz, 2002; id., "Montaigne et les 'practiques' politiques de son temps." In Philippe Desan, ed., *Montaigne politique*. Paris: H. Champion, 2006, 95–112.

96. *Essais* EB, II, 17, f. 281v. Frame, p. 498.

97. *Essais* EB, I, 26, f. 66v. Frame, p. 130.

98. *Essais* 80, I, 28, pp. 251–52. Frame, p. 135.

99. *Essais* 80, I, 29, p. 277. Frame, p. 144.

100. Ibid.

101. On the place of women in the *Essais*, see Cecile Insdorf, *Montaigne and Feminism*. Chapel Hill: University of North Carolina Press, 1977; Cathleen Bauschatz, "The gender of genre: A study in the reception of Montaigne's *Essais*." *Montaigne Studies*, vol. II, 1990, 26–24; Françoise Charpentier, "L'absente des *Essais*: Quelques questions autour de l'essai II-8." *Bulletin de la Société des amis de Montaigne*, no. 17–18, 1984, 7–16; Dorothy Coleman, "Montaigne's 'Sur des vers de Virgile': Taboo subject, taboo author." In R. Bolgar, ed., *Classical Influences on European Culture: A.D. 1500–1700*. Cambridge: Cambridge University Press, 1976, 135–40; Philippe Desan, "The book, the friend, the woman: Montaigne's circular exchanges." In Marie-Rose Logan and Peter Rudnytsky, eds., *Contending Kingdoms:*

Historical, Psychological and Feminist Approaches to the Literature of Sixteenth-Century France and England. Detroit: Wayne State University Press, 1991, 225–62; Richard Regosin, *Montaigne's Unruly Brood: Textual Engendering and the Challenge to Paternal Authority.* Berkeley: University of California Press, l996.

102. *Essais* 80, I, 28, p. 253. Frame, p. 136. "That was all I could recover of what he left" ("C'est tout ce que j'ay peu recouvrer de ses reliques").

103. *Mesnagerie de Xénophon,* 321.

104. On this point, see Philippe Desan, "La place de La Boétie dans les *Essais* ou l'espace problématique du chapitre 29." In Zoé Samaras, ed., *Montaigne: Espace, voyage, écriture.* Paris: H. Champion, 1995, 181–89.

105. *Essais* 80, I, 28, p. 260. Frame, p. 138

106. Ibid.

107. *Essais* 88, III, 3, f. 367v–368r. Frame, p. 625.

108. *Essais* 80, I, 28, p. 254. Frame, p. 136.

109. *Essais* 80, I, 28, pp. 254–55. Frame, p. 136.

110. *Essais* 80, II, 8, p. 85. Frame, p. 291.

111. *Essais* 88, III, 3, f. 358r. Frame, p. 623.

112. *Essais* 80, I, 28, pp. 268–69. Frame, p. 141.

113. *Essais* 88, III, 3, f. 358r. Frame, p. 623.

114. *Essais* 80, I, 28, p. 258. Frame, p. 137.

115. *Essais* 80, I, 28, 256–57. Frame, pp. 136–37.

116. *Essais* 80, I, 28, 258–59. Frame, p. 137.

117. *Essais* 80, I, 28, 265. Frame, p. 140.

118. *Essais* 80, I, 28, 265, Frame, p. 141.

119. *Essais* 80, I, 28, 268. Frame, p. 141.

120. *Essais* 80, I, 28, 266. Frame, p. 141.

121. *Essais* 88, III, 9, f. 430v. Frame, p. 746.

Chapter 4. "Witness My Cannibals": The Encounter with the Indians of the New World

1. On the brief French colonial adventure in Brazil, see Paul Gaffarel, *Histoire du Brésil français au seizième siècle.* Paris: Maisonneuve, 1878. See also Frank Lestringant's studies, *Le Huguenot et le Sauvage: L'amérique et la controverse coloniale, en France, au temps des guerres de Religion (1555–1589).* Paris: Aux amateurs de livres, 1990; *L'Atelier du cosmographe ou l'image du monde à la Renaissance.* Paris: Albin Michel, 1991; and chapter 5 in Michel de Certeau's book *L'Écriture de l'histoire.* Paris: Gallimard, 1975. See in addition the two laconic but profound pages Claude Lévi-Strauss devotes to this disastrous colonial experiment in *Tristes tropiques.* Paris: Plon, 1955, 91–92; and Olivier Reverdin, *Quatorze calvinistes chez les Topinambous: Histoire d'une mission genevoise au Brésil (1556–1558).* Geneva: Éditions du Journal de Genève, 1957.

2. Frank Lestringant, "Fictions de l'espace brésilien à la Renaissance: L'exemple de

Guanabara." In Christian Jacob and Frank Lestringant, eds., *Arts et légendes d'espaces. Figures du voyage et rhétoriques du monde*. Paris: Presses de l'École normale supérieure, 1981, 207–56.

3. *Essais* 80, I, 23, p. 137. Frame, p. 82.

4. George Hoffmann, "Anatomy of the Mass: Montaigne's Cannibals." *PMLA*, vol. 117, no. 2, 2002, 207–21.

5. *Essais* 88, III, 9, f. 421v. Frame, p. 730.

6. *Essais* EB, I, 23, f. 39r. Frame, p. 81.

7. This Brazilian celebration has been commented upon by José Alexandrino de Souza Filho in his thesis, "Civilisation et barbarie en France au temps de Montaigne." Lille: ANRT, 2003, 48–88; see the same author's *Projeto "Livraria" de Montaigne: Um passeio ao universo do escritor francês Michel de Montaigne*. João Pessoa: Editora Universitária, 2007, 44–57. See also André Pottier, "L'entrée de Henri II à Rouen en 1550." *Revue de Rouen*, vol. V, 1835, 18–108; Fernand Denis, "Une fête brésilienne célébrée à Rouen en 1550." *Bulletin du bibliophile*, 1849, 332–402; Margaret McGowan, "Henri's entry into Rouen." *Renaissance Drama*, 1968, 199–225; Jean-Marie Massa, "Le monde luso-brésilien dans la Joyeuse entrée à Rouen." In *Les Fêtes de la Renaissance*, vol. III. Paris: Éditions du CNRS, 1975, 105–16.

8. *C'est la déduction du sumptueux ordre plaisantz spectacles et magnifiques théâtres dressées, et exhibés par les citoiens de Rouen ville métropolitaine du pays de Normandie, A la sacré Maiesté du Treschristian Roy de France, Henry second leur souverain Seigneur, Et à Tresillustre dame, ma Dame Katherine de Medicis, la Royne son espouze, lors de leur triumphant ioyeuls et nouvel advènement en icelle ville, qui fut es jours de Mercredy et jeudy premier et second jours d'octobre 1550*. Rouen: Robert Le Hoy, 1551, f. 41v.

9. Ibid.

10. Ibid.

11. Ibid., f. 42r.

12. Ibid.

13. *Essais* 80, I, 31, p. 300. Frame, p. 150.

14. Andrea Frisch, *The Invention of the Eyewitness: Witnessing and Testimony in Early Modern France*. Chapel Hill: University of North Carolina Press, 2004.

15. Frank Lestringant, *Le Brésil de Montaigne: Le Nouveau Monde des "Essais" (1580–1592)*. Paris: Chandeigne, 2005.

16. *Essais* 80, I, 31, p. 329. Frame, p. 159.

17. *Essais* 88, III, 6, f. 400r. Frame, p. 696.

18. *Essais* 80, I, 31, p. 327. Frame, p. 158.

19. Letter from the Spanish ambassador, Thomas Perrenot de Chantonnay, to Philip II, dated August 19, 1563. In Hector de La Ferrière, *Le XVIᵉ siècle et les Valois d'après les documents inédits du British Museum*. Paris: Imprimerie nationale, 1879, 164.

20. Sarah Hanley Madden, "L'idéologie constitutionnelle en France: le lit de justice." *Annales. Économie, sociétés, civilisations*, vol. 37, no. 1, 1982, 32–63.

21. See in particular *L'Entrée faicte au Roy treschrestien Charles neuviesme: A Rouen, le*

XII jour d'Aoust, l'An mil cinq cens Soixante troys, de son regne le troisiesme. Rouen: Martin le Mesgissier, 1563.

22. *La Declaration faicte par le Roy, de sa majorité, tenant son lict de justice en sa Cour de Parlement de Rouen: Et Ordonnance par luy faicte pour le bien et repos public de son Royaume: Et ce qu'il dict en ladicte Cour avant la publication de ladicte Ordonnance.* Paris: Robert Estienne, 1563. See also François-Léon Réguis, *Le Lit de justice tenu à Rouen par Charles IX.* Rouen, 1902; Elizabeth Brown and Richard Famiglietti, *The Lit de justice: Semantics, Ceremonial, and the Parlement of Paris—1300–1600.* Sigmaringen: Jan Thorbecke, 1994, 90–96.

23. *Archives historiques du département de la Gironde,* vol. XXVIII, 1893, no. LVIII, 145.

24. Abel Jouan, *Recueil et discours du voyage du Roy Charles IX de ce nom à present regnant, accompagné des choses dignes de memoire faictes en chacun endroit faisant sondit voyage en ses païs et provinces de Champaigne, Bourgoigne, Daulphiné, Provence, Languedoc, Gascoigne, Baïonne, et plusieurs autres lieux, suyvant son retour depuis son partement de Paris jusques à son retour audit lieu, és annees Mil cinq cens soixante quatre et soixante cinq.* Paris: Jean Bonfons, 1566.

25. Charles IX's royal entry into Bordeaux in 1565 is described in *L'Entrée du Roy à Bordeaux, avecques les Carmes Latins qui luy ont esté presentez, et au Chancelier.* Paris: Thomas Richard, 1565; also in *La Royale reception de leurs majestez treschrestiennes en la ville de Bourdeaus ou le siecle d'or ramené par les Alliances de France et d'Espaigne. Recueilli par le commandement du Roy.* Bordeaux: Simon Millanges, 1615; *Prosphonematon, sive de adventu Christianissimi Regis Caroli IX in suam urbem Burdigalam Mauricii Marcii Burdigalensis: Ad eundem.* Paris: Thomas Richard, 1565. See also Estienne de Cruseau, *L'Entrée de Charles IX à Bordeaux,* ed. Philippe Tamizey de Larroque. Bordeaux: Chollet,1882; Gabriel de Lurbe, *Chronique bordeloise.* Bordeaux: Simon Millanges, 1619, f. 32r; and Darnal's *Supplément,* 1666, f. 77v; Jean de Gaufreteau, *Chronique bordeloise, 1240–1638,* ed. Jules Delpit. Bordeaux: Société des bibliophiles de Guyenne, 1876–78, vol. 1, 136–37; Dom Devienne, *Histoire de la ville de Bordeaux.* Bordeaux: Simon de la Court, 1771, 146–48; Jacques Baurein, *Variétés bordeloises ou essai historique et critique sur la topographie ancienne et moderne du diocèse de Bordeaux.* Bordeaux, 1876, vol. 2, 223–33.

26. Theodore Godefroy, *Le Ceremonial François contenant les cérémonies observées en France aux Sacres & Couronnemens de Roys, & Reynes, & de quelques anciens Ducs de Normandie, d'Aquitaine, & de Bretagne: Comme aussi à leurs Entrées solennelles: Et à celles d'aucuns Dauphins, Gouverneurs de Provinces, & autres Seigneurs, dans diverses Villes du Royaume* [1619]. 2 vols. Paris: Sebastien et Gabriel Cramoisy, 1649.

27. François Hauchecorne, "Une intervention ignorée de Montaigne au parlement de Bordeaux." *Bibliothèque d'Humanisme et Renaissance,* vol. IX, 1947, 164–68.

28. Bibliothèque municipale de Bordeaux, Fonds patrimoniaux, ms. 369 (1), f. 68r.

29. Theodore Godefroy, *Le Ceremonial François,* op. cit., 913.

30. C.B.F. Boscheron des Portes, *Histoire du parlement de Bordeaux depuis sa création*

jusqu'à sa suppression (1451–1790). 2 vols. Bordeaux: Ch. Lefèvre, 1878, vol. 1, 189–90.

31. Lancelot de La Popelinière, *L'Histoire vulgairement dite*, vol. I, bk. X; Michel de L'Hospital, "Harangue devant le Parlement de Bordeaux en 1565." In Theodore Godefroy, *Le Ceremonial François*, op. cit.

32. *L'Entrée du Roi à Bordeaux, avecques les Carmes Latins qui ont été présentez, et au Chancelier*. Paris: Thomas Richard, 1565, "Au lecteur."

33. Agrippa d'Aubigné, *Histoire universelle*, vol. II, bk. IV, chap. V.

34. Jean-Marie Chartrou, "Les entrées solennelles à Bordeaux au XVIᵉ siècle." *Revue historique de Bordeaux et du département de la Gironde*, vol. XXIII, 1930, 99–102.

35. Theodore Godefroy, *Le Ceremonial François*, op. cit., 907.

36. *L'Entrée du Roi à Bordeaux*, op. cit., 9.

37. Ibid., 10.

38. Theodore Godefroy, *Le Ceremonial François*, op. cit., 915.

39. Ibid., 910.

40. Michel de L'Hospital, "Discours devant le parlement de Bordeaux," 12 avril 1565. In Loris Pétris, *Michel de L'Hospital: Discours et correspondance: La plume et la tribune II*. Geneva: Droz, 2013, 74. Pétris reproduced the text in the BNF, ms. fr. 16518, f. 1r–12r.

41. Ibid.

42. Ibid.

43. Ibid., p. 78.

44. Ibid.

45. Text in the Dupuy collection, reproduced by Auger de Mauléon, *Recueil de divers Mémoires, Harangues, remonstrances, et lettres servans à l'histoire de nostre temps*. Paris: Pierre Chevalier, 1623. This version bears the title "Lit de justice teneu par le roy Charles IX, en sa court de Parlement de Bordeaux, le 12 avril 1563 [1565], avant Pasques, ensemble la harangue qu'y prononça le chancelier de L'Hospital." In *Œuvres complètes de Michel de L'Hospital, Chancelier de France*. Paris: A. Boulland, 1824, vol. II, 114.

46. *Registre Secret du Parlement de Bordeaux commençant le 16 novembre 1564 et finissant le 1er septembre 1576, copie de Monsieur de Poitevin, avocat, qui la tenait de feu Monsieur le Premier Président Daulede, ce 30 aoust 1720, De Savignac*. Bibliothèque municipale de Bordeaux, Fonds patrimoniaux, ms. 369 (3), f. 638r.

47. On the Protestants' political situation in Bordeaux and the measures taken by the parlement against them, see Dom Devienne, *Histoire de la ville de Bordeaux*, op. cit., 148–50.

48. Philip Benedict, *Rouen during the Wars of Religion*. Cambridge: Cambridge University Press, 1981.

49. Louis Desgraves, *Inventaire des fonds Montaigne conservés à Bordeaux*. Paris: H. Champion, 1995, 142 (A. D. IB9, f. 113).

50. *Essais* 80, I, 31, p. 327. Frame, p. 158.

51. *Essais* 80, I, 31, p. 308. Frame, p. 153.

52. *Essais* 80, I, 31, p. 309. Frame, p. 153.

53. Pierre d'Origny, *Le Herault de la noblesse de France.* Reims: J. de Foigny, 1578, 20.

54. *Essais* 80, I, 31, p. 319. Frame, p. 156.

55. *Essais* 80, I, 31, p. 328. Frame, p. 159.

56. *Essais* 80, I, 31, p. 329. Frame, p. 159.

57. Ibid.

58. This important point is made by Loris Pétris, *Michel de L'Hospital: Discours et correspondancè; La plume et la tribune II*, op. cit., 72n216. Pétris remarks that Montaigne "listens to L'Hospital's speech but masks this borrowing by seeking in Plutarch the words he heard L'Hospital utter." See Montaigne, *Essais* 80, I, 31, p. 300. Frame, p. 150.

59. *Essais* 80, I, 31, p. 328. Frame, p. 159.

60. Archives nationales, Registres du Parlement de Paris, X, 1602, f. 384; quoted by Paul Bonnefon, *Montaigne, l'homme et l'œuvre.* Bordeaux; Paris: G. Gounouilhou; J. Rouam, 1893, 83. See Émile Dupré-Lasale, "Montaigne au Parlement de Paris en 1562." *Bulletin de la Société des amis de Montaigne*, no. 10, 1941, 3; id., *Bulletin du bibliophile*, 1887, 23–25; André Lelarge, "Autour du serment de Montaigne devant le Parlement de Paris en 1562." *Bulletin de la Société des amis de Montaigne*, no. 11, 1941, 40–42.

61. Pierre Villey, "Montaigne au Parlement de Paris en 1562." *Bulletin de la Société des amis de Montaigne*, no. 10, 1941, 4.

62. On Montaigne's heroic culture, see Jean Balsamo, " 'Et me contente de gémir sans brailler': Montaigne et l'humanité héroïque." In Pierre Magnard and Thierry Gontier, eds., *Montaigne.* Paris: Éditions du Cerf, 2010, 133–53; and Daniel Ménager, "La culture héroïque de Montaigne." *Bulletin de la Société des amis de Montaigne*, no. 9–10, 1998, 39–52.

63. *Essais* 80, I, 31, p. 304. Frame, pp. 151–52.

64. *Essais* 80, I, 31, p. 305. Frame, p. 152.

65. *Essais* 80, I, 31, p. 306. Frame, p. 152.

66. *Essais* 80, I, 31, p. 310. Frame p. 153.

67. *Essais* 80, I, 31, p. 329. Frame, p. 159. Gérard Defaux has noted all the instances where Montaigne certifies his credibility as a witness. See "Un cannibale en haut de chausses: Montaigne, la différence et la logique de l'identité." *Modern Language Notes*, vol. 97, 1982, 919–57.

68. François Roussel, *Montaigne: Le Magistrat sans juridiction.* Paris: Michalon, 2006.

69. *Essais* 80, I, 9, p. 32. Frame, p. 21.

Chapter 5. The Making of a Gentleman (1570–1580)

1. *Mémoire* of August 23, 1568, quoted by Vittorio de Caprariis, *Propaganda e pensiero politico in Francia durante le guerre di Religione*, vol. I: *1559–1572*. Naples: Edizioni scientifiche italiane, 1959, 416.

2. Bibliothèque municipale de Bordeaux, ms. 370, f. 873–74, November 14, 1569.

3. Roger Trinquet, "Le quatrième centenaire de la retraite de Montaigne." *Bulletin de*

la Société des amis de Montaigne, no. 25–26, 1971, 67–69. See also the article published in *Le Temps* (August 3, 1911) on the basis of a document discovered by Paul Courteault and reprinted in *Revue de la Renaissance* under the title "Montaigne, fonctionnaire mécontent: Un document inédit," vol. XII, 1911, 176–79.

4. *Registre secret du Parlement de Bordeaux commençant le 16 novembre 1564 et finissant le 1er septembre 1576, copie de Monsieur de Poitevin, avocat, qui la tenait de feu Monsieur le Premier Président Daulede, ce 30 aoust 1720, De Savignac.* Bibliothèque municipale de Bordeaux, Fonds patrimoniaux, ms. 369 (3), f. 85r.

5. *Essais* 80, II, 6, p. 51. Frame, p. 269.

6. *Registre secret du Parlement de Bordeaux*, op. cit., f. 86r.

7. Ibid. A practically identical version of this decision is given by François-Martial de Verthamon d'Ambloy, *Registre secret du Parlement de Bordeaux, recueilli et mis en ordre par les soins de François-Martial de Verthamon d'Ambloy commençant le 12 novembre 1569 et finissant le 12 janvier 1570*, 1770. Archives municipales de Bordeaux, ms. 775, f. 696–697.

8. *Registre secret du Parlement de Bordeaux*, op. cit., f. 90v.

9. François-Martial de Verthamon d'Ambloy, *Registre secret du Parlement de Bordeaux*, op. cit., ms. 775, f. 717r.

10. *Archives historiques du département de la Gironde*, vol. XVII, 1877, no. CXXV, 338–39.

11. On Florimond de Raemond's parlementary career, see Philippe Tamizey de Larroque, *Essai sur la vie et les ouvrages de Florimond de Raymond, conseiller au Parlement de Bordeaux.* Paris: A. Aubry, 1867.

12. Claire Chatelain, *Chronique d'une ascension sociale: Exercice de la parenté chez de grands officiers (XVIᵉ–XVIIᵉ siècles).* Paris: Éditions EHESS, 2008, 162.

13. *Archives départementales de la Gironde*, 1B11, f. 213r–241r. Cited by Gérard Morisse, "Sur les traces de Florimond de Raemond (Agen 1540–Bordeaux 1601)." *Revue française d'histoire du livre*, no. 122–25, 2004, 136.

14. Gaston Zeller, "Une notion de caractère historico-social, la dérogeance." *Cahiers internationaux de sociologie*, vol. 22, 1957, 40–74; Étienne Dravasa, "'Vivre noblement': Recherches sur la dérogeance de noblesse du XIVᵉ au XVIᵉ siècle." *Revue juridique et économique du Sud-Ouest, série juridique*, vol. 16, no. 3–4, 1965, 135–93; and vol. 17, no. 1–2, 1966, 23–129.

15. Pierre Barrière, *Montaigne gentilhomme français.* Bordeaux: Delmas, 1940.

16. *Archives historiques du département de la Gironde*, vol. XXV, 1887, no. CLXXXVI, 410–11.

17. Bibliothèque municipale de Bordeaux, ms. 738 (3), f. 11.

18. Ibid., f. 110.

19. Alexandre Nicolaï, *Montaigne intime.* Paris: Aubier, s.d., 75–78; Maurice Rat, "Le ménage de Montaigne." *Bulletin de la Société des amis de Montaigne*, no. 15, 1949–52, 4–23; Donald Frame, *Montaigne: A Biography*, op. cit., 89–91.

20. Donald Frame, op. cit., 89.

21. *Essais* 88, III, 5, f. 371r. Frame, pp. 645–46.

22. *Essais* 88, III, 5, f. 371r. Frame, p. 646.

23. *Essais* 88, III, 5, f. 373r. Frame, p. 649.

24. *Essais* 80, I, 30, p. 296. Frame, p. 147.

25. *Essais* 88, III, 5, f. 381r. Frame, p. 663.

26. *Essais* 88, III, 5, f. 381r. Frame, p. 647.

27. "A Madamoiselle de Montaigne ma femme," *Mesnagerie de Xénophon*, 185.

28. Ibid.

29. *Essais* 80, II, 17, p. 452. Frame, p. 493.

30. *Essais* EB, III, 3, f. 362r. Frame, p. 629.

31. See Alain Legros, *Essais sur poutres: Peintures et inscriptions chez Montaigne*. Paris: Klincksieck, 2000.

32. "*Si te fata fervnt fer fata ferere ferentes fata fervnt rapivnt sin minvs illa feras.*" See Alain Legros, "Buchanan et Cicéron chez Montaigne: Deux sentences inédites de sa 'librairie.'" *Montaigne Studies*, vol. XXVI, 2014, 171–75.

33. Roland Mousnier, "Les concepts d'ordres, 'd'états,' de 'fidélité' et de 'monarchie absolue' en France de la fin du XVᵉ à la fin du XVIIIᵉ siècle." *Revue historique*, no. 247, 1972, 289–312.

34. Christophe Piel, "Les clientèles, entre sciences sociales et histoire." In *Hypothèses: Travaux de l'École doctorale d'Histoire*. Paris: Publications de la Sorbonne, 1998, 119–29. On the clientele system, also see S. W. Schmidt, ed., *Friends, Followers and Factions: A Reader in Political Clientelism*. Berkeley: University of California Press, 1977; and S. N. Eisenstadt and Louis Roniger, "Patrons-Clients Relations as a Model of Structuring Social Exchange." *Comparative Studies in Society and History*, vol. 22, no. 1, 1980, 42–77; id., *Patrons, Clients, and Friends: Interpersonal Relations and the Structure of Trust in Society*. Cambridge: Cambridge University Press, 1984.

35. Nussy Saint-Saens, "Montaigne au Parlement de Bordeaux." *Revue historique de Bordeaux et du département de la Gironde*, new series II, 1953, 119–35; and Georges Hubrecht, "Montaigne juriste." In *IVᵉ Centenaire de la naissance de Montaigne*. Bordeaux: Delmas, 1933, 239–98.

36. Joseph Dumoulin, *Vie et œuvres de Federic Morel imprimeur à Paris*. Paris: Dumoulin et Picard, 1901, 55.

37. See Philippe Desan, "La Boétie poète et ses deux éditeurs: Federic Morel et Montaigne." In Denis Bjaï and François Rouget, eds., *Les Poètes français de la Renaissance et leurs libraires*. Geneva: Droz, 2015, 485–505.

38. Loys Le Roy, *Avertissement sur la fausseté de plusieurs mémoires*. Paris: Federic Morel, 1562; id., *Discours sur ce qui est advenu à Vassy*. Paris: Federic Morel, 1562.

39. *Mesnagerie de Xénophon*, 61.

40. Ibid., 62.

41. Jacques-Auguste de Thou, *Histoire universelle*. Basel: Jean Louis Brandmuller, 1742, vol. III, book XXXV, 464.

42. The expression is Michel Simonin's: "Œuvres complètes ou plus que complètes?: Montaigne éditeur de La Boétie." *Montaigne Studies*, vol. VII, 1995, 16.

43. Alain Legros, "Dix-huit volumes de la bibliothèque de La Boétie légués à Montaigne et signalés par lui comme tels." *Montaigne Studies*, vol. XXV, 2013, 177–87.

44. *Essais* 80, I, 28, pp. 252–54. Frame, pp. 135–36.

45. "Advertissement au lecteur par M. de Montaigne," 61.

46. "A Monsieur Monsieur de Foix." *Vers françois*, 249.

47. "A Monseigneur Monsieur de L'Hospital Chancelier de France." *Mesnagerie de Xénophon*, 205.

48. "A Monsieur Monsieur de Foix." *Vers françois*, 248.

49. *Essais* EB, I, 26, f. 64r. Frame, p. 127.

50. *Essais* 80, II, 17, p. 438. Frame, p. 483.

51. "A Monsieur de Lansac." *Mesnagerie de Xénophon*, 63.

52. Michel Magnien remarks that in 1571 the eulogy of La Boétie is "hyperbolic and absolute," while "in 1580 the enthusiasm has greatly diminished." See his "De l'hyperbole à l'ellipse: Montaigne face aux sonnets de La Boétie." *Montaigne Studies*, vol. II, no. 1, 1990, 24n65.

53. "A Monsieur de Lansac." *Mesnagerie de Xénophon*, 64.

54. Ibid.

55. Charles Sauzé de Lhoumeau, "Un fils naturel de François Ier, Louis de Saint-Gelais, baron de la Mothe-Saint-Héray." *Mémoires de la société des antiquaires de l'Ouest*, vol. XVI, 1940, 5–175.

56. François de Lorraine, duc de Guise, *Mémoires-journaux de François de Lorraine*, eds. Joseph-François Michaud, Jean-Joseph Poujoulat, Jacques-Joseph Champollion Figeac, and Aimé Champollion-Figeac. Paris: Nouvelle collection des mémoires pour servir à l'histoire de France, 1839, vol. VI, 76.

57. Ernest Gaullieur, *Histoire de la Réformation à Bordeaux et dans le ressort du Parlement de Guienne*. Paris; New York: H. Champion; J. W. Bouton, 1884.

58. Brantôme (Pierre de Bourdeille), "Discours sur les Rodomontades." In *Œuvres complètes*, ed. Ludovic Lalanne. Paris: Jules Renouard, 1873, vol. VII, 76.

59. Charles Sauzé de Lhoumeau, "Un fils naturel de François Ier, Louis de Saint-Gelais, baron de la Mothe-Saint-Héray," art. cit., 37–38.

60. *Essais* 80, I, 48, p. 445. Frame, p. 210.

61. Philippe Tamizey de Larroque, *Antoine de Noailles à Bordeaux, d'après des documents inédits*. Bordeaux: C. Lefebvre, 1878, 66.

62. See Nicolas Le Roux, "Guerres civiles, entreprises maritimes et identité nobiliaire: Les imaginations de Guy de Lansac (1544–1622)." *Bibliothèque d'Humanisme et Renaissance*, vol. LXV, no. 3, 2003, 529–69.

63. In his *Mémoires inédits*, Henri de Mesmes confesses his political disillusions and expresses his desire to be remembered as a man of letters.

64. François de L'Alouëte, *Traité des nobles et des vertus dont ils sont formés*. Paris: Guillaume de La Nouë, 1577, f. 13v.

65. Henri de Mesmes, *Mémoires inédits*, op. cit., 9.

66. Janet G. Espiner-Scott, "Note sur le cercle de Henri de Mesmes et sur son influence." In *Mélanges offerts à M. Abel Lefranc*. Paris: Droz, 1936, 354–61.

67. Katherine Almquist, "Montaigne judging with Henri de Mesmes (May–June 1565)." *Montaigne Studies*, vol. XVI, 2004, 37–40.

68. BNF, ms. fr. 839.

69. Henri de Mesmes, "Contre La Boétie." In Nadia Gontarbert, ed., *La Boétie: De la servitude volontaire ou Contr'un*. Paris: Gallimard, 1993, 203.

70. "A Monseigneur Monsieur de Mesmes." *Mesnagerie de Xénophon*, 159.

71. Ibid., 160.

72. "A Monsieur Monsieur de Foix." *Vers françois*, 249–50.

73. Ibid., 249.

74. "A Monseigneur Monsieur de Mesmes." *Mesnagerie de Xénophon*, 159.

75. A hypothesis proposed by Roger Trinquet, "Le quatrième centenaire de la retraite de Montaigne," art. cit., 67–69.

76. Loris Petris, *La Plume et la tribune. Michel de L'Hospital et ses discours (1559–1562). Suivi de l'édition du De sacra Francisci II. Galliarum regis initiatione, regnique ipsius administrandi providentia, Mich. Hosp. Sermo (1559) et des discours de Michel de L'Hospital (1560–1562)*. Geneva: Droz, 2002.

77. Denis Crouzet, *La Sagesse et le Malheur: Michel de L'Hospital chancelier de France*. Seyssel: Champ Vallon, 1998.

78. "A Monseigneur Monsieur de L'Hospital Chancelier de France." *Mesnagerie de Xénophon*, 205–6.

79. Jean Bodin, *Juris universi distributio*. In *Œuvres philosophiques de Jean Bodin*, ed. Pierre Mesnard. Paris: Presses Universitaires de France, 1951, 71–80 (table of universal law, 83–97).

80. The publishing history of the *Discourse on Voluntary Servitude* in the *Mémoires* has been studied by Joseph Calemard, "L'édition originale de 'La Servitude volontaire.'" *Bulletin du bibliophile et du bibliothécaire*, May–June 1947, 209–29 and 269–82. See also Jean-Eudes Girot, "Une version inconnue du *Discours de la servitude volontaire* de La Boétie." *Bibliothèque d'Humanisme et Renaissance*, vol. LXIII, no. 3, 2001, 551–65; and Renzo Ragghianti, *Rétablir un texte: Le Discours de la servitude volontaire d'Étienne de La Boétie*. Florence: Leo Olschki, 2010.

81. "Arrêt du Parlement de Bordeaux ordonnant de brûler les livres intitulés *Mémoires de l'Estat de France*—7 mai 1579," transcribed and published by Gabriel Loirette. In *Archives historiques du département de la Gironde*, new series, vol. I, 1933–36, no. XVIII, 52–53.

82. On the circumstances of this ruling by the Bordeaux parlement and its political consequences, see Nicola Panichi, *Plutarchus redivivius? La Boétie e i suoi interpreti*. Naples: Vivarium, 1999.

83. Michel Simonin, "Œuvres complètes ou plus que complètes? Montaigne éditeur de La Boétie," art. cit., 6–11.

84. Michel Magnien, "Discours de la servitude volontaire." In Philippe Desan, ed., *Dictionnaire de Michel de Montaigne*. Paris: H. Champion, 2007, 273.

85. See Claude Barmann, "Exemplaires uniques ou rarissimes conservés à la B. M. de Grenoble." *Bibliothèque d'Humanisme et Renaissance*, vol. LI, no. 1, 1989, 139–46.

86. *Essais* 80, II, 17, p. 459. Frame, p. 497.

87. Nadine Kuperty-Tsur, "La notion de serviteur de l'État entre éthos et pratique à la fin du XVIᵉ siècle en France." In Jean Céard, Marie-Christine Gomez-Géraud, Michel Magnien, and François Rouget, eds., *Cité des hommes, cité de Dieu: Travaux sur la littérature de la Renaissance en l'honneur de Daniel Ménager.* Geneva: Droz, 2003, 63–74.

88. Jean Balsamo, "Un gentilhomme et ses patrons: Remarques sur la biographie politique de Montaigne." In Philippe Desan, ed., *Montaigne politique.* Paris: H. Champion, 2006, 223–42.

89. Letter from Gaston de Foix, January 6, 1561, quoted by Alexandre Nicolaï, "Germain-Gaston de Foix, marquis de Trans." *Bulletin de la Société des amis de Montaigne*, no. 19, 1956, 12.

90. Agrippa d'Aubigné, *Histoire universelle.* Maille: Jean Moussat, 1616, vol. I, 204.

91. Philippe Tamizey de Larroque, "Christophe et François de Foix-Candalle." *Revue de Gascogne*, vol. XVIII, 1877, 57–62, 138–45, 158–65, 285–86.

92. Léonie Gardeau, *Les Comtes de Foix-Gurson et la cause royale au XVIᵉ siècle.* Périgueux: Imprimerie Pierre Fanlac, 1969; Alexandre Nicolaï, "Germain-Gaston de Foix, marquis de Trans," art. cit., 7–26; and Jean-Marie Compain, "Les relations de Montaigne avec son voisin et son protecteur le marquis de Trans." In Claude-Gilbert Dubois, ed., *Les Écrivains et la politique dans le sud-ouest de la France autour des années 1580.* Talence: Presses Universitaires de Bordeaux, 1982, 101–11.

93. Letter from Charles IX discovered by the canon Prunis (probably among the papers accompanying the manuscript of Montaigne's journal of his journey to Italy), today lost, but reproduced by Prunis in the introduction that he wrote for the 1774 edition of the *Journal de voyage.* This letter was later published by Payen, *Nouveaux documents inédits ou peu connus sur Montaigne.* Paris: P. Jannet, 1850, 46. Jean Balsamo rightly notes that the letter from the king "gives few details regarding the reasons for granting this exceptional distinction, never accorded a member of the parlement, mentioning only the recipient's "merits and virtues," along with an assurance of the king's good will" (cf. "Un gentilhomme et ses patrons: Remarques sur la biographie politique de Montaigne." In Philippe Desan, ed., *Montaigne politique*, op. cit., 223–42).

94. *Éphéméride*, October 28, 86.

95. *Essais* 80, II, 7, p. 62. Frame, p. 276.

96. *Essais* 88, II, 12, f. 244r. Frame, p. 434.

97. Jean Le Laboureur, *Additions aux Mémoires de Castelnau.* In *Les Memoires de messire Michel de Castelnau, seigneur de Mauvissiere, illustrez et augmentez de plusieurs commentaires & manuscrits, tant lettres, instructions, traitez, qu'autres pieces secrettes & originales, servans à donner la verité de l'histoire des regnes de François II, Charles IX & Henry III, & de la regence & du gouvernement de Catherine de Medicis.* 3 vols. Brussels: L. Leonard, 1731, vol. 1, 336.

98. Ludovic de Colleville and François Saint-Christo, *Les Ordres du Roi. Répertoire général contenant les noms et qualités de tous les chevaliers des Ordres royaux, militaires et chevaleresques ayant existé en France de 1099 à 1830. Avec une Histoire des Ordres du Saint-Esprit, de Saint-Michel, de Saint-Louis, etc.* Paris: Jouve, 1924.

99. Arlette Jouanna, "Montaigne et la noblesse." In Claude-Gilbert Dubois, ed., *Les Écrivains et la politique dans le sud-ouest de la France autour des années 1580. Quatrième centenaire de l'accession de Montaigne à la mairie de Bordeaux, 1581–1981.* Talence: Presses Universitaires de Bordeaux, 1982, 113–23.

100. Brantôme, *Œuvres du seigneur de Brantôme.* Paris: Jean-François Bastien, 1787, vol. VI, 456.

101. Ibid., vol. IX, 84. Original French text:

> Si je suis de petite taille,
> Pour prendre au col ce beau collier,
> Prenez que d'un homme de paille,
> L'on en façonne un chevalier.

102. *Remontrance au roy par des abbayans à l'Ordre.* Original French text:

> Puisque chascun dit ses mérites,
> Pour parvenir à cest honneur,
> Je sçay bien faire les pratiques
> Pour l'amour de quelque seigneur.

103. Xavier Le Person, *"Practiques" et "practiqueurs": La vie politique à la fin du règne de Henri III (1584–1589).* Geneva: Droz, 2002.

104. Reported by Michel de Castelnau, *Les Mémoires de Messire Michel de Castelnau, seigneur de Mauvissiere.* Brussels: Jean Léonard, 1731, vol. I. 356.

105. François de L'Alouëte, *Traité des nobles et des vertus dont ils sont formés,* op. cit., f. 46v.

106. See Hervé Pinoteau, *Étude sur les ordres de chevalerie du roi de France, et tout spécialement sur les ordres de Saint-Michel et du Saint-Esprit.* Paris: Le Léopard d'or, 1995, 43.

107. *Le Livre des Statuts et ordonnances de l'ordre Sainct Michel, estably par le treschrestien Roy de France Loys unzieme de ce nom.* Paris: [c. 1550], f. C2r.

108. Jacob Vance, "Duty, Conciliation, and Ontology in the *Essais.*" In Zahi Zalloua, ed., *Montaigne after Theory, Theory after Montaigne.* Seattle: University of Washington Press, 2009, 75–99.

109. *Le Livre des Statuts et ordonnances de l'ordre Sainct Michel,* op. cit., article LXXXI, f. I4v.

110. *Mémoires de Messire Philippe Hurault, comte de Cheverny,* in *Collection universelle des Mémoires particuliers relatifs à l'histoire de France.* London: 1789, vol. L, 105.

111. Ibid., 107.

112. The St. Bartholomew's Day massacre has been given many interpretations. See in particular Denis Crouzet, *La Nuit de la Saint-Barthélemy: Un rêve perdu de la Renaissance.* Paris: Fayard, 1994; id., "La nuit de la Saint-Barthélemy: Confirmations et compléments." In Chantal Grell and Arnaud Ramière de Fontanier, eds., *Le Second Ordre: L'idéal nobiliaire; Hommage à Ellery Schalk.* Paris: Presses de l'Université Paris-Sorbonne, 1999, 55–81; Barbara B. Diefendorf, "La Saint-Barthélemy et la bourgeoisie parisienne." *Histoire, économie et société,* vol. 17, no. 3, 1998, 341–52.

113. On St. Bartholomew's Day in Bordeaux, see Henri Hauser, "Le père Emond Auger

et le massacre de Bordeaux (1572)." *Bulletin de la Société d'histoire du protestantisme français*, July–August 1911, 1–23.

114. Letter from President Lagebaston to Charles IX, Bordeaux, October 7, 1572. BNF, ms. fr. 15 555. Extracts reproduced by Grégory Champeaud, *Le Parlement de Bordeaux et les paix de religion (1563–1600)*. Bordeaux: Éditions d'Albret, 2008, 407–8.

115. *Traduction d'une Epistre latine d'un excellent personnage de ce Royaume faicte par forme de discours, sur aucunes choses depuis peu de temps advenues en France*. Paris: Federic Morel, 1573.

116. Edmé Cougny, *Pibrac: Sa vie et ses écrits; Fragments d'une étude historique et littéraire*. Versailles: Aubert, 1869; Édouard Faye de Brys, *Trois magistrats francais du seizième siècle (Antoine Duprat, Guy du Faur de Pibrac, Jacques Faye d'Espeisses)*. Paris: Comptoir des imprimeurs-unis, 1844; Alban Cabos, *Guy du Faur de Pibrac, un magistrat poète au XVIᵉ siècle (1529–1584)*. Paris: E. Champion; Auch: F. Cocharaux, 1922.

117. Jean-Louis Bourgeon, "Montaigne et la Saint-Barthélemy." *Bulletin de la Société des amis de Montaigne*, nos. 37–38, 1994, 101–12.

118. Alexandre Nicolaï, "Germain-Gaston de Foix, marquis de Trans," art. cit., 7–26.

119. On the exchange of favors in the sixteenth century, see Nicolas Le Roux, *La Faveur du roi: Mignons et courtisans au temps des derniers Valois (vers 1547–vers 1589)*. Seyssel: Champ Vallon, 2000.

120. Jean-François Médard, "Le rapport de clientèle, du phénomène social à l'analyse politique." *Revue française de science politique*, no. 26, 1976, 103–31.

121. Philippe Desan, "Éléments d'une sociologie des *Essais*." In Thierry Gontier and Pierre Magnard, eds., *Montaigne*. Paris: Éditions du Cerf, 2010, 45–66.

122. *Lettres de Montaigne*, from Montaigne to Matignon, February 2, 1585, 687.

123. Ibid., from Montaigne to Matignon, February 9, 1585, 689.

124. Ibid., from Montaigne to Matignon, February 12, 1585, 693.

125. *Essais* 80, I, 23, p. 144. Frame, p. 85.

126. Charles Loyseau, *Du Droict des offices*. In *Œuvres de Charles Loyseau*. Geneva: Estienne Gamonet, 1636, Book IV, chap. III, 579.

127. Ibid.

128. *Ordonnances du Roy Henry troisiesme de ce nom, Roy de France et de Pologne: sur les plainctes et doléances faictes par les députez des Estats de son Royaume convoquez et assemblez en la ville de Bloys. Publiées en la court de Parlement, le 25e jour de janvier 1580*. Lyon: Jean Pillehotte, 1582, article 259.

129. *Éphéméride*, 29 juillet, 94.

130. *Essais* 80, I, 26, p. 191. Frame, p. 109.

131. *Essais* 88, III, 9, f. 425v. Frame, p. 739.

132. *Essais* 88, II, 8, f. 163r. Frame, p. 285.

133. Quoted by Manfred Orléa, *La Noblesse aux États généraux de 1576 et 1588: Étude politique et sociale*. Paris: Presses Universitaires de France, 1980.

134. Robert Descimon, "Chercher de nouvelles voies pour interpréter les phénomènes

nobiliaires dans la France moderne: La noblesse, 'essence' ou rapport social?" *Revue d'histoire moderne et contemporaine,* vol. 46, no. 1, 1999, 17–18.

135. Jehan Bacquet, *Quatriesme traicté des droicts des domaines de la couronne de France: Concernant les Francs Fiefs, Nouveaux Acquests, Anoblissements & Amortissements.* Paris: Sébastien Nivelle, 1582, f. 2v.

136. Jean-Marie Constant, "Les partis nobiliaires et le développement de l'État moderne: Le rôle de la noblesse seconde." In Jean-Philippe Genet and Daniel Tollet, eds., *L'État moderne: Genèse, bilan et perspectives.* Paris: Éditions du CNRS, 1990, 175–84.

137. Jehan Bacquet, *Quatriesme traicté des droicts des domaines de la couronne de France,* op. cit., f. 10r.

138. *Archives historiques du département de la Gironde,* vol. I, 1859, no. CXCVIII, 406–22.

139. Jean-Marie Constant, "Les barons français pendant les guerres de religion." In *Quatrième centenaire de la bataille de Coutras.* Biarritz: J & D Éditions, 1989, 49–62.

140. Serge Brunet, *"De l'Espagnol dedans le ventre!" Les catholiques du sud-ouest de la France face à la Réforme (vers 1540–1589).* Paris: H. Champion, 2007, 139.

141. Véronique Larcade, "La clientèle du duc d'Épernon dans le sud-ouest du royaume." *Annales du Midi,* vol. 108, no. 213, 1996, 29–37.

142. On the nobility of Guyenne, see Henri Gabriel O'Gilvy and Jules de Bourrousse de Laffore, *Nobiliaire de Guienne et de Gascogne: Revue des familles d'ancienne chevalerie ou anoblies de ces provinces, antérieures à 1789, avec leurs généalogies et armes, suivie d'un traité héraldique sous forme de dictionnaire.* Paris: Dumoulin, 1856–1883; Badier de La Chesnaye-Desbois, *Dictionnaire de la noblesse contenant les généalogies, l'histoire & la chronologie des familles nobles de la France, l'explication de leurs armes et l'état des grandes terres du royaume, possédées à titre de principautés, duchés marquisats, comtés, vicomtés, baronnies.* Paris: Schlesinger frères, 1863–77.

143. *Essais* 80, I, 26, p. 225. Frame, p. 125.

144. François de L'Alouëte, *Traité des nobles et des vertus dont ils sont formés,* op. cit., f. 15r.

145. *Essais* 88, I, 46, f. 116v. Frame, p. 202.

146. *Essais* 88, I, 46, f. 116v. Frame, p. 203.

147. *Essais* 88, I, 46, f. 117r. Frame, p. 203.

148. David Posner, *The Performance of Nobility in Early Modern European Literature.* Cambridge: Cambridge University Press, 1999. On Montaigne and Castiglione, see Marcel Tetel, "The Humanistic Situation: Montaigne and Castiglione." *Sixteenth Century Journal,* vol. X, no. 3, 1979, 69–84.

149. Paul Courteault, "Une mission de Montaigne en 1574." *Bulletin de la Société des amis de Montaigne,* no. 8, 1940, 4.

150. Bibliothèque municipale de Bordeaux, Fonds patrimoniaux, ms. 369 (4), f. 344r.

151. *Éphéméride,* 87.

152. Jean Plattard, "Montaigne à Poitiers." *Bulletin de la Société des antiquaires de l'Ouest,* 1930, 679–81.

153. P. Gambier, "Montaigne a-t-il assiégé Fontenay?" *Bulletin de la Société des amis de Montaigne*, no. 25–26, 1971, 117–19.

154. Bibliothèque municipale de Bordeaux, Fonds patrimoniaux, ms. 738 (3), f. 130.

155. *Éphéméride*, November 29, 88.

156. Archives nationales, ms. fr. 32866 (1568), 280; quoted by Jean-Marie Compain, "Montaigne et Henri de Navarre avant Coutras." In *Quatrième centenaire de la bataille de Coutras*. Pau: J. & D. Éditions, 1989, 42.

157. Jacqueline Boucher, *Société et mentalité autour de Henri III*. Paris: H. Champion, 2007.

158. James Supple, *Arms versus Letters: The Military and Literary Ideals in the "Essais" of Montaigne*. Oxford; New York: Clarendon Press, 1984.

159. François Billacois, *Le Duel dans la société française des XVIᵉ–XVIIᵉ siècles: Essai de psychosociologie historique*. Paris: Éditions de l'EHESS, 1986.

160. *Essais* 80, I, 20, p. 99. Frame, p. 58.

161. Catherine Magnien, "Montaigne historien de 'l'expédition' de Henri d'Anjou en Pologne (1573–1574)? Hypothèses . . ." In Françoise Argod-Dutard, ed., *Histoire et littérature au siècle de Montaigne: Mélanges offerts à Claude-Gilbert Dubois*. Geneva: Droz, 2001, 195–206.

162. *Recueil de plusieurs pieces, des Sieurs de Pybrac, d'Espeisses, Presidents au Parlement de Paris, et de Bellieve Chancelier de France non encore imprimées*. Paris: Pierre Blaise, 1635, 149.

163. *Archives historiques du département de la Gironde*, vol. I, 1859, no. XXVI, 41.

164. Jean Balsamo "Foix (famille)." In Philippe Desan, ed., *Dictionnaire de Michel de Montaigne*. Paris: H. Champion, 2007, 468–70.

165. On this token (*jeton*), see Alain Brieux, "Petit trésor de souvenirs de Montaigne." *Bibliothèque d'Humanisme et Renaissance*, vol. XIX, 1957, 265–93; id., "Autres souvenirs de Michel de Montaigne." *Bibliothèque d'Humanisme et Renaissance*, vol. XX, 1958, 370–76. For a description of the mold, see the catalog of the bookseller Jean-Claude Vrain, *Catalogue année 2000: Livres anciens, atlas, histoire naturelle, belles reliures, illustrées modernes*, no. 20, 30–31.

166. Richard A. Sayce, "L'ordre des *Essais* de Montaigne." *Bibliothèque d'Humanisme et Renaissance*, vol. XVIII, 1956, 7–22; Pierre Villey, *Les Sources et l'évolution des Essais de Montaigne*. 2 vols. Paris: Hachette, 1933.

167. On Montaigne and his secretaries, see Alain Legros, *Essais sur poutres: Peintures et inscriptions chez Montaigne*, op. cit., 217–19; id., "Petit 'eB' deviendra grand . . . : Montaigne correcteur de l'exemplaire 'Lalanne' (Bordeaux: S. Millanges, 1580, premier état)." *Montaigne Studies*, vol. XIV, 2002, 179–210; George Hoffmann, *Montaigne's Career*. Oxford: Clarendon Press, 1998, 53–78; George Hoffmann and Alain Legros, "Secrétaire(s)." In Philippe Desan, ed., *Dictionnaire de Michel de Montaigne*, op. cit., 1051–54. On the role of the secretaries Montaigne employed, see also Craig B. Brush, "La composition de la première partie du *Journal du voyage* de Montaigne." *Revue d'histoire littéraire de la France*, vol. 71, no. 3, 1971, 369–84; id., "The secretary, again." *Montaigne Studies*, vol. V, 1993, 113–18.

168. *Essais* 88, II, 9, f. 168r. (Not translated by Frame.)

169. *Essais* 80, II, 17, p. 453. Frame, p. 495.

170. *Essais* 88, III, 3, f. 362r. Frame, p. 629.

171. See Ingrid A. R. De Smet and Alain Legros, "Un manuscrit de François Baudouin dans la 'librairie' de Montaigne." *Bibliothèque d'Humanisme et Renaissance*, vol. LXXV, no. 1, 2013, 105–11.

172. *Essais* 80, II, 10, p. 418. Frame, p. 305.

173. John R. Cole, "Montaigne's dead babies." *Montaigne Studies*, vol. XII, 2000, 167–84.

Chapter 6. The *Essais* of 1580: Moral, Political, and Military Discourses

1. *Declaration, et Protestation du Roy de Navarre, sur les justes occasions qui l'ont meu de prendre les armes, pour la defense et tuition des Eglises reformees de France*, 1580. Text reproduced in M. L. Cimber, ed., *Archives curieuses de l'Histoire de France depuis Louis XI jusqu'à Louis XVIII*. Paris: 1836, vol. X, 1–52.

2. Ibid., 27.

3. *Archives historiques du département de la Guyenne*, vol. XIV, 1873, no. XCV, April 25, 1580, 154.

4. Ibid., vol. IV, 1863, 175–78, no. CXXI.

5. Catherine de Medici to Henry of Navarre, April 21, 1580, *Lettres de Catherine de Medici*, ed. Comte Baguenault de Puchesse. Paris: Imprimerie nationale, 1899, vol. 7, 1579–81, 252.

6. Géralde Nakam, *Les* Essais *de Montaigne, miroir et procès de leur temps: Témoignage historique et création littéraire*. Paris: A.-G. Nizet, 1984.

7. On the composition of the text of 1580, see Jeanne Veyrin-Forrer, "La composition par forme et les *Essais* de 1580." In Claude Blum and André Tournon, eds., *Éditer les* Essais *de Montaigne*. Paris: H. Champion, 1997, 23–44.

8. Michel Simonin, "Le Périgourdin au Palais: Sur le voyage des *Essais* de Bordeaux à Paris." In Marcel Tetel and Mallary Masters, eds., *Le Parcours des* Essais: *Montaigne 1588–1988*. Paris: Aux amateurs de livres, 1989, 17–30.

9. Claude Blum, "Dans l'atelier de Millanges: Les conditions de fabrication des éditions bordelaises des *Essais* (1580, 1582)." In Claude Blum and André Tournon, eds., *Éditer les* Essais *de Montaigne*, op. cit., 82.

10. This essential point has been analyzed by George Hoffmann (*Montaigne's Career*. Oxford: Clarendon Press, 1998, 63–83) and Michel Simonin ("Poétiques des éditions 'à l'essai' au XVIᵉ siècle." In Elio Mosele, ed., *Riflessioni teoriche e trattati di poetica tra Francia et Italia nel Cinquecento*. Fasano: Schena Editore, 1999, 17–33).

11. The *Essais* of 1580 contain 180,562 words, 66,313 in the first book and 114,249 in the second.

12. See Ruggero Campagnoli, "Girolamo Naselli primo traduttore italiano di Montaigne (1590)." *Studi Francesi*, vol. 47–48, 1972, 214–31.

13. This first partial translation of the *Essais* into Italian was censured in 1600. How-

ever, Jean-Louis Quantin has shown that this censure "is connected with a purely fortuitous circumstance, the discovery of a copy by an inquisitor who was zealous or wanted to pass for such in the eyes of the cardinals." Montaigne was reproached chiefly for having attributed miracles to natural forces (notably the force of the imagination), a common accusation that amounted to proof of heterodoxy at that time. See "Les censures de Montaigne à l'Index romain: Précisions et corrections." *Montaigne Studies*, vol. XXVI, 2014, 152.

14. On the reception of Montaigne in the late sixteenth and early seventeenth century in England, see Warren Boutcher, *The School of Montaigne in Early Modern Europe*, 2 vols. Oxford: Oxford University Press, 2016. On the influence of Montaigne on Shakespeare, see Peter Mack, *Reading and Rhetoric in Montaigne and Shakespeare*. London: Bloomsbury, 2010; Jean-Marie Maguin, ed., *Shakespeare et Montaigne: Vers un nouvel humanisme*. Montpellier: Société française Shakespeare, 2003.

15. "Preface to the Essays of Michel de Montaigne by His Adoptive Daughter, Marie le Jars de Gournay." Trans. Richard Hillman and Colette Quesnel. Tempe, AZ: Medieval and Renaissance Texts and Studies, 1998, p. 75. On Montaigne and Montluc's *Commentaires*, see Jean Balsamo, "Montaigne et les *Commentaires* de Monluc: Deux notes de philologie." *Montaigne Studies*, vol. XXII, 2010, 207–21.

16. George Hoffmann, "From Amateur Gentleman to Gentleman Amateur." In Zahi Zalloua, ed., *Montaigne after Theory / Theory after Montaigne*. Seattle: University of Washington Presss, 2009, 24.

17. Robert J. Sealy, *The Palace Academy of Henri III*. Geneva: Droz, 1981.

18. These speeches delivered at the Académie du Palais have been studied by Édouard Frémy, *L'Académie des derniers Valois*. Paris: E. Leroux, 1887. On the eloquence of passions at the Académie du Palais, see Mark Greengrass, *Governing Passions: Peace and Reform in the French Kingdom, 1576–1585*. Oxford: Oxford University Press, 2007, especially Chapter II: "Comprehending passions."

19. François de La Croix du Maine, *Premier volume de la bibliotheque du sieur de La Croix du Maine: Qui est un catalogue general de toutes sortes d'Autheurs, qui ont escrits en François depuis cinq cents ans et plus, jusques à ce jourd'huy* ... Paris: Abel L'Angelier, 1584, 328.

20. Ibid.

21. *Essais* 88, I, 23, f. 42r. Frame, p. 87.

22. *Essais* 80, II, 12, p. 345. Frame, p. 428.

23. See the reading of this chapter by David Quint, *Montaigne and the Quality of Mercy: Ethical and Political Themes in the* Essais. Princeton, NJ: Princeton University Press, 1998.

24. *Essais* 80, I, 1, p. 6. Frame, p. 5.

25. Frieda Brown, " 'Si le chef d'une place assiegée doit sortir pour parlementer' and 'L'heure des parlemens dangereuses': Montaigne's political morality and its expression in the early essays." In Raymond C. La Charité, ed., *O un amy! Essays on Montaigne in Honour of Donald M. Frame*. Lexington, KY: French Forum, 1977, 72–87.

26. Pierre Goumarre, "Montaigne et Gentillet." *Romance Notes*, vol. 13, 1971, 322–25. On the development of anti-Machiavellianism in France, see Jean Balsamo, "'Un livre écrit du doigt de Satan': La découverte de Machiavel et l'invention du machiavélisme en France au XVIe siècle." In Dominique de Courcelles, ed., *Le Pouvoir des livres à la Renaissance*. Geneva: Droz, 1998, 77–92.

27. *Essais* 80, II, 17, pp. 459–60. Frame, p. 497.

28. Donald R. Kelly, "'Fides Historiae': Charles Dumoulin and the Gallican View of History." *Traditio*, vol. XXII, 1966, 347–402.

29. Jean Bodin, *La Méthode de l'Histoire*, ed. Pierre Mesnard. In *Œuvres philosophiques de Jean Bodin*. Paris: Presses Universitaires de France, 1951, 349.

30. C. Edward Rathé, "Innocent Gentillet and the First 'Anti-Machiavel.'" *Bibliothèque d'Humanisme et Renaissance*, vol. XXVII, 1965, 186–225; and Antonio d'Andrea, "The Political and Ideological Context of Innocent Gentillet's Anti-Machiavel." *Renaissance Quarterly*, vol. XXIII, no. 4, 1970, 397–411.

31. Agrippa d'Aubigné, *Les Tragiques*, II, v. 651–54.

32. René Pintard, "Une adaptation de Machiavel au XVIe siècle: Le 'Prince nécessaire de Jean de La Taille." *Revue de littérature comparée*, vol. XIII, 1933, 385–402.

33. Alexandre Nicolaï, "Le 'machiavélisme' de Montaigne." *Bulletin de la Société des amis de Montaigne*, no. 4, 1957, 11–21; no. 7, 1958, 2–8; no. 9, 1959, 18–30.

34. This emphasis on prudence in Montaigne has been studied by Francis Goyet, *Les Audaces de la prudence: Littérature et politique aux XVIe et XVIIe siècles*. Paris: Classiques Garnier, 2009.

35. *Essais* 80, "Au lecteur." Frame, p. 2.

36. On the Court as a school of discipline and the obligation of courtiers and gentlemen of the king's chamber to be constant, see Norbert Elias, *The Court Society*, trans. Edmund Jephcott. New York: Pantheon, 1983.

37. *Essais* 88, III, 9, f. 436v. Frame, p. 756.

38. *Essais* 80, I, 24, p. 161. Frame, p. 93.

39. *candide lecteur*. *Essais* 80, I, 26, p. 227. Frame renders this as "gentle reader," p. 125.

40. *Essais* EB, I, 26, f. 64r. Frame, p. 127.

41. *Essais* EB, III, 9, f. 439v. Frame, p. 761.

42. *Essais* EB, III, 13, f. 472r. Frame, p. 817.

43. Michel Simonin, "*Rhetorica ad lectorem*: Lecture de l'avertissement des *Essais*." *Montaigne Studies*, vol. I, 1989, 71.

44. *Essais* 88, III, 9, f. 424v. Frame, p. 736.

45. *Essais* 88, III, 9, f. 425r. Frame, p. 737.

46. On the social symbolism of giving a book in the Renaissance, see Natalie Zemon Davis, "Beyond the Market: Books as Gifts Sixteenth-Century France." *Transactions of the Royal Historical Society*, no. 33, 1983, 69–88. This study was reprinted in Davis's book *The Gift in Sixteenth-Century France* (The Curti Lectures). Madison: University of Wisconsin Press, 2000.

47. Léonie Gardeau, "La bibliothèque du marquis de Trans et de son petit-fils Frédéric de Foix." *Bulletin de la Société des amis de Montaigne*, no. 20, 1970, 51–61.

48. See Geneviève Guilleminot-Chrétien, "Michel de Montaigne, *Essais*." In Marie-

Hélène Tesnière, ed., *Trésors de la Bibliothèque nationale de France*, vol. 1, *Mémoires et merveilles VIIIe–XVIIIe siècle*. Paris, 1996, 151; Jean Marchand, "Le Montaigne de la reine Élisabeth d'Angleterre." *Bulletin de la Société des amis de Montaigne*, no. 22, 1962, 23–27. On De Thou's famous library, see Antoine Coron, "*Ut prosint aliis:* Jacques-Auguste de Thou et sa bibliothèque." In Claude Jolly, ed., *Histoire des bibliothèques françaises: Les bibliothèques sous l'Ancien Régime*. Paris: Promodis, 1988, 101–26; and Ingrid De Smet, "Montaigne et Jacques-Auguste de Thou: Une ancienne amitié mise à jour." *Montaigne Studies*, vol. XIII, 2001, 223–40. De Thou's copy of the *Essais* passed through the libraries of Soubise, Didot, Nodier, and Pichon before joining the Dutuit collection at the Petit Palais.

49. The six engravings are reproduced in Philip Benedict, *Graphic History: The Wars, Massacres, and Troubles of Tortorel and Perrissin*. Geneva: Droz, 2007.

50. See the detailed analysis of this battle by the Commander de Coynart, *L'Année 1562 et la bataille de Dreux: Étude historique et militaire*. Paris: Firmin-Didot, 1894.

51. Ronsard, *Remonstrance au peuple de France*. Paris: Gabriel Buon, 1563, v. 218.

52. On these negotiations, see André Robinet, "Prisons et tractations de la bataille de Dreux à la Paix d'Orléans (18 décembre 1562–12 mars 1563)." *Bulletin de la Société archéologique et historique de l'Orléanais*, new series, vol. VIII, no. 62, 1983, 1–52.

53. Agrippa d'Aubigné, *Histoire universelle*, book III, chapter IV.

54. *Essais* 80, I, 45, p. 418. Frame, p. 200.

55. Éric Durot, *François de Lorraine, duc de Guise entre Dieu et le Roi*. Paris: Classiques Garnier, 2013.

56. *Essais* 88, III, 9, f. 439r. Frame, p. 760.

57. *Essais* EB, II, 10, f. 173v. Frame, p. 303.

58. *Essais* EB, III, 10, f. 447v. Frame, pp. 774–75.

59. *La Théologie naturelle de Raymond Sebon, traduicte nouvellement en françois par Messire Michel, Seigneur de Montaigne, Chevalier de l'ordre du Roy, et Gentilhomme ordinaire de sa chambre*. Paris: Michel Sonnius, 1581, 8.

60. Margaret of Valois, *Mémoires et autres écrits 1574–1614*, ed. Éliane Viennot. Paris: H. Champion, 1999, 133. See Joseph Coppin, "Margaret de Navarre et le *Livre des créatures* de Raimond Sebond." *Revue du seizième siècle*, vol. 10, 1923, 57–66.

61. *Essais* 80, II, 12, p. 325. Frame, p. 419.

62. *Essais* 80, II, 12, 324. Frame, p. 418.

63. Henri Busson doubts Montaigne's statements regarding religious practice. For him, nothing authorizes us to believe, for example, that Montaigne heard mass every day. To him, Montaigne seems to be "lukewarm with respect to the great duties of a Christian life" (p. 93); see "La pratique religieuse de Montaigne." *Bibliothèque d'Humanisme et Renaissance*, vol. XVI, 1954, 86–95. On the practice of prayer, see Léon Ernest Halkin, "Montaigne et la prière." In Henri Limet and Julien Ries, eds., *L'Expérience de la prière dans les grandes religions*. Louvain: Centre d'histoire des religions, 1980, 411–17.

64. *Essais* 80, I, 32, 331. Frame, p. 160.

65. *Essais* 80, I, 32, 331–32. Frame, p. 160.

66. *Essais* 80, I, 32, 332. Frame, p. 160.

67. *Essais* 80, I, 32, 333. Frame, p. 160.

68. *Essais* EB, I, 32, f. 91v. Frame, p. 161.

69. Jean Balsamo, "Montaigne et Pierre Eyquem: Le meilleur des fils du meilleur des pères." In Julia Chamard-Bergeron, Philippe Desan, and Thomas Pavel, eds., *Les Liens humains dans la littérature (XVIᵉ–XVIIᵉ siècle)*. Paris: Classiques Garnier, 2012, 13–31.

70. André Tournon has pointed out Montaigne's frequent deviations from Sebond's text. In fact, there are numerous traces of distancing between the Catalan theologian and the translator that, to adopt Tournon's expression, show "brief spurts of intellectual autonomy" ("Un théologien par procuration." In Philippe Desan, ed., *"Dieu à nostre commerce et société": Montaigne et la théologie*. Geneva: Droz, 2008, 23). Jean Céard thinks that the attenuations of the text found in Montaigne's translation were already present in a manuscript copied from a printed edition ("Montaigne traducteur de Raimond Sebond: Positions et propositions." *Montaigne Studies*, vol. V, 1993, 11–26). On Montaigne's translation, see Philip Hendrick, *Montaigne et Sebond: L'art de la traduction*. Paris: H. Champion, 1996; Mireille Habert, "L'inscription du sujet dans la traduction par Montaigne de la *Theologia naturalis*." *Montaigne Studies*, vol. V, 1993, 27–47; and François Rigolot, "Editing Montaigne's Translation of Sebond's *Theologia*: Which Latin Text Did the Translator Use?" *Montaigne Studies*, vol. VII, 1995, 53–67.

71. Prologue to the *Theologia naturalis* (Montaigne's translation).

72. Paul F. Grendler, "The Roman Inquisition and the Venetian Press, 1540–1605." *Journal of Modern History*, vol. 47, 1975, 48–65.

73. Joseph Coppin observes that the prologue to the *Theologia naturalis* had been voluntarily modified by Montaigne (Cf. *Montaigne traducteur de Raymond Sebon*. Lille: H. Morel, 1925, 65–80).

74. All these revisions made in the prologue to Sebond's book have been studied in detail by Terence McQueeny, "Montaigne et la 'Theologia naturalis.'" *Bulletin de la Société des amis de Montaigne*, no. 9, 1967, 41–45.

75. *Essais* 80, I, 27, pp. 249–50. Frame, pp. 134–35.

76. *Essais* 80, I, 56, p. 485. Frame, p. 234.

77. Alain Brieux, "Autres souvenirs de Montaigne." *Bibliothèque d'Humanisme et Renaissance*, vol. XX, 1958, 370–76.

78. *La Theologie naturelle de Raymond Sebon, traduicte nouvellement en françois par messire Michel, Seigneur de Montaigne, Chevalier de l'ordre du Roy, & Gentilhomme ordinaire de sa chambre*. Paris: Michel Sonnius [Gilles Gourbin, Guillaume Chaudière], 1581, f. 8r.

79. *Essais* 80, II, 12, p. 151. This passage was excised in the Bordeaux Copy, and was thus not translated by Frame. [Trans.]

80. *Essais* 80, II, 12, p. 161. Again, this passage was excised in the Bordeaux Copy, and was not translated by Frame. [Trans.]

81. That is what was proposed by Michel Simonin, "La préhistoire de l'Apologie de Raimond Sebond." In Claude Blum, ed., *Montaigne, Apologie de Raymond Sebond: De la Theologia à la Théologie*. Paris: H. Champion, 1990, 85–116. Also see Marcel Françon, "Montaigne et François d'Amboise." *Bulletin de la Société des amis de Montaigne*, no. 5–6, 1981, 115; Pierre Michel, "La suppression du sonnet de François d'Amboise dans l'édition de 1581 de la *Théologie naturelle*." *Bulletin de la Société des amis de Montaigne*, no. 5–6, 1981, 116–17; and Daniela Costa, "Montaigne et François d'Amboise." *Montaigne Studies*, vol. XIII, 2001, 175–86.

82. Dante Ughetti, *François d'Amboise (1550–1619)*. Rome: Bulzoni Editore, 1974.

83. *Essais* 80, I, 26, p. 210. Frame, p. 117.

84. *Essais* 80, I, 26, pp. 210–11. Frame, pp. 117–18.

85. Raymond Sebond, *La Théologie naturelle*, "Preface de l'autheur." Paris: Michel Sonnius, 1569, f. B2v.

86. Ibid.

87. *Essais* 80, II, 12, p. 149. Frame, p. 320.

88. *Essais* 80, II, 12, p. 148. Frame, p. 318.

89. *Mémoires inédits de Henri de Mesmes, seigneur de Roissy et de Malassise*, ed. Edouard Frémy. Paris: E. Leroux, 1886, 142.

90. *Essais* 80, II, 12, p. 149. Frame, p. 320.

91. *La Theologie naturelle de Raymond Sebon*, op. cit., f. a2r.

92. *Essais* 80, II, 12, pp. 149–150. Frame, p. 320.

93. *Essais* 80, II, 12, pp. 150–51. Frame, p. 320.

94. Terence McQueeny, "Montaigne et la 'Theologia naturalis,'" art. cit. According to McQueeny, the translation of the *Theologia naturalis* required "at least the better part of a year" (p. 41).

95. *Essais* 80, II, 12, p. 152. Frame, p. 321.

96. On this point, see Joseph Coppin, *Montaigne traducteur de Raymond Sebon*, op. cit., 37.

97. *Essais* 80, II, 12, p. 151. Frame, p. 320.

98. *Essais* 80, I, 56, p. 487. Frame, p. 235. Montaigne replaces "mystères" ("mysteries") by "matières" ("matters") in the Bordeaux Copy. On Montaigne's female readers, see François Rigolot, "D'une Théologie 'pour les dames' à une Apologie 'per le donne,'" In *Montaigne, Apologie de Raymond Sebond: De la Theologia à la Théologie*, op. cit., 261–90.

99. *Essais* 80, II, 12, p. 149. Frame, p. 320.

100. On Montaigne's relationship to theology and the importance of religion in Montaigne's biography, see Hans-Peter Bippus, *In der Theologie nicht bewandert?: Montaigne und die Theologie*. Tübingen; Bâle: Tübinger Studien zur Theologie und Philosophie, 2000.

101. *Essais* 80, II, 12, p. 153. Frame, p. 321.

102. *Essais* 80, II, 12, p. 151. Frame, p. 320.

103. *Essais* 80, II, 12, p. 154. Frame, p. 321.

104. *Essais* 80, II, 12, p. 157. Frame, p. 323.
105. *Essais* 80, II, 12, pp. 158–59. Frame, p. 324.
106. *Essais* 80, II, 12, p. 159. Frame, p. 325.
107. *Essais* 80, II, 12, p. 162. Frame, p. 327.
108. *Essais* 80, II, 12, p. 163. Frame, p. 327.
109. Ibid.
110. *Essais* 80, II, 12, p. 164. Frame, p. 328.
111. *Essais* 80, II, 12, p. 166. Frame, p. 329.
112. François de La Croix du Maine, *Premier volume de la bibliothèque du sieur de La Croix du Maine*. Paris: Abel L'Angelier, 1584, 329.
113. Pierre de L'Estoile, *Mémoires-journaux de Pierre de L'Estoile*, ed. G. Brunet, A. Champollion, E. Halphen, P. Lacroix, C. Read, T. de Laroque, and E. Tricotel. Paris: Librairie des Bibliophiles, 1825, vol. I, 361.
114. Ibid., July 1580.
115. Émile Galtier, *Histoire de Saint-Maur-des-Fossés, depuis son origine jusqu'à nos jours: L'abbaye, le château, la ville*. Saint-Maur-des-Fossés: Société d'histoire et d'archéologie de Saint-Maur-des-Fossés, 1989.
116. "A Monsieur d'Abin." In *Lettres de Catherine de Medici (1579–1581)*, op. cit., June 24, 1580, p. 266.
117. François de La Croix du Maine, *Bibliotheque françoise*, op. cit., p. 328.
118. Alain Legros, "Montaigne, son livre et son roi." *Studi Francesi*, vol. XLI, fasc. II, 1997, 259–74.
119. Monique Chatenet, "Henri III et 'l'ordre de la cour.' Évolution de l'étiquette à travers les règlements généraux de 1578 et 1585." In Robert Sauzet, ed., *Henri III et son temps*. Paris: J. Vrin, 1992, 133–39.
120. Maurice Rat, "Madame d'Estissac, son fils et Montaigne." *Bulletin de la Société des amis de Montaigne*, no. 16, 1953–54, 24–33; Lauro-Aimé Colliard, "Un jeune ami de Montaigne: Charles d'Estissac." In Enrica Galassi and Giuseppe Bernardelli, eds., *Lingua, cultura e testo: Miscellanea di studi francesi in onore di Sergio Cigada*. Milan: Gemelli, 2003, 273–84.
121. Henry III to Marshal Biron, May 15, 1579, Paris. In *Lettres de Henri III roi de France*, ed. Pierre Champion and Michel François. Paris: Klincksieck, 1984, vol. IV, p. 195, no. 3373.
122. *Archives historiques du département de la Gironde*, vol. XIV, 1873, no. XCV, April 25, 1580, p. 153.
123. Pierre de L'Estoile, *Journal de L'Estoile pour le règne de Henri III (1574–1589)*, entry for June, 1580. Paris: Gallimard, 1943.
124. Maximilien Melleville, *Histoire de la Ville et des Sires Coucy-le-Château*. Laon: Fleury & A. Chevergny, 1848, 294–95.
125. *Éphéméride*, August 6.
126. Raymond Ritter, "Un ami de Montaigne, Philibert de Gramont (1552–1580)." In Georges Palassie, ed., *Mémorial du 1er congrès international des études montaignistes*. Bordeaux: Taffard, 1964, 136–45.

127. *Essais* 88, III, 4, f. 366r. Frame, p. 637.

128. *Journal de voyage*, p. 3. *The journal of Montaigne's travels in Italy by way of Switzerland and Germany in 1580 and 1581*, trans. W. G. Waters. London: Murray, 1903, 26.

129. *Journal de François de Syrueilh*, op. cit., 322. This figure seems greatly exaggerated. See *Copie d'une missive envoyée de Paris à Lyon . . . sur la contagion de Paris en 1580*. Lyon, 1580, Archives curieuses, vol. X.

130. On the d'Estissac family, see Maurice Campagne, *Histoire de la Maison de Madaillan*. Bergerac: J. Castanet, 1900, chap. IV.

131. See Roger Trinquet, "En marge des *Essais*: La vraie figure de Madame d'Estissac ou les pièges de l'homonymie." *Bibliothèque d'Humanisme et Renaissance*, vol. XVII, 1956, 23–36.

132. These letters are in the archives of Modena (Cancell. Duc. Lett. Di Princ. Est.). In his edition of the *Journal de voyage de Montaigne*, Alessandro d'Ancona reproduces them. Letter from Henry III: "*Mio zio. Il signore d'Estissac desiderando di rendersi di più in più degno di continuare il servitio, che tutti li suoi predecessori hanno sempre et anticamente fatto a questo regno, se ne va di presente in Italia affin di fermarvisi qualche tempo et attendere fra tanto a' più virtuosi et honesti esercitij che vi si fanno ciascun giorno, et perchè io desidero in tutto quello che mi è possibile favorir il suo viaggio, et accompagnarlo in questo suo desiderio, io vi prego, mio zio, mentre ch'egli starà nelle vostre bande fargli fare tutte le gratiose et migliori accoglienze che voi potrete, in maniera ch'egli conosca per affetto in quale raccomandatione havete tutto quello che vi è raccomandato da parte mia, essendo un gentilhuomo che merita che gli sia fatto favore. Pregando Dio, mio zio, havervi in sua santa et degna custodia, Di San Mauro di Fossati a' 27 d'Agosto 1580, vostro bon nipote Henrico.*" Letter from Catherine de Medici: "*Mio cugino. Havendo saputo che il signore Destissac se n'andava in Italia con intentione di fermarsi qualche giorno nelle terre di vostro dominio, io ho ben voluto testimoniarvi con la presente il contento che il Re, monsignor mio figliuolo, ha delli servitij di tutti li suoi, et pregarvi quanto più m'è possibile che mentre egli potrà essere alle bande vostre, che vi piaccia haverlo in vostra buona et favorevole protettione, gratificandolo et favorendolo in quanto si potrà offrire per suo contento, della medesima affectione come il Re, monsignor mio figliuolo, et io siamo accostumati fare quelli che ci sono raccomandati da parte vostra. Nè essendo la presente ad altro fine, prego Dio, mio cugino, che vi habbia in sua santa et degna guardia. Di San Mauro di Fossati ai 29 agosto 1580. Vostra buona cugina Caterina.*" Alessandro d'Ancona, *L'Italia alla fine del secolo XVI: Giornale del viaggio di Michele de Montaigne in Italia nel 1580–1581*. Castello: S. Lapi, 1895, 708–9.

133. On this hypothesis, see Émile Picot, *Les Français italianisants au XVIe siècle*. Paris: H. Champion, 1906, vol. II, p. 201.

134. On Du Hautoy, who may or may not have accompanied Montaigne and d'Estissac on their trip to Rome, see Jean Balsamo, "Montaigne, Charles d'Estissac et le sieur du Hautoy." In P. Desan, L. Kritzman, R. La Charité, and M. Simonin, eds., *Sans autre guide: Mélanges de littérature française de la Renaissance offerts à Marcel Tetel*. Paris: Klincksieck, 1999, 117–28.

Chapter 7. The Call of Rome, or How Montaigne Never Became an Ambassador (1580–1581)

1. Jean-Michel Ribera, *Diplomatie et espionnage: Les ambassadeurs du roi de France auprès de Philippe III; Du traité de Cateau-Cambrésis (1559) à la mort de Henri III (1589)*. Paris: H. Champion, 2007; Lucien Bely, ed., *L'Invention de la diplomatie, Moyen Âge–Temps modernes*. Paris: Presses Universitaires de France, 1998; Pierre Blet, *Histoire de la représentation diplomatique du Saint-Siège des origines à l'aube du XIXe siècle*. Vatican City: Collectana Archivi Vaticani 9, 1982; René Maulde-La-Clavière, *La Diplomatie au temps de Machiavel*. 3 vols. Paris: E. Leroux, 1892.

2. *Archives historiques du département de la Gironde*, vol. III, 1861–62, no. LXXXVI, February13, 1580, 210.

3. *Journal de François de Syrueilh*. In *Archives historiques du département de la Gironde*, vol. XIII, 1871–72, 320.

4. George Hoffmann goes in this direction when he remarks that the chapters "Whether the governor of a besieged place should go out to parley," "Parley time is dangerous," "Of prompt or slow speech," and "A trait of certain ambassadors" show Montaigne's interest in diplomacy (*Montaigne's Career*. Oxford: Clarendon Press, 1998, 151).

5. See our introduction to the facsimile reproduction of the *Journal du voyage de Michel de Montaigne en Italie et en Allemagne en 1580 et 1581*, ed. Philippe Desan. Paris: Société des Textes Français Modernes, 2014, pp. vii–lxx.

6. *Essais* EB, I, 18, f. 26v. Frame, p. 53.

7. George Hugo Tucker, "'Homo viator' and the Liberty of Exile (Du Bellay, Montaigne, Belon)." *Studies in Early Modern France*, vol. 2, 1996, 29–66.

8. *Journal de voyage*, 13–14. Waters, vol. 1, 57–58.

9. On the succession of the abbey's doyenne, see Jean Balsamo, "Montaigne, Charles d'Estissac et le sieur du Hautoy." In P. Desan, L. Kritzman, R. La Charité, and M. Simonin, eds., *Sans autre guide: Mélanges de littérature française de la Renaissance offerts à Marcel Tetel*. Paris: Klincksieck, 1999, 127. See also Odile Boulard, "Les chanoinesses de Remiremont du XIVe au début du XVIIe siècle." In Michel Parisse, *Remiremont. L'abbaye et la ville*. Nancy: Service des Publications de Nancy II, 1980, 61–69.

10. *Journal de voyage*, 14. Waters, vol. 1, 59.

11. *Journal de voyage*, 15. Waters, vol. 1, 60.

12. *Journal de voyage*, 15. Waters, vol. 1, 62.

13. René Bernoulli, "Montaigne rencontre Félix Platter." In François Moureau and René Bernoulli, eds., *Autour du* Journal de voyage *de Montaigne 1580–1980*. Geneva: Slatkine, 1982, 88–103. Waters, vol. 1, 65.

14. *Journal de voyage*, 16. Waters, vol. 1, 65.

15. Pierre Danès, *Conseils à un ambassadeur*. Text reproduced by L. Delavaud, "La diplomatie d'autrefois." *Revue d'histoire diplomatique*, vol. XXVIII, 1914, 602–12, 608.

16. *Journal de voyage*, 32. Waters, vol. 1, 110.

17. *Journal de voyage*, 31. Waters, vol. 1, 105–6.

18. *Journal de voyage*, 38. Waters, vol. 1, 127.

19. *Journal de voyage*, 31. Waters, vol. 1, 106.

20. *Essais* 88, III, 13, f. 472v. Frame, p. 818.

21. *Journal de voyage*, 41. Waters, vol. 1, 136.

22. *Journal de voyage*, 40. Waters, vol. 1, 133.

23. *Journal de voyage*, 47. Waters, vol. 1, 152.

24. On Montaigne in Germany, see particularly Jean-Marie Compain, "Montaigne en Allemagne." In Claude-Gilbert Dubois, ed., *Montaigne et l'Europe*. Mont-de-Marsan: Éditions InterUniversitaires, 1992, 211–22; Wolfgang Leiner, "Du voyage en pays germaniques: Intertextualité et portée du *Journal de voyage* de Montaigne." In Zoé Samaras, ed., *Montaigne: Espace, voyage, écriture*. Paris: H. Champion, 1995, 55–64; and Wolfgang Adam, " 'Si grand plaisir à la visitation d'Allemaigne': Montaigne en terres germaniques." In Philippe Desan, ed., *Montaigne à l'étranger: Voyages avérés, possibles et imaginés*. Paris: Classiques Garnier, 2016, 67–88.

25. Marcel Françon, "Sur l'entrevue de Montaigne et Maldonat à Epernay et à Rome." *Quaderni di filologia e lingue romanze*, vol. V, 1983, 39–40; Alain Legros, "Montaigne et Maldonat." *Montaigne Studies*, vol. XIII, 2001, 65–98; Camille Aymonier, "Un ami de Montaigne: Le jésuite Maldonat." *Revue historique de Bordeaux et du département de la Gironde*, vol. XXVIII, 1935, 5–35.

26. Fausta Garavini, "Montaigne rencontre Theodor Zwinger à Bâle: Deux esprits parents." *Montaigne Studies*, vol. V, 1993, 191–206.

27. Michel Hermann, "L'attitude de Montaigne envers la Réforme et les Réformés dans le *Journal de voyage*." In François Moureau and René Bernoulli, eds., *Autour du* Journal de voyage *de Montaigne 1580–1980*. Geneva: Slatkine, 1982, 37–54; id., "L'attitude de Montaigne envers la réforme et les Réformés dans les *Essais* de 1580 et le *Journal de voyage*." In François Moureau, Robert Granderoute, and Claude Blum, eds., *Montaigne et les* Essais *1580–1980: Actes du Congrès de Bordeaux (juin 1980)*. Paris; Geneva: Champion; Slatkine, 1983, 352–67; Marie-Christine Gomez-Giraud, "Autour du catholicisme de Montaigne: perspectives depuis le *Journal de voyage*." *Montaigne Studies*, vol. XV, 2003, 31–41.

28. Concetta Cavallini, "Montaigne à Venise: Rencontres et hypothèses." *Montaigne Studies*, vol. XXIV, 2012, 163–74.

29. A felicitous phrase by Frank Lestringant. Cf. "Montaigne et les protestants." In Philippe Desan, ed., *Montaigne politique*. Paris: H. Champion, 2006, 360.

30. Michel Hermann, "L'attitude de Montaigne envers la Réforme et les Réformés dans le *Journal de voyage*," art. cit., 352–67.

31. Daniel Ménager, *Diplomatie et théologie à la Renaissance*. Paris: Presses Universitaires de France, 2001; Timothy Hampton, *Fictions of Embassy: Literature and Diplomacy in Early Modern Europe*. Ithaca, NY: Cornell University Press, 2009.

32. De Lamar Jensen, "French Diplomacy and the Wars of Religion." *Sixteenth Century Journal*, no. 2, 1974, 23–46.

33. Édouard Frémy, *Essai sur les diplomates du temps de la Ligue*. Paris: E. Dentu, 1873, 98.

34. Ernest Nys, "Les origines de la diplomatie et du droit d'ambassade jusqu'à Grotius." *Revue de droit international et de législation comparée*, vol. XV, 1883, 577–86; vol. XVI, 1884, 167–89.

35. Matthieu Gellard, "Une reine épistolaire: Les usages de la lettre et leurs effets dans l'action diplomatique de Catherine de Medicis (1559–1589)." PhD diss., Université Paris-Sorbonne, 2010, chapter 3: "Les grandes caractéristiques du réseau diplomatique français." An edited version of this dissertation was recently published under the title *Une reine épistolaire: Lettres et pouvoir au temps de Catherine de Médicis*. Paris: Classiques Garnier, 2015.

36. Jean-Michel Ribera, *Diplomatie et espionnage*, op. cit., 118.

37. *Mémoires de Jean Choisnin*. In *Collection universelle des Mémoires particuliers relatifs à l'histoire de France*. London: 1789, vol. LIV, 214–17.

38. Ibid., 213.

39. On Fourquevaux's career, see Matthieu Gellard, "Le Métier d'ambassadeur pendant les Guerres de Religion: Raymond de Fourquevaux, représentant de Charles IX à Madrid (1565–1572)." Master's thesis, Université Paris-Sorbonne, 2001.

40. Jean-François Labourdette, "Le recrutement des ambassadeurs sous les derniers Valois." In Lucien Bély, ed., *L'Invention de la diplomatie*, op. cit., 99–114.

41. Jacqueline Boucher, "La diplomatie de Henri III (1574–1589)." In *La Diplomatie au temps de Brantôme, Cahiers Brantôme*. Bordeaux: Presses Universitaires de Bordeaux, 2007, vol. III, 39–54.

42. Matthieu Gellard, "*Une reine épistolaire,*" op. cit., 208.

43. E. Charrière, *Négociations de la France dans le Levant ou correspondances, mémoires et actes diplomatiques des ambassadeurs, envoyés ou résidents à divers titre à Venise, Raguse, Rome, Malte et Jérusalem, en Turquie, Perse, Géorgie, Crimée, Syrie, Égypte, etc., et dans les États de Tunis, d'Alger et du Maroc*. Paris: Imprimerie impériale, 1853, vol. III, 289–90.

44. See *État des gages et pensions des membres du Parlement de Bordeaux pour l'année 1569*. BNF, pièces originales, ms. 2525, Roffignac, f. 55; *Archives historiques du département de la Gironde*, vol. XXIX, 1894, no. CCLXVI, 459–78.

45. Letter to Monsieur de Dacqs, February 7, 1573. *Lettres de Catherine de Medicis*, ed. Gustave Baguenault de Puchesse. Paris: Imprimerie nationale, 1880–1909, vol. X, 305.

46. Letter to Monsieur de Dacqs, July 24, 1573, ibid., vol. X, 327.

47. These instructions for the ambassador to the Levant are found in the manuscript of the "Dépôt de la Guerre" (298–302).

48. See *Registre Secret du Parlement de Bordeaux commençant le 16 novembre 1564 et finissant le 1er septembre 1576, copie de Monsieur de Poitevin, avocat, qui la tenait de feu Monsieur le Premier Président Daulede, ce 30 aoust 1720, De Savignac*. Bibliothèque municipale de Bordeaux, Fonds patrimoniaux, ms. 369 (3), f. 13r.

49. Archives départementales de la Gironde, ruling of April 6, 1566, liasse 1B 291, item 142.

50. Catherine Magnien, "Montaigne historien de 'l'expédition' de Henri d'Anjou en Pologne (1573–1574)? Hypothèses . . ." In Françoise Argod-Dutard, ed., *Histoire*

et littérature au siècle de Montaigne: Mélanges offerts à Claude-Gilbert Dubois. Geneva: Droz, 2001, 195–206.

51. Matthieu Gellard, "Une reine épistolaire," op. cit., 202.

52. Nicolas Le Roux, "Les négociateurs royaux en France pendant les guerres de Religion." In Heinz Duchhardt and Patrice Veit, eds., *Guerre et paix du Moyen Âge aux Temps modernes: Théorie—Pratiques—Représentations*. Mainz: Philipp von Zabern, 121.

53. Thierry Wanegffelen, *Catherine de Medicis, le pouvoir au féminin*. Paris: Payot, 2005, 377.

54. Édouard Frémy, *Un ambassadeur libéral sous Charles IX et Henri III: Ambassades à Venise d'Arnaud du Ferrier, d'après sa correspondance inédite (1563–1567, 1570–1582)*. Paris: E. Leroux, 1880, 363–65, note 2.

55. Philippe Hurault, *Mémoires de Messire Philippe Hurault, comte de Cheverny*. In *Collection universelle des Mémoires particuliers relatifs à l'histoire de France Mémoires*. Vol. L, 56–59.

56. Hugues Daussy, "Un diplomate protestant au service d'un roi catholique: Charles de Danzay, ambassadeur de France au Danemark (1515–1589)." In Frédérique Pitou, ed., *Élites et notables de l'Ouest: XVIᵉ–XXᵉ siècle: Entre conservatisme et modernité*. Rennes: Presses Universitaires de Rennes, 2003, 277–94.

57. Charles de Danzay, *Correspondance de Charles de Danzay, ministre de France à la Cour de Danemark*. Stockholm: Elmen and Granberg, 1824. Cited by Alfred Richard, *Charles de Danzay, ambassadeur de France en Danemark*. Poitiers: Imprimerie Blais et Roy, 1910, 176.

58. Ibid., 179.

59. Saint-Gouard (Jean de Vivonne) to the duke of Anjou, September 19, 1572. BNF, ms. fr. 16104, cited by Guy Bremond d'Ars, *Jean de Vivonne, sa vie et ses ambassades près de Philippe II et à la cour de Rome, d'après des documents inédits*. Paris: Plon, 1884, 97.

60. Saint-Gouard to Catherine de Medici, August 28, 1581. In *Lettres de Catherine de Medicis*, op. cit., vol. VII, 104.

61. Catherine de Medici to Monsieur du Ferrier, September 19, 1579, ibid., 135–36.

62. *Scoevolae Sammarthani lucubrationem pars altera, qua continentur gallorum doctrina illustrium, qui nostras patrunque memoria florverunt elogia*. Augustoriti Pictonum, 1606.

63. Correspondence of Du Ferrier, BNF, ms. fr. 3321. Document reproduced by Édouard Frémy, *Un ambassadeur libéral sous Charles IX et Henri III*, op. cit., 406–13.

64. Letter from Arnaud Du Ferrier to Catherine de Medici, September 4, 1579. Cited by Matthieu Gellard, "*Une reine épistolaire*," op. cit., 249.

65. Quoted by Édouard Frémy, *Un ambassadeur libéral sous Charles IX et Henri III*, op. cit., 363–64.

66. Jean Nicot to the cardinal of Lorraine, September 26, 1560. Cited by Edmond Falgairolle, *Jean Nicot, ambassadeur de France au Portugal au XVIᵉ siècle: Sa correspondance diplomatique*. Paris: A. Challamel, 1897, 58.

67. Cited by David Vanoverberghe, "L'Ambassade de Bertrand de Salignac de La Mothe-Fénelon en Angleterre (1568–1574)." Master's thesis, Université de Lille, 1994, 10.

68. Letter from Raymond de Fourquevaux to Catherine de Medici, from Madrid, July 26, 1568. Cited by abbé Douais, *Dépêches de M. de Fourquevaux, ambassadeur du roi Charles IX en Espagne, 1565–1572*. 3 vols. Paris: E. Leroux, 1896–1904, vol. III, 95–96.

69. Matthieu Gellard gives the examples of Raymond de Fourquevaux and Jean de Vulcob, ambassadors to the emperor. "Une reine épistolaire," op. cit., 244.

70. Nicola Mary Sutherland, *The French Secretaries of State in the Age of Catherine de Medicis*. London: Athlone Press, 1962.

71. Laurent Bouchel, *La Bibliothèque ou thrésor du droict françois recueilly et mis en ordre*. Paris: Baillet, 1629. Cited by Édouard Frémy, *Essai sur les diplomates du temps de la Ligue*. Paris: E. Dentu, 1873, 76.

72. Edmond Cabié, *Ambassade en Espagne de Jean Ebrard, seigneur de Saint-Sulpice, de 1562 à 1565 et mission de ce diplomate dans le même pays en 1566*. Albi: Nouguiès, 1903.

73. Guy de Brémond d'Ars, *Le Père de Mme Rambouillet, Jean de Vivonne, sa vie, ses ambassades près de Philippe II et à la cour de Rome, d'après des documents inédits*. Paris: E. Plon, 1884.

74. This figure is given by Jean-François Labourdette, "Le recrutement des ambassadeurs sous les derniers Valois," art. cit., 111.

75. Marie-Noëlle Baudouin-Matuszek, "Un ambassadeur en Écosse au XVIᵉ siècle, Henri Clutin d'Oisel." *Revue historique*, vol. 281, no. 1, 1989, 78–131.

76. Letter to Villeroy, December 25, 1586. In *Lettres de Catherine de Medicis*, op. cit., vol. IX, 128. Cited by Nicolas Le Roux, "Les négociateurs royaux en France pendant les guerres de Religion," art. cit., 130.

77. *Essais* 80, I, 17, p. 85. Frame, p. 26. On the status of speech and "speaking" in the *Essais*, see Bruno Méniel, "La notion de 'parler' chez Montaigne." *Bulletin de la Société des amis de Montaigne*, no. 41–43, 2006, 119–30.

78. *Essais* 80, II, 12, p. 180. Frame, p. 336.

79. Jean Hotman de Villiers, *L'Ambassadeur*, s.l., 1603, 18.

80. *Mémoires inédits de Henri de Mesmes, seigneur de Roissy et de Malassise*, ed. Édouard Frémy. Paris: E. Leroux, 1886, 168.

81. *Essais* 88, I, 17, f. 25 r–v. Frame, p. 50.

82. *Essais* 80, I, 17, p. 85. Frame, p. 51.

83. *Essais* 80, I, 17, pp. 85–86. Frame, p. 51.

84. *Essais* 80, I, 9, pp. 37–38. Frame, p. 24.

85. *Essais* 88, I, 17, f. 25v. Frame, p. 51.

86. L. Delavaud, "La diplomatie d'autrefois." *Revue d'histoire diplomatique*, nos. 28–29, 1914–15, 602–12; René Maulde-La-Clavière, *La Diplomatie au temps de Machiavel*, op. cit.

87. Cited by Jean-Michel Ribera, *Diplomatie et espionnage*, op. cit., 39.

88. Brantôme, *Hommes illustres et grands capitaines françois*. In *Œuvres complètes de Pierre de Bourdeille abbé séculier de Brantôme*. Paris: Auguste Desrez, 1839.

89. Fleury Vindry, *Les Ambassadeurs français permanents au XVIe siècle*. Paris: H. Champion, 1903. Figures presented by Jean-Michel Ribera, *Diplomatie et espionnage*, op. cit., 54–55.

90. Figures given by Matthieu Gellard, "Une reine épistolaire," op. cit., chapter III: "Les grandes caractéristiques du réseau diplomatique français."

91. *Lettres de Messire Paul de Foix archevesque de Tolose et ambassadeur pour le Roy auprès du pape Grégoire XIII, écrites au roi Henri III*, éd. Auger de Mauléon. Paris: C. Chappellain, 1628, f. ê3r.

92. On sincerity and dissimulation in Montaigne, see Margaret McGowan, *Montaigne's Deceits: The Art of Persuasion in the* Essais. London: University of London Press, 1974.

93. *Essais* 88, I, 14, f. 21r. Frame, p. 43.

94. *Essais* 80, I, 9, pp. 32–33. Frame, p. 21.

95. *Essais* EB, I, 9, f. 11v. Frame, p. 23.

96. Jean Hotman de Villiers, *L'Ambassadeur*, op. cit., 12.

97. Marc-Antoine Muret, *Harangue funebre sur le trespas de Messire Paul de Foix*... *faite en Latin par Marc Antoine Muret, & traduite en François par A. de M. [Auger deMauléon]*. Rome, 1584.

98. Ibid., 17.

99. Ibid., 71.

100. *Essais* 88, I, 40, f. 105r. Frame, p. 185.

101. *Essais* 80, II, 17, p. 451. Frame, p. 492.

102. On the tradition of the humanist letter in the Renaissance, see Guy Gueudet, *L'Art de la lettre humaniste*. Paris: H. Champion, 2004; Marc Fumaroli, "Genèse de l'épistolographie classique: Rhétorique humaniste de la lettre, de Pétrarque à Juste Lipse." *Revue d'histoire littéraire de la France*, vol. 78, no. 6, 1978, 886–900.

103. *Essais* 88, I, 40, f. 105v. Frame, p. 186.

104. *Le Grant Stille et protocolle de la Chancellerie de France* (1514), Fabri's treatise on the *Protocolle des secretaires et aultres gens desirans savoir L'art et maniere de dicter en bon Françoys toutes lettres missives et epistres en prose* (1534), and *Le stile et maniere de composer, dicter, et escrire toutes sortes d'epistres, ou lettres missives* (1553). See Claude La Charité, "Le stile et maniere de composer, dicter, et escrire toutes sortes d'epistres, ou lettres missives (1553). De la *Dispositio* tripartite de Pierre Fabri au poulpe épistolaire d'Érasme." In Frank Lestringant, ed., *L'Épistolaire au XVIe siècle*. Paris: Presses de l'École normale supérieure, 2001, 17–32.

105. *Essais* 80, II, 17, p. 445. Frame, p. 487.

106. *Essais* 88, I, 40, f. 105v–106r. Frame, pp. 186–87.

107. *Essais* EB, I, 40, f. 105v. Frame, pp. 185–86.

108. Daniel Ménager, "Lettres d'ambassadeurs." In *L'Épistolaire au XVIe siècle*, op. cit., 227–36.

109. *Trésor politique divisé en trois livres: Contenant les relations, instructions, traictez, et divers discours appartenans à la parfaicte intelligence de la raison d'Estat & de tres-*

*grande importance à l'entiere cognoissance des interests, pretentions, desseins, & reve-
nus des plus grands princes & seigneurs du monde.* Paris: Rollin Thierry, 1608, 748.

110. Philippe Desan, "Introduction." In Philippe Desan, ed., *Reproduction fac-similé du
Journal du voyage de Michel de Montaigne en Italie et en Allemagne en 1580 et 1581.*
Paris: Société des Textes Français Modernes, 2014, vii–lxx.

111. Antoine de Laval, *Desseins des professions nobles et publiques contenans plusieurs
traictez divers & rares. Et entre autres, l'histoire de la maison de Bourbon: avec autres
beaux secrets historiques, extraicts de bons & authentiques memoires & manuscripts*
[1605]. Paris: Abel L'Angelier, 1611, f. 201r.

112. Ibid.

113. Ibid., f. 295r.

114. Guy de Brémond d'Ars, *Le Père de Mme de Rambouillet*, op. cit.

115. Letters from Catherine de Medici to Saint-Gouard, August 29, 1572. In *Lettres de
Catherine de Medicis*, op. cit., vol. IV, 115.

116. Letter from Saint-Gouard to Charles IX, September 12, 1572. Cited by Jean-
Michel Ribera, *Diplomatie et espionnage*, op. cit., p. 156–57.

117. Letter to Charles IX, October 2, 1572. In *Lettres de Catherine de Medicis*, op. cit.,
vol. IV, 134.

118. Letter to Saint-Gouard, December 5, 1572. In *Lettres de Catherine de Medicis*,
ibid., vol. IV, 148.

119. Letter to the duke of Savoy, August 13, 1573. In *Lettres de Catherine de Medicis*,
ibid., vol. X, 329.

120. BNF, Nouvelles acquisitions françaises, no. 9175, f. 379, and ms. fr. 7854, f.
13–36.

121. Archives nationales de France, Maison de Catherine de Medicis, 1579–1585,
K388–423. État des gages des domestiques de la Reine mère [Catherine de Medi-
cis], 1585; distribution des sommes laissées par la Reine à ses domestiques par testament, 1589 (3 bound paper signatures), K. 502.

122. *Essais* 88, III, 13, f. 487r–v. Frame, p. 841.

123. Letter to Henry III, March 16, 1579, sent from Agen. In *Lettres de Catherine de
Medicis*, op. cit., vol. VI, 305.

124. Letter to Monsieur de Bellièvre, September 17, 1579, from La Côte-Saint-André,
near Vienne in Isère. In *Lettres de Catherine de Medicis*, op. cit., vol. II, 133.

125. Jean-François Payen, *Recherches sur Montaigne: Documents inédits*. Paris: Techener, 1856, 10.

126. Letter to Villeroy, April 8, 1584. In *Lettres de Catherine de Medicis*, op. cit., vol.
VIII, 179.

127. *Essais* 80, I, 14, p. 71. Frame, p. 41. On Iberian images and reflections in the *Essais*,
see Géralde Nakam, "Ibériques de Montaigne: Reflets et images de la péninsule
Ibérique dans les *Essais*." In Claude-Gilbert Dubois, ed., *Montaigne et l'Europe*, op.
cit., 153–75.

128. Figures provided by Matthieu Gellard, "Une reine épistolaire," op. cit., 190–98.

129. Henry III to the duke of Anjou, between October 20 and October 22, Ollainville.

In *Lettres de Henri III roi de France*, ed. Jacqueline Boucher. Paris: H. Champion, 2000, vol. V, 113–14, no. 4018.

130. Henry III to Pomponne de Bellièvre, May 27, 1581, Blois. In *Lettres de Henri III roi de France*, op. cit., 183–84, no. 4235.

131. *Mémoires et lettres de Marguerite de Valois*. Paris: Jules Renouard, 1842, 150.

132. Henry III to Marshal Matignon, October 12,1581, Paris. In *Lettres de Henri III roi de France*, op. cit., 224, no. 4351.

133. Henry III to Pomponne de Bellièvre, October 27, 1581, Paris. In *Lettres de Henri III roi de France*, op. cit., 229, no. 4365.

134. André du Chesne, *Histoire généalogique de la maison des Chasteigners, seigneurs de la Chasteigneray, de la Rochepozay, de St-Georges de Rexe, de Lindoys, de la Rochefaton et autres lieux, justifiés par chartes diverses, églises, arrests à la cour de Parlement, lettres domestiques et autres bonnes preuves*. Paris: Sébastien Cramoisy, 1634. P. de Chasteigner de La Rochepozay, *Montaigne et l'ambassadeur de France à Rome en 1580: Portrait, deux lettres inédites de Henri III et de Catherine de Medicis* (facsimile). Bayonne: A. Lamaignère, 1895.

135. Léon Petit, "Montaigne à Rome et deux ambassadeurs amis, Louis Chasteigner, seigneur d'Abain et de La Rocheposay, et Paul de Foix." *Bulletin de la Société des amis de Montaigne*, no. 56, 1958, 924.

136. Jean Balsamo, "Deux gentilshommes 'nécessiteux d'honneur': Montaigne et Pressac. *Montaigne Studies*, vol. XIII, 2001, 141–74.

137. *Archives historiques du département de la Gironde*, vol. XXIV, 1884, no. CXXIV, May 14, 1587, 367–68.

138. *Journal de voyage*, 94. Waters, vol. 2, 79–80.

139. Jean-François Labourdette, "Le recrutement des ambassadeurs sous les derniers Valois," art. cit., 102.

140. See the letter from Salviati at Como, October 18, 1574. Cited by Noël Didier, "Paul de Foix et Grégoire XIII (1572–1584): Une suite de la mercuriale de 1559." *Annales de l'université de Grenoble*, section lettres-droit, vol. XVII, 1941, 169.

141. *Journal de voyage*, 94–95. Waters, vol. 2, 81–82.

142. Antoine de Laval, *Desseins des professions*, op. cit., f. 186r.

143. De Thou, *Mémoires*, collection universelle, op. cit., vol. LIII, 66.

144. *Journal de voyage*, 99–100. Waters, vol. 2, 94–95.

145. Thomas Ashby, *Topographical Study in Rome in 1581, a Series of Views with a Fragmentary Text by Étienne du Pérac*. London: Roxburghe Club, 1916. On the perception of Rome in Montaigne's time, see Margaret M. McGowan, *The Vision of Rome in Late Renaissance France*. New Haven, CT: Yale University Press, 2000.

146. *Journal de voyage*, 99. Waters, vol. 2, 92.

147. *Journal de voyage*, 126. Waters, vol. 2, 161.

148. Ibid.

149. *Journal de voyage*, 91. Waters, 74.

150. *Journal de voyage*, 91. Waters, 73.

151. These figures are provided by Jean Delumeau, *Vie économique et sociale à Rome dans la seconde moitié du XVIᵉ siècle*. 2 vols. Paris: E. de Boccard, 1957, vol. I, 139.

152. *Journal de voyage,*112. Waters, vol. 2, 120.

153. *Journal de voyage,* 112–13. Waters, vol. 2, 121.

154. Catherine de Medici to Monsieur du Ferrier, January 19, 1580. In *Lettres de Catherine de Medicis*, op. cit., vol. VII, 222.

155. Catherine de Medici to Monsieur d'Abin, January19, 1580, op. cit., 221–22.

156. Roland Mousnier, "Les fidélités et les clientèles en France aux XVIe, XVIIe et XVIIIe siècles." *Social History*, vol. 15, 1982, 35–46.

157. Henry III to Lord Abain, November 28, 1578, Paris. In *Lettres de Henri III, roi de France*, ed. Pierre Champion. Paris: Klincksieck, 1984, vol. IV, 107–8, no. 3182.

158. Henry III to Lord Abain, April 7 1579. Ibid., 184–85, no. 3357.

159. Stanislas Grzybowski, "Henri III et Étienne Bathory." In Robert Sauzet, ed., *Henri III et son temps*. Paris: J. Vrin, 1992, 93–101.

160. See the letter of May 18, 1577, sent from Chenonceaux.

161. Warren Boutcher, " 'Le moyen de voir ce Senecque escrit à la main': Montaigne's *Journal de voyage* and the Politics of *Science* and *Faveur* in the Vatican Library." In John O'Brien, ed., *(Ré)interprétations: Études sur le seizième siècle*. Ann Arbor: Michigan Romance Studies, 1995, 177–214; François Rigolot, "Curiosity, Contingency, and Cultural Diversity: Montaigne's Readings at the Vatican Library." *Renaissance Quarterly*, vol. 64, no. 3, 2011, 847–74.

162. Du Chesne, *Histoire générale de la maison des Chasteigners*, op. cit., 125.

163. Charles-Martial de Witte, "Notes sur les ambassadeurs de France à Rome et leur correspondance sous les derniers Valois (1556–1589)." *Mélanges de l'École française de Rome (Moyen Âge-Temps modernes)*, vol. 83, 1971, 89–121; Fleury Vindry, *Les Ambassadeurs français permanents au XVIe siècle*, op. cit.

164. Nicolas Le Roux, "Négociateurs royaux en France . . . ," art. cit., 133.

165. This hypothesis has been proposed by Daniel Ménager, "La diplomatie de Montaigne." In Philippe Desan, ed., *Montaigne politique*, op. cit., 152.

166. *Essais* 80, I, 1, p. 6. Frame, p. 5.

167. According to David Maskell, this activity as a mediator between Navarre and Guise took place between Janurary and March 1578. "Montaigne médiateur entre Navarre et Guise." *Bibliothèque d'Humanisme et Renaissance*, vol. XLI, 1979, 541–53.

168. Catherine de Medici to Cardinal d'Este, March 13, 1581. In *Lettres de Catherine de Medicis*, op. cit., 366.

169. Cité par Noël Didier, "Paul de Foix et Grégoire XIII, 1572–1584," art. cit., 188.

170. Catherine de Medici to Henry III, March15, 1581. In *Lettres de Catherine de Medicis*, op. cit., 366–67.

171. See NF 15, f. 113–15. Cited by Ivan Cloulas, *Correspondance du nonce en France Anselmo Dandino (1578–1581)*. Rome: Presses de l'Université grégorienne, 1970, 822. Also see NF 15, f. 110 and 111, letters from Henry III and Catherine de Medici, dated from Blois April 21, 1581, announcing this nominaiton to the cardinal of Como.

172. On the Maugirons, see Nicolas Le Roux, *La Faveur du roi: Mignons et courtisans au temps des derniers Valois (vers 1547–vers 1589)*. Paris: Champ Vallon, 2001, 229–31.

173. Letter of May 4, 1581, NF 15, f. 118–19. Cited by Ivan Cloulas, *Correspondance du nonce en France Anselmo Dandino (1578–1581)*, op. cit., 824.

174. I thank Anna Bettoni for these details regarding Du Ferrier's "conversion." On this episode and more generally on Du Ferrier's embassy to Venice, see Anna Bettoni, "Arnaud du Ferrier et les Français de Venise à l'époque de la peste de 1576." In Jean Balsamo and Chiara Lastraioli, eds., *Chemins de l'exil: Havres de paix; Migrations d'hommes et d'idées au XVIᵉ siècle*. Paris: H. Champion, 2009, 261–88; id., "Duplessis-Mornay et la 'famille' de l'ambassade d'Arnaud du Ferrier à Venise." In Hugues Daussy and Véronique Ferrer, eds., *Servir Dieu, le Roi et l'État: Philippe Duplessis-Mornay (1549–1623)*. Paris: H. Champion, 2006, 381–407. On the friendsgip between Montaigne and Du Ferrier, see Alexandre Nicolaï, "Un autre ami de Montaigne: Arnaud du Ferrier." *Bulletin de la Société des amis de Montaigne*, no. 19, 1956, 37–39; Alain Tallon, "Diplomate et 'politique': Arnaud du Ferriet." In Thierry Wanegffelen, ed., *De Michel de L'Hospital à l'édit de Nantes: Politique et religion face aux Églises*. Clermont-Ferrand: Presses Universitaires Blaise-Pascal, 2002, 305–33.

175. Jane Crawford, "Diplomacy for the Honor of God: A Study of the Papal Nunciature in France (1572–1590)." PhD diss., Brigham Young University, 1974.

176. On the *mercuriale* of 1559, see Noël Didier, "Paul de Foix à la mercuriale de 1559, son procès, ses idées religieuses." *Mélanges d'archéologie et d'histoire publiés par l'École française de Rome*, vol. LVI, 1939, 396ff.

177. Catherine de Medici to the pope, October 22, 1579. In *Lettres de Catherine de Medicis*, op. cit., vol. VII, 182.

178. Auger de Mauléon, ed., *Les Lettres de Messire Paul de Foix*, op. cit.

179. *Miscell.* II, 117, f. 162–70. Cited by Robert Toupin, ed., *Correspondance du nonce en France Giovanni Battista Castelli (1581–1583)*. Rome: Presses de l'Université grégorienne, 1967, 101: "Se a V. S. [Vostra Signoria] fosse parlato da le lor Maestà sopra il fatto di Mons. di Fois, è necessario che ella sia informata di ciò che passa per poter dare conveniente risposta. Saprà adunque che questo gentil'huomo fu inquisito più anni sono per certi sospetti d'heresia, de li quali, per dir il vero, egli si è purgato qui in Roma, et così resta libero, et senza nota. Ma perché il Re vorebbe che N. S. lo promovesse a l'arcivescovato di Tolosa, et S. S. [Sua Santità] giudica che per quella suspitione che si hebbe di lui, la quale non fu leggeria, sia espediente di non mandarlo a una chiesa tanto insigne, et forse la più cattolica che sia in tutta Francia, tanto più essendo S. S. stata pregata da alcumi principali del luogo a non consentirvi, di qui è che il Re, et molto maggiormente la Madre si sono tal volta doluti di questa esclusione, et hanno fatti far molti officii per spuntar la cosa. N. S. [Nostro Signore: le pape] ha offerto che se il Re vorrà nominarlo a una chiesa che sia ne i contorni di Parigi, lo promoverà volentieri, et così il negotio resta suspeso, et Mons. di Fois è tuttavia in Roma. V. S. potrà mostrar' a Mons. Dandino tutta la presente Instruttione, pigliando da lui, come da persona informatissima, consiglio in tutto quello che haverà a trattare. Dio Nostro Signore la conduchi a buon viaggio, et le doni prosperità. Datum Romae in Palatio Apostolico kal. Aprilis, 1581. Il Cardinale di Como."

180. NF 15, f. 83–84. In *Correspondance du nonce en France Anselmo Dandino (1578–1581)*, op. cit., 809.

181. Ibid., NF 15, f. 86–88, p. 810.

182. *Annales Ecclesiastici*, ed. Augustin Theiner. Rome: Ex Typographia Tiberina, 1856, LII, 1581, § 42, 708.

183. Ibid.

184. Jean Delumeau, *Vie économique et sociale de Rome dans la seconde moitié du XVIe siècle*, op. cit., vol. I, 39–55. See also E. P. Rodocanachi, "Les courriers pontificaux du quatorzième au dix-septième siècle." *Revue d'histoire diplomatique*, vol. 26, no. 3, 1912, 392–428; John B. Allen, "Les courriers diplomatiques à la fin du XVIe siècle (1560–1600)." *Revue d'histoire diplomatique*, 1972, 226–36; Eugène Vaillé, *Histoire générale des Postes françaises*, vol. II, *De Louis XI à la création de la Surintendance générale des postes, 1477–1630*. Paris: Presses Universitaires de France, 1948.

185. *Les Lettres de Messire Paul de Foix, Archevesque de Toulouse, & ambassadeur pour le roy auprés de Pape Gregoire XIII escrites au roy Henry III*, ed. Auger de Mauléon. Paris: Charles Chappellain, 1628, letter dated Monday, May 15, 1581, p. 1.

186. Ibid., p. 3.

187. Cardinal of Como to Dandino, from Rome, April 17, 1581, NF 16, f. 40–43. Cited by Ivan Cloulas, *Correspondance du nonce en France Anselmo Dandino (1578–1581)*, op. cit., 819.

188. See, for example, *Le Cose maravigliose dell'Alma Città di Roma*, by Girolamo Franzini (Venice, 1575).

189. In the archives of the Santa Casa there is a series of ancient registers of gifts (*Registro Doni*) that offer a few details concerning these good works. In volume VIII (1576–99), we read the following entry in Italian: "*A di 26 maggio 1581—Intro in Sma Capella un homo d'arg-to fatto lama sottile in genocchio sopra uno scubello con ltre a piede che dicono Michael Montanus Gallus Vasco, eques Regii ordinis, con una donna drieto pur d'arg-to della medema lania con ltre che dicono Francisca Casaniana uxor, cô una putta, con ltre Leonora Montana filia unica, quale cose sono poste in un' quadretto di noce, attacato nella porta che esce Capella, nella quale ancora, swi [= Sonvi], e, una Mad. d'arg-to picciola*" (f. 74v). See Mathurin Dréano, "Note sur l'ex-voto laissé par Montaigne à Notre-Dame-de-Lorette." *Bulletin de la Société des amis de Montaigne*, no. 9, 1940, 59–60; André Rebsomen, "Un ex-voto de Montaigne au sanctuaire de Notre-Dame-de-Lorette." *Revue historique de Bordeaux*, vol. XX, no. 7, 1934, 133–34; Concetta Cavallini, "Encore une note sur Lorette et Montaigne." *Annali della Facoltà di Lingue e Letteratura Straniere*, vol. XIV, 2000, 277–85; and Philippe Desan, *Portraits à l'essai: Iconographie de Montaigne*. Paris: H. Champion, 2007, 61–62.

190. *Négociations de la France dans le Levant ou correspondances, mémoires et actes diplomatiques des ambassadeurs de France à Constantinople*. Paris: Imprimerie impériale, 1860, 31–32.

191. Rudolf Braun, "'Rester au sommet': Modes de reproduction socioculturelle des élites du pouvoir européennes." In Wolfgang Reinhard, ed., *Les Élites du pouvoir et*

la construction de l'État en Europe. Paris: Presses Universitaires de France, 1996, 323–54.

192. *Journal de voyage,* 123. Waters, vol. 2, 151.

193. *Journal de voyage,* 127. Waters, vol. 2, 165.

194. See Jean-François Payen, *Recherches sur Montaigne: Documents inédits.* Paris: J. Techener, 1856, 61–64.

195. This letter in Italian, preserved in Rome (*Registro di Privilegi di Cittadini Romani Creati,* Archivio Storico Capitolino, cred. IV, vol. 64, f. 176r), noted by Paola Pavan, "Cives origine vel privilegio." In Luigi Spezzaferro and Maria Elisa Tittoni, eds., *Il campidoglio e Sisto V.* Rome: Ed. Carte Segrete, 1991, 37, is reproduced by Alain Legros, *Montaigne manuscrit.* Paris: Classiques Garnier, 2010, 665. Here is the text: "[on the reverse side:] *Alli Ill.mi SS.ri miei . . . li SS.ri Conservatori di Roma Michel Montaigne 13 mars 1581.* / [on the obverse:] *Ill.mi SS.ri Desiderando da V. S. Ill.me et da cotesto inclito Popolo essere aggregato nel numero delli altri loro Cittadini, vengo a supplicarle, che si degnino conumerare me, et miei figlioli, fra loro cittadini con concedermi li soliti privileggi, che tutto ripportero per gratia singulare, offerendomi a VV. SS. Ill.me et a cotesto inclito Popolo espore la propria vita in loro servitio. Di casa al di XII di Marzo 1581 / Di VV. SS. Ill.me* / [the rest written in Montaigne's hand:] *Servitore Michele di Montaigna cavallier de l'ordine del re christianissimo & gentillomo ordinario de la su camera.*" I owe this transcription to Jean-Robert Armogathe, who presented the documents relating to Montaigne's Roman citizenship at the Académie des inscriptions et belles-lettres on January 17, 2014.

196. *Essais* 80, II, 12, p. 228. Frame, p. 354.

197. *Journal de voyage,* 127. Waters, vol. 2, 164–65.

198. *Journal de voyage,* 127. Waters, vol. 2, 165.

199. Ibid.

200. I thank Jean-Robert Armogathe for pointing out to me that the register of the Roman Senate is now available online. The list drawn up by Magni in 1736 has been published by Claudio De Dominicis, consulted on September 27, 2013, *Repertorio delle creazioni di cittadinanza romana (secoli XIV–XIX).* Rome: 2007, https://docs.google.com/viewer?url=http://www.accademiamoroniana.it/indici/Cittadinanza+romana.pdf.

201. *Registro di Privilegi di Cittadini Romani Creati,* Archivio Storico Capitolino, cred. I, vol. 22, f. 161r.

202. Elisabetta Mori, " 'Tot reges in Urbe Roma quot cives.' Cittadinanza e nobiltà a Roma tra Cinque e Seicento." *Roma moderna e contemporanea,* vol. IV, no. 2, 1996, 379–401, especially 384–87; Ferdinand Gregorovius, "Alcuni cenni storici sulla cittadinanza romana." Rome: *Reale Accademia dei Lincei, Memorie della Classe di scienze morali, storiche e filologiche,* series 3, vol. I, 1877, 314–46.

203. "Decreto di consiglio segreto, che per l'avvenire li chierici non si ammettessero alla C[ittadinanza] R[omana], confermato dal susseguente publico consiglio." Archivio Storico Capitolino, cred. I, vol. 27, f. 255v. On Roman citizenship, see also Gaetano Moroni, *Dizionario di erudizione storico-ecclesiastica.* Venice: Tipografia Emiliana, 1840–79.

204. *Registro di Privilegi di Cittadini Romani Creati*, Archivio Storico Capitolino, cred. I, vol, 1, f. 91v–92r.

205. Maria Luisa Napolitano, "Hubertus Goltzius e la Civitas almae urbis Romae." *Anabases* [online], vol. 11, 2010, 55–94, put online March 1, 2013, consulted on October 5, 2013, http://anabases.revues.org/769.

206. These figures are given by Elisabetta Mori, " 'Tot reges in Urbe Roma quot cives': Cittadinanza e nobiltà a Roma tra Cinque e Seicento," art. cit., 388. Paola Pavan lists 580 Roman citizenships granted (but with only 321 privileges sent) between 1580 and 1595. In "Cives origine vel privilegio," art. cit., 38.

207. "*Pri[vilegium] ro[manae] Civitatis obtentum per Ill.mum Michaelem Montagna equitem Scti. Michaelis et a Cubiculo Regis christianissimi Quod Horatius Maximus, Martius Ciocius, Alexander Mutus, Almae urbis Conss. [= Consultores] incipienti privilegio ut sequitur: Cum e veteri more et instituto cupide illi semper studioseque suscepti sint . . .* ," Archivio Storico Capitolino, cred. I, vol. 1, f. 154.

208. Maria Luisa Napolitano, "Hubertus Goltzius e la Civitas almae urbis Romae," art. cit., § 27. On this point, see also Elisabetta Mori, " 'Tot reges in Urbe Roma quot cives': Cittadinanza e nobiltà a Roma tra Cinque e Seicento," art. cit.

209. *Essais* 88, III, 9, f. 441v. Frame, p. 765.

210. *Essais* 88, III, 9, f. 442v. Frame, p. 766.

211. *Journal de voyage*, 127. Waters, vol. 2, 165–66.

212. Mary McKinley, "Vanity's Bull: Montaigne's Itineraries in III, 9." In Marcel Tetel and Mallary Masters, eds., *Le Parcours des* Essais: *Montaigne 1588–1988*. Paris: Aux amateurs de livres, 1989, 196–98; F. Caldari Bevilacqua, "Montaigne alla Biblioteca vaticana." In Enea Balmas, ed., *Montaigne e l'Italia*. Geneva: Slatkine, 1991, 363–90; Concetta Cavallini, *L'Italianisme de Michel de Montaigne*. Fasano; Paris: Schena Editore, 2003, 159–90.

213. Frame, III: 9, p. 765. Original Latin text: "*Cum e veteri more et instituto cupide illi semper studioseque suscepti sint, qui virtute ac nobilitate praestantes, magno Reipubl. Nostrae usui atque ornamento fuissent, vel esse aliquando possent, nos maiorum more exemplo atque authoritate permoti, praeclaram hanc consuetudinem nobis imitandam ac servandam fore censemus. Quamobrem cum Illmus Michael Montanus Eques sancti Michaelis et a Cubiculo Regis Christianissimi, Romani nominis studiosissimus et familiae laude ac splendore et propriis virtutum meritis dignissimus sit, qui summo Senatus Populique Romani judicio ac studio in Romanam Civitatem adsciscatur, placere Senatui PQR Illmum Michaelem Montanum rebus omnibus ornatissimum atque huic inclito populo charissimum, ipsum, posterosque eius in Romanam Civitatem adscribi, ornarique omnibus et praemiis et honoribus, quibus illi fruuntur, qui Cives Patritiique Romani nati aut jure optimo facti sunt, in quo censere Senatum PQR se, non tam illi jus civitatis largiri quam debitum tribuere, neque magis beneficium dare quam ab ipso accipere, qui hoc civitatis munere accipiendo, singulari civitatem ipsa ornamento atque honore affecerit. Quam quidem SC auctoritatem Iidem Coss. per Senatus PQR scribas in Acta referri atque in Capitoliis curiae servari privilegiumque hujusmodi fieri solitoque urbis sigillo communiri curarunt, anno ab Urbe condita 2331, post Xtum natum 1580.*" In Archivio Storico Capitolino, cred. I, vol. 28, f. 30r.

214. This was pointed out to me by Jean-Robert Armogathe.

215. Paul F. Grendler, "The Roman Inquisition and the Venetian Press—1540–1605." *Journal of Modern History*, vol. 47, 1975, 48–65. These decrees are summed up in a law of the *Consiglio dei Dieci* passed on June 28,1569.

216. *Journal de voyage*, 92. Waters, vol. 2, 76–78.

217. *Journal de voyage*, 119. Waters, vol. 2, 138–39.

218. *Journal de voyage*, 119–20. Waters, vol. 2, 140. The French text reads: "et Sebon, il me dirent que la preface estoit condamnée," but this does not appear in Waters's translation. [Trans.]

219. Malcolm Smith, *Montaigne and the Roman Censors*. Geneva: Droz, 1981; and Enea Balmas, "Montaigne et l'Inquisition." In Marcel Tetel and G. Mallary Masters, eds., *Le Parcours des* Essais *de Montaigne 1588–1988*. Paris: Klincksieck, 1989, 239–49.

220. Jean-Robert Armogathe, "Montaigne et la censure romaine: Julien l'Apostat." In Philippe Desan, ed., *"Dieu à nostre commerce et société": Montaigne et la théologie*. Geneva: Droz, 2008, 251–58. More generally, on censure and reading in Montaigne's time, see Emily Butterworth, "Censors and Censure: Robert Estienne and Michel de Montaigne." In Maria Jose Vega, Julian Weiss, and Cesc Esteve, eds., *Reading and Censorship in Early Modern Europe*. Barcelona: Universitat Autònoma de Barcelona, 2010, 161–79.

221. Peter Godman found two censures from 1581 in the archives of the Congregation of the Index. These documents have been reproduced—with errors of transcription—in Godman's *The Saint as Censor: Robert Bellarmine between Inquisition and Index*. Leiden; Boston; Cologne: Brill, 2000, 339–42. These reports submitted by *consultores* have also been commented upon by Godman in his introduction ("Montaigne und die römischen Zensoren") to *Michel de Montaigne: Tagebuch einer Reise nach Italien über die Schweiz und Deutschland*. Wiesbaden: Marix Verlag, 2005, 5–9. The corrections of these *Protocolli* have been given by Jean-Louis Quantin, "Les censures de Montaigne à l'Index romain: Précisions et corrections." *Montaigne Studies*, vol. XXVI, 2014, 145–62.

222. Jean-Robert Armogathe and Vincent Carraud, "Les *Essais* de Montaigne dans les archives du Saint-Office." In Jean-Louis Quantin and Jean-Claude Waquet, eds., *Papes, princes et savants dans l'Europe moderne: Mélanges à la mémoire de Bruno Neveu*. Geneva: Droz, 2006, 79–96.

223. "*Et nel primo libro pag. 180: dice che la theologia non insegna ne a ben fare ne a ben pensare.*" *Indice*, *Protocolli* C, f. 346r–347r. Quoted by Peter Godman, *The Saint as Censor: Robert Bellarmine between Inquisition and Index*, op. cit., 339–42: "*In librum sermone Gallico impressum Abourdeaus 1580 auctore Michaele de Montaigne.*"

224. "*Forse risponderà l'autore che quelle dice per ironia burlandosi di Parigini, ma ancor che fosse cosi, quel luogho è molto periculoso, per esser la cosa si brutta et la ironia si nascosta.*"

225. *Essais* 80, II, 3, pp. 31–32. Frame, p. 257.

226. "*Et pag. 32: Approva un detto del buon Marot et lo chiama buono, essendo egli here-tic—questi autori o sono heretici o sono poco boni.*"

227. "*Già dissi che luogo si puo pigl[i]are per ironia, ma non tutti il pigleranno cosi forse.*"

228. As Frank Lestringant remarks ("Montaigne et les protestants." In Philippe Desan, ed., *Montaigne politique*, op. cit., 353–72), the satirical dimension of the *Essais* may also have pleased the first Protestant readers who were versed in this literary genre. On satire in Montaigne, see Ruth Calder, "Montaigne as satirist." *Sixteenth Century Journal*, vol. 17, no 2, 1986, 225–35; Élisabeth Caron, *Les Essais de Montaigne ou les échos satiriques de l'humanisme.* Paris: Éditions CERES, 1993; Jean Balsamo, "Montaigne 'admirable,' les libertins et l'esprit 'satyrique.'" *Montaigne Studies*, vol. 19, 2007, 57–66.

229. "*Et cap. 12: Defende Raymondo Sebondo.*"

230. "*È vero che defende Raymondo Seboni, ma in quel autore non vè altro prohibito che la prefatione.*"

231. *Journal de voyage*, 120. Waters, vol. 2, 140.

232. *Journal de voyage*, 131. Waters, vol. 2, 175–76.

233. *Journal de voyage*, 120. Waters, vol. 2, 176.

234. Jean-Robert Armogathe and Vincent Carraud, "Les *Essais* de Montaigne dans les archives du Saint-Office," art. cit.

235. On the relation between Montaigne and the representatives of the Church during his sojourn in Rome, see Saverio Ricci, *Inquisitori, censori, filosofi sullo scenario della Controriforma.* Rome: Salerno Editrice, 2008, 99–220.

236. On Montaigne's relation to this illness, see Olivier Pot, *L'Inquiétante étrangeté: Montaigne, la pierre, le cannibale, la mélancolie.* Paris: H. Champion, 1993.

237. *Essais* 88, II, 37, f. 337v. Frame, p. 589.

238. Frank Fürberth, "L'essor de la balnéologie dans le monde germanique à la fin du Moyen Âge." In Didier Boisseuil and Marilyn Nicoud, eds., *Séjourner au bain: Le thermalisme entre médecine et société (XIVᵉ–XVIᵉ siècle).* Lyon: Presses de l'université de Lyon, 2010, 99–109. See also Birgit Studt, "Les joies du thermalisme: Nouvelles pratiques thermales et sociabilité dans l'Allemagne de la fin du Moyen Âge," ibid., 113–29.

239. *Essais* 88, II, 37, f. 338r. Frame, p. 590.

240. Matteo Corti, *De balneis omnia quae extant* (Venice, 1553); Gabriele Falloppia, *De medicatis acquis atque de fossilibus* (Venice, 1564); Andrea Bacci, *Discorso delle Acque, bagni di Cesare Augusto a Tivoli* (Rome, 1567); Ventura Minardo, *Compendio delle regole date da diversi eccellentissimi autori intorno ai bagni di Caldiero* (Verona, 1594); William Turner, *A Booke of the nature and properties as well of the bathes in England as of other bathes in Germanye and Italye* (Cologne, 1568). On the importance of the Italian baths in the Renaissance, see Richard Palmer, "'In this our lightye and learned tyme': Italian baths in the era of the Renaissance." *Medical History*, supplement, no. 10, 1990, 14–22.

241. On the baths in Antiquity and in the Middle Ages, see Augustin Cabanès, *La Vie thermale au temps passé.* Paris: A. Michel, 1934; Catherine Gouedo-Thomas, "Le

thermalisme médiéval de Flamenca à Michel de Montaigne." *Villes d'eaux, histoire du thermalisme*. Paris: Éditions du CDHS, 1994, 11–26; Didier Boisseuil, *Le Thermalisme en Toscane à la fin du Moyen Âge: Les bains siennois de la fin du XIIIe siècle au début du XVIe siècle*. Rome: École française de Rome, 2002.

242. *Journal de voyage*, 11. Waters, vol. 1, 52.

243. *Journal de voyage*, 239. Waters, vol. 3, 67–68.

244. *Journal de voyage*, 239. Waters, vol. 3, 68.

245. Xavier Le Person, "Montaigne et les pratiques politiques de son temps." In Philippe Desan, ed., *Montaigne politique*, op. cit., 95–112; and *"Practiques" et "practiqueurs": La vie politique à la fin du règne de Henri III (1584–1589)*. Geneva: Droz, 2002.

246. *Journal de voyage*, 240. Waters, vol. 2, 69.

247. Ibid.

248. *Journal de voyage*, 244. Waters, vol. 2, 80.

249. *Journal de voyage*, 242. Waters, vol. 2, 75.

250. *Journal de voyage*, 274. Waters, vol. 2, 144.

251. Richard Palmer, " 'In this our lightye and learned tyme': Italian baths in the era of the Renaissance." In Roy Porter, ed., *The Medical History of Waters and Spas*. London: Wellcome Institute for the History of Medicine, 1990, 14–22.

252. *Essais* 88, II, 37, f. 337v. Frame, pp. 589–90.

253. *Essais* 88, II, 37, f. 337v. Frame, p. 590.

254. Ibid.

255. Ibid.

256. On the importance of gardens in Montaigne's work, see Philippe Desan, "Montaigne paysagiste." In Dominique de Courcelles, ed., *Éléments naturels et paysages à la Renaissance*. Paris: Études et rencontres de l'École des chartes, 2006, 39–49.

257. Warren Boutcher " 'Le pauvre patient': Montaigne agent dans l'économie du savoir." In Philippe Desan, *Montaigne politique*, op. cit., 243–61.

258. *Journal de voyage*, 243. Waters, vol. 2, 78–79.

259. *Journal de voyage*, 276. Waters, vol. 2, 148.

260. *Journal de voyage*, 276. Waters, vol. 2, 147.

261. On Montaigne's visits to the baths, see Anna Bettoni, Massimo Rinaldi, and Maurizio Rippa Bonati, eds., *Michel de Montaigne e il Termalismo*. Florence: Leo S. Olschki, 2010.

262. Fausta Garavini, "Montaigne e il suo biografo: doppia esposizione." In Massimo Colesanto, ed., *Scritti in onore di G. Macchia*. 2 vols. Milan: Mondadori, 1983, vol. I, 100–113.

263. Concetta Cavallini, *"Cette belle besogne": Étude sur le* Journal *de voyage de Montaigne avec une bibliographie critique*. Fasano; Paris: Schena Editore; Presses de l'Université Paris-Sorbonne, 2005.

264. See "Introduction." In Philippe Desan, ed., *Reproduction fac-similé du Journal du voyage de Michel de Montaigne en Italie et en Allemagne en 1580 et 1581*, op. cit.

265. See Philippe Desan and Carl Frayne, "Données quantitatives sur le *Journal du voyage* de Montaigne." In Philippe Desan, ed., *Montaigne à l'étranger: Voyages avérés, possibles et imaginés*. Paris: Classiques Garnier, 2016, 41–65.

266. *Essais* 88, III, 9, f. 429r. Frame, p. 744.

267. *Journal de voyage*, 309.

268. See Fausta Garavini, "Sull'italiano del *Journal de voyage*." In *Itinerari a Montaigne*. Florence: Sansoni Editore, 1983, 119–32; and Concetta Cavallini, "Giuseppe Bartoli et le *Journal de voyage* de Montaigne." *Studi di Letteratura Francese*, vol. XXVIII, 2003, 19–29.

269. *Essais* 88, III, 5, f. 382v. Frame, p. 685.

270. Craig B. Brush, "La composition de la première partie du *Journal de voyage* de Montaigne." *Revue d'histoire littéraire de la France*, vol. 73, no. 3, 1971, 369–84; id., "The secretary, again." *Montaigne Studies*, vol. V, 1993, 113–38; George Hoffmann, *Montaigne's Career*, op. cit., 39–62; Richard Keatley, "Le statut du valet dans le *Journal du voyage de M. de Montaigne en Italie, par la Suisse et l'Allemagne en 1580 et 1581*. L'édition B de Querlon." Master's thesis, Université Paris-Sorbonne, 1997, 8–32.

271. Concetta Cavallini, "Le tourisme religieux en Italie dans la deuxième moitié du XVIᵉ siècle: Montaigne et les Français à Lorette." In Philippe Desan and Giovanni Dotoli, eds., *D'un siècle à l'autre: Littérature et société de 1590 à 1610*. Fasano; Paris: Schena Editore; Presses de l'université Paris-Sorbonne, 2001, 133–52.

272. *Essais* 88, III, 13, f. 477v. Frame, p. 826.

273. Gabriel Chappuys, *L'Art des Secretaires*. Paris: Abel L'Angelier, 1588, f. 17v. See Patrick Mula, "De Venise à Paris: *L'Art des Secretaires* de Gabriel Chappuys entre traduction et création." In *La Lettre, le Secrétaire, le Lettré: De Venise à la cour de Henri III, Francesco Sansovino—Gabriel Chappuys*. Grenoble: HURBI, Filigrana, no. 6, 2000–2001, 115–82.

274. Gabriel Chappuys, op. cit., f. 1r.

275. Ibid., f. 4r.

Chapter 8. "Messieurs of Bordeaux Elected Me Mayor of Their City" (1581–1585)

1. *Essais* 88, III, 10, f. 444r. Frame, p. 768.

2. *Journal de voyage*, 275–76. Waters, vol. 3, 146.

3. *Journal de voyage*, 274. Waters, vol. 3, 143.

4. *Journal de voyage*, 284. Waters, vol. 3, 167.

5. Letter from Henry III, July 2, 1577. In *Lettres de Henri III roi de France*, vol. III, 309–10, no. 2540.

6. Ibid., 314–15, no. 2553.

7. Jean-Pierre Levraud, "La lieue de Montaigne." *Bulletin de la Société des amis de Montaigne*, no. 15–16, 1999, 99–122.

8. On this banker originally from Lucca, see Émile Picot, *Les Italiens en France au XVIᵉ siècle*. Bordeaux: Feret et fils, 1901, 133–34.

9. *Journal de voyage*, 228. Waters, vol. 3, 198–99. See Marcel Françon, "Remarques

sur l'itinéraire d'Italie adopté par Montaigne." *Romance Notes*, vol. IX, 1966–67, 299–301.

10. On this incident, see Lauro-Aimé Colliard, "Le thème du duel chez Montaigne: L'affaire Mattecoulon." *Montaigne Studies*, vol. XV, 2003, 159–68; id., "Montaigne et l'affaire Mattecoulon: Dernières trouvailles." *Montaigne Studies*, vol. XIX, 2007, 213–24.

11. This letter, discovered by Jean Alexandre Buchon in the Bordeaux archives, was first published in 1841 in his notice on *Chronique des comtes de Foix en langue béarnaise* (*Choix de chroniques et mémoires sur l'histoire de France*. Paris: Le Panthéon littéraire, 1841). It is also found in Paul Bonnefon, *Montaigne et ses amis: La Boétie, Charron, Mlle de Gournay*. 2 vols. Paris: A. Colin, 1898, vol. II, 45–46.

12. Henri de Mesmes, *Mémoires inédits*. Paris: E. Leroux, 1886, 185–86.

13. *Registre secret de la cour du parlement de Bordeaux commençant le douzième de novembre 1580 et finissant en décembre 1613*. Bibliothèque municipale de Bordeaux, ms. 369 (5), f. 219v.

14. Ibid., f. 221v.

15. *Anciens et nouveaux statuts de la ville et cité de Bourdeaus. Esquels sont contenues les Ordonnances requises pour la police de ladicte ville, & de tous les estats & maistrises d'icelle*. Bordeaux: S. Millanges, 1612, 5.

16. Letters to the jurats from Montaigne, May 21, 1583. In *Lettres de Montaigne*, 670.

17. We have only one copy (Harvard University) of the book of poetry by De Thou printed "as a trial" (*à l'essai*) by Millanges. In a letter dated May 1, 1583, and addressed to Pierre Pithou, De Thou indicates that only a few copies were printed and then sent to a handful of friends in order to receive their commentaries before a more official publication (see Samuel Kinser, *The Works of Jacques-Auguste de Thou*. The Hague: M. Nijhoff, 1966, 206–7).

18. On the political specificity of this edition, see the introduction to my photographic reproduction of the 1582 edition, *Reproduction fac-similé de l'édition de 1582 des* Essais *de Montaigne*, ed. Philippe Desan. Paris: Société des Textes Français Modernes, 2005.

19. François de La Croix du Maine, *Premier volume de la bibliotheque du sieur de La Croix du Maine*. Paris: Abel L'Angelier, 1584, 328–29.

20. See the works by Guillaume Rouillé, *Promptuarium inconum insigniorum e seculo Hominum, Promptuaire des médailles, huit cent portraits de personnages célèbres de l'antiquité à l'époque de François I gravures sur bois* (Lyon, 1553); Hubert Goltzius, *Les Images presque de tous les empereurs* (Antwerp, 1557); Théodore de Bèze, *Les Vrais Portraits des hommes illustres* (Paris, 1581); André Thevet, *Vrais Pourtraits et vies des hommes illustres grecz, latins et payens, recueilliz de leurs tableaux, livres médailles antiques et modernes* (Paris, 1584); Jacques de Bie, *Les Vrais Portrais des rois de France* (Paris, 1634); and also the series of engravings better known as the *Chronologie collée*, which appeared in 1628 and consisted of about five hundred portraits.

21. A systematic inventory of the variants from the 1580 and 1582 editions was carried out by Reinhold Dezeimeris and H. Barckhausen in their critical edition of

the *Essais* of 1580, 1582, and 1587. It is also found in the most recent Pléiade edition of Montaigne's works. See the studies by Marcel Françon and, more recently, Concetta Cavallini, *L'Italianisme de Michel de Montaigne*. Fasano; Paris: Schena Editore; Presses de l'Université Paris-Sorbonne, 2003.

22. *Archives historiques du département de la Gironde*, vol. VI, 1864, no. VI, June 12, 1582, 9.

23. François Moureau, "Sur des exemplaires des *Essais* en vente à la Foire de Francfort (automne 1581)." *Bulletin de la Société des amis de Montaigne*, no. 9, 1974, 57–59.

24. *Essais* 88, II, 17, f. 278r. Frame, p. 493.

25. This point has already been stressed—perhaps with some exaggeration—by Marcel Françon, for whom the 1582 edition "testifies, above all, to the influence of Montaigne's journey to Italy and to his desire to conform to the principles of the Catholic religion, while at the same time retaining a certain freedom of literary expression." *Pour une édition critique des* Essais. Cambridge, MA: Schoenhof's Foreign Books, 1965, 49.

26. *Essais* 82, I, 56, pp. 296–97. Frame, p. 229.

27. *Essais* 88, II, 12, f. 240r. Frame, p. 428.

28. Alain Legros, "Édition de 1582." In Philippe Desan, ed., *Dictionnaire de Michel de Montaigne*. Paris: H. Champion, 2007, 303.

29. On Montaigne's encounter with Tasso, see Jean Balsamo, "Montaigne et le 'saut' du Tasse." *Rivista di Letterature moderne e comparate*, vol. 54, fasc. 4, 2001, 389–407.

30. *Essais* 82, II, 12, p. 495. Frame, p. 363.

31. *Essais* 82, I, 49, p. 279. Frame, p. 217.

32. As Concetta Cavallini (*L'Italianisme de Michel de Montaigne*, op. cit., p. 227) observes, the anecdotes about Italy in the 1582 edition concern mainly contemporary history.

33. See Alexander H. Schutz, *Vernacular Books in Parisian Private Libraries of the Sixteenth Century According to the Notarial Inventories*. Chapel Hill: University of North Carolina Press, 1955.

34. Richard Sayce and David Maskell (*A Descriptive Bibliography of Montaigne's* Essais *1580–1700*. London: The Bibliographic Society, 1983) list thirty-eight copies of the 1580 edition in public collections and only twenty-three of the 1582 edition. However, these figures do not necessarily reflect the print runs for these editions. See also Philippe Desan, *Bibliotheca Desaniana: Catalogue Montaigne*. Paris: Classiques Garnier, 2011, 39.

35. Montaigne's four years as mayor of Bordeaux have been studied by Anne-Marie Cocula, *Montaigne: Les années politiques*. Bordeaux: Confluences, 2011.

36. Christian Taillard, *Bordeaux à l'âge classique*. Bordeaux: Mollat, 1997.

37. Richard Cooper, "Montaigne dans l'entourage du maréchal de Matignon." *Montaigne Studies*, vol. XIII, 2001, 99–140.

38. Roger Trinquet, "Montaigne et le maréchal de Matignon." *Bulletin de la Société des amis de Montaigne*, no. 14–15, 1975, 11–34.

39. Letter to Matignon from Montaigne, February 2, 1585. In *Lettres de Montaigne*, 687.

40. Brantôme, *Hommes illustres et grands capitaines françois*. In *Œuvres complètes de Pierre de Bourdeille, abbé séculier de Brantôme*. Paris: Auguste Desrez, 1839, 529.

41. *Journal de François de Syrueilh*. In *Archives historiques du département de la Gironde*, vol. XIII, 1871–72, no. CIII, 340.

42. The map of Bordeaux reproduced here was published in George Braun and Frans Hogenberg, *Civitates Orbis Terrarum*, 6 vols., 1572–1617. On the topography of Bordeaux in Montaigne's time, see Marc Favreau, *Les "Portraits" de Bordeaux: Vues et plans gravés de la capitale de la Guyenne du XVIe au XVIIIe siècle*. Camiac-et-Saint-Denis: Éditions de l'Entre-deux-Mers, 2007.

43. Philip Benedict, "French Cities from the Sixteenth Century to the Revolution: An Overview." In Philip Benedict, ed., *Cities and Social Change in Early Modern France*, London: Unwin Hyman, 1989, 7–64.

44. Document reproduced by Grégory Champeaud, *Le Parlement de Bordeaux et les Paix de religion (1563–1600)*. Bordeaux: Éditions d'Albret, 2008. Letter from the first president of the parlement, Benoist de Lagebaston.

45. *Archives historiques du département de la Gironde*, vol. XIV, 1873, no, XCVI, 154–56.

46. Jean Darnal, *Supplement des chroniques de la Noble Ville & Cité de Bourdeaux*. Bordeaux: Jacques Mongiron Millanges, 1666, 16.

47. *Anciens et nouveaux statuts de la ville et cité de Bourdeaus*, op. cit., 3.

48. *Livre des Privilèges*. Bordeaux: Imprimerie G. Gounouilhou, 1878, no. XIX, June 1556, 121–22.

49. Ibid., no. XXII, April 22, 1558, 133–36.

50. *Archives historiques du département de la Gironde*. vol. VIII, 1866, no. LXXXI, 245.

51. *Essais* 88, III, 10, f. 447v. Frame, p. 774. [English trans. modified.]

52. Gabriel de Lurbe, *Chronique bourdeloise*. Bordeaux: Simon Millanges, 1619, 47. On Gabriel de Lurbe, see Catherine Magnien, "Un Bordelais convaincu: Le procureur syndic Gabriel de Lurbe (1538–1613)." In Jean Mondot and Philippe Loupès, eds., *Provinciales: Hommage à Anne-Marie Cocula*. 2 vols. Bordeaux: Presses Universitaires de Bordeaux, 2009, vol. II, 857–67.

53. *Essais* 88, III, 10, f. 444r. Frame, p. 768.

54. Laurent Coste, "Les jurats de Bordeaux et Montaigne (1581–1585)." *Nouveau bulletin de la Société internationale des amis de Montaigne*, no. 2, 2008, 301–23.

55. Laurent Coste, *Messieurs de Bordeaux: Pouvoirs et hommes de pouvoirs à l'Hôtel de Ville 1548–1789*. Bordeaux: Fédération historique du Sud-Ouest, 2006.

56. Laurent Coste, "Les jurats de Bordeaux et Montaigne," art. cit., 310.

57. *Anciens et nouveaux statuts de la ville de Bourdeaus*, op. cit., 41.

58. Ibid., 105.

59. *Livre des Privilèges*, op. cit., no. XXIX, June 1565, 168–80.

60. Ibid., no. XXX, December 26, 1576, 181–85.

61. *Anciens et nouveaux statuts de la ville et cité de Bourdeaus*, op. cit., 143.

62. *Privilèges des Bourgeois de la ville et cité de Bourdeaux, octroyez et approuvez par les*

Rois Tres-Chrestiens, Henry II, Charles IX, Henry III, Henry IV & Louys XIII d'heureuse memoire. Avec les Sentences & Arrests, par lesquels est ordonné que lesdits Bourgeois peuvent tenir franc-fiefs, toutes Terres Nobles & de franc alleu, sans estre tenus d'en payer aucune chose. Bordeaux: Jacques Mongiron Millanges, 1667.

63. *Archives historiques du département de la Gironde*, vol. III, 1861, no. LXXXI, 203–4.

64. Ibid., no. LXXXII, 204–5.

65. Ibid., vol. VIII, 1866, no. CXIII, 336–37.

66. *Privilèges des Bourgeois de la ville et cité de Bourdeaux*, op. cit., 17.

67. *Livre des Privilèges, op. cit.*, no. XI, July 2, 1551, 75.

68. Ibid., no. XV, June 11, 1554, 100.

69. Letter to Matignon, from Bordeaux, October, 30, 1582. In *Lettres de Montaigne*, 668.

70. Pierre Damas, *Histoire de la juridiction consulaire de Bordeaux.* Paris: Delmas, 1947, 82.

71. *Livre des Privilèges*, op. cit., no. XL, August 6, 1581, 227–31.

72. Ibid., no. VII, August 1550, 59.

73. Letter to Matignon from Montaigne, February 9, 1585. In *Lettres de Montaigne*, 692.

74. *Articles proposez et mis en avant en l'assemblee & Conference faicte au lieu de Flex pres la ville Saincte-Foy, entre Monsieur le Duc d'Anjou, Frere unicque du Roy, en vertu du pouvoir que sa Majesté luy a donné, & le Roy de Navarre, siisté des deputez de la Religion pretendue reformee.* Lyon: Jean Pillehotte, 1581.

75. This edict was transcribed at the beginning of the Registers of the chamber of justice established in Bordeaux in 1582 (*Registre de l'audience de la Chambre de Justice et Registre du Conseil*), a manuscript held at the Bordeaux municipal library. The text was reproduced by Émile Brives-Cazes, *Le Parlement de Bordeaux et la Chambre de justice de Guyenne en 1582.* Bordeaux: G. Gounouilhou, 1887.

76. On the chamber of justice of Guyenne established by the king in 1582, see Émile Brives-Cazes, *Le Parlement de Bordeaux et la Chambre de justice de Guyenne en 1582,* op. cit.; id., *La Chambre de justice de Guyenne en 1583–1584.* Bordeaux: G. Gounouilhou, 1874.

77. Jacques-Auguste de Thou, *La Vie de Jacques-Auguste de Thou,* éd. Anne Teissier-Ensminger. Paris: H. Champion, 2007, 415.

78. *Archives historiques du département de la Gironde*, vol. XLI, 1906, no. XXXVIII, January 17, 1582, 73.

79. *Articles proposez et mis en avant en l'assemblée & Conference faicte au lieu de Flex pres la ville Saincte-Foy*, op. cit.

80. *Essais* 88, III, 10, f. 451v. Frame, p. 781.

81. *Journal de François de Syrueilh*, op. cit., 341.

82. This dedication was transcribed by Dr. Payen, *Bulletin du bibliophile*, 1855, 398–400. See Catherine Magnien-Simonin, "Loisel, Antoine." In Philippe Desan, ed., *Dictionnaire de Michel de Montaigne.* Paris: H. Champion, 2007, 696–97.

83. *Journal de François de Syrueilh*, op. cit., 342.

84. Remonstrances June 9, 1582, Archives municipales de Bordeaux.

85. *Archives de la Commission des monuments historiques*, 1855, 40.

86. George Hoffmann, "Le roi 'débonnaire': Duplessis-Mornay, Montaigne et l'image de Henri de Navarre en 1583–1584." In Philippe Desan, ed., *Montaigne politique*. Paris: H. Champion, 2006, 289–304.

87. *Statuts de la ville de Bordeaux*, op. cit., 146–50.

88. *Archives historiques du département de la Gironde*, vol. XIII, 1871–72, no. CIII, 343. For a detailed account of this trial, see Émile Brives-Cazes, *Le Parlement de Bordeaux et la Chambre de justice de Guyenne en 1582*, op. cit.

89. De Thou, *Mémoires*, op. cit., 174–75.

90. Letter from Henry III to Henry of Navarre, November 23, 1582, reproduced in *Bulletin de la Société historique du Périgord*, vol. XXIX, 1902, 164–69.

91. *Essais* 88, III, 1, f. 344v. Frame, p. 601.

92. *Journal de François de Syrueilh*, op. cit., 347.

93. Ibid., 348.

94. *Anciens et nouveaux statuts de la ville et cité de Bourdeaus*, op. cit., 134.

95. Ibid., 107.

96. Ibid., 315.

97. Sentence issued by the jurade, quoted by Alphonse Grün, *La Vie publique de Michel Montaigne*. Paris: Librairie d'Amyot, 1855, 267.

98. *Essais* 80, I, 39, p. 366. Frame, p. 177.

99. Jean Darnal, *Supplément des chroniques de la Noble Ville & Cité de Bourdeaux*, op. cit., 94.

100. *Essais* EB, III, 10, f. 446v. Frame, p. 773.

101. *Essais* EB, III, 11, f. 461v. Frame, p. 784.

102. Xavier Védère, "Deux ennemis de Montaigne, le sénéchal Merville et le capitaine Vaillac." *Revue historique de Bordeaux*, vol. 36, 1943, 88–97; and Roger Trinquet, "La réélection de Montaigne à la mairie de Bordeaux en 1583." *Bulletin de la Société des amis de Montaigne*, no. 10–11, 1974, 17–35.

103. *Essais* 88, III, 10, f. 451r. Frame, p. 781.

104. *Mémoire présenté à Monsieur Matignon, par les Maires et Jurats de Bordeaux au sujet du droit qu'avait la ville de placer des sentinelles du côté des châteaux et fortifications*. BNF, collection Payen, no. 690. Text reproduced by Roger Trinquet, "La réélection de Montaigne à la mairie de Bordeaux en 1583," art. cit., 36–38.

105. *Mémoire des gouverneurs des châteaux du Hâ et Trompette en réponse aux Remontrances faites par le Maire et les jurats de Bordeaux, contre leurs prétendues entreprises*. Archives municipales de Bordeaux, DD4, padouens, text reproduced in Roger Trinquet, art. cit., 38–43.

106. Agnès Marcetteau-Paul, *Montaigne propriétaire foncier: Inventaire raisonné du Terrier de Montaigne conservé à la Bibliothèque municipale de Bordeaux*. Paris: H. Champion, 1995.

107. *Mémoire des gouverneurs des châteaux du Hâ et Trompette*, op. cit., 39.

108. *Mémoire des Maires et Jurats de Bordeaux adressé au Maréchal de Matignon, pour se plaindre des entreprises des Gouverneurs des Châteaux du Hâ et Trompette sur les privileges de la Ville*. Archives municipales de Bordeaux, DD4, padouens, in Roger

Trinquet, "La réélection de Montaigne à la mairie de Bordeaux en 1583," art. cit., 44.

109. *Archives historiques du département de la Gironde*, vol. XIX, 1879, no. CXIII, 270–71; Francis Loirette, "Un transport de vin pour le compte de Montaigne en 1588." *Société archéologique de Bordeaux: Bulletin et Mémoire*, vol. LXVI, 1965–70, *Groupe Jules Delpit*, vol. III, 43–44.

110. BNF, ms. fr. 3357, f. 3v. Letter reproduced by Paul Bonnefon, *Montaigne: L'homme et l'œuvre*. Bordeaux; Paris: G. Gounouilhou; J. Rouam, 1893, 329–30.

111. Jean Darnal, *Supplement des chroniques de la Noble Ville & Cité de Bourdeaux*, op. cit., 52.

112. Gilles André de Laroque, *Traité de la noblesse*. Paris: E. Michallet, 1678, chap. 39.

113. *Privilèges de la ville de Bordeaux*. In *Privileges des Bourgeois de la ville et cité de Bourdeaux*, op. cit., 17.

114. *Essais* 88, III, 10, f. 444r. Frame, p. 768.

115. Archives municipales de Bordeaux, série FF, liasse 12, transcribed by Xavier Védère. In *Archives historiques du département de la Gironde*, new series, vol. 1, 1933–36, 63–64.

116. Ruling of the Council of State, reproduced by Alphonse Grün, *La Vie publique de Michel Montaigne*, op. cit., 256–57.

117. Ibid., 258–60.

118. Machiavelli, *The Prince*, trans. James B. Atkinson, Indianapolis: Bobbs-Merrill, 1976, chap. XXV, 365.

119. According to the *Coustumier de Guyenne*, called *Rolle de la ville de Bourdeaux: Contenant partie des privilèges, franchises, lois, moeurs et forme de vivre des Anciens Bordelais; Sur lequel la coustume réformée en l'an 1520 a été extraite. Taken from L'Estude de Messire Michel de Montaigne, autheur des essais..., par Monsieur Estienne Cleirac*, discovered in the University of Bordeaux's law library by André Tournon and quoted by Géralde Nakam, "Michel de Montaigne maire de Bordeaux: À la mairie et dans les *Essais*." *Bulletin de la Société des amis de Montaigne*, no. 13–14, 1983, 17.

120. *Remontrance de la jurade de Bordeaux, adressée au roi*, 1583. This remonstrance was discovered by the city of Bordeaux's archivist, M. d'Etcheverry, and published by Jules Delpit in the *Courrier de la Gironde* on January 21, 1856. Cited by Jean-François Payen, *Documents inédits ou peu connus sur Montaigne*. Paris: Techener, 1856, 60.

121. Ibid., 58.

122. Ibid., 59.

123. Ibid., 58–59.

124. Ibid., 59.

125. Ibid.

126. Ibid., 60.

127. Ibid.

128. Gustave Labat, *Documents sur la ville de Royan et la Tour de Cordouan*. Bordeaux: G. Gounouilhou, 1884.

129. Robert Boutruche, ed., *Bordeaux de 1453 à 1715*. Bordeaux: Fédération historique du Sud-Ouest, 1966, 138.

130. *Archives historiques du département de la Gironde*, vol. X, 1868, no. CLXXXVI, August 15, 1583, 399–401.

131. Roger Trinquet, "Quand Montaigne défendait les privilèges des vins de Bordeaux." *Revue historique de Bordeaux et du département de la Gironde*, 1956, 263–66.

132. *Anciens et nouveaux statuts de la ville et cité de Bourdeaus*, op. cit., 179.

133. Ibid., p. 186.

134. Archives départementales de la Gironde, série E. Notaires, Delaville no. 173.8. Document reproduced in *Archives historiques du département de la Gironde*, vol. XII, 1870, no. CXLVII, 369–72. See Philippe Desan, *Portraits à l'essai: Iconographie de Montaigne*. Paris: H. Champion, 2007, 38–39.

135. *Anciens et nouveaux statuts de la ville et cité de Bourdeaus*, op. cit., 121.

136. Roger Trinquet, "Quand Montaigne défendait les privilèges des vins de Bordeaux," art. cit.

137. Letter to the jurats from Montaigne, December 10, 1584. In *Lettres de Montaigne*, 681.

138. Alexandre Nicolaï, *Les Belles Amies de Montaigne*. Paris: Éditions Dumas, 1950.

139. *Essais* 80, I, 29, p. 277. Frame, p. 145.

140. Jean Balsamo, "Montaigne, le 'sieur de Poiferré' et la comtesse de Guiche: Documents nouveaux." *Montaigne Studies*, vol. XVI, 2004, 75–91.

141. *Éphéméride*, December 19, 92.

142. Anne-Marie Cocula, "Henri de Navarre et la noblesse de Guyenne (1576–1589)." In Jean-Pierre Poussou, Roger Baury, and Marie-Catherine Vignal-Souleyrou, eds., *Monarchies, noblesses et diplomaties européennes: Mélanges en l'honneur de Jean-François Labourdette*. Paris: Presses de l'université Paris-Sorbonne, 2005, 405–20.

143. *Essais* 88, III, 1, f. 345r. Frame, p. 600.

144. Letter to the jurats from Montaigne, February 8, 1585. In *Lettres de Montaigne*, 689.

145. Charlotte Duplessis-Mornay, *Les Mémoires de Madame de Mornay*, éd. Nadine Kuperty-Tsur. Paris: H. Champion, 2010, 178.

146. Letter to Matignon from Montaigne, January 18, 1585. In *Lettres de Montaigne*, 683.

147. Letter to Matignon from Montaigne, February 9, 1585. Ibid., 691.

148. Nicolas Le Roux, "Les négociateurs royaux en France pendant les guerres de Religion." In Heinz Duchhardt and Patrice Veit, eds., *Guerre et Paix du Moyen Âge aux Temps modernes. Théorie—Pratiques—Représentations*. Mainz: Philipp von Zabern, 2000, 119–36.

149. Hugues Daussy, *Les Huguenots et le Roi: Le combat politique de Philippe Duplessis-Mornay (1572–1600)*. Geneva: Droz, 2002.

150. Hugues Daussy, "Montaigne et Duplessis-Mornay: Les mystères d'une correspondance." *Montaigne Studies*, vol. XVIII, 2006, 169–82.

151. Bibliothèque de la Sorbonne, ms. 362, f. 1v (copy). Cited by Hugues Daussy, ibid., 179.

152. Ibid., letter of November 25, 1583, 178.

153. Ibid., letter of December 31, 1583, 181.

154. Ibid., letter of January 25, 1584, 182.

155. Letter published by Jean-François Payen, *Nouveaux documents inédits ou peu connus sur Montaigne.* Paris: Jannet, 1850, 49–50.

156. *Archives historiques du département de la Gironde*, vol. XV, 1874, no. LXXI, September 13, 1584, 261–62.

157. Letter to Matignon from Montaigne, January 18, 1585. In *Lettres de Montaigne*, 683.

158. On la Belle Corisande, see Raymond Ritter, *Cette grande Corisande.* Paris: Albin Michel, 1936.

159. *Essais* 88, I, 24, f. 48r. Frame, p. 96.

160. Letter to Matignon from Bordeaux, May 27, 1585. In *Lettres de Montaigne*, 706.

161. *Anciens et nouveaux statuts de la ville et cité de Bordeaux*, op. cit., 136.

162. Catherine Magnien-Simonin, "'Des senteurs' (*Essais*, I, 55): Un chapitre exemplaire, délaissé par la critique." In Philippe Desan, ed., *Les Chapitres oubliés des Essais de Montaigne.* Paris: H. Champion, 2011, 167–79.

163. Letter to the jurats from Libourne, July 30, 1585. In *Lettres de Montaigne*, 709.

164. *Essais* 88, III, 9, f. 426r. Frame, p. 738.

165. Jean-Louis Guez de Balzac, "Entretien 18." In *Les Entretiens* [1654]. Paris: M. Didier, 1972, 293.

166. *Essais* 88, III, 10, f. 451r. Frame, p. 781.

167. Ibid.

168. Letter to Matignon from Montaigne, July 12, 1584. In *Lettres de Montaigne*, 677–78.

169. This has been pointed out by Anne-Marie Cocula, "Le rôle politique de Montaigne, maire de Bordeaux (1581–1585), en faveur du rétablissement de la paix civile." *Revue française d'histoire du livre*, no. 78–79, 1993, 155–62.

170. *Essais* 88, III, 10, f. 451v. Frame, p. 781.

171. *Essais* 88, III, 10, f. 443r. Frame, p. 766.

172. *Essais* 88, III, 10, f. 443r. Frame, p. 767.

173. *Essais* 88, III, 10, f. 445r. Frame, p. 769.

174. *Essais* 88, III, 10, f. 447v. Frame, p. 774.

175. *Essais* 88, III, 10, f. 443v. Frame, p. 767.

176. Ibid.

177. *Essais* 88, III, 10, f. 444v. Frame, p. 768.

178. *Essais* 88, III, 10, f. 445v. Frame, p. 770.

179. Ibid.

180. *Essais* 88, III, 10, f. 447r. Frame, p. 773.

181. Ibid.

182. Ibid.

183. *Essais* 80, II, 17, p. 459. Frame, p. 497.

184. *Essais* 88, III, 9, f. 419v. Frame, p. 727.

185. Ibid.

186. *Essais* 88, III, 10, f. 450v. Frame, p. 780.
187. *Essais* 88, III, 10, f. 452v. Frame, p. 783.
188. *Essais* EB, III, 10, f. 445v. Frame, p. 770.
189. *Essais* 88, III, 10, f. 453r. Frame, p. 783.
190. *Essais* 88, III, 12, f. 461r. Frame, p. 796.
191. Ibid.
192. *Essais* 88, III, 2, f. 355r–v. Frame, pp. 617–8.
193. *Essais* 80, II, 8, p. 66. Frame, p. 278.

Chapter 9. "Benignity of the Great" and "Public Ruin" (1585–1588)

1. Pierre de L'Estoile, *Registre-journal du règne de Henri III*, ed. Madeleine Lazard and Gilbert Schrenck. Vol. V (1585–1587). Geneva: Droz, 2001.
2. François Racine de Villegomblain, *Les Memoires des troubles arrivez en France, sous les regnes des roys, Charles IX, Henry III & Henry IV: Avec les voyages des sieurs de Mayenne & de Joyeuse au Levant & en Poictou. Par Monsieur de Villegomblain.* Paris: Guillaume de Luyne, 1598, vol. II, 2.
3. *Essais* EB, III, 13, f. 476v. Frame, p. 825.
4. Nicolas Le Roux, *Un régicide au nom de Dieu: L'assassinat de Henri III*. Paris: Gallimard, 2006, 41.
5. Denis Crouzet, *Le Haut Cœur de Catherine de Médicis: Une raison politique aux temps de la Saint-Barthélemy*. Paris: Albin Michel, 2005.
6. Nicolas Le Roux, "Servir un roi méconnaissable: Les incertitudes de la noblesse au temps de Montaigne." In Philippe Desan, ed., *Montaigne politique*. Paris: H. Champion, 2006, 155–74.
7. *Essais* 80, I, 27, p. 249. Frame, p. 134.
8. *Essais* 80, II, 6, p. 49. Frame, p. 268.
9. Alphonse Grün, *La Vie publique de Michel Montaigne: Étude biographique*. Paris: Librairie d'Amyot, 1855, 359.
10. *Essais* 88, III, 9, f. 425v. Frame, p. 737.
11. Brantôme, *Grands Capitaines*, éd. Lalanne. Vol. V, 163.
12. Ibid., 168.
13. See Duplessis-Mornay, *Fidelle Exposition sur la declaration du duc de Mayenne tenant les exploicts de guerre qu'il a fait en Guyenne*. La Rochelle: Jérôme Haultin, 1587.
14. René de Lucinge, *Lettres sur les débuts de la Ligue, 1585*, ed. Alain Dufour. Geneva: Droz, 1964, 24 (March 25, 1585).
15. BNF, ms. fr. 5045, f. 185–186 (memoir on the principal lords following the king, the king of Navarre, and the duke of Mayenne). Cited in Nicolas Le Roux, *Un régicide au nom de Dieu. L'assassinat de Henri III*, op. cit., 194.
16. *Essais* 88, III, 9, f. 439r. Frame, p. 760. On this point see the analysis by James J. Supple, "Montaigne and the French Catholic League." *Montaigne Studies*, vol. IV, 1992, 111–26.

17. Jean-Marie Constant, "La noblesse protestante en France pendant les guerres de religion," *La Noblesse en liberté (XVIe–XVIIe siècles)*. Rennes: Presses Universitaires de Rennes, 2004, 201.

18. Jean-Marie Constant, "Les barons français pendant les guerres de religion," *La Noblesse en liberté (XVIe–XVIIe siècles)*, ibid., 103–13.

19. Janine Garrisson-Estèbe, *Protestants du Midi, 1559–1598*. Toulouse: Privat, 1980. On the genesis of the Reformation in France, see Denis Crouzet, *Genèse de la réforme française (1520–1562)*. Paris: SEDES, 1996; and Arlette Jouanna, *Le Devoir de révolte: La noblesse française et la gestation de l'État moderne, 1559–1661*. Paris: Fayard, 1989. For the southwest of France, see Edmond Cabié, *Guerres de Religion dans le sud-ouest de la France et principalement dans le Quercy*. Paris: Champion, 1906.

20. *Essais* 88, III, 1, f. 345v. Frame, p. 601.

21. René de Lucinge, *Lettres sur la cour de Henri III en 1586*, ed. Alain Dufour. Geneva: Droz, 1966, 104, Paris, March 13, 1586.

22. *Essais* 88, III, 7, f. 403v. Frame, p. 700.

23. *Ibid.*

24. *Essais* EB, II, 10, f. 173v. Frame, p. 303.

25. Transcript given by Alain Legros, *Montaigne manuscrit*. Paris: Classiques Garnier, 2010, 623.

26. See Jean Balsamo, "Des *Essais* pour comprendre les guerres civiles." *Bibliothèque d'Humanisme et Renaissance*, vol. LXXII, no. 3, 2010, 521–40.

27. *Essais* 88, III, 9, f. 416v. Frame, p. 722.

28. *Essais* 88, III, 9, f. 462r. Frame, p. 798.

29. Ibid.

30. *Essais* 88, III, 12, f. 462r. Frame, p. 799.

31. *Essais* 88, III, 12, f. 468v. Frame, p. 812.

32. *Essais* 88, III, 12, f. 469r. Frame, p. 813.

33. *Essais* 88, III, 12, f. 469v. Frame, p. 814.

34. *Essais* 88, III, 12, f. 469r. Frame, p. 813.

35. Ibid.

36. Ibid.

37. Ibid.

38. *Essais* 88, III, 12, f. 461v. Frame, p. 796.

39. *Essais* 88, III, 9, f. 425v. Frame, p. 737.

40. *Essais* 88, III, 9, f. 421r–v. Frame, p. 730.

41. Denis Crouzet has analyzed this concept of "political necessity" in the time of Montaigne; see *Le Haut Cœur de Catherine de Médicis*, op. cit.

42. Roger Trinquet, "Aperçus généraux sur l'attitude politique de Montaigne après la Mairie de Bordeaux (1585–1592)." *Bulletin de la Société des amis de Montaigne*, no. 11, 1967, 3–22.

43. *Essais* 88, III, 12, f. 461v. Frame, p. 796.

44. *Essais* 88, III, 12, f. 463r. Frame, p. 801.

45. *Essais* 88, III, 12, f. 463v. Frame, pp. 801–2.

46. *Essais* 88, III, 12, f. 463v. Frame, p. 802.

47. Pierre de L'Estoile, *Registre-journal du règne de Henri III*. Vol. V, op. cit., 201.

48. *Essais* 88, III, 9, f. 425v–426r. Frame, p. 738.

49. *Essais* 88, III, 12, f. 462r–v. Frame, p. 799.

50. *Essais* EB, II, 8, f. 163r. Frame, p. 285.

51. Alan M. Boase, "Montaigne annoté par Florimond de Raemond." *Revue du seizième siècle*, vol. XV, 1928, 253–54.

52. Guy de Brémond d'Ars, "Les conférences de Saint-Brice entre Henri de Navarre et Catherine de Médicis, 1586–1587." *Revue des questions historiques*, vol. XXXVI, 1884, 496–523.

53. Sully, *Mémoires des sages et royales oeconomies d'estat, domestiques, politiques et militaires*. In *Collection des Memoires relatifs à l'histoire de France*, ed. M. Petitot. Paris: Foucault, 1820, vol. I, 58.

54. Letter of December 13, "Au roy monsieur mon fils." In *Lettres de Catherine de Médicis*, ed. Gustave de Puchesse. Paris: Imprimerie nationale, 1880–1909, vol. IX, 115.

55. Ibid., 132.

56. BNF, Nouvelles acquisitions françaises, no. 9175, f. 379; and ms. fr. 7854, f. 13–36.

57. *Lettres de Catherine de Médicis*, op. cit., vol. II, 46, 90, and 95. Jean-François Payen had a document signed by François Montaigne and dated 1572. In 1851, Lucas Montigny had two documents written by this secretary dated 1574. Cf. *Documents inédits ou peu connus sur Montaigne*, 1856, vol. IV, 10.

58. *État des gages des domestiques de la Reine mère [Catherine de Médicis], 1585, distribution des sommes laissées par la Reine à ses domestiques par testament, 1589*. Archives nationales, série K, monuments historiques, Comptes, K502; and *Maison de Catherine de Médicis, 1579–1585*, K388–423.

59. Donald M. Frame, *Montaigne: A Biography*. New York: Harcourt, Brace and World, 1965, 268.

60. For complete information on this document and why it might in fact refer to Michel de Montaigne, see Roger Trinquet, "Du nouveau dans la biographie de Montaigne." *Revue d'histoire littéraire de la France*, vol. LIV, 1953, 1–22. More recently, and after Donald Frame, Amy Graves has adopted Trinquet's arguments and shown that it was probably Montaigne and not one of Catherine de Medici's secretaries who bore the same name: "Crise d'engagement: Montaigne et la Ligue." In *Montaigne politique*, op. cit., 340–41.

61. *Lettres de Catherine de Médicis*, op. cit., vol. II, 131.

62. Ibid., vol. IX, 176.

63. Letter from Henry III to Catherine de Medici (late January 1587). In *Lettres de Henri III roi de France*, ed. Pierre Champion et Michel François. Paris: Klincksieck, 1984, vol. IX, 436.

64. *Lettres de Montaigne*. Letter from Montaigne to Matignon, June 12, 1587, p. 712.

65. On the importance of this Protestant victory, see Antoine de Lévis-Mirepoix,

"Montaigne et le secret de Coutras." *Revue des Deux Mondes*, October 1950, 461–72; and Jean-Marie Compain, "Montaigne et Henri de Navarre avant Coutras." In *Avènement d'Henri IV: Quatrième centenaire de la bataille de Coutras*. Pau: Association Henri IV, 1989, 39.

66. *Recueil des lettres missives de Henri IV*, ed. Jules Berger de Xivrey. 9 vols. Paris: Imprimerie royale, 1843–76, vol. II (1585–89), 309–11.

67. On the role of Cyprien de Poiferré in the transmission to Montaigne of La Boétie's love sonnets, see Jean Balsamo, "Montaigne, le 'sieur de Poyferré' et la comtesse de Guiche: documents nouveaux." *Montaigne Studies*, vol. XVI, 2004, 75–92.

68. Letter from Stafford to Lord Burghley, February 20, 1588. Cited by Donald Frame, *Montaigne: A Biography*, op. cit., 272.

69. *Recueil des lettres missives de Henri IV*, op. cit., 348 (March 15, 1588).

70. Duplessis-Mornay to his wife. In *Mémoires de Madame de Mornay*, edition revised in accord with the manuscripts, published with the variants and accompanied by previoiusly unpublished letters from Mr and Mme Du Plessis Mornay and their children, ed. Madame de Witt. 2 vols. Paris: For the Société de l'histoire de France, 1868, vol. II, 148.

71. *Essais* 88, III, 13, f. 476v. Frame, p. 825.

72. *Essais* EB, III, 5, f. 384r. Frame, p. 667.

73. Estienne Pasquier, "A Monsieur de Pelgé." In *Les Œuvres d'Estienne Pasquier*, 2 vols. Amsterdam [Trévoux]: Aux Depens de la compagnie, 1723, vol. II, book XVIII, letter 1, col. 517. The letter to Pellejay is reproduled in Catherine Magnien, "Étienne Pasquier 'familier' de Montaigne." *Montaigne Studies*, vol. XIII, 2001, 277–313.

74. *Calendar of State Papers, Foreign Series of the Reign of Elizabeth, 1586–1588*. Vol. XXI, Part I. London: Stationery Office, 1927, 488.

75. *Essais* 88, II, 6, f. 154r. Frame, p. 370.

76. Alain Legros has shown that "le Lignou" refers to a robber who was operating in the forest of Loches and who was the subject of a work titled *Les Inhumanitez et sacrileges du capitaine Lignou, envers les Religieux de la Chartreuse du Liget, place en Thouraine par luy prise: Avec l'emprisonnement de Chicot par ledict Lignou. Suyvant la coppie d'une Missive envoyée de Tours à un Religieux de Paris*. Paris: Denis Binet, 1589.

77. René de Lucinge, *Lettres de 1588*, ed. James J. Supple. Geneva: Droz, 2006, 88 (Mondragon [?] to Lucinge, February 16, 1588).

78. *Les Inhumanitez et sacrileges du capitaine Lignou*, op. cit., 7.

79. *Lettres de Montaigne*, 714–15. Donald Frame commented on this letter to Matignon, sent from Orléans and dated "this 16th of February, in the morning," in "Du nouveau sur le voyage de Montaigne à Paris en 1588." *Bulletin de la Société des amis de Montaigne*, no. 22, 1962, 3–22.

80. Ibid.

81. *Calendar of letters, despatches, and state papers relating to the negotiations between England and Spain preserved in the archives at Simancas and elsewhere: Elizabeth, 1586–1588*. London: Longman, 1862–99, 510.

82. René de Lucinge, *Lettres de 1588*, op. cit., 92 (letter sent to Lucinge, Paris, February 25, 1588).

83. Raymond Ritter discovered these letters in the *Archivos generales de Salamanca*, Estado K. 1567, nos. 24–27 and 29. I give Ritter's translation, somewhat revised by Donald Frame, *Montaigne: A Biography*, op. cit., 273.

84. De Lamar Jensen, *Diplomacy and Dogmatism: Bernardino de Mendoza and the French Catholic League.* Cambridge, MA: Harvard University Press, 1964.

85. Pierre de L'Estoile, *Journal de L'Estoile pour le règne de Henri III (1574–1589)*. Paris: Gallimard, 1943, 618.

86. Quoted in Frame, *Montaigne: A Biography*, op. cit., 273.

87. Letter of March 8. Unpublished letter to Henry III. Cited by Roger Trinquet, "Aperçus généraux sur l'attitude politique de Montaigne après la mairie de Bordeaux," art. cit., 13.

88. *Essais* 80, II, 17, p. 459. Frame, p. 497.

89. This similarity has been pointed out by Michel Magnien, "Juste Lipse et Pierre de Brach: Regards croisés sur Montaigne." In Claude-Gilbert Dubois, ed., *Montaigne et Henri IV*. Biarritz: J & D Éditions, 1996, 125–49.

90. Jean Balsamo and Michel Simonin, *Un couple de libraires au Palais: Abel L'Angelier et Françoise de Louvain (1574–1620), suivi du catalogue des livres publiés par Abel L'Angelier (1574–1610) et la veuve Abel L'Angelier (1610–1620)*. Geneva: Droz, 2001, nos. 100 and 131.

91. Jean Marchand, "Hypothèse sur la quatrième édition des *Essais* de Montaigne." *Bulletin de la Société des bibliophiles de Guyenne*, vol. 27, 1937, 97–104; id., "L'édition des *Essais* de 1587." *Bulletin de la Société des amis de Montaigne*, no. 9, 1940, 57–58.

92. François de La Croix du Maine, *Premier volume de la bibliothèque du sieur de La Croix du Maine*. Paris: Abel L'Angelier, 1584, 328.

93. *Essais* 88, III, 9, f. 439v. Frame, p. 761.

94. See Robert Garapon, "Quand Montaigne a-t-il écrit les 'Essais' du Livre III?" In *Mélanges de Langue et de Littérature du Moyen Age et de la Renaissance offerts à Jean Frappier*. Geneva: Droz, 1970, vol. I, 321–27. See also Philippe Desan, "De la nature du troisième livre des *Essais* de Montaigne." In Philippe Desan, ed., *Lectures du Troisième livre des* Essais *de Montaigne*. Paris: H. Champion, 2016, 7–24.

95. Marie de Gournay, "Vie de la Demoiselle de Gournay." In *Les Advis ou les Presens de la Demoiselle de Gournay*. Paris: Jean Du Bray, 1641, 993.

96. Jean Balsamo, "Les *Essais* de Montaigne et leurs premiers lecteurs: Exemplaires annotés (1580–1598)." *Montaigne Studies*, vol. XVI, 2004, 143–50.

97. *Essais* 88, III, 13, f. 477v. Frame, p. 826.

98. Jean Balsamo, "Les premières éditions de Giordano Bruno et leur contexte éditorial." *Filologia antica e moderna*, vols. V–VI, 1994, 100–102.

99. *Essais* EB, III, 2, f. 352v. Frame, p. 614.

100. *Essais* 88, III, 1, f. 344r. Frame, p. 599.

101. Ibid.

102. *Essais* 88, I, 14, f. 21r. Frame, p. 43.

103. Philippe Desan, "L'avarice chez Montaigne." *Seizième siècle*, no. 4, 2008, 113–24.

104. *Essais* 88, I, 14, f. 21v. Frame, p. 45.

105. Roger Trinquet, "Montaigne et l'argent." In Raymond La Charité, ed., *O un amy! Essays on Montaigne in Honor of Donald M. Frame*. Lexington, KY: French Forum, 1977, 290–313.

106. *Essais* 88, I, 14, f. 22r. Frame, p. 44.

107. *Essais* 88, I, 14, f. 22v. Frame, p. 45.

108. Ibid.

109. Ibid.

110. These accusations were made by Roger Trinquet, "Montaigne et l'argent," art. cit.

111. On moderation in Montaigne, see the studies by John O'Brien, "L'immodération d'un modéré: Montaigne, la règle et l'exception." *Journal of the Institute of Romance Studies*, vol. 6, 1998, 151–60; and Claire Couturas, "'De la modération' (I, 30): Vertu 'affaireuse' ou principe vital?" *Bulletin de la Société des amis de Montaigne*, no. 29–30, 2003, 59–74.

112. See Emmanuel Naya, "De la 'médiocrité' à la 'mollesse': Prudence montaignienne." In Emmanuel Naya and Anne-Pascale Pouey-Mounou, eds., *Éloge de la médiocrité: Le juste milieu à la Renaissance*. Paris: Éditions Rue d'Ulm, 2005, 195–216.

113. *Essais* 88, II, 17, f. 277v–278r. Frame, p. 492.

114. Tabourot des Accords, *Les Touches*, book V:

> Quiconque voit la nette pureté
> De tes écrits, les lit de tel courage
> Que si c'était quelque gentil ouvrage
> Qu'il eût jadis lui-même medité:
> Puis tout ravi de sa simplicité,
> Reconnaissant ton style inimitable,
> T'adore ainsi qu'une divinité
> Te voyant seul à toi-même semblable.

115. *Essais* 88, I, 40, f. 105r. Frame, p. 186.

116. *Essais*, III, 5, f. 384r. Frame, p. 667

117. *Essais* 88, III, 13, f. 472v. Frame, p. 819.

118. *Essais* 88, III, 10, f. 447r. Frame, p. 773.

119. René de Lucinge, *Lettres de 1588*, op. cit., 107 (Paris, March 16, 1588).

120. Ibid., p. 135 (Paris, May 11, 1588).

121. *Essais* EB, III, 10, f. 447v. Frame, p. 775.

122. Robert Descimon, *Qui étaient les Seize? Étude sociale de 225 cadres laïcs de la Ligue radicale parisienne (1585–1594)*. Paris: Fédération des sociétés historiques et archéologiques de Paris et Île-de-France, 1983.

123. Elie Barnavi, *Le Parti de Dieu: Étude sociale et politique des chefs de la Ligue parisienne, 1585–1596*. Louvain: Nauwelaerts, 1980, 14–15.

124. Pierre de L'Estoile, *Registre-journal de Henri III*. In *Nouvelle collection des Mémoires pour servir à l'Histoire de France*, ed. Michaud et Poujoulat. Paris, 1837, 87.

125. Jacques Carorguy, *Recueil des choses les plus mémorables advenues dans le royaume de France (1582–1595)*, ed. Jacky Provence. Paris: H. Champion, 2011, 52.

126. Sully, *Mémoires des sages et royales œconomies d'estat, domestiques*, op. cit., vol. I, 95. This list is provided by Cheverny, *Mémoires de Cheverny*, ibid., vol. XXXVI, 110. Cheverny adds "and several other gentlemen of the Court and the council with me, the lord of Bellievere and the state secretaries Villeroy and Brulard; and as for Pinard, who was also with us, the King sent him to find the queen his mother, who was with the said Lord of Guise to pacify everything, so as to make her understand the reasons for his sudden departure."

127. René de Lucinge, *Lettres de 1588*, op. cit., 138 (Paris, after May 18, 1588).

128. *Histoire de Sébastien Le Pelletier: Prêtre ligueur et Maître de grammaire des enfants de chœur de la cathédrale de Chartes pendant les guerres de la Ligue (1579–1592)*, ed. Xavier Le Person. Geneva: Droz, 2006, 84.

129. Jean-Marie Le Gall, "Paris à la Renaissance: Capitale ou première des bonnes villes?" In Jean-Marie Le Gall, ed., *Les Capitales de la Renaissance*. Rennes: Presses Universitaires de Rennes, 2011, 45–69.

130. Pierre de L'Estoile, *Journal de Henri III et de Henri IV*. In Petitot, op. cit., 1825, vol. XLV, 367.

131. *Recueil des lettres missives de Henri IV*, op. cit., 383 (late June 1588).

132. René de Lucinge, *Lettres de 1588*, op. cit., 182 (Paris, June 25, 1588).

133. Roger Trinquet suggests that Montaigne accompanied the king in his flight at the request of the queen mother. See "Du nouveau dans la biographie de Montaigne," art. cit.

134. Michel Magnien, "Juste Lipse et Pierre de Brach: Regards croisés sur Montaigne." In Claude-Gilbert Dubois, ed., *Montaigne et Henri IV*, op. cit., 126. See also Reinhold Dezeimeris, "Recherches sur la vie de Pierre de Brach." In Pierre de Brach, *Œuvres poétiques*. Paris: A. Aubry, 1861–62, vol. II, lxiv. In this letter to Justus Lipsius, Brach says this about his portrait: "To show you that I seek every mark to engrave a testimony of friendship, I send you my portrait, which I have had engraved to put at the front of her *tombeau* [a collection of poems in memory of de Brach's late wife], which I shall have printed with about a thousand French verses of my own composition" (From Rouen, at the Court, July 6, 1588).

135. Philippe Desan, *Portraits à l'essai: Iconographie de Montaigne*. Paris: H. Champion, 2007, no. 82.

136. René de Lucinge, *Lettres de 1588*, op. cit., 214 (Paris, July 9, 1588).

137. Several studies provide accounts of this arrest. See in particular Donald Frame, *Montaigne: A Biography*, op. cit., 280–81.

138. *Éphéméride*, 96. On this episode, see Amy Graves, "Crises d'engagement: Montaigne et la Ligue," art. cit., 329–52.

139. *Journal de voyage*, 139. Waters, vol. 2, 197.

140. On the meeting between Marteau and Montaigne at Loretto, see Concetta Cavallini, *L'Italianisme de Michel de Montaigne*. Fasano; Paris: Schena Editore; Presses de l'Université Paris-Sorbonne, 2003, 197–212.

141. "Édit du roi sur l'Union de ses sujets Catholiques." In *Des États généraux, et autres assemblées nationales*. The Hague: Buisson, 1789, vol. XIV, October 18, 1588, 418.

142. *Essais* EB, III, 12, f. 462r. Frame, p. 799.

143. On the biography of Marie de Gournay, see Michèle Fogel, *Marie de Gournay: Itinéraire d'une femme savante*. Paris: Fayard, 2004.

144. Marie de Gournay, *Les Advis ou les Presens de la Demoiselle de Gournay*, op. cit., 993.

145. Marie de Gournay, "Copie de la vie de la Damoiselle de Gournay." In Marie de Gournay, *Fragments d'un discours féminin*, ed. Elyane Dezon-Jones. Paris: José Corti, 1988, 138.

146. Estienne Pasquier, "A Monsieur de Pelgé." In *Les Œuvres d'Estienne Pasquier*, op. cit., vol. II, book XVIII, letter 1, col. 518.

147. Marie de Gournay, "Copie de la vie de la Damoiselle de Gournay," op. cit., 138.

148. *Essais* 88, I, 24, f. 47r. Frame, p. 94.

149. *Essais* EB, I, 24, f. 47r. Frame, p. 94.

150. Alain Legros, "Montaigne et Gournay en marge des *Essais*: Trois petites notes pour quatre mains." *Bibliothèque d'Humanisme et Renaissance*, vol. LXV, 2003, 613–30.

151. Quoted by Alan M. Boase, "Montaigne annoté par Florimond de Raemond," art. cit., 263.

152. Mario Schiff comments on the meeting between Montaigne and Gournay: "Everything leads us to think that the master and the pupil read the best pages of this book together. Montaigne, already discontent and looking for something better, loaded the margins of the work with corrections, supplements, and various notes. Two of the most important additions were written by Marie de Gournay under his dictation and later completed or corrected by him." In *La Fille d'alliance de Montaigne, Marie de Gournay*. Paris: Champion, 1910, 6. These additions in Marie de Gournay's hand are found on folios 42v and 47r.

153. *Essais* EB, I, 40, f. 20r. Frame, p. 41.

154. On this editorial deception, see Paul Bonnefon, "Une supercherie de Mlle de Gournay." *Revue d'Histoire Littéraire de la France*, vol. III, 1896, 70–89; and more recently Claude Blum, "La Pléiade en habits de Gournay." *Nouveau Bulletin de la Société des amis de Montaigne*, no. 3, 2008, 55–70.

155. *Essais* 95, II, 17, 661. Frame, p. 502.

156. Marie de Gournay, *L'Ombre de la Damoiselle de Gournay*. Paris: Jean Libert, 1626, 658.

157. Catherine Martin, "Le premier testament de Marie de Gournay." *Bibliothèque d'Humanisme et Renaissance*, vol. LXVII, no. 3, 2005, 653–58.

158. Estienne Pasquier, "A Monsieur de Pelgé." In *Les Œuvres d'Estienne Pasquier*, op. cit., vol. II, book XVIII, letter 1, col. 519–20.

159. Annotation by Florimond de Raemond, quoted by Alan M. Boase, "Montaigne annoté par Florimond de Raemond," art. cit., 239–40.

160. *Essais* 80, I, 28, pp. 259–60. Frame, pp. 137–38.

161. *Essais* 88, III, 5, f. 370v. Frame, p. 645.

162. Ibid.

163. *Essais* 88, III, 13, f. 487r. Frame, p. 840.

164. Justus Lipsius, letter to Moretus, December 27, 1601. In *Iusti Lipsi Epistolae: Pars*

XIV (1601), ed. Jeanine De Landtsheer. Brussels: Koninklijke Vlaamse Academie van België voor Wetenschappen en Kunsten, 2006.

165. Georges M. R. Picot, *Histoire des États généraux*, 5 vols. Paris: Hachette, 1872.

166. *Journal du chanoine Nicolas Brulart*. In *Journal d'un ligueur parisien des barricades à la levée du siège de Paris par Henri IV (1588–1590)*, ed. Xavier Le Person. Geneva: Droz, 1999, 107.

167. Étienne Bernard, *Journal des États de Blois*. In *Des États généraux, et autres assemblées nationales*. The Hague: Buisson, 1789, vol. XIV, 551.

168. On these meetings, see George Hoffmann, "Croiser le fer avec le Géographe du Roi: L'entrevue de Montaigne avec Antoine de Laval aux États généraux de Blois en 1588." *Montaigne Studies*, vol. XIII, 2001, 207–22.

169. Jacques-Auguste de Thou, *La Vie de Jacques-Auguste de Thou*, ed. Anne Teissier-Ensminger. Paris: H. Champion, 2007, 659–61. On the friendship between De Thou and Montaigne, see Ingrid De Smet, "Montaigne et Jacques-Auguste de Thou: Une ancienne amitié mise à jour." *Montaigne Studies*, vol. XIII, 2001, 223–40.

170. On Montaigne's mediation between the duke of Guise and Henry of Navarre, see David Maskell, "Montaigne médiateur entre Navarre et Guise." *Bibliothèque d'Humanisme et Renaissance*, vol. XLI, 1979, 541–53; and Marcel Françon, "Montaigne, J.-A. de Thou et les 'guerres de religion.'" *Bulletin de la Société des amis de Montaigne*, no. 18, 1969, 35–39.

171. De Thou, *Histoire universelle*, op. cit., vol. 1, 136.

172. Estienne Pasquier, "A Monsieur de Pelgé." In *Les Œuvres d'Estienne Pasquier*, op. cit., vol. II, book XVIII, letter 1, col. 518.

173. The expression is that of Jacques-Auguste de Thou, *La vie de Jacques-Auguste de Thou*, op. cit., 667.

174. Étienne Bernard, *Journal des États de Blois*, op. cit., 23.

175. Ibid.

176. Georges M. R. Picot, *Histoire des États généraux*, op. cit., vol. 3, 374–75.

177. Étienne Bernard, *Journal des États de Blois*, op. cit., 25–26.

178. Sully, *Mémoires des sages et royales oeconomies d'estat, domestiques*, op. cit., 112.

179. *Essais* 88, EB, III, 9, f. 438r. Frame, p. 758.

180. *Éphéméride*, 98.

181. *Essais* 88, III, 1, f. 347r. Frame, p. 603.

182. Malcolm Smith, "Lost Writings by Montaigne." *Bibliothèque d'Humanisme et Renaissance*, vol. XLIX, no. 2, 1987, 309–18.

183. *Essais* EB, I, 21, f. 37r. Frame, p. 76.

Chapter 10. The Marginalization of Montaigne

1. *Essais* EB, III, 10, f. 446v. Frame, p. 773.

2. *Essais* 80, II, 37, p. 598. Frame, p. 576.

3. *Essais* EB, I, 39, f. 102r. Frame, p. 180.

4. Estienne Pasquier, "A Monsieur de Pelgé." In *Les Œuvres d'Estienne Pasquier*, 2

vols. Amsterdam [Trévoux]: Aux Depens de la compagnie, 1723, vol. II, book XVIII, letter 1, col. 517.

5. *Essais* EB, III, 8, f. 415v. Frame, p. 720.

6. Montaigne made this separation clear in *Essais* EB, III, 5, f. 384r. Frame, p. 667.

7. *Essais* EB, III, 10, f. 447v. Frame, p. 774.

8. *Essais* EB, II, 16, f. 266r. Frame, p. 471.

9. *Mémoires de Marguerite de Valois, reine de France et de Navarre.* In *Collection complète des mémoires relatifs à l'histoire de France*, ed. Claude Bernard Petitot. Paris: Foucault, 1823, vol. XXXVII, 152–53.

10. *Essais* EB, III, 13, f. 476v. Frame, p. 825. For an assessment and discussion of the role of the *raison d'état* in Montaigne, see Doug Thompson, "Montaigne's Political Education: *raison d'état* in the Essais." *History of Political Thought*, vol. XXXIX, no. 2, 2013, 195–224; Nicola Panichi, "Au-delà de la vertu 'innocente': Montaigne et les théoriciens de la raison d'état." In Philippe Desan, ed., *Montaigne politique*, Paris: H. Champion, 2006, 73–91; and Anna Maria Battista, *Alle origini della pensiero politico libertino: Montaigne e Charron*. Milan: A. Giuffrè, 1966.

11. On Henry of Navarre's religion, see Christian Desplat, "La religion d'Henri IV." In *Henri IV, le roi et la reconstruction du royaume*. Pau: J & D Éditions, 1989, 223–67.

12. *Essais* EB, II, 15, f. 264r. Frame, p. 467.

13. *Essais* EB, II, 15, f. 264r. Frame, pp. 467–68.

14. *Essais* EB, II 2, f. 141r. Frame, p. 245. On the relationship between politics and self-government, see Paolo Slongo, *Governo della vita e ordine politico in Montaigne*. Milan: Franco Angeli, 2010.

15. Montaigne considers Epaminondas not only a great general but also places him in "the first rank of outstanding men" (*Essais* 88, III, 1, f. 349v. Frame, p. 608). On several occasions he identifies himelf with this great commander famed for his magnanimity, kindness, and humanity. See Kyriaki Christodoulou, "Le portrait d'Epaminondas chez Montaigne et chez Pascal." In I. Zinguer, ed., *Le Lecteur, l'auteur et l'écrivain: Montaigne, 1492–1592–1992.* Paris: H. Champion, 1993, 121–36.

16. *Essais* EB, III, 13, f. 472v. Frame, p. 818.

17. *Essais* EB, I, 39, f. 100v. Frame, p. 178.

18. *Essais* EB, III, 9, f. 438v. Frame, p. 759.

19. *Essais* EB, III, 9, f. 439v. Frame, p. 761.

20. *Essais* EB, I, 17, f. 25v. Frame, p. 51.

21. Ibid.

22. *Essais* EB, I, 13, f. 15v. Frame, p. 33.

23. On Montaigne's ambivalent attitude toward the Jesuits, see Alain Legros, "Jésuites ou Jésuates? Montaigne entre science et ignorance." *Montaigne Studies*, vol. XV, 2003, 131–46.

24. *Articles sur l'union des manans et habitans de la ville de Tolose, et des autres villes et lieux de Languedoc, et de la Guienne, qui seront par eux jurez: Pour le soustenement et défense de la Religion Catholique, Apostolique, et Romaine, et extirpation des her-*

esies, et Arrest de la Cour de Parlement dudit Tolose donné sur iceux. Toulouse: J. Pillehotte, 1589.

25. Brantôme, *Grands capitaines Français de son temps*, ed. Lalanne. Paris: Renouard, 1866, vol. V, 161.

26. Gérard Jubert, *Ordonnances enregistrées au parlement de Paris sous le règne de Henri IV*. Paris: Archives nationales, 1993, 15, no. 6.

27. *Archives historiques du département de la Gironde*. Vol. IV, letter from Matignon to the king of Navarre, August 18, 1589, no. CXXXV, 206.

28. Ibid., vol. XLIV, letter from Henry IV to Matignon, December 4, 1589, no. CLII, 208.

29. Tax of "15 *sous* per bale of pastel, 15 *sous* per *pipe* [about 400 liters] and 6 *deniers* per *livre* for other merchandise entering Bordeaux or Bayonne by water," June 12, 1590. *Archives historiques du département de la Gironde*, B 43, f. 138v. This new tax was allocated to the parlement's wages on June 14, 1590.

30. Jean-Baptiste de Sainte-Anne Pradillon, *La Conduite de dom Jean de La Barrière, premier abbé et instituteur des Feuillants, durant les troubles de la Ligue et son attachement au service du roi Henri III par un religieux feuillent*. Paris: Muguet, 1699.

31. Édouard Frémy, "La médiation de l'abbé des Feuillants entre la Ligue et Henri III (1588–1589)." *Revue d'histoire diplomatique*, no. 6, 1892, 449–78.

32. See the report of October 14, 1589, BNF, Fonds Dupuy, vol. LXI, f. 55. Cited by François Gébelin, *Le Gouvernement du Maréchal de Matignon en Guyenne pendant les premières années du règne de Henri IV (1589–1594)*. Bordeaux: Marcel Mounastre-Picamilii, 1912, 50.

33. On Montaigne and the Feuillants, see Michel Simonin, "Montaigne et les Feuillants." In *L'Encre et la Lumière*, Geneva: Droz, 2004, 571–96.

34. Bayle, *Dictionnaire critique*, 1720, vol. 1, 852.

35. Gabriel de La Rochemaillet, "Éloge veritable ou sommaire discours de la vie de Pierre Charron parisien vivant Docteur és droicts," published at the beginning of his *Traicté de Sagesse*. Paris: David Leclerc, 1606, f. B3v.

36. On Charron and the League, see Ernest Mourin, "Note relative à Charron, à sa conduite et à ses écrits du temps de la Ligue." *Mémoires de la Société académique de Maine et Loire*, 1858, 53–59.

37. Letter of May 12, 1589, to Gabriel de La Rochemaillet. The originals of Charron's letters have disappeared, and today we have only partial copies made by Gabriel Naudé in 1628. These copies of the letters were published, with an introduction by Lucien Auvray. *Revue d'histoire littéraire de la France*, 1894, 308–29.

38. Ibid.

39. Extract from a letter sent in April 1589 to a doctor at the Sorbonne. An extract from this letter was published by Charron under the title *Discours chrestien, qu'il n'est permis ny loisible a un subject, pour quelque cause & raison que ce soit, de se Liguer, bander & rebeller contre son Roy*. This *Discours* was printed following the *Petit traicté de Sagesse*. Paris: David Le Clerc, 1606, 73.

40. Pierre Villey, *Les Sources et l'évolution des* Essais *de Montaigne*. 2 vols. Paris: Hachette, 1933, vol. I, 177–83.

41. Michel Magnien, "Trois lettres de Lipse à Montaigne (1587 [?]–1589)." *Montaigne Studies*, vol. XVI, 2004, 103–11.

42. Juste Lipse, *Epistolarum Centuria Secunda*. Leiden: Plantin, 1590, epistles XLV, LIX, and XCVI.

43. *Essais* EB, I, 26, f. 54r. Frame, p. 108.

44. George Hoffmann, "Was Montaigne a Good Friend?" In Lewis C. Seifert and Rebecca M. Wilkin, eds., *Men and Women Making Friends in Early Modern France*. London; New York: Routledge, 2015, 31–60. Michel Magnien has also suggested that Montaigne had tried to dissociate himself from Lipsius: "Montaigne et Juste Lipse: Une double méprise?" In Christian Mouchel, ed., *Juste Lipse (1547–1606) en son temps*. Paris: H. Champion, 1996, 423–52; id., "*Aut sapiens, aut peregrinator*: Montaigne *vs.* Lipse." In Marc Laureys, ed., *The World of Justius Lipsius: A Contribution towards Intellectual Biography*. Brussels; Rome: Institut historique belge de Rome, 1998, 209–32. Paul J. Smith notes other criticisms made by Montaigne against Justus Lipsius, notably regarding his conception of travel. See Paul Smith's *Dispositio: Problematic Ordering in French Renaissance Literature*. Leiden: Brill, 2007, 203–19.

45. Letter from Montaigne to Henry IV, January 18, 1590. In *Lettres de Montaigne*, 720.

46. Ibid.

47. Ibid.

48. *Archives historiques du département de la Gironde*, vol. IV, 1863, no. CXLIX, 234–35.

49. Marriage contract reproduced by Jean Marchand, "Documents originaux relatifs à Montaigne et à sa famille." *Bulletin de la Société des amis de Montaigne*, no. 19, 1969, 14–16.

50. *Recueil des lettres missives de Henri IV*, ed. Berger de Xivrey. Paris: Imprimerie royale, 1846, vol. III, 218–19.

51. Ibid., 219–26.

52. Letter from Montaigne to Henry IV, September 2, 1590. In *Lettres de Montaigne*, 724.

53. Anne-Marie Cocula, "Montaigne et Henri IV: Une impossible rencontre." In Claude-Gilbert Dubois, ed., *Montaigne et Henri IV*. Biarritz: Terres et Hommes du Sud, 1996, 29–37.

54. *Discours au vray de l'entreprise faicte par le roy de Navarre sur la ville de Paris dont elle a esté miraculeusement delivrée, avec l'estat où est à présent la dicte ville*. Lyon: Jean Pillehotte, 1591.

55. *Archives historiques du département de la Gironde*, October 30, 1590, vol. VI, no. LXXIV, 210.

56. Estienne de Cruseau, *Chronique*, ed. Jules Delpit. Bordeaux: G. Gounouilhou, 1879–81, 16.

57. Ibid., 19.

58. Ibid.

59. Léonie Gardeau, "Le testament du marquis de Trans." *Bulletin de la Société histo-*

rique et archéologique du Périgord, vol. LXXXIII, 1956, 125–32; id., "La bibliothèque du marquis de Trans et de son petit-fils Frédéric de Foix." *Bulletin de la Société des amis de Montaigne*, no. 20, 1970, 51–61.

60. Ibid., "Le testament du marquis de Trans," art. cit., 132.

61. Louis Audiat, "Un neveu de Montaigne, Raymond de Montaigne, évêque de Bayonne." *Revue de Gascogne*, no. 18, 1877, 201–17, 356–78.

62. Estienne de Cruseau, *Chronique*, op. cit., 39–42.

63. Philippe Desan, *Montaigne: Les formes du monde et de l'esprit*. Paris: Presses de l'Université Paris–Sorbonne, 2008.

64. Alfred Glauser, *Montaigne paradoxal*. Paris: A.-G. Nizet, 1972.

65. *Essais* EB, II, 8, f. 358r. Frame, p. 278.

66. *Essais*, III, 9, f. 424v. Frame, p. 736.

67. *Essais*, III, 9, f. 439v. Frame, p. 762.

68. *Essais* EB, III, 3, f. 362r. Frame, p. 629.

69. Marie de Gournay, "Préface de 1595." *Montaigne Studies*, vol. I, 1989, 46.

70. Ibid., 23–24.

71. Estienne Pasquier, "A Monsieur de Pelgé," op. cit., col. 518.

72. *Essais* EB, III, 9, f. 438r. Frame, p. 759. On Montaigne's idleness, see Virginia Krause, *Idle Pursuits: Literature and Oisiveté in the French Renaissance*. Newark: University of Delaware Press, 2003.

73. *Essais* 80, II, 10, p. 119. Frame, p. 305.

74. Gilbert de Botton and Francis Pottiée-Sperry, "À la recherche de la 'librairie' de Montaigne." *Bulletin du bibliophile*, no. 2, 1997, 254–96. A more recent and more detailed survey of this library has been made by Barbara Pistilli and Marco Sgattoni, *La Biblioteca di Montaigne: Catalogo ragionato dei libri ritrovati*, preface by Nicola Panichi. Pisa: Edizioni della Normale, 2014.

75. *Essais* EB, III, 11, f. 457v. Frame, p. 790.

76. *Essais* 80, I, 28, p. 273. Frame, p. 144.

77. *Essais* 88, I, 29, f. 74v. Frame, p. 145.

78. *Essais* EB, III, 2, f. 350v. Frame, p. 611.

79. *Essais* EB, II, 12, f. 228r. Frame, p. 409.

80. *Essais* 80, 88, EB, "Au lecteur." Frame, p. 2.

81. *Essais* EB, III, I, f. 345v. Frame, p. 601.

82. *Essais* 88, III, 5, f. 834r. Frame, p. 667.

83. *Essais* EB, III, 9, f. 424v. Frame, p. 736.

84. *Essais* EB, flyleaf.

85. Ibid.

86. On the publishing history of the *Essais* and the representation of the text of the *Essais*, see Philippe Desan, "Brève histoire de Montaigne dans ses couches." *Montaigne Studies*, vol. VII, 1995, 35–52.

87. On the errors of transcription from the Bordeaux Copy, see Yasuaki Okubo, "Quelques transcriptions erronées de l'Exemplaire de Bordeaux dans les éditions modernes des *Essais*." *Bulletin de l'Association d'étude sur l'Humanisme, la Réforme, et la Renaissance*, vol. XXVI, 1988, 23–24.

88. On Montaigne's handwritten corrections of the punctuation, scansion, and segmentation of the Bordeaux Copy, see André Tournon, "La segmentation du texte: Usages et singularités." In Claude Blum, ed., *Éditer les* Essais *de Montaigne*. Paris: H. Champion, 1997, 173–83; id., "Syntaxe et scansion: L'énergie du 'langage coupé' et la censure éditoriale." In John O'Brien, Malcom Quainton, and James Supple, eds., *Montaigne et la rhétorique*. Paris, H. Champion, 1995, 117–33.

89. *Essais* 80, I, 26, p. 186. Frame, p. 107.

90. *Essais* 80, II, 10, p. 112. [This sentence was later altered to read (in Frame's translation) "The historians come right to my forehead"; the translation of the earlier text is mine.—Trans.]

91. *Essais* 80, I, 17, p. 82–83. Frame, p. 50.

92. On Montaigne as a reader of Commynes, see Jeanne Demers, "Montaigne lecteur de Commynes." In Franco Simone, ed., *Seconda miscellanea di studi e ricerche sul Quattrocento francese*. Ann Arbor; Chambéry: University Microfilms International; Centre d'études francoitalien, 1981, 206–16; and Marcel Tetel, "Montaigne's glances at Philippe de Commynes." *Bibliothèque d'Humanisme et Renaissance*, vol. LX, no. 1, 1998, 25–40.

93. Philippe de Commynes, *Mémoires*, éd. Joël Blanchard. Geneva: Droz, 2007, vol. 1, V, XIII, 372. English translation, *The Historie of Philip de Commines, Lord of Argenton*, trans. Thomas Danett. London, 1596, Book V, chap. 13, 180.

94. On the memoir genre in the sixteenth and seventeenth centuries, see Nadine Kuperty-Tsur, *Se dire à la Renaissance: Les mémoires au XVIᵉ siècle*. Paris: Vrin, 1997; Marie-Sol Ortola and Maria Roig Miranda, eds., *Mémoire, récit, histoire dans l'Europe des XVIᵉ et XVIIᵉ siècles*. 2 vols. Nancy: Groupe XVIᵉ–XVIIᵉ siècle en Europe, Université Nancy-II, 2007; and especially Marc Fumaroli, "Les Mémoires au carrefour des genres en prose." In *La Diplomatie de l'esprit de Montaigne à La Fontaine*. Paris: Gallimard, 2001. For a study of seventeenth- and eighteenth-century memoirs, see Rolf Wintermeyer, ed., *Moi public et Moi privé dans les mémoires et les écrits autobiographiques du XVIIᵉ siècle à nos jours*. Mont-Saint-Aignan: Publications des universités de Rouen et du Havre, 2008.

95. *Essais* 80, I, 21, p. 132. Frame, p. 75.

96. *Essais* 88, III, 8, f. 414r. Frame, p. 718.

97. Francis Goyet, *Les Audaces de la prudence: Littérature et politique aux XVIᵉ et XVIIᵉ siècles*. Paris: Classiques Garnier, 2009.

98. Alain Malissart, "Montaigne lecteur de Tacite." In Raymond Chevallier and Rémy Poignault, eds., *Présence de Tacite. Hommage au professeur G. Radke*. Tours: Caesarodunum, Bulletin de l'Institut d'études latines, 1992, 157–64. On the reception of Tacitus in France and Italy in the late Renaissance, see Rosanna Gorris, "'La France estoit affamée de la lecture d'un tel historien': Lectures de Tacite entre France et Italie." In Danièle Bohler, ed., *Écritures de l'Histoire: XIVᵉ XVIᵉ siècles*. Geneva: Droz, 2005, 113–41.

99. *Essais* 88, III, 8, f. 414v. Frame, p. 718. This anecdote is reported by Antoine de Laval in *Les Desseins des professions nobles et publiques* (Paris: Abel L'Angelier 1605, f. 189r–197r).

100. *Essais* 88, III, 8, f. 414v. Frame, pp. 718–19.
101. Malcolm Smith, "Montaigne and the Christian foes of Tacitus." In I. D. McFarlane, ed., *Acta Conventus Neo-latini Sanctandreani: Proceedings of the Fifth International Congress of Neo-Latin Studies*. Binghamton, NY: Medieval and Renaissance Texts and Studies, 1986, 379–89.
102. José Ruysschaert, "Une édition du Tacite de Juste Lipse, avec annotations de Muret, conservée à la Mazarine." *Revue belge de philologie et d'histoire*, vol. 23, 1994, 251–54.
103. Tacitus, *Œuvres de Tacite*. Paris: Abel L'Angelier, 1582, f. a2r.
104. *Essais* 88, III, 8, f. 414v. Frame, p. 719.
105. Ibid.
106. *Essais* 88, II, 3, 942. Frame, p. 720.
107. Floyd Gray, *Montaigne et les livres*. Paris: Classiques Garnier, 2013, 205–12. Montaigne's sources regarding the person and the life of Socrates have been studied by Frederick Kellermann, "The *Essais* and Socrates." *Symposium*, vol. 10, 1956, 204–16; Floyd Gray, "Montaigne and the *Memorabilia*." *Studies in Philology*, no. 58, 1961, 130–39; and John O'Brien, "'Autheur de merveilleux poids': Montaigne et Xénophon." *Montaigne Studies*, vol. XVII, 2005, 17–34. See also the studies collected by Thierry Gontier and Suzel Mayer, eds., *Le Socratisme de Montaigne*. Paris: Classiques Garnier, 2010; and Claudie Martin-Ulrich, "'Je pareillement': La figure de Socrate dans les *Essais* de Montaigne." In Alexis Tadié, ed., *La figure du philosophe dans les lettres anglaises et françaises*. Paris: Presses Universitaires de Paris-Ouest, 2010, 25–38.
108. *Essais* EB, II, 12, f. 213r. Frame, p. 377.
109. Plato, *Apology*, trans. Hugh Tredennick, in *The Collected Dialogues of Plato*, ed. E. Hamilton and H. Cairns. Princeton, NJ: Princeton University Press, 1961, 16 (29 e).
110. *Essais* EB, II, 6, f. 155v. Frame, p. 273.
111. *Essais* 80, II, 11, p. 126. Frame, p. 307.
112. Plato, *Apology*, op. cit., 4 (17 c).
113. Ibid., 18 (33 a).
114. *Essais* 80, I, 26, p. 226. Frame, p. 125.
115. *Essais* EB, III, 8, f. 407r. Frame, pp. 705–6.
116. *Essais* 88–EB, III, 9, f. 438r. Frame, p. 758.
117. *Essais* 88–EB, I, 11, f. 14v. Frame, p. 29.
118. *Essais* 88–EB, I, 11, f. 14v. Frame, pp. 29–30.
119. *Essais* 80, II, 11, p. 125. Frame, p. 308
120. *Essais* 80, II, 12, p. 162. Frame, pp. 326–27.
121. *Essais* 88, II, 12, f. 178r. Frame, p. 322.
122. Ibid.
123. *Essais* EB, II, 12, f. 178v. Frame, p. 322.
124. *Essais* 80, I, 51, p. 467. Frame, p. 222.
125. *Essais* 88, II, 12, f. 221v. Frame, p. 395.
126. Plato, *Apology*, op. cit., 18 (31 c).

127. Ibid., 17 (31 d–e).

128. *Essais* 88–EB, III, 12, f. 466v. Frame, p. 808.

129. *Essais* EB, I, 21, f. 37r. Frame, p. 75.

130. *Essais* 88, III, 12, f. 467r. Frame, p. 809.

131. *Essais* EB, III, 9, f. 429r. Frame, p. 743.

132. *Essais* 88, III, 12, f. 459r. Frame, p. 792.

133. Lawrence Kritzman, "The Socratic Makeover: Montaigne's 'De la physionomie' and the Ethics of the Impossible." *L'Esprit créateur*, vol. 46, no. 1, 2006, 79. I agree with Kritzman when he says that, "Montaigne describes himself as strikingly unsocratic in his ability to adapt to the vicissitudes of human existence" (81).

134. *Essais* 88, III, 9, f. 439v. Frame, p. 761.

135. *Essais* 88, III, 3, f. 357v. Frame, p. 622.

136. *Essais* EB, III, 12, f. 466r. Frame, p. 807.

137. Plato, *Apology*, op. cit., 19 (33 b).

138. *Essais* EB, I, 20, f. 31v. Frame, p. 62.

139. *Essais* 88, III, 9, f. 416r. Frame, p. 721.

140. Estienne Pasquier, "A Monsieur de Pelgé," op. cit., col. 518.

141. A. Eyquem, "La mort de Michel de Montaigne: Ses causes rediscutées par la consultation posthume de médecins spécialistes de notre temps; M. Daudon, J. Thomas, P. Trotot, R. Bernouli, P. Albou, A. Eyquem, F. Pottiée-Sperry." *Bulletin de la Société des amis de Montaigne*, no. 4, 1996, 7–16.

142. *Journal de voyage*, 250. Waters, vol. 3, 91.

143. Estienne Pasquier, "A Monsieur de Pelgé," op. cit., col. 518.

144. Nicola Panichi, "Morte 'muette' e morte 'parlante': Montaigne e La Boétie." *Rivista di storia della filosofia*, vol. 67, no. 1, 2012, 35–58.

145. Bernard Automne, *Commentaire sur les coustumes generales de la ville de Bourdeaux et pays Bordelois* [1621], Bordeaux, Jacques Mongiron Millanges, 1666, 330. On Bernard Automne and Montaigne, see Michel Simonin, "Bernard Automne (1564–après 1628), témoin et lecteur de Montaigne." *Montaigne Studies*, vol. XIII, 2001, 315–60.

146. Marie de Gournay, "Sommaire recit sur la vie de Michel Seigneur de Montaigne, extraict de ses propres Escrits." In *Les Essais de Michel, seigneur de Montaigne: Édition nouvelle exactement corrigee selon le vray exemplaire*. Paris: Jean Camusat, 1635, f. 3¶5v.

147. For a complete description and other similar representations, see Philippe Desan, *Portraits à l'essai: Iconographie de Montaigne*. Paris: H. Champion, 2007, 108–9, no. 44.

148. Estienne Pasquier, "A Monsieur de Pelgé," op. cit., col. 520.

149. See the letters from Françoise de La Chassaigne to Marc-Antoine de Saint-Bernard, reproduced in Gabriel Richou, *Inventaire de la collection des ouvrages et documents réunis par J.-F. Payen et J.-B. Bastide sur Michel de Montaigne*. Paris: Techener, 1878, 279–324.

150. See Philippe Desan, *Portraits à l'essai: Iconographie de Montaigne*, op. cit., 279–84, no. 287.

151. Translation of Pierre Bernadau, *Le Viographe bordelais ou revue historique des monuments de Bordeaux*. Bordeaux: Gazay et Compagnie, 1845, 275–80. On these epitaphs, see Reinhold Dezeimeris, *Recherches sur l'auteur des épitaphes du tombeau de Montaigne: Lettres à M. le Dr J.-F. Payen*. Paris: Librairie Auguste Aubry, 1861; Jean Lapaume, *Le Tombeau de Montaigne, étude philosophique et archéologique*. Rennes: Imprimerie Oberthur, 1859; Aubin-Louis Millin, "Le tombeau de Montaigne." *Voyage dans les départements du Midi de la France*, s.l., 1807, vol. IV, part 2, 634–42.

152. Jean Lapaume, *Le Tombeau de Montaigne*, op. cit., 97–98; *Compte rendu des travaux de la commission des monuments et documents historiques et des bâtiments civils du département de la Gironde*. Paris: Librairie archéologique de Victor Didron, 1855, 22.

Chapter 11. Montaigne's Political Posterity

1. *Essais* EB, II, 18, f. 285r. Frame, p. 504.

2. La Croix du Maine, *Premier volume de la bibliotheque du sieur de La Croix du Maine*. Paris: Abel L'Angelier, 1584, 329.

3. Olivier Millet, *La Première Réception des* Essais *de Montaigne (1580–1640)*. Paris: H. Champion, 1995.

4. Paul J. Smith and Karl A. E. Enenkel, eds., *Montaigne and the Low Countries (1580–1700)*. Leiden: Brill, 2007.

5. Max Weber, *The Protestant Ethic and the Spirit of Capitalism* [1905]. Trans. Talcott Parsons. New York: Scribner's, 1958.

6. For example, George Hoffmann maintains that, at the end of the sixteenth century, France remained Catholic in religion, even though culturally and ideologically its intelligentsia was perhaps closer to Protestant values and ideas: *Alone unto Their Distance: French Reformers, Satiric Alienation, and the Creation of Religious Foreignness*, forthcoming.

7. Philippe Desan, "Simon Goulart, éditeur de Montaigne." In Olivier Pot, ed., *Simon Goulart, un pasteur aux intérêts vastes comme le monde*. Geneva: Droz, 2013, 289–305.

8. Frank Lestringant, "Montaigne et les protestants." In Philippe Desan, ed., *Montaigne politique*. Paris: H. Champion, 2006, 353–72; and especially chapter VII, "The legacy of French Reformation satire." In George Hoffmann, *Alone unto Their Distance: French Reformers, Satiric Alienation, and the Creation of Religious Foreignness*, op. cit.

9. On satire in Montaigne, see Ruth Calder, "Montaigne as Satirist." *Sixteenth Century Journal*, vol. 17, no. 2, 1986, 225–35; Élisabeth Caron, *Les* Essais *de Montaigne ou les échos satiriques de l'humanisme*. Paris: Éditions CERES, 1993; Jean Balsamo, "Montaigne 'admirable,' les libertins et l'esprit 'satyrique.'" *Montaigne Studies*, vol. XIX, 2007, 57–66.

10. François Rigolot, "Saint-Barthélemy l'Indien: Montaigne, la 'loy d'oubliance' et la

Légende dorée." *Bulletin de la Société des amis de Montaigne*, no. 37–38, 2005, 51–65.

11. See Warren Boutcher, *The School of Montaigne in Early Modern Europe: The Reader-Writer*. Oxford: Oxford University Press, 2016.

12. William Hamlin, *Montaigne's English Journey: Reading the* Essays *in Shakespeare's Day*. Oxford: Oxford University Press, 2013.

13. Marie de Gournay, "Préface de 1595." *Montaigne Studies*, vol. I, 1989, 45.

14. Letter from Marie de Gournay to Justus Lipsius, April 25, 1593. In *Justi Lipsi Epistolae—1594*, ed. Jeanine de Landtsheer. Brussels: Paleis der Academiën, 1994, no. 1418, 145.

15. *Justi Lipsi Epistolae*, 1594, op. cit., 145.

16. See Philippe Desan, "Petite histoire des réinventions et des récupérations de Montaigne au cours des siècles." *Australian Journal of French Studies*, vol. 52, no. 3, 2015, 229–42.

17. Catherine Magnien-Simonin, *Une vie de Montaigne ou le sommaire discours sur la vie de Michel Seigneur de Montaigne (1608)*. Paris: H. Champion, 1992.

18. *Éloges des hommes illustres qui depuis un siècle ont fleuri en France dans la profession des lettres* (1598, trans. G. Colletet in 1644). This relatively short biography that associates Montaigne with La Boétie runs to only six pages in quarto format.

19. Ibid., 154–55.

20. This identification is due to Jean-Louis Quantin, "Les censures de Montaigne à l'Index romain: Précisions et corrections." *Montaigne Studies*, vol. XXVI, 2014, 145–62.

21. Antoine Gilles' *votum* has been reproduced by Jean-Robert Armogathe and Vincent Carraud, "Les *Essais* de Montaigne dans les archives du Saint-Office." In Jean-Louis Quantin and Jean-Claude Waquet, eds., *Papes, princes et savants dans l'Europe moderne: Mélanges à la mémoire de Bruno Neveu*. Geneva: Droz, 2006, 79–96. On censorship in the seventeenth century, see also Saverio Ricci, "La censura romana e Montaigne, con un documento relativo alla condanna del 1676." *Bruniana & Campanelliana*, vol. 15, 2008, 59–79; and especially Jean-Louis Quantin, "Les censures de Montaigne à l'Index romain: Précisions et corrections," art. cit.

22. François de Grenaille, *L'Honneste Garçon, ou l'Art de bien élever la noblesse à la vertu, aux sciences et à tous les exercices convenables à sa condition . . .* Paris: Quinet, 1642, Book I, chap. V, 189.

23. *Pensées de Montaigne, propres à former l'esprit et les moeurs*. Paris: Anisson, 1700, f. ã2v–ã3r.

24. Ibid., f. ã1r–v.

25. Ibid., f. ã2r–v.

26. *Les Essais de Michel seigneur de Montaigne*, ed. Pierre Coste. London: J. Tonson and J. Watts, 1724, vii.

27. François-Xavier Talbert, *Éloge de Michel Montagne*. Published in London, sold in Paris by Moutard, 1775, 34–35.

28. Ibid., 35.

29. Ibid., 53.

30. Ibid., 98.

31. On the transformation of Montaigne into a moralist, see Jean Balsamo, "L'invention d'un moraliste: Montaigne." In Volker Kapp and Dorothea Scholl, eds., *Literatur und Moral*. Berlin: Duncker & Humblot, 2011, 65–93.

32. For example, Guillaume Bérenger's book published in 1667: *Response a plusieurs injures et railleries, Ecrites contre Michel seigneur de Montagne, dans un livre intitulé La Logique ou l'Art de penser, contenant, outre les regles generales, plusieurs observations particulieres, propres à former le jugement, de la 2. Edition. Avec un beau traité de l'éducation des Enfans, & cinq cens Excellens passages tirez du Livre des Essais, pour montrer le merite de cet Autheur.* See Philippe Desan, "Les *Essais* en cinq cents pensées ou la réponse de Guillaume Bérenger aux 'injures et railleries' d'Arnauld et Nicole contre Montaigne (1667)." *Renaissance Journal*, vol. II, no. 4, 2005, 6–13.

33. See Philippe Desan, " 'Cette espece de manuscrit des *Essais*': L'édition Naigeon de 1802 et son 'avertissement' censuré." *Montaigne Studies*, vol. X, 1998, 7–34.

34. *L'Esprit de Montaigne*, ed. Laurentie. Paris: 1829, 1.

35. Ibid., 2.

36. Ibid., 3.

37. See in particular the popular books by Sarah Bakewell, *How to Live: A Life of Montaigne in One Question and Twenty Attempts at an Answer*. London: Chatto & Windus, 2010; and Antoine Compagnon, *Un été avec Montaigne*. Sainte-Margurite-sur-Mer: Éditions des Équateurs, 2013.

38. See Paul J. Smith, "Montaigne in the World." In Philippe Desan, ed., *Oxford Handbook of Montaigne*. Oxford: Oxford University Press, 2016, 287–305.

Epilogue

1. *Essais* EB, II, 18, f. 285v. Frame, p. 504.

2. *Essais* 88, III, 13, f. 478r. Frame, p. 827.

BIBLIOGRAPHY

Manuscript Sources

État des gages des domestiques de la Reine mère [Catherine de Médicis], 1585, distribution des sommes laissées par la Reine à ses domestiques par testament, 1589. Archives nationales, série K, monuments historiques, Comptes, K502.

Extraits des registres secrets de la Cour: 1462 à 1582. Bibliothèque municipale de Bordeaux, Fonds patrimoniaux, ms. 368.

Extraits des registres secrets du Parlement de Bordeaux. BNF, Fonds français, ms. 22.369–22.370.

Extraits des registres secrets de la Cour. Archives départementales de la Gironde, ms. 3JB1.

Fontainemarie, *Recueil*. 2 vols. Livre noir de l'Hôtel de Périgueux, Bibliothèque municipale de Bordeaux, ms. 380.

Labat de Savignac, M., *Registres secrets du Parlement* 1734. 27 vols. Bibliothèque municipale de Bordeaux, Fonds patrimoniaux, ms. 369.

La Roche-Posay, "Lettres au Roi et à la Reine sa mère." BNF, coll. Dupuy, ms. 351.

Maison de Catherine de Médicis, 1579–1585. Archives nationales, série K, monuments historiques, Comptes, K388–423.

Registres secrets du Parlement de Bordeaux. BNF, Fonds français, ms. 22.371–22.377.

Registres secrets du Parlement de Bordeaux. November 14, 1531–September 1582, BNF, Z Payen 1393.

Verthamon d'Ambloy, François-Martial de, *Registre secret du Parlement de Bordeaux, recueilli et mis en ordre par les soins de François-Martial de Verthamon d'Ambloy*, 1770. 48 vols. Bordeaux: Archives municipales de Bordeaux, ms. 764–72.

Printed Sources

Anciens et nouveaux statuts de la ville de Bourdeaus. Esquels sont contenues les Ordonnances requises pour la police de ladicte ville, & de tous les estats & maistrises d'icelle. Bordeaux: Simon Millanges, 1612.

Annales Ecclesiastici, ed. Augustin Theiner. Rome: Ex Typographia Tiberina, 1581.

Archives historiques du département de la Gironde. 59 vols. Paris: Aubry, Picard, Champion; Bordeaux: Gounouilhou, Lefebvre, Feret, 1859–1936.

Articles sur l'union des manans et habitans de la ville de Tolose, et des autres villes et lieux de Languedoc, et de la Guienne, qui seront par eux jurez: pour le soustenement et defense de la Religion Catholique, Apostolique, et Romaine, et extirpation des heresies, et Arrest de la Cour de Parlement dudit Tolose donné sur iceux. Toulouse: J. Pillehotte, 1589.

Aubigné, Agrippa d', *Histoire universelle*. Maille: Jean Moussat, 1616.

Automne, Bernard, *Commentaire sur les coustumes generales de la ville de Bourdeaux et pays Bordelois* [1621]. Bordeaux: Jacques Mongiron Millanges, 1666.

Bacci, Andrea, *Discorso delle Acque, bagni di Cesare Augusto a Tivoli*. Rome, 1567.

Bacquet, Jehan, *Quatriesme traicté . . . des droicts des domaines de la couronne de France. Concernant les Francs Fiefs, Nouveaux Acquests, Anoblissements & Amortissements*. Paris: Sébastien Nivelle, 1582.

———, *Trois premiers traictez . . . des droicts du domaine de la couronne de France. Avec l'establissement et jurisdiction de la Chambre du Tresor*. Paris: Sebastien Nivelle, 1580.

Bernard, Étienne, *Journal des États de Blois, dans Des états généraux, et autres assemblées nationales*. The Hague: Chez Buisson, 1789, vol. XV.

Bodin, Jean, *Œuvres philosophiques de Jean Bodin*, ed. Pierre Mesnard. Paris: Presses Universitaires de France, 1951.

Bonne, François de [Lesdiguières], *Actes et Correspondance du Connétable*. Grenoble: Édouard Allier, 1878.

Bouchel, Laurent, *La Bibliothèque ou thrésor du droict françois recueilly et mis en ordre*. Paris: Baillet, 1629.

Brantôme, *Œuvres completes de Pierre de Bourdeille abé séculier de Brantôme*. Paris: Auguste Desrez, 1839.

Calendar of Letters and State Papers relating to English affairs preserved in, or originally belonging to, the archives of Simancas: Elizabeth. 4 vols. London: Stationery Office, 1892–1899.

Castelli, Giovanni Battista, *Correspondance du nonce en France Giovanni Battista Castelli (1581–1583)*, ed. Robert Toupin. Rome: Presses de l'Université Grégorienne, 1967.

Castelnau, Michel de, *Les Mémoires de Messire Michel de Castelnau, seigneur de Mauvissiere*. Brussels: Jean Léonard, 1731.

C'est la déduction du sumptueux ordre plaisantz spectacles et magnifiques théâtres dressés, et exhibés par les citoiens de Rouen ville métropolitaine du pays de Normandie, A la sacré Maiesté du Treschristian Roy de France, Henry second leur souverain Seigneur, Et à Tresillustre dame, ma Dame Katharine de Medicis, la Royne son espouze, lors de leur triumphant ioyeuls et nouvel advènement en icelle ville, qui fut es jours de Mercredy et jeudy premier et second jours d'octobre 1550. Rouen: Robert Le Hoy, 1551.

Chappuys, Gabriel, *L'Art des secrétaires*. Paris: Abel L'Angelier, 1588.

Choisnin, Jean de, *Mémoires*. In *Collection universelle des Mémoires particuliers relatifs à l'histoire de France*. London: 1789, vol. LIV.

Coras, Jean de, Arrest *memorable du Parlement de Tolose. Contenant une Histoire prodigieuse d'un supposé mari advenue de nostre temps: enrichie de cent et onze belles et doctes annotations*. Lyon: Antoine Vincent, 1561.

Correspondance du nonce en France Anselmo Dandino (1578–1581), ed. Ivan Cloulas. Rome: Presses de l'Université Grégorienne, 1970.

Corti, Matteo, *De balneis omnia quae extant*. Venice, 1553.

Cotgrave, Randle, *Dictionarie of the French and English Tongues*. London: Adam Islip: 1611.

Cruseau, Étienne de, *Chronique*, ed. Jules Delpit. Bordeaux: G. Gounouilhou, 1879–1881.

———, *L'Entrée de Charles IX à Bordeaux*, ed. Philippe Tamizey de Larroque. Bordeaux: Chollet, 1882.

Danès, Pierre, *Conseils à un ambassadeur*, ed. L. Delavaud, "La diplomatie d'autrefois." *Revue d'histoire diplomatique*, vol. XXVIII, 1914, 602–12.

Darnal, Jean, *Supplément Chronique bordelaise* [1620]. Bordeaux: J. Montgiron-Millange, 1666.

De Lurbe, Gabriel and Jean Darnal, *Chronique bourdeloise*. Bordeaux: Simon Millanges, 1619.

De Thou, Jacques-Auguste, *Histoire universelle*. Basel: Jean Louis Brandmuller, 1742.

———, *Mémoires*. In *Collection complète des mémoires relatifs à l'histoire de France*, ed. Claude Bernard Petitot. Paris: Libraire Foucault, 1823.

Discours au vray de l'entreprise faicte par le roy de Navarre sur la ville de Paris dont elle a esté miraculeusement delivrée, avec l'estat où est à présent la dicte ville. Lyon: Jean Pillehotte, 1591.

Dom Devienne, *Histoire de la ville de Bordeaux*. Bordeaux: Simon de la Court, 1771.

Du Chesne, André, *Histoire généalogique de la maison des Chasteigners, seigneurs de la Chasteigneray, de la Rochepozay, de St-Georges de Rexe, de Lindoys, de la Rochefaton et autres lieux, justifiés par chartes diverses, églises, arrests à la cour de Parlement, lettres domestiques et autres bonnes preuves*. Paris: Sébastien Cramoisy, 1634.

Du Fossé, Nicolas, *Trésor politique divisé en trois liures: contenant les relations, instructions, traictez, et divers discours appartenans à la parfaicte intelligence de la raison d'Estat & de tres-grande importance à l'entiere cognoissance des interests, pretentions, desseins, & reuenus des plus grands princes & seigneurs du monde*. Paris: Rollin Thierry, 1608.

Ernaud, Loys, *Discours de la noblesse, et des justes moyens d'y parvenir*. Caen: Benedic Macé, 1584.

Falloppia, Gabriele, *De medicatis acquis atque de fossilibus*. Venice, 1564.

Foix, Paul de, *Lettres de Messire Paul de Foix, Archevesque de Toulouse, & ambassadeur pour le roy auprés de Pape Gregoire XIII escrites au roy Henry III*, ed. Auger de Mauléon, sieur de Granier. Paris: Charles Chappellain, 1628.

Franzini, Girolamo, *Le Cose maravigliose dell'Alma Città di Roma*. Venice, 1575.

Gaufreteau, Jean de, *Chronique bordeloise, 1240–1638*, ed. Jules Delpit. 2 vols. Bordeaux: Société des Bibliophiles de Guyenne, 1876–78.

Godefroy, Theodore, *Le Ceremonial François contenant les cérémonies observées en France aux Sacres & Couronnemens de Roys, & Reynes, & de quelques anciens Ducs de Normandie, d'Aquitaine, & de Bretagne: Comme aussi à leurs Entrées solennelles: Et à celles d'aucuns Dauphins, Gouverneurs de Provinces, & autres Seigneurs, dans diverses Villes du Royaume* [1619]. 2 vols. Paris: Sebastien et Gabriel Cramoisy, 1649.

Goulart, Simon, *Memoires de l'estat de France sous Charles IX, contenans les choses plus notables, faites & publiées tant par les Catholiques que par ceux de la Religion, depuis le troisiesme Edit de pacification fait au mois d'Aoust 1570 jusques au regne de Henry Troisiesme, & réduite en trois volumes, chacun desquels a un indice des principales matières y contenues.* Meidelbourg [Geneva]: Henry Wolf, 1577, 1578.

Gournay, Marie de, *Les Advis ou, les presens de la demoiselle de Gournay.* Paris: Toussainct Du Bray, 1641.

———, "Copie de la vie de la Damoiselle de Gournay." In Marie de Gournay, *Fragments d'un discours féminin*, ed. Elyane Dezon-Jones. Paris: José Corti, 1988.

———, *L'Ombre de la Damoiselle de Gournay.* Paris: Jean Libert, 1626.

Henri III, *Lettre de Henri III, roi de France*, ed. Pierre Champion and Michel François. Paris: Klincksieck, 1984.

Hobbes, Thomas, *The Elements of Law Natural and Politic* [1650], ed. F. Tönnies. London: Simpkin, Marshall, 1889.

Hurault, Philippe, *Mémoires de Messire Philippe Hurault, comte de Cheverny.* In *Collection universelle des Mémoires particuliers relatifs à l'histoire de France.* London, 1789, vol. L.

Inventaire sommaire des registres de la jurade 1520–1783. Bordeaux: Archives municipales de Bordeaux, 1909.

Jubert, Gérard, ed., *Ordonnances enregistrées au parlement de Paris sous le règne de Henri IV.* Paris: Archives nationales, 1993.

Jouan, Abel, *Recueil et discours du voyage du Roy Charles IX de ce nom à present regnant, accompagné des choses dignes de memoire faictes en chacun endroit faisant sondit voyage en ses païs et provinces de Champaigne, Bourgoigne, Daulphiné, Provence, Languedoc, Gascoigne, Baïonne, et plusieurs autres lieux, suyvant son retour depuis son partement de Paris jusques à son retour audit lieu, és annees Mil cinq cens soixante quatre et soixante cinq.* Paris: Jean Bonfons, 1566.

La Declaration faicte par le Roy, de sa majorité, tenant son lict de justice en sa Cour de Parlement de Rouen: et Ordonnance par luy faicte pour le bien et repos public de son Royaume: Et ce qu'il dict en ladicte Cour avant la publication de ladicte Ordonnance. Paris: Robert Estienne, 1563.

La Ferrière, Hector de, *Le XVIᵉ siècle et les Valois d'après les documents inédits du British Museum.* Paris: Imprimerie nationale, 1879.

L'Alouëte, François de, *Traité des nobles et des vertus dont ils sont formés.* Paris: Guillaume de La Noue, 1577.

La Boétie, Étienne de, *Œuvres complètes d'Estienne de La Boétie*, ed. Paul Bonnefon. Bordeaux; Paris: G. Gounouilhou and J. Rouam, 1892.

La Croix du Maine, François de, *Bibliotheque françoise*, Paris: Abel L'Angelier, 1584.

Lamothe, Alexis, *Coutumes du ressort du Parlement de Guyenne; avec un commentaire pour l'intelligence du texte, et les arrest rendus en interprétation.* Bordeaux: Chez les Frères Labottiere, 1769.

Larivey, Pierre de, *L'Institution morale du Seigneur Alexandre Piccolomini . . .* Paris: Abel L'Angelier, 1581.

La Roche Flavin, Bernard de, *Treize livres des parlemens de France, esquels est amplement traicté de leur origine et institution, et des présidens, conseillers, gens du roy, greffiers, secrétaires, huissiers et autres officiers . . .* Bordeaux: Simon Millanges, 1617.

La Rochemaillet, Gabriel, "Eloge veritable ou sommaire discours de la vie de Pierre Charron parisien vivant Docteur és droicts." In Pierre Charron, *Traicté de Sagesse.* Paris: David Leclerc, 1606.

Laroque, Gilles André de, *Traité de la noblesse.* Paris: E. Michallet, 1678.

La Royale reception de leurs majestez tres-chrestiennes en la ville de Bourdeaus ou le siecle d'or ramené par les Alliances de France et d'Espaigne. Recueilli par le commandement du Roy. Bordeaux: Simon Millanges, 1615.

Laval, Antoine de, *Desseins des professions nobles et publiques contenans plusieurs traictez divers & rares: et entre autres, l'histoire de la maison de Bourbon: avec autres beaux secrets historiques, extraicts de bons & authentiques memoires & manuscripts.* Paris: Abel L'Angelier, 1605.

Le Laboureur, Jean, *Additions aux Mémoires de Castelnau, dans Les Memoires de messire Michel de Castelnau, seigneur de Mauvissiere, illustrez et augmentez de plusieurs commentaires & manuscrits, tant lettres, instructions, traitez, qu'autres pieces secrettes & originales, servans à donner la verité de l'histoire des regnes de François II, Charles IX & Henry III, & de la regence & du gouvernement de Catherine de Medicis.* 3 vols. Brussels: L. Leonard, 1731.

L'Entrée du Roy à Bordeaux, avecques les Carmes Latins qui luy ont esté presentez, et au Chancelier. Paris: Thomas Richard, 1565.

Le Pelletier, Sébastien, *Histoire de Sébastien Le Pelletier. Prêtre ligueur et Maître de grammaire des enfants de chœur de la cathédrale de Chartes pendant les guerres de la Ligue (1579–1592),* ed. Xavier Le Person. Geneva: Droz, 2006.

Les Inhumanitez et sacrileges du capitaine Lignou, envers les Religieux de la Chartreuse du Liget, place en Thouraine par luy prise: Avec l'emprisonnement de Chicot par ledict Lignou. Suyvant la coppie d'une Missive envoyée de Tours à un Religieux de Paris. Paris: Denis Binet, 1589.

L'Estoile, Pierre de, *Journal de l'Estoile pour le règne de Henri III (1574–1589).* Paris: Gallimard, 1943.

———, *Registre-journal du règne de Henri III,* vol. V (1585–87), ed. Madeleine Lazard and Gilbert Schrenck. Geneva: Droz, 2001.

Le Sueur, Guillaume, *Histoire admirable d'un faux et supposé mary, advenue en Languedoc, l'an mil cinq cens soixante.* Paris: Vincent Sertenas, 1561.

L'Hospital, Michel de, *Œuvres complètes de Michel de l'Hospital, Chancelier de France.* Paris: A. Boulland, 1824.

Lipsius, Justus, *Epistolarum Centuria Secunda.* Leiden: Plantin, 1590.

———, *Justi Lipsi Epistolae—1594,* ed. Jeanine de Landtsheer. Brussels: Paleis der Academiën, 1994.

Livre des Privilêges. Bordeaux: G. Gounouilhou, 1878.

Livre des statuts & ordonnances de l'ordre sainct Michel, establi par le treschrestien Roy de France Loys unzieme de ce nom. [Paris: circa 1550].

Lorraine, François de, duc de Guise, *Mémoires-journaux de François de Lorraine,* ed. Joseph-françois Michaud, Jean-Joseph Poujoulat, Jacques-Joseph Champollion

Figeac and Aimé Champollion-Figeac. Paris: Nouvelle collection des mémoires pour servir à l'histoire de France, 1839.

Loyseau, Charles, *Du Droict des offices*. In *Œuvres de Charles Loyseau*. Geneva: Estienne Gamonet, 1636.

Lucinge, René de, *Lettres de 1588*, ed. James J. Supple, Geneva: Droz, 2006.

———, *Lettres sur la cour de Henri III en 1586*, ed. Alain Dufour. Geneva: Droz, 1966.

———, *Lettres sur les débuts de la Ligue, 1585*, ed. Alain Dufour. Geneva: Droz, 1964.

Machiavelli, *The Prince*, trans. James B. Atkinson. Indianapolis: Bobbs-Merrill, 1976.

Magni, Francesco, *De Dominicis, Claudio, Repertorio delle creazioni di cittadinanza romana (secoli XIV–XIX)*. Rome: Archivio Storico Capitolino, 2007; https://docs.google.com/viewer?url=http://www.accademiamoroniana.it/indici/Cittadinanza+romana.pdf.

Mauro, Lucio, *Le antichita de la citta di Roma*. Venice: Giordanno Ziletti, 1556.

Medici, Catherine de, *Lettres de Catherine de Médicis*, ed. Gustave Baguenault de Puchesse. Paris: Imprimerie nationale, 1880–1909.

Mémoire présenté à Monsieur Matignon, par les Maires et Jurats de Bordeaux au sujet du droit qu'avait la ville de placer des sentinelles du côté des châteaux et fortifications. BNF, coll. Z. Payen, no. 690.

Mémoire sur la constitution politique de la ville et cité de Périgueux, où l'on développe l'origine, le caractère & les droits de la seigneurie qui lui appartient, & dont tous ses citoyens & bourgeois sont propriétaires par indivis. Paris: Imprimerie de Quillau, 1775.

Mémoires de Madame de Mornay, ed. Madame de Witt. 2 vols. Paris: Société de l'histoire de France, 1868.

Mesmes, Henri de, *Mémoires inédits de Henri de Mesmes, seigneur de Roissy et de Malassise*, ed. Édouard Frémy. Paris: E. Leroux, 1886.

Métivier, Jean de, *Chronique du Parlement de Bordeaux*, ed. Arthur de Brezetz and Jules Delpit. 2 vols. Bordeaux: G. Gounouilhou, 1886–87.

Minardo, Ventura, *Compendio delle regole date da diversi eccellentissimi autori intorno ai bagni di Caldiero*. Verona, 1594.

Muret, Marc-Antoine, *Harangue funebre sur le trespas de Messire Paul de Foix . . . faite en Latin par Marc Antoine Muret, & traduite en François par A. de M. [Auger de Mauléon]*. Rome, 1584.

Ordonnances du Roy Henry troisiesme de ce nom, Roy de France et de Pologne: sur les plainctes et doléances faictes par les députez des Estats de son Royaume convoquez et assemblez en la ville de Bloys. Publiées en la court de Parlement, le 25ᵉ jour de janvier 1580, Lyon: Jean Pillehotte, 1582.

Origny, Pierre d', *Le Herault de la noblesse de France*. Reims: J. de Foigny, 1578.

Paradin, Guillaume, and Jean Bouchet, *La Révolte de la Gabelle en Guienne l'an mil cinq cens quarante-huit, tiree de l'Histoire de notre temps de maitre Guillaume Paradin, doyen de Beaujeu*. Bordeaux: Atelier Aldo Manuzio, 1981.

Pasquier, Estienne, *Les Œuvres d'Estienne Pasquier*. Amsterdam [Trévoux]: Aux dépens de la Compagnie des libraires associez, 1723.

Prosphonematon, sive de adventu Christianissimi Regis Caroli IX in suam urbem Burdigalam Mauricii Marcii Burdigalensis. Ad eundem. Paris: Thomas Richard, 1565.

Recueil des lettres missives de Henri IV, ed. Jules Berger de Xivrey. 9 vols. Paris: Imprimerie royale, 1843–76, vol. II (1585–89).

Sainte-Anne Pradillon, Jean-Baptiste de, *La Conduite de dom Jean de La Barrière, premier abbé et instituteur des Feuillents, durant les troubles de la Ligue et son attachement au service du roi Henri III par un religieux feuillent*. Paris: Muguet, 1699.

Sauzé De Lhoumeau, Charles, *Correspondance politique de M. de Lanssac (Louis de Saint-Gelais), 1548–1557*. Poitiers: Société française d'imprimerie et de librairie, 1904.

Savaron, Jean, *Traicté de l'annuel et vénalité des offices*. Paris: Pierre Chevalier, 1615.

Scaliger, *Scaligerana editio altera*. Cologne: G. Scagen, 1667.

Sebond, Raymond, *La Théologie naturelle de Raymond Sebon, traduicte nouvellement en françois par Messire Michel, Seigneur de Montaigne, Chevalier de l'ordre du Roy, et Gentilhomme ordinaire de sa chambre*. Paris: Michel Sonnius, 1581.

Sully, *Mémoires des sages et royales œconomies d'estat, domestiques, politiques et militaires*. In *Collection des Memoires relatifs à l'histoire de France*, ed. M. Petitot. Paris: Foucault, 1820.

Syrueilh, François de, *Journal [1568–1585]*. In *Archives historiques du département de la Gironde*, vol. XIII, no. CIII, 244–357.

Tarneau, Jean, *Stile et usage observé au parlement de Bourdeaux, touchant l'exercice de la justice. Avec la forme de ses entrées, sceances, et audiances. Et une table des jours des roolles ordinaires de châque seneschaussée du resort* . . . Bordeaux: C. de la Court, s. d.

Turner, William, *A Booke of the nature and properties as well of the bathes in England as of other bathes in Germanye and Italye*. Cologne: 1568.

Valois, Marguerite de, *Mémoires et autres écrits 1574–1614*, ed. Éliane Viennot. Paris: Honoré Champion, 1999.

Vinet, Élie, *Schola Aquitanica*. Bordeaux: Simon Millanges, 1583. In Louis Massebieau ed., *Schola Aquitanica: programme d'études du Collège de Guyenne au XVIᵉ siècle*. Paris: C. Delagrave, 1886.

Critical Bibliography

Abel, Günter, "Juste Lipse et Marie de Gournay: Autour de l'exemplaire d'Anvers des *Essais* de Montaigne." *Bibliothèque d'Humanisme et Renaissance*, vol. XXX, 1971, 117–29.

Adam, Wolfgang, " 'Si grand plaisir à la visitation d'Allemaigne': Montaigne en terres germaniques." In Philippe Desan, ed., *Montaigne à l'étranger: Voyages avérés, possibles et imaginés*. Paris: Classiques Garnier, 2016, 67–88.

Almquist, Katherine, "Examining the evidence: Montaigne in the *Registres Secrets* du Parlement de Bordeaux." *Montaigne Studies*, vol. XVI, 2004, 45–74.

———, "Montaigne et la politique du Parlement de Bordeaux." In Philippe Desan, ed., *Montaigne politique*. Paris: Honoré Champion, 2006, 127–38.

———, "Montaigne judging with Henri de Mesmes (May–June 1565)." *Montaigne Studies*, vol. XVI, 2004, 37–40.

———, "Quatre arrêts du Parlement de Bordeaux, autographes inédits de Montaigne (mai 1566–août 1567)." *Bulletin de la Société des amis de Montaigne*, nos. 9–10, 1998, 13–38.

———, "Writing pluralist biography of Montaigne's legal career." In George Hoffmann, ed., *The New Biographical Criticism*. Charlottesville, VA: Rookwood Press, 2004, 58–76.

Armogathe, Jean-Robert, "Montaigne et la censure romaine: Julien l'Apostat." In Philippe Desan, ed., *"Dieu à nostre commerce et société": Montaigne et la théologie*. Geneva: Droz, 2008, 251–58.

Armogathe, Jean-Robert, and Vincent Carraud, "Les *Essais* de Montaigne dans les archives du Saint-Office." In Jean-Louis Quantin and Jean-Claude Waquet, eds., *Papes, princes et savants dans l'Europe moderne. Mélanges à la mémoire de Bruno Neveu*. Geneva: Droz, 2006, 79–96.

Ashby, Thomas, *Topographical Study in Rome in 1581, a Series of Views with a Fragmentary Text by Étienne du Pérac*. London: Roxburghe Club, 1916.

Audiat, Louis, "Un neveu de Montaigne, Raymond de Montaigne, évêque de Bayonne." *Revue de Gascogne*, no. 18, 1877, 201–17, 356–78.

Auvray, Lucien, "Lettres de Pierre Charron à Gabriel Michel de la Rochemaillet." *Revue d'histoire littéraire de la France*, 1894, 308–29.

Aymard Saint-Saud (Count), Jean-Marie Hippolyte, *Magistrats des sénéchaussées, présidiaux et élections, fonctionnaires des vices-sénéchaussées du Périgord*. Bergerac: Imprimerie générale du Sud-Ouest, 1931.

Aymonier, Camille, "Un ami de Montaigne: le jésuite Maldonat." *Revue historique de Bordeaux et du département de la Gironde*, vol. XXVIII, 1935, 5–35.

Azéma, Béatrice, "Les jurats de Bordeaux au XVIᵉ siècle: Étude prosopographique." Master's thesis, Université de Bordeaux 3, 2003.

Baguenault de Puchesse, Gustave, *Jean de Morvillier, évêque d'Orléans, garde des Sceaux de France, étude sur la politique française au XVIᵉ siècle d'après des documents inédits*. Paris: Didier, 1869.

Bakewell, Sarah, *How to Live: A Life of Montaigne in One Question and Twenty Attempts at an Answer*. London: Chatto & Windus, 2010.

Ballagny, Paul, "La sincérité de Montaigne." *Mercure de France*, August 1, 1933, 547–75.

Balmas, Enea, "Montaigne et l'Inquisition." In Marcel Tetel and G. Mallary Masters, eds., *Le Parcours des Essais de Montaigne 1588–1988*. Paris: Klincksieck, 1989, 239–49.

Balsamo, Jean, "Biographie, philologie, bibliographie: Montaigne à l'essai d'une 'nouvelle histoire' littéraire." In George Hoffmann, ed., *The New Biogtraphical Criticism*. Charlottesville, VA: Rookwood Press, Studies in Early Modern France, 2004, 10–29.

———, "Le destin éditorial des 'Essais' (1580–1598)." In *Montaigne, Les Essais*, ed. Jean Balsamo, Michel Magnien, and Catherine Magnien-Simonin. Paris: Gallimard, "La Pléiade," 2007, xxxii–lv.

———, "Deux gentilshommes 'necessiteux d'honneur': Montaigne et Pressac." *Montaigne Studies*, vol. XIII, 2001, 141–73.

———, "Des *Essais* pour comprendre les guerres civiles." *Bibliothèque d'Humanisme et Renaissance*, vol. LXXII, no. 3, 2010, 521–40.

———, " 'Et me contente de gémir sans brailler': Montaigne et l'humanité héroïque." In Pierre Magnard and Thierry Gontier, eds., *Montaigne*. Paris: Éditions du Cerf, 2010, 133–53.

———, "Foix (famille)." In Philippe Desan, ed., *Dictionnaire de Michel de Montaigne*. Paris: Honoré Champion, 2007, 468–70.

———, "Un gentilhomme et ses patrons: Remarques sur la biographie politique de Montaigne." In Philippe Desan, ed., *Montaigne politique*. Paris: Honoré Champion, 2006, 223–42.

———, "L'invention d'un moraliste: Montaigne." In Volker Kapp and Dorothea Scholl, eds., *Literatur und Moral*, Berlin: Duncker & Humblot, 2011, 65–93.

———, " 'Un livre écrit du doigt de Satan': La découverte de Machiavel et l'invention du machiavélisme en France au XVIe siècle." In Dominique de Courcelles, ed., *Le Pouvoir des livres à la Renaissance*. Geneva: Droz, 1998, 77–92.

———, " 'Ma fortune ne m'en a fait voir nul': Montaigne et les grands hommes de son temps." *Travaux de littérature*, vol. XVIII, 2005, 139–55.

———, "Montaigne 'admirable,' les libertins et l'esprit 'satyrique.' " *Montaigne Studies*, vol. XIX, 2007, 57–66.

———, "Montaigne avant Montaigne ou les scénarios de Roger Trinquet." *Montaigne Studies*, vol. XX, 2008, 129–44.

———, "Montaigne, Charles d'Estissac et le sieur du Hautoy." In P. Desan, L. Kritzman, R. La Charité and M. Simonin, eds., *Sans autre guide: Mélanges de littérature française de la Renaissance offerts à Marcel Tetel*. Paris: Klincksieck, 1999, 117–28.

———, "Montaigne et le 'saut' du Tasse." *Rivista di Letterature moderne e comparate*, vol. 54, fasc. 4, 2001, 389–407.

———, "Montaigne et les *Commentaires* de Monluc: deux notes de philologie," *Montaigne Studies*, vol. XXII, 2010, 207–21.

———, "Montaigne et Pierre Eyquem: Le meilleur des fils du meilleur des pères." In Julia Chamard-Bergeron, Philippe Desan, and Thomas Pavel, eds., *Les Liens humains dans la littérature (XVIe–XVIIe siècle)*. Paris: Classiques Garnier, 2012, 13–31.

———, "Montaigne, le 'sieur de Poyferré' et la comtesse de Guiche: Documents nouveaux." *Montaigne Studies*, vol. XVI, 2004, 75–92.

———, " 'Le plus grand bien que j'atande de cete miene charge publique': Montaigne entre vie publique et vie privée." *Nouveau Bulletin de la Société des amis de Montaigne*, no. IV, 2008, 359–75.

Balsamo, Jean, and Michel Simonin, *Abel L'Angelier & Françoise de Louvain (1574–1620), suivi du catalogue des ouvrages publiés par Abel L'Angelier (1574–1610) et la veuve L'Angelier (1610–1620)*. Geneva: Droz, 2002.

Barbier, Jean-Paul, *Ma Bibliothèque poétique*, vol. II: *Contemporains et successeurs de Ronsard. De Desportes à La Boétie*. Geneva: Droz, 2001.

————, *Ma bibliothèque poétique*, vol. III: *La Boétie. 1530–1563*. Geneva: Droz, 2000.

Barrière, Pierre, *Montaigne gentilhomme français*. Bordeaux: Delmas, 1940.

Barnavi, Elie, *Le Parti de Dieu: Étude sociale et politique de la Ligue parisienne*. Louvain: B. Nauwelaertz, 1980.

Bastard d'Estang, Henri de, *Les Parlements de France: Essai historique sur leurs usages, leur organisation et leur autorité*. 2 vols. Paris: Didier, 1857.

Battista, Anna Maria, *Alle origini della pensiero politico libertino: Montaigne e Charron*. Milan: A. Giuffrè, 1966.

Baudouin-Matuszek, Marie-Noëlle, "Un ambassadeur en Écosse au XVIᵉ siècle, Henri Clutin d'Oisel." *Revue historique*, vol. 281, no. 1, 1989, 78–131.

Baurein, Jacques, *Variétés bordeloises ou essai historique et critique sur la topographie ancienne et moderne du diocèse de Bordeaux*. Bordeaux, 1876.

Bauschatz, Cathleen, "The Gender of Genre: A Study in the Reception of Montaigne's *Essais*." *Montaigne Studies*, vol. II, 1990, 26–47.

Bège-Seurin, Denise, "La Cour des aides de Périgueux (1553–1561)." In *Sarlat et le Périgord*. Périgueux: Société historique et archéologique de Périgueux, 1987, 321–30.

Bely, Lucien, ed., *L'Invention de la diplomatie, Moyen Âge-Temps modernes*. Paris: Presses Universitaires de France, 1998.

Benedict, Philip, "French Cities from the Sixteenth Century to the Revolution: An Overview." In Philip Benedict, ed., *Cities and Social Change in Early Modern France*. London: Unwin Hyman, 1989, 7–64.

————, *Graphic History: The Wars, Massacres and Troubles of Tortorel and Perrissin*. Geneva: Droz, 2007.

————, *Rouen during the Wars of Religion*. Cambridge: Cambridge University Press, 1981.

Bernadau, Pierre, *Le Viographe bordelais ou Revue historique des monuments de Bordeaux*. Bordeaux: Gazay et Compagnie, 1845.

Bernoulli, René, "Montaigne rencontre Félix Platter." In François Moureau and René Bernoulli, eds., *Autour du Journal de voyage de Montaigne 1580–1980*. Geneva: Slatkine, 1982, 88–103.

Bettoni, Anna, "Arnaud Du Ferrier et les Français de Venise à l'époque de la peste de 1576." In Jean Balsamo and Chiara Lastraioli, eds., *Chemins de l'exil: Havres de paix; Migrations d'hommes et d'idées au XVIᵉ siècle*. Paris: Honoré Champion, 2009, 261–88.

————, "Duplessis-Mornay et la 'famille' de l'ambassade d'Arnaud du Ferrier à Venise." In Hugues Daussy and Véronique Ferrer, eds., *Servir Dieu, le Roi et l'État. Philippe Duplessis-Mornay (1549–1623)*. Paris: Honoré Champion, 2006, 381–407.

————, Rinaldi, Massimo, and Maurizio Rippa Bonati, eds., *Michel de Montaigne e il Termalismo*. Florence: Leo S. Olschki, 2010.

Billacois, François, *Le Duel dans la société française des XVIᵉ–XVIIᵉ siècles: Essai de psycho-sociologie historique*. Paris: Éditions de l'EHESS, 1986.

Bippus, Hans-Peter, *In der Theologie nicht bewandert?: Montaigne und die Theologie*. Tübingen; Basel: Tübinger Studien zur Theologie und Philosophie, 2000.

Birnstiel, Eckart, "Les chambres mi-parties: Les cadres institutionnels d'une juridiction spéciale (1576–1679)." In *Les Parlements de Province, pouvoirs, justice et société du XVe au XVIIIe siècle*. Toulouse: Framespa, 1996,121–40.

Blet, Pierre, *Histoire de la représentation diplomatique du Saint-Siège des origines à l'aube du XIXe siècle*. Vatican City: Collectana Archivi Vaticani 9, 1982.

Bloch, Jean-Richard, *L'Anoblissement en France au temps de François Ier*. Paris: Félix Alcan, 1934.

Bloch, Marc, *Les Caractères originaux de l'histoire rurale française*. Paris: Armand Colin, 1952.

Blum, Claude, "Dans l'atelier de Millanges: Les conditions de fabrication des éditions bordelaises des *Essais* (1580, 1582)." In Claude Blum and André Tournon, eds., *Éditer les Essais de Montaigne*. Paris: Honoré Champion, 1997, 79–96.

———, "La Pléiade en habits de Gournay." *Nouveau Bulletin de la Société des amis de Montaigne*, no. 3, 2008, 55–70.

Boase, Alan M., "Montaigne annoté par Florimond de Raemond." *Revue du seizième siècle*, vol. XV, 1928, 253–54.

Boisseuil, Didier, *Le Thermalisme en Toscane à la fin du Moyen Âge. Les bains siennois de la fin du XIIIe siècle au début du XVIe siècle*. Rome: École française de Rome, 2002.

Boltanski, Luc, and Laurent Thevenot, *De la justification: Les économies de la grandeur*. Paris: Gallimard, 1991.

Bonnefon, Paul, "Cinq arrêts du Parlement de Bordeaux rendus au rapport de Michel de Montaigne." *Archives historiques du département de la Gironde*, vol. XXVIII, 1893, 121–47.

———, *Montaigne et ses amis: La Boétie-Charron-Mlle de Gournay*. 2 vols. Paris: Armand Colin, 1898.

———, *Montaigne, l'homme et l'œuvre*. Bordeaux; Paris: G. Gounouilhou; J. Rouam, 1893.

———, "Une supercherie de Mlle de Gournay." *Revue d'Histoire Littéraire de la France*, vol. III, 1896, 70–89.

Boscheron des Portes, C.B.F., *Histoire du Parlement de Bordeaux*. Bordeaux: C. Lefebvre, 1878.

Boucher, Jacqueline, "La diplomatie de Henri III (1574–1589)." In *La Diplomatie au temps de Brantôme, Cahiers Brantôme*. Bordeaux: Presses Universitaires de Bordeaux, 2007, 39–54.

———, *Société et mentalité autour de Henri III*. Paris: Honoré Champion, 2007.

Boulard, Odile, "Les chanoinesses de Remiremont du XIVe au début du XVIIe siècle." In Michel Parisse, ed., *Remiremont: L'abbaye et la ville*. Nancy: Service des publications de Nancy-II, 1980, 61–69.

Bourdieu, Pierre, "L'illusion biographique." *Actes de la recherche en sciences sociales*, nos. 62–63, 1986, 69–72.

———, *The Logic of Practice* [1980], trans. Richard Nice. Stanford, CA: Stanford University Press, 1990.

Bourgeon, Jean-Louis, "Montaigne et la Saint-Barthélemy." *Bulletin de la Société des amis de Montaigne*, nos. 37–38, 1994, 101–12.

Bourquin, Laurent, *La Noblesse dans la France moderne (XVIe–XVIIIe siècles)*. Paris: Belin, 2002.

Boutcher, Warren, " 'Le moyen de voir ce Senecque escrit à la main': Montaigne's Journal de voyage and the Politics of Science and Faveur in the Vatican Library." In John O'Brien, ed., *(Ré)interpretations: Études sur le seizième siècle*. Ann Arbor: Michigan Romance Studies, 1995, 177–214.

———, " 'Le pauvre patient': Montaigne agent dans l'économie du savoir." In Philippe Desan, ed., *Montaigne politique*. Paris: Honoré Champion, 2006, 243–61.

———, *The School of Montaigne in Early Modern Europe*. 2 vols. Oxford: Oxford University Press, 2016.

Braun, Rudolf, " 'Rester au sommet': Modes de reproduction socioculturelle des élites du pouvoir européennes." In Wolfgang Reinhard, ed., *Les élites du pouvoir et la construction de l'état en Europe*. Paris: Presses Universitaires de France, 1996, 323–54.

Brahami, Frédéric, " 'Être à soi': La place du politique dans les *Essais*." In Philippe Desan, ed., *Montaigne politique*. Paris: Honoré Champion, 2006, 39–56.

———, "Montaigne et la politique." *Bulletin de la Société des amis de Montaigne*, nos. 33–34, 2004, 15–37.

Braye, L., "Le premier voyage de Montaigne à Bar-le-Duc en 1559." *Bulletin de la Société des Lettres de Bar-le-Duc*, 1938–39, 184–86.

Brémond d'Ars, Guy de, "Les Conférences de Saint-Brice entre Henri de Navarre et Catherine de Médicis, 1586–1587." *Revue des questions historiques*, vol. XXXVI, 1884, 496–523.

———, *Le Père de Mme Rambouillet, Jean de Vivonne, sa vie, ses ambassades près de Philippe II et à la cour de Rome, d'après des documents inédits*. Paris: E. Plon, 1884.

Brezetz, Eugène de, *Essais historiques sur le parlement de Bordeaux*. Bordeaux: Crugy, 1856.

Brieux, Alain, "Autres souvenirs de Michel de Montaigne." *Bibliothèque d'Humanisme et Renaissance*, vol. XX, 1958, 370–76.

———, "Petit trésor de souvenirs de Montaigne." *Bibliothèque d'Humanisme et Renaissance*, vol. XIX, no. 2, 1957, 265–93.

Brives-Cazes, Émile, *La Chambre de justice de Guyenne en 1583–1584*. Bordeaux: G. Gounouilhou, 1874.

———, *Origines du Parlement de Bordeaux (1370–1462)*. Bordeaux: G. Gounouilhou, 1887.

———, *Le Parlement de Bordeaux et la Chambre de justice de Guyenne en 1582*. Bordeaux: G. Gounouilhou, 1866.

———, *Le Parlement de Bordeaux et la cour des Commissaires de 1549*. Bordeaux, 1870.

Brown, Elizabeth, and Richard Famiglietti, *The Lit de justice: Semantics, Ceremonial, and the Parlement of Paris, 1300–1600*. Sigmaringen: Jan Thorbecke Verlag, 1994.

Brown, Frieda, *Religious and Political Conservatism in the* Essais *of Montaigne*. Geneva: Droz, 1963.

———, " 'Si le chef d'une place assiegée doit sortir pour parlementer' and 'L'heure des parlemens dangereuses': Montaigne's political morality and its expression in the early essays." In Raymond C. La Charité, ed., *O un amy! Essays on Mon-*

taigne in Honour of Donald M. Frame. Lexington, KY: French Forum, 1977, 72–87.

Brunet, Serge, *"De l'Espagnol dedans le ventre!" Les catholiques du Sud-Ouest de la France face à la Réforme (vers 1540–1589)*. Paris: Honoré Champion, 2007.

Brush, Craig B., "La composition de la première partie du Journal de voyage de Montaigne." *Revue d'histoire littéraire de la France*, vol. 71, no. 3, 1971, 369–84.

———, "The Secretary, Again." *Montaigne Studies*, vol. V, 1993, 113–18.

Buffum, Imbrie, *L'Influence du voyage de Montaigne sur les Essais*. Princeton, NJ: Princeton University Press, 1946.

Busson, Henri, "La pratique religieuse de Montaigne." *Bibliothèque d'Humanisme et Renaissance*, vol. XVI, 1954, 86–95.

Butterworth, Emily, "Censors and censure: Robert Estienne and Michel de Montaigne." In Maria Jose Vega, Julian Weiss, and Cesc Esteve, eds., *Reading and Censorship in Early Modern Europe*. Barcelona: Universitat Autònoma de Barcelona, 2010, 161–79.

Cabanès, Augustin, *La Vie thermale au temps passé*. Paris: Albin Michel, 1934.

Cabié, Edmond, *Ambassade en Espagne de Jean Ebrard, seigneur de Saint-Sulpice, de 1562 à 1565 et mission de ce diplomate dans le même pays en 1566*. Albi: Nouguiès, 1903.

———, *Guerres de Religion dans le Sud-Ouest de la France et principalement dans le Quercy*. Paris: Champion, 1906.

Cabos, Alban, *Guy du Faur de Pibrac, un magistrat poète au XVIᵉ siècle (1529–1584)*. Paris; Auch: E. Champion; F. Cocharaux, 1922.

Caldari Bevilacqua, Franca, "Montaigne alla Biblioteca vaticana." In Enea Balmas, ed., *Montaigne e l'Italia*. Geneva: Slatkine, 1991, 363–90.

Calder, Ruth, "Montaigne as Satirist." *Sixteenth Century Journal*, vol. 17, no. 2, 1986, 225–35.

Calemard, Joseph, "L'édition originale de 'La Servitude volontaire.'" *Bulletin du bibliophile et du bibliothécaire*, May–June 1947, 209–29, 269–82.

Campagne, Maurice, *Histoire de la Maison de Madaillan*. Bergerac: J. Castanet, 1900.

Campagnoli, Ruggero, "Girolamo Naselli primo traduttore italiano di Montaigne (1590)." *Studi Francesi*, vol. 47–48, 1972, 214–31.

Caron, Élisabeth, *Les Essais de Montaigne ou les échos satiriques de l'humanisme*. Paris: Éditions CERES, 1993.

Cassan, Michel, "Pour une enquête sur les officiers 'moyens' de la France moderne." *Annales du Midi*, vol. 108, no. 213, 1996, 89–112.

Cassirer, Ernst, *The Individual and the Cosmos in Renaissance Philosophy* [1927], trans. Mario Domandi. New York: Harper Torchbooks, 1963.

Catusse, A., "Michel Montaigne, meunier." *La France de Bordeaux*, March 27, 1933.

Cavallini, Concetta, *"Cette belle besogne": Étude sur le Journal de voyage de Montaigne avec une bibliographie critique*. Fasano; Paris: Schena Editore; Presses de l'université Paris-Sorbonne, 2005.

———, "Giuseppe Bartoli et le *Journal de Voyage* de Montaigne." *Studi di Letteratura Francese*, vol. XXVIII, 2003, 19–29.

———, *L'Italianisme de Michel de Montaigne*. Fasano; Paris: Schena Editore; Presses de l'université Paris-Sorbonne, 2003.

———, "Montaigne à Venise: Rencontres et hypothèses." *Montaigne Studies*, vol. XXIV, 2012, 163–74.

———, "Le tourisme religieux en Italie dans la deuxième moitié du XVIᵉ siècle: Montaigne et les Français à Lorette." In Philippe Desan and Giovanni Dotoli, eds., *D'un siècle à l'autre: Littérature et société de 1590 à 1610*. Fasano; Paris: Schena Editore; Presses de l'Université Paris-Sorbonne, 2001, 133–52.

Céard, Jean, "Montaigne traducteur de Raimond Sebond: Positions et propositions." *Montaigne Studies*, vol. V, 1993, 11–26.

Chambrun, L., *Giovanni Florio*. Paris: Payot, 1921.

Champeaud, Grégory, *Le Parlement de Bordeaux et les paix de religion (1563–1600)*. Bordeaux: Éditions d'Albret, 2008.

Charpentier, Françoise, "L'absente des *Essais*: Quelques questions autour de l'essai II-8." *Bulletin de la Société des amis de Montaigne*, nos. 17–18, l984, 7–16.

———, "Accepter la mairie: Un déchiffrement." In Claude-Gilbert Dubois, ed., *Les Écrivains et la politique dans le Sud-Ouest de la France autour des années 1580: Quatrième centenaire de l'accession de Montaigne à la mairie de Bordeaux, 1581– 1981*. Talence: Presses Universitaires de Bordeaux, 1982, 37–44.

Chartrou, Jean-Marie, "Les entrées solennelles à Bordeaux au XVIᵉ siècle." *Revue historique de Bordeaux et du département de la Gironde*, vol. XXIII, 1930, 99–102.

Chasteigner de La Rochepozay, P. de, *Montaigne et l'ambassadeur de France à Rome en 1580: Portrait, deux lettres inédites de Henri III et de Catherine de Médicis*. Bayonne: A. Lamaignère, 1895.

Chatelain, Claire, *Chronique d'une ascension sociale: Exercice de la parenté chez de grands officiers (XVIᵉ–XVIIᵉ siècles)*. Paris: Éditions EHESS, 2008.

Chatenet, Monique, "Henri III et 'l'ordre de la cour': Évolution de l'étiquette à travers les règlements généraux de 1578 et 1585." In Robert Sauzet, ed., *Henri III et son temps*. Paris: J. Vrin, 1992, 133–39.

Christodoulou, Kyriaki, "Le portrait d'Épaminondas chez Montaigne et chez Pascal." In Ilana Zinguer, ed., *Le Lecteur, l'Auteur et l'Écrivain; Montaigne, 1492–1592–1992*. Paris: Honoré Champion, 1993, 121–36.

Clastres, Pierre, "Liberté, malencontre, innommable." In Étienne de La Boétie, *Le Discours de la servitude volontaire*, ed. P. Léonard, preceded by "La Boétie et la question du politique," texts by Lamennais, P. Leroux, A. Vermorel, G. Landauer, S. Weil, P. Clastres, and C. Lefort. Paris: Payot, 1976, 229–46.

Cocula, Anne-Marie, "L'événement bordelais de la Saint-Jean 1570 et le clan Montaigne." In *Regards sur les sociétés modernes, XVIᵉ–XVIIIᵉ siècle: Mélanges offerts à Claude Petitfrère*. Tours: Université de Tours, 1997, 71–81.

———, "Formation et affirmation d'un patriciat: Le Parlement de Bordeaux au XVIᵉ siècle." In Claude Petitfrère, ed., *Construction, reproduction et representation des praticiats urbains de l'Antiquité au XXᵉ siècle*. Tours: CEHVI, 1999, 283–97.

———, "Henri de Navarre et la noblesse de Guyenne (1576–1589)." In Jean-Pierre Poussou, Roger Baury and Marie-Catherine Vignal-Souleyrou, eds., *Monarchies, noblesses et diplomaties européennes: Mélanges en l'honneur de Jean-François Labour-dette.* Paris: Presses de l'Université Paris-Sorbonne, 2005, 405–20.

———, " 'Je vis en mon enfance un Gentilhomme commandant à une grande ville . . .': Montaigne et la révolte bordelaise de 1548." In Bernard Barbiche, Jean-Pierre Poussou, and Alain Tallon, eds., *Pouvoirs, contestations et comportements dans l'Europe moderne: Mélanges en l'honneur du professeur Yves-Marie Bercé.* Paris: Presses de l'Université Paris-Sorbonne, 2005, 531–47.

———, *Montaigne: Les années politiques.* Bordeaux: Confluences, 2011.

———, "Montaigne et Henri IV: Une impossible rencontre." In Claude-Gilbert Dubois, ed., *Montaigne et Henri IV.* Biarritz: Terres et Hommes du Sud, 1996, 29–37.

———, "Le Parlement de Bordeaux au milieu du XVIᵉ siècle." In Marcel Tetel, ed., *Étienne de La Boétie: Sage révolutionnaire et poète périgourdin.* Paris: Honoré Champion, 2004, 421–36.

———, "Le parlement de Bordeaux et les présidiaux de Guyenne: Quelques tracasseries de mise en place." In Michel Cassan, ed., *Les Officiers "moyens" à l'époque moderne.* Limoges: Presses Universitaires de Limoges, 1998, 247–59.

———, "Le rôle politique de Montaigne, maire de Bordeaux (1581–1585), en faveur du rétablissement de la paix civile." *Revue française d'histoire du livre,* nos. 78–79, 1993, 155–62.

Cocula, Anne-Marie, and Alain Legros, *Montaigne aux champs.* Bordeaux: Sud-Ouest Éditions, 2011.

Cole, John R., "Montaigne's Dead Babies." *Montaigne Studies,* vol. XII, 2000, 167–84.

Coleman, Dorothy, "Montaigne's 'Sur des vers de Virgile': Taboo Subject, Taboo Author." In R. Bolgar, ed., *Classical Influences on European Culture: A.D. 1500–1700.* Cambridge: Cambridge University Press, 1976, 135–40.

Coleman, James, "Montaigne and the Wars of Religion." In Keith Cameron, ed., *Montaigne and His Age.* Exeter: University of Exeter, 1981, 107–19.

Colleville, Ludovic de, and François Saint-Christo, *Les Ordres du Roi: Répertoire général contenant les noms et qualités de tous les chevaliers des Ordres royaux, militaires et chevaleresques ayant existé en France de 1099 à 1830; Avec une Histoire des Ordres du Saint-Esprit, de Saint-Michel, de Saint-Louis, etc.* Paris: Jouve, 1924.

Colliard, Lauro-Aimé, "Un jeune ami de Montaigne: Charles d'Estissac." In Enrica Galassi and Giuseppe Bernardelli, eds., *Lingua, cultura e testo: Miscellanea di studi francesi in onore di Sergio Cigada.* Milan: Gemelli, 2003, 273–84.

———, "Montaigne et l'affaire Mattecoulon: Dernières trouvailles." *Montaigne Studies,* vol. XIX, 2007, 213–24.

———, "Le thème du duel chez Montaigne: L'affaire Mattecoulon." *Montaigne Studies,* vol. XV, 2003, 159–68.

Combes, François, *Essai sur les idées politiques de Montaigne et La Boétie.* Bordeaux: Duthu, 1882.

Communay, Arnaud, *Le Parlement de Bordeaux: Notes bibliographiques sur ses principaux officiers.* Bordeaux: Olivier-Louis Favraud, 1886.

Compain, Jean-Marie, "Montaigne en Allemagne." In Claude-Gilbert Dubois, ed.,

Montaigne et l'Europe. Mont-de-Marsan: Éditions InterUniversitaires, 1992, 211–22.

———, "Montaigne et Henri de Navarre avant Coutras." In *Avènement d'Henri IV: Quatrième Centenaire de la bataille de Coutras*. Pau: J.&D. Éditions, 1989, 39–48.

———, "Les relations de Montaigne avec son voisin et son protecteur le marquis de Trans." In Claude-Gilbert Dubois, ed., *Les Écrivains et la politique dans le sud-ouest de la France autour des années 1580*. Talence: Presses Universitaires de Bordeaux, 1982, 101–11.

Constant, Jean-Marie, "Les barons français pendant les guerres de Religion." In *Quatrième centenaire de la bataille de Coutras*. Biarritz: J. & D. Éditions, 1989, 49–62.

———, *La Noblesse en liberté (XVIe–XVIIe siècles)*. Rennes: Presses Universitaires de Rennes, 2004.

———, "Les partis nobiliaires et le développement de l'État moderne: Le rôle de la noblesse seconde." In Jean-Philippe Genet and Daniel Tollet, eds., *L'État moderne: Genèse, bilan et perspectives*. Paris: Éditions du CNRS, 1990, 175–84.

Cooper, Richard, "Montaigne dans l'entourage du maréchal de Matignon." *Montaigne Studies*, vol. XIII, 2001, 99–140.

Coppin, Joseph, "Marguerite de Navarre et le Livre des créatures de Raimond Sebond." *Revue du Seizième Siècle*, vol. 10, 1923, 57–66.

———, *Montaigne traducteur de Raymond Sebon*. Lille: H. Morel, 1925.

Coron, Antoine, "Ut prosint aliis: Jacques-Auguste de Thou et sa bibliothèque." In Claude Jolly, ed., *Histoire des bibliothèques françaises: Les bibliothèques sous l'Ancien Régime*. Paris: Promodis, 1988, 101–26.

Corraze, Raymond, "Les Lopez, ancêtres maternels de Michel de Montaigne." *Bulletin philologique et historique du comité des travaux historiques et scientifiques*, 1932–33, 283–98.

———, "Le père de Michel de Montaigne à l'Université de Toulouse." *Bulletin philologique et historique du comité des travaux historiques et scientifiques*, 1940, 191–96.

Costa, Daniela, "Montaigne et François d'Amboise." *Montaigne Studies*, vol. XIII, 2001, 175–86.

Coste, Laurent, "Les jurats de Bordeaux et Montaigne (1581–1585)." *Nouveau bulletin de la Société internationale des amis de Montaigne*, no. 2, 2008, 301–23.

———, *Messieurs de Bordeaux: Pouvoirs et hommes de pouvoirs à l'Hôtel de Ville, 1548–1789*. Bordeaux: Fédération historique du Sud-Ouest, 2006.

Cottrell, Robert, "An Introduction to La Boétie's Three Latin Poems Dedicated to Montaigne." *Montaigne Studies*, vol. III, no. 1, 1991, 3–14.

Cougny, Edmé, *Pibrac. Sa vie et ses écrits: Fragments d'une étude historique et littéraire*. Versailles: Aubert, 1869.

Courteault, Paul, "Les clefs des portes de Bordeaux de 1548 à 1566." *Revue historique de Bordeaux*, vol. XXXV, 1942, 71–77.

———, *Geoffroy de Malvyn, magistrat et humaniste bordelais*. Paris: Champion, 1907.

———, "La mère de Montaigne." *Revue de Bordeaux*, vol. 27, no. 1, 1934, 5–14; vol. 27, no. 2, 49–60.

———, "Une mission de Montaigne en 1574." *Bulletin de la Société des amis de Montaigne*, no. 8, 1940, 4.

———, "Montaigne, fonctionnaire mécontent: Un document inédit." *Revue de la Renaissance*, vol. XII, 1911, 176–79.

———, "Montaigne maire de Bordeaux." In Henri Teulié, ed., *IVᵉ centenaire de la naissance de Montaigne, 1533–1933: Conférences organisées par la ville de Bordeaux et catalogue des éditions françaises des* Essais. Geneva: Slatkine, 1969, 72–162.

Couturas, Claire, " 'De la modération' (I, 30): vertu 'affaireuse' ou principe vital?" *Bulletin de la Société des amis de Montaigne*, nos. 29–30, 2003, 59–74.

Crawford, Jane, *Diplomacy for the Honor of God: A Study of the Papal Nunciature in France (1572–1590)*. Doctoral dissertation, Brigham Young University, 1974.

Cremer, Albert, "La genèse de la notion de noblesse de robe." *Revue d'histoire moderne et contemporaine*, vol. 46, no. 1, 1999, 22–38.

Cremona, Isida, "La pensée politique de Montaigne et les guerres civiles." *Studi Francesi*, vol. 69, 1979, 432–48.

Crouzet, Denis, "Les fondements idéologiques de la royauté d'Henri IV." *Avènement d'Henri IV: Quatrième centenaire*. Pau-Nérac: J.&D. Éditions, 1989, vol. III, 165–94.

———, *Genèse de la réforme française (1520–1562)*. Paris: Sedes, 1996.

———, *Les Guerriers de Dieu: La violence au temps des troubles de religion (vers 1525–vers 1610)*. Seyssel: Champ Vallon, 1990.

———, *Le Haut Cœur de Catherine de Médicis: une raison politique aux temps de la Saint-Barthélemy*. Paris: Albin Michel, 2005.

———, "La nuit de la Saint-Barthélemy: Confirmations et compléments." In Chantal Grell and Arnaud Ramière de Fontanier, eds., *Le Second Ordre: L'idéal nobiliaire; Hommage à Ellery Schalk*. Paris: Presses de l'Université Paris-Sorbonne, 1999, 55–81.

———, *La Nuit de la Saint-Barthélemy: Un rêve perdu de la Renaissance*. Paris: Fayard, 1994.

———, *La Sagesse et le Malheur: Michel de L'Hospital chancelier de France*. Seyssel: Champ Vallon, 1998.

Damas, Pierre, *Histoire de la juridiction consulaire de Bordeaux*. Paris: Delmas, 1947.

D'Andrea, Antonio, "The Political and Ideological Context of Innocent Gentillet's Anti-Machiavel." *Renaissance Quarterly*, vol. XXIII, no. 4, 1970, 397–411.

Dargenty, G., *Le Baron Gros*. Paris: Librairie de l'Art, 1887.

Dast Le Vacher de Boisville, "Liste générale et alphabétique des membres du parlement de Bordeaux depuis la foundation de cette cour souveraine en 1462 jusqu'à sa suppression en 1790." *Archives historiques du département de la Gironde*, vol. XXXI, 1896, 1–62.

———, "Simon Millanges, imprimeur à Bordeaux de 1572 à 1623." *Bulletin historique et philologique du comité des travaux historiques et scientifiques*, 1896, 788–812.

Daubresse, Sylvie, "Christophe de Thou et Charles IX: Recherche sur les rapports entre le parlement de Paris et le Prince (1560–1574)." *Histoire, économie & société*, vol. 17, no. 3, 1998, 389–422.

Daussy, Hugues, "Un diplomate protestant au service d'un roi catholique: Charles de Danzay, ambassadeur de France au Danemark (1515–1589)." In Frédérique Pitou, ed., *Élites et notables de l'Ouest: XVIᵉ–XXᵉ siècle: Entre conservatisme et modernité*. Rennes: Presses Universitaires de Rennes, 2003, 277–94.

———, *Les Huguenots et le Roi: Le combat politique de Philippe Duplessis-Mornay (1572–1600)*. Geneva: Droz, 2002.

———, "Montaigne et Duplessis-Mornay: Les mystères d'une correspondance." *Montaigne Studies*, vol. XVIII, 2006, 169–82.

Davis, Natalie Zemon, "Beyond the Market: Books as Gifts in Sixteenth-Century France." *Transactions of the Royal Historical Society*, 5th series, no. 33, 1983, 69–88.

———, *The Gift in Sixteenth-Century France*. The Curti Lectures. Madison: University of Wisconsin Press, 2000.

———, *The Return of Martin Guerre*. Cambridge, MA: Harvard University Press, 1984.

De Boer, Cornelis, *Montaigne als "Apologeet" van Raymond Sebond: Een moreel probleem*. Amsterdam: Uitgevers Maatschappij, 1940.

De Botton, Gilbert, and Francis Pottiée-Sperry, "À la recherche de la 'librairie' de Montaigne." *Bulletin du bibliophile*, no. 2, 1997, 254–96.

De Caprariis, Vittorio, *Propaganda e pensiero politico in Francia durante le guerre di Religione*. Vol. I: *1559–1572*. Naples: Edizioni scientifiche italiane, 1959.

De Certeau, Michel, *L'Écriture de l'histoire*. Paris: Gallimard, 1975.

Defaux, Gérard, "Un cannibale en haut de chausses: Montaigne, la différence et la logique de l'identité." *Modern Language Notes*, vol. 97, 1982, 919–57.

———, *Montaigne et le travail de l'amitié*. Orléans: Éditions Paradigme, 2001.

De Lamar, Jensen, *Diplomacy and Dogmatism: Bernardino de Mendoza and the French Catholic League*. Cambridge, MA: Harvard University Press, 1964.

———, "French Diplomacy and the Wars of Religion." *Sixteenth Century Journal*, vol. 2, 1974, 23–46.

Delavaud, Louis, "La diplomatie d'autrefois." *Revue d'histoire diplomatique*, no. 28–29, 1914–15, 602–12.

Delhaume, Bernard, "Note sur quelques impressions bordelaises inconnues, provenant de l'atelier de Simon Millanges." *Revue française d'histoire du livre*, vol. 62, no. 3, 1989, 5–40.

Delumeau, Jean, *Vie économique et sociale à Rome dans la seconde moitié du XVIᵉ siècle*. 2 vols. Paris: E. de Boccard, 1957.

Demers, Jeanne, "Montaigne lecteur de Commynes." In Franco Simone, ed., *Seconda miscellanea di studi e ricerche sul Quattrocento francese*. Ann Arbor; Chambéry: University Microfilms International; Centre d'études franco-italien, 1981, 206–16.

Demerson, Guy, "Les exempla dans le *Discours de la servitude volontaire*: Une rhétorique datée?" In Marcel Tetel, ed., *Étienne de la Boétie: Sage révolutionnaire et poète périgourdin*. Paris: H. Champion, 2004, 195–224.

Denis, Fernand, "Une fête brésilienne célébrée à Rouen en 1550." *Bulletin du biblio-phile*, 1849, 332–402.

Desan, Philippe, "L'avarice chez Montaigne." *Seizième Siècle*, no. 4, 2008, 113–24.

———, *Bibliotheca Desaniana: Catalogue Montaigne*. Paris: Classiques Garnier, 2011.

———, "La Boétie poète et ses deux éditeurs: Federic Morel et Montaigne." In Denis Bjaï and François Rouget, eds., *Les Poètes français de la Renaissance et leurs "librai-res."* Geneva: Droz, 2015, 485–505.

———, "The Book, the Friend, the Woman: Montaigne's Circular Exchanges." In Marie-Rose Logan and Peter Rudnytsky, eds., *Contending Kingdoms: Historical, Psychological, and Feminist Approaches to the Literature of Sixteenth-Century France and England*. Detroit: Wayne State University Press, 1991, 225–62.

———, "Brève histoire de Montaigne dans ses couches." *Montaigne Studies*, vol. VII, 1995, 35–52.

———, " 'Cette espece de manuscrit des *Essais*': L'édition Naigeon de 1802 et son 'aver-tissement' censuré." *Montaigne Studies*, vol. X, 1998, 7–34.

———, *Les Commerces de Montaigne: Le discours économique des* Essais. Paris: A.-G. Nizet, 1991.

———, "Le Discours *de la servitude volontaire* et la cause protestante: Les paradoxes de la réception de La Boétie." *Studi Francesi*, vol. 180, no. 3, 2016.

———, "Eléments d'une sociologie des *Essais*." In Thierry Gontier and Pierre Magnard, eds., *Montaigne*. Paris: Éditions du Cerf, 2010, 45–66.

———, "Les *Essais* en cinq cents pensées ou la réponse de Guillaume Bérenger aux 'in-jures et railleries' d'Arnaud et Nicole contre Montaigne (1667)." *Renaissance Jour-nal*, vol. II, no. 4, 2005, 6–13.

———, *L'Imaginaire économique de la Renaissance*. Paris: Presses de l'Université Paris-Sorbonne, 2002.

———, "Introduction." In Philippe Desan, ed., *Reproduction fac-similé du Journal du voyage de Michel de Montaigne en Italie et en Allemagne en 1580 et 1581*. Paris: So-ciété des Textes Français Modernes, 2014, vii–lxx.

———, "Le *Journal du voyage* de Montaigne est-il un journal de voyage?" In Véronique Ferrer, Olivier Millet, and Alexandre Tarrête, eds., *La Renaissance au grand large: Mélanges en l'honneur de Frank Lestringant*. Geneva: Droz, 2017.

———, *Montaigne dans tous ses états*. Fasano: Schena Editore, 2001.

———, "Montaigne et la théâtralité du politique." In Concetta Cavallini and Philippe Desan, eds., *Le texte en scène: Littérature, théâtre et théâtralité à la Renaissance*. Paris: Classiques Garnier, 2016, 131–49.

———, *Montaigne, les Cannibales et les Conquistadores*. Paris: A.-G. Nizet, 1994.

———, *Montaigne: Les formes du monde et de l'esprit*. Paris: Presses de l'Université Paris-Sorbonne, 2008.

———, "Montaigne paysagiste." In Dominique de Courcelles, ed., *Éléments naturels et paysages à la Renaissance*. Paris: Études et rencontres de l'École des chartes, 2006, 39–49.

———, "De la nature du troisième livre des Essais de Montaigne." In Philippe Desan, ed., *Lectures du Troisième livre des* Essais *de Montaigne*. Paris: Honoré Champion, 2016, 7–24.

———, "Nommer, dénommer et renommée: Le nom propre de Montaigne." *Corpus, revue de philosophie*, no. 50, 2006, 9–28.

———, *Penser l'histoire à la Renaissance*. Caen: Éditions Paradigme, 1993.

———, "Petite histoire des réinventions et des récupérations de Montaigne au cours des siècles," *Australian Journal of French Studies*, vol. 52, no. 3, 2015, 229–42.

———, "La place de La Boétie dans les *Essais* ou l'espace problématique du chapitre 29." In Zoé Samaras, ed., *Montaigne: Espace, voyage, écriture*. Paris: Honoré Champion, 1995, 181–89.

———, *Portraits à l'essai: Iconographie de Montaigne*. Paris: Honoré Champion, 2007.

———, "Simon Goulart, éditeur de Montaigne." In Olivier Pot, ed., *Simon Goulart, un pasteur aux intérêts vastes comme le monde*. Geneva: Droz, 2013, 289–305.

Desan, Philippe, ed., *Oxford Handbook of Montaigne*. Oxford: Oxford University Press, 2016.

———, *Montaigne politique*. Paris: Honoré Champion, 2006.

———, *"Dieu à nostre commerce et société": Montaigne et la théologie*. Geneva: Droz, 2008.

———, *Dictionnaire de Michel de Montaigne*. Paris: Honoré Champion, 2007.

Desan, Philippe, and Carl Frayne, "Données quantitatives sur le *Journal du voyage* de Montaigne." In Philippe Desan, ed., *Montaigne à l'étranger: Voyages avérés, possibles et imaginés*. Paris: Classiques Garnier 2016, 41–65.

Descimon, Robert, "Chercher de nouvelles voies pour interpréter les phénomènes nobiliaires dans la France moderne: La noblesse, 'essence' ou rapport social?" *Revue d'histoire moderne et contemporaine*, vol. XLVI, no. 1, 1999, 5–21.

———, "Les De Thou au miroir des archives notariales du XVIᵉ siècle: Les chemins de la haute robe." In *Jacques-Auguste de Thou: Écriture et condition robine*. Paris: Presses de l'Université Paris-Sorbonne, 2007, 13–35.

———, "La haute noblesse parlementaire parisienne: La production d'une aristocratie d'État aux XVIᵉ et XVIIᵉ siècles." In Philippe Contamine, ed., *L'État et les aristocraties XIIᵉ–XVIIᵉ siècles: France, Angleterre, Écosse*. Paris: Presses de l'ENS, 1989, 357–84.

———, "Modernité et archaïsme de l'État monarchique: Le Parlement de Paris saisi par la vénalité (XVIᵉ siècle)." In Jean-Philippe Genet, ed., *L'État moderne, genèse: Bilan et perspectives*. Paris: Éditions du CNRS, 1990, 147–61.

———, *Qui étaient les Seize? Mythes et réalités de la Ligue parisienne, 1585–1594*. Paris: Mémoires de la Fédération des sociétés historiques et archéologiques de Paris et de l'Île-de-France, 1983.

———, "La vénalité des offices et la construction de l'État dans la France moderne: Des problems de la représentation symbolique aux problèmes du coût social du pouvoir." In Robert Descimon, Jean-Frédéric Schaub, and Bernard Vincent, eds., *Les Figures de l'administrateur: Institutions, réseaux, pouvoirs en Espagne, en France et au Portugal, XVIᵉ–XIXᵉ siècles*. Paris: Éditions de l'EHESS, 1997, 78–93.

Descimon, Robert, and Élie Haddad, eds., *Épreuves de noblesse: Les expériences nobiliaires de la haute robe parisienne (XVIᵉ–XVIIIᵉ siècle)*. Paris: Les Belles Lettres, 2010.

Desgraves, Louis, *Bibliographie bordelaise: Bibliographie des ouvrages imprimés à Bordeaux au XVIe siècle par Simon Millanges (1572–1623)*. Baden-Baden: Valentin Koerner, 1971.

———, *Dictionnaire des imprimeurs, libraires et relieurs de Bordeaux et de la Gironde*. Baden-Baden: Valentin Koerner, 1995.

———, *Inventaire des fonds Montaigne conservés à Bordeaux*. Paris: Honoré Champion, 1995.

De Smet, Ingrid, "Montaigne et Jacques-Auguste de Thou: Une ancienne amitié mise à jour." *Montaigne Studies*, vol. XIII, 2001, 223–40.

———, *Thuanus: The Making of Jacques-Auguste de Thou (1553–1617)*. Geneva: Droz, 2006.

De Smet, Ingrid, and Alain Legros, "Un manuscrit de François Baudouin dans la 'librairie' de Montaigne." *Bibliothèque d'Humanisme et Renaissance*, vol. LXXV, 1, 2013, 105–11.

De Souza Filho, José Alexandrino, *Civilisation et barbarie en France au temps de Montaigne*. Lille: ANRT, 2003.

———, *Projeto "Livraria" de Montaigne: Um passeio ao uni-verso do escritor francês Michel de Montaigne*. João Pessoa: Editora Universitária, 2007.

Desplat, Christian, "La religion d'Henri IV." In *Henri IV, le roi et la reconstruction du royaume*. Pau: J. & D. Éditions, 1989, 223–67.

Devienne, Don, *Histoire de la ville de Bordeaux*. Bordeaux: Simon de la Court, 1771.

De Witte, Charles-Martial, "Notes sur les ambassadeurs de France à Rome et leur correspondance sous les derniers Valois (1556–1589)." *Mélanges de l'École française de Rome (Moyen Âge-Temps modernes)*, vol. 83, 1971, 89–121.

De Waele, Michel, "Les relations entre le Parlement de Paris et les Parlements de province à l'époque des guerres de religion." In Jacques Poumarède and Jack Thomas, eds., *Les Parlements de province, pouvoirs, justice et société du XVIe au XVIIIe siècle*. Toulouse: Framespa, 1996, 427–35.

Dewald, Jonathan, *The Formation of a Provincial Nobility: The Magistrates of the Parlement of Rouen (1499–1610)*. Princeton, NJ: Princeton University Press, 1980.

Dezeimeris, Reinhold, *Recherches sur l'auteur des épitaphes du tombeau de Montaigne: Lettres à M. le Dr J.-F. Payen*. Paris: Librairie Auguste Aubry, 1861.

———, *De la Renaissance des Lettres à Bordeaux*. Bordeaux: P. Chaumas, 1864.

D'Hozier, Jean-François Louis, and Michel Popoff, *Recueil historique des chevaliers de l'ordre de Saint-Michel*. Paris: Le Léopard d'or, 1998.

Didier, Noël, "Paul de Foix et Grégoire XIII (1572–1584). Une suite de la mercuriale de 1559." *Annales de l'université de Grenoble*, section lettres-droit, vol. XVII, 1941, 93–245.

———, "Paul de Foix à la mercuriale de 1559, son procès, ses idées religieuses." *Mélanges d'archéologie et d'histoire publiés par l'École française de Rome*, vol. LVI, 1939, 396–435.

Diefendorf, Barbara B., *Paris City Councillors in the Sixteenth Century: The Politics of Patrimony*. Princeton, NJ: Princeton University Press, 1983.

————, "La Saint-Barthélemy et la bourgeoisie parisienne." *Histoire, économie et société*, vol. 17, no. 3, 1998, 341–52.

Douais, abbé, *Dépêches de M. de Fourquevaux, ambassadeur du roi Charles IX en Espagne, 1565–1572*. 3 vols. Paris: E. Leroux, 1896–1904.

Dravasa, Étienne, " 'Vivre noblement': Recherches sur la dérogeance de noblesse du XIVᵉ au XVIᵉ siècle." *Revue juridique et économique du Sud-Ouest*, série juridique, vol. 16, nos. 3–4, 1965, 135–93; vol. 17, nos. 1–2, 1966, 23–129.

Dreano, Maturin, *La Pensée religieuse de Montaigne*. Paris: Gabriel Beauchesne, 1936.

Dufour, Alain, "Le colloque de Poissy." In *Mélanges d'histoire du XVIᵉ siècle offerts à Henri Meylan*. Geneva: Droz, 1970, 127–37.

Dumoulin, Joseph, *Vie et œuvres de Federic Morel imprimeur à Paris*. Paris: Dumoulin et Picard, 1901.

Dupèbe, Jean, "Un poète néo-latin: Jean Binet de Beauvais." In *Mélanges sur la littérature à la mémoire de V.-L. Saulnier*. Geneva: Droz, 1984, 613–28.

Dupré-Lasale, Émile, *Michel de L'Hospital avant son élévation au poste de Chancelier de France 1505–1558*. 2 vols. Paris: Thorin, 1875.

————, "Montaigne au Parlement de Paris." *Bulletin du bibliophile*, 1887, 23–25.

Durkan, John, "John Rutherford and Montaigne: An Early Influence." *Bibliothèque d'Humanisme et Renaissance*, vol. XLI, 1979, 115–22.

Durkheim, Émile, *The Rules of Sociological Method* [1894], trans. W. D. Halls. 2nd ed. Houndmills: Palgrave Macmillan, 2013.

Durot, Éric, *François de Lorraine, duc de Guise entre Dieu et le Roi*. Paris: Classiques Garnier, 2013.

Eberl, Dominik A., *Michel de Montaigne und das Politische in den* Essais. Würzburg: Ergon Verlag, 2009.

Eisenstadt, S. N., and Louis Roniger, *Patrons, Clients, and Friends: Interpersonal Relations and the Structure of Trust in Society*. Cambridge: Cambridge University Press, 1984.

————, "Patrons-Clients Relations as a Model of Structuring Social Exchange." *Comparative Studies in Society and History*, vol. 22, no. 1, 1980, 42–77.

Elias, Norbert, *The Court Society* [1939], trans. Edmund Jephcott. New York: Pantheon, 1983.

Espiner-Scott, Janet G., "Note sur le cercle de Henri de Mesmes et sur son influence." *Mélanges offerts à M. Abel Lefranc*. Paris: Droz, 1936, 354–61.

Etchechoury, Maïté, *Les Maîtres des requêtes sous les derniers Valois (1553–1589)*. Paris: Honoré Champion, 1991.

Eyquem, A., "La mort de Michel de Montaigne: Ses causes rediscutées par la consultation posthume de médecins spécialistes de notre temps; M. Daudon, J. Thomas, P. Trotot, R. Bernouli, P. Albou, A. Eyquem, F. Pottiée-Sperry." *Bulletin de la Société des amis de Montaigne*, no. 4, 1996, 7–16.

Falgairolle, Edmond, *Jean Nicot, ambassadeur de France au Portugal au XVIᵉ siècle: Sa correspondance diplomatique*. Paris: A. Challamel, 1897.

Favreau, Marc, *Les "portraits" de Bordeaux: Vues et plans gravés de la capitale de la Guy-*

enne du XVIe au XVIIIe siècle. Camiac-et-Saint-Denis: Éditions de l'Entre-deux-Mers, 2007.

Faye de Brys, Édouard, *Trois magistrats francais du seizieme siècle (Antoine Duprat, Guy Du Faur De Pibrac, Jacques Faye d'Espeisses)*. Paris: Comptoir des imprimeurs-unis, 1844.

Ferguson, Gary, *Queer (re)readings in the French Renaissance: Homosexuality, Gender, Culture*. Hampshire: Ashgate, 2008.

Fèvres, Jessica, "À propos de la maison de Montaigne." *Revue archéologique de Bordeaux*, vol. XCV, 2004, 131–42.

Fogel, Michèle, *Marie de Gournay: Itinéraire d'une femme savante*. Paris: Fayard, 2004.

Fontana, Biancamaria, *Montaigne's Politics: Authority and Governance in the* Essais. Princeton, NJ: Princeton University Press, 2007.

Ford, Philip, "La bibliothèque grecque de Montaigne." In Philip Ford and Neil Kenney, eds., *La Librairie de Montaigne*. Cambridge: Cambridge French Colloquia, 2012, 25–38.

———, "George Buchanan et Montaigne." *Montaigne Studies*, vol. XIII, 2001, 45–63.

Forton, René, *La Maison familiale de Montaigne à Bordeaux*. Bordeaux: J. Bière, 1935.

Frame, Donald, "Did Montaigne Betray Sebond?" *Romanic Review*, vol. XXXVIII, 1947, 297–329.

———, *Montaigne: A Biography*. New York: Harcourt, Brace & World, 1965.

———, "Du nouveau sur le voyage de Montaigne à Paris en 1588." *Bulletin de la Société des amis de Montaigne*, no. 22, 1962, 3–22.

Françon, Marcel, "Les guerres de religion et Montaigne." *Bulletin de la Société des amis de Montaigne*, no. 20, 1970, 39–47.

———, "Montaigne et François d'Amboise." *Bulletin de la Société des amis de Montaigne*, nos. 5–6, 1981, 115–16.

———, "Montaigne et Philippe Du Plessis-Mornay." *Bulletin de la Société des amis de Montaigne*, no. 12, 1974, 56.

———, "Montaigne, J.-A. de Thou et les 'guerres de religion.'" *Bulletin de la Société des amis de Montaigne*, no. 18, 1969, 33–42.

———, "Remarques sur l'itinéraire d'Italie adopté par Montaigne." *Romance Notes*, vol. IX, 1966–67, 299–301.

———, "Sur le rôle de conseiller et d'intermédiaire joué par Montaigne." *Bulletin de la Société des amis de Montaigne*, nos. 14–15, 1975, 114.

———, "Sur l'entrevue de Montaigne et Maldonat à Epernay et à Rome." *Quaderni di filologia e lingue romanze*, vol. V, 1983, 39–40.

———, "Sur Montaigne et les Jésuites." *Bulletin de la Société des amis de Montaigne*, vol. 11–12, 1982, 107–8.

Frémy, Edouard, *L'Académie des derniers Valois*. Paris: E. Leroux, 1887.

———, *Un ambassadeur libéral sous Charles IX et Henri III: Ambassades à Venise d'Arnaud du Ferrier d'après sa correspondance inédite (1563-1567-1570-1582)*. Paris: Ernest Leroux, 1880.

———, *Essai sur les diplomates du temps de la Ligue*. Paris: E. Dentu, 1873.

———, "La médiation de l'abbé des Feuillants entre la Ligue et Henri III (1588–1589)." *Revue d'histoire diplomatique*, no. 6, 1892, 449–78.

Friedrich, Hugo, *Montaigne* [1949], ed. Philippe Desan, trans. Dawn Eng. Berkeley, CA: University of California Press, 1991.

Frisch, Andrea, *The Invention of the Eyewitness: Witnessing and Testimony in Early Modern France*. Chapel Hill: University of North Carolina Press, 2004.

Fumaroli, Marc, *La Diplomatie de l'esprit de Montaigne à La Fontaine*. Paris: Gallimard, 2001.

———, "Genèse de l'épistolographie classique: Rhétorique humaniste de la lettre, de Pétrarque à Juste Lipse." *Revue d'histoire littéraire de la France*, vol. 78, no. 6, 1978, 886–900.

Fürberth, Frank, "L'essor de la balnéologie dans le monde germanique à la fin du Moyen Âge." In Didier Boisseuil and Marilyn Nicoud, eds., *Séjourner au bain: Le thermalisme entre medicine et société (XIVe–XVIe siècles)*. Lyon: Presses de l'Université de Lyon, 2010, 99–109.

Gaffarel, Paul, *Histoire du Brésil français au seizième siècle*. Paris: Maisonneuve, 1878.

Galtier, Émile, *Histoire de Saint-Maur-des-Fossés, depuis son origine jusqu'à nos jours: L'abbaye, le château, la ville*. Saint-Maur-des-Fossés: Société d'histoire et d'archéologie de Saint-Maur-des-Fossés, 1989.

Gambier, P., "Montaigne a-t-il assiégé Fontenay?" *Bulletin de la Société des amis de Montaigne*, nos. 25–26, 1971, 117–19.

Garapon, Robert, "Quand Montaigne a-t-il écrit les 'Essais' du Livre III?" In *Mélanges de langue et de littérature du Moyen Âge et de la Renaissance offerts à Jean Frappier*. 2 vols. Geneva: Droz, 1970, vol. 1, 321–27.

Garavini, Fausta, "Montaigne rencontre Theodor Zwinger à Bâle: Deux esprits parents." *Montaigne Studies*, vol. V, 1993, 191–205.

———, "Montaigne e il suo biografo: Doppia esposizione." In *Scritti in onore di G. Macchia*. Milan: Mondadori, 1983, vol. I, 100–113.

———, "Sull'italiano del *Journal de voyage*." In *Itinerari a Montaigne*. Florence: Sansoni, 1983, 119–32.

Garde, J. A., "Montaigne notre voisin," *Revue historique et archéologique du Libournais*, vol. XIX, 1951, 11–20, 60–68, 81–84.

Gardeau, Léonie, "La bibliothèque du marquis de Trans et de son petit-fils Frédéric de Foix." *Bulletin de la Société des amis de Montaigne*, no. 20, 1970, 51–61.

———, *Les Comtes de Foix-Gurson et la cause royale au XVIe siècle*. Périgueux: Imprimerie Pierre Fanlac, 1969.

———, *Gurson Montaigne: Terres d'histoire*. Bayac: Éditions du Roc de Bourzac, 1992.

———, "Les moulins de la seigneurie de Montaigne." *Bulletin de la Société historique et archéologique du Périgord*, vol. LXXXVII, 1960, 177–82.

———, "Le testament du marquis de Trans." *Bulletin de la Société historique et archéologique du Périgord*, vol. LXXXIII, 1956, 125–32.

Garrisson-Estèbe, Janine, *Protestants du Midi, 1559–1598*. Toulouse: Privat, 1980.

Gaullieur, Ernest, *Histoire de la Réformation à Bordeaux et dans le ressort du Parlement de Guienne*. Paris; New York: Honoré Champion; J. W. Bouton, 1884.

————, *Histoire du Collège de Guyenne d'après un grand nombre de documents inédits*. Paris: Sandoz et Fischbacher, 1874.

Gébelin, François, *Le Gouvernement du Maréchal de Matignon en Guyenne pendant les premières années du règne de Henri IV (1589–1594)*. Bordeaux: Marcel Mounastre-Picamilii, 1912.

Gellard, Matthieu, "Le Métier d'ambassadeur pendant les Guerres de Religion: Raymond de Fourquevaux, représentant de Charles IX à Madrid (1565–1572)." Master's thesis in History, Université Paris-Sorbonne, 2001.

————, "Une reine épistolaire: Les usages de la lettre et leurs effets dans l'action diplomatique de Catherine de Médicis (1559–1589)." Doctoral dissertation in History, Université Paris-Sorbonne, 2010.

Geonget, Stéphan, "L'arrêt notable entre droit et littérature, les choix de Jean Papon." In Laurence Giavarini, ed., *L'Écriture des juristes (XVe–XVIIIe siècles)*. Paris: Classiques Garnier, 2010, 206–22.

————, "L'humanisme littéraire de Jean de Coras: Un juriste lecteur de Budé et de Rabelais." In Nathalie Dauvois-Lavialle, ed., *L'Humanisme à Toulouse (1480–1580)*. Paris: Honoré Champion, 2006, 271–87.

Gigon, Stéphane Claude, *Contribution à l'histoire de l'impôt sous l'Ancien Régime: La révolte de la Gabelle en Guyenne (1548–1549)*. Paris: Honoré Champion, 1906.

Gionet, Arthur J., "Les idées de Montaigne sur la capacité de raisonner du peuple." *Kentucky Foreign Language Quarterly*, vol. 10, no. 1, 1963, 140–44.

Glauser, Alfred, *Montaigne Paradoxal*. Paris: A.-G. Nizet, 1972.

Godman, Peter, "Montaigne und die römischen Zensoren." In Michel de Montaigne, *Tagebuch einer Reise nach Italien über die Schweiz und Deutschland*. Wiesbaden: Marix Verlag, 2005, 5–9.

————, *The Saint as Censor: Robert Bellarmine between Inquisition and Index*. Leiden; Boston; Cologne: Brill, 2000.

Goldmann, Lucien, *Le Dieu caché: Étude sur la vision tragique dans les Pensées de Pascal et dans le théâtre de Racine*. Paris: Gallimard, 1959.

Gontier, Thierry, "Entre les 'Politiques' et Montaigne: Le théologico-politique chez Pierre Charron." *Montaigne Studies*, vol. XII, 2000, 105–22.

————, and Suzel Mayer, eds., *Le Socratisme de Montaigne*. Paris: Classiques Garnier, 2010.

Gorris, Rosanna, " 'La France estoit affamée de la lecture d'un tel historien': Lectures de Tacite entre France et Italie." In Danièle Bohler, ed., *Écritures de l'Histoire: XIVe–XVIe siècles*. Geneva: Droz, 2005, 113–41.

Gouedo-Thomas, Catherine, "Le thermalisme médiéval de Flamenca à Michel de Montaigne." Paris: Éditions du CDHS, 1994, 11–26.

Gourgues, Alexis de, *Réflexions sur la vie et le caractère de Montaigne*. Bordeaux: G. Gounouilhou, 1856.

Goyet, Francis, *Les Audaces de la prudence: Littérature et politique aux XVIe et XVIIe siècles*. Paris: Classiques Garnier, 2009.

Graves, Amy, "Crise d'engagement: Montaigne et la Ligue." In Philippe Desan, ed., *Montaigne politique*. Paris: Honoré Champion, 2006, 340–41.

Gray, Floyd, *Montaigne et les livres*. Paris: Classiques Garnier, 2013.

———, "Montaigne and the Memorabilia." *Studies in Philology*, no. 58, 1961, 130–39.

Greenblatt, Stephen, *Renaissance Self-Fashioning: From More to Shakespeare*. Chicago: University of Chicago Press, 2005.

Greengrass, Mark, *Governing Passions: Peace and Reform in the French Kingdom, 1576–1585*. Oxford: Oxford University Press, 2007.

Gregorovius, Ferdinand, *Alcuni cenni storici sulla cittadinanza romana*. Rome: Reale Accademia dei Lincei, Memorie della Classe di scienze morali, storiche e filologiche, series 3, vol. I, 1877, 314–46.

Grendler, Paul F., "The Roman Inquisition and the Venetian Press, 1540–1605." *Journal of Modern History*, vol. 47, 1975, 48–65.

Grün, Alphonse, *La Vie publique de Michel Montaigne: Étude biographique*. Paris: Librairie d'Amyot, 1855.

Grzybowski, Stanislas, "Henri III et Étienne Bathory." In Robert Sauzet, ed., *Henri III et son temps*. Paris: J. Vrin, 1992, 93–101.

Gueudet, Guy, *L'Art de la lettre humaniste*. Paris: Honoré Champion, 2004.

Guilhiermoz, Paul, *Enquêtes et procès: Étude sur la procédure et le fonctionnement du Parlement au XIVe siècle, suivie du style de la Chambre des enquêtes, du style des commissaires du Parlement et de plusieurs autres textes et documents*. Paris: A. Picard, 1892.

Guilleminot-Chrétien, Geneviève, "Michel de Montaigne, *Essais*." In Marie-Hélène Tesnière, ed., *Trésors de la Bibliothèque nationale de France*, vol. 1: *Mémoires et merveilles VIIIe–XVIIIe siècle*. Paris, 1996.

Gutwirth, Marcel, "Montaigne pour et contre Sebond." *Revue des sciences humaines*, vol. 34, 1969, 175–88.

Habert, Mireille, "L'inscription du sujet dans la traduction par Montaigne de la *Theologia naturalis*." *Montaigne Studies*, vol. V, 1993, 27–47.

———, "Pierre Bunel." In Philippe Desan, ed., *Dictionnaire de Michel de Montaigne*. Paris: Honoré Champion, 2007, 151–52.

——— "Théologie naturelle." In Philippe Desan, ed., *Dictionnaire de Michel de Montaigne*. Paris: Honoré Champion, 2007, 972–76.

Halkin, Léon Ernest, "Montaigne et la prière." In Henri Limet and Julien Ries, eds., *L'Expérience de la prière dans les grandes religions*. Louvain: Centre d'histoire des religions, 1980, 411–17.

Hall, Marie-Louise, "Montaigne et ses traducteurs." Doctoral dissertation, University of Wisconsin–Madison, 1940.

Hamlin, William M., *Montaigne's English Journey: Reading the* Essays *in Shakespeare's Day*. Oxford: Oxford University Press, 2013.

Hampton, Timothy, *Fictions of Embassy: Literature and Diplomacy in Early Modern Europe*. Ithaca, NY: Cornell University Press, 2009.

———, "'Tendre negociateur': La rhétorique diplomatique dans les *Essais*." In John O'Brien, Malcolm Quainton, and James Supple, eds., *Montaigne et la rhétorique*. Paris: Honoré Champion, 1995, 189–200.

Hauchecorne, Francis, "Le Parlement de Bordeaux pendant la première guerre civile, décembre 1560–mars 1563." *Annales du Midi*, vol. 62, no. 4, 1950, 329–40.

———, "Une intervention ignorée de Montaigne au parlement de Bordeaux." *Bibliothèque d'Humanisme et Renaissance*, vol. IX, 1947, 164–68.

Hendrick, Philip, *Montaigne et Sebond: L'art de la traduction*. Paris: Honoré Champion, 1996.

Hermann, Michel, "L'attitude de Montaigne envers la Réforme et les réformés dans les *Essais* de 1580 et le *Journal de voyage*." In François Moureau, Robert Granderoute, and Claude Blum, eds., *Montaigne et les Essais 1580–1980*. Paris; Geneva: Honoré Champion; Slatkine, 1983, 352–67.

———, "L'attitude de Montaigne envers la Réforme et les réformés dans le *Journal de voyage*." In François Moureau and René Bernoulli, eds., *Autour du Journal de voyage de Montaigne 1580–1980*. Geneva: Slatkine, 1982, 37–54.

Hirstein, James S., and Robert D. Cottrell, "La Boétie, *Poemata*," *Montaigne Studies*, vol. III, no. 1, 1991, 21–25.

Hoffmann, George, "About Being about the Renaissance: Bestsellers and Booksellers." *Journal of Medieval and Renaissance Studies*, vol. 22, no. 1, 1992, 75–88.

———, *Alone unto Their Distance: French Reformers, Satiric Alienation, and the Creation of Religious Foreignness*, forthcoming.

———, "Anatomy of the Mass: Montaigne's Cannibals." *PMLA*, vol. 117, no. 2, 2002, 207–21.

———, "Croiser le fer avec le Géographe du Roi: L'entrevue de Montaigne avec Antoine de Laval aux États généraux de Blois en 1588." *Montaigne Studies*, vol. XIII, 2001, 207–22.

———, "From Amateur Gentleman to Gentleman Amateur." In Zahi Zalloua, ed., *Montaigne after Theory / Theory after Montaigne*. Seattle: University of Washington Press, 2009, 19–38.

———, "Le monopole Montaigne." In Claude Blum and André Tournon, eds., *Éditer les* Essais *de Montaigne*. Paris: Honoré Champion, 1997, 99–131.

———, *Montaigne's Career*. Oxford: Clarendon Press, 1998.

———, "Montaigne's Lost Years." *Bulletin de la Société internationale des amis de Montaigne*, no. 55, 2012, 121–41.

———, "Le roi 'débonnaire': Duplessis-Mornay, Montaigne et l'image de Henri de Navarre en 1583–1584." In Philippe Desan, ed., *Montaigne politique*. Paris: Honoré Champion, 2006, 289–304.

———, "Self-Assurance and Acting in the *Essais*." *Montaigne Studies*, vol. XXVI, 2014, 55–78.

———, "Was Montaigne a Good Friend?" In Lewis C. Seifert and Rebecca M. Wilkin, eds., *Men and Women Making Friends in Early Modern France*. London; New York: Routledge, 2015, 31–60.

Hoffmann, George, and Alain Legros, "Secrétaire(s)." In Philippe Desan, ed., *Dictionnaire de Michel de Montaigne*. Paris: Honoré Champion, 2007, 1051–54.

Hubrecht, Georges, "Montaigne juriste." In *IVᵉ Centenaire de la naissance de Montaigne*. Bordeaux: Delmas, 1933, 239–98.

Huppert, George, *Les Bourgeois Gentilshommes: An Essay on the Definition of Elites in Renaissance France*. Chicago: University of Chicago Press, 1977.

————, *Public Schools in Renaissance France*. Urbana: University of Illinois Press, 1984.

Insdorf, Cecile, *Montaigne and Feminism*. Chapel Hill: University of North Carolina Press, 1977.

Jama, Sophie, *L'Histoire juive de Montaigne*. Paris: Flammarion, 2001.

Janssen, Herman, *Montaigne fidéiste*. Nijmegen; Utrecht: N. V. Dekker & van de Vegt en J. W. van Leeuwen, 1930.

Jouanna, Arlette, *Le Devoir de révolte: La noblesse française et la gestation de l'État moderne, 1559–1661*. Paris: Fayard, 1989.

————, "Montaigne et la noblesse." In Claude-Gilbert Dubois, ed., *Les Écrivains et la politique dans le sud-ouest de la France autour des années 1580: Quatrième centenaire de l'accession de Montaigne à la mairie de Bordeaux, 1581–1981*. Talence: Presses Universitaires de Bordeaux, 1982, 113–23.

————, *Ordre social, mythes et hiérarchies dans la France du XVIᵉ siècle*. Paris: Hachette, 1977.

————, "Perception et appréciation de l'anoblissement dans la France du XVIᵉ et du début du XVIIᵉ siècle." In *L'Anoblissement en France, XVᵉ–XVIIIᵉ siècles: Théories et réalités*. Bordeaux: Publications de la Maison des sciences de l'homme d'Aquitaine, 1985, 1–37.

Jullian, Camille, *Histoire de Bordeaux depuis les origines jusqu'en 1895*. Bordeaux: Feret et fils, 1895.

Keatley, Richard, "Le statut du valet dans le *Journal de voyage* de M. de Montaigne en Italie, par la Suisse et l'Allemagne en 1580 et 1581: L'édition B de Querlon." Master's thesis, Université Paris-Sorbonne, 1997.

Kellermann, Frederick, "The *Essais* and Socrates." *Symposium*, vol. 10, 1956, 204–16.

Kelly, Donald R., " 'Fides Historiae': Charles Dumoulin and the Gallican View of History." *Traditio*, vol. XXII, 1966, 347–402.

————, "Jurisconsultus perfectus: The Lawyer as Renaissance Man." *Journal of the Warburg Courtauld Institutes*, vol. 51, 1998, 84–102.

Kinser, Samuel, *The Works of Jacques-Auguste de Thou*. The Hague: M. Nijhoff, 1966.

Koyré, Alexandre, *Études d'histoire de la pensée scientifique*. Paris: Gallimard, 1985.

————, *From the Closed World to the Infinite Universe*. New York: Harper Torchbook, 1958.

Krause, Virginia, *Idle Pursuits: Literature and Oisiveté in the French Renaissance*. Newark: University of Delaware Press, 2003.

Kritzman, Lawrence, "The Socratic Makeover: Montaigne's 'De la physionomie' and the Ethics of the Impossible." *L'Esprit créateur*, vol. 46, no. 1, 2006, 75–85.

Kuperty-Tsur, Nadine, *Se dire à la Renaissance: Les mémoires au XVIᵉ siècle*. Paris: Vrin, 1997.

Labourdette, Jean-François, "Le recrutement des ambassadeurs sous les derniers Valois." In L. Bély, ed., *L'Invention de la diplomatie: Moyen Âge-Temps modernes*. Paris: Presses Universitaires de France, 1998, 99–114.

Lagrée, Marie-Clarté, *"C'est moy que je peins": Figures de soi à l'automne de la Renaissance*. Paris: Presses de l'Université Paris-Sorbonne, 2011.

Langer, Ullrich, "Montaigne's Customs." *Montaigne Studies*, vol. IV, 1992, 81–96.

———, *Perfect Friendship: Studies in Literature and Moral Philosophy from Boccaccio to Corneille*. Geneva: Droz, 1994.

Lapaume, Jean, *Le Tombeau de Montaigne: Étude philosophique et archéologique*. Rennes: Imprimerie Oberthur, 1859.

Larcade, Véronique, "La clientèle du duc d'Épernon dans le Sud-Ouest du royaume." *Annales du Midi, Revue de la France méridionale*, vol. 108, no. 213, 1996, 29–37.

Lavergne, Géraud, "Les conflits de la Cour des aides de Périgueux avec les Cours des aides de Paris et de Montpellier (1554–1557)." *Bulletin philomatique et historique*, 1936–37, 37–45.

La Ville de Mirmont, H. de, "George Buchanan à Bordeaux." *Revue philomatique de Bordeaux et du Sud-Ouest*, 1906, 289–312.

Lazard, Madeleine, "Montaigne diplomate." In Zoé Samaras, ed., *Espace, voyage, écriture*. Paris: Honoré Champion, 1995, 22–33.

Lebrun, François, *La Vie conjugale sous l'Ancien Régime*. Paris: Armand Colin, 1975.

Legros, Alain, "Buchanan et Cicéron chez Montaigne: Deux sentences inédites de sa 'librairie.'" *Montaigne Studies*, vol. XXVI, 2014, 171–75.

———, "Dix-huit volumes de la bibliothèque de La Boétie légués à Montaigne et signalés par lui comme tels." *Montaigne Studies*, vol. XXV, 2013, 177–87.

———, "Édition de 1582." In Philippe Desan, ed., *Dictionnaire de Michel de Montaigne*. Paris: Honoré Champion, 2004, 301.

———, *Essais sur poutres: Peintures et inscriptions chez Montaigne*. Paris: Klincksieck, 2000.

———, "Jésuites ou Jésuates? Montaigne entre science et ignorance." *Montaigne Studies*, vol. XV, 2003, 131–46.

———, "La main grecque de Montaigne." *Bibliothèque d'Humanisme et Renaissance*, vol. LXI, no. 2, 1999, 461–78.

———, *Montaigne, Essais, I, 56 "Des prieres": Édition annotée des sept premiers états du texte avec étude de genèse et commentaire*. Geneva: Droz, 2003.

———, "Montaigne et Gournay en marge des *Essais*: Trois petites notes pour quatre mains." *Bibliothèque d'Humanisme et Renaissance*, vol. LXV, no. 3, 2003, 613–30.

———, "Montaigne et Maldonat." *Montaigne Studies*, vol. XIII, 2001, 65–98.

———, "Montaigne face à ses censeurs romains de 1581 (mise à jour)." *Bibliothèque d'Humanisme et Renaissance*, vol. LXXI, no. 1, 2009, 7–33.

———, *Montaigne manuscrit*. Paris: Classiques Garnier, 2010.

———, "Montaigne politique malgré lui? Réticences et aveux." In Philippe Desan, ed., *Montaigne politique*. Paris: Honoré Champion, 2006, 113–26.

———, "Montaigne, son livre et son roi." *Studi Francesi*, vol. XLI, fasc. II, 1997, 259–74.

———, "Petit 'eB' deviendra grand . . . : Montaigne correcteur de l'exemplaire 'Lalanne' (Bordeaux: S. Millanges, 1580, premier état)." *Montaigne Studies*, vol. XIV, 2002, 179–210.

Leiner, Wolfang, "Du voyage en pays germaniques: Intertextualité et portée du *Journal de voyage* de Montaigne." In Zoé Samaras, ed., *Montaigne: Espace, voyage, écriture*. Paris: Honoré Champion, 1995, 55–64.

Lelarge, André, "Autour du serment de Montaigne devant le Parlement de Paris en 1562." *Bulletin de la Société des amis de Montaigne*, no. 11, 1941, 40–42.

Le Mao, Caroline, *Parlement et parlementaires: Bordeaux au Grand Siècle*. Seyssel: Champ Vallon, 2007.

Lemoine, Yves, *La Grande Robe, le Mariage et l'Argent: Histoire d'une grande famille parlementaire*. Paris: Michel de Maule, 2000.

Le Person, Xavier, "Montaigne et les 'practiques' politiques de son temps." In Philippe Desan, ed., *Montaigne politique*. Paris: Honoré Champion, 2006, 95–112.

———, *"Practiques" et "practiqueurs": La vie politique à la fin du règne de Henri III (1584–1589)*. Geneva: Droz, 2002.

Le Roux, Nicolas, *La Faveur du roi: Mignons et courtisans au temps des derniers Valois (vers 1547–vers 1589)*. Paris: Champ Vallon, 2001.

———, "Guerres civiles, entreprises maritimes et identité nobiliaire: Les imaginations de Guy de Lansac (1544–1622)." *Bibliothèque d'Humanisme et Renaissance*, vol. LXV, no. 3, 2003, 529–69.

———, "Les négociateurs royaux en France pendant les guerres de Religion." In Heinz Duchhardt and Patrice Veit, eds., *Guerre et paix du Moyen Âge aux temps modernes: Théorie—Pratiques—Représentations*. Mainz: Philipp von Zabern, 2000, 119–136.

———, *Un régicide au nom de Dieu: L'assassinat de Henri III*. Paris: Gallimard, 2006.

Lestringant, Frank, *L'Atelier du cosmographe ou l'image du monde à la Renaissance*. Paris: Albin Michel, 1991.

———, *Le Brésil de Montaigne: Le Nouveau Monde des "Essais" (1580–1592)*. Paris: Chandeigne, 2005.

———, "Fictions de l'espace brésilien à la Renaissance: L'exemple de Guanabara." In Christian Jacob and Frank Lestringant, eds., *Arts et légendes d'espaces: Figures du voyage et rhétoriques du monde*. Paris: Presses de l'École normale supérieure, 1981, 207–56.

———, *Le Huguenot et le Sauvage: L'Amérique et la controverse coloniale, en France, au temps des guerres de Religion (1555–1589)*. Paris: Aux amateurs de livres, 1990.

———, "Montaigne et les protestants." In Philippe Desan, ed., *Montaigne politique*. Paris: Honoré Champion, 2006, 353–72.

Levi, Giovanni, "Les usages de la biographie." *Annales: Économies, sociétés, civilisations*, no. 6, 1989, 1325–36.

Lévi-Strauss, Claude, *Tristes Tropiques*. Paris: Plon, 1955.

Lévis-Mirepoix, Antoine de, "Montaigne et le secret de Coutras." *Revue des Deux Mondes*, October 1950, 461–72.

Losse, Deborah, *Montaigne and Brief Narrative Form: Shaping the Essay*. London: Palgrave Macmillan, 2013.

Loussouarn, Olivier, "Les Milieux parlementaires bordelais: 1520–1550." T.E.R. in History, Université Bordeaux-3, 1996.

Lowenthal, Martin, *The Autobiography of Michel de Montaigne*. London: Routledge and Sons, 1935.

Mack, Peter, *A History of Renaissance Rhetoric, 1380–1620*. Oxford: Oxford University Press, 2011.

———, *Reading and Rhetoric in Montaigne and Shakespeare*. London: Bloomsbury, 2010.

Madden, Sarah Hanley, "L'idéologie constitutionnelle en France: Le lit de justice." *Annales: Économie, sociétés, civilisations*, vol. 37, no. 1, 1982, 32–63.

Magnien, Michel, "Aut sapiens, aut peregrinator: Montaigne vs. Lipse." In Marc Laureys, ed., *The World of Justius Lipsius: A Contribution towards Intellectual Biography*. Brussels; Rome: Institut historique belge de Rome, 1998, 209–32.

———, *"Discours de la servitude volontaire."* In Philippe Desan, ed., *Dictionnaire de Michel de Montaigne*. Paris: Honoré Champion, 2007, 316–19.

———, *Étienne de La Boétie*. Paris; Rome: Memini, coll. "Bibliographie des Écrivains Français," 1997.

———, "Juste Lipse et Pierre de Brach: Regards croisés sur Montaigne." In Claude-Gilbert Dubois, ed., *Montaigne et Henri IV*. Biarritz: J.&D. Éditions, 1996, 125–49.

———, "Pour une attribution définitive du *Memoire* à E. de La Boétie." In Jean Céard, Marie-Christine Gomez-Géraud, Michel Magnien and François Rouget, eds., *Cité de Dieu, cité des hommes*. Geneva: Droz, 2003, 133–142.

———, "Trois lettres de Lipse à Montaigne (1587 [?]–1589)." *Montaigne Studies*, vol. XVI, 2004, 103–11.

Magnien-Simonin, Catherine, "Étienne Pasquier familier de Montaigne." *Montaigne Studies*, vol. XIII, 2001, 277–313.

———, "Etienne Pasquier (1529–1615) lecteur de Montaigne." In Claude-Gilbert Dubois, ed., *Montaigne et Henri IV*. Biarritz: Terres et Hommes du Sud, 1996, 67–85.

———, "Loisel, Antoine." In Philippe Desan, ed., *Dictionnaire de Michel de Montaigne*. Paris: Honoré Champion, 2007, 696–97.

———, "Montaigne historien de 'l'expédition' de Henri d'Anjou en Pologne (1573–1574)? Hypothèses . . ." In Françoise Argod-Dutard, ed., *Histoire et littérature au siècle de Montaigne: Mélanges offerts à Claude-Gilbert Dubois*. Geneva: Droz, 2001, 195–206.

———, " 'Des senteurs' (*Essais*, I, 55): Un chapitre exemplaire, délaissé par la critique." In Philippe Desan, ed., *Les Chapitres oubliés des* Essais *de Montaigne*. Paris: Honoré Champion, 2011, 167–79.

———, *Une vie de Montaigne ou le sommaire discours sur la vie de Michel Seigneur de Montaigne (1608)*. Paris: Honoré Champion, 1992.

Maguin, Jean-Marie, ed., *Shakespeare et Montaigne: Vers un nouvel humanisme*. Montpellier: Société Française Shakespeare, 2003.

Malvezin, Théophile, *Michel de Montaigne, son origine, sa famille*. Bordeaux: Charles Lefebvre, 1875.

———, *Note sur la maison d'habitation de Michel de Montaigne à Bordeaux*. Bordeaux: Feret et fils, 1889.

Malissart, Alain, "Montaigne lecteur de Tacite." In Raymond Chevallier and Rémy Poi-

gnault, eds., *Présence de Tacite: Hommage au professeur G. Radke*. Tours: Caesarodunum, Bulletin de l'Institut d'études latines, 1992, 157–64.

Marcetteau-Paul, Agnès, *Montaigne propriétaire foncier*. Paris: Honoré Champion,
1995.

Marchand, Jean, "Documents originaux relatifs à Montaigne et à sa famille." *Bulletin de
la Société des amis de Montaigne*, no. 19, 1969, 9–42.

———, "L'édition des *Essais* de 1587." *Bulletin de la Société des amis de Montaigne*, no.
9, 1940, 57–58.

———, "Hypothèse sur la quatrième édition des *Essais* de Montaigne." *Bulletin de la
Société des bibliophiles de Guyenne*, vol. 27, 1937, 97–104.

———, "Le Montaigne de la reine Elisabeth d'Angleterre." *Bulletin de la Société des
amis de Montaigne*, no. 22, 1962, 23–27.

Martin, Catherine, "Le premier testament de Marie de Gournay." *Bibliothèque
d'Humanisme et Renaissance*, vol. LXVII, no. 3, 2005, 653–58.

Martin-Ulrich, Claudie, " 'Je pareillement': La figure de Socrate dans les *Essais* de Montaigne." In Alexis Tadié, ed., *La Figure du philosophe dans les lettres anglaises et françaises*. Paris: Presses Universitaires de Paris-Ouest, 2010, 25–38.

Maskell, David, "Montaigne médiateur entre Navarre et Guise." *Bibliothèque
d'Humanisme et Renaissance*, vol. XLI, 1979, 541–53.

Massa, Jean-Marie, "Le monde luso-brésilien dans la Joyeuse entrée à Rouen." In *Les
Fêtes de la Renaissance*, vol. III. Paris: Éditions du CNRS, 1975, 105–16.

Maugis, Édouard, *Histoire du parlement de Paris de l'avènement des rois Valois à la mort
d'Henri IV*. 3 vols. Paris: Picard, 1913.

Maulde-La-Clavière, René, *La Diplomatie au temps de Machiavel*. 3 vols. Paris: E. Leroux, 1892.

Mauss, Marcel, "Essai sur le don." In *Sociologie et anthropologie*. Paris: Presses Universitaires de France, 1968, 145–84.

McFarlane, Ian D., "George Buchanan and France." In J. C. Ireson, Ian D. McFarlane,
and Garnet Rees, eds., *Studies in French Renaissance presented to H. W. Lawton*.
Manchester; New York: Manchester University Press; Barnes and Noble, 1970,
295–320.

McGowan, Margaret, "Henri's Entry into Rouen." *Renaissance Drama*, no. 1, 1968,
199–225.

———, *Montaigne's Deceits: The Art of Persuasion in the* Essais. London: University of
London Press, 1974.

———, *The Vision of Rome in Late Renaissance France*. New Haven, CT: Yale University Press, 2000.

McKinley, Mary, "Vanity's Bull: Montaigne's Itineraries in III, 9." In Marcel Tetel and
Mallary Masters, eds., *Le Parcours des* Essais: *Montaigne, 1588–1988*. Paris: Aux
amateurs de livres, 1989, 196–98.

McQueeny, Terence, "Montaigne et la 'Theologia naturalis.' " *Bulletin de la Société des
amis de Montaigne*, no. 9, 1967, 41–45.

Meauldre de Lapouyade, Count of Saint-Saud, M., *Les Makanam, les Ayquem de Montaigne, recherches historiques*. Bordeaux: Féret, 1943.

Médard, Jean-François, "Le rapport de clientèle, du phénomène social à l'analyse politique." *Revue française de science politique*, no. 26, 1976, 103–31.

Meller, Pierre, *Les Anciennes familles dans la Gironde*. Bordeaux: E. Grugy, 1895.

———, *Notes pour servir à l'histoire de la famille de Pontac*. Tarbes: Imprimerie Croharé, 1910.

Melleville, Maximilien, *Histoire de la ville et des sires Coucy-le-Château*. Laon: Fleury & A. Chevergny, 1848.

Ménager, Daniel, "La culture héroïque de Montaigne." *Bulletin de la Société des amis de Montaigne*, nos. 9–10, 1998, 39–52.

———, "La diplomatie de Montaigne." In Philippe Desan, ed., *Montaigne politique*. Paris: Honoré Champion, 2006, 139–53.

———, *Diplomatie et théologie à la Renaissance*. Paris: Presses Universitaires de France, 2001.

———, "Lettres d'ambassadeurs." In Frank Lestringant, ed., *L'Épistolaire au XVIᵉ siècle*. Paris: Presses de l'École normale supérieure, 2001, 227–236.

———, "Montaigne et la philosophie de l'ambassade." *Bulletin de la Société des amis de Montaigne*, no. 17–18, 2000, 55–67.

Méniel, Bruno, "La notion de 'parler' chez Montaigne." *Bulletin de la Société des amis de Montaigne*, nos. 41–43, 2006, 119–30.

Michel de Montaigne et son temps: Collection Francis Pottiée-Sperry. Sotheby's sale catalog. Paris: November 27, 2003.

Michel, Pierre, "La suppression du sonnet de François d'Amboise dans l'édition de 1581 de la *Théologie naturelle*." *Bulletin de la Société des amis de Montaigne*, 1981, nos. 5–6, 116–17.

———, "Les visiteurs champenois de Montaigne." *Bulletin de la Société des amis de Montaigne*, 1971, 75–106.

Miernowski, Jan, *L'Ontologie de la contradiction sceptique: Pour l'étude de la métaphysique des* Essais. Paris: Honoré Champion, 1998.

Millet, Olivier, *La Première Réception des* Essais *de Montaigne (1580–1640)*. Paris: Honoré Champion, 1995.

Millin, Aubin-Louis, *"Le tombeau de Montaigne": Voyage dans les départements du midi de la France*. s. l., 1807, vol. IV, 2ᵉ partie, 634–42.

Mori, Elisabetta, "Tot reges in Urbe Roma quot cives: Cittadinanza e nobiltà a Roma tra Cinque e Seicento." *Roma moderna e contemporanea*, vol. IV, no. 2, 1996, 379–401.

Morisse, Gérard, "Sur les traces de Florimond de Raemond (Agen 1540–Bordeaux 1601)." *Revue française d'histoire du livre*, nos. 122–25, 2004, 121–46.

Moroni, Gaetano, *Dizionario di erudizione storico-ecclesiastica*. Venice: Tipografia Emiliana, 1840–79.

Moureau, François, "La copie Leydet du 'Journal de voyage.'" In François Moureau and René Bernouli, eds., *Autour du* Journal de voyage *de Montaigne, 1580–1980*. Geneva; Paris: Slatkine, 1982, 107–85.

———, "Le sens du titre: Typographie et gravure dans les premières éditions des *Es-*

sais." In Marcel Tetel and G. Mallary Masters, eds., *Le Parcours des Essais: Montaigne, 1588–1988*. Paris: Aux amateurs de livres, 1989, 13–16.

Mourin, Ernest, "Note relative à Charron, à sa conduite et à ses écrits du temps de la Ligue." *Mémoires de la Société académique de Maine-et-Loire*, 1858, 53–59.

Mousnier, Roland, "Les concepts 'd'ordres,' 'd'états,' 'de 'fidélité' et de 'monarchie absolue' en France de la fin du XVᵉ à la fin du XVIIIᵉ siècle." *Revue historique*, no. 247, 1972, 289–312.

———, "Les fidélités et les clientèles en France aux XVIᵉ, XVIIᵉ et XVIIIᵉ siècles." *Histoire sociale*, vol. XV, 1982, 35–46.

———, *Les Institutions de la France sous la monarchie absolue* [1974]. Paris: Presses Universitaires de France, 2005.

———, *La Vénalité des offices sous Henri IV et Louis XIII*. Rouen: Maugard, 1945.

Mula, Patrick, "De Venise à Paris: *L'Art des secrétaires* de Gabriel Chappuys entre traduction et création." In *La Lettre, le Secrétaire, le Lettré: De Venise à la cour de Henri III, Francesco Sansovino—Gabriel Chappuys*. Grenoble: HURBI, Filigrana, no. 6, 2000–2001, 115–82.

Nagle, Jean, *Un orgueil français: La vénalité des offices sous l'Ancien Régime*. Paris: Odile Jacob, 2008.

Nakam, Géralde, *Le Dernier Montaigne*. Paris: Honoré Champion, 2002.

———, *Les Essais de Montaigne: Miroir et procès de leur temps*. Paris: A.-G. Nizet, 1984.

———, "Ibériques de Montaigne: Reflets et images de la péninsule Ibérique dans les *Essais*." In Claude-Gilbert Dubois, ed., *Montaigne et l'Europe*. Mont-de-Marsan: Éditions InterUniversitaires, 1992, 153–75.

———, "La mairie de Bordeaux dans les *Essais*: Quelques grands principes de la conduite politique de Montaigne." In Claude-Gilbert Dubois, ed., *Les Écrivains et la politique dans le sud-ouest de la France autour des années 1580: Quatrième centenaire de l'accession de Montaigne à la mairie de Bordeaux, 1581–1981*. Talence: Presses Universitaires de Bordeaux, 1982, 23–32.

———, *Montaigne et son temps: Les événements et les* Essais; *l'histoire, la vie, le livre*. Paris: A.-G. Nizet, 1982.

Napolitano, Maria Luisa, "Hubertus Goltzius e la Civitas almae urbis Romae." *Anabases* online, vol. 11, 2010, 55–94, put online March 1, 2013, consulted on October 5, 2013, http://anabases.revues.org/769.

Naya, Emmanuel, "De la 'médiocrité' à la 'mollesse': Prudence montaignienne." In Emmanuel Naya and Anne-Pascale Pouey-Mounou, eds., *Éloge de la médiocrité: Le juste milieu à la Renaissance*. Paris: Éditions Rue d'Ulm, 2005, 195–216.

Nicolaï, Alexandre, "Un autre ami de Montaigne: Arnaud du Ferrier." *Bulletin de la Société des amis de Montaigne*, no. 19, 1956, 37–39.

———, "Germain-Gaston de Foix, marquis de Trans." *Bulletin de la Société des amis de Montaigne*, no. 19, 1956, 7–26.

———, "Les grandes dates de la vie de Michel de Montaigne." *Bulletin de la Société des amis de Montaigne*, no. 13–14, 1948–49, 24–27.

———, "Le 'machiavélisme' de Montaigne." *Bulletin de la Société des amis de Montaigne*, no. 4, 1957, 11–21; no. 7, 1958, 2–8; no. 9, 1959, 18–30.

————, *Montaigne intime*. Paris: Aubier, s.d.

————, "Où Montaigne logeait-il dans ses séjours à Bordeaux?" *Bulletin de la Société des amis de Montaigne*, no. 10, 1941, 5–6.

————, "Le serment de Montaigne au Parlement de Paris en 1562." *Bulletin de la Société des amis de Montaigne*, no. 11, 1941, 39–40.

Norton, Grace, *Studies in Montaigne: Early Writings of Montaigne and Other Papers*. 2 vols. New York: Macmillan, 1904.

Nys, Ernest, "Les origines de la diplomatie et du droit d'ambassade jusqu'à Grotius." *Revue de droit international et de législation comparée*, vol. XV, 1883, 577–586; vol. XV, 1884, 167–89.

O'Brien, John, "'Autheur de merveilleux poids': Montaigne et Xénophon." *Montaigne Studies*, vol. XVII, 2005, 17–34.

————, "Comment estre un bon juge?" *Bulletin de la Société des amis de Montaigne*, no. 21–22, 2001, 185–92.

————, "L'immodération d'un modéré: Montaigne, la règle et l'exception." *Journal of the Institute of Romance Studies*, vol. 6, 1998, 151–60.

————, "L'oubli comme mémoire: À propos de l'amitié politique." In Stéphan Geonget and Laurent Gerbier, eds., *Amitié & Compagnie: Autour du* Discours de la servitude volontaire *de La Boétie*. Paris: Classiques Garnier, 2012, 95–111.

————, "Retrait." In Philippe Desan, ed., *Montaigne politique*. Paris: Honoré Champion, 2006, 203–22.

————, "Suspended Sentences." In Keith Cameron and Laura Willett, eds., *Le Visage changeant de Montaigne / The Changing Face of Montaigne*. Paris: Honoré Champion, 2003, 195–206.

————, "La Transparence et l'ombre: L'énigme du sujet politique." In Daniel Martin, Pierre Servet, and André Tournon, eds., *L'Énigmatique à la Renaissance*. Paris: Honoré Champion, 2008, 489–503.

O'Brien, John, ed., *Pour une réévaluation de la diffusion manuscrite et imprimée du* Discours de la servitude volontaire. Paris: Honoré Champion, 2017.

O'Gilvy, Henri Gabriel, *Nobiliaire de Guienne et de Gascogne*. 4 vols. Bordeaux: G. Gounouilhou, 1856.

Okubo, Yasuaki, "Quelques transcriptions erronées de l'Exemplaire de Bordeaux dans les éditions modernes des *Essais*." *Bulletin de l'Association d'étude sur l'Humanisme, la Réforme, et la Renaissance*, vol. XXVI, 1988, 23–24.

Orléa, Manfred, *La Noblesse aux États généraux de 1576 et 1588: Étude politique et sociale*. Paris: Presses Universitaires de France, 1980.

Ortola, Marie-Sol, and Maria Roig Miranda, eds., *Mémoire, récit, histoire dans l'Europe des XVIᵉ et XVIIᵉ siècles*. 2 vols. Nancy: Université Nancy-II, 2007.

Padgett, John F., and Christopher K. Ansell, "Robust Action and the Rise of the Medici, 1400–1434." *American Journal of Sociology*, vol. 98, no. 6, 1993, 1259–319.

Palmer, Richard, "'In This Our Lightye and Learned Tyme': Italian Baths in the Era of the Renaissance." In Roy Porter, ed., *The Medical History of Waters and Spas*. London: Wellcome Institute for the History of Medicine, 1990, supplement no. 10, 14–22.

Panichi, Nicola, "Au-delà de la vertu 'innocente': Montaigne et les théoriciens de la raison d'état." In Philippe Desan, ed., *Montaigne politique*, Paris: Honoré Champion, 2006, 73–91.

———, "La boiterie de la raison: Le cas Martin Guerre." *Bulletin de la Société des amis de Montaigne*, no. 21–22, 2001, 171–83.

———, *Les Liens à renouer: Scepticisme, possibilité, imagination politique chez Montaigne*, trans. J.-P. Fauquier. Paris: Honoré Champion, 2008.

———, "Morte 'muette' e morte 'parlante': Montaigne e La Boétie." *Rivista di storia della filosofia*, vol. 67, no. 1, 2012, 35–58.

———, *Plutarchus redivivus? La Boétie e i suoi interpreti*. Naples: Vivarium, 1999.

Pavan, Paola, "Cives origine vel privilegio." In Luigi Spezzaferro and Maria Elisa Tittoni, eds., *Il campidoglio e Sisto V*. Rome: Ed. Carte Segrete, 1991, 37–41.

Payen, Jean-François, *Documents inédits ou peu connus sur Montaigne*. Paris: Techener, 1847.

———, *Nouveaux documents inédits ou peu connus sur Montaigne*. Paris: P. Jannet, 1850.

———, *Recherches sur Montaigne: Documents inédits*. Paris: Techener, 1856.

Petit, Léon, "Montaigne à Rome et deux ambassadeurs amis, Louis Chasteigner, seigneur d'Abain et de la Rocheposay, et Paul de Foix." *Bulletin de la Société des amis de Montaigne*, no. 5–6, 1958, 9–24.

Petris, Loris, *Michel de L'Hospital: Discours et correspondance; La plume et la tribune II*. Geneva: Droz, 2013.

———, *La Plume et la tribune: Michel de L'Hospital et ses discours (1559–1562)*. Followed by an edition of *De sacra Francisci II: Galliarum regis initiatione, regnique ipsius administrandi providentia, Mich. Hosp. Sermo* (1559) and discourses by Michel de L'Hospital (1560–62). Geneva: Droz, 2002.

Peyrecave, Mathe, *Arnauld Le Ferron conseiller au Parlement de Guyenne*. Bordeaux: G. Gounouilhou, 1877.

Picot, Émile, *Les Français italianisants au XVIᵉ siècle*. 2 vols. Paris: Champion, 1906.

Picot, Georges M. R., *Histoire des États généraux*. 5 vols. Paris: Hachette, 1872.

Piel, Christophe, "Les clientèles, entre sciences sociales et histoire." In *Hypothèses: Travaux de l'École doctorale d'Histoire*. Paris: Publications de la Sorbonne, 1998, 119–29.

Pinoteau, Hervé, *Étude sur les ordres de chevalerie du roi de France, et tout spécialement sur les ordres de Saint-Michel et du Saint-Esprit*. Paris: Le Léopard d'or, 1995.

Pintard, René, "Une adaptation de Machiavel au XVIᵉ siècle: Le 'Prince nécessaire' de Jean de la Taille." *Revue de littérature comparée*, vol. XIII, 1933, 385–402.

Pistilli, Barbara, and Marco Sgattoni, *La Biblioteca di Montaigne: Catalogo ragionato dei libri ritrovati, préface de Nicola Panichi*. Pisa: Edizioni della Normale, 2014.

Plattard, Jean, "Montaigne à Poitiers." *Bulletin de la Société des antiquaires de l'Ouest*, 1930, 679–81.

Posner, David, *The Performance of Nobility in Early Modern European Literature*. Cambridge: Cambridge University Press, 1999.

Pot, Olivier, *L'Inquiétante étrangeté: Montaigne, la pierre, le cannibale, la mélancolie*. Paris: Honoré Champion, 1993.

Pottier, André, "L'entrée de Henri II à Rouen en 1550." *Revue de Rouen*, vol. V, 1835, 18–108.

Powis, Jonathan, "Aristocratie et bureaucratie dans la France du XVIᵉ siècle." In Philippe Contamine, ed., *L'État et les aristocraties XIIᵉ–XVIIᵉ siècle: France, Angleterre, Écosse*. Paris: Presses de l'École normale supérieure, 1989, 230–43.

———, "The Magistrates of the Parliament of Bordeaux c. 1500–1563." Doctoral thesis, Oxford University, 1975.

———, "Officers and Gentilshommes: A parlementaire class in Sixteenth-Century Bordeaux?" In *Bordeaux et les îles britanniques du XIIIᵉ au XXᵉ siècle*. Bordeaux: Fédération historique du Sud-Ouest, 1975, 27–36.

Quantin, Jean-Louis, "Les censures de Montaigne à l'Index romain: Précisions et corrections." *Montaigne Studies*, vol. XXVI, 2014, 145–62.

Quet, Simone, "La Cour des aides de Guyenne, ses rapports avec le Parlement de Bordeaux." *Revue historique de Bordeaux*, vol. XLIII, 1939, 97–111, 167–82.

Quint, David, *Montaigne and the Quality of Mercy: Ethical and Political Themes in the Essais*. Princeton, NJ: Princeton University Press, 1998.

Ragghianti, Renzo, "*Discours de la servitude volontaire* et Étienne de La Boétie: D'une énigme à l'autre." *Rinascimento*, vol. XLIII, 2003, 507–52.

———, *Rétablir un texte: Le* Discours de la servitude volontaire *d'Étienne de La Boétie*. Florence: Leo Olschki, 2010.

Rat, Maurice, "Le ménage de Montaigne." *Bulletin de la Société des amis de Montaigne*, no. 15, 1949–52, 4–23.

Rathé, C. Edward, "Innocent Gentillet and the First 'Anti-Machiavel.'" *Bibliothèque d'Humanisme et Renaissance*, vol. XXVII, 1965, 186–225.

Regosin, Richard, *Montaigne's Unruly Brood: Textual Engendering and the Challenge to Paternal Authority*. Berkeley: University of California Press, 1996.

Réguis, François-Léon, *Le Lit de justice tenu à Rouen par Charles IX*. Rouen, 1902.

Reiss, Timothy, "Montaigne et le sujet politique." *Œuvres et critiques*, vol. 8, no. 1–2, 1983, 127–52.

Reverdin, Olivier, *Quatorze Calvinistes chez les Topinambous: Histoire d'une mission genevoise au Brésil (1556–1558)*. Geneva: Éditions du Journal de Genève, 1957.

Ribera, Jean-Michel, *Diplomatie et espionnage: Les ambassadeurs du roi de France auprès de Philippe II; Du traité du Cateau-Cambrésis (1559) à la mort de Henri III (1589)*. Paris: Honoré Champion, 2007.

Ricci, Saverio, "La censura romana e Montaigne, con un documento relativo alla condanna del 1676." *Bruniana & Campanelliana*, vol. 15, 2008, 59–79.

———, *Inquisitori, censori, filosofi sullo scenario della Controriforma*. Rome: Salerno Editrice, 2008.

Richard, Alfred, *Charles de Danzay, ambassadeur de France en Danemark*. Poitiers: Imprimerie Blais et Roy, 1910.

Richou, Gabriel, Jules Delpit, and Francois de Lachassaigne, *Inventaire de la collection des ouvrages et documents réunis par J.-F. Payen et J.-B. Bastide sur Michel de Montaigne. Rédigé et précédé d'une Notice par Gabriel Richou. Suivi de lettres inédites de Françoise de Lachassaigne.* Paris: Techener, 1878.

Rigolot, François, "Curiosity, Contingency, and Cultural Diversity: Montaigne's Readings at the Vatican Library." *Renaissance Quarterly*, vol. 64, no. 3, 2011, 847–74.

———, "Editing Montaigne's Translation of Sebond's *Theologia*: Which Latin Text Did the Translator Use?" *Montaigne Studies*, vol. VII, 1995, 53–67.

———, "Friendship and Voluntary Servitude: Plato, Ficino, and Montaigne." *Texas Studies in Literature and Language*, vol. 47, no. 4, 2005, 326–44.

———, "Saint-Barthélemy l'Indien: Montaigne, la 'loy d'oubliance' et la *Légende dorée*." *Bulletin de la Société des amis de Montaigne*, no. 37–38, 2005, 51–65.

———, "D'une Théologie 'pour les dames' à une Apologie 'per le donne.'" In Claude Blum, ed., *Montaigne, Apologie de Raymond Sebond: De la Theologia à la Théologie*. Paris: Honoré Champion, 1990, 261–90.

Ritter, Raymond, "Un ami de Montaigne, Philibert de Gramont (1552–1580)." In Georges Palassie, ed., *Mémorial du 1er congrès international des études montaignistes*. Bordeaux: Taffard, 1964, 136–45.

———, *Cette grande Corisande*. Paris: Albin Michel, 1936.

Roudière-Dejean, Simone, "Le rôle politique du Parlement de Bordeaux sous le règne de Henri III de 1574 à 1582." Thesis, École des Chartes, 1963.

Rouméjoux, Anatole de, "Essai sur les guerres de Religion en Périgord." *Bulletin de la Société historique et archéologique du Périgord*, vol. XXIX, 1902, 111–64, 221–56, 336–99, 428–71, 543–51.

Roussel, François, *Montaigne. Le Magistrat sans juridiction*. Paris: Michalon, 2006.

Rouxel, Marcel, *La Compétence de la cour des jurats de Bordeaux*. Bordeaux: Bière, 1949.

Russel-Major, James, *The Deputies of the Estates General in Renaissance France*. Madison: University of Wisconsin Press, 1960.

Ruysschaert, José, "Une édition du Tacite de Juste Lipse, avec annotations de Muret, conservée à la Mazarine." *Revue belge de philologie et d'histoire*, vol. 23, 1994, 251–54.

Saint John, Bayle, *Montaigne the Essayist*. 2 vols. London: Chapman and Hall, 1858.

Saint-Saens, Nussy, "Montaigne au Parlement de Bordeaux." *Revue historique de Bordeaux et du département de la Gironde*, new series II, 1953, 119–35.

Sauzé de Lhoumeau, Charles, *Correspondance politique de M. de Lanssac (Louis de Saint-Gelais), 1548–1557*. Poitiers: Société française d'imprimerie et de librairie, 1904.

———, "Un fils naturel de François Ier, Louis de Saint-Gelais, baron de la Mothe-Saint-Héray." *Mémoires de la Société des antiquaires de l'Ouest*, vol. XVI, 1940, 5–175.

Sayce, Richard, and David Maskell, *A Descriptive Bibliography of Montaigne's* Essais, *1580–1700*. London: Bibliographic Society, 1983.

———, "L'ordre des *Essais* de Montaigne." *Bibliothèque d'humanisme et Renaissance*, vol. XVIII, 1956, 7–22.

Schachter, Marc, "Presentation of a Newly Discovered Manuscript of La Boétie's *Dis-*

cours de la servitude volontaire and Hypotheses on the Datation of the BNF Manuscripts." *Montaigne Studies*, vol. XX, 2008, 185–206.

Schalk, Ellery, *From Valor to Pedigree: Ideas of Nobility in France in the Sixteenth and Seventeenth Centuries*. Princeton, NJ: Princeton University Press, 1986.

Schiff, Mario, *La Fille d'alliance de Montaigne, Marie de Gournay*. Paris: Champion, 1910.

Schmidt, S. W., ed., *Friends, Followers, and Factions: A Reader in Political Clientelism*. Berkeley: University of California Press, 1977.

Schutz, Alexander H., *Vernacular Books in Parisian Private Libraries of the Sixteenth Century According to the Notarial Inventories*. Chapel Hill: University of North Carolina Press, 1955.

Screech, Michael A., *Montaigne: The Complete Essays*. Harmondsworth: Penguin Classics, 1993.

Sealy, Robert J., *The Palace Academy of Henry III*. Geneva: Droz, 1981.

Simonin, Michel, "Bernard Automne (1564–après 1628), témoin et lecteur de Montaigne." *Montaigne Studies*, vol. XIII, 2001, 315–60.

———, "Françoise (de La Chassaigne) et (son?) Michel." In François Lecercle and Simone Perrier, eds., *La Poétique des passions à la Renaissance: Mélanges offerts à Françoise Charpentier*. Paris: Honoré Champion, 2001, 155–70.

———, "Montaigne et les Feuillants." In *L'Encre et la Lumière*. Geneva: Droz, 2004, 571–96.

———, "Montaigne et ses frères: Un poème inédit de George Buchanan conservé par Henri de Mesmes." In Philippe Desan, ed., *"Sans autre guide": Mélanges de littérature française de la Renaissance offerts à Marcel Tetel*. Paris: Klincksieck, 1999, 97–115.

———, "Œuvres complètes ou plus que complètes? Montaigne éditeur de La Boétie." *Montaigne Studies*, vol. VII, 1995, 5–34.

———, "Le Périgourdin au Palais: Sur le voyage des *Essais* de Bordeaux à Paris." In Marcel Tetel and Mallary Masters, eds., *Le Parcours des* Essais: *Montaigne 1588–1988*. Paris: Aux amateurs de livres, 1989, 17–30.

———, "Poétiques des éditions 'à l'essai' à la Renaissance." In Elio Mosele, ed., *Riflessioni teoriche e trattati di poetica tra Francia e Italia nel Cinquecento*. Fasano: Schena, 1999, 17–33.

———, "Poétique(s) du politique: Montaigne et Ronsard prosopographes de François de Guise." In Michel Dassonville, ed., *Ronsard et Montaigne écrivains engagés?* Lexington, KY: French Forum, 1989, 83–101.

———, "La préhistoire de l'Apologie de Raimond Sebond." In Claude Blum, ed., *Montaigne, Apologie de Raymond Sebond: De la Theologia à la Théologie*. Paris: Honoré Champion, 1990, 85–116.

———, "Des projets littéraires et de leurs réalisations éditoriales à la Renaissance." *Cahiers de l'Association internationale des études françaises*, no. 51, 1999, 183–203.

Slongo, Paolo, *Governo della vita e ordine politico in Montaigne*. Milan: Franco Angeli, 2010.

Smith, Malcolm, "Lost Writings by Montaigne." *Bibliothèque d'humanisme et Renaissance*, vol. XLIX, no. 2, 1987, 309–18.

———, "Montaigne and the Christian Foes of Tacitus." In I. D. McFarlane, ed., *Acta Conventus Neo-latini Sanctandreani: Proceedings of the Fifth International Congress of Neo-Latin Studies*. Binghamton, NY: Medieval & Renaissance Texts & Studies, 1986, 379–89.

———, *Montaigne and the Roman Censors*. Geneva: Droz, 1981.

Smith, Paul J., *Dispositio: Problematic Ordering in French Renaissance Literature*. Leiden: Brill, 2007.

———, "Montaigne in the World." In Philippe Desan, ed., *Oxford Handbook of Montaigne*. Oxford: Oxford University Press, 2016, 287–305.

Smith, Paul J., and Karl A. E. Enenkel, eds., *Montaigne and the Low Countries (1580–1700)*. Leiden: Brill, 2007.

Souza Filho, José Alexandrino de, *Civilisation et barbarie en France au temps de Montaigne*. Lille: ANRT, 2003.

———, *Projeto 'Livraria' de Montaigne: Um passeio ao universe do escritor francês Michel de Montaigne*. João Pessoa: Editora Universitária, 2007.

Starobinski, Jean, *Montaigne in Motion* [1982], trans. Arthur Goldhammer. Chicago: University of Chicago Press, 1985.

———, "'To Preserve and to Continue': Remarks on Montaigne's Conservatism." *Diogenes*, no. 118, 1982, 03–20.

Strowski, Fortunat, *Montaigne*. Paris: Éditions de la Nouvelle Revue critique, 1938.

Studt, Birgit, "Les joies du thermalisme: Nouvelles pratiques thermales et sociabilité dans l'Allemagne de la fin du Moyen Âge." In Didier Boisseuil and Marilyn Nicoud, eds., *Séjourner au bain: Le thermalisme entre medicine et société (XIVᵉ–XVIᵉ siècle)*. Lyon: Presses de l'Université de Lyon, 2010, 113–29.

Supple, James, *Arms versus Letters: The Military and Literary Ideals in the* Essais *of Montaigne*. Oxford; New York: Clarendon Press, 1984.

———, "Montaigne and the French Catholic League." *Montaigne Studies*, vol. IV, 1992, 111–26.

Sutherland, Nicola Mary, *The French Secretaries of State in the Age of Catherine de Medicis*. London: Athlone Press, 1962.

Taillard, Christian, *Bordeaux à l'âge classique*. Bordeaux: Mollat, 1997.

Tallon, Alain, "Diplomate et 'politique': Arnaud du Ferrier." In Thierry Wanegffelen, ed., *De Michel de L'Hospital à l'édit de Nantes: Politique et religion face aux Églises*. Clermont-Ferrand: Presses Universitaires Blaise Pascal, 2002, 305–33.

Tamizey de Larroque, Philippe, *Antoine de Noailles à Bordeaux, d'après des documents inédits*. Bordeaux: C. Lefebvre, 1878.

———, "Christophe et François de Foix-Candalle." *Revue de Gascogne*, vol. XVIII, 1877, 57–62, 138–45, 158–65, 285–86.

———, *Essai sur la vie et les ouvrages de Florimond de Raymond, conseiller au Parlement de Bordeaux*. Paris: A. Aubry, 1867.

Tetel, Marcel, "The Humanistic Situation: Montaigne and Castiglione." *Sixteenth Century Journal*, vol. X, no. 3, 1979, 69–84.

———, "Montaigne's Glances at Philippe de Commynes." *Bibliothèque d'Humanisme et Renaissance*, vol. LX, no. 1, 1998, 25–40.

Thireau, Jean-Louis, "Le conseil du roi au XVIᵉ siècle." *Revue administrative*, no. 3, 1999, 10–19.

Thompson, Doug, "Montaigne's Political Education: *Raison d'État* in the *Essais*." *History of Political Thought*, vol. XXXIX, no. 2, 2013, 195–224.

Tournon, André, *Montaigne: La glose et l'essai*. Lyon: Presses Universitaires de Lyon, 1983.

———, "La segmentation du texte: Usages et singularités." In Claude Blum, ed., *Éditer les* Essais *de Montaigne*. Paris: Honoré Champion, 1997, 173–83.

———, "Syntaxe et scansion: L'énergie du 'langage coupé' et la censure éditoriale." In John O'Brien, Malcom Quainton, and James Supple, eds., *Montaigne et la rhétorique*. Paris: Honoré Champion, 1995, 117–33.

———, "Un théologien par procuration." In Philippe Desan, ed., *"Dieu à nostre commerce et société": Montaigne et la théologie*. Geneva: Droz, 2008, 13–23.

Trani, Camille, "Le Grand Conseil de Henri II à Henri IV (1547–1610)." Thesis in the faculty of law. Paris, 1969.

———, "Les magistrats du Grand Conseil au XVIᵉ siècle (1547–1610)." *Mémoires publiés par la fédération des sociétés archéologiques de Paris et de l'Île-de-France*, vol. 42, 1991, 61–218.

Trinquet, Roger, "Aperçus généraux sur l'attitude politique de Montaigne après la mairie de Bordeaux (1585–1592)." *Bulletin de la Société des amis de Montaigne*, no. 11, 1967, 3–22.

———, "La lettre sur la mort de La Boétie ou Lancelot de Carle inspirateur de Montaigne." *Mélanges d'histoire littéraire (XVIᵉ–XVIIᵉ siècle) offerts à Raymond Lebègue par ses collègues, ses élèves et ses amis*. Paris: A.-G. Nizet, 1969, 115–25.

———, "En marge des *Essais*: La vraie figure de Madame d'Estissac ou les pièges de l'homonymie." *Bibliothèque d'Humanisme et Renaissance*, vol. XVII, 1956, 23–36.

———, "Montaigne Chevalier de l'ordre de Saint-Michel—octobre 1571." *Bulletin de la Société des amis de Montaigne*, 1971, 7–17.

———, "Montaigne et l'argent." In Raymond La Charité, ed., *O un amy! Essays on Montaigne in Honor of Donald M. Frame*. Lexington, KY: French Forum, 1977, 290–313.

———, "Montaigne et la divulgation du Contr'un." *Bulletin de la Société des amis de Montaigne*, no. 29, 1964, 1–12.

———, "Montaigne et le maréchal de Matignon." *Bulletin de la Société des amis de Montaigne*, nos. 14–15, 1975, 11–34.

———, "Du nouveau dans la biographie de Montaigne." *Revue d'histoire littéraire de la France*, vol. LIV, 1953, 1–22.

———, "Problèmes posés par la révision de la biographie de Montaigne." *Bulletin de la Société des amis de Montaigne*, nos. 23–24, 1962, 12–21.

———, "Quand Montaigne défendait les privilèges des vins de Bordeaux." *Revue historique de Bordeaux*, vol. V, 1956, 263–66.

———, "Le quatrième centenaire de la retraite de Montaigne." *Bulletin de la Société des amis de Montaigne*, nos. 25–26, 1971, 67–69.

———, "La réélection de Montaigne à la mairie de Bordeaux en 1583." *Bulletin de la Société des amis de Montaigne*, nos. 10–11, 1974, p. 17–46.

Tucker, George Hugo, "'Homo viator' and the Liberty of Exile (Du Bellay, Montaigne, Belon)." *Studies in Early Modern France*, vol. 2, 1996, 29–66.

Turchetti, Mario, "Une question mal posée: La 'tolérance' dans les édits de Janvier (1562) et d'Amboise (1563); les premiers commentaires et interprétations: Jean Bégat." In Henry Méchoulan et al., eds., *La Formazione storica dell'alterita: Studi di storia della tolleranza nell'età moderna offerti a Antonio Rotondò*. 3 vols. Florence: Leo S. Olschki, 2001, vol. I, 245–94.

Ughetti, Dante, *François d'Amboise (1550–1619)*. Rome: Bulzoni Editore, 1974.

Vacant, Alfred, and Eugène Mangenot, *Dictionnaire de théologie catholique, contenant l'exposé des doctrines de la théologie catholique: Leurs preuves et leur histoire*. 18 vols. Paris: Letouzey et Ané, 1908–72.

Vance, Jacob, "Duty, Conciliation, and Ontology in the *Essais*." In Zahi Zalloua, ed., *Montaigne after Theory, Theory after Montaigne*. Seattle: University of Washington Press, 2009, 75–99.

Vanoverberghe, David, "L'Ambassade de Bertrand de Salignac de La Mothe-Fénelon en Angleterre (1568–1574)." Master's thesis, Université de Lille, 1994.

Védère, Xavier, "Deux ennemis de Montaigne, le sénéchal Merville et le capitaine Vaillac." *Revue historique de Bordeaux*, vol. 36, 1943, 88–97.

Veyrin-Forrer, Jeanne, "La composition par forme et les *Essais* de 1580." In Claude Blum and André Tournon, eds., *Éditer les Essais de Montaigne*. Paris: Honoré Champion, 1997, 23–44.

Villey, Pierre, *Les Essais de Michel de Montaigne*. Paris: A.-G. Nizet, 1967.

———, "Montaigne en Angleterre." *Revue des Deux Mondes*, vol. XVII, 1913, 115–50.

———, *Les Sources et l'évolution des* Essais de Montaigne. 2 vols. Paris: Hachette, 1933.

Vindry, Fleury, *Les Ambassadeurs français permanents au XVIe siècle*. Paris: Champion, 1903.

———, *Les Parlementaires français au XVIe siècle*. Paris: Champion, 1909–10.

Voizard, Eugène, "Les relations de Montaigne avec la cour." *Revue d'histoire littéraire de la France*, 1894, 446–50.

Weber, Max, *The Protestant Ethic and the Spirit of Capitalism* [1905], trans. Talcott Parsons. London; Boston: Unwin Hyman, 1930.

Willett, Laura, "Rue de la Rousselle: Domicile conjugal." *Nouveau bulletin de la Société internationale des amis de Montaigne*, no. IV, 2008, 19–40.

Wintermeyer, Rolf, ed., *Moi public et Moi privé dans les mémoires et les écrits autobiographiques du XVIIe siècle à nos jours*. Mont-Saint-Aignan: Publications des universités de Rouen et du Havre, 2008.

Zeller, Gaston, "Une notion de caractère historico-social, la dérogeance." *Cahiers internationaux de sociologie*, no. XXII, 1957, 40–74.

TRANSLATIONS CITED

All quotations from Montaigne's *Essais* cite the translation by Donald M. Frame, *The Complete Essays of Montaigne*. Stanford, CA: Stanford University Press (1958) rpt. 1965.

All quotations from Montaigne's *Travel Journal* cite the translation by W. G. Waters, *The Journal of Montaigne's Travels in Italy by Way of Switzerland and Germany*. London: John Murray, 1903.

All quotations from La Boétie's *Discourse on Voluntary Servitude* cite the translation by Harry Kurz. New York: Columbia University Press, 1942.

Machiavelli, *The Prince*, trans. James B. Atkinson. Indianapolis: Bobbs-Merrill, 1976.

Norbert Elias, *The Court Society*, trans. Edmund Jephcott. New York: Pantheon, 1983.

Émile Durkheim, *The Rules of Sociological Method*, trans. W. D. Halls. 2nd ed. Houndmills: Palgrave Macmillan, 2013.

Pierre Bourdieu, *The Logic of Practice*, trans. Richard Nice. Stanford, CA: Stanford University Press, 1990.

Unless otherwise noted, all other translations are those of the translator of this book.

INDEX